PRIVATE EQUITY

Founded in 1807, John Wiley & Sons is the oldest independent publishing company in the United States. With offices in North America, Europe, Australia and Asia, Wiley is globally committed to developing and marketing print and electronic products and services for our customers' professional and personal knowledge and understanding.

The Wiley Finance series contains books written specifically for finance and investment professionals as well as sophisticated individual investors and their financial advisors. Book topics range from portfolio management to e-commerce, risk management, financial engineering, valuation and financial instrument analysis, as well as much more.

For a list of available titles, visit our website at www.WileyFinance.com.

PRIVATE EQUITY

IN HEALTHCARE AND LIFE SCIENCES

Strategies, Cases, and Industry Insights

MARC KITTEN AND GILLES CHEMLA

WILEY

Registered Office(s)

John Wiley & Sons, Inc., 111 River Street, Hoboken, NJ 07030, USA
John Wiley & Sons Ltd, New Era House, 8 Oldlands Way, Bognor Regis, West Sussex, PO22 9NQ, UK
John Wiley & Sons Singapore Pte. Ltd, 134 Jurong Gateway Road, #04-307H, Singapore 600134

For details of our global editorial offices, customer services, and more information about Wiley products visit us at www.wiley.com.

The manufacturer's authorized representative according to the EU General Product Safety Regulation is Wiley-VCH GmbH, Boschstr. 12, 69469 Weinheim, Germany, e-mail: Product_Safety@wiley.com.

Wiley also publishes its books in a variety of electronic formats and by print-on-demand. Some content that appears in standard print versions of this book may not be available in other formats.

Library of Congress Cataloging-in-Publication Data has been applied for:

Print ISBN: 9781394292592
ePDF ISBN: 9781394292646
ePub ISBN: 9781394292653

Cover Design: Wiley
Cover Image: © JihanFahri/stock.adobe.com

Typesetting: Set in 10/12 Sabon LT Std by Lumina Datamatics
Printed and bound by CPI Group (UK) Ltd, Croydon, CR0 4YY

C9781394292592_130826

This book is dedicated to our late friend Denis Gromb (1966–2022),
professor of finance at MIT, LBS, LSE, INSEAD, and HEC.

Contents

Foreword

When someone you love is unwell, nothing else matters. Deadlines fade. Ambitions pause. All you want is for them to get better. In these moments, the complexity of life reduces to a single, universal truth: good health is the foundation upon which every dream, every relationship, and every achievement rests.

Healthcare is not just an industry; it is humanity's most enduring act of collective hope. It is where science meets compassion, where innovation meets need, and where the measure of progress is not only efficiency but empathy. For decades, this sector existed largely within the domain of the state.

Today, healthcare is changing faster than at any point in modern history. What was once a fragmented network of public institutions has become one of the most dynamic and consequential sectors in global private markets. Yet, despite its scale and social importance, few have explored healthcare through the lens of private equity—as both a financial discipline and a force for human progress. This book does exactly that, and it does so with clarity and conviction.

At Quadria Capital, we have long believed that the rise of healthcare in Asia is one of the defining economic and social transformations of our lifetime. Across this region, home to a third of the world's population and more than half its disease burden, the need for accessible and affordable care is growing exponentially. At the same time, incomes are rising, innovation is accelerating, and expectations are changing. The convergence of affluence and illness has created a structural shift—one that demands both investment and imagination.

By the end of this decade, total healthcare spending in Asia will exceed five trillion dollars, surpassing that of the United States and Europe combined today. Yet government spending still falls short, leaving an estimated $80 billion gap every year just to meet minimum care standards. It is the private sector—and in particular private equity—that must help bridge this divide. Eight out of ten new hospital beds in Asia are now being built by private operators. Nearly 70% of the world's generic medicines are produced in the region. Nearly two-thirds of all FDA-registered pharmaceutical manufacturing sites outside the United States are located in Asia, underscoring the region's importance in the global healthcare supply chain.

What makes healthcare remarkable as an investment is its rare balance of resilience and growth. It is almost a defensive industry—stable, reliable, and persistent across economic cycles—but it also delivers consistent and compelling expansion. Demand for care does not fade with market volatility. It grows with population, innovation, and longevity. Few sectors can offer investors this combination of predictability and growth: the assurance of steady returns alongside the promise of long-term impact.

But beyond the numbers, healthcare speaks to something deeper—a shared responsibility. When capital is applied thoughtfully, it can transform not just companies but entire systems of care. The most successful healthcare enterprises are built not only on sound strategy and disciplined operations but on a sense of purpose. They are institutions that endure because they matter.

This book captures that intersection of purpose and performance. It provides practical frameworks, grounded case studies, and clear explanations of how private equity can drive meaningful change in healthcare. It reminds us that the role of investors is not only to deploy capital, but to direct it toward progress—to ensure that growth and good coexist.

To those who believe that capital should serve as a force for healing—for societies, systems, and people—this book is both a guide and a call to action. The next era of healthcare investing is being written now. Let this book be your compass as you navigate it: to invest wisely, to grow responsibly and to leave the system better than you found it.

Abrar Mir
Cofounder, Managing Partner, and IC Member, Quadria Capital
Cofounder and IC Member, HealthQuad

The authors of this book have a unique combination of relevant qualifications in business and academia. With decades of experience in private equity, they have seen the best, the worst, and what is considered industry standard in what you are about to read.

This makes the book particularly relevant for all of the following:

- A company **manager or entrepreneur**, because PE firms are a major and growing contributor to reshaping the corporate world. They can finance your business, they can help grow and sometimes save it, or they can hire you to run theirs
- A manager or **employee at a PE firm**, because they represent a growing segment of the asset management industry, offer rewarding careers, both economically and in terms of interesting experience
- An **advisor to PE firms**—investment banker, management consultant, lawyer or other specialist—because we will clarify concepts that will help you provide the support your clients need
- An individual involved in the setup or management of a **regional PE ecosystem** (industry body, regulator, state)
- A **wealthy investor**, because PE investments are expected to provide high returns, as well as diversification, and because we hope to help the reader triage good investments from bad
- A **future pensioner**, as pension funds have been significantly raising their allocation to PE in the last decades
- A **technology enthusiast** who would like to explore the role of technology in both private equity and in the health sector
- Project or **infrastructure developers** and managers
- Investors, managers, employees, and other **stakeholders of the healthcare sector**, as PE is now one of the most important forms of investment in that sector

Ultimately, this book applies to readers interested in private equity and those interested in healthcare finance. We believe there is a lot more than just focusing on one important private equity sector in writing a book on private equity with healthcare sector in mind. On the contrary, many unique features of private equity and many controversies on value creation and on societal implications are exacerbated when one considers them through the lens of healthcare. Our coverage of all topics has benefited greatly from the many years we have spent confronting and combining academic and practitioner perspectives.

Caveat: We have used AI tools the same way we invite our students to use them: mostly to enhance language, to help identify any missing sources, to help careful cross-checking of sources and logic, to ensure accuracy, clarity, and for comprehensive analysis while maintaining the rigor and depth expected in financial education.

Acknowledgments

We would like to thank in priority the main contributors to this book, starting with two beautiful spirits, Dr. Marco Mazevet, a caffeinated owl at Candesic who did not hesitate to pull all-nighters crashing the index and whose rigor and insightful recommendations have considerably helped in this protracted process, and Anna Silvestri at PAI Partners, who tirelessly reviewed our work, made countless valuable recommendations, and was a key contributor to the development of our investment frameworks.

Other significant contributors are Marc Julien, at En Carta, for his eagle eye and critical review of our frameworks; Dr. Isaac Liu, our MBA student at Imperial, who took the lead in refining our LBO model; the support of Matt Ng, Mario El Asmar, Javier Garcia-Perez, and Chris Nasseh from Candesic; Johannes Natterer, former managing director at HIG, who shared his experience on value creation and helped with the LBO model; Mike Mortimer, founding partner at GHO Capital, and Herb Hooper, managing partner at Ampersand Capital, who shared their wealth of experience as specialist investors; and Alessandro Moretti at PIF, who shared his long experience of value creation in the portfolio.

We also want to thank Robin Jakubowski on expanding investor access and for mastering waterfalls, Philipp Khokhlov on the specific role of private equity in pharma, Ruby Wang at Lintris who reviewed the key section on China, Matthias Chemla who helped with the literature review, and Aldous Mitchell at Candesic New York for his critical reading.

Many academic colleagues have also contributed generously. Ludovic Phalippou kindly authorized us to borrow from his own work. We are also highly grateful to Mike Ewens (Columbia), Antoinette Schoar (MIT), Steven Kaplan (Chicago), Gordon Philips (Dartmouth), Jose Scheinkman (Columbia), Paolo Fulghieri (UNC), David Robinson (Duke), Caroline Genc (Michigan State), Paul Beaumont (McGill), Katrin Tinn (McGill), Patrick Bolton (Imperial), Claudia Custodio (Imperial), Ailsa Roell (Imperial), Ramana Nanda (Imperial), Marco di Maggio (Imperial), Magda Rola-Janicka (Imperial), Christopher Hennessy (LBS), Clara Martinez-Toledano (Imperial), David Licher (Imperial), Naveed Sultan (Imperial CFT), Anne-Louise Burnett (Imperial CFT), Charlotte Crosswell (Imperial CFT), and Jean Tirole (Toulouse), who contributed very helpful feedback on various drafts and conversations throughout the years. Alassane Sangare (Imperial), Simeng Li (Imperial), Zhengming Li (Oxford), and Aude Chevalier (Imperial) contributed stunning research assistance.

And of course, Abrar Mir, cofounder and managing partner of Quadria Capital, who kindly agreed to write the foreword for this book. We also appreciate his thoughtful contributions on the evolution of private equity in healthcare.

We also express our sincere gratitude to the following individuals, thoughtfully listed in alphabetical order: Scott Adelson at Houlihan Lokey, Ludovic Alonzi at ARCHIMED, Rajib Arjun at Altius, Souleymane Ba at LeapFrog, Gauthier Baijot at Clearwater, Carl Berglind at GT Law, Nikhil Chadha at EQT, Nora Colton at UCL GBSH, Elena Coluccelli at Rothschild, Andrew Connelly at Fremman Capital, Ivan Coulter at Eden Biopharma, Quentin de Labarre at Merieux Equity Partners, Marie-Eve de Saint-Florent, Laurent Dethomas at Vivalto Partners, Mansuy Dieudonné at Bridgepoint, Estelle Dolla at Private Corner, Arnaud Dufer at Ardian, Elad Duschak, advisor to healthcare PortCos, Thomas Goudriaan at Gimv, Daniel Green at Audax Private Equity, Philipp von Hammerstein at Gimv, Jannick Hunecke at DBAG, Nicole Jones at Advent International, Kapil Kachru at Altius, Christoph Kausch at MTIP, Michael Healy at Keensight Capital, Milan Kulich at Advent International, Dr Bruno Ladriere at Ardian, Jon Laifer at Cobepa, Jean-Francois Le Ruyet at Quilvest, Rachel Lewis at Mergermarket, Alessandra Mazzuchelli at Soledar Partners, Mauro Moretti at Three Hills, Ingrid Mueller at Evotec, Marc Nahum formerly at Carlyle, Dr. Felix Olale at LeapFrog, Richard Olson at 88capital, Vikrant Parashar at Quadria Capital, Estelle Pfitzer at MTIP, Stephane Pichon at YourCare, Alessio Piccoli at PI Health Sciences, Nicolas Ploquin at Acteon, Nico Prokop at AGIC Capital, Marek Rodak at MidEuropa, Noé Richard at Astorg, Barbara Roversi at Three Hills, Dominik Schwartz at Verdane, Youssef Sebban at Eckuity Capital, Prateek Sharma at Cipla, Bo Shi at Pall Mall Capital, Alex Slack at Lauxera, Michael Thanner at Triton Partners, Paul Tomasic at Houlihan Lokey, Toni Torra at Miura, Eric Trüeb at eevolve, Nikki Walker at RLDatix, Yaoyao Wang at DC Advisory, Dr Sam Winward at Pastel Health, Yangshen Yang at Imperial, Sheryl Young formerly at Cross Atlantic Capital Partners, Tad Zindi at Datasite, Joseph Zipfel at SFC Capital, our former students Linus Baumann, Peiyuan Li, Maximilian Mayr, Dr. Dev Pannu, Jine Wu, and Gordon Zhu.

Acknowledgments are also due to the following:

Our combined 30,000 former and current students at Imperial and other institutions (UCL, Columbia, LBS, LSE, Bayes, Renmin, EDHEC, ESCP, ENPC, Sciences-Po, GSOM, Loughborough London, PSL Research University, ENSAE ...), for their curiosity, enthusiasm, and challenging questions.

Marc's partners and colleagues at Candesic who have jointly delivered about 1,000 engagements on six continents for private equity investors and their portfolio companies over 20 years.

Stephanie from Preqin (part of Blackrock), Terri from Dealogic (Ion Group), Shyan from PitchBook, Helen from Private Equity International, Anjana from Real Deals, and Nicola from Gain.pro who generously allowed us to use their industry data.

Gemma, Alice, and Richard at Wiley for their support and patience.

Our parents and our immediate families, in particular Angie, Antoine, Ariana, Enza, Corinne, Oriane, Cloe, Matthias, for reminding us there is life beyond writing a book.

About the Authors

MARC KITTEN

Marc is a visiting professor of finance at Imperial Business School in London, in charge of private equity courses for Master in Management, MBA, Executive MBA, and executive education programs. He is a founding partner at Candesic, a leading strategy consultancy in London and New York, focused on healthcare and life sciences, where he advises private equity investors on their investments and senior executives in healthcare companies on their strategies. He has advised on several hundred transactions, from healthtech startups to pharmaceutical and medtech multinationals. He serves on several advisory boards across the EMEA region.

Marc holds an MBA from Chicago Booth, a masters in management with a concentration in finance from EDHEC Business School and attended the Young Manager Program at INSEAD. He is a doctoral candidate at UCL Global Business School for Health. He has also lectured in private equity and corporate finance at Columbia, Renmin, UCL, Bayes, Loughborough, ESCP, EDHEC, Sciences Po Paris, ENPC, IUM Monaco, and GSOM St. Petersburg.

Marc's research interests include corporate finance, mergers and acquisitions, private equity and venture capital, with a focus on the health sector. He is the author of the *Vault Guide to Careers in Private Equity in Europe* and of a dozen case studies published at the Case Centre, including "Bain Capital's 'Take Private' of China Fire" with HEC, Prize Winner in 2021 and 2022.

GILLES CHEMLA

Gilles is a professor of finance at Imperial Business School and co-director of Imperial's Centre for Financial Technology. He is also a research fellow at Centre National de la Recherche Scientifique, a research fellow at Centre for Economic Policy Research (CEPR), a senior research fellow at the Rimini Centre for Economic Analysis (RCEA), and a member of the American Finance Association, American Economic Association, Western Finance Association, and European Finance Association. He currently serves as an associate editor at the *Journal of Empirical Finance* and is a visiting scholar at Harvard University.

Gilles holds a PhD in economics from the London School of Economics, an MSc in economics from the Paris School of Economics, and he is a graduate engineer from the Ecole Nationale des Ponts et Chaussées. Prior to joining Imperial, Gilles was an assistant professor of finance at the Sauder School of Business, University of British Columbia.

Gilles' research interests include financial technology and data science, private equity and venture capital, corporate governance and mergers and acquisitions, healthcare, energy markets, securitization, debt markets, pension funds, and financial regulation and policymaking. Gilles' research has been published in top academic journals and has been presented at many of the best institutions around the world.

Infographics

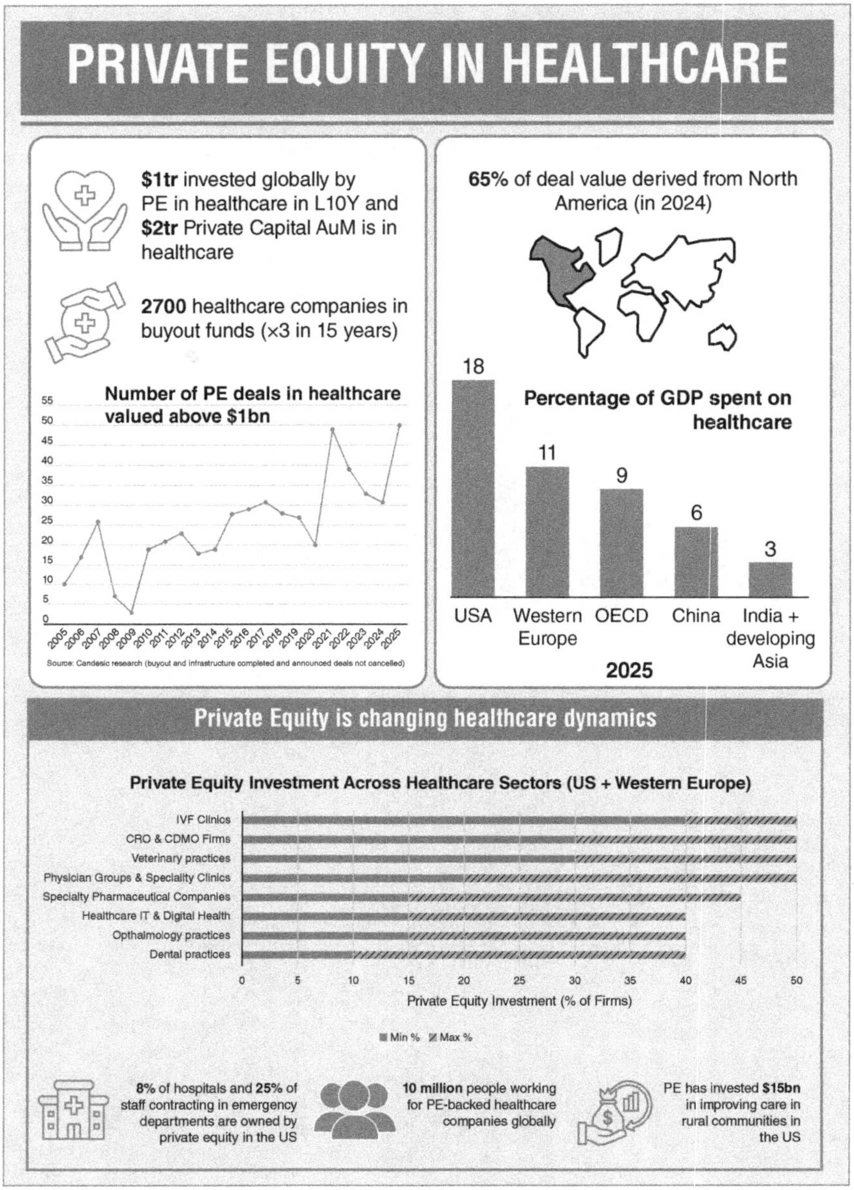

Source: Candesic research

Introduction

WHY PRIVATE EQUITY?

Welcome to the world of private equity—or PE—a dynamic, fast-growing field with a historical track record of creating long-term value in all kinds of business environments. In case the title was not a dead giveaway to even the most casual observer, this book delves into the exciting world of PE with a practical focus on healthcare: products and services, life sciences and healthcare services, infrastructure, and technology.

PE is an important form of investment whereby specialized firms acquire companies and then fuel growth, improve operations, or restructure finances in order to sell them at a profit. To this end, PE firms may use their control rights to shape strategy, which may include financing schemes such as leveraged buyouts (LBOs) to generate higher returns.

PE firms control trillions of dollars across countries and sectors, driving innovation and operational efficiency while transforming jobs, corporate governance, and capital allocation on a global scale. Healthcare is one of the most important PE sectors across the world. Analyzing PE through its prism will enable us to illustrate starkly the impact of PE on value creation and on society.

WHY HEALTHCARE?

Healthcare is one of the largest industries globally. Since 2010, it is the top employer in the United States, ahead of retail and manufacturing, accounting for 13% of the total workforce in 2023.[1] The share of healthcare in PE is in line with its share of GDP: around 20% in the United States, closer to 10% in Europe. Further, while increasingly more data are generated across sectors, 10% to 15% of all data are generated by healthcare alone.[2]

Healthcare is perhaps the most fascinating and complex sector: it deals with life and death, nondiscretionary spending, and significant capital expenditures with long horizons of funding of essential innovation, in particular in biotech. It is subject to a sensitive balance of public and private funding, with two separate populations of patients and caregivers, and with complex, diverse, and evolving regulations. In times of ageing populations, considerable increases in research and development costs, and constrained public investment due to spiraling government debt in most developed countries, private investment is of the utmost importance to the healthcare sector. In

[1] US Quarterly Census of Employment and Wages.

[2] Chris, M. (2024, June). No, healthcare isn't 30% of the world's data. https://www.extractsystems.com/no-healthcare-isnt-30-of-the-worlds-data.

the United States and Europe, about two-thirds of healthcare innovation is funded by the private sector (Moses et al., 2015; Research America, 2022; EFPIA, 2023). Together with the decades-long shift of research and development from the largest listed firms to privately held firms (Acharya and Xu, 2017; Gao et al., 2018; Atanasova and Chemla, 2026), the case for PE is reinforced by the sale of business divisions to PE firms to fund innovation. In addition, many business owners or medical practice owners reaching retirement age are looking to sell, which creates an opportunity for PEs to buy. Further, younger healthcare practitioners' reluctance to take on practice ownership debt creates opportunities for PE to buy the practices of baby boomer doctors. As a result, PE-funded investment is essential to the healthcare sector. As an illustration, HolonIQ (2023) listed 140 healthtech unicorns, those famous privately held firms with an estimated value in excess of $1 billion, in 2023.

From the origins and types of funds to the stages of the investment process and financial modelling, to the impact on stakeholders and society across subsectors including products, services, infrastructure, and technology, we cover it all. You will explore PE's role in healthcare, including in emerging markets, and see how it has fared during various periods of crisis.

We have always been fascinated by how PE integrates multiple disciplines and is thus even more an "art" than a science. That is why we must emphasize—PE is not just finance! It also combines strategy, economics, operations, and even behavioral psychology—it is a comprehensive approach to business growth and ultimate success.

The book leverages the authors' decades of experience advising investors and executives in healthcare and in other sectors, researching, developing case studies, and teaching PE, finance, and corporate strategy across all populated continents.

WHY PE AND HEALTHCARE?

Many challenges within PE investment appear to be exacerbated when considering PE in the healthcare sector. For example, valuation is a notoriously complex challenge for many payors, and even more so when what is being valued is not easy to substantiate and when it is not listed. As investments in healthcare are so essential to our life, erroneous valuations can generate dramatic investment inefficiencies.

Investments in many areas of healthcare, whether they need research and development or infrastructure development, are long-term projects while the investment horizon of PE investors appear to be shorter. Can these differences in horizon be overcome?

Innovation is critical and perhaps even more so in healthcare: while many researchers seem convinced that scientific discovery and technology development are innovation, these are only a first step. They require a lot of effort in development and an application that addresses a problem important enough for payors to consider worth funding, making it profitable for the healthcare system or for society. Technology alone rarely fulfills an existing need. Unlike in consumer industries, it is difficult to imagine a healthcare entrepreneur like Steve Jobs deciding which people will use what technology. Many new healthcare products or services must satisfy a complex regulatory process upward and a "go to market" process downward.

The prescriber is generally not the direct payor or the end user. An innovation that is too disruptive will rarely find an easy channel to the market. Payors have already lost money on many innovations, including some that have turned out to be successful.

SUMMARY OF CONTENTS

Chapter 1 provides a broad overview of the PE industry, exploring its definitions, origins, and evolution first as an industry, then in the healthcare sector. Chapter 2 covers the various segments that make up the PE industry. PE encompasses many alternative investment strategies in addition to the highly publicized LBOs.

Chapter 3 discusses several important attributes of PE as an asset class, including its performance and the metrics used to measure this, while considering how these attributes are unique to PE as well as pitfalls and alternative performance metrics. Chapter 4 explains how PE funds are structured and organized and outlines the full investment process. It describes how carried interest for general partners (GPs) is calculated and distributed, identifies where attractive deal opportunities come from, and highlights the key features of a strong business plan and the importance of the due diligence process. Chapter 5 develops a full LBO analysis model and discusses different approaches to valuation used in LBO situations.

Chapter 6 examines what happens after a company is acquired, focusing on how PE funds create value during the ownership period. It explores value creation from a financial perspective, including how portfolio companies are managed, how managers and co-investors are coordinated, and how human factors contribute to performance. The chapter concludes with a discussion of exit management and an introduction to the UNITE framework. Chapter 7 focuses specifically on 31 value creation strategies organized into five categories in the healthcare sector. It takes into account all types of healthcare deals (LBOs, add-ons, growth investments, secondary buyouts), and it develops the H.E.A.L. framework.

Chapter 8 discusses the impact of PE deals on stakeholders, which is hotly debated, and this debate is exacerbated in the healthcare sector. We examine the impact of PE on owners, other investors, workers, patients, the environment, society, and economic sovereignty. Chapter 9 examines the growth of PE in emerging and developing markets. Finally, Chapter 10 reviews recent developments and major trends in the PE industry, including fundraising, investment activity, fee structures, and the key forces shaping its future. It then introduces the main players in the PE healthcare specialization and provides insight into the daily work of PE professionals.

CHAPTER 1

Introduction and History

This chapter provides a broad overview of the private equity industry, exploring its definitions, origins, and evolution. We begin by examining the various ways private equity is defined and understood before tracing its historical roots—stretching as far back as Christopher Columbus—and focusing on its development, particularly from the latter half of the twentieth century onward.

Next, we examine the diverse landscape of private equity investors, analyzing what drives their investment decisions as well as the constraints they face. We then explore the different stages of private equity investment and how these map onto a company life cycle. In doing so, we examine how private equity funds work: who runs them, how do they make money, and how are they set up and structured. As we answer these questions, we examine the roles of both limited partners (LPs) and general partners (GPs) in the investment process.

Beyond its general principles, private equity has played a significant role in the healthcare sector. We identify key investment trends in healthcare and life sciences, exploring why the sector has been attractive to private equity firms and how different investment models have evolved over time. We also analyze the resilience of healthcare investments through various economic crises.

Finally, we present case studies of landmark transactions like STADA Arzneimittel that highlight key lessons, strategic approaches, and challenges in private equity investments within healthcare. Alongside this, we examine key metrics that provide insights into the current state of the private equity industry worldwide and how it has evolved over time.

1.1 AN INITIAL DEFINITION

There is often confusion when it comes to defining private equity. It was once simple:

> *Any equity investment in a company which is not quoted on a stock exchange.*

However, as Guy Fraser-Sampson once pointed out in 2007, this definition is no longer sufficient. Before we explore why, we start with an alternative definition provided by the BVCA, now renamed British Private Equity & Venture Capital Association:

> *Private equity provides long-term, committed share capital, to help unquoted companies grow and succeed. If you are looking to start up, expand, buy into a business, buy out a division of your parent company, turnaround or revitalize a company, private equity could help you to do this.*

An alternative definition was provided by the American Investment Council is even longer:

> *Private equity invests capital in companies that are perceived to have growth potential and then works with these companies to expand or turnaround the business. This capital is contributed by large institutional investors and is organized into a fund. After three to seven years of ownership and working with the company, the fund manager will seek to "exit" the company by taking the business public or selling it for a higher valuation than it was purchased. This exit distributes profits from the sale ("returns") to the investors in the fund and the fund manager. At the end of this process, private equity investments usually result in better jobs, stronger companies, and healthier communities.*

Why do we rely on such long definitions? Obviously, there are many concepts to include, and it is easy to overlook an element. Some definitions in other books, in their pursuit of brevity, miss key components. While it is true that private equity can be defined in opposition to public equity—simply as equity not listed on an exchange—this does not capture the full picture, if only because private equity often acquires public companies, taking them private.

It is important to keep in mind the difference between **profitability** and **cash generation:** profitability measures the surplus of revenues over expenses, including non-cash items, while cash generation reflects the actual movement of cash in and out of the business, determining its liquidity.

For example, a healthcare startup in the United Kingdom might report **annual revenues** of £500,000 from providing health services, with **expenses** of £400,000 (including staff salaries, equipment, and facility costs). On paper, this results in a **profit** of £100,000. However, if only £300,000 of the revenue was collected in cash during the year (due to delayed payments from clients or insurance providers), while the company paid out £380,000 in cash for expenses, its **cash flow** would be **negative £80,000**, despite being profitable. This shows how cash generation and profitability can diverge, especially in industries like healthcare, where payment delays are common.

Private equity was once described as providing capital to companies that do not have access to traditional capital markets (such as debt capital markets [DCM] and equity capital markets [ECM]).

> ***Debt capital markets*** *(DCM) involve raising funds by issuing bonds, notes and large loans offered to investors, while* ***equity capital markets*** *(ECM) involve raising funds by selling ownership shares in the company to institutional investors and to the wider public.*
>
> *Debt creates a repayment obligation with interest, whereas equity gives investors ownership stakes without requiring repayment. Small or young firms often struggle to access debt capital markets due to limited credit history and higher perceived risk, while equity capital markets can be out of reach because*

these firms may lack the scale, track record, or investor confidence necessary for public listings or significant equity investment.

Hence, private equity is not just about "equity," and it is not necessarily "private" either! Before we can provide a more appropriate definition of private equity, it is important to delve into its history.

1.2 ORIGINS AND HISTORY OF PRIVATE EQUITY

Let's explore the history and origins of private equity. In reality, much of what is considered historical private equity is actually venture capital, i.e., private equity investment in early-stage companies.

The history of private equity dates back centuries, even millennia, evolving alongside the changing needs of entrepreneurs and financiers.

In ancient Persia, India, and China, wealthy individuals, including merchants and aristocrats, often funded trade expeditions and business ventures, much like the early European merchant families. The Silk Road, for instance, was a major network for trade, with financiers backing traders and explorers in the hope of receiving profits from goods transported between China and the rest of the world. These early investments were highly speculative but could yield large rewards, similarly again to a venture capital model.

This pattern of private financing in China continued during the Tang Dynasty (618–907 AD) and later in the Ming Dynasty (1368–1644), when wealthy financiers supported commercial and industrial ventures. The funding, often informal and based on personal relationships, was particularly prominent in industries such as silk, tea, and ceramics. These early forms of financing, though not structured like today's private equity, also shared similarities with modern-day venture capital.

Similar patterns can be observed in medieval Europe, where merchant banks began providing capital for trade expeditions, setting the stage for modern venture investment with more structured financial mechanisms. The Silk Road laid the groundwork for risk-sharing trade models, but structured venture capital as we understand it today—with formalized investments, stock issuance, and equity partnerships—emerged much later in Europe. For example, wealthy families, such as the Medicis in Italy, were early pioneers in the private financing of businesses and trade ventures.

Moving into the late fifteenth century, Queen Isabella of Spain could be considered one of the earliest Western venture capitalists when she financed Christopher Columbus's voyages.[1] By providing capital in the form of money, ships, supplies, and crew, Isabella took on a significant risk to support Columbus's expedition to find a westward route to Asia. Given the widespread belief at the time that the venture would fail, her investment was seen as highly speculative. However, if successful, the rewards—such as control over new trade routes and riches from uncharted territories—would be disproportionately high compared to the initial investment, embodying the high-risk, high-reward nature of venture capital. Spain would ultimately keep nearly 90% of the profits from the successful expeditions.

[1] https://msh.councilforeconed.org/documents/978-1-56183-758-8-activity-lesson-18.pdf.

Fast forward to the eighteenth century, wealthy investors were instrumental in the financing of the Industrial Revolution. For example, Britain's 65-kilometer-long Bridgewater canal, which was inaugurated in 1761, is named after its financier, the Duke of Bridgewater, while the Liverpool and Manchester Railway, dating back to 1830, was funded by a group of merchants and industrialists including George Stephenson. In the early nineteenth century again, the American whaling industry provides another example of a financial structure strikingly similar to modern venture capital.[2] Whaling agents in New Bedford raised capital from wealthy individuals, local merchants, and even small investors much like today's venture capitalists pool funds from limited partners. These agents then financed high-risk whaling voyages, hoping for substantial returns, similar to the way venture capitalists invest in startups. Crew members were compensated through a system of "lays," where they earned a share of the voyage's profits, which is analogous to modern stock options. This method ensured that everyone, from the lowest ranked crew members to the ship's captain, had aligned incentives, fostering a shared interest in the success of the venture. Much like today's entrepreneurs who transition into venture capitalists, successful whaling captains often reinvested their earnings into future voyages, further aligning their interests with the agents and the crews they led. Whaling agents also provided more than just funding; they acted as mentors, guiding captains through the challenges of running high-risk ventures, much like venture capitalists do for startup CEOs today. Though there are differences between the two models, the lay/agent structure of the whaling industry serves as an early precursor to the venture capital system, with its similar dynamics of aligning risk, reward, and leadership for navigating uncertain and potentially lucrative undertakings.

As the Industrial Revolution progressed, the increasing demand for private capital to fund new technologies and businesses led to a rise in private partnerships for financing industrial ventures. By the late nineteenth century, during a period of significant industrial development, wealthy families and individuals, like J.P. Morgan, were investing directly in private companies. This era also saw the rise of "merchant banking,"[3] where banks invested their own capital in businesses.

In the early twentieth century, groups of wealthy investors would create investment syndicates, pooling resources to fund private companies. The 1920s brought the popularity of holding companies, which controlled stakes in other companies, while investment trusts, similar to modern closed-end funds, provided a way for smaller investors to access private investments.

During the Great Depression in the United States, the Securities Act of 1933 and Securities Exchange Act of 1934 were enacted, increasing regulation of public markets. This, in turn, indirectly spurred the development of private investment vehicles. During this time, some investors specialized in buying and reorganizing distressed companies, a practice that can be seen as an early form of "turnaround investing" in private equity.

It is worth noting that the term "private equity" was not used during this period. These historical practices, while distinct from modern private equity in terms of structure, regulation, and scale, laid the foundation for the industry as we know it today.

---

[2] https://nha.org/research/nantucket-history/history-topics/short-lays-on-greasy-voyages-whaling-and-venture-capital.

[3] The topic of merchant banking actually traces back to the Medici family, who established one of Europe's first and most influential banking empires in the fifteenth century.

Before World War II, it was referred to as "development capital" and primarily involved wealthy individuals and families.

The industry as we know it today began to take shape in the aftermath of World War II. Here we list the defining moments in the modern history of private equity:

- In 1946, French General Georges Doriot and his two partners at Harvard created the American Research and Development Corporation (ARDC). It was a pioneering venture capital firm that played a key role in the development of private equity. Unlike previous family-funded investment ventures, ARDC was unique in raising capital from institutional investors and the public, specifically to fund early-stage companies, particularly in technology. ARDC aimed to support the commercialization of innovations, contribute to economic growth in New England, and demonstrate that venture capital could be profitable. Its success, particularly its early investment in Digital Equipment Corporation (DEC), which grew to be a major company, established ARDC as a model for modern venture capital practices, even though it eventually struggled to compete with newer models like the limited partnership.[4]
- Starting in the 1960s, there was a surge in attempts to acquire companies, particularly conglomerates, with the goal of asset stripping. Asset stripping involved selling off the valuable parts of a company while shutting down the less profitable or nonessential segments, thereby unlocking value from the idea that the whole company was worth less than the sum of its individual parts. While this approach generated significant returns for some, it also led to several disastrous outcomes, as the long-term sustainability of the business was often compromised in the pursuit of short-term profits.
- A defining moment occurred in 1968 with the first attempt to raise money on a deal-by-deal basis when funds such as AEA, one of the most prominent private equity firms of its time, began investing alongside founding families in a deal-by-deal investing structure, called AEA Investment Programs.[5] AEA's strategy allowed them to raise capital only when a specific investment opportunity arose, instead of locking in capital for a set fund duration. This flexibility became increasingly popular in the years that followed, particularly after the 2000s credit crisis.
- Founded in 1966, Warburg Pincus was one of the earliest PE firms to raise institutional capital into a committed fund rather than relying solely on deal-by-deal financing. By the 1970s, it had already moved away from the merchant banking tradition of funding one deal at a time, securing capital upfront from investors for multiple investments, focused on growth capital and venture investments, rather than purely LBOs,[6] which would later become the dominant segment of PE.
- In 1974, Thomas H. Lee Partners set up the first dedicated LBO fund, marking a significant development in the private equity landscape. LBOs or leveraged buyouts are acquisitions heavily financed with expensive debt. The firm became

[4] https://kenney.faculty.ucdavis.edu/wp-content/uploads/sites/332/2018/03/Organizing-Venture-Capital_-The-Rise-and-Demise-of-American-Research-and-Development-Corporation.pdf.

[5] https://www.aeainvestors.com/our-history.

[6] A leveraged buyout (LBO) is a transaction where a company is acquired using a higher proportion of debt than would typically be used for such a company, with the expectation that the acquired company's cash flows will service the debt.

highly influential over the next 30 years, pioneering and perfecting the LBO model. This innovative approach allowed Thomas H. Lee Partners to acquire companies with relatively little upfront equity, enabling higher returns on investment. One of the firm's most notable early successes came in the 1980s with the leveraged buyout of Snapple Beverage Corporation. Acquired for $135 million in 1992, Snapple was sold just two years later to Quaker Oats for $1.7 billion, generating a staggering 32 times return on equity. This deal became a landmark in private equity history, solidifying Thomas H. Lee Partners' reputation as a leader in the field.

- In 1978, perhaps the most famous name in the private equity history, Kohlberg Kravis Roberts (KKR), set up the first institutional LBO fund of investor commitments with several insurance companies, pension funds, and other institutional investors pooling their resources together to invest in private equity. This structure provided a more formal and scalable way for private equity to grow, moving further away from the earlier deal-by-deal model.
- The 1970s saw the end of the era of asset stripping. After about 10 years of widespread use, many developed countries began to outlaw asset stripping, making it illegal or at least significantly more difficult to acquire companies solely to liquidate their most valuable assets. This shift forced private equity firms to reconsider their investment strategies, as the focus moved toward long-term value creation rather than short-term profits from dismantling companies.
- In the 1980s, several significant legal developments shaped the landscape of private equity. One key piece of legislation was the introduction of laws related to financial assistance, which allowed for the rescue of viable companies. In the United Kingdom, the 1981 Companies Act required directors to make a statutory declaration stating that, as far as they knew, the company would remain solvent for at least 12 months after the completion of the transaction. If the declaration was knowingly false, it would become a criminal offense. This legal framework becomes particularly relevant in the context of private equity transactions, where the acquiring company often uses the target company's assets as collateral for the acquisition financing. The laws surrounding financial assistance and solvency were crucial in ensuring the integrity of such transactions and protecting both creditors and investors.

ASSET STRIPPING IN HEALTHCARE: A COMPLEX PRACTICE WITH ONGOING IMPACTS ON COMMUNITIES

A notable real-life example of asset stripping in healthcare is the case of **Hahnemann University Hospital** in Philadelphia. In 2018, the hospital was purchased by a private equity firm, Paladin Healthcare, led by Joel Freedman. After acquiring the hospital, the new owners sold the valuable real estate on which the hospital sat, while the hospital itself faced severe financial issues. The stripping of assets, including the sale of the property, contributed to the closure of the

171-year-old hospital in 2019, leaving thousands of healthcare workers without jobs and limiting healthcare services for the local community, particularly for low-income patients. This example has been widely criticized as a case of private equity prioritizing profits over patient care and community health needs. In all fairness, it is not clear what would have happened to the hospital had it not been acquired. The extant debate on the impact of private equity on business and society is particularly vivid in the healthcare sector and will be the subject of Chapter 8.

From then on, the history of private equity can perhaps be better demonstrated through the accelerated development of LBOs, which represent the bulk of private equity in value.

For this we need to go back in time again. Depending on what are considered "true" LBOs, their prehistory arguably goes back to 1919 with Henry Ford's leveraged transaction to regain control of his company, buying out minority shareholders. Other examples include the buyout of UPS by its founder, which occurred during the Great Depression in 1933, or the takeover more than 20 years later of Pan-Atlantic Steamship Company by its management using a publicly traded holding company, McLean Industries, in 1955. We consider the modern LBO to have taken shape in the 1960s and 1970s, with Jerome Kohlberg, and two cousins, Henry Kravis and George Roberts, pioneering the LBO model at Bear Stearns before founding KKR in 1976. KKR launched many of the first modern LBOs including the takeover of Houdaille Corp in 1979. A significant milestone came in 1982 with the buyout by Wesray Capital Corporation, led by US Treasury Secretary William E. Simon and Ray Chambers, of Gibson Greetings, for $80 million, contributing only $1 million in equity and financing the rest through debt. In just 18 months, they took the company public, generating more than $290 million in proceeds. This equated with a 200-time return on their initial equity investment, making it one of the most profitable LBOs of its time. It consequently showcased the potential for high returns and helped popularize the LBO strategy.

In the 1980s, Michael Milken, the famous junk bond king, helped develop that activity further by providing financing to investors. Before Michael Milken's influence, LBOs were primarily funded through traditional bank loans or private equity, limiting them to well-established, low-risk companies. Milken, working at Drexel Burnham Lambert, revolutionized the industry by popularizing the use of high-yield (junk) bonds, allowing companies with lower credit ratings to secure financing in exchange for higher returns to investors. This innovation expanded LBO opportunities to a wider range of highly leveraged, undervalued, or underperforming companies that had previously been overlooked.[7]

The historical takeover of RJR Nabisco by KKR happened in 1989 and would remain the largest LBO for two decades, becoming the subject of the international

[7] Nicholas, T. and Preble, M. G. (2016, rev. 2021). *Michael Milken: The junk bond king.* Harvard Business School Case 816-050.

bestseller book *Barbarians at the Gate*. The RJR Nabisco deal featured an intense bidding war between KKR, the company's management, and other contenders, epitomizing the aggressive tactics of 1980s private equity. It became a public symbol of the excess and risks of LBOs, even earning a *Time Magazine* cover titled "A Game of Greed." Despite its mixed financial outcomes, the deal significantly influenced the private equity industry by demonstrating the viability of large-scale LBOs and solidifying private equity's role in corporate takeovers. It also drew increased scrutiny of the sector, highlighting both the substantial rewards and the inherent risks of highly leveraged acquisitions.[8]

During the 1980s, the junk bond market expanded dramatically, surging from just \$10 billion in 1979 to an astonishing \$189 billion by 1989. In that year, Milken's legal issues, coupled with the growing instability of the junk bond market and associated default rates, provoked the collapse of Drexel Burnham Lambert (Hurduzeu and Popescu, 2015). The US congress ended the ability of savings and loans to invest in lower than investment grade securities, ending the era of junk-bond-driven LBOs.[9]

The modern era of private equity started in the 1990s and was marked by a decisive shift from purely financial engineering toward value creation through operational improvement.[10] One of the emblematic transactions of this era was Bain Capital's 1997 leveraged buyout, with co-investors, of Sealy Corporation, the world's largest bedding manufacturer. The deal, valued at approximately \$300 million, was notable not only for its structure but also for the strategic transformation that followed.

Bain Capital implemented a hands-on operational approach that involved streamlining Sealy's manufacturing footprint, optimizing its distribution channels, and professionalizing its management. Rather than relying solely on financial leverage to generate returns, Bain focused on improving supply chain efficiency and product innovation, helping Sealy regain market leadership. Over the course of the investment, EBITDA increased substantially, driven by margin expansion and cost control, not just revenue growth.

The transaction reflected the broader evolution in private equity toward "operational alpha"—the ability to drive performance through active governance, strategic oversight, and performance monitoring. When Sealy was eventually sold to KKR in 2004 for approximately \$1.5 billion, it delivered strong returns to Bain's investors and set a precedent for later buyouts in the consumer and manufacturing sectors.

This deal exemplified the private equity industry's transition from the high-leverage strategies of the 1980s to a more hands-on, value-creation model that would come to define the asset class in the decades that followed.

[8] Nicholas, T. and Masko, J. (2021). Barbarians at the gate or turnaround gurus? Private equity and the rise of the LBO. Harvard Business School Case 821-016.

[9] H.R.1278—Financial Institutions Reform, Recovery, and Enforcement Act of 1989. https://www.congress.gov/bill/101st-congress/house-bill/1278/text.

[10] Capital Dynamics & Center for Entrepreneurial and Financial Studies (CEFS), Technische Universität München (2009). "Value Creation in Private Equity."

The turn of the millennium ushered in the mega-buyout era, with deals like the $33 billion acquisition of HCA in 2006 by Bain Capital, KKR, and Merrill Lynch setting new records. The 2007 buyout of TXU (Energy Future Holdings) for $45 billion by KKR, TPG, and Goldman Sachs Capital Partners marked the peak of this trend. The 2008 financial crisis temporarily halted mega LBO activity, but the industry's resilience was proven by deals like the $27 billion Heinz buyout in 2013 by 3G Capital and Berkshire Hathaway. Post-crisis, new strategies emerged, such as the $67 billion acquisition of EMC by Dell and Silver Lake in 2015, blurring the lines between strategic and financial buyers.

These mega deals resulted from a combination of macroeconomic and industry-specific forces. Key drivers included low interest rates making debt financing cheaper, abundant private equity and corporate cash reserves, slow economic growth pushing firms to seek inorganic growth, high levels of competition, strategic attempts at consolidation, tax arbitrage opportunities, and the search for innovation. Companies facing weak demand and limited organic growth looked to large acquisitions for scale, efficiency, and access to new markets. We will discuss more recent developments in Chapter 10.

In Europe, private equity truly took off in the early 1980s, initially fueling the rise of venture capital. This was followed by the emergence of dedicated buyout funds in the 1990s, which later led to increasing sector specialization and market consolidation by the mid-1990s. The next phase was characterized by rapid globalization, a trend that continued until the initial disruptions brought by the COVID-19 pandemic.

It is interesting to note how private equity has expanded significantly over time. We have already discussed this in part, but a good metric to illustrate the growth of the private equity sector is the number of participants in the sector.

The evolution of the members of Invest Europe (formerly the European Venture Capital Association) sheds light on how the private equity industry has evolved in Europe. Private equity has matured over a period of about 25 years during which the number of participants went from 37 in 1983 to more than 600 in 2008, a number that has remained stable since then (although the balance has shifted from venture capital to private equity).

Taking these historical developments into perspective, it appears that as for other areas in finance such as mergers and acquisitions or venture capital, private equity experiences cycles. To illustrate, we propose five phases to understand the evolution of private equity in modern history (Figure 1.1). Note that each of the last four phases lasts approximately 10 years:

- 1946–1981: Setting the scene of modern private equity
- 1982–1992: First boom and bust cycle
- 1993–2002: Technology boom and bust. Separation of venture capital and LBO segments
- 2003–2012: Credit boom and bust, hangover
- 2013–2022: Buildup of *dry powder* and integration of private capital

The sixth phase, which likely started in 2022, will be discussed in the last chapter.

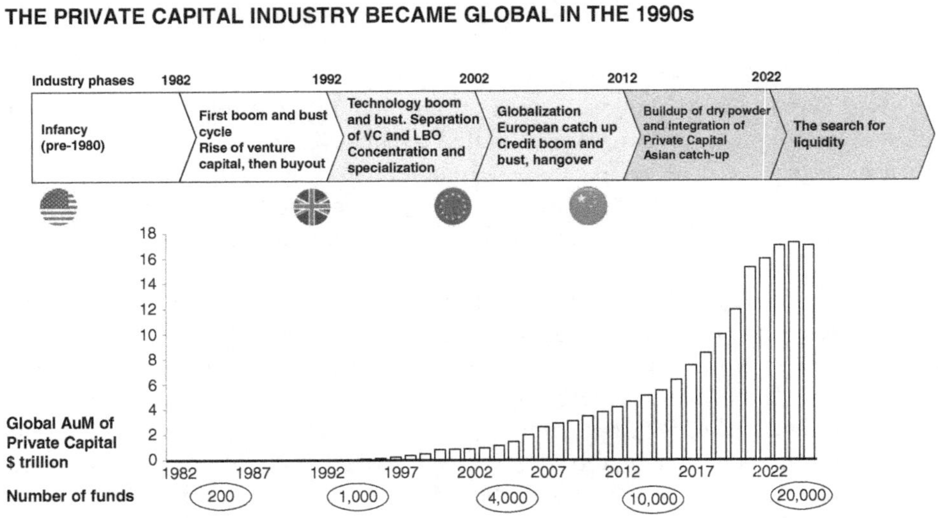

FIGURE 1.1 History of private capital.
Source: Authors' research.

1.3 DEFINITIONS AND SEGMENTATIONS

While **formal private equity (PE) is** a segment that is well documented with thousands of firms accounting for most industry statistics, the **informal segment** of investments financed by family members and/or business angels, is difficult to track as there is no official reporting. The distinction between the two is increasingly difficult to track with easier access to technology and the professionalization of many informal players. In venture capital, which we will define later, there is now a significant quasi formal segment of early-stage investors: super angels, angel clubs, and family offices.

We consider five main approaches to PE segmentation that can help us better understand what PE is about.

1.3.1 By Stages of Financing

Figure 1.2 illustrates the company life cycle that usually ranges from a startup phase to a stable, slower growth, mature position in the market. We distinguish between a private capital first phase and a subsequent capital markets one. Although most companies never go public and some private companies issue bonds (debt securities), the usual path of development is such that, traditionally, most successful companies, i.e., reaching a significant market value, would opt to sell some of their shares in a stock exchange through an initial public offering (IPO) and get continuous access to capital markets.

Within private capital, it is important to distinguish between the initial stages and the subsequent stages of principal investing (see Figure 1.3). Note that the expression *principal investing* has been—mostly—gradually replaced with *private equity*. They do overlap, but venture capital starts from a very early stage, with seed capital, and then goes on to the first, second, and third stages, also called Series A, B, C …, and sometimes include bridge capital. These stages are relevant to companies that start being merely an idea on paper, or startups, which may create revenue and ultimately become profitable.

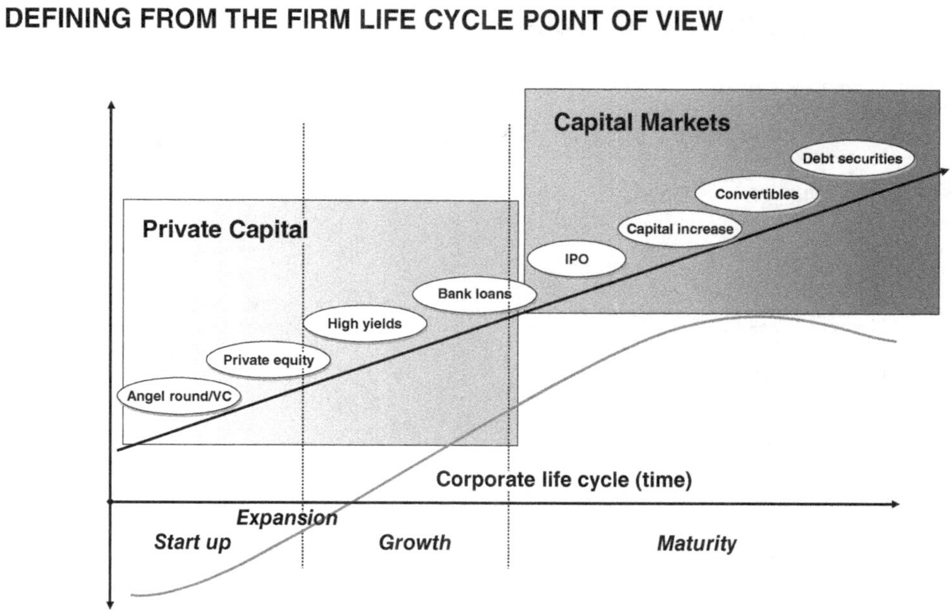

FIGURE 1.2 Financing stages from firm life cycle point of view.
Source: Adapted from Paul Achleitner in Frank Bancel—Investment Banking—January 2004.

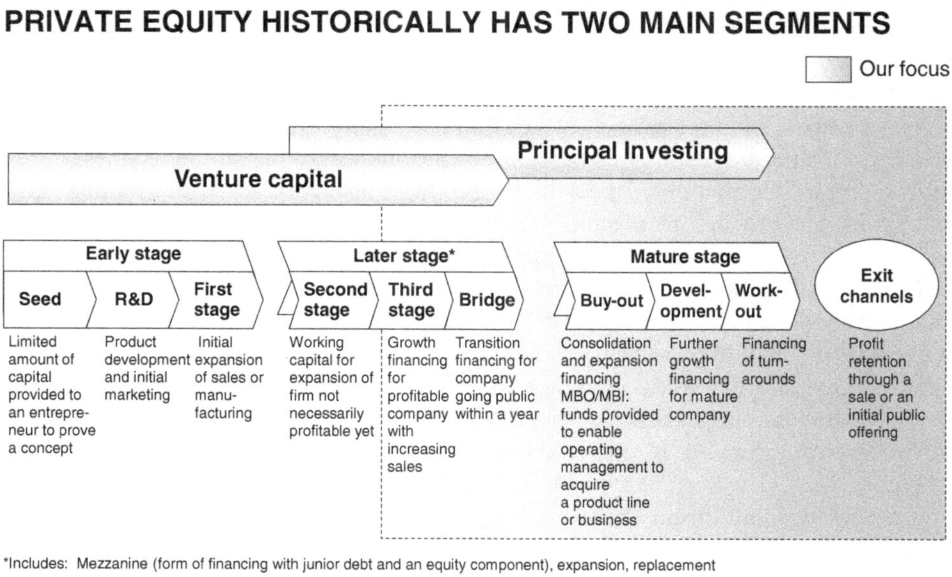

FIGURE 1.3 Venture capital vs. principal investing.
Source: Candesic analysis.

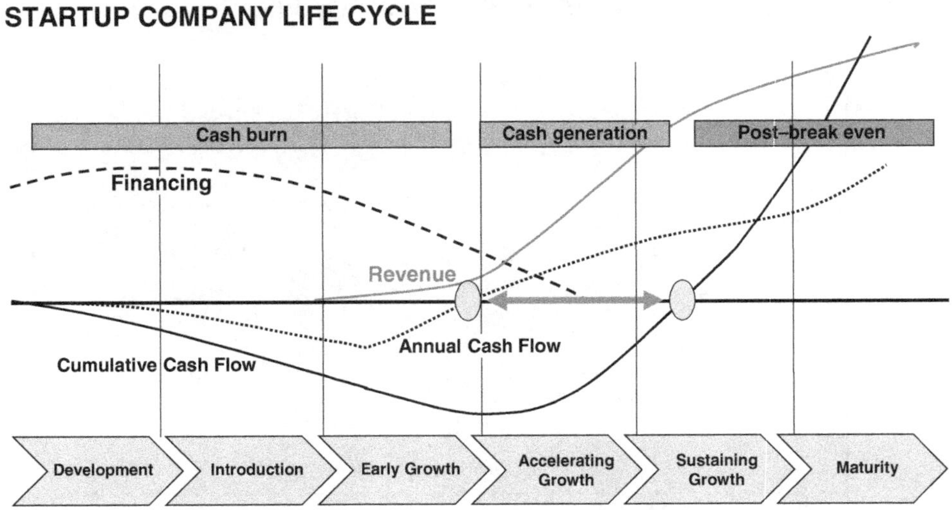

FIGURE 1.4 Startup company life cycle.

Figure 1.4 focuses on the early stages of a company's life cycle, from inception to maturity. We distinguish **revenues**, as the total income from sales in a given year, **cash flow** as the net movement of cash in and out of the business in a given year, and **cumulative cash flows** as the overall total of these net cash movements accumulated over time. When mapping the evolution of revenue and cash flows, we identify some key moments. The first one is when the annual cash flow turns positive, marking the transition from cash burn to cash generation. The second one is when the cumulated cash flows turn positive, sort of making it break even. The distance between the two points is a period of accelerating growth that is critical to the success and value of the company. This period demonstrates the viability and scalability of the business model. Many successful companies, especially in technology sectors, go through longer periods of high growth before reaching cumulative positive cash flows. They prioritize scaling and market dominance over early profitability.

Principal investing, however, is relevant to companies that are at later stages (sustaining growth to maturity), ultimately called growth capital. These companies are expected to be profitable and they may reach a more mature stage that may lead to a buyout—often an LBO—but also some other forms of development capital, as well as the very particular stage known as the work-out, which means financing with private equity companies that are in financial difficulty.

Figure 1.5 illustrates the typical rounds of financing associated with each phase of development from inception to maturity, associating an indicative expected return (the IRR or internal rate of return) to each phase. The IRR, which is certainly the most common performance measure in private equity, represents the discount rate that an investor would apply to the free cash flows. Note this describes mostly the rounds of financing in venture capital (VC) but is essential to understand the relationship between business maturity and return expectations.

In simple terms, a **discount rate** is used to estimate how much future money is worth today. When investing in a startup, in particular in healthcare, the future can be particularly uncertain, and a discount rate is used to estimate the value of potential future earnings in today's terms.

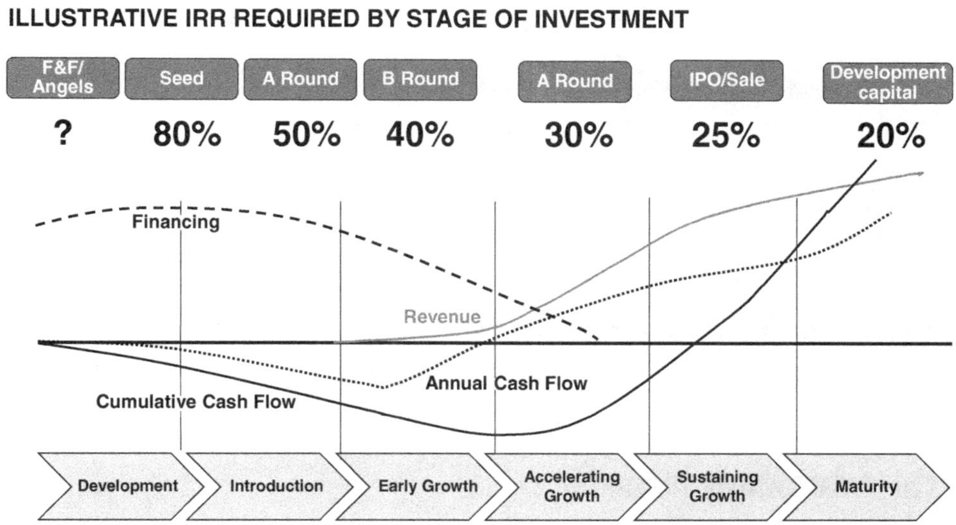

FIGURE 1.5 Illustrative IRR required by stage of investment from early stage.

Different phases of a company's growth, such as early development and product testing (development) or market launch (introduction), are associated with different risks so the discount rate changes across phases. Early on, when the startup is merely an idea, the discount rate is higher because the risk is higher—there is a bigger chance the company will not succeed. As the company evolves toward later stages and becomes more stable, the discount rate becomes lower because the risk decreases and future earnings are less uncertain.

The internal rate of return or **IRR** attempts to measure the profitability of an investment, with some limitations that we will develop in Chapter 3. It is the discount rate at which the present value of future cash flows from the investment equals the amount of money initially invested. In other words, the IRR is the break-even discount rate, and investors use it to evaluate whether an investment will be profitable—if the IRR is higher than the required discount rate, the investment is likely to be a good one. However, as we will explain later, it is not the return on investment.

You are considering investing in the development of a new drug that requires an initial investment of $10,000. The project is expected to generate annual cash inflows of $2,500 for 10 years from the sale of the drug.

- **Initial Investment** (Year 0): –$10,000
- **Annual Cash Inflows** (Years 1–10): +$2,500 each year

STEP 1: USING THE DISCOUNT RATE

You set your required rate of return, or **discount rate**, at 10%, which reflects the risk of investing in drug development and your cost of capital.

(*Continued*)

(Continued)

To calculate the **net present value (NPV)** at this discount rate, you discount each of the annual cash inflows back to the present value:

$$NPV = \sum_{t=1}^{10} \frac{2{,}500}{(1 + 0.10)^t} - 10{,}000$$

After calculating the discounted cash flows for each year and summing them up:

- **NPV at a 10% discount rate** ≈ $5,361

Since the NPV is positive, the project is expected to generate more than your required 10% return, making it an attractive investment based on your criteria.

STEP 2: CALCULATING THE IRR

The **IRR** is the rate that makes the NPV of the project equal to zero. This is found by solving for the rate that satisfies the following equation:

$$NPV = \sum_{t=1}^{10} \frac{2{,}500}{(1 + IRR)^t} - 10{,}000 = 0$$

Using a financial calculator or Excel, we find that the **IRR** for this project is approximately **21.4%**.

Interpretation:

- The **discount rate** of 10% represents your required return for investing in the new drug. Since the NPV at this rate is positive ($5,361), the project is expected to meet your required return and add value.
- The **IRR** of 21.4% indicates that the project is expected to generate an annual return of 21.4%, which is significantly higher than your required 10%. This makes the project even more attractive.

In summary:

- Your **discount rate** (10%) is a benchmark for deciding if the investment is worth pursuing.
- The **IRR** (21.4%) shows a possible actual return on the project, which is higher than your required rate, suggesting that the investment in the drug development project is financially sound. Note that it generously assumes that you can reinvest all intermediary cash flows at this rate, which can be a misleading assumption in some cases. We will discuss this important point later.

The discount rate varies with market conditions and company specificities. The earlier and less proven the business opportunity, the higher the risk associated with the future cash flows and the lower the net present value. A pre-seed company that plans to IPO in 10 years at a valuation of, say, $100 million, may be worth surprisingly little. The present value of the business when applying a rather fair discount rate of 80% is a mere $280,000. Raising millions of dollars on that basis is highly unlikely.

1.3.2 By Asset Class Differentiation

Many investors hold primarily traditional asset classes such as stocks and bonds. PE (and VC) investments belong to the segment of "traditional alternative investments," together with real estate and commodities. Other alternatives include hedge funds, infrastructures, and digital assets. Refer to Figure 1.6.

Alternative investments differ significantly from traditional investments—public equity, bonds, and cash equivalents—in terms of asset types, liquidity, risk-return profiles, regulatory oversight, and accessibility. Traditional investments are widely accessible, highly liquid, and subject to strict regulatory and transparency requirements. These factors provide investors with clear insights into potential risks and returns.

In contrast, alternative investments encompass a diverse range of assets, including private equity (and venture capital), real estate, commodities, and hedge funds (and more recently, cryptocurrencies, with total capitalization of around $4 trillion at the time of writing). These investments are often **illiquid**, requiring long holding periods with limited opportunities for early exit. While they are expected to offer the potential for **higher returns**, they also come with **greater risk and return volatility** due to their complex structures and exposure to less conventional markets. Additionally, alternative investments are typically subject to **less regulation and transparency**, making risk assessment more challenging.

Access to these investments is generally **restricted** to accredited—mostly high net worth individuals and families—investors or institutions with substantial capital, limiting participation from retail investors. Despite these challenges, alternative investments play a crucial role in **portfolio diversification**, offering opportunities for **enhanced growth** and acting as a hedge against market volatility.

1.3.3 By Acquisition Motives

Barber and Goold (2007) proposed an intriguing framework (Figure 1.7), mapping the intention (keep or sell) against the nature of the involvement in the target company (from investing passively to investing to influence and build synergies). This allows us

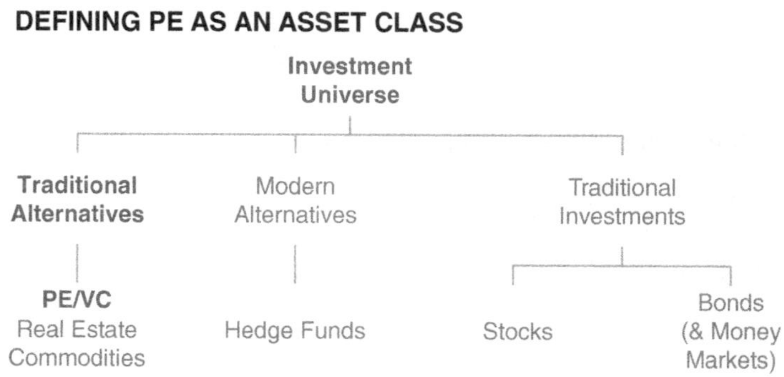

FIGURE 1.6 Asset classes.

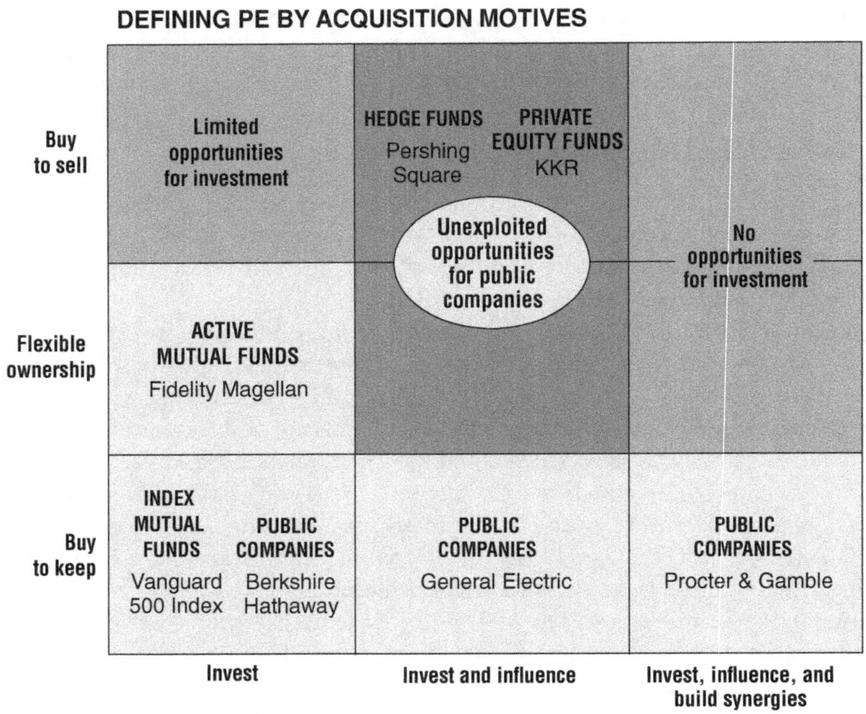

FIGURE 1.7 Influence vs. intent.
Source: HBR, the strategic secret of private equity, by Felix Barber and Michael Goold (2007)

to position different types of investors in their specific position, with private equity at the intersection of "*buying to sell*" and "*investing to influence*."

While hedge funds appear adjacent to private equity funds in Barber and Goold's segmentation, this proximity primarily applies to activist hedge funds, which may seek to influence management or strategy. However, the majority of hedge funds—including macro, quantitative, and arbitrage funds—tend to invest passively, diversify across many assets, and focus on capitalizing on market movements or inefficiencies rather than engaging directly with company operations. Even activist hedge funds, while sometimes influential, rarely become as operationally involved as private equity sponsors, whose value creation is rooted in hands-on management and long-term transformation. Moreover, for obvious liquidity reasons, they tend to invest in listed companies. First Light Asset Management is an example of such a healthcare specialist hedge fund investor.

1.3.4 By Characteristics of the Investment Vehicle

As we will establish later, private equity funds are set up in a very specific way that distinguishes them from mutual funds, hedge funds, and most other specialist funds. We identify four main characteristics of a direct private equity fund:[11]

[11] As opposed to funds of funds and secondary funds.

- The fund serves as a financial intermediary, directly investing capital into companies that become **portfolio companies (PortCos).**
- It exclusively invests in private companies or acquires public companies with the intention of immediately privatizing them.
- The fund takes an active role in overseeing and providing support to the PortCos.
- Its main objective is to optimize investor returns through either selling the invested companies or guiding them through an IPO process.

1.3.5 By Investment Constraints

A discussion we regularly hold in our classes consists of asking which type of investor invests in which asset class and why. To that end it is helpful to list all types of investors, institutional and retail. A possible list includes the following:

- Insurance companies
- Pension funds
- Endowments and foundations
- Corporates
- Mutual funds
- Other institutional asset managers
- Family offices
- Sovereign funds
- Funds of funds
- HNWI (high net worth individuals)
- Retail investors
- Central banks

The next step is to list common investment constraints:

- Regulatory and ethical constraints
- Access or control
- Return (level and nature)
- Risk profile
- Diversification (hence risk reduction)
- Liquidity
- Timing of payouts

Finally, we can match investors and investments for each type of constraint (Figure 1.8)

- Regulatory and ethical constraints (e.g., tobacco, weapons, gambling, North Korea …) will affect all investors in various combinations
- Control: Corporate M&A, sometimes a HNWI who wants to be a decision-maker
- Return: Family offices and endowments tend to look for absolute returns
- Risk profile: Retail investors may need to protect their capital
- Liquidity: Mutual funds in particular may face large immediate redemptions
- Timing of payouts: Insurance companies want reserves of non-taxed profits …

SENSITIVITY TO CONSTRAINTS BY TYPE OF INVESTOR

	Sensitivity to constraints						
Investors	Regulatory & Ethical Constraints	Access or Control	Return (Level & Nature)	Risk Profile	Diversification (Risk Reduction)	Liquidity	Timing of Payouts
Insurance	High	Medium	Medium	High	High	High	High
Pension Funds	High	Low	High	High	High	Medium	Medium
Endowments	High	Low	High	High	High	Medium	Medium
Corporates	High	High	Medium	Medium	High	Medium	Low
Mutual Funds	High	Low	High	Medium	High	High	Low
Other Institutional	High	Low	High	Medium	High	Medium	Low
Family Offices	Medium	High	High	Medium	Medium	Low	Medium
Sovereign Funds	High	Medium	Medium	Medium	High	Low	Low
Funds of Funds	Medium	Low	High	Medium	High	Medium	Low
HNWI	Medium	High	High	Medium	Medium	Low	Low
Retail Investors	Medium	Low	Medium	High	Medium	High	Low
Central Banks	High	Low	Low	Low	Medium	High	Low

FIGURE 1.8 Mapping investors constraints.
Source: Candesic analysis

What does PE offer to investors with regard to these constraints? This will be the subject of the next chapters, but it will not be a surprise that PE investment is first and foremost defined by its lack of liquidity.

1.3.6 By Relationship to Liquidity

Many investors view private equity investment as an opportunity to seek superior returns, as discussed earlier, and to diversify from public equity markets. While private equity does provide diversification benefits, some sectors, e.g., infrastructures, offer lower correlation with stock markets than others, especially in well-developed markets. For all the previous investor types, PE offers access to investments not easily accessible through public equity markets. That can be the case, for example, because the number of—and the industry diversification among—listed firms in Western countries has declined significantly in the past decades, or because the number of listed firms is limited, e.g., in emerging markets. As the highly regulated IPO process and stringent information disclosure requirements in public markets have pushed the cost of being public higher, firms tend to be increasingly funded by private equity and tend to go public at later stages of their development than a few decades ago. Institutions such as insurance companies, pension funds, and endowment companies face regulatory constraints inherent to their needs to invest to meet current and future liabilities. For example, while early researchers such as Black (1991) pointed out that pension funds had to invest in fixed income to take advantage of their tax exemption, it is now well established that they need to invest in public and private equity that are correlated with wage growth in the long run (Lucas and Zeldes, 2006; Atanasova and Chemla, 2026).

Another way of understanding private equity is that it involves sacrificing liquidity, which selects investors who are patient, informed, and able to bear the risks associated with information risk—where one party, typically the seller, has more or better information than the buyer (investor) (Lerner and Schoar, 2004). As pointed out by Kaplan and Stromberg (2003, 2009), PE contracts design cash flow, control, and liquidation rights so that control rights vest as information is revealed. By sacrificing liquidity, PE firms engage in deep due diligence and develop long-term relationships with the companies they invest in (Gompers and Lerner, 2001). The illiquid nature of PE gives investors the time to conduct thorough investigations into the company's operations, finances, and market position, thereby reducing the information asymmetry. They may gain access to internal data, meet with management frequently, and even take active roles in shaping the company's strategy. This intensive involvement helps PE firms gather better information, monitor the company more closely, and ultimately make more informed investment decisions. This also implies that they should expect an illiquidity premium. Although this leads us directly to the intricacies of performance measure in private equity, there is some evidence of such an illiquidity premium (Franzoni et al., 2012), although the presence of non-monetary benefits, e.g. for informal private equity investments, can also challenge this view (Moskowitz and Vissing-Jorgensen, 2002).

In the healthcare sector, private equity firms often face significant information asymmetry due to the complex nature of medical technologies, regulatory landscapes, and market dynamics. Here is a specific example illustrating how a private equity firm might sacrifice liquidity to solve information asymmetry in a healthcare context.

SCENARIO: INVESTMENT IN A BIOTECH COMPANY

Company Background: Consider "BioInnovate," a biotech company that specializes in developing gene therapies for rare genetic disorders. BioInnovate has developed a promising new therapy that has shown potential in early-stage clinical trials but needs substantial funding to proceed through the costly and lengthy process of late-stage clinical trials and regulatory approvals.

Private Equity Firm: "HealthVenture Capital" is a private equity firm with a focus on innovative healthcare solutions. HealthVenture recognizes the potential in BioInnovate's new therapy but understands the risks associated with the biotech field, particularly the regulatory hurdles and the scientific validity of the treatments in larger, diverse populations.

SOLVING INFORMATION ASYMMETRY THROUGH STRATEGIC INVESTMENT

Due Diligence and Expert Engagement: HealthVenture Capital conducts extensive due diligence, involving scientific experts who assess the validity and reproducibility of the clinical trial results. They also engage regulatory consultants to evaluate the likelihood of obtaining FDA approval.

Equity Investment and Board Involvement: To mitigate the information asymmetry, HealthVenture decides to invest a significant amount of capital in exchange for a major equity stake in BioInnovate. This investment includes conditions that allow HealthVenture to place its members on BioInnovate's board of directors. This board involvement ensures HealthVenture has a say in strategic decisions, closer oversight of the operational progress, and better access to internal data.

(*Continued*)

(*Continued*)

SACRIFICING LIQUIDITY

Capital Lock-up: The investment in BioInnovate is highly illiquid. HealthVenture's capital is locked up in the biotech firm, with no easy or immediate exit strategy. The funds are committed through the various stages of clinical trials, which can take several years, and until a liquidity event such as an IPO or acquisition by a pharmaceutical giant occurs.

POTENTIAL OUTCOMES

Successful Therapy Launch: If BioInnovate's therapy successfully passes through clinical trials and receives FDA approval, its value could skyrocket. HealthVenture might see a significant return on investment during an IPO or acquisition, rewarding their patience and risk.

Regulatory or Clinical Failure: If the therapy fails to meet clinical efficacy or safety standards or does not receive regulatory approval or is outperformed in the market by a superior product, HealthVenture could face substantial financial losses. This risk is inherent in biotech investments and represents the trade-off for the potential high rewards.

Conclusion: In this healthcare example, HealthVenture Capital sacrifices liquidity to address the information asymmetry by gaining an insider's perspective through board involvement and direct influence over BioInnovate's operations. This strategic placement helps it manage the risks associated with the high-stake biotech investment, aligning its interests closely with the success of BioInnovate, and leveraging its expertise to guide the company toward achieving regulatory and commercial milestones. This is a common approach in healthcare private equity, reflecting a balance between high risk and potentially high returns in a sector where outcomes are highly uncertain but can be transformationally profitable.

Thinking about which businesses need private equity provides additional insight into the nature of the industry. As mentioned by BVCA, "*many small companies are 'lifestyle' businesses whose purpose is to provide a good standard of living and job satisfaction for their owners. These businesses are not generally suitable for private equity investment as they are unlikely to provide the potential growth and financial returns to make them interesting to an external investor.*" We agree with this statement with three caveats:

First, a business with limited growth opportunities can still provide a platform for operational and financial engineering with value creation opportunity, it is a question of buying it at the right price. Second, many less attractive stand-alone businesses become appropriate if they bring synergies to an existing portfolio company. Third, the new owner may be able to create the conditions for value creation. This may happen, for example, in some "take-privates," when acquiring a listed company that is underperforming.

As many other financiers, PE investors are constantly looking to create value, including by being at the forefront of financial innovation. This may include, for example, financing projects through securitization, the issuance of tradable securities granting their holders cash flow rights attached to pooled illiquid assets, or investing in innovative projects co-funded or previously successfully funded on crowdfunding platforms. Chapters 6 and 7 will describe these innovative forms of financing in greater detail.

1.3.7 Private Markets and Private Capital

1.3.7.1 Private Capital: A New Name for the Industry? Private credit has recently emerged as another significant segment of formal activity, with $3 trillion AuM by 2025. David Rubenstein, cofounder of the Carlyle Group, was among the first to acknowledge the expanding landscape of private investments beyond traditional private equity. He has highlighted the significant opportunities presented by noninstitutional and private wealth capital pools, describing them as "gigantic." This perspective aligns with the industry's broader shift toward embracing the term "private capital," which encompasses a range of investment strategies, including private equity, venture capital, private credit, real estate, and infrastructure.

1.3.7.2 The Diverging Paths of Private Markets: Traditional Enterprises and Technologically Enabled Capital Markets The term "private markets" has historically referred to a wide range of economic activity outside the scope of public exchanges, from family-owned businesses and informal lending to sophisticated private equity vehicles and institutional alternative asset platforms. However, this broad label increasingly obscures an important structural divergence. As private capital markets mature and absorb new technologies, a fork is emerging: one branch will remain resolutely traditional, relationship-based, and illiquid; the other will evolve rapidly toward greater standardization, accessibility, and market-like liquidity. It is the "private capital" universe we have introduced here.

At one end of the spectrum lies traditional private markets, including many family-owned healthcare businesses such as local clinics, specialist practices, and regional long-term care operators. These entities rely heavily on personal relationships, historical ownership, and reinvested earnings. Their capital structures are simple, and their legal and reporting frameworks are not designed for external scrutiny or fluid investment. While some have started using digital tools to improve operations—such as electronic medical records or cloud-based payroll systems—these technological advances rarely translate into greater participation in formal capital markets. For these businesses, illiquidity is often deliberate, preserving control and community ties. They typically remain outside the reach of professional private equity except in cases of consolidation or generational transition.

In contrast, sophisticated private capital markets—which include private equity, private debt, infrastructure funds, and the secondary markets that support them—are on a clear path toward partial convergence with public market dynamics. This trajectory is being driven by three forces: the institutionalization of capital, the digitization of assets, and the rising demand for liquidity among both asset owners and allocators. In the healthcare sector, for example, large private equity-backed hospital groups, diagnostics chains, health IT platforms, and biopharma services are increasingly structured with levels of financial and operational transparency that resemble publicly listed firms. Fund administrators, data providers, and regulatory bodies are progressively imposing frameworks that facilitate valuation, benchmarking, and risk management, all of which are prerequisites for liquidity.

Technological advances—particularly in tokenization, blockchain-based registries, AI-enhanced due diligence, and digitally native secondary trading platforms—are enabling a transformation in how private assets are issued, owned, and exchanged. These tools promise to reduce friction in capital formation, enhance price discovery, and allow for fractional ownership that could bring in a broader range of investors. In this sense, private capital markets are converging with public markets not in governance or regulation, but in function: capital becomes more mobile, pricing becomes more responsive, and information becomes more accessible.

However, this convergence is neither total nor inevitable. Structural barriers remain that limit the extent to which private markets—even technologically advanced ones—can mimic the full liquidity of public markets. For instance, the underlying assets in PE remain illiquid: hospitals, clinics, life sciences service firms, and even healthtech platforms are not easily bought or sold without considerable transaction costs, operational disruption, and in some cases regulatory approvals. Even where tokenization is feasible, the lack of homogeneous assets and the complexity of underwriting in healthcare make continuous pricing and real-time trading difficult to sustain. Moreover, legal frameworks governing investor protections, disclosures, and fiduciary responsibilities in private markets are still fundamentally different from those of public exchanges, and for good reason. Investors in PE remain exposed to higher risk and lower liquidity, and this asymmetry cannot be fully mitigated by technology alone.

In sum, the future of private markets in healthcare will not be uniform. A meaningful subset—those aligned with institutional capital and technological infrastructure—will *likely* increasingly exhibit characteristics associated with public markets, including faster capital rotation, broader access, and more responsive pricing. Others will remain deeply rooted in traditional private ownership structures, with capital flows defined by trust, local knowledge, and long-term control rather than market mechanisms. Understanding this bifurcation will help assess both the opportunities and the constraints in the evolving financial landscape of healthcare.

1.4 GP AND LP

PE investments are typically made through an investment fund organized as a limited partnership. In this structure, the general partner (GP)—also known as the investment manager—is responsible for managing the fund and investing capital on behalf of the limited partners (LPs). Common LPs include pension funds, life insurance companies, funds of funds, and high-net-worth individuals or families. Historically, pension funds account for just under half of the total capital committed to these funds. The next largest contributors are financial institutions and endowments/foundations, each comprising approximately one-sixth of the overall capital. The balance of capital is provided by individuals, families, and corporations, whose investment activity tends to fluctuate more than that of other investor groups.

Managers use operational improvement, synergies, and/or leverage to create profit. LPs are not actively involved and receive a percentage of the profits. GPs receive compensation in two main forms: an **annual management fee**, typically set at approximately 2% of committed capital, and a share of the realized investment gains, known as **carried interest** or **carry**. This carried interest usually amounts to 20% of the profits, provided that returns exceed a predefined **hurdle rate**. Figure 1.9 provides a simplified

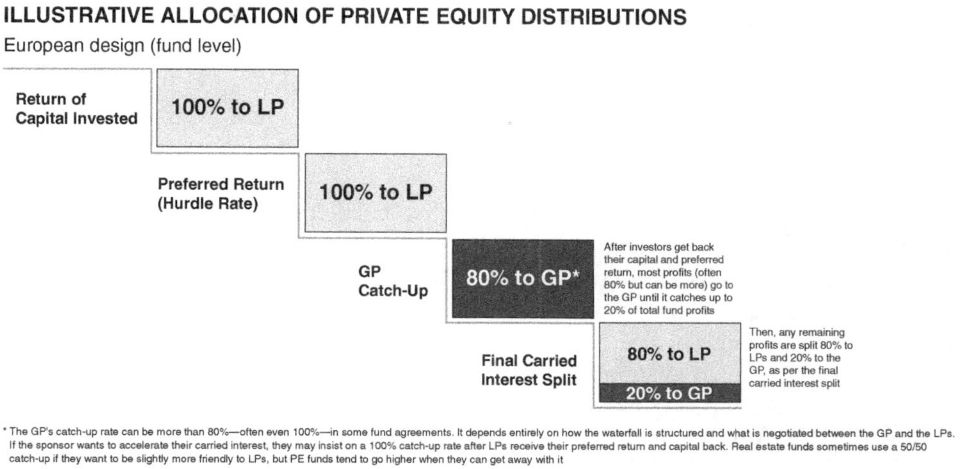

FIGURE 1.9 Simple European waterfall.
Source: Candesic analysis.

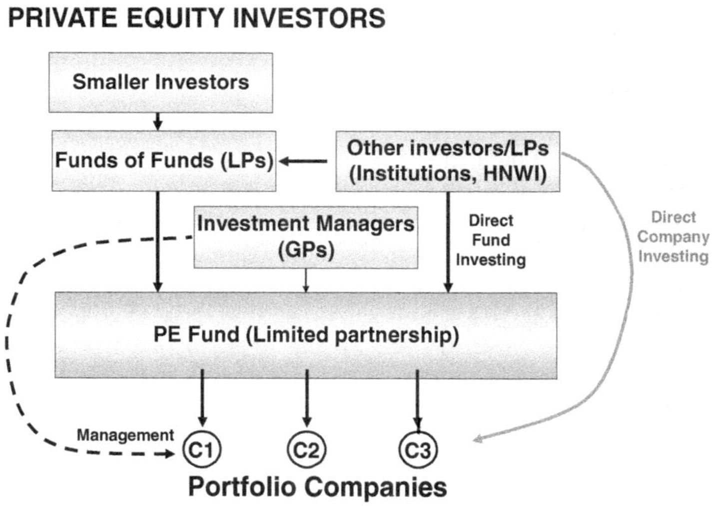

FIGURE 1.10 Investors in PE.

view of the allocation of the profits between GPs and LPs, in a European waterfall allocating at fund level. These concepts will be explored in greater detail in subsequent sections.

LPs invest in the fund with committed capital, which the GP then draws down as needed to make investments. Returns to the LPs are distributed proportionally as they are realized, typically following a liquidity event or exit, such as a trade sale or an IPO. Distributions to the LPs include the original purchase cost plus the gains net of the carry, so typically 80% of the gains.

Figure 1.10 shows the different types of investors and partners who are involved. Numerous stakeholders interact with the investment managers. The GPs manage the

PE fund, which is itself invested in several portfolio companies, sometimes directly, sometimes partially. GPs invest the money of various interested investors and sometimes invite them to invest directly into the portfolio companies too.

At Eckuity Capital for example, LPs benefit from guaranteed co-investment capacity across all portfolio companies, on a no-fee, *pari passu* basis with their fund commitments.

While access may vary slightly depending on participation timing or check size, they make every effort to ensure equitable and consistent participation—especially when the fund reaches its 10% concentration threshold and cannot allocate more capital. This structure has become a cornerstone of their LP relationships, aligning interests and reinforcing transparency.

THE CANADIAN MODEL

Canadian pension funds are globally distinctive because they can invest directly in private markets (Chemla, 2004a)—an ability that sets them apart from most US pension funds, which generally rely on external asset managers or fund investments. This approach, known as the "Canadian model," allows major funds such as CPP Investments, CDPQ, and Ontario Teachers' to act more like PE firms, deploying large pools of patient capital directly into assets like infrastructure, real estate, and private equity deals.

Their structure combines internal investment teams, independent governance, and long-term funding horizons, enabling them to build in-house expertise and bypass the high fees associated with traditional private equity partnerships. This combination of autonomy and scale has made Canada's "Maple Eight" pension funds some of the world's most sophisticated institutional investors—effectively operating hybrid models that bridge public pension management and PE investing (World Bank, 2017).

Lastly, it is important to be familiar with the main metrics and industry statistics used to measure and evaluate the performance of private equity firms. The three main metrics relate to fundraising, activity, and assets under management. Within fundraising, we need to distinguish between two key terms: commitments versus called-up capital. When talking about activities, we'll distinguish between deals, investments, and exits. And when talking about assets under management (AuM), we should understand the difference between unrealized value and "dry powder" versus distributed capital.

The **unrealized value** represents the portion of the fund's investments that have not yet been exited (sold or liquidated). This value is based on the current valuation of these investments, but no actual returns have been realized. It is subject to change until the investments are liquidated. The **dry powder** refers to the capital reserves that a private equity firm has raised but has not yet invested. Essentially, it is unallocated capital that is available to fund new investments or follow-on investments in existing portfolio companies. **Distributed capital** represents the cash or profits that a private equity firm has returned to its investors after exiting investments. This is the portion of capital that has been realized and paid out to investors, typically in the form of distributions or dividends.

1.5 THE PE CYCLE

We now introduce the PE cycle: fundraising, investing, and exiting to return the capital invested (Figure 1.11). In today's environment, PE fund managers continuously consider all three phases as part of their strategy.

In the realm of philosophy, the meaning of life has often been described as the ability to fully appreciate three dimensions of experience: the anticipation of future joy, the enjoyment of the present moment, and the recollection of past happiness. True fulfilment, it is argued, lies in holding these three experiences in dynamic tension, each enriching the other—not merely enduring them in a linear sequence, but savoring them simultaneously.

This model, oddly enough, bears a striking resemblance to the rhythms of PE.

At first glance, PE may appear to be a straightforward sequence where one first, raises a fund (anticipation), then invests the capital raised (enjoyment), and then exit investments and distribute returns (fond memory with some IRR manipulation for good measure). But as any seasoned practitioner will confirm, PE life is far from linear. It is cyclical, overlapping, and best appreciated when all phases are considered in tandem.

To illustrate, **fundraising** is the hopeful stage—the equivalent of dreaming about a perfect future holiday while sitting in a rainy office. A PE firm tells a compelling story of its investment philosophy, team cohesion, and track record, all designed to awaken a sense of anticipation in LPs. The mood is optimistic, forward-looking, and often painted in the soft-focus glow of past successes. Yet good fundraising is not just about the future; it requires tangible signs of present competence and reassuring echoes of past wisdom.

Next, **investing**—the present-tense action—is the thrill of doing deals, supporting portfolio companies, deploying capital with strategic flair, hopefully not overpaying. If fundraising is the dream of the meal, investing is the dinner itself. But beware: just as overeating at a banquet leads to indigestion, reckless investing leads to subpar returns and awkward investor updates. Successful GPs are those who remain mindful of the exit even as they take their first bite. They invest not simply for today's returns, but with an eye toward tomorrow's value creation.

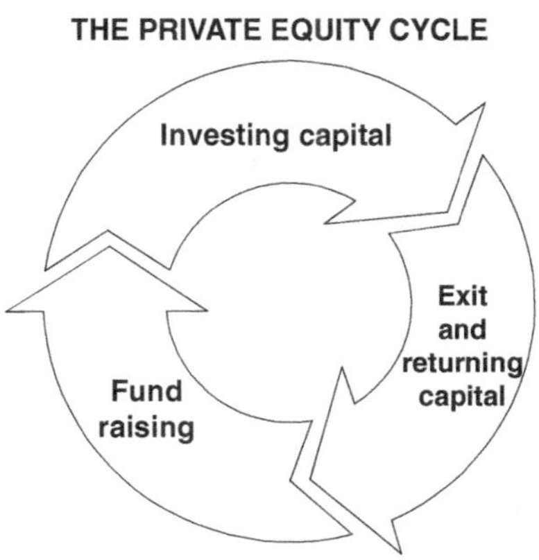

FIGURE 1.11 The PE cycle.

Finally, when **exiting**—the reflective phase—memories are monetized. The GP looks back on the journey with a mix of nostalgia and spreadsheet precision, crafting narratives for the investment committee and IR deck alike. This is the time for harvesting the rewards of foresight and hard work. Yet even at this stage, the seeds of the next cycle are sown: the strength of an exit fuels the credibility of the next fundraise.

Just as life is best lived when we can dream about tomorrow, savor today, and reflect fondly on yesterday—all at once, so too is PE best practiced with continuous attention to all three phases: fundraising, investing, and exiting. Each informs the other. Exits shape fundraising narratives. Fundraising determines investment firepower. Investments affect exit outcomes. The most successful firms do not compartmentalize these phases but weave them into a coherent and simultaneous strategy.

While PE may not provide the ultimate answer to the meaning of life, it certainly mirrors the structure of a well-lived one—just with more spreadsheets.

To summarize. When we look at definitions of PE, PE touches on several interesting topics. PE is related to growing unquoted, unlisted companies. It relates to equity but is not listed on an exchange. It is also meant to support companies that tend to not have access, or have limited access, to capital markets. It is a very precise moment in the life cycle of most companies. It is typically given with the intent of reselling the company after influencing its development, so it is quite hands-on. It is also managed by a certain type of fund, for the formal part. It can be considered as an asset class, and it is characterized by a limited liquidity.

To conclude, we propose the following definition:

"Private Equity" refers to institutional equity and equity-linked investments in unlisted companies or companies that will be delisted.

1.6 EUROPE AND THE GLOBALIZATION OF PE

Relative to the United States, Europe, led by the United Kingdom, was a latecomer to the PE market, with a slow start in the 1990s, but it has become a very mature market since then. Asia followed another 15 years later, albeit less integrated so far. Other parts of the world, which will be covered in Chapter 9, are less developed to date. The global number of funds with more than $1 billion in assets under management illustrates that competition in the PE industry has grown (Figure 1.12). The number of such funds increased from five in 1989 to 14 six years later to more than 100 by 2005 and about 800 PE and infrastructure funds in 2025 (VC not included). Further, the metric by then had changed as PE firms had multiplied the number of funds they would launch and there were more than 2,000 PE and infrastructure firms with this amount under management according to Pitchbook.

A macroeconomic metric, the proportion of GDP, illustrates the economic importance of PE.

Over 2015–2020, the United States remained the largest market with 1.5% of GDP invested in PE (Figure 1.13), considerably more than the EU average of 0.3%. Israel has been an anomaly due to the oversized VC activity, while Luxembourg manages funds for other countries. In Europe, the United Kingdom has had the strongest historical exposure and culture of PE, not far behind the United States.

The "addition" of Europe to the already sizable US PE market was the first step in the globalization of the industry. The next development in the 1990s was mostly

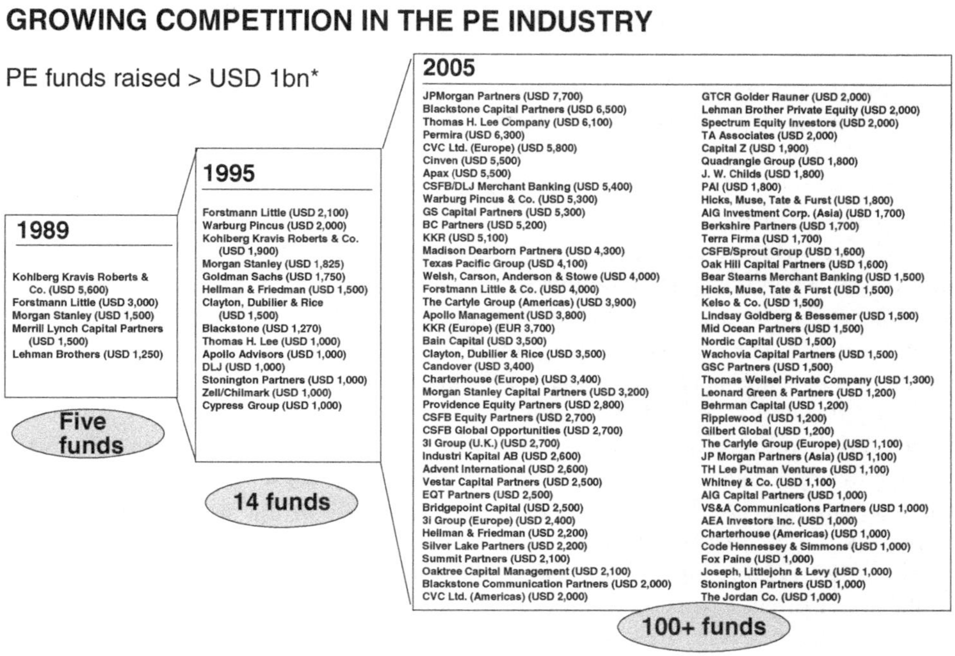

FIGURE 1.12 Large funds in history.

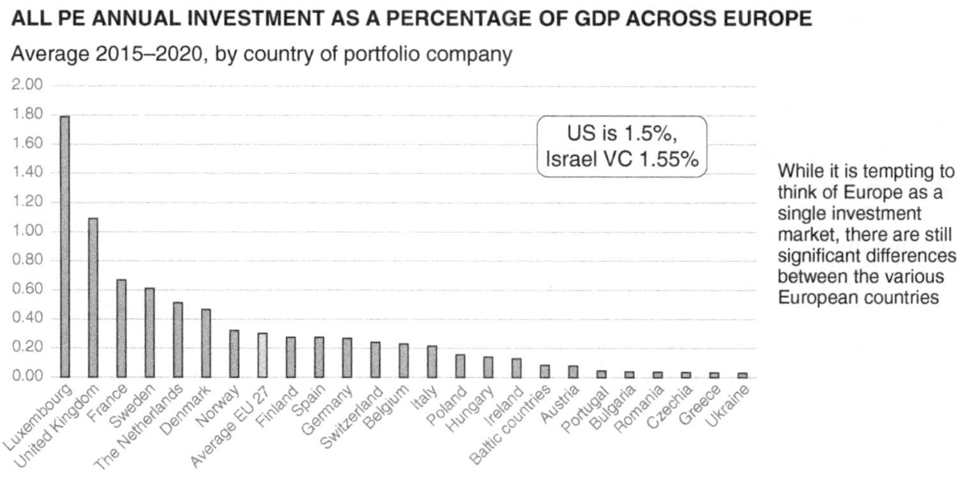

FIGURE 1.13 PE investment as percentage of GDP.
Source: Candesic research.

in Asia. However, the region's development has been markedly uneven, with China emerging as the standout success story while Japan has remained a persistent laggard.

China's PE transformation began slowly but accelerated dramatically after joining the Word Trade Organization (WTO) in 2001. The sector experienced tremendous growth over the next 15 years, driven by two pivotal factors: WTO membership and financial market liberalization. By 2007, when China Investment Corporation invested $3 billion for nearly 10% of Blackstone, the country signaled its commitment to understanding and embracing private equity.

Numbers are remarkable. Dominated by China, Asian PE investments grew from $4 billion annually in 2000–2004 to more than $60 billion in 2010–2015, achieving a 15-year CAGR of 19%—double the global average of 9%. The Asian-Pacific market grew further and is forecast to reach $3 to 5 trillion by 2030. This growth reflects not just China's expansion but increasing sophistication across the region.

In stark contrast, Japan has long remained the "sleeping giant" of Asian PE. Despite being Asia's second-largest economy with sophisticated corporations and abundant capital, several structural factors have constrained this development, including cultural barriers, a preference for cash, and regulatory and structural hurdles. Since 2020 however, Japan has experienced record and growing PE activity.

Asia's uneven PE development reflects broader economic and cultural differences. China's rapid embrace of market mechanisms and foreign capital contrasted sharply with Japan's gradual, consensus-driven approach. Southeast Asia followed China's path but with a 5- to 10-year lag, while countries like India developed significant growth equity markets by the mid-2000s.

The result is an Asian PE landscape where China dominates deal flow and innovation, Japan offers compelling but complex opportunities, and smaller markets like Southeast Asia provide growth-stage investment platforms. This fragmentation—unlike the more integrated US and European markets—continues to characterize Asian PE, though increasing cross-border activity and regional fund strategies are gradually building connections across the diverse markets. Chapter 9 will further explore the development of PE in Asia and in the rest of the world.

While private equity was once a small asset class compared to traditional ones, it has grown fast and has captured adjacent areas (such as infrastructure, private credit, and even real estate funds) and brought them into what is now called private capital, which altogether grew from $600 billion in 2000 to $15–20 trillion AuM in 2025, depending on what we take into account.[12]

As a comparison, Figure 1.14 shows that pension funds managed about $55 trillion and mutual funds managed $60 trillion. Without counting the dry powder, i.e. the part that is not yet invested, or the adjacent segments, PE was almost $7 trillion in 2024. Overall, PE amounts to 6% of the world's assets under management in traded securities and 13% of all stock markets.

One of our students once observed that the growth of aggregate private capital assets under management was broadly similar to the average returns of its main segments, wondering if the industry's growth was simply the compounding of its returns. Starting from less than $1 trillion in 2000, private capital achieved a CAGR of about 13% over the next 25 years (Figure 1.15). This view suggests that funds paid out over time were broadly in line with new funds invested.

However, this apparent similarity with typical private equity returns is misleading for several fundamental reasons. First, AuM growth combines two distinct components: returns on existing investments (value creation) and net new capital flows (new

[12]Typically, this will not even include a growing portion of co-investments in large buyouts, and, of course, the informal market of private transactions not conducted by professional firms. Dry powder is sometimes omitted.

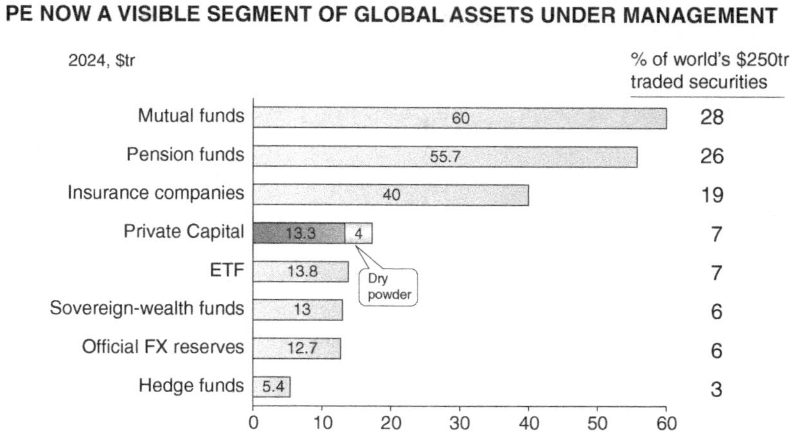

FIGURE 1.14 Global AuM by investor category.
Source: Candesic research.

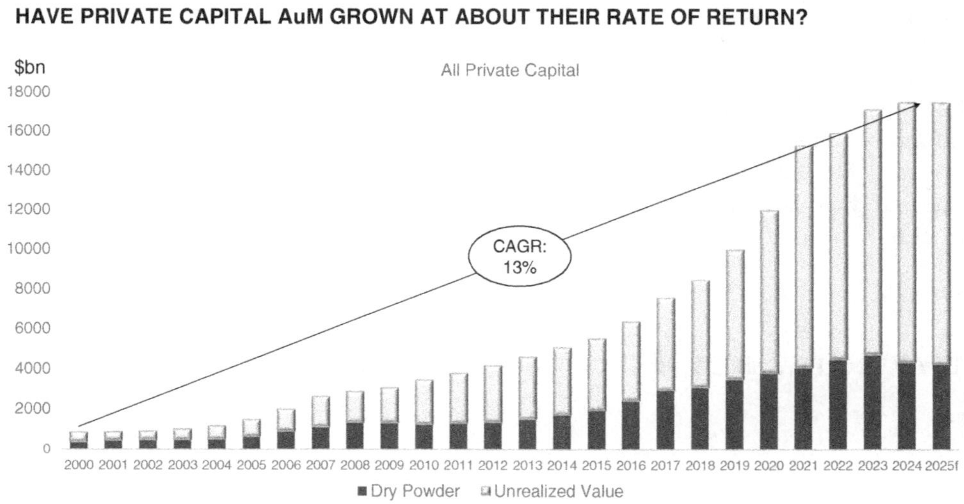

FIGURE 1.15 Historical growth of private capital.
Source: Preqin (part of Blackrock) (Global PE including RE and infrastructure).

fundraising minus distributions to investors). Second, even when considering returns alone, the relationship between AuM growth and returns is complex: a 2× multiple can represent very different annual returns depending on the investment period, and high IRRs can coexist with modest money multiples due to shorter holding periods. Moreover, reported AuM includes unrealized returns that may not materialize. Finally, structural industry factors have significantly influenced AuM growth, including increasing allocations to private markets by institutional investors, expansion into new strategies like private credit and infrastructure, and longer holding periods in some segments affecting capital recycling. Therefore, the industry's growth reflects a much more complex dynamic than simple return compounding, including increasing allocations to private markets by institutional investors, expansion into new strategies like private credit and infrastructure, and longer holding periods in some segments affecting capital recycling.

Why has PE grown so much? Kaplan and others list four main reasons:

1. Strong performance of the buyout segment relative to the stock market
2. Diversification opportunities
3. Less regulation and compliance
4. A business model that is better suited to managerial talent

We will discuss each of those in later chapters.

Analyzing performance by vintage year (the year in which the fund was first raised) is crucial, especially in private equity, because it helps account for varying market and economic conditions at the time investments are made. It allows investors to compare funds launched in the same year, offering a fair assessment of managers' abilities under similar market environments. Vintage year analysis also highlights how well funds navigate risks related to specific periods and provides insights into the effectiveness of investment strategies. Additionally, it clarifies the timing of cash flows, enabling a more accurate understanding of returns over the life cycle of the fund.

A snapshot of recent years and developments up to 2022 (Figure 1.16) shows that most of the capital raised three years earlier, in 2019, has been deployed—though not entirely. Some funds remained uninvested for various reasons (the dry powder). This is a normal occurrence, as it takes time to identify the right opportunities, and the life cycle of private equity funds is structured to accommodate this process.

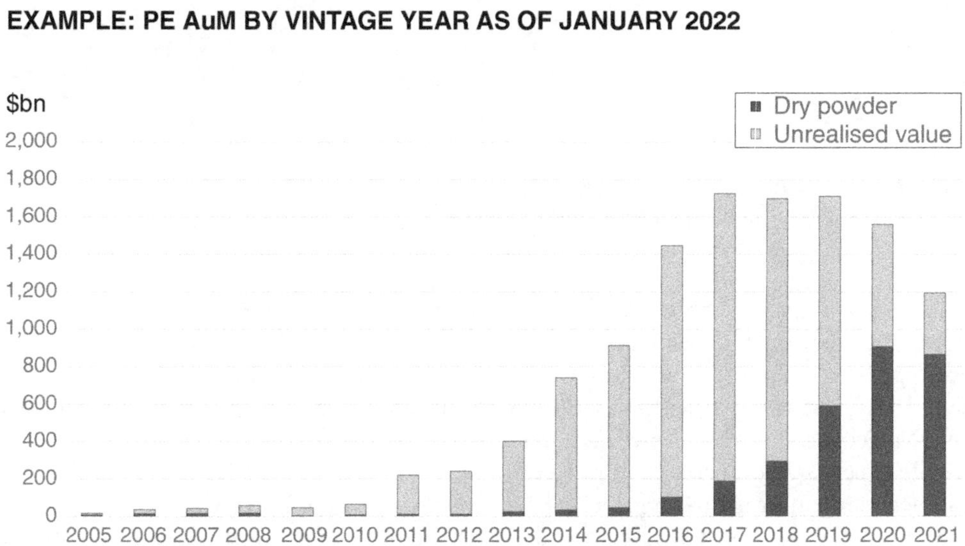

FIGURE 1.16 Evolution of PE AuM by vintage year.
Source: Preqin (part of Blackrock).

1.7 THE INVESTMENT CASE FOR HEALTHCARE AND LIFE SCIENCES

1.7.1 Investing in Health

We now turn to the second component of this book: health, which we view as healthcare (services) and life sciences (products and services).

Healthcare and life sciences present PE investors with a structurally resilient but intricately complex sector. Demand is inelastic and growing, yet exposed to technology shifts and political disruption, making it hard to forecast. Value creation requires deep regulatory and go-to market expertise, long-term capital commitment, resilience to delays and setbacks, and alignment across fragmented stakeholder groups. From patient demand to payer dynamics, each layer of the sector presents unique risks and structural barriers—requiring deep domain expertise and close proximity to industry realities.

- **An industry serving a fundamental, unpredictable, and irreplaceable need**
  The healthcare sector addresses a unique issue: human health. This comes with inherent characteristics:
  - Unpredictable: No one can predict the timing or severity of a pathology.
  - Nondiscretionary nature: Getting sick is not a choice, nor are the treatment options always voluntary.
  - Complex: Each patient and treatment involves biological, psychological, social, economic—and at times, ethical—dimensions.

→ For the investor: demand in healthcare is str ucturally s trong, often price-inelastic, and on a long-term growth trend, but it is difficult to mode l in the short term.

- **Pooled and heavily regulated care mechanisms**
  This inherent characteristic leads directly to the following:
  - The need for expert intervention: for diagnosis, treatment, and patient support
  - Risk pooling through public or private insurance systems
  - Guaranteed access to safe, effective treatments, regardless of individual financial means

→ For the investor: the patient (end user) is rarely the payer or decision-maker. Business models depend on buy-in from multiple parties—physicians, insurers, and regulators—resulting in longer sales cycles but more durable revenue stream once established.

- **High demands for science-based evidence and evaluation**
  To operate in this environment, companies—and health systems—the following are required (to varying degrees depending on geography):
  - Strong clinical evidence: efficacy, safety, and comparator data
  - Health-economic rationale: demonstrating system-wide value
  - Strict regulatory oversight: to ensure safety, uphold ethical standards and effective access to treatment

→ For the investor: these demands create formidable barriers to entry driven by high fixed costs. Obtaining reimbursement or regulatory approval—requiring significant investment with no short-term revenue—becomes a critical inflection point in value creation.

- **A capital-intensive industry, with long cycles, high risk, and high volatility**
  These structural demands shape the industry's operations:
  - Heavy investment requirements in R&D and infrastructure (CapEx)

  - Extended development timelines: from trials to approval to market adoption
  - High uncertainty: in success rates, access, and product diffusion

  → For the investor: value is tied to managing long timelines, mastering regulatory and go-to market turning points, and executing disciplined, risk-aware strategies.
- **A fragmented ecosystem with diverging interests**

  Finally, treatment decisions involve multiple stakeholders:
  - Patients and families (need, acceptance, adherence)
  - The medical community (clinical relevance and prescription behavior)
  - Public and private payers
  - The State (ensuring equitable access, safety—and often acting as financier)

  → For the investor: the value chain is decentralized, asymmetric, and highly political. Success depends not just on technical merit, but on demonstrated and perceived value across all these constituencies.

Building on these industry fundamentals, investment in healthcare and life sciences is driven by multiple long-term growth levers—demographics, innovation, and new models of care—that directly exploit the structural context described above.

1.7.1.1 Demographic and Macroeconomic Drivers Demographic shifts, particularly aging populations in developed economies, reinforce the sector's structural growth and nondiscretionary character. With increasing life expectancy, the prevalence of chronic diseases such as diabetes, cardiovascular conditions, and neurodegenerative disorders is rising, necessitating sustained medical intervention. Concurrent with this, healthcare spending has expanded significantly: Annual per capita healthcare expenditure in the United States increased from $8,877 in 2012 to $13,493 in 2022,[13] demonstrating both the scale and upward trajectory of financial flows into the sector. Emerging markets also present diversified investment opportunities due to rising middle-class populations, urbanization, and expanding access to care.

1.7.1.2 Innovation as a Growth Catalyst Beyond demographics, continuous technological innovation is amplifying both the complexity and potential for value creation within healthcare. Advances in biotechnology, genomics, telemedicine, AI-driven diagnostics, and personalized medicine are reshaping both patient care and operational efficiencies. Given high barriers to entry and regulatory complexity noted previously, these innovations are capital and expertise intensive—playing to PE's strengths in strategic investment, operational scale-up, and risk management. By investing in companies capable of integrating new technologies, PE firms can both drive and benefit from the sector's transformation.

Rapid growth of healthcare expenditures has become one of the main challenges for the sustainability of public finances worldwide (Meskarpour Amiri et al., 2021). As traditional models strain under these costs, private investors—including PE—expand their role in supporting shifts toward value-based care, digital health, and new service models emphasizing patient outcomes and cost-efficiency. This transition presents investment opportunities in data-driven healthcare platforms, digital health solutions, and outpatient care models, directly aligned with PE strategies geared toward

[13] *Source:* www.healthsystemtracker.org.

performance optimization and market expansion. These shifts also illustrate how PE supports both sustaining innovations (such as operational optimization) and disruptive ones (such as digital therapeutics or AI-enabled diagnostics).

1.7.1.3 Operational Efficiencies and Market Consolidation The sector's fragmentation—see earlier—creates scope for consolidation and operational professionalization. Subsectors such as diagnostics or outpatient clinics offer distinct opportunities for streamlining processes, integrating platforms, and professionalizing management—core elements of the PE playbook. By doing so, PE firms can unlock value beyond financial engineering, transforming fragmented systems into scalable and efficient networks.

1.7.1.4 Regulatory Complexity and Competitive Advantages Although the regulatory landscape is complex, it creates a "moat" favoring experienced sector specialists. PE firms with deep sector expertise are able to navigate reimbursement structures, licensing processes, and data privacy requirements, translating compliance mastery into deal-sourcing and execution advantages. As governments increasingly turn to public-private partnerships to modernize healthcare systems, PE's combination of capital, operational rigor, and regulatory awareness positions it as a valuable partner in healthcare infrastructure and modernization initiatives.

We should add that a strong sense of mission permeates the healthcare industry. It is not merely a commercial field but one deeply anchored in purpose, empathy, and public service. This pervasive ethos is evident across physicians, entrepreneurs, executives, and investors, who often share a conviction that their work contributes meaningfully to human well-being. In our discussions with healthcare investors, we have repeatedly encountered deeply personal testimonies describing how individual experiences have shaped their professional motivations, reinforcing the idea that healthcare investing is as much about purpose as it is about performance. Thomas Goudriaan at Gimv shares that sense of a mission: "We believe that private equity can be part of the driving force to make healthcare more accessible, affordable and of higher quality. This will be essential to provide sustainable solutions to the challenges in healthcare today, but also for the next generations. Gimv is proud to be a part of the solution."

For many healthcare investors, the motivation that extends beyond financial returns includes personal experiences that shape their professional mission. Youssef Sebban, co-founder of Eckuity Capital, a growth investor in healthcare, explains: "I lost my father at a young age to a cancer that, today, would have been easily detected and treated. That experience shaped my commitment to ensuring that the future of healthcare is more equitable, efficient, and preventive. Having grown up in a developing country where care standards lag far behind, I built Eckuity around three pillars—improving efficiency, democratizing access, and lowering the cost of care. My mission is to leave a tangible mark on the future of health—across prevention, diagnosis, treatment, and monitoring."

This example reflects a broader trend among healthcare investors whose strategic focus is anchored in purpose-driven goals. Beyond performance metrics and deal structures, many view their role as advancing systemic progress—helping shape a more inclusive, sustainable, and high-impact healthcare environment. Such alignment between personal conviction and investment purpose is a distinctive characteristic of the sector, perhaps even stronger than in education and environment.

1.7.2 A History of PE in Healthcare and Life Sciences

The relationship between PE and healthcare has evolved from early venture capital investments in medical technology to today's sophisticated ecosystem of buyouts, growth equity, and sector-specialist funds.

1.7.2.1 Early Capital Formation (1925–1970s) The intersection of private equity and healthcare is a relatively young phenomenon, given the complex regulatory environment and high-risk, long-term nature of life sciences investments. The roots of this relationship can be traced back to the early twentieth century, though it was not recognized as "private equity" at the time. At a stretch, one of the earliest examples was the creation of IG Farben in 1925, a conglomerate of German chemical and pharmaceutical companies, which could be seen as an early form of industry consolidation and private investment.

In the United States, in 1946, the ARDC made one of the first venture capital investments in the medical field by funding Digital Equipment Corporation (DEC), which would later become a player in medical imaging technology, among other technologies.

The 1950s and 1960s saw the emergence of more formalized venture capital, with significant implications for healthcare. In 1959, Fairchild Semiconductor laid the groundwork for Silicon Valley and future medical technology innovations. Two of its senior executives went to launch Kleiner Perkins and Sequoia Capital.

The 1960s and 1970s witnessed the emergence of specialized venture capital firms that focused on the burgeoning field of biotechnology. The establishment of Kleiner Perkins in 1972, for instance, marked a significant development in the financing of healthcare innovations. The firm's investment in Genentech in 1976 is often cited as a groundbreaking moment for biotech venture capital. Genentech's success not only demonstrated the potential of recombinant DNA technology but also validated the role of venture capital in accelerating medical advancements. Genentech's 1980 IPO thus marked a turning point for venture capital in life sciences. Venture capital actually had many specialized players early on, like Sofinnova Partners in France (1972), Abingworth in the United Kingdom (1973), and Healthcare Ventures in the United States (1985). The Bayh-Dole Act of 1980, which allowed universities to patent and retain ownership to inventions developed with federal funding, was a pivotal moment in fostering innovation and creating opportunities for private investment. Increasingly more venture-backed biotech companies emerged in the 1980s, focusing on areas such as recombinant DNA technology and monoclonal antibodies.

1.7.2.2 Emergence of Healthcare LBOs and Specialized PE (1980s–2000s) The 1980s saw an explosion of activity. Notably, in 1989, the $5.1 billion management-led take-private of Hospital Corporation of America (HCA) in response to two successive hostile takeover attempts signaled private equity's growing interest in large-scale healthcare deals. This interest in consolidation of hospitals in particular was driven in the United States by federal legislation pushing for adoption of health IT solutions to facilitate more consistent and scalable delivery. The adoption of DRG-based payment systems reinforced this trend with the need for economies of scale, streamlined operational efficiency, and increased market power (Ma et al., 2024).

The late 1980s saw the emergence of specialized healthcare investment teams. Notably, Ampersand Capital Partners was established in 1988 and began investing in life sciences companies in the early 1990s. Ampersand's healthcare focus originated from their relationship with Fisher Scientific, who served as an LP in 1992. Fisher Scientific requested the creation of a dedicated lab product-focused fund in 1994, making Ampersand one of the first healthcare specialists in the field. Their early success in focused niches of laboratory tools, diagnostics, and pharmaceutical services demonstrated the value of deep sector expertise, particularly in complex segments requiring scientific and regulatory knowledge. Under private ownership, Ampersand has maintained this specialized focus, reaching close to $3 billion AuM.

The 1990s brought further sophistication to healthcare private equity. In 1993, Welsh, Carson, Anderson & Stowe (WCAS) raised the first private equity fund dedicated exclusively to healthcare and have since then stuck to healthcare and technologies.

The 1990s marked a significant expansion in healthcare private equity, with large firms like Carlyle, TPG, and VC-veteran Warburg Pincus developing dedicated healthcare teams. This period saw increased interest in pharmaceutical services, medical devices, and healthcare providers, driven by the sector's defensive characteristics and fragmented nature. DLJ Merchants Banking Partners (now MidOcean) emerged as another significant player, particularly in pharmaceutical services and medical devices. Meanwhile, Bain Capital started looking into healthcare services during the 1990s, leveraging its expertise in operations to improve efficiency in acquired companies.

The European healthcare private equity market developed later than its American counterpart, due to stronger public healthcare systems and less developed private markets but gaining momentum in the late 1990s and early 2000s. Nordic Capital became one of the first European firms to develop a strong healthcare focus, followed by EQT, Permira, and Cinven. These firms benefited from Europe's diverse healthcare systems and the opportunity to consolidate fragmented markets across different countries, also targeting pharmaceutical companies and medical device manufacturers as privatization and market liberalization created opportunities.

The late 1990s and early 2000s saw increased LBO activity in healthcare. The 2000s witnessed the era of mega-buyouts, including in healthcare. We mentioned in the introduction the pivotal moment that came in 2006 with the massive $33 billion buyout of US hospital group HCA Healthcare, by then with 176 hospitals and 92 surgery and outpatient centers,[14] by KKR, Bain Capital, and Merrill Lynch. It was then the largest and remains one of the largest healthcare LBOs in history.[15] Part of the equity story was the opportunity to raise prices in markets where they would be the sole player. The 2007 $4.5 billion take-private of Bausch & Lomb by Warburg Pincus marked a significant move in the medical device and eye care space. In 2007, KKR defeated rival Terra Firma and took Alliance Boots private for £11.1 billion ($22 billion), the largest LBO ever in Europe at the time.

This period also witnessed increased specialization, with, on one hand, the launch of PE firms focusing exclusively on healthcare and life sciences while, on the other hand, traditional generalist firms expanded their healthcare teams significantly, with firms like Bain Capital and Advent International building substantial healthcare portfolios.

[14]Following its first LBO in 1989, HCA went public again in 1992 and later combined with Columbia Healthcare.

[15]An analysis by *Fortune* conducted shortly after the 2011 IPO found that Bain Capital ultimately realized approximately $1.2 billion from an initial equity investment of just $64 million.

Venture capital in healthcare also evolved, with firms like New Enterprise Associates, Kleiner Perkins, and OrbiMed making significant investments in healthtech startups. Years later, the complete sequencing of the human genome in 2003 spurred a new wave of investments in genomics and personalized medicine.

1.7.2.3 The Modern Era: Digital Health, Global Expansion, and a New Reality (2010s–Present) The 2008 financial crisis temporarily slowed activity, but healthcare proved resilient. Post-crisis, interest in healthcare services renewed, exemplified by the 2011 $6.3 billion acquisition of Kinetic Concepts by Apax Partners. Buy-and-build strategies were by then ubiquitous, and it is worth noting that, by February 2011, PE firms owned 10 of the 15 largest for-profit hospital chains in the United States.

Ma et al. (2024) identify three key reasons for the increased attractiveness of healthcare for PE during this period: economic resilience, growing need for capital and management expertise, and regulatory shifts. These regulatory shifts have collectively created an environment ripe for innovation and investment, enabling PE firms to explore diverse opportunities and play a significant role in reshaping the healthcare landscape (see Chapter 7).

The 2010s also saw a boom in healthtech investments. The Affordable Care Act in the United States passed in 2010 spurred investments in health insurance technology and value-based care models. The 2018 $5.7 billion take-private of Athenahealth by Veritas Capital and Elliott Management represented a major private equity move into healthcare technology.

Venture capital in digital health exploded, with companies like 23andMe ($860 million over nine rounds of financing before IPO by SPAC in 2021 and later collapse), Noom ($624 million over 12 rounds), Guardant Health ($557 million over six rounds before IPO), Amwell, Flatiron Health, Doctolib, and Oscar Health raising hundreds of millions of dollars. Some of these companies would later reach profitability and attract growth capital.

The decade also saw the rise of corporate venture capital, with pharmaceutical giants like Novartis, Johnson & Johnson, and Roche launching their own CVC arms, some of them adding digital health to their portfolio. While Johnson & Johnson Innovation—JJDC, Inc.—has invested $3.5 billion across all segments of life sciences, many of the other CVCs are approaching $1 billion AuM: Novartis Venture Fund has more than $750 million of committed capital and made 346 investments between 2007 and 2025; Roche Venture Fund is a $850 million evergreen fund investing in life science companies in pharmaceuticals, diagnostics, and digital health; Pfizer Ventures is a $600 million fund focused on potentially transformative therapeutics; while Sanofi Ventures recently increased its fund to $650 million.[16]

In Asia, healthcare private equity developed later but has grown rapidly since the 2010s. Firms like Hillhouse Capital and PAG from Hong Kong have built significant

[16] Most large pharmaceutical companies now run a CVC fund, including Amgen Ventures; AstraZeneca's BioVentureHub; Baxter Ventures; Boehringer Ingelheim Venture Fund; J&J Development Corp; Leaps by Bayer; Lilly Ventures; M Ventures (Merck KGaA); MP Healthcare Venture Management (Mitsubishi Tanabe); MRL Ventures Fund (Merck & Co), Novartis Venture Fund, Novo Ventures, Pfizer Ventures, Roche Venture Fund, Sanofi Ventures, SR One Capital Management (GSK), and Takeda Ventures.

healthcare expertise, focusing on opportunities in China's expanding healthcare market. However, the region has fewer pure-play healthcare investors compared to North America and Europe. It is telling that one of the most significant Chinese healthcare LBOs was the $3.3 billion take-private in 2015 of WuXi PharmaTech, an open-access R&D capability and technology platform serving the pharmaceutical, biotechnology, and medical device industries. While headquartered in Shanghai, the company was actually listed on the NYSE. It was acquired and delisted by a consortium composed of Ally Bridge Group, Boyu Capital, Temasek Life Sciences, and Ping An Insurance, as well as existing investor Hillhouse Capital.

The 2020s experienced a frenzy of mega deals, with significant concentration in 2021 (Figure 1.17). Hellman & Friedman and Bain Capital took over Athenahealth from Veritas and Elliott, this time for $17 billion. It also included one of the two largest healthcare private equity deals in history—the Medline acquisition for some $34 billion by a consortium including Blackstone, Carlyle, and Hellman & Friedman. This transaction not only set a new scale benchmark but also highlighted the growing importance of medical supply chain assets. One mega deal fell through though: Swedish Orphan Biovitrum AB (Sobi) agreed to be acquired by Advent International and GIC for nearly $8 billion, but the deal was torpedoed when AstraZeneca decided to withhold its 8% stake from the buyout offer, probably to keep the option to increase its investment later.

The COVID-19 pandemic in 2020 accelerated major trends in telemedicine and digital health, exemplified by Teladoc's $18.5 billion merger with Livongo, which created a combined entity valued at $37 billion, and the $4 billion SPAC listing of British firm Babylon Health. While neither transaction was a leveraged buyout, both highlighted the growing strategic and financial importance of digital health solutions. The pandemic also spurred unprecedented investment in vaccine development and biotechnology.

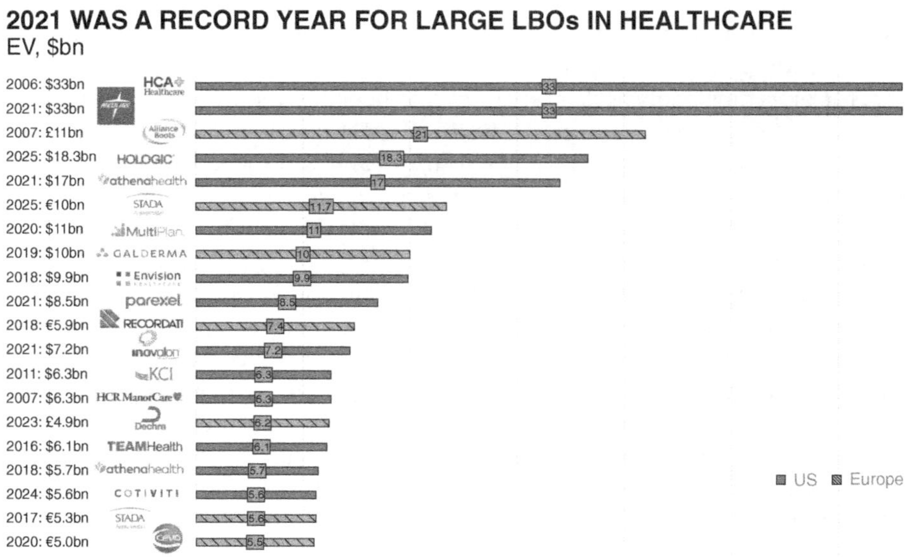

FIGURE 1.17 Largest LBOs in healthcare as of 2025.
Source: Candesic research.

This period was further characterized by a low-interest rate environment that facilitated a wave of roll-up activity in healthcare services, as cheap financing and fragmented markets made consolidation particularly attractive.

In the years that followed, private equity interests increasingly took on board broader societal concerns. Impact investing gained momentum, with attention turning to health equity, climate resilience, and access to care. Meanwhile, advancements in machine learning and artificial intelligence (AI) have created new investment opportunities in areas such as drug discovery, diagnostics, and personalized medicine.

By 2022, the return of inflation and rising interest rates began to reshape investment strategies. Investors increasingly favored asset-light, digital-first business models and sought shorter holding periods, often at the expense of capital-intensive sectors such as biotechnology and hospitals. A notable exception was digital imaging, where adoption of teleradiology and AI-driven analysis supported continued investment despite broader market pressures. In healthcare services, the post-COVID-19 shift also marked a turning point in private equity's roll-up playbook: investors became less willing to rely solely on multiple expansion and demanded tangible operational improvements, platform integration, and realized synergies to justify value creation. In Chapter 10, we will review later developments and industry outlook.

The evolution of PE investment represents a fascinating journey of increasing specialization and sophistication, especially over the past four decades. Throughout this history, PE in healthcare and life sciences has evolved from simple stand-alone leveraged buyouts to a complex ecosystem of venture capital, growth equity, buyouts, and specialized investment strategies, playing a crucial role in funding innovation and shaping the healthcare landscape. These transactions also contribute to bringing together healthcare and life sciences—services and products—reflecting accelerating shifts in technology, regulation, and market dynamics over the last five decades.

1.7.3 Enduring Themes in Healthcare PE and Strategic Implications

The historical evolution of PE in healthcare reveals several enduring themes that continue to shape investment strategy today.

First, the preceding analysis demonstrates that healthcare's sheer scale and noncyclical demand make it a resilient cornerstone for PE portfolios. Accounting for 10–20% of GDP in many developed economies, the sector provides stable demand for essential services, a quality that has proven invaluable during economic downturns.

Second, history highlights that healthcare's complexity is both a challenge and an opportunity. The intricate interplay among providers, payors, and patients, combined with long development timelines and a highly regulated environment, demands deep expertise. This complexity creates a high barrier to entry, allowing specialist investors to carve out defensible niches and generate alpha. This has driven the rise of pure-play healthcare firms with the domain knowledge to navigate these challenges effectively.

Third, private capital has repeatedly acted as a catalyst not just for individual companies, but for entire new markets. The archetypal example is Genentech (Figure 1.18). Early venture funding from Kleiner Perkins came when the biotech sector barely existed. Genentech's subsequent success validated the entire field of genetic engineering, fueled massive VC interest, and laid the groundwork for the genomics revolution. Its eventual $46.8 billion acquisition by Roche in 2009 illustrates the complete life cycle of how private capital can identify, fund, scale, and ultimately institutionalize a new healthcare paradigm.

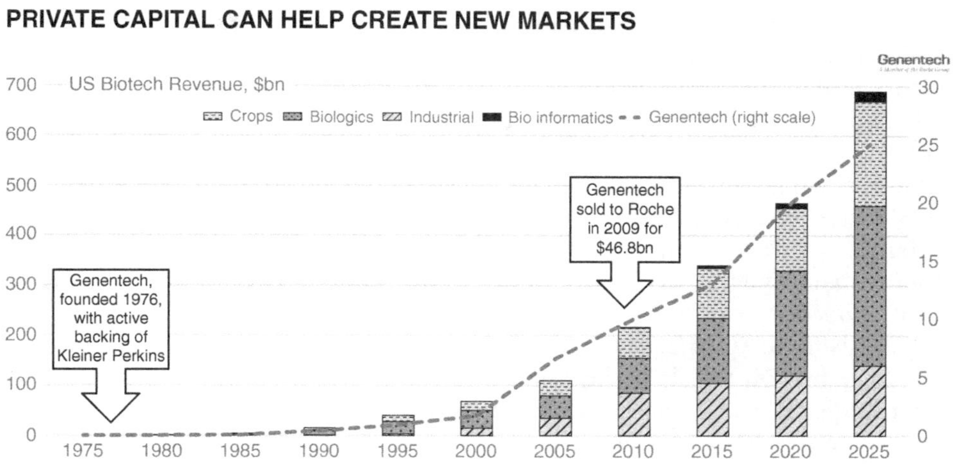

FIGURE 1.18 Evolution of US biotech industry.
Source: Nature; Candesic research (estimates).

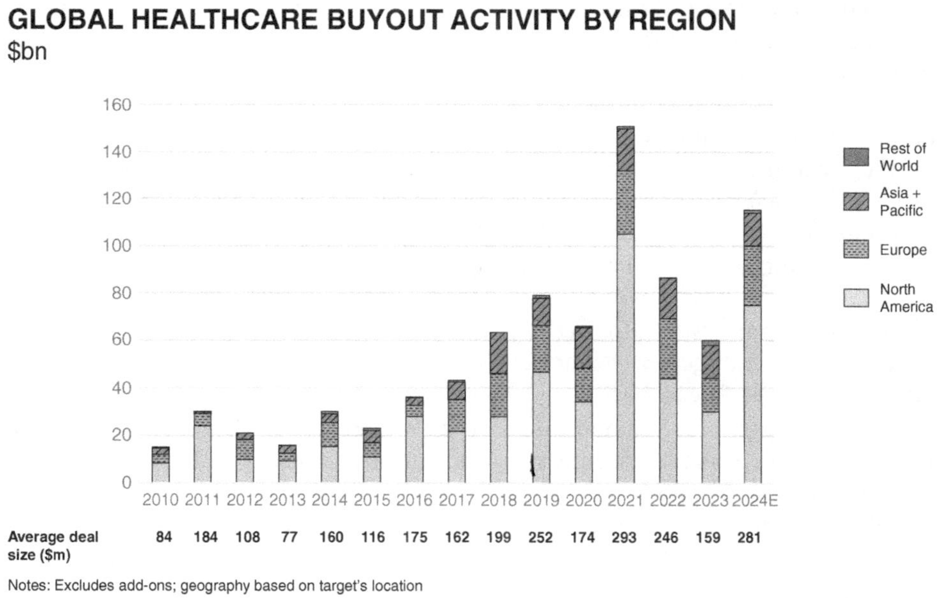

FIGURE 1.19 Global healthcare buyout activity by world region.
Source: Dealogic.

Fourth, healthcare is increasingly being treated as a strategic national priority. Disruptions to global supply chains, public health threats, and geopolitical tensions have led many governments to rethink healthcare infrastructure, access, and innovation—often opening new avenues for public-private collaboration.

1.7.4 Geographical Patterns of Growth

Significant differences exist across regions in how private equity engages with the healthcare and life sciences sectors (Figure 1.19).

The United States remains the most developed and dynamic PE healthcare market. Its predominantly private healthcare system, robust biotech ecosystem, and deep exit markets via IPOs or strategic sales have long attracted domestic and global investors. Specialized firms and diversified platforms thrive in both healthcare services and life sciences.

Europe, while slower to develop, has focused more on life sciences, medtech, and health services consolidation. Strong public healthcare systems and supportive R&D environments have fostered specialized mid-market firms like GHO and ARCHIMED. European markets tend to favor cross-border consolidation and investment in capital-efficient models.

Asia is still an emerging PE healthcare market but has grown rapidly in the last decade. The focus is largely on healthcare infrastructure and delivery, with increasing interest in digital health and insurance platforms. Growth is driven by demographic trends, rising middle-class demand, and underdeveloped public health infrastructure. Significant investors include Hillhouse Capital, PAG, and TPG. While Asia still lacks the density of specialized healthcare PE players seen in the United States or Europe, firms like TPG and KKR have targeted hospital networks and insurance platforms, addressing the region's structural healthcare deficits. Among other examples, TPG Growth established AHH (Asia Healthcare Holdings) as a platform to manage and expand its healthcare investments across Asia. In 2019, KKR, alongside GIC, Singapore's sovereign wealth fund, invested $680 million in Metro Pacific Health, the largest private healthcare provider in the Philippines, operating 24 hospitals and numerous outpatient centers, growing the value to over $3 billion.

Other regions, such as Africa and Latin America, present significant long-term healthcare investment needs, but lower PE penetration. Challenges include political risk, fragmented health systems, and smaller deal sizes. However, these regions may become more important as impact investing and blended finance gain momentum globally.

Looking forward, while the sector has proven its resilience, it is not immune to market pressures. Subsectors reliant on essential, reimbursed services tend to be more durable than those driven by elective procedures or consumer spending. In a high-interest-rate environment, capital-intensive areas like hospitals become more challenging, while investors increasingly favor businesses where AI and data can enhance clinical or operational performance. As capital becomes more selective, investors are demanding tangible improvements and strategic synergies, not just multiple expansion. This shift underscores the continued evolution of PE in healthcare as a dynamic and complex ecosystem of innovation, specialization, and value creation.

1.7.5 The Role of Private Equity in Pharma[17]

1.7.5.1 Where PE Plays Across the Pharma Value Chain

R&D Finance and Risk-sharing At the upstream end, investors use asset-centric and virtual models to ring-fence one or two programs, reducing organizational overhead while aligning capital to decision gates. Pharmas complement this with corporate venture capital (CVC) and portfolio constructs that externalize early risk while preserving

[17] A contribution by Philipp Khokhlov, DBA candidate and visiting lecturer at UCL GBSH.

options to reacquire or codevelop later. Academic work shows CVC activity rises when incumbents' internal innovation wanes, consistent with pharma's use of mirror funds and optioned collaborations. Royalty and revenue-interest financings—traditional and synthetic—have matured into a nondilutive toolkit spanning clinical- to commercial-stage assets. These structures let developers trade a slice of future sales for upfront capital, often with downside protection and milestone-based step-ups.

CRO/CDMO/Tools In development and manufacturing, PE concentrates on scaled platforms that monetize outsourcing and regulatory complexity. Reviews document the rise of end-to-end CDMOs (contract development and manufacturing organizations) and preferred-provider CRO (contract research organization) models; value creation comes from specialization (biologics DS/DP, sterile operations), right-first-time quality systems, and commercial focus on top accounts. Modality specialization—encompassing antibodies, ADCs, cell and gene therapy—raises barriers but rewards capacity and expertise.

Drug Delivery and Containment Fill-finish, device components, and primary containers have become chokepoints—most visibly for GLP-1s, where demand spikes meet pen assembly and aseptic bottlenecks. Academic and regulatory sources note persistent GLP-1 shortages and the implementation of targeted mitigation measures, while the bioprocess literature highlights the capital-intensive and compliance-heavy nature of sterile operations. These dynamics underpin PE theses in delivery systems, containment, and capacity debottlenecking.

Branded/Consumer/Specialty Carve-outs of noncore portfolios (e.g., consumer health, legacy brands, standalone plants) create focused growth stories. Governance resets, separation capital expenditures, and bolt-ons can unlock mix and margin. Empirical finance literature generally finds positive announcement effects for carve-outs/spin-offs, with improved focus and capital allocation as mechanisms—a rationale that translates well to pharma's fragmented adjacencies.

Clinical-trial/Provider IT Workflow software (eSource/eClinical, site enablement), e-prescribing infrastructure, and payment-integrity analytics are asset-light wedges with recurring revenue and data moats. Peer-reviewed studies and guidance chronicle the steady adoption of eSource and e-prescribing, improving safety, auditability, and cycle time. Meanwhile, health-system research quantifies waste and improper payments as durable cost pools for analytics platforms.

1.7.5.2 Why Pharma Attracts PE Now Private equity has reasserted itself as a structural force across pharma post-COVID-19. After a 2021 risk peak and a 2022–2023 slowdown amid inflation and rate hikes, global healthcare PE rebounded in 2024 to about $115 billion—the second highest on record—driven by megadeals in biopharma, manufacturing, and enabling infrastructure. Europe outpaced its 2021 surge with record activity in cross-border CDMO, CRO, and medtech platforms offering compliance moats and operational levers. In Asia-Pacific, India's expanding CDMO/API capacity and hospital platforms drew record capital, reflecting "China-plus-one" strategies and domestic demand. The PE playbook remains operational—quality upgrades, capacity debottlenecking, disciplined pricing, and mix optimization—underwritten by

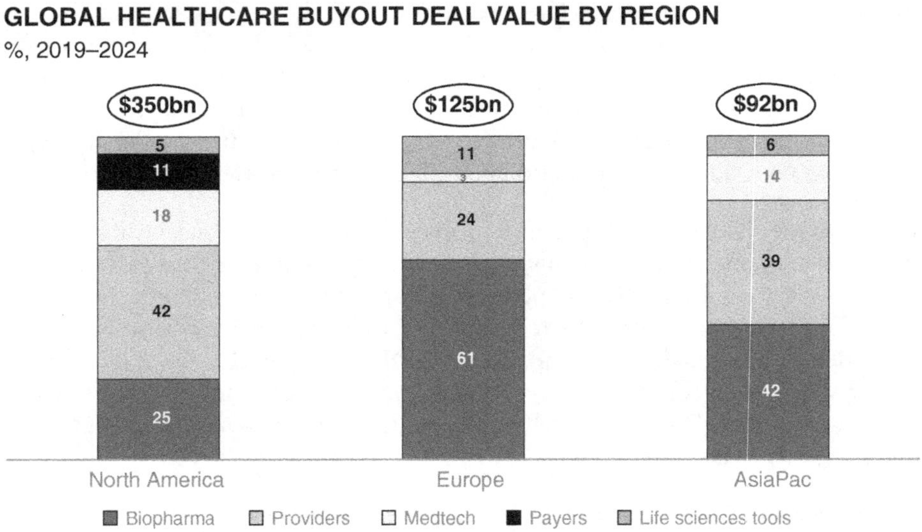

FIGURE 1.20 Six-year global healthcare buyout deal value by region.
Source: Dealogic.

tailwinds in biologics, GLP-1s, and ADCs. Pharma's structural pressures—Eroom's law, patent cliffs, and capacity bottlenecks—continue to fuel deal activity, with the largest share in Europe, followed by AsiaPac regions, and the third one in North America (Figure 1.20). Cyclicality affects timing, not thesis: PE continues to monetize complexity through scale, quality, and execution.[18]

1.7.5.3 PE Strategies, Playbook, and Business Models in Pharma PE has become a defining force in reshaping the pharmaceutical industry's structure and value creation playbook. Through buy-and-build platforms, carve-outs, and growth-equity investments, sponsors are scaling specialized CDMOs, CROs, and healthcare information-technology (IT) tools, unlocking value via operational excellence, utilization gains, and commercialization discipline. Modality specialization—particularly in biologics, antibody-drug conjugates (ADCs), and sterile injectables—drives pricing power and scarcity value, while royalty and revenue-backed monetizations offer creative, nondilutive funding for innovation. Carve-outs and partnerships with Big Pharma illustrate how governance resets and focused incentives can rejuvenate legacy assets, as shown by case studies such as Novo Holdings–Catalent, Clayton Dubilier & Rice (CD&R)–Opella, and Warburg Pincus–Simtra. Across transactions, a distinct "PE operating playbook" emerges: regulatory readiness, quality-system reinforcement, pricing discipline, throughput acceleration, and rapid bolt-on integration. The coming decade will see deeper integration of data, sustainability, and patient-access imperatives into PE's

[18]Eroom's law observes that the inflation-adjusted cost of developing a new drug doubles approximately every nine years, despite advances in technology—making drug discovery slower and more expensive over time. The term is "Moore's law" spelled backward and was coined by Jack Scannell et al. in 2012.

approach—aligning financial engineering with scientific rigor. These themes, strategies, and case studies will be developed in Chapter 7.

1.8 LESSONS FROM THE CRISES AND HEALTH SECTOR RESILIENCE

This section examines how the private equity industry has fared during a few crises.

Private equity has been impacted and shaped by crises going all the way back to the eighteenth century. Here, our focus will be on some more recent crises, including the global financial crisis of 2007–2012, which was a defining moment for the economies of the developed world, but in particular for private equity and its LBO segment. In addition, we will consider the impact of the COVID-19 pandemic on private equity in the early 2020s.

Finally, taking into account the various crises considered, we will try to draw some lessons for the future, and in the process consider some related issues of ethics and regulation.

1.8.1 Junk Bonds and Michael Milken

Though this topic does not represent a crisis per se nor directly address healthcare resilience, it is essential to include as a defining moment in private equity's history. Michael Milken's pioneering development of the high-yield bond market in the 1970s and 1980s at Drexel Burnham Lambert fundamentally transformed the financing landscape, establishing the capital structures and investment practices that underpin modern private equity.[19] By championing high-yield bonds, commonly known as "junk bonds," Milken created a powerful new financing mechanism for high-growth but high-risk firms expanded access to capital for smaller and less established technology companies that were often excluded from traditional financing avenues.

This innovation proved particularly valuable to early-stage life sciences and biotech firms, which typically lacked both revenues and tangible assets, making them ineligible for traditional bank loans or investment-grade debt. Groundbreaking companies such as Genentech, Amgen, and Cetus Corporation were able to tap the high-yield market to fund costly R&D programs and scale manufacturing. These firms, despite their scientific potential, faced significant capital constraints prior to Milken's intervention. In parallel, companies like Biogen and Immunex also benefited from this evolving capital market architecture, enabling them to accelerate clinical development and expand commercial capacity.

Milken's innovation thus helped catalyze the emergence of the modern biotechnology sector, laying the financial groundwork for VC participation.

This innovation was also beneficial to PE, as high-yield bonds became a critical tool for funding LBOs. With this financing option, PE firms could raise substantial amounts of debt capital to fund acquisitions, significantly increasing the size and scale of potential deals. The rise of high-yield bonds enabled the era of mega-buyouts, allowing PE to target much larger acquisitions than previously possible.

---

[19] We strongly recommend reading *Den of Thieves*, by James B. Stewart (Simon and Schuster, 1992).

Milken's efforts also enhanced liquidity in the high-yield debt market, making these instruments more appealing for LBO financing. His innovative financing structures supported more complex and flexible transactions, later on offering PE firms new opportunities for structuring acquisitions. Additionally, Milken's advocacy attracted institutional investors to the high-yield bond market, effectively expanding the capital pool available for PE investments.

The accessibility of high-yield debt was instrumental in fueling the leveraged buyout boom of the 1980s, which included high-profile transactions like the RJR Nabisco buyout. Milken's contributions also shifted corporate perspectives on debt, normalizing leveraged transactions as a strategic business approach.

Milken further propelled the PE industry through his famous "Predators' Ball" conferences, which served as networking hubs for PE professionals, corporate raiders, and institutional investors. These gatherings helped strengthen relationships within the industry and facilitated deal-making. Moreover, Milken's work reshaped risk assessment and pricing in the financial markets, leaving a lasting influence on how PE transactions were evaluated and structured.

Although Milken's career ended amid controversy, his contributions to the high-yield market and the PE industry remain enduring. The financial frameworks and markets he helped establish have evolved into essential components of today's financial landscape, continuing to play a vital role in private equity long after his direct involvement ended.

1.8.2 Global Financial Crisis

The Global Financial Crisis—referred to as the GFC—profoundly impacted the private equity industry across several key areas. First and foremost, the crisis triggered a severe credit crunch, which sharply curtailed the availability of new loans essential for leveraged buyouts. A simultaneous decline in asset values meant there was less available collateral, further restricting access to credit. For existing portfolio companies, their debt became highly problematic as declining earnings led to widespread breaches, or near-breaches, of loan covenants.

The collapse in public market valuations—with indices like the S&P 500 and MSCI Europe falling by 37% and 46%, respectively—directly reduced both the volume and value of new PE deals. This market turmoil also limited exit opportunities, which in turn restricted cash distributions back to LPs.

Finally, institutional investors such as pension funds experienced the "denominator effect." As the value of their listed assets plummeted, their allocation to PE as a percentage of their total portfolio rose above target levels. This unintended overallocation forced many LPs to halt new commitments and rebalance their portfolios, further straining the PE ecosystem.

Were there any signs of the incoming crisis and how it was going to impact the PE industry? With the perspective provided by time and history, we can identify several signs that, in retrospect, should have told us that something bad was looming.

First, there was the increasing number of large PE funds. Back in 1996, there were just 19 PE funds with more than $1 billion under management, but we had 170 of them in 2006.

Another warning sign was the surge in IPOs of private equity and hedge funds themselves. The annual number of such IPOs, which had been between one and three from 1996 to 2003, jumped to 15 in 2006 alone. This trend indicated a strong appetite to source capital from any available channel, perhaps signaling that market discipline was weakening.

A further indicator was the growth of the global capital overhang: an excess of dry powder (committed but uninvested capital) relative to the number of quality investment opportunities. The growth of this overhang was clearly visible: it grew from nearly zero in 1998 to almost $100 billion by 2000. After remaining stable for two years, it surged to nearly $150 billion in 2004 and continued to climb thereafter.

Additionally, the nature of typical private equity acquisitions shifted between 2000 and 2007. While in 2000 and 2001 most deals were corporate divestitures of business units, by 2007 the majority had become public-to-private transactions. This shift suggested an excess of capital competing for a limited pool of opportunities, ultimately targeting the most accessible assets: entire public companies.

The escalating size of leveraged buyouts (LBOs) also pointed to a potential loss of market discipline. Before 2000, LBOs with an enterprise value exceeding $10 billion were virtually nonexistent, yet by 2006, five to six such deals were occurring annually. Post-2006, the market saw the emergence of $20 billion and then $30 billion transactions, culminating in at least two attempted deals valued at more than $50 billion between 2007 and 2008. In total, approximately 25 deals exceeding $10 billion were completed between 2005 and 2008, representing an unprecedented scale of activity.

The onset of the global financial crisis dealt a particularly severe blow to the buyout segment. Once the downturn took hold, the industry's structural dependence on readily available leverage became starkly evident. Buyout fund managers customarily follow a sequential investment rhythm—typically closing a new transaction every 6–12 months—because they lack the operational capacity and capital to acquire and oversee multiple targets simultaneously.

When credit markets froze, the supply of acquisition financing contracted sharply, curtailing the managers' ability to deploy committed capital. At the same time, the valuations of portfolio companies purchased at the market peak deteriorated markedly. Public-equity indices declined by approximately 35–50%, offering a rough proxy for the magnitude of unrealized losses within private-equity portfolios.

Consequently, limited partners—many of whom had aggressively increased their allocations to the asset class in the preceding expansion—reassessed the risk-return profile of private equity. Faced with declining net-asset values and heightened liquidity concerns, they deferred or reduced new commitments, exacerbating the industry's short-term funding constraints.

Figure 1.21 shows the impact the crisis had on the deal value in 2007 for global lending to LBOs, which fell from more than $600 billion to $144 billion, a decrease of 77%.

Another metric is provided by the number of deals, the deal volume. Industry went from 712 deals in 2007 to 281 in 2008, a 60% decrease, and the banks were finding it increasingly difficult to lend to buyouts because their own capital position was endangered and constrained, so they would shy away from lending money.

The hung loans—debt that banks had underwritten for leveraged transactions but were unable to syndicate to other investors—were also quite enormous. Citygroup especially suffered quite a lot at the time, with $43 billion of hung loans in early 2008. There was about $200 billion of leverage loans held by the syndicating banks in July 2007, and the crunch lasted beyond 2010, even though the crisis started more or less in 2007 with a peak in 2008.

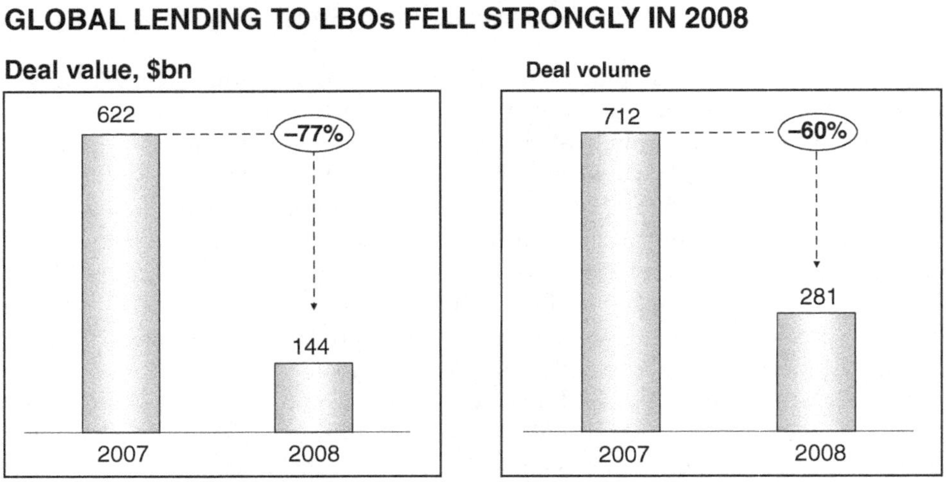

FIGURE 1.21 Global lending to LLBOs in 2007 and 2008.
Source: Dealogic.

Another important metric is the average write-down, the adjustment of book value for unrealized loss in marked downturns, of private portfolios, which was 44% in 2008. According to *Financial News*, 550 redundancies were announced by buyout firms globally between September 2008 and March 2009. The Boston Consulting Group, together with IESE, produced an alarming report announcing that almost 50% of the companies in the portfolios of private equity companies could default within three years (Boston Consulting Group, 2008). Credit rating agencies Moody's and Standard and Poor's also predicted that the default rate would rise significantly during the recession.

When the largest US LBO funds showed their performance in June 2009, six to nine months after the peak of the crisis, actually only 20% of them at most had incurred strong difficulties; not as severe as what had been predicted. In early 2010, the Private Equity Council[20] argued that companies backed by private equity demonstrated superior resilience during the financial crisis. According to their research, among more than 3,200 PE-backed firms acquired in the 2000–2009 period, the annual default rate reached just 2.8% during the recession, significantly below the 6.2% rate observed among comparable non-PE companies with similar financing structures.[21] However, it is undeniable that the overall performance had declined sharply.

Figure 1.22 illustrates this with the State Street private equity index. Even though it is not representative of the entire industry, it gives us a useful benchmark, and the quarterly IRR for all private equity that used to perform at between 5% and 10% in their sample became negative in 2008. It was at –8% in September 2008.

[20]The American Investment Council (AIC), formerly the Private Equity Growth Capital Council (PEGCC), is a lobbying, advocacy, and research organization based in Washington, DC, that was launched by a consortium of leading private equity firms in February 2007.

[21]https://www.investmentcouncil.org/private-equity-backed-companies-weathered-great-recession-better-than-peers-new-pec-study-finds/?utm_source=chatgpt.com.

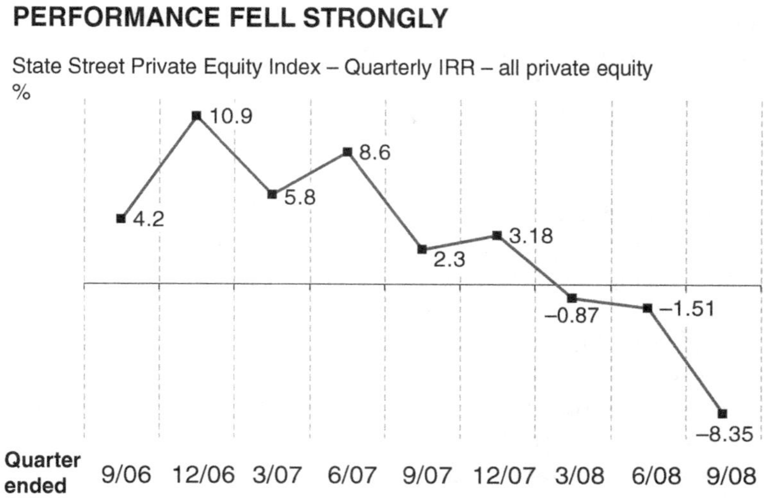

FIGURE 1.22 State street private equity index during the global financial crisis.
Source: State street.

There was still a huge, immediate impact, and several agreed deals were aborted at that time. The terms were renegotiated, break-off fees of up to 1% were incurred, and a few potential investors invoked the so-called Material Adverse Change (MAC) clause to renege from the deals and that included what would have been the largest deal ever. In effect, the symbolic end of the pre-crisis "golden age" of mega-buyouts was the collapse of the proposed acquisition of BCE Inc. (Bell Canada). Announced in June 2007 at the peak of the market, the transaction was valued at approximately $52 billion and was set to be the largest leveraged buyout in history, led by a private equity consortium that included the Ontario Teachers' Pension Plan (OTPP). The deal ultimately became a direct casualty of the Global Financial Crisis. By the time it was scheduled to close in late 2008, the seizure of global credit markets made its massive debt structure untenable, leading auditors to conclude that the new, heavily indebted entity would fail to meet legal solvency requirements. Its cancellation definitively signaled that the era of abundant, cheap debt that had fueled ever-larger LBOs was over.

While trailing the United States by a far margin, European activity had benefited a lot from the boom years of the 1990s. Buyouts and buy-ins in Europe went from less than $30 billion in transactions in 1996 to about 200 billion in 2007. As in the United States, Europe was hit hard by the crisis. At Candesic, we saw the overall LBO market divided by 10 in Europe. While that was not the case in Candesic's core industry sector of healthcare, the next two years were very difficult ones, particularly for advisors. As for the investment banks that had once ridden high on the wave of lucrative PE mandates, they suddenly faced the stark reality of being unable to cover their basic fixed costs.

Most stakeholders were hit severely by the crisis. Investors in PE funds particularly struggled if they needed to exit. Many funds went bust. An unusually large number of portfolio companies went bust—nothing like the 50% that was predicted by BCG,[22] but still enough to make the life of PE investors difficult.

[22] See report published by the Boston Consulting Group and IESE in 2008.

The GFC uncovered several ethical issues motivated by greed. Excesses that test the legal limits—fraud, collusion, and manipulation—were not new but were starkly revealed under the heightened scrutiny of the crisis, with LBO transactions attracting particular attention. We will discuss them in Chapter 8 and extend the discussion to other controversies in the relationships among stakeholders.

1.8.2.1 After the Financial Crisis After the financial crisis, many were left with the same question. As Joe Rice, chairman of CD&R, a major operating player, put it: "Is private equity just about financial engineering, or is it really an ownership model able to produce sustainable improvement in business?"

The financial crisis blurred people's perspective by bringing lots of companies to the verge of bankruptcy, companies that might otherwise have had a bright future. Any form of debt was suddenly toxic, masking, or undoing the operational improvements achieved by many portfolio companies, temporarily highlighting the financial engineering side of private equity.

Four major factors should be considered when understanding the credit crisis. First, increasing public scrutiny: as individuals suffered financial losses, fears of further deterioration mounted, prompting demands for tighter regulations and higher taxes on those who had benefited from historically favorable tax conditions. The second factor was a severe freeze in the LBO market following the credit crunch, which sharply restricted access to financing for large transactions, effectively halting deal activity for a significant period. Third, the collapse of multiple stock markets exacerbated economic instability, contributing directly to the onset of a global recession by eroding household wealth and corporate investment appetite. Finally, many potential sellers in the market were reluctant to divest their holdings during this turbulent period, recognizing that market conditions were too unfavorable to realize optimal value.

In spite of those challenges, private equity was still a great model for owning businesses, with a great track record of creating value over the long term. But it became affected by short-term events, and it needed more governance.

With regard to the credit crunch, the LPs had become more cautious (and who wouldn't), but their initial objective of increasing or at least maintaining their allocation to PE remained firmly in place.

Regarding the stock market collapse, two factors guaranteed that the credit markets would recover, perhaps not to the conditions of 2007 before the crisis but to something more like normality, if any year would be indicative of normality. First, there was a substantial influx of capital seeking high-yield investment opportunities, and second, there were low historical default rates in PE.

Regarding the issue with vendors not being ready to sell, well, private equity represented only one or two trillion dollars of assets under management back in 2007, compared to $60 trillion in stocks.

Importantly, there were winners as well as losers: it is all a question of timing. Those who had raised enough money but not invested it just before the crisis were the clear winners; those who had invested everything, especially just before the crisis, and who had paid high multiples and now needed to raise the next fund, they were the clear losers. Those who were cash rich were ready to seize all the best opportunities—they might have had to wait a year or two until things settled a little bit, but it was a time when they had little competition. The other funds were unable to raise money into 2009 and 2010.

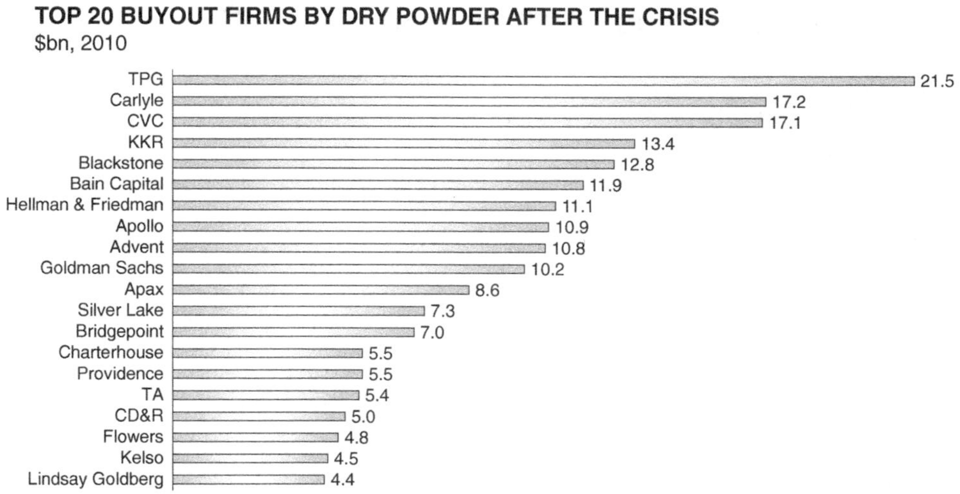

FIGURE 1.23 Top 20 buyout firms by dry powder after the global financial crisis.
Source: Candesic research.

The funds, like TPG, Carlyle, CVC, KKR, Blackstone, Bain Capital, who had more than £10 billion each in dry powder right after the crisis, were the cash kings of the after crisis (Figure 1.23). They may or may not have been the best investors, but their timing was perfect, and their timing was perfect partially because they were so big, so there is again an advantage for the largest players.

In 2009, Guy Hands, CEO of buyout firm Terra Firma, famously said: "Private equity should not expect sizeable leverage in new deals until 2011—2012. Deals in 2009 will be like picking claret in 2003—a lot will look promising but end up disappointing with only a few stars. 2010 deals will, however, be like 1982 clarets, difficult to find a poor one and with a lot of stars."

Some evidence suggests that the best deals are done during downturns such as this. In this study (Figure 1.24) that shows the net IRR of US-focused buyout funds in vintage years during the decades before the crisis, a clear correlation is shown between downturn periods and increased returns. This illustrates the advantage that can be gained by having cash available when the crisis strikes.

1.8.3 COVID-19 and Disruptions of the Supply Chain

We now discuss some effects of the COVID-19 pandemic on PE.

First, private equity often becomes a target of political scrutiny during episodes of turmoil or societal disruption. In the United States, for example, in the spring of 2020, a number of senators from the left of the Democratic Party, such as Elizabeth Warren and Alexandria Ocasio-Cortez, stated that they wanted to go after or even ban some private equity firms for profiting excessively from businesses hit hard by COVID-19. They aimed to combat predatory mergers during this period. Although their efforts did not lead to significant immediate changes, this sort of scrutiny is sometimes justified, given the documented abuses and predatory behaviors of some private equity players.

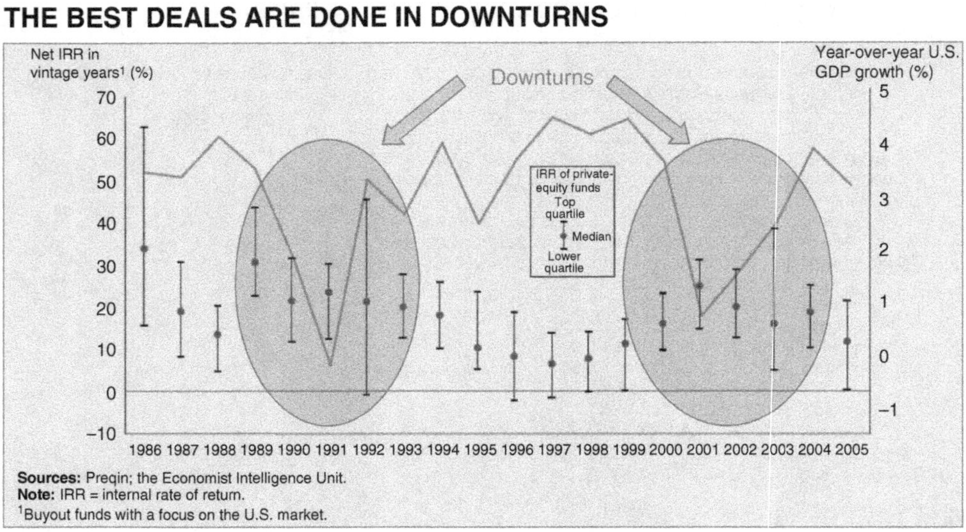

FIGURE 1.24 IRR of PE funds by quartile in 1986–2005.
Source: IESE-BCG report (2008).

More significant than the politics, however, was the disruption to supply chains. These were impacted more than they had been for many years and not just by the pandemic but also subsequently by a combination of other disruptions, including transport disruptions in many parts of the world, such as the blockage of the Suez Canal and issues around Iran, the Indian Ocean, and the South China Sea with lots of skirmishes between China and its neighbors. And in addition to all that, the increasing costs of energy affect global transportation.

An awful lot of oil was needed to move the 20,000 tankers that cross the world daily and which themselves transport a significant part of that same oil. If these supply chains are disrupted, we do not really have a good alternative. If we cannot transport that oil, the economy ceases to function, or at least a very large part of it cannot function anymore. This affects PE portfolio companies and other small to medium-size enterprises (SMEs), which often have fewer alternatives or resources to adapt than large multinationals.

Other global challenges that impact private equity include the rise of autocracies, the rivalry between the United States and China, and the establishment of new currency zones with several parts of the world essentially trying to eradicate the hegemony of the dollar. These events had various consequences, including the strategic repatriations in areas like microchips, vaccines, APIs (active pharmaceutical ingredients), and ammunition for the defense industry. And it has also highlighted the long-term need to reduce transport costs and enhance geographical proximity. It no longer makes sense to transport pretty much everything, including sand and water, across the entire world.

So, that will all have an impact on private equity, but private equity can also play a positive role in that transformation of the world. We should assume PE owners are sophisticated and run well-connected organizations, good not only at lobbying, but able to help their companies adapt faster and better to a changing world.

1.8.4 Silicon Valley Bank

Silicon Valley Bank (SVB) was a prominent bank that primarily served the technology startup ecosystem, accounting for up to 70% of the venture debt market. Its collapse in March 2023 was a shock to the financial industry (Figure 1.25). Several factors contributed to its downfall, starting with significant concentration risk. SVB had a highly concentrated customer base, primarily tech startups. When most of these companies suddenly faced funding challenges and withdrew their deposits, the bank faced a liquidity crisis. This was coupled with interest rate risk: as interest rates rose, the value of SVB's bond holdings declined significantly. This mismatched asset-liability position exacerbated the bank's financial troubles. Some argue that less stringent regulations on banks, particularly those deemed to be less risky, also contributed to the crisis.

The collapse of SVB had significant implications for the private equity industry, but more specifically in the VC segment. It led to reduced debt funding for startups and increased scrutiny. As a primary lender to startups, SVB's collapse temporarily restricted the flow of capital to this relatively small but crucial segment of the economy. This had the potential to slow down the creation of new, disruptive businesses. The crisis also highlighted the risks associated with the factors we mentioned. This led to increased regulatory scrutiny of financial institutions, including those serving the private equity industry.

The implications were particularly significant for the health sector, considering SVB had worked with three quarters of all US healthcare-related IPOS since 2020. Many companies involved in clinical trials or drug development were unable to access their funds and faced difficulties in paying suppliers and employees, potentially disrupting ongoing research and development activities. Large banks that were called to fill the gap often lacked the specialized services and understanding of the unique needs of healthcare startups that SVB provided. It was less of an issue in other sectors.

The collapse of SVB created opportunities for private credit firms to fill the financing gap left by traditional banks, especially in the startup and growth equity space, but HSBC, JPMorgan, Stifel, and other banks moved fast to hire SVB's employees and

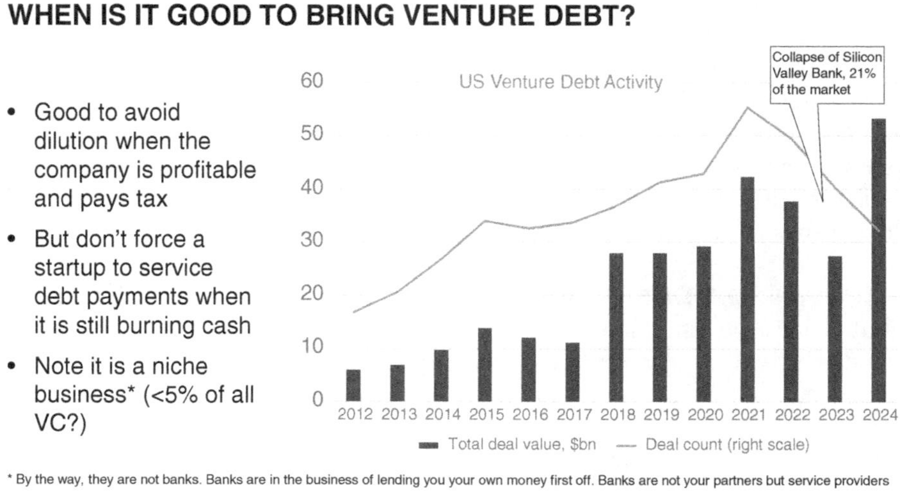

FIGURE 1.25 US venture debt activity.
Source: Candesic analysis.

capture part of the business. Many of SVB's assets and deposits were transferred to the Federal Deposit Insurance Corporation (FDIC) for management. The FDIC then facilitated the transfer of certain assets and liabilities to other banks. Two years later, while the market had not fully returned to its pre-SVB state, the absence of a single dominant player had led to a more diversified and balanced ecosystem, with both traditional banks and nonbank lenders coexisting and offering unique debt solutions. Against all odds, 2024 was marked by a historical record of venture debt, more than $50 billion, still a very marginal component of VC and PE financing.

1.8.5 High Inflation

Inflation in 2022 was a "long-awaited surprise" and a major headache for the private equity industry. Central banks responded to rising prices by increasing interest rates, which substantially elevated the cost of debt financing. This environment rendered LBOs more complex to execute. Concurrently, the escalating inflationary pressures eroded the valuation of target companies, complicating exit strategies.

Portfolio companies grappled with increased operational costs and the pressure to adjust pricing without deterring customers. These factors, combined with ongoing supply chain disruptions, further strained profitability. Investor sentiment was impacted as well, with a growing preference for less risky assets.

The industry demonstrated resilience. Firms adapted by prioritizing operational efficiency, diversifying investment strategies, extending investment horizons, and enhancing risk management practices. But the distress frontier had shifted, and the firms that had undergone an LBO with variable debt prior to 2022 were now struggling.

1.8.6 The Impact of Tariffs and Trade Policy Under Trump's Second Term

Trade policies, particularly tariffs and regulatory barriers, have become significant factors shaping private equity strategies in healthcare. Trump's second presidency, launched in 2025, revived and intensified protectionist measures, including steep tariffs, reshoring mandates, and executive orders affecting pricing and manufacturing. For PE-backed healthcare companies operating across borders or reliant on global supply chains, these policies altered cost structures, investment strategies, and exit valuations. They translated into higher diligence thresholds, longer holding periods, a trend toward continuation vehicles capturing approximately half of all PE deal flow, and a clear strategic shift toward domestic, digital, or vertically integrated assets, and assets that were not exposed to government reimbursement or global supply chain risks. Trade policy, once peripheral to healthcare investment, became a core consideration in portfolio construction, value creation planning, and exit timing.

1.8.6.1 Tariffs and Supply Chain Disruption In the United States, renewed tariffs—including (initially) 10% on Chinese imports and 25% on selected products from Mexico and Canada—raised input costs for medical device manufacturers, pharmaceutical firms, diagnostics companies, and CDMOs. Many of these firms rely on imported APIs, reagents, packaging materials, or electronic components. As a result, cost inflation compressed EBITDA margins, especially for mid-market portfolio companies lacking vertical integration.

These effects were particularly acute for PE-owned firms assembling devices or pharmaceuticals in the United States but sourcing critical components abroad. Longer lead times, higher compliance burdens, and pricing volatility disrupted product launch timelines and regulatory filings. This, in turn, delayed value creation milestones and heightened execution risk.

CROs and manufacturers also faced increased prices on imported lab equipment and consumables. Combined with new FDA inspection fees for foreign facilities and customs delays, these pressures contributed to operational unpredictability—a critical concern for investors targeting margin expansion or rapid scale-up.

1.8.6.2 Onshoring, Industrial Policy, and Capital Expenditure Pressures In parallel with tariffs, Trump's May 2025 Executive Order (EO) directed the FDA and EPA to fast-track permits and reviews for new US-based drug manufacturing facilities, in an effort to "restore a robust domestic pharmaceutical base." These policy shifts supported PE theses focused on domestic infrastructure build-out but introduced capital intensity and timeline risks incompatible with shorter fund cycles.

While long-term reshoring may benefit firms able to invest in US API or device manufacturing, construction lead times of 5–10 years, skilled labor shortages, and CapEx intensity pose significant hurdles. For many sponsors, the near-term implication is a strategic pivot: investing in contract manufacturers, logistics firms, and supply chain visibility platforms that support localization, rather than owning manufacturing assets outright.

1.8.6.3 Sector Rotation and Portfolio Repositioning Faced with rising material costs and regulatory volatility, US-based PE funds increasingly reoriented toward subsectors with minimal tariff exposure—such as domestic healthcare services, healthcare IT, AI-enabled platforms, and IP-driven biotech ventures in early-stage R&D. For these assets, geopolitical risk is lower, and digital scalability remains intact.

Still, growth equity investments in life sciences at the scale-up stage—where clinical development converges with manufacturing—became more exposed to trade risk. This forced PE sponsors to conduct deeper diligence on component sourcing, regulatory pathways, and pricing models in anticipation of ongoing trade policy turbulence.

1.8.6.4 Drug Pricing and Distribution Disruption In parallel with trade frictions, Trump's 2025 Executive Order (EO) targeting PBMs (pharmacy benefit managers) and drug pricing intermediaries added uncertainty to the pharmaceutical value chain. The EO instructed Health and Human Services and the Department of Labor to enforce greater transparency in PBM fee structures and to accelerate generic and biosimilar approval pathways, aiming to "knock out the middleman" and reduce patient drug prices.

For PE investors in specialty pharma, generics, or distribution platforms, these reforms created a dual dynamic: potential margin compression for intermediaries, but also new investment opportunities in cost-efficient or vertically integrated models aligned with lower out-of-pocket drug costs.

Additionally, the planned implementation of a "Most-Favored Nation" (MFN) drug pricing model, benchmarking US drug prices against Organisation for Economic Co-operation and Development (OECD) countries, created downward pricing pressure on branded drugs. Although legal and regulatory hurdles remain, this direction of travel affected revenue forecasting, particularly for PE-owned commercial-stage biopharma firms reliant on US pricing power.

1.8.6.5 European Impacts and Retaliatory Risks In Europe, the implications were different but equally disruptive. Many European portfolio companies in life sciences and medical technology serve US markets through exports or licensing arrangements.

Retaliatory tariffs, customs friction, and regulatory divergence under the revived Trump trade agenda raised operational risks.

For example, a PE-backed biotech firm in Germany or France licensing to a US distributor could face pricing renegotiations or delayed regulatory clearance if tariff burdens increase end-user costs. Exporters of diagnostics or imaging equipment also encountered new FDA review protocols and import delays, creating liquidity strains and disrupting cash flow forecasts.

Moreover, European firms reliant on Asian supply chains—particularly for APIs and electronic subcomponents—found themselves indirectly affected by US-China tensions. In response, several PE sponsors initiated reshoring or nearshoring initiatives, albeit cautiously, as these typically required fresh capital injection and longer payback periods.

1.8.6.6 Implications for Exits and Portfolio Valuation Across regions, the compounded uncertainty—tariffs, PBM reform, price controls, and geopolitical tension—slowed down M&A exits. Public markets began discounting companies with high exposure to global supply chains, while strategic acquirers applied deeper scrutiny to potential CapEx liabilities and sourcing fragility.

Exit valuations were revised downward for firms with exposure to tariffed goods or requiring significant supply chain restructuring. Value creation shifted away from multiple expansion and toward operational resilience, integration, and localization. Sponsors with a playbook focused on efficiency, self-sufficiency, and digital transformation were better positioned to withstand this phase.

1.8.7 Key Learnings

What have past crises taught us? Setting aside the 1720 South Sea Bubble, private-equity shocks appear roughly every decade: junk-bond turmoil in the late 1980s, the internet bubble in 2000, the Global Financial Crisis in 2008, and the COVID-19 disruption in 2020.

First, it helps to distinguish "accidents" from structural shifts. The dot-com crash was an accident—including too much internet-capacity built too quickly—whereas the post-2008 leverage unwind reflected deeper changes in credit markets.

Second, the best PE deals often happen in downturns. Seasoned sponsors deploy dry powder to buy high-quality assets at distressed prices. As a result, senior investors with crisis experience tend to outperform during market turmoil.

Third, crises spark a race between regulation and technology, especially when innovation enables new abuses. From insider-trading booms to AI-driven fraud, each wave of disruptive tech triggers a regulatory response. Private-equity firms that anticipate when rules will tighten or loosen can ride these cycles to their advantage.

Finally, recent events suggest the era of ever-expanding globalization may be ending. Geopolitical tensions, energy-security risks, and climate shocks are pushing toward regionalization—a world divided between free-market democracies and controlled autocracies. Private equity, which thrives on entrepreneurial dynamism and open capital flows, must adapt to invest in regions that uphold transparent rule-of-law and market freedoms.

We started out by looking at some historical crises, which demonstrated that such events are nothing new but rather come round periodically in some form or another, and the private equity industry needs to be prepared for when they do.

We then looked in some detail at the events of the financial crisis that hit in 2007–2008. We saw that, although private equity was perhaps not hit as hard as some predicted at the time, there were both winners and losers, and the crisis uncovered several issues around greed, excess, and regulation.

Lastly, we looked at some more recent crises, particularly those triggered by the COVID-19 pandemic and other geopolitical events that followed it.

This review of crises that have impacted private equity over the years can help anticipate what could happen again and how best to deal with such crises when they do occur.

1.9 CASE STUDY: STADA ARZNEIMITTEL TAKE-PRIVATE LBO

1.9.1 Case Study: STADA Arzneimittel—Reinvigorating a German Pharmaceutical Icon

The STADA case study highlights how two PE firms successfully collaborated to take private and transform the company into a leading healthcare platform through strategic acquisitions and operational improvements. Although the anticipated IPO did not materialize, the partnership between the investors culminated in the sale of a majority stake to a specialist healthcare investor, ensuring continuity and positioning STADA for further growth. This example illustrates the effectiveness of PE collaboration in driving long-term value creation and operational excellence in the healthcare sector.

1.9.2 From Pharmacists' Cooperative to European Powerhouse

Founded in 1895 in Dresden, STADA Arzneimittel began life as a cooperative of German pharmacists committed to ensuring affordable access to standardized medicines. Over the twentieth century, the company transitioned into a leading producer of generic prescription drugs and over-the-counter (OTC) products. By the early 2000s, STADA had become a recognized name across Germany and parts of Europe, particularly for its branded generics and consumer health lines, including cold and flu remedies, pain relievers, and cardiovascular treatments.

As it expanded internationally through organic growth and acquisitions, the company built a strong commercial presence in Central and Eastern Europe. However, despite a broad portfolio and solid market presence, STADA remained fundamentally a volume-driven generics business, with limited pricing power and few innovation-led growth levers.

1.9.3 Losing Ground: Margin Pressure and Strategic Drift

By the 2010s, STADA faced a challenging environment. Germany's statutory health insurers imposed increasing cost constraints, while price competition across Europe intensified. Global players like Teva and Mylan applied pressure on margins, and STADA's own operational structure remained fragmented.

Between 2014 and 2016, the company listed on the Frankfurt stock exchange entered a period of drift. Revenue growth slowed, earnings came under pressure, and strategic initiatives lacked cohesion. Shareholders began losing patience, and activist investors, led by Active Ownership Capital, initiated campaigns to restructure the board and improve governance. STADA's long-serving management resisted at first but eventually conceded to a strategic review process. What had once been a stable, if unspectacular, pharmaceutical stalwart was now openly considering a change in ownership.

1.9.4 A Bold Bet: Bain Capital and Cinven Take Control

In 2017, a consortium formed by Bain Capital and Cinven acquired STADA for €5.3 billion EV in one of the largest healthcare buyouts in Germany's history. The deal followed a competitive process and closed at €66 per share, representing a premium of nearly 50% over the company's preannouncement share price.

To the new owners, STADA represented a classic value opportunity: a strong brand with consistent revenues but underwhelming profitability, burdened by operational inefficiencies and outdated systems. By taking the company private, Bain Capital and Cinven could implement the transformation without public scrutiny. The private equity thesis centered on cost optimization, portfolio rationalization, and growth through select acquisitions, particularly in the less price-sensitive OTC segment.

1.9.5 Operational Overhaul and Targeted Expansion

Following the buyout, the PE firms moved quickly. A new CEO and senior management team were brought in, tasked with executing a wide-reaching operational reset. Manufacturing was consolidated, redundant facilities were shuttered, and procurement processes were overhauled. Investments in automation and digitization further improved the company's cost base.

Meanwhile, STADA began shifting emphasis away from low-margin generics toward branded consumer health. This included a few well-timed acquisitions: Takeda's European OTC portfolio, GSK's off-patent brands, and Walmark, a Central European supplements manufacturer. Each acquisition expanded the company's footprint in defensible, high-margin categories with strong brand loyalty.

These changes paid off. By 2023, EBITDA had more than doubled, rising from approximately €364 million in 2017 to over €800 million, while the company's product mix became more resilient and strategically focused. Though revenue growth remained modest, the margin expansion created significant enterprise value.

1.9.6 A Return to Market: Preparing for IPO

By early 2024, with the operational turnaround largely complete and financial performance substantially improved, Bain Capital and Cinven began preparing STADA for a public listing. Reports suggested then that a Frankfurt IPO could value the company at close to €10 billion, nearly double its 2017 acquisition price. In parallel, they were negotiating a sale to another PE firm, CapVest, but as reported by Bloomberg, the discussions broke down over differences in valuation and the structure of the bid.

The timing aligned with renewed investor appetite for profitable mid-cap healthcare companies, and STADA's streamlined structure, consistent earnings, and growth story made it an attractive listing candidate. The IPO market window was favorable in mid-2025, with STADA positioned as a prime candidate alongside other German mid-caps like Ottobock. While the exact exit structure had yet to be finalized, it was clear that the PE owners were preparing for a monetization event that could mark one of Europe's more successful healthcare turnarounds of the past decade.

On August 31, 2025, after eight years of active ownership, Bain Capital and Cinven announced the sale of a majority stake in STADA to CapVest, valuing the enterprise around $10 billion. The two firms would retain a minority stake in the company. They seem to have executed a dual-track process exceptionally well, using IPO preparation as negotiating leverage.

A back-of-the-envelope calculation indicates they achieved an estimated IRR below 14%, which is modest by PE standards, but in line with the real average performance of the industry. They are likely to have extracted interim dividends, though specific amounts are not disclosed. The initial 2017 takeover offer included paying shareholders the 2016 dividend of €0.72 per share. The debt reduction strategy near exit was partly financed through "shareholder equity contribution," which could indicate either additional equity injections or foregone distributions.

The debt story reveals a more complex strategy than simple reduction. Initially, leverage likely increased as the sponsors executed more than 25 targeted acquisitions during their ownership. The debt reduction was primarily executed near the exit to enable the sale, not as a consistent deleveraging strategy throughout ownership. The timing suggests this was primarily an exit preparation strategy rather than consistent deleveraging. They refinanced debt earlier in 2025 with a portability clause, meaning CapVest wouldn't need to refinance again, smoothing the transaction path.

1.9.7 Lessons from the STADA Deal

STADA illustrates the kind of platform that PE firms favor in mature European markets: an operationally sound company with brand strength and scale, but with untapped potential due to inertia, inefficiencies, or strategic misalignment. Bain Capital and Cinven's approach, based on disciplined execution, strong governance, and focused M&A, created a more competitive and profitable business without relying on radical transformation or speculative growth.

CapVest's willingness to pay full IPO valuations in a private transaction reflects the scarcity value of scaled healthcare platforms. This represents a "strategic buyer premium" where PE buyers pay public market multiples to avoid execution risk and market volatility.

While it may not have generated the headlines of a high-multiple tech exit, the STADA deal reminds us that PE investors can create real value in established, low-glamour sectors like generics and OTC health, and do so with relatively low risk.

1.10 CHAPTER SUMMARY

In summary, we have seen various definitions of private equity. We have considered a number of these definitions to grasp an overall idea of what PE is about.

We have discussed who invests in PE, what their general motives are, and the constraints that shape the investment decisions of different types of investors. We have considered the importance of LBOs, which constitute the main and most discussed segment of the PE world, though not the only one. We have also explored the history of PE, from the twentieth century to more recent times.

In addition, we have examined the various stages of PE investing and considered the way in which PE funds are typically set up and structured. We have also discussed the distribution of PE commitments and PE deals, and the tight relationship between the three phases of the PE cycle: fundraising, investment, and exit.

We have introduced the investment case in healthcare and reviewed the impact of the crises of the last 50 years, before wrapping up with the case of the STADA LBO.

CHAPTER 2

Types and Economics of Private Equity

This chapter covers the various segments that make up the private equity (PE) industry. While leveraged buyouts are the most prominent, widely studied, and scrutinized segment, PE encompasses many alternative investment strategies. We will examine these alternatives, including secondaries, funds of funds, and listed PE. Additionally, this chapter provides an opportunity to introduce real-world situations we have encountered, both as consultants advising PE investors and through our interactions with PE firms over the past 20 years. We will continue to illustrate the concepts with examples from healthcare and life sciences. Finally, we will conclude the chapter with a special case study.

Figure 2.1 introduces the different types of funds and segments in PE.

The largest segment by far is leveraged buyouts (LBOs). Real estate also represents a significant segment, though it is not always classified strictly as PE—many, however, include it within the broader PE landscape. Growth capital is a smaller segment, both in terms of unrealized value and available capital (dry powder).

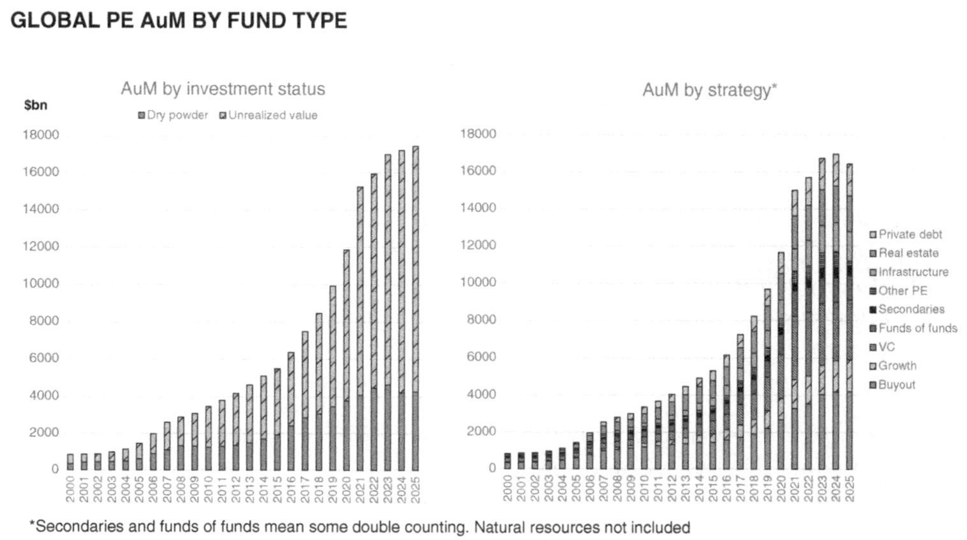

FIGURE 2.1 Global PE AuM by fund type.
Source: Preqin (part of Blackrock).

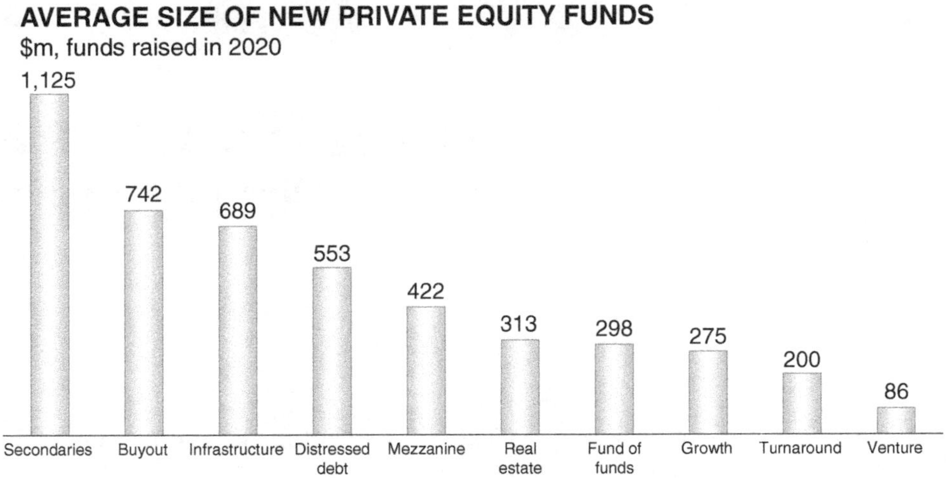

FIGURE 2.2 Average size of new PE funds raised in 2020.
Source: Candesic research.

We can also observe the average size of newly created PE funds at the time they are raised (Figure 2.2). While these data are from 2020, it remains highly representative. The largest funds tend to be in secondaries, buyouts, infrastructure, and distressed debt—topics we will discuss later. In contrast, smaller funds typically include venture funds, as well as funds of funds and turnaround funds.

2.1 VENTURE CAPITAL

2.1.1 Venture Capital as an Asset Class

Venture capital (VC) is now a topic in itself, usually treated as a separate asset class by investors. We discussed how it separated from the rest of PE in the late 1990s. It cannot be ignored in the wider PE context—the VC segment is often included in PE statistics—but we will only view it as a segment of PE. We start with a definition provided by once almighty Silicon Valley Bank, one of our preferred ones.

> *The funding VCs provide nascent businesses—and industries—the chance to flourish. They help to bring ideas to life and fill the void that capital markets and traditional bank debt leave due to the high risk associated with limited operating history, lack of collateral and unproven business models.*

A few additional definitions can be useful food for thought. Note the keywords:

- *Money that is invested or is available for investment in a new company, especially one that involves risk* (Cambridge)
- *Capital that is invested in projects that have a high risk of failure, but that will bring large profits if they are successful* (Collins)
- *Money invested in an innovative enterprise in which both the potential for profit and the risk of loss are considerable* (YourDictionary)
- *A temporary quasi-equity or equity investment provided to small businesses and startup firms that are expected to have long-term growth* (Bankrate)

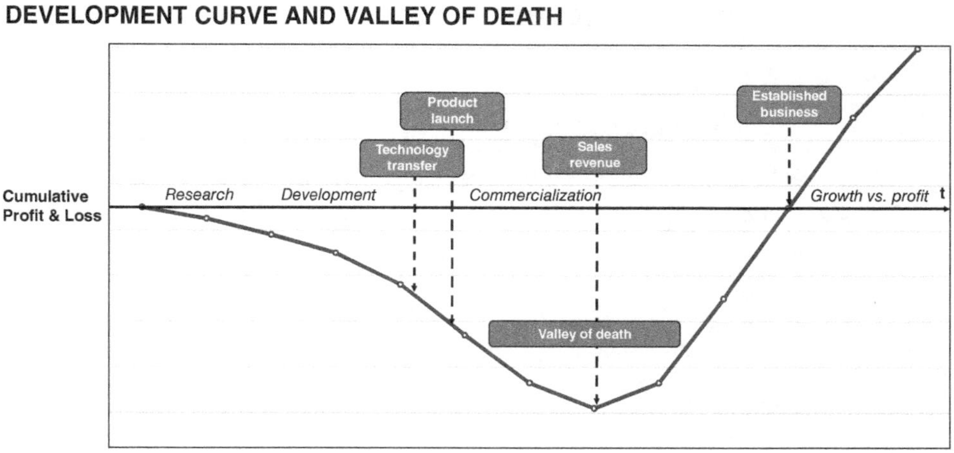

FIGURE 2.3 Startup company development curve.
Source: Candesic analysis.

To help us frame it more finely, where does VC start? We have mentioned the existence of an informal segment of investors. This is actually mostly relevant for VC. Not only do we identify a significant informal segment of financing by friends and family members as well as angel investors providing generally smaller and longer term, "pre-seed" equity investments, but we can also define an intermediary, semiformal segment of financing by corporations and nontraditional asset managers: CVCs (corporate venture capitalists), "Micro VCs" and "Angel Clubs." Those segments have been traditionally less well reported but play an important role in funding startups, potentially preparing them for the next, more formal stages of VC financing.

A closer look at the startup company life cycle we introduced earlier can be useful. The "*valley of death*" curve (Figure 2.3) refers to the period during the initial investment in a startup when the organization is not generating sufficient revenues to meet the expenses and could result in a negative cash flow if it does not raise more capital. There are predictable costs, like rent and salaries, and harder to predict R&D and marketing costs. The longer this period, the higher the probability of premature failure. It is an assumed risk of entrepreneurship and almost unavoidable for any new business. It is also a useful reminder that, in the first years of a company, there is no time to rest; one must plan the next stages of financing as accurately as possible.

2.1.2 Stages of Financing

Within VC, various stages of financing are distinguished, typically beginning at the Seed level. At this stage, companies are pre-revenue but have a tested concept or prototype that is ready for commercialization. The seed funding typically ranges from $1 to 5 million as of 2025, with amounts increasing over time.

The next stages of financing are referred to as Series A, Series B, Series C, and so forth (Figure 2.4). Series A generally involves funding between $4 million and $15 million, Series B ranges from $15 million to $40 million, and Series C typically sees investments in the range of $40 million to $100 million (Figure 2.5).

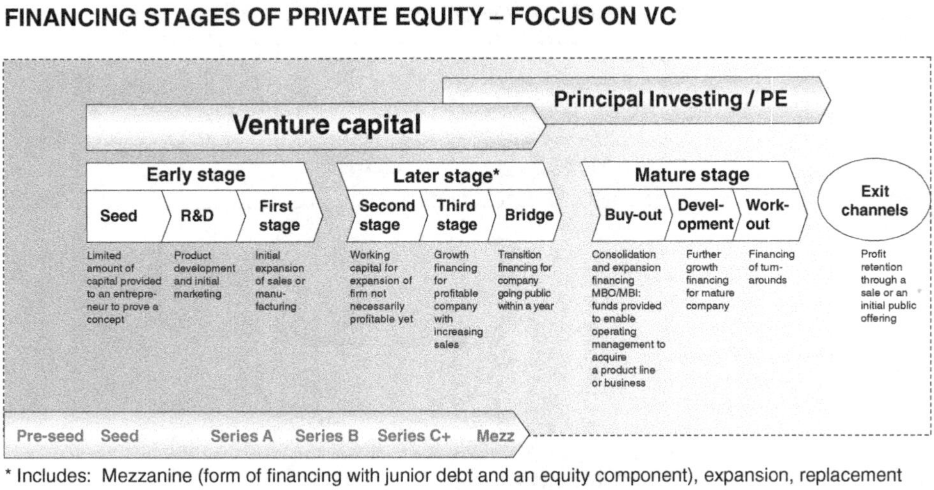

FIGURE 2.4 Financing stages of VC within PE.
Source: Candesic analysis.

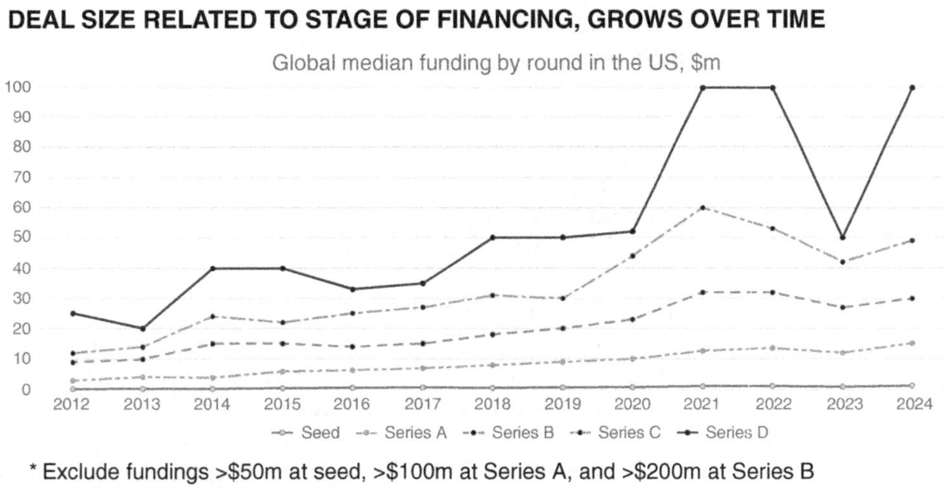

FIGURE 2.5 Global median funding by round.
Source: Crunchbase; Candesic (Series D).

Rounds beyond Series C are often called mega rounds, with investments starting at approximately $100 million. The size of the average investment grows logically as the company progresses through each financing stage, reflecting its maturity and the increased capital needs of the business.

2.1.3 Convertible Loan Notes

Convertible loan notes (CLNs) have become increasingly popular in startup financing as a bridge between early seed capital and formal equity rounds, particularly in Europe. Unlike traditional venture debt, which functions as pure debt requiring regular interest payments and eventual repayment, CLNs are designed to convert into equity during a subsequent funding round, avoiding immediate cash servicing obligations. This fundamental difference makes CLNs more suitable for cash-strapped startups that cannot afford regular debt payments, while venture debt typically serves growth-stage companies with predictable revenue streams needing nondilutive capital alongside equity financing.

The primary advantages of CLNs include speed of execution (often closing within days versus months for equity rounds), lower legal costs ($1,500–$2,000 versus $10,000–$30,000 for equity), delayed valuation negotiations, and minimal founder dilution until conversion.

However, CLNs carry significant risks: if the startup fails to raise follow-on funding, founders may face forced repayment or liquidation; valuation caps can result in excessive dilution if the company significantly outperforms expectations; and the accrued interest (typically 6–8% in EUR and USD) compounds the conversion cost, effectively increasing the equity stake granted to investors. Additionally, CLNs can create a "floor valuation" effect where the conversion terms influence subsequent funding round pricing, potentially limiting the startup's negotiating power with future investors.

While CLNs offer tactical advantages for bridging funding gaps and capitalizing on time-sensitive opportunities, they work best in favorable market conditions with strong investor demand and clear paths to subsequent equity rounds—making them powerful but potentially dangerous instruments that require careful structuring and realistic exit planning.

2.1.4 Venture Debt

Venture debt represents a further step away from the core PE topic, as it involves a different form of financing for startups (Figure 2.6). While debt is generally not an ideal or natural financing option for most early-stage companies due to the high risk, lack

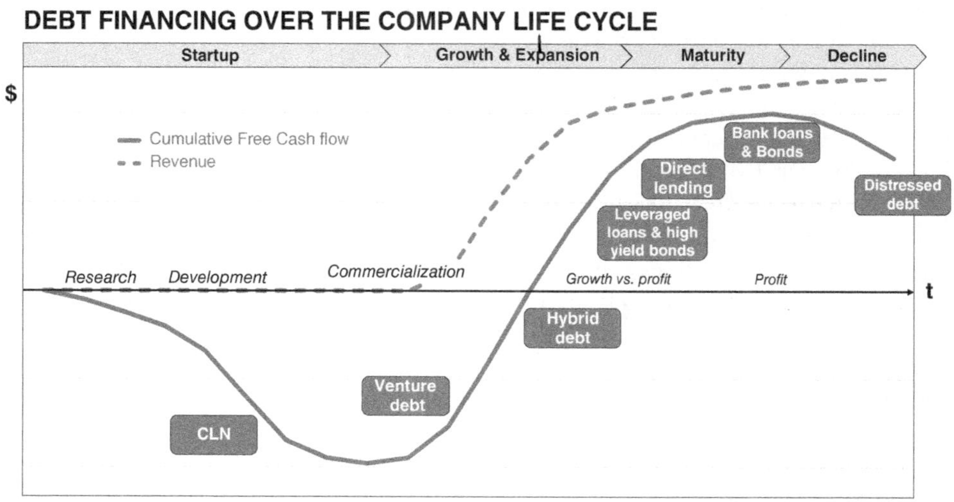

FIGURE 2.6 Debt financing over the PE life cycle.
Source: Candesic analysis.

of visibility on future cash flows, and absence of collateral, there exists a niche market for venture debt. This form of financing is primarily aimed at tech companies that have intellectual property (IP), equipment, or other forms of collateral, particularly in the United States.

While CLNs are often used as bridge funding between rounds and can happen from an early seed stage, venture debt tends to come later. In Europe, it is often offered to companies showing a decent level of recurring revenue (£1m+), and typically at Series A-stage at the earliest.

Unlike high-yield ("junk") bonds, which are unsecured debt instruments issued by more mature companies with lower credit ratings, venture debt is typically secured by tangible assets such as IP or equipment. This distinction makes venture debt an appealing option for certain startups that are not yet ready for equity funding but still need capital to grow and scale.

Venture loans are provided specifically to startup companies as a complement to the equity funding they have already raised, typically shortly after a VC round, allowing them to extend their runway, invest in growth, or reach key milestones without diluting existing shareholders. The loans are usually for one to three years and may include warrants as part of the financing deal, giving lenders some upside if the company succeeds.

In 2021, the venture debt deal value reached a peak of $35 billion in the United States and less than half that across Europe according to Pitchbook.

2.1.5 Venture Capital for Biotech, Medtech, Healthtech

Venture capital and venture debt are essential in the biotech, medtech, and healthtech sectors, where high research and development costs, lengthy timelines, and regulatory hurdles make financing particularly challenging. Biotech and medtech companies often start at the seed stage, with VC providing the necessary funds to advance innovative therapies, medical devices, or diagnostic technologies from concept to clinical trials. Series A and B rounds follow as companies progress and achieve proof of concept, often targeting large amounts of funding to navigate the expensive stages of product development and regulatory approvals.

Additionally, biotech companies typically advance through clearly defined clinical trial phases—Phase I (safety and dosage testing with 20–100 patients), Phase II (efficacy and side effects evaluation with 100–300 patients), and Phase III (large-scale testing with 1,000–3,000 patients to confirm effectiveness and monitor adverse reactions). Series B and C funding rounds often coincide with these costly clinical milestones, providing the $50–$100 million+ capital necessary to conduct expansive, multicenter trials that are essential for FDA or EMA regulatory approval. Medtech startups may similarly raise subsequent rounds as they approach regulatory clearances such as FDA 510(k) or CE marking, reflecting increasing product validation and market readiness. Healthtech companies, while often avoiding lengthy clinical trials, might use Series B and C rounds to scale technology infrastructure, enhance regulatory compliance (such as HIPAA or GDPR adherence), and expand customer acquisition efforts.

Venture debt also plays a crucial role in these sectors, especially for companies that have valuable intellectual property or equipment but may not yet be generating significant revenue. For instance, a biotech company with promising drug candidates or a medtech company with patented medical devices can use venture debt to secure additional working capital without further diluting equity. This approach is especially helpful in healthtech, where technology-driven solutions, such as AI in diagnostics or digital health platforms, require substantial investment to scale. Overall, both VC and venture debt are pivotal in propelling biotech, medtech, and healthtech innovations to market, enabling companies to navigate the financial complexities of these high-risk, high-reward industries.

DEFINING BIOTECH, MEDTECH, AND HEALTHTECH

Biotech (Biotechnology): Biotech refers to the use of biological organisms, systems, or processes to develop products and technologies that address medical, agricultural, and environmental challenges. In the medical field, biotechnology primarily focuses on developing innovative treatments, therapies, and drugs by manipulating biological systems or organisms at the molecular and cellular level. Examples include gene therapy, monoclonal antibodies, and personalized medicine.

Medtech (Medical Technology): Medtech refers to the design, development, and manufacturing of medical devices, equipment, and diagnostic tools used to treat, monitor, and diagnose medical conditions. Medtech products can range from simple devices like bandages to complex machinery such as MRI machines, pacemakers, or robotic surgical instruments. Medtech innovations are vital in improving patient care, enhancing the efficiency of healthcare systems, and enabling precise diagnostics and treatments.

Healthtech (Health Technology): Healthtech refers to the application of technology to improve healthcare delivery, management, and outcomes. It encompasses a wide range of digital health solutions, including telemedicine, health apps, electronic health records (EHR), wearable health devices, and AI-powered diagnostics. Healthtech aims to enhance the quality of care, increase accessibility, and reduce healthcare costs by integrating innovative technologies and data-driven solutions into healthcare practices.

A further layer of complexity in biotech VC lies in the presence of not just one, but two distinct "valleys of death" that critically shape financing decisions and risk management. While most innovation sectors must contend with the difficulties of funding unproven technologies, biotech entrepreneurs and investors face a uniquely protracted and hazardous path. The first valley of death emerges early, as companies navigate the costly and uncertain terrain of discovery research and clinical validation, during which capital is primarily consumed by R&D and regulatory expenses without any commercial traction. Even after successfully crossing this initial chasm—often marked by regulatory approval—a second valley appears: the post-approval, pre-commercialization stage. Here, products, though technically de-risked, encounter delays and hurdles related to reimbursement, market access, and physician or patient adoption, often requiring further substantial funding and strategic persistence. Both valleys are characterized by extended timelines, high burn rates, and the need for specialized capital, underscoring why biotech investment demands both risk tolerance and a long-term perspective.

2.1.6 Technology Readiness Levels for Healthcare Innovations

Technology readiness levels (TRLs) provide a standardized nine-level framework (Figure 2.7) that enables investors and entrepreneurs to objectively assess the maturity of healthcare innovations, creating alignment between funding stages and technical milestones.

TRLs serve as the compass for navigating the complex journey from laboratory bench to patient bedside in healthcare ventures. Originally developed by NASA and now widely adopted across industries, the TRL framework uses nine distinct levels to measure technological maturity, from basic principles observed (TRL 1) through system proven in operational environment (TRL 9). This standardized approach proves particularly valuable in biotech/medtech/healthtech sectors where technical risk assessment can make or break investment decisions.

The TRL framework aligns naturally with funding stages in healthcare ventures, though the relationship is not always linear. Early-stage companies at TRL 2–4 typically seek seed funding while proving fundamental concepts and conducting initial feasibility studies. Series A investments generally correspond to TRL 4–6, where companies demonstrate technology functionality in relevant environments. For instance, a medtech startup securing Series A funding at TRL 5 might have validated its device concept through laboratory testing and begun animal studies, while a biotech company at TRL 6 could be completing preclinical studies and preparing IND filings.

The developmental stages of biotech/medtech/healthtech companies for seed, Series A funding, Series B funding, and Series C funding can be very specific. Series A funding for a medtech startup is triggered when it has demonstrated a viable product concept, a clear market opportunity, and a promising go-to-market strategy. Similarly, biotech companies typically secure Series A funding after completing preclinical studies and IND filing, while Series B coincides with positive Phase I/II results. Healthtech companies may raise Series A upon achieving product-market fit and initial customer traction, with Series B focused on scaling and geographic expansion.

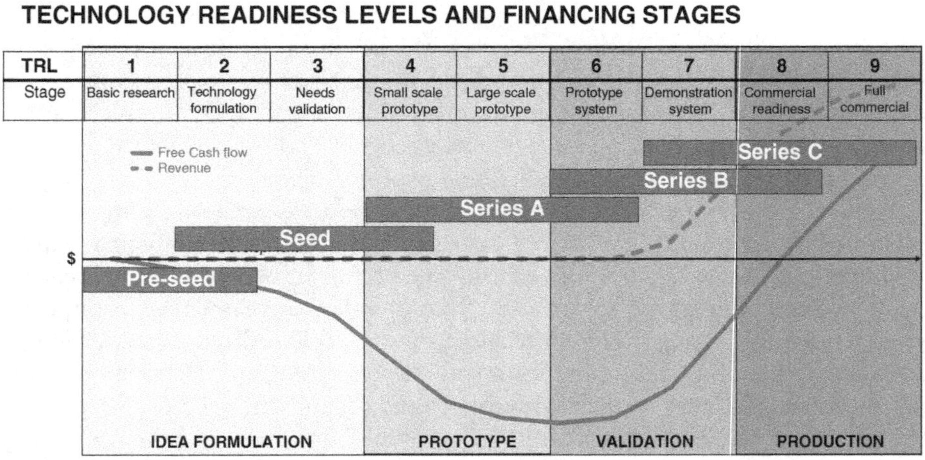

FIGURE 2.7 TRLs against VC financing stages.
Source: Candesic research and analysis.

Series B rounds typically occur at TRL 6–8, coinciding with human trials for biotech companies or clinical validation for medical devices. By Series C, companies often operate at TRL 7–9, having demonstrated system functionality in operational environments and moving toward commercialization. Smart investors use TRL assessments to benchmark technical progress against comparable companies and identify potential red flags when funding stages do not match technological maturity levels.

2.2 GROWTH CAPITAL AND DEVELOPMENT CAPITAL

Now, a few words about growth capital, which is a fascinating segment because it allows companies that have already proven that they have a right to exist, to develop and potentially become large players. Growth capital is important during the period of a company's life where it is going international and launching new products but typically has already proven that it can create revenue and perhaps even profit.

2.2.1 Characteristics and Maturity of the Segment

This subsection presents a few specific characteristics of the growth capital industry. First is the fact that it is an old segment, a sizable one (Figure 2.8), but it is not very well defined and historically has not been well organized. It is also usually focused on minority investments, often structured as preferred equity, but half of them are technology investments similar to—but less than—within the world of VC.

Growth capital investments are less risky than both VC and even LBOs. There is more predictability and stability than with startups but no exposition to financial leverage. The returns are, in theory, less attractive but are still expected to be higher than those in public equity. In growth capital, we would typically expect to get 1% or 2% higher return than in public equity (small to mid-caps) to compensate for the lack of liquidity.

There are not that many pure players in growth capital—historically.

Dedicated growth capital funds remain relatively uncommon in the PE landscape, with most growth financing actually provided by traditional buyout funds supporting their

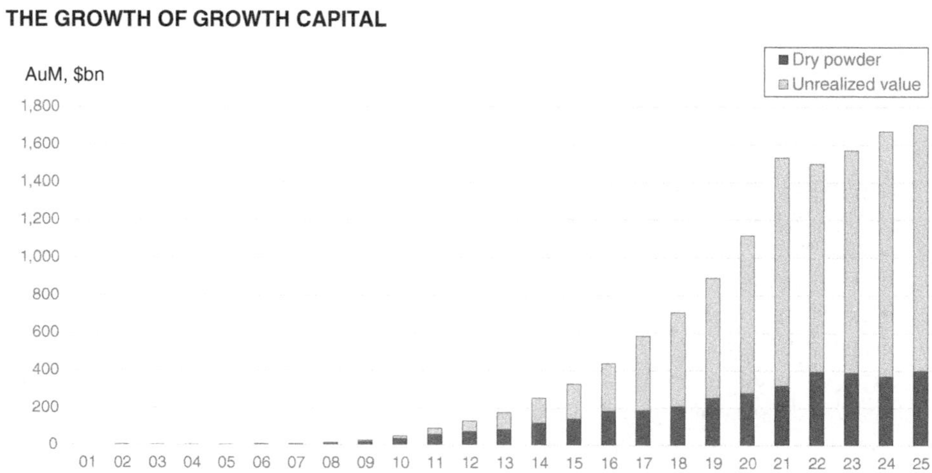

FIGURE 2.8 Evolution of global growth capital AuM.
Source: Preqin (part of Blackrock).

portfolio companies' expansion post-acquisition. We have not met many people who said, "I'm working in the growth capital industry and managing a growth capital fund." The apparent scarcity of pure-play growth capital specialists stems partly from historical market dynamics where merchant banking divisions traditionally filled this niche.

Growth capital proves less critical as a standalone strategy in PE compared to VC, where early-stage companies desperately need expansion funding before achieving profitability. Established PE targets typically possess stronger cash generation capabilities and debt capacity, reducing their reliance on pure equity growth financing. This fundamental difference explains why buyout shops can effectively handle growth capital needs within their existing operational frameworks.

Beyond the core growth capital provided to entrepreneurs and family businesses, and the follow-on capital deployed by sponsors to expand their PortCos post-buyout, a specialized strategy has emerged where investors like Audax Strategic Capital (part of Audax Private Equity) inject equity into companies already owned by PE sponsors who are constrained from committing additional funds. This "mid-hold" financing model allows incumbent sponsors to maintain control while accessing incremental capital to execute on M&A pipelines or organic growth initiatives, with interests remaining aligned through bespoke structures that balance continued ownership with the flexibility of external growth equity.

Market maturity significantly influences growth capital fund prevalence. Less developed financial markets often feature more growth capital funds because limited debt markets prevent traditional leveraged buyout structures from functioning effectively. Companies in these regions require equity-based growth financing since bank lending infrastructure cannot support LBO transactions.

Looking ahead, growth capital should expand even in developed markets due to regulatory pressure affecting traditional lending. Basel III restrictions have tightened bank lending standards, creating opportunities for alternative financing sources across the PE spectrum. This regulatory shift supports broader PE growth while specifically benefiting the growth equity segment, as companies seek nondebt expansion capital in an increasingly constrained lending environment.

The evolution suggests growth capital will carve out a more distinct identity, though buyout funds will likely continue dominating the space through their existing portfolio company relationships and operational expertise.

The North American Venture Capital Association has its own definition of growth equity investments:

- Company's revenues are growing rapidly.
- Company is cash flow positive, profitable, or approaching profitability.
- Company may be founder-owned and often has no prior institutional investment.
- Investor is agnostic about control and purchases minority ownership positions more often than not.
- Industry investment mix is similar to that of VC investors.
- Capital is used for company needs or shareholder liquidity, and additional financing rounds are not usually expected until exit.
- Investments are unlevered or use light leverage at purchase.
- Investment returns are primarily a function of growth, not leverage.

Growth equity investments include companies with fast-growing revenues that are already cash flow positive, potentially profitable or near profitable. They may not have been held by an institutional investor so far. And the investors, as we mentioned, are likely to accept being minority investors, but that does not mean they cannot take control. Some say the investment mix is similar to that of VC investors, although we beg to differ here. We feel it is less technological. As we mentioned before, the capital is used for all the needs that we have listed. We may not expect additional financing rounds before the exit of those investors. There's no leverage, or if there is any, it will be extremely light—and so the performance, the expected return, will typically be linked to growth opportunities rather than leverage.

The growth capital industry has continued to attract renewed interest, not just as a result of the Basel regulatory changes, but also due to several other factors. The first is that NVCA finally created a growth equity group, acknowledging the growing importance of the segment. Second, a company called Cambridge Associates decided to issue a quarterly benchmark, which is a very strong sign of the maturity of the segment. And third, a player called Insight Venture Partners managed to raise an impressive—at the time—two and a half billion dollars in 2013. In addition, in 2017, SoftBank raised $93 billion for its Vision Fund, and then planned to create a new $100 billion fund every two to three years and invest $50 billion annually. That did not happen, but Insight raised another $6.3 billion in 2018, which was followed by record fundraising in the following years: TA Associates with $12.5 billion, and Insight again with $17.2 billion, in 2021; Blue Owl with $12.9 billion in 2022; and Warburg Pincus with $17.3 billion in 2023. All this has been very promising for the growth capital segment, which we believe is the most interesting segment of all, but also the most difficult to tackle.

In healthcare, growth capital is unique because it not only fuels expansion but also supports the adoption of cutting-edge technologies and compliance with strict regulatory standards. Unlike other sectors, growth capital in healthcare must balance scaling operations with patient safety, quality of care, and evolving reimbursement models. This specialized focus means investors must often engage deeply with clinical expertise and long development timelines, making healthcare growth capital a blend of strategic funding and operational partnership.

2.2.2 Growth Capital vs. Venture Capital

Growth capital and venture capital have a lot in common. What are the differences?

- VCs—generally—invest in loss-making businesses, in any case cash flow negative (unlike "growth stage").
- VC targets mostly tech companies. In growth capital, these constitute about half of the investments.
- PE investors tend to pursue CEOs to invest in their business; VCs are pursued by entrepreneurs.
- VCs typically take minority positions in the cap table, whereas growth capital often follows a transfer of ownership, for example through a buyout.
- VC investments typically represent a smaller ticket size because the company being younger tends to be smaller, on average.
- It can be argued that VC deals are often less complex in terms of structuring. On the other hand, they need to take into account the next stages of financing, which is not always simple as we will see when we discuss the term sheets.
- Many observers have commented that "PE guys wear suits and ties while VCs wear jeans!"

Yet, there is this grey area between late-stage growth of scale-ups and growth equity for profitable companies. Eckuity Capital for example defines growth equity as investments in commercial-stage healthcare and life sciences companies that have achieved regulatory approval, are generating revenue, and are positioned for sustainable profitability and near-term liquidity. They look for the following:

- Demonstrated revenue traction and product-market fit
- Category leadership potential
- Regulatory approval and proven efficacy
- Twenty to thirty percent organic growth with visibility to profitability within 18 months
- Defensible models supported by data, IP, or switching costs
- Clear dual-track exit optionality within 18–36 months post-investment

For Youssef Sebban, co-founder of the firm, "our strategy aims to capture the innovation upside typical of VC while maintaining the risk discipline and governance rigor of buyouts—targeting superior risk-adjusted returns through a concentrated portfolio of high-conviction investments."

Pfitzer et al. (2025) identified a recurring theme in their interviews with 29 executives and founders of European healthtech companies: many successful entrepreneurs treat fundraising not as a one-off milestone but as a continuous process of selecting and engaging with investors who can deliver both resources and strategic value. Access to capital is not optional; it is a precondition for survival and growth. But capital alone is not sufficient. As a PE-backed CEO explained, "You need to understand the philosophy of the investor and why this specific partner is right for your stage of growth. Early investors often take higher risks because the company is small and unproven, while later investors bring the capital and capabilities needed to scale. Most will only stay for three to seven years, so alignment on timing and objectives is just as important as the money."

2.3 BUYOUTS AND THE VALUE CREATION FRAMEWORK

2.3.1 Definitions and Types of Buyouts

Buyouts involve the acquisition of a controlling stake in a company, typically addressing ownership transition or strategic restructuring needs in established businesses. These situations often arise from various circumstances: succession planning when founders want to retire, generational transfers within family enterprises, partnership dissolutions, or ownership disputes stemming from divorces or disagreements between co-owners. Beyond ownership changes, buyouts can also facilitate major strategic initiatives like implementing costly enterprise resource planning (ERP) systems, funding modernization efforts, or enabling industry consolidation through acquisitions. In emerging markets, buyouts may serve as a crucial mechanism for corporate restructuring, especially in regions with limited access to debt financing due to underdeveloped financial systems or restrictive regulatory environments.

So how does growth capital differ from buyouts? Many will highlight the use of leverage. While true, this can be misleading. The confusion stems from comparing them as two major segments of PE investment, which they are. There is, however, a fundamental difference in the purpose of each investment. Unlike growth capital investments, which typically involve minority stakes designed to fund expansion without changing control, buyouts fundamentally alter ownership structure. Growth capital provides companies with additional funds to accelerate their development—whether through market expansion, new product development, or operational scaling—while leaving existing owners in control. In contrast, buyouts signify a complete ownership transition. While not inherently a financing tool, buyouts can include cash injections to support growth initiatives post-acquisition. This distinction is critical: growth capital supports growth from a minority position, while buyouts deliver both control and the opportunity to drive transformative strategies.

Buyouts come in several variants, distinguished by two key variables: management origin and leverage use. They are often combined. Leveraged buyouts (LBOs) emphasize the use of debt financing to enhance returns. Management buyouts (MBOs) involve the existing management team acquiring or sharing control, often partnering with PE firms. Management buy-ins (MBIs) bring in external management teams to take control.

2.3.2 MBI: A Matter of Preference and Expertise

The choice between an MBO or MBI depends on the PE firm's strategy, the company's needs, and the available talent pool. It often reflects specific circumstances, such as when taking a public company private requires different management expertise, or when preparing a company for an eventual IPO necessitates public company management experience.

Appetite for MBIs varies among PE firms. Some actively avoid them, citing risks associated with introducing external management into unfamiliar organizations. These firms prefer working with incumbent management who thoroughly understand the business. Other PE firms specialize in MBIs, maintaining networks of experienced executives ready to lead newly acquired companies. These firms often build substantial internal teams dedicated to identifying and supporting external management talent. They view MBIs as an opportunity to implement transformative strategies and unlock significant value.

A few years ago, the Candesic team advised a PE fund on the potential buyout of a European CDMO. They ultimately decided not to proceed, despite being aligned with the CEO and business plan, not because of price, but because they lacked confidence in the CFO's seniority. The firm did not want to take on the responsibility of recruiting a suitable CFO in an unfamiliar country, illustrating the operational challenges that can arise in buyouts.

Several other factors characterize modern buyouts. Industry specialization has become increasingly important, with many PE firms focusing on specific sectors where they have developed deep expertise and valuable networks. This is particularly visible in healthcare with all its complexities. The role of value creation has evolved beyond financial engineering to include operational improvements, digital transformation, and strategic repositioning. Add-on acquisitions are increasingly prevalent, making platform-building capabilities essential for success. Additionally, regulatory considerations, particularly in cross-border transactions, have gained significance in buyout structuring, influencing deal timelines and execution strategies.

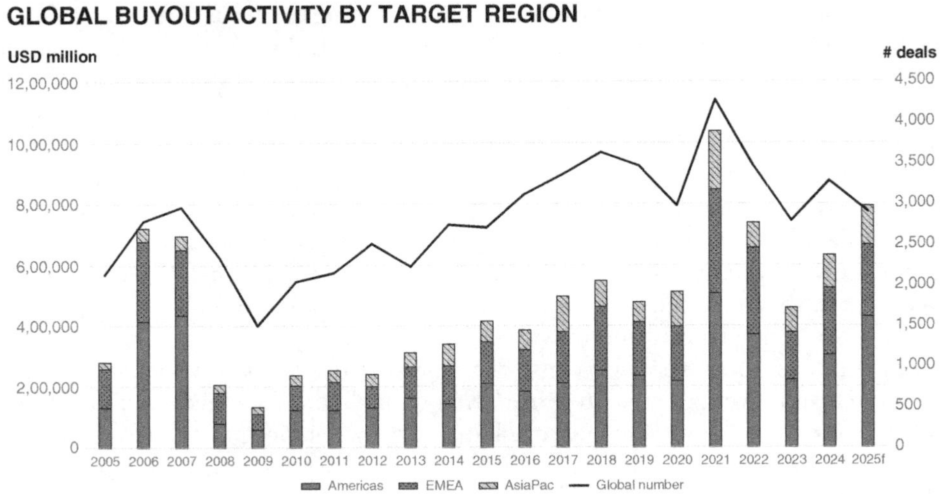

FIGURE 2.9 Global buyout activity by target region.
Source: Dealogic (Candesic forecast for 2025).

Figure 2.9 shows the evolution of the global buyout activity from the mid-2000s to the 2020s. As in the other segments of PE, there was a record growth of activity up until the global financial crisis: in late 2008–2009, as we have seen, the market collapsed. It took a while for the market to recover.

2.3.3 Drivers of Value Creation in Buyouts

Historically, beyond financial leverage, buyouts have been perceived as an organizational efficiency tool. They were used to streamline processes, reduce the workforce, and decrease costs in general. A good example of this is the acquisition of Safeway by KKR through an LBO in 1986. Through a combination of rationalization of distribution and negotiation of contracts, a more performance-related remuneration for the managers, and a focus on the core businesses, KKR were able to raise the operating profit margin from 1% to 4.4%. It took time, but that created substantial value. But note that this came with a 50% reduction in the workforce.

There are many other examples of early LBOs, and they typically focus on active ownership. That was the case with the acquisition of OM Scott by CD&R. OM Scott was a subsidiary of ITT, then a famous conglomerate, which started to unload many of their businesses in the 1980s. The changes that were brought by the PE investor enabled them to enhance several performance drivers, increasing the sales by 25%, the working capital by 40%, and, ultimately, the EBIT by more than 50%. So, the investment return appeared considerable: an IRR of 40% at a time where the S&P 500 was producing an average of 10%.

Before we delve into the economics of an LBO, we examine the drivers of value creation in the process of investing in companies.

It should be useful to remember that the drivers of value creation in an acquisition by a PE fund will be related not only to the ability to use leverage, but also to assets, both financial assets and the ability to raise money with track record and reputation, to competencies, which are a combination of skills and processes, and to relationships, in particular the ability to source deals (Figure 2.10).

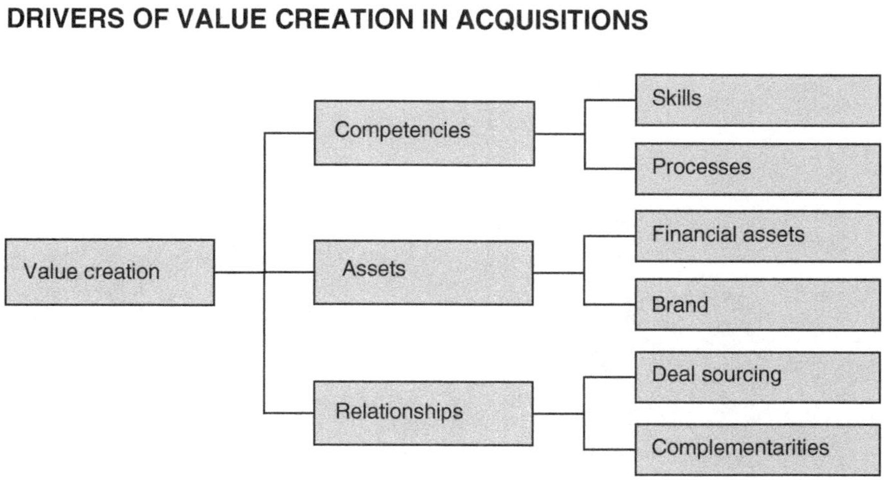

FIGURE 2.10 Drivers of value creation in acquisitions.

It is worth mentioning, however, that deals can be opportunistic as well as strategic. As an example, at the end of the Cold War, in 1989, investments in defense were suddenly completely out of fashion. The Berlin Wall was down, and everybody expected that there would be no more Cold War. In the following years, a major operating investor, Carlyle, decided to buy numerous arms companies, and they bought them at an incredibly low multiple, two times EBITDA. They did not have to wait very long for their investment to pay off. At the beginning of the 1990s, we had the First Gulf War. After a few years, Carlyle was able to sell those investments at a multiple of eight or nine times, well above the purchase multiple at two times. Carlyle recognized that the fall of the Berlin Wall did not mean that military operations were consigned to the dustbin of history.

So, over time we have seen a shift in possible investment strategies. What was an external set of improvement levers focusing on the targets became a new value proposition, where the value creation levers would go beyond the target itself and sometimes change the rules and conduct of a whole industry.

2.3.4 Economics of an LBO

Have a quick look at Figure 2.11. It conceptualizes all the angles Candesic explores with its PE clients to help them create value. Pause and check if it makes sense to you before we apply it to an LBO situation. Note that deleveraging creates additional value beyond the replacement of debt by equity thanks to the tax shield.

Four levers are particularly important for increasing the equity value in an LBO (Figure 2.12).

We consider hereafter the acquisition of a company with an enterprise value (EV) of \$1 billion. We plan to finance it with 70% debt. It is aggressive but could be warranted by stable cash flows—for example thanks to long-term contracts or a monopolistic position—and good collateral to reduce the risks of the lenders. This means we will need to finance the rest with \$300 million in equity. We will show the impact of the four levers on both the EV and the capital structure of the target company until we exit.

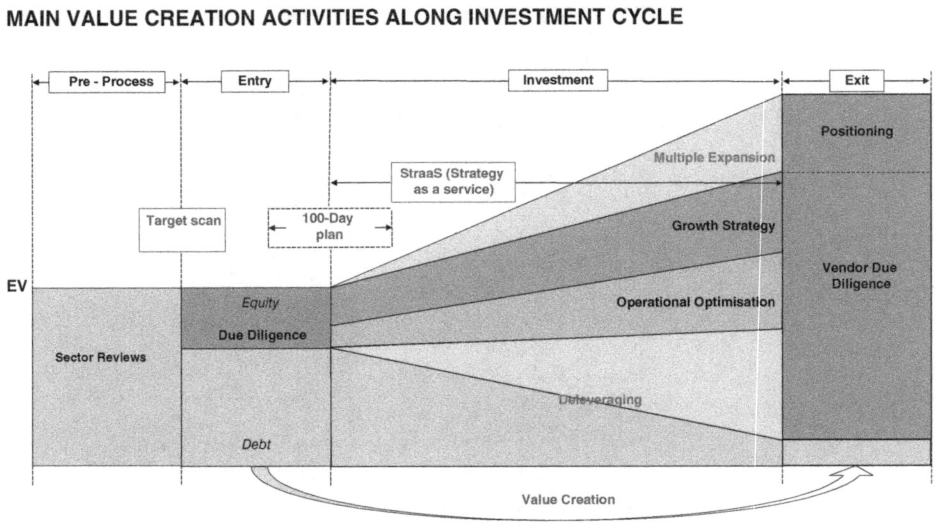

FIGURE 2.11 Value creation activities along the investment cycle.

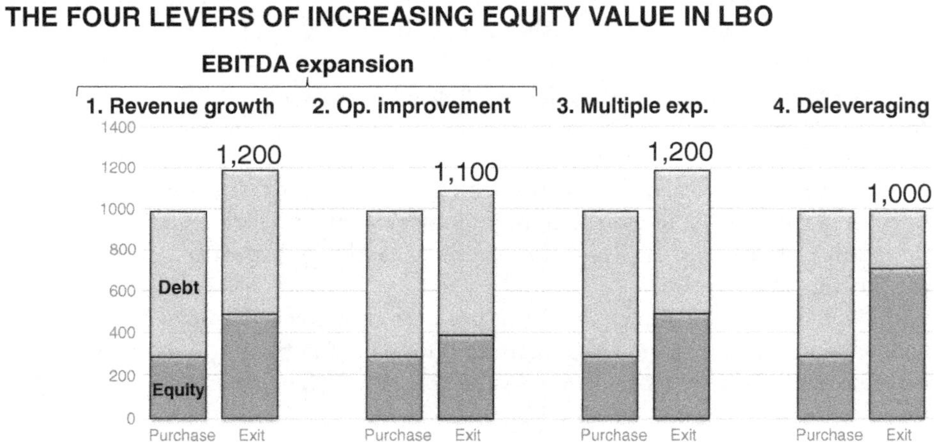

	Purchase	Exit	Purchase	Exit	Purchase	Exit	Purchase	Exit
EBITDA	100	120	100	110	100	100	100	100
EV/EBITDA	10x	10x	10x	10x	10x	12x	10x	10x
Debt	700	700	700	700	700	700	700	280
Equity	300	500	300	400	300	500	300	720

FIGURE 2.12 Four levers of value creation in an LBO.

The first two levers concentrate on EBITDA expansion. Here we do not look at any change in the capital structure. One lever is about selling more; the other is about selling at a lower cost; each has an impact on EBITDA. In the case of 20% revenue growth, it leads to similar increase in EBITDA from 100 to 120, the margin being unchanged. In the separate case of operational improvement, the EBITDA increase this time is led by an increase in margin, lifting it from 100 to 110. That is a 20% and a 10% improvement respectively. But for a constant multiple and a constant debt value, we are able to increase the value of the equity from 300 to 500 in the first case and to

400 in the second case. Those two increases are additive and, combined, will lead to a doubling of the equity, from 300 to 600.

The third lever is the possibility for multiple expansion. Here we assume both the EBITDA and the amount of debt remain unchanged. This time, it is the multiple that increases. It goes from 10 times to 12 times. We will discuss in more detail what the trigger of that increase could be, but if that happens, it will create a substantial additional value, lifting the equity value from 300 to 500.

The final lever is deleveraging. Whereby the large amount of debt is repayed quickly. This example illustrates that, if we keep EBITDA and the multiple unchanged and aggressively amortize debt over five years, it will be reduced from 700 to 280 over three years. Equity more than doubles during this period, up from 300 to 720. This lever comes last because (1) it is not always there, (2) there is decreasingly less of it, and (3) it only works if the company is creating value that it helps boost.

The first and last levers are related. It is rather common to read that a business is cash generative. This means it can reliably produce surplus cash from its normal operating activities, beyond what is required to cover ongoing expenses and capital investments. In the context of an LBO, such companies are particularly desirable because their strong and consistent cash flows are essential for supporting and repaying the substantial debt incurred during the acquisition. The steady generation of cash enables the acquired business to meet regular interest and principal payments on its borrowings, often allowing the investors to reduce leverage ("deleveraging") as the debt is paid down over time. Mature businesses with stable revenues and manageable capital expenditure needs typically qualify as cash generative and thus present robust targets for LBO transactions.

Now, if we consider the impacts of those four levers on the value creation, imagine what would happen if we were able to combine them in the same deal—we would be able to multiply the value by several times as shown in Figure 2.13.

We can show this combined value here. We increase the EBITDA from 100 to 130 through a combination of higher revenue and higher EBITDA margin. We decrease debt from 700 to 280 and we apply an EBITDA multiple of 12× instead of 10×. We

IMPACT OF COMBINED LEVERS ON THE EQUITY VALUE IN LBO

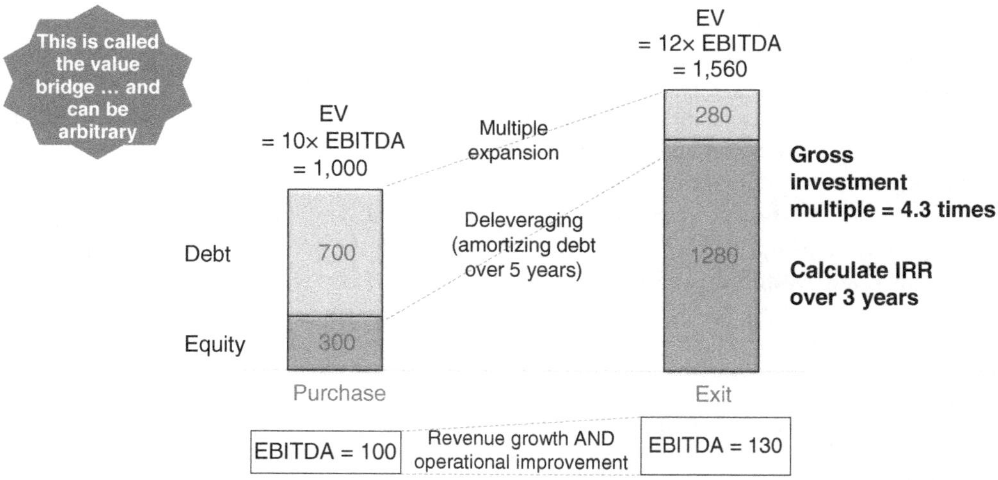

FIGURE 2.13 Combined levers of value creation in an LBO.

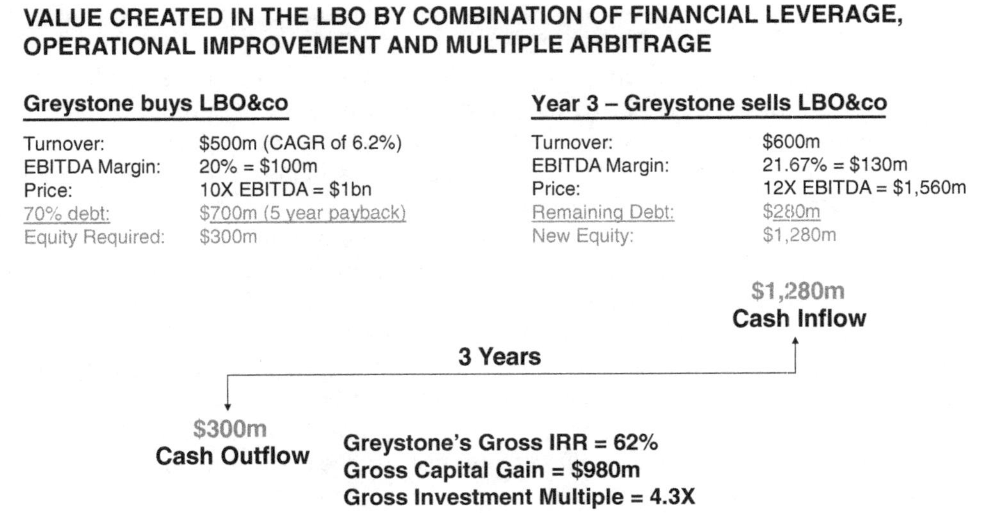

FIGURE 2.14 Alternative example of combined value creation in an LBO.
Source: After Ed Miller.

obtain an impressive level of value creation that can be estimated in terms of IRR over three years before looking at the next figure.

Figure 2.14 provides an additional figure depicting the economics of the LBO value creation in a specific setting.

And that's not the full story. There is something else. There is also the fact that PE investors, the GPs, are generally taxed at a lower capital gains rate than normal investments. For a long time, this rate has been only 15% to 20% in the United States, and there has been a lot of discussion around changing that. Since the 2017 Tax Cuts and Jobs Act, carried interest qualifies for long-term capital gains treatment (20% federal rate) if the investment is held for more than three years. An additional 3.8% Net Investment Income Tax (NIIT) often applies. This remains significantly lower than the top ordinary income tax rate of 37%.

In the United Kingdom, it used to be 18% but was increased to 28% in 2015, which still compared very favorably to the combined corporate and individual tax rates. A 4% surcharge was introduced in 2022 but was not universally applied, depending on the individual's overall tax situation and residency. This changed in 2025, when a single unified rate of 32% was implemented, after intense lobbying of the British PE industry that was facing the threat of a higher rate and warned against the risk of most GPs leaving Britain.

If we look again at our example LBO, we have 30% of equity and 70% of other forms of capital (Figure 2.15). That could be, for example, 45% of senior debt (including Term Loan A[1] and a revolving credit facility that may or may not be drawn) and

[1] In most LBOs

- **Term Loan A** or TLA is the senior term loan in the capital structure, meaning it usually ranks just below revolving credit facilities or asset-based loans, if they exist.
- **Term Loan B** is generally junior to TLA within the term loan structure but still considered senior debt overall, ranking above subordinated debt or mezzanine financing.

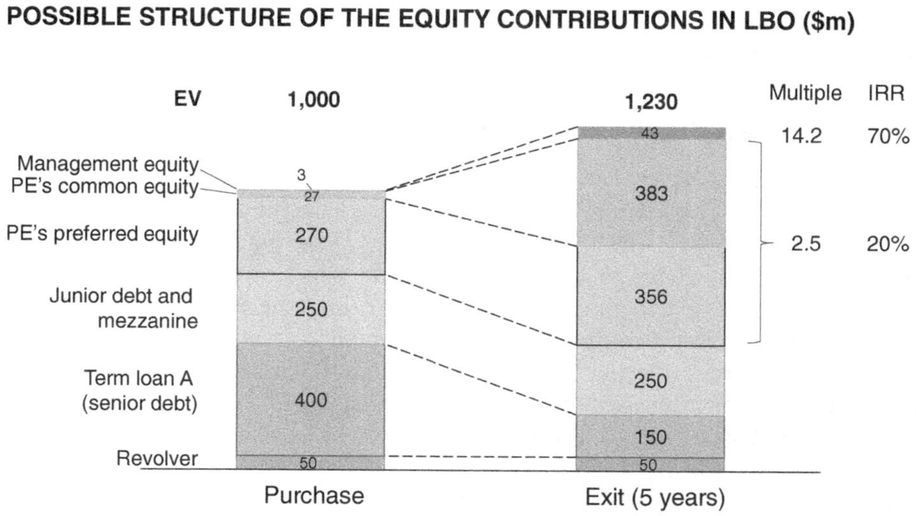

FIGURE 2.15 Example of structure of capital in an LBO.

25% of junior debt, which might include a smaller part of mezzanine financing (intermediate capital). The composition of the capital structure will be dictated by market conditions such as pricing, ease of issuance, and potential refinancing needs. The equity portion (here 30%) typically consists of common and preferred equity, with management usually holding around 10% of the common equity.

The proportion of common equity will be related to the absolute amount of common equity held by management. For example, should management have $10 million out of $1 billion in total equity, it can be split $900 million preferred and $100 million common, of which management is allocated 10%. This calibration ensures management is highly motivated by the success of the LBO, thanks to an inflated target IRR. It is important to note that the total financing must also cover transaction fees and expenses, which can amount to approximately 5% of the total deal value.

What does this structure mean for the performance in each tranche of financing? We assume here an exit in five years. Apart from the revolver, our senior debt is a Term Loan A of $400 million that will be repaid as fast as possible. After five years, thanks to a successful free cash flow generation, we have only $150 million of TLA outstanding. This is the cash sweep we will study in Chapter 5. It is very different for the next layer of debt, the junior debt, which is made of unsecured debt, subordinate debt, and payment in-kind (so-called PIK). That part will typically not see its nominal amount change: here we start and finish with $250 million. We may not even have paid some of the interest, that may be accumulated at the end. Then we have the layer of preferred stock. In this example, we start with $270 million and we end up with $356 million. This is the accumulated value, and we'll see what it represents in performance. The final part of this example is extremely small, accounting for only $30 million of common equity, of which 10% is for the management, and the other 90% is in the fund. The common equity will see its value increase by a staggering 14.2 multiple, going from $30 million to more than $400 million. This grants common shareholders an IRR of 70% while the preferred investor did well as well. Other than management, shareholders are invested in both preferred stock and equity and achieve a combined IRR of 20%. The return is lower, obviously, for junior debt and even lower for the senior debt.

2.3.5 Debt Terms in an LBO

2.3.5.1 Syndicated Loans vs. Bonds In LBOs, syndicated loans are a cornerstone of acquisition financing, allowing PE firms to raise significant amounts of debt from a group of lenders under a unified loan agreement. These loans distribute risk across multiple institutions while giving the borrower access to capital at scale. In Europe, syndicated loans are particularly dominant, providing the bulk of the initial capital injected into portfolio companies. Banks compete aggressively to underwrite and arrange these facilities, offering committed financing that allows PE sponsors to make binding bids with funding certainty. Once a deal is signed, however, the structure is often revised and syndicated out to a broader group of lenders, including institutional investors such as credit funds and CLOs.

The loan package may include the tranches presented in the previous section, commonly Term Loan A (amortizing), Term Loan B (bullet repayment), and revolving credit facilities, each with different risk-return characteristics. The lead arranger, usually a major bank, coordinates the syndication and pricing, while tranches can later be traded in the secondary market. These loans are generally senior in the capital structure, often secured by the company's assets, and typically contain financial covenants that offer lenders early warning signals and a basis for renegotiation if performance diverges from plan.

While syndicated loans are used in both Europe and the United States, the financing mix in LBOs diverges between the two regions. In the United States, high-yield bonds are more frequently used alongside institutional term loans, especially in larger transactions. The US capital markets offer greater depth, liquidity, and investor appetite for bonds, making it easier for sponsors to access long-dated, fixed-rate financing with fewer covenants. European deals, by contrast, lean more heavily on bank-led debt, with bond issuance often playing a secondary role or coming post-close as a refinancing tool. This reflects not only market maturity but also legal and regulatory environments, where loan enforcement mechanisms are generally more efficient than bondholder coordination in Europe. As a result, while both regions utilize broadly similar instruments, the composition and sequencing of LBO financing often differ significantly, depending on the market context. Credit ration, on the other hand, remain relatively consistent between the two regions (Figure 2.16).

2.3.5.2 Cost of Debt What is the cost of debt? Considering the complexity of the financing structure of large LBOs, there is no single answer, each tranche having its specific conditions. Professor Phalippou (2009, 2021) tracked average costs (Figure 2.17). While most premia increase in turbulent and inflationary markets, the levels presented remain representative.

Some other important elements of debt in LBOs include the following.

2.3.5.3 Covenants Senior lenders closely assess a variety of financial ratios and performance measures before agreeing to extend a loan. These conditions, which are contractual obligations in the loan agreement, are known as covenants. Covenants serve as protective measures for lenders, ensuring that the borrower maintains financial health and the ability to repay the debt.

KEY TO ASSESS THE VIABILITY OF THE PROPOSED CAPITAL STRUCTURE

Key credit ratios include:

- ✓ EBIT/Interest: > 2× for BB, >4× for BBB
- ✓ EBITDA/Interest: > 3.5× for BB, > 6× for BBB
- ✓ Debt/EBITDA: < 5× for BB, < 3× for BBB
- ✓ FCFF/Debt Service: > 1× for viability, > 1.5× for BBB

And don't forget there are variable rates!

FIGURE 2.16 Key credit ratios for LBOs.

FIFTY SHADES OF DEBT

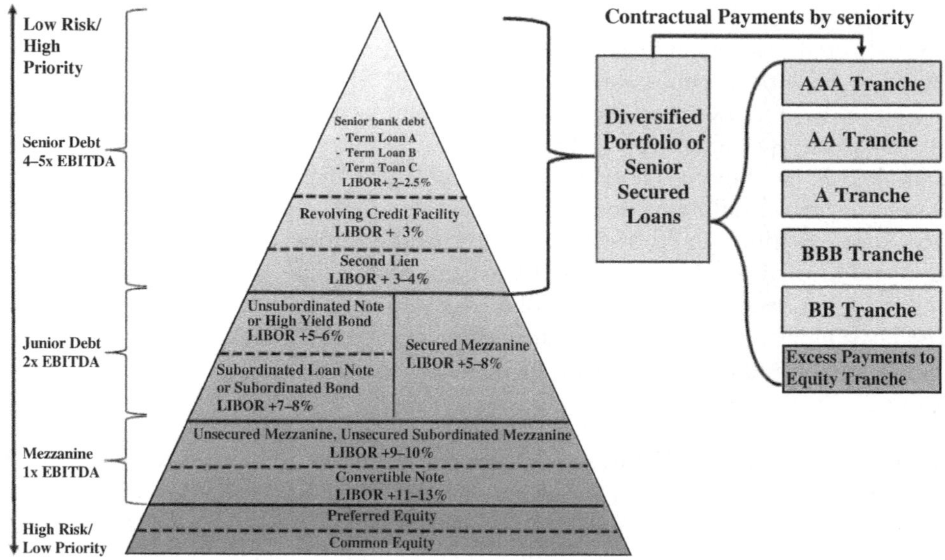

FIGURE 2.17 Fifty shades of debt.
Source: L. Phalippou, Private Equity Laid Bare.

There are two broad categories of covenants:

- **Affirmative covenants** require the borrower to take certain actions—such as delivering audited financial statements or maintaining adequate insurance.
- **Negative covenants** restrict certain activities—such as incurring additional debt, making significant asset sales, or distributing dividends without lender approval.

Some of the most critical covenants in the context of senior loans focus on the company's ability to generate cash flow and manage debt levels. In particular, lenders will pay close attention to EBITDA or free cash flow projections, as these metrics help to gauge the company's ability to meet debt service obligations. Lenders will also scrutinize the senior debt to enterprise value (EV) ratio, which should not exceed certain thresholds, such as 50%. This ratio measures how much debt the company is carrying relative to its total enterprise value, and a lower ratio generally indicates a lower risk to the lender. Finally, the presence of collateral is often a key covenant, especially for riskier loans, as it provides additional security to the lender in case the borrower defaults.

These covenants are critical for senior lenders to manage their risk, and borrowers must carefully adhere to these terms to avoid triggering default clauses or penalties.

2.3.5.4 Unitranche Debt Unitranche debt is a hybrid loan structure that combines elements of both senior and subordinated debt into a single instrument. The borrower enters into one credit agreement, pays a blended interest rate, and faces a single maturity date, typically ranging from five to seven years, with repayment often made in fine (i.e., at maturity). Originally developed in the United States in 2005, unitranche financing gained traction in Europe from 2012, particularly during periods when troubled or sub-investment-grade companies were unable to access traditional syndicated loans or high-yield bond markets. It is provided primarily by nonbank lenders, such as private credit funds, and has become especially popular among middle-market borrowers, often with revenues under $100 million or EBITDA below $50 million.

While the borrower experiences a single, simplified facility, the underlying loan may still involve a hidden split between senior-like and junior-like tranches, governed by an Agreement Among Lenders (AAL). This keeps inter-creditor issues away from the borrower while allowing different lenders to earn risk-adjusted returns. Unitranche offers speed, flexibility, and execution certainty and is now a widely accepted alternative to traditional multi-tranche LBO financing—particularly in mid-market buyouts or transactions requiring rapid, bespoke structuring. Although typically more expensive than senior bank loans, unitranche is often cheaper and less complex than layering separate senior and mezzanine debt, further contributing to its rise in both the US and European PE ecosystems.

2.3.5.5 Resetting Creditor Hierarchies When LBOs face distress, creditors increasingly find themselves battling shareholders to protect their interests. Post-2022 interest rate spikes have intensified these conflicts, with restructuring practices "*blowing up a foundational debt-market rule*" by subverting traditional creditor hierarchies.

Bloomberg reported that "*PE owners and aggressive creditors, including gatecrashing hedge funds, have been able to exploit lax legal wording on loan terms signed when money was cheap.*[2]" This often occurs when a creditor group offers new financing in exchange for preferential terms—such as debt swaps or collateral reallocations—that structurally subordinate other lenders. The disparity in outcomes has grown extreme: while primary creditors negotiate haircuts capped at 5%, junior tiers face losses of some 60%, with residual claims sometimes recovering just as little as 30%.

Buyout firms now voice concerns about reputational damage in credit markets, though they argue these clashes are often instigated by dominant debtholders seeking to maximize their recoveries at others' expense.

---

[2] Basu, R., Bloomberg, Private Equity Shoves Angry Lenders to the Back of the Line, May 7, 2025. https://www.bloomberg.com/news/features/2025-05-07/private-equity-firms-prioritize-their-own-returns-costing-lenders-billions.

2.3.6 Mini Case: Medline LBO

Remember Medline (Chapter 1), the top-tier, privately held medical supply organization that found itself at the center of a landmark transaction when a consortium of renowned PE organizations, namely Blackstone Group Inc., Carlyle Group Inc., and Hellman & Friedman LLC, orchestrated its acquisition? This substantial deal, unveiled in June 2021, propelled Medline to a staggering valuation of approximately $34 billion (including debt), solidifying its status as one of the most substantial LBOs in recent memory and the largest since the 2008 financial crisis. The transaction involved approximately $17 billion in equity contributions from the three PE firms, with the remaining $17+ billion financed through debt markets, including $14.77 billion raised across bond and loan markets plus $2.1 billion from commercial mortgage bonds. Singapore's sovereign wealth fund GIC also participated as a co-investor, underscoring the deal's strategic significance. The Mills family, which founded Medline in 1966, received more than $22 billion in pre-tax proceeds while retaining 20–25% ownership and remaining the largest single shareholder, with CEO Charlie Mills, President Andy Mills, and COO Jim Abrams continuing in their leadership roles.

Three years post-acquisition, the Medline LBO demonstrated mixed results that illustrate common PE execution challenges. Revenue grew from $17.5 billion in 2020 to $25.5 billion in 2024, driven by aggressive M&A activity—four add-on acquisitions in 12 months, including Ecolab's surgical solutions business for $950 million. However, the company may have seemed to struggle with debt management, requiring a massive $6.14 billion term loan repricing in 2024 to reduce margins from 300 bps to 275–300 bps, highlighting the refinancing pressures inherent in mega-LBOs.

Key success factors included Medline's dominant market position as the largest privately held medical supply distributor in the United States, serving more than 110 countries with products ranging from surgical equipment to personal protection equipment. The deal also reflected a degree of "pandemic opportunism"—PE firms capitalizing on supply chain disruptions while valuations remained attractive. Healthcare supply costs had increased 15.9% from 2019 to 2021, creating both revenue opportunities and operational challenges. Medline's $2.5 billion Healthcare Resilience Initiative (launched in 2018) proved prescient, positioning the company to benefit from pandemic demand while competitors struggled with capacity constraints.

Post-acquisition strategies focused on international expansion, product-portfolio diversification, and supply chain infrastructure investments, including seven new medical-grade distribution centers planned for 2021 alone. Early risk concerns materialized predictably: supply chain normalization delivered margin compression as pandemic-driven spikes receded, and rapid M&A integration strained organizational bandwidth. Debt service pressures surfaced quickly—the need to refinance within three years underscored the importance of conservative leverage assumptions in deal structuring.

The platform strategy worked. Systematic add-ons strengthened Medline's market moat, and consolidation in a highly fragmented medical-supply industry continued to create roll-up opportunities. The Medline LBO represented the "platformization" of healthcare—PE firms building diversified infrastructure plays rather than traditional single-asset roll-ups. This shift reflected healthcare's broader move toward integrated supply chain management platforms, where scale and technology created competitive moats that pure-play distributors could not replicate.

Following years of operational improvement and some deleveraging, Medline successfully went public in 2025 at a valuation of roughly $38 billion (vs. $17 billion equity value in 2021). The IPO marked a strong (if partial) exit for its sponsors who realized significant gains on their original investment while retaining minority stakes alongside the Mills family. The successful listing confirmed investor confidence in Medline's integrated supply chain model and the long-term strength of the platform developed under PE ownership.

The few discussion questions that follow will be left for the reader to assess:

- Was the $34 billion EV justified, or did temporary pandemic-driven revenue inflation distort Medline's true underlying value?
- How does a 50% debt-to-enterprise-value ratio compare to leverage norms in 1980s LBOs, and what does this suggest about evolving sponsor risk tolerance?
- What does Medline's need for rapid refinancing reveal about the initial capital-structure assumptions and market conditions at deal close?

2.4 INFRASTRUCTURE EQUITY FUNDS

Infrastructure (equity) funds represent a distinct investment approach within PE, particularly relevant to healthcare given the sector's capital-intensive nature and essential service characteristics. While traditionally focused on transportation, utilities, and energy assets, infrastructure funds have increasingly expanded into healthcare infrastructure, recognizing similarities in stable cash flows and critical social function.

The modern infrastructure fund model was pioneered by Macquarie Group in Australia during the 1990s, initially focusing on privatized government assets like roads, airports, and utilities. Macquarie's success in developing a systematic approach to infrastructure investment—emphasizing stable, long-term yields from regulated assets—created a template that others would follow. The model proved particularly successful in Australia due to the country's mandatory pension system creating strong demand for yield-generating assets. As the model gained traction globally, infrastructure funds began exploring adjacent sectors sharing similar characteristics, including healthcare infrastructure. Over the last 20 years, they have spread across developed markets as traditional buyout houses moved into the segment (Figure 2.18).

Infrastructure funds differ from traditional LBO funds in several crucial aspects:

- **Investment horizon:** While even long-dated PE funds typically target 10–15 year holds rather than the usual 3–7, infrastructure funds often maintain investments for 20+ years or establish permanent ("evergreen") capital vehicles.
- **Return profile:** Infrastructure funds generally target lower but more stable returns (8–12% IRR) compared to traditional LBO funds (20%+ IRR), with a greater emphasis on yield rather than capital appreciation.
- **Risk profile:** Core infrastructure assets share characteristics such as predictable cash flows, regulatory protection or contracted revenue streams, high barriers to entry, essential service characteristics, monopolistic or oligopolistic dynamics, and high asset longevity. These features are common in healthcare infrastructure as well.
- **Leverage profile:** While both use leverage, infrastructure funds typically employ lower-risk debt structures with longer tenors and often include inflation-linked components to match their cash flow profiles and risk tolerance.

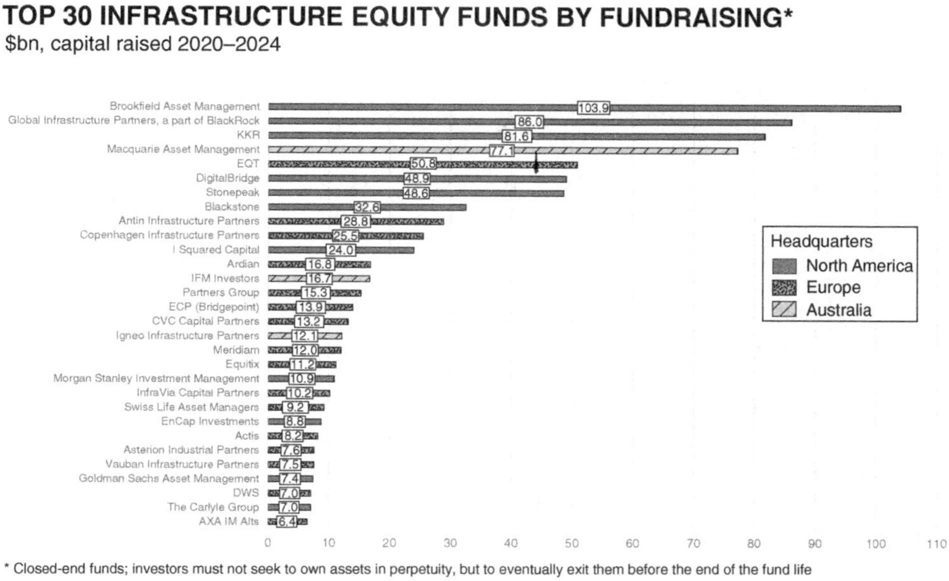

FIGURE 2.18 Top 30 infrastructure equity funds by fundraising amount, 2020–2024.
Source: 2025 infrastructure investor 100, PEI group.

FIVE CRITERIA FOR HEALTHCARE INFRASTRUCTURE FUND INVESTMENTS

- **Essentiality:** Does the asset provide critical care or underpin care delivery?
- **Regulated revenue:** Are cash flows backed by government contracts, insurance reimbursement, or long-term leases?
- **Longevity:** Can the asset deliver stable value over decades?
- **Low volatility:** Is demand predictable regardless of macro cycles?
- **Social impact:** Does the investment align with ESG or public good mandates?

Infrastructure investors identify long-term investment themes. For instance, DWS, Deutsche Bank's asset management division, has identified five major long-term investment themes supported by durable positive macroeconomic, regulatory, and demographic conditions. While only one theme focuses exclusively on healthcare, several others intersect with it, highlighting the sector's centrality to future infrastructure investment. The five themes are as follows:

1. Energy Transition

   Aligned with the EU's "Fit for 55" initiative which targets a 55% reduction in greenhouse gas emissions by 2035, this theme emphasizes investments in decarbonization infrastructure. Notable examples include Weltec, a German producer of biogas and biomethane, and Vertex, a bioethanol producer with operations in Spain and France.

2. Urbanization and Sustainable Mobility

   Continued urban growth in Europe is driving demand for efficient and low-emission public transport. This is reinforced by regulatory initiatives and a generational shift away from private vehicle ownership.
3. Supply Chain Resilience

   With decarbonization goals extending across entire value chains, investment is shifting toward cleaner logistics and infrastructure, such as a modal shift from road to rail.
4. Digitalization

   With data traffic growing at over 20% CAGR, the EU is prioritizing investments to bridge the digital divide. Healthcare infrastructure, including electronic health records and telemedicine platforms, is a key beneficiary of this digital expansion.
5. Demographic Change and the Impact on Healthcare

   Europe's aging population, combined with rising multimorbidity and mounting pressure on public healthcare budgets, is accelerating the shift toward preventive care and more efficient service delivery. DWS's investments in this space include Althea, a UK-based provider of managed medical equipment services, and RON, a German network of radiotherapy clinics.

While this thematic segmentation is one of many, the themes are relatively consistent, with some variations. Macquarie and Antin identify social infrastructure as a key segment, while Infravia adds education to the list. Brookfield Infrastructure Partners defines it differently, focusing on "critical global infrastructure networks which facilitate the movement and storage of energy, water, freight, passengers and data."

Healthcare is increasingly viewed as "infrastructure-like" by institutional investors, recognizing its essential service characteristics. Hospitals share core infrastructure traits: high barriers to entry, essential community services, and predictable demand patterns. This recognition has led infrastructure funds to move beyond traditional "no blood" PPP structures into direct healthcare operations.

In healthcare, infrastructure funds typically focus on the following:

- **Physical infrastructure**, which includes hospitals, surgical centers, rehabilitation facilities, long-term care homes, diagnostic imaging centers, and laboratories

  In a typical example, in 2025, Candesic advised Macquarie on their investment in Luz Saude, leading Portuguese hospitals. In accordance with the expectations of a long-term investor, the due diligence confirmed that Luz Saúde operated a modern and operationally fit-for-purpose imaging fleet, with quantified investment requirements over the next five years to keep it competitive and up to date. Candesic also confirmed that the group was efficiently equipped when benchmarked against international hospitals of comparable size.

  Another example is provided by NorthWest Healthcare Properties REIT and partners investing in multi-jurisdictional hospital portfolios in Canada, Australia, and Europe since 2012 and until today. You notice that the investor here is a real estate specialist, which shows the blurred boundary between infrastructure and real estate investing. NorthWest and its peers do not just buy buildings—they acquire large portfolios and typically sign long-term leases with operating hospital groups, blending real estate, infrastructure, and healthcare exposure in a single vehicle. This hybrid approach is increasingly common, especially as infrastructure investors seek stable, asset-backed yields and real estate specialists look to tap healthcare's demographic opportunities.

We think the historical evidence supports the thesis that traditional LBOs have been a poor match for hospital investments, creating a natural evolution toward infrastructure funds that better align with healthcare's capital-intensive, long-term realities. Infrastructure funds represent a structural evolution that directly addresses LBO failures in healthcare. Their investment approach aligns much better with hospital economics across three dimensions: an extended time frame that allows for proper equipment replacement cycles, facility renovations, and staff development programs without the pressure of quick exits, a lower hurdle rate that means less aggressive cost-cutting and more sustainable operational improvements, and less reliance on debt financing, reducing the operational stress that plagued hospital LBOs.

- **Digital infrastructure,** which covers health data centers, telemedicine platforms, cloud-based electronic health records (EHR), and digital payment platforms

  A good example here is DigitalBridge's investment in health data infrastructure supporting large-scale telehealth deployments in the United States and Europe. DigitalBridge has invested in digital infrastructure critical to health technology primarily from the early 2020s onward. Its portfolio includes Vantage Data Centers, which through multiple funding rounds since 2020 operates hyperscale facilities across North America and Europe, and AtlasEdge, launched in 2022 as a joint venture managing over 100 edge data centers in Europe for latency-sensitive medical applications. Additional investments like Scala Data Centers in Brazil and Leading Edge Data Centres in Australia have been made during the same period, supporting regional telehealth and digital health needs. This infrastructure underpins cloud-based healthcare services without directly operating these platforms.
- **Research infrastructure**, which encompasses drug discovery labs and other life sciences research facilities, clinical trial sites, GMP-certified biotech manufacturing facilities, and genomics platforms

  The creation of Oxford Biomedica's advanced therapy manufacturing hub supported by infrastructure-oriented capital is a typical example. Oxford Biomedica has developed advanced manufacturing infrastructure to support gene and cell therapy production, including multiple GMP-certified facilities in the United Kingdom, United States, and France. Starting in the late 2010s, the company expanded its capacity through phased construction of cleanroom suites, bioreactors, and fill-finish lines to meet growing demand for viral vector manufacturing. By 2025, these facilities support both clinical development and commercial supply, reflecting sustained investments in scalable, compliant biomanufacturing environments critical for advanced therapy medicinal products.

Infrastructure funds bring several advantages to healthcare investments. Their patient capital approach, characterized by long investment horizons, aligns well with healthcare's need for sustained capital to support development cycles and facility maintenance. Their focus on operational stability rather than aggressive growth suits the essential service nature of healthcare. Additionally, infrastructure funds' emphasis on social infrastructure dovetails with growing ESG mandates from institutional investors. Their experience with public-private partnerships also translates effectively to healthcare settings, especially in systems with significant public sector involvement.

The healthcare infrastructure sector is evolving rapidly, driven by several notable trends. There is increasing convergence as traditional infrastructure funds compete with specialized healthcare real estate investment trusts (REITs) and long-dated PE funds in certain segments. Digital transformation is accelerating, with growing investment in digital health infrastructure reflecting the sector's technological evolution. Specialization is increasing, with healthcare-specific infrastructure funds emerging that combine sector expertise with infrastructure investment principles. Examples include Everstone Capital in India, which focuses on healthcare and technology, and Medical Properties Trust, which, while technically a healthcare REIT, operates similarly to an infrastructure fund, specializing in sale-leaseback transactions with hospital operators across the United States and Europe, offering a model of permanent capital focused exclusively on acute care infrastructure. The greater emphasis placed by investors on social impact metrics and sustainability in healthcare infrastructure reinforces the need for ESG integration. Measurement of accessibility, carbon footprint, and clinical outcome metrics are becoming central to capital deployment.

Despite these opportunities, infrastructure investors in healthcare face several challenges. The sector's heavy regulation varies significantly by jurisdiction and demands specialized expertise to navigate complex compliance requirements. Rapid technological change can affect the longevity and value of infrastructure assets, requiring ongoing adaptation. Political risk is significant, as healthcare's essential nature makes it subject to policy shifts and government intervention. Finally, evolving healthcare delivery models can alter infrastructure needs and valuations, necessitating flexible investment strategies.

The expansion of infrastructure funds into healthcare represents a natural evolution, aligning patient capital with a sector that requires long-term, stable investment. As healthcare continues to grow and demand substantial capital, infrastructure funds are poised to play an increasingly vital role in shaping the sector's future.

2.5 FUNDS OF FUNDS AND SECONDARIES

2.5.1 Funds of Funds

The segment of PE funds of funds[3] appeared in the late 1980s in the United States and the United Kingdom (e.g., Pantheon Ventures), but really took off in the 1990s, with growth partially correlated with the financial liberalization in Europe. It represented about 10% to 15% of PE commitments worldwide at the peak, but the proportion has declined. This slower growth and shrinking market share are largely due to institutional investors like pensions, endowments, and sovereign wealth funds increasingly building their own in-house teams for direct fund selection, bypassing funds of funds

[3]While we focus on PE funds of funds, similar structures exist across multiple asset classes, including hedge funds, real estate, infrastructure, commodities, ETFs, and target date used in retirement plans.

to reduce fees and gain more control. There have been about 100 significant players in this segment, although the number may have slightly decreased due to these difficulties.

Funds of funds are like a one-stop shopping place as opposed to direct fund investing. What are the pros and cons? In terms of positive elements, we as an investor get access to top-tier managers, and we can diversify across geographies, sectors, vintages, and industries. We may benefit from more information advantage due to the established resources and in-depth market knowledge. This also allows investors' exposure in a diversified manner. We have lower commitment levels. It allows us to consolidate cash management and reporting, and it has the potential for accelerated returns through secondaries.

What are the downsides of funds of funds? Well, three things. First, an extra layer of fees and additional carry need to be paid. The 2% management fees when investing in a product fund typically comes with another 1% if investing in the fund that invests in those funds. Same for the carry. Second, the investors are exposed to a long-term investment with a commitment that spans several years. They are bound to a commitment to invest in several partnerships over five years. That becomes complicated with the different layers of investment. Finally, investors have a complete lack of control over the investments that will be made.

As shown in Figure 2.19, PE funds of funds increased their fundraising quite rapidly until the global financial crisis, as did other segments. And like all other segments of PE, funds of funds got hit by the crisis and took a long while to recover, achieving record years from 2016.

Based on industry definitions and common usage, "fund of funds" traditionally refers to primary fund investments only—funds that invest in other funds' primary fundraising rounds. Twenty years ago, leading investor Ardian introduced a further segmentation of primary, early secondary, and secondary funds of funds that, while not widely adopted across the industry, remains conceptually interesting (Figure 2.20).

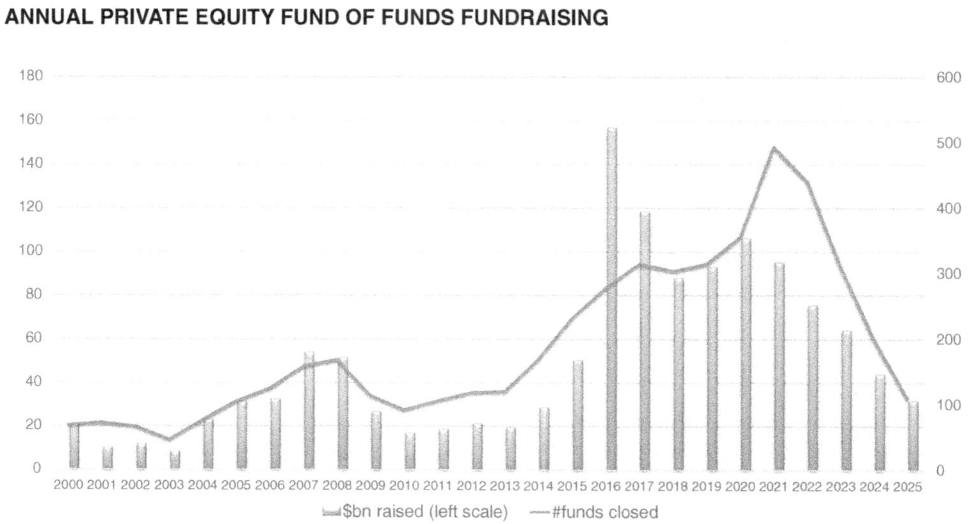

FIGURE 2.19 Annual fundraising by PE funds of funds.
Source: Preqin (part of Blackrock).

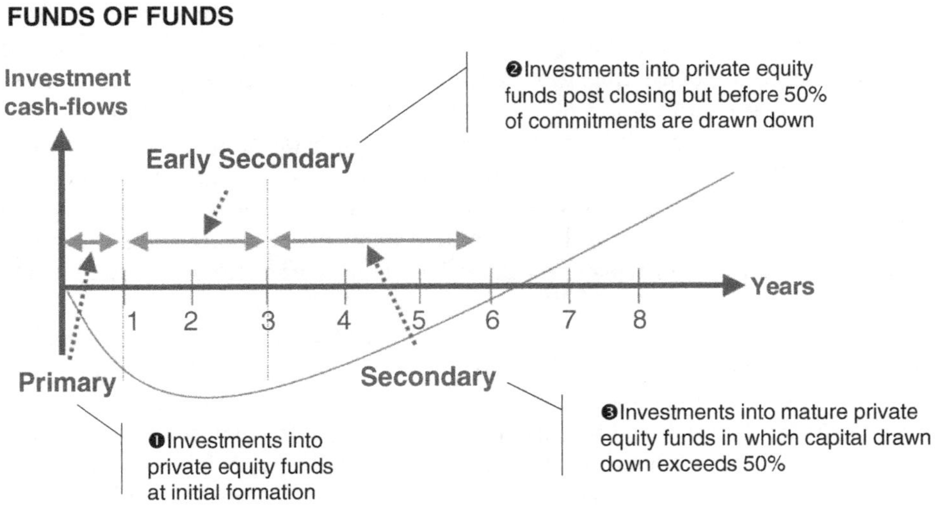

FIGURE 2.20 Possible segmentation of funds of funds.

According to Ardian's framework, primary funds of funds invest directly into PE funds from the beginning. Early secondary funds of funds target "funds of which less than 50% is invested," focusing on PE funds post-closing but before half the commitments are drawn down. Plain secondary funds of funds invest into mature PE funds where capital drawn down exceeds 50%. The distinction matters because the work differs significantly—early secondary investing sits between the long-term commitment horizons of primary investing and the more opportunistic nature of traditional secondary investing, with different risk-return profiles and portfolio company maturity levels.

While these secondary funds of funds invest in existing LP interests across multiple funds, they differ from the wider category of secondary funds or "secondaries"—which represent direct secondary investing without the fund-of-funds layer. This creates a more nuanced landscape where "funds of funds" can operate across primary and secondary markets, while "secondary funds" represent direct secondary investing strategies. We detail it in the next separate section.

2.5.2 Secondaries

Secondary funds can take the form of either "LP interests," the acquisition of the interests of a specific LP in a PE fund, the most common form, and "direct secondaries," also called "GP-led secondaries," "secondaries direct GPs," or sometimes "direct managers," which are funds that acquire many or all the companies from other PE funds (Figure 2.21).

We distinguish between "early secondaries," where acquisition occurs during the first three years of the fund's existence when typically less than 50% of commitments are funded, and "mature secondaries," occurring after three years when funds are more seasoned and often 50–80% funded. This timing distinction is important because early secondary investments retain some characteristics of primary investing with less portfolio visibility, while mature secondaries benefit from established track records and the potential for immediate cash flows.

IS PE REALLY AN ILLIQUID ASSET CLASS? SECONDARY INVESTING

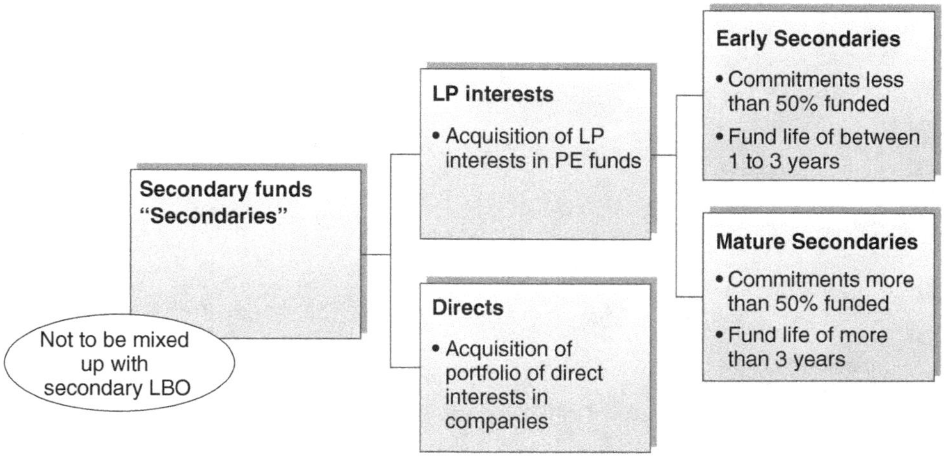

FIGURE 2.21 Segmentation of secondaries.

We now turn to what fuels that secondaries market and what benefits it brings for investors.

The secondaries market is driven by a combination of meeting liquidity needs, satisfying new regulatory constraints, and optimizing asset allocation. The key benefits of investing in the secondaries market are accelerated cash flows in the case of the acquisition of mature portfolios, which allows the investor to minimize the J-curve effect that we will discuss later. You might also find diversification benefits through assets, GPs, and geographies, but also through different types of businesses and vintages—i.e., when those investments were made. Investors also benefit from more asset transparency and fund access, and in financial terms, they would expect an 8–12% discount to the net asset value and an IRR that would typically be between 12% and 20%.

This has fueled the development of this new segment of the market, which barely existed before 2002 (Figure 2.22). But it has been growing relatively fast. In spite of this fast development, we had not reached the point where there would be healthcare-focused secondaries by the mid-2020s.

We propose several explanations. First, the specialized expertise and concentrated exposures required in healthcare assets ran counter to the broad, diversified portfolio profiles that fueled the mainstream secondaries market. Dedicated buyers of mature, multi-segment buyout stakes sought scale and liquidity, which meant they preferred large portfolios spanning multiple sectors rather than niche bundles of clinic- or biotech-only interests. In addition, the regulatory complexity of life-science and healthcare businesses—ranging from FDA-approval pipelines to payer-contract negotiations—made due diligence more time-consuming and costly. Finally, healthcare deal flow often skews toward earlier-stage or growth-equity financings rather than the mature buyout stakes that dominate secondaries. As a result, until sufficient scale of seasoned healthcare portfolios emerged, specialized secondaries buyers have largely steered clear of the sector, delaying the rise of healthcare-focused secondary transactions.

If we look at 10 years of fundraising for the period of 2015 to 2025, comparing funds of funds with secondaries funds (Figure 2.23), we observe that they are of a

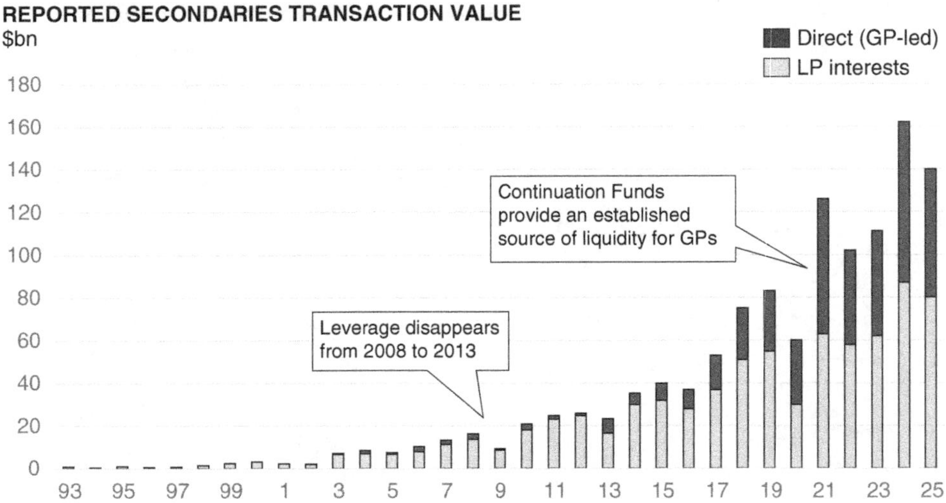

FIGURE 2.22 Estimated secondaries transactions value.
Source: Press search; Candesic research.

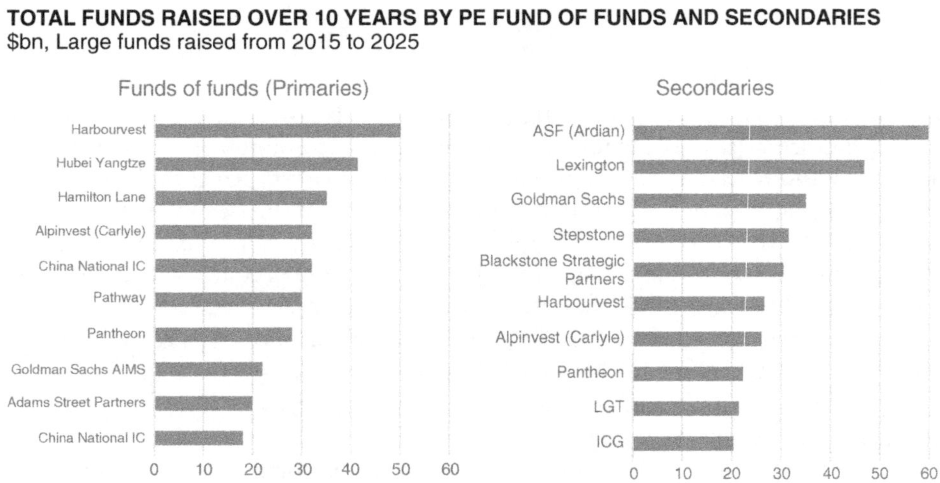

FIGURE 2.23 Comparing fundraising by PE funds of funds and secondaries.
Source: Candesic research (as of September 2025. Does not include infrastructure).

similar size. Funds of funds used to be larger because they predated secondaries by decades. Secondaries have caught up in recent years, evolving according to J.P. Morgan "from an outlet for distressed LPs to a widely utilized portfolio management tool." Among the largest players, Harbourvest, Alpinvest, and Pantheon have significant presence in both segments. Note also the recent emergence of large Chinese primary funds of funds.

2.5.2.1 Direct or GP-led Secondaries We have introduced the GP-led secondaries. They have become a mainstream and high-volume segment of the PE secondaries market. These funds buy entire companies, minority stakes, full portfolios, or even single assets, often through continuation vehicles or restructuring transactions. Sellers can include PE firms but also financial institutions or corporations seeking strategic divestments or liquidity.

The landscape features both specialized mid-market players focused significantly to almost exclusively on GP-led transactions, such as Vision Capital, Verdane, Nova, Evoco, and Tempo, and large, diversified secondaries firms that operate across LP-led and GP-led deals. The larger firms include Ardian, Blackstone Strategic Partners, HarbourVest, Lexington, Goldman Sachs, and StepStone, among others.

These prominent players have recognized the strategic and financial importance of GP-led secondaries, which now represent roughly half of the secondary market volume. GP-led transactions provide flexibility for GPs to manage portfolio liquidity and extend asset hold periods while offering LPs tailored exit opportunities.

Investor interest and capital commitments to this space have grown substantially, with dedicated GP-led secondaries funds regularly exceeding $2 billion in fund size, signaling the maturity and scale of this once-niche market segment. Consequently, GP-led secondaries have transitioned from a niche strategy to a core pillar of the PE ecosystem, involving a broad spectrum of investors and deal structures.

A specific form of GP-led secondaries fund is the continuation fund, where a new vehicle is created to hold and manage a selected subset of portfolio assets—rather than the entire fund—so that the GP can continue owning and growing those assets beyond the original fund's life. They are typically set to last up to six to seven years. There is some controversy associated with their recent success, which we will cover in Chapter 10.

To conclude this section, the secondaries markets in general have grown strongly but not steadily over 25 years (Figure 2.24). They are expected to grow further for three main reasons. One is regulatory, with a combination of Basel rules and the Volcker rule that led to portfolio sales by banks and IAS 27 leading to the consolidation of portfolios. The second reason is related to financial requirements for liquidity management,

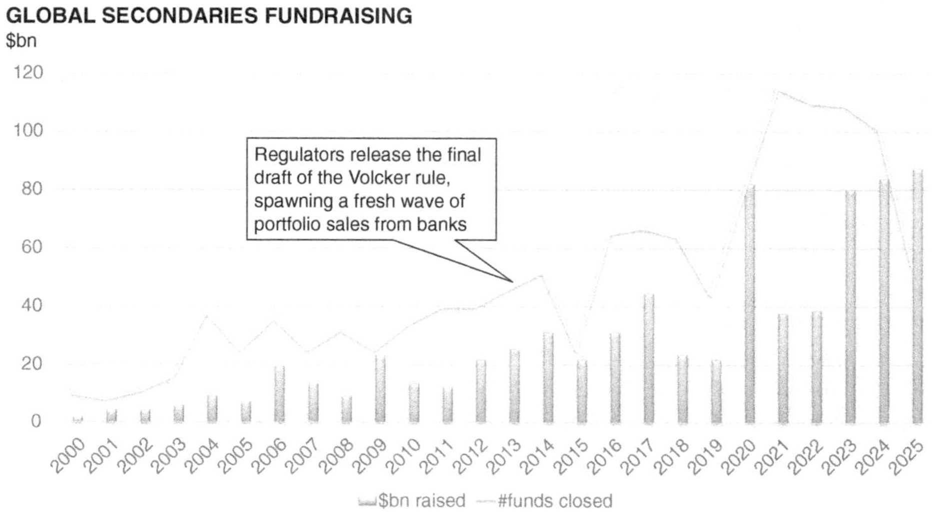

FIGURE 2.24 Evolution of global secondaries fundraising.
Source: Candesic Research.

portfolio management, and financial distress. And as for the third reason, there are strategic changes such as a focus on core or more profitable GP-leveraged finance relationships; asset relocation driven by financial institutions, as well as M&A activity and post-merger asset management; or general corporate strategy changes.

2.5.2.2 Fund Recap A recent segment, or subsegment of the secondaries segment, is the "fund recap," similar to the continuation fund but broader in scope, involving restructuring of the entire original fund to provide liquidity and extend the investment period, typically for all portfolio companies. This has always existed but was kind of a one-off event here and there. Now it seems to have become an industry in itself. In a fund recapitalization, a PE firm restructures an existing fund, typically toward the end of its investment period, to provide liquidity options for current LPs while allowing for continued investment in the portfolio. In this process, some LPs may choose to exit, while new investors are brought in to recapitalize the fund and support the further growth of the portfolio companies. It essentially refreshes the capital base of the fund, giving the GPs more time and flexibility to manage the assets without selling them prematurely. It can be complex because of all the parties involved. These include the GPs, who may sometimes agree to reset the fund's economics, like the management fees, but it is not very easy to get that from them—they may have had an easy life with that 2% management fee so far. On the contrary, the LPs must decide whether they want to exit the fund through a sale to a new investor or accept to roll the interest into a new vehicle at a predetermined valuation.

This involves lots of discussion and negotiation. Some of the transactions, by the way, will involve replacing the GP altogether, something they do not accept easily. The fund recap market is relatively recent; it appeared as a market only around 2013 but has grown to tens of billions of dollars since then. That is only a fraction of the total market, perhaps even smaller than the segment of the zombie funds, which represented some $100 billion in assets under management after the financial crisis. Zombie fund refers to funds that performed very poorly then and whose GPs had little hope to ever be able to raise money again. But they refused to disband and continued to manage their investments for as long as possible to continue capturing the management fees. LPs have learnt from this and are more careful now.

2.5.2.3 Mini Case on Fund Recap: Perseus Partners[4] Perseus' struggles emerged after the May 2012 death of its founder Frank Pearl. Founded in 1995, the firm raised $1.6 billion in capital across seven funds, of which $602.5 million for its last fund, Perseus Partners VII LP, in 2006. Pearl's estate was quickly embroiled in lawsuits, both with banks and with Perseus itself over Pearl's assets transfers prior to his death. For its part, Perseus sued the estate for claims related to Pearl's commitment to invest alongside the investors in the Perseus funds, and those related to his obligations to repay carried interest distributions that were made to him with the understanding they would be repaid.

The legal wrangling added to the challenges Perseus faced, which included poor performance. As of June 30, 2013, Perseus Partners VII LP had generated a net IRR of minus 22.4%. Perseus Market Opportunity Fund (2002 vintage) generated a –10.2%

[4] *Sources:* Dow Jones Private Equity Analyst; Lexington Partners; Secondaries Investor; CalPERS performance data; *Wall Street Journal.*

net IRR and 0.6× investment multiple, while Perseus 2000 Expansion delivered a catastrophic –16.9% net IRR and 0.4× investment multiple as of June 2014. Perseus initially sought to recapitalize five of its funds with a secondary firm, but the steep discounts proposed—more than 60% to the portfolio's underlying NAV—angered investors.

In 2012–2013, NewGlobe Partners offered to pay $240 million for 100% interests in all five funds, representing a 60% discount to NAV. However, this uncompetitive process ultimately failed. Pricing was not the only impediment. Another LP objected to the lack of a broad auction process to maximize value for LPs. He said he was told that such a process would have been too "complicated" due to the ongoing litigation and several cross fund investments. In addition, no formal adviser was attached to the deal to ensure fair valuation.

The situation deteriorated further when Perseus hired Cogent Partners at the end of 2013 to conduct a formal two-round secondary process in Q1 2014. After six months, Centre Lane Partners emerged as the acquirer of Perseus' five remaining funds: Perseus Capital ($102 million, 1997 vintage), Perseus 2000 ($222 million), Perseus Market Opportunity Fund ($340 million, 2002 vintage), Perseus 2000 Expansion ($153 million, 2004 vintage), and Perseus VII ($602.5 million, 2006 vintage).

The final outcome was even more punishing for LPs: Centre Lane offered liquidation at discounts of roughly 85–90% to NAV, far steeper than the initial 60% discounts that had previously angered investors. LPs could alternatively roll their stakes into new vehicles (CLP 2014-A, CLP 2014-B, and CLP 2014-LT) to continue backing specific portfolio companies. Only 11 portfolio companies remained across all five funds, with Perseus Books—Frank Pearl's personal publishing venture—being sold outright to Centre Lane.

Key remaining assets included Haggar Corporation (valued at $100 million), German environmental company Twintec (57% Perseus stake), and Perseus Books ($70 million valuation). The overwhelming majority of LPs accepted Centre Lane's terms, effectively ending Perseus' 19-year run as an independent PE firm. By early 2015, Perseus began winding down operations, with only chairman Ken Socha and a few executives remaining.

This case is quite uncommon, but useful to illustrate how founder dependency, poor performance, and legal complications can create a "death spiral" in PE. The 85–90% discounts to NAV represent among the steepest write-downs in PE secondary market history, demonstrating how operational disruption and performance failures compound to destroy LP value almost entirely.

2.5.2.4 Conclusion on Secondaries For Alessandra Mazzuchelli, co-founder of Soledar Partners, a placement agent operating out of Switzerland, secondaries' liquidity is now strategic: "... with distributions slowing and many LPs overallocated, secondaries have become a powerful portfolio management tool. Whether LP-led (selling fund interests) or GP-led (continuation vehicles), these solutions provide flexibility without fully exiting the asset class."

COVID-era vintages, which saw quick deployments but slow exits, have led many LPs to explore secondaries more proactively. Liquidity management is no longer just a back-office function—it has become part of the capital allocation strategy.

2.6 CLOSER TO DEBT: MEZZANINE, DISTRESSED DEBT AND TURNAROUND

We have looked at the core segments of non-VC PE, including growth capital and LBOs. We have also examined the segments of funds of funds and secondaries. We now discuss the debt-related segments of PE, including the mezzanine, distressed debt, and turnaround segments. We do not cover the largest segment of debt here, that of the credit funds providing term loans because it doesn't qualify as "quasi equity."

2.6.1 Mezzanine

Mezzanine financing sits between senior debt and equity in the capital structure, offering a middle ground in terms of risk and return. It typically accounts for 10–20% of total capital structure in larger LBOs, with 7+ year terms and bullet repayment at maturity.

Mezzanine is less risky than equity because it provides fixed interest payments and often includes equity kickers such as warrants, giving lenders upside potential. However, it ranks below senior debt, meaning mezzanine lenders are repaid after senior lenders in liquidation scenarios.

Default rates historically range 1–4% in normal periods, spiking above 10% during crisis periods like 2008–2009. Loss given default (LGD) averages around 50%, meaning investors typically recover half their investment upon default.

Second lien debt represents a distinct category—it is secured debt subordinated only by lien priority, not payment subordination like traditional mezzanine. Second lien ranks behind senior debt but typically ahead of mezzanine, offering lower pricing (variable benchmark + 6% vs. 15–18% fixed rates) due to its secured characteristics.

Both structures allow companies to raise capital without surrendering control, making them valuable tools for expansion, acquisitions, or leveraged buyouts, though they come with higher costs and greater risk compared to senior debt.

Figure 2.25 shows total funds raised over 10 years by leading mezzanine players. Goldman Sachs and HPS Investment Partners, a subsidiary of Blackrock, have been the largest players in this field for some time.

2.6.2 Distressed Debt and Turnaround

The second major segment of debt-related PE is distressed debt, though it is closely linked to the third segment, turnaround investing (Figure 2.26). Distressed debt involves acquiring the debt of struggling companies before they enter bankruptcy. Traditional banks often prefer to sell these troubled loans to specialist investors—typically PE or hedge funds—who purchase them at a discount and actively work to restructure the business.

Turnaround investing, by contrast, focuses on acquiring the equity rather than the debt of distressed companies. Given the financial distress, the distinction between equity and debt can sometimes be minimal; a company may have little or no debt but still face severe operational or financial difficulties. In this case, PE investors—sometimes referred to as workout funds—aim to restore profitability and revive the business.

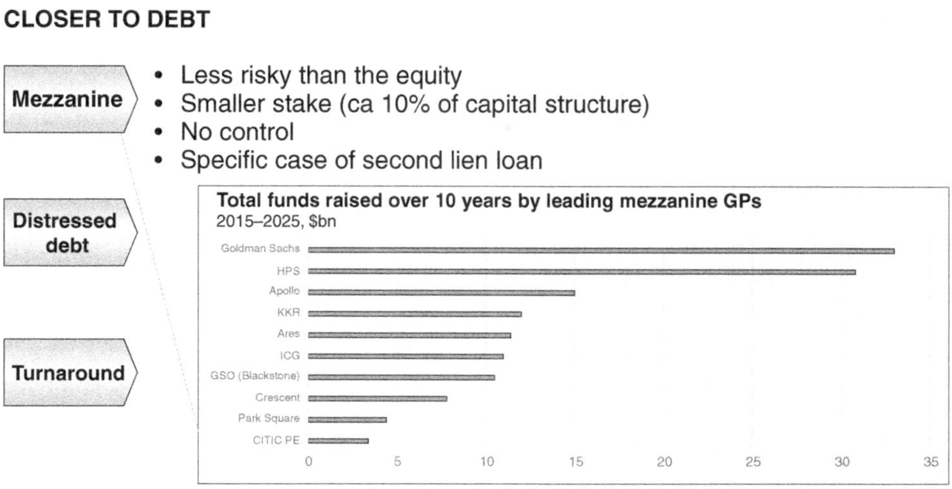

FIGURE 2.25 Fundraising by mezzanine funds.
Source: Company announcements; Candesic research.

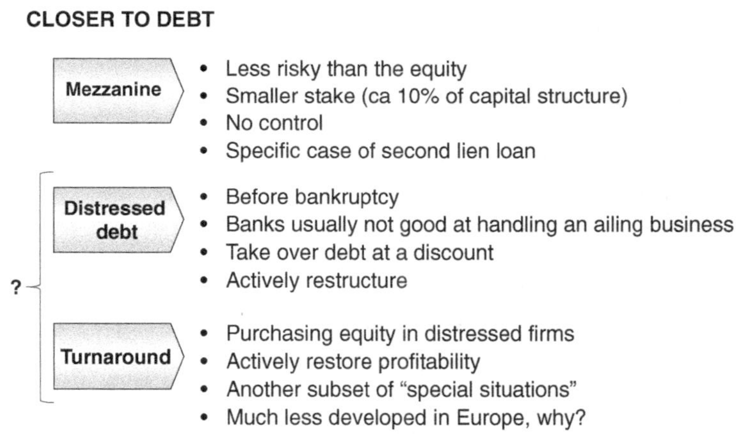

FIGURE 2.26 Distressed dent funds vs. turnaround funds.
Source: Candesic.

While turnaround investing is well-established in the United States, it is less prevalent in Europe due to stricter bankruptcy laws. In many Southern European countries in particular, bankruptcy can have long-lasting consequences for entrepreneurs, whereas in the United States, more forgiving legal frameworks allow business owners to recover and start anew more quickly, sometimes by simply relocating to another state.

In healthcare, true "turnaround" PE deals are less frequent than safe-sound buyouts or growth-driven roll-ups. Regulatory scrutiny, reimbursement constraints, and mission-driven governance make distressed assets risky and hard to fix. For example, PE firms have systematically acquired distressed nursing homes, but these typically involve asset purchases rather than equity stakes. There are however some examples in pharma, like Famar, a European CDMO that was diligenced by Candesic. We present the three phases of the operation next:

The Distressed Breakup (2019–2020)

Famar faced a €200 million debt crisis in 2019, forcing KKR's Pillarstone subsidiary to dismantle the Greek pharmaceutical manufacturer's 12 European sites. The company split into two transactions: According to FiercePharma, French competitor Fareva acquired five profitable French/Dutch/Canadian facilities for over €250 million with 1,300 employees, while ECM Partners and York Capital, two PE firms, bought the struggling "southeastern perimeter"—six plants in Italy, Greece, and Spain generating €210 million revenue with 1,900 employees, maintaining the legacy of the company's name.

The PE Turnaround (2020–2024)

ECM implemented classic CDMO restructuring across the distressed assets. The firm invested in R&D to shift toward higher-value products, improved operations across six manufacturing sites, and diversified the client base to serve pharmaceutical companies in more than 80 markets. This represented genuine equity turnaround work on assets acquired during financial distress.

The Successful Exit (2024)

ECM sold majority control to MidEuropa in 2024, with EBRD co-investing €24 million alongside the buyer. The exit valuation substantially exceeded ECM's 2020 distressed purchase price. Under new ownership, Famar acquired a German sterile manufacturing facility in May 2025 and planned major R&D investments in Greece, demonstrating continued growth momentum.

Figure 2.27 illustrates the security value provided by the assets of a failing company. Cash would obviously be up to 100% because one can be confident to have access to it. Land would typically be estimated at about 70%. Buildings as freehold property is still above 50%, but finished goods are closer to 25%, and work in progress, equity, and goodwill will be closer to zero. But bear in mind that what looks reasonable for a manufacturer will obviously be very different for a retailer.

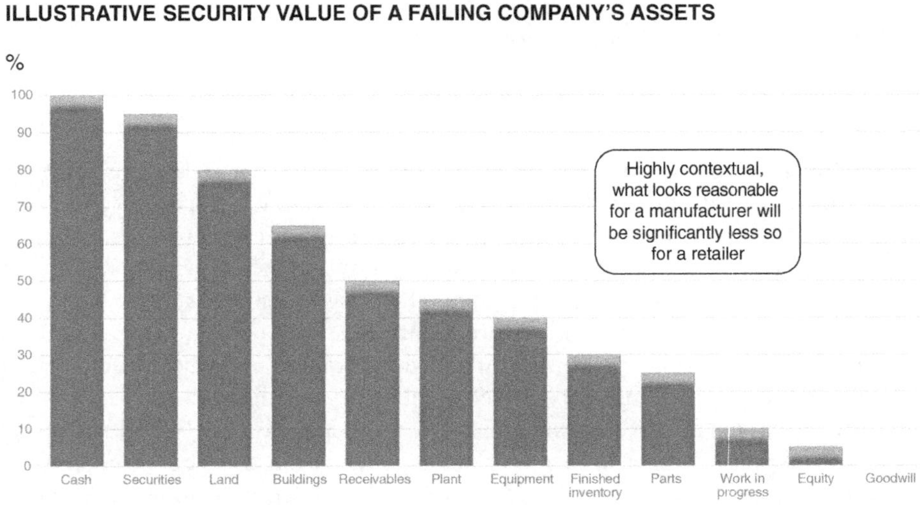

FIGURE 2.27 Illustrative value of a company's assets in bankruptcy.

Distressed debt investing is an alternative strategy to take advantage of distress. It is considered a PE investment strategy because distressed PE firms pursue control-oriented strategies, acquiring equity stakes or convertible debt to gain controlling interests, then actively restructuring operations over three- to seven-year periods. Distressed hedge funds are another player in the segment. While both invest in troubled companies, they differ in approach and timeline. Distressed hedge funds focus on short-term trading of discounted debt securities (typically 30–40% below par), seeking quick profits from price recovery within months to two years. However, these distinctions have increasingly blurred as hedge funds adopt "loan-to-own" strategies seeking control, while PE firms operate trading-focused distressed arms, creating a convergent landscape where strategy matters more than structural classification.

The segment of distressed debt has sometimes raised almost $50 billion a year (Figure 2.28). Between 2012 and 2016, a growing amount of high yield LBO and corporate debt was maturing, which meant that distressed funds were expecting lots of opportunities. Many LBO firms, like Blackstone and Apollo, diversified into distressed debt in the United States because they were expecting a great opportunity from that event.

This wall of debts actually became a refinancing hill only, through a combination of long-term amendments, extensions, refinancings, and payments by portfolio companies thanks to low-interest rates. So, we never faced a huge problem.

In the meantime, a few special opportunities, distressed, and turnaround funds raised money successfully. In 2014–2015, at a time when many wanted to capitalize on a recovery phase in the aftermath of the GFC, several funds like Alchemy Special Opportunities Three were oversubscribed. Endless, also oversubscribed that same year, reached fame for flipping Kiddicare after a record 11 weeks. Large players then entered the market with multi-billion funds, like Pimco (Bonds), CQS (Hedge funds), and Hayfin (Special opportunities).

Then, in the 2020s, huge, distressed debt funds were raised, sometimes more than $10 billion and often under the name "special opportunities" or, later on, "opportunistic credit." Oaktree raised $16 billion, West Street $14 billion, and Starwood

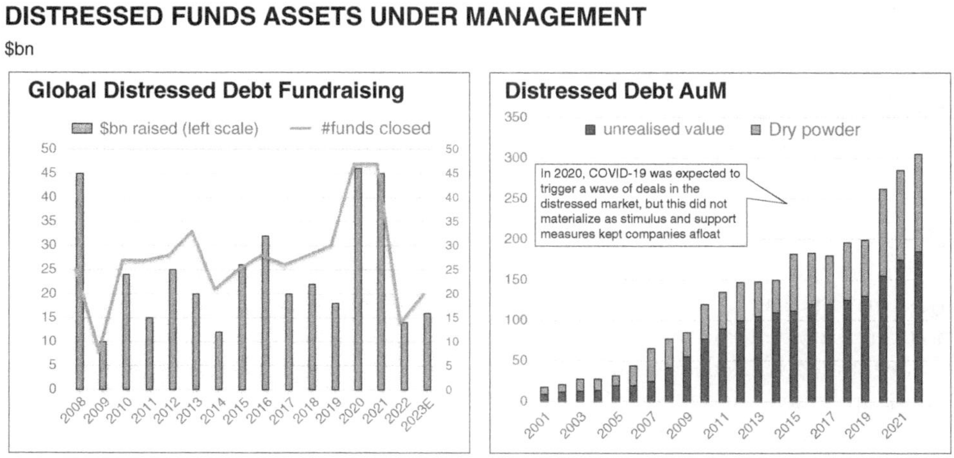

FIGURE 2.28 Distressed debt funds' fundraising and AuM.
Source: Preqin (part of Blackrock).

$10 billion. It helped that central banks had flooded the market with liquidity during the pandemic, eliminating "distress."

Leading distressed GPs have raised significant amounts of money in the last 20 years. Large players with more than $15 billion AuM include Apollo, Oaktree, Cerberus, Lone Star, Blackstone, CarVal, and Avenue Capital.

Several specialized PE distressed debt funds have emerged to target healthcare companies facing financial stress, capitalizing on a sector that has become increasingly leveraged and vulnerable to bankruptcy. In 2025, healthcare companies represented some of the riskiest borrowers in leveraged lending, with nearly 88% of the most distressed healthcare firms being PE-owned, leveraged at debt-to-EBITDA ratios often exceeding 7:1 compared to historical averages of 5:1. Specialist funds like CRG ($4+ billion), Deerfield Management ($3+ billion), and Athyrium Capital ($2+ billion) focus specifically on distressed healthcare debt, targeting companies struggling with reimbursement rate changes, labor shortages, rising interest costs, and excessive leverage from previous buyouts. These funds benefit from deep healthcare sector expertise, understanding complex regulatory environments, and the ability to navigate bankruptcy proceedings while potentially gaining control through debt-to-equity conversions in companies providing essential healthcare services that cannot simply disappear.

2.7 PRIVATE CREDIT

It is well known that bad times have virtues, and this applies to the fostering of financial innovation during financial crises (Aghion et al., 2012). Like crowdfunding, private debt, which is privately negotiated and originated by nonbank lenders such as private debt funds, asset managers, and business development companies to corporate borrowers, has emerged during the 2008 Great Financial Crisis. Credit funds have experienced a remarkable rise in recent years according to Moody's, evolving from a niche asset class in 2008 into a $3 trillion industry that now rivals traditional bank lending. This explosive growth stems from several converging factors: post-2008 financial reforms like Basel III and Dodd-Frank have imposed stricter capital requirements on banks, limiting their ability to lend to middle-market firms; institutional investors desperately seeking higher yields in persistently low-interest-rate environments have flocked to credit funds offering 5–8% returns; and the massive expansion of PE has created unprecedented demand for flexible, nontraditional financing sources. Today, private debt is an important part of the macroeconomic rise of shadow banking and the decline of banks which currently only originate 40% of the loans in the United States (Buchak et al., 2024).

For borrowers, private debt is a more flexible alternative to bank debt. For PE funds, private debt is a convenient way to finance growth by limiting dilution and benefiting from the flexibility of privately negotiated repayment terms that can also be renegotiated if needed (Gompers et al., 2016). It can be tailored to the long term, illiquid, and uncertain nature of project and infrastructure finance. It is also financing vehicle to raise both senior and mezzanine debt in leveraged transactions, and it can take full advantage of its flexibility in restructuring and distressed PE investments.

Credit funds get their own section, although they find other ways to "get closer to equity." Here is a comment made by an industry veteran who will remain anonymous:

> *Credit gets to mid-teens [returns] in 3 ways: lending to crap/high risk, with back-leverage or spec-sits restructuring. The last two are riskier than they look, the first one is doomed to fail unless there is a massive market upturn hiding monsters. And in credit funds, when you have a full default and are in a subordinated position (those are the mid-double digit ones), you are looking at a total write-off in most cases. See a couple of those in a portfolio and all of your return (and carry) are gone.*

Like PE versus listed stocks, investors view private debt as an attractive alternative to listed fixed income securities, which they expect to provide both superior returns and welcome diversification. Given this interest from LPs, many of these credit funds have been launched by PE firms themselves, such as Blackstone, KKR, and Apollo (Figure 2.29), capitalizing on their insider industry knowledge, proprietary deal flow, and deep understanding of borrower needs to structure tailored financing solutions that traditional banks cannot match. However, to navigate potential conflicts of interest and regulatory scrutiny, these firms maintain strict Chinese walls between their PE investment teams and credit fund managers, ensuring arm's-length transactions and compliance with fiduciary duties. These credit funds have increasingly replaced traditional lenders in middle-market and leveraged transactions, offering borrowers greater certainty on deal closure, more financing options, faster execution, and the ability to work with fewer lenders while providing stronger covenant protection than the "covenant-lite" public markets.

The US Federal Reserve estimates that loan commitments from large banks to PE and private credit funds surged from approximately $10 billion in 2013 to $300 billion in 2023—a 30-fold increase that underscores this fundamental shift in the lending landscape.

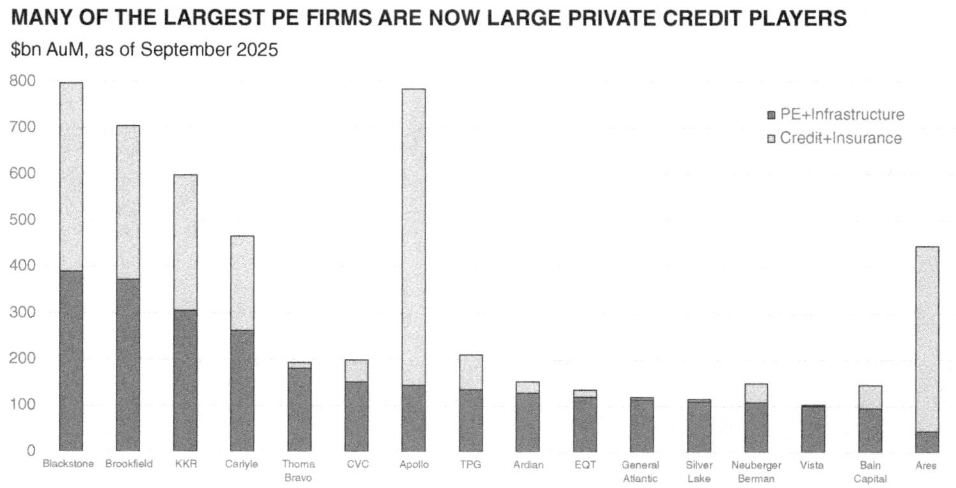

FIGURE 2.29 Largest private credit players by AuM.
Source: Company websites; Candesic research.

This $300 billion represented 14% of large banks' total loan commitments to nonbank financial institutions as of 2023, up from about 1% in 2013. This transformation has created a more competitive environment where credit funds can provide capital to high-quality companies without forcing share price resets or generating meaningful dilution, while regulators increasingly monitor these opaque lending relationships for potential systemic risks.

These concerns have only intensified as rising interest rates exposed underlying credit quality issues across private lending portfolios, with default rates climbing materially through 2025 and into 2026 — prompting a wave of fund-level gate mechanisms that have restricted investor redemptions and raised broader questions about liquidity mismatches at the heart of the private credit model.

2.8 PRIVATE AND PUBLIC EQUITY

We now consider the various ways in which the boundaries between private and public equity can be crossed. First, in Figure 2.30, we introduce three types of funds that toy with the public markets: private investment in public equity, crossover funds, and interval funds.

2.8.1 Private Investment in Public Equity

A private investment in public equity (PIPE) refers to a transaction where private investors, typically private accredited investors, purchase shares of a publicly traded company through a private placement rather than a public offering. They do so below the current market price. It is not limited to PE firms; hedge funds are also regular investors. It can be raised in complement to a public offering. Note that while the majority of the PIPE transactions raise equity, there are various segments of convertible and straight debt.

PIPE transactions seem to be associated with exuberant markets as shown by Figure 2.31.

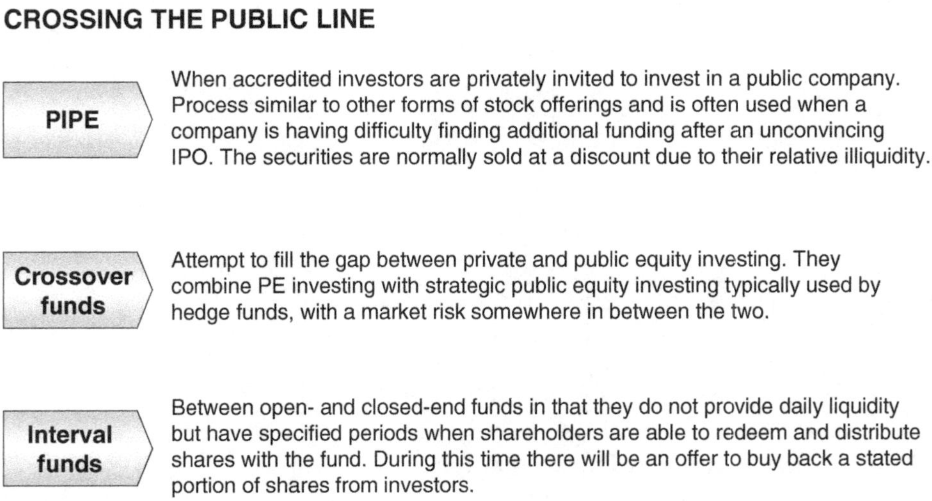

FIGURE 2.30 PIPE, crossover, and interval funds.
Source: Candesic.

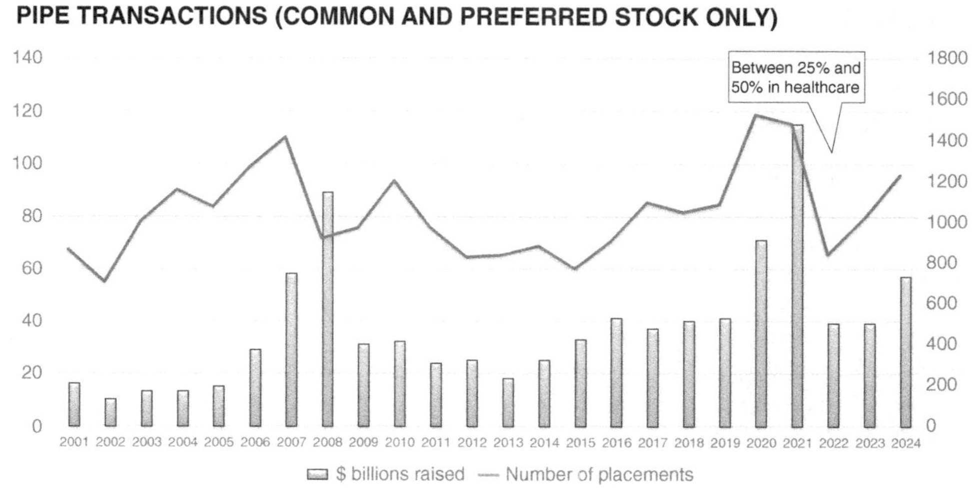

FIGURE 2.31 PIPE transactions in value and placement count.
Source: PrivateRaise; PlacementTracker; Candesic.

In 2023, according to PrivateRaise, about half of all PIPE transactions were in healthcare: about 30% in biotech, more than 10% in pharmaceuticals, and almost 10% in medtech. In healthcare, such PIPE deals are indeed often associated with biotechs and other startups. They are often used for balance sheet support, clinical trial funding, or strategic acquisitions, rather than early-stage venture investments. They can become a lifesaver when other fundraising options have dried up.

After signing an NDA, investors can gain early access to sensitive data like positive trial results, enabling them to predict stock increases and invest. That can be perceived as unfair to other investors. This access may also allow for negotiating larger discounts and additional warrants.

Famous transactions include the 2021 US SPAC of UK-headquartered Babylon Health,[5] where a significant part of the funding came through a PIPE of $230 million. In another example, in 2023, BridgeBio Pharma, a commercial-stage biotech company, announced a $250 million PIPE fundraising led by Qatar Investment Authority (QIA), with significant participation from four of the largest US investment management firms, to support the company's ongoing commercial and development activities.

2.8.2 PEBCI or "PE + Listed Company" Model

PEBCI stands for PE-Backed Corporate Incubation and refers to a model sometimes called "PE + Listed Company." It is effectively a hybrid approach combining PIPE-like arrangements, SPV fund incubation, and roll-up style consolidation. A listed company partners with a PE fund to incubate off-balance sheet assets and later integrate them via M&A. We describe the approach in Chapter 9, in the section on China, where it has been implemented most often. The term to describe it is not fully fixed. Alternative

[5] See Kitten M., Babylon's SPAC Opera, Imperial College, The Case Centre (2026). We discuss this transaction in our section on SPACs.

terms like "PIPE-based roll-up model," "public-private M&A incubator," "listed sponsor PE Roll-up structure" can frame it in familiar global PE terminology.

2.8.3 Crossover Funds

Crossover funds occupy a distinctive position—more VC than PE—at the intersection of private and public markets, offering a hybrid investment strategy into high-growth companies. Managed primarily by public-market investors—such as hedge funds, mutual funds, or late-stage VC firms—these funds invest in companies both before and after their IPO, effectively straddling the transition from private to public ownership. Their approach allows them to build substantial stakes in promising companies shortly before they go public, capturing the potential upside at the IPO while retaining the flexibility to maintain or adjust their positions after listing.

The strategy is especially influential in sectors like healthcare and life sciences, where companies often remain private for extended periods during intensive research and development phases. Here, crossover funds act as a crucial bridge, providing not only much-needed capital but also a form of market validation: their participation signals credibility to future public investors and can accelerate a company's path to IPO. Notable players in healthcare include Sands Capital Life Sciences Pulse Fund III, with $555 million raised in 2024 for this strategy, and Sofinnova Crossover Fund, the largest one in Europe with €445 million raised in 2021.

This unique positioning comes with its own challenges. The liquidity expectations of public-market investors can conflict with the longer-term horizons typical of PE, sometimes leading to misalignments or heightened volatility, particularly in turbulent markets. This tension is especially evident when market sentiment shifts, as crossover funds may be more exposed to sudden changes in risk appetite compared to traditional, buy-and-hold PE strategies.

Traditional boundaries between asset classes tend to blur, and the rise of crossover funds reflects this broader evolution in the investment landscape. Driven by the relentless pursuit of yield in an increasingly competitive and mature market, these funds exemplify a growing appetite for flexible, outcome-oriented strategies that blend the best of public and private investing.

2.8.4 Interval Funds

They are regulated investment vehicles that bridge the gap between open-end (mutual) funds and traditional closed-end private funds by offering periodic, but not daily, liquidity. They continuously offer shares to an unlimited number of investors. The liquidity is provided through scheduled repurchase offers, typically quarterly, semi-annually, or annually, where the fund offers to buy back a stated percentage (usually between 5% and 25%) of its outstanding shares at net asset value (NAV). Investors are notified in advance of these intervals and can choose to participate. If redemption requests exceed the stated amount, shares are repurchased on a pro rata basis.

Their structure is generally codified in the United States under the 1940 Act and the Securities Act of 1933, providing a regulatory framework and investor protections similar to mutual funds, but allowing for investment in less liquid assets. This enables broader investor access to private and illiquid markets, while maintaining regulatory oversight and periodic redemption opportunities.

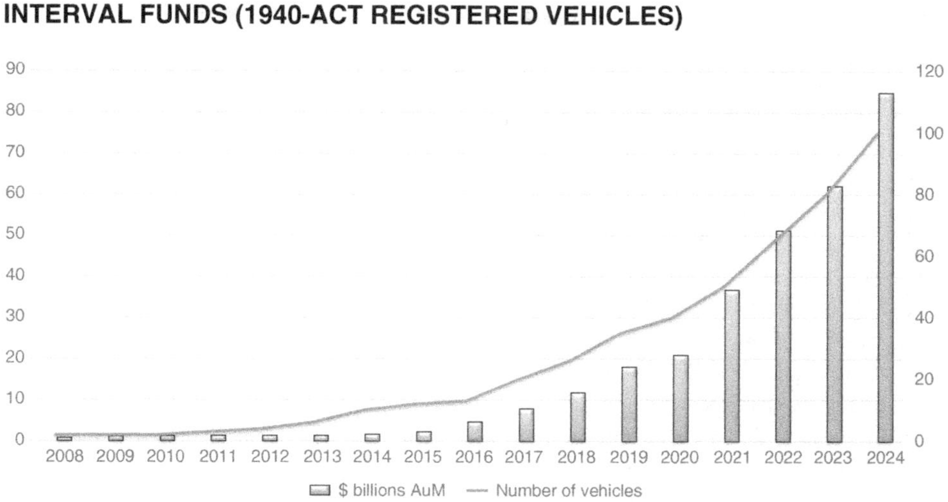

FIGURE 2.32 Interval funds by AuM and number of vehicles.
Source: Candesic research.

Designed to expand access to private market and alternative investment strategies, especially for high-net-worth investors and their advisors, interval funds have become a popular "evergreen" structure for asset managers seeking to broaden their investor base beyond institutions. As of 2025, interval funds had surpassed $100 billion in assets under management, reflecting their growing role in the alternative investment landscape (Figure 2.32). They became a visible component of the new trend of "democratization of PE" in the 2020s.

2.8.5 LPE

We now discuss the broader segment of listed PE, which we call LPE. This refers to PE vehicles that are quoted on stock exchanges, typically international ones. It is both a defined strategy for PE investing and a commitment to the investment process that is typical of PE.

The theoretical advantages of LPE investment vehicles center on accessibility, liquidity, and transparency mechanisms that traditional PE structures cannot provide. LPE offers market access to retail investors who would otherwise be excluded from PE allocations due to minimum investment thresholds and accredited investor requirements. The vehicles provide daily liquidity through exchange trading, theoretical transparency through regulatory disclosure requirements, portfolio diversification across multiple PE strategies, and potential tax optimization benefits exemplified by specialized structures such as UK Venture Capital Trusts.

However, empirical evidence reveals significant structural limitations that constrain these theoretical advantages. Academic research demonstrates persistent NAV-to-price discounts in listed PE vehicles, with some studies documenting discount persistence over extended periods regardless of underlying performance. Investors face limited control over critical investment parameters including leverage deployment and capital allocation timing, while remaining exposed to "overhang" risk when underlying fund managers fail to deploy committed capital efficiently. Furthermore, the liquidity premium comes at the cost of surrendering the illiquidity premium that compensates traditional PE investors, potentially creating a structural return disadvantage relative to direct PE investment.

The market capitalization of the listed PE worldwide can be easily tracked once the main funds are identified. The market capitalization is public information. That is another advantage of this segment: it can easily be tracked without having to buy expensive databases. If we exclude special local segments like UK VCTs, we could identify about 100 such listed funds as of 2025, with about half of the asset allocation to North America. Tracking the Top 50, we see their total market capitalization has fluctuated a lot. It went up just before the internet bubble crashed, then decreased by half, then went up again to another peak in 2006 and 2007. This was followed by the global financial crisis, which caused a significant drop to only €23 billion. One of us was invested in several of those funds and saw their money disappear very quickly. Figure 2.33 illustrates that the market seemed to have recovered by 2013 and continued to grow, reaching record levels. The chart needs to be looked at with sufficient care. In fact, this was fueled by a wave of IPOs of many of the largest PE funds more than the performance of the sector. In 2021, we almost reached €400 billion, and while 2022 suffered somewhat from the surge in interest rates, 2023 set a new record, in line with the surprising performance of the stock market.

Note that, over the period 2013 to 2023, the sector allocation has changed. While the exposure to industrials decreased substantially, the exposure to healthcare in those portfolios increased from 10% to 13%.

Is LPE really PE? Well, it first depends on the definition and would benefit to be called listed private capital, considering how diversified the firms are, whether in private credit, mezzanine, or less relevant segments. In any case, its promoters allege that it comes with a few key advantages. The organization LPEQ, for example, gives three reasons why LPE is such an attractive investment vehicle. First, the cash flows are managed by the company rather than being distributed in an unpredictable way. Second, the investor does not suffer from the J-curve effect, so they are not paying fees on the committed but uninvested capital—that is true. Third, they offer daily liquidity, which is attractive to a certain number of institutional investors, like defined contribution

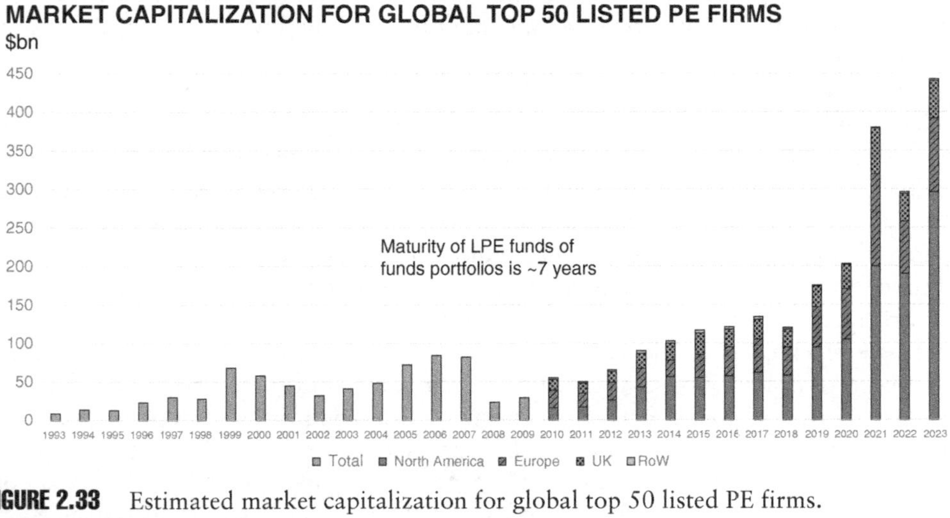

FIGURE 2.33 Estimated market capitalization for global top 50 listed PE firms.
Source: Candesic research.

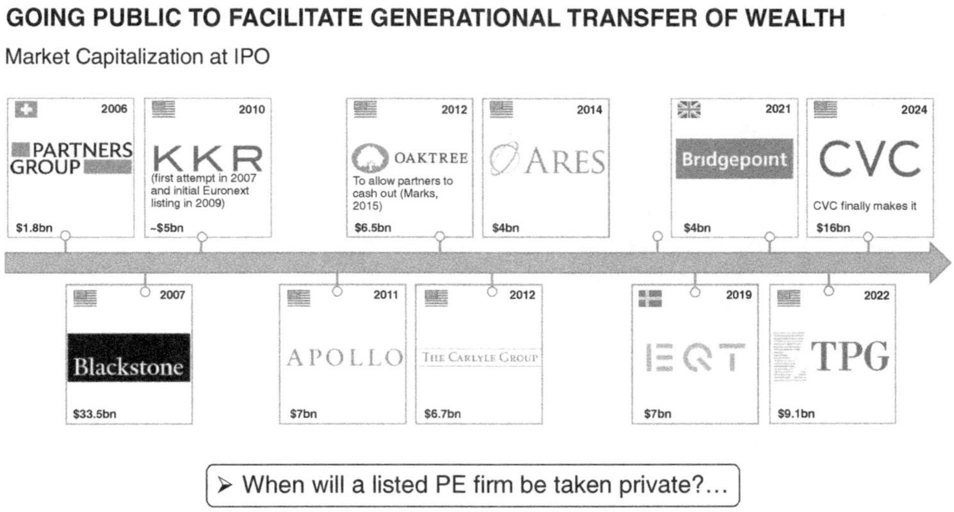

FIGURE 2.34 Main IPOs of PE firms.

pension plans in the United Kingdom, but also private banks and family offices. That is also true to an extent. Normally, PE investors accept that their investment will be blocked for many years. So, there is a liquidity advantage in case a shock happens in the market altogether.

Back in 1980, the number of LPEs was very small: there were just three at that time. That number rose quickly, and by 2008, we could identify more than 50 of them including, notably, Blackstone, and alongside other listed alternative fund managers. Two-thirds of them at that point were direct PE investment companies. After the interruption of the global financial crisis, most large PE firms that had not yet done so decided to go public.

Figure 2.34 shows 11 PE firms that have gone public over the years. But what are the reasons for going public? A major one is that it can facilitate generational transfer of wealth. For example, Oaktree went public in 2012, at least partially to allow some of its senior partners to cash out—something that is always sensitive in private funds.

In the next sections, we will explore the back and forth between public and private markets, through SPACs and "take-privates." In Chapter 6, we will also discuss dual-track processes.

2.9 INTERMITTENT TRADING OF SHARES IN PRIVATE COMPANIES

The Private Intermittent Securities and Capital Exchange System (PISCES) was launched in June 2025 as a new, regulated UK market infrastructure designed to facilitate the intermittent trading of shares in private companies. Unlike traditional public stock exchanges, PISCES operates through scheduled "trading windows"—for example, on a quarterly or biannual basis—during which eligible investors can buy and sell existing shares in private companies. It is important to note that PISCES does not allow for the issuance of new shares or company share buybacks; its sole function is to provide a secondary market for existing private company equity. The system is overseen by the

TABLE 2.1 Summary of PISCES Characteristics vs. Public and Private Markets

Feature	PISCES Approach	Public Markets	Private Markets (Current)
Liquidity	Intermittent, scheduled trading windows	Continuous	Illiquid, bilateral
Investor Access	Institutional, HNW, sophisticated, employees	Public/retail	Closed/private
Disclosure	Bespoke, event-specific, lighter than public	Full, ongoing	Minimal
Capital Raising	Not permitted	Yes	Yes (private rounds)
Buybacks	Not permitted (initially)	Yes	Yes (sometimes)
Taxation	Stamp duty exempt	Stamp duty applies	Stamp duty applies

UK Financial Conduct Authority (FCA) with a five-year regulatory sandbox, during which its rules and market impact are evaluated before any permanent adoption.

PISCES is globally innovative and widely recognized as the first initiative of its kind. While other private share trading platforms existed, such as the NASDAQ Private Market in the United States, PISCES is unique in being a regulator-backed, intermittent, multilateral trading system with a bespoke legal and disclosure regime.

The system operates through scheduled trading events, during which only existing shares in companies not listed on any public market may be traded. Note that participation is limited to institutional investors, high-net-worth individuals, sophisticated investors, and employees of participating companies rather than the general retail public. Companies must provide tailored, event-specific disclosures to eligible investors, though these requirements are lighter than those for public markets. Companies also retain control over when shares are traded, who can buy, and the price parameters.

PISCES promised several potential benefits. It provides a long-missing liquidity path for early investors, founders, and employees in private companies, which is especially valuable as companies remain private for longer (Table 2.1). By opening private company shares to a wider pool of sophisticated investors, PISCES partially democratizes access to PE and VC-backed growth companies, moving beyond the closed networks of traditional PE. The platform's structured disclosures and regulatory oversight improve transparency compared to purely bilateral private transactions. Furthermore, PISCES may help companies transition more smoothly to public markets by familiarizing them with periodic disclosure and trading requirements, and the ability to exercise share options on PISCES—with preserved tax advantages—may make equity compensation more attractive for employees.

Its intent was to bridge the gap between private and public capital markets, increasing liquidity for founders, employees, and early investors, while broadening access for a wider pool of sophisticated investors. The platform aims to support company growth, rationalize shareholder bases, and serve as a "stepping-stone" to public markets, all while reducing transaction costs through stamp duty and SDRT exemptions.

However, from the start PISCES has drawn significant controversy for its abandonment of many protections traditionally associated with public markets. Disclosure requirements are notably light: companies are not required to disclose ongoing or past litigation nor to apply any specific accounting standards. There is no obligation to be audited—only to state whether an audit has occurred. Major shareholders (more than 25%) are not required to announce their dealings, and directors need only declare their intentions at the start of a trading window; if they change their mind after the window opens, no update is required. Initial proposals for clear, comprehensive, and easily analyzable disclosures were dropped after industry opposition.

Market monitoring has been left to participants under what the FCA calls an "ask-model," a vaguely defined approach that places the burden on investors to request information. There were no statutory powers for platform operators to enforce disclosure, nor a right of private action for breaches of disclosure rules. As the *Financial Times* observed, PISCES widens the pool of investors, allowing many to "cosplay as PE funds," but does so by creating a buyer-beware marketplace that embraces information asymmetry and bypasses the banks, advisers, and intermediaries whose reputations have traditionally protected market integrity.

PISCES is not a fundraising platform, but PE firms are expected to use it as a new channel for liquidity, portfolio management, and shareholder base diversification in their private company investments. The platform may also stimulate greater activity in the UK's PE ecosystem by lowering barriers to secondary trading and providing new exit options, but it does not replace traditional fundraising or public capital markets.

While PISCES promised to partially democratize access to PE and venture-backed companies, its impact has been limited by investor eligibility, intermittent liquidity, and—most critically—the absence of many investor protections. Five years of sandbox operation should determine whether PISCES can deliver on its promise and become a permanent fixture in the UK's capital markets landscape.

2.10 SPECIAL PURPOSE ACQUISITION COMPANY

Special purpose acquisition companies (SPACs) are shell companies established to merge with or acquire private companies, enabling them to go public without undergoing the traditional IPO process.

We have seen in the case of Babylon how a SPAC transaction can be paired with a PIPE. But the SPAC itself has been called a hybrid between IPO and PE. The SPAC vehicle raises cash for a listed shell company with no assets. Within a defined period that can be as long as one to two years, the sponsors promise to acquire/merge it with an established (private) company. Investors normally do not know the type of company in which the sponsors might invest their cash, although it is usually in high-tech. Once shareholders approve the deal, the acquired business will be publicly traded through the SPAC, and the company name can be changed.

Every investor can individually request their money to be returned. They get two protections. The first one is a veto power, whereas the proposed transaction requires approval of the majority of investors above a specified threshold, often 60–80%. The second one is time insurance: the money is held in a trust until an acquisition is made and returned to investors if no suitable company was identified or approved by the end of the stated period. Sponsors typically put up their own cash, typically 3–4%, as part of the original amount raised at the flotation but receive a 10–20% stake.

A SPAC looks similar to a reverse merger with two significant differences of context: in a reverse merger, the owners and the management of the company lead the entire process, and no capital is raised (Figure 2.35). In a SPAC transaction, the owners and the management of the target company are on the sell side and will organize the sale of part of the company against the capital raised by the SPAC. Moreover, SPACs

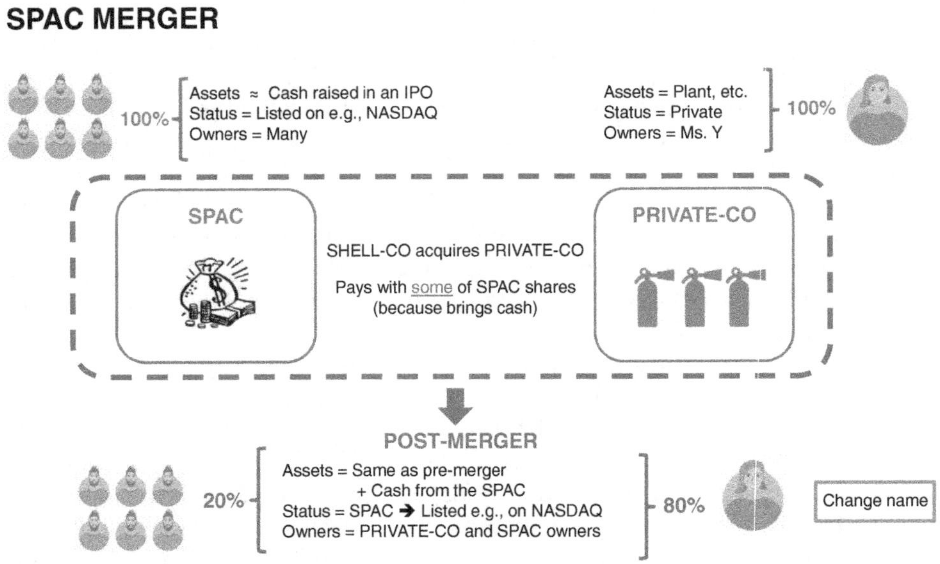

FIGURE 2.35 Design of a SPAC merger.
Source: Denis Gromb.

are created from scratch specifically for the purpose of going public and finding an acquisition target. Unlike the shells acquired for the purpose of reverse mergers, they are "clean shells" with no previous operational history, assets, or liabilities, and conduct their own IPO to raise capital and become publicly traded.

Proponents see SPACs as serving an important role in bringing new technology to the market. Others see them as asymmetrical, allowing management and investment bankers to collect large fees leaving most of the risk to investors.

SPACs surged during the COVID-19 era due to a perfect storm of unprecedented market conditions: massive government stimulus and near-zero interest rates flooded markets with liquidity while investors sought higher yields and alternative routes to public markets amid traditional IPO volatility. The speculative environment, fueled by retail investors with stimulus cash and institutional endorsement from celebrity sponsors, drove SPAC IPOs to account for 39% of the global IPO market by 2021, with first-day pops quadrupling from pre-2020 levels.

However, this boom spectacularly collapsed by 2022–2024 as the SEC implemented stricter regulatory oversight, market saturation led to declining deal quality and valuations divorced from fundamentals (Klausner and Ohlrogge, 2022). Catastrophic performance emerged with 90% of SPACs underperforming equity markets by up to 70%, culminating in 21 SPAC-backed bankruptcies destroying $46 billion in equity value in 2023 alone (Insurance Journal, 2023). The DeSPAC index lost 80% of its value between February 2021 and early 2023 and did not recover, while the NASDAQ Composite was up 25% over the same period.

Moreover, the Federal Reserve's interest rate hikes from 2022 onward eliminated the cheap money that fueled speculation, forcing investors to demand better risk-adjusted returns and making refinancing difficult for cash-burning SPAC targets, ultimately reducing SPAC IPO activity from hundreds at peak to just 11 filings in Q1 2023 according to Russell Investments, representing one of the most dramatic boom-bust

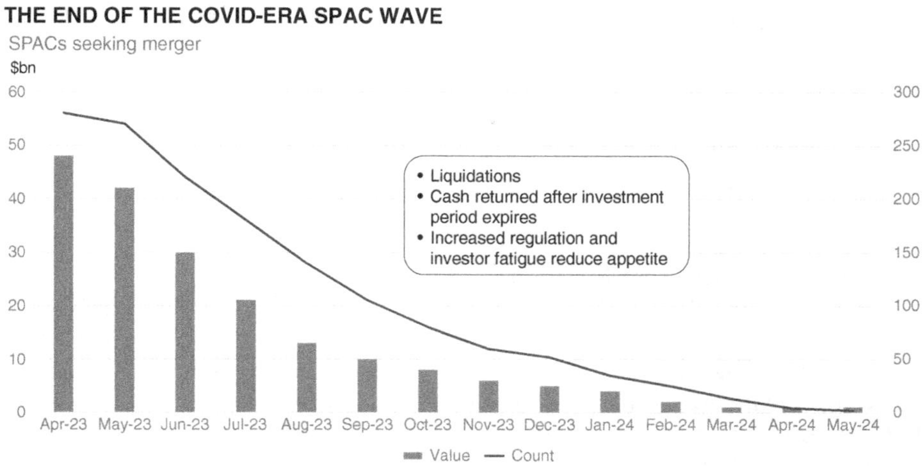

FIGURE 2.36 Evolution of the number of SPACs seeking merger 2023–2024.
Source: Candesic research.

cycles in modern financial markets. From that moment, the total number of SPACs looking for a merger with a target private company fell from close to 300 to just a few in May 2024 (Figure 2.36).

In 2025, Guy Semmens, cofounder of Gyrus Capital, declared: "SPACs in 2020–2021 were 90% BS. If they are back, we should be concerned!"

2.11 TAKE-PRIVATE

We have explored the various ways to take a company public or mingle with public status. Conversely, why would we take a public company private? Well, the reasons for taking a public company private are at the very heart of our discussions on PE.

Of course, a very good reason is the confidence that a public company is undervalued and can be bought cheap, even when adding the typical acquisition premium of 20–30%. One may wonder what drives this confidence.

We can list at least five reasons. The first one is related to all the measures to protect the minority shareholders in a public company, like SOX (Sarbanes-Oxley). They can be expensive and unforgiving. Once private this no longer needs to be a cause of concern. The second one is that managing quarterly earnings and being exposed to the short-termism of some investors can be exhausting. This is not ideal for implementing a long-term strategy and many CEOs suffer from it—being fired just because the next earnings do not meet expectations. A third reason is that sometimes quick unpleasant decisions need to be made, like outsourcing some activities, which will make less noise and will be easier to do within a private company. Fourth, there are some secondary reasons, like creating an attractive package for the managers. Lastly, some may be tempted to hid negative information, something that would need to be disclosed by a public company and could jeopardize its future. What could be so bad that it would lead someone to take a public company private? Well, think about severe pending liabilities, like litigation, environmental hazard, safety hazard, a major labor issue ...

Note that there is an overemphasis on public-to-private transitions in the press and in academic literature due to a greater availability of data on public companies. In the United Kingdom, for example, those deals represent a relatively small proportion by number—2% to 8% of the total volume of the overall PE market. But because the data are available, we have more reasons to look at it.

We will cover take-privates in more detail in Chapter 7 on investment strategies.

TAKE-PRIVATE OF ALLOCATE SOFTWARE

An interesting take-private of a publicly listed software company took place in October 2014. Hg Capital, a PE fund we were advising, offered to take Allocate Software private. The transaction valued Allocate at £110 million, with shareholders receiving 153.55 pence per share. This represented a 35% premium over the prior day's closing price—a notable, but not extraordinary, premium.

The offer gained rapid support, with 56% of shareholders quickly endorsing the bid. The board of Allocate Software recommended the transaction, and acceptance was swift.

Contrary to the press release's "done deal" bravado, the announcement opened the door for late bidders. Two investors requested access to the company's accounts, leveraging their financial capacity and the legal protections afforded to minority holders. In theory, their involvement could have halted the process, pending their review.

Their rationale was clear: if Hg Capital saw value at this price, perhaps even more value could be extracted at a higher bid. One investor deployed a veritable battalion—many advisers crossed the Atlantic to tackle due diligence. Despite caffeine and jet lag, they could not complete their analysis in time. The accelerated timetable prevented any higher competing bid.

Hg Capital completed the acquisition. Allocate Software was delisted and entered a new phase, away from the scrutiny and disclosure requirements of the public market. This illustrates how, even at the eleventh hour, the public-to-private process remains exposed to opportunistic bids, shareholder protection, and a robust due diligence scramble.

2.12 CASE STUDY: THE RISE AND FALL OF BABYLON

2.12.1 Babylon Health's SPAC IPO in the United States

We start exploring the rise and fall of Babylon in more detail (Kitten, 2026).

Babylon initially surfed the wave of teleconsultation that was boosted by the pandemic. They were not the only company offering that service but were quite a powerful player.

Prior to the COVID-19 pandemic, approximately 15% of consultations were conducted remotely through teleconsultation platforms, but during the pandemic, this proportion increased dramatically to 37%. While initial projections anticipated a partial reversion to pre-pandemic patterns as in-person consultations resumed, the

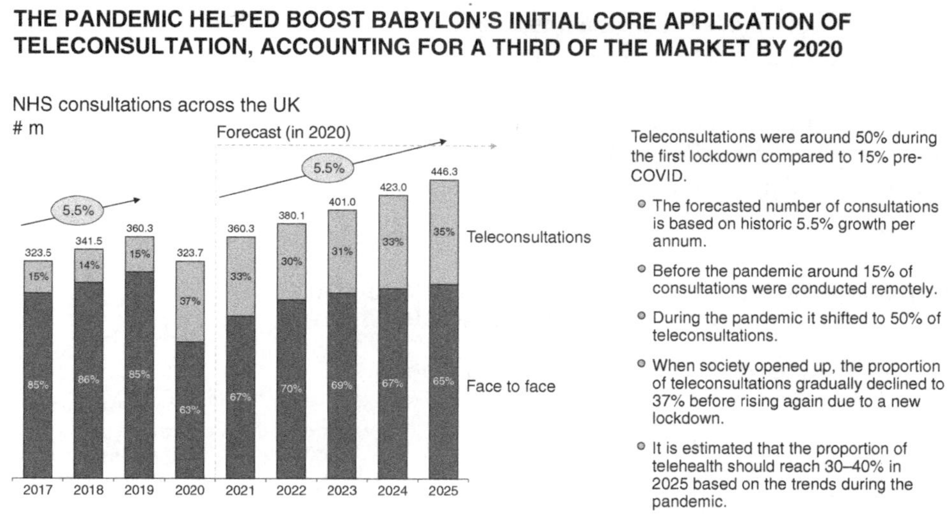

FIGURE 2.37 Share of NHS teleconsultations.
Source: NHS Digital; Candesic research and analysis.

sustained behavioral changes among younger demographics suggested that telehealth adoption would stabilize between 30% and 40% by the mid-2020s (Figure 2.37). Current empirical data from 2025 indicates that telehealth now accounts for approximately 23% of healthcare encounters nationwide, with certain specialties reporting virtual visit rates exceeding 50%, validating these earlier projections.

Babylon's technological approach centered on the application of artificial intelligence and automation within their mobile health platform. From a strategic perspective, AI should function as an efficiency enhancement tool and complement to human healthcare services rather than serving as the primary care delivery mechanism unless technological mastery has been definitively established. However, the absence of such mastery and widespread skepticism regarding the platform's capabilities generated significant controversy surrounding the application's deployment. While patient satisfaction surveys revealed a bifurcated response pattern with some users expressing high satisfaction levels, many others reported substantial dissatisfaction with the service quality. The optimal solution framework suggests implementing a hybrid care model that systematically integrates automated services with supplementary information sources and human clinical oversight.

Babylon claimed that its technology could lower the overall cost of delivering primary care by around 30% under value-based care models. However, their foundational business models presented significant challenges in terms of economic justification and sustainable revenue generation, ultimately undermining the viability of their cost reduction claims.

Their initial pay-as-you-go pricing model established a £25 consultation fee, which was priced for growth but proved economically unviable when benchmarked against traditional GP consultation costs of approximately £20. The fundamental profitability challenge emerged from the customer acquisition cost (CAC) parameters, which were estimated to range between £140 and £150 per user. Given the nominal profit margin differential, the payback period extended to approximately seven years to recover initial acquisition investments, assuming optimistic annual profit margins of £20 per customer (Figure 2.38). This cost structure represented a fundamentally unsustainable unit economics framework that precluded scalable profitability.

Their secondary strategic focus on NHS contracts presented equally challenging profitability dynamics (Figure 2.39). Despite the potential for enhanced credibility and market validation within the UK healthcare system, founder Ali Parsa ultimately

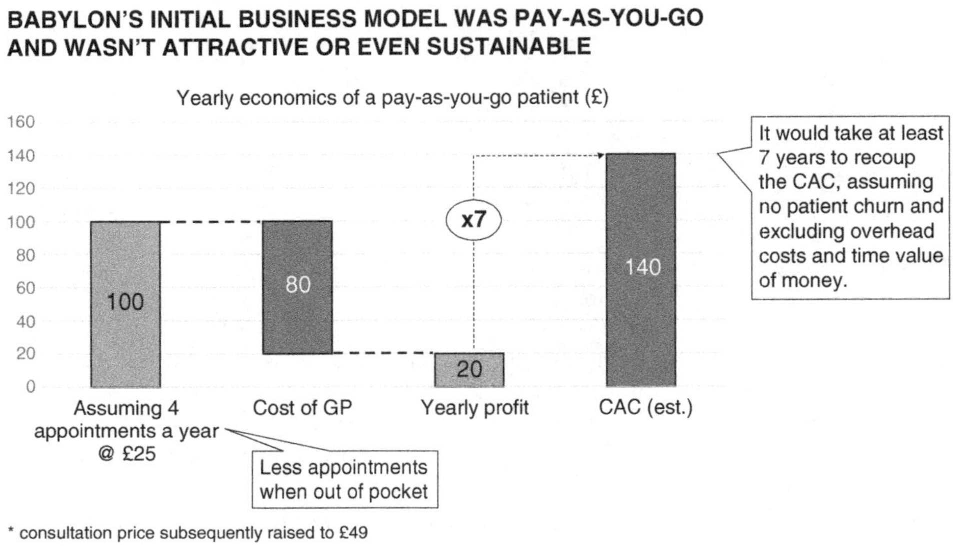

FIGURE 2.38 Estimated yearly economics of a pay-as-you-go patient for Babylon.
Source: Interviews; Candesic research.

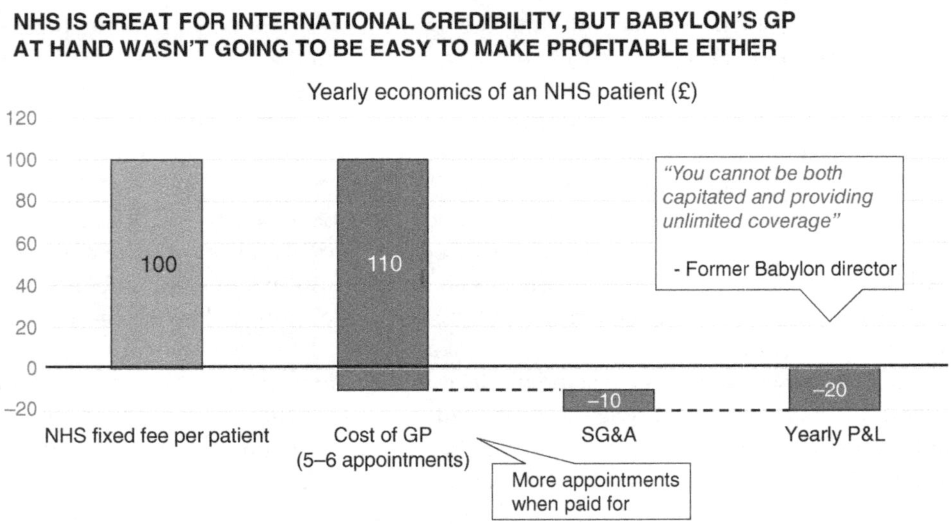

FIGURE 2.39 Estimated yearly economics of a NHS patient for Babylon.
Source: Interviews; Candesic research.

acknowledged the inability to achieve sustainable profitability within this segment. While NHS partnerships provided significant, valuable international credibility and regulatory validation for global expansion initiatives, they failed to generate sufficient financial returns to support the organization's operational requirements and growth objectives.

The private medical insurance business could be more attractive, but the problem was that most of the markets they targeted, including the United Kingdom, were not large enough. The only very large private medical insurance market in the world is the US one.

US contracts were a different model of value-based care, i.e., taking risk for a population. These contracts take time and investment to get going (adoption of course, but also interventions that are not immediate). This requires both time and cash to work.

However, Babylon's US business was not immediately profitable. It is a very large, complex, and competitive market, and Babylon's UK-trained technology did not work well in an environment with a different epidemiology, like in the United States. Some mistakes were also made at the local level. For example, in Missouri, they had patients with only low-tech phones that were not compatible with Babylon's app, so they had to train people to use it on a computer instead. In some places, people had poor internet, so Babylon had to look at more analogue models.

Despite their challenges, Babylon's number of registered app users was rising fast. As of 2020, they were planning to have close to 8 million users by the end of 2021 (Figure 2.40). They planned to have exponential growth by 2022. And their plan was that the American market would become the largest one after a few years.

By 2021, they did have significant revenue to show coupled with stellar growth, but they were losing a lot of money, as can be seen from their P&L and EBITDA, which were negative (Figure 2.41). They were hoping that the EBITDA would turn positive by 2024.

They had financed their growth with VC money and multiple rounds of financing. They valued the company at $100 million in 2016, at $200 million in the next year, and at about $2 billion by the fourth year. They raised £25 million in their first round

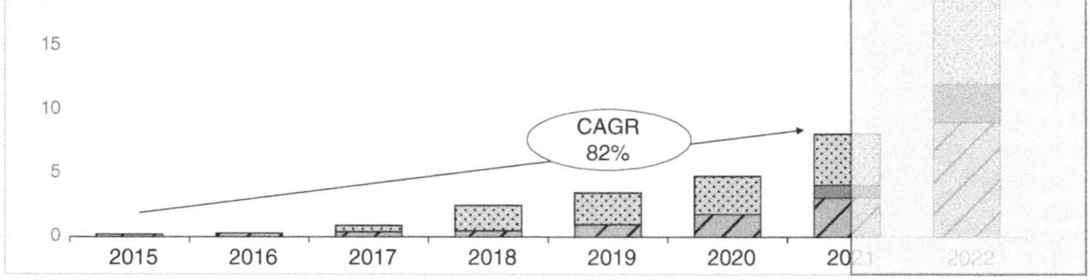

FIGURE 2.40 Number of registered users.
Source: Kinnevic; VNV; Candesic research and analysis.

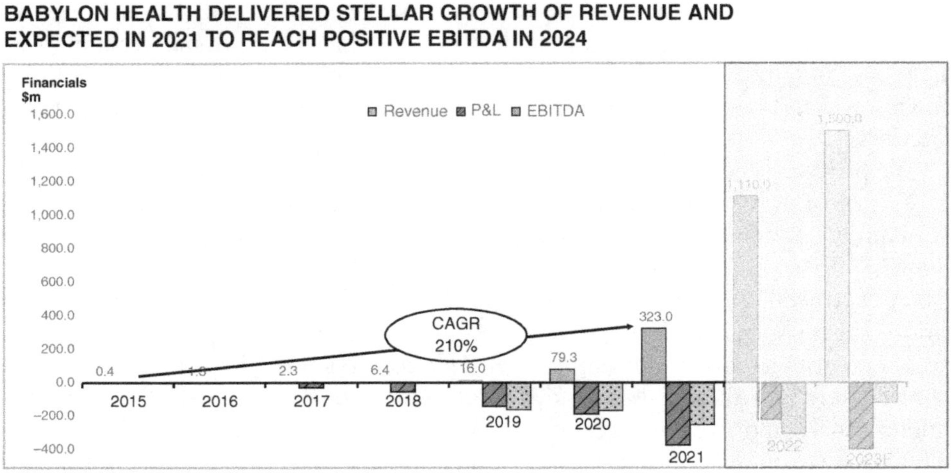

FIGURE 2.41 Revenue and profitability of Babylon health.
Source: Candesic research and analysis.

of funding in 2016, \$60 million in 2017, and somewhere up to \$550 million in 2019—we say "up to" as it is not entirely clear what had been raised by that time.

In 2021, the founder decided to go for a SPAC IPO on the New York Stock Exchange, combined with a PIPE, a private investment in a public entity. To do this, Babylon merged with the SPAC in June 2021, in a transaction that valued Babylon at \$4.2 billion (Figure 2.42).

As of June 30, 2021, Babylon Holdings cash and cash equivalents amounted to \$42.4 million.

> *On a pro forma basis [...], the transaction was expected to deliver up to \$575 million in gross proceeds, including \$345 million in gross proceeds from cash held in Alkuris trust account, assuming no redemptions. In addition, the Business Combination was further supported by a \$230 million PIPE Investment.*
>
> *In addition, [...], Babylon Holdings previously acquired an option to purchase Higi, a consumer health engagement company, and intended to acquire the remaining equity it did not already own, which would reduce Babylon Holdings cash needs by approximately \$40 million.*
>
> *Assuming no redemptions, and taking transaction costs and strategic investments into account, Babylon was expected to have approximately \$540 million in cash and cash equivalents assuming no redemptions by Alkuri Stockholders.*[6]

[6] *Source:* Babylon Health.

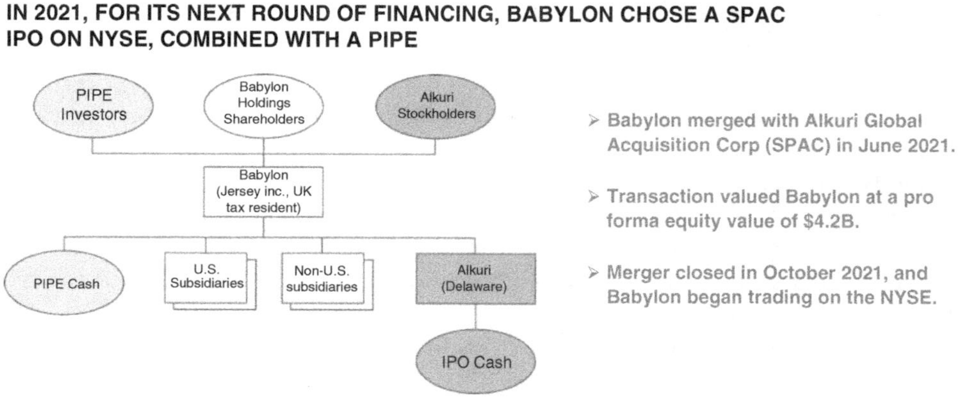

FIGURE 2.42 Babylon's SPAC and PIPE.
Source: Candesic research.

But when the date to vote on the merger approached, around 90 percent of shareholders asked to redeem their shares despite approving the deal, which left Babylon with only $275 million in cash, mostly from the PIPE.

A few months after the SPAC IPO, the share price started to fall, with significant activity by short sellers (the stock market was otherwise relatively stable). Around May 2022, when the stock had lost more than 80% of its value, falling from $10 to $2, the Berenberg analyst reported: "Investors are likely under-estimating the benefits of a digital-first care model, while healthcare stakeholders are widely adopting it. Hold." (price target: $5.5). The price continued to fall, under $1. A few months later, interviewed by the *Financial Times,* Ali Parsa declared: "What an unbelievable, unmitigated disaster, with the benefit of hindsight it is super simple to understand. We learnt a big lesson, which is we should have done a lot more thinking through SPACs."

For more than a year, the management team explored every option to stop the fall. In April 2023, Babylon hired consultants Alvarez & Marsal to help restructure and secure financing after being left with less than 13 weeks of cash flow. In May 2023, 18 months after the SPAC IPO, AlbaCore Capital, a European credit fund and Babylon's main lender, forced a restructuring and recapitalization of the business, wiping out the shareholders and taking the company private as it tried to recoup some of the $380.5 million it had lent, of which only $34.5 million were secured. The shareholders lost all their money. VNV Global lost all of its investment, $125 to $163 million.

Albacore tried to merge Babylon with another healthtech company, Swiss-based PE-owned digital therapeutics company MindMaze. The merger fell through in early August:

> *... on August 9, Babylon filed for Chapter 7 bankruptcy protection for two of its U.S. subsidiaries with the intention of liquidating. Babylon Inc. reported $309.3 million in assets and $389 million in liabilities, including $34.9 million in secured liabilities. (Forbes)*

2.13 CHAPTER SUMMARY

In this chapter, we have covered a lot of concepts and explored all the major segments that make up PE. In particular, we have considered growth capital, LBOs, and all the ways of making money in an LBO. We have looked at various types of secondary funds and funds of funds, and how PE uses various forms of debt and intermediary financing to structure investments and drive value creation. We have also examined examples of when PE goes public and when public companies are taken private.

We finished with a review of a major healthtech venture that promised to revolutionize value-based care. Babylon Health's SPAC-fueled IPO unlocked significant capital, but it also steered the company headlong into the US market—where scale meets scrutiny. In chasing America's healthcare goldmine, Babylon underestimated the regulatory gauntlet and payer complexities that turned its "value-based care revolution" into a textbook lesson on the perils of exuberant growth.

We hope the readers now have a better understanding of the diverse segments and strategies within the PE sector, how they can be effectively leveraged to optimize investment return, and, most importantly, how they each contribute to specific market needs, allowing supply and demand to meet in a naturally illiquid asset class.

CHAPTER 3

Opportunities and Risks for Investors

In this chapter, we examine several key attributes of PE as an asset class. We begin by discussing how PE performance is evaluated and the metrics commonly used for this purpose while highlighting how these measures differ from those applied to more traditional asset classes such as stocks and bonds. We then review the benchmarks typically used to compare PE with alternative investments. The chapter also addresses some of the less favorable aspects of PE, showing that, as in any industry, not everything is without drawbacks. We also discuss the role of PE in portfolio allocation and the rise in data, AI, and tokenization.

PE lies between two extreme forms of firm ownership. On the one hand, many private firms are owned and managed by a single individual. Such owners are often highly committed to the firm's performance but face strong constraints on diversification, as their wealth is largely tied to a single asset. As a result, they are highly exposed to firm-specific risk. On the other hand, shareholders of publicly listed firms typically hold diversified portfolios, which allows them to largely eliminate idiosyncratic risk. However, this dispersion of ownership leads to a separation between ownership and control that gives rise to corporate governance problems (Tirole, 2006; Hart and Zingales, 2022).

PE occupies an intermediate position between these two extremes. PE portfolios are more concentrated than public equity portfolios, as they contain fewer assets, but they are still more diversified than firms owned by a single individual. In this sense, PE offers investors access to a diversified portfolio of actively managed firms. However, this comes at a cost: investors pay management and performance fees and face significant illiquidity. Because PE investments cannot be easily sold without affecting their value, this illiquidity creates important challenges when assessing their performance and overall attractiveness.

3.1 THE LIQUIDITY FACTOR

Illiquidity is a fundamental characteristic of PE that significantly shapes its structure, investment strategies, returns, and overall appeal to investors. It affects not only portfolio construction and risk management but also the expectations of both investors and fund managers.

Illiquidity is a double-edged sword in PE. While it constrains investor flexibility and complicates portfolio management, it also enables many of the strategies that underpin PE's potential for outperformance. Understanding and managing the implications of illiquidity is therefore central to evaluating PE as an asset class.

Illiquidity is a defining characteristic of PE and shapes the asset class along several key dimensions, including investment horizon, valuation, risk and return profile, diversification, fund structure, and liquidity management.

- **Investment horizon and exit constraints**
  PE investments are typically held over long investment horizons and are plagued by limited exit possibilities. While the historical average holding period is around five years, it increased to nearly six years by 2025, with approximately 25% of investments held for eight years or more. Importantly, these figures exclude the pre-investment phase during which committed capital must remain available before being drawn down. When this period is included, the effective commitment often extends close to eight years on average (Bain & Company, 2025c). This long horizon allows fund managers to implement strategic and operational changes, but it also prevents investors from easily liquidating their positions. Unlike publicly traded assets, PE investments can only be exited through mergers and acquisitions, initial public offerings, or secondary transactions, all of which require time and favorable market conditions. As a result, capital is effectively locked in for the life of the fund, typically around 10 years and often extended to 12.
- **Valuation and pricing**
  Illiquidity also strongly affects how PE investments are valued. Unlike public assets, which are priced continuously by the market, PE valuations are conducted periodically, often quarterly or annually. They rely on internal models or third-party assessments and therefore involve a degree of subjectivity. Valuations are based on assumptions regarding future performance and market conditions, making the precise value of an investment at any point in time inherently uncertain.
- **Risk and return profile**
  Illiquidity plays a central role in shaping the risk–return trade-off of PE. Investors demand an illiquidity premium to compensate for the inability to exit investments quickly. This premium reflects both the opportunity cost of locked capital and the additional risk associated with long holding periods and economic cycles. As a result, PE investors must tolerate higher risk and accept periods of volatility without the option of rapid divestment.
- **Diversification and portfolio construction**
  From a portfolio perspective, illiquidity leads to higher concentration. PE portfolios typically contain fewer assets than public equity portfolios, increasing exposure to firm-specific or sector-specific risk. Investors therefore seek diversification across funds, vintages, industries, and geographic regions. However, such diversification is more difficult to achieve and less flexible than in public markets, where assets can be rebalanced quickly and at low cost.
- **Fund structure and secondary markets**
  Most PE funds are organized as closed-end vehicles with fixed lifetimes and no redemption options. Investors cannot withdraw capital at will. Although secondary markets have expanded—supported by continuation funds, fund recapitalizations, and the growth of listed PE managers—transactions often occur at discounts to net asset value. Emerging innovations such as tokenization and

semi-liquid fund structures may improve liquidity, but they are unlikely to eliminate the fundamental illiquidity of the asset class. Historically, this illiquidity has also justified regulatory restrictions on retail investor access. However, since the 2020s, the industry has increasingly developed evergreen and semi-liquid vehicles to broaden access beyond closed-end funds.

- **Liquidity management**
  Taken together, these characteristics make liquidity management a central challenge in PE. Fund managers must coordinate capital calls, distributions, and cash reserves to meet obligations while minimizing idle capital. This often involves maintaining dedicated liquidity buffers and aligning cash availability with the fund's life cycle. Effective liquidity management helps reduce operational risk, smooth cash flows, and enhance overall portfolio efficiency.

In sum, illiquidity is a defining feature of PE that shapes investment horizons, valuation practices, risk exposure, portfolio construction, and fund design. While it imposes significant constraints on investors, it is also a key source of the return premium associated with PE. Understanding and managing illiquidity is therefore essential for assessing both the risks and the potential rewards of this asset class.

3.2 J-CURVE AND IRR

Measuring performance in PE constitutes one of the main challenges of the asset class. Unlike publicly traded assets, PE performance depends on several specific factors. In particular, four elements play a central role: the J-curve, vintage years, the time value of money, and valuation methods. The J-curve has already been mentioned, but its meaning and implications will now be explained in more detail.

3.2.1 J-curve

We begin by considering periodic—typically annual—returns, which are commonly used to measure the performance of assets, sectors, or markets. For example, if the FTSE index starts the year at 1,000 and ends it at 1,100, its annual return is 10%. While this approach is standard for publicly traded assets, it is poorly suited to PE.

Indeed, annual returns are not only uninformative in the context of PE but can also be misleading. A PE fund represents an investment in a stream of cash flows rather than in a continuously priced asset. These cash flows consist of multiple capital outflows and inflows whose timing and magnitude are uncertain. As a result, performance cannot be accurately captured by simple year-to-year price changes.

Moreover, valuation in PE relies heavily on net asset value (NAV), which is typically self-reported and updated infrequently. This makes NAV more susceptible to estimation error or manipulation than market prices. Consequently, conventional annual return measures fail to provide a reliable assessment of PE performance.

While the return on a bond can be calculated on the day of purchase, the return on the PE investment will generally be known only at the end of the fund's life.

The cumulative cash flows of a PE investment are typically negative over the first several years. It often takes a considerable amount of time before these initial outflows are offset by returns, meaning that early performance is typically negative. In Figure 3.1, it takes approximately five years before the investment generates positive net returns. To properly assess performance, one must consider the compounded return of all cash flows over time. This is precisely what the internal rate of return (IRR) measures: the overall performance of the investment by accounting for both the magnitude and timing of cash flows. For instance, achieving an IRR of 25% implies roughly doubling the invested capital over three years or tripling it over five years. It should be noted that what is shown here are the cumulative cash flows, not the J-curve, even though the two exhibit a similar shape.

The J-curve shown in Figure 3.2 shows the evolution of the IRR over time, the compound annual return from inception to exit. There are two distinct periods. The first—the

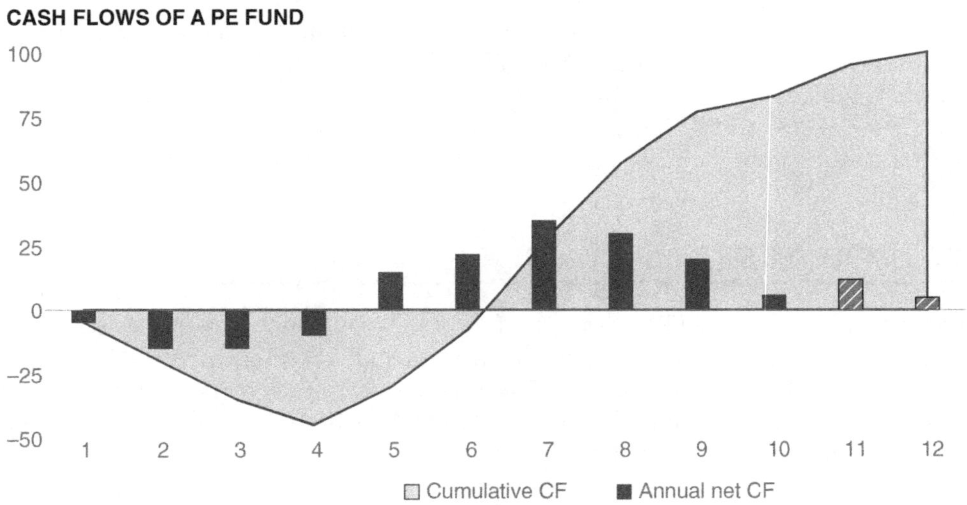

FIGURE 3.1 Typical cash flows of a PE fund.

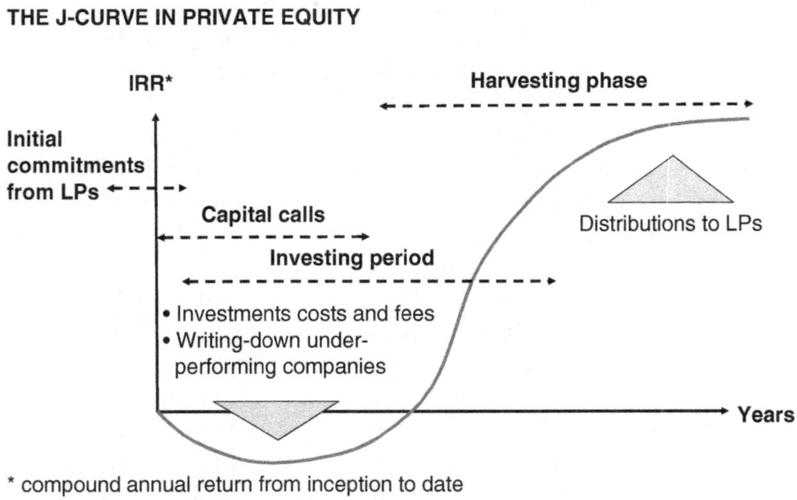

FIGURE 3.2 J-curve.

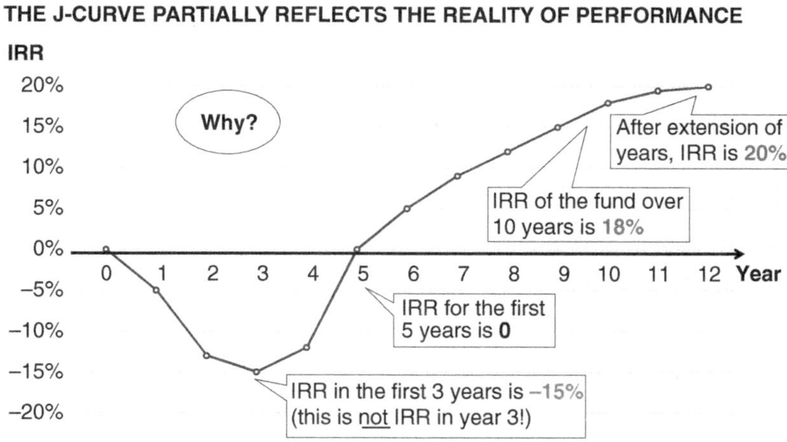

FIGURE 3.3 Performance along the J-curve.
Source: Allen Latta; Candesic analysis.

early years—is made up of drawdowns for investments, fees, and costs incurred, including some potential write-downs of poorly performing companies. They tend to occur in the first years. The second period, after the performance becomes positive, is marked by several distributions to the LPs, as we are selling some of the investments.

The J-curve is illustrated in Figure 3.3. In the first three years of the fund's life, the IRR is –20%. Importantly, this figure represents the IRR calculated over the first three years, not the IRR in year three alone—a distinction that is often missed by practitioners unfamiliar with PE. Similarly, the IRR over the first six years is zero, meaning that it takes six years for cumulative returns to offset initial losses. By year 12, the fund achieves an IRR of 20%. A 20% annual return sustained over 12 years represents substantial value creation. However, this figure only partially reflects reality: as long as all investments have not yet been exited, valuations rely on interim estimates rather than realized cash flows.

The IRR alone is an imperfect performance measure in several respects. First, it does not distinguish between realized and unrealized investments. Second, it fails to account for the remaining time horizon of an investment. Third, as with many traditional corporate valuation metrics, it does not differentiate between cash flows distributed to investors and cash flows that are reinvested at the fund level (Hennessy and Whited, 2005; Phalippou, 2020). Finally, the IRR does not explicitly adjust for risk, which further limits its usefulness as a standalone performance measure.

There are several alternatives to the standard since-inception IRR. In what follows, we focus on three main approaches commonly used to measure performance using IRR-based metrics.

3.2.2 Return Since Inception

First, the since-inception return, which is typically used by GPs to showcase performance, can be reported using either IRR or multiples, and in practice both should be considered together. Within this category, several measures are commonly used. These include simple multiples, vintage-year returns that group funds according to their year of inception, and pooled IRR, which combines cash flows across multiple funds into a single performance measure. Accordingly, we distinguish between cumulative returns, vintage-year IRRs that reflect performance based on the start year of funds, and pooled IRRs that aggregate cash flows across funds.

3.2.3 Investment Horizon IRR

Second, the investment horizon IRR (sometimes referred to as end-to-end IRR) is particularly useful when assessing the performance of a single fund or a portfolio over a defined subperiod. Although not without limitations, horizon IRR is generally less misleading than since-inception IRR for evaluating performance over a specific time frame. We recommend *The Tyranny of IRR: A Reality Check on Private Market Returns* for a clear explanation of why IRR should not be interpreted as a true rate of return and how it can overstate performance. An example later in this text further illustrates how misleading IRR can be as a performance measure.

3.2.4 Period IRR

For asset-class or segment-level analysis, horizon IRR is sometimes used, but period IRRs are generally more informative. Period IRRs measure performance over a specific calendar window—such as 1, 3, 5, or 10 years—and are particularly useful for evaluating shorter, well-defined intervals in a fund's or asset class's performance.

A since-inception IRR can be viewed as a special case of horizon IRR, where the horizon runs from the fund's launch to the reporting date. However, when assessing asset-class performance, period IRRs are typically preferred, as they provide a clearer picture of performance over comparable time spans.

3.2.5 Vintage Year Return

We have seen that PE returns are measured as the IRR of all cash flows and any remaining net asset value. PE returns are thus measured on a vintage-year basis, and for benchmarking purposes, we group all the funds in a selected sample for the same year so that the combined returns of all those funds are called that year's vintage year return. Remember that the vintage year return of 2015 is not the return for that year. It is the return for all constituent funds formed in 2015, from 2015 to the valuation date. Also remember, young vintage year returns are expected to be low or negative and are unreliable because of the effects of the J-curve discussed above. Hence, a fund's performance is extremely noisy during its first three to five years. Those who overlook this distinction draw incorrect conclusions from traditional performance measures.

In addition, J-curves from different vintage years are often aggregated to produce a single J-curve intended to represent the performance of the PE industry as a whole. Each vintage contributes to this aggregate based on the timing and magnitude of its cash flows. The resulting industry-level IRR can therefore be interpreted as an estimate of compounded performance across vintages, reflecting both reinvestment over time and the aggregation of cash flows from multiple investment cohorts.

Similarly, a fund-level J-curve is derived by aggregating the cash flows of all investments within the fund. Each individual investment has its own J-curve, and the fund's overall J-curve reflects the net cash flows between the fund and its investors.

It is important to note, however, that a fund's IRR is not a simple average or compounding of the IRRs of its individual investments. Instead, it is calculated from the aggregate timing and magnitude of all cash flows, capturing their combined effect on performance.

Here too, the illiquid nature of PE investment has consequences. For example, suppose an LP who has allocated and committed one billion dollars to PE has to choose between two mutually exclusive and sufficiently attractive projects with different investment horizons: the first project is a three-year investment returning an IRR of 35% and the second one a five-year investment returning 25% IRR. While it is tempting to choose the higher IRR, the investment horizon matters. Investing for three years requires confidence to find a future two-year investment project starting in three years that will return at least 10% to match the alternative five-year investment opportunity.[1]

3.3 EMPIRICAL PERFORMANCE

3.3.1 Common Performance Measures

3.3.1.1 Benchmarking Performance Benchmarking performance raises a number of difficulties inherent in the valuation of nontraded assets and to differences across segments. We have already discussed some of the challenges associated with IRR. Here, we discuss limits and controversies in comparing PE IRRs with the performance of stock markets before discussing an alternative performance measure provided by value multiples.

As discussed earlier, the illiquidity of PE investments raises specific issues relative to as public market when estimating returns. Before we discuss how adjustments can be made in order to estimate returns for end investors, it is useful to shed light on three additional controversies regarding the choice of the public benchmark, the sector comparativeness, and the illiquidity of PE investment.

When tracking stock market's performance, there is an apparent embarrassment of stock indices. In the United States, examples include the Dow Jones, the S&P 500, and the MSCI. Importantly, they do not track the same companies, and they weigh firms differently. GPs have long used the S&P 500 as a benchmark but perhaps unsurprisingly their reliance on this index has been reduced as the S&P 500 performed well. Many have switched to MSCI, or even to Russell 2000, arguing the size of firms in these indices was more comparable to that of PE investments. The timing may be suspicious, and the mere choice of the benchmark must be scrutinized (Phalippou, 2014, 2025).

Next comes the sector composition of the index. While healthcare has a relatively constant weight of 15% in most indices, the overall composition of the Cambridge Associates PE index makes it highly skewed toward IT when compared to the Russell 2000,[2] helping PE outperform public equity in recent decades. Phalippou observes that the difference is even higher in Europe, with almost no large tech companies in the public index, which explains the better performance of PE. He also questions the absence of

[1] Of course, if your target IRR is superior to 25%, you cannot choose the second option.

[2] It has been argued that they are not the same type of IT companies, but they still have something in common, and that would be true in other sectors too.

the low performing real estate, energy, and utilities companies in the PE index, under the pretense that the investors are called REITS or infrastructure, not LBO funds.

Beyond the index benchmarking and the sector composition, the illiquidity of PE investment discussed in the previous section creates fundamental performance benchmarking problems (Lerner and Schoar, 2005; Phalippou, 2009, 2021; Gornall and Strebulaev, 2020) that have led to a significant literature and that will be addressed in greater depth in Section 3.3.2. In summary, there are many reasons to be circumspect when comparing percentage returns.

An alternative assessment of the return is provided by the value multiples. There are several such performance metrics used in the industry. We present them here and will discuss their merits and pitfalls in Section 3.3.2.

The most common one is the TVPI (total value to paid-in capital). This is also called the investment multiple, or the multiple of money. It measures the overall value generated by a fund relative to the total capital invested by its LPs.

TVPI divides the total value of a fund by the initial capital investment made by limited partners. It can also be estimated by adding the realized value multiple and the unrealized value multiple. The realized value multiple is simply the total distribution to the investors divided by the invested capital plus the management fees, whereas the unrealized value multiple is the value of unrealized investments divided by the invested capital and the management fees.

An alternative metric for multiples is provided by the "distributed over paid in" or DPI. This is useful at the end of the fund's life. Another metric, the DCC, "distributed over committed capital," is used in case there is not enough investment.

Remember MOIC, which measures the multiple of money returned to investors relative to the amount of capital they invested. Unlike TVPI, MOIC can refer to individual investments or the overall fund, and it doesn't distinguish between realized and unrealized value.

We have shown how IRR can be extraordinarily deceptive. For decades, Phalippou (2014, 2020) has been leading the crusade against manipulation of the performance measures by some GPs. In this simple example, he shows very clearly how this can be done.

IS DPI THE NEW IRR?

It is fortunate that more people have become aware that "you cannot eat IRR." A simple cash measure like multiple is generally useful. However, it is also helpful to bear in mind that:

1. DPI is the amount distributed over invested. Is a 0.8 DPI good? If the fund is four years old, it is probably excellent. If it is eight years old, it is probably not, unless it has a large number of great un-exited investments. DPI is useless since that, unless it is above 2×, one cannot conclude whether the fund is doing well. For a performance measure, it is not enough.
2. Now consider instead TVPI, which is not subject to the criticism above. A TVPI of 1.5 is approximately the US equity market return over any four years period and so this is barely enough: below 1.5 is insufficient whereas above 1.8× is often considered good. However, TVPI has two big problems.

GP sets the NAV and can thus have any TVPI it wants. This is why many investors like DPI—NAV does not come in. However, importantly but often ignored, multiples like DPI and TVPI can also be manipulated like IRR.

Manipulation of multiples 101: Have a recycling close, net out cash flows, and your multiple will magically improve.

Example:

1. You invest 100, exit 150 year 4, invest 100 that same year, and exit for 200 year 10. TVPI is 350/200 = 1.75×. Fine.
2. Net out these cash flows and tell investors you invested 100, distributed 50 in year four and then 200 in year 10. Now your DPI is 250/100 = 2.5×. Now you are a superstar!!
3. You do not like the net out/cannot easily do it, have a recycling close, will do the same thing.

So, like IRR, you can juice your DPI. Maybe not as ridiculously as an IRR, but pretty good. And like with IRR, there is a cheating inequality. It is mostly the large LBO funds that have recycling clauses and can juice up their DPI.

According to Phalippou, assessing PE financial performance involves several other critical challenges.

3.3.1.2 Benchmark Selection Issues The widespread use of the S&P 500 as a PE benchmark is fundamentally flawed. First, it covers very large firms in sectors that are generally not comparable with those of PE investments. Second, while the S&P 500 has experienced only one 10-year period with returns below the risk-free rate (1998–2008), a period after which that benchmark was perhaps ironically very commonly used in PE circles, PE holding periods vary significantly, making 10-year comparisons arbitrary. Alternative indices starting with S&P 600, which covers the small cap range of American stocks, offer a more appropriate comparison given that it covers companies whose size is comparable with those of many PE investments. However, it does not solve the holding period conundrum, and it requires paid access. Alternative indices or portfolios of comparison firms, such as the Fama-French datasets dear to academics, can be chosen to represent tailor-made comparison firms in sectors, locations, and sizes closer to those of the PE investments being evaluated. However, the mere fact that these stocks are listed makes them fundamentally different from PE investments and subject to the challenges addressed in this chapter.

3.3.1.3 Geographic Composition Mismatches Stark differences exist between US and European public benchmarks that distort PE comparisons. Nowadays, US public indices are dominated by technology companies, while European benchmarks heavily weight oil and gas and banking sectors—with most European tech remaining private. Healthcare presents a notable exception, offering cleaner PE-to-public comparisons due to more similar company profiles across both markets (Figure 3.4).

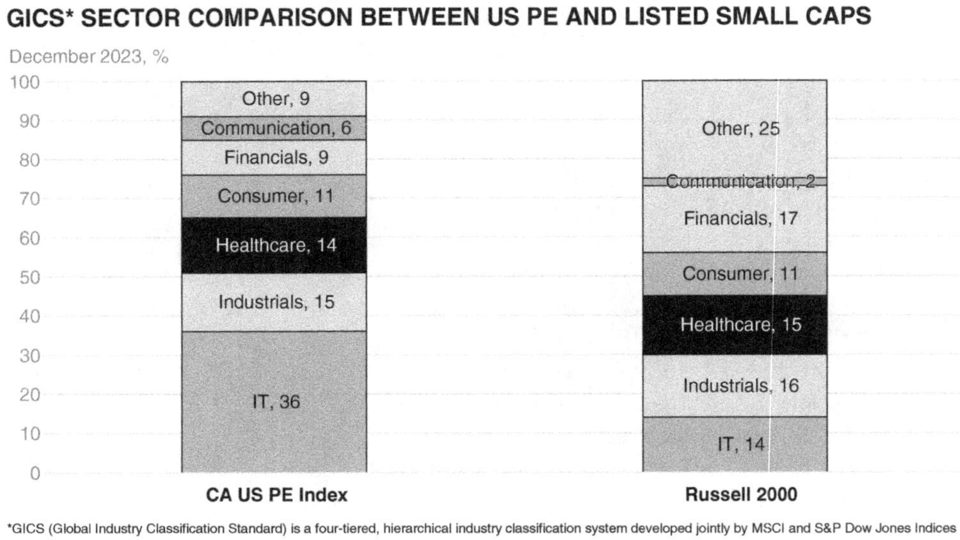

FIGURE 3.4 Comparing US PE and listed small caps by sector.
Source: Candesic research and analysis.

3.3.1.4 Survivorship and Selection Biases PE funds suffer from survivorship bias because failed fundraising attempts remain invisible—identifying these would require comprehensive collection of all Private Placement Memos, not just successful raises. Additionally, managers selectively present track records, creating further distortions in reported performance data.

3.3.1.5 The Reality Behind Performance Metrics Despite IRR manipulation concerns, the core PE metric remains simple (Phalippou, 2020): funds typically exit at 2× multiples, regardless of whether this takes 10+ years. Interestingly, PE in Africa provides an exception with transparent reporting—Anne Fossemale from EBRD reports 10% IRRs and 1.5× TVPI over 10 years, figures that align closely with CalPERS' and KKR's actual global PE returns, suggesting these may reflect more realistic industry performance expectations.

Even the best databases are highly incomplete regarding benchmarking. When VentureXpert once listed 525 US venture funds as having raised capital in 2005, it showed the performance of only 118. Thankfully, things have improved over time as increasingly more participants agree to disclose information to those databases. In addition, the PE figures can be very misleading if taken out of context—as for the J-curve. A general principle in PE, perhaps even more than in other areas of finance due to the illiquidity of PE investments, is the requirement to think carefully behind raw figures.

This can be illustrated with PE indices such as the State Street GX PE Index.

Figure 3.5 shows the composition and long-term IRR as of September 30, 2008, during the 2008 financial crisis. Then, buyouts were represented through 665 funds versus 590 for venture capital. The long-term IRR for buyout at that time was 13% versus 12% for venture capital. This is useful information as unlike many other indices, the State Street Index does not rely on voluntary reporting. By 2023, State Street had

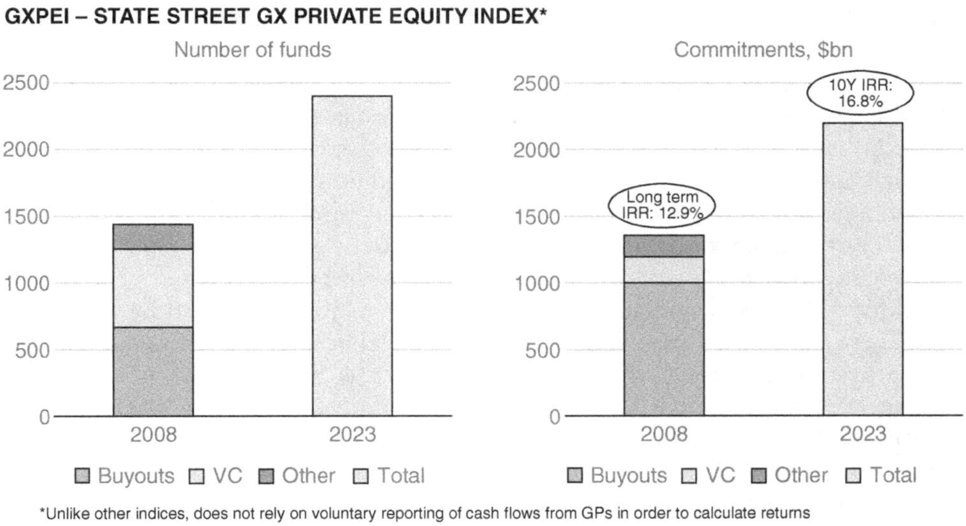

FIGURE 3.5 State street PE index.
Source: State street; American Investment Council; IFSWF.

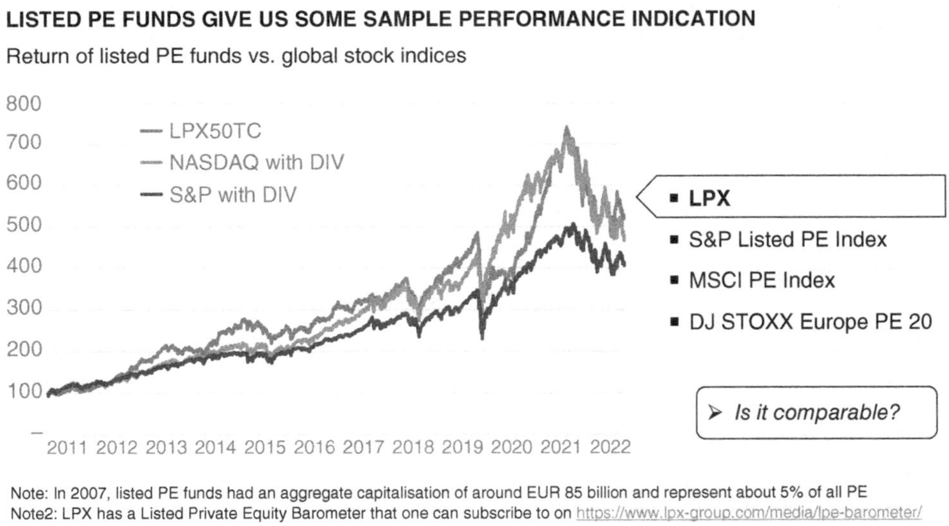

FIGURE 3.6 Historical performance of top 50 listed PE firms vs. global stock indices.
Source: LPX (www.lpx.ch): WRDS (CRSP).

included more than 2,400 funds representing more than $2.2 trillion in capital commitments. That is a very sizable part of the market—but it ignores many smaller funds.

Listed PE funds provide a compelling alternative in that they benchmark the performance of PE investments. There is a growing number of indices that track the performance of listed PE funds. However, their risks and valuation drivers are inherently different from those of many LP investors, not to mention that they are exposed to fee income and some carry.

Figure 3.6 compares the performance of the LPX 50 with that of the NASDAQ and the S&P 500 with all series shown on a total-return basis including dividends.

While the NASDAQ outperforms in certain periods, the LPX 50 generally exhibits strong long-term performance. However, an important limitation of such indices is that they often include publicly listed firms that are not pure PE players. These may include companies with significant exposure to real estate, credit, or hedge fund activities, which can distort the interpretation of returns. As a result, although these indices are widely used, they provide an imperfect representation of PE as an asset class. IRR and multiples are useful tools for comparing PE investments with one another, but they are poorly suited for comparisons with other asset classes, which typically rely on time-weighted returns. To address this mismatch, researchers have developed methods that adjust public market returns to replicate the timing and magnitude of PE cash flows. These approaches are collectively known as Public Market Equivalents (PME).

The first such method, the Long–Nickels PME (LNPME or ICM), was introduced in 1996 but suffers from its failure to account for liquidation timing. Kaplan and Schoar (2005) proposed the KS-PME, which expresses performance as a multiple rather than an IRR. Rouvinez's PME+ (2003) addressed some of these issues but introduced new limitations and is not directly replicable. More recently, Cambridge Associates developed the modified PME (mPME), which applies a time-varying scaling factor based on interim NAVs.

Despite these refinements, all PME methods rely on approximations and remain imperfect. This led to the development of *Direct Alpha*, which can be viewed as the PME analogue of IRR and provides a more consistent framework for performance comparison. A detailed discussion can be found in *Benchmarking PE: The direct alpha method* (Gredil et al, 2023), from which Figure 3.7 is taken.

In summary, benchmarking PE performance requires understanding the complexities of metrics such as TVPI and the limitations of databases, while also recognizing

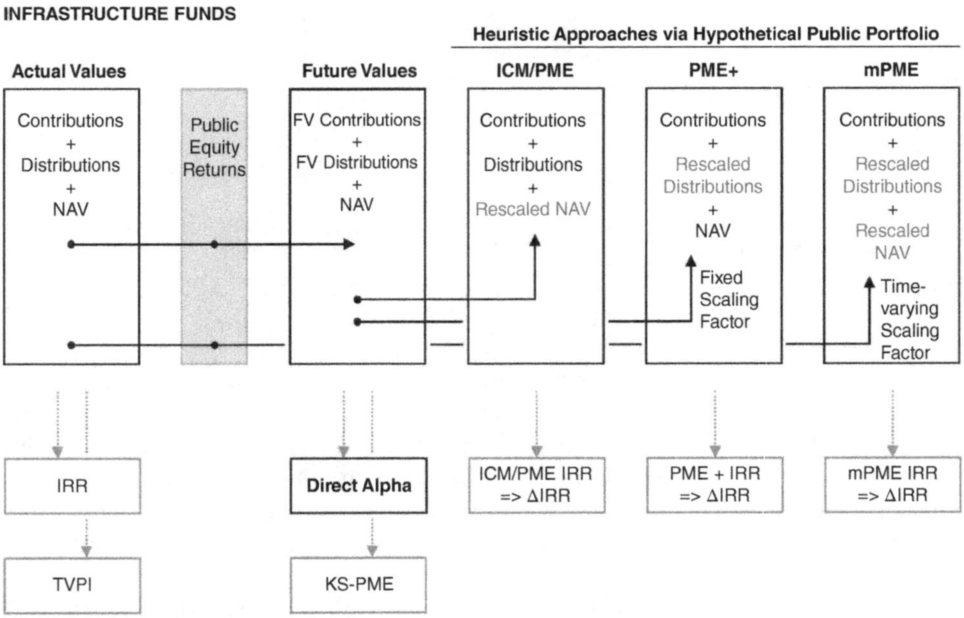

FIGURE 3.7 The direct alpha method.

that PE figures must be contextualized for accurate analysis, and that PE and public market returns cannot be directly compared.

3.3.2 Advanced Performance Measures

The difficulties inherent to illiquidity, sector composition, and index benchmarking have spurred a large academic literature attempting to provide better PE performance measures at the cost of rich but often conflicting set of findings. These disagreements stem not only from differences in data and methodology, but also from deeper conceptual challenges related to benchmarking illiquid investments, measuring risk, and interpreting cash-flow-based returns (Phalippou, 2014, 2021; Korteweg and Westerfield, 2022). This section presents the diverse set of methodologies and findings and aims to reconcile apparently conflicting results while clarifying what different performance measures actually capture and where their limitations lie.

In a paper that focuses on VC but applies to PE, Cochrane (2005) challenges optimistic interpretations of VC returns by correcting for selection bias. Since failed investments are rarely observed, naïve return estimates are overstated. Once corrected, VC returns decline substantially, and much of the apparent outperformance is shown to stem from extreme firm-specific risk rather than superior growth. VC returns resemble those of option-like investments rather than skilled active management.

Using their KSPME approach discussed previously, Kaplan and Schoar (2005) find that venture capital funds featured in the Thomson Venture Economics dataset underperform the S&P500 on an equal-weighted basis, while buyout funds perform roughly in line with this reference large stock index. They also provide evidence that performance improves when weighted by fund size, suggesting that larger funds perform better. Their most important contribution, however, is the discovery of strong performance persistence: top-performing funds are much more likely to remain top performers, highlighting the importance of manager selection rather than broad exposure to the asset class.

Lerner et al. (2007) shift attention to investor heterogeneity, showing that performance differs dramatically across limited partners. Endowments significantly outperform other investors due to superior fund selection and reinvestment strategies, reinforcing the idea that PE outcomes depend heavily on investor sophistication.

Using Thomson Venture Economics data as well, Phalippou and Gottschalg (2009) adjust for NAV reporting bias, inappropriate weighting of cash flows, and insufficient risk adjustment and find that on average PE underperforms public markets by 3–6% per year. However, they confirm strong persistence among top funds. This pessimistic view is challenged by Stucke (2011) and Higson and Stucke (2012), who argue that data errors in Venture Economics drive earlier underperformance results. Using cleaner datasets, they find that buyout funds outperform public markets by 4–5% annually. Harris, Jenkinson, and Kaplan (2014) reach similar conclusions using Burgiss data, showing consistent buyout outperformance, though venture capital results remain mixed.

Robinson and Sensoy (2016) add nuance by showing that PE cash flows are procyclical, undermining the idea of a universal liquidity premium. Only funds that invest countercyclically earn excess returns, and even these explain only part of overall performance.

As discussed earlier, benchmark choice is of paramount importance when evaluating the performance of PE investments. Phalippou (2014) argues that when buyouts are compared to small-cap value stocks with similar leverage, alpha largely vanishes. In their synthesis, Korteweg and Westerfield (2022) also find that disagreements in the literature are largely driven by benchmark choice, perhaps even more than data quality.

Driessen et al. (2012) introduce a framework that estimates PE risk and return directly from cash flows and decompose PE returns into systematic risk and managerial skill. Their method recovers a single risk–return profile that best explains observed fund cash flows. They find evidence that VC funds exhibit extremely high market risk ($\beta \approx 2.7$) and significantly negative alpha after fees, while buyout funds display more moderate risk ($\beta \approx 1.3$) and statistically insignificant alpha. Here again, fund selection appears to be an essential driver of PE investment performance.

Korteweg and Nagel (2016) develop the Generalized Public Market Equivalent (GPME), which corrects two major flaws of traditional PME measures. First, it adjusts for the time variation in market risk using a stochastic discount factor (SDF), which captures how much investors value one dollar received in the future under different economic conditions. One dollar received in good times is generally worth less than one dollar received in bad times. Hence, using the SDF prevents artificial outperformance during bull markets. Second, Korteweg and Nagel enable formal statistical inference through a Generalized Method of Moments (GMM) framework, a statistical estimation technique that allows researchers to estimate parameters relying on empirical observations implied by economic theory rather than a full, complete dataset that does not exist in the PE space (Chemla and Hennessy, 2021). Their GPME retains the advantages of PME for handling irregular cash flows while providing a theoretically sound risk-adjusted benchmark. They find that buyout fund returns are highly sensitive to market risk and exhibit an alpha close to 0 on average.

Ang et al. (2018) construct a time series of PE returns and decompose PE performance into systematic risk exposure and a time-varying alpha component. They find that PE returns are more volatile and less smoothed than industry indices suggest, and that buyout performance is closely linked to credit market conditions, which implies that PE risk is often understated when observing raw conventional data.

Gredil et al. (2023) propose Direct Alpha, a performance metric that computes alpha as the IRR of benchmark-adjusted cash flows. Direct Alpha avoids the distortions of traditional PME methods and provides a clean, annualized measure of excess return. Using a large dataset, the authors show that Direct Alpha often produces markedly different results from commonly used PME variants, especially for venture capital funds, demonstrating that performance conclusions are highly sensitive to the chosen metric.

Korteweg and Nagel (2025) show that once time-varying risk, leverage, and cash-flow timing are properly accounted for, PE does not deliver robust alpha on average. Apparent outperformance is largely explained by exposure to systematic risk factors and by cyclicality, with PE cash flows tending to be procyclical rather than providing insurance in downturns. Their analysis further shows that illiquidity is not reliably rewarded on average and that performance persistence reflects access to better funds rather than manager skill. Overall, PE behaves like a leveraged public equity investment rather than a distinct alpha-generating asset class. Further, benchmark choice is central to understanding performance differences reported in the literature.

Together, these studies confirm the view that PE performance cannot be reliably measured by LPs using IRR or multiples alone and that risk adjustment is essential and materially changes conclusions. Traditional PME methods improve comparability but depend heavily on benchmark choice and are often biased or incomplete. More recent approaches such as GPME and Direct Alpha provide a more accurate and theoretically grounded assessment of PE performance.

This literature reinforces the view that measurement methodology drives much of the disagreement in the PE performance literature. Several studies show that after proper risk adjustment, average PE performance is close to zero and that performance depends on fund selection, just like the performance of stock portfolios depends largely on stock selection. Outperformance is concentrated among a small subset of managers. Across funds, much of PE's apparent success reflects leverage, risk exposure, and illiquidity rather than persistent alpha.

3.3.3 Controversies with LPs

The difficulty in establishing a consensus performance measure is, of course, not just a methodological issue. LPs want to follow closely the performance of their PE investment and may be concerned with illiquidity and, as in delegated portfolio management in other asset classes, agency conflicts, information asymmetries, and possibly misaligned incentives. Sophisticated LPs will be aware of the intricacies of performance measures. Indeed, reported IRRs and multiples of invested capital can be manipulated by timing cash flows and leverage. IRR reporting may rely on unrealistic reinvestment assumptions. Capital calls and distributions may be timed to inflate IRRs before fundraising. Further, LPs may have limited information on the fund's performance, valuation methods, and even operations (Ang et al., 2018). Finally, LPs will understand that as they commit capital for a long period that can exceed 10 years, they will still have little control on the timing of investment and distributions (Robinson and Sensoy, 2013).

Chapter 8 will delve deeper into the economic consequences of the difficulty for LPs to measure PE performance and to control investments and distributions.

3.3.4 Does PE Create Financial Value?

In 2014, after underperforming its PE benchmark, CalPERS created controversy in announcing its intention to lower its benchmark. The rationale was to better reflect the actual performance of the PE asset class. Previously, the benchmark had been set too high, creating an unrealistic expectation and making it difficult to accurately assess the performance of CalPERS' PE investments. On one hand, this could be seen as a way to mask underperformance. On the other hand, as a more realistic reflection of current market conditions and return expectations, also reflecting a more cautious approach in setting performance expectations.

Over the last decades, Preqin has accumulated significant data on the performance of funds. Using their Private Capital Benchmarks, we mapped the evolution of the performance of a few selected segments of PE for three decades of vintages, comparing vintages 1995–2004 with 2005–2014 and 2015–2024 (see Figure 3.8).

The VC outlier in the 1995–2004 period includes the full impact of the internet bubble burst in 1999, with a poor performance expressed through both low returns and high volatility. VC will not recover for a while.

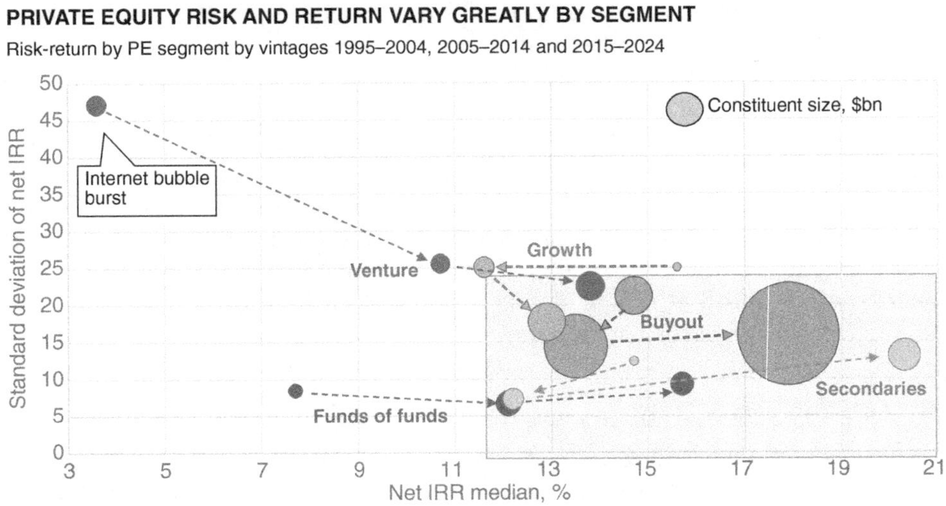

FIGURE 3.8 Risk and return by PE segment over time.
Source: Preqin Private Capital Benchmarks, accessed August 2024 (reported performances only, to be updated).

The growth segment is quasi-invisible first as it was not a recognized formal segment in the 1990s. It has grown significantly since and exhibits consistent performance.

In spite of the impact of the GFC, buyout performance has been relatively stable. However, the Preqin database is not exhaustive, and there is a likely selection bias with the worst performing funds less likely to be reported.

Secondaries and funds of funds appeared strikingly similar for the vintages 2005–2014. Behind these raw statistics, the GFC hit funds of funds hard while secondaries ended up providing one of the most attractive performances in the asset class.

We have seen how the inclusion of a major event like an economic crisis or methodological challenges can temper the interpretation of raw data. The horizon IRR of the different segments is often represented over several defined periods of 1, 3, 5, 10 (Figure 3.9), and sometimes 15 or even 25 years, but this is at best noisy information.

Again, horizon IRRs are computed by considering the fund's NAV as a negative cash flow at the start of the period, including any cash payments or receipts during the period, and the fund's residual value as a positive cash inflow at the end of the period. Preqin calculates horizon IRRs by analyzing cash flow data from more than 3,000 private capital funds.

However, horizon IRRs for private capital should be interpreted with caution. These returns are based on both actual cash transactions and portfolio valuations, the latter of which are estimates provided by GPs. Given that private capital is an illiquid asset, investors are typically committed for extended periods and are unable to realize their returns over short time frames.

When used with caution, the horizon IRR offers a comparison across different PE segments, but not with other asset classes. As mentioned earlier, direct comparison of performance is unfair considering the poor liquidity provided by PE relative to most other asset classes.

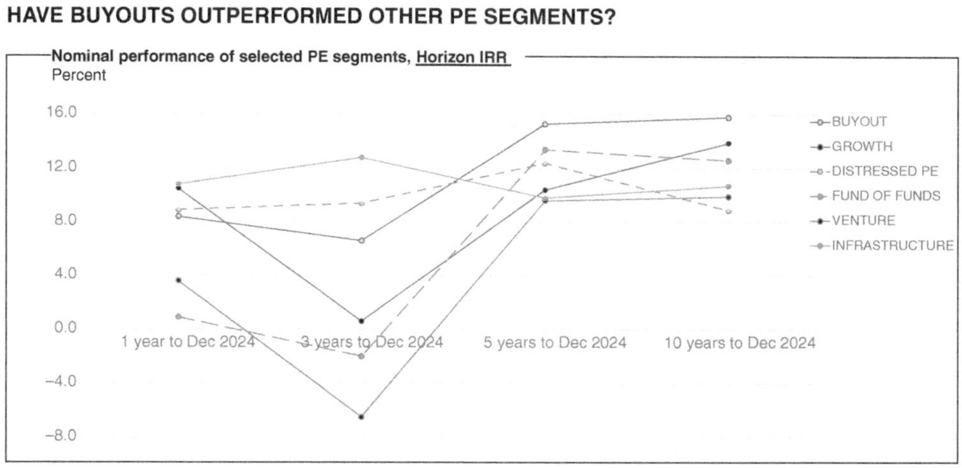

FIGURE 3.9 Horizon IRR performance by PE segment.
Source: Preqin (net-to-LP PE fund performance), database of 3,000 funds. Includes cash component and GP valuations.

We have seen how we can transform the return of public markets with state-of-the-art PME and alpha approaches to make them "PE-like." A less common alternative is to transform the PE returns, measuring them on a time-weighted basis rather than on a money-weighted IRR basis to eliminate possible distortions.[3] The formula for TWR (time-weighted return) eliminates the effect of cash flows and measures the performance of the underlying investments over time. We can calculate a TWR from the NAV and periodic valuations of the PE portfolio. For example, one can break the PE investment period into intervals where NAV is reported and calculate the return for each interval, then chain-link them to derive the overall TWR.

Figure 3.10 shows that, for most rolling periods, PE net of fees appears to outperform public markets, although due to differences in selection bias across these measures, this is no definitive comparison.

3.3.4.1 Performance of the First Quartile Figure 3.11 illustrates the performance dispersion within PE in Europe, highlighting the exceptional returns achieved by top-quartile managers across three segments, notably buyouts. This now historical data reveals that during the 1990s vintage years, the performance gap between first quartile and median funds reached levels that significantly exceeded typical quartile differentials but are still not at the level of VC performance dispersion (Kerr et al., 2014; Lerner and Nanda, 2020, 2023).

3.3.4.2 Successes and Failures PE is a world replete with stories, some successful and others less so. In the 1970s, PE was largely domestic in scope. Success depended primarily on access to capital and the ability to identify financial value in potential

[3] Note that Evergreen fund returns can be naturally measured via TWR.

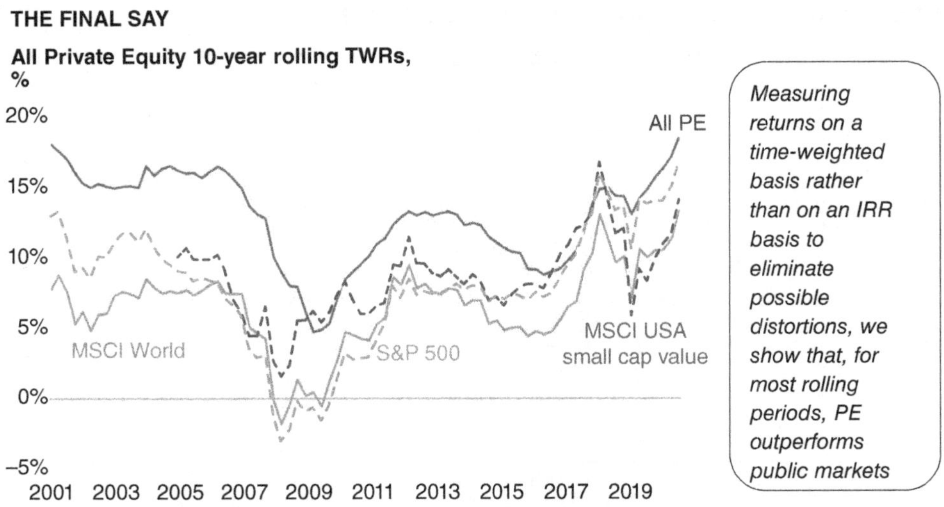

FIGURE 3.10 10-year rolling TWR of PE vs. stock indices.
Source: Hamilton Lane; Cobalt; Bloomberg (January 2022).

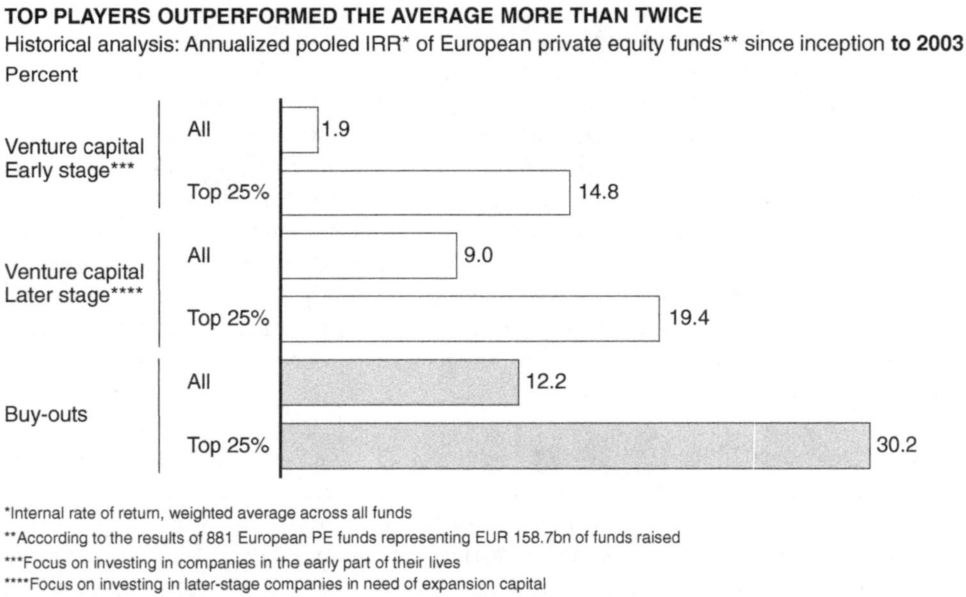

FIGURE 3.11 Historical comparison of performance between VC and buyouts.
Source: Invest Europe.

transactions. Over time, this changed. By the 1990s, particularly in Europe, firms had begun to complement deal-making capabilities with restructuring expertise, while the geographical scope of investments expanded from national to regional markets.

More recently, the focus has shifted toward strategic growth. Today, PE combines deal execution and restructuring with active ownership. Although portfolio companies may still operate locally or regionally, the largest PE funds now invest on a global scale.

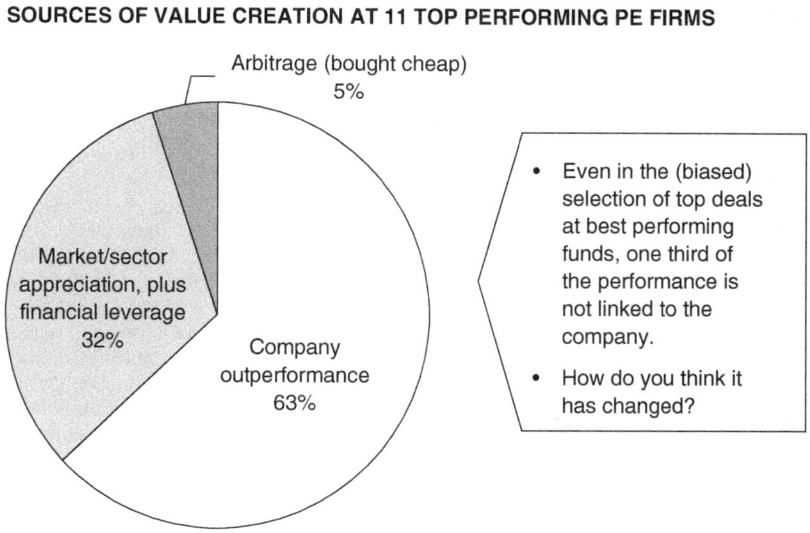

FIGURE 3.12 Source of value creation at top performing PE firms (2005).
Source: McKinsey Quarterly 2005-1.

As a result, firms are required to manage their investments far more actively if they are to generate sustained value.

Until the 2010s, value creation at top-performing PE firms came mostly from company outperformers.

In 2005, McKinsey estimated that, for a sample of top performing PE funds, more than a quarter, perhaps a third of the value was created by financial leverage and, to an extent, multiple appreciation or sector appreciation (Figure 3.12). A small part was pure arbitrage, which is more common in the hedge fund space. This involves simply identifying and buying an undervalued asset and then selling it at a higher price or instead short-selling an overvalued asset and buying it back at a lower price. Even for top performers, up to one-third of the performance is not linked to the company, so two-thirds are.

These days are gone. A 2022 Goldman Sachs analysis (Figure 3.13) highlighted a fundamental shift in the sources of value creation in LBOs. Prior to the 2008 Global Financial Crisis (GFC), financial leverage was a primary driver of returns. In the subsequent era (2008–2021), its contribution was minimal, while a significant driver of performance was market-based multiple expansion. Revenue growth has been a significant driver all along, but thanks mostly to acquisitions, and EBITDA margin expansion has been conspicuously lagging.

Looking forward, relying on mere multiple expansion is untenable. With the levers of financial engineering and market beta largely exhausted and the opportunity to consistently "buy cheap" being rare in competitive markets, value creation will likely be driven by operational and strategic improvements. A strong, thesis-driven investment case is therefore necessary to justify the high valuations demanded by most vendors. As Guy Semmens of Gyrus Capital succinctly puts it, "You need to have a clear view on what to do with the asset to accept to pay a high multiple."

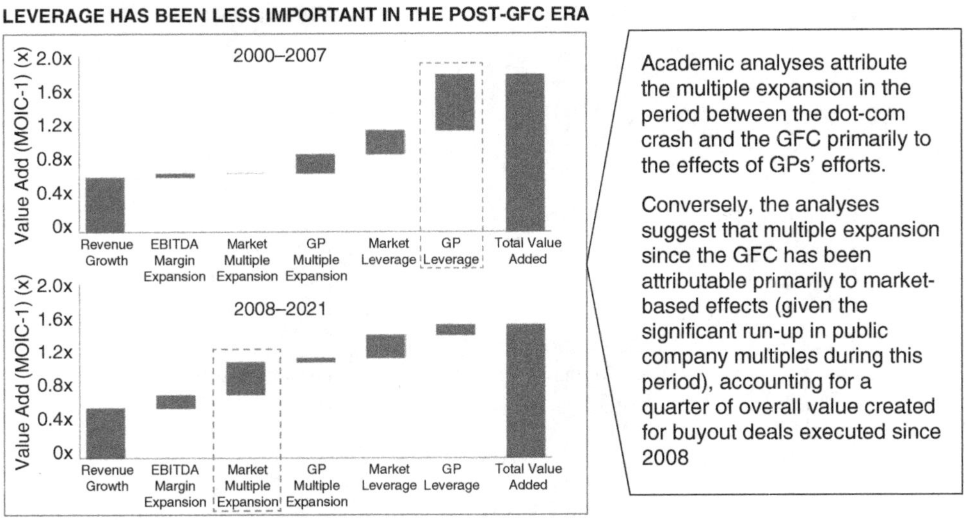

FIGURE 3.13 Performance analysis and attribution with alternative investments (2022).
Source: Matteo Binfare, Gregory Brown, Andra Ghent, Wendy Hu, Christian Lundblad, Richard Maxwell, Shawn Munday, and Lu Yi, "Performance Analysis and Attribution with Alternative Investments," as of January 24, 2022; Goldman Sachs.

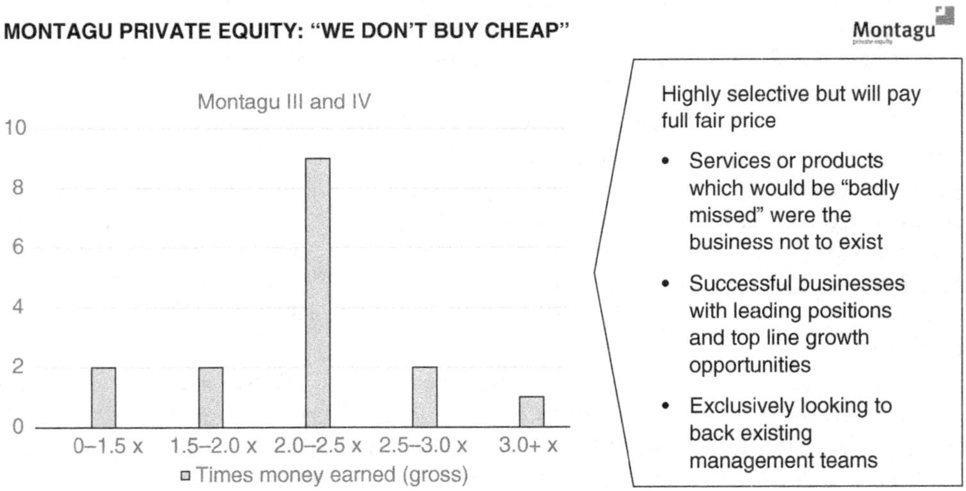

FIGURE 3.14 Montagu PE.
Source: Montagu.

An example of success we would like to highlight (Figure 3.14) is Montagu PE, who a few years ago had a very clear motto: "We do not buy cheap." They preferred to jump in with full force and deploy all necessary resources as soon as they spotted an investment opportunity. They were very selective and did not push as hard as others to reduce the price once they liked a business. They focused on services and products that would be missed if they did not exist, and they also focused on businesses that had attained a leading position but could still provide additional growth opportunities.

In addition, they would not invest in a business that did not come with a successful management team. No MBI please.

The result was very positive. Not only have they provided a very high return—the average return on investments was two-and-a-half times, and an average investment was around three years—but the distribution was quite narrow compared to most of their competitors. As you can see, they have a couple of investments that have returned little of the money invested—but they did not really lose money. While there are a couple of investments that have provided very high returns, around three times or more of what was invested, the majority of their investments return a two to two-and-a-half times multiple over about three years. This strategy allowed Montagu to achieve top quartile performance for a while.

Now turn to failure in PE. The type of PE acquisition that is most likely to be a guaranteed failure is one where buyers have no understanding of the business they are buying.

The cartoon from Roger Beale (Figure 3.15), published in the *Financial Times* a long time ago, reminds us that there have been and probably still are situations where some buyers impose their absurd misconceptions about the business with disastrous consequences.

Bad timing also doesn't help. For example, Darwin PE was a mid-market buyout fund launched in 2007 by a trio of seasoned PE veterans from Permira and CVC. They attracted other high-caliber investment professionals from Silverfleet and Citigroup. The fund quickly gained traction, securing a cornerstone investment from Lord Rothschild's RIT Capital Partners. With an ambitious target of £250 million, Darwin aimed to carve a niche in the small to mid-market buyout space.

* Historically, clowns and court jesters often served as tolerated truth-tellers who helped maintain social equilibrium; investor relations can play a comparable intermediary role between GPs, LPs, and management teams.

FIGURE 3.15 The Show Must Go On: An Iconic Cartoon on MBI.

However, the fund's trajectory was short-lived. The GFC of 2008 hit the PE industry hard, and Darwin was no exception. The dramatic downturn in economic conditions, coupled with the freezing of credit markets, made it extremely challenging for the fund to deploy its capital and generate returns.

After two years, the fund had lost almost a third of its value. After four years, it had lost two-thirds of its value, and one of the major investments, Fenn Wright Manson, went into administration. By 2014, it was assumed that there was no more value left in the PE fund. The members of the team left, and many of them joined other PE funds. Having the best team members does not guarantee success.

3.4 PERSISTENCE OF PERFORMANCE

The 1990s saw the emergence of the concept of performance persistence in PE. During this time, not only was there a substantial gap between the top-performing funds and the rest, but as discussed earlier, research also provided strong empirical evidence that certain PE firms consistently outperformed their peers across multiple funds. This finding was significant as it challenged the efficient market hypothesis common in public equity markets as well as research on mutual funds, suggesting that past PE performance could predict future success. The persistence observed was largely attributed to factors such as the experience of the GPs, their access to deal flow, and their ability to enhance operational value. Furthermore, top talent tended to concentrate within high-performing firms, further reinforcing the persistence of their success.

During the early 2000s, academic understanding of performance persistence in PE advanced significantly (Figure 3.16). Seminal research by Kaplan and Schoar (2005) discussed above, employing larger datasets and more rigorous performance measurement techniques, provided strong evidence that top-quartile funds were more likely to maintain their outperformance in subsequent funds, with persistence rates estimated between 35% and 45%. This finding directed scholarly attention toward identifying

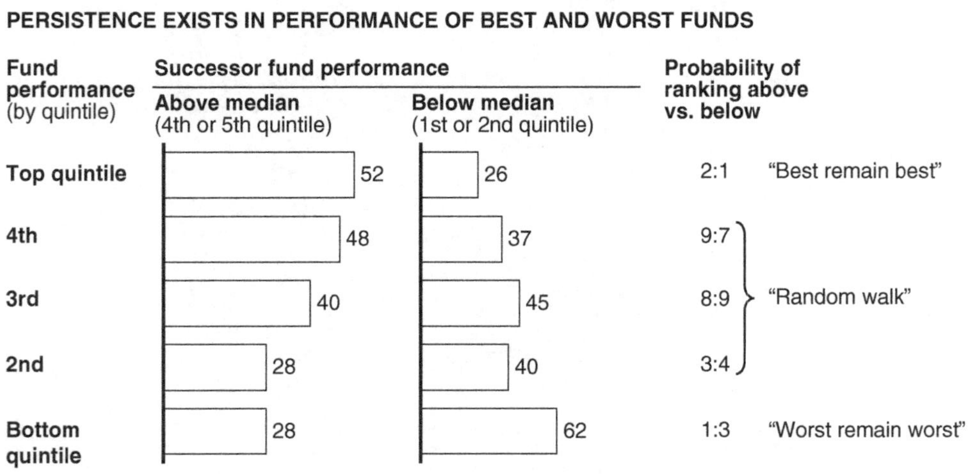

FIGURE 3.16 Persistence of performance by quartile in PE.
Source: Candesic analysis (2003 example).

the sources of this persistence, with GP skill, proprietary networks, and reputational advantages emerging as key factors. Nevertheless, by the close of the decade, evidence suggested this persistence was declining, a trend attributed to heightened competition for deals and a greater volume of capital flowing into the industry.

By the 2010s, the persistence of performance in PE began to noticeably decline. Research from this period, such as the work by Harris et al. (2014), indicated that while persistence was still observed, it had weakened over time. Factors such as the industry's expanding size, heightened competition, better data accessibility and analytics reducing information asymmetry, and the influx of new players all contributed to this trend, leading to a more competitive environment.

In the 2020s, this trend continued as the persistence that once defined the industry diminished further, influenced by the democratization of information, the widespread adoption of best practices across firms, and the increasing sophistication of LPs in their fund selection. Nevertheless, certain niche areas, like sector-specific or region-focused funds, may still exhibit higher persistence due to specialized knowledge and networks. This pattern is especially pronounced in venture capital, where the dispersion of returns is broader, making the selection of fund managers even more crucial.

However, Phalippou (2021) reminded us that the persistence of performance in PE can be understood—at least partially—as a consequence of managers consistently applying the same investment strategy with a stable team over successive funds, which is structurally easier for smaller and more specialized vehicles that can maintain focus and cohesion than for large, diversified platforms that frequently change scope, scale, or personnel.

3.5 ASSET ALLOCATION AND DIVERSIFICATION

So far, we have discussed the performance of PE, the persistence of performance, as well as some of the risks attached. Now, we turn to how PE fares in asset allocation. If we take the view of portfolio choice on the efficient frontier, the value of PE investments will come from either a higher expected return for higher risk than traditional assets such as stocks and bonds or diversification benefits. Assessing correlations between PE and other asset classes is also challenging as they vary across time, horizons, and sectors. However, history suggests that including PE in traditional investment portfolios can be valuable. Diversification benefits also require PE investments not highly correlated with LP portfolios or liabilities. And as we will see in Chapter 8, some LPs do tend to invest in PE sectors that are related to sectors they are familiar with but that is ultimately costly (Atanasova and Chemla, 2026). LPs need to avoid this mistake.

The evolution of PE allocation by investor type in Figure 3.17 shows that over the five-year period from 2009 to 2014, right after the GFC, nearly all the investor types increased their investments. Some started from a very low level, particularly the insurance companies and private pensions, but they substantially raised the bar, both in terms of current allocation and target allocation. The one category of investors that still had a long way to go was family offices, that are typically keen on investing in PE but had yet to do so. They invested only 9% of their portfolio in 2009 but increased their allocation to 28%, so almost a third of their portfolio, by 2014.

Allocations vary by geography. In their 2025 Global Family Office Report, UBS provided statistics on 317 of the world's wealthiest families who managed a combined

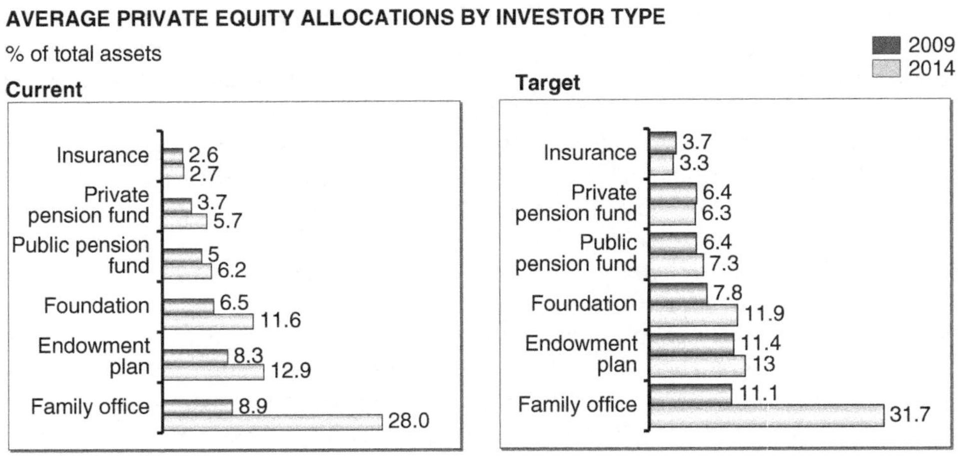

FIGURE 3.17 PE allocations by type of investor.
Source: Preqin (part of Blackrock).

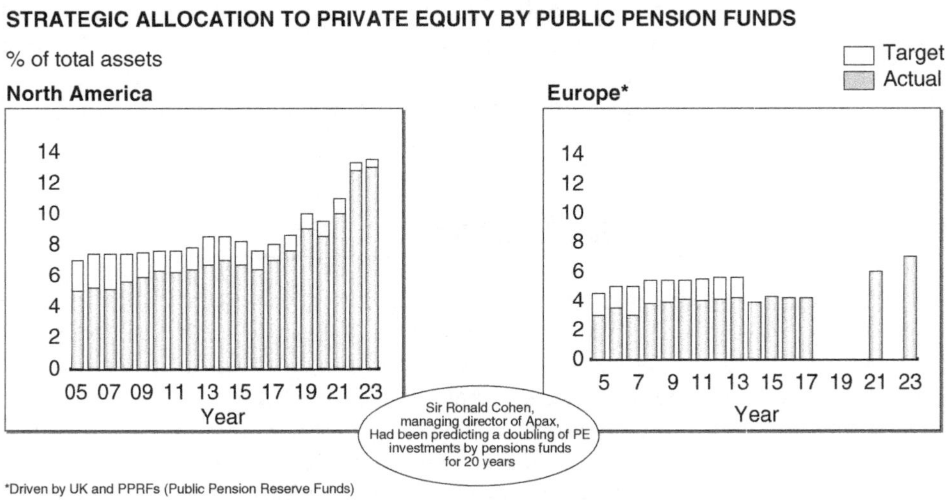

FIGURE 3.18 Strategic allocation to PE by public pension funds.
Source: Adveq, American Investment Council; Preqin (part of Blackrock); EPRA; Equable; OECD.

$650 billion in assets. Their allocation to PE was 27% in the United States and Europe, but below 15% in most of Asia.

Globally, family offices allocated 21% to PE, down from 22% the year before, still substantially higher than pension funds and endowments that have been trying to reduce their exposure to illiquid assets in an increasingly uncertain global environment.

The same goes for pension funds. North America has a long tradition of pension funds investing in PE. Public pension funds specifically reached an actual level of investment above 6% in 2013, whereas their European counterparts were still below 5% at the time (Figure 3.18). This is not like, for example, the Yale Investment Fund, which at one point raised its stake to an unusually high 20–25%.

Overall, the increase in investment in PE has been less visible since 2014 because most categories of investors had caught up by then, but there is still a debate. In 2024, for example, the state pension fund of Norway decided not to invest in PE—a setback for the PE industry.

Ronald Cohen, cofounder of Apax, predicted in the early 2000s that the allocation for pension funds would reach 10%. At the time this appeared unlikely, but this did happen in the 2020s for US public pension funds and might happen shortly in Europe.

The differences are manifest when comparing the allocation to PE of typical profiles—US endowments and European LPs—in the 2020s, shown in Table 3.1.

We have seen how US endowments—particularly Ivy League schools—were early champions of PE. But even they are reassessing in today's environment. Liquidity needs, high valuations, and a desire for flexibility have led to more emphasis on secondaries and direct investments.

We now turn to examples of large pension funds in both America and Europe (Figure 3.19). In the United States, CalPERS had a formal 17% asset allocation target in 2024, which is about $76 billion out of the $500 billion it managed then. The actual allocation was closer to 14%. In Europe, the largest public pension fund is ABP, with

TABLE 3.1

Dimension	US Endowments	European LPs
Allocation	Often 20%+	Typically, 5–10%
Strategy Focus	Aggressive: venture, growth, buyout	More conservative, income-focused
Liquidity Tolerance	High—long-term capital	More cautious
Diversification	Global, multi-asset	Often regional and less diversified

Source: Soledar partners.

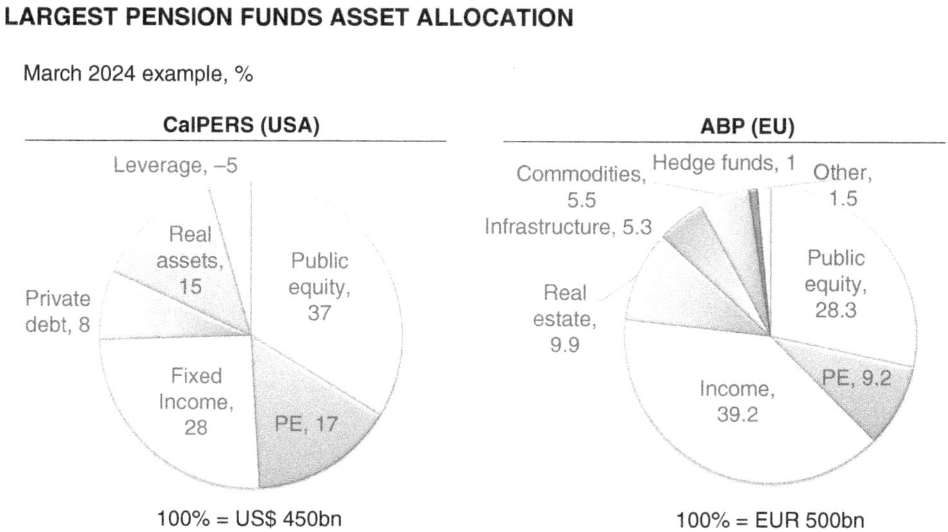

FIGURE 3.19 Comparing asset allocation of CalPERS and ABP.
Source: Candesic research.

500 billion euros under management in 2024. ABP had less than 10% invested in PE, likely due to the lack of tradition—meaning Europe came to investing in PE later than America did. It is also probably more difficult to find the right opportunities in Europe, where the markets are less homogenous. But they are slowly getting there, and ABP is leading the way.

Over the years, CalPERS provided interesting measures of its PE investments' performance when comparing it to the public equity market—the benchmark being the S&P 500.

CalPERS' PE performance has been historically high (Figure 3.20). It has generally beaten its PE benchmark, and, as you can see, its PE investments tend to outperform its other asset classes in the medium to long run.

Moreover, a yearly comparison shows that, at least until the GFC, PE investment offered a countercyclical performance opportunity. Not that PE was always performing very well, but this low correlation with public equity markets provided investors with meaningful diversification benefits. During this period, the PE market was smaller and less mature, with fewer funds and less synchronization to broader capital market cycles. Studies from this time (e.g., Gompers et al., 2005; Kaplan and Schoar, 2005) documented this weak correlation, reflecting the niche and idiosyncratic nature of PE investments.

As the market expanded, PE investments, especially buyout strategies, became more closely linked to the performance of public equity markets. The larger scale of PE funds, greater use of leverage, and increased focus on established companies have contributed to higher correlations between PE returns and public market fluctuations. Factors such as more frequent mark-to-market valuations, exit multiples influenced by public market conditions, and liquidity constraints that affect fundraising and deal activity simultaneously have further aligned PE outcomes with stock market movements. Recent empirical research supports this trend, indicating that the diversification benefits once associated with PE have diminished (Braun et al., 2017).

In contrast, VC investments have generally maintained lower correlations with public equity markets. Research indicates that VC returns continue to reflect a high

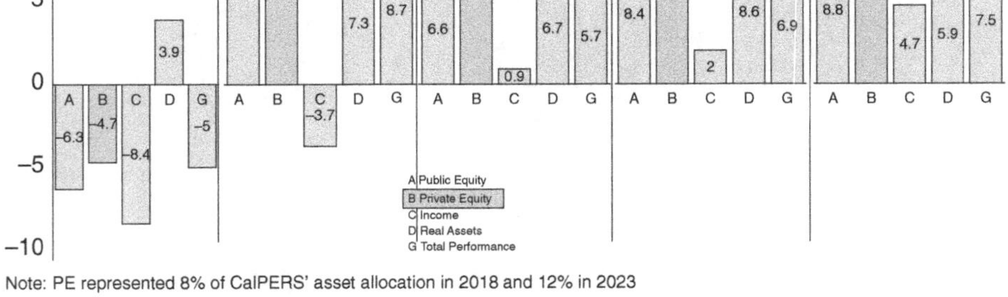

FIGURE 3.20 CalPERS PE performance as of 2023.
Source: CalPERS.

degree of idiosyncratic risk driven by factors such as innovation cycles, the capabilities of startup founders, and technological breakthroughs. As a result, VC performance tends to be less sensitive to short-term market fluctuations and overall stock market trends (Xu, 2004; Gompers et al., 2005).

Importantly, during major market disruptions such as the 2008 GFC, PE returns showed a setting of distress aligned with public equities, though typically with a lag and less immediate volatility. VC, by contrast, was less influenced by day-to-day market movements and more characterized by illiquidity and longer investment horizons, making its returns relatively insulated during the crisis period (Gompers et al., 2005).

3.6 DATA AND AI ADOPTION

Both investors and modern PE firms already sit on large amounts of data collected through past investments, due diligence, financial statements, market research, and portfolio reporting.

Technology adoption in PE spans the entire investment life cycle, from origination to exit, and can help with performance forecasting and with decision-making across the deal life cycle (Fernández Tamayo et al., 2023; Robin AI, 2025). Specifically, use cases for data are numerous:

- To identify good PE funds and promising targets and do so earlier than competitors (Gompers et al., 2016; Lerner et al., 2021; Deloitte, 2023). To this end, they use data such as past performance, web traffic, hiring patterns, and patent filings, which enables predictive sourcing as well as natural language processing and machine learning models in order to improve target screening efficiency and reduce bias.
- To improve valuation and due diligence (Barber et al., 2021; KPMG, 2022; Kaplan and Sensoy 2015). Adequate data analytics are intended to enhance valuation precision and identify hidden risks. These include transaction-level data, alternative datasets, and machine learning improve earnings forecasts as well as text analytics on contracts, news, and filings help detect legal or ESG (environmental, social, and governance) risks.
- To monitor portfolio and measure performance (Phalippou and Gottschalg, 2009; Phalippou, 2020; EY, 2024a). After the acquisition, firms use real-time data feeds to monitor performance and risk. In particular, data integration platforms and key performance indicators (sales, churn, ESG metrics) allow dynamic dashboards while predictive analytics flag operational bottlenecks or liquidity risks earlier.
- To create value through operational improvements (Acharya et al., 2013; Bain & Company, 2024b). Typically, this involves predictive analytics for pricing, marketing, and supply chain optimization and performance dashboards to measure efficiency and ESG impact.
- To optimize exit strategies (Jenkinson et al., 2013; McKinsey & Company, 2023a). This includes choosing the best route, e.g., IPO or trade sale, and choosing an optimal time to exit. This can be achieved by analyzing market sentiment and comparable transaction data.

In today's AI-driven environment, any advantage in speed, precision, or forecasting can provide a competitive edge in sourcing and winning high-quality deals.

Unsurprisingly, whenever they expect AI can outperform standard data analytics, many PE firms now turn to AI (including generative AI) and other advanced machine learning technologies to support smarter investment decisions, optimize exit strategies, and unlock operational value within their portfolio companies.

Use cases for AI abound. For example, before 2021, the median time from fund launch to final close was around 10 months (PE International, 2021), but timelines have stretched to 18–19 months nowadays (Pitchbook, 2024) due to a decrease in exit opportunities and lower LP distributions. Building digital processes, modernizing legacy systems, and gradually adopting AI can help streamline the repetitive aspects of fundraising. For example, AI tools can assist with the following:

- Due diligence questionnaires
- LP onboarding including subscription agreements, know your client (KYC) documents, and limited partner agreements
- Side letter management and MFN elections
  - Side letters have grown very long and complex; De Fontenay and Nili (2023) document that average side letter length rose from 659 words before 2005 to 4,983 words after 2014.
  - The MFN election process which requires heavy clause comparison is highly manual as well. AI especially NLP can build clause repositories, compare terms, and flag duplicates, which frees legal specialists for higher-value work.

In dealmaking, time really is money, and AI can speed up by automating manual work:

- Deal origination and pipeline management
- Pre-transaction document review
- Due diligence
  - SS&C Intralinks (2025) found that the average due diligence processing time rose from 124 to 203 days between 2013 and 2023, driven by regulatory and ESG complexity.
- Investment decisions
  - Predictive models can simulate revenue scenarios, forecast sensitivities, and exit timing strategies.

To sum up, on the dealmaking side, AI supports decision-making across the investment life cycle. Firms use machine learning to scan diverse datasets ranging from news, filings, social media, and job postings to patent databases and web signals, uncovering potential targets or sector trends that might otherwise remain unexplored. NLP and generative AI are applied to contract and legal document review, accelerating due diligence while reducing human error. Predictive models help forecast revenue, run scenario analyses, and optimize exit strategies by identifying the best timing and potential buyers. Some firms go further by developing proprietary scoring algorithms that combine structured and unstructured data to rank and prioritize acquisition targets.

The scale of AI adoption is significant. According to FTI Consulting (2024), 75% of surveyed PE firms (around 200 respondents) already use AI in their investment and value creation processes or plan to within the next 12 months. The most common use cases include data analysis/summarization (68%), document scanning and processing (61%), investor profile summarization (41%), market scanning (40%), trends and investment monitoring (31%), etc. These technologies are already improving efficiency across the deal life cycle. World Economic Forum (2025) reports that more than 80% of PE firms now deploy AI/machine learning for deal sourcing, due diligence, and portfolio management. Pictet Group (2025) reports that more than 40% of 22 PE firms (19 of which manage more than US $1 billion) have a formal AI strategy at the GP level. More than 60% of respondents observed revenue increases in their portfolio companies due to AI strategies. EY (2024) reports that 84% of the funds they interviewed expect AI to have a significant to transformational impact on their business. They note that AI is being adopted both at the GP level to streamline deal processes, uncover investment opportunities, and improve information flows between LPs and GPs, and at the portfolio company level to grow revenue, reduce costs, and improve productivity. Their case studies include a portfolio company improving call center agent efficiency by 15% and a global fund reducing credit contract processing time by about 75% with AI.

Research also confirms the potential of such approaches. Petersone et al. (2022) show that data-driven, automated screening tools indeed improve finding promising companies by increasing coverage, speed, and consistency and reducing human bias. Traditionally, PE firms relied on manual review financials, metrics, and management quality together with human intuitions. As the number of potential companies and the volume of available data grow, such approach gradually becomes infeasible. Their framework combines multiple data sources to score and rank companies and applies explainable AI techniques so that predictions are transparent and interpretable. They further validate the framework empirically using UK data, showing it is practically feasible. At the fund selection level, Fernández Tamayo et al. (2023) show that while traditional quantitative metrics (reputation proxies, fund size, prior performance, etc.) used by LPs fail to predict PE fund performance, AI tools can extract information from qualitative narratives (fundraising prospectuses) to predict future fund performance: the performance spread among the funds within the top and bottom terciles of predicted probability of success is about 25%, which suggests the value of AI in selecting fund and allocating capital.

3.7 DIGITAL PLATFORMS, CROWDFUNDING, AND TOKENIZATION

We have seen that PE's AI adoption is moving beyond experimentation. From fundraising automation to dealmaking acceleration to portfolio optimization, AI can reshape how PE firms compete and create value. But another technology is also transforming the structure and liquidity of PE as an asset class. New forms of financing on digital platforms can also transform PE and, meanwhile, create value, reduce liquidity, and facilitate exit.

Crowdfunding platforms enable equity investors, debt investors, or future users to fund projects (Chemla and Tinn, 2020, 2021). Reward-based platforms such as Kickstarter allow entrepreneurs not only to fund projects, but also to find out whether there is enough demand from consumers or patients. Equity and lending platforms show investor valuation for such projects, which may provide valuable information to PE funds not only regarding value at the time they invest and at the time of exit. This may allow PE funds to either share project funding alongside backers or crowdfunding investors or to invest after investors on platforms successfully endorsed a project.

Unsurprisingly, there is an abundance of examples, including in the healthcare sector. For example, Capital Cell, Europe's first equity-crowdfunding platform for biotech and healthcare startups, has co-funded firms such as Peptomyc and InBrain Neuroelectronics that have subsequently successfully raised millions from PE investors such as Alta Life Sciences or Asabys Partners (Capital Cell, 2024). Relatedly, €238 million were raised by health startups in Catalonia including €187 from VC and PE funds and a relatively important share through crowdfunding platforms such as Capital Cell (Genesis Biomed, 2021). Given the long development phases, crowdfunding proves to be a convenient funding model for seed and pre-clinical stages, while VC and PE focus on funding scale-up and clinical phases. These hybrid financing strategies enable PE funds from observing a successful proof-of-concept or regulatory milestone while or before they invest (Chemla and Tinn, 2020, 2021).

Crowdfunding shares some features with PE and VC. First, it tends to finance new ventures, which makes it closer to venture capital. Second, the equity component is typically a small fraction (20–25%) of the funds raised. While equity crowdfunding is investing in the equity of private companies, it is generally not considered part of the PE asset class in the traditional sense because of the different retail investor base and the different regulatory framework focused on protecting retail investors, such as the JOBS Act in the United States. However, PE funds can also invest at the crowdfunding stage, often through tokenization (Cong et al., 2021; Lewis, 2023; Chemla and Tinn, 2026).

Tokenization, which is a fast-growing process that is widely expected to reach multiple trillions of dollars (Chemla et al., 2025), converts ownership interests in funds or portfolio companies into digital tokens recorded on a distributed ledger such as blockchain platforms. These tokens can represent fractional ownership, embed contractual rights through smart contracts, and are traded on secondary markets. All these feature lower barriers to entry for smaller investors and are expected to increase liquidity. This would, of course, be a blessing for the industry. First, this may open wide the PE market to households, which could foster considerable PE growth. Second, many existing LPs will likely welcome the increased liquidity embedded in tokenized LP stakes provided by the public disclosure of asset characteristics and ownership histories on blockchain and other digital ledger technology platforms.

But how would this work? After all, PE investment requires constant due diligence and monitoring, which requires the acquisition of forward-looking information that is not easy to substantiate or to record on a blockchain. Still, track records and verifiable project characteristics and history of ownership are valuable sources of information that can reassure would-be secondary investors. Further, smart contracts can include royalties that can provide GPs with incentives, meanwhile modernizing the good old carry (Chemla and Tinn, 2026).

In practice, many tokenization pilots exhibit thin secondary markets and limited price discovery, with slow adoption due to legacy systems and cultural resistance. Still, case studies demonstrate progress. In 2022, KKR partnered with Securitize to tokenize part of its $4 billion Health Care Strategic Growth Fund II on the Avalanche blockchain. In 2024, Citi ran a pilot tokenizing a hypothetical PE fund issued by Wellington on Avalanche to test smart contract-based distributions and secondary transferability. These examples suggest that while tokenization is at an earlier stage than AI, it represents a complementary frontier. Traditional PE vehicles require large capital commitments and long lock-up periods, which effectively exclude retail investors. Tokenized PE structures—such as those offered by Moonfare, Titanbay, and Securitize—reduce these barriers by allowing investors to purchase small, divisible shares of private fund interests, sometimes starting at €10,000 rather than the conventional €250,000 threshold (Bain & Company, 2024b).

Moreover, blockchain-based fund administration can improve transparency and efficiency by automating capital calls, performance reporting, and secondary transfers through smart contracts (Chemla et al., 2025). Arguably, the tokenization of illiquid assets could reshape household exposure to private markets by embedding them within fixed-income and mixed-asset portfolios, potentially aligning illiquidity premia with long-term savings needs. However, democratization through tokenization also raises new regulatory and distributional challenges. Lower entry barriers may expose retail investors to valuation opacity, high effective fees with complex fee structures, and cyber risk, while liquidity via secondary markets remains contingent on thin trading volumes and uncertain legal frameworks (World Economic Forum, 2023).

Overall, tokenization presents a paradigm shift in PE accessibility, balancing inclusion with investor protection. When governance, custody, and settlement infrastructures mature, tokenized PE could narrow the wealth gap in access to alternative assets—though current adoption remains dominated by affluent individuals and institutional feeders (Lerner, 2023; Phalippou, 2020).

3.8 THREE EPISODES OF LIQUIDITY CONSTRAINTS

Illiquidity often defines outcomes for both managers and investors. Three episodes—across different geographies and periods—illustrate how liquidity constraints shape returns, governance, and risk perception.

1. **The Global Financial Crisis and the 2006–2007 Vintage Funds**
   Funds raised in the buyout boom immediately before the 2008 GFC were heavily exposed when credit markets froze and IPO windows shut. Managers struggled to exit portfolio companies, forcing extended holding periods and delayed distributions. Many funds had to seek term extensions beyond the typical 10-year life, depressing IRRs as cash flow timing was pushed out. Bain & Company's *Global PE Report 2010* highlighted that these vintages delivered significantly weaker performance than funds raised earlier or later, underscoring how liquidity conditions in exit markets directly influence returns.
2. **Blackstone BREIT and the Limits of Semi-liquidity**
   Blackstone Real Estate Income Trust (BREIT) was designed as a semi-liquid vehicle, offering investors quarterly redemption windows. Yet in 2022–2023, amid rising interest rates and declining real estate valuations, redemption requests exceeded the set thresholds. Blackstone imposed "gates," restricting withdrawals to protect the vehicle's stability. While the structure promised flexibility, the episode revealed the tension between investors' desire for liquidity and the illiquid nature of the underlying assets. As the *Financial Times* reported (December 2022), this highlighted a fundamental truth: no structure can fully reconcile private-market assets with public-market liquidity expectations.
3. **The Collapse of Abraaj (2018)**
   Abraaj, once the largest PE firm in emerging markets, imploded in 2018 after revelations that it had misused client funds, partly to manage liquidity shortfalls.

The firm had raised billions for healthcare and infrastructure investments, but chronic delays in exits and fundraising pressures led to commingling of investor capital and operational cash needs. The scandal, widely covered by *The Wall Street Journal* (2018), demonstrated the darker side of illiquidity: when cash flows are uncertain, even large managers may resort to opaque practices, eroding investor trust and ultimately collapsing under liquidity strain.

3.8.1 Takeaways

These cases underscore that illiquidity is not an incidental risk but a structural feature of PE. Whether through delayed exits, gated redemptions, or governance failures, liquidity constraints shape investor experience, fund performance, and even firm survival. They also explain why LPs demand an illiquidity premium—and why due diligence on structures, fund terms, and manager practices remains essential.

3.9 CHAPTER SUMMARY

Chapter 3 explains how illiquidity fundamentally shapes PE as an asset class. Unlike public markets, PE commitments remain locked up for the fund's life—typically 10 to 12 years—plus an undrawn drawdown period, extending the effective horizon to 8 years or more (Bain & Company, 2025c). This extended lockup underpins the illiquidity premium investors demand but also necessitates closed-end fund structures, subjective valuation processes, and concentrated portfolios that require careful diversification across vintages, sectors, and geographies.

Measuring performance in PE diverges sharply from public-market metrics. The J-curve effect illustrates early negative cumulative cash flows from drawdowns and fees, followed by distributions that eventually drive positive IRRs over time. Yet IRR's assumption of reinvestment at the same rate and its sensitivity to early exits can distort true return. Horizon IRRs, vintage-year analyses, and value multiples such as TVPI and MOIC each offer alternative lenses, with PME methods like KS-PME and mPME enabling more meaningful comparisons to equities.

The chapter also uncovers PE's "dark side." Performance metrics can be manipulated through timing, recycling clauses, and selective data reporting, while benchmarking against indices is fraught with sector-weight and size-bias distortions. High IRRs may mask survivorship bias, and multiples can be juiced by netting or recycling cash flows. Understanding these pitfalls is critical before drawing conclusions from headline numbers.

PE's role in institutional portfolios is considered. Despite higher expected returns and diversification potential—particularly when correlations with public markets were historically low—growing fund sizes and mark-to-market influences have increased PE's alignment with broader equity cycles. Asset-allocation decisions must balance illiquidity risks against the illiquidity premium, with secondaries and hybrid fund structures emerging to address investors' desire for shorter lockups or semi-liquidity in an evolving market landscape.

Finally, the chapter concludes on the initial topic of liquidity, exploring the impact of tokenization on PE investment in healthcare and discussing three notable episodes of liquidity constraints.

CHAPTER 4

Investment Process

This chapter explores the set-up and organization of private equity (PE) funds and the investment process as shown in Figure 4.1. It explains how the carried interest paid to general partnerships (GPs) is allocated and calculated, where to find good deal opportunities, and the characteristics of a good business plan. Lastly, it covers due diligence and several real-life examples.

4.1 INVESTMENT STRATEGY

Like any business, a PE fund needs an investment strategy aligned with the firm's strategy. Limited partnerships (LPs) are likely to scrutinize it before signing in. The investment strategy is the foundation of a fund's operations. It guides decision-making, ensures alignment with fund objectives and investors, and helps manage risks effectively, all of which are essential for achieving long-term success in a highly competitive world.

Moreover, sectoral or geographic focus or business model specialization helps a fund develop expertise and competitive advantages. This helps the investment process in every step, from instilling investor confidence, to attracting the right types of deals and partners, and streamlining the rest of the process.

The investment strategy generally starts with boundaries. Philipp von Hammerstein shares Gimv's simple filter for healthcare investments. Every company they invest in

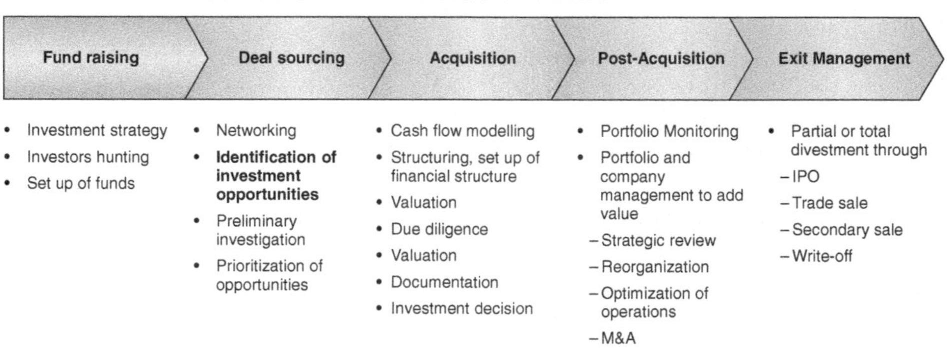

FIGURE 4.1 Investment process of PE firms.
Source: Candesic.

must meet at least one of three criteria: better quality of care, better access to care, or same outcomes at lower cost to the system. For Alessio Piccoli, CCO PI Health Sciences, "Any M&A transaction requires a careful assessment of strategic fit. In the CDMO sector, understanding of business dynamics by PE has sometimes been lacking, leading to poorly aligned deals."

The strategic fit is a critical consideration throughout every stage of the transaction process. Abrar Mir, cofounder of Quadria Capital, describes the company's investment philosophy as based on four enduring pillars: deep conviction built on domain expertise, value creation through operating excellence, focus on businesses destined to be future giants, and clarity on exit discipline:

> *Investing today demands not just capital, but an industrial approach—to innovate, to scale, and to institutionalize alpha.*

- Develop early a strong conviction on sectors and subsectors, start with deep domain knowledge, and understand what we invest in.
- Focus on industry leaders: We invest in strong businesses with robust fundamentals that we believe will be either leaders or the future industry giants and where we believe we can bring value to make them an industry leader.
- Be prepared to add critical operating value: One can no longer be a successful investor with a purely financial approach. One has to have an industrial approach to investing, with strong operating capability to help grow the revenue, drive the margin, and expand the product portfolio or geographically.
- Have a clear early view on the exit: Know how we are going to return the investors' money. DPI is more critical now than it has ever been.

Too often, investing is viewed through a distinctly US-centric lens—one that is relentlessly value and price-driven. For Abrar, however, returns in Asia are not earned in the margins of financial engineering; rather, the real driver of success lies in the underlying quality of the business and the hard work adding operational value. That quality is measured not just in numbers but in the ability to outpace peers in growth and profitability, and above all, in the capacity to transform more lives. Hence, paying a premium for excellence is not a risk—it is a recognition of enduring value.

To truly capture value in Asia, presence is not optional—it is essential. Success in PE cannot be achieved from a distance; it demands proximity. One must be close to the ground, immersed in the nuances of local markets, and alive to the regulatory and social context in which businesses operate. Abrar Mir noted:

> *Being based in Asia allows us to see opportunities as they emerge, not as they are reported months later in data. It enables us to sit across the table from entrepreneurs and speak in a language they understand—not only linguistically, but in terms of shared experience and mutual trust.*

In a region as diverse and dynamic as Asia, execution rests on empathy, insight, and credibility—qualities that can only be earned by being physically present and deeply engaged.

Guy Semmens, co-founder of Gyrus Capital, a Swiss PE firm focused on healthcare and sustainability, also argues for the need to specialize:

> *The best strategy must first be repeatable. The outcome must be linked to your own capabilities, limiting the negative impact of external events. A highly competitive world requires differentiation. Due diligence and modelling are completely commoditized and that is no longer where you can differentiate. Healthcare requires properly assessing the impact of technology in a highly regulated market.*

4.2 FUNDRAISING AND FUND SETUP

We now explore the beginning of the investment process for PE firms, which includes the set-up of funds. This setup involves addressing several critical organizational issues. We group them into six main categories:

- Fund structure characteristics
- Specialized fund structures
- Fundraising
- Capital structure models
- Organizational and compensation models
- Investment and value creation models

Each of these categories addresses key aspects of how a PE fund operates, ensuring a correct structure and positioning it for success.

4.2.1 Fund Structure Characteristics

The characteristics of a PE fund's structure are foundational to its operation and long-term viability. Key elements include **fund life, tax status, management,** and **liquidity.**

4.2.1.1 Fund Life

Traditional Fixed-term Structures Typically, a PE fund has a lifespan of around 10 years, divided into an *investment period* (usually the first five years) and a *harvesting period* (concentrated in the final five years). During the investment period, the fund actively seeks and makes investments, while the harvesting period is focused on managing exits and realizing returns. Extensions beyond the 10-year period may be necessary if the portfolio is not fully liquidated and there is typically an option to do so for another two years.

Perpetual Capital and Evergreen Funds As mentioned earlier, the traditional drawdown model we just described is starting to get slightly eroded by an alternative evergreen model. It is tempting for GPs to try to get a break from the constant fundraising pressure. After all, perpetual capital suggests perpetual fees.

The shift represents what many consider the next era of modernization for the investment industry, driven partly by the maturation of institutional LP allocations—many have reached their exposure limits and pulled back commitments, forcing GPs to seek new capital sources.

Investors benefit too. Evergreen funds offer limited liquidity with regular—typically quarterly—subscriptions and redemptions windows.

While they target wealthy individuals in priority, they can be attractive to some institutional investors among traditional LPs. In fact, according to PitchBook's 2029 Private Market Horizons report, institutional and retail-focused evergreen structures were projected to reach, respectively, 3.6% and 2.8% of PE's overall AuM by 2029.

In 2024, PitchBook estimated that nearly $400 billion was managed in private-wealth-targeted evergreen structures (interval funds, tender offer funds, non-listed REITs and BDCs), with more than 230 fund launches since 2019 targeting this channel. Overall evergreen LP funds reached approximately $1 trillion AuM (250 billion for PE and VC), though traditional drawdown funds still dominate at nearly $15 trillion globally.

4.2.1.2 Tax Status

Pass-through Entities PE funds are often established as limited partnerships, a structure that is tax transparent. This means that profits and losses are passed through directly to the investors, who then pay taxes in their own jurisdictions, avoiding double taxation. This structure is favored not for tax avoidance, but to streamline tax liabilities and enhance efficiency (Figure 4.2).

Regulatory Considerations A typical PE fund is a carefully engineered machine designed to optimize tax benefits, shield investors from liability, and tightly align the interests of fund managers and backers.

At its heart lies an LP, the principal investment vehicle where the investors—known as limited partners—commit their capital. These LPs are usually institutional giants or high-net-worth individuals who provide the fuel but stay out of the driver's seat, leaving day-to-day management strictly to the GP.

The GP usually takes the form of a limited liability company (LLC), owned by the fund's management team. This GP entity steers all investment decisions and handles operations, bearing full responsibility for the fund's obligations.

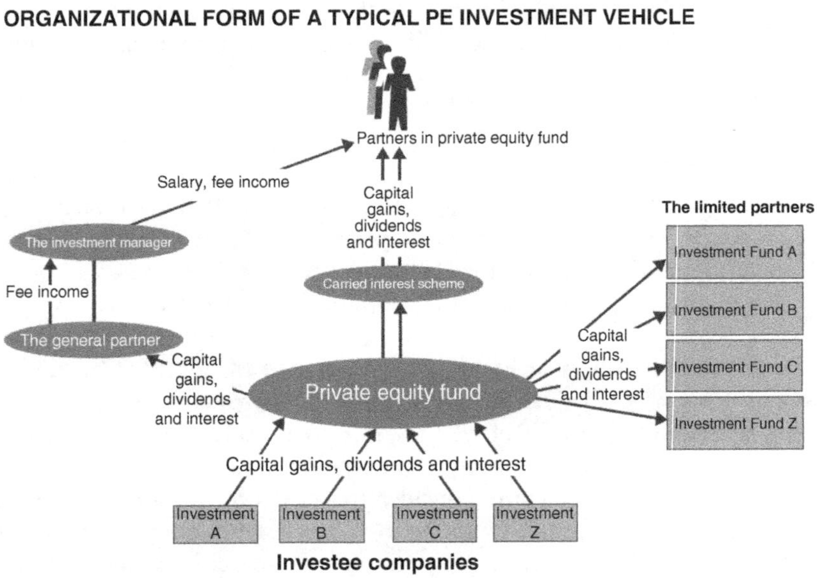

FIGURE 4.2 PE investment vehicle.
Source: Gilligan and wright.

To underline skin in the game, the GP typically invests between half a percent and 5% of the total capital. In return for managing the complex engine of deals and operations, the GP earns an annual management fee—commonly around 1.5% to 2% of committed capital—covering overhead and salaries.

Performance incentives come via "carried interest," a share of profits—often 20%—granted once the fund meets a hurdle rate, usually around 8%. This profit share is funneled through a specialized entity called the carried interest partner, allowing flexibility for the GP to split rewards among the team.

Tax-wise, structuring carried interest to be treated as capital gains offers significant savings and ensures that the GP's upside is not taxed as ordinary income—a crucial benefit in many jurisdictions.

Supporting this architecture, a separate investment advisory company is often established, employing the investment professionals and advising the GP. This entity is typically funded through management fees and handles the analytical and advisory workload. Finally, each portfolio company investment is often housed in its distinct LP or LLC, isolating liabilities and facilitating co-investments while maintaining operational clarity.

Together, this layered, intricate design balances legal protections, economic incentives, and operational flexibility—allowing PE funds to navigate complex markets, optimize returns, and remain aligned with investor interests over the fund's life cycle. It is worth noting that specific structures can vary based on legal jurisdictions, tax considerations, and the particular needs of the fund and its investors.

4.2.1.3 Management

Governance Structures Like for firms and other financial institutions, governance is essential in PE. Governance is meant to balance control and provide appropriate incentives to the GPs who make investment decisions, manage the funds, and control exit decisions, and to the LPs who supply capital, are protected by limited liability, and cannot interfere with fund management, with the complexities inherent to illiquid investments governed by long-term contracts signed under asymmetric information.

Most PE funds are set up as Limited Partnerships (LPs), with an LP agreement (LPA) that is intended to ensure strong contractual governance and shares many features with standard shareholder agreements (Chemla et al., 2007). The contract typically specifies governance rights, reporting duties, conflicts procedures, and fees (Kaplan and Stromberg, 2003). It lasts 10 to 12 years, with a five-year investment period and a five- to seven-year divestment period. LPs commit capital upfront while GPs "call" capital gradually as needed.

4.2.1.4 Liquidity

Investor Entry and Exit Provisions Liquidity in PE funds is limited, as these are generally closed-ended structures where investors' capital is locked in for the duration of the fund's life. Secondary market options for liquidity are typically restricted and may come with certain conditions.

The lock-in relates to the liquidity provided to investors. It refers to the restriction placed on the investors (the LPs) that prevents them from selling or withdrawing their shares or investment in a fund for a specified period. The lock-in for PE funds is typically five to seven years. However, there are sometimes exceptions—for example, the British PE firm Alchemy was quite unusual in offering participants a 12-month rolling notice period, in contrast to the usual requirement for a lock-in.

Commitment Periods and Capital Calls The commitment period typically spans the first three to five years of a fund's life. During this window, GPs can legally call capital from LPs to finance new investments. Most funds require LPs to fund capital calls within 10–30 business days of notice, creating pressure for institutions to maintain ready liquidity.

Capital calls follow a just-in-time approach rather than requiring upfront funding. When the GP identifies an investment opportunity, they issue a capital call notice specifying the amount needed and the funding deadline. LPs cannot refuse these calls without risking default, which may result in forfeiture of their investment and dilution of their ownership percentage.

The commitment period can be extended under specific circumstances, typically for another one to two years. Extensions usually require LP approval or occur automatically if certain deployment thresholds haven't been met. After the commitment period expires, GPs can generally only call additional capital for follow-on investments in existing portfolio companies, bridge financing, or to cover expenses and fees.

Some funds implement recycling provisions during the commitment period. When portfolio companies generate proceeds through dividends or early exits, these amounts can be "recycled"—called again for new investments rather than distributed to LPs. This mechanism helps GPs deploy capital more efficiently while maintaining their target fund size.

4.2.2 Specialized PE Vehicles

Finder's funds and search funds offer two special cases of fundraising.

4.2.2.1 Finder's Funds: Selective Capital Deployment Models Deal-by-deal Investment Model. Finder's funds, alternatively termed pledge funds or deal-by-deal funds, represent a distinctive approach to PE capital formation that traces its lineage to the earliest manifestations of the industry. In this model, rather than committing capital to a blind investment pool, LPs reserve discretion to evaluate and participate in individual transactions presented by the GP.

The operational mechanics of finder's funds involve a GP who identifies potential acquisition opportunities and subsequently presents these prospects to a preestablished network of investors. Each investor independently determines whether to allocate capital to specific transactions based on their individual assessment of the opportunity's merits. This structure contrasts sharply with traditional PE vehicles where initial capital commitments are irrevocable and investment decisions remain the exclusive province of the GP.

A distinguishing characteristic of finder's funds is the absence of committed capital for preliminary opportunity identification activities. Additionally, GPs typically maintain a financial advisory role rather than assuming operational leadership within portfolio companies. This arrangement provides investors with enhanced flexibility, permitting selective participation across the opportunity spectrum while potentially facilitating more diverse investment exposure.

Investor Selection Rights. This third vehicle feature highlights how GPs tailor their LP base—just as finder's funds narrow deal rights and search funds focus on entrepreneur-led acquisitions, investor selection rights ensure a cohesive, aligned investor group for niche vehicles.

In many specialized vehicles, the GP reserves the right to approve or decline any prospective investor to ensure alignment of interests and maintain a cohesive investor base. These **investor selection rights** typically appear in the side-letter or limited partnership agreement and grant the GP sole discretion to reject LPs who might conflict with fund strategy, risk tolerance, or reputation standards. For example, a search fund may stipulate that only accredited individual investors with direct industry experience may participate, allowing the entrepreneur to build a supportive network rather than a passive capital pool.

Beyond outright approval rights, the GP may also negotiate preemptive and co-investment rights, enabling existing LPs to upsize their allocations before new investors are admitted. This protects the economic interests of cornerstone backers and reinforces long-term support. Conversely, transfer restrictions prevent secondary sales of interests to unvetted parties, ensuring that any incoming LP meets the fund's governance and confidentiality requirements. By codifying these selection and transfer controls, GPs preserve strategic flexibility, safeguard the fund's culture, and reduce the risk of future conflicts that can distract from value creation.

4.2.2.2 Search Funds: Entrepreneurial Acquisition Vehicles

Entrepreneurial Acquisition Vehicles. Search funds represent a specialized PE structure that emerged in 1984 and has gained significant traction since 2013 (Figure 4.3). They are designed to enable aspiring entrepreneurs, frequently recent MBA graduates, to identify, acquire, and subsequently lead a single privately held enterprise. The model effectively synthesizes entrepreneurial ambition with institutional investment discipline.

Two-stage Funding Process. The search fund framework employs a bifurcated capital formation approach. Initially, the entrepreneur secures modest funding to support a comprehensive acquisition search process, historically spanning 18–24 months. This phase encompasses systematic opportunity identification, rigorous due diligence, and transaction negotiation. Upon identifying a suitable acquisition candidate, the entrepreneur solicits additional investment capital to execute the transaction.

Following acquisition completion, the entrepreneur transitions to the chief executive role within the acquired entity, assuming responsibility for strategic direction and operational execution over a typical five- to seven-year investment horizon before pursuing liquidity alternatives. Search funds predominantly target established small and medium-sized enterprises operating in fragmented industry sectors with identifiable growth catalysts.

Investors in search funds frequently contribute strategic guidance beyond capital, often serving in formal advisory capacities including board directorships. The economic structure typically incorporates liquidation preferences for investors while providing the entrepreneur with meaningful equity participation contingent upon successful acquisition and subsequent value creation. This alignment mechanism rewards entrepreneurial execution while preserving investor downside protection.

This model affords entrepreneurially oriented professionals accelerated pathways to executive leadership while simultaneously providing institutional investors access to smaller-capitalization opportunities with attractive growth characteristics. However, search funds present distinct challenges, including potentially protracted search periods with uncertain outcomes and concentrated dependence on a single entrepreneur's capabilities.

Despite these inherent complexities, search funds have evolved into an increasingly significant PE segment, effectively bridging traditional VC and conventional buyout approaches through their unique entrepreneurial acquisition methodology.

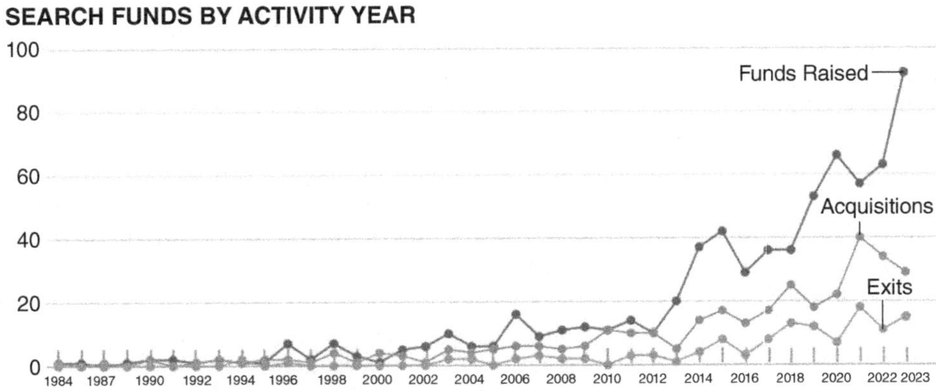

FIGURE 4.3 Evolution of search funds' activity.
Source: Stanford Graduate School of Business, Search Fund Study 2024.

In contrast to finder's funds that may pursue multiple investments across various companies or sectors, search funds typically focus on acquiring and operating a single company.

4.2.3 Fundraising

4.2.3.1 Traditional Capital Sources and Process Institutional investors constitute the foundational capital base for PE fundraising, with pension funds, sovereign wealth funds, endowments, and insurance companies traditionally providing the bulk of industry capital. Family offices and high-net-worth individuals represent secondary but increasingly important sources, each bringing distinct investment preferences, time horizons, and risk tolerance parameters.

The GP must demonstrate sophisticated understanding of these nuanced investor profiles when structuring fundraising approaches. Regulatory compliance forms an essential component of the fundraising framework, with jurisdictional variations requiring meticulous attention to securities laws and investor protection statutes. The legal architecture surrounding private capital formation continues to evolve, necessitating ongoing vigilance from fund managers.

Capital formation methodologies vary across the spectrum, from traditional limited partnership structures relying exclusively on external capital to captive arrangements funded by corporate sponsors. Hybrid models synthesize these approaches, potentially offering enhanced flexibility while introducing governance complexities that require careful consideration.

A GP's historical performance metrics, investment philosophy coherence, and reputation for fiduciary responsibility significantly influence fundraising outcomes. External market conditions further modulate investor receptivity, with macroeconomic factors and asset class sentiment playing decisive roles in allocation decisions.

The fund's ultimate capitalization not only determines its investment capacity but fundamentally shapes its strategic orientation, organizational structure, and economics. Appropriately sized funds optimize the alignment of interests between GPs and LPs while establishing realistic parameters for value creation and performance distribution throughout the investment life cycle.

Fee structures have evolved significantly beyond the traditional "2 and 20" model. As funds have gotten larger, fees have come under pressure. Following the GFC peak in 2009, certain PE firms had lowered their fees to reassure investors. For example, TPG Capital reduced management fees by 10%, while Madison Dearborn Partners chose to postpone collecting theirs. Since then, while the traditional "2 and 20" model still exists, large funds (especially $10B+) often agree to 1.0–1.25% management fees for cornerstone or returning investors. Carried interest remains in place but is more frequently subject to hurdles, catch-ups, and custom waterfalls for key LPs.

Publicly listed firms like CVC offer transparency into this shift: in 2024, for example, the vast majority of its revenues came from management fees rather than carry, showing how fee-based, recurring revenue has become the core business model for many.

Figure 4.4 shows a recent example of the basic terms for a fundraising campaign by a leading LBO firm.

4.2.3.2 The Evolution of Private Equity Fundraising Since 2000 *[With the contribution of Alessandra Mazzuchelli]*

PE fundraising has significantly matured over the past decades. In the early 2000s, capital was raised largely through informal networks and longstanding relationships. GPs with strong reputations could often close a fund quickly, especially among pension funds, endowments, and a few institutional family offices. Placement agents were essential intermediaries, especially for newer or niche managers.

This changed dramatically after the GFC in 2008. Institutional investors began demanding much more in terms of transparency, operational robustness, and governance. As LPs became more selective, larger GPs gained an edge, while first-time funds and smaller managers had to work harder and wait longer to secure commitments.

By the mid-2010s, the market was booming again. Cheap capital and low rates led to a rush into private markets. New strategies emerged—from sector-focused buyout funds to continuation vehicles and impact funds—and the investor base widened. Alongside institutional capital, the rise of secondaries and co-investments provided LPs with tools to manage liquidity and optimize allocations.

EXAMPLE OF FUNDRAISING BY MAJOR LBO FIRM IN 2020

Geography	US/Europe
Target size	$15–20 billion
Ticket	Minimum ticket is 15 million. Possibility to invest through private bank with minimum ticket of 250K (with additional fees)
Management fees	1.5% of committed capital for the first five years and then 0.75% of investments.
Carried interest	90% of amounts attributable to investors will be subject to a European style fund distribution waterfall, with 8% preferred return, 100% GP catch-up and 20% carried interest, with the remaining 10% subject to a realized deals waterfall (also with 8% preferred return, 100% GP catch-up and 20% carried interest)

FIGURE 4.4 Fundraising terms for a large LBO fund.
Source: Investment offer.

Technology started to influence the fundraising process more heavily. From customer relationship management systems and digital roadshows to automated investor portals and virtual due diligence, GPs began running more structured, data-driven processes. Many also built in-house capital formation teams, minimizing the need for external agents—especially for larger, recurring fundraises.

After 2020, capital formation became increasingly complex. Fundraising cycles extended significantly, with mid-market funds (roughly $1–5 billion AuM) often requiring 24–36 months to complete raises, compared to 12–18 months historically, at least in boom phases. Competition intensified across all fund sizes, while macroeconomic uncertainty and rising interest rates affected investor sentiment and allocation timing.

Role of Intermediaries The role of intermediaries has also evolved. Traditional placement agents remain important, particularly for specialized mandates or accessing new geographies, but they are no longer just "connectors." Many now provide strategic advisory services: helping GPs shape their pitch, segment their LP universe, and refine their capital-raising strategy.

Whereas many firms historically relied on placement agents, it is now standard practice for mid-to-large GPs to have dedicated in-house fundraising and investor relations teams. For funds with over $5B AuM, it is not unusual for 80–90% of capital to come in via internal efforts. External agents are often used only for specific investor types or niche regional coverage.

This shift reflects cost efficiency, control over messaging, and the growing complexity of investor expectations around reporting, ESG, and co-investment opportunities.

On the other side, digital platforms such as iCapital, CAIS, and Moonfare are creating new distribution channels for PE access, particularly targeting the individual wealth segment. These are not classic placement agents—they are digital distribution networks with strong relationships across wealth managers, private banks, and registered investment advisors. We will analyze their offering in the next sections of this chapter.

4.2.3.3 Expanding Investor Access *[With the contribution of Robin Jakubowski, formerly at Rothschild]*

The evolution of PE fundraising reflects an ongoing attempt to address structural limitations in traditional capital formation models. However, this expansion toward private wealth raises questions about investor protection, market stability, and the fundamental suitability of illiquid investments for less sophisticated participants.

The Transformation of Private Equity Fundraising—From Institutional Dominance to Private Wealth Expansion Traditionally backed by institutional investors, the industry has been undergoing a significant structural shift in the 2020s. As legacy capital providers encounter cyclical pressures and macroeconomic challenges, the private markets ecosystem is evolving from a predominantly institutional fundraising model toward a more inclusive, technology-driven architecture for capital mobilization. GPs increasingly target not just high-net-worth individuals (HNWIs), but also less wealthy investors through financial intermediaries and digital platforms.

This shift reflects both institutional constraints and market opportunities. Institutional LPs are reducing commitments due to the denominator effect, illiquidity premiums, and declining distributions. Simultaneously, private wealth is growing globally, with increasing demand for alternative asset exposure. According to Blackstone, these dual pressures have catalyzed GPs to redesign product structures and develop new distribution capabilities. Firms like Blackstone and Apollo have invested heavily in building wealth teams targeting financial advisors and family offices with tailored products.

Critical concerns emerge regarding investor protection, as regulatory frameworks remain incomplete for retail participants in illiquid markets. The complexity of PE investments may exceed many individual investors' sophistication levels, potentially creating systemic risks if market conditions deteriorate.

The Emergence of Private Wealth as a Capital Channel In the mid-2020s, private wealth, comprising HNWIs, mass-affluent investors, and family offices, but excluding retail investors, controlled US$130 to 150 trillion and over half of all investable assets globally according to iCapital Network, growing at a faster pace than institutional pools. Despite this, barriers such as high minimum investments, complex subscriptions, and limited liquidity historically excluded these investors from PE.

If 5% to 10% of this private wealth were allocated to private markets, depending how much is already invested in them, this could represent an additional $10 trillion in potential capital formation. Moreover, if 5% of the estimated $450 trillion in total global wealth (including retail), where approximately 90% is held by those with at least $100K in assets, were invested that way, it would represent more than $20 trillion in potential capital formation, dwarfing current drawdown fund AuM.

Product Innovation: Fund Structures Designed for Individuals. PE firms have deployed semi-liquid and evergreen vehicles to accommodate liquidity expectations of wealthy clients. In the United States, interval and tender offer "40 Act funds" have enabled firms such as Blackstone, KKR, and Apollo to offer PE access with quarterly or semi-annual redemption windows. In real estate, BREIT had raised $60–70 billion by 2023 and offered monthly liquidity features within NAV-capped thresholds.

In Europe, the revised ELTIF 2.0 regulation—effective from 2024—removed the €10,000 minimum investment threshold entirely, broadened eligible asset classes, and introduced conditional liquidity windows. However, these structures necessitate advanced operational frameworks and may present liquidity mismatches during market stress and valuation challenges.

Evergreen structures address portfolio management challenges in individual investors' PE allocations. Unlike drawdown funds requiring unpredictable capital calls, evergreen funds provide immediate NAV exposure that compounds continuously, eliminating complex cash flow forecasting. PitchBook data showed annualized returns since inception of approximately 11% for direct PE and 10% for infrastructure evergreen fund indexes. Industry analysis demonstrates that an evergreen fund generating consistent 10% annual returns can be equivalent to a drawdown fund showing 20% IRR over a decade, primarily due to reinvestment friction in traditional structures (Pitchbook, 2024).

Distribution Transformation: From Relationships to Scale. Private wealth fundraising requires fundamentally different distribution mechanics than institutional models. Leading firms have built dedicated wealth divisions: Blackstone's Private Wealth Solutions, KKR, and Apollo have institutionalized wealth distribution through partnerships with wirehouses and digital platforms.

Platforms such as iCapital and CAIS have enabled PE firms to scale distribution by facilitating compliance, onboarding, and reporting infrastructure for retail investors, bridging the gap between PE firms and retail clients and accelerating the shift toward a more inclusive fundraising approach.

4.2.3.4 Fundraising Process and Strategy: Evolving Approaches in a Changing Market Modern fundraising requires systematic coordination across multiple phases while accommodating diverse investor requirements and regulatory frameworks. Contemporary approaches emphasize process standardization and investor segmentation rather than traditional relationship-based models.

Fundraising timelines have lengthened significantly: mid-market funds already typically needed 18–24 months to close a few years ago, and they often take even longer today, especially for first-time vehicles. This extension reflects increased market competition, more rigorous due diligence requirements, and greater regulatory complexity.

The process follows a systematic four-phase approach: preparation, marketing, due diligence, and closing. Effective execution requires clear narrative development, targeted investor segmentation, and operational capabilities.

Preparation Phase GPs must articulate their differentiated value proposition through compelling narrative development and market positioning before engaging with prospective LPs. This storytelling element has become crucial as investors evaluate not just historical performance but also the fund's strategic vision and market opportunity assessment.

During the preparation phase, funds develop comprehensive due diligence packages including audited track records, reference portfolios, and operational frameworks. ESG policies, diversity initiatives, and risk management protocols now constitute essential components of any institutional-grade presentation. Marketing materials require regulatory compliance across multiple jurisdictions, particularly when targeting cross-border LP bases.

Marketing Phase The marketing phase involves systematic outreach through both existing relationships and new prospect development. Digital roadshows have become standard practice, supplementing traditional face-to-face presentations rather than replacing them. LPs increasingly conduct preliminary screening through online platforms and automated due diligence systems before committing to detailed evaluation processes.

Investor categorization determines fundraising approach, with distinct methods for pension funds, sovereign wealth funds, family offices, and insurance companies. Each category requires tailored messaging, fee structures, and reporting requirements. Anchor investors often receive preferential terms in exchange for early, substantial commitments that provide credibility and momentum for subsequent fundraising efforts.[1]

Due Diligence Phase The due diligence phase has intensified significantly, with LPs conducting operational due diligence, cybersecurity assessments, and detailed reference calls. Fund managers must demonstrate institutional-quality operations including

[1] This is not fundraising advice, but a regular observation by GPs and LPs.

compliance frameworks, portfolio monitoring systems, and investor reporting capabilities. This phase often extends 6–12 months for institutional investors.

Closing Phase Closing sequences require careful coordination to manage LP expectations and maintain fundraising momentum. Multiple closings allow funds to begin investing while continuing to raise capital, though this creates complexity around fee calculations and investment allocation rights. Final closing typically occurs 12–18 months after initial marketing launch.

The increasing focus on private wealth investors has introduced several key changes to the traditional fundraising process. The need to engage with a broader and more diverse range of investors led PE firms to invest in technology platforms and digital tools to streamline their fundraising efforts. Digital onboarding, automated compliance checks, and online reporting have all played a part in enabling firms to scale their distribution efforts to a larger investor base, while simultaneously improving efficiency and reducing overheads.

PE firms are also increasingly focusing on tailoring their fundraising strategies to different investor segments. For instance, firms targeting mass-affluent investors may emphasize the flexibility and liquidity features of their fund vehicles, such as quarterly redemption options, while firms focused on ultra-high-net-worth (UHNW) clients may market bespoke co-investment opportunities and tailored portfolio strategies. The move to semi-liquid and evergreen vehicles also reflects a strategic response to the increased demand for liquidity from private wealth investors who have historically been excluded from such investments.

4.2.3.5 Investor Relations and Reporting: Building Trust in a More Transparent Environment Contemporary investor relations encompass continuous engagement through digital platforms, proactive communication, and customized reporting frameworks. Effective programs require specialized teams, advanced technology infrastructure, and transparent performance attribution methodologies.

Reporting frameworks must accommodate diverse LP requirements across multiple jurisdictions. Standard reports include fund performance, portfolio company updates, market commentary, and regulatory compliance summaries. However, LPs increasingly demand customized reporting covering ESG metrics, diversity statistics, and portfolio-level impact measurements.

In the United States, regulatory reforms, including the 40 Act funds, have forced PE firms to enhance their reporting standards to comply with SEC guidelines. This includes more frequent disclosure of net asset value, fund performance, and asset valuations (Blackstone, 2023). Moreover, firms must be prepared to address the specific concerns of retail investors—particularly around liquidity, fees, and risk—by providing clear, accessible reports that demystify the complexities of PE investments.

Digital investor portals have become essential infrastructure, providing secure access to documents, performance data, and portfolio information. These platforms enable LPs to conduct independent analysis while reducing administrative burden on fund managers. Integration with LP systems allows automated data feeds for institutional investors' internal reporting requirements.

Performance reporting requires careful attention to valuation methodologies, particularly for unrealized investments. Independent valuation providers increasingly supplement internal assessments, providing third-party credibility for NAV calculations. Transparent discussion of valuation changes and methodology adjustments builds LP confidence and reduces due diligence friction for subsequent fundraises.

Proactive communication around portfolio developments, market conditions, and strategic adjustments distinguishes superior fund managers. LPs value early notification of challenges, detailed explanation of value creation initiatives, and honest assessment of market risks. This transparency builds trust and strengthens relationships for future fundraising cycles.

Co-investment opportunities represent increasingly important LP relationship management tools. Providing attractive co-investment access can justify higher fees while strengthening LP loyalty. However, managing allocation across LPs requires careful attention to conflicts of interest and fairness principles.

Crisis communication protocols ensure effective LP management during challenging periods. Whether addressing portfolio company difficulties, market dislocations, or internal personnel changes, funds must maintain transparent dialogue while protecting confidential information and portfolio company relationships.

4.2.3.6 Technology Platforms in Private Equity: History, Economic Models, and Market Impact Technology platforms represent a structural shift in PE distribution, introducing new intermediation models between fund managers and individual investors. While these platforms have expanded access, they also create new risks and dependencies that merit careful analysis.

The Evolution of Digital Access One of the first platforms to gain global institutional traction was iCapital Network, founded in New York in 2013. iCapital pioneered a digital aggregation model, pooling smaller investor allocations into institutional-grade PE funds. By creating feeder funds and offering a white-labeled platform to wealth managers and private banks, iCapital enabled minimum investments as low as $100,000—substantially less than the multi-million-dollar thresholds previously required. Over the following decade, iCapital expanded rapidly, partnering with industry giants such as Blackstone and Goldman Sachs, and by 2025, it reported more than $250 billion in alternative platform assets, serving more than 100,000 financial professionals and over 1,600 funds globally. CAIS, founded in New York earlier in 2009, reported more than $25 billion in platform assets the same year. iCapital and CAIS do not limit themselves to PE. Both also offer access to hedge funds, structured credits, and real assets.

Inspired by these early platforms, a wave of platforms emerged in Europe and beyond. Moonfare, founded in Germany in 2016, targeted high-net-worth individuals, offering a fully digital experience and minimums initially at €50,000, later reduced to €10,000. Moonfare positioned low minimums as a key differentiator and promoted its platform as streamlining onboarding, compliance, and reporting, while advertising its rigorous fund selection process—claiming to approve fewer than 5% of funds reviewed—as a trust-building mechanism. By 2024, Moonfare had attracted over 60,000 registered users and managed more than €3 billion in assets.

Other notable entrants include Titanbay, which launched in the United Kingdom in 2019 with a focus on partnerships with wealth advisors, and Private Corner, a French platform established in 2020 to serve wealth managers and their clients, authorized by the French regulator (AMF). Both have reached $1 billion AuM. In the United States, Opto Investments took a slightly different approach, targeting registered investment advisors (RIAs) and emphasizing co-investment alignment and educational tools. Yieldstreet, also US-based, broadened access to alternatives beyond PE, including real estate and litigation finance, with minimums as low as $500. Yieldstreet and Opto Investments have not publicly disclosed their AuM but are recognized for their reach and product innovation.

Operational Mechanisms, Business Models, and Platform Features Digital platforms operate through capital aggregation mechanisms. This typically occurs through feeder fund structures or special purpose vehicles (SPVs) that consolidate individual commitments into single, larger investments acceptable to PE fund managers.

The platforms' core value proposition rests on three operational pillars: capital aggregation, technology infrastructure, and regulatory compliance. Capital aggregation allows platforms to bundle smaller investments from individual investors to meet institutional minimums. Technology infrastructure provides digital onboarding, portfolio management, and reporting systems that replace traditional paper-based processes. Regulatory compliance services navigate complex securities regulations across multiple jurisdictions while providing investor protection mechanisms.

Revenue models vary across platforms but typically include management fees charged to investors, often lower than those of traditional private banks,[2] revenue sharing arrangements with fund providers, and platform fees for technology services. These fee structures often represent lower total costs compared to traditional private banking relationships, though they introduce new intermediation layers between investors and fund managers.

iCapital's model is primarily business-to-business (B2B), offering its software-as-a-service (SaaS) platform to wealth managers and private banks, who in turn serve their clients. The platform earns revenue through fee-sharing arrangements with fund providers and financial institutions. Moonfare, by contrast, operates a direct-to-consumer model, managing its own feeder funds and charging management fees directly to individual investors. Titanbay and Private Corner blend these models, focusing on partnerships with advisors and wealth managers, while Opto Investments and Yieldstreet further diversify the landscape with unique approaches to product offerings and investor education.

The private wealth targeting has crystallized into four distinct structural approaches, each addressing different investor preferences and regulatory requirements. Interval funds ($78.8 billion AuM) and tender offer funds ($80.9 billion) focus on periodic liquidity windows, while non-listed BDCs ($115.1 billion) and REITs ($106.4 billion) emphasize income generation with limited redemption features (Pitchbook, 2024). These vehicles typically offer minimum investments ranging from $1,000 to 50,000—dramatically lower than traditional PE minimums—while providing varying degrees of

[2] While platform fees are often lower than those of private banks, total costs (including underlying fund fees) should still be considered by investors.

liquidity, fee structures, and regulatory oversight tailored to individual investor sophistication levels.

Structural Implications for the Industry and Comparison with Private Banking Platform intermediation introduces new dependencies and potential points of failure in PE capital formation. Unlike direct LP-GP relationships, platform-mediated investments create additional layers of legal structure, operational risk, and potential conflicts of interest. Platform business models may prioritize revenue generation over investor suitability, particularly when targeting retail investors unfamiliar with PE complexities.

The aggregation model also concentrates investor flows through relatively few platforms, potentially creating systemic risks if platforms experience operational difficulties or if their business models prove unsustainable during market downturns. The sector's relative youth means long-term viability remains untested through full market cycles.

Investing in PE through a private bank has traditionally involved far higher minimums—often €1 million or more-along with bespoke advisory services and less transparent fee structures. Investors relied heavily on the expertise and discretion of their bankers, with limited visibility into fund selection and underlying costs. The process was paper-heavy, slow, and often reserved for the wealthiest clients.

In contrast, technology platforms have lowered minimums dramatically, sometimes to as little as €10,000 or even $500 (Figure 4.5), and offer a digital, streamlined experience. Investors benefit from transparent dashboards, standardized reporting, and curated fund selections, often with lower fees. The platforms' use of feeder funds and digital workflows not only reduces administrative overhead but also makes PE accessible to a much broader audience. Furthermore, the democratization of access has prompted private banks to adapt, with many now partnering with platforms like iCapital or developing their own digital solutions.

Is that a good thing? It is a controversial topic, and we will raise it again.

Market Impact and Access to Healthcare Investments The emergence of technology platforms has expanded the investor base beyond institutions and ultra-wealthy

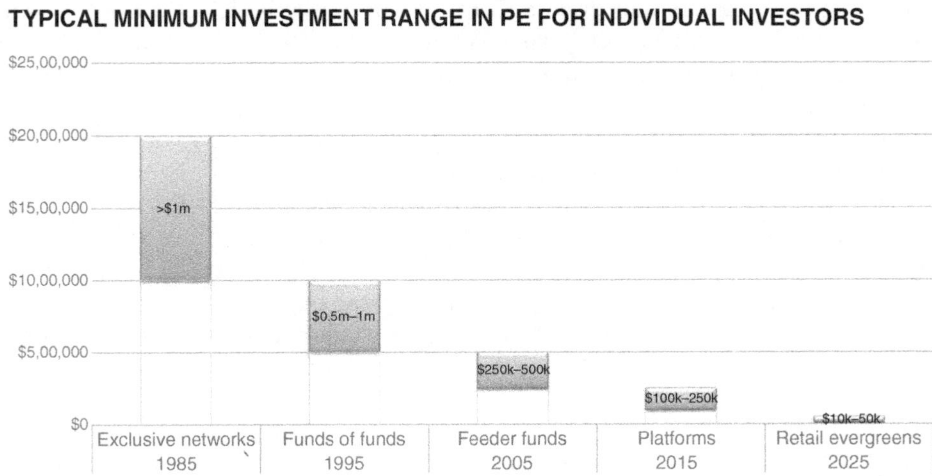

FIGURE 4.5 Lowering the entry ticket for individual investors.
Source: Candesic research.

families to include mass-affluent individuals and their advisors. While proponents argue this expansion has increased transparency, efficiency, and competition, critics point to potential risks for less sophisticated investors and questions about long-term market stability.

Collectively, these platforms appear to manage or facilitate access to substantial private market assets, representing a potentially significant development in PE distribution, though the permanence and sustainability of this transformation remain to be established through full market cycles.

Over time, the platforms have widened their offering and started to provide access to sector-focused funds, including those in healthcare.

A notable example is the partnership between iCapital and AXA IM Alts, which launched the Global Health Private Equity strategy on the iCapital platform. This fund is specifically focused on healthcare innovation, investing in areas such as medical devices, biopharmaceuticals, vaccines, and diagnostics. The strategy aims to provide exposure to private healthcare companies delivering accessible healthcare solutions globally. It also seeks to align with impact goals, addressing United Nations Sustainable Development Goals related to health and equality.

Risks Significant risks are associated with expanded access to PE through digital platforms, particularly regarding less sophisticated retail investors. PE investments are inherently illiquid and complex, characteristics that may be poorly understood by individual investors accustomed to liquid public markets. Platform-mediated investments can suffer from information asymmetries compared to public markets, where pricing, fees, and underlying investment details may be less readily available or more difficult for inexperienced investors to interpret.

Regulatory oversight remains limited in many jurisdictions, potentially inadequate for protecting retail investors from risks they may not fully comprehend. This regulatory gap increases the likelihood of misunderstandings about investment terms, liquidity constraints, and risk characteristics. Such misalignments could result in liquidity pressures if retail investors attempt to exit investments during market stress, potentially creating broader market disruptions.

Platform dependency also introduces operational risks. Investors relying on platforms for access, reporting, and liquidity may find themselves disadvantaged if platforms experience financial difficulties, operational failures, or changes in business strategy. The sector's relative immaturity means these risks remain largely untested.

A potential selection bias may emerge if platforms increasingly target retail investors as more sophisticated investors reduce their allocations to the asset class. This could raise further suitability and reputational risks, particularly given that most retail investors rarely read the full prospectus.

Digital platforms have expanded access to PE investments through technological infrastructure and capital aggregation models, potentially altering the distribution landscape. However, this expansion raises important questions about investor protection, market stability, and the appropriateness of illiquid investments for retail participants. Ludovic Phalipppou in particular has repeatedly warned regulators and the wider public about excessive cumulative fees, misunderstood historical performance, exaggerated liquidity, and a potential looming disaster. As regulation and investor experience develop, the sector will likely continue evolving, with both opportunities and challenges for platforms and investors alike.

4.2.3.7 Strategic Outlook and Future of PE Fundraising Leading asset managers have committed substantial resources to capture this private wealth opportunity, fundamentally restructuring their organizations beyond traditional institutional focus. Apollo exemplifies this transformation, expanding its private wealth team from minimal staffing to 150 professionals between 2019 and 2024—a 10-fold increase reflecting the operational intensity required to serve thousands of individual investors versus dozens of institutions, according to Pitchbook. This pattern extends across major platforms, with firms like Blackstone, KKR, and Blue Owl now deriving 20–40% of total AuM from perpetual capital structures, demonstrating how private wealth has evolved from supplementary to core revenue streams.

PE firms are developing broader product offerings and distribution capabilities as they adapt to changing investor demographics and regulatory environments. Table 4.1 provides a comparison of the basic features of the main vehicles while Table 4.2 provides a list of the main private wealth distribution alternatives. However, this evolution creates new challenges around operational complexity, regulatory compliance, and investor suitability.

Competition is intensifying. Fintech entrants, asset managers, and universal banks are all vying for dominance in the distribution race for alternative investments. For Moonfare, differentiation increasingly hinges on client experience, brand trust, regulatory sophistication, and operational resilience.

To remain competitive, GPs must invest in product innovation aligned with the evolving preferences of individual investors, including liquidity solutions, thematic portfolios, ESG alignment, and digital reporting interfaces. Tokenization and secondary liquidity platforms are also emerging as areas of strategic focus.

TABLE 4.1 Comparison of Institutional vs. Private Wealth Vehicles

Feature	Traditional PE Fund	Interval Fund (US)	ELTIF 2.0 (EU)
Liquidity	None	Quarterly (2–5%)	Conditional
Investor Type	Institutional	Accredited/Retail	Retail with €1k+
Regulatory Framework	AIFMD (EU), Exempt (US)	40 Act (US)	ELTIF Regulation (EU)
Reporting	Quarterly	Monthly/Quarterly	Semi-Annual
Minimum Investment	$5 million+	$25,000–$100,000	€1,000+

Source: SEC, ESMA, Blackstone and ELTIF Regulation websites

TABLE 4.2 Private Wealth Distribution Ecosystem

Channel	Role
Wirehouses (e.g., Morgan Stanley)	Mass affluent access via financial advisors
RIAs	Independent advisors managing HNW clients
Digital Platforms (e.g., iCapital)	Aggregators; automate onboarding & reporting
Private Banks	Serve UHNW clients with bespoke portfolios

Source: iCapital Network website

Brand credibility and investor trust have become essential as retail investors allocate capital to illiquid vehicles. This requires firms to operate with transparency and accountability standards typically associated with consumer-facing financial institutions, representing a significant departure from traditional institutional-focused practices.

Over the next decade, the central strategic question will be whether the shift toward private wealth becomes a stable second pillar of PE fundraising or proves cyclically fragile. PE firms will need to demonstrate that semi-liquid and evergreen structures can withstand periods of market stress without resorting to gatekeeping, side-pockets, or ad hoc suspensions that damage trust and draw regulatory scrutiny.

At the same time, competition for private wealth is likely to intensify as universal banks, asset managers, and fintech platforms converge on the same client base. Success will depend less on engineering ever more complex products and more on building scalable operating models, credible governance, and genuinely investor-centric economics that can survive closer public, media, and regulatory attention than the industry has historically faced.

For Guy Semmens, co-founder of Gyrus Capital,

> *There is no reason why HNWI investors should not get access to PE but once you are in you do not get out. The democratization of PE is squeezing the Funds-of-funds to save the fees but opens the door to people who don't understand the mechanics of PE and there is a substantial risk here. PE is complex and should be left to professionals. The FOF ought to be the gateway for HNWIs—otherwise regulation of less sophisticated capital becomes important.*

4.2.4 Capital Structure Models

The capital structure of a PE fund determines how the fund is financed and identifies its investors. Several models are commonly used in the industry:

- **Traditional Limited Partner Funds (Third-party Investor Funds)** are the most common model, where institutional investors, such as pension funds, endowments, and family offices, commit capital to be managed by the PE firm. These funds are structured with GPs who manage the fund and LPs who provide the capital. Blackstone and KKR both operate extensive limited partner structures with a wide range of institutional investors.
- **Captive Funds** are when a corporation or financial institution establishes its own PE fund, which is financed with the company's capital. These funds are typically used to make strategic investments aligned with the parent company's business interests. Like GE Capital previously, Intel Capital operates as a captive fund, investing in startups and companies that can benefit Intel's strategic goals. An interesting alternative motivation is to leverage the entrepreneurial spirit of employees, funding internal venture projects that would be too early stage for the company but could be acquired and reintegrated as a core business in case of successful development. Captive funds managers do not usually charge any management fees.

- **Captive Funds with External Limited Partners (Hybrid Funds)** provide a variation of the captive fund model. This structure involves a parent company—also called a sponsor, which can be a family office, insurance company, asset management firm, etc.—creating a PE fund that also raises capital from external investors, including institutional investors or high-net-worth individuals. This approach allows the parent company to leverage outside capital while maintaining significant control over the fund's operations. Goldman Sachs and Morgan Stanley have both used this model for some of their PE activities, combining internal and external capital.
- **Independent Funds with Shared Ownership (Spinout Funds)** emerge when formerly captive funds become independent, often a result of a management buyout or strategic divestiture. The management team may retain minority ownership, or external investors may purchase stakes. This approach allows the fund to operate independently while benefiting from its previous association with the parent organization. In the United States, firms like Vista Equity Partners started as captive or semi-captive entities before fully establishing themselves as independent PE powerhouses. In Europe in particular, the model was extremely common in the 1990s when most financial institutions decided to spinout their principal investing activities, due to the joint pressure of regulators worried about the nature of the risk and PE clients unwilling to compete with their suppliers of advisory, financing, and administrative services. Most people have forgotten or never knew the origins of Bridgepoint (Natwest), Charterhouse (Charterhouse Bank), CVC (Citibank), Equistone (Barclays), Montagu (HSBC), One Equity Partners (JPMorgan), Permira (Schroder), Terra Firma (Nomura), or West Street Capital Partners (Goldman Sachs). Unlike captive funds, independent funds are usually closed-ended. This means that once the fund has raised capital, no further commitments are accepted from third parties. Typically, third-party commitments expire according to a timescale based on a use-it-or-lose-it principle once a maximum drawdown period expires.
- **Direct Investment Funds** are typically managed by large institutional investors like sovereign wealth funds, pension funds, or even insurance companies, which choose to bypass traditional PE funds and invest directly in companies. This allows them to avoid management fees and carry interest associated with typical PE funds. The Canada Pension Plan Investment Board and Singapore's GIC often engage in direct investments, deploying significant capital without intermediaries.

Each of these models has its own implications for control, investor relationships, and the degree of independence from the parent company or external investors.

4.2.5 Organizational and Compensation Models

The structure and incentives of a PE firm are crucial for aligning interests and ensuring performance. This includes team structures and compensation mechanisms.

PE firms can adopt different organizational models, from centralized structures where decisions are made collectively, to more decentralized models where individual partners or teams manage specific investments. The choice of structure can affect decision-making speed, risk management, and the distribution of profits.

4.2.5.1 Fees An important aspect of the set-up of funds is deciding what fees will be paid to whom. Compensation in PE is typically composed of management fees and carried interest. But first, how did these fees originate? In some sense, they date back to ancient times, when, typically, a merchant and an investor agreed on a fee and a share of the bounty. Thousands of years ago, funders would offer captains a modest fee to manage the voyage and allow them to take about a fifth of the bounty when they returned. The practice spread in Asia as well as in the Mediterranean world, then in medieval and Renaissance Italy.

> *If you were going to operate a ship and drive it from, say, the New World back to Europe with some valuable cargo, you and the captain of the ship would keep an interest of 20% for whatever you carried. So it's called the carried interest.*[3]

We still see this 20% fee in PE, and our fees model has very deep roots.

The annual management fees were historically around 2% of either committed or drawn-down capital. While they sometimes reach 5% of the committed capital, the trend has been down—slightly below 2%. They have decreased in the 2020s due to a combination of discounts and the rise of co-investments that by-pass the fees.

Carry is about 20% of the proportion of the performance above a certain hurdle that goes to the GPs. The hurdle will generally be between 5% and 8% ROI. In environments with very low risk-free rates, it might be a little bit lower.

The industry norm is to charge management fees on all committed capital. In 2015, Terra Firma Chairman and CIO Guy Hands announced that the firm would only charge investors on money that has been invested in deals, an approach described as a "radical break with industry conventions" by the *Financial Times*.

Other costs include transaction costs, monitoring costs, and costs for paying non-executive directors, as well as potentially unspecified costs, such as those for travel, subsistence, or advisors for legal auditing or taxes or requirements for bridge financing or contractual bias in favor of the GP. Moreover, costs might be incurred from ignoring unrealized gains and losses and focusing only on the realized investments.

The IRRs discussed in the previous session can be easily manipulated and diluted by significant fund management fees and expenses. So, the net of all those fees should be included in the calculation of the management fee and should not increase the overall rewards of the PE fund managers, which makes it quite complicated.

4.2.5.2 Waterfall Structures: European vs. American PE distribution models typically follow one of two main "waterfall" structures: the European waterfall and the American waterfall, each defining how and when profits are shared between LPs and the GP.

The American waterfall, or "deal-by-deal" model, allows the GP to receive carried interest on individual profitable deals as soon as they clear the hurdle rate, without waiting for the entire fund to achieve a full return of capital. While this permits earlier GP remuneration, it introduces the risk that investors might not be made whole if later deals underperform. To mitigate this, American-style funds often include a clawback provision, requiring the GP to return excess carried interest if, upon final liquidation, LPs have not received their full entitlement.

---

[3] *Source:* The Family.

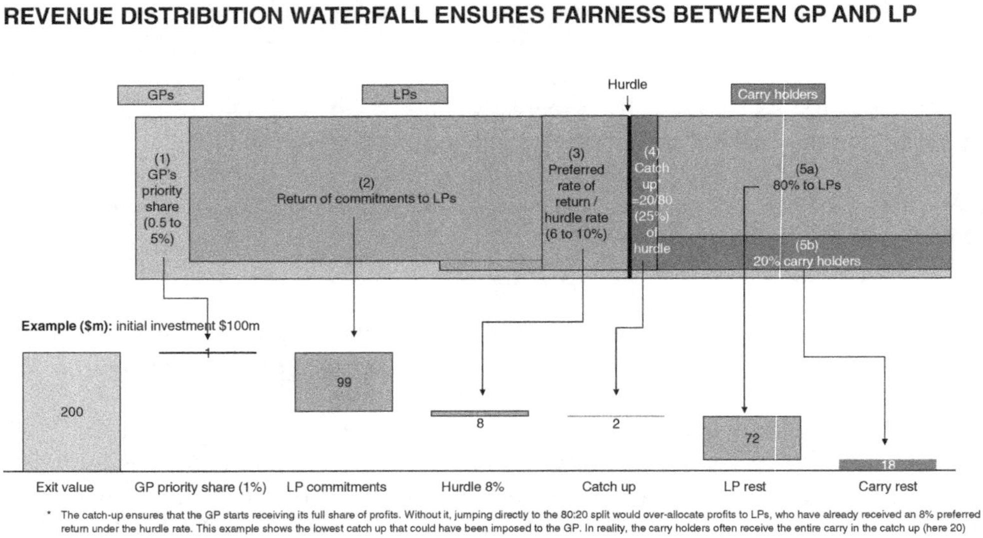

FIGURE 4.6 American waterfall.
Source: Adam Frais; Candesic analysis.

Figure 4.6 is the diagram of an American (or hybrid) waterfall that shows how we progress from the proceeds from the sale of investment to the profit that we split between the GP and the LP. There are four or five steps to this. In step 1, the GP first receives a priority share of the partnership returns each year. Then, in step 2, the investors are reimbursed 100% of their initial capital commitments, and in step 3 they earn a preferred rate of return, typically around 8%. Upon achieving this preferred rate (the hurdle), step 4 activates, where the GP enters the so-called "catch-up" phase, receiving 100% of distributions until they match an agreed percentage of the total preferred return to the investors. Finally, in step 5, any surplus profits are divided, with 80% going to the investors and 20% to the GP as carried interest.

In contrast, the European waterfall, also known as the "whole-of-fund" model or "global-style" schedule, is applied at an aggregate fund level. It is LP-friendly and widely adopted, particularly in Europe and increasingly in global funds. In a large sample of 2019 vintage funds, 88% of European funds and 40% of American funds had European waterfalls (MJ Hudson, 2021).

Under this model, LPs must first receive full return of their contributed capital plus the preferred return (typically 8%) before the GP is entitled to any carried interest. This approach ensures that investors are comprehensively compensated before any performance-based fees are paid to the GP, though it may delay the GP's incentive compensation until later in the fund's life: the majority of the manager's profits may not be realized for several years after the initial investment. This is less incentivizing in early years.

- LPs are first returned all their invested capital.
- Then LPs receive the full preferred return (usually 8% per annum).
- Once these hurdles are cleared, GPs receive 20% of the profits (carry), including a catch-up phase to rebalance past underpayments.

Please bear in mind that every waterfall structure can be subject to legal interpretation. Slight variations of interpretations can result in large differences. Each LPA is different, and close examination of the LPA is the only way to determine the specific terms of each component. For example, some LPAs return capital as first priority of distributions while others may pay preferred returns ahead of capital. GP catch-ups in particular are commonly miscalculated because it is easy to misinterpret the GP catch-up section (see EisnerAmper article).

Supercarry represents a significant deviation from the traditional PE fee structure, where GPs command carried interest rates exceeding the industry standard of 20%. These elevated carry rates, typically ranging from 25% to 30%, are usually implemented through tiered or ratchet structures that reward exceptional performance once specific hurdle rates or return thresholds are achieved (P+P Pöllath + Partners, 2016). Major PE firms including Bain Capital, the Carlyle Group, Vista Equity Partners, EQT Partners, and Eurazeo have successfully negotiated such arrangements in recent funds, leveraging their strong track records and market positioning (Primack, 2019; *Financial Times*, 2019). For instance, as shown on the Growth Equity Interview Guide website, a GP might earn the standard 20% carry until achieving a 2.0× money multiple, then escalate to 25% carry for returns between 2.0× and 2.5×, and ultimately reach 30% carry for returns exceeding 2.5×. Importantly, supercarry arrangements are often accompanied by lower management fees or offered as alternative investment structures, allowing LPs to choose between traditional "2 and 20" models versus reduced management fees with higher performance-based compensation—a structure designed to better align GP and LP interests while rewarding truly exceptional performance. The prevalence of supercarry reflects the competitive dynamics in PE fundraising, where established managers with proven track records can command premium terms from investors eager to access top-tier funds, though this trend has generated debate about fee escalation and appropriate alignment of interests between GPs and LPs.

4.2.5.3 Allocation Model The compensation structure will also depend on the allocation models. The structure of these payments can vary significantly. For example, KKR used to pool all fees and carry for all the partners and all the employees and allocate them based on individual performance, while Apax Partners pre-allocated carry at fund closing to split it equally within each class of partners, and CVC allocated carry on a deal-by-deal basis, more of an eat-what-you-kill type of system. These models reflect different philosophies about teamwork, risk-sharing, and rewarding individual contributions. PE firms may change their model over time, but the diversity remains.

Both models aim to align the interests of GPs and LPs by emphasizing investor returns, but they differ significantly in the timing and risk allocation of profit sharing. The choice of structure can influence fundraising, deal pacing, and internal economics of the fund.

4.2.5.4 Carried Interest and Waterfall Calculations

Exercise 1: MedGrowth Healthcare Capital III
Fund Details

- Fund size: $500 million
- Management fee: 2% per annum (on committed capital for years 1–5, then on cost basis)—assumes fee paid after exit to avoid mid-period cash-flow timing.
- Carried interest (carry): 20% (after an 8% preferred return hurdle—hard hurdle)

- Investment period: 5 years
- Holding period: 5 years (exit in Year 10)
- Fund lifespan: 10 years

Investment Scenario

- The fund invests \$200 million in HealthCo, a fast-growing healthcare services provider.
- After five years, HealthCo is sold for \$600 million, generating a 3× return.
- The fund has no other investments (for simplicity).

Questions

1. Calculate total management fees over fund life.
2. Calculate net proceeds available for distribution.
3. Apply a distribution waterfall with a hard hurdle rate and a full catch-up structure where GP gets 100% of next distributions until they reach their 20% share of total profits paid so far (including catch-up).
4. Calculate total carry.
5. Calculate the investment returns.

Solution to Exercise 1

Step 1: Calculate Total Management Fees Over Fund Life
Management fees are typically charged throughout the fund's life:

- Years 1–5 (Investment Period): 2% × \$500M = \$10M per year
- Years 6–10 (Harvest Period): 2% × \$200M (invested capital) = \$4M per year
- Total Management Fees over 10 Years: (5 × \$10M) + (5 × \$4M) = \$50M + \$20M = \$70M

Step 2: Calculate Net Proceeds Available for Distribution

- Gross Exit Proceeds: \$600M
- Less: Management Fees: \$70M
- Net Proceeds for Distribution: \$600M – \$70M = \$530M

Step 3: Apply Distribution Waterfall
Tier 1: Return of Capital to LPs

- Return the initial \$200M investment to LPs first
- Remaining After Capital Return: \$530M – \$200M = \$330M

Tier 2: Preferred Return to LPs (8% Hurdle)

- LPs receive 8% annual compounded return on their \$200M investment over five years
- Preferred Return Calculation: \$200M times [(1.08)^5 – 1] = \$200M times 0.4693 = \$93.86M
- Remaining After Preferred Return: \$330M – \$93.86M = \$236.14M

Tier 3: GP Catch-up (Full Catch-up)

- Total profit above capital = $330M
- GP's 20% entitlement = 20% times 330M = $66M
- GP gets 100% of next distributions until $66M is paid
- Remaining = $236.14M – $66M = $170.14M

Tier 4: Remaining Split 80/20

- LP share = 80% times 170.14M = $136.11M
- GP share = 20% times 170.14M = $34.03M

Step 4: Total Carry Calculation

- GP Catch-up = $66M
- GP Split Share = $34.03M
- Total GP Carry = $100.03M

Step 5: Final Distribution Summary

Component	LPs ($M)	GP ($M)	Total ($M)
Return of Capital	$200.00	$0.00	$200.00
Preferred Return (8%)	$93.86	$0.00	$93.86
Catch-up	$0.00	$66.00	$66.00
Remaining Profits (80/20)	**$136.11**	**$34.03**	**$170.14**
Management Fees	$0.00	$70.00	$70.00
TOTAL	**$429.97**	**$170.03**	**$600.00**

Step 6: Calculate Investment Returns

- LP Net Proceeds (after fees & carry): $429.97M
- Capital committed: $500M
- Capital actually drawn: $200M

So:

- MOIC on committed = 429.97 ÷ 500 = 0.86 times
- MOIC on drawn = 429.97 ÷ 200 = 2.15 times
- LP IRR (200 → 429.97 in five years): (429.97 ÷ 200)^(1/5) – 1 ≈ 16.0%
- GP Compensation: Carry $100.03M + Fees $70M = $170.03M
- Gross MOIC (before fees & carry): 600 ÷ 200 = 3.0 times
- Gross IRR: ≈ 24.6% annually over five years

This shows how the **hard hurdle protects LPs** by requiring their 8% annual return before GP is paid, while the **full catch-up rewards the GP generously once the hurdle is met.** The GP ends up with $100M in carry on one deal—highlighting how powerful the catch-up phase can be.

Exercise 2: MedGrowth Evaluating Two Different Carried Interest Structures
Structure A: 25% carry calculated on committed capital basis
Structure B: 20% carry calculated on invested capital basis

Fund Parameters

- Committed capital: $500 million
- Annual management fee: 2.0% of committed capital
- Fund life: 10 years

Questions

1. Compare the carry for each structure when the fund has no hurdle rate and the total distributions are $800 million.
2. What is the breakeven total distribution amount between the two structures in the absence of hurdle?
3. Compare the carry for each structure when the fund has an 8% hurdle rate and the total distributions are $1,500 million.
4. What is the breakeven total distribution amount between the two structures in the case of the 8% hurdle?

Solution to exercise 2

Question 1: Carry comparison at $800M total distributions and no hurdle

Annual management fee = 2.0% × $500M = $10M per year

Total lifetime management fees = $10M × 10 years = $100M

Invested Capital = Committed Capital – Total Management Fees Invested Capital = $500M – $100M = $400M

Assuming total cumulative distributions over 10 years = $800M

Structure A (25% carry on committed capital basis):

- Profit calculation = $800M – $500M = $300M
- Carried interest = 25% × $300M = $75M

Structure B (20% carry on invested capital basis):

- Profit calculation = $800M – $400M = $400M
- Carried interest = 20% × $400M = $80M

Analysis: Structure B generates higher carry ($80M vs. $75M) because the lower capital basis allows carry to accrue more quickly, offsetting the reduced carry percentage.

Question 2: Breakeven distribution analysis with no hurdle

To find the distribution level where both structures yield equal carry:

Let X = total distribution amount

Structure A carry = Structure B carry (X – $500M) × 0.25 = (X – $400M) times 0.20

Solving for X: 0.25X – $125M = 0.20X – $80M 0.05X = $45M X = $900M

Interpretation: At total distributions of $900M, both carry structures provide identical compensation to the GP. Above $900M in total distributions, the GP would prefer Structure A (higher carry rate), while below $900M, Structure B (lower basis) is more advantageous.

Question 3: Carry comparison at $1,500M total distributions and 8% hurdle

Hurdle Rate Calculation

The 8% annual hurdle rate creates minimum return thresholds that must be met before carry is earned:

Structure A hurdle threshold = $500M × (1.08)^10 = $500M × 2.159 = $1,079.5M
Structure B hurdle threshold = $400M × (1.08)^10 = $400M times 2.159 = $863.6M

Assuming total cumulative distributions over 10 years = $1,500M

Structure A (25% carry on committed capital basis):

- Distributions above hurdle = $1,500M – $1,079.5M = $420.5M
- Carried interest = 25% × $420.5M = $105.1M

Structure B (20% carry on invested capital basis):

- Distributions above hurdle = $1,500M – $863.6M = $636.4M
- Carried interest = 20% × $636.4M = $127.3M

Analysis: At $1,500M distributions, Structure B generates higher carry ($127.3M vs. $105.1M) due to its lower hurdle threshold, despite the reduced carry percentage.

Question 4: Breakeven distribution analysis with 8% hurdle

To find the distribution level where both structures yield equal carry (above their respective hurdles):

Let X = total distribution amount

For distributions above both hurdle thresholds: Structure A carry = Structure B carry (X – $1,079.5M) × 0.25 = (X – $863.6M) × 0.20

Solving for X: 0.25X – $269.9M = 0.20X – $172.7M 0.05X = $97.2M X = $1,944M

Interpretation: At total distributions of $1,944M, both carry structures provide identical compensation to the GP ($216.1M each). Above $1,944M, the GP would prefer Structure A (higher carry rate), while between the hurdle thresholds and $1,944M, Structure B is more advantageous.

Key Impact of 8% Hurdle Rate: The hurdle significantly increases the breakeven point from $900M (without hurdle) to $1,944M (with hurdle), and eliminates carry entirely for distributions below $863.6M–$1,079.5M range.

Exercise 3: Comparing American and European waterfall structures

This exercise shows how profit distributions differ under the American (deal-by-deal) and European (fund-as-a-whole) waterfall models.

The purpose is to highlight how the **timing and amount of GP carry** changes depending on whether distributions are calculated per deal or across the full fund.

Fund Overview

To illustrate the mechanics, we assume the fund invests in two companies with very different outcomes:

- **Investment 1 (HealthCo):** $200M invested, later sold for $600M (profit $400M)
- **Investment 2 (MediHalf):** $300M invested, later sold for $250M (loss $50M)
- **Total proceeds:** $850M, so the fund overall makes a net profit of $350M.

Other assumptions:

- Carried interest: 20%
- Hurdle rate: 8% per annum (hard hurdle, compounded, over five years)
- Carry mechanic: Full catch-up (GP takes 100% of cash flow until their share of overall profits is reached)
- Management fees: Ignored in this example to keep the focus on the waterfall itself.

Step 1: Preferred Return (Hurdle)

Before the GP can receive any carry, LPs must first receive both their invested capital and their hurdle return. Over five years, the 8% annual compound return amounts to:

- On $200M (HealthCo): **$93.86M**
- On $300M (MediHalf): **$140.79M**
- **Total hurdle return required:** $234.65M

This hurdle serves as a **minimum performance threshold** that protects LPs. Only after this return is paid does the GP begin to earn carried interest.

Step 2: American Waterfall (Deal-by-deal)

Under the American model, each investment is treated separately. The GP can earn carry on a winning deal without waiting for the rest of the portfolio to be realized.

Investment 1: HealthCo ($200M → $600M)

1. LPs first recover their $200M capital.
2. LPs then receive their hurdle return of $93.86M.
3. The GP enters the **catch-up phase** and receives $80M (20% of the $400M profit).
4. The remaining $226.14M is split 80/20, giving $180.91M to LPs and $45.23M to the GP.

Result HealthCo: LPs = $474.77M, GP = $125.23M.

At this stage, the GP has already crystallized substantial carry, even though the fund is only halfway through its life.

Investment 2: MediHalf ($300M → $250M)

Here the picture changes. The investment returns less than the capital put in.

- All $250M goes back to LPs as a partial return of capital.
- There is no surplus to pay the hurdle, and therefore no carry for the GP.

Result MediHalf: LPs = **$250M,** GP = **$0M.**

American Totals

- LPs = **$724.77M**
- GPs = **$125.23M**
- **Grand Total** = **$850M**

Interpretation

The GP already secured $125M from the first deal. The later loss did not affect that payout. Unless a clawback mechanism is enforced at the end of the fund's life, LPs effectively bear the downside while GPs keep their early carry. This is why the American model is considered **GP-friendly**.

Step 3: European Waterfall (Fund-as-a-whole)
In the European model, all proceeds are pooled, and the waterfall is applied at the **fund level**. This ensures that GPs only earn carry if the **entire fund** clears the hurdle.

1. LPs recover their full $500M capital first.
2. LPs then receive their hurdle return of $234.65M. At this point, from the $350M total profit, only $115.35M remains after paying LPs their preferred return.
3. GP enters catch-up: they are entitled to 20% of total profits ($70M). They receive this amount.
4. The final $45.35M is split 80/20: LPs $36.28M, GP $9.07M.

European Totals

- LPs = **$770.93M**
- GPs = **$79.07M**
- **Grand Total** = **$850M**

Interpretation

Because the second investment underperformed, the fund overall only just cleared the hurdle. The GPs' carry is reduced to $79M—significantly less than the $125M they collected under the American system.

Step 4: Comparison & Lessons

Structure	LPs ($M)	GPs ($M)	Comment
American	724.77	125.23	GP crystallizes carry early from HealthCo, unaffected by MediHalf's later loss
European	770.93	79.07	GP's carry reduced because fund performance as a whole matters

- **American:** GP-friendly. Carry is paid on each profitable deal. If early wins are followed by later losses, GPs can still walk away with large payouts.
- **European:** LP-friendly. Carry is only paid if the whole fund performs above hurdle, protecting investors from overpaying carry on partial success.
- **Key insight:** Both structures produced the same overall fund result ($850M). But the **distribution between LP and GP differs dramatically** depending on the waterfall model chosen.

Note on Clawback Provisions

In practice, American waterfalls are usually combined with a **clawback clause.** A clawback requires the GP to return excess carried interest if, at the end of the fund's life, they have received more carry than they are ultimately entitled to on a whole-fund basis.

- **Why it matters:** Without clawback, the GP in an American structure could keep carry from early successful exits even if later deals lose money and the fund underperforms.
- **How it works:** At fund termination, the total carry entitlement is recalculated based on the **final overall profits.** If the GP has been overpaid relative to that final entitlement, they must refund the difference to the LPs.
- **Practical issues:** Clawback is protective in theory, but in practice it can be hard to enforce (e.g., if distributions have already been spent by individual partners). For this reason, many LPs prefer the European waterfall, where carry is naturally deferred until the fund as a whole clears the hurdle.

4.2.6 Investment and Value Creation Models

The approach to finding investment opportunities and creating value from them is central to the success of any PE fund. We retrieve here the PE investment cycle. Apologies for insisting on it, but in theory, all PE investors should excel in each step:

- **Deal Sourcing:** PE firms must have a robust strategy for sourcing deals, which includes leveraging networks, industry expertise, and market research. The ability to identify undervalued or high-potential companies is a key differentiator in the competitive PE landscape.
- **Value Creation:** Beyond simply acquiring companies, PE firms must have a clear strategy for enhancing the value of their portfolio companies. This can involve operational improvements, strategic repositioning, financial restructuring, or preparing the company for an eventual sale. The ultimate goal is to exit investments at a higher value than the initial purchase price, generating returns for the investors.
- **Exit Strategies:** The process of exiting investments, whether through IPOs, sales to strategic buyers, or secondary buyouts, is where the value created is realized. A well-planned exit strategy is critical for maximizing returns and managing the fund's overall performance.

Remember how understanding these organizational issues is crucial for anyone involved in setting up or managing a PE fund, as they define the operational framework within which the fund will operate.

4.2.7 Main Fund Documentation

There are typically four to six main documents.

The **Offering Memorandum,** also called Private Placement Memorandum, is a document issued by the GP on behalf of the fund to prospective investors. The extent to which it may constitute any sort of contractual undertaking is a grey area. At one extreme, it can be argued that it is incorporated by reference into the LPA. Despite legal boilerplate, it might also be subject to public offering regulations. At other extreme, it can be considered just a marketing document.

The **LPA or Limited Partnership Agreement** is the key document. It is a long (often more than 200 pages) contract between all the LPs and the GP establishing the fund and defining each party's rights and liabilities. If something is not mentioned in the LPA, it is irrelevant.

The **IMA or Investment Management Agreement** is a contract between the fund and the GP management entity. It sets out entitlement to management fee and carry (though carry often goes to a separate vehicle under a separate agreement). No fault divorce is customary.

The **subscription agreement** is the contract between the fund and its investors (LPs), specifying the terms under which the investors agree to commit capital to the fund. It includes representations and warranties from the investor, confirms the amount of capital committed, and outlines the payment schedule for capital contributions. The subscription agreement also typically includes important regulatory and tax-related disclosures that the investor must acknowledge.

If the PE fund is structured with a separate management company, an **operating agreement** will govern the management company's internal operations. This agreement outlines the ownership structure, the roles and responsibilities of the management team, decision-making processes, profit distribution, and other governance matters. It ensures that the management company operates in a manner consistent with the fund's objectives and the interests of the investors.

Finally, **Side Letters** are sometimes given to specific LPs confirming that certain terms will or will not apply as against them. Legally, this is very unsatisfactory as it is typically used to get around an amendment to the LPA. An investor must systematically ask to see all side letters that have been issued.

Here is a typical extract of key terms in an LPA (Phalippou, 2021):

- Up to [10%] of total commitments (TC) may be invested in quoted securities or convertible into quoted securities, and in debt-related instruments …
- No investment in excess of [15%] of the TC in the securities of any single Portfolio company …
- Up to 50% of the TC may be invested outside of [the USA] …
- … no investment in any company engaged in [war material], [oil and gas exploration], [tobacco-related products], [business of gambling (unless they have the required license!)], [production of pornography], [child labor], [incorporated in Japan, except if it is a non-hostile transaction], etc.
- Key man clause if, during the investment period, [GP] is unable to devote the majority of his business time and fewer than [3 of the other 5] Principals are unavailable, GP must nominate suitable replacement …

What about terms and restrictions specific to healthcare and life sciences?

Given the heavily regulated nature of healthcare and life sciences, the LPA may include specific provisions requiring compliance with relevant healthcare regulations, such as the US Food and Drug Administration (FDA) regulations, European Medicines Agency (EMA) guidelines, or other local regulatory bodies. The LPA may detail additional risk management protocols, including regular assessments of regulatory risks, clinical trial risks, and market risks associated with healthcare investments. Given the sensitive nature of healthcare and life sciences, the LPA may also include ethical investment guidelines. These could restrict investments in areas that are controversial or ethically challenging, such as certain types of clinical trials, genetic manipulation, or investments in countries with poor regulatory oversight. The LPA may even outline flexible exit strategies. This could include provisions for holding periods that extend beyond the typical PE fund duration to accommodate the long timelines often required for successful exits in life sciences.

Outside of the LPA, strategic investors, such as large pharmaceutical companies or healthcare systems, may negotiate side letters for preferential treatment. These might include co-investment rights, early access to deal flow, or specialized reporting on regulatory developments affecting the fund's portfolio.

Finally, the fund will often establish a (specialized) scientific advisory board with healthcare or life sciences experts to provide oversight and guidance on investments. The structure and role of this board may be detailed in the fund's operating agreements or other governing documents.

4.3 SOURCING DEALS

One of the key ways to add value in the investment process is to source the right investment opportunities. When sourcing a deal, GPs may benefit from a certain level of expertise in a geographical region, an industry sector, or a corporate function. Or perhaps your specialty will be related to the size of the deal—scouting a company that has a \$10 million turnover is not the same as scouting a company with a \$10 billion turnover. Whatever the case, the ability to source the appropriate deals is a driver of value creation. But where do they come from? Figure 4.7 proposes a continuum of sourcing situations from fully competitive to proprietary (more desirable).

Sourcing high-quality deals is a critical differentiator in a competitive PE environment, where there is typically an excess of capital pursuing too few opportunities. While intimate knowledge and expertise in a particular industry sector, business model, or geography are valuable, they are often not sufficient to source the right deal at the right price.

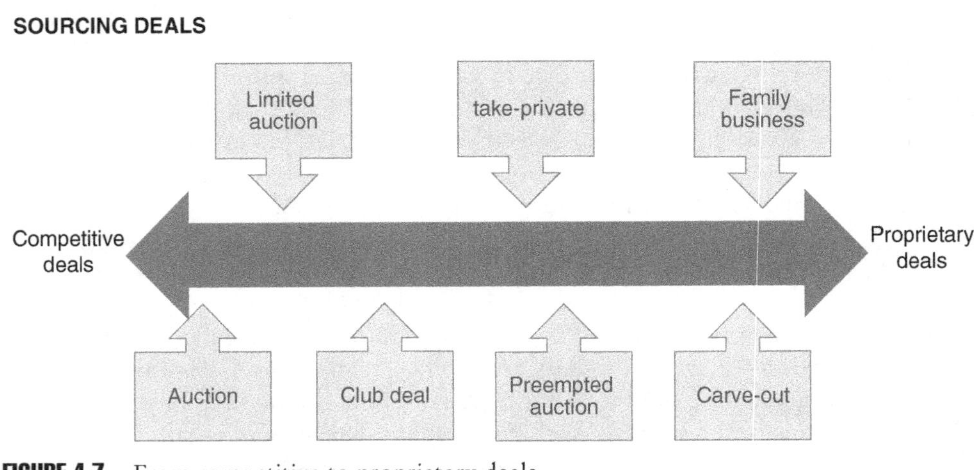

FIGURE 4.7 From competitive to proprietary deals.

Therefore, investors actively seek proprietary, bilateral, or less competitive situations, for example by engaging with a family owner who values discretion and a trusted partner over the publicity and uncertainty of a broad auction. Many PE investors claim to pursue only proprietary deals. While there are exceptions, it is often an exaggeration, partially motivated to convince LPs during fundraising. However, the ability to genuinely source such opportunities is directly tied to a GP's reputation.

Systematically seeking proprietary deals can backfire: some sellers may enter bilateral discussions solely to secure an initial offer, which they then use as a stalking horse to shop the deal to other bidders. Building a longstanding relationship mitigates this risk.

At GHO, it takes an average of 18 months to build a relationship and actually close the deal. Mike Mortimer reckons that

> *... seventy percent of our deals are proprietary or bilateral. Our two largest deals were proprietary with teams that reached out to us directly. We only go for bank processes if we have a clear competitive angle.*

These metrics demonstrate the intensely relationship-driven nature of specialized healthcare investing. The 18-month timeline appears to contrast sharply with auction processes that can close in three to six months but consistently yields higher-quality opportunities with substantially less competition. Some investors however prepare up to several years before the sale process, as they need the access to the internal data to make an investment decision. Their level of preparation allows them to make a faster decision, within one or two weeks.

Miura, a Spanish mid-market PE fund active in healthcare and other sectors, sources 80% of its deals proprietarily. As Toni Torra explains: "For the remaining 20%, we work hard to build relationships with management and, more often than not, succeed in securing exclusivity."

Fremman Capital, a pan-European PE firm created in 2020, is another one of those outliers who really focus on proprietary deals and succeed at it. As of mid-2025, from eleven investments in their debut fund, eight had been sourced without the pain of a competitive process. Six of the investments were in healthcare. Palex, Medinet, HT Medica, and Diesse were proprietary deals, while Rehaneo and Amethyst were acquired in limited auctions.

The team shared their approach for Palex' proprietary transaction:

> *Fremman had identified the MedTech sector as attractive and overlapping with the team's experience. Through a market screening, Fremman identified and approached several potential sector consolidators, with Palex standing out as the most interesting opportunity. The company was the Iberian market leader operating in the attractive and growing MedTech sector. It had a proven track record of organic and inorganic growth, was well diversified both in terms of customers and suppliers, with significant barriers to entry, and was well positioned to lead further consolidation of the European market. The company had an excellent management team widely recognised across the industry. Ricardo de Serdio was introduced to Palex's CEO through a mutual personal connection and set out his vision for Palex, the sector and Palex's potential role as a consolidator, which resulted in him and the Fremman team developing a strong and close relationship with the CEO and the company's management*

team. Palex's management team had ambitious growth plans (continue Iberian consolidation and international expansion) and considered Fremman the right partner to help them achieve these objectives. With the management team's backing, Fremman then convinced the then financial shareholders to engage with Fremman on a fully bilateral and off-market basis. In December 2021, Fremman acquired Palex in a fully proprietary transaction and became the majority shareholder of the company.

ARCHIMED regularly mentions in public disclosures and news releases their MedDiscover and MedValue proprietary tools. MedDiscover is designed to identify and approach leading companies operating in their prioritized healthcare subsectors. It enables systematic sector analysis, tracking hundreds of subsegments worldwide to spot high-potential investment opportunities. For example, ARCHIMED used MedDiscover to identify and engage companies like Irrimax and BioVendor, facilitating acquisitions through its MED Platform funds.

Over 20 years, Ampersand developed internal business development capabilities including trade shows, cold calling, and networking. They maintain a comprehensive database of healthcare assets and typically track companies for multiple years before initiating investment processes. This longitudinal approach provides cycle-aware perspectives and enables quick elimination of unsuitable opportunities.

The investment process follows a gated structure with continuous evolution. Starting with business development, deals proceed through deal team screening, exploratory investment committee (IC) votes, negotiation phases with additional votes, LOI[4] signing, and due diligence with subcommittee involvement. The process requires three formal votes plus intermediary IC and deal team engagements before closing.

Ampersand's investment criteria reveal a deliberate focus on execution risk over market risk. By systematically avoiding management buy-ins, turnarounds, and companies facing binary regulatory outcomes, they concentrate their efforts on operational improvement rather than financial engineering.

For Abrar Mir, the true driver of value is the essential quality of the business itself:

In the end, you want to own companies not because of clever structures or market timing, but because their fundamentals set them apart from the rest. Quality reveals itself in businesses that are leaders in fast-emerging sectors—leadership that must be defined with precision, segment by segment and geography by geography.

[4] The Letter of Intent (LOI) is a preliminary, usually nonbinding document exchanged in M&A transactions, outlining core terms like price, structure, and timeline before parties dive deeper into due diligence and final agreements. It's rarely legally binding, except for confidentiality or exclusivity, but it serves as formal evidence of intent and shapes negotiations. The Non-binding Offer (NBO) is a cousin to the LOI—an initial written proposal put forward by a buyer, stating headline terms without legal commitment and aiming to spark negotiations. The NBO often precedes the LOI, signaling serious interest and starting the process before everyone's ready for handshakes or lawyers.

It also emerges in markets where the imbalance between demand and supply is so profound that even significant capital deployment barely scratches the surface.

Mir adds:

> *The philosophy is simple: own businesses that endure. Businesses that can grow faster, withstand cycles and compound value over time. Price matters, but quality matters more. If you back companies with durable advantages, deep fundamentals and the ability to touch more lives than their peers, value creation becomes not a gamble but an inevitability.*

In any case, the reputation of the GP is a significant factor in attracting the best deals. As the market becomes more competitive and value creation opportunities become more elusive, this reputational capital becomes paramount. This dynamic enforces a unique level of accountability on PE investors. Eric Trüeb, co-founder and partner at eevolve, a Swiss small and mid-cap firm that counts healthcare as one of its main sectors, explains this mechanism:

> *PE investors are more professional because they are more exposed to scrutiny: each deal is visible in the community. If things go wrong, it will tarnish the reputation and may hinder the ability to access other good deal opportunities, and ultimately to raise the next fund. It's different for corporate investors who can bury the acquisition in the wider corporation and for family businesses that are not monitored.*

Another sought-after situation is the carve out of a noncore division of a multinational. The deal can rely on a manager or management team in the division who knows how to create value once the business becomes autonomous. Assume the manager of a noncore division of a large company has a great idea that could double the value of the business. What should they do?

- Tell their boss and hope to convince them to let you implement it, with hopes for an extra bonus and perhaps a promotion.
- Bypass their boss and take it directly to the CEO or the board.
- Discreetly offer it to a PE fund that will make an offer difficult to refuse to the company and task them as the CEO to capture the value of the MBO.
- Do nothing perhaps because they are well paid and will not take such a risk.

In class, this little exercise and the debate that ensues help raise awareness of some ethical issues. We will not disclose the detailed results of the votes in our classes, but they are very consistent and predictable within specific demographics (type of program and cultural background).

Most GPs would prefer to stay away from competitive auctions but do not have enough alternatives. Some GPs, however, identify value creation opportunities early on and do not hesitate to pay a high price if they think it justified, sometimes pre-empting the auction. In 2016, ARCHIMED bought +90% of Polyplus Transfection, a small French biotech company developing and manufacturing reagents for nucleic acid transfection and gene editing, for less than €10 million at an apparently extravagant multiple of +20X EBITDA. Such a multiple wouldn't be a surprise for a VC transaction but remains rare in the PE universe, and many bidders just weren't prepared to even consider it. In 2020, ARCHIMED sold half of it to Warburg Pincus at a valuation of more than $€550 million for a reported 70X multiple on invested capital.

In 2023, after integrating a few bolt-on acquisitions, they jointly sold the company for €2.4 billion ($2.6 billion), to listed Sartorius Stedim Biotech SA, this time returning more than 300 times the cost of investment for the part in ARCHIMED's inaugural fund. According to ARCHIMED and based on data from Preqin and other sources, that multiple represents an all-time record return for a PE investment from a buyout fund.[5]

Mike Mortimer from GHO emphasizes that successful healthcare PE investing demands transformational thinking rather than incremental improvement. His firm's approach deliberately challenges the common PE practice of backing companies with established track records. Instead, they place their bets on potential and management's proven ability to execute a compelling vision. "For the majority of deals we look at, we wouldn't invest on the basis of where they are today. It requires a vision." He adds: "We look for management teams we can truly back—no MBIs, no turnarounds. We also avoid binary product risk and payor risk."

AI is also promising to reshape how investors identify and evaluate companies, especially in healthcare. A forthcoming study (Pfitzer et al., 2025) presents an AI-based screening model that integrates financing history, regulatory milestones, patents, clinical trial activity, and growth indicators. By applying large language models to extract domain-specific features, such as therapeutic focus, reimbursement potential, and target users, the system captures dimensions of healthcare ventures that traditional databases often overlook.

The model shows encouraging early results, outperforming the average healthtech investor in predicting which companies will achieve a successful exit. For venture capital investors, such tools provide a scalable way to benchmark opportunities, extend coverage, and reduce reliance on intuition alone. For PE firms, they offer early signals of which companies are most likely to mature into sustainable scale-up candidates, thereby refining sourcing and long-term investment strategies.

The example of the VC and growth capital deal funnel in Figure 4.8 shows that for one completed deal, several hundred business plans could be received. Only a portion of the business plans will be read—typically 30% to 50%—and only a small proportion, say 10%, will lead to a meeting to assess the opportunity. However, since the COVID-19 pandemic, one observes an increase in online meetings with GPs (Alekseeva et al., 2022), meetings are still predominantly in person.

In other PE segments, GPs will receive fewer business plans, which will not always be received directly from the owners as in VC. Still, PE fund managers receive information memoranda, or at least teasers, through financial advisors on a daily basis. Having good information memoranda, business plans, or teasers is very important. To identify the right deal opportunities, they will then be included in a long,

[5] It is a bit misleading as it is more a VC investment in a PE fund but shows the ability of a specialist investor to recognize and capture opportunities.

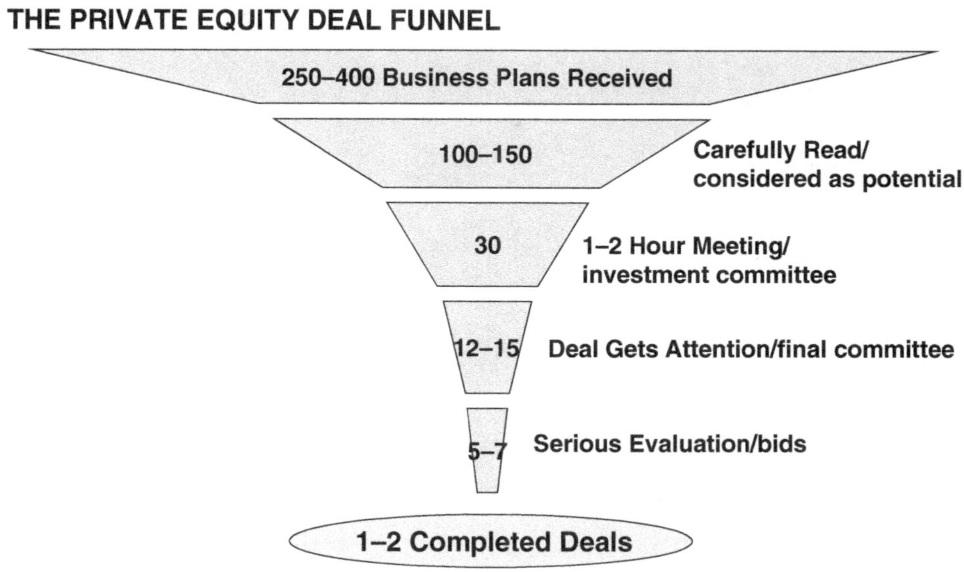

FIGURE 4.8 PE deal funnel.

thorough process that will typically require six months of work and involve some professionals and advisors.

The Eckuity team, for example, reviews more than 1,000 opportunities annually, ultimately investing in three or four. Their disciplined funnel is guided by 27 qualitative and quantitative criteria, ensuring consistency and selectivity. Beyond financial metrics, the human element—leadership credibility, cultural fit, and mission alignment—is often the deciding factor. The aim is to back not only great companies, but great teams capable of executing at scale.

The typical process shown in Figure 4.9 assumes that the business plan is worth it. If the information is not properly prepared, the process will be stopped after a couple of weeks.

Some small companies are geared toward providing a good standard of living and job satisfaction for their owners. Of course, these businesses are not generally suitable for PE investment. They are unlikely to provide the growth and the potential financial returns that will make them interesting to an institutional investor.

The basic attributes of a good LBO candidate are (1) a good position in the industry with a solid profit history, but also good growth to come; (2) a relatively low level of debt so one can add more and a high level of potential collateral that will also allow us to raise more debt; and last but not least, (3) stable and predictable cash flows that will be sufficient to meet the minimum debt servicing, which includes the payment of the interest and the principal repayments that will be included in the capital structure. Other attributes include not being in a largely cyclical or technological industry with a high disruption risk. You also need to be able to find performance improvement opportunities, like a strategic repositioning, improved marketing or offering, better operational efficiency, and better cash management. The loosening of corporate constraints may also indicate a good LBO candidate, as could the ability to sell undervalued or underperforming assets. Underperforming or poorly incentivized management could be a good attribute too because they may not have seized all value-creating

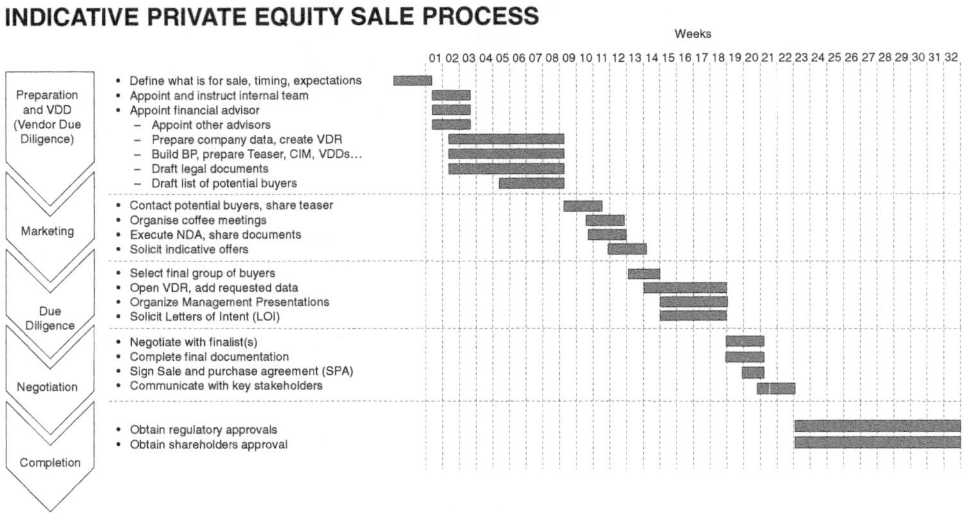

FIGURE 4.9 PE sale process.
Source: Candesic analysis.

opportunities. Finally, some specialist investors will be looking for an undervalued company, especially one that is either distressed or exposed to a forced sale.

Sometimes, circumstances dictate the choice of investment over the fit with the fund's investment strategy. A common specific situation is the temptation of the secondary buyout (SBO) at the end of the investment period. GPs may be tempted to invest in an SBO and burn money because it is immediately available, it means lower search costs and lower adverse selection risk, and it will help to both raise the next fund and get more management fees. It could also backfire, but this is an example of agency cost for LPs.

4.4 STRUCTURING THE INVESTMENT

PE investment structuring involves five critical areas: valuation and pricing terms, capital structure design, governance and control mechanisms, legal protections, and exit arrangements. The key is balancing investor protection with management incentives while ensuring operational flexibility for value creation.

4.4.1 Valuation and Deal Economics

The foundation starts with getting the valuation methodology right. PE firms typically use multiple approaches: discounted cash flow analysis, comparable company multiples, and precedent transaction analysis. The purchase price directly impacts potential returns, making this the most contentious negotiation point.

Capital structure optimization requires balancing debt and equity components. In leveraged buyouts, debt-to-equity ratios typically range from 50% to 75% debt, depending on the target's cash flow predictability and asset base. The structure affects both risk profile and return potential significantly.

4.4.2 Management Incentive Structures and Sweat Equity

The most essential features of an LBO management package revolve around strong incentives to align management's interests with those of the PE investors, primarily through equity participation that drives performance and value creation. Sweat equity, often acquired at a discounted price, ensures management personally invests in the company's success, fostering ownership mentality. Ratchets are performance-triggered adjustments that increase management's stake if certain return hurdles are met, often linked to multiples or IRRs. Retrocession thresholds set specific performance levels management must reach before earning additional upside, safeguarding the PE firm's downside. These elements work together to motivate management to improve operational efficiency, maximize cash flows, and achieve exit targets within typical three to seven years. The package also usually includes retention and lock-up periods, veto rights, and anti-dilution provisions to ensure management stability and protect their holdings, while the entire structure is designed to promote long-term value creation instead of short-term gains.

Beyond these core features, the management package often encompasses a variety of supplementary elements. These include vesting schedules to incentivize retention, performance thresholds escalating management participation upon exceeding baseline targets, and specific governance rights, such as board representation or veto powers on key decisions. The equity is usually structured as a mix of common shares, options, or warrants, with participation levels calibrated to the company's growth prospects and the risk appetite of the PE sponsor. Additional protections like anti-dilution clauses, clawback provisions, and tax-efficient arrangements help optimize overall incentives and alignment. While the approach might differ across deals, the overarching goal remains consistent: motivate management to deliver operational improvements while maintaining their long-term commitment, all within a carefully negotiated contractual framework.

This is where PE deals get particularly interesting. Management sweat equity requirements ensure skin in the game that goes far beyond typical employment arrangements. In LBOs, top managers are often expected to contribute substantial personal wealth—typically 20% to 50% of their net worth—directly into the equity of the company they are running.

Consider the psychology here: a CEO who invests $2M of their own money (representing 40% of their personal wealth) into a $50M LBO will think twice before pursuing empire-building activities or excessive perks. They lose their investment if they do not reach minimum performance hurdles, creating powerful alignment with PE sponsors.

Stock option plans complement sweat equity by providing upside participation tied to specific performance targets. These plans typically vest based on achieving revenue growth, EBITDA margins, or return thresholds rather than simple time-based vesting. A software company buyout might include options that vest only if the company achieves 20% annual revenue growth and maintains 25% EBITDA margins.

The combination creates a risk-return profile vastly different from public company management. Public company CEOs might lose their jobs for poor performance, but PE-backed managers lose substantial personal wealth. This explains why empire building and excessive spending are less common in PE-backed companies—managers have real money at stake.

Exercise: Suppose there is a 15-people management team with access to equity:

- CEO
- CFO
- COO
- Eight VPs
- Four other key employees
  - *How would you divide the equity between those 15 people and why?*
  - *Who decides?*

Figure 4.10 shows a possible but very rough example and should not be considered final!

- First, it depends on the size and nature of the business, on the criticality of each role, and on the track-record and skills of each manager.
- Second, it may be skewed by out-of-pocket personal investments by some managers.
- Ultimately, it is the PE investor who decides. They have a usual model, and the shareholder agreement is rarely negotiable.

4.4.3 Governance and Control Framework

Board composition typically gives PE investors control or significant influence through carefully structured representation. Standard arrangements include PE-appointed directors (often two or three seats), management directors (one or two seats), and independent directors (one seat). The exact composition depends on ownership percentage and the complexity of operational oversight required.

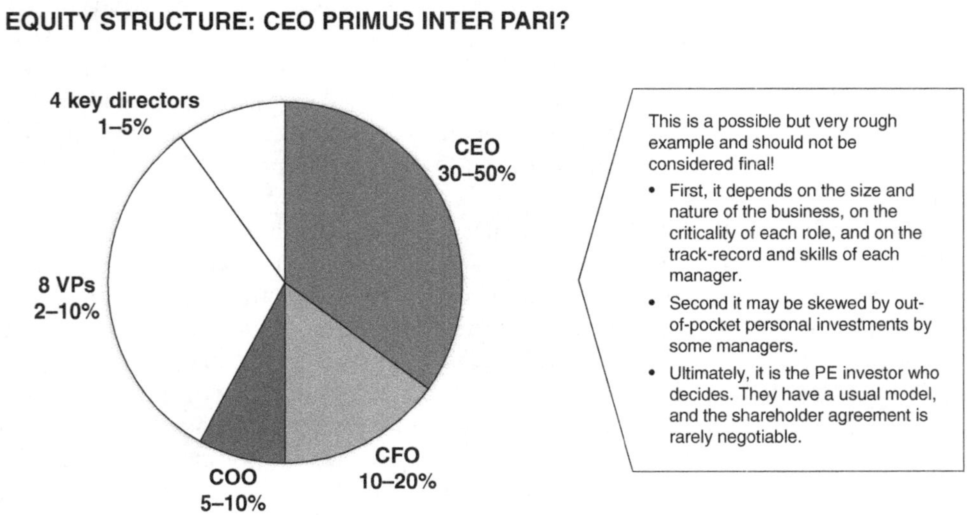

FIGURE 4.10 Primus inter Pari.

However, effective governance goes beyond board seats. Communication protocols between investors and managers require formal structure to avoid micromanagement while ensuring transparency. Many deals establish monthly operating review meetings, quarterly strategy sessions, and annual planning processes. This creates predictable touchpoints that satisfy PE oversight needs without hampering day-to-day operations.

Reserved matter provisions grant PE investors veto rights over major decisions: capital expenditures above thresholds (often \$500K to \$2M), acquisitions and disposals, changes to business strategy, additional debt issuance, and management compensation changes. These protections prevent management from taking actions that could harm investor interests.

Transaction example: In a recent healthcare services deal, the PE sponsor negotiated veto rights over any acquisition above \$1M, new debt exceeding 4 times EBITDA, and any management compensation increases above 10% annually. Monthly board packages included detailed financial reporting, pipeline updates, and operational metrics. This structure proved crucial when management proposed an expensive acquisition that would have stretched the balance sheet.

4.4.4 Debt Structuring and Banking Negotiations

Bank financing negotiations represent a critical component often overlooked in academic discussions. The debt structure directly impacts equity returns and operational flexibility. Senior debt typically provides 4–6 times EBITDA at attractive rates, while mezzanine financing fills gaps at higher costs but with equity participation.

Financial covenants require careful consideration during structuring. Common covenants include maximum debt-to-EBITDA ratios (often stepping down over time), minimum interest coverage ratios, and maximum capital expenditure limits. These covenants should provide adequate operational flexibility while satisfying lender risk requirements.

Nonfinancial covenants can be equally important. These might include restrictions on dividend payments, limitations on additional debt, requirements for key person life insurance, and restrictions on material contract changes. A manufacturing company LBO might include covenants preventing the sale of key production facilities without lender consent.

The negotiation process involves balancing multiple competing interests. Lenders want maximum protection through tight covenants, PE sponsors need operational flexibility for value creation initiatives, and management requires certainty that reasonable business decisions won't trigger covenant violations.

Transaction example: A consumer goods LBO included stepping debt covenants starting at 6.0 times EBITDA and declining to 4.5 times over four years. Nonfinancial covenants restricted capital expenditures above \$3M annually without lender consent. The structure provided growth capital flexibility while satisfying lender requirements for gradual deleveraging.

4.4.5 Equity Structure and Investor Rights

PE investments rarely involve simple common stock purchases. Instead, firms structure preference shares that provide downside protection and upside participation. These typically include liquidation preferences (often 1× nonparticipating preferred), antidilution provisions, and conversion rights to common shares upon exit.

Shareholder agreement terms establish the framework for ongoing relationships between investors and management. These agreements specify information sharing requirements, approval thresholds for major decisions, and procedures for resolving disputes. Well-structured agreements prevent conflicts while maintaining operational efficiency.

Consider the case of a typical mid-market buyout: A PE firm acquires a $100M revenue software company for $50M using $35M debt and $15M equity. Management rolls over $2M of their existing equity and receives options on an additional $3M, giving them roughly 15% of the post-transaction equity. This structure ensures management remains motivated while providing PE investors with control and preferential returns.

4.4.6 Exit Strategy Integration and Shareholder Provisions

Exit clauses require particular attention for minority shareholders who lack control over timing and process. Tag-along rights protect minority investors by ensuring they can participate in any sale of control blocks at the same terms. This prevents majority shareholders from excluding minorities from attractive exit opportunities.

Drag-along rights enable PE investors to force management and other shareholders to participate in exit transactions, preventing holdout situations that could derail value-maximizing exits. These provisions become crucial when strategic buyers require 100% ownership or when IPO processes need clean cap tables.

Preemptive rights give existing shareholders first refusal on new equity issuances, protecting against dilution. However, these rights typically include exceptions for employee option plans and certain strategic initiatives to maintain operational flexibility.

For founder shareholders who remain as minorities post-transaction, liquidity provisions often include rights to sell portions of their holdings in secondary transactions or tag along with PE exits. A founder might negotiate rights to sell up to 20% of their holdings annually after year three, providing some liquidity while maintaining alignment incentives.

4.4.7 Legal Protections and Risk Allocation

Representations and warranties from selling shareholders and target companies provide crucial protections. These typically cover financial statement accuracy, legal compliance, material contracts, and absence of undisclosed liabilities. The scope and survival periods (usually 12–24 months) vary based on deal size and risk profile.

Indemnification arrangements allocate risk between buyers and sellers. Sellers typically provide escrow accounts (5–15% of purchase price) and may give personal guarantees up to certain caps. However, PE investors should avoid over-relying on indemnities since recovering from selling shareholders can prove challenging.

Due diligence findings inform the final contract terms and pricing adjustments. Buyers typically negotiate purchase price reductions or additional protections based on issues discovered during the review process. This creates a feedback loop between investigation findings and deal structure.

The complexity stems from balancing competing interests while maintaining operational flexibility. PE investors need control and protection, management requires incentives and autonomy, and the company needs capital structure optimization for growth. Getting these elements right from the start creates the foundation for successful value creation and attractive returns.

The personal wealth requirements for management create a fundamentally different dynamic than public company governance. When a CEO has $2M of personal money at risk, board discussions about strategy and spending take on entirely different urgency. This alignment mechanism, combined with sophisticated governance and exit provisions, explains much of PE's operational effectiveness compared to public market alternatives.

4.5 INTELLIGENCE AND DUE DILIGENCE

4.5.1 Biases and Challenges in Data, Both in PE and in Healthcare

As pointed out in Chapter 3, data are increasingly abundant and increasingly easy to access, organize, and observe and provide PE funds with valuable information. In many cases, they are indeed a very valuable source of information, and it is no surprise that PE funds use them more and more because they may seem objective and provide a sound basis for sound decision-making.

However, they too can be subject to biases and misunderstanding. First, companies may be more prone to communicate about success, less about failure. Several datasets will show firms still alive at the time we look at them, which generates a so-called survivorship bias. Hence, success may be overrepresented in data. They can also be overemphasized in our memory or our attention. For example, we may view an extraordinarily but highly unlikely successful venture as a success that was more predictable than it was, which is referred to as an outcome bias or an attribution bias. In addition, GPs are well aware that entrepreneurs tend to be overconfident regarding the success of their venture (Landier and Thesmar, 2009).

More generally, the outcome of a PE-funded project may be determined by the time and the location it was started and the management team that led it. Hence, past observations may not always be good indicators for what one would expect to observe in another environment, let alone future projects. In technical terms, we say past observations may lack external validity. These and many other biases are the subject of a considerable literature (Angrist and Pischke, 2009; Imbens and Rubin, 2015; Chemla and Hennessy, 2019, 2020, 2021, 2022, 2025).

Health data, like other types of data, are also subject to a wide range of biases. Here are a few examples: First, they are often plagued by selection bias, where the sample is not representative of the target population (Heckman, 1979; Hernán and Robins, 2020; Todd and Wolpin, 2023). For example, health studies based on hospitalized patients exclude patients who were not hospitalized. Since healthy people are less likely to buy health insurance, insurance datasets tend to overrepresent high risk, less healthy people. During a clinical trial, if patients on whom the treatment being tested is ineffective are more likely to drop out of trials and are omitted from the reports, the test results suffer from a so-called attrition bias. There is also a survivorship bias when, say, one compares two treatments and forgets that bias can arise from the fact that patients must survive long enough to receive treatment (Hernán, 2010). There can be a measurement error when subjects are asked to self-report their physical activity or their alcohol consumption (Bound et al., 2001). A publication bias arises when tests, including clinical trials, are more likely to be published and advertised when they are statistically significant (Ioannidis, 2005).

4.5.2 Due Diligence

We now introduce an essential aspect of the investment process: due diligence. The negotiation of a deal depends largely on the intelligence that has been gathered before and during the process. Good intelligence requires a trusting relationship between the management and the investors. The intelligence gathering needed to gain a sustainable competitive advantage will be achieved through due diligence and sometimes the use of a corporate investigation agency, to learn more, for example, about the whereabouts of a CEO or an owner. That will be more important in emerging markets, for example, where an investor may be a little bit worried about where they are investing. Another element of gathering intelligence is the establishment of a clean team within the company—a clean team facilitates the exchange of sensitive information between merging companies, thus preserving confidentiality and integrity during the merger process.

Due diligence should be considered in every business transaction, but it is vital to the PE process. But who must carry it out, and why?

Due diligence is particularly important when there is leverage involved—the sponsor is taking additional risk, and that risk is shared with the lenders, who want to be reassured with a credible third-party opinion. The sponsor and their advisors will need to provide the banks with information to give them that reassurance. The second reason to perform due diligence in PE is to gather more industry knowledge. A financial investor may know less than most strategic buyers. A third reason relates to cases when the targets are still immature—when their cash flows are not as stable as one would like to add debt in the context of an LBO. All that speaks for why buyers should systematically conduct a due diligence, and why it is important to hire outside professionals to do it.

When does due diligence happen? Well, officially speaking, it is the last step in the acquisition process shown in Figure 4.11. The official due diligence comes after the letter of intent and the potential exclusivity that would be granted to the investor once the initial conditions have been pre-agreed. In reality, however, due diligence will start much earlier. In fact, it begins even before there is an investment process in place. A good, intelligent investor will scout the market on a regular basis and gather information about potential targets that may at some point become available.

4.5.2.1 Areas of Due Diligence The scope of due diligence in any transaction encompasses several critical domains (Figure 4.12). Most notably, financial due diligence examines a company's internal data and historic performance, with a focus on verifying accounts, assessing sustainability of earnings, and identifying risks tied to assets, liabilities, and cash flows. Commercial due diligence is distinct in its focus on external market conditions, competitive landscape, and the business's future prospects, including market share, customer dynamics, and growth opportunities. In addition, comprehensive due diligence routinely covers legal matters, operations, technology or scientific capabilities, environmental exposures, human resources, and—where relevant—pensions. Each component is essential for building a reliable risk-adjusted view of the target company, and their relative emphasis may vary by sector and jurisdiction.

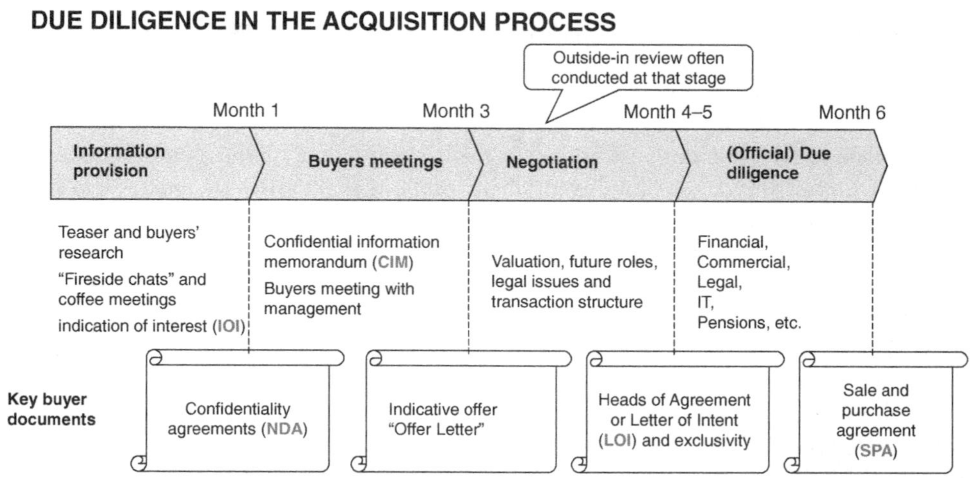

FIGURE 4.11 Due diligence process.
Source: Candesic analysis.

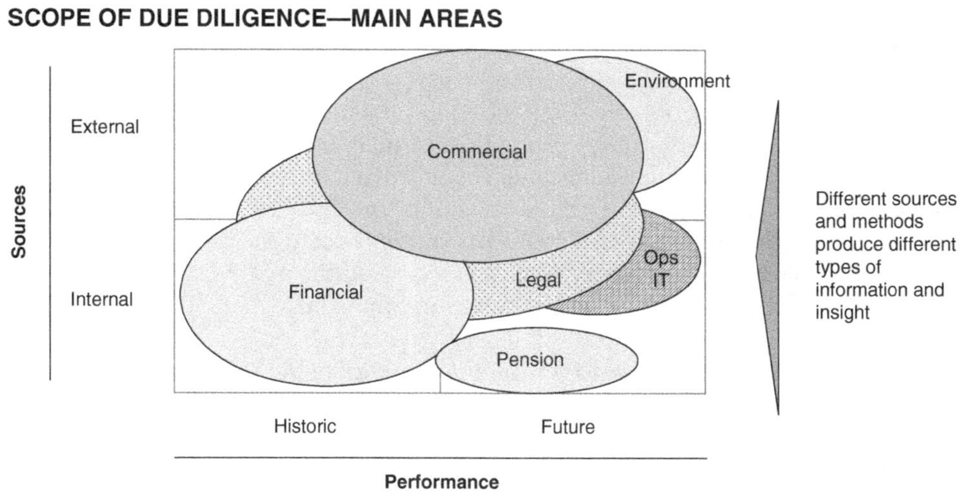

FIGURE 4.12 Main areas of due diligence.
Source: Candesic analysis.

Coordination of due diligence typically involves a range of specialists covering areas such as commercial, financial, legal, and IT matters. While it is best practice for the client to directly oversee this process, in reality, investment bankers frequently assume a coordinating role on the client's behalf. This arrangement can introduce conflicts of interest, as bankers' incentives may be aligned with deal completion rather than thorough risk identification. The robustness and independence of the due diligence process ultimately depend on the client's level of active engagement and oversight throughout the transaction.

Paul Tomasic, managing director of Healthcare at Houlihan Lokey, notes that, over time, M&A bankers have become more integrated with other advisors throughout the due diligence process and are now brought in much earlier to prepare businesses for sale. "While some might argue this is typically the domain of management consultants, we bankers maintain a unique relationship with both strategic and financial buyers—a connection that consultants do not consistently possess."

4.5.2.2 Data Room The data room is a central component of the due diligence process. Before granting access, all potential buyers and their advisors (such as lawyers, accountants, and consultants) must sign a non-disclosure agreement (NDA), forming a single "confidentiality circle." Historically, this process took place in a physical data room, often organized by lawyers. In these secure environments, participants were invited into a locked room after leaving all personal items outside. With only pen and paper, they would review thousands of physical documents, with strict limitations on what could be noted or photocopied.

This process has been fundamentally transformed by the advent of the virtual data room (VDR). Nowadays, data rooms are almost exclusively virtual, at least in developed markets. A VDR is a secure online repository where sellers can grant controlled access to sensitive documents. Security features remain paramount; access is often restricted to screen-viewing only, with printing or saving disabled. When printing is permitted, documents are typically watermarked with the name of the potential investor and the date to deter unauthorized distribution. Despite these controls, the efficiency and accessibility of VDRs represent a significant improvement over their physical predecessors.

Data rooms are particularly important in competitive sale processes, such as auctions. The primary function of a VDR in this context is to provide fair and equal treatment to all potential buyers by giving them simultaneous access to the same comprehensive set of information. This allows the seller to manage a high number of possible acquirers efficiently. In a typical acquisition timeline, the data room is opened during the marketing phase, approximately two months into the process.

The VDR market itself is highly concentrated. As of the mid-2020s, two providers had historically dominated the space: Datasite and Intralinks.

Digital Traceability in the Diligence Process: A Case Example Tad Zindi of Datasite recalls a revealing case that highlights how digitalization has transformed the due diligence process in M&A. In this instance, a bidder attempted to claw back part of the transaction price, claiming that a critical document had not been made available during due diligence. In the predigital era—particularly when physical data rooms were the norm—such a claim would have been nearly impossible to refute. Sellers had limited means to prove whether or when a document had been disclosed.

However, in this case, the attempt failed. Datasite's advanced platform—which has benefited from more than $100 million in investment into document tracking, real-time analytics, translation, and redaction tools—was able to provide precise evidence. The platform's analytics demonstrated that the buyer's own user credentials had accessed the disputed document, complete with a timestamp showing the exact date, time, and page view.

These tracking capabilities, particularly useful during Phase I of auction processes—where some prospective bidders enter the process primarily to gain intelligence on a target's supplier costs or pricing strategy—now serve as a powerful deterrent against bad-faith tactics. This example underscores how digital platforms not only enhance efficiency but also strengthen auditability, compliance, and legal defensibility during transactions.

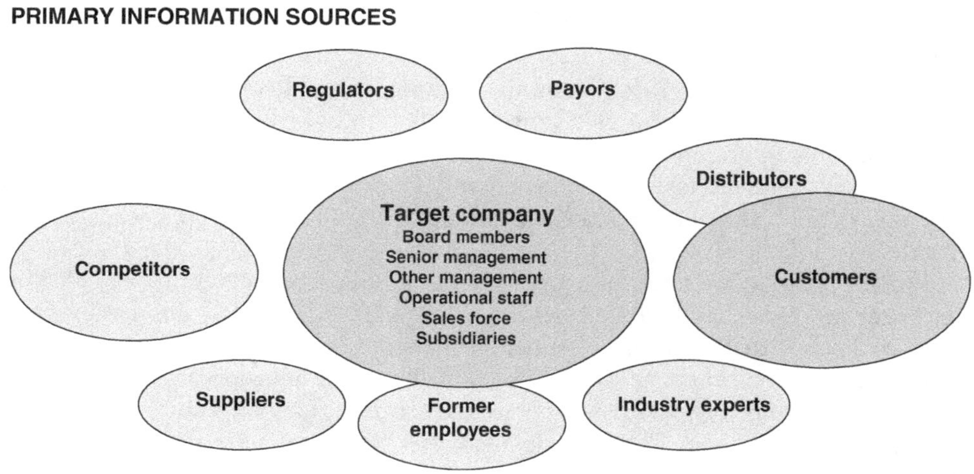

FIGURE 4.13 Sources of primary information in due diligence.

4.5.2.3 Information Sources Primary information sources for due diligence are everywhere: they can be data provided by the company itself, conversations with management, employees, key salespeople, suppliers, clients, regulators, distributors—any stakeholder, including sometimes former employees and competitors. However, the main source of information for due diligence will always remain customers, as shown in Figure 4.13. We will discuss in greater detail in the section on commercial due diligence.

There is a little-known source of information that is often exploited by sophisticated investors, directly or more commonly through their advisors: the Freedom of Information Act (FOIA) that exists in the United States and the United Kingdom, or equivalent in many other countries.[6] This is a law that gives the public the right to access information held by public authorities, often previously unreleased. Hedge funds have been early users and have been shown to generate abnormal returns (Gargano et al., 2017).

During the due diligence process, stakeholders must understand the terms of reference. They must provide a very clear definition of and guidance on the strategy because the transaction is designed to fit that strategy. So, the due diligence team needs to understand the context of the business. The terms of reference also need to be clear about the scope—the focus on certain areas. Conversely, the vendor due diligence means preparing everything for the seller, they may ask us to concentrate on one aspect of the business and forget another, which is not very transparent. When performing due diligence for a buyer, one cannot forget anything, and the scope must be very precisely defined. Timing responsibilities and the nature of reporting will also need to be well defined.

What makes a successful due diligence? It is one where the seller is prepared, the buyer is prepared, and the buyer's team is coordinated. In addition, a very key thing is

---

[6] One of the oldest ones is the Freedom of the Press Act in Sweden, dating back to 1766. In France, the Loi n° 78-753 (1978) provides for access to administrative documents while, in Germany, the Informationsfreiheitsgesetz (IFG) (2006) allows access to federal-level information.

to ensure confidentiality. The buyer's due diligence team must maintain this throughout the process. Another success factor would be that disclosures are kept current as the transaction progresses. Renegotiations resulting from due diligence findings, and that are handled fairly and in good faith by both parties, are also a good sign. The engagement of a competent financial person to assist the seller during the entire process is also key. A full disclosure should, in theory, be practiced by both parties, but that is not always the case. And lastly, the aim should be for all the due diligence efforts to end with a win-win conclusion.

By contrast, what are some of the reasons for due diligence failures? We can identify three key issues. First, bad faith. For example, this might include refusal to use external resources, a scope that is wrongly defined, denying access to the target, or refusal to accept the conclusions of the advisors. Those are all reasons linked to negative behavior that we have encountered as advisors. A second set of reasons for failure is related to a poorly organized process. For example, there may be no proper terms of reference, a poor estimation of the time and resources needed, a lack of coordination between the advisors, or sometimes the wrong incentivization of advisors. As consultants, we are uncomfortable when clients want to pay us a success fee, as if we were M&A bankers. This is inappropriate. We are performing almost an audit, a strategic and commercial audit, so should be working without an incentive. If we get paid only if the deal happens, we may, consciously or not, view the target as very attractive, no matter how honest we try to be. Another set of causes for due diligence failures relates simply to doing a sloppy job. One may hire the wrong advisor, one may be a bad fit with the management, or one may make a mistake when prioritizing issues or even procrastinate.

Since the massive introduction of chatbots in 2023, AI has been transforming the way and speed at which the different parts of the due diligence can be conducted. Investors no longer need to turn to the specialists to validate their first findings. They can immediately check whether the target company's product will be compliant with the Canadian regulation, benchmark the historical CapEx, synthesize the patterns from thousands of company presentations collected by the firm, perform a first analysis of the business plan and benchmark it against all previous investments. Many investment opportunities will be discarded early without much investment in external advice. The process becomes faster, with less waste.

To summarize, due diligence is extremely important. It is complex because it has many, diverse aspects. It brings together lots of people, lots of specialists, and it is absolutely essential to coordinate them effectively because due diligence is a structured process.

4.5.2.4 Commercial Due Diligence Commercial due diligence is at the very core of the process of value creation in PE investments. The commercial due diligence process is intended to assess the future cash flows of a company to assess how much value will be created. This requires a clear understanding of the revenue in the existing portfolio of activities, but also the associated costs, and hence the profitability—the revenue minus the costs. But understanding the growth opportunities—the pipeline of new projects, for example—is very important.

So, how do PE companies use the information that we gather?

At this stage, value creation can be maximized in three key ways (Figure 4.14). First, identify reasons to minimize the price to pay. This can be achieved by challenging overly optimistic forecasts, whether they are due to optimistic sales figures or conservative expected CapEx. This process can also help reduce the volatility of

HOW PRIVATE EQUITY COMPANIES USE THE INFORMATION GATHERED DURING COMMERCIAL DUE DILIGENCE

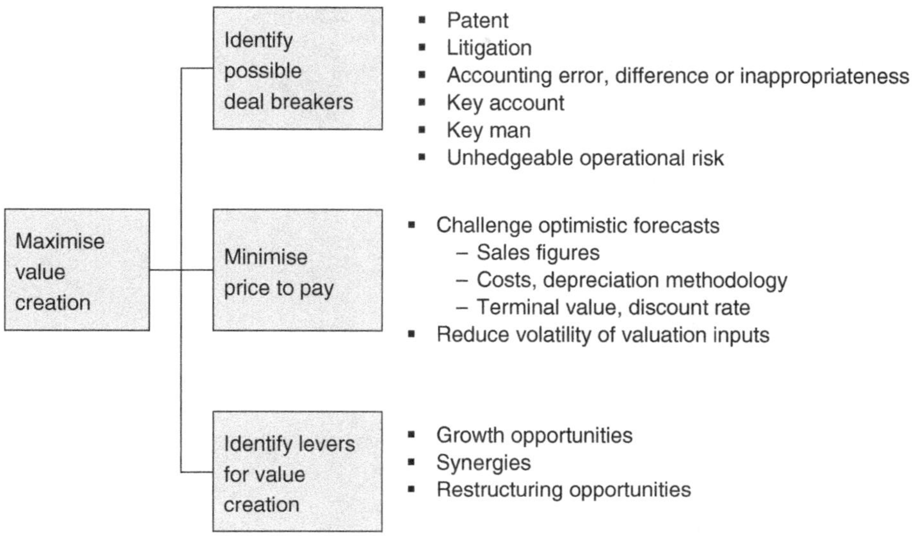

FIGURE 4.14 Three ways to maximize value creation during negotiations.
Source: Candesic analysis.

valuation inputs with a better understanding of the underlying data. Second, due diligence information can maximize value creation and prevent the buyer from completing a bad deal. The legal team could identify possible deal breakers such as litigation risks or the accountants could identify an accounting error. Alternatively, there could be an issue with a key person or a key account. For example, losing the top salesman might jeopardize the relationship with top clients and negate a significant part of the value creation plan. Third, information can be leveraged to find new sources of value creation—the growth opportunities that we mentioned. These may include synergies: although PE is not like corporate M&A, work with the client will lead to business growth and synergetic value. Alternatively, these may be restructuring opportunities.

We now examine the process of gathering commercial due diligence. This requires looking for both upside opportunities and downside risk. These include five key areas: the market, industry dynamics, competition, customers, and the company itself.

What does this process look like in practice? There are three key steps. In step one, we analyze the industry attractiveness (Figure 4.15). This is based on the assessment of the industry structure, of the evolution of the profit pool, and of the structure of the competition.

The second step assesses competitive positioning (Figure 4.16). First, this involves benchmarking the performance of the target in terms of growth, cost structure, productivity, and the margins they can capture. We will need to understand some rankings, which might be related to market share. Some clients will consider a company only if it is a leader, or at least in the top three, in the market. We work hard at understanding reputation and the international reach of the company. We will also identify competitive advantages. Those could be linked to patents or to relationships with authorities, regulators, or other partners or they could be a customer franchise. Alternatively, they

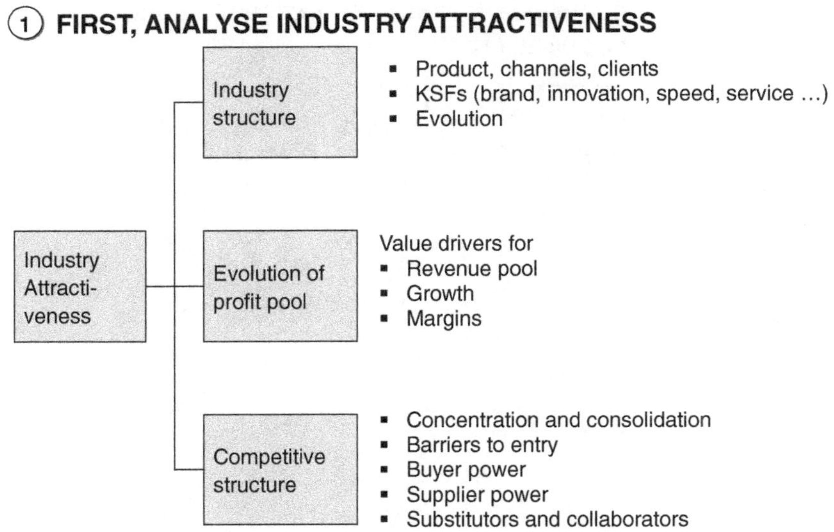

FIGURE 4.15 Analyze industry attractiveness.
Source: Candesic analysis.

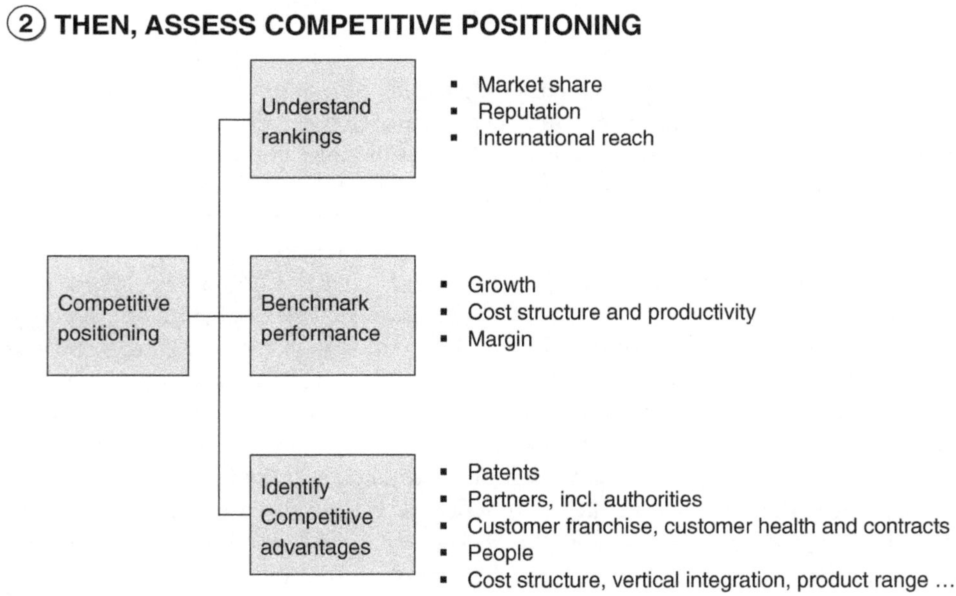

FIGURE 4.16 Assess strength of competitive positioning.
Source: Candesic analysis.

could come from the kind of people who they are able to attract and retain, or from a different cost structure.

The rise of AI has introduced a new, critical dimension to the due diligence process. Investors must now assess not only a company's current competitive position but also its long-term viability in an AI-driven future. This has fundamentally changed the initial screening questions for potential investments.

The third step in the process is to review the business plan (Figure 4.17) So, are the risks properly identified? Are the targets achievable and in line with what we can see in the market? And are there any other upsides that could have been forgotten in the business plan?

In Figure 4.18, we show a typical example of a CDD conducted over three weeks.

Examples of Commercial Due Diligence We describe three transactions on which we have worked and that, we believe, illustrate some interesting elements.

The first case study examines a proposed $150-million investment in a medical digitizer company. Years ago, we were hired to assess a company offering a technology related to PACS (picture archiving and communication system) equipment.

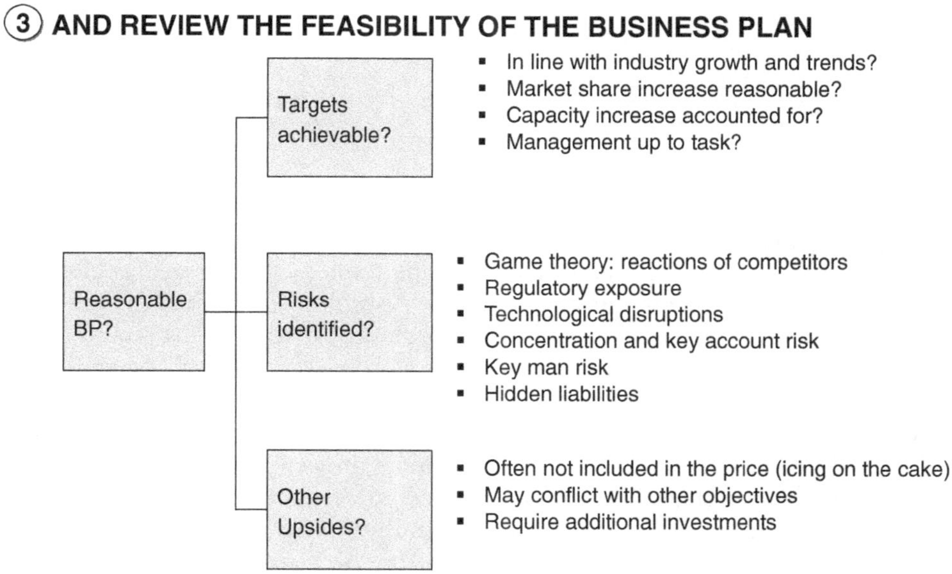

FIGURE 4.17 Assess feasibility of management plan.
Source: Candesic analysis.

THE COMMERCIAL DUE DILIGENCE TYPICALLY LASTS ONLY THREE WEEKS

Terms of reference	Frame problem	Develop hypothesis	Interview experts	Synthesize results → Final report
Timing	2 days	3 days	2 weeks	3 days
Objectives	• Tease out "what you have to believe" for the investment to be successful	• Prioritize and lay out roadmap for testing assumptions	• Test key findings with key opinion leaders, regulators, stakeholders, and customers	• Summarize learnings from all available data and make recommendations • Get buy-in from stakeholders
Activities	• Prepare interview guide • Interview key members of management • Review company's existing data • Discuss with investors	• Review external and company papers • Conduct press and industry report research • Write interview guides • Set up interviews	• Interview experts, key opinion leaders and regulators • Synthesize key reports • Summarize learnings and highlight potential obstacles/opportunities	• Document evidence for our view • Suggest ways to mitigate deal breakers and/or refine data • Discuss with management and investors

FIGURE 4.18 Activities in a typical three-week CDD.
Source: Candesic.

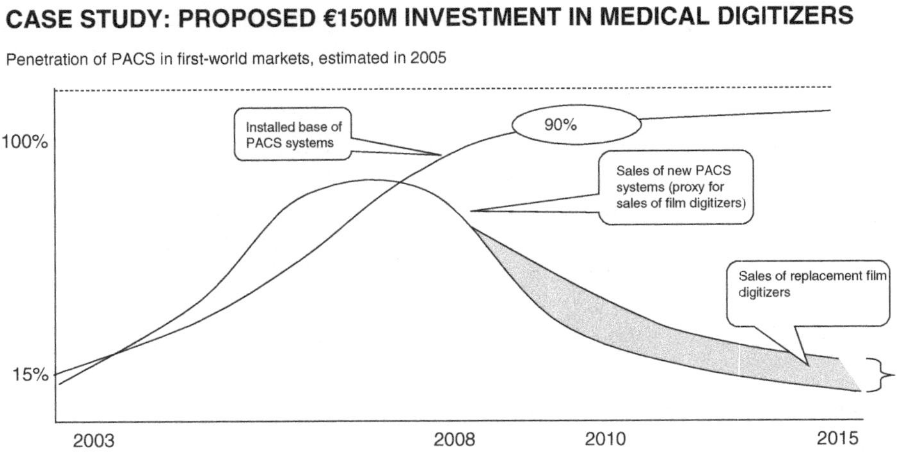

FIGURE 4.19 CDD of medical digitizers.
Source: Candesic analysis; interviews.

The investment thesis was based on the transition from physical to digital medical imaging. Traditionally, X-rays were provided on large plastic sheets that were difficult to manipulate, store, and maintain. Furthermore, the legacy imaging machines that produced them were expensive assets, amortized over very long periods. The target company proposed a (then) novel solution: a professional scanner that could digitize these physical films, offering the benefits of digital files—easy storage, magnification, electronic sharing for second opinions, and the potential for AI analysis.

The company attempted to assess its market size, but as Figure 4.19 illustrates, it used a fatally flawed proxy. The company based its projections on the total installed base of all imaging systems. This approach ignored the fact that the product was a bridge technology designed exclusively for a rapidly shrinking market of legacy, non-digital equipment. A correct analysis, based on the decaying installed base of these older machines, revealed a market that would virtually disappear within a few years. The valuation the company derived from this flawed analysis was completely exaggerated, a fact our client had not identified in its initial review of the information memorandum.

This discovery, made within the first few days of our work, led to a clear recommendation to terminate the deal. The company was seeking hundreds of millions for a business whose reasonable value was a fraction of that, given its limited market lifespan. Our primary research had uncovered a second critical issue: the adoption of the scanners was partially an illusion. Interviews with end users in hospitals revealed the machines were hardly ever used, a very negative signal for future sales.

In this case, the due diligence process fulfilled its primary function: preventing a potentially significant capital loss by uncovering fatal flaws in the investment's core assumptions.

In the second example (Figure 4.20), we looked at a medtech company in IVD, and here we gave our client very thorough assessments of the expected growth—around 6% for the legacy business, achieved through drivers like population growth, an increase in referrals, and automation. But there was also an additional 5% growth forecast. If our client wanted to invest, they would need to believe two things in particular: that the

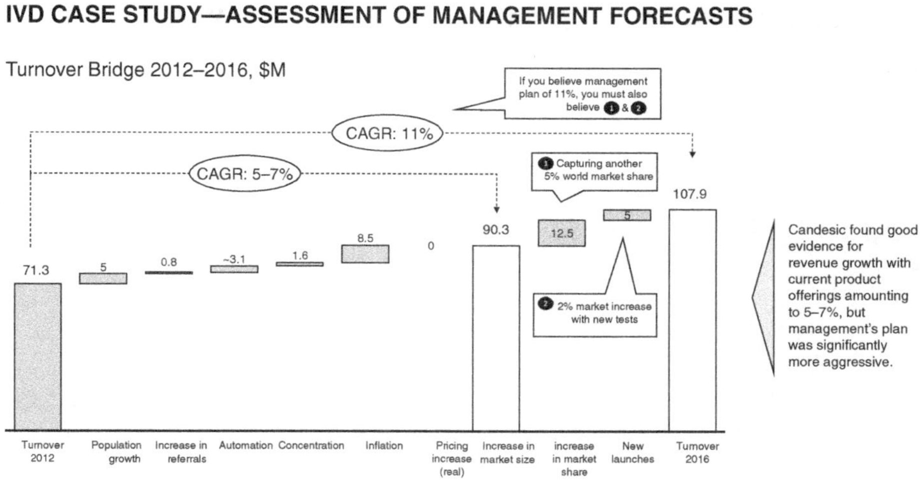

FIGURE 4.20 CDD of IVD equipment company.
Source: Interviews; Candesic analysis.

company would capture another 5% world market share, and that there would be a 2% increase achieved through the launch of new tests. We told our client that we were very comfortable with the first 6%. But we warned them to be careful about the other 5% of growth—they would need to be comfortable with the two points mentioned. We couldn't validate either after interviewing dozens of lab biologists and procurement executives.

In the third example, the team assessed Mediwound's forecasts. Mediwound (not the actual name), had successfully developed a range of advanced wound care products and was planning to develop a hemostat segment. Note that Mediwound had been many years an unprofitable startup. By 2015, the company could have been profitable but had to decide whether to continue investing to grow faster. This is a typical zone where the difference between a scaled-up startup and a growth company is blurred.

The team could validate the development of a sizable segment for hemostat use in cardiothoracic procedures (Figure 4.21), which management argued in an old plan would guarantee the successful launch of VasoMW, Mediwound's brand new hemostat.

However, the opportunity was not substantial. After interviewing 20 cardiothoracic surgeons, the team concluded that only a small portion of the segment was addressable and obtainable (Figure 4.22).

Through the surgeons' interviews, the team also found that VasoMW worked particularly well when there was bleeding over a large area and could be used immediately, saving precious seconds; however, the method of application and lack of published literature to demonstrate clinical evidence made it weak compared to current agents that surgeons were familiar with. "A lot of surgeons are creatures of habit and will stick with existing products until the literature clearly demonstrates an improvement of some sort," said one of the interviewees. The management forecasts for VasoMW could not be validated at all.

One can understand the type of analysis that is being conducted on behalf of the investor and how conclusions are drawn after a critical and thorough review of the

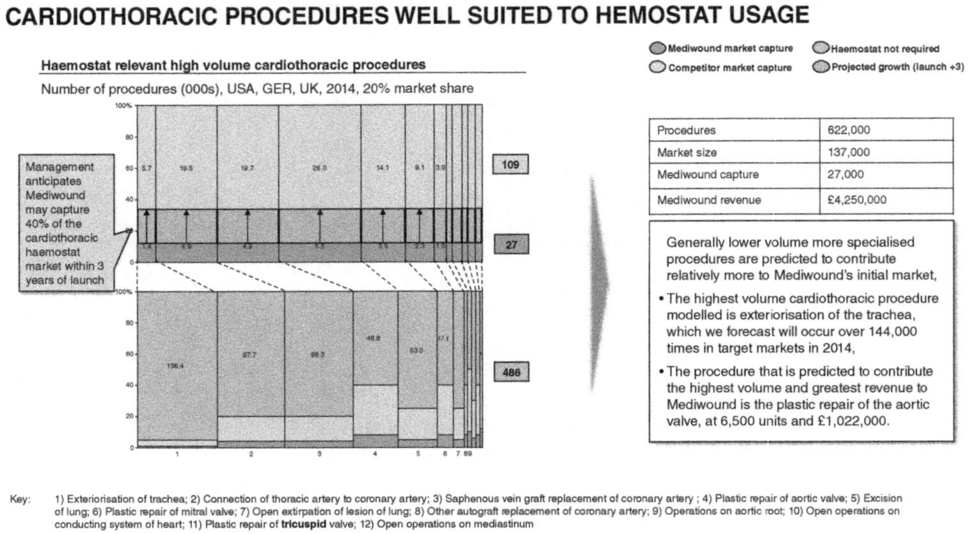

FIGURE 4.21 CDD of Mediwound (1/2).
Source: Health and Social Care Information Centre; US Census Bureau; Federal Statistics Office (Destatis); UK Office for National Statistics; World Bank; UN Department of Economics & Social Affairs; Candesic interviews; Candesic analysis.

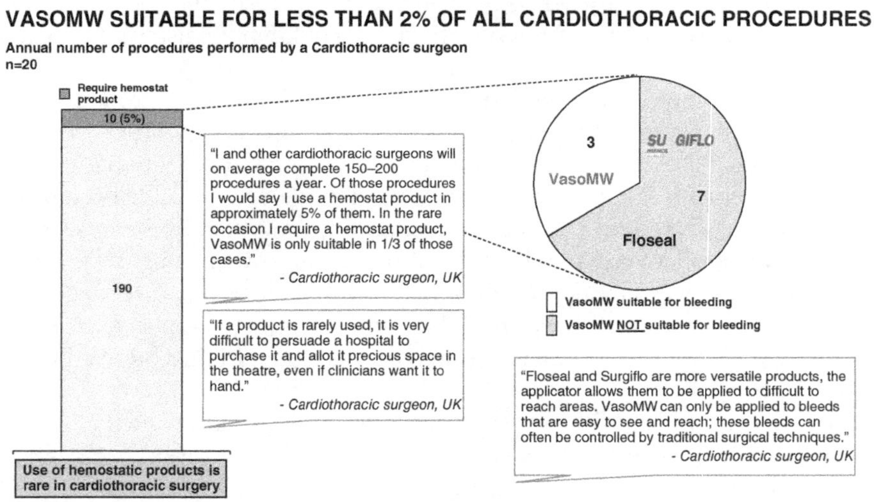

FIGURE 4.22 CDD of Mediwound (2/2).
Source: Candesic interviews, research and analysis.

management forecasts. The investor will never be able to get an absolute conviction. Their decision to invest will be based on reasonable appreciation of the information available. Here, in spite of the poor prospects for the hemostat opportunity, the conclusions were cautiously optimistic and led to an investment. Then came COVID-19 that completely rewrote the rules of the surgery market for a few years.

Those are just a couple examples out of a very long list—the team at Candesic has performed more than 800 due diligence projects over the last 20 years.

4.5.2.5 Legal Due Diligence in Healthcare[7] In M&A transactions, the bulk of the legal due diligence typically follows the execution of the LOI and is completed prior to the signing of the definitive agreements, with few exceptions. LOIs, while largely nonbinding, set forth the basic parameters of the legal due diligence, such as the period in which legal due diligence is conducted, and articulates the seller's commitment to provide due diligence information in the transaction. Buyers wish to have comfort that the seller is committed to a transaction with the buyer before incurring the expenses—often significant—that full legal due diligence entails. Sellers are in turn comfortable proceeding on the basis of NDAs that protect their disclosure from misappropriation or misuse.

The legal due diligence process has multiple objectives: (1) identify whether there are unknown liabilities and legal risks that are unacceptable to the buyer's risk profile—and therefore a reason not to pursue the transaction; (2) ascertain information about the target company that can be used to craft deal terms in the definitive agreements, and the covenants, indemnification, and escrow provisions in particular; (3) pave the way for a transaction that is both structured permissibly and does not trigger unaddressed requirements, such as third-party contractual or regulatory consents; and (4) confirm the buyer's expectation of what it is actually acquiring and its risk assessment of the target company.

For timing reasons, legal due diligence is commonly conducted concurrently with negotiation of the core definitive documents, and buyers habitually reserve the right to revise legal terms pending completion of due diligence. Notably, in deals without representations and warranties insurance, the diligence process provides buyers with the intelligence they need to seek enhanced recourse provisions in purchase agreements, such as special escrows, increased indemnification "caps" and special indemnification provisions to offset risk, extended indemnification survival periods, and lower indemnification baskets. When the offer in the LOI reflects the buyer's valuation prior to knowledge of specific diligence issues, these are ways for a buyer to protect its valuation when confronting previously unknown significant due diligence issues.

In US healthcare transactions, diligence by experienced healthcare counsel early in the process is critical in assessing the viability of the parties' business terms within the complex healthcare regulatory framework and determining whether a legally compliant structure is available to execute them. The parties otherwise risk wasting resources and incurring costs only to learn later in the deal that they need to revise the transaction structure or, worse, finding out after the closing that they structured the deal in a violative manner with significant consequences.

In transactions in which the target company receives US federal reimbursement for its services, buyers additionally often engage the services of healthcare compliance consultants to assess the target company's billing and coding practices and the integrity of its compliance framework. Noncompliance with billing practices and regulatory requirements carries steep potential penalties with regulatory authorities, and incorrect billing practices may reveal that the target company's valuation

[7] This section in this book was contributed by Carl Berglind at Greenberg Traurig. It reflects opinions of the author and not necessarily of Greenberg Traurig. It is presented for informational purposes only and is not intended and should not be construed or relied upon as legal advice. Greenberg Traurig is not sponsoring or recommending any business venture or legal position included in this section. This section does not create an attorney-client relationship with anyone and is not a solicitation of any kind.

ultimately cannot be supported. Legal due diligence works in tandem with the compliance diligence: poor compliance practices are often addressed by crafting covenants (such as requiring the seller to address compliance issues in connection with the transaction) and special indemnification and escrow to protect against the specific risks revealed by the due diligence.

Buyer's counsel typically generates a bespoke due diligence request list that seeks a broad range of legal information from the seller, and the back-and-forth nature of the requests and responses is one of the most iterative parts of the legal due diligence process between the parties. The buyer's request list covers various specific legal subject matter areas from the target company, such as general corporate and organizational matters, healthcare legal/regulatory matters, litigation, contracts, employment matters, employee benefits information, intellectual property, real property, environmental, and data privacy/information technology. The precise due diligence requests will vary to some extent depending both on the buyer's priorities and the attributes of the target company. The target then generally generates responses and produces materials in consultation with its counsel and advisers. The seller's ability to provide robust due diligence information promptly is a key factor in keeping the deal moving swiftly to closing and keeping pressure on the buyer to close on the desired timeline.

Additionally, legal due diligence encompasses reviewing publicly available information. For example, buyers customarily obtain and review third-party record searches that reveal whether the target company carries liens on its assets, which would need to be addressed prior to the closing, and whether there is public record of litigation against the target company. Some buyers may obtain tax clearance certificates from local tax authorities prior to closing, and various additional materials are sought in transactions in which owned real estate is conveyed in the transaction.

4.5.3 Case Study: Using Due Diligence as a Strategic Weapon in Competitive Bids

In a competitive PE bidding process, access to the target company's confidential information for due diligence is not merely a procedural step; it is a critical dependency. PE bidders are generally unable to secure debt financing without their lenders first reviewing a comprehensive due diligence report. A sophisticated rival bidder can exploit this dependency, turning the granting of due diligence into a strategic weapon to disrupt or dismantle a competing offer, particularly when that rival appears to have a structural advantage.

A compelling example of this tactic occurred during the 2018 bidding war for Healthscope, a major Australian hospital operator. The initial front-runner was a consortium led by the PE firm BGH Capital, which had secured a powerful advantage by signing a binding agreement with AustralianSuper, a pension fund that owned 14% of Healthscope. This "lock-up" agreement committed AustralianSuper's significant stake to the BGH bid, making it large enough to block any competing offer that required a shareholder vote.

A rival bidder, Brookfield Asset Management from Canada, emerged with a higher but highly conditional offer. To counteract BGH's blocking stake, Brookfield introduced a "level playing field" condition in its proposal. This condition stipulated that Healthscope's board could not grant due diligence access to any potential acquirer—namely BGH—if that acquirer was party to an agreement (the lock-up with AustralianSuper) that prevented its members from supporting a superior proposal.

This created an intractable dilemma for Healthscope's board. If they granted BGH access to the data room, they would violate Brookfield's condition, potentially causing the higher offer to evaporate. However, if they denied BGH access, BGH's bid would likely collapse, as its lenders would not provide the necessary financing without a full due diligence investigation. Brookfield's strategic objective was to use this condition to force BGH to release AustralianSuper from its restrictive lock-up agreement in order to gain the due diligence access it needed to proceed.

The tactic, combined with Brookfield's superior offer price, ultimately proved successful. The pressure created by the conditional offer gave the Healthscope board the leverage it needed to negotiate more freely. The BGH consortium's bid eventually failed, and Brookfield was granted the access it needed to conduct its due diligence, leading to its successful acquisition of Healthscope in 2019. This case illustrates how access to due diligence is a crucial vulnerability for a PE bidder, which can be strategically exploited by a competitor to neutralize a seemingly decisive advantage.[8]

4.6 INTRODUCTION TO VALUATION

The next chapter is dedicated to valuation. We need, however, to introduce a few concepts here as it relates to due diligence and negotiation.

Valuation represents the critical juncture where all parties in a PE transaction must reconcile their competing perspectives on worth. Unlike public markets where prices emerge from continuous trading, PE valuations require constructing defensible estimates in the absence of ready market signals. This inherent challenge transforms valuation from a mechanical exercise into something resembling both analytical craft and strategic positioning.

The fundamental difficulty lies in the forward-looking nature of investment decisions. Every valuation ultimately rests on assumptions about future performance, market conditions, and exit possibilities that cannot be known with certainty. Private companies present particular challenges because they lack the transparent financial reporting and market benchmarks available for public entities. This uncertainty creates legitimate space for disagreement—and strategic maneuvering.

What makes PE valuation particularly complex is how different stakeholders approach the same company with entirely different objectives and constraints. The sponsor needs a valuation that supports acceptable returns to LPs while remaining competitive in auction processes. Management seeks validation of their growth

[8] Success in the acquisition process does not always guarantee ultimate success. Brookfield reportedly injected more than AUD 200 million in additional equity throughout 2024 to address operational losses stemming from COVID-19's impact on elective surgeries, rising inflation and interest rates, and a strategic misstep involving the imposition of facility fees that severed relationships with major insurers. These challenges occurred against an unsustainable debt load of AUD 1.4 billion. In 2025, a tragic death linked to a misdiagnosis prompted a Serious Adverse Event Review that confirmed multiple systemic failures, followed by a New South Wales government inquiry that considered the future of public-private hospital partnerships. Despite Brookfield's further emergency funding injections during negotiations, lenders ultimately withdrew support, leading to Healthscope entering receivership.

projections and strategic vision. Lenders require conservative estimates that support debt service coverage. Investment bankers balance maximizing seller proceeds against maintaining credibility for future mandates. Each party's valuation reflects not just their analytical conclusions but their institutional requirements.

This multiplicity of perspectives explains why valuation disagreements are standard rather than exceptional in PE transactions. The same financial projections can yield vastly different conclusions depending on discount rates, multiple selection, and terminal value assumptions. Sponsors might emphasize discounted cash flow analysis when market multiples seem high, while sellers favor comparable transactions during active periods. These aren't necessarily acts of bad faith—they often reflect genuinely different assessments of risk and opportunity.

The timing of valuation work also matters enormously. Initial sponsor valuations during sourcing focus on identifying attractive opportunities and setting bid parameters. Due diligence valuations involve deeper analysis but remain influenced by confirmation bias—having invested significant time and resources, deal teams naturally lean toward conclusions that support transaction completion. Lender valuations typically occur later in the process and emphasize downside protection over upside potential. Bank credit committees often receive completely different valuation ranges than those presented to PE investment committees for the same deal.

Perhaps most critically, PE valuations must serve multiple purposes simultaneously. They inform investment decisions, support fee calculations, guide portfolio company reporting, and ultimately determine LP returns. This creates inherent tensions of interest that regulatory bodies increasingly scrutinize. When management fees are calculated on invested capital, there may be subtle pressure to avoid write-downs. When carried interest depends on unrealized gains, optimistic valuations become financially attractive to sponsors.

The rise of continuation funds and GP-led secondary transactions has intensified these dynamics. When the same manager effectively sells assets to itself, valuation becomes both the mechanism and the battleground for allocating value between exiting and continuing investors. The challenge of maintaining arm's-length objectivity becomes particularly acute.

Yet for all its complexity and potential for manipulation, valuation ultimately serves as the essential common language for PE transactions. It forces all parties to make their assumptions explicit and creates a framework for productive disagreement. The best valuations do not eliminate uncertainty—they help quantify and allocate it fairly among sophisticated parties who understand the stakes.

The key insight for practitioners is that valuation in PE contexts is rarely about finding a single "correct" answer. Instead, it is about constructing defensible ranges that reflect genuine uncertainty while serving legitimate commercial purposes. This requires technical competence, certainly, but also judgment about which assumptions matter most and how different stakeholders will interpret the results. Getting valuation right—or at least getting it reasonable—often determines whether deals happen at all and on what terms.

This conceptual backdrop sets the stage for a technical chapter, where these competing perspectives and conflicting incentives get translated into specific methodologies, discount rates, and multiple selections. The mathematics matter enormously, but understanding why different parties care about different aspects of that mathematics matters even more. Chapter 5 will investigate this thoroughly.

4.7 NEGOTIATION

We now turn to the documentation involved, which is an important part of the negotiation process and the investment decision.

4.7.1 Investment Recommendation

First, we consider a typical investment presentation template, which could be used to prepare an investment recommendation and presented to the "IC," the investment committee. It starts with an executive summary, which includes the investment recommendation itself, prepared by an analyst within the PE fund. This is followed by a few slides listing the qualitative factors supporting your recommendation. Then, the numbers include the valuation, a review of the revenue, and the scenario presented—this is the output of the LBO model, the first page produced in the initial model. Some commentaries and some downside scenarios are important as well.

The next part of the document explains the reasons why a recommendation might be wrong or could change. This serves as a useful hedge and helps readers understand how confident one is in our view. Then we conclude. A blank template for this type of presentation is included as supplementary material. Sources such as the Mergers & Inquisitions website, which offers detailed industry commentary, may be useful.

After the investment recommendation is accepted, potential investors will negotiate with the vendor and much of the negotiation will occur through the documentation where most negotiations really happen. Some of the examples below are specific to VC funding, where it is crucial to find the right balance between the entrepreneur and the investor(s), but most issues remain similar in other segments of PE.

4.7.2 Investment Committee

4.7.2.1 The Art and Substance of Convincing an IC A note of caution. ICs serve as critical gatekeepers, demanding that deal teams demonstrate not only financial potential but also the long-term viability of a business.

As IC members note, pitching is an art: deal teams must be persuasive without appearing to "sell" and must bring forward concise, focused papers—ideally under 20 pages—that explain sector dynamics, unit economics, and key risks. The best IC papers avoid excessive optimism and focus on balanced insight, particularly around market positioning. Importantly, the best performing ICs place more weight on market understanding than on financial models, which are often inaccurate in hindsight.

At a recent industry event, a participant cautioned that too many deal teams over-rely on numbers, which are often misleading. He argued that understanding the market and the business's positioning is far more predictive of outcomes. Deals that failed often lacked a clear grasp of the market dynamics or overestimated the company's competitive edge.

Another participant added that ICs are increasingly interested in market durability and business purpose rather than just spreadsheet outcomes.

Our students will recognize the mantra: success hinges less on dense numerical analysis and more on a clear understanding of why a business deserves to exist now and a decade from now. What legitimizes the existence of this business? Why and where does it have the right to play?

Pre-IC reviews and early engagement with the business can help IC members ask deeper, more meaningful questions when it matters most. But deal teams must also remain vigilant of non-deal-related pressures—such as being the first or last investment in a fund cycle—which can distort decision-making. In the end, the winning formula is to frame the business's long-term relevance, communicate with precision, and resist overconfidence or pressure-led choices.

4.7.3 Term Sheets

One starts with the term sheet, which is a preliminary document that outlines the main terms and conditions of the proposed investment or transaction. Although it is not legally binding it sets the stage for drafting the final agreements. That will lead to documents such as the new articles of association, a shareholders' agreement, the management service agreement, share subscription agreement, and potentially a warrantors' disclosure letter.

Some key documents and agreements will help when managing conflicts during negotiations. For example, managers, founders, and entrepreneurs may aim to build a successful business, raise only the necessary money, and maintain control while financial investors may want to maximize financial return, seek control to impose their decisions, and aim to achieve liquidity within a reasonable time.

Term sheets are not systematically mentioned in the PE-focused literature. They are less important than with VC, but this varies by segment. They are not that relevant for LBOs, more in growth capital, although less than in VC, and remain critical in turnaround deals. Some PE firms treat term sheets more as practical checklists or summaries rather than negotiation tools once internal approvals are complete.

There are three characteristics that define the level of importance of term sheets for a given type of deal:

1. Standardization and Maturity

   In PE deals, especially LBOs, many terms have become relatively standardized over decades of industry practice. The core economic and control provisions tend to follow established patterns, particularly for straightforward buyouts. In contrast, VC deals often require more creative structuring due to the uncertainty around early-stage companies.
2. Due Diligence Focus

   PE deals typically involve mature companies with operating histories, making due diligence the more complex and critical phase. PE books tend to focus more on operational analysis, financial modeling, and value creation strategies rather than deal documentation. The term sheet, while important, is often seen as a more mechanical step after the key business decisions are made.
3. Deal Complexity Differences

   PE deals, particularly LBOs, tend to have their complexity in the capital structure (senior debt, mezzanine, etc.) rather than in shareholder rights and preferences that dominate VC term sheets. The debt documents often receive more attention than the equity terms.

Consequently, term sheets remain crucial in specific PE contexts:

- VC: Early-stage investments involve higher risk, less-established companies, and significant negotiation over control rights, protections, and upside sharing.

Startups' futures are highly uncertain, so term sheets play a vital role in defining how future uncertainties will be managed. Anti-dilution, liquidation preferences, voting rights, board composition, and founder vesting are highly negotiated to manage risks and align incentives.

- **Growth Capital:** The investee companies are typically more established, with proven revenue and profitability models. The focus is often on valuation, governance, and minority/majority ownership rather than detailed protective provisions. However, term sheets remain important as these deals often involve minority stakes and need careful structuring of governance rights, exit provisions, and anti-dilution protections—similar to VC deals.
- **LBOs:** PE firms usually acquire full control of the target company and don't require extensive protective provisions. The emphasis is on financing structures (debt-to-equity ratios), covenants in financing agreements, and operational improvement plans rather than negotiation of term sheets. Deal documentation focuses more on purchase agreements, financing agreements, and operational restructuring plans.
- **Turnarounds:** In distressed situations, the focus shifts to restructuring debt, injecting new capital, or negotiating with creditors rather than negotiating equity investment terms. The priority is stabilizing the business and negotiating with lenders, which overshadows traditional equity-related term sheet discussions. Term sheets can thus be quite complex due to the need to address existing creditor rights, potential debt-for-equity swaps, and complex governance arrangements during the turnaround period.

4.7.4 Other Documents

Various mechanisms can be introduced in the **share subscription agreement** to minimize such potential conflicts, such as equity share structure and liquidation preferences that incentivize entrepreneurs to maximize value and remain with the company, while also rewarding investors for taking risks. Liquidation preferences and anti-dilution are VC staples; in PE, control is achieved via majority ownership and debt covenants rather than preferred equity waterfalls or anti-dilution ratchets. Minority PE or growth equity rounds can resemble VC in adopting such rights, especially with minority protective provisions.

In VC, the share subscription agreement will also manage the balance of control between entrepreneurs and investors, through anti-dilution agreements/share price protections. PE buyouts emphasize **management incentive plans** (often outside these core docs) and rollover equity for key management as distinct motivators. Management incentive plans typically include short-term and long-term incentives (cash bonuses, stock options, restricted shares), designed to align management's interests with PE sponsors and retain key talent.

- The **shareholders and debt agreements** will provide additional support on interest coverage ratios, minimum earnings, CapEx limit and more, which is central in buyouts. Shareholders' agreements in PE often include robust governance and reserved matters provisions reflecting sponsor control and operational oversight. Debt financing agreements (loan agreements, security agreements) deserve more emphasis as these often occupy the deal's complexity in PE buyouts.

Exit provisions are addressed in the shareholder agreement, which provides incentives for all parties to achieve a liquidity event. The rationale differs: VC uses them to align diverse constituencies; PE uses them to tidy minority holdouts. Drag-along, tag-along, and IPO/M&A processes appear in both VC and PE, but VC docs often embed investor-protective exit timing incentives and preferred waterfalls, while PE relies on sponsor control to run a sale without needing liquidation-preference triggers. PE exit documents sometimes also include sale process control measures like drag-along rights backed by sponsor ownership, reducing need for preferred liquidation waterfalls.

- **Management incentive plans (MIP)** or equity incentive plans are crucial PE docs often separate from subscription agreements.
- **Purchase agreements (SPA)** or business transfer agreements are critical in PE buyouts; these cover acquisition terms beyond share subscription. We describe them in the Closing section.

Due diligence reports and **disclosure schedules/backstops** are essential documents that underpin risk assessment and negotiation, supporting the main transaction agreements by detailing the company's financial, legal, operational, and compliance status.

4.7.5 Covenants

We introduced covenants in Chapter 2. Beyond their role in risk mitigation, covenants are powerful instruments in the negotiation and control of LBO financing structures, particularly from the perspective of the lender.

Covenants typically fall into two types, each with distinct strategic implications:

- **Incurrence covenants** apply only when a borrower takes a specific action (e.g., issuing new debt, making an acquisition, or paying dividends). These are **trigger-based** and act as guardrails at key decision points.
- **Maintenance covenants** are more prevalent in traditional leveraged loan structures, require the borrower to continually meet financial performance tests, typically on a quarterly basis, and regardless of specific events. These include the following ratios:
  - Interest coverage ratio (EBIT/Interest expense)
  - EBITDA coverage ratio (Total debt/EBITDA)
  - Cash flow coverage (Operating cash flow/Total debt or Interest payments)
  - Fixed charge coverage ratio (in some structures)

Maintenance covenants serve two main purposes. They function as early warning mechanisms, alerting lenders if the company is drifting off its projected performance path. More critically, they offer negotiation leverage—if breached, they can trigger a restructuring or repricing of the debt or allow lenders to impose tighter controls or extract concessions from sponsors.

In strong credit markets, sponsors often push back on these provisions. This led to the rise of "covenant-lite" loans, especially before the 2008 financial crisis. These loans contained only incurrence covenants (or severely diluted maintenance covenants), limiting lenders' ability to intervene before a payment default. Covenant-lite structures are typically seen in borrower-friendly conditions, when competition among lenders is high and credit risk is underpriced. Whenever a borrower is in a position of strength, they are tempted to try to remove or weaken the covenants.

Nevertheless, when properly structured, covenants can serve the interests of both parties. They provide early signals to lenders while giving sponsors room to manage operations without excessive interference, until performance meaningfully diverges from plan. In distressed scenarios, covenants offer a pre-default checkpoint at which capital structure can be renegotiated proactively, often preserving more value than a post-default resolution.

4.8 CLOSING

Closing a direct PE transaction, whether buying a company or investing growth capital, is a critical phase that requires careful attention to detail and thorough preparation, like any M&A transaction. After the due diligence process is completed, several key steps must be managed effectively to ensure a successful closing.

Firstly, finalizing the transaction documents is paramount. The primary document is the **purchase agreement** (or **investment agreement** in the case of growth capital). This contract outlines the terms of the transaction, including the purchase price, representations and warranties, covenants, indemnities, and closing conditions. It is essential that all terms are carefully negotiated and agreed upon to avoid disputes post-closing. Other key documents—often called ancillary documents—may include shareholders' agreements, employment agreements for key management, noncompete agreements, and any necessary financing documents, including, depending on the nature of the operation, the allocation of shares or equity interests, the valuation of the company, the terms of the capital infusion, and the terms of the loan agreements. These documents need to be carefully reviewed and negotiated to ensure they accurately reflect the agreed-upon terms and protect the interests of all parties involved.

Secondly, securing necessary approvals and consents is crucial. This may involve obtaining regulatory approvals, such as antitrust clearances or industry-specific regulatory consents or licenses (especially relevant in healthcare) and filing with securities regulators. Additionally, third-party consents may be required, such as from key customers, suppliers, or lenders, particularly if there are change of control provisions in existing contracts. Shareholder approvals may also be necessary, depending on the company's structure and the nature of the transaction. Both parties also need to ensure that all legal obligations are fulfilled before closing, including compliance with local, state, and federal regulations, depending on the country. This might involve clearing any outstanding liabilities or resolving legal disputes that were identified during due diligence.

Lastly, the closing process involves coordinating the transfer of funds and, in the case of a buyout, the transfer of ownership. This requires careful timing and coordination with banks and other financial institutions participating to the financing. It is also important to ensure that all closing conditions specified in the transaction documents are met or waived. These may include the delivery of certain certificates, the resolution of any outstanding legal issues, the achievement of specific financial or operational targets, or the arrangement of **Escrow and Holdbacks.**

- Often, a portion of the purchase price is held in escrow to cover potential post-closing claims, such as breaches of representations and warranties. The terms of the escrow, including the duration and conditions for release of funds, should be clearly defined.
- Similar to escrows, holdbacks involve retaining a portion of the purchase price until certain conditions or milestones are met post-closing. This provides protection for the buyer and incentivizes the seller to ensure a successful transition.

The closing typically culminates in a "signing ceremony" where final documents are executed and the transaction is formally completed.

Throughout this process, effective communication and project management are essential to keep all parties aligned and to address any last-minute issues that may arise. Legal counsel plays a crucial role in managing these aspects and ensuring a smooth closing process. The closing would also often include some preparation of post-closing integration planning (culture and operations). We will discuss this in Chapter 6.

4.9 CHAPTER SUMMARY

Chapter 4 walks through the six sequential stages of a PE transaction. It begins with defining the investment strategy, where the GP crystallizes target sectors, geographies, and return objectives. Next comes fundraising and fund setup, detailing LP outreach, governance design, fee economics, and legal structuring of the vehicle. We have seen how funds are set up and how compensation structures work, in particular in relation to the carry, the carried interest. The third stage, deal sourcing, covers proprietary origination, auction processes, and initial screening against the strategy.

Once a target is identified, structuring the investment addresses financing mix, transaction-level debt terms, equity waterfall mechanics, governance rights, and management incentives. A brief valuation introduction then situates the philosophical role of valuation—aligning diverse perspectives, surfacing assumptions, and framing negotiation ranges—setting up the deep dive in Chapter 5.

The fifth phase, due diligence, spans commercial, financial, legal, operational, and ESG vetting, culminating in detailed data-room analysis and confirmatory modeling. We focused on how it goes to the core of value creation and examined what is actually involved in carrying it out. Examples like the Commercial Due Diligence of Mediwound for a growth investor and the take-private of Acorn case studies illustrate these principles in action, showing how the business plan prepared by management was thoroughly assessed to justify the injection of capital.

Finally, negotiation and closing brings together SPA negotiation, covenant packages, legal sign-off, antitrust filings, and closing deliverables. Throughout, Chapter 4 emphasizes the interplay of strategic discipline, stakeholder coordination, and rigorous analysis that underpins a successful PE deal.

CHAPTER 5

Leveraged Buyout Analysis and Valuation

In this chapter, we develop a full leverage buyout (LBO) analysis model. Then, we discuss some of the different approaches to valuation that are used in LBO situations. Finally, we present advanced concepts such as cash sweeps and the adjusted present value (APV).

5.1 VALUATION 101

Valuation, while not rocket science, requires practice. There are two complementary approaches to valuation, a market-based one and a fundamental one that requires a detailed understanding of the future activities and performance of the company. They are respectively called relative valuation and discounted cash flow (DCF) methods.

In private equity (PE), relative valuation methods typically focus on Earnings Before Interest, Taxes, Depreciation, and Amortization aka EBITDA—which is derived from the Earnings Before Interest and Taxes (EBIT) that is found in the income statement. Rather, the most common DCF approach for LBO modeling uses free cash flows to the firm (FCFF). FCFF is also derived from EBIT. To obtain FCFF from EBIT, operational taxes and accounts are imputed for both short-term financing needs pinned down with working capital changes and long-term financing requirements, that is capital expenditures net of depreciation.

5.1.1 Relative Valuation

Relative valuation is easy to understand and apply. Although it is imperfect, it is used in almost every company valuation. The idea of the relative valuation approach is to identify a common denominator to the industry and then apply a multiple to measure performance (profit, EBITDA, sales, etc.) in order to obtain either the enterprise value—including debt—or the equity value only.

Figure 5.1 shows a simple example of such a relative valuation. We identified three listed companies in the same industry and line of business, of similar size, and with a similar business model that we then deemed comparable to the private company we wanted to value, Snoozy. We simply divide the EV (enterprise value) of each company by the EBITDA figure for the same period. The result is called the EBITDA multiple. If we have enough such comparable companies, we will be able to calculate an average, or

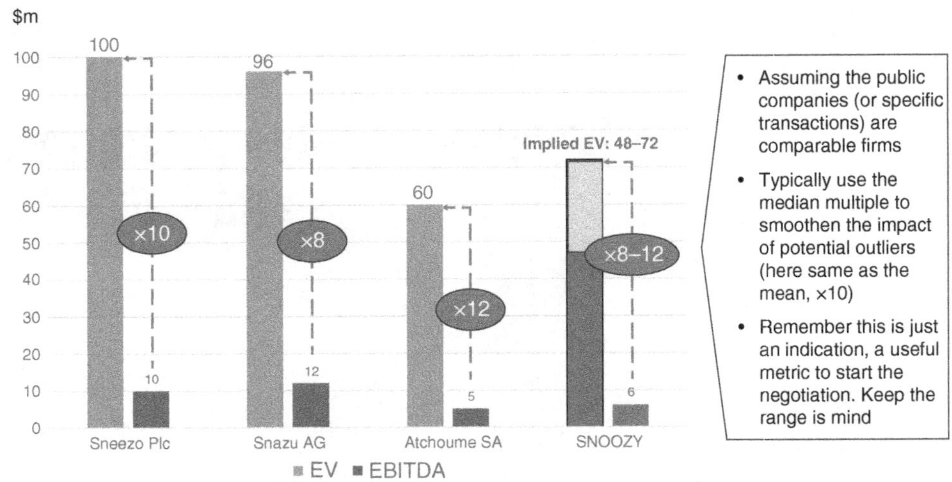

FIGURE 5.1 Relative valuation of Snoozy.

even better, a median multiple, which we will apply to Snoozy's EBITDA to estimate a relative EV.

In Figure 5.1, multiples range from 8× to 12×, with an average and a median at 10×. Applying these multiples to the $6 million EBITDA, Snoozy's EV lies in an estimated range of $48–$72 million, or approximately $60 million. In practice, we will often make additional adjustments to compensate for the imperfect comparability, starting with the fact that listed companies typically trade at a premium over their private equivalent. There are several reasons for this, which include greater information availability, a liquidity premium, and different contractual provisions (Gornall and Strebulaev, 2020).

5.1.1.1 Relative Valuation Pros and Cons

Pros

- *Market-based*: Values companies by comparing them to peers using multiples like P/E or EV/EBITDA, reflecting current market sentiment.
- *Simplicity*: Often easier and quicker to apply using available market data, also easier to communicate and use in negotiations.
- *Useful for sanity checks*: Shows how similar companies are valued, helping to validate or question other valuation methods.

Cons

- *Dependent on comparables*: If no good peers exist, the valuation can be misleading.
- *Market mood influences*: It reflects market sentiment that can be irrational or temporary.
- *Less detailed*: Does not explain why a company differs fundamentally from its peers.

5.1.2 DCF

The various approaches to DCF use different cash flows and discount rates. The weighted average cost of capital (WACC) methods discounts FCFF, which represents the cash generated by the business that is available to all providers of capital—both debt and equity—after covering operating expenses, taxes, and necessary investments in working capital and fixed assets. Expected FCFFs are discounted to their present value using WACC:

$$\text{Present Value of FCFF}_t = \frac{\text{FCFF}_t}{(1 + \text{WACC})^t}$$

Here, t represents the period (usually years).

The WACC remains the weighted cost of equity and debt capital, adjusted for the company's capital structure and tax shield benefits on debt interest.

The total enterprise value is obtained by adding *the discounted FCFFs for all forecast years* and the present value of the terminal value—which estimates the value of cash flows beyond the explicit forecast period. This can be expressed as follows:

$$\text{EnterpriseValue} = \sum_{t=1}^{n} \frac{\text{FCFF}_t}{(1 + \text{WACC})^t} + \frac{\text{Terminal Value}}{(1 + \text{WACC})^n}$$

Here, n is the final forecast year (typically $n = 5$).

The *terminal value* using the perpetuity growth method (also called the Gordon growth model) is calculated as follows:

$$\text{Terminal Value} = \frac{\text{FCFF}_n \times (1 + g)}{\text{WACC} - g}$$

where:

- FCFF_n is the free cash flow to the firm in the last forecast year,
- g is the constant growth rate expected to continue indefinitely beyond year n,
- WACC is the weighted average cost of capital.

Once the total firm value is estimated, net debt can be subtracted from the enterprise value to obtain the equity value.

The sum of FCFFs discounted with WACC aligns the valuation with all cash flows available before debt payments, thus matching the discount rate that blends costs of both debt and equity capital. This method results in a comprehensive intrinsic valuation of the firm's total value.

5.1.2.1 DCF Pros and Cons

Pros

- *Intrinsic valuation*: DCF focuses on a company's future free cash flows discounted to present value, reflecting its fundamental worth based on explicit financial assumptions like revenue growth and margins.
- *Market-independence*: It does not rely on current market prices or comparables, so temporary market mispricing doesn't distort the valuation.
- *Detailed and defendable*: Since the valuation depends on concrete assumptions, each driver can be examined and justified closely.

Cons

- *Highly assumption-dependent*: Errors or overconfidence in projecting future cash flows or the terminal value or discount rates can drastically change valuation. The WACC too, as it is often used, relies on assumptions that debt ratios remain constant. It also ignores the risk of tax shields as well as costs of financial distress, which explains that it is common to use the WACC formula without debt tax shields. To address this, one often performs a sensitivity analysis to estimate how sensitive results are to changes in assumptions to cash flows and to the WACC.
- *Complexity*: Gathering necessary data and modeling projections can be time-consuming and complex.

5.1.3 Comparison

These approaches are meant to answer different questions. DCF tells you, "What is the company really worth based on its own fundamentals?" Relative valuation asks, "What is the market currently willing to pay relative to others?"

Using both methods together is prudent. When their outputs align, confidence in the valuation increases. Comparable firms' valuations reflect investor assumptions on the cost of capital, growth rates, and ROI of comparable firms, which is often relevant to the valuation of the private firm. When they differ significantly, it signals a need to revisit assumptions or understand market dynamics better. Hence, DCF and relative valuation complement each other by providing a fuller picture, blending intrinsic economic value and market perspectives. One may expect relative valuations to yield higher values than a DCF. Indeed, transaction comparables tend to trade at an average premium of around 25% in take-private transactions, and trading comparables benefit from an additional premium of about 20% for being publicly listed, again because listed firms were listed because they were successful and they benefit from higher information disclosure and from a liquidity premium. Yet, the DCF approach often produces the higher valuation. This may be because despite weighting multiple scenarios, DCFs may not fully capture the numerous internal and external risks faced by a company, whereas these risks tend to be priced into relative valuations.

5.1.3.1 Valuation of Small Companies The valuation of a small company typically commands a lower multiple of EBITDA compared to larger, more established firms. There are several reasons for this. Small companies often exhibit higher reliance on their founder-CEOs, which raises key-person risk and raises concerns about leadership continuity. They tend to have higher customer concentration, exposing them to revenue volatility if one major client departs. Financial statements of smaller companies are often less reliable or accurate, due to less rigorous accounting controls and fewer resources for financial management. Additionally, working capital management is frequently weaker, causing cash flow unpredictability and operational inefficiencies that can impair value. Other factors include limited scale and scope, less diversified product and service offerings, vulnerability to market and competitive pressures, and generally lower bargaining power with suppliers and customers. In contrast, large, listed firms are subject to strict information disclosure requirements, not to mention analyst and media coverage that contain valuable information. All these issues increase the perceived risk and reduce forecast reliability to small private firms, leading investors to apply lower EBITDA multiples to compensate for the heightened uncertainty and potential value erosion.

This fundamental risk profile translates to typical EBITDA multiples for small businesses often ranging between 2× and 5×, depending on industry and growth prospects, compared to higher multiples often above 10× as seen in larger companies with proven management teams, diversified customers, and strong financial controls.

5.2 VALUATION OF STARTUPS

To determine the worthiness of any venture capital (VC) deal, VC organizations employ a variety of financial metrics and figures. The process of determining value and investability in mature organizations is relatively simple because established businesses generate sales, profits, and cash flow that can be used to calculate a reasonably reliable measure of value. However, to understand the business and the opportunity for early-stage ventures, VCs must place greater emphasis on their expectations of the value creation potential of management teams than on past cash flows (Gompers et al., 2016). Here, we examine the most commonly used metrics for measuring a VC investment's performance.

Valuation in venture capital is more challenging due to the lack of historical financial data for the firm being valued and the high uncertainty surrounding early-stage companies. Rather than relying solely on traditional financial metrics like revenue or profit, VCs focus on potential growth, scalability, market opportunity, and the ability to achieve a successful exit. They often employ specialized valuation methods tailored for startups, such as the venture capital method, which focuses on estimating the future exit value and calculating the current value by applying discount rates that reflect high risk.

Moreover, qualitative factors like the strength of the founding team, product viability, competitive landscape, and market traction play a critical role in assessing value, as they signal the startup's potential to scale and create returns. Other approaches like the Berkus method and the scorecard method incorporate these qualitative and comparative metrics to supplement financial data, particularly when early-stage startups have limited quantifiable performance.

In addition to direct valuation methods, VCs closely track performance metrics such as customer acquisition cost (CAC), lifetime value (LTV) of customers, burn rate, and runway, since these indicate how efficiently the startup is functioning and how soon it might need additional funding.

In summary, VC valuation blends financial projections, qualitative assessments, and market dynamics, recognizing that early-stage investing involves higher uncertainty but also substantial upside potential. This combined approach enables VCs to systematically evaluate an investment's risk and expected return despite a lack of traditional financial history.

5.3 THE BETA IN PRIVATE EQUITY

One could argue that a beta requires a fluctuating and observable price. This is not the most obvious characteristic of PE, on the contrary. We often circumvent this issue by adjusting the betas of the stocks of comparable public companies. But what do we observe? Can we assume an average beta for each segment of PE?

As discussed in Section 3.3 of Chapter 3, earlier research attributes an average beta of about 2.5 to VC. This seems sensible. But what is the beta for LBOs? The intuition would suggest more than one because of their higher leverage (around 50%) than public companies (about 30%).

However, empirical estimates using cash flows consistently place LBO beta closer to one (Franzoni et al., 2012; Ang et al., 2018). This often leads to positive alpha for LBO funds. For venture capital, beta is higher (over 2.5 in some periods), implying lower or even negative alpha. LBO leverage functions far more flexibly than simple levered stock positions, thanks to evolving debt terms, credit lines, and payment options, making LBOs less cyclical and bankruptcy-prone than one may expect; this pattern persists regardless of the estimation method (Phalippou, 2021; Korteweg and Nagel, 2025). These give us useful orders of magnitude, notwithstanding that every LBO deal will have its own beta.

Secondary market price-based betas can be much higher but rely on noisy, recent data. In the end, LBOs act more like stable operating businesses than leveraged stock bets, implying risk and required return for LBOs should not be blindly scaled from public equities.

5.4 TARGET IRR AND CASH SWEEP

As we discussed earlier, PE firms usually think in terms of a target overall return from their investments. Return is typically the annual internal rate of return, the IRR (Gompers et al., 2020), and it is calculated over the life of the investment. Remember that the overall return takes into account capital redemptions, possible capital gains, and income through fees and dividends. As a rough guide, the average return required in LBOs used to exceed 25% a year before the Global Financial Crisis. Many firms now target closer to 15–20%. Several PE firms including very top ones acknowledged that their target was now lower than 25%.

The target IRR is assessed using an iterative calculation that will include the valuation of the initial investment, the desired return, and the valuation of the firm at exit. It is particularly relevant to investors in VC, but also in buyouts.

We value the investment project from the initial investment to the value at exit (Figure 5.2).

We evaluate the IRR through the cash sweep method.[1] A cash sweep applies some or all surplus cash flows directly to paying down debt faster in an LBO model, which impacts the returns and IRR calculation for equity investors. We want to reproduce a simple pattern: shareholders invest at year 0 and then receive nothing before exit, at which point they receive a single cash payment. In most cases, we will use all the excess cash flows to reduce debt.

[1] This little exercise was initially developed together with Denis Gromb.

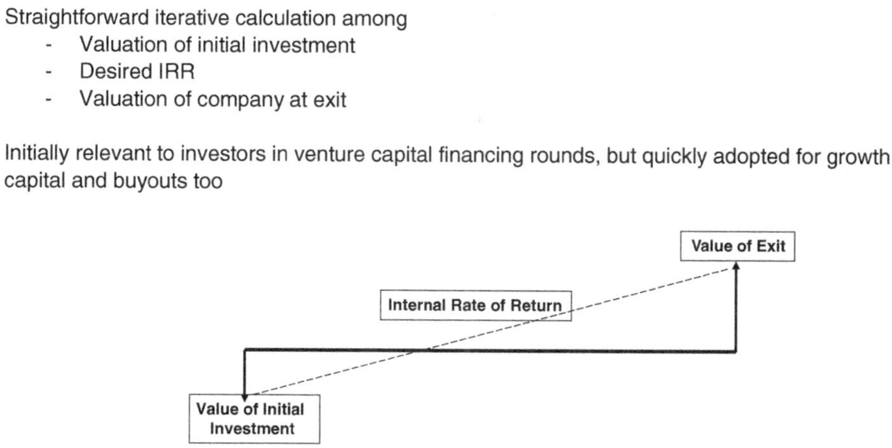

FIGURE 5.2 Target IRR approach.

TABLE 5.1 Starting with $780 Million of Debt

	Year 1	Year 2	Year 3	Year 4	Year 5
FCFF	61.4	82.8	91.0	97.4	110.2
Initial debt	780.0	778.5	755.5	722.5	680.6
Interest rate	12%	12%	12%	12%	12%
Interest payment	93.6	93.4	90.7	86.7	81.7
Tax rate	36%	36%	36%	36%	36%
Interest tax shield	33.7	33.6	32.6	31.2	29.4
Cashflow available	1.5	23.0	33.0	41.9	57.9
Debt principal repayments	1.5	23.0	33.0	41.9	57.9
Net cash flow	0.0	0.0	0.0	0.0	0.0
Final debt	778.5	755.5	722.5	680.6	622.7

For example, assume we are buying a company at $70.00 per share and there are 10 million shares outstanding—that is about $700 million in equity value. Debt is worth $300 million so the enterprise value is $1 billion. We consider an LBO with a maximum debt-to-value ratio of 75%—we assume lenders would not lend more—and a high yield interest rate of 12%. We plan to exit in five years through a trade sale with a debt-to-value ratio of 33% in line with the industry and help secure the industry multiple. We forecast this multiple at exit to be eight times so the future EV will be eight times the future EBITDA. The PE investor requires an IRR of 35%.

We estimate that free cash flows to the firm will increase from $60 to $110 million (Table 5.1). We can calculate an EBITDA of $200 million at exit so the exit value will be eight times that EBITDA, that is $1.6 billion. A target debt ratio of one-third yields a debt level of $528 million dollars.

To guess a starting debt level in year 0, we try an initial debt level, work out cash flows and debt repayments, and compare our debt level at exit with our target \$528 million. We plug debt at the beginning of every year and forecast cash flow available for the cash sweep. That is all available cash flow after paying interest to reduce debt. This allows us to iteratively forecast debt at exit.

We forecast cash flows available to make debt principal repayments with

$$\text{FCFF} - \text{Interest payments} + \text{Tax shield}$$

In practice, one can use the forecast of actual tax and interest payments, for example:

$$\text{NI} + \text{Deferred tax} + \text{Other non-cash expenses} + \text{Dep.} - \text{CAPX} -$$
$$\Delta_{\text{NWC}} + \text{Other cash inflows not in NI (e.g., after-tax asset sales)}$$

First, we try a debt level of \$780 million—this is our first guess for our starting debt level. With a 12% interest rate, interest payment is \$94 million. With a tax rate of 36%, the tax yield is 33.7 million. We then calculate the available cash flow worth \$1.5 million left that is used for debt principal repayments. This reduces the end of year principal by \$1.5 million and leaves zero cash flow.

The principal is reported at the beginning of year 2. We iterate and obtain a slightly higher cash flow of \$23 million to deduct from debt. Debt then decreases to \$755 million. We iterate over five years, and we end up with about \$623 million. This exceeds our target debt level of \$528 million by \$95 million.

We then try an initial debt level lower than \$780 million by, say, \$80 million, hoping that with added interest and the cash sweep we will decrease debt at exit by \$95 million. With an initial debt level of \$700 million, the cash flow available at the end of year 1 is \$7.6 million (Table 5.2). This helps us to reduce debt faster to \$692 million in the second year. We iterate and end up with debt worth \$507 million at exit. That is too low compared to our target \$528 million. We can optimize our return by choosing a higher initial debt level.

TABLE 5.2 Adjusting to a Lower 700 Million Debt

	Year 1	Year 2	Year 3	Year 4	Year 5
FCFF	61.4	82.8	91.0	97.4	110.2
Initial debt	700.0	692.4	662.7	622.6	573.0
Interest rate	12%	12%	12%	12%	12%
Interest payment	84.0	83.1	79.5	74.7	68.8
Tax rate	36%	36%	36%	36%	36%
Interest tax shield	30.2	29.9	28.6	26.9	24.8
Cashflow available	7.6	29.6	40.1	49.6	66.2
Debt principal repayments	7.6	29.6	40.1	49.6	66.2
Net cash flow	0.0	0.0	0.0	0.0	0.0
Final debt	692.4	662.7	622.6	573.0	**506.9**

TABLE 5.3 Finetuning to the Optimal Level of Debt

	Year 1	Year 2	Year 3	Year 4	Year 5
FCFF	61.4	82.8	91.0	97.4	110.2
Initial debt	714.6	708.1	679.7	640.9	592.7
Interest rate	12%	12%	12%	12%	12%
Interest payment	85.8	85.0	81.6	76.9	71.1
Tax rate	36%	36%	36%	36%	36%
Interest tax shield	30.9	30.6	29.4	27.7	25.6
Cashflow available	6.5	28.4	38.8	48.2	64.7
Debt principal repayments	6.5	28.4	38.8	48.2	64.7
Net cash flow	0.0	0.0	0.0	0.0	0.0
Final debt	708.1	679.7	640.9	592.7	528.0

After several trials, we find an optimal debt level of $715 million, which yields our target debt level at exit of $528 million (Table 5.3).

After deducting this debt amount from the enterprise value we had calculated, we are left with $1.072 billion. Since we started with a debt level of $714 million and the enterprise value used to be $1 billion, the equity should be $285.4 million. This gives us a debt to value of 71.4%. This is a cash multiple of 1,072/285.4 = 3.76, which corresponds to an IRR of $3.76^{1/5}$ = 30%. Have we met our objectives given our constraints? The debt to value is below 75%, but the IRR is lower than the required 35%.

To make this work, we can use our value creation framework. We examine every variable in the IRR calculation and look for any legitimate room for improvement. We list common value drivers here.

1. Buy cheaper (negotiate less than $70 per share).
2. Improve cash flow generation
   - to accelerate cash sweep
   - to increase EBITDA at exit
3. Renegotiate debt interest rate below 12%.
4. Sell noncore or nonperforming assets.
5. Look for any way to reduce taxes, e.g. think of inversion deals to reduce the tax rate.
6. Renegotiate minimum IRR with your investment committee.
7. Increase debt and delay exit? (unlikely)
8. Reduce debt and accelerate exit? (unlikely)
9. Increase the multiple at exit is also unlikely, unless ...
   - We bought cheap.
   - We know we have a buyer above market price.
   - We have repositioned/strategically augmented the asset and are playing in a different league, where the multiple is higher.

We will revisit all these options in the UNITE playbook in Chapter 6.

It is tempting to forecast several small improvements that will jointly meet the 35% IRR target. Unfortunately, this can become an exercise of manipulation. Stretching each variable to the limit is inappropriate because the likelihood that you can simultaneously improve in all dimensions is low.

5.5 APV AND RELATIVE VALUATIONS

In the DCF method, the WACC is commonly used as the discount rate to discount future free cash flows to the firm. The WACC method is easy to use and does well for moderate and stable debt ratios. However, it is often not convenient to analyze firms with high debt ratios that vary over time, which is often the case in LBOs. In our previous examples we assumed a stable capital structure, which allowed us to use a constant WACC. In an LBO with accelerated repayment of high yield debt and the subsequent expected yearly boost of the equity value, using the WACC is not impossible, but it requires additional effort. First, the WACC formula generally does not adjust for costs of debt, which can be high for high debt ratios. Second, whenever the debt ratio is not too high and time-varying, the WACC also varies with time so using the WACC method requires adjusting and recalculating the debt ratio, the cost of equity, and ultimately the WACC itself every year. In LBOs, we start highly levered, and we end the investment period with much less debt and typically much more equity, as we hope we have increased its value every year.

Fortunately, there is an elegant solution called the adjusted present value (APV) method. It is a valuation approach that breaks down a company's value into two main parts: the value if it were financed entirely by equity (unlevered value) and the net value of financing effects, mainly the present value of tax shields from debt.

Unlike the standard DCF using WACC, APV discounts the project's free cash flows at the unlevered cost of equity to find the base value of the business without debt. Then it separately adds the benefits of debt financing, such as tax deductibility of interest payments, which reduces the company's tax burden and increases its value. The tax shield's present value is typically discounted at the cost of debt, reflecting its risk level.

Formally, it can be expressed as follows:

$$\text{Value}_{levered} = \text{Value}_{unlevered} + \text{PV of tax shield} - \text{PV of financial distress costs}$$

APV's strength lies in its ability to clearly separate operating performance from financing decisions. It offers detailed insight into how financing affects firm value, which is why it is favored for LBOs and other transactions where debt levels and financing terms evolve significantly. Unlike the WACC, it offers a clear, easy-to-use method to capture various costs and benefits of leverage such as debt issuance costs or costs of financial distress.

This method was introduced by Stewart Myers in 1974 and is particularly favored for complex capital structures where separating operating and financing effects brings clarity and precision.

The relative valuation, whether based on trading comparables or on recent transactions, offers the most common measures for LBOs. EBITDA multiples are used most often as they remove the direct impact of debt interest. We will also discuss the net asset value (NAV) as well as shorthand or industry valuation benchmarks, which are shortcuts to assess the value without going through the traditional financial metrics. We will explore this later, after the APV method.

5.5.1 Step-by-step APV Valuation: Example of "DealCo" LBO

Here, we conduct a straightforward APV valuation to illustrate the method.

Step 1: Calculate Present Value of Unlevered Cash Flows (Years 1–5)

- Assume DealCo generates unlevered free cash flows (UFCF[2]) of $100 million in year 1, growing at 5% annually for five years:

Year	UFCF ($M)
1	100
2	105
3	110.25
4	115.76
5	121.55

- Using an unlevered cost of capital R_0 of 12%, we discount each UFCF to present value:

$$PV_{UFCF} = \sum_{t=1}^{5} \frac{UFCF_t}{(1 + 0.12)^t}$$

- Calculating yields approximately $394 million.

Step 2: Calculate Terminal Value of Unlevered Firm Beyond Year 5

- Assume UFCF grows at a constant rate $g = 3\%$ beyond year 5.
- Terminal value at year 5 (value of the unlevered firm VU_5):

$$TV_{Unlevered} = \frac{UFCF_5 \times (1 + g)}{R_0 - g} = \frac{121.55 \times 1.03}{0.12 - 0.03} = \frac{125.2}{0.09} = 1{,}391.07 \text{ million}$$

- Discount back to present value:

$$PV_{TV} = \frac{1{,}391.07}{(1 + 0.12)^5} = \frac{1{,}391.07}{1.7623} = 789.33 \text{ million}$$

- Total present value of unlevered firm:

$$394 + 789.1 = 1{,}183.33 \text{ million}$$

[2]UFCF = FCFF. The term UFCF highlights the fact that this cash flow is calculated without accounting for interest expense (i.e., unlevered).

Step 3: Compute Present Value of Interest Tax Shields (Years 1–5)

- DealCo issues debt of \$700 million at 8% interest rate with the view of keeping the debt level constant for five years so the decrease in the debt ratio is driven by cash flow growth.
- Annual interest payment = \$700M × 8% = \$56 million.
- The corporate tax rate is assumed at 35%, so annual tax shield = \$56M × 35% = \$19.6 million.
- With a fixed debt repayment schedule, we discount tax shields at the cost of debt, 8% (NOT the unlevered cost of capital):

$$PV_{TaxShield} = \sum_{t=1}^{5} \frac{19.6}{(1 + 0.08)^t}$$

- Calculation yields approximately \$78.26 million.

Step 4: Calculate Terminal Value of Tax Shields Beyond Year 5

- There is an elegant way shown by Ross et al. (2002). It calculates it as the difference between the value of the levered firm in year 5 (VL_5) and the value of the unlevered firm in year 5 (VU_5).
- Assume a target debt-to-value ratio of 40% stabilized from year 5. The levered cost of equity in year 5 is:

$$r_E = r_0 + \frac{D}{E}(1 - T_c)(r_0 - r_D) = 13.73\%$$

- We then calculate WACC (also from year 5) and use it to estimate VL_5 as a terminal value:

$$WACC_5 = r_E \frac{E}{D+E} + r_D(1 - T_c)\frac{E}{D+E} = 10.32\%$$

$$VL_5 = UCFF_{Year5} \times \frac{1+g}{WACC - g} = \frac{121.55(1.03)}{(0.1032 - 0.03)} = 1{,}710.33 \text{ million}$$

- Terminal value of tax shield at year 5 is thus:

$$TV_{TaxShield} = VL_5 - VU_5 = 1{,}710.33 - 1{,}391.07 = 319.26 \text{ million}$$

- Discount terminal tax shield back to present at the cost of unlevered equity[3]:

$$PV_{TV\,TaxShield} = \frac{319.26}{(1 + 0.1032)^5} = \frac{319.26}{1.6341} = 181.16 \text{ million}$$

- Total tax shield value:

$$78.26 + 181.16 = 259.42 \text{ million}$$

[3] Practitioners often use the cost of debt by default for convenience, although academic literature shows the unlevered cost of equity is theoretically more appropriate when the firm maintains a constant leverage ratio, which is the case here from year 5.

Final Step: Calculate Total Firm and Equity Value

- Total enterprise value (levered) = unlevered firm value + tax shield value:

$$1{,}183.33 + 259.42 = 1{,}442.75 \text{ million}$$

- Subtract debt principal ($700 million) to get equity value:

$$1{,}442.75 - 700 = 742.75 \text{ million}$$

This APV valuation provides a clear breakdown of how the unlevered operations and debt financing tax benefits contribute to DealCo's value.

Recall, we have applied the APV to this LBO in four steps. That may look slightly tedious. However, it is simpler than with a WACC that we would need to recalculate every year in which the debt ratio evolves. With the APV, we have avoided that.

5.5.2 More About Relative Valuations

When selecting comparables for valuation, whenever possible, we choose companies that operate in the same industry as the target company. There are often many transactions in the same sector, which will help us. In addition, one will find comparables in an area where PE funds already operate because they tend to operate in similar sectors and similar types of firms.

However, more often than not, you will have to look beyond the usual metrics. This will require to pick comparables that have the same types of customers, a similar cost structure, a similar growth trajectory or projected growth, or that may be exposed to similar payment terms, and so on. One might also consider factors like seasonality, trends, rollout schemes, and market multiples (Figure 5.3).

EBITDA is the preferred and most common measure of relative valuation in the universe of PE. It started being adopted during the 1980s and gained widespread popularity in the 1990s. It replaced EBIT as the metric of choice for several reasons. EBITDA allows for better comparison between companies with different capital structures, tax situations, and depreciation policies, and neutralizes differences in capital intensity; it is considered a closer approximation of operating cash flow; it provides a clearer picture of a company's ability to service debt; and it is easier to calculate from financial statements while requiring fewer adjustments than EBIT.

Selection criteria

- Same line of business
- Same customers
- Same cost structure
- Same past and/or projected growth
- Similar payment terms
- Following the same business and economic cycles

Factors to consider

- Seasonality
- Financial ratios
- Trends in numbers or ratios over time
- Roll out schedule
- Market multiples

FIGURE 5.3 Criteria and factors for the selection of comparables.

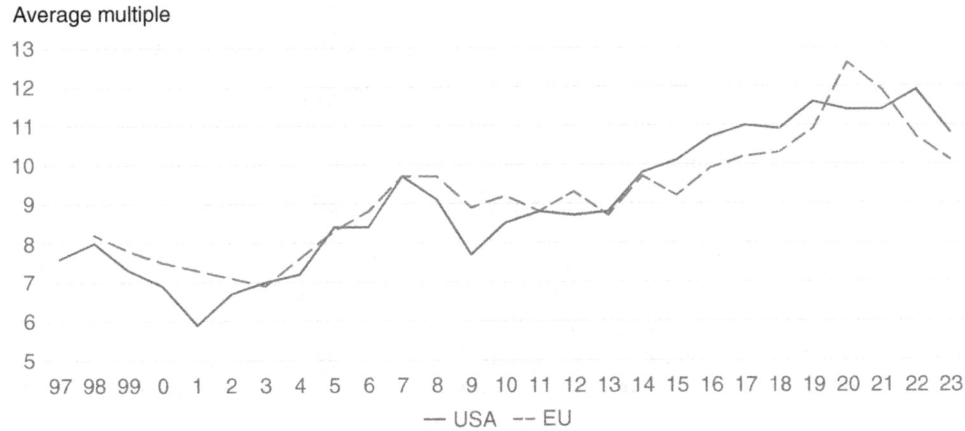

Note: Based on pro forma trailing EBITDA. Including fees

FIGURE 5.4 Evolution of LBO purchase price/EBITDA multiples in the United States and Europe. Source: Candesic research.

However, EBITDA has limitations and can sometimes overstate a company's financial health. Some regulatory bodies, like the Securities and Exchange Commission, have expressed concerns that it is not defined by Generally Accepted Accounting Principles (GAAP) or International Financial Reporting Standards (IFRS). This lack of standardization means different companies can calculate their EBITDA differently. Without strict guidelines, they can potentially manipulate EBITDA by classifying regular expenses as "extraordinary" to exclude them, aggressively recognizing revenue or understating expenses. Additionally, by excluding depreciation and amortization, EBITDA ignores the real costs of maintaining and replacing assets.

The "adjusted EBITDA" has become a regular joke in the industry, with many cases of overly optimistic financial pictures. As usual, investors should exercise caution. EBITDA is an appropriate and convenient measure but should not be used in isolation.

General partners often start working with **EBITDA minus maintenance CapEx** but, once they have determined EV, tend to express it as a multiple of the full EBITDA.

Historically, average EBITDA multiples have increased significantly over 25 years (Figure 5.4). This can be attributed to several factors: tech-driven efficiency and scalability that have enhanced growth prospects for many businesses, prolonged periods of low interest rates, abundant capital, globalization and increased competition between strategic and financial buyers, shift to asset light businesses. As we have seen in our cash sweep exercise, it is not appropriate to continue the trend in the future, whether we look at it from the perspective of mean reversion (valuation metrics tend to revert to long-term averages over time) or the financial law of gravity (the factors that helped raise multiples historically).

5.6 LBO ANALYSIS

We now highlight some of the issues one may face in an LBO valuation. To start with, unlike in many other acquisitions and apart from bolt on acquisitions following an initial buyout, there are no synergies because the acquirer is a financial investor. In addition, managers often have access to significant information about the company's debts that investors do not have—this can lead to information asymmetry in the case of a management buyout. While management will not change, the financing decisions will. This mismatch can result in management not being fully equipped to handle the new financing structure. As LBOs are financed disproportionately with debt, we will need to handle riskier cash flows and a variable cost of capital that may require adjustments or alternative valuation measures. Finally, the financial investor may not have the same sector expertise as a competing strategic investor, but they can mitigate this problem by hiring expert advisors.

5.6.1 Introduction to the Modelling Process

A full LBO analysis is quite a lengthy process. Some readers will skim through instructions to get a high-level overview of what is involved in such an exercise and why it is important in PE. Others will follow instructions closely and fill out the entire spreadsheet themselves, step by step, experimenting and playing with the inputs to assess the impact on the outputs. That will take more time, but it is worth it.

We will use the book's model. There are countless other models that circulate between investment banks, as bankers move between houses. Some are more sophisticated than others. A good model that can flexibly incorporate various cash flow scenarios and financing structures can take months to develop. The model we use is by no means the most comprehensive one in the market, but it gives access to detailed revenue forecasting for a hospital.

Note that some i-bankers do not rely on a generic model. According to a managing director at Stifel, a leading advisor in healthtech M&A, "My team and I develop a new model for each transaction. Yes, we have templates, but our transactions are simple from a valuation perspective, and I'd rather not take any risk with a model I don't fully understand." This is indeed more common for smaller and less complex transactions. There is some value in this approach as long as the user is rigorous and competent. AI tools can also significantly accelerate the modelling process. For mid to large LBOs however, it is often inefficient and risky to build from scratch.

This type of exercise is typically done by leverage finance teams in investment banks in order to develop a viable financing structure that will be presented to PE investors, the so-called sponsors. The leverage finance team does not normally provide the financing itself, although they often introduce their colleagues from the lending department. They play an advisory role and get paid a fee. The analysis might also be used in other contexts, by a strategic buyer who wants to understand how much a potential rival PE bidder can afford to pay for a company, for example.

5.6.2 Structure of the Model

Some best practices when building a model in a spreadsheet are worth mentioning here.

1. Create different sheets to separate assumptions from intermediary calculations and from outputs. Create an executive summary sheet with key outputs (IRR, cash-on-cash, exit multiples).
2. Include a "user manual" sheet.
3. Include a dedicated sources and uses sheet for transaction mechanics.
4. Build separate debt schedules for each tranche with detailed amortization.
5. Color-code your cells to distinguish variables, parameters, and results.

6. *Never* embed a variable assumption into a formula; this is a recipe for disaster.
7. Use consistent referencing (avoid circular references in leverage calculations).
8. Build flexibility for multiple exit scenarios and sensitivity analysis.
9. Consider building in covenant testing throughout the projection period.
10. Add scenario toggles for base/upside/downside cases.
11. Consider operating in manual calculation mode to choose when to see the impact of your changes.

The model is built around the financial statements projected into the future. Two levels of assumptions pages feed forecasting pages, which in turn generate two levels of summary (Figure 5.5).

Assumptions are divided between an **operating model** (a detailed review of all the components of the financial statements, typically done by the management team of the company, which includes a revenue model,[4] a balance sheet model, and a cash flow model) and an **LBO model** that defines in particular the capital structure (adding a debt schedule to the three financial statements).

The initial operating model projects the company's financial statements (income statement, balance sheet, cash flow statement) based purely on management's operational plans without considering the new LBO debt. This isolates the "business as usual" scenario and provides clear visibility into the underlying business performance

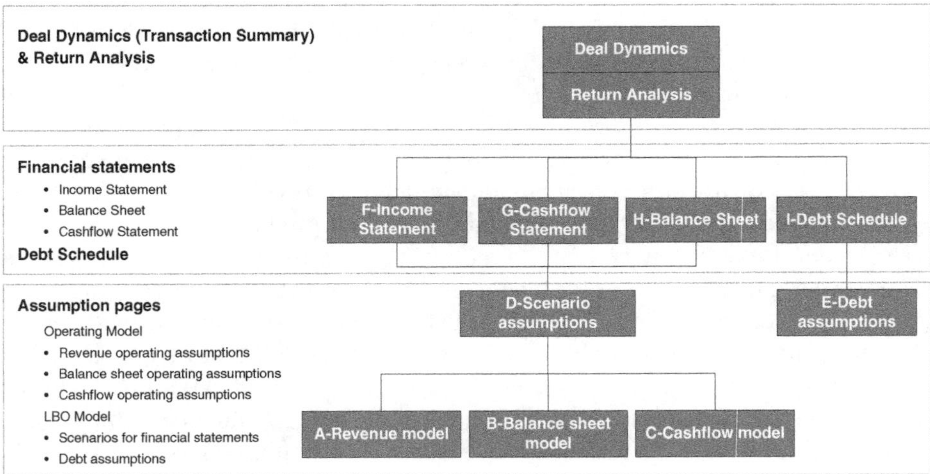

FIGURE 5.5 LBO model structure.

[4]The main reason it is often called the "revenue model" is that revenue is the primary driver for the entire operating forecast. In most financial models, the detailed assumptions start with the top line (revenue). You will build out projections based on key operational metrics like price, volume, customers, or locations. Nearly all the major variable costs that follow, such as Cost of Goods Sold (COGS) and variable Selling, General, & Administrative (SG&A) expenses, are then forecast as a percentage of that revenue.

Because the revenue build-up is the most complex and foundational part of the forecast from which everything else flows, the entire section informally takes its name. It's industry shorthand.

and cash flow generation capacity. The expected profitability is shown only for information but is not fully relevant as the management plan is generally not supposed to be implemented without the LBO. Profitability here is not finalized but serves as a base case for operating performance.

The second part then takes the operating forecasts as an input but replaces the capital structure with the LBO structure, which often includes higher-cost debt, amortization schedules, interest payments, and cash sweeps for debt repayment. This allows the model to capture the leverage impact on profitability, cash flow, and balance sheet dynamics. Such separation also facilitates analyzing scenarios and sensitivities: the standalone business performance can be analyzed independently of financing considerations, and different capital structures can be tested without rebuilding the entire operating forecast.

5.6.3 The Process Step by Step

We will explain how an LBO analysis can be carried out in five key steps.

1. Data gathering and operating model
2. Pre-LBO statements
3. Deal structure
4. Post-LBO statements
5. Deal dynamics

It involves first collecting or generating assumptions and other inputs, then in step 2, working on the pre-LBO model, followed by the transaction structure in step 3. After that we look at the post-LBO model and then conduct our analysis and valuation. We will explore each step at a time.

We provide the reader with the template model which accompanies the book. The fundamental structure is in place, and any reader can fill in the cells on their own. *The input cells should be limited to the cells with a yellow background only*. Other cells should not be overwritten.

It is a reasonably comprehensive model that can be used in many circumstances with a few adjustments for specific situations, including replacing the operating model for a company other than a UK general hospital. Of course, readers can play with all the inputs and assess how they impact the end product. However, we do not accept responsibility for the accuracy of these calculations. This model has not been validated for every possible scenario and should be used with caution when making decisions.

5.6.3.1 Step 1—Data Gathering and Operating Model In this approach, we prioritize revenue forecasting over cost and investment projections. This does not imply that costs and investments lack significance; rather, it reflects the perspective most relevant to investors. We need both, but once future revenues for growth or mature companies can be anticipated with reasonable accuracy, costs and CapEx become largely predictable. The resources required to achieve those revenue figures are, to a great extent, already known.

Considerable attention should be devoted to developing detailed insights into the fundamental drivers of revenue performance. These include volume versus pricing dynamics, timing of new product or service introductions, distribution channel strategies, modifications in reimbursement frameworks, specialty mix within healthcare facilities, bundled service offerings, and the balance between public and private payer sources. Our hospital model provides this level of detail and, from that perspective, is not adapted to modelling a CDMO or a healthcare software company. You would need to develop an alternative appropriate operating model, replacing the A, B, and C sheets that we describe hereafter.

First Level of Assumptions: Operating Model If we were to build the forecasts together with the company's management, we would first decompose the forecast revenue into all its components. Here is an example of building the revenue components for our hospital, followed by the costs, then the cash flow components, and the current assets and the liabilities in the balance sheet which provide the components of the working capital (short-term investments), and the CapEx (long-term investments).

Following, we share 14 screenshots that show the level of detail necessary to build such an operating model. A hospital is a complex set of businesses, with many layers of activity, both horizontally (medical specialties) and vertically (e.g., admissions, diagnostic, therapy, pharmacy). We have kept it simple. It can be more granular. The same is true for a diversified pharma specialty company, a CDMO, or an integrated provider of outsourcing services to medtech companies.

Operating Revenue Model We start by defining the characteristics of the hospital (Figures 5.6 to 5.8) and the pricing parameters by type of payor (Figure 5.9).

Building inputs

Theatres

Theatre type	Units	Input
		-
Number of operating theatres	#	9
Number of Cath labs	#	1

Procedure rooms

Procedure rooms	Units	Input
		-
Number of endoscopy suite	#	3

Rooms

Rooms/chairs	Units	Input
		-
Number of chemotherapy chairs	#	10
Number of radiotherapy theatres	#	1
Number of aesthetics rooms	#	1
Number of dentistry rooms	#	1

Diagnostics

Scanner type	Units	Input
		-
Number of CT scanners	#	2
Number of MRI scanners	#	2
Number of X-ray scanners	#	1

FIGURE 5.6 Operating model assumptions (IS)—sizing the hospital.

Capacity

Other inputs

-	Units	Input
		-
Weeks in a year	#	52

Theatres

Metric	Units	Input >> Weekdays	Saturday	Sunday	Extra hours
Available hours	Hours	60	8	0	0
Inpatient average theatre time	Hours	1.9	1.9	1.9	1.9
Outpatient average theatre time	Hours	0.9	0.9	0.9	0.9

Cath lab

Metric	Units	Input >> Weekdays	Saturday	Sunday	Extra hours
Cath lab availability	Hours	60	8	0	0
Average procedure time	Hours	1.5	1.5	1.5	1.5

Endoscopy

Metric	Units	Input >> Weekdays	Saturday	Sunday	Extra hours
Endoscopy availability	Hours	60	8	0	0
Average procedure time	Hours	0.5	0.5	0.5	0.5

CT

Metric	Units	Input >> Weekdays	Saturday	Sunday	Extra hours
Scanner availability	Hours	60	8	0	0
Average diagnostic time	Hours	0.25	0.25	0.25	0.25

MRI

Metric	Units	Input >> Weekdays	Saturday	Sunday	Extra hours
Scanner availability	Hours	60	8	0	0
Average diagnostic time	Hours	0.6	0.6	0.6	0.6

X-ray

Metric	Units	Input >> Weekdays	Saturday	Sunday	Extra hours
Scanner availability	Hours	60	8	0	0
Average diagnostic time	Hours	0.1	0.1	0.1	0.1

Chemotherapy

Metric	Units	Input >> Weekdays	Saturday	Sunday	Extra hours
Room availability	Hours	60	8	0	0
Average chemotherapy infusion time	Hours	3	3	3	3

Radiotherapy

Metric	Units	Input >> Weekdays	Saturday	Sunday	Extra hours
Room availability	Hours	60	8	0	0
Average treatment time	Hours	0.25	0.25	0.25	0.25

Aesthetics

Metric	Units	Input >> Weekdays	Saturday	Sunday	Extra hours
Room availability	Hours	60	8	0	0
Average aesthetics procedure time	Hours	0.3	0.3	0.3	0.3

Dentistry

Metric	Units	Input >> Weekdays	Saturday	Sunday	Extra hours
Room availability	Hours	60	8	0	0
Average dentistry procedure time	Hours	0.5	0.5	0.5	0.5

FIGURE 5.7 Operating model assumptions (IS)—defining the hospital capacity.

Utilisation

Ramp up period

-	Units	Input
		-
Years to maturity	Years	5

Utilisation inputs

		Inputs >>	
Category	Units	Current utilisation	Max utilisation
Theatre and procedure rooms	%	60.0%	75.0%
CT	%	60.0%	75.0%
MRI	%	60.0%	75.0%
X-ray	%	25.0%	25.0%
Chemotherapy and radiotherapy	%	40.0%	75.0%

Hospital wide utilisation

		0	1	2	3	4	5	6	7
Category	Units	2023	2024	2025	2026	2027	2028	2029	2030
Theatre and procedure rooms	%	60.0%	63.0%	66.0%	69.0%	72.0%	75.0%	75.0%	75.0%
CT	%	60.0%	63.0%	66.0%	69.0%	72.0%	75.0%	75.0%	75.0%
MRI	%	60.0%	63.0%	66.0%	69.0%	72.0%	75.0%	75.0%	75.0%
X-ray	%	25.0%	25.0%	25.0%	25.0%	25.0%	25.0%	25.0%	25.0%
Chemotherapy and radiotherapy	%	40.0%	47.0%	54.0%	61.0%	68.0%	75.0%	75.0%	75.0%

Other assumptions

Other assumptions

-	Units	Input
		-
Price inflation	%	3.0%
Year 1 inpatient share of hours	%	40.0%
Rest of time inpatient share of hours	%	60.0%

FIGURE 5.8 Operating model assumptions (IS)—utilization parameters.

Price assumptions

Payor splits

		Input >>			
Payor	Units	ting theatres & diagn	Cath lab	Endoscopy	erapy, aesthetics and dentistry
Self-pay	%	18.4%	19.3%	16.8%	50.0%
PMI	%	73.7%	77.3%	67.2%	50.0%
NHS	%	7.9%	3.4%	16.0%	0.0%

Average theatre procedure price

		Input >>	
Payor	Units	Inpatient	Outpatient
Self-pay	GBP	14,896	3,454
PMI	GBP	11,171	2,591
NHS	GBP	7,149	1,658
Weighted average	**GBP**	**11,538**	**2,676**

Average other procedure price

		Input >>	
Payor	Units	Endoscopy	Cath lab
Self-pay	GBP	1,918	5,842
PMI	GBP	1,439	4,382
NHS	GBP	921	2,804
Weighted average	**GBP**	**1,437**	**4,610**

Average diagnostic procedure price

		Input >>			
Payor	Units	CT scan	MRI	X-ray	Pet-CT
Self-pay	GBP	435	418	109	2,000
PMI	GBP	326	314	82	1,500
NHS	GBP	209	201	52	811
Weighted average	**GBP**	**337**	**324**	**84**	**1,537**

Average chemotherapy sessions price

		Input >>	
Payor	Units	Chemotherapy	Radiotherapy
Self-pay	GBP	1,800	800
PMI	GBP	1,350	600
NHS	GBP	-	-
Weighted average	**GBP**	**1,575**	**700**

Average aesthetics procedure price

		Input >>
Payor	Units	Aesthetics
Self-pay	GBP	948
PMI	GBP	711
NHS	GBP	455
Weighted average	**GBP**	**830**

Average dentistry procedure price

		Input >>
Payor	Units	Dentistry
Self-pay	GBP	2,468
PMI	GBP	1,851
NHS	GBP	1,185
Weighted average	**GBP**	**2,160**

FIGURE 5.9 Operating model assumptions (IS)—pricing parameters.

In Figures 5.10 to 5.13, we show the main cost assumptions to finish defining the operating model assumptions at the level of the Income Statement. Some of the data will vary over time and require historical figures. Here, we look at the last three years, which is generally sufficient.

Consultant fee assumptions

Average procedure/session consultant fee

Procedure type	Units	Input >>	Average consultant fent fee % of total procedure fee
Inpatient	GBP	1,102	9.5%
Outpatient	GBP	971	36.3%
Endoscopy	GBP	348	24.2%
Cath lab	GBP	730	15.8%
Radiotherapy	GBP	0	0.0%
Chemotherapy	GBP	543	34.5%
Aesthetics	GBP	434	52.3%
Dentistry	GBP	455	21.1%

Proportion of consultants employed

Scenario picker: 1 - Full employed by maturity

Category	Units	0 2023	1 2024	2 2025	3 2026	4 2027	5 2028	6 2029	7 2030
Proportion of consultants employed	%	0.0%	10.0%	30.0%	35.0%	40.0%	50.0%	60.0%	70.0%
Doctor retention bonus	%	0.0%	0.0%	50.0%	0.0%	0.0%	0.0%	0.0%	0.0%

Proportion of consultants employed (scenarios)

Category	Units	0 2023	1 2024	2 2025	3 2026	4 2027	5 2028	6 2029	7 2030
1 - Full employed by maturity	%	0.0%	10.0%	30.0%	35.0%	40.0%	50.0%	60.0%	70.0%
2 - 30% employment	%	0.0%	0.0%	0.0%	0.0%	0.0%	30.0%	30.0%	30.0%

FIGURE 5.10 Operating model assumptions (IS)—consultant fees.

Staffing cost assumptions

Assumptions

Metric	Units	Input >> -
On cost % of salary	%	20%
Staff pay rises	%	2.50%
Staffing over capacity of 75%	#	1.00
Staffing needs if more than 12 hours a day	#	0.0
Staffing needs if more than 8 theatres	#	0.1

Clinical

Category	Units	Data>> staff at maturity with	mber of staff at matu	Salary	Ramp up	g needs at 8 theatre plus cath lab
Director of Clinical Services	**# of staff**	1	1	102,000	No	1
Theatres	**# of staff**	**61**	**61**	**41,107**		**56**
Theatre Manager	# of staff	1	1	75,000	No	1
Deputy Theatre Manager	# of staff	1	1	62,500	No	1
Scrub	# of staff	20	20	47,500	Yes	18
Anaesthetics	# of staff	14	14	45,000	Yes	13
Recovery	# of staff	11	11	40,000	Yes	10
Healthcare assistants	# of staff	14	14	25,000	Yes	13
Imaging	**# of staff**	**14**	**14**	**40,750**		**14**
Imaging Manager	# of staff	1	1	68,000	No	1
Radiographers	# of staff	8	8	47,500	No	8
Healthcare assistant	# of staff	5	5	24,500	No	5
Physiotherapy	**# of staff**	**26**	**26**	**42,500**		**26**
Inpatient	# of staff	13	13	45,000	Yes	13
Outpatient	# of staff	13	13	40,000	Yes	13
Pharmacy	**# of staff**	**4**	**4**	**40,625**		**4**
Pharmacist	# of staff	1	1	52,000	No	1
Dosimetrists	# of staff	2	2	43,000	No	2
Technician	# of staff	1	1	24,500	No	1
Inpatient and outpatient	**# of staff**	**229**	**229**	**33,074**		**200**
Registered general nurse	# of staff	156	156	36,500	Yes	134
Senior medical physicist	# of staff	1	1	65,000	No	1
Medical physicist	# of staff	1	1	43,000	No	1
Radiation therapist	# of staff	2	2	58,000	No	2
Healthcare assistant	# of staff	69	69	24,000	Yes	62
Pre-admission	**# of staff**	**23**	**23**	**33,326**		**21**
Registered general nurse	# of staff	14	14	39,000	Yes	13
Healthcare assistant	# of staff	9	9	24,500	Yes	8

FIGURE 5.11 Operating model assumptions (IS)—staffing costs (1/2).

Non-clinical

Category	Units	Data>> staff at maturity with	mber of staff at matu	Salary	Ramp up	g needs at 8 theatre plus cath lab
Management	**# of staff**	**2**	**2**	**94,500**		**2**
Managing & Hospital Director	# of staff	1	1	149,000	Yes	1
Physician associates	# of staff	1	1	40,000	Yes	1
Bookings	**# of staff**	**18**	**18**	**36,000**		**18**
Reservations	# of staff	9	9	36,000	Yes	9
Certified surgical assistant	# of staff	6	6	36,000	Yes	6
Medical records	# of staff	3	3	36,000	Yes	3
Facilities	**# of staff**	**6**	**6**	**47,333**		**6**
Engineer	# of staff	2	2	60,000	No	2
Radiotherapy technologist	# of staff	2	2	42,000	No	2
Engineering support	# of staff	2	2	40,000	No	2
Catering	**# of staff**	**17**	**17**	**32,176**		**17**
Head Chef	# of staff	1	1	50,000	No	1
Chef	# of staff	3	3	40,000	No	3
Catering support	# of staff	10	10	29,000	Yes	10
Coffee shop	# of staff	3	3	29,000	No	3
Hotel	**# of staff**	**92**	**92**	**28,500**		**77**
Housekeeper	# of staff	46	46	28,500	Yes	31
Hostess	# of staff	31	31	28,500	Yes	31
Porters	# of staff	15	15	28,500	Yes	15
Theatre Admin	**# of staff**	5	5	30,000	Yes	5
Procurement	**# of staff**	**7**	**7**	**34,286**		**7**
Manager	# of staff	1	1	60,000	No	1
Stores	# of staff	6	6	30,000	Yes	6
Reception	**# of staff**	3	3	30,000	No	3
IT support	**# of staff**	4	4	42,000	Yes	4
Business Development Manager	**# of staff**	2	2	75,000	No	2
HR	**# of staff**	6	6	60,000	Yes	6
Finance	**# of staff**	**13**	**13**	**44,308**		**13**
Financial Management	# of staff	1	1	90,000	No	1
Financial planning and analysis	# of staff	2	2	68,000	No	2
Billers	# of staff	4	4	35,000	Yes	4
Credit Control	# of staff	3	3	35,000	Yes	3
Purchase Ledger	# of staff	3	3	35,000	Yes	3

FIGURE 5.12 Operating model assumptions (IS)—staffing costs (2/2).

Direct cost assumptions

		Historical >>			Forecast >>				
Category	Units	2023	2024	2025	2026	2027	2028	2029	2030
Medical supplies	% of revenues	18.0%	15.0%	15.0%	15.0%	15.0%	15.0%	15.0%	15.0%
Cost of tests, procedures, and billing	% of revenues	5.0%	4.0%	4.0%	4.0%	4.0%	4.0%	4.0%	4.0%
Facility expenses related to patient care	% of revenues	5.0%	4.0%	4.0%	4.0%	4.0%	4.0%	4.0%	4.0%
Medical records and billing	% of revenues	1.0%	1.0%	1.0%	1.0%	1.0%	1.0%	1.0%	1.0%
Food and dietary services	% of revenues	1.0%	1.0%	1.0%	1.0%	1.0%	1.0%	1.0%	1.0%
Employee training and education	% of revenues	1.0%	1.0%	1.0%	1.0%	1.0%	1.0%	1.0%	1.0%

Indirect cost assumptions

		Historical >>			Forecast >>				
Category	Units	2023	2024	2025	2026	2027	2028	2029	2030
Utilities	% of revenues	4.0%	3.0%	3.0%	3.0%	3.0%	3.0%	3.0%	3.0%
Legal & Professional Fees	% of revenues	2.5%	2.0%	2.0%	2.0%	2.0%	2.0%	2.0%	2.0%
Marketing and advertising	% of revenues	5.0%	4.0%	3.0%	2.0%	2.0%	2.0%	2.0%	2.0%
Transport	% of revenues	1.0%	1.0%	1.0%	1.0%	1.0%	1.0%	1.0%	1.0%
Printing, Postage, & Stationary	% of revenues	1.0%	1.0%	1.0%	1.0%	1.0%	1.0%	1.0%	1.0%
Service charges	GBP	280,000	280,000	280,000	280,000	280,000	280,000	280,000	280,000
Insured value	GBP	80,000,000							
Insurance cost per GBP insured	GBP	0.003							

Rent and council rates

Scenario picker: Case 1

		Historical >>			Forecast >>				
Category	Units	2023	2024	2025	2026	2027	2028	2029	2030
Rent (active)	GBP	**15000000**	**15,000,000**	**15,000,000**	**15,300,000**	**15,606,000**	**15,918,120**	**16,236,482**	**16,561,212**
Case 1	GBP	15,000,000	15,000,000	15,000,000	15,300,000	15,606,000	15,918,120	16,236,482	16,561,212
Case 2	GBP	15,000,000	15,000,000	15,000,000	15,750,000	16,537,500	17,364,375	18,232,594	19,144,223
Case 3	GBP	15,000,000	15,000,000	15,000,000	16,200,000	17,496,000	18,895,680	20,407,334	22,039,921
Council rates	GBP	5,000,000	5,000,000	5,000,000	5,000,000	5,000,000	5,000,000	5,000,000	5,000,000

FIGURE 5.13 Operating model assumptions (IS)—other costs.

The operating model must be extended to the other financial statements, fortunately requiring typically less assumptions than the income statement (Figures 5.14 to 5.19).

Balance Sheet Operating Model

Current assets

Accounts receivable/DSO

Breakdown by payor

		0	1	2	3	4	5	6	7
Category	Units	2023	2024	2025	2026	2027	2028	2029	2030
Self pay	%	21.6%	21.9%	21.8%	22.0%	22.2%	22.4%	22.4%	22.4%
PMI	%	70.4%	70.2%	70.3%	70.2%	70.0%	69.9%	69.9%	69.9%
NHS	%	8.0%	7.9%	7.9%	7.8%	7.7%	7.7%	7.7%	7.7%
Total	%	100.0%	100.0%	100.0%	100.0%	100.0%	100.0%	100.0%	100.0%

Days Sales Outstanding (DSO) by payor

		0	1	2	3	4	5	6	7
Category	Units	2023	2024	2025	2026	2027	2028	2029	2030
Self pay	Days	30.0	30.0	30.0	30.0	30.0	30.0	30.0	30.0
PMI	Days	75.0	75.0	75.0	75.0	75.0	75.0	75.0	75.0
NHS	Days	45.0	45.0	45.0	45.0	45.0	45.0	45.0	45.0
Weight average	Days	62.9	62.8	62.8	62.7	62.7	62.6	62.6	62.6

Inventory

Calculation

		0	1	2	3	4	5	6	7
Category	Units	2023	2024	2025	2026	2027	2028	2029	2030
Days Inventory Held (DIH)	Days	105.8	105.8	105.8	105.8	105.8	105.8	105.8	105.8
Supply expense	GBP	29,359,484	32,079,102	38,110,912	41,354,459	44,757,344	48,328,970	49,778,839	51,272,204
Inventory	GBP	8,510,228	9,298,545	11,046,944	11,987,128	12,973,499	14,008,781	14,429,044	14,861,916

Prepaid expenses

Calculation

		0	1	2	3	4	5	6	7
Category	Units	2023	2024	2025	2026	2027	2028	2029	2030
Proportion of revenue	%	2.0%	2.0%	2.0%	2.0%	2.0%	2.0%	2.0%	2.0%
Prepaid expenses	GBP	2,552,999	2,789,487	3,313,992	3,596,040	3,891,943	4,202,519	4,328,595	4,458,453

Non-current assets

Breakdown

PPE

		0	1	2	3	4	5	6	7
Category	Units	2023	2024	2025	2026	2027	2028	2029	2030
PPE	GBP	30,000,000	28,122,866	26,693,519	25,695,391	25,111,420	24,924,030	25,115,119	25,666,042

Goodwill

Assumption

		0	1	2	3	4	5	6	7
Category	Units	2023	2024	2025	2026	2027	2028	2029	2030
Assumption	GBP	1,000,000	1,000,000	1,000,000	1,000,000	1,000,000	1,000,000	1,000,000	1,000,000

Intangible assets

Intangible assets

		0	1	2	3	4	5	6	7
Category	Units	2023	2024	2025	2026	2027	2028	2029	2030
Intangible assets	GBP	6,000,000	6,060,000	6,169,800	6,318,894	6,496,461	6,691,355	6,892,095	7,098,858

FIGURE 5.14 Operating model assumptions (B/S)—assets.

Current liabilities

Accounts payable/DPO

Calculation

		Historical >>			Forecast >>				
Category	Units	2023	2024	2025	2026	2027	2028	2029	2030
Days Payable Outstanding (DPO)	Days	37.9	37.9	37.9	37.9	37.9	37.9	37.9	37.9
Supply expense	GBP	29,359,484	25,739,881	29,800,185	31,561,242	33,400,238	35,323,115	37,330,154	39,425,313
Inventory	GBP	3,048,560	2,672,716	3,094,321	3,277,181	3,468,134	3,667,797	3,876,200	4,093,752

Current liabilities excluding accounts payable

Current liabilities as a proportion of revenue

		Historical >>			Forecast >>				
Category	Units	2023	2024	2025	2026	2027	2028	2029	2030
Accrued expenses/liabilities	%	5.0%	5.0%	5.0%	5.0%	5.0%	5.0%	5.0%	5.0%
Bonus accrual	%	5.0%	5.0%	5.0%	5.0%	5.0%	5.0%	5.0%	5.0%
Tax accrual	%	5.0%	5.0%	5.0%	5.0%	5.0%	5.0%	5.0%	5.0%
Other current liabilities	%	5.0%	5.0%	5.0%	5.0%	5.0%	5.0%	5.0%	5.0%
Current liabilities excluding accounts pa	%	20.0%	20.0%	20.0%	20.0%	20.0%	20.0%	20.0%	20.0%

Current liabilities as a proportion of revenue

		Historical >>			Forecast >>				
Category	Units	2023	2024	2025	2026	2027	2028	2029	2030
Accrued expenses/liabilities	%	6,382,496	6,773,653	7,842,154	8,305,590	8,789,536	9,295,557	9,823,725	10,375,082
Bonus accrual	%	6,382,496	6,773,653	7,842,154	8,305,590	8,789,536	9,295,557	9,823,725	10,375,082
Tax accrual	%	6,382,496	6,773,653	7,842,154	8,305,590	8,789,536	9,295,557	9,823,725	10,375,082
Other current liabilities	%	6,382,496	6,773,653	7,842,154	8,305,590	8,789,536	9,295,557	9,823,725	10,375,082
Current liabilities excluding accounts pa	%	25,529,986	27,094,611	31,368,615	33,222,360	35,158,145	37,182,226	39,294,899	41,500,329

FIGURE 5.15 Operating model assumptions (B/S)—current liabilities.

Pro-forma balance sheet

Balance sheet

Category	Units	Historical >> 2023	2024	2025	Forecast >> 2026	2027	2028	2029	2030
Assets									
Cash	Millions of GBP	10.00	16.17	23.68	28.05	35.46	45.51	52.43	60.41
Accounts receivable	Millions of GBP	21.99	23.99	28.52	30.91	33.41	36.04	37.12	38.23
Inventory	Millions of GBP	8.51	9.30	11.05	11.99	12.97	14.01	14.43	14.86
Prepaid expenses	Millions of GBP	2.55	2.79	3.31	3.60	3.89	4.20	4.33	4.46
Current assets	**Millions of GBP**	**43.06**	**52.24**	**66.56**	**74.54**	**85.73**	**99.76**	**108.30**	**117.96**
PPE	Millions of GBP	30.00	28.12	26.69	25.70	25.11	24.92	25.12	25.67
Goodwill	Millions of GBP	1.00	1.00	1.00	1.00	1.00	1.00	1.00	1.00
Intangible assets	Millions of GBP	6.00	6.06	6.17	6.32	6.50	6.69	6.89	7.10
Other assets	Millions of GBP	10.00	10.00	10.00	10.00	10.00	10.00	10.00	10.00
Total non-current assets	**Millions of GBP**	**47.00**	**45.18**	**43.86**	**43.01**	**42.61**	**42.62**	**43.01**	**43.76**
Total assets		**90.06**	**97.43**	**110.42**	**117.55**	**128.34**	**142.37**	**151.31**	**161.72**
Liabilities									
Accounts payable	Millions of GBP	3.05	3.33	3.96	4.29	4.65	5.02	5.17	5.32
Accrued expenses/liabilities	Millions of GBP	1.28	1.39	1.66	1.80	1.95	2.10	2.16	2.23
Bonus accrual	Millions of GBP	1.28	1.39	1.66	1.80	1.95	2.10	2.16	2.23
Tax accrual	Millions of GBP	1.28	1.39	1.66	1.80	1.95	2.10	2.16	2.23
Other current liabilities	Millions of GBP	1.28	1.39	1.66	1.80	1.95	2.10	2.16	2.23
Total current liabilities	**Millions of GBP**	**8.15**	**8.91**	**10.59**	**11.49**	**12.43**	**13.42**	**13.83**	**14.24**
Debt	Millions of GBP	10.00	10.00	10.00	10.00	10.00	10.00	10.00	10.00
Deferred income tax	Millions of GBP	2.00	2.00	2.00	2.00	2.00	2.00	2.00	2.00
Other long-term liabilities	Millions of GBP	20.00	20.00	20.00	20.00	20.00	20.00	20.00	20.00
Total non-current liabilities	**Millions of GBP**	**32.00**	**32.00**	**32.00**	**32.00**	**32.00**	**32.00**	**32.00**	**32.00**
Total liabilities	**Millions of GBP**	**40.15**	**40.91**	**42.59**	**43.49**	**44.43**	**45.42**	**45.83**	**46.24**
Equity									
Contributed capital	Millions of GBP	42.35	52.43	64.76	71.22	77.67	87.75	97.21	105.75
Retained Earnings	Millions of GBP	7.55	4.08	3.08	2.85	6.23	9.20	8.27	9.73
Total equity	**Millions of GBP**	**49.90**	**56.52**	**67.84**	**74.06**	**83.91**	**96.95**	**105.48**	**115.48**
Equity + liabilities	**Millions of GBP**	**90.06**	**97.43**	**110.42**	**117.55**	**128.34**	**142.37**	**151.31**	**161.72**
Net working capital (excluding cash)	**Millions of GBP**	**24.90**	**27.17**	**32.29**	**35.00**	**37.84**	**40.82**	**42.05**	**43.31**
Change in net working capital	Millions of GBP		2.26	5.13	2.71	2.84	2.98	1.22	1.26
Balance check		*0.00*	*0.00*	*0.00*	*0.00*	*0.00*	*0.00*	*0.00*	*0.00*

FIGURE 5.16 Operating model assumptions (B/S)—additional inputs and summary.

Cash Flow Operating Model

Depreciation and amortization schedule

Depreciation schedule

CapEx

Category	Units	0 2023	1 2024	2 2025	3 2026	4 2027	5 2028	6 2029	7 2030
Medical equipment	GBP	1,276,499	1,314,794	1,354,238	1,394,865	1,436,711	1,479,813	1,524,207	1,569,933
Facilities & infrastructure	GBP	1,276,499	1,314,794	1,354,238	1,394,865	1,436,711	1,479,813	1,524,207	1,569,933
Furniture & fixtures	GBP	1,276,499	1,314,794	1,354,238	1,394,865	1,436,711	1,479,813	1,524,207	1,569,933
Land & buildings	GBP	1,276,499	1,314,794	1,354,238	1,394,865	1,436,711	1,479,813	1,524,207	1,569,933
Vehicles & buildings	GBP	1,276,499	1,314,794	1,354,238	1,394,865	1,436,711	1,479,813	1,524,207	1,569,933
Other	GBP	1,276,499	1,314,794	1,354,238	1,394,865	1,436,711	1,479,813	1,524,207	1,569,933
Cumulative CapEx	**GBP**	**7,658,996**	**7,888,766**	**8,125,429**	**8,369,191**	**8,620,267**	**8,878,875**	**9,145,241**	**9,419,599**

FIGURE 5.17 Operating model assumptions (CFS)—CapEx.

Depreciation schedule

Depreciation years	10

Year	Units	0 2023	1 2024	2 2025	3 2026	4 2027	5 2028	6 2029	7 2030
2023	GBP	10,000,000	9,000,000	8,000,000	7,000,000	6,000,000	5,000,000	4,000,000	3,000,000
2024	GBP		765,900	765,900	765,900	765,900	765,900	765,900	765,900
2025	GBP			788,877	788,877	788,877	788,877	788,877	788,877
2026	GBP				812,543	812,543	812,543	812,543	812,543
2027	GBP					836,919	836,919	836,919	836,919
2028	GBP						862,027	862,027	862,027
2029	GBP							887,888	887,888
2030	GBP								914,524
2031	GBP								
2032	GBP								
2033	GBP								
2034	GBP								
2035	GBP								
2036	GBP								
Cumulative depreciation	GBP	10,000,000	9,765,900	9,554,776	9,367,319	9,204,238	9,066,265	8,954,152	8,868,677

FIGURE 5.18 Operating model assumptions (CFS)—depreciation schedule.

Amortization schedule

Additions

Category	Units	0 2023	1 2024	2 2025	3 2026	4 2027	5 2028	6 2029	7 2030
Licenses & permits	GBP	400,000	412,000	424,360	437,091	450,204	463,710	477,621	491,950
Software & IT systems	GBP	400,000	412,000	424,360	437,091	450,204	463,710	477,621	491,950
Intellectual property	GBP	400,000	412,000	424,360	437,091	450,204	463,710	477,621	491,950
Contracts & relationships	GBP	400,000	412,000	424,360	437,091	450,204	463,710	477,621	491,950
Research & education assets	GBP	400,000	412,000	424,360	437,091	450,204	463,710	477,621	491,950
Cumulative Additions	**GBP**	**2,000,000**	**2,060,000**	**2,121,800**	**2,185,454**	**2,251,018**	**2,318,548**	**2,388,105**	**2,459,748**

Amortization schedule

Amortization years: 5

Year	Units	0 2023	1 2024	2 2025	3 2026	4 2027	5 2028	6 2029	7 2030
2023	GBP	2,000,000	1,600,000	1,200,000	800,000	400,000	-	-	-
2024	GBP		400,000	400,000	400,000	400,000	400,000		
2025	GBP			412,000	412,000	412,000	412,000	412,000	
2026	GBP				424,360	424,360	424,360	424,360	424,360
2027	GBP					437,091	437,091	437,091	437,091
2028	GBP						450,204	450,204	450,204
2029	GBP							463,710	463,710
2030	GBP								477,621
2031	GBP								
2032	GBP								
2033	GBP								
2034	GBP								
2035	GBP								
2036	GBP								
Cumulative depreciation	**GBP**	**2,000,000**	**2,000,000**	**2,012,000**	**2,036,360**	**2,073,451**	**2,123,654**	**2,187,364**	**2,252,985**

FIGURE 5.19 Operating model assumptions (CFS)—amortization schedule.

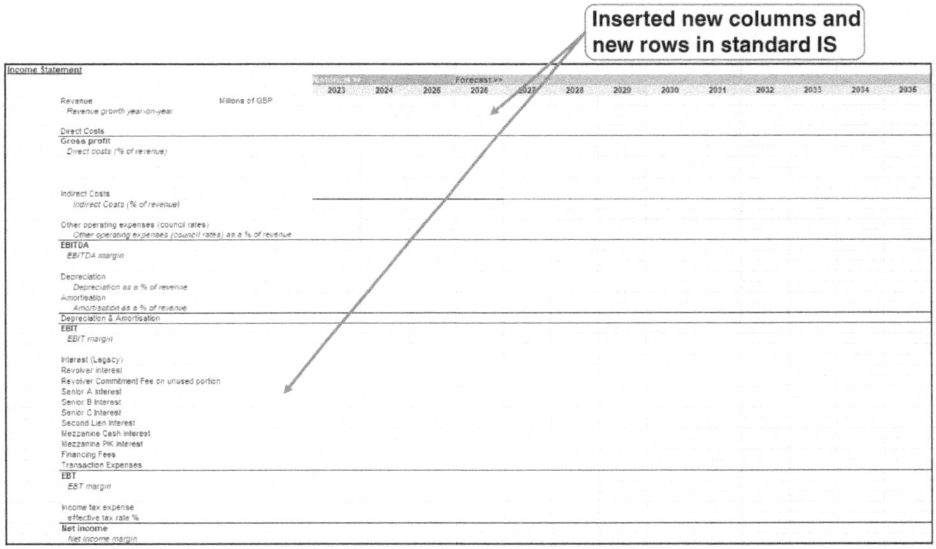

FIGURE 5.20 Income statement template.

Structure of the Financial Statements for the LBO Now that we have all the information from the management plan, we will fill out the LBO model with current and historical data from the financial statements. Again, we examine the last three years of the Income Statement (Figure 5.20), which is generally sufficient.

At the top of each tab in the spreadsheet, there are four buttons that allow us to choose a scenario for the financial forecasts and a debt structure (both are relevant for the second part of the modelling).

We assume that the valuations will be performed as of January 1, 2026. For the Balance Sheet, which is a picture of a firm's assets and liabilities at one point of time, there is no need to go back in the past; we are only interested in the starting date. As it is unlikely to match the year end, we will need a pro forma column to take us to the end of the current year and start our forecasts anew. Similar to the Income Statement, we need to make room for the LBO capital structure (Figure 5.21).

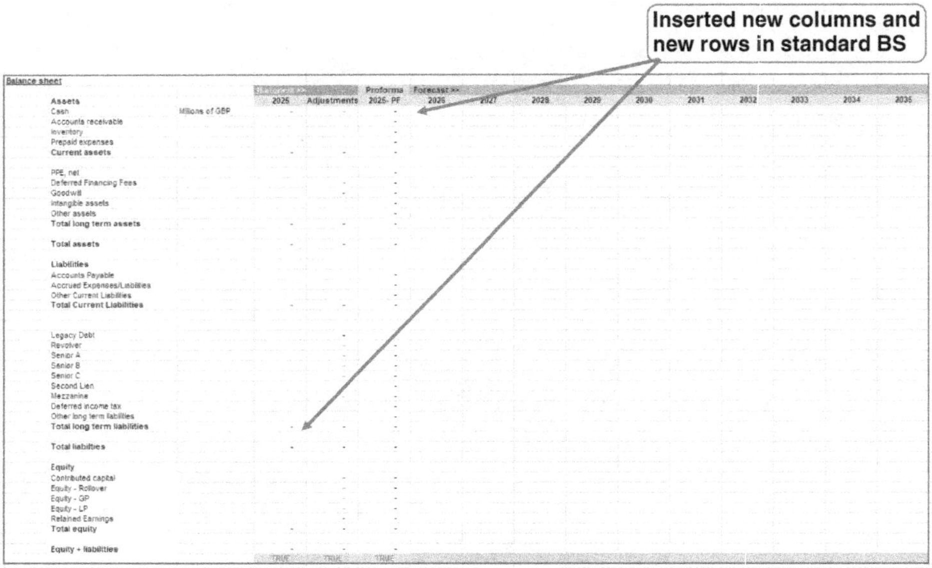

FIGURE 5.21 Balance sheet template.

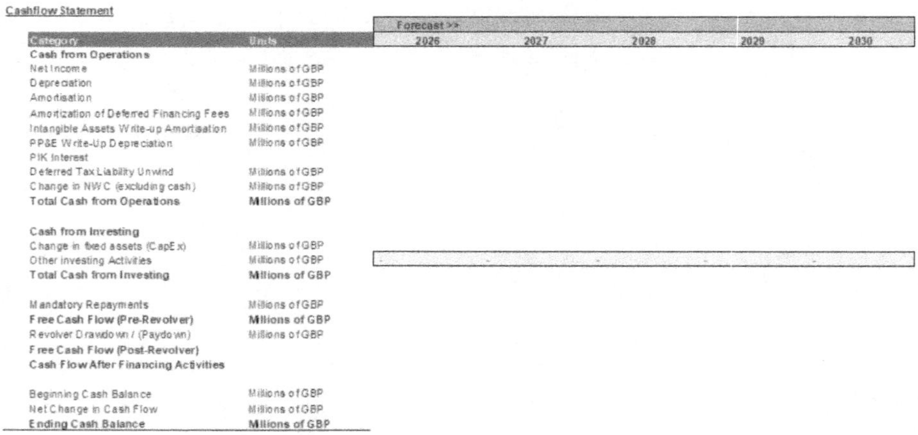

FIGURE 5.22 Cash flow statement template.

The Cash Flow Statement (Figure 5.22) results mostly from the reconciliation of the Income Statement and the Balance Sheet. The only significant adjustment needed are the CapEx assumptions (done in the operating model).

The Debt Schedule will be built around combinations of debt tranches (Figure 5.23). In a typical LBO capital structure, debt is arranged in multiple tranches with varying seniority, terms, and pricing. Here's the standard hierarchy from most to least senior:

- **Senior Secured Debt/Revolver** (Revolving Credit Facility)
  Seniority: First lien, pari passu with Term Loan A
  Maturity: 5–6 years
  Interest Rate: Floating (SOFR + spread, typically 200–300 bps)
  Purpose: Working capital and letters of credit; drawn as needed

Cash available for Sweep

Category	Units	2026	2027	2028	2029	2030
		Forecast >>				
£ / SONIA	%	3.85%	4.00%	4.15%	4.30%	4.35%
Cash Flow from Operating Activities		18.22	20.86	22.65	25.29	28.07
Cash Flow from Investing Activities		(8.37)	(8.62)	(8.88)	(9.15)	(9.42)
Cash Available for Debt Repayment		**9.85**	**12.24**	**13.77**	**16.15**	**18.65**
Total Mandatory Repayments						
Cash from Balance Sheet						
Cash Available for Optional Debt Repayment		**9.85**	**12.24**	**13.77**	**16.15**	**18.65**

Revolving Credit Facility

		2026	2027	2028	2029	2030
Revolving Credit Facility Size/Capacity	10.00					
Spread	3.00%					
Floor	2.00%					
Term	6 years					
Commitment Fee on Unused Portion	0.50%					
Beginning Balance		10.00	4.95	-	-	-
Drawdown/(Repayment)		(5.05)	(4.95)	-	-	-
Ending Balance		**4.95**	-	-	-	-
Total Revolver Capacity		10.00	10.00	10.00	10.00	10.00
Beginning Available Capacity		-	5.05	10.00	10.00	10.00
Ending Available Capacity		15.05	14.95	10.00	10.00	10.00
Revolver Interest Rate		6.85%	7.00%	7.15%	7.30%	7.35%
Revolver Interest Expense		0.51	0.17	-	-	-
Unused Revolver Commitment Fee		0.50%	0.50%	0.50%	0.50%	0.50%
Unused Commitment Fee		0.04	0.05	0.05	0.05	0.05

Senior Tranche A

Size	20.00					
Spread	3.50%					
Floor	2.00%					
Term	7 years					
Repayment Schedule	*20.00%*					
		Forecast >>				
		2026	2027	2028	2029	2030
Beginning Balance		20.00	16.00	12.00	8.00	4.00
Mandatory Repayments		(4.00)	(4.00)	(4.00)	(4.00)	(4.00)
Ending Balance		**16.00**	**12.00**	**8.00**	**4.00**	-
Interest Rate		7.35%	7.50%	7.65%	7.80%	7.85%
Interest Expense		1.32	1.05	0.77	0.47	0.16

Senior Tranche B

Size	80.00					
Spread	4.00%					
Floor	2.00%					
Term	8 years					
Repayment Schedule	*1.00%*					
		Forecast >>				
		2026	2027	2028	2029	2030
Beginning Balance		80.00	79.20	78.40	77.60	76.80
Mandatory Repayments		(0.80)	(0.80)	(0.80)	(0.80)	(0.80)
Ending Balance		**79.20**	**78.40**	**77.60**	**76.80**	**76.00**
Interest Rate		7.85%	8.00%	8.15%	8.30%	8.35%
Interest Expense		6.25	6.30	6.36	6.41	6.38

Mezzanine Debt

Size	20.00					
Spread (Cash interest)	10.50%					
Floor	0.00%					
PIK Interest Rate	10.00%					
Term	10 years					
Repayment Schedule	0.00%					
		Forecast >>				
		2026	2027	2028	2029	2030
Beginning Balance		20.00	22.00	24.20	26.62	29.28
Mandatory Repayments		-	-	-	-	-
PIK interest		2.00	2.20	2.42	2.66	2.93
Ending Balance		**22.00**	**24.20**	**26.62**	**29.28**	**32.21**
Cash Interest Rate		14.35%	14.50%	14.65%	14.80%	14.85%
PIK Rate		10.00%	10.00%	10.00%	10.00%	10.00%
Cash Interest Expense		3.01	3.35	3.72	4.14	4.57
PIK Interest Expense		2.00	2.20	2.42	2.66	2.93

FIGURE 5.23 Debt schedule.

- Term Loan A (TLA)
  - Seniority: First lien, pari passu with revolver
  - Maturity: 5–7 years
  - Interest Rate: Floating (SOFR + spread, typically 250–350 bps)
  - Amortization: Modest amortization (10–20% annually)
- Term Loan B (TLB)
  - Seniority: First lien, but junior to TLA/revolver in some structures
  - Maturity: 7–8 years

Interest Rate: Floating (SOFR + spread, typically 350–500 bps)
Amortization: Minimal (1% annually), with bullet payment at maturity
Most common tranche in modern LBOs

- **Second Lien Debt** (Less common post-2008)
  Seniority: Second lien on same collateral
  Maturity: 8 years
  Interest Rate: Floating (SOFR + 700–900 bps)
  Amortization: None; bullet payment
- **Unsecured/Subordinated Debt**
  Senior Notes
  Seniority: Unsecured, senior to subordinated debt
  Maturity: 8–10 years
  Interest Rate: Fixed (7–10%)
  Structure: High-yield bonds
- **Subordinated Notes/Mezzanine Debt**
  Seniority: Subordinated to all senior debt
  Maturity: 9–10 years
  Interest Rate: Fixed or PIK (payment-in-kind), 10–14%
  Equity kicker: Often includes warrants

Note that we haven't integrated unsecured subordinated debt in our model. It is not systematically issued.

Once the financial statements and the debt schedule are filled, we automatically generate the returns on investment analysis, in the lower part of the **Deal Dynamics**, which is the overall summary of the transaction.

Second Level of Assumptions: Scenarios for LBO Model Our operating model assumptions have generated aggregated assumptions for the financial statements. They feed the "management case" in the next level of assumptions, at LBO model level. This management case is one of five scenarios, the other ones being typically—but not necessarily—defined relatively to it.

Here are the five scenarios for our forecasts:

- **Management case:** the case of the sellers, assuming management represents them.
- **Sponsor case:** the case of the buyers, often but not necessarily in between management case and base case. Sometimes actually more aggressive than the management if they have clever ideas of value creation. They often do not share them, even with their own advisors.
- **Base case:** a more conservative operating case.
- **Downside case 1:** under internal stress (e.g., the unlikely loss of a key contract).
- **Downside case 2:** under external stress (e.g., a severe economic crisis).

A typical approach for stress testing and defining downside cases is to consider two levels of severity. We prefer to identify two very separate events that are unlikely to happen together; examples would be a fire destroying the manufacturing capacity (internal event) and war cutting access to a main market (external event). But you are free to adopt the approach you are most comfortable with.

Where does the information come from? If the company is public, one can have access to detailed information on a yearly basis, and some update on a quarterly basis.

In a PE setting, we are more likely to deal with a private company. Ahead of any access to the company's books, the data are estimated on an outside-in basis, through a combination of secondary research and interviews of insiders. Later on, most of the information will be provided at the discretion of the owners or management, generally in the context of a process or a bilateral discussion. This should include the most important information, the management forecasts.

We fill the forecasts for the other scenarios in relation to the management forecasts. In the Income Statement, the calculations stop at EBIT because we don't know yet the debt structure (Figure 5.24).

Assumptions for the Income Statement

I/S assumptions

		Historical >>			Forecast >>				
Category	Case	2023	2024	2025	2026	2027	2028	2029	2030
Revenue growth (yoy)	**Active**		**6.1%**	**15.8%**	**5.9%**	**5.8%**	**5.8%**	**5.7%**	**5.6%**
Management case	1		6.1%	15.8%	5.9%	5.8%	5.8%	5.7%	5.6%
Sponsor case	2		6.1%	15.8%	6.9%	6.8%	6.8%	6.7%	6.6%
Base case	3		6.1%	15.8%	3.0%	4.0%	4.8%	4.7%	4.7%
External shock	4		6.1%	15.8%	0.0%	0.0%	0.0%	0.0%	0.0%
Internal crisis	5		6.1%	15.8%	-4.0%	-4.0%	-4.0%	-4.0%	-4.0%
Direct costs (% revenue)	**Active**	65.5%	**60.2%**	**58.7%**	**55.6%**	**55.4%**	**55.5%**	**55.4%**	**55.2%**
Management case	1		60.2%	58.7%	55.6%	55.4%	55.5%	55.4%	55.2%
Sponsor case	2		60.2%	58.7%	50.0%	50.0%	50.0%	50.0%	50.0%
Base case	3		60.2%	58.7%	61.1%	61.0%	61.1%	60.9%	60.8%
External shock	4		60.2%	58.7%	65.0%	65.0%	65.0%	65.0%	65.0%
Internal crisis	5		60.2%	58.7%	67.0%	67.0%	67.0%	67.0%	67.0%
Indirect costs (% revenue)	**Active**	18.8%	**16.1%**	**14.6%**	**13.4%**	**13.3%**	**13.6%**	**13.4%**	**13.3%**
Management case	1		16.1%	14.6%	13.4%	13.3%	13.6%	13.4%	13.3%
Sponsor case	2		16.1%	14.6%	15.0%	15.0%	15.0%	15.0%	15.0%
Base case	3		16.1%	14.6%	13.4%	13.3%	13.6%	13.4%	13.3%
External shock	4		16.1%	14.6%	22.0%	22.0%	22.0%	22.0%	22.0%
Internal crisis	5		16.1%	14.6%	25.0%	25.0%	25.0%	25.0%	25.0%
EBITDA Margin (%)	**Active**	0.0%	**9.0%**	**14.0%**	**18.8%**	**19.5%**	**19.7%**	**20.4%**	**21.0%**
Management case	1		9.0%	14.0%	18.8%	19.5%	19.7%	20.4%	21.0%
Sponsor case	2		9.0%	14.0%	19.8%	20.6%	20.7%	21.4%	22.0%
Base case	3		9.0%	14.0%	17.1%	17.7%	17.9%	18.5%	19.1%
External shock	4		9.0%	14.0%	2.0%	2.0%	2.0%	2.0%	2.0%
Internal crisis	5		9.0%	14.0%	0.0%	0.0%	0.0%	0.0%	0.0%
Depreciation (% revenue)	**Active**	7.8%	**7.2%**	**6.1%**	**5.6%**	**5.2%**	**4.9%**	**4.6%**	**4.3%**
Management case	1		7.2%	6.1%	5.6%	5.2%	4.9%	4.6%	4.3%
Sponsor case	2		7.2%	6.1%	5.6%	5.2%	4.9%	4.6%	4.3%
Base case	3		7.2%	6.1%	5.6%	5.2%	4.9%	4.6%	4.3%
External shock	4		7.2%	6.1%	5.6%	5.2%	4.9%	4.6%	4.3%
Internal crisis	5		7.2%	6.1%	5.6%	5.2%	4.9%	4.6%	4.3%
Amortization (% revenue)	**Active**	1.6%	**1.5%**	**1.3%**	**1.2%**	**1.2%**	**1.1%**	**1.1%**	**1.1%**
Management case	1		1.5%	1.3%	1.2%	1.2%	1.1%	1.1%	1.1%
Sponsor case	2		1.5%	1.3%	1.2%	1.2%	1.1%	1.1%	1.1%
Base case	3		1.5%	1.3%	1.2%	1.2%	1.1%	1.1%	1.1%
External shock	4		1.5%	1.3%	1.2%	1.2%	1.1%	1.1%	1.1%
Internal crisis	5		1.5%	1.3%	1.2%	1.2%	1.1%	1.1%	1.1%

FIGURE 5.24 Income statement scenario assumptions.

Assumptions in the Balance Sheet The Income Statement was the most demanding part, at least from our perspective. The balance sheet assumptions are simpler (Figure 5.25).

We mostly need to make assumptions on the components of the working capital. We could have used absolute numbers (Accounts Receivable, Inventory, Accounts Payable) but have chosen instead to work with metrics.

The most commonly used metrics are the following:

- DSO (Days Sales Outstanding): Accounts Receivable ÷ Sales × 360 days
- DIH (Days Inventory Held): Inventory ÷ COGS × 360 days
- DPO (Days Payable Outstanding): Accounts Payable ÷ COGS × 360 days

This approach offers several key benefits over absolute numbers:

1. Scalability: Working capital components automatically scale with revenue and COGS changes.
2. Operational logic: Ratios reflect actual business operations—how long it takes to collect receivables, turn inventory, and pay suppliers.
3. Historical consistency: Based on the company's established operational patterns rather than arbitrary absolute amounts.

Assumptions on BS

		Historical >>			Forecast >>				
Category	Case	2023	2024	2025	2026	2027	2028	2029	2030
Days Sales Outstanding (DSO)	**Active**	62.89	**62.83**	**62.91**	**62.86**	**62.82**	**62.78**	**62.74**	**62.70**
Management case	1		62.83	62.91	62.86	62.82	62.78	62.74	62.70
Sponsor case	2		62.83	62.91	60.00	60.00	60.00	60.00	60.00
Base case	3		62.83	62.91	69.15	69.10	69.06	69.01	68.97
External shock	4		62.83	62.91	80.00	80.00	80.00	80.00	80.00
Internal crisis	5		62.83	62.91	80.00	80.00	80.00	80.00	80.00
Days Inventory Held (DIH)	**Active**	105.80	**105.80**	**105.80**	**105.80**	**105.80**	**105.80**	**105.80**	**105.80**
Management case	1		105.80	105.80	105.80	105.80	105.80	105.80	105.80
Sponsor case	2		105.80	105.80	150.00	150.00	150.00	150.00	150.00
Base case	3		105.80	105.80	126.96	126.96	126.96	126.96	126.96
External shock	4		105.80	105.80	200.00	200.00	200.00	200.00	200.00
Internal crisis	5		105.80	105.80	200.00	200.00	200.00	200.00	200.00
Supply expense (% of revenue)	**Active**	**23.0%**	**19.0%**	**19.0%**	**19.0%**	**19.0%**	**19.0%**	**19.0%**	**19.0%**
Management case	1		19.0%	19.0%	19.0%	19.0%	19.0%	19.0%	19.0%
Sponsor case	2		19.0%	19.0%	20.0%	20.0%	20.0%	20.0%	20.0%
Base case	3		19.0%	19.0%	20.0%	20.0%	20.0%	20.0%	20.0%
External shock	4		19.0%	19.0%	30.0%	30.0%	30.0%	30.0%	30.0%
Internal crisis	5		19.0%	19.0%	30.0%	30.0%	30.0%	30.0%	30.0%
Prepaids and Other Current Assets (% revenue)	**Active**	5.0%	**5.0%**	**5.0%**	**5.0%**	**5.0%**	**5.0%**	**5.0%**	**5.0%**
Management case	1		5.0%	5.0%	5.0%	5.0%	5.0%	5.0%	5.0%
Sponsor case	2		5.0%	5.0%	10.0%	10.0%	10.0%	10.0%	10.0%
Base case	3		5.0%	5.0%	5.0%	5.0%	5.0%	5.0%	5.0%
External shock	4		5.0%	5.0%	15.0%	15.0%	15.0%	15.0%	15.0%
Internal crisis	5		5.0%	5.0%	15.0%	15.0%	15.0%	15.0%	15.0%
Days Payable Outstanding (DPO)	**Active**	37.90	**37.90**	**37.90**	**37.90**	**37.90**	**37.90**	**37.90**	**37.90**
Management case	1		37.90	37.90	37.90	37.90	37.90	37.90	37.90
Sponsor case	2		37.90	37.90	40.00	40.00	40.00	40.00	40.00
Base case	3		37.90	37.90	34.45	34.45	34.45	34.45	34.45
External shock	4		37.90	37.90	20.00	20.00	20.00	20.00	20.00
Internal crisis	5		37.90	37.90	20.00	20.00	20.00	20.00	20.00
Accrued Liabilities (% revenue)	**Active**	5.0%	**5.0%**	**5.0%**	**5.0%**	**5.0%**	**5.0%**	**5.0%**	**5.0%**
Management case	1		5.0%	5.0%	5.0%	5.0%	5.0%	5.0%	5.0%
Sponsor case	2		5.0%	5.0%	10.0%	10.0%	10.0%	10.0%	10.0%
Base case	3		5.0%	5.0%	8.0%	8.0%	8.0%	8.0%	8.0%
External shock	4		5.0%	5.0%	20.0%	20.0%	20.0%	20.0%	20.0%
Internal crisis	5		5.0%	5.0%	20.0%	20.0%	20.0%	20.0%	20.0%
Bonus accrual (% revenue)	**Active**	5.0%	**5.0%**	**5.0%**	**5.0%**	**5.0%**	**5.0%**	**5.0%**	**5.0%**
Management case	1		5.0%	5.0%	5.0%	5.0%	5.0%	5.0%	5.0%
Sponsor case	2		5.0%	5.0%	10.0%	10.0%	10.0%	10.0%	10.0%
Base case	3		5.0%	5.0%	8.0%	8.0%	8.0%	8.0%	8.0%
External shock	4		5.0%	5.0%	20.0%	20.0%	20.0%	20.0%	20.0%
Internal crisis	5		5.0%	5.0%	20.0%	20.0%	20.0%	20.0%	20.0%
Tax accrual (% revenue)	**Active**	5.0%	**5.0%**	**5.0%**	**5.0%**	**5.0%**	**5.0%**	**5.0%**	**5.0%**
Management case	1		5.0%	5.0%	5.0%	5.0%	5.0%	5.0%	5.0%
Sponsor case	2		5.0%	5.0%	10.0%	10.0%	10.0%	10.0%	10.0%
Base case	3		5.0%	5.0%	8.0%	8.0%	8.0%	8.0%	8.0%
External shock	4		5.0%	5.0%	20.0%	20.0%	20.0%	20.0%	20.0%
Internal crisis	5		5.0%	5.0%	20.0%	20.0%	20.0%	20.0%	20.0%
Other Current Liabilities (% revenue)	**Active**	**5.0%**	**5.0%**	**5.0%**	**5.0%**	**5.0%**	**5.0%**	**5.0%**	**5.0%**
Management case	1		5.0%	5.0%	5.0%	5.0%	5.0%	5.0%	5.0%
Sponsor case	2		5.0%	5.0%	5.0%	5.0%	5.0%	5.0%	5.0%
Base case	3		5.0%	5.0%	2.9%	2.9%	2.9%	2.9%	2.9%
External shock	4		5.0%	5.0%	10.0%	10.0%	10.0%	10.0%	10.0%
Internal crisis	5		5.0%	5.0%	10.0%	10.0%	10.0%	10.0%	10.0%

FIGURE 5.25 Balance sheet scenario assumptions.

Assumptions on CF

		Historical >>			Forecast >>				
Category	Case	2023	2024	2025	2026	2027	2028	2029	2030
CapEx (% sales)	**Active**	**6.0%**	**5.8%**	**5.2%**	**5.0%**	**4.9%**	**4.8%**	**4.7%**	**4.5%**
Management case	1		**5.8%**	**5.2%**	**5.0%**	**4.9%**	**4.8%**	**4.7%**	**4.5%**
Sponsor case	2		5.8%	5.2%	7.0%	7.0%	7.0%	7.0%	7.0%
Base case	3		5.8%	5.2%	7.0%	7.0%	7.0%	7.0%	7.0%
External shock	4		5.8%	5.2%	9.0%	9.0%	9.0%	9.0%	9.0%
Internal crisis	5		5.8%	5.2%	10.0%	10.0%	10.0%	10.0%	10.0%
Additions (% sales)	**Active**	**1.6%**	**1.5%**	**1.4%**	**1.3%**	**1.3%**	**1.2%**	**1.2%**	**1.2%**
Management case	1		**1.5%**	**1.4%**	**1.3%**	**1.3%**	**1.2%**	**1.2%**	**1.2%**
Sponsor case	2		1.5%	1.4%	2.0%	2.0%	2.0%	2.0%	2.0%
Base case	3		1.5%	1.4%	2.0%	2.0%	2.0%	2.0%	2.0%
External shock	4		1.5%	1.4%	3.0%	3.0%	3.0%	3.0%	3.0%
Internal crisis	5		1.5%	1.4%	4.0%	4.0%	4.0%	4.0%	4.0%

FIGURE 5.26 Cash flow statement scenario assumptions.

Assumptions in the Cash Flow Statement Here, our only significant variable is CapEx, which appears under investing activities. It is capitalized on the balance sheet within PP&E, and its impact subsequently flows through the income statement via depreciation rather than as CapEx itself (Figure 5.26).

5.6.3.2 Step 2—Pre-LBO Model In our workshops, we populate the statements one by one, entering all the parameters required for intermediary calculations up to the summary of the deal dynamics. This includes, mostly in the <Scenario assumptions> sheet,

- Having forecasted the aggregate figures for revenue and operational costs in the income statement for each of the five scenarios, we add EBITDA margin, depreciation and amortization forecasts for each scenario (Figure 5.27).
- Adding the tax rates in the income statement.
- Checking the opening balances in the balance sheet, then adjusting Pro Forma to the beginning of the next tax year. The Pro Forma balance sheet is thus built

based on adjustments to historical balance sheet. Here too, the data for capital structure hasn't yet appeared.

Pre-LBO Model—Income Statement

Income Statement

Category	Units	Historical >> 2023	2024	2025	Forecast >> 2026	2027	2028	2029	2030
Revenue	Millions of GBP	127.65	135.47	156.84	166.11	175.79	185.91	196.47	207.50
Revenue growth year-on-year	%		*6.1%*	*15.8%*	*5.9%*	*5.8%*	*5.8%*	*5.7%*	*5.6%*
Direct Costs	Millions of GBP	83.66	81.52	92.07	92.28	97.41	103.21	108.78	114.61
Direct costs (% of revenue)	%	*65.5%*	*60.2%*	*58.7%*	*55.6%*	*55.4%*	*55.5%*	*55.4%*	*55.2%*
Gross profit	**Millions of GBP**	**43.99**	**53.95**	**64.77**	**73.83**	**78.38**	**82.70**	**87.70**	**92.89**
Indirect Costs	Millions of GBP	24.05	21.82	22.84	22.34	23.46	25.23	26.42	27.70
Indirect Costs (% of revenue)	%	*18.8%*	*16.1%*	*14.6%*	*13.4%*	*13.3%*	*13.6%*	*13.4%*	*13.3%*
Other operating expenses (council rates)	Millions of GBP	20.00	20.00	20.00	20.30	20.61	20.92	21.24	21.56
Other operating expenses (council rates)	%								
EBITDA	**Millions of GBP**	**(0.06)**	**12.13**	**21.93**	**31.19**	**34.32**	**36.55**	**40.04**	**43.64**
EBITDA margin	%	*0.0%*	*9.0%*	*14.0%*	*18.8%*	*19.5%*	*19.7%*	*20.4%*	*21.0%*
Depreciation	Millions of GBP	10.00	9.77	9.55	9.37	9.20	9.07	8.95	8.87
Depreciation as a % of revenue	%	*7.8%*	*7.2%*	*6.1%*	*5.6%*	*5.2%*	*4.9%*	*4.6%*	*4.3%*
Amortization	Millions of GBP	2.00	2.00	2.01	2.04	2.07	2.12	2.19	2.25
Amortization as a % of revenue	%	*1.6%*	*1.5%*	*1.3%*	*1.2%*	*1.2%*	*1.1%*	*1.1%*	*1.1%*
Intangible Assets Write-up Amortization	Millions of GBP	-	-	-	1.26	1.26	1.26	1.26	1.26
PP&E Write-up Depreciation	Millions of GBP	-	-	-	3.79	3.79	3.79	3.79	3.79
Depreciation & Amortization	Millions of GBP	12.00	11.77	11.57	16.46	16.33	16.24	16.19	16.17
EBIT	**Millions of GBP**	**(12.06)**	**0.36**	**10.37**	**14.74**	**17.99**	**20.31**	**23.85**	**27.46**
EBIT margin	%	*-9.4%*	*0.3%*	*6.6%*	*8.9%*	*10.2%*	*10.9%*	*12.1%*	*13.2%*
Revolver	Millions of GBP								
Senior A	Millions of GBP								
Senior B	Millions of GBP								
Senior C	Millions of GBP								
Second Lien	Millions of GBP								
Mezzanine	Millions of GBP								
Amortization of Financing Fees	Millions of GBP								
EBT	**Millions of GBP**								
EBT margin	%								
Income tax expense	Millions of GBP								
Effective tax rate %	%								
Net income	**Millions of GBP**								
Net income margin	%								

Not showing up yet

FIGURE 5.27 Income statement: historical and forecasts.

Pre-LBO Model—Balance Sheet

- Insert new lines for financing structure:
  - Long-term liabilities: new debt
  - Long-term assets: for example, amortizing of financing fees
- Insert two columns between the opening column and the first forecast year:
  - Adjustments/bridge column to account for changes to opening B/S as a result of the LBO (to be calculated from sources and uses)
  - Pro forma column to account for the adjustments applied to the opening balance (same year but appropriate starting point for forecasts)

(These changes are already made in the model, as shown in Figure 5.28.)

Pre-LBO Model—Cash Flow Statement Here, there is nothing to do if CapEx has been analyzed carefully (very important in an LBO). We observe how it links to the Income Statement and to the Balance Sheet. In particular, the ending cash balance should be equal to the cash position in the balance sheet. The cash flows for operating and investing activities are the FCFF.

5.6.3.3 Step 3—Structuring the Transaction We assume a purchase price expressed as a multiple of the EBITDA of the target company. (For the acquisition of a public company, we would need to assume a premium over an undisturbed price per share.) We will then choose a financing structure among four options and apply it to the Sources & Uses, including the one-off financing fees and any other transaction fees and expenses. Financing structures can be made of any working combinations of financing tranches (Figure 5.29).

Balance sheet

		Historical >>			Forecast >>				
Category	Units	2025	Transaction	2025-post	2026	2027	2028	2029	2030
Assets									
Cash	Millions of GBP	18.35	(4.67)	13.68	13.68	16.17	25.14	36.49	50.34
Accounts receivable	Millions of GBP	27.03		27.03	28.61	30.26	31.98	33.77	35.65
Inventory	Millions of GBP	8.64		8.64	9.15	9.68	10.24	10.82	11.43
Prepaid expenses	Millions of GBP	7.84		7.84	8.31	8.79	9.30	9.82	10.38
Current assets	**Millions of GBP**	**61.86**	**(4.67)**	**57.19**	**59.74**	**64.90**	**76.65**	**90.90**	**107.78**
PPE	Millions of GBP	26.69	37.89	64.58	59.79	55.42	51.44	47.85	44.61
Goodwill	Millions of GBP	1.00	143.53	144.53	144.53	144.53	144.53	144.53	144.53
Intangible assets	Millions of GBP	6.17	18.94	25.11	21.81	18.48	15.09	11.64	8.12
Other assets	Millions of GBP	10.00		10.00	10.00	10.00	10.00	10.00	10.00
Total non-current assets	**Millions of GBP**	**43.86**	**200.36**	**244.23**	**236.14**	**228.43**	**221.07**	**214.02**	**207.27**
Total assets		**105.72**	**195.70**	**301.42**	**295.88**	**293.33**	**297.72**	**304.92**	**315.05**
Liabilities									
Accounts payable	Millions of GBP	3.09		3.09	3.28	3.47	3.67	3.88	4.09
Accrued expenses/liabilities	Millions of GBP	7.84		7.84	8.31	8.79	9.30	9.82	10.38
Bonus accrual	Millions of GBP	7.84		7.84	8.31	8.79	9.30	9.82	10.38
Tax accrual	Millions of GBP	7.84		7.84	8.31	8.79	9.30	9.82	10.38
Other current liabilities	Millions of GBP	7.84		7.84	8.31	8.79	9.30	9.82	10.38
Total current liabilities	**Millions of GBP**	**34.46**		**34.46**	**36.50**	**38.63**	**40.85**	**43.17**	**45.59**
Debt	Millions of GBP	10.00							
Revolver	Millions of GBP								
Senior A	Millions of GBP								
Senior B	Millions of GBP								
Senior C	Millions of GBP								
Second Lien	Millions of GBP								
Mezzanine	Millions of GBP								
Capitalized Financing Fees	Millions of GBP								
Deferred income tax	Millions of GBP	2.00							
Other long-term liabilities	Millions of GBP	20.00							
Total non-current liabilities	**Millions of GBP**	**32.00**							
Total liabilities	**Millions of GBP**	**66.46**							
Equity									
Contributed capital	Millions of GBP	31.07							
Transaction fees	Millions of GBP								
Equity—rollover (Seller)	Millions of GBP								
Equity—Sponsor (GP)	Millions of GBP								
Equity—LP	Millions of GBP								
Retained Earnings	Millions of GBP	8.19							
Total equity	**Millions of GBP**	**39.26**							
Equity + liabilities	**Millions of GBP**	**105.72**							
Net working capital (excluding cash)	**Millions of GBP**	**9.05**							
Change in net working capital	Millions of GBP								

Not showing up yet

FIGURE 5.28 Balance sheet: historical and forecasts.

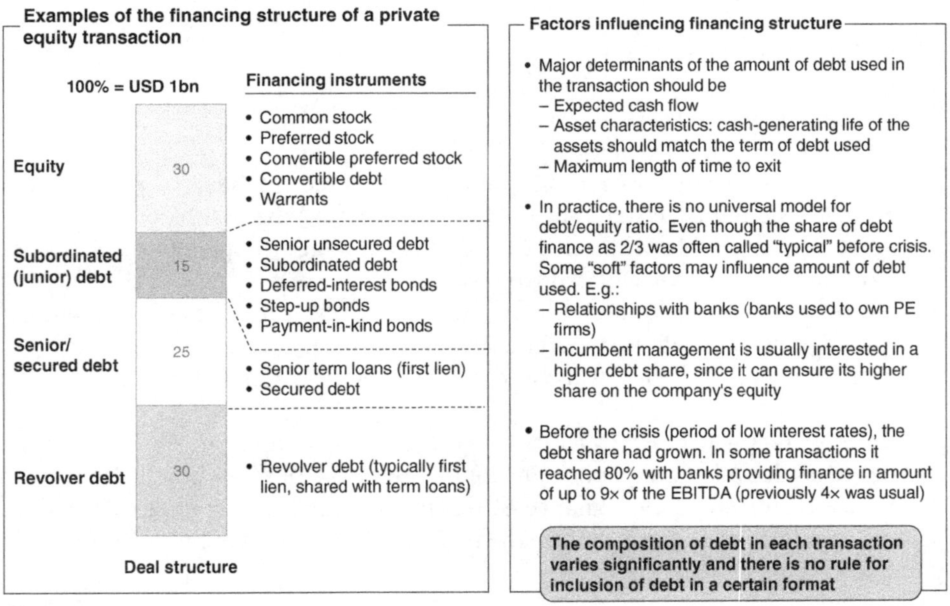

FIGURE 5.29 Example of LBO capital structure.

Entry and Exit Multiples Entry and exit values will define most of the performance of the investment, together with the changes in the capital structure and any intermediary payments to the shareholders.

First, enter an entry multiple and a reasonable target exit multiple in the Return on Investment Analysis part of Deal Dynamics. In our example we use 10× entry multiple and expect the same fair multiple of 10× at exit. As discussed previously, the exit multiple shouldn't normally be expected to be higher, unless you bought cheap or plan to reposition the company to make it more attractive.

Transaction Structure In <Deal Dynamics>, we input four possible debt structures before choosing one (Figure 5.30). They are structures that the leveraged finance team believes are negotiable with the various lenders at the conditions given in the financing fees. We chose the first structure.

Financing Fees (One-off Fees) They must be entered in <Deal Dynamics> (Figure 5.31). They are NOT the yearly interest, please don't get confused! Let's use

- 1.0% for revolver and term loans,
- 1.75% for second lien, and
- 2.00% for mezzanine.

Transaction Fees: This includes fees for M&A advisory and other professional services, like financial audit, legal and consulting. We input them in the sources and uses of funds in <Deal Dynamics> (Figure 5.32).

Debt Selector	1	<< Do not touch			
	Debt Options	**Debt 1**	**Debt 2**	**Debt 3**	**Debt 4**
Revolver	Millions of GBP	10.00	6.00	6.00	10.00
Senior TLA	Millions of GBP	20.00	20.00	20.00	24.00
Senior TLB	Millions of GBP	80.00	70.00	90.00	76.00
TLC	Millions of GBP	-	-	-	-
Second Lien	Millions of GBP		14.00	-	-
Mezzanine	Millions of GBP	20.00	20.00	14.00	20.00

FIGURE 5.30 Debt structure.

Financing fees based on transaction debt

		Finance fees >>		
Category	**Units**	**Size of loan**	**Fee as a proportion of total loan value (%)**	**Total fee cost**
Revolver	Millions of GBP	10.00	1.00%	0.10
Senior A	Millions of GBP	20.00	1.00%	0.20
Senior B	Millions of GBP	80.00	1.00%	0.80
Senior C	Millions of GBP	-	1.00%	-
Second Lien	Millions of GBP	-	1.75%	-
Mezzanine	Millions of GBP	20.00	2.00%	0.40
Total financing fees	**Millions of GBP**			**1.50**

FIGURE 5.31 Financing fees.

Sources of funds

		SOURCES >>					
Category	**Units**	**Pro Forma Equity Post T**	**Capacity**	**EBITDA multiple**	**mulative EBITDA mul**	**% total source**	**Amount**
Revolver	-		10.00	0.5×	0.5×	4.2%	10.00
Senior A	-			0.9×	1.4×	8.4%	20.00
Senior B	-			3.6×	5.0×	33.7%	80.00
Senior C	-			0.0×	5.0×	0.0%	-
Second Lien	-			0.0×	5.0×	0.0%	-
Mezzanine	-			0.9×	5.9×	8.4%	20.00
Equity—Seller rollover / management equity	-	9%				4.2%	10.00
Equity—GP	-	9%				4.2%	10.00
Equity—LP	-	81%				36.8%	87.52
Total Sources	-				**10.8×**	**100.0%**	**237.52**

Uses of funds

		USES >>
Category	**Units**	**Amount used**
Purchase equity value	Millions of GBP	227.69
Existing net debt—payback	Millions of GBP	(8.35)
Transaction fees	Millions of GBP	3.00
Financing fees	Millions of GBP	1.50
Cash to Balance Sheet of NewCo	Millions of GBP	13.68
Total Uses	**Millions of GBP**	**237.52**

FIGURE 5.32 Sources and uses of funds.

The M&A advisory fees often represent the main part of the fees. They are mostly success fees and can vary significantly. Paul Tomasic is well placed to compare the evolution of the M&A market in the United States and Europe, particularly regarding differences in fee structures: "European clients are used to pay less fees on average, perhaps up to 30% less, both in M&A and for IPOs. Europe remains more relationship-based, while the US is marginally more transactional."

5.6.3.4 Step 4—Post-LBO Model Once the capital structure for the LBO is chosen, all missing calculations follow using cash sweeps, where all excess free cash flow (operating + investing CF) after paying interest is used to reduce the part of the debt that can be repaid early without penalty. The typical order would be revolver first, then Term Loan A, B, C, ...

We need to input financial terms for each component of debt.

Forward Interest Rates This raises an important question: *How should we account for the interest expenses on floating-rate debt instruments?*

We need forward interest rates, which represent the market's consensus on the expected future levels of interest rates (Figure 5.33). For many years, LIBOR was the primary benchmark, calculated daily for the most liquid currencies. However, following a scandal involving rate manipulation by some London market makers, LIBOR was finally phased out in 2023 and replaced by term rates such as SOFR for USD, €STR for the euro (alongside the remaining Euribor), SONIA for GBP, and others. Indicative values as of the time of editing are provided in <D-debt Assumptions>, but these should be updated manually.

Financial Terms for Debt We input the terms in <D-debt Assumptions> with the following characteristics (Figure 5.34):

- The revolver typically includes a commitment fee for unused portion (0.5%).
- The term loans may have a floor, a short option that reduces slightly the variable rate, at the cost of always paying that minimum floor rate, even if the interest rate falls below.
- Term loans are expected to have an amortization schedule with a small, here 0.5%, mandatory annual minimum repayment.
- The interests on each debt tranche are calculated based on the average outstanding debt over the year (not the opening or ending balance).

The expected evolution of the chosen debt structure appears in Figures 5.35 and 5.36

Active debt curve

		1	Historical >>			Forecast >>				
Curve	Units		2023	2024	2025	2026	2027	2028	2029	2030
£/SONIA	%		4.00%	3.65%	3.75%	3.85%	4.00%	4.15%	4.30%	4.35%

Debt rates and financing overview

		Historical >>			Forecast >>				
Curve	Units	2023	2024	2025	2026	2027	2028	2029	2030
£/SONIA	%	4.00%	3.65%	3.75%	3.85%	4.00%	4.15%	4.30%	4.35%
$/SOFR	%	4.30%	5.32%	4.32%	3.51%	2.94%	3.03%	3.22%	3.40%
€STR	%	1.90%	3.90%	2.92%	1.87%	1.78%	1.99%	2.19%	2.37%
€/EURIBOR	%	1.98%	3.87%	2.79%	1.98%	1.91%	2.11%	2.31%	2.48%
$/AMERIBOR	%	4.62%	5.43%	4.42%	3.61%	3.04%	3.14%	3.33%	3.50%
¥/TONAR	%								
CHF/SARON	%								

FIGURE 5.33 Forward interest rate curves.

Debt rates and financing overview—debt taken	
Revolving Credit Facility	
Revolving Credit Facility Size/Capacity	10.00
Spread	3.00%
Floor	2.00%
Term	6 years
Commitment Fee on Unused Portion	0.50%
Senior Tranche TLA	
Size	20.00
Spread	3.50%
Floor	2.00%
Term	7 years
Repayment Schedule	20.00%
Senior Tranche TLB	
Size	80.00
Spread	4.00%
Floor	2.00%
Term	8 years
Repayment Schedule	1.00%
Senior Tranche TLC	
Size	0.00
Spread	5.00%
Floor	2.00%
Term	8 years
Repayment Schedule	0.00%
Second Lien	
Size	0.00
Spread	8.000%
Floor	2.00%
Term	8 years
Mezzanine Debt	
Size	20.00
Spread (Cash interest)	10.500%
Floor	0.00%
PIK Interest Rate	10.000%
Term	10 years
Repayment Schedule	0.00%

FIGURE 5.34 Debt terms.

The three financial statements should now look as shown in Figures 5.37, 5.38, and 5.39 (management case).

5.6.3.5 Step 5—Deal Dynamics

- Analyze financing structure
- Perform return analysis
- Valuation
- Summarize Deal Dynamics

By now we should have solved the circularity issue

Cash available for Sweep	Units	Forecast >> 2026	2027	2028	2029	2030
Category	Units	2026	2027	2028	2029	2030
£/SONIA	%	3.85%	4.00%	4.15%	4.30%	4.35%
Cash Flow from Operating Activities		18.22	20.86	22.65	25.29	28.07
Cash Flow from Investing Activities		(8.37)	(8.62)	(8.88)	(9.15)	(9.42)
Cash Available for Debt Repayment		**9.85**	**12.24**	**13.77**	**16.15**	**18.65**
Total Mandatory Repayments						
Cash From Balance Sheet						
Cash Available for Optional Debt Repayment		**9.85**	**12.24**	**13.77**	**16.15**	**18.65**

Revolving Credit Facility		2026	2027	2028	2029	2030
Revolving Credit Facility Size/Capacity	10.00					
Spread	3.00%					
Floor	2.00%					
Term	6 years					
Commitment Fee on Unused Portion	0.50%					
Beginning Balance		10.00	4.95	-	-	-
Drawdown/(Repayment)		(5.05)	(4.95)	-	-	-
Ending Balance		**4.95**	-	-	-	-
Total Revolver Capacity		10.00	10.00	10.00	10.00	10.00
Beginning Available Capacity		-	5.05	10.00	10.00	10.00
Ending Available Capacity		15.05	14.95	10.00	10.00	10.00
Revolver Interest Rate		6.85%	7.00%	7.15%	7.30%	7.35%
Revolver Interest Expense		0.51	0.17	-	-	-
Unused Revolver Commitment Fee		0.50%	0.50%	0.50%	0.50%	0.50%
Unused Commitment Fee		0.04	0.05	0.05	0.05	0.05

Senior Tranche A		Forecast >> 2026	2027	2028	2029	2030
Size	20.00					
Spread	3.50%					
Floor	2.00%					
Term	7 years					
Repayment Schedule	20.00%					
Beginning Balance		20.00	16.00	12.00	8.00	4.00
Mandatory Repayments		(4.00)	(4.00)	(4.00)	(4.00)	(4.00)
Ending Balance		**16.00**	**12.00**	**8.00**	**4.00**	-
Interest Rate		7.35%	7.50%	7.65%	7.80%	7.85%
Interest Expense		1.32	1.05	0.77	0.47	0.16

FIGURE 5.35 Debt structure (1/2).

Senior Tranche B		Forecast >> 2026	2027	2028	2029	2030
Size	80.00					
Spread	4.00%					
Floor	2.00%					
Term	8 years					
Repayment Schedule	1.00%					
Beginning Balance		80.00	79.20	78.40	77.60	76.80
Mandatory Repayments		(0.80)	(0.80)	(0.80)	(0.80)	(0.80)
Ending Balance		**79.20**	**78.40**	**77.60**	**76.80**	**76.00**
Interest Rate		7.85%	8.00%	8.15%	8.30%	8.35%
Interest Expense		6.25	6.30	6.36	6.41	6.38

Mezzanine Debt		Forecast >> 2026	2027	2028	2029	2030
Size	20.00					
Spread (Cash interest)	10.50%					
Floor	0.00%					
PIK Interest Rate	10.00%					
Term	10 years					
Repayment Schedule	0.00%					
Beginning Balance		20.00	22.00	24.20	26.62	29.28
Mandatory Repayments		-	-	-	-	-
PIK interest		2.00	2.20	2.42	2.66	2.93
Ending Balance		**22.00**	**24.20**	**26.62**	**29.28**	**32.21**
Cash Interest Rate		14.35%	14.50%	14.65%	14.80%	14.85%
PIK Rate		10.00%	10.00%	10.00%	10.00%	10.00%
Cash Interest Expense		3.01	3.35	3.72	4.14	4.57
PIK Interest Expense		2.00	2.20	2.42	2.66	2.93

Interest Expense Calculation	Forecast >> 2026	2027	2028	2029	2030
Revolver	0.51	0.17	-	-	-
Senior A	1.32	1.05	0.77	0.47	0.16
Senior B	6.25	6.30	6.36	6.41	6.38
Senior C	-	-	-	-	-
Second Lien	-	-	-	-	-
Mezzanine	5.01	5.55	6.14	6.80	7.49
Total Interest Expense	**13.10**	**13.08**	**13.26**	**13.67**	**14.03**

FIGURE 5.36 Debt structure (2/2).

Income Statement

Category	Units	Historical >> 2023	2024	2025	Forecast >> 2026	2027	2028	2029	2030
Revenue	Millions of GBP	127.65	135.47	156.84	166.11	175.79	185.91	196.47	207.50
Revenue growth year-on-year	%		*6.1%*	*15.8%*	*5.9%*	*5.8%*	*5.8%*	*5.7%*	*5.6%*
Direct Costs	Millions of GBP	83.66	81.52	92.07	92.28	97.41	103.21	108.78	114.61
Direct costs (% of revenue)	%	*65.5%*	*60.2%*	*58.7%*	*55.6%*	*55.4%*	*55.5%*	*55.4%*	*55.2%*
Gross profit	**Millions of GBP**	**43.99**	**53.95**	**64.77**	**73.83**	**78.38**	**82.70**	**87.70**	**92.89**
Indirect Costs	Millions of GBP	24.05	21.82	22.84	22.34	23.46	25.23	26.42	27.70
Indirect Costs (% of revenue)	%	*18.8%*	*16.1%*	*14.6%*	*13.4%*	*13.3%*	*13.6%*	*13.4%*	*13.3%*
Other operating expenses (council rates)	Millions of GBP	20.00	20.00	20.00	20.30	20.61	20.92	21.24	21.56
Other operating expenses (council rates)	%								
EBITDA	**Millions of GBP**	**(0.06)**	**12.13**	**21.93**	**31.19**	**34.32**	**36.55**	**40.04**	**43.64**
EBITDA margin	%	*0.0%*	*9.0%*	*14.0%*	*18.8%*	*19.5%*	*19.7%*	*20.4%*	*21.0%*
Depreciation	Millions of GBP	10.00	9.77	9.55	9.37	9.20	9.07	8.95	8.87
Depreciation as a % of revenue	%	*7.8%*	*7.2%*	*6.1%*	*5.6%*	*5.2%*	*4.9%*	*4.6%*	*4.3%*
Amortization	Millions of GBP	2.00	2.00	2.01	2.04	2.07	2.12	2.19	2.25
Amortization as a % of revenue	%	*1.6%*	*1.5%*	*1.3%*	*1.2%*	*1.2%*	*1.1%*	*1.1%*	*1.1%*
Intangible Assets Write-up Amortization	Millions of GBP	-	-	-	1.26	1.26	1.26	1.26	1.26
PP&E Write-up Depreciation	Millions of GBP	-	-	-	3.79	3.79	3.79	3.79	3.79
Depreciation & Amortization	Millions of GBP	12.00	11.77	11.57	16.46	16.33	16.24	16.19	16.17
EBIT	**Millions of GBP**	**(12.06)**	**0.36**	**10.37**	**14.74**	**17.99**	**20.31**	**23.85**	**27.46**
EBIT margin	%	*-9.4%*	*0.3%*	*6.6%*	*8.9%*	*10.2%*	*10.9%*	*12.1%*	*13.2%*
Revolver	Millions of GBP	-	-	-	0.51	0.17	-	-	-
Senior A	Millions of GBP	-	-	-	1.32	1.05	0.77	0.47	0.16
Senior B	Millions of GBP	-	-	-	6.25	6.30	6.36	6.41	6.38
Senior C	Millions of GBP	-	-	-	-	-	-	-	-
Second Lien	Millions of GBP				-	-	-	-	-
Mezzanine	Millions of GBP	-	-	-	5.01	5.55	6.14	6.80	7.49
Amortization of Financing Fees	Millions of GBP	-	-	-	0.21	0.21	0.21	0.21	0.21
EBT	**Millions of GBP**	**(12.06)**	**0.36**	**10.37**	**1.43**	**4.71**	**6.83**	**9.97**	**13.22**
EBT margin	%	*-9.4%*	*0.3%*	*6.6%*	*0.9%*	*2.7%*	*3.7%*	*5.1%*	*6.4%*
Income tax expense	Millions of GBP	-	*0.08*	*2.18*	*0.30*	*0.99*	*1.43*	*2.09*	*2.78*
Effective tax rate %	%	*21.0%*	*21.0%*	*21.0%*	*21.0%*	*21.0%*	*21.0%*	*21.0%*	*21.0%*
Net income	**Millions of GBP**	**(12.06)**	**0.29**	**8.19**	**1.13**	**3.72**	**5.40**	**7.87**	**10.45**
Net income margin	%	*-9.4%*	*0.2%*	*5.2%*	*0.7%*	*2.1%*	*2.9%*	*4.0%*	*5.0%*

FIGURE 5.37 Finalizing the income statement.

Balance sheet

Category	Units	Historical >> 2025	Transaction	2025-post	Forecast >> 2026	2027	2028	2029	2030
Assets									
Cash	Millions of GBP	18.35	(4.67)	13.68	13.68	16.17	25.14	36.49	50.34
Accounts receivable	Millions of GBP	27.03		27.03	28.61	30.26	31.98	33.77	35.65
Inventory	Millions of GBP	8.64		8.64	9.15	9.68	10.24	10.82	11.43
Prepaid expenses	Millions of GBP	7.84		7.84	8.31	8.79	9.30	9.82	10.38
Current assets	**Millions of GBP**	**61.86**	**(4.67)**	**57.19**	**59.74**	**64.90**	**76.65**	**90.90**	**107.78**
PPE	Millions of GBP	26.69	37.89	64.58	59.79	55.42	51.44	47.85	44.61
Goodwill	Millions of GBP	1.00	143.53	144.53	144.53	144.53	144.53	144.53	144.53
Intangible assets	Millions of GBP	6.17	18.94	25.11	21.81	18.48	15.09	11.64	8.12
Other assets	Millions of GBP	10.00		10.00	10.00	10.00	10.00	10.00	10.00
Total non-current assets	**Millions of GBP**	**43.86**	**200.36**	**244.23**	**236.14**	**228.43**	**221.07**	**214.02**	**207.27**
Total assets		**105.72**	**195.70**	**301.42**	**295.88**	**293.33**	**297.72**	**304.92**	**315.05**
Liabilities									
Accounts payable	Millions of GBP	3.09		3.09	3.28	3.47	3.67	3.88	4.09
Accrued expenses/liabilities	Millions of GBP	7.84		7.84	8.31	8.79	9.30	9.82	10.38
Bonus accrual	Millions of GBP	7.84		7.84	8.31	8.79	9.30	9.82	10.38
Tax accrual	Millions of GBP	7.84		7.84	8.31	8.79	9.30	9.82	10.38
Other current liabilities	Millions of GBP	7.84		7.84	8.31	8.79	9.30	9.82	10.38
Total current liabilities	**Millions of GBP**	**34.46**		**34.46**	**36.50**	**38.63**	**40.85**	**43.17**	**45.59**
Debt	Millions of GBP	10.00	(10.00)	-	-	-	-	-	-
Revolver	Millions of GBP		10.00	10.00	4.95	-	-	-	-
Senior A	Millions of GBP		20.00	20.00	16.00	12.00	8.00	4.00	-
Senior B	Millions of GBP		80.00	80.00	79.20	78.40	77.60	76.80	76.00
Senior C	Millions of GBP		-	-	-	-	-	-	-
Second Lien	Millions of GBP		-	-	-	-	-	-	-
Mezzanine	Millions of GBP		20.00	20.00	22.00	24.20	26.62	29.28	32.21
Capitalized Financing Fees	Millions of GBP		(1.50)	(1.50)	(1.29)	(1.08)	(0.87)	(0.66)	(0.47)
Deferred income tax	Millions of GBP	2.00	11.93	13.93	12.87	11.81	10.75	9.69	8.63
Other long-term liabilities	Millions of GBP	20.00		20.00	20.00	20.00	20.00	20.00	20.00
Total non-current liabilities	**Millions of GBP**	**32.00**	**130.43**	**162.43**	**153.73**	**145.33**	**142.10**	**139.11**	**136.37**
Total liabilities	**Millions of GBP**	**66.46**	**130.43**	**196.90**	**190.23**	**183.96**	**182.95**	**182.28**	**181.97**
Equity									
Contributed capital	Millions of GBP	31.07	(31.07)	-	-	-	-	-	-
Transaction fees	Millions of GBP		(3.00)	(3.00)	(3.00)	(3.00)	(3.00)	(3.00)	(3.00)
Equity—rollover (Seller)	Millions of GBP		10.00	10.00	10.00	10.00	10.00	10.00	10.00
Equity—Sponsor (GP)	Millions of GBP		10.00	10.00	10.12	10.50	11.05	11.86	12.93
Equity—LP	Millions of GBP		87.52	87.52	88.54	91.87	96.72	103.78	113.16
Retained Earnings	Millions of GBP	8.19	(8.19)	-	-	-	-	-	-
Total equity	**Millions of GBP**	**39.26**	**65.26**	**104.52**	**105.65**	**109.37**	**114.77**	**122.64**	**133.09**
Equity + liabilities	**Millions of GBP**	**105.72**	**195.70**	**301.42**	**295.88**	**293.33**	**297.72**	**304.92**	**315.05**
Net working capital (excluding cash)	**Millions of GBP**	**9.05**		**9.05**	**9.56**	**10.10**	**10.66**	**11.24**	**11.85**
Change in net working capital	Millions of GBP				(0.51)	(0.54)	(0.56)	(0.58)	(0.61)
Balance check		-		-	-	-	-	-	-

FIGURE 5.38 Finalizing the balance sheet.

Financing Structure First, can we serve debt interests? Repay the principal? Credit statistics will be scrutinized by the lenders (Figure 5.40).

- Evolution of capital structure ("capitalization").
- Credit statistics in <Deal Dynamics> (we show eight years): Leverage and coverage ratios (e.g., debt-to-EBITDA, debt-to-total capitalization, and EBITDA-to-interest expense).

- As expected, credit statistics improve over the projection period. TLA is fully repaid by end of 2030E and TLB has been reduced by the mandatory amortization. Debt to total capitalization decreases from 56% at entry to 22% in 2030. EBITDA to interest expense increases from 2.3× to 3.3×.

Returns Analysis Do we meet the return expectations of the sponsor? Remember the main drivers of the IRR:

- Projected financial performance
- Purchase price
- Financing structure
- Exit multiple
- Exit year

Look at the IRR and the cash return in Figure 5.41, and then in Figure 5.42, from <Deal Dynamics>. (One enters manually the entry and exit multiples in each sensitivity matrix; they do not automatically use the multiples you entered in the equity value section.) The predicted IRR in the management case is 28.6%. Remember that is the yearly return for each of the five years (if everything goes well). It corresponds to a multiple of 3.5×. You can see the returns are lower if you select the base case.

We can play with the entry and exit EBITDA multiples and the exit year in <Deal Dynamics> to observe the impact on the returns.

Keeping 28.6% IRR and five years to exit, we can also vary the equity contribution to assess a range of EV.

The model also includes a <Management Package> sheet that can be used to run a simulation with sweat equity, ratchets, retrocession thresholds, and other characteristics as described in Chapter 4.

Cashflow Statement

Category	Units	Forecast >> 2026	2027	2028	2029	2030
Cash from Operations						
Net Income	Millions of GBP	1.13	3.72	5.40	7.87	10.45
Depreciation	Millions of GBP	9.37	9.20	9.07	8.95	8.87
Amortization	Millions of GBP	2.04	2.07	2.12	2.19	2.25
Amortization of Deferred Financing Fees	Millions of GBP	0.21	0.21	0.21	0.21	0.19
Intangible Assets Write-up Amortization	Millions of GBP	1.26	1.26	1.26	1.26	1.26
PP&E Write-up Depreciation	Millions of GBP	3.79	3.79	3.79	3.79	3.79
PIK Interest		2.00	2.20	2.42	2.66	2.93
Deferred Tax Liability Unwind	Millions of GBP	(1.06)	(1.06)	(1.06)	(1.06)	(1.06)
Change in NWC (excluding cash)	Millions of GBP	(0.51)	(0.54)	(0.56)	(0.58)	(0.61)
Total Cash from Operations	**Millions of GBP**	**18.22**	**20.86**	**22.65**	**25.29**	**28.07**
Cash from Investing						
Change in fixed assets (CapEx)	Millions of GBP	(8.37)	(8.62)	(8.88)	(9.15)	(9.42)
Other investing Activities	Millions of GBP	-	-	-	-	-
Total Cash from Investing	**Millions of GBP**	**(8.37)**	**(8.62)**	**(8.88)**	**(9.15)**	**(9.42)**
Mandatory Repayments	Millions of GBP	(4.80)	(4.80)	(4.80)	(4.80)	(4.80)
Free Cash Flow (Pre-revolver)	**Millions of GBP**	**5.05**	**7.44**	**8.97**	**11.35**	**13.85**
Revolver Drawdown/(Paydown)	Millions of GBP	(5.05)	(4.95)	-	-	-
Free Cash Flow (Post-revolver)		**-**	**2.49**	**8.97**	**11.35**	**13.85**
Cash Flow After Financing Activities		-	2.49	8.97	11.35	13.85
Beginning Cash Balance	Millions of GBP	13.68	13.68	16.17	25.14	36.49
Net Change in Cash Flow	Millions of GBP	-	2.49	8.97	11.35	13.85
Ending Cash Balance	**Millions of GBP**	**13.68**	**16.17**	**25.14**	**36.49**	**50.34**

FIGURE 5.39 Finalizing the cash flow statement.

Credit statistics

Category	Units	Debt Statistics >>	1	2	3	4	5	6	7	8
		Year	2026	2027	2028	2029	2030	2031	2032	2033
EBITDA/Total Interest Expense			2.34x	2.58x	2.75x	3.01x	3.28x	3.55x	3.83x	4.50x
EBITDA/Total Cash Interest Expense			2.81x	3.16x	3.37x	3.64x	3.93x	4.15x	4.25x	4.75x
EBITDA—CapEx/Total Interest Expense			1.72x	1.93x	2.08x	2.32x	2.57x	2.82x	3.08x	3.72x
EBITDA—CapEx/Total Cash Interest Expense			2.06x	2.36x	2.55x	2.81x	3.08x	3.30x	3.42x	3.93x
Total debt/EV (EoY)			38%	32%	29%	25%	22%	20%	19%	16%
Senior Debt/EBITDA			3.05x	2.63x	2.34x	2.02x	1.74x	1.59x	1.46x	1.23x
Total Debt/EBITDA			4.93x	4.23x	3.89x	3.47x	3.13x	2.91x	2.74x	2.36x
Net Debt/EBITDA			4.49x	3.76x	3.20x	2.56x	1.97x	1.42x	0.92x	0.34x

FIGURE 5.40 Credit statistics.

Equity value

EBITDA Multiple At Entry	10.0x
EBITDA Multiple At Exit	10.0x
Exit year	2030

		Historical >>	Forecast >>				
Category	**Units**	**2025**	**2026**	**2027**	**2028**	**2029**	**2030**
Revenue	Millions of GBP	156.84	166.11	175.79	185.91	196.47	207.50
EBITDA	Millions of GBP	21.93	31.19	34.32	36.55	40.04	43.64
EBITDA margin	%	*14.0%*	*18.8%*	*19.5%*	*19.7%*	*20.4%*	*21.0%*
Enterprise Value at Entry/Exit	**Millions of GBP**	**219.34**	**311.91**	**343.22**	**365.48**	**400.43**	**436.35**
Debt							
Revolver		10.00	4.95	-	-	-	-
Senior A		20.00	16.00	12.00	8.00	4.00	-
Senior B		80.00	79.20	78.40	77.60	76.80	76.00
Senior C		-	-	-	-	-	-
Second Lien		-	-	-	-	-	-
Mezzanine Debt		20.00	22.00	24.20	26.62	29.28	32.21
Total Debt		130.00	122.15	114.60	112.22	110.08	108.21
Cash		13.68	13.68	16.17	25.14	36.49	50.34
Net debt		**116.32**	**108.47**	**98.43**	**87.08**	**73.60**	**57.88**
Equity value at exit		**103.02**	**203.44**	**244.79**	**278.40**	**326.83**	**378.48**

Returns analysis

	Historical >>	Forecast >>				
	2025	**2026**	**2027**	**2028**	**2029**	**2030**
Initial investment	(107.52)	(107.52)	(107.52)	(107.52)	(107.52)	(107.52)
		203.44	-	-	-	-
			244.79	-	-	-
				278.40	-	-
					326.83	-
						378.48
IRR		**89.2%**	**50.9%**	**37.3%**	**32.0%**	**28.6%**
MoM		**1.9x**	**2.3x**	**2.6x**	**3.0x**	**3.5x**

FIGURE 5.41 Return analysis.

=TABLE(E9,E6) (exit and entry multiples)

Return on investment sensitivity analysis

Exit year	2030

IRR sensitivity analysis—assuming exit in 2030

Multiple steps	1.0x

		Exit multiple						
		7.0x	8.0x	9.0x	10.0x	11.0x	12.0x	13.0x
Entry multiple	7.0x	42.8%	47.5%	51.7%	55.4%	58.9%	62.0%	64.9%
	8.0x	31.2%	35.5%	39.4%	42.8%	46.0%	48.9%	51.6%
	9.0x	23.7%	27.7%	31.4%	34.6%	37.6%	40.3%	42.9%
	10.0x	18.2%	22.1%	25.5%	**28.6%**	31.5%	34.1%	36.5%
	11.0x	13.8%	17.6%	20.9%	23.9%	26.7%	29.2%	31.5%
	12.0x	10.3%	14.0%	17.2%	20.1%	22.8%	25.2%	27.5%
	13.0x	7.4%	10.9%	14.1%	16.9%	19.5%	21.9%	24.1%

MoM sensitivity analysis—assuming exit in 2030

Multiple steps	1.0x

		Exit multiple						
		7.0x	8.0x	9.0x	10.0x	11.0x	12.0x	13.0x
Entry multiple	7.0x	5.9x	7.0x	8.0x	9.1x	10.1x	11.2x	12.2x
	8.0x	3.9x	4.6x	5.3x	5.9x	6.6x	7.3x	8.0x
	9.0x	2.9x	3.4x	3.9x	4.4x	4.9x	5.4x	6.0x
	10.0x	2.3x	2.7x	3.1x	**3.5x**	3.9x	4.3x	4.7x
	11.0x	1.9x	2.2x	2.6x	2.9x	3.3x	3.6x	3.9x
	12.0x	1.6x	1.9x	2.2x	2.5x	2.8x	3.1x	3.4x
	13.0x	1.4x	1.7x	1.9x	2.2x	2.4x	2.7x	2.9x

Sources of return

		Historical >>	Forecast >>					
Category	**Units**	**2025**	**2026**	**2027**	**2028**	**2029**	**2030**	**2031**
EBITDA growth	Millions of GBP		92.57	123.88	146.14	181.08	217.01	253.46
De-leverage	Millions of GBP		7.85	17.89	29.24	42.72	58.44	76.14
Multiple expansion	Millions of GBP		-	-	-	-	-	-
Total returns	**Millions of GBP**		**100.42**	**141.77**	**175.38**	**223.81**	**275.45**	**329.59**
Balance check			-	-	-	-	-	-

Currently showing sources of return for 2030

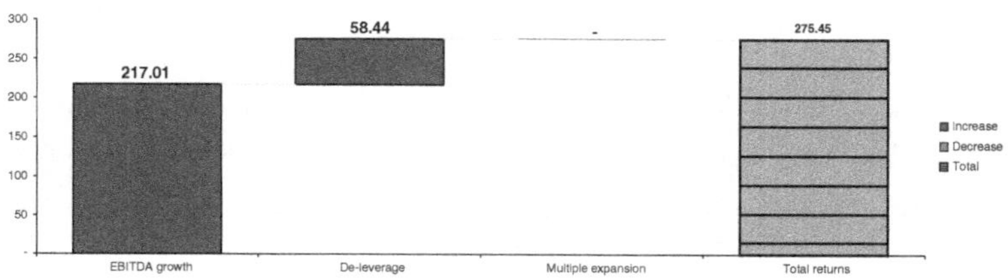

FIGURE 5.42 Sensitivity analysis.

5.7 EQUITY STORY AND INVESTMENT CASE

There is a fine distinction to make here, and you will be forgiven if it is not immediately clear, as many practitioners do not really make the difference.

The **Equity Story** is the compelling narrative that articulates why an investment is attractive and how value will be created. It is essentially the strategic vision and growth narrative that will be used throughout the investment life cycle—from fundraising through exit. It targets a certain type of investor, depending on the situation. A strong equity story will have to include the following:

1. Market positioning and competitive advantages
2. Growth opportunities and expansion potential
3. Value creation levers and operational improvement plans
4. Management team capabilities and track record
5. Clear path to exit and potential future owners

The **Investment Case** is the more detailed, analytical framework that supports the equity story with specific data, assumptions, and financial projections. It includes the following:

1. Detailed market analysis and industry trends
2. Historical financial performance and projected returns
3. Specific value creation initiatives with quantified impact
4. Risk assessment and mitigation strategies
5. Entry and exit multiples analysis
6. Returns modeling under different scenarios

The relationship between the two is important: the Equity Story needs to be supported by a robust Investment Case, while the Investment Case needs to tell a coherent story that aligns with the broader narrative. Both evolve throughout the investment period (Figure 5.43).

Pre-acquisition:	**During ownership:**	**Toward exit:**
• Used to secure internal investment committee approval	• Serves as a roadmap for value creation initiatives	• Refined to appeal to potential buyers or public markets
• Guides price negotiations and deal structure	• Provides benchmarks for measuring progress	• Updated to reflect achieved milestones
• Helps align management team around the vision	• Gets updated as market conditions change	• Used to demonstrate value creation track record
• Supports debt fundraising with lenders	• Helps communicate with key stakeholders	• Supports exit valuation discussions

FIGURE 5.43 Equity Story and Investment Case evolve throughout investment period.

A well-crafted Equity Story and Investment Case are particularly important for several reasons:

- Create alignment between PE firm, management, and other stakeholders
- Provide clear metrics for measuring success
- Help maintain focus during challenging periods
- Support consistent communication with all parties
- Form the foundation for exit planning from day one

5.8 CHAPTER SUMMARY

We have examined further valuation methods and what is involved in a full LBO analysis. We have developed a model from the pre-LBO stage to the post-LBO stage to provide the reader with a better understanding of the key steps in an LBO analysis.

We also discussed cash sweeps, and we looked at the most appropriate way of valuing an LBO in both a relative valuation, and in a DCF, which typically involves using the APV approach. Later, we explained what is included in a typical investment presentation. We ended with a review of some of the elements of the documentation that are used in the final negotiation, once the decision has been taken to invest in a company.

Some readers may have struggled a bit with the wealth of information here, but valuation is typically the most challenging part of this process for those who have little or no exposure to it as there are many parameters to digest. As with everything, it is a question of practice. To practice, the reader can replace the hospital operating model with their preferred healthcare business.

CHAPTER 6

Value Creation and Exit

This chapter considers what happens once we have acquired a company: How do we manage the PE fund beyond investments? This is commonly referred to as "value creation," meaning once in the portfolio, and focuses on the financial impact. To address this question, we discuss managing not only the company, but also people, in particular managers and co-investors. We finish with managing exits and conclude with the introduction to the UNITE playbook.

6.1 STEPS IN VALUE CREATION

Once a company is bought, there should be a plan for value creation (Figure 6.1).

First, the investment must fit an investment strategy. We may want to redefine or redesign the strategy for the company and very often it will be followed immediately by a so-called 100-day plan where we will transform the business, preparing it for growth. Throughout the life of the business, we will continuously try to improve its operational efficiency, looking for opportunities to grow organically and through acquisitions, and we will prepare the exit.

Throughout this process we will have to manage separately the sellers, the managers, and the investors (the LPs and sometimes other co-investors).

We also find that the focus and backgrounds of the GPs may influence the outperformance of the investment. Academic research shows that abnormal post-deal performance can be explained partially through human factors. Those deals that focus exclusively on internal value creation improve the EBITDA margins, and GPs with operational backgrounds generate significantly higher outperformance in those deals. The deals with an M&A focus grow EBITDA multiples more substantially, and GPs with a background in finance tend to outperform in those deals (Acharya et al., 2013). It does not remove the necessity to manage all stakeholders but can change the priorities.

6.2 100-DAY PLAN

No successful firm in the PE world would really dare to acquire a business without having a clear strategic roadmap. A roadmap should include a thesis for the investment, something that they should have from the very beginning, even before they have started discussions with the target's management. It should also include a post-deal

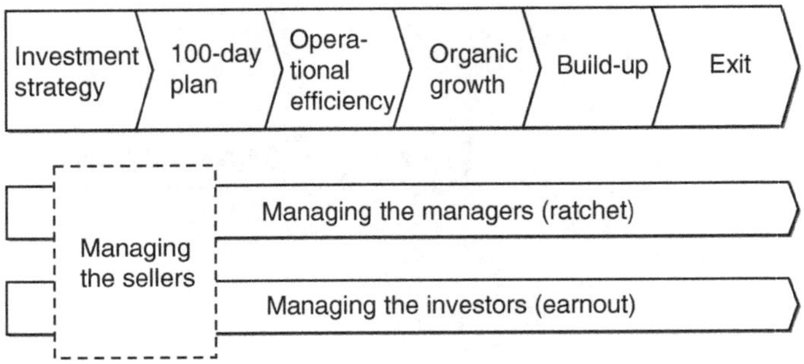

FIGURE 6.1 Managing the investment—what it entitles.

strategy and the 100-day plan I mentioned earlier, which is inherited from the turnaround world and before that from the military world. It is something developed early, during due diligence, and it will involve advisors like consultants. This plan is crucial for stabilizing the acquired business. The activities that will be performed in those first three months constitute the setup of a value creation roadmap, pertaining to cost assets and sales. The roadmap lays out a plan for capturing quick wins first, but also tracking progress and benefits, managing the risks and protecting the revenues while potentially restructuring the business.

Kravis and Roberts initiated a multi-faceted approach. They decided each investment would have a 100-day plan, like General Electric had for its businesses, forcing the dealmakers to think beyond the closing dinner. The pair, who'd been content to have every partner be a generalist, organized executives into industry teams (initially 12 groups, later pared to 9). "We made it clear that we expected them to understand an industry from the bottom up," Kravis said. "Go to trade shows, meet with purchasing managers, marketing and sales managers, really get into the flow of whatever the business was."

Source: A.T. Kearney.

Another benefit of the plan is to help focus. Gadiesh and MacArthur (2008) warned us that "planning to do a dozen things simultaneously usually turns into a recipe for disappointment." Instead, astute PE owners will want the management to focus on critical initiatives, up to five, while making it clear what the company should not spend time on.

Based on BCG's extensive experience supporting CEO transitions, a robust 100-day plan should integrate six critical facets (Boston Consulting Group, 2023). First, conduct an unbiased, multidimensional, fact-based analysis covering operational efficiency, market positioning, and competitor dynamics—ensuring the CEO and CFO understand what drives stock price multiples and can identify focused value-creation opportunities. Second, articulate a strategic narrative and ambition that tells investors and employees where the company is headed, which paths it will pursue, and crucially, which it will not. Third, develop a financial and transformation roadmap projecting revenue, costs, and operational improvements over two to four years, with both upside and downside scenarios to provide transparency on capital allocation and the pace of value creation. Fourth, establish a stakeholder alignment and management plan that intentionally engages the board, management team, frontline employees, and external parties, including activists and nongovernmental organizations. Fifth, design a communications plan with tailored content strategies, cadences, and channels for key audiences—recognizing that CEOs are increasingly expected to be visible, authentic public figures. Finally, assess talent and organizational readiness by evaluating the top leadership, cultural health, and alignment of resources to strategic priorities, preparing to reshuffle roles and establish accountability systems within the first 100 days.

GHO Capital does not have a one-size-fits-all value creation plan. Instead, a critical early focus during the 100-day plan is identifying who will execute on key initiatives and whether they bring the right skills. To support this, GHO now conducts management team assessments, a practice highly valued by CEOs who appreciate the clarity and insight it brings to strengthening leadership and aligning capabilities with strategic goals.

6.3 DRIVERS OF VALUE CREATION IN PORTFOLIO

Let's go back to the Candesic framework for value creation we discussed in Chapter 2. How does it apply post-transaction?

From the framework, post-transaction value creation can be organized into five complementary drivers that work in concert throughout the holding period (Figure 6.2).

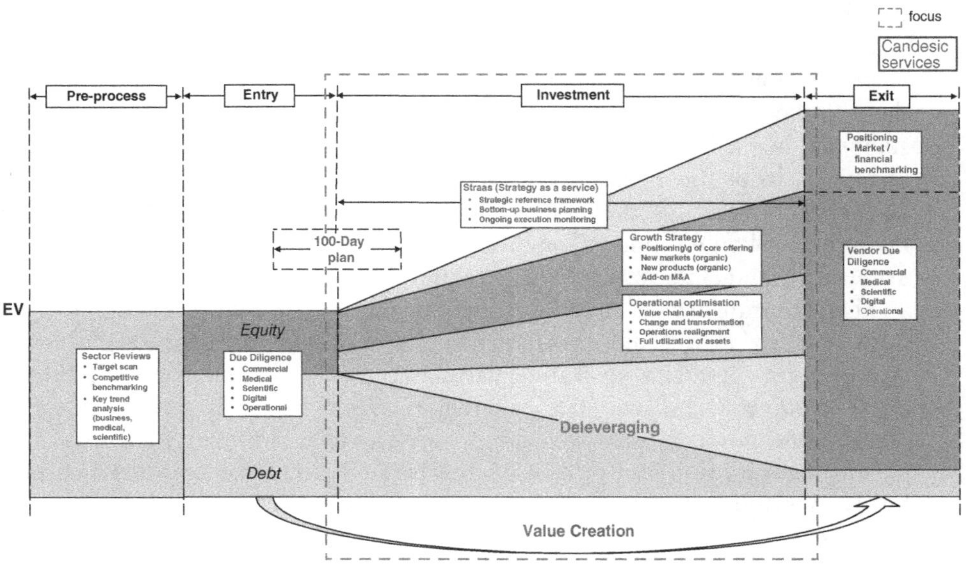

FIGURE 6.2 Drivers of post-deal operational improvements.
Source: Candesic analysis.

- Margin Improvement

  Sponsors maintain relentless focus on every margin lever, ensuring each initiative is tied to a specific EBITDA uplift. In healthcare, this begins with renegotiating supplier contracts for high-cost clinical consumables and extending group-purchasing arrangements across hospital networks to secure volume discounts. Operational programs—such as lean process redesign in operating theatres or automating patient-registration and claims management—can reduce cycle times and administrative errors. In a Candesic project, one hospital platform introduced barcode-driven medication administration and cut pharmacy dispensing costs by 10%, lifting overall margins by 200 bps within 18 months.
- Asset Utilization

  Maximizing returns from existing assets often outperforms large capital outlays. A common approach is sale-and-leaseback of medical real estate—freeing tied-up capital in outpatient clinics and redeploying it to fund growth initiatives. Alternatively, sponsors may outsource noncore diagnostic labs or imaging services to specialized partners, thus converting fixed costs to variable fees and improving utilization rates of high-value equipment such as MRI or CT scanners.
- Human-capital Optimization

  Building a result-driven culture anchored by aligned incentives delivers sustained performance improvements. Sponsors require key executives to rollover equity and supplement this with performance-based stock-option plans vesting against EBITDA, patient-throughput, or quality-metric targets. Governance checkpoints—including monthly operating-committee sessions and quarterly board deep dives—ensure accountability without micromanagement. In a dialysis provider transaction, Candesic was asked to review tying medical-director bonuses to both ethical treatment-volume growth and reductions in hospital readmissions to drive a 10% uplift in operating metrics and strengthen payer partnerships.
- ESG Integration

  Environmental, social, and governance programs ideally evolve into strategic value-creation levers rather than compliance afterthoughts. From the outset of the 100-day plan, sponsors conduct ESG due diligence—auditing energy consumption in facilities, assessing board diversity, and reviewing labor practices in supply chains for medical devices. They set quantifiable targets (for instance, 20% reduction in carbon emissions, 30% female board representation) linked to management bonuses and LP reporting.
- Technology and Data-driven Value Creation

  Digital transformation now underpins both cost reduction and revenue growth. Early in due diligence and the 100-day plan, sponsors deploy data-science teams or digital operating partners to assess IT architectures, cybersecurity readiness, and analytics capabilities. Common initiatives include ERP upgrades to automate order-to-cash processes, advanced analytics for dynamic patient-segmentation and pricing, and integrated electronic health record platforms. A Candesic customer is deploying a unified records system to reduce administrative overhead while improving patient throughput and lifting EBITDA margins substantially. Real-time dashboards for clinical and financial key performance indicators (KPIs) enable more agile decision-making and continuous performance refinement.

These five drivers form the backbone of both the initial value-creation roadmap and the ongoing operational agenda. As Roberto Quarta of CD&R reminds us, "The first 100 days are simply not enough." True transformation requires sustained effort: sponsors must embed these disciplines into the fabric of the business, continually engage management and co-investors, and adapt initiatives as market conditions evolve—ensuring full value is realized at exit. It is like a kick start, but many responsibilities will continue and sometimes even intensify beyond those first three months.

We presented ARCHIMED's MedDiscover proprietary tool to identify and approach target companies operating in its prioritized healthcare subsectors. MedValue complements this by serving as a "playbook" for accelerating growth in portfolio companies through international expansion, innovation, product range expansion, capacity expansion, and business development.

While the exact contents of the MedValue approach are not fully disclosed, it can be inferred that it includes dedicated operating support and detailed frameworks for value creation, commercial and operational excellence, sustainability and impact objectives, market prioritization, and the deployment of healthcare sector expertise to drive growth and exits. This aligns with ARCHIMED's reputation for combining hands-on business builder support with healthcare investment specialization to achieve top-tier returns and impact.

References to MedDiscover and MedValue appear in ARCHIMED's public disclosures and news releases related to acquisitions such as Irrimax (2024), BioVendor (2025), Arkstone (2025), and others, illustrating their central role in ARCHIMED's investment strategy and operational model.

6.4 MANAGING THE MANAGEMENT AND THE GROWING ROLE OF THE OPERATING PARTNER

6.4.1 Management Oversight and Control

PE firms typically maintain close oversight of their PortCos while carefully balancing hands-on involvement with management autonomy (Figure 6.3). Their management style is driven by the need to achieve specific value creation goals within a defined investment horizon. The relationship between PE investors and portfolio company CEOs is crucial yet delicate, requiring clear governance frameworks and communication channels. Most PE firms hold board seats and establish regular monitoring through monthly or quarterly board meetings, preferably supplemented by weekly or biweekly informal check-ins on key initiatives and performance metrics, where the CEO is expected to provide detailed updates on progress and challenges.

PE firms are not universally hands-on; their involvement varies depending on the complexity of the business, the CEO's competence, and the stage of the investment. Early in the ownership period, firms are typically more hands-on, focusing on setting the strategy, implementing critical changes, and assembling the right leadership team. As the business stabilizes and demonstrates progress, PE investors may take a more high-level approach, stepping in only to address major decisions or unexpected issues. By then, the intensity of PE involvement often follows a "trust but verify" approach.

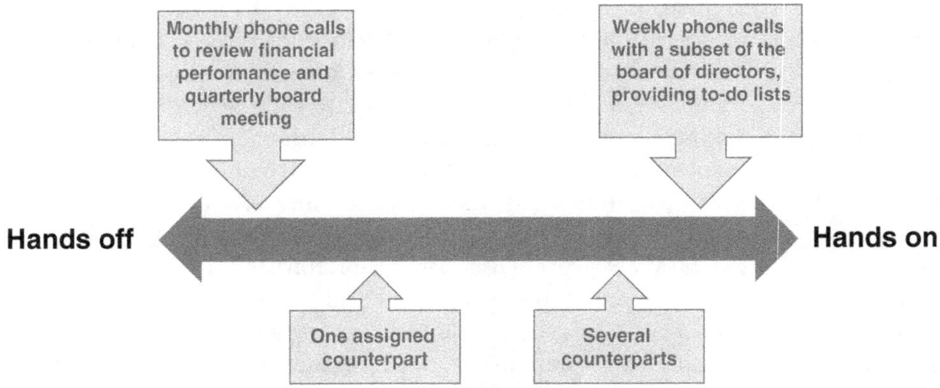

FIGURE 6.3 Different management styles of PE investors.

When performance meets or exceeds expectations and management executes effectively on the agreed-upon value creation plan, PE firms typically maintain a lighter touch. Conversely, they become more actively involved when companies miss targets, face unexpected challenges, or require significant strategic shifts. This increased engagement might involve more frequent meetings, detailed operational reviews, or direct intervention in specific areas like cost reduction programs or acquisition integration.

In any case, PE-ownership generally brings a faster pace of change. For Elad Duschak, advisor to healthcare PortCos,

> *When you are PE owned, there is a constant sense of urgency, the underlying driver is to continuously think of new ways of growing, demonstrating scalable and sustainable paths for growth while at the same time also driving operational efficiencies and improved profitability.*

That tension between growth and profitability can be quite challenging and at times conflicting particularly considering the typical timelines of PEs and the relatively long sales cycles in the healthcare sector.

Management consultants are often hired to work alongside the management team and the operating partner. Rajib Arjun, cofounder of Altius, explains the importance of making difficult decisions sooner than later:

> *Often there's hidden comfort working as part of the larger parent company versus adopting an agile start-up mindset in carve-outs. Not all executive DNAs are designed to approach a lean, agile fail-fast approach. Several executives may be doing it for the one and only time in their career. Sponsors need to recognize that across the value chain, and to protect the core, move in and make the changes sooner than later, whether it's in key markets, product development, go-to-market, manufacturing and G&A organizations.*

With the emergence of AI as a step-function disruptor, more functions will be impacted, and sponsors need to identify those tee-off points and make appropriate changes in people, process, and/or technology sooner than later.

Eckuity's value creation model seems to set them further apart. Each of their funds has a dedicated, wholly owned subsidiary designed to accelerate commercial growth across their portfolio. This platform actively connects portfolio companies with more than 100 health systems in 38 international markets, helping them scale revenues and validate their products globally. The result is a measurable impact on their top line—while creating an embedded liquidity pathway that benefits both the PortCos and the LPs. According to Youssef Sebban, "This model has proven instrumental in winning highly competitive transactions and delivering tangible, quantifiable outcomes."

H.I.G. Capital is another PE firm that consistently prioritizes proprietary, or "primary," deal sourcing—and it succeeds at it most of the time. Several managing directors at the firm have shared that management teams that they collaborate with often have limited prior experience with PE investors and sometimes struggle to understand their role in the partnership. The CEO's skill set must be broad, but one frequently overlooked ability is managing the sponsor relationship—developing an intuition for what the PE firm truly wants and needs. Mastering this dynamic is crucial for navigating the partnership effectively.

CEO replacement is common in PE-backed companies, despite typically being viewed as a last resort due to its disruptive nature. In reality, high turnover of CEOs is a known feature of the PE ownership model, particularly in LBOs. Academic research has highlighted this trend early: Gong and Wu (2011), examining 126 PE-sponsored LBOs in the United States between 1990 and 2006, reported a CEO turnover rate of 51% within two years of an LBO announcement. Similarly, a 2018 survey by Alix Partners found that 58% of CEOs were replaced within two years of investment, rising to 73% over the full holding period. These findings suggest that CEO turnover is more widespread than the often-cited 30–40% figure, which may understate the frequency by focusing on broader PE categories or shorter time frames.

There are exceptions, though. Michael Healy from Keensight Capital commented:

> *It's important to talk the language of the founder or manager. Over 70 investments, Keensight has never changed the CEO. What we do is professionalize the finance function, create a BD function. We give them all the support they need to succeed.*

In contrast to public companies, most PE-backed firms do not offer golden parachutes to underperforming senior executives. They have a lot to lose, including sometimes their own savings. Boards in post-LBO companies tend to act decisively, replacing entrenched CEOs, especially when agency problems are apparent—for example, where pre-LBO return on assets is low, or where capital structure fails to impose sufficient discipline. In many cases, the plan to replace the CEO exists from the outset of the investment, even if it is not shared with the incumbent. It happened to the CEO of a newly acquired PortCo of a Candesic PE client under due diligence for a take-private. We worked with the CEO on the new strategy for the private company. To our surprise, the CEO got replaced within three months of closing the transaction. That was a surprise for the CEO too, but we learned the investor had made the decision prior to the closing.

Spencer Stuart, in a 2011 study, found that about half of CEO replacements were actively planned by PE firms and typically occurred within the first 6–18 months post-acquisition. Early changes can reflect planned transitions—such as the exit of a founder-owner—or rapid responses to post-deal discoveries. Later changes are usually driven by company underperformance relative to the investment thesis. Common triggers for CEO replacement include persistent failure to meet financial targets, inability to execute key strategic initiatives, erosion of credibility with the board, or deep misalignment over the company's direction. Cultural incompatibility and difficulty adapting to the speed, transparency, and reporting rigor required by PE ownership can also prompt leadership change. An IPO can also be a catalyst for CEO replacement, particularly when the incumbent lacks the profile, experience, or credibility required to lead a listed company through the scrutiny of public markets and institutional investors.

Finding the right senior talent for value creation roles can be hard and extends beyond the CEO. As Nicole Jones, talent director at Advent International put it,

> *CFOs who combine technical excellence with strategic and commercial instincts are difficult to find and highly sought after. The same is true for truly transformational commercial directors – the people who can design a scalable sales organisation and then actually run it day to day are some of the scarcest profiles in the market.*

6.4.2 The Operating Partner Model: Evolution and Reality Gap

The PE operating model has evolved significantly over the past decade, with many firms building dedicated operating teams to support portfolio companies. This allows investment managers to focus primarily on the transaction itself—deal sourcing, due diligence, and exit strategy—while operating partners handle the day-to-day interaction with the portfolio company. Many PE firms trumpet their operating partner (OP) model, with glossy organizational charts and big claims of "core capability." Yet, as several PE veterans have pointed out, the reality is often more muddled than majestic.

OPs typically have extensive C-suite experience in relevant industries or functional expertise in areas like digital transformation, supply chain optimization, or commercial excellence. They come from diverse backgrounds but often share certain characteristics: successful track records as CEOs or senior executives, experience managing through different business cycles, and strong networks in relevant industries. Their roles vary by PE firm but typically include conducting operational due diligence on new investments and bolt-on acquisitions, developing value creation plans, monitoring performance, and providing strategic counsel to management teams.

As PE owners expect management teams to execute strategic initiatives rapidly and professionally, operating partners often take responsibility for ensuring management implements techniques to test these initiatives—like lean testing with tools such as MVP/MVS design, smokescreen testing, Fishbone analysis, A/B testing, and cohort analysis—among many others in the PE value creation arsenal (Sola & Couturier, 2014).

Some firms employ full-time operating partners, while others maintain networks of experienced executives who serve as part-time advisors or board members across multiple portfolio companies. OPs are sometimes asked to step in to fill a C-level position.

However, in some shops, OPs are brought in post-deal as glorified consultants, expected to miraculously turn around a PortCo without the authority or resources to make decisions, essentially doing "consulting theatre" instead of genuine transformation. Bad implementations are common: one frequent mistake is dropping generalist OPs into highly technical sectors, hoping they will "move the needle," when sector experts should have been engaged or trust-based relationships with management been built from the outset. Another misfire: giving OPs advisory board seats but no budget, decision-making power, or team support, expecting them to deliver results despite being hands-off when it matters. OPs live in the grey zone: half COO, half management consultant, half firefighter, expected to drop into any company, any situation, any sector and somehow outperform, given all the responsibility for growth, with none of the actual authority to make decisions.

6.4.3 What Works: Best Practice Implementation

The best performing PE funds have figured out that the key is to treat value creation as a contact sport—integrating OPs directly from deal inception through exit, giving them real workstream ownership, budget, and the authority to challenge or collaborate with management (McKinsey & Company, 2019). KKR Capstone and Bain Portfolio Group, for example, deploy cross-functional OP teams who work side-by-side with deal partners and management, embedding expertise in digital, pricing, HR, and go-to-market, and crucially, earning the respect of strong-minded CEOs by providing actionable playbooks and repeatable systems—rather than parachuting in to "fix" things reactively. Nordic Alpha Partners goes one step further, making their value creation partner a daily contact and board vice chair. This elevated approach doesn't just professionalize processes and sharpen decisions—it actively manages egos, aligning incentives and building a culture that encourages transparency rather than turf wars (McKinsey & Company, 2024a).

Maximilian K. E. Mayr, one of our former students, exemplifies the "CEO for hire" model. After learning the tricks of the trade as a management consultant, he became independent after 10 years in senior positions as fund manager, operating partner, and interim C-level for PortCos. He describes himself as the Swiss Army knife of the sponsor:

> *My job is to execute anything my client wants, from integrating bolt-on acquisitions to implementing cost cutting or managing insolvency. I was once put in charge of a value creation plan. By the time I came in, a large specialist team focused on growth had already been hired, and then the company unexpectedly went into insolvency. I had to change the entire plan in less than a week, with all the wrong profiles in the team. That also makes me realize there is a common pattern in these projects: they always call me later than they should have.*

6.4.4 Managing Egos and Human Capital Dynamics

Underestimating the importance of human capital is another classic error. OPs who specialize in HR can be game-changers—they audit, upgrade, and fine-tune leadership teams, resolve talent mismatches, and work through the delicate task of reigning in alpha CEOs and founders with strong egos. When OPs are shut out of talent management decisions, or relegated to generic "advice" roles, PE firms miss out on substantial long-term value creation. Empowered HR OPs can mentor first-time CEOs, coach senior execs through automation and digital transformation, and design incentive plans that actually stick—preventing the parade of cost-cutter CEOs who neglect organizational health and talent development.

For CEOs working with PE owners, several key success factors emerge. First, maintaining transparent communication about both successes and challenges is crucial. PE firms value early warnings about potential issues more than positive surprises. Second, CEOs should expect to focus heavily on cash flow management and working capital optimization, as these metrics often receive more attention than in non-PE-owned companies. Third, successful CEOs learn to balance short-term performance requirements with long-term value creation initiatives. Finally, CEOs should proactively leverage their PE firm's resources, including operating partners' expertise and cross-portfolio learning opportunities. CEOs should view OPs as allies rather than overseers, leveraging their expertise to drive success.

PE firms increasingly emphasize talent development and succession planning within portfolio companies, often working with CEOs to strengthen the management team and develop future leaders. This focus reflects the recognition that strong management teams are crucial for successful exits and that developing internal talent can reduce dependence on external hiring for key roles.

6.4.5 Recommendations for PE Firms

To avoid these pitfalls, GPs should integrate OPs early—ideally during diligence—not just at post-close crisis points. Make OPs true owners: give them budget, real decision rights, and a seat at the table for both strategy and execution. Specialize: build HR, digital, and sector OP benches to suit portfolio needs, not a one-size-fits-all team. Encourage humility and open communication, especially when dealing with high emotional intelligence, high ego founders, or C-suite leaders. Use incentive alignment and multi-year onboarding, spreading value creation across cycles rather than limiting it to the mythical 100-day plan. Above all: staff, fund, and incentivize value creation with the same urgency and seniority as deal execution. No theatre, just traction, as the best firms prove every quarter.

6.5 PERFORMANCE MONITORING AND METRICS

In a PortCo, financial monitoring focuses on ensuring value creation, liquidity control, and covenant compliance across both operating and strategic dimensions. Commonly tracked metrics can be grouped into four categories: profitability, cash flow, growth, and leverage efficiency.

6.5.1 Examples of Financial Metrics

These include profitability and efficiency, cash flow and liquidity, value creation, and capital structure metrics.

6.5.1.1 Profitability and Efficiency Metrics The following are mostly concerned with revenues, costs, and operating margins and profitability:

- *Revenue* and *Revenue Growth* are typically captured by examining total sales and growth rates often segmented by product line, geography, or contract type.
- *Gross Margin* and *EBITDA Margin* track cost efficiency and earnings before non-operating expenses; as before, EBITDA is a key proxy for operational health in PE.
- *Operating Margin* and *Net Income* measure how efficiently the company converts revenue into bottom-line profit.
- *EBITDA per Employee/Operating Leverage* is often used to assess productivity gains and scaling efficiency over time.

6.5.1.2 Cash Flow and Liquidity Metrics These metrics include familiar operating cash flows and free cash flows as well as the cash conversion ratio and working capital days:

- *Operating Cash Flow (OCF)* and *Free Cash Flow (FCF)* are core indicators of liquidity available for debt servicing and reinvestment.
- *Cash Conversion Ratio* (CCR = OCF ÷ Net Income, or FCF ÷ EBITDA) reflects cash quality of earnings and is closely monitored after leveraged buyouts.
- The number of *Working Capital Days* measures how effectively receivables, inventory, and payables are managed.
- The *Cash Burn Rate* monitors monthly cash depletion relative to funding runway; it is used mostly for early-stage companies.

6.5.1.3 Growth and Value Creation Metrics These growth metrics are typically focused on revenue growth:

- *Organic Revenue Growth* and *Add-on Impact* distinguish between operational expansion and acquisition-driven growth.
- *Return on Invested Capital (ROIC)* is a key measure of efficiency in deploying capital for value creation.
- *Customer Acquisition Cost (CAC)* and *Lifetime Value (LTV)* are used mostly in service-based or tech-enabled businesses; these customer unit economics drive valuation and FCF potential.
- *Annual Recurring Revenue (ARR)* is a useful metric for subscription-based models, such as healthcare or software services.

6.5.1.4 Leverage and Capital Structure Metrics These include specific commonly used financial metrics:

- *Debt-to-EBITDA* and *Interest Coverage Ratios* monitor leverage levels and debt service capacity.
- *Net Debt* and *Cash Conversion Cycle* assess financial flexibility and working capital strain.
- *Covenant Headroom* ensures compliance with financing terms across the LBO structure.

CASH CONVERSION RATIO AS A COMPLEMENTARY METRIC TO FCF

The cash conversion ratio (CCR) evaluates how effectively a company transforms its accounting profits into actual cash generation. It is calculated by comparing OCF to net income. A CCR above 1 indicates robust cash conversion performance, while a value below 1 can signal inefficiencies or working capital friction.

In LBOs, a persistently low CCR may serve as an early indicator of liquidity strain, suggesting that earnings are not translating into sufficient cash flow to service debt. Since FCF equals OCF minus capital expenditures, weak cash conversion reduces OCF and consequently limits the cash available for reinvestment, debt repayment, and other financial obligations after an LBO.

6.5.2 Operational Metrics

PE firms also closely monitor operational metrics in their PortCos, alongside financial performance, as these metrics directly reflect the operational sources of value creation as well as the efficiency, scalability, and execution quality of management's value-creation plan. Typical ones include the following.

6.5.2.1 Efficiency and Productivity Metrics These focus on the timeliness of resource churning, productivity, and operating margin improvements:

- *Inventory Turnover* and *Production Cycle times* measure how efficiently resources are used.
- *Employee Productivity* and *Output per Labor Hour* indicate workforce efficiency.
- *Operating Margin Improvements* capture the results of process optimization and cost management.

6.5.2.2 Commercial and Customer Metrics These focus on customer acquisition and retention and revenue growth:

- *CAC* and *LTV* (again) primarily quantify marketing and retention efficiency.
- *Churn Rate* and *Net Promoter Score (NPS)* are tracked to evaluate satisfaction and loyalty, especially in recurring-revenue models.
- *Sales Pipeline Velocity* and *Revenue by Channel* monitor commercial execution and forecast accuracy.

6.5.2.3 Operational Flow and Supply Chain Metrics These are focused on vendors, costs, and implications for working capital:

- *Order Fulfillment Time* and *On-time Delivery rate* signal supply chain reliability.
- *Procurement Efficiency* and *Vendor Consolidation* metrics are used to control costs.
- *Cash Conversion Cycle* also tracks the speed at which working capital turns into cash inflows.

6.5.2.4 Technology and Process Indicators These are particularly important for technology-intensive firms:

- *Automation Rate* and *System Uptime* evaluate process digitization and IT reliability.
- Lean operations metrics like *Defect Rates* or *Downtime* highlight operational excellence initiatives.

Not all PE firms monitor the same metrics, and the most successful ones differentiate themselves by focusing on operational metrics that provide early insights into a company's progress toward strategic goals—often well before these efforts are reflected in financial performance. Tracking these leading indicators allows PE firms to identify opportunities, address challenges, and recalibrate strategies proactively, staying ahead of financial outcomes rather than reacting to lagging financial indicators.

Equally important, managers in top-performing PE firms recognize that a one-size-fits-all approach to measurement is ineffective. Instead of imposing a standard set of metrics across their entire portfolio, they develop tailored performance indicators for each business. This customization ensures that metrics are closely aligned with the unique dynamics of each company, including its industry, growth stage, operational priorities, and competitive environment. By taking a bespoke approach to performance monitoring, these firms not only capture the nuances of individual portfolio companies but also foster collaboration with management teams, enhancing buy-in and execution.

In practice, this means that a PE firm might track customer acquisition costs and churn rates in a tech-enabled business, while focusing on throughput and equipment utilization in a manufacturing company. Even within a company, the metrics can be tailored to the various customer segments: retention rates for cash cows, cross-selling for rising stars, and customer acquisition or penetration for nascent segments. Such nuanced tracking ensures that portfolio companies are evaluated and supported based on the most relevant and actionable metrics, which drives sustainable value creation across diverse investments. This strategic balance between forward-looking operational metrics and tailored measurement frameworks is a hallmark of leading PE firms.

Quoting James Coulter, founding partner of TPG,

> *We use their metrics, not our metrics. You have to use performance measures that make sense for the business unit itself, rather than some preconceived notion from the corporate center. (Gadiesh and McArthur, 2008)*

In Asia, the focus can be different. At Quadria Capital, Abrar Mir believes that value in any enduring business rests on four foundations: revenue, costs, management with strong governance, and social value. Of these, the company focuses first on revenue—on growth and scale—because leadership knows that "if the fundamentals are strong, costs ultimately take care of themselves."[1]

When it comes to financial value creation and impact, Quadria Capital takes a perspective that is different from many of its peers. Leadership emphasizes that, in Asia, the two cannot be separated. They are not parallel goals; they are a single mission.

[1] Interview of Abrar Mir, co-founder of Quadria Capital (September 2025).

> *This is a region that carries the world's largest disease burden and population, yet where the average individual earns barely ten to fifteen dollars a day, with little or no access to social security or private insurance.*

For most people, healthcare is paid for out of pocket.

That reality is what unites Quadria Capital's investment thesis with its impact thesis. To lead in this market is to touch as many lives as possible. Mir said,

> *Our philosophy has always been to invest in high-quality, industry-leading businesses that deliver world-class healthcare at prices people can afford. We have never invested in businesses that cater only to the privileged few.*

Leadership also holds a simple discipline of no dividends. Every profit is reinvested into the business to build scale, to drive down costs, and to reach more patients. Over time, this creates a virtuous cycle—greater access, greater affordability, and ultimately, stronger profitability: "At the heart of it all lies a principle we never compromise on: no one is ever turned away from any of our hospitals."

Finally, many GPs stress the importance of consistency. For Mir,

> *We've learnt that investors reward conviction, but they demand consistency. For us, consistency means holding to a simple truth: DPI-led. IRR-first. Consistency of our returns means discipline in process, repeatability in execution and depth in value creation. In a world of volatility, consistency with our financial returns is how we want to earn trust.*

At Ampersand, success measurement follows traditional metrics: performance relative to vintage year, public markets, and peer groups. However, according to Herb Hooper,

> *Consistency takes precedence over home runs. Investors typically choose between 2–3 funds and prioritize consistent performance with loss ratios below 10%—explicitly rejecting the venture capital model of accepting high failure rates for outsized winners.*

6.5.3 Working with the CEO

In any case, the performance metrics must be agreed with management. Drawing from discussions with PE investors and insights from Candesic's tech-enabled strategic planning program implemented at corporate customers, we recommend six foundational instructions for portfolio company CEOs. First, align fully with the value creation plan by understanding the PE firm's vision, committing to shared strategic KPIs, and ensuring the entire team communicates progress effectively against operational improvements, strategic priorities, and financial goals. Second, focus relentlessly on operational excellence by identifying opportunities to optimize costs, enhance productivity, and streamline processes while monitoring key metrics that serve as early indicators of success or challenge. Third, adopt a data-driven approach through rigorous performance monitoring and transparent reporting systems that track both financial and operational metrics, enabling informed decision-making and regular board discussions. Fourth, embrace change and adaptability by proactively driving restructuring, technology adoption, or cultural shifts, building a team capable of executing strategy under tight timelines. Fifth, maintain strong, strategic communication with the PE firm, board, and leadership team—sharing updates on successes, challenges, and risks transparently, as lack of transparency is almost unthinkable in a PE context and erodes the trust essential to effective partnership. Finally, prepare continuously for the exit by recognizing that PE ownership is temporary, understanding the timeline and milestones, and aligning actions to enhance the company's attractiveness to buyers or public markets, as exit opportunities may materialize faster than expected.

A DISCUSSION WITH ALESSANDRO MORETTI, HEAD OF OPERATIONAL VALUE CREATION FOR DIRECT INVESTMENTS AT PIF, THE KSA PUBLIC INVESTMENT FUND

ORCHESTRATING VALUE CREATION THROUGH COLLABORATION

Alessandro emphasizes that successful value creation requires orchestrated teamwork rather than individual expertise. "Value creation is like conducting an orchestra," he explains, "combining strategic, organizational, operational, technology, and infrastructure elements in one unified approach. The deal team person remains the conductor—accountability cannot be delegated to value creation specialists alone, or buyers would acquire anything without proper strategic alignment." This collaborative approach ensures that value creation plans emerge from joint assessment rather than isolated analysis, creating unified vision between investors and portfolio company management from day one.

THE 100-DAY FRAMEWORK: ASSESSMENT TO ACTION

Alessandro advocates for a structured 100-day approach focused on rapid organizational assessment, potential identification, and pathway development:

> *"We conduct rapid assessment of current organizational status, understand the company's true potential, and develop the target business shape through concrete initiatives," he notes. However, he cautions against confusing activity with progress: "You must distinguish between movement and action when prioritizing initiatives. Impact, risk, and strategic relevance should drive discussions when management bandwidth is limited."*

The key lies in creating granular roadmaps that maintain constant coordination with all stakeholders while ensuring management teams can realistically execute identified opportunities.

TECHNOLOGY AS STRATEGIC ENABLER

Regarding technology's role in value creation, Alessandro views it as pervasive but purposeful:

> *Technology should have an angle in every investment, or there will be missed opportunities. Whether through digital transformation, reporting innovation, or process automation—it's a critical enabler but not the objective itself.*

He emphasizes that technology must maximize value through operational efficiencies and competitive positioning rather than being pursued for its own sake. This perspective aligns with modern PE's recognition that technological integration often determines whether portfolio companies can achieve sustainable competitive advantages in their respective markets.

BUILDING CAPABILITIES FOR VALUE CREATION SUCCESS

For professionals entering value creation roles, Alessandro stresses different skill sets for different career stages. Graduate students should master "strong analytical and financial modeling skills, develop deep understanding of business operations, and build communication abilities for internal and external teamwork." For seasoned executives transitioning into value creation, the requirements shift:

> *Build networks within the investment community, develop both strategic and investor mindsets, and manage personality dynamics effectively when working with portfolio company leadership.*

He particularly emphasizes the importance of sector specialization, especially in regulated industries like healthcare, where deep domain expertise becomes essential for navigating both operational improvements and regulatory compliance requirements.

6.6 VALUE CREATION WITH DATA AND AI

In addition to creating value across the deal life cycle, data and AI have become mainstream to generate operational improvements in portfolio companies through several channels (RobinAI, 2025):

1. Performance tracking: machine learning algorithms can analyze a wide range of datasets to identify sources of risks and growth opportunities, predict asset performance, identify potential targets, and assess exit timing. In addition, natural language processing and large language models can be used to track growth potential and operational improvements from qualitative reports.
2. Compliance: fine-tuned AI models for legal work can help firms to keep up with complex regulation.

PE firms use data from diverse sources to manage and enhance portfolio companies: financial statements, market research, regulatory filings, industry datasets, and deal documentation. Traditionally, processing such data is inefficient, error-prone, and difficult to scale, which often delays critical decisions.

Robotic process automation (RPA), which automates rule-based tasks, is increasingly used in PE operations as a practical way to improve efficiency, reduce costs, and increase transparency, particularly in back-office and middle-office roles, so humans can focus on analysis, decision-making, and value creation. Specifically, RPA is often used to automate accounts payable, accounts receivable, journal entry posting, and expense validation and reporting. Although machine learning (ML) is rarely used at the fund level, mostly due to data constraints, it is typically used within portfolio companies for specific tasks such as the detection of historical patterns; demand, revenue, and cash flow forecasting; pricing and supply chain optimization; inventory management; and error and fraud detection.

PE firms can automate repetitive tasks such as extracting data from multiple sources, scanning and reviewing contracts, and flagging anomalies. Importantly, Baik et al. (2024) find that PE investors often act as active intermediaries of digital transformation for private firms: following a PE acquisition, portfolio firms increase the share of digital job posting by 1.5% on average, and IT budgets rise by around 20.5% which is equivalent to about $2.64 million relative to matched non-PE controls. Chapter 8 discusses how AI adoption affects jobs and wages. RPA and ML are often combined with other tools such as natural language processing (NLP) and large language models (LLM), which can process unstructured information, accelerate knowledge work, and improve document understanding. However, strategic judgment and decision-making in value creation priorities, risk assessment, and investment and exit decisions are always left to humans.

6.7 INVESTOR RELATIONS

Investor relations (IR) in PE is no longer ancillary—it is integral to both fundraising success and portfolio value creation. Effective IR teams coordinate fundraising, deepen LP engagement, and unlock strategic support for portfolio companies. Conversely, poor IR can hinder capital raising and stifle growth opportunities.

6.7.1 The Evolution of PE Investor Relations

In the early days of PE, IR was a part-time or shared responsibility. Today, most firms appoint dedicated IR professionals—or entire teams—to partner closely with deal teams. This shift reflects LPs' demand for transparency, rapid responsiveness, and evidence of value-creation credentials. IR specialists now coauthor pitch books, present at roadshows, and maintain ongoing dialogue with existing and prospective investors.

6.7.2 Synergies Between Fundraising and IR

Integrating IR into fundraising brings two advantages. First, seasoned IR professionals understand LP priorities—risk controls, sector expertise, and co-investment terms—so they tailor fund marketing to resonate with investor mandates. Second, by cultivating relationships during the hold period, IR lays the groundwork for follow-on funds, smoothing subsequent closes. For example, a healthcare-focused PE fund might leverage IR's deep ties with a major life-science LP to secure both primary commitments and board-level introductions at a biotech portfolio company.

6.7.3 LP Engagement as a Value-creation Lever

Savvy IR teams do more than report performance—they facilitate LP contributions to portfolio companies. In healthcare deals, LPs with hospital networks or payer contacts can open doors for pilot programs or preferred contracting. For example, an IR team might arrange an introduction between a portfolio specialty-clinic platform and an LP's affiliated insurer or provider network, accelerating contracting and driving measurable EBITDA growth within a year. By matching portfolio needs with LP expertise—whether regulatory insights, distribution channels, or M&A sourcing—the IR function transforms investors into value-creation allies.

6.7.4 The Risks of Weak IR

Neglecting IR can have tangible downsides. LPs may reduce allocations if they feel under-informed, raising costs for future funds. In crisis scenarios—such as regulatory setbacks at a portfolio healthtech company—IR must act swiftly to calm LP nerves. Failure to do so can trigger redemption pressures or co-investor withdrawal, constraining equity calls and forcing suboptimal financing decisions.

6.7.5 Differentiating IR in Public vs. Private Markets (PE)

Unlike public companies bound by SEC disclosure schedules, PE firms control the timing, content, and audience of their communications. IR in PE emphasizes customized, qualitative updates—deep dives into operational KPIs, board-level developments, and thematic research on (healthcare) trends. Public-company IR focuses on quarterly earnings calls, broad analyst coverage, and compliance with continuous disclosure rules. PE IR, by contrast, orchestrates board meetings, LP advisory committees, and bespoke sessions on topics like FDA approval pathways or hospital contracting dynamics (Figure 6.4).

6.7.6 Crisis Response and Institutional Memory

Since placement agents retrenched after the GFC, IR teams absorbed capital-raising and LP servicing duties. Today's IR professionals maintain institutional memory—tracking which LPs prefer co-investments in medtech carve-outs or which retract in

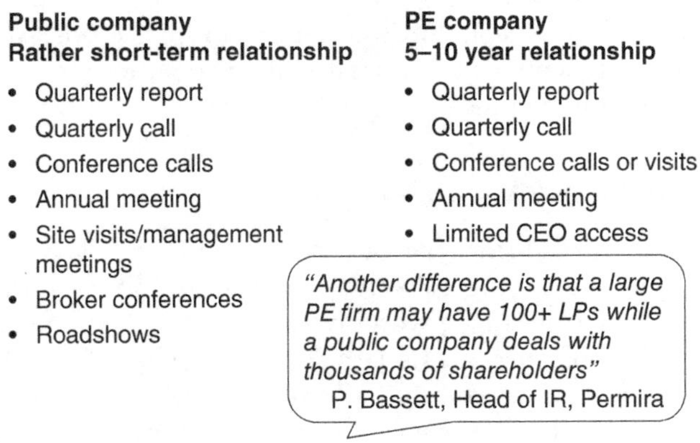

FIGURE 6.4 IR–investor relations.

downturns. When a hospital-management portfolio company faced litigation over accreditation, IR coordinated a joint conference call with legal counsel, the GP, and key LPs, promptly addressing concerns and averting co-investor drop-outs.

6.8 MANAGING THE LENDERS

In an LBO context, cultivating a strong partnership with debt providers is as vital as guiding the management team or satisfying LPs. Effective lender engagement secures the debt structure's durability, preserves access to future financings, and underpins value creation through the investment's life.

6.8.1 Deal Inception and Financing Negotiations

At the outset, the GP negotiates tranche sizes—senior debt, second-lien loans, mezzanine financing—and crafts covenant packages. This requires balancing flexible amortization schedules with lenders' appetite for coverage ratios and maintenance tests. Clear covenant-tracking responsibilities are set here, creating mutual accountability.

6.8.2 Ongoing Covenant Management

After closing, the GP acts as a conduit between management and the syndicate. Monthly covenant certificates and quarterly compliance reports become standard. If shortfalls emerge, the sponsor works with management to prepare variance analyses and action plans—whether by trimming CapEx or accelerating receivables—to secure waivers or forbearance with minimal fees.

6.8.3 Structured Communication Cadence

Transparent dialogue cements trust. PE firms schedule monthly performance calls, biannual strategy reviews, and annual site visits that include facility tours and presentations by the CEO and CFO. These forums let bankers validate progress early and raise concerns before they escalate.

6.8.4 Strategic Capital Requests and Amendments

When pursuing bolt-on acquisitions, dividend recaps, or refinancings, the GP presents robust pro forma covenant tests and debt service models. Demonstrating that new borrowing accelerates deleveraging convinces lenders to amend terms. This positions banks as co-investors in growth rather than mere creditors.

6.8.5 Crisis Management and Default Avoidance

In downturns or unexpected EBITDA dips, timely disclosure and recovery blueprints prevent technical defaults. Contingency plans—such as dividend blocks, equity injections, or covenant resets—reassure lenders. The sponsor's proactive stance avoids punitive default consequences that can derail exits.

6.8.6 The Cost of Default

If a GP backs a company that defaults, future financings grow more expensive. Lenders remember past defaults. The GP–bank interaction is a repeated game. Over time, experienced sponsors earn better terms because they

- work harder to avoid default,
- are more experienced and proactive at managing the debt covenants, and
- can inject more equity to avert breaches.

The interaction between GPs and lenders is a repeat game. Treating lenders as partners rather than adversaries preserves the financing optionality necessary for aggressive value creation and a smooth exit.

6.9 MANAGING OTHER STAKEHOLDERS

Beyond co-investors, lenders, and management, PE sponsors must engage payors, regulatory bodies, local communities, and the broader public to protect the company's license to operate and sustain long-term value creation. This subsection focuses on the management of the relationship with these stakeholders. Chapter 8 will cover the impact of PE on stakeholders.

6.9.1 Stakeholder Mapping and Prioritization

Effective engagement begins with mapping all relevant stakeholders and assessing their influence and interests. Payors—whether insurance companies in healthcare or distributors in consumer products—directly affect revenue. Regulators oversee compliance with industry standards, licensing, and antitrust rules. Local communities and advocacy groups can impact reputation and social license, especially in sectors sensitive to environmental or labor issues.

6.9.2 Strategic Communication and Relationship Building

Regular, tailored communication maintains alignment and trust. With payors, sponsors collaborate on contracting strategies, reimbursement frameworks, and performance-based pricing models. In heavily regulated industries, the PE firm supports the portfolio company's regulatory affairs function by ensuring timely filings, transparent reporting, and proactive dialogue with oversight agencies. This includes briefing regulators on quality improvements, safety initiatives, and compliance milestones to smooth inspections and approvals.

6.9.3 Corporate Social Responsibility and Community Engagement

Local communities and the public often judge PE-backed companies through the lens of job creation, environmental stewardship, and civic contribution. Sponsors can guide management to launch community advisory panels, host open houses, or support local development projects. Demonstrating a commitment to social responsibility not only mitigates activism risk but also strengthens brand loyalty and employee morale.

6.9.4 Crisis Preparedness and Rapid Response

No stakeholder engagement plan is complete without crisis protocols. Whether a product recall, compliance breach, or environmental incident, the sponsor works with management to activate rapid response teams. Clear roles, pre-approved messaging, and designated spokespeople ensure consistent communication to payors, regulators, media, and the public. Prompt transparency and remediation plans limit reputational damage and reduce regulatory scrutiny.

6.9.5 Continuous Feedback and Adaptation

Once systems are in place, sponsors institute regular reviews of stakeholder sentiment through surveys, advisory board feedback, and regulatory trend monitoring. This ongoing feedback loop enables the PE firm and management team to refine strategies—adjusting payment terms, updating compliance programs, or expanding community investments—as the external environment evolves.

6.10 MANAGING THE EXIT

The natural investment horizon of the PE investor is a few years. Managing the PortCo and all stakeholders is ultimately directed at managing the exit. Figure 6.5 shows us where we should focus.

6.10.1 Exit Strategy

Managing the exit is something that we do throughout the life of the portfolio, and it involves considering the fund strategy in terms of liquidity, performance, and what we signal to investors about our position toward taxes. Additionally, we need to decide on our exit strategy: do we prefer a trade sale or secondary sale, perhaps an IPO, or partial exit through a leverage recapitalization? And finally, how do we manage the exit process, when do we hire advisors and which ones? Do we want to commission a sell-side due diligence? Do we want to provide a staple debt opportunity to the investors?

On the last points, they depend on the context and the exit strategy. The VDD (Vendor Due Diligence) in particular has the advantage of compelling management to

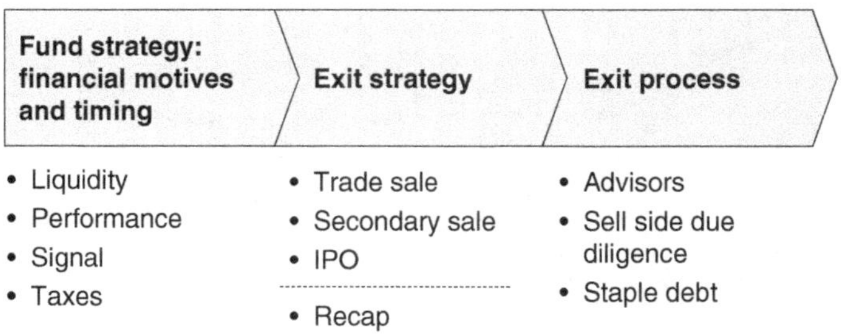

FIGURE 6.5 Managing the exit—what to care about.
Source: Candesic.

collect the company data for the VDR, build a robust business plan, and prepare for the tough questions of the investors. Despite these obvious advantages, it is not universal, especially on the commercial side. As Paul Tomasic at Houlihan Lokey puts it: "VCDD is not as common of a US product, in part, because buyers would not entirely rely on material provided by vendors."

There are three main exit options. We talk at length about IPOs, but trade sales and secondary or tertiary buyouts are more common. This comparison of exits is most relevant for buyouts. The most common exit for growth capital investments is a secondary sale, selling one's minority stake to another investor who may be a better owner considering the augmented size and the next ambitions.

Figure 6.6 shows the evolution of buyouts' exits globally. IPOs represent a very small part of it, at least in deal count (more in value); they also come very irregularly. There was a surge of IPOs during the internet bubble before 2000, then another one before the credit crisis, further spikes in the record years of 2014 and 2021, followed by a multi-year drought. Everyone talks a lot about IPOs, some market veterans lament that IPOs are no longer a viable exit for PE portfolio companies, but the bulk of the exits was and will likely continue to be in trade sales and secondary buyouts.

PE investors tend to be savvy owners who know how to professionalize their portfolio companies and prepare them for the next owner. Strategic buyers know they will have to pay a high price, but often they don't mind that much. PE delivers what they need. For Prateek Sharma, Head of M&A at Cipla, a leading Indian branded generic pharma company: "PE prepares and cleans up the marketing, lays the compliance and reinforces the processes for strategic buyers."

We do not show partial exits here but will discuss recaps and refinancings. A substantial part of the "exits" are shown as receivership or other write-off, especially right after the GFC in 2009, in 2020 during the pandemic, and in 2023 following the surge of inflation.

Figure 6.7 highlights the evolution of exit distribution over time, here comparing 2010, right after the crisis, with 2023. The proportion of IPOs went from 10% down to 4%. The proportion of trade sales, meanwhile, went up from 41% to 50%.

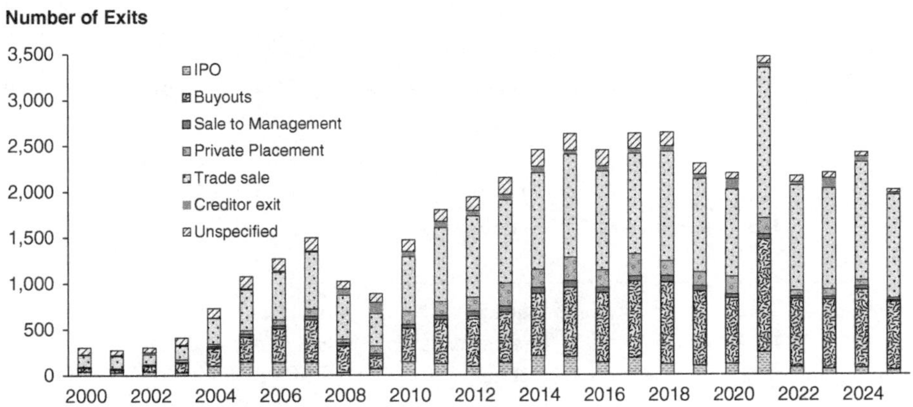

FIGURE 6.6 Buyouts and buy-ins by type of exit globally.
Source: Preqin (part of Blackrock).

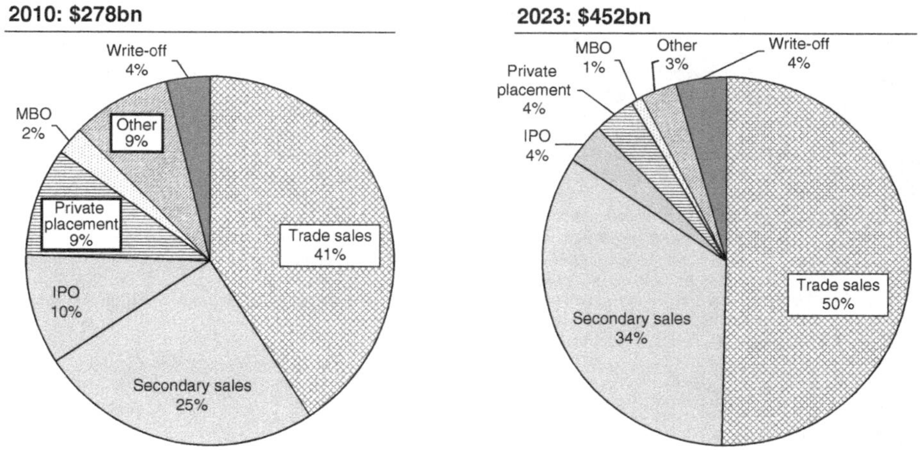

FIGURE 6.7 Exit distribution varies significantly over time.
Source: Preqin (part of Blackrock).

Some market observers see the reduction of IPOs as a sign that PE assets have become too expensive and that the PE industry is churning artificial gains. We will discuss this later but, hopefully, the lower proportion of IPOs is a temporary issue. From an historical perspective, IPOs come and go, with windows of opportunity generated by a combination of macroeconomic factors.

In any case, it will be critical to first consider whether an IPO is suitable and if the timing is right for the business. This is particularly the case for life sciences companies expecting clinical or regulatory results.

Second, the proportion of the shares tendered to the public needs to be carefully evaluated. There are financial but also legal considerations in the case of a full exit, for example pertaining to buyer representations and warranties insurance.

Third, to test if the timing is right, "pre-IPO companies should take the opportunity to assess market receptivity by taking advantage of confidential meetings with investors known as 'testing-the-waters' meetings in the United States or 'early look' or 'pilot fishing' meetings in Europe, which may be conducted concurrently with SEC review of a confidentially submitted draft registration statement."[2]

The road to the IPO is a complex, highly regulated, cumbersome, risky, and expensive process. It typically requires at least six months, with the timetable influenced by the preparation of the registration statement, going back and forth with the SEC or another local regulator. It is different from the SPAC IPO, which was used extensively during the pandemic, and which we will discuss later.

The usual IPO process goes through three phases: first, one needs to hire managers. Second, one runs due diligence. Third, one engages in a long marketing campaign. This can be decomposed into 12 steps, which requires much effort (Figure 6.8).

---

[2]McDermott Will & Emery. Dual track reboot. https://www.mwe.com/insights/five-key-considerations-for-supercharging-your-life-science-company-exit.

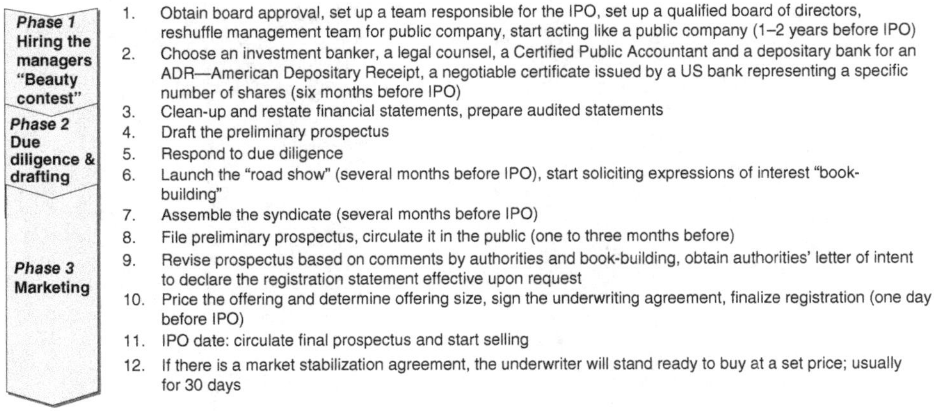

FIGURE 6.8 The road to public offering.
Source: NASDAQ; Ross et al. (2002).

6.10.2 Dual-track Process

IPOs can also go through a dual-track process, which involves the combination of an IPO with, for example, a trade sale or a secondary buyout. This approach maximizes the seller's options. It provides flexibility to choose the best path based on market conditions and business objectives. In creating more competition among the potential buyers, it should lift up the price.

We list a few examples of dual-track processes. Few end up with an IPO.

TeamHealth, a provider of outsourced healthcare professional staffing backed by Blackstone, pursued a dual-track process before its December 2009 IPO on the NYSE. With demand softer than expected, Blackstone withdrew the secondary shares it had planned to sell, and the offering was reduced to a primary-only issuance that raised approximately $159 million. Blackstone did not cash out any of its holding, but the primary issuance diluted its stake from essentially 100% to 71%. Blackstone took the company private again in early 2017 for $6.1 billion.

In another case, in 2013, Surgical Care Affiliates (SCA), one of the largest providers of outpatient surgery in the United States, backed by TPG Capital, pursued a dual-track process. The company ultimately went public in 2013 on the NASDAQ. It was later acquired by UnitedHealth's Optum in 2017 in a $2.3 billion deal, highlighting how dual-track processes can still lead to strategic sales post-IPO.

In contrast, Thomas H. Lee Partners took a different approach in 2016 when exploring exit options for US outsourced pharma services company inVentiv Group through a dual-track process, ultimately choosing to sell a significant stake to Advent International instead of completing the planned IPO.

In Europe, similarly, in 2017, PAI Partners launched a dual-track sale process for Cerba Healthcare, a French medical diagnostics company it had acquired from IK Investment Partners in 2010. Eventually, Cerba was sold to another private equity firm, Partners Group, and to Canadian pension fund PSP Investments for over €1.8 billion.

In another example, in 2021, Igenomix, a Spanish reproductive genetics company backed by EQT since 2019, hired J.P. Morgan and Morgan Stanley to pursue a dual-track exit strategy with a potential IPO on the New York Stock Exchange. The company was rapidly snapped by Vitrolife, a Swedish company, in a €1.25 billion deal.

The growing appetite for a dual-track process is not universal, particularly in China, where there is a natural preference for IPOs over selling a company through M&A. Several factors contribute to this tendency. First, the Chinese government and regulatory authorities actively promote IPOs as part of a national agenda to develop domestic capital markets and support the growth of homegrown companies. Listing on a Chinese exchange is often seen as a mark of prestige and a tacit endorsement by the state, enhancing a company's visibility and reputation. Second, IPOs typically allow founders and early investors to retain greater control and autonomy post-listing compared to M&A, where an outright sale often leads to a loss of control and integration into another firm.

Additionally, IPOs in China frequently offer higher valuations than private M&A transactions, particularly during bullish market conditions, driven by strong retail investor demand and government incentives to encourage public listings. Cultural factors also play a significant role. In China, and much of East Asia, selling a company to another controller through M&A can be perceived as "surrendering," undermining the legacy, reputation, and brand of the original owners. IPOs, in contrast, are often seen as a means to preserve the company's identity and maintain its standing as an independent entity.

It is worth noting that this preference for IPOs over M&A may also reflect differences in capital market structures and investor dynamics across regions. For example, public markets in China are often characterized by a higher proportion of retail investors, whose enthusiasm can drive valuations beyond what strategic or financial buyers are willing to pay in an M&A scenario. Furthermore, regulatory frameworks in China tend to favor IPOs, sometimes making M&A transactions more complex or less attractive.

Several challenges can arise in a dual-track process. First, it can become costly and time-consuming, as preparing for both paths can strain the company's time and resources, including regulatory filings for an IPO and negotiations for a private sale. The demands of both tracks can distract management from day-to-day operations, potentially impacting the company's short-term performance. There is also the delicate balance of information disclosure, as IPOs require extensive public disclosure while private sales involve confidential information sharing. This can create legal risks and potential conflicts as confidentiality can be compromised, especially with more parties involved. Additionally, it can create uncertainty within the company and among potential buyers or investors, as the firm may struggle to signal a clear strategic direction. Finally, market volatility may affect the IPO track, and if not well-managed, the dual-track approach becomes difficult to coordinate and can erode the firm's leverage during private sale negotiations, potentially leading to lower valuations.

That seems like a long list of challenges to secure, perhaps, a higher valuation. But there is also the optionality value, and that can be in the form of a negotiation tool. A *Financial News* article once made the link with *The Game*, Neil Strauss's popular handbook on picking up women. The best way to attract someone you fancy is to get their friends to fall in love with you first. The same logic applies here. The dual-track process flushes out potential bidders and helps to achieve the seller's real goal, which is an outright sale.

A failed IPO is also an opportunity for a secondary transaction. In 2015, Cinven conducted the buyout of Labco, a large pan-European provider of blood analysis services. 3i wanted to IPO the company after failing to secure a high enough price from

PE investors. Cinven didn't raise its price but was ready to come back into the process. When the owners of Labco understood that the IPO process was going nowhere, Cinven provided an acceptable alternative and acquired the company. Cinven merged Labco into Synlab and organized the IPO of the merged companies in 2021.[3]

6.10.3 Recaps and Refinancing

Similarly, when an IPO or other exit strategy is not viable, companies can consider leveraged recapitalizations (recaps) and refinancing as valuable partial exit strategies, allowing them to extract cash from portfolio companies without fully divesting.

A recap typically involves restructuring the company's capital structure, often by increasing debt to pay a special dividend to the PE owner, in which case the leveraged recap is called a dividend recap. This allows the firm to recover a portion of its initial investment while maintaining ownership and potential future upside. In a leveraged recap, the funds will be able to pull out some residual equity without losing the ownership of the portfolio company. It can be done through bonds, sometimes through hybrid financing. Recaps can also be used to optimize the company's capital structure, potentially increasing its value for a future full exit. In the specific case of the dividend recap, the combination of the increased debt and the payment of a dividend to the shareholders will increase the financial risk of the company and may affect future performance or limit operational flexibility.

Refinancing, on the other hand, primarily focuses on replacing existing debt with new debt on more favorable terms. As part of the refinancing, a portion of the new debt might be used to pay out dividends to the PE firm and other shareholders, functioning as a partial exit. Like in a recap, the PE firm still maintains ownership but gains liquidity without a full sale of its stake. Note that a refinancing doesn't always result in a dividend payout to the PE firm, and its main benefits can just be reduced interest rates, extended maturities, or improved covenants.

In some cases, particularly with large dividends, there is a risk that the IRS could recharacterize the dividend as a disguised sale, which could result in less favorable tax treatment. Additionally, if the dividend is deemed excessive, it could potentially be treated as a return of capital, which would reduce the tax basis of the PE firm's investment. International tax considerations can add further complexity, especially if the portfolio company is foreign or if there are non-US investors in the PE fund. Withholding taxes and tax treaties may come into play in these scenarios.

Both strategies provide PE firms with flexibility in timing their exits, demonstrate investment performance to LPs, and can serve to realign equity stakes with management. These partial exit methods are particularly useful when market conditions aren't ideal for a full exit, allowing PE firms to make some returns while continuing to hold and potentially grow their investments.

Historically, dividend recaps have been used in periods of cheap debt. In spite of high interest rates, the recent years have seen a surge of large dividend recaps as PE firms are holding on to their portfolio companies longer. In 2024, the D'Ieteren Group in Belgium announced that it would increase the debt of its Belron subsidiary (in which it holds a 50% stake) to a record €8.1 billion. This move was aimed at financing a €4.3 billion special dividend, which would be distributed among its shareholders,

[3] In 2023, they offered in a controversial move to buy back the public shares and took the company private again after the price had fallen by more than 60%.

including D'Ieteren Group and private equity sponsors such as CD&R and Hellman & Friedman who backed the company in 2018 and in 2021 and would recoup 35% of their investment.

The previous records were set in 2021 by Hellman & Friedman with Verisure's \$6.35 billion dividend recap and in 2019 by Sycamore Partners with a \$5.3 billion refinancing package with dividend recap of Staples in the United States. This surge is controversial as overleveraging portfolio companies in highly uncertain economic times increases the risk of default. In 2024, credit rating agencies downgraded Belron to junk after the announcement of the proposed transaction.

Bhardwaj et al. (2025) highlighted those risks but pointed out that, compared to a full exit, the sponsors are giving themselves more time to create value. While all stakeholders share an interest in the success of the company, shareholders have the most to gain. In addition, this partial exit boosts their IRR, increasing their chances to raise the next fund.

It is difficult to track precisely the dividend recaps since financial data providers tend to focus on the debt issued, not the portion that is ultimately used for the payment of the dividends.

6.10.4 Write-Off

While not an exit "strategy," write-offs or "creditor exits" just happen.

Several high-profile LBO deals turned sour for the shareholders, including LifeCare Holdings, and Four Seasons Health Care.

LifeCare Holdings was a Texas-based chain of long-term acute care hospitals. In 2005, it was acquired in an LBO by the Carlyle Group, one of the largest private equity firms, for approximately \$555 million. Carlyle financed the deal with a significant amount of debt, typical of LBO transactions at the time. Over the years, LifeCare Holdings struggled with rising healthcare costs, changes in reimbursement rates under Medicare, lower patient volumes, and the high debt load from the buyout. The company faced increasing financial stress, and the debt became unsustainable. In 2012, the company started facing liquidity issues and, in December, filed for Chapter 11 bankruptcy. As part of the bankruptcy restructuring, the lenders, which included distressed debt investors, took control of the company. Carlyle Group effectively lost its entire equity stake in the company as the debt holders became the new owners through the bankruptcy process.

There are famous stories of LBOs that collapsed from too much debt that had been raised in recapitalizations to pay significant dividends to the sponsor and the management team. The goal was not to make the company insolvent, but the extreme leverage made it much more likely to happen.

Complex and creative refinancing aims to improve the return of the owner. While it is often undertaken on the back of a successful business, it can also be the expression of desperate attempts to fend off a bankruptcy. The limit is not always clear and can be fast changing.

Four Seasons Healthcare was a leading provider of elderly care homes in the United Kingdom. It was acquired in 2006 by Qatari-based Three Delta for £1.4 billion in a highly leveraged (12×) LBO. Terra Firma Capital Partners, a leading UK-based PE firm, had offered £900 million. In 2008, Three Delta was unable to refinance £1.24 billion of debt maturing. Four Seasons went through years of defaults, debt-to-equity swap, loan extensions, and other negotiations that left it with £780 million of debt in the ownership of the lenders.

In 2012, Terra Firma acquired Four Seasons from the lenders for a total consideration of £825 million, of which £255 million from Terra Firma. The new debt for the deal was arranged by Barclays and Goldman Sachs and amounted to £725 million. Four Seasons had to borrow £220 million from Terra Firma subsidiaries at 15% yearly interest, over 10 years. By 2022, when it was due to be repaid, Four Seasons would have owed its controlling shareholder four times the original sum. In addition, this loan and complex financial engineering across geographies might have allowed Terra Firma to sell the business largely tax-free.[4]

However, after the takeover, Four Seasons continued to struggle. Most of its income was from the public sector, and local authority care spending had been falling in the years of austerity in the United Kingdom, while increases to the minimum wage had pushed up its payroll costs. Terra Firma decided to reorganize the Group into three separate businesses, with the main part, publicly funded care homes, supporting the debt.

In 2014, Terra Firma slashed the value of its investment. The £220 million deeply discounted bond was reduced to a new principal amount of £72 million. In 2015, the value of the loan was further cut, to £20 million. Terra Firma was still hoping to recoup a larger part of its investment should the fortunes of the company improve.

In 2015, Terra Firma had to call PJT Partners to review its £513.7 million net debt package. H/2 Capital, a secretive American distressed debt fund, began buying the company's debt at a sharp discount and snapped up both senior and junior debt. Terra Firma's hope was to turn around the business and buy back the debt from H/2 at a reasonable discount. H/2, however, had their own plans for the company.

In 2017, Terra Firma and H/2 spent months accusing each other of failing to come to an agreement as to how to proceed with the debt-laden care home group. In November, Terra Firma agreed to cede control and transfer their interest in the High Yield Bond Group to the creditors for a nominal sum as part of the restructuring led by main creditor H/2 Capital. In December, Terra Firma asked H/2 to accept its stake "for a nominal sum, with immediate effect." But the companies couldn't agree on resolving a £26 million interest payment due within days by Four Seasons. Without this payment, Four Seasons could be broken and forced by the UK Care Quality Commission to stop accepting new residents from local councils. After the payment was missed, Terra Firma was no longer in operational control. H/2 was effectively in control.

Four Seasons' holding companies collapsed into administration in April 2019.[5] Alvarez & Marsal were appointed as administrators in connection with the sale of the

[4] Garside, J. (2017, November 8). Private equity firm made struggling care home operator take costly loan. *The Guardian*.

[5] Administration in the United Kingdom is a legal process used when a company is insolvent and unable to pay its debts, similar to Chapter 11 bankruptcy in the United States. The aim is to rescue the company as a going concern, if possible, or to achieve a better result for creditors than they would receive from an outright liquidation. An administrator, who is an insolvency practitioner, takes control of the company's affairs, managing it with the goal of either restructuring, selling assets, or finding a buyer. Administration provides the company with a temporary reprieve from creditor actions, allowing time to reorganize and stabilize. In contrast, Chapter 11 focuses on restructuring the company's debts while allowing management to retain control under court supervision.

bond-financed part of the Four Seasons Health Care Group. As a result, in September, H/2 took over Four Seasons for an estimated £400 million.

Four Seasons was not a "bad" business. Terra Firma paid a reasonable price and had sound views on how to run it. But the drastic budget reductions from the main (public) payor over many years and the exposure to unforgiving fixed rent[6] and debt servicing made it just unsalvageable for the PE investor.

There are situations where the GPs don't lose everything, at the expense of the LPs. In a bankruptcy, the LPs normally lose their money while the lenders may lose some of theirs and gain control. However, the GPs often continue to make money as they work on the restructuring or pursue add-on acquisitions.

6.10.4.1 Fund Liquidation A single write-off of a key investment can have catastrophic effects on a PE fund, potentially triggering the liquidation of the entire fund. This was the case of Montreux Capital Management's GBP 425 million healthcare fund, which entered liquidation after losing control of its major portfolio company, Active Care Group (Risner, 2025). The collapse of this investment, burdened by high inflation and operational challenges, undermined the fund's viability despite the firm continuing to raise capital through other vehicles. This case highlights the high stakes and illiquidity risks inherent in PE funds, where a single failure can imperil the whole portfolio.

6.11 CASE STUDY: GENESISCARE—A GLOBAL ONCOLOGY VISION THAT FALTERED

6.11.1 From Local Clinic to National Leader

GenesisCare was founded in 2005 in Australia, born out of a desire to consolidate the country's fragmented oncology services. Radiotherapy had long been dominated by public hospitals and small private clinics with inconsistent quality and technology. GenesisCare's founders—including doctors and business operators—believed they could deliver better patient outcomes and higher efficiency by bringing services under a single, quality-focused brand.

Over the next decade, the company rapidly expanded across Australia through acquisitions and organic growth. It developed a national footprint of cancer centers, cardiology services, and imaging facilities, becoming a household name in private oncology care. The capital-intensive model relied on advanced equipment, private payer partnerships, and physician referral networks.

6.11.2 KKR and China Resources Back a Global Ambition

In 2012, KKR acquired a 63% stake in the company valuing the equity at about AUD 600 million. KKR's entry marked the beginning of a bold international expansion strategy.

[6] Many investors argue operations and real estate management are very different activities that should be kept separated, the so-called OpCo/PropCo model. It is, however, another layer of fixed costs.

Following a refinancing in 2013 and an aborted attempt to IPO in 2015 at AUD 800 million to 1 billion, KKR sold its by then 45% diluted stake in the company in 2016 in a deal reportedly valued at AUD 1.7 billion EV to a consortium led by China Resources, a large state-backed conglomerate investor who took the control. The remaining ownership was retained by founders and staff. GenesisCare expanded into the United Kingdom and Spain, acquiring clinics and cardiology services. The company marketed itself as a clinical leader, focusing on advanced equipment, rapid treatment access, and physician-led governance. It differentiated itself from hospital-based oncology by emphasizing convenience, consistency, and patient experience. KKR reinvested as a minority shareholder in 2018–2019.

The ultimate goal, however, was to crack the US market—the largest and most profitable healthcare system in the world. While fragmented and complex, the US oncology sector had many independent providers and legacy assets, making it attractive to a well-funded consolidator.

In 2020, GenesisCare made its boldest move yet: it acquired 21st Century Oncology, one of the largest private cancer clinic networks in the United States, which had recently emerged from bankruptcy. The deal added 293 locations and gave GenesisCare immediate national presence. At the time, CEO Dan Collins described it as a transformative acquisition that would allow the company to operate more than 440 locations across four countries.

The acquisition was funded through a combination of debt and internal capital, with GenesisCare reportedly taking on hundreds of millions of dollars in additional leverage. The strategy depended on achieving operational synergies and raising performance across a portfolio of historically underperforming assets.

6.11.3 Integration Challenges and Mounting Pressure

The integration proved far more difficult than anticipated. Many of the acquired US clinics were outdated, under-invested, or struggling with reimbursement issues. GenesisCare faced challenges aligning technology platforms, standardizing protocols, and retaining key medical personnel.

At the same time, the company's ambitious expansion had stretched management bandwidth and capital reserves. Back in Australia and Europe, growth slowed, and COVID-19 disrupted patient volumes and delayed elective procedures. The debt taken on to fund US expansion became harder to service as cash flow fell short of expectations.

Despite efforts to restructure operations and exit underperforming markets, the situation continued to deteriorate. By 2023, GenesisCare's US business was facing serious financial stress. With repayment deadlines looming and no clear recovery path, the company made the decision to separate the troubled US division from its healthier international operations. In March 2023, founder Dan Collins stepped down from his executive role.

6.11.4 Collapse in the US Market

In June 2023, GenesisCare's US business filed for Chapter 11 bankruptcy. The filing listed more than $1.7 billion in liabilities, including bank debt and lease obligations. The company announced it would seek to sell its US assets and refocus on its operations in Australia, the United Kingdom, and Spain.

As part of the Chapter 11 proceedings, Oaktree Capital emerged as a key stakeholder. Holding a large portion of GenesisCare's debt, Oaktree took a leading role in negotiating the restructuring terms. Ultimately, it assumed ownership of the reorganized US business—effectively wiping out the equity held in the US subsidiary by earlier investors including KKR and China Resources. The recapitalization left Oaktree in control of what remained of GenesisCare's US footprint, while the Australian parent attempted to continue independently abroad.

The bankruptcy marked a dramatic fall for what had once been seen as a model for global oncology consolidation. It also underscored how even sophisticated sponsors like KKR and China Resources could miscalculate the operational and financing risks of cross-border healthcare expansion.

Though the bankruptcy was largely confined to the US unit, the damage to GenesisCare's global brand and the value of its equity was significant.

6.11.5 Lessons from the GenesisCare Deal

GenesisCare's downfall illustrates the risks of rapid global expansion in capital-intensive, locally regulated healthcare sectors. The company had a credible business in Australia and promising early steps in Europe, but its attempt to become a global leader in cancer care was undercut by overleveraging, poor asset selection, and a failure to manage operational complexity across borders.

The acquisition of 21st Century Oncology—a company that had already gone through bankruptcy once—was a high-risk bet that did not pay off. Rather than integrating a complementary business, GenesisCare took on a troubled asset base that dragged down its entire platform.

PE investors often talk about creating global leaders in healthcare delivery, but GenesisCare shows how hard that is in practice. Healthcare remains highly local, culturally specific, and operationally complex. When strategy outpaces execution, even the best capitalized and most mission-driven platforms can stumble.

6.12 TYING IT ALL TOGETHER

[A contribution by Johannes Natterer]

In the previous chapters, we have attempted to provide a comprehensive overview of the various components of a PE investment in its lifetime: the valuation at entry, the Due Diligence, getting financing in place, the 100-day plan, management incentives, business plans, exit preparation, etc.

Not unique to PE investment, 100-day plans should be employed in any business upon a change or updated strategy. Incentive systems likewise are nothing unique to PE and any listed or unlisted business has them. Doing a Due Diligence is actually nothing else than checking carefully before you buy something—any house buyer is doing that.

But if all the tools are known and all the methods have been described, what is missing then to make a good deal? After diligently and completely applying all tools that we described, one must get two priorities right in order for a deal to be successful: (1) the timing and (2) the priorities.

Get the timing wrong for entry or exit or both and the most diligently conducted Due Diligence and 100 days plans will likely not help. Prioritize incorrectly and again the deal will almost certainly not work out.

6.12.1 Getting the Timing Right

Few people like to admit it, but timing is arguably the single most important factor in generating strong returns in a PE investment—even more so than valuation, management teams, incentive systems, or operational improvements. Timing affects both the entry and the exit, and while finding the right timing will likely be different for every investment, we can offer some guidelines to help you get it right.

In order to achieve a good exit, here are key internal factors you want to have in place at the time of exit:

- The business should demonstrate consistent improvement of performance over time and show that budgets and targets were achieved. The performance improvement needs to be derived from management action, be it internal business optimization or value-added M&A or product development. Ideally the business outperforms its markets.
- The management team must be on board, both in supporting the value creation plan and in expressing a willingness to continue under new ownership and to roll the lion's share of their proceeds into the new investment.
- The business should show an ambitious and achievable business plan with upsides. The business plan should be based on credible, achievable projects and initiatives and there needs to be a track record of implementing initiatives and reaping their benefits.

While each individual component is not straightforward to achieve, achieving all three of them is even more difficult. We explain below what can be done when only two of the three are implemented.

- Just like with the sale of any good or service, the sale of a business benefits from having competitive tension. Such a tension is either explicit when the business is sold in an auction or implicit when a buyer tries to snatch up an asset before it goes into an auction, or the tension can show up in many other forms. In fact, that buyers believe there is competitive tension is sufficient.
- The difference in financing packages offered to a buyer by lending banks between a good or a bad financing environment can be most significant.
- All businesses are sold on the basis of expected future earnings, so visibility of such earnings is indispensable for achieving a good sales price.

When looking at these three factors, it is clear that they are linked and rarely does one have attractive financing markets in times of insecure business outlooks and strong competitive tension is unlikely to happen if the financing markets are weak. Nonetheless, these three factors matter individually and need to be considered upon starting an exit process.

It is important that all these criteria hold not only at the start of a sales process but also during the entire sales process until closing—a period that can easily span 9–12 months. There is nothing more confusing to buyers during a sales process than misses to the monthly budgets as well as announcements about tariffs or other macro trends that are likely to affect the business under consideration.

From the outside, it may seem bewildering that buyers can be put off by missing a monthly budget and can change their entire view on a business, a business they have spent multiple 100k on Due Diligence costs. However, upon closer inspection, this is not so surprising:

1. All purchase prices are justified by future performance and hence the business plan. If therefore, during the relatively short period of a sales process, the business does not perform according to plan, what confidence can one then have in the achievability of a three-year business plan?
2. On the buyer side, multiple stakeholders need to like the deal and support it. The investment team, financing banks, the investment committee, co-investors, etc. No deal is liked by everyone, and many stakeholders will be on the fence about the deal; some others may outright not like it. A deviation in performance during a sales process can easily change the odds in the stakeholder group about a deal. The result can be a loss of interest or a price adjustment.

When considering entry, the dynamics are somewhat the opposite for all the internal and external requirements listed earlier. However, during periods of instability or when financing is scarce, sellers may hold off on selling, and price expectations between buyers and sellers can easily misalign so that no transaction can be realized. The most successful private equity funds often excel at acquiring businesses at the very beginning of an upturn, when sellers are ready to sell and business plans can be credibly supported. At this stage, banks may not yet offer attractive financing terms, so market-clearing prices are depressed, and deals are often structured with all-equity or bridge financing, with refinancing options explored later as debt markets improve. Having such an ability (and the guts to employ it ...) is a key component to reducing competitive tension, which is of course exactly what one wants on entry.

Entry, thus, truly is the moment when business savviness pays off. Guessing that the market will recover when sellers still see gloom is tricky. A further complication is that at that moment banks are not yet willing to finance businesses, but you convince your investment committee that this is the moment to go all in and finance the acquisition with 100% equity and refinance it later in better financing markets, when you see that a budget miss can be rectified going forward by implementing initiatives only you know, and so on. These are all the hallmarks of a good entry and this is what you need to look for if you want to have a chance for a stellar deal.

An honest assessment would likely conclude that *timing is the single most critical component* to get right in a private equity investment.

6.12.2 Getting the Priorities Right

When one thinks about everything that needs to happen for a PE investment to succeed, it is quite overwhelming.

Sourcing the investment

- The investment opportunity must be sourced, and the business must be up for sale.

Buying the business

- Due diligence must be conducted, with multiple service providers coordinated and kept informed.
- While due diligence is ongoing, the management team must be evaluated, augmented, or replaced. Internal stakeholders must also be kept in the loop.
- A financing package must be negotiated in parallel.
- All documents and communications must be continuously updated as new information emerges.
- The SPA must be negotiated and finalized.
- Management incentive systems must be designed and implemented.
- Between signing and closing, antitrust filings must be submitted and processed. Other closing conditions, including approvals by suppliers and/or customers, must be met.

Upon buying the business

- Operations
  - At closing, employee communications must be handled.
  - The 100-day plan must be developed and executed.
  - Operational improvement programs must be rolled out, depending on the complexity of the business.
  - Stakeholders must be regularly updated on progress.
- M&A
  - M&A activity often plays a key role in value creation, so each transaction must be managed with the same rigor as the initial acquisition.
  - M&A targets must be integrated, and synergies must be realized.
- Financing
  - During the holding period, the financing package may be adjusted, or dividends may be paid out.
- Communication
  - Investors must continuously inform about the state of the investment.
  - Depending on the structure of the private equity funds, regular valuation of the individual investments must be conducted.

Exit preparation and exit

- As the exit process begins, banks must be selected, business plans finalized, and management succession plans put in place.
- The data room needs to be prepared.
- Sales documents need to be produced.
- Sales contracts need to be negotiated.

It is easy to see that such long list of tasks can get overwhelming. It can be overwhelming for the investment team, but even more so it can be overwhelming for the management team who in addition to supporting all of the above still has to run the normal operations of the business—which usually already is a full-time job. Different

PE funds run different models to manage this complexity. Some have dedicated staff working at all times at the company's premises as operating partners. Others initiate the holding period with their own dedicated staff as management or as topic owner to drive certain initiatives and only later change to permanent management.

To tackle that problem of prioritization, it has proven most useful to work backward and to determine fairly early on during the holding period what shape the business that is up for sale needs to have. If the exit story is to be tailored around the accretion of M&A, then focus should be set on executing add-on acquisitions early on during the holding period. If the managers at entry are already at an age that makes it unlikely for them to last two more PE cycles and sale to a strategic is not a preferred option or one to be solely relied upon, then consider changing management early on during the holding period. Effectively, the suggestion is to work backward from the three criteria we established earlier, which need to be in place at the time of exit.

Getting priorities right is crucial to preparing businesses for a successful exit. Even more so, getting them right early on is even more important!

6.13 THE UNITE PLAYBOOK

We now introduce the **UNITE** value creation playbook (Figure 6.9), which lists five categories of actions to identify and deliver value from deal cultivation ("U") through value creation in the portfolio ("N" & "I") to exit ("T" & "E"). UNITE just does that: it brings together our suggestions to PE investors at each step of the process and provides an integrated framework for the investor.

For this, we built on the initial framework that we introduced in Chapter 2 to illustrate the drivers of value creation in an LBO and used again in this chapter, this time to illustrate the value creation in the portfolio. This is the third and last version.

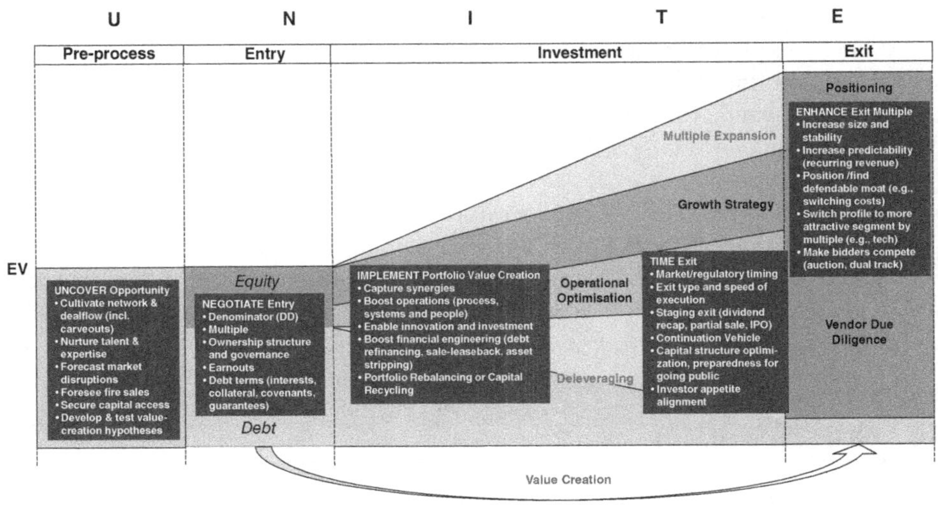

FIGURE 6.9 UNITE—aligning PE strategies with actionable phases in the investment life cycle.
Source: Kitten M. (n.d.). UNITE Playbook. Working Paper.

The main actions in each category include the following:

- UNCOVER (investment opportunity)
  - Cultivate network and dealflow, including carve-outs
  - Nurture talent and expertise
  - Forecast market disruptions
  - Develop and test value-creation hypotheses
  - Secure capital access
  - Foresee fire sales
- NEGOTIATE (at entry)
  - Negotiate the denominator
  - Negotiate the multiple
  - Negotiate the ownership structure (e.g., seller reinvesting) and governance
  - Negotiate earnouts
  - Negotiate debt terms (interests, collaterals, covenants, guarantees)
- IMPLEMENT (value creation in portfolio)
  - Capture synergies
  - Boost operations (process, systems, and people)
  - Enable innovation and investment
  - Boost financial engineering (debt refinancing, sale-leaseback, asset stripping)
  - Portfolio rebalancing or capital recycling
- TIME (exit)
  - Market/regulatory timing
  - Exit type
  - Staging exit (dividend recap, partial sale, IPO)
  - Continuation vehicle
  - Capital structure optimization, preparedness for going public
  - Investor appetite alignment
- ENHANCE (exit multiple)
  - Increase size and stability
  - Increase predictability (recurring revenue)
  - Position/find defendable moat (e.g., switching costs)
  - Switch profile to more attractive segment by multiple (e.g., tech)
  - Make bidders compete (auction, dual track)

UNITE was designed for LBO investors first. It remains useful for other direct PE investors, less so for other asset classes. UNITE does not pretend to teach much to the veterans of the LBO industry who breathe the concepts in every deal they work on. Finally, UNITE is not specific to healthcare or any industry sector. There will be another framework for that purpose in Chapter 7.

6.14 CHAPTER SUMMARY

Chapter 6 provides a comprehensive roadmap for value creation and exit management once a PE firm has acquired a company. It begins with the 100-day plan that stabilizes the business through strategic focus, organizational alignment, quick-win initiatives, and detailed roadmaps. This early work lays the foundation for deeper operational improvements and prepares the company for sustainable growth. It also reminds us of the importance of moving fast past the acquisition. Here we would like to emphasize again the importance of KPIs. According to Nikhil Chadha, Head of Operations Europe at EQT, "*The industry typically focuses on revenue and EBITDA. At EQT, we added three leading indicators post-acquisition: free cash flow including NWC, customer satisfaction, and quality. I see many other PE firms following our example.*"

The chapter then explores a first set of five core drivers of value creation—margin improvement, asset utilization, human-capital optimization, and the growing roles of ESG and technology. Margin initiatives such as supply chain renegotiations and lean process redesign deliver immediate EBITDA uplifts, while asset-light strategies like sale-and-leasebacks free capital for reinvestment. Aligning management incentives to clinical- and financial-performance targets fosters a results-driven culture, systematic ESG programs can mitigate risk and unlock exit-multiple premiums, while digital transformation underpins both cost and revenue levers.

Effective stakeholder management extends beyond internal operations to include investor relations, lender partnerships, management teams, regulators, payors, and communities. Dedicated IR teams now drive fundraising synergies and activate LP expertise—such as hospital-network introductions—that translate directly into portfolio growth. Lender relationships in LBOs demand rigorous covenant management, structured communication, and contingency planning to avoid defaults and maintain financing optionality. Engaging payors and regulators through targeted communication and ESG reporting safeguards licenses to operate and supports premium exit valuations.

The chapter then addresses exit preparation and execution, emphasizing continuous planning for trade sales, secondary buyouts, IPOs, dual-track processes, and recaps. Success at exit depends on aligning internal performance benchmarks—historic budget achievements, management commitment, and a tangible equity story—with external factors like competitive tension and financing market conditions.

The GenesisCare case study provides a warning that ambitious cross-border expansion in healthcare can quickly unravel when overleveraging meets poor asset selection and complex local integration challenges, even for top-tier PE sponsors.

Finally, the chapter synthesizes all the key learnings, first through the closing remarks of an industry practitioner, then introducing the UNITE playbook, which integrates all the steps of the PE investment process until exit.

CHAPTER 7

Investing in Health—Investment Strategies and a Dedicated Playbook

This chapter develops a playbook to invest in the healthcare sector that includes 31 strategies in five categories:

> *Taking into account all types of healthcare deals (LBOs, add-ons, growth investments, secondary buyouts), PE capital invested in healthcare grew from less than $5 billion per year in 2000 to $100 billion in 2018—a 20-fold increase. Cumulatively, PE firms closed roughly 7,300 'deals' totaling $833 billion from 2000 to 2018, with 70% of these investments occurring since 2010. (Appelbaum and Batt, 2020)*

To produce this list, we have interviewed dozens of PE practitioners all over the world and reviewed over one hundred transactions to identify the most compelling ideas of value creation they have implemented or encountered. Our objective was to isolate each approach to value creation and assess how specific they could be to the health sector, even though they may have been originally generated in other sectors.

We then categorized them from the perspective of the main owner or stakeholder in charge (investor, CEO, CFO, COO, and CTO), as this could be useful to the investor. While this is a simplification—an initiative can have several owners, or the main owner may change depending on context—this approach has the merit to align with decision-making.

These strategies may not be specific to healthcare, but we aim to show how PE firms have often adapted their value creation playbook to the unique characteristics of the healthcare and life sciences sectors. The securitization of healthcare receivables, in particular, demonstrates a creative financing approach that leverages the predictable cash flows typical in healthcare, similar to how Terra Firma considered leveraging EMI's music catalog.

Such strategies allow PE firms to potentially increase their returns while managing risk in a sector that is both highly regulated and critical to public welfare. However, these approaches also come with their own set of challenges and risks, including regulatory scrutiny and the need to balance profit motives with quality-of-care considerations.

While we have already presented many successful case studies of PE investment in health, we wish to categorize them here by underlying ideas of value creation.

TAXONOMY: 31 STRATEGIES OF VALUE CREATION IN HEALTHCARE INVESTMENT

Investor Playbook (ownership, capital structure, and portfolio-level investment strategies)

- S01. Roll-up and Buy-and-build
- S02. Dismantling/ De-conglomeration/ Carve Outs
- S03. Take-Private
- S04. Portfolio Synergies & Cross-platform Value Creation
- S05. Governance & Leadership (New leadership, physician alignment)
- S06. Tax Arbitrage

CEO Playbook (Strategic growth, market positioning, and integration initiatives the CEO would drive)

- S07. Turnaround
- S08. Specialization and Focus
- S09. Health System Integration and Vertical Integration
- S10. Cross-Sector Integration (e.g., Health and Social Care)
- S11. International Expansion, Globalization and Cross-border Arbitrage
- S12. Human Capital
- S13. Payer-provider Partnerships & Risk Sharing
- S14. Behavioral Health Integration

CFO Playbook (Financial operations, funding structures, and revenue-focused strategies)

- S15. Real Estate Optimization (OpCo/PropCo)
- S16. Manufacturing Infrastructure & Capacity Expansion
- S17. Refinancing with Securitization
- S18. Revenue Cycle Optimization (Improving billing, coding, collections)
- S19. Other Opportunistic Competitive Moves
- S20. Contract Structuring & Bundled Payments

COO Playbook (Operational efficiency, clinical quality, human capital, and patient experience)

- S21. Cost & Supply Chain Optimization
- S22. Alternative Sites of Care (Moving care to outpatient/home settings)
- S23. Clinical Excellence: Quality, Safety, & Pathway Optimization
- S24. Regulatory Strategy and Policy Navigation
- S25. Patient-centric & Experience-focused Models
- S26. Impact-driven Sustainability vs. ESG Compliance

CTO Playbook (Technology-driven innovation, digital transformation, and IP monetization)

- S27. Data Strategies: Analytics and Monetization
- S28. Intellectual Property (IP) Monetization & Licensing
- S29. Precision Medicine & Personalized Care
- S30. Patient acquisition and engagement (Patient Funnel Innovation/Direct-to-consumerization, Digital Front Door)
- S31. Technology-enabled Care Delivery and Life Sciences Development Models

FIGURE 7.1 Thirty-one strategies of value creation in healthcare.

The following taxonomy thus organizes 31 identified strategies into five coherent categories, providing a comprehensive overview of PE levers in the sector (Figure 7.1). Note that many of these strategies are not specific to PE. They are also not mutually exclusive. Often, investors will pursue several of them, simultaneously or sequentially.

From this list, we then developed a brand-new playbook dedicated to healthcare: H.E.A.L., which we present at the end of this chapter.

7.1 INVESTOR PLAYBOOK

(Ownership, capital structure, and portfolio-level investment strategies)

7.1.1 S01: Roll-up and Other Buy-and-build Strategies in Fragmented Markets

Buy-and-build remains the most common and successful value creation strategy in PE historically, and that extends to the health sector. Gain.pro reported that 65% of PE exits in 2025 had a buy-and-build component, up from 53% in 2020. They also identified HUB International, a Hellman & Friedman PortCo, as a record aggregator at the time with 108 acquisitions over five years. But many small deals are just not widely reported, and PHM Group, a PE-backed BnB within residential property services, reported 184 acquisitions over five years. Horizontal and vertical integration are not new concepts—they were flagged by US regulators more than one hundred years ago with a battery of antitrust measures. Firms typically acquire—or occasionally establish—a platform company with the critical scale, systems, and leadership to integrate other businesses efficiently. From there, they pursue two complementary paths: a buy-and-build strategy that expands capabilities and adjacencies (for instance, adding a clinical research site network to a contract research organization [CRO]), and a roll-up, which focuses on pure horizontal consolidation of similar entities to gain market share and operational leverage. PE firms excel at consolidating fragmented segments with easy access to cheaper add-ons, generally staying under the radar of antitrust regulators[1] because each individual acquisition falls below their jurisdiction thresholds. In the specific case of a roll-up, much of the value creation stems from multiple arbitrage: the average differential between established, dominant, diversified platforms trading at 8–12× EBITDA and smaller acquisitions in the same line of business purchased at 2–8× EBITDA.[2]

Several studies provide evidence that PE-led buy-and-build strategies deliver meaningful return uplifts through multiple and operational synergies. For example, Hammer et al. (2022) find that PE-backed buy-and-build transactions achieve, on average, a 17% higher IRR compared with standalone buyouts, driven by valuation multiple arbitrage and post-deal integration gains. Bain's 2024 Global Private Equity Report shows that platforms executing four or more add-ons within a three-year hold period outperform comparable standalone investments by approximately 300 basis points in exit multiples. McKinsey (2024c) further documents that front-loading add-on acquisitions and rigorously capturing revenue and cost synergies can boost portfolio companies' EBITDA growth by 20–35% versus organic growth alone.

Referring to Ampersand's acquisition strategy, Herb Hooper explains: "With add-ons, we do not simply buy EBITDA. Add-ons help our platform companies expand our product offerings, enable geographic reach and average down our entry multiples."

In 2019, PitchBook reported that the proportion of PE-backed companies undertaking at least one add-on acquisition had increased from less than 20% in the early 2000s to nearly 30% (Appelbaum and Batt, 2020). In 2024, PitchBook reported new data showing the proportion had increased further to nearly 60%. Six hundred and twenty-one add-on acquisitions occurred across 383 unique PE-backed healthcare platform companies, with at least 13 PE-owned platforms making five or more add-on acquisitions.

Moreover, VC firms are increasingly adopting PE-style roll-up strategies, acquiring fragmented small businesses in sectors like healthcare and IT services to consolidate operations and deploy AI tools for enhanced efficiency and scale.

In **healthcare services**, PE-driven consolidation began with hospitals in the United States, later expanding to nursing homes, medical laboratories, and dentistry. Over time, this trend extended to specialty clinics, including rehabilitation, psychiatry, ophthalmology, in vitro fertilization, orthopedics, dermatology, radiology, and radiotherapy, as well as multi-specialty clinics. More recently, PE activity has encompassed veterinary clinics, primary care, medical aesthetics, dental labs, and occupational health services. The preference remains for highly fragmented niche markets where operational synergies and economies of scale can be readily achieved. For example, Kitten and Mazevet (2026) demonstrate this pattern across every segment of dentistry, including practices, laboratories, and suppliers.

Arnaud Dufer at Ardian testifies that

> *... PE has progressively driven the buy-and-build consolidation of healthcare specialty practices, as we have been able to do in the following sectors over*

---

[1] FTC in the United States, CMA in the United Kingdom, European Commission in the European Union.

[2] Some segments, for instance veterinary clinics and select add-on platforms during peak consolidation periods, can be in high demand for a while and command higher multiples.

the past decade: medical testing laboratories, clinics, radiology, radiotherapy, orthopedics, dental practices, home care and veterinary. Scale unlocks clear value through economies of scale, lower overhead costs, stronger positioning with hospitals and payers, improved operational efficiency and a more holistic approach to the patient journey. Larger platforms also enable sustained investment both in equipment and consumables with an increased purchasing power as well as in technology, which is increasingly critical to quality of care and long-term competitiveness.

In the United States as in most of Europe, despite significant capital deployment, PE has neither dominated healthcare historically nor does it today. According to recent analysis, PE firms owned approximately 4% of US hospitals and 11% of US nursing homes as of 2021. While these figures reflect PE's presence, they underscore its relatively modest market share compared to the broader healthcare landscape.

This limited ownership stems from several factors: the heavily regulated nature of healthcare, high barriers to entry, and the complex, mission-driven goals of many nonprofit and public healthcare institutions. However, PE firms have demonstrated growing interest in specialty care, outpatient services, and ancillary healthcare businesses, where operational efficiencies and innovative care models present clearer value creation opportunities.

While PE sometimes reaches 20% market share in specific healthcare service specialties—such as dentistry, ophthalmology, or psychiatry—this concentration rarely persists long term, as the ultimate goal remains selling to strategic investors or pursuing public offerings. This approach has been seen not only in physician practice management, but also in revenue cycle management and clinical trial technology, where PE firms aggregate assets to create dominant regional or national players, sometimes outmaneuvering slower-moving corporate consolidators.

Roll-up strategies can, however, trigger antitrust enforcement when market concentration becomes excessive. In 2023, the FTC sued Welsh, Carson, Anderson & Stowe (WCAS) over its creation of US Anesthesia Partners in 2012, alleging that the PE firm violated the Sherman, Clayton, and FTC Acts by acquiring anesthesia practices across Texas to control nearly 70% of the commercial-insured, hospital-only anesthesia market in Houston and Dallas (Ma et al., 2024). The FTC's complaint detailed how US Anesthesia Partners increased prices by 26% post-acquisition and gained 18.8% and 22.0% shares of the anesthesia and emergency medicine markets, respectively, by 2019. Although the court dismissed WCAS from the lawsuit in May 2024, the case underscores the risks of unchecked roll-ups and their potential to undermine competitive dynamics (Ma et al., 2024).

Another issue stems from aggressive cost management that can compromise patient safety in healthcare settings. Bain Capital's CRC Health Group investment exemplifies financial success overshadowed by operational controversy. Acquired for $720 million in 2006, CRC nearly doubled revenue under Bain's ownership before selling to Acadia Healthcare for $1.2 billion in 2015. However, as reported by *Time*, aggressive cost-cutting compromised patient safety, leading to multiple facility closures including Mount Bachelor Academy, shut down for student abuse, and SageWalk Wilderness School, closed after a 16-year-old's heat stroke death. Staff reported reduced staffing levels and eliminated essential supplies like drug testing kits. While Bain Capital successfully identified a fragmented market ripe for roll-up strategies, achieved substantial scale economies, and created the largest provider of specialized behavioral health services in the United States at the time, the regulatory scrutiny and safety failures demonstrate how prioritizing financial engineering over quality care can create significant reputational and operational risks in healthcare investments.

Buy-and-build strategies thrive in low-interest environments, but rising variable rates have exposed highly leveraged companies to financial strain. France's largest dental center network, Dentego, struggled under an LBO burden exceeding €200 million in unitranche debt from Tikehau Capital. Its EBITDA collapsed to less than a tenth of its debt, forcing G Square to cede ownership to Tikehau in 2025.

Similarly, the **pharmaceutical services** sector has also seen significant roll-up activity. PE has been systematic in consolidating activities that big pharma companies have carved out (a phenomenon we describe in the next section on de-conglomeration). The strategy began with US CDMOs in the 1980s, targeting aging manufacturing sites operating at low capacity and opening them to multiple customers. This approach led to the creation of industry giants: Catalent emerged from Cardinal Health's pharmaceutical technologies division in 2007 through Blackstone's acquisition, growing through serial acquisitions to become a $4.3 billion revenue CDMO before Novo Holdings's $16.5 billion acquisition in December 2024.

CordenPharma is a typical example of a CDMO built through systematic acquisition of pharmaceutical sites over time. Originally established in 2006 by International Chemical Investors Group (ICIG), CordenPharma grew by acquiring manufacturing facilities divested by major pharmaceutical companies. Notable acquisitions included Vifor Pharma's finished drug product manufacturing operations in Switzerland and Portugal in 2021. Astorg acquired CordenPharma from ICIG in 2022 for approximately €2.5 billion, gaining control of 11 manufacturing facilities across Europe and the United States serving over 250 pharmaceutical customers. ICIG had been convinced that CordenPharma was no longer a core business. Dr. Signe Michel, director of Healthcare Investments at Astorg, said:

> *Knowing that CordenPharma is in professional hands with Astorg will give ICIG the opportunity to focus and pursue new opportunities in its core chemical businesses. We will leverage our expertise in pharma services and our global network to help further develop the company through both organic and external initiatives. (Astorg.com, 2022)*

The consolidation phenomenon extends across the entire pharmaceutical value chain. In CROs, the latest trend involves creating therapeutic area champions: Sanos Group adopted this approach, operating three specialized CROs focused on musculoskeletal disorders (NBCD), neurological conditions (NeuroScios), and dermatological diseases (Blueskin). Under Investcorp's ownership since 2020, Sanos systematically acquired complementary capabilities, including the 2024 acquisition of NeuroScios GmbH to expand into Alzheimer's and CNS research. ARCHIMED has pursued similar strategies across therapeutic areas, building platforms in biosafety testing (Clean Cells, now Clean Biologics), diagnostics (BioVendor Group), and health safety testing (CARSO), with each platform making multiple add-on acquisitions to achieve market leadership.

Other areas of consolidation include specialty distribution (e.g., rare disease drugs, cold-chain logistics), clinical trial site networks which provide recurring revenues, high barriers to entry, and growing outsourcing demand from pharma and biotech, regulatory and pharmacovigilance services, and medical communications and real-world evidence providers. These segments are often fragmented but benefit from strong structural growth drivers, making them ideal for buy-and-build strategies.

7.1.1.1 Case Study: Charterhouse and SERB In specialty pharmaceuticals, firms like SERB Pharmaceuticals have built global platforms, in this case through targeted acquisitions in rare diseases, conditions, and emergencies (Figure 7.2). Charterhouse's investment in SERB began in 2017 when the firm acquired a majority stake in the small specialty pharma business that distributed critical antidotes and antitoxins to hospital emergency wards in Belgium and France, negotiating a valuation that reflected SERB's narrow product base and structuring earn-outs tied to new product approvals. Charterhouse implemented a rapid roll-up strategy, first across Europe, acquiring niche distributors to capture distribution synergies and licenses for orphan-drug designations for treatments of rare metabolic disorders, all while modernizing quality-management systems to satisfy FDA and other regulatory requirements.

Recognizing the US market's growth potential, Charterhouse then orchestrated in 2021 a landmark $800 million acquisition in cash of BTG Specialty Pharmaceuticals from Boston Scientific. BTG was a perfect strategic fit as it provided antidotes and rescue medicines typically used in emergency rooms and intensive care units to treat patients with critical conditions, including market-leading products such as CroFab®, DigiFab®, and Voraxaze®. While SERB was exclusively operating in Europe, the BTG products were sold primarily in the United States and gave SERB a $210 million direct sales, marketing, and medical affairs presence in the United States, helping to build a global platform. A pool of super senior lenders provided financing of EUR 900 million structured in the form of a senior unitranche debt and a super senior revolving facility.

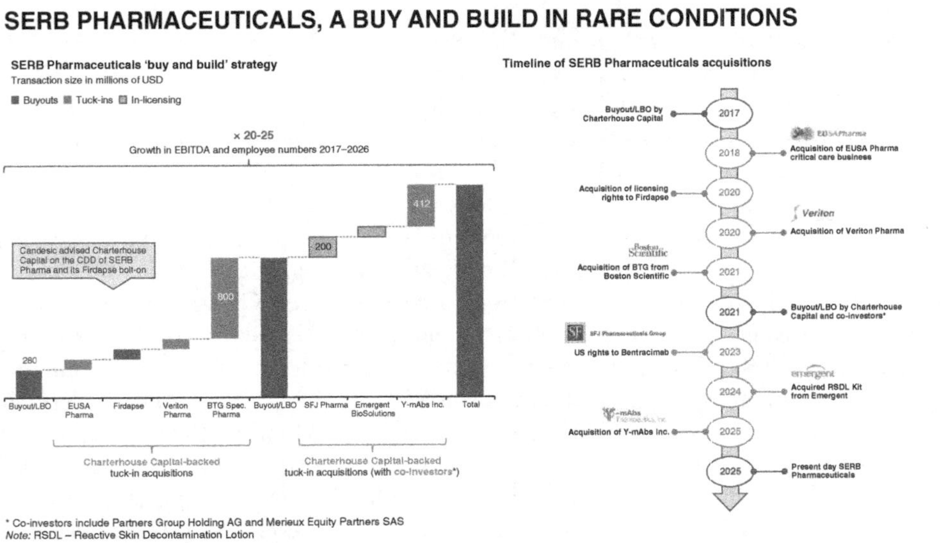

FIGURE 7.2 Serb Pharmaceuticals buy and build strategy.
Source: Mergermarket; PitchBook; Interviews; Candesic analysis.

In May 2023, Charterhouse moved SERB into a single-asset continuation fund at a reported valuation of €700 million, backed by Goldman Sachs, CPP Investments, and Hamilton Lane. The continuation fund included €200 million for the acquisition of US rights to Bentracimab, a blood-thinning reduction drug. SERB later acquired the RSDL® (Reactive Skin Decontamination Lotion) kit from Emergent BioSolutions in 2024, and in August 2025, SERB completed its acquisition of Y-mAbs Therapeutics from NASDAQ for $412 million, adding the pediatric oncology drug Danyelza® (naxitamab-gqgk) to strengthen its rare oncology portfolio.

In **medtech**, consolidation has accelerated across distribution and manufacturing. Palex Medical, backed by Apax Partners, exemplifies the distributor roll-up model. Following Apax's and Fremman's 2023 acquisition of a shared controlling stake at a €1 billion valuation, Palex systematically acquired distributors across Europe; this includes the €100+ million acquisition of Werfen's distribution businesses (Izasa Medical, Izasa Scientific, MC Medical) and the planned acquisition of Belgium's Duomed Group to create a truly pan-European medtech distribution platform spanning Northern, Western, and Southern Europe. The vertical integration of manufacturers with their local distributors has also accelerated, as PE-backed platforms seek to capture more value across the supply chain while achieving operational synergies.

Our examples are mostly in the Western world. How is it in Asia? Quadria Capital provides good cases of sophisticated buy-and-build strategy execution across the region by systematically acquiring and consolidating scalable healthcare companies in high-growth markets, including India, Indonesia, Malaysia, Vietnam, and Singapore. The firm's portfolio demonstrates strategic sector diversification, including hospital networks like NephroPlus (Asia's largest dialysis network with more than 450 centers), and Hermina Hospital (Indonesia's largest BPJS-focused hospital group), alongside specialty pharmaceuticals, digital health platforms like MediBuddy, and healthcare services companies. What distinguishes Quadria's Asian approach is its emphasis on addressing massive healthcare access gaps in markets where social impact and financial returns converge—leveraging Asia's demographic dividend and rapidly expanding middle class while partnering with development finance institutions, including the US International Development Finance Corporation, Asian Development Bank, and International Finance Corporation. The firm targets both substantial minority and majority stakes in approximately 10 companies per fund, focusing on operational excellence and scale to improve healthcare delivery across underserved populations. This strategy capitalizes on Asia-specific dynamics: fragmented healthcare markets ripe for consolidation, regulatory environments favoring local champions, and the region's projected healthcare sector growth to $5 trillion by 2030 while currently representing only 22% of global healthcare spending.

These examples demonstrate how PE buy-and-build strategies have matured from opportunistic asset aggregation to systematic market consolidation, leveraging operational expertise, multiple arbitrage, and patient capital to create industry-leading platforms across healthcare's most fragmented sectors.

7.1.2 S02: Carve-outs and Conglomerate Dismantling

The strategic dismantling of conglomerates through carve-outs represents one of PE's most enduring value creation strategies. There is a continuum of situations. At one end, selective carve-outs represent surgical removal of noncore assets to generate cash and allow the parent company to refocus investment on its core operations. At the other end, complete de-conglomeration involves breaking apart entire corporate structures into multiple independent entities—a wholesale transformation that redistributes capital and management focus across newly autonomous businesses.

Both approaches exploit the same fundamental principle: when negative synergies outweigh consolidation benefits, the sum of the parts exceeds the whole. Yet the execution challenges differ dramatically. Complete de-conglomeration requires orchestrating multiple simultaneous separations while maintaining operational continuity across diverse business units. Selective carve-outs demand precision in identifying which assets to shed while ensuring the remaining business benefits from improved focus and capital allocation.

Modern PE practitioners have refined both playbooks considerably since the crude asset stripping of the 1980s. Today's successful carve-outs require surgical precision rather than blunt force, with particular success emerging in specialized sectors like healthcare and life sciences where regulatory complexity and operational specialization create natural separation opportunities.

7.1.2.1 The Strategic Distinction: Complete Transformation vs. Focused Optimization The difference between complete de-conglomeration and selective carve-outs goes beyond mere scale—it reflects fundamentally different strategic objectives and value creation mechanisms. Complete de-conglomeration transforms the entire corporate structure, often triggered by persistent conglomerate discounts that can reach 10–15% of market value. Companies like General Electric, Johnson & Johnson, and Toshiba exemplify this approach, splitting themselves into focused entities that can pursue distinct capital allocation strategies aligned with their specific industry dynamics.

Selective carve-outs, by contrast, serve as portfolio optimization tools that allow companies to monetize noncore assets while strengthening their core business focus. The parent company typically retains the majority of operations and uses proceeds to invest in higher-return opportunities or reduce leverage. This approach proves particularly effective when companies identify specific business units that would benefit from different ownership structures or management approaches while the core business remains strategically sound.

The financial implications differ substantially. Complete de-conglomeration often requires significant transaction costs—averaging 1% of consolidated revenue—and extended timelines of 12–18 months. Selective carve-outs can move more quickly but require careful analysis of stranded costs and operational dependencies that may not be immediately apparent.

7.1.2.2 The Nature of Negative Synergies Negative synergies manifest in several distinct forms that PE practitioners must identify and quantify. Operational inefficiency occurs when diverse business units compete for management attention, resulting in mediocre oversight across all divisions rather than excellence in any single area. Cultural misalignment creates internal friction when incompatible business cultures are forced under one roof, leading to confused decision-making and employee disengagement. Capital misallocation represents perhaps the most damaging form, where resources flow from high-performing units to subsidize underperforming divisions, destroying shareholder value in the process. Finally, strategic distraction dilutes leadership focus, preventing management from capitalizing on genuine growth opportunities within individual business units.

These negative synergies often compound over time, creating what researchers term the "conglomerate discount"—the valuation penalty that diversified firms typically suffer relative to their focused peers. This discount provides the fundamental arbitrage opportunity that PE firms exploit through strategic separations, whether complete or selective.

7.1.2.3 Historical Evolution: From Raiders to Regulators The carve-out strategy originated in the aggressive 1980s, when pioneering raiders like Carl Icahn, Victor Posner, and Nelson Peltz developed what became known as asset stripping. These early practitioners operated in a regulatory environment that provided few protections for employees or communities, leading to substantial public backlash. The regulatory response was swift and decisive, with lawmakers implementing stronger oversight mechanisms to prevent wanton destruction of industrial assets.

The 1980s wave of de-conglomeration coincided with three critical regulatory changes that supported LBO activity: the failure of Carter's tax reforms, ERISA modifications allowing pension fund investment in PE, and Reagan's Economic Recovery Tax Act lowering capital gains taxes. These changes created the perfect storm for conglomerate breakups, as PE funds suddenly had both the capital and tax incentives to pursue aggressive acquisition strategies.

However, the crude asset stripping of the 1980s gave way to more sophisticated approaches as regulations tightened and institutional investors demanded better stewardship. Modern carve-outs require careful attention to transition service agreements, IT disentanglement, and operational continuity—areas where the early raiders often left destruction in their wake.

7.1.2.4 The Modern Pharma Opportunity Biopharma has emerged as particularly fertile ground for PE carve-outs, driven by the sector's inherent specialization requirements and regulatory complexity. Pharmaceutical companies have led this trend, with major players like Sanofi, Novartis, and others systematically divesting noncore assets to focus on high-margin innovative medicines.

The outsourcing wave in pharmaceuticals has created numerous carve-out opportunities through both complete de-conglomeration and selective divestitures. Large pharmas have spun out manufacturing facilities to create independent CDMOs (contract development and manufacturing organizations), breathing new life into aging assets while reducing fixed costs.

The dynamics of patent cliffs create particularly compelling opportunities for this transformation (Figure 7.3). Patent cliffs leave single-product manufacturing sites underutilized, creating stranded assets.

The problem becomes acute because pharmaceutical production lines are typically configured for specific drugs, making retooling complex and expensive. Unlike the original owner, who faces declining volumes and shrinking margins for the off-patent product, an independent CDMO can transform these underutilized assets by offering manufacturing services across the entire pharmaceutical industry. This expanded customer base allows CDMOs to target full capacity utilization, breathing commercial life back into plants that would otherwise become liability drains for their former parents.

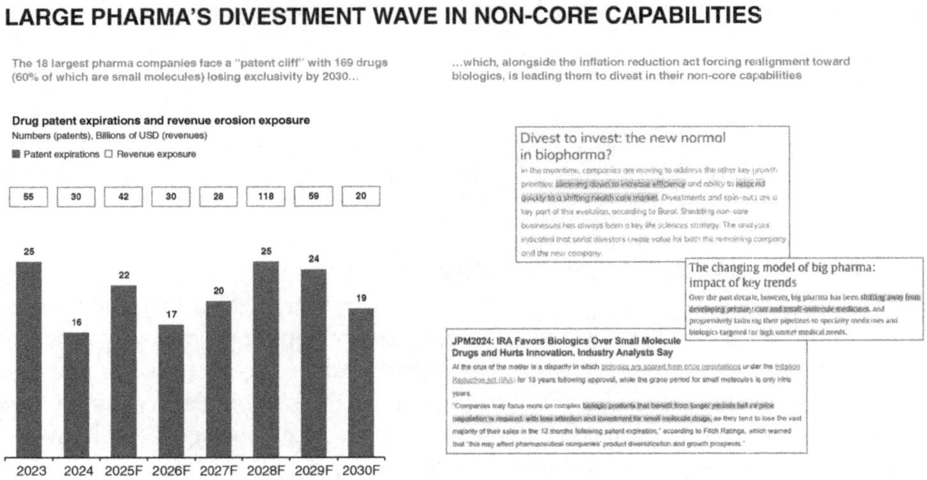

FIGURE 7.3 Large pharma's divestments.
Source: Market reports; Candesic analysis.

In one notable case we worked on, a global pharma attempted to bind the buyer to exclusive production.

PE investors are particularly eager to invest and support the management team in an MBO when they can negotiate keeping a few years of business from the original owner, creating some recurring revenue.

The strategic advantage becomes clear when considering operational flexibility. A pharmaceutical company managing its own plant for an off-patent drug must balance the declining economics of that specific product against the fixed costs of maintaining the facility. CDMOs eliminate this constraint by serving multiple clients with varying production schedules, allowing them to optimize capacity utilization across their entire portfolio. This model proves particularly effective for specialized manufacturing capabilities—such as sterile injectables, high-potency APIs, or complex biologics—where the CDMO can leverage expensive, purpose-built infrastructure across numerous customer relationships rather than being locked into a single product's declining trajectory.

Simtra BioPharma Solutions is a prominent recent example. Created in 2023 from Baxter's BioPharma Solutions business, Advent International and Warburg Pincus acquired the assets for \$4.25 billion. The new CDMO operates manufacturing sites in Bloomington, Indiana, and Halle, Germany, with approximately 1,700 employees providing sterile contract manufacturing solutions and parenteral delivery systems (Advent, n.d.).

Recipharm represents a major platform and compelling story in the pharmaceutical CDMO sector. The company systematically expanded by acquiring pharmaceutical sites, including Sanofi's CMO business in Holmes Chapel, United Kingdom, in 2018. EQT took the Swedish CDMO private in 2021, completing the acquisition at a premium price of approximately \$2.9 billion, and continued to develop Recipharm as a buy-and-build platform. In 2022, Recipharm announced several acquisitions in the advanced therapeutics market, including American CDMO Arranta Bio Holdings and German CDMO Vibalogics—both backed by Ampersand—expanding its capabilities in biologics and viral vector manufacturing. In 2024, having reinforced its core activities, EQT optimized Recipharm's portfolio by carving out the inhaled and nasal drug delivery devices and drug-device combination products under Bespak, which remained an EQT-owned global CDMO. Simultaneously, seven Recipharm sites across Europe focused on oral solid dosage forms were sold to Blue Wolf Capital, who combined them with Synerlab to form Meribel Pharma Solutions. These facilities were specifically carved out to create a more focused and operationally efficient platform (EQT, n.d.).

PCI Pharma Services is a textbook example of how a carve-out can rapidly evolve under successive PE owners with a deliberate M&A playbook. The company took shape in 2012 when Frazier Healthcare Partners led the acquisition of US commercial pharmaceutical packaging operations from Catalent Pharma Solutions Inc., owned by the Blackstone Group.

Partners Group, which had served as an LP of Frazier on the initial PCI deal, became the majority owner of PCI in 2016, at a valuation of just over $1 billion. During this period, the company focused on expanding its packaging and manufacturing capabilities, primarily through acquisition of additional assets and sites.

In 2020, as reported by Private Equity Insights, in concert with ongoing investors Thomas H. Lee Partners and Frazier Healthcare Partners, Partners Group sold a majority stake in PCI to Kohlberg & Co. and Mubadala Investment Co. These new owners accelerated PCI's buy-and-build strategy. Over the next several years, PCI expanded internationally and doubled its site count, notably through the acquisition and integration of additional pharmaceutical manufacturing facilities.

By 2025, Bain Capital—together with Kohlberg—had taken a controlling interest in PCI through a strategic investment round. Mubadala also reinvested alongside them in a deal that valued the company at $10 billion. The other prior investors retained minority positions. PCI operated 30 sites spread across North America, Europe, and Australia. The company had more than doubled its scale through this highly PE-driven growth and acquisition model but had seen its value multiplied by 10 in nine years. PCI's valuation surge reflects a transition from a commodity-driven aggregator to a sophisticated, global CDMO platform, precisely the type of transformation that PE loves (and pays up for).

The trend has expanded beyond traditional manufacturing into specialized services. Pharma companies now routinely carve out medical affairs, regulatory affairs, pharmacovigilance, and medical communications functions, as well as entire verticals such as consumer health. These separations allow both the parent company and the carved-out entity to pursue focused strategies—the parent concentrates on drug discovery and development, while the service provider develops expertise across multiple therapeutic areas and client relationships.

7.1.2.5 The Medtech Opportunity The medical technology sector also presents some attractive carve-out opportunities as large corporations struggle to maintain focus across diverse product portfolios. Companies like Medtronic, Edwards Lifesciences, and Baxter regularly announce plans to divest noncore units, creating opportunities for PE firms to acquire potentially undervalued assets through selective carve-outs. These divestitures often involve respiratory, monitoring, or renal care businesses that, while profitable, lack strategic importance within the parent company's core focus areas.

PE firms have shown remarkable success in revitalizing these carved-out medtech assets through focused operational improvements, strategic investments in neglected product lines, and subsequent roll-up opportunities. The fragmented nature of many medtech subsectors provides abundant targets for consolidation, allowing PE-backed platforms to negotiate better terms with hospitals and payers while achieving operational synergies.

7.1.2.6 Regional Success Stories North America provides compelling examples of successful healthcare carve-outs across both complete and selective approaches. Johnson & Johnson's announced split into consumer healthcare and pharmaceutical segments in 2021 represents complete de-conglomeration, recognizing that the businesses require fundamentally different strategic approaches and capital allocation frameworks.

Europe has witnessed equally dramatic success stories, with the Menix case serving as a textbook example of systematic value creation through strategic carve-outs. Turenne Capital, a small French PE firm, initially merged two rival implant companies, Dedienne Sante and SERF, in 2009. It sold a majority stake to LBO Partners and Keensight in 2014, who passed it in 2017 to Five Arrows, a Rothschild investment subsidiary. In 2024, Menix found it difficult to attract a new investor. Our PE clients could not justify synergies between dental and orthopedic implants. In fact, they had not materialized in 15 years of PE ownership. Guided by Natixis Partners' advisory expertise, the company split to maximize value for all stakeholders. SERF, the orthopedic division, was sold to Stryker for more than €200 million, allowing the global medical device leader to expand its European presence while providing SERF with resources for international growth. Global D, the dental implant specialist, found a new home with Naxicap Partners at a valuation between €100 and 200 million, enabling aggressive expansion plans including buy-and-build strategies across multiple geographies.

Asia-Pacific has produced notable successes despite recent market volatility, with both complete transformations and selective divestitures creating value. South Korea's healthcare sector has attracted significant PE interest, while Japan's regulatory reforms have—finally—made carve-outs from large conglomerates more feasible. India continues to offer robust opportunities, particularly in the provider space and CDMO sector, where PE firms are building platforms through strategic acquisitions and targeted carve-outs.

7.1.2.7 Learning from Mistakes For a start, some carve-outs that look good on paper never get a chance to happen. They get canceled due to fierce internal resistance because someone from corporate realizes they will lose some P&L. It is a battle that the CEO may decide is not worth starting.

Michael Thanner, from Triton Partners, mentioned that about 50% of their PortCos were carve-outs and shared his experience that "during due diligence of a carveout, it is important to spend time not only with the C-suite but to involve the next level of management."

For Rajib Arjun at Altius,

PE-backed carve-outs are anything but cozy and slow-moving. One global mid-market fund, with a significant US presence, we've been associated with since 2014 always has Executive team A, B and C. The shelf life to deliver results was 1–2 quarters, else it was rip-and-replace Team A, with B, and so on.

Then, once started, not every carve-out succeeds, and understanding failure modes is crucial for PE practitioners pursuing either complete de-conglomeration or selective divestitures. Operational entanglement represents the most common pitfall, where carved-out businesses remain dependent on parent company systems, creating ongoing vulnerabilities and transition costs. Loss of scale advantages can devastate businesses that relied upon the parent's bargaining power or shared services, particularly in procurement and distribution.

Talent drain poses another significant risk, as uncertainty during carve-out transitions often drives key employees to competitors. Underestimated standalone costs frequently catch buyers off-guard, as businesses that appeared profitable within a conglomerate structure struggle to cover previously shared overhead expenses.

The complexity varies significantly between complete de-conglomeration and selective carve-outs. Complete breakups face the additional challenge of managing multiple simultaneous separations while maintaining operational continuity across all business units. Some GE breakup units have struggled without the conglomerate's financial backing and supply chain advantages, highlighting the importance of thorough due diligence and realistic standalone planning for each separated entity.

What next?

Healthcare and life sciences continue to offer compelling opportunities for carve-out and sometimes full dismantling, driven by specialization requirements and the ongoing trend toward outsourcing noncore functions. However, the margin for error has narrowed considerably as competition intensifies and regulatory oversight increases. The most successful carve-outs combine operational expertise, patient capital, and deep sector knowledge—attributes that separate sophisticated PE operators from mere financial engineers.

The Menix example demonstrates that thoughtful carve-out strategies can create value for all stakeholders when executed with precision and market insight. As conglomerates continue to face pressure to optimize their portfolios, PE firms that master both the art of complete transformation and the precision of selective divestiture will find abundant opportunities to generate superior returns while creating more efficient market structures.

7.1.3 S03: Take-Private

As we discussed in Chapter 2, take-privates are an opportunity to buy compagnies that are struggling or disappointing in public markets. Hg's acquisition of Allocate Software in 2013 was a case in point. There was limited financial market activity, and the share price was perceived as lagging, offering ample room for a 35% premium (Figure 7.4).

IK Partners' 2023 take-private strategy for Medica focused on leveraging its strong position in the United Kingdom and Ireland's teleradiology market and expanding its clinical trials division in the US, enabling multi-year growth strategies that are less feasible in public markets (Lewis, 2023b). We share more case studies illustrating the angles of value creation typically developed during the bidding process.

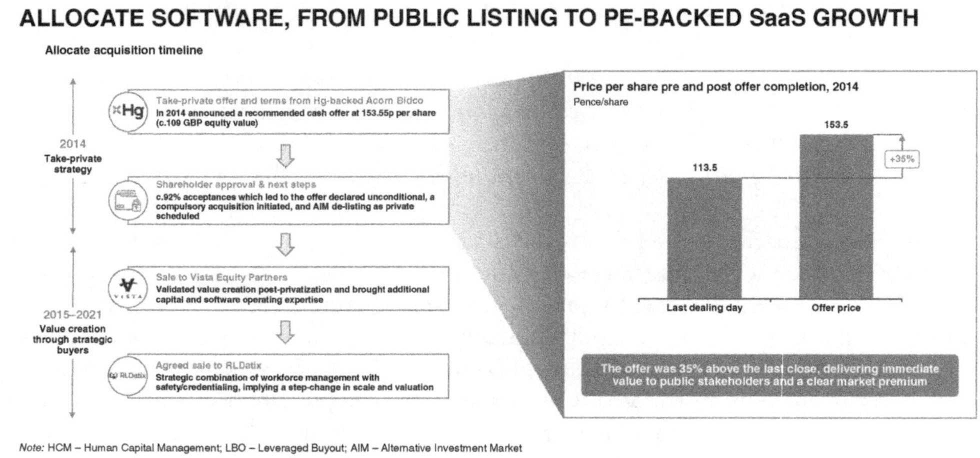

FIGURE 7.4 Allocate Software take-private.
Source: London South East; *The Wall Street Journal*; Candesic analysis.

7.1.3.1 Representative Examples

Case Study 1: Alliance Boots (KKR & Stefano Pessina, 2007–2015) KKR's £11.1 billion leveraged buyout of Alliance Boots in 2007—Europe's largest LBO at the time—demonstrates how PE can transform a fragmented healthcare player into a global leader. Before the LBO, Alliance Unichem (a wholesale pharmaceutical distributor) had merged with Boots (a UK pharmacy retailer) to create vertical integration. The company was listed on the London Stock Exchange (LSE) and was the first Financial Times Stock Exchange 100 firm to be taken private by a PE group. Following the LBO, KKR and Stefano Pessina (Alliance Boots' largest shareholder) expanded into emerging markets, acquiring a 12% stake in China's Nanjing Pharmaceutical and extending Almus, a proprietary generics division, beyond its UK origins to establish operations in France, Spain, Italy, and Portugal by 2013. Operational improvements, including centralized procurement and store modernization, boosted EBITDA from £1.1 billion (2007) to £2.3 billion (2014). The exit via a two-stage sale to Walgreens (45% in 2012, 55% in 2014) generated a 3× return for KKR, validating the strategy of leveraging mergers and internationalization to create value in healthcare.

We identify here some of the other levers of value creation that were implemented by KKR:

- Vertical integration: Merging complementary businesses to capture margin expansion (Alliance Boots achieved cumulative synergies of ~£300 million through procurement integration and distribution scale-ups) while expanding control over key supply chain assets across Europe. Building on the foundational 2006 merger between Alliance UniChem (wholesale distribution) and Boots (retail pharmacy), KKR and Stefano Pessina recognized that vertical integration represented a core competitive advantage in healthcare retail.
- International expansion in core markets: Strategic acquisitions and organic growth opportunities across Europe, building on Alliance UniChem's existing wholesale distribution network. This geographic diversification reduced dependence on the UK market and created opportunities for cross-border synergies.

- Emerging market expansion: Targeting high-growth regions (e.g., China, India) to offset saturated domestic markets, as seen in Alliance Boots' 50:50 joint venture with Guangzhou Pharmaceuticals Corporation in 2008, followed by a 12% stake acquisition in Nanjing Pharmaceutical in 2012 (completed in 2014). By then, Alliance Boots had stakes in both China's fourth and fifth largest pharmaceutical wholesalers through these two distinct transactions. Stefano Pessina stated at the time that he expected these investments to eventually lead to a 20–30% share of China's pharmaceutical distribution market.
- Operational streamlining: Centralizing procurement, improving inventory management systems, modernizing IT systems, digitizing supply chain.
- Store modernization: Upgrading Boots' retail locations, improving store layouts, product merchandising, and customer experience. These improvements helped drive same-store sales growth and enhanced the brand's competitive position against other UK pharmacy chains.
- Financial engineering and debt management: KKR demonstrated sophisticated financial management during the global financial crisis by purchasing Alliance Boots' own debt at substantial discounts in secondary markets. This opportunistic move reduced the company's debt burden while creating immediate equity value for shareholders. The strategy proved particularly effective given Alliance Boots' strong cash generation capabilities during the economic downturn. The firm also optimized the capital structure throughout the holding period, refinancing debt at favorable rates and managing leverage ratios to maximize financial flexibility.
- Strategic exits via trade sale: Aligning with industry consolidators seeking global scale to monetize scaled platforms. Here, ideal timing with Walgreens generated 3×+ returns.

The absence of major sales of noncore assets during KKR ownership (Almus would be sold later by new owner Walgreens) contrasts with typical take-private strategies that often involve aggressive portfolio rationalization. Instead, according to Mergermarket on organic growth, KKR's approach centered on operational improvements and strategic expansion.

Overall, these drivers highlight PE's ability to unlock value in healthcare by combining financial engineering with operational expertise, particularly in fragmented markets ripe for consolidation.

Case Study 2: Medica Group (IK Partners, 2023) With the support of Candesic, IK Partners acquired UK-listed teleradiology leader Medica Group Plc (LSE: MGP) in July 2023 for £269 million, at a 33% premium to the pre-announcement closing price. Founded in 2004 and headquartered in Hastings, Medica provided teleradiology reporting to more than 100 NHS trusts and the Irish HSE, alongside imaging services for clinical trials in the United States through its RadMD subsidiary. Public-market scale had become a constraint rather than a platform: the company struggled to attract investor attention and trading liquidity on the LSE despite its market-leading position in a structurally attractive niche.

Key value-creation levers implemented post-close included the following:

- International expansion: Accelerating growth of RadMD in the US imaging-trial market and broadening the teleradiology network beyond the UK and Ireland

- M&A acceleration: Deploying capital to pursue bolt-on acquisitions—such as Axon Diagnostics—without public-market scrutiny of short-term dilution
- Technology investment: Committing capital to workflow automation, AI-enabled reporting tools, and clinician-network platforms that required multi-year payback profiles
- Operational focus: Removing the cost and distraction of LSE disclosure requirements and aligning management incentives with long-term value creation through private equity structures

By taking Medica private, IK created room for a longer-dated, M&A-heavier growth agenda than public markets would reward—a classic take-private logic where the sponsor's ability to invest through earnings cycles outweighs the premium paid at entry.

7.1.3.2 Drivers of Success in Take-Private Key drivers of successful healthcare take-privates include specialized repositioning away from diversified public company structures toward focused, high-margin segments, operational transformation enabled by private ownership's longer investment horizons, and strategic expansion unconstrained by quarterly earnings pressures. Scale-driven consolidation through vertical integration and geographic expansion creates defensible competitive positions that justify premium valuations at exit. Portfolio optimization through strategic divestitures focuses resources on core assets while eliminating public market complexity. These strategies leverage PE's ability to make long-term investments, pursue complex restructuring, and execute multi-year transformation plans that would face resistance from public market shareholders focused on quarterly performance.

7.1.3.3 CBPO and the Case of the Chinese Orphans Headquartered in Beijing, China, China Biologic Products (CBPO) initially entered the US market by merging into Logic Express in July 2006. This initial reverse merger provided an active SEC-reporting vehicle and over-the-counter market trading. On November 25, 2009, the common stock of CBPO was approved for listing on the NASDAQ. This at a time of broader skepticism of Chinese backdoor listings that was creating a market of undervalued, neglected firms—often called "Chinese orphans."

Chinese reverse mergers faced heavy scrutiny from 2009, following financial restatements and growing suspicions of frauds. There were close to 500 Chinese companies listed in the United States at the time, most of them through the backdoor. Their share prices would soon halve on average, leading some PE firms to consider them to be bargain acquisitions paired with direct access to the Chinese market. The first to be taken private was a company called China Fire & Security, successfully acquired by Bain Capital in 2011 and delisted in 2012 (Gromb and Kitten, 2016).

CBPO allegedly navigated this environment through a combination of robust due diligence, strong sponsor backing, and adherence to US listing standards. Its success was built on several key factors: a reverse merger vehicle with clean financials and up-to-date SEC filings; full US GAAP financial statements audited by one of the "Big Four" accounting firms to assuage concerns about opaque Chinese accounting practices; and anchor PIPE (Private Investment in Public Equity) investors—namely, US and global institutional funds—with experience in Chinese healthcare. The company also publicly disclosed detailed information on its plasma-collection network, including regulatory approvals from China's National Medical Products Administration. By meeting—and in some cases exceeding—the SEC's disclosure requirements, CBPO differentiated itself from earlier shell-backed frauds.

The plasma-based biopharmaceutical company operated on NASDAQ for nearly a decade. In spite of some corporate governance issues (founder disputes, inventory management challenges), it benefited from China's plasma market expansion and the company's operational scale-up, with the share price climbing from $10 to over $80. In September 2019, a buyer consortium led by Centurium Capital, along with CITIC Capital, Hillhouse Capital, Temasek, and management, sent a preliminary nonbinding proposal to privatize the company, at a 21% premium to the one-month volume-weighted average price (VWAP). Following an initial rejection, it finally completed in April 2021 at $120 per share, a $4.76 billion valuation. The privatization was one of the largest healthcare deals in China at the time and won AVCJ's "Deal of the Year—Large Cap" award.

The consortium based its investment thesis on three pillars: the secular growth of China's plasma-based therapy market, CBPO's underleveraged balance sheet and ability to accelerate facility rollouts, and the opportunity to enhance R&D pipelines away from quarterly reporting pressures. Post-take-private, management consolidated manufacturing into three regional hubs, secured exclusive plasma-collection partnerships, and initiated a late-stage trial for an IVIG (intravenous immunoglobulin) next-generation formulation. Since delisting, CBPO has completed two capacity expansions in Hebei and Sichuan provinces, increasing output by 60%, and was on track to file a BLA (Biologics License Application) in China by 2026 under its new private ownership.

Chinese orphans in healthcare/life sciences available at steep discounts for PE investors are scarce, but this reflects the sector's unique regulatory complexity rather than effective fraud filtering. Healthcare companies face heightened FDA scrutiny requiring multiregional trials, different patient population considerations, and more complex regulatory pathways that make successful US listings inherently more challenging for Chinese firms, regardless of corporate governance quality.

7.1.4 S04: Portfolio Synergies and Cross-platform Value Creation

This strategy involves structural coordination and integration across portfolio companies to create value through the following:

- Shared services platforms
- Cross-portfolio procurement and supply chain optimization
- Knowledge and best practice transfer
- Cross-selling opportunities between portfolio companies
- Consolidated back-office functions

Rather than viewing each investment in isolation, PE firms leverage synergies that emerge when portfolio companies collaborate or share resources, thereby generating operational efficiencies, cost reductions, and revenue enhancements at a broader scale.

One key area of synergy is the establishment of shared services platforms. By consolidating functions such as human resources, IT, finance, or legal services across several portfolio companies, PE firms can significantly reduce overhead costs and improve service quality through centralized expertise and technology. This approach eliminates duplicated efforts while allowing portfolio companies to maintain their core operational focus.

Procurement and supply chain optimization represent another fruitful synergy avenue. Coordinated buying across portfolio companies can boost bargaining power with suppliers, streamline inventory management, and lower operational risks. For example, a PE firm that owns several manufacturing businesses might consolidate supplier contracts, reducing the number of vendors and gaining volume discounts, thereby improving margins across the portfolio. Such procurement synergies can also extend to logistics and distribution networks, allowing companies to leverage scale.

Knowledge transfer and best practice sharing promote value creation by spreading operational, strategic, and managerial insights throughout the portfolio. This could take the form of cross-company workshops, internal consulting teams, or centralized data analytics functions that identify successful growth levers or productivity enhancements applied by one portfolio company and replicate them elsewhere. The dissemination of talent and innovation boosts overall portfolio resilience and performance.

Cross-selling opportunities between portfolio companies further enhance revenue. Companies with complementary products or service lines can introduce each other's offerings to their customer bases, expanding market reach without incurring additional customer acquisition costs. A PE investor may facilitate joint sales efforts or bundled product offerings to accelerate growth organically.

Finally, many PE investors pursue consolidation of back-office functions to drive scale benefits. Areas such as accounting, compliance, and administrative tasks can be centralized to avoid redundant staffing and overhead, improving cost efficiency while allowing portfolio leadership teams to focus on strategic growth initiatives.

All these initiatives can be identified and implemented dynamically by a PE firm through a typical strategic planning program where the strategic priorities get implemented at portfolio level, as opposed to business level in a corporate (Figure 7.5).

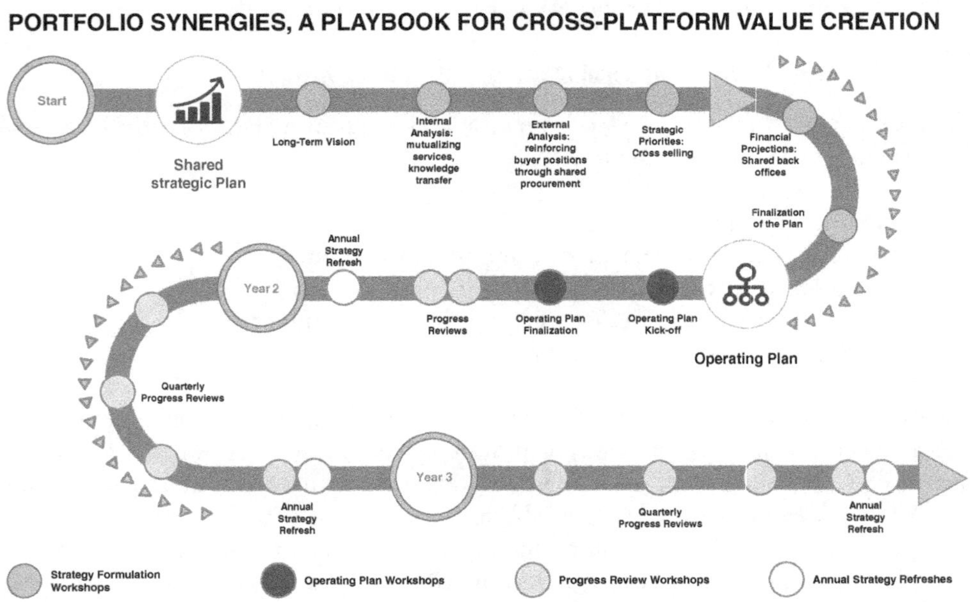

FIGURE 7.5 Candesic tech-enabled strategic planning program.
Source: Candesic strategy in action.

7.1.4.1 Case Study 1: Manufacturing Shared Services Center A PE-backed manufacturing company, as documented by advisory firm Alvarez & Marsal, established a shared services center in Eastern Europe covering finance, customer service, and order management functions across multiple portfolio companies. The captive center allowed the PE firm to control key customer-facing processes while achieving substantial cost savings through geographic arbitrage. By standardizing processes and implementing automation across the shared platform, the company achieved measurable improvements in both service quality and cost benchmarks. This centralized approach eliminated redundant back-office operations while maintaining dedicated customer relationships, demonstrating how operational synergies can simultaneously reduce costs and enhance service delivery.

This portfolio synergy strategy leverages the collective scale and expertise of the PE firm's portfolio and transforms it into a competitive advantage. It requires active portfolio management and coordination, often supported by dedicated operating teams or value creation groups within the PE firm. Research by Alvarez and Marsal (2023) shows that PE-backed shared services centers in low-cost regions can reduce back-office FTE costs by 20–30% while improving process cycle times by up to 40%. Anna Silvestri from PAI Partners remains prudent and cautions against forgetting the limits of this approach: "A crucial point is what the fund will do when it wants to exit one of the portfolio companies sharing the service or benefiting from sharing services. How to allocate the value there?"

7.1.4.2 Case Study 2: Procurement at Scale (Blackstone, Carlyle, Hellman and Friedman, and Medline) In Chapter 2, we analyzed the 2021 acquisition of Medline Industries for $34 billion by a consortium of Blackstone, Carlyle, and Hellman & Friedman. This landmark deal centered on supply chain excellence. Medline is one of the largest manufacturers and distributors of medical supplies in the United States, and it also operates a major GPO (group purchasing organization). The investment thesis was not just about Medline's own operations, but about its strategic position at the heart of the healthcare supply chain. For the PE sponsors, Medline serves as a platform to drive procurement efficiencies across their extensive healthcare portfolios. By encouraging their other portfolio companies (e.g., hospital systems, physician groups) to leverage Medline's purchasing power and distribution network, the firms can achieve significant cost savings at scale, creating a powerful portfolio-wide synergy.

7.1.4.3 Case Study 3: Montagu's Three-way Portfolio Merger (Intech, Resolve Surgical, and Tyber Medical) The ultimate portfolio strategy is to merge portfolio companies that were not necessarily designed to be combined, unlocking hidden synergies and value through strategic integration. Montagu's 2025 three-way merger—uniting Intech, Resolve Surgical, and Tyber Medical—is a textbook case in the art (and agony) of complex portfolio integration. By anticipating multilayered synergies—across footprints, capabilities, and product lines—Montagu positioned the combined group—$300 million revenue—to lead the OEM outsourcing wave in MedTech, promising clients faster innovation, broader supply chain coverage, and one-stop regulatory expertise. Sassi, who led the original deals and this new merger, said:

> *Engagement and commitment to the transaction was actually led by [management] in the first place. It has been a very collaborative effort and they all share our conviction in industry trends to bring together a unique actor in the space, and they are all meaningfully financially participating in the transaction.*

Orchestrating such a deal was no walk in the park. Aligning French and US teams, weaving together management's buy-in, and carefully pacing every step, underscores not just financial engineering, but diplomatic choreography. Getting all stakeholders—including innovative clients—on board was not just a checkbox; it was the linchpin that made the anticipated synergies both credible and executable. In a market still full of corporate orphans and shifting industry boundaries, this deal proves that value creation hinges as much on people and timing as on spreadsheets and synergies (Lewis, 2025).

7.1.5 S05: Governance and Leadership

Beyond financial engineering or operational spreadsheets, the most impactful value creation lever in healthcare PE is often the strategic management of human capital at the highest levels. Strong governance and effective leadership are not just support functions; they are the core drivers that enable the successful execution of any investment thesis. This section explores two of the most critical and sensitive dimensions of this strategy: the decision to install new leadership and the essential process of achieving physician alignment.

7.1.5.1 New Leadership The central debate often revolves around a single question: should the CEO have a medical background? On one hand, a CEO with clinical training can inspire trust among staff, understand regulatory nuance, and navigate complex care delivery. This is especially relevant in hospital groups or advanced specialty clinics. For example, a study of US hospital systems found that organizations led by physician-CEOs frequently scored higher on quality metrics (Tasi et al., 2019). On the other hand, many healthcare businesses, particularly large-scale roll-ups or diagnostics platforms, require deep operational or financial expertise at the helm. In these cases, a nonclinical CEO can drive efficiencies and scale the business, typically by partnering closely with a strong chief medical officer (CMO) to ensure clinical integrity.

Strong leadership correlates with portfolio outperformance. Sponsors often establish internal "leadership academies" to rotate high-potential executives across assets, accelerating capability transfer and fostering a unified culture. For example, CD&R's 2022 "Leadership Pipeline" program placed 25 alumni into C-suite roles across its healthcare platforms, driving an average 12% uplift in EBITDA at successor-led companies.

Developing a culture-driven performance is part of this leadership development. The chief people officer has moved into the C-suite, partnering with CEOs and CFOs to drive productivity, compliance, and resource management. Insights from the Compass Carter Osborne 2025 CPO Roundtable Report highlight practical initiatives such as mapping career paths via "tube-map" models, deploying self-service rostering tools that boost payroll efficiency by up to 10%, and using colleague-experience metrics (e.g., NPS) to forecast top-line growth—a 7–8% NPS lift correlates with roughly 20% revenue growth.

Case Study: The Two CEOs of Athenahealth The case of Athenahealth, a leading provider of electronic health records (EHR) and practice management software, illustrates this tension. The company was cofounded and led for over two decades by Jonathan Bush, a charismatic leader with deep family roots in politics and business but not a clinical background, who built it into a major industry player before stepping down in 2018.

Shortly after Bush's departure and the 2019 take-private by Veritas Capital and Evergreen Coast Capital, the PE sponsors installed Bob Segert, a seasoned executive with a strong track record in software and healthcare IT, as chairman and CEO to bring strategic direction and operational discipline, focusing on product innovation and market expansion under proven nonclinical leadership. This strategy proved successful, culminating in a $17 billion sale to Hellman & Friedman and Bain Capital in 2022, demonstrating the value that can be created by installing an operationally focused leader in a complex healthcare technology company.

7.1.5.2 Physician Alignment Many PE investors have struggled with their doctors and other health practitioners when trying to modernize and optimize health operations. There is an inherent conflict between the search for profit and the Hippocratic Oath. The savvy investors recognize this and are careful to establish the right balance, leaving a lot of decision-making to the health practitioners, mostly the physicians, and getting their buy-in.

In healthcare, governance involving physicians is critical since they have a unique expertise in assessing the essential quality stakes. As Laurent Dethomas from Vivalto Partners emphasizes, "those who generate the revenue are often visionary shareholders in the organization they work for." Their strategy prioritizes partnerships with entrepreneurial physicians who "put their shoulder to the wheel" by sharing ownership and governance. This approach not only signals sector expertise at entry and builds trust with stakeholders beyond price but also ensures sustained quality of products and services—a key success factor—and naturally aligns interests between investors and physician-managers through co-ownership.

This strategy aims to leverage the physicians' expertise and relationships to drive growth and improve operational efficiency, while also increasing their engagement and retention. Vivalto's co-ownership model is a typical case in point (Figure 7.6).

Successful Case Study: Audax Group and Gastro Health In 2016, Audax Group invested in Gastro Health, a platform of gastroenterology practices. A core element of the strategy

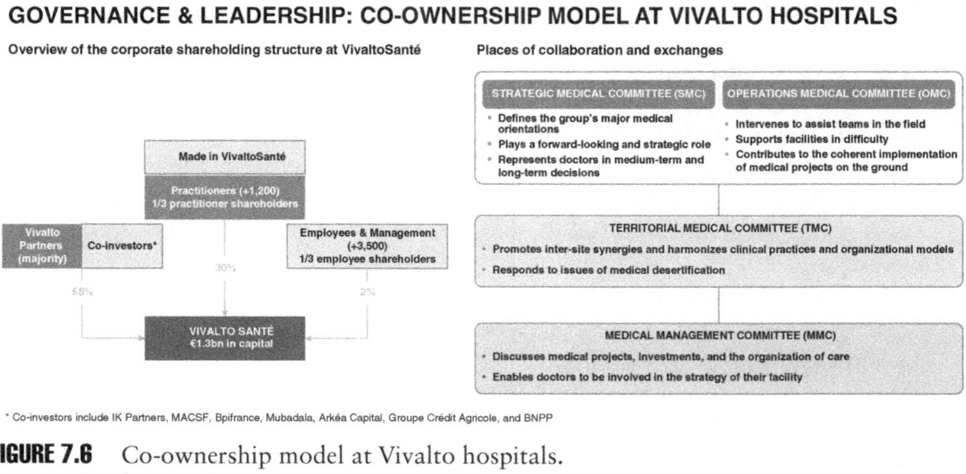

FIGURE 7.6 Co-ownership model at Vivalto hospitals.
Source: Candesic analysis.

was a deep partnership with the physicians. Doctors were given a significant equity stake in the combined enterprise and a strong voice in clinical governance. This alignment of interests fueled rapid growth through a disciplined buy-and-build strategy, expanding from 21 locations in South Florida to over 150 locations across six states and growing from 30+ to over 250 physician partners, as physicians became motivated partners in identifying and integrating new practices. The model was highly successful, leading to a sale of the company to OMERS Private Equity in 2021 at a significantly higher valuation (approximately $950 million EV, roughly 16× EBITDA), demonstrating how a true physician partnership can drive both clinical and financial success.

Cautionary Case Study: Blackstone and TeamHealth The case of TeamHealth introduced in Chapter 6 illustrates the risks of failed physician alignment in PE-backed healthcare ventures. Taken private again by Blackstone in a $6.1 billion leveraged buyout in 2016–2017, TeamHealth operates emergency rooms across 3,300 facilities with 16,000 healthcare providers through a controversial business model that has generated significant physician resistance. Emergency medicine physicians have actively challenged the company's practices through multiple lawsuits, arguing that TeamHealth's corporate structure violates state "corporate practice of medicine" laws by using physician professional associations as shell entities to circumvent regulations prohibiting corporate control of medical practices. The American Academy of Emergency Medicine has filed lawsuits in multiple states specifically targeting TeamHealth's ownership structure, while physicians like Dr. Marco Fernandez formed the Association for Independent Medicine to push back against such PE acquisitions. This physician resistance has contributed to operational disruptions, with hospitals losing anesthesia coverage during transitions. Combined with mounting debt pressures ($714 million in maturing obligations out of $2 billion debt) and the loss of surprise billing revenues following federal No Surprises Act legislation, TeamHealth has been labeled "at risk" by credit rating agencies, demonstrating how physician misalignment can compound financial vulnerabilities and threaten the sustainability of PE healthcare investments.

Outlook and Recommendations for Investors The importance of governance and leadership as a value creation strategy will only intensify as healthcare becomes more complex and competitive. PE investors should do the following:

- Develop a "leadership thesis": For every deal, have a clear and explicit thesis on whether the existing management team has the right skills for the next phase of growth and be prepared to make changes quickly if necessary.
- Prioritize physician alignment in due diligence: The quality of the physician partnership model should be a key diligence item. Investors should assess the culture, governance structure, and economic alignment of any physician group they plan to acquire.
- Build a bench of talent: Top-tier PE firms cultivate a network of proven healthcare executives who can be deployed into portfolio companies to drive change and provide expert oversight.
- Structure for true partnership: Move beyond simple equity offerings to create governance structures that give physicians a genuine voice in the strategic direction of the company, ensuring that the pursuit of financial returns does not compromise clinical quality.

By treating leadership and physician alignment as central pillars of their investment strategy, PE firms can build more resilient, reputable, and ultimately more valuable healthcare enterprises.

7.1.6 SO6: Tax Arbitrage

Tax arbitrage in healthcare-focused investing remains real but narrower post-BEPS, ATAD I/II, and GloBE.[3] It thrives in transfer pricing around CROs and IP (intellectual property) holding, timing/character of carry, and jurisdictional incentives (Ireland R&D/KDB, Singapore Pioneer/DEI). Several classic European structures (Luxembourg hybrids, Dutch CV–BV, Double Irish) have been curtailed, but legacy outcomes and successor incentives still matter. Transfer pricing scrutiny in life sciences is intense, with DEMPE and realistic-alternatives tests constraining aggressive profit shifting. UK reforms to non-dom status and carried interest materially changed manager-level arbitrage from 2025 to 2026. Australia's stapled structure reforms curtailed flow-through recharacterization that some PE-backed platforms used in health-adjacent infrastructure.

7.1.6.1 Opening Windows Sometimes, authorities will inadvertently open a window of opportunity in a tax jurisdiction. PE investors have access to sophisticated advice, they are astute and agile, and they will jump on the opportunity faster than most other institutional investors. We have seen how the carried interest provision in the United States has allowed PE firms to significantly reduce their tax liabilities on a large portion of their earnings. In a more specific example to health, PE-backed life sciences platforms and CRO groups face—and sometimes test—the limits of transfer pricing to shift profits to lower-tax jurisdictions, with tax authorities increasingly tying IP returns to DEMPE functions rather than nominal IP ownership. For instance, intellectual property developed through clinical trials might be held in a low-tax country, with higher-tax subsidiaries paying royalties for its use, but EU proposals to harmonize TP and growing audit intensity raise the bar on documentation and substance.

[3] Here is a quick decoder for all those alphabet soups—because tax folks really do speak their own language: BEPS (Base Erosion and Profit Shifting) is the OECD's crusade to stop companies from quietly siphoning profits to low-tax havens, while ATAD I/II (Anti-tax Avoidance Directives) are the EU's rulebooks to plug loopholes and harmonize anti-avoidance measures across member states. GloBE (Global Anti-base Erosion) sits at the heart of the OECD's Pillar Two minimum tax effort, making sure everyone pays at least a sliver of tax somewhere. CROs are contract research organizations—think outsourced laboratories and trial managers—while IP holding refers to the special legal boxes companies use to park patents and trademarks where the tax rate is friendliest. R&D/KDB (Research & Development tax credits and Korea's Knowledge Development Box) and Singapore's Pioneer/DEI (Development and Expansion Incentive) are just two examples of government bribes for innovating in their backyards. DEMPE (Development, Enhancement, Maintenance, Protection, and Exploitation) tests force life-science firms to prove where real value is created, and realistic-alternatives tests make them justify why profits should not rest where the R&D happens. Finally, UK non-dom (non-domiciled) tweaks reshaped expatriate tax breaks, and Australia's stapled structure reforms snapped shut a popular trick for flowing income through infrastructure vehicles.

Many other examples also relate to the VC stages: the Qualified Small Business Stock (QSBS) Exclusion in the United States allows for potentially significant capital gains tax savings on the sale of stock in certain small businesses, including many early stage biotech companies. VC firms investing in early stage life sciences companies have sometimes structured their investments to potentially qualify for this benefit. In Singapore, the Pioneer Status and the Development and Expansion Incentive have been particularly interesting for VC investors in the biotech and medical technology sectors. Companies granted Pioneer Status can enjoy full or partial exemption from corporate tax for up to 15 years. The Development and Expansion Incentive provides a concessionary tax rate of 5% or 10% on incremental income from qualifying activities.

Practical healthcare angle: CROs, CDMOs, specialty pharma, and medtech often centralize patents, software, data assets, or clinical know-how in IP vehicles in favorable regimes, while operating companies in major markets book routine returns; however, enforcement trends mean royalties, cost-sharing, and intercompany contract R&D charges must align to DEMPE, realistic alternatives, and local incentives interaction (e.g., France's R&D credit) to withstand audits.

7.1.6.2 Europe: Jurisdiction-specific Plays (and Their Closure) PE firms have also benefited from multiple opportunities linked to a specific jurisdiction, especially in Europe. We list some examples here.

In Luxembourg, the use of hybrid mismatch arrangements created temporary tax opportunities for PE firms. Hybrid mismatches involve financial instruments that are treated differently for tax purposes in two different jurisdictions. For example, an instrument might be treated as debt in one country (leading to interest deductions) and as equity in another (leading to tax-exempt dividends). This created a "double non-taxation" scenario, where income was untaxed in both jurisdictions. These outcomes have been targeted and neutralized via ATAD I (implemented December 2018) and ATAD II (effective 2020; reverse hybrids from 2022).

Also in Luxembourg, the IP box regime, introduced in 2008, allowed companies to benefit from an 80% tax exemption on income derived from the use and licensing of software copyrights, patents, and trademarks. This created opportunities for PE firms to structure investments in tech companies to take advantage of this regime. However, this regime was phased out in 2016 and replaced with a new IP regime in 2018 that is more restrictive. PE healthcare platforms with software and data assets took note, but newer rules require closer nexus to local R&D and are less generous.

In the Netherlands, PE firms have historically used CV-BV structures to reduce taxes. Under this structure, a limited partnership (CV) would be tax transparent in the Netherlands, meaning it was not taxed at the corporate level. The BV (limited liability company) could then receive dividends tax-free under Dutch participation exemption rules. This allowed PE firms to structure deals in a way that minimizes taxation. These structures allowed PE investors to shift income to low-tax jurisdictions, effectively reducing their tax burden. However, ATAD II reverse hybrid rules, and subsequent Dutch reforms have made this structure nonviable from 2022 onward, with further classification changes set for 2025.

In the United Kingdom, PE firms have historically benefitted from favorable tax treatment for non-domiciled individuals. Those who resided in the United Kingdom but had their permanent home outside the United Kingdom were able to use their "non-dom" status to shelter foreign earnings from UK taxes. This created opportunities for PE managers, who often structured themselves or their funds to benefit from this. The UK government has since moved to abolish non-dom status from April 2025, replacing it with a residence-based regime. In parallel, carried interest rules are being overhauled: a transition to 32% CGT in 2025/2026 and full income-tax treatment as deemed trading receipts from April 2026, with territorial safe harbors for nonresidents' limited UK workdays.

Ireland's Double Irish tax structure allowed many multinational corporations and PE firms to lower their tax burden by shifting IP to Irish and Dutch subsidiaries and using intra-company payments to move profits to low or no-tax jurisdictions like Bermuda. Before reforms closed this loophole in 2020, some PE investors took advantage of Ireland's favorable tax laws by structuring acquisitions in the healthcare (pharma) and technology sectors around Irish-based IP holding companies. They benefitted from favorable rates on royalties and other income streams generated by IP holdings. The Double Irish was grandfathered until end-2020; Ireland now competes with a 25% R&D tax credit (recently enhanced in payability) and a Knowledge Development Box at 6.25% effective rate, albeit with restrictive nexus. In addition, companies can claim a 25% tax credit on qualifying R&D expenditure, which can be used to offset corporation tax or, in some cases, claimed as a payable credit, making Ireland attractive for pharma and biotech R&D footprints.

In Australia, Stapled Structures allowed companies to separate their trading income from passive property income, often resulting in lower overall tax rates. They were particularly popular in the infrastructure and real estate sectors. While not exclusively a PE strategy, many PE firms investing in these sectors used stapled structures. In 2018, the government introduced an integrity package increasing the withholding tax rate on trading income (as opposed to passive investment income) to 30% and curtailing recharacterization; the Australian Taxation Office has maintained guidance and administration on these trading income provisions.

7.1.6.3 PE Examples in Healthcare-adjacent Tax Structuring

- CRO/CDMO transfer pricing scrutiny: Global life sciences groups—common PE targets—face heightened TP examination tying profits to DEMPE, affecting how IP centralization and intercompany royalties are priced, with extensive EU policy movement toward harmonization to reduce abuse and double taxation. This is not a loophole; it is a compliance battleground that narrows arbitrage.
- UK PE managers and carry: UK-based PE healthcare specialists have been directly affected by non-dom abolition in 2025 and the carried interest redesign toward income-tax treatment from April 2026, altering manager-level net outcomes even when portfolio companies remain abroad.
- Ireland R&D/KDB for pharma/biotech platforms: PE-backed pharma services and medtech platforms with Irish R&D footprints can benefit from the 25% R&D credit and KDB's 6.25% rate on qualifying income, subject to nexus and evolving Pillar Two interactions, a frequent structuring lever in post–Double Irish Ireland.

While claims of "double nontaxation" via hybrids and CV–BV are historically documented, transaction-level case studies of specific named PE deals with their tax structures are typically private. We provide here some brief case-style illustrations:

- A PE-backed CDMO migrates process patents to a Luxembourg IP company in 2014 and charges royalties to German and French ops. After ATAD I/II, deductions are challenged; DEMPE analysis reallocates more profit to operating entities, reducing royalty base, with hybrid denial rules preventing deduction-without-inclusion.
- A UK-based healthcare GP with non-dom partners historically remits minimal foreign tax on carry. From April 2025/2026, partners face non-dom abolition and carry taxed as deemed trading income; the fund introduces workday tracking and apportionment to leverage the 60-day safe harbor and mitigate double taxation for non-resident partners.
- A PE roll-up in diagnostics shifts incremental R&D to Ireland to utilize the 25% credit and evaluates KDB for software-related analytics IP; after Double Irish closure, structure relies on onshore substance with payable R&D credit mechanics to smooth cash flows.

In spite of tax authorities systematically closing loopholes, healthcare tax arbitrage has matured into a standalone PE investment strategy that exploits jurisdictional incentives and regulatory gaps to enhance risk-adjusted returns. It now demands not only creative structuring but also robust substance, meticulous documentation, and ongoing alignment with evolving global rules—success hinges on pairing technical expertise with genuine operational presence, because the window has not shut, it just swings on a sturdier hinge.

7.2 CEO PLAYBOOK

(Strategic growth, market positioning, and integration initiatives the CEO would drive)

7.2.1 S07: Turnaround

Turnaround is more than an investment strategy; it is a niche but full segment of PE, with its dedicated funds.

True turnarounds in healthcare are rare because distress often implies compromised clinical safety or regulatory failure, making equity recovery difficult.

7.2.1.1 Evotec AG and TVM Capital (2009): A Classic Life Sciences Turnaround TVM Capital's turnaround of Evotec AG represents an exemplary case of distressed life sciences investing that transformed a near-bankrupt company into a profitable enterprise. In March 2009, Evotec—a German drug discovery and development company—was trading at a market capitalization of just €60 million, having burned through cash and faced potential bankruptcy. TVM Capital, as a major shareholder, led a comprehensive restructuring under CEO Dr. Werner Lanthaler.

The turnaround strategy centered on transforming Evotec from a traditional R&D-focused biotech into a revenue-generating CRO. The "Evotec 2012—Action Plan to Focus and Grow" achieved dramatic results: R&D expenses were slashed by 50% and SG&A costs by 15%, while the company pivoted toward fee-for-service drug discovery partnerships. Despite significant restructuring, Evotec actually increased headcount by 300 people to 500 employees, demonstrating growth in core revenue-generating activities.

The financial transformation proved spectacular. Within nine months, Evotec's market capitalization surged from €60 million to €240 million—a 300% increase that validated the turnaround strategy. The company secured eight new collaborations or research agreements and completed two strategic acquisitions to enhance research capabilities, all while moving from cash burn to sustainable profitability. This performance earned Evotec the M&A Advisor Healthcare Turnaround Company of the Year award in 2010.

The company secured multiple high-profile collaborations, including strategic alliances with Genentech, extended partnerships with CHDI for Huntington's Disease research, and new agreements with Almirall and Shionogi. This partnership-driven model provided recurring revenue streams while reducing dependency on internal R&D funding.

Evotec's post-turnaround performance proved highly successful for a while, sustaining rapid growth for more than a decade and transforming into a major drug discovery platform with revenues exceeding €780 million by 2023.

TVM Capital's success stemmed from recognizing that Evotec's core drug discovery platform retained significant value despite financial distress. Rather than liquidating assets, TVM restructured operations around recurring revenue streams from pharmaceutical partnerships while maintaining essential R&D capabilities. The turnaround demonstrated how specialized life sciences expertise and patient capital can revive distressed biotech companies by repositioning business models rather than simply cutting costs. Evotec's transformation from near bankruptcy to industry recognition illustrates the potential for value creation in distressed life sciences investing when combined with operational expertise and strategic vision.

More common than true turnarounds are cases of low performing companies that a new PE owner will successfully revitalize. In this case, it is perhaps more appropriate to talk about transformation than turnaround.

7.2.1.2 Max Healthcare and KKR (2018–2024): A Remarkable Transformation in Healthcare KKR's turnaround of Max Healthcare in India stands as one of the most successful PE healthcare transformations on record. In 2018, this premium-branded hospital chain in North India had solid assets but disappointing margins. The company was struggling with cost inefficiencies, low profitability, and operational fragmentation across its 15 hospitals. EBITDA margins were stuck at a low 9.7%, despite commanding premium valuations in the market.

KKR deployed its signature "investor-operator" model. They acquired a 49.7% stake in the combined entity of Radiant Life Care and Max Healthcare for $200 million (valuing the business at $900 million). The decisive move was bringing in Abhay Soi, a proven turnaround specialist, and giving him a 23.1% equity stake to align his interests with value creation. According to *Forbes*, Soi had already demonstrated his skills by successfully turning around BLK Hospital and Nanavati Hospital in Mumbai.

Soi executed a comprehensive restructuring program across multiple dimensions:

- Cost cutting and supply chain optimization: Consolidated procurement across facilities, renegotiated supplier contracts, and eliminated corporate overhead redundancies. Agency labor usage was dramatically reduced from 40% of wages to minimal levels.
- Operational synergies: Merged previously separate medical tourism offices and streamlined back-office functions. The combined scale allowed for economies that neither entity could achieve independently.
- Revenue mix enhancement: Shifted focus to high-margin specialized services like knee replacements, spinal surgeries, and complex procedures. This significantly increased average revenue per occupied bed (ARPOB).
- Workforce restructuring: Realigned roles and responsibilities, reduced minimum guarantees in doctor fees, and optimized staffing levels to match occupancy patterns.

The transformation was remarkable. EBITDA margins surged almost threefold to 27.2% by FY2022. The company achieved a 32% compound annual growth rate in sales over three years. By 2024, Max Healthcare had become India's second-largest hospital chain by revenue and market capitalization, with more than 3,400 beds across 17 facilities.

In August 2024, KKR executed one of India's most successful PE exits, selling its remaining 27.5% stake and delivering a stunning 4.5× return in just four years. This represented KKR's most lucrative exit in India since entering the market 27 years earlier and set a new benchmark for PE returns in the country.

7.2.2 S08: Specialization and Focus

In an increasingly complex and competitive healthcare landscape, one of the most potent PE value creation strategies is Specialization and Focus. This approach involves concentrating resources, expertise, and capital on a narrow clinical, technological, or patient subsector to build a differentiated, high-value platform. Unlike broad diversification or horizontal integration, this strategy is about achieving market leadership and operational excellence through depth, not breadth. By creating "Centers of Excellence" or dominating a specific niche, PE sponsors can drive superior clinical outcomes and command premium valuations.

This strategy is distinct from a generic buy-and-build; while it often uses a platform-and-add-on consolidation model, the acquisitions are strictly curated to deepen expertise within a single, well-defined vertical. This section deconstructs this strategy into its three core pillars: clinical subsector specialization, high-acuity and high-volume models, and niche market domination.

7.2.2.1 The Three Pillars of the Specialization Strategy

Clinical Subsector Specialization The first and most common pillar involves identifying a fragmented but high-margin clinical specialty and consolidating it into a scaled, professionally managed platform. The thesis is that a focused provider network can achieve efficiencies and a level of clinical quality that is difficult for a generalist hospital system to replicate. Key specialties that have attracted PE investment include ophthalmology, dermatology, gastroenterology, and dentistry.

This approach creates a specialized asset that is highly attractive to strategic acquirers or for a public market listing.

High-acuity and High-volume Models (Centers of Excellence) This pillar focuses on creating highly efficient, specialized facilities for specific complex procedures or R&D, often in an outpatient setting or CROs (Figure 7.7). By concentrating surgical or procedural volume, these "Centers of Excellence" can standardize protocols, attract top clinical talent, and achieve superior efficiency and outcomes compared to generalist hospitals. For example, Bain Capital's backing of Surgery Partners from 2017 helped create a leading platform of ambulatory surgery centers (ASCs) that achieved superior efficiency for specific procedures compared to traditional hospital-based surgery departments. The core of this strategy is operational innovation to drive down costs while maintaining or improving quality. This involves standardizing workflows, optimizing the care pathway, and leveraging data.

Ampersand's investments often involve supply chain consolidation that improves efficiency for larger players. Operating primarily in B2B markets, Ampersand focuses on quality and service reliability rather than direct health outcomes. We mentioned in Chapter 8 their 2015 acquisition of Brammer Bio, whose reputation centered on scientific expertise, quality systems, and reliability. Thermo Fisher acquired more than a leading position in viral vectors; Brammer Bio also reinforced the efficiency of the company's supply chain.

These models demonstrate how specialization can lead to genuine productivity gains and create highly profitable, defensible businesses.

Niche Market Domination (Super-specialization) The third and most sophisticated pillar involves focusing on ultra-specialized, high-value areas of healthcare, such as

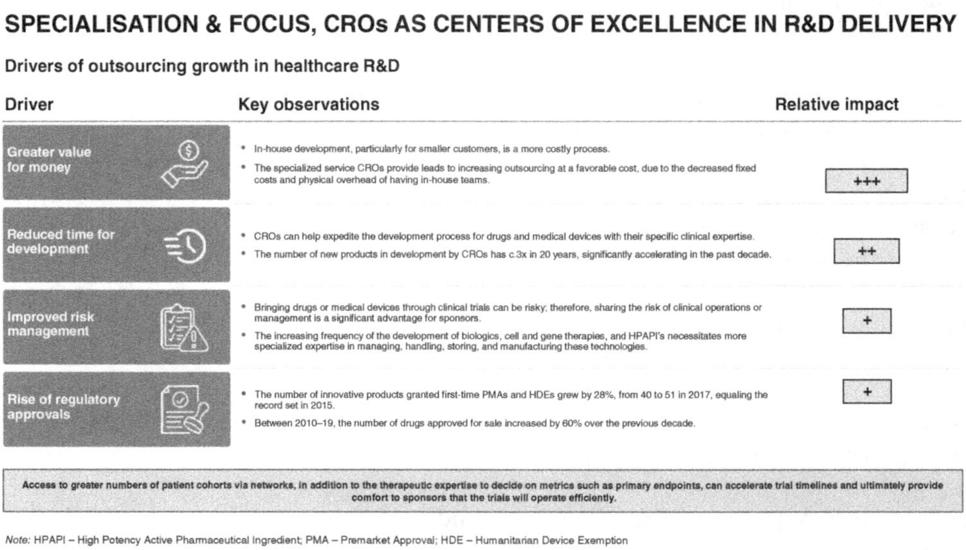

FIGURE 7.7 CROs as centers of excellence in R&D delivery.
Source: CBO.gov; Evaluate MedTech; Evaluate Pharma; Candesic analysis.

biologics, rare diseases, specific gene therapies, or niche diagnostics. The investment thesis here is to dominate a small but highly profitable market where deep scientific or clinical expertise creates a formidable barrier to entry. This strategy often involves investing in novel therapeutics for rare diseases, building longitudinal care platforms that manage the entire life cycle of a patient with a specific rare or chronic condition, or backing a niche service provider of highly specialized, critical service to the life sciences industry, such as medical imaging analysis for clinical trials.

On the manufacturing side, sterile fill-finish and device/containment (e.g., pens, autoinjectors) remain chokepoints, particularly under pressure from rising demand for GLP-1 therapies. Regulatory agencies have repeatedly highlighted these bottlenecks and encouraged manufacturers to prioritize medical-need products. Aseptic processing standards explain this scarcity: they demand heavy CapEx, validated clean environments, media fills, and rigorous quality assurance and quality control. Such requirements reward well-run, scaled contract CDMOs that can combine compliance, reliability, and throughput at scale.

This "super-specialization" allows PE firms to capture value from areas of deep unmet medical need, often with less direct competition.

7.2.2.2 Case Studies in Action

Case Study 1: Clinical Subsector (OMERS Private Equity and Forefront Dermatology) In 2016, OMERS Private Equity, the PE arm of a major Canadian pension plan, acquired Forefront Dermatology, one of the largest dermatology practice groups in the United States. The investment exemplified the clinical subsector consolidation strategy. At the time of acquisition, the US dermatology market was highly fragmented, composed mostly of small, physician-owned practices. OMERS' strategy was to provide capital and operational support to accelerate Forefront's growth through a disciplined buy-and-build approach, acquiring smaller practices and integrating them into its centralized platform. This allowed the company to achieve economies of scale in administration and procurement while building a leading brand in a specialized clinical field.

Case Study 2: High-volume Model (J.P. Morgan Partners and Narayana Health) In India, Narayana Hrudayalaya (now Narayana Health) pioneered a high-volume, "assembly-line" model for cardiac surgery. The model was financed pre-IPO by investors including J.P. Morgan Partners, which invested in 2008. As reported by the Commonwealth Fund, by standardizing workflows and batching procedures, Narayana was able to perform coronary artery bypass surgery at a cost of around $2,000, compared to over $70,000 in US hospitals, while maintaining strong quality outcomes. The high volume—Narayana surgeons perform 400–600 surgeries annually compared to 100–200 for their American counterparts—demonstrates genuine productivity gains through operational innovation. This case illustrates how private capital can support the creation of highly specialized Centers of Excellence that achieve both scale and radical cost reduction, particularly in emerging markets.

Case Study 3: Super-specialization (Cinven and BioClinica) A clear example of niche market domination is the European PE firm Cinven's 2016 acquisition of BioClinica, a company that provides highly specialized medical imaging and eClinical services for pharmaceutical clinical trials. Rather than investing in a drug developer, Cinven's thesis was to build a market leader in a critical, outsourced niche of the R&D process. BioClinica was strategically combined with another PE-owned specialized clinical trial services company, ERT, in 2021 to form a new entity, Clario. This merger created a global leader in clinical trial endpoint technology and services, dominating the specialized market for collecting and analyzing clinical trial data. The strategy demonstrates how PE can create value by identifying and scaling a "super-specialized" service provider that is essential to the broader life sciences ecosystem.

Risks and Outlook for Investors Over-concentration in a single specialty can expose a platform to sudden changes in reimbursement policy or the emergence of a disruptive new technology that renders a specific procedure obsolete. Furthermore, the success of a clinical roll-up hinges on the ability to truly integrate practices, not just aggregate them, which is a significant operational challenge.

Despite these risks, the strategy of Specialization and Focus will remain a potent value creation lever in healthcare. As the healthcare system becomes more complex, the demand for deep, specialized expertise will only grow. Successful execution of this strategy hinges on deep industry expertise and a disciplined approach to building a truly integrated platform. For those who get it right, the rewards can be substantial.

Learning from Mistakes Specialization requires expertise. PE investors reinforce it when needed with external hires and operating partners. They also sometimes invite expertise at the investment level. That is the case of club deals organized by growth investors pairing with successful executives to bring specialist advisory capabilities into the governance.

However, even specialist investors can get it wrong. Mike Mortimer from GHO has not forgotten:

> *Consumer health is really hard. We wouldn't do another direct-to-consumer investment—we simply don't have that expertise. We had the head of marketing from Pepsi helping us, which was valuable, but we still didn't truly understand the customer base.*

This candid admission illustrates how even healthcare specialists can overestimate their domain expertise and how hiring highly qualified external talent might not fully compensate for their lack of sector-specific knowledge.

7.2.3 S09: Health System Integration and Vertical Integration

While many PE strategies focus on optimizing a single type of asset, Health System Integration is a more complex and ambitious approach aimed at acquiring and combining different, complementary components of the healthcare value chain. This strategy, often referred to as vertical integration, seeks to control the entire patient journey to improve care coordination, reduce costs, and capture value that is typically lost between disconnected stages of care.

This strategy is fundamentally different from a horizontal "buy-and-build" roll-up, which consolidates similar assets (e.g., multiple dermatology clinics). Vertical integration, in contrast, combines dissimilar assets—such as primary care clinics with specialty physician groups or a health insurer with a network of providers. For PE sponsors, the thesis is that by owning and coordinating multiple stages of the value chain, they can build a more efficient, defensible, and ultimately more valuable healthcare enterprise. This section deconstructs this strategy into its three core pillars: provider-side integration, payer-provider integration, and the integration of life sciences with care delivery.

7.2.3.1 The Three Pillars of Vertical Integration Strategy

Provider-side Integration (the Clinical Value Chain) The first and most common form of vertical integration focuses on building a seamless clinical pathway by combining different types of healthcare providers. The goal is to create a "one-stop-shop" for patients with specific conditions, ensuring better care coordination and keeping the patient within a single, controlled network. Key combinations include the following:

- Primary care and specialty care: Acquiring primary care practices to act as a referral engine for a network of higher-margin specialty services like cardiology, oncology, or orthopedics
- Diagnostics and treatment: Integrating diagnostic imaging centers or pathology labs with physician practices to streamline the diagnostic process and speed up time-to-treatment
- Acute and post-acute care: Combining surgical centers or hospitals with post-acute care providers like skilled nursing facilities or home health agencies to manage the patient's recovery more effectively and reduce costly hospital readmissions

This pillar aims to create a clinically integrated network that can manage a patient's entire episode of care more efficiently than a fragmented system. In the United Kingdom, many of the largest healthcare groups have vertically integrated from primary and secondary care to community health or occupational health offerings, such as Bupa and Spire Healthcare (Figure 7.8).

Payer-provider Integration (the Financial Value Chain) A more advanced and complex form of vertical integration involves combining the health insurer (the payer) with the

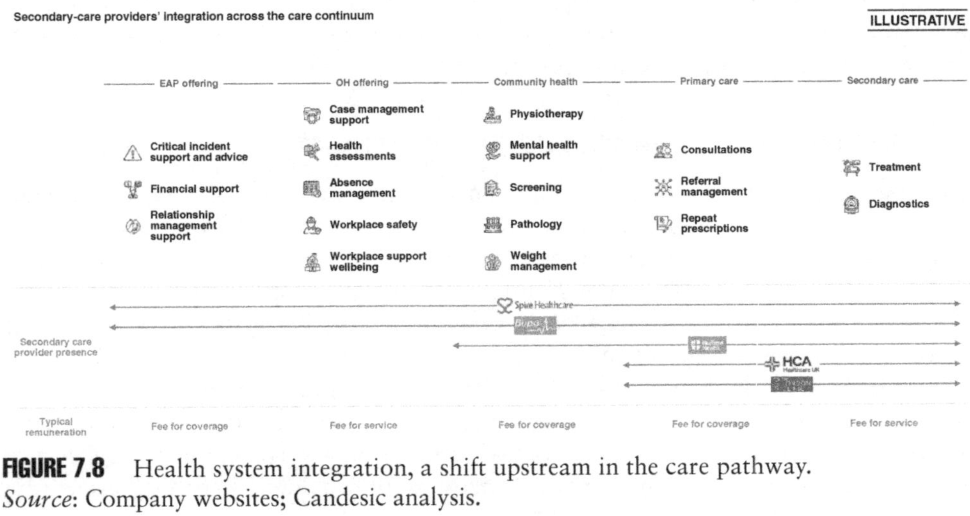

FIGURE 7.8 Health system integration, a shift upstream in the care pathway.
Source: Company websites; Candesic analysis.

care delivery network (the provider). This is the ultimate play in value-based care, as it directly aligns the financial incentives of paying for care with the act of providing it. The strategic goal is to take on full financial risk for a patient population and generate returns by keeping them healthy and out of high-cost settings. This involves the following:

- Acquiring Medicare Advantage plans: PE firms may acquire a private Medicare insurer and then build or buy a network of providers to serve those members.
- Building full-risk provider networks: Creating large, integrated provider groups that are capable of taking on capitated contracts from payers, where they receive a fixed fee per member per month to manage all of their healthcare needs.

This strategy is exceptionally difficult to execute but offers the potential for outsized returns by fundamentally changing the economic model of healthcare from fee-for-service to population health management.

Life Sciences and Provider Integration (the Supply Chain) The third pillar involves integrating the "product" side of healthcare (pharmaceuticals, medical devices) with the "service" side (care delivery). The goal is to create a closed-loop system that can control the use of high-cost products, ensure patient adherence, and capture value across the supply chain. Following are some examples:

- Specialty pharmacy and infusion centers: Combining a specialty pharmacy that dispenses high-cost biologic drugs with a network of infusion centers where those drugs are administered
- Medical device manufacturers and surgical centers: Creating partnerships or integrated models between device makers and ambulatory surgery centers to streamline the supply chain and promote the use of specific technologies

This form of integration is focused on managing the high and rising costs of medical technology and specialty drugs.

7.2.3.2 Case Studies in Action

Case Study 1: Provider-side Integration (Warburg Pincus and Summit Health/CityMD) The 2019 merger of Summit Medical Group, a large multispecialty physician practice, and CityMD, a leading urgent care provider, backed by Warburg Pincus, is a prime example of provider-side vertical integration. The strategy was to create a comprehensive, integrated network where a patient could enter through a low-cost "front door" (an urgent care clinic), be seamlessly referred to a primary care physician or a specialist (like a cardiologist or an orthopedic surgeon) within the same system, and receive coordinated care throughout their journey. By controlling the different stages of the outpatient care pathway, the combined entity aimed to keep patients within its network, improve care coordination, and offer a more convenient experience than a traditional, fragmented health system. This integration created a highly valuable asset, which was subsequently acquired by VillageMD in 2022 for $8.9 billion with participation from Cigna's Evernorth.

Case Study 2: Payer-provider Integration (Clayton, Dubilier & Rice and Agilon Health) Agilon Health, a company that partners with primary care physician groups to help them transition to a full-risk, value-based care model, received significant growth investment from Clayton, Dubilier & Rice (CD&R) after formation.[4] Agilon's model was a form of payer-provider integration; it provided the capital, technology, and expertise for physician groups to take on full financial risk for their senior patients, primarily through Medicare Advantage. In essence, Agilon created a platform that turns independent provider groups into integrated delivery systems capable of managing population health. CD&R's investment was a bet on this asset-light model of enabling payer-provider integration at scale. The company's successful IPO in 2021 demonstrated the strong market appetite for business models that facilitate the shift to risk-based, integrated care.

Case Study 3: Integrating Comorbidities (Quadria and AIG-Asia Institute of Gastroenterology) "When we invested in AIG, they were just in that single morbidity, which was gastric sciences," explained Abrar Mir, managing partner. Quadria identified a fundamental opportunity: patients with gastric diseases often had related cardiovascular and diabetic conditions but were being referred elsewhere after treatment, representing lost value and fragmented care.

The solution involved building "a full healthcare ecosystem around comorbidity" by adding centers of excellence in cancer, cardiovascular, and diabetes care around the existing gastric specialty. This approach retained patients within their system while providing comprehensive care. The management team acknowledged the idea's merit but lacked execution capability: "Great idea, but how do you do it? We've never done that." Quadria's operational expertise filled this gap, transforming AIG into probably the world's largest gastric sciences hospital group in terms of value as well as volume.

Case Study 4: Life Sciences and Provider Integration (TPG Capital and Kadiant) In 2019, TPG Capital launched Kadiant, a platform focused on providing Applied Behavior Analysis (ABA) therapy for individuals with autism spectrum disorder. This represents a more subtle form of vertical integration. The value creation plan involved not just providing the core therapy (the "service") but also integrating diagnostic and assessment services to create a more comprehensive care pathway. By building a platform that could manage the entire patient journey from initial diagnosis to ongoing treatment, TPG aimed to create a more efficient and clinically effective model. This strategy of integrating the diagnostic "product" (the assessment) with the therapeutic "service" (the ABA therapy) within a single, controlled system is a key tenet of vertical integration in specialized healthcare services.

7.2.3.3 Outlook and Recommendations for Investors The strategic imperative to manage costs and improve outcomes will continue to drive interest in health system integration. As the healthcare industry moves inexorably toward value-based care, owning and coordinating multiple parts of the value chain will become an increasingly

[4] CD&R had initially formed Agilon Health in 2016 through the combination of PPMC, a Californian Management Service Organization (MSO), and Cyber-Pro, a data and tech company service MSOs.

powerful source of competitive advantage. However, this strategy comes with significant challenges. PE investors should address the following:

- Anticipate and manage antitrust scrutiny: Vertical integration is facing intense scrutiny from regulators, particularly in the United States, who are concerned that it can be used to build local monopolies, reduce patient choice, and increase prices. A core part of any investment thesis must be a clear plan to demonstrate that the integration will lead to lower costs and better outcomes for patients.
- Prioritize IT and data integration: True vertical integration is impossible without a sophisticated IT and data analytics platform that can connect disparate systems and provide a single view of the patient. This is a major capital expense and a significant execution risk that must be underwritten upfront.
- Master clinical and cultural integration: Merging different types of healthcare organizations—with their distinct cultures, workflows, and physician compensation models—is exceptionally difficult. A successful strategy requires a robust change management plan and a deep commitment to physician alignment.
- Focus on a specific population or condition: The most successful vertical integration strategies are often those that focus on managing the complete care pathway for a specific, high-cost patient population (e.g., seniors on Medicare Advantage, patients with complex cancer, or individuals with chronic kidney disease).

While the execution risk is high, for those firms that can successfully navigate these challenges, vertical integration offers the potential to build truly transformative and highly valuable healthcare enterprises.

7.2.4 S10: Cross-sector Integration (e.g., Health and Social Care)

While vertical integration focuses on combining different stages *within* the traditional healthcare value chain, cross-sector integration connects the formal medical system with adjacent, nonclinical sectors that drive health outcomes. This thesis is built on the importance of the Social Determinants of Health (SDoH)—conditions like housing, nutrition, and transport that often dictate clinical results.

Dr. Michelle Tempest from Candesic argues that primary care provides the perfect opportunity for cross-sector integrated joined-up care, across health and social care. Linking care coordination is an effective methodology to deliver better clinical outcomes with efficient cost base (Tempest and Funa, 2024).

For PE firms, this represents a frontier of value creation. The core thesis is that by investing in platforms that address nonmedical needs—such as nutrition, housing, transportation, and social support—it is possible to improve patient health, dramatically reduce costly medical events (like emergency department visits and hospitalizations), and generate significant returns, particularly in value-based care models. This strategy is distinct from clinical integration; its goal is to build a bridge between the medical and social ecosystems to create a more holistic and efficient system of care. Elysium healthcare in the United Kingdom, part of Ramsay (Figure 7.9), has expanded into care homes, providing a holistic approach to specialist rehabilitation.

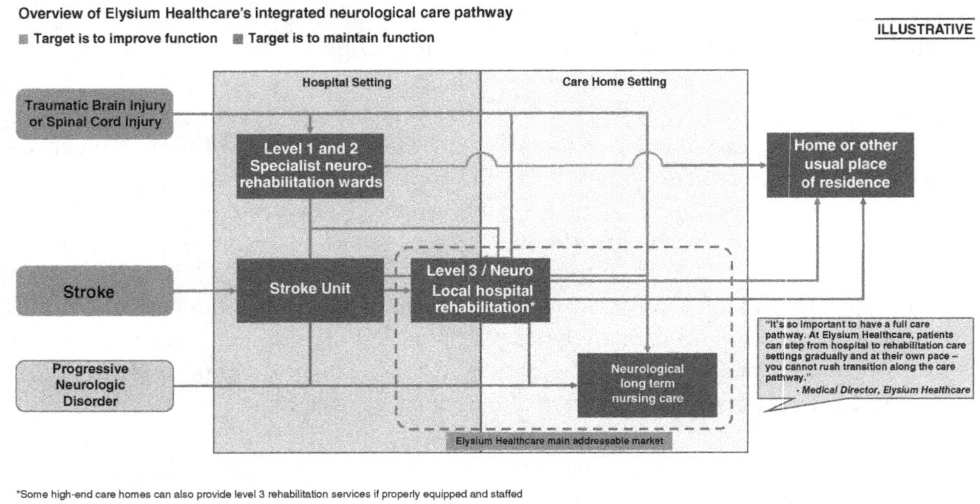

FIGURE 7.9 Cross sector integration, a bridge from hospital to long-term care.
Source: Candesic analysis.

7.2.4.1 The Three Pillars of Cross-sector Integration Strategy

Integrating Health and Social Care: This pillar targets complex populations, such as "dual eligibles" (Medicare/Medicaid), who require both medical treatment and social support. The PE playbook involves investing in platforms that coordinate this complex web of services. Key initiatives include managed care for complex populations (MCOs specializing in long-term care), home and community-based services (HCBS) that combine medical care with daily living assistance, and behavioral health integration, as mental health issues are often intertwined with social challenges. By managing the full spectrum of needs, PE-backed companies can take on financial risk and drive margins through better coordination.

Integrating Health and Nutrition: "Food as Medicine" Growing evidence suggests medically tailored meals can improve outcomes for chronic conditions like diabetes and heart failure. The "Food as Medicine" thesis invests in scalable providers of medically tailored meals (delivered meals covered by Medicare Advantage/Medicaid) and nutritional counseling (access to dietitians).

Integrating Health and Enabling Services: Transportation and Housing Access to care is a fundamental SDoH; patients lacking transport or housing often miss appointments or medication. PE firms address this by investing in nonemergency medical transportation (NEMT) brokerage platforms that contract with payers, and social service coordination technology that connects members with community housing and food assistance.

By solving these basic logistical challenges, PE-backed platforms can improve patient adherence to treatment, reduce missed appointments (a major source of inefficiency), and ultimately improve health outcomes.

7.2.4.2 Case Studies in Action

Case Study 1: Integrating Health and Social Care (Humana and WCAS—CenterWell Senior Primary Care Joint Ventures) In 2020, Humana Inc. and WCAS formed their first joint venture to develop senior-focused, value-based primary care clinics, committing $800 million to open 67 clinics by early 2023. Building on this success, in May 2022, the companies announced a second joint venture with an additional $1.2 billion investment to develop approximately 100 new CenterWell Senior Primary Care clinics between 2023 and 2025.

WCAS held majority ownership while Humana operated the clinics under the CenterWell brand. The model demonstrates how PE can scale value-based care that addresses the medical, behavioral, and social needs of seniors while generating returns through reduced total cost of care.

Case Study 2: Integrating Health and Nutrition (SoftBank Vision Fund 2 and Papa's Social Determinants Platform) In November 2021, Papa, a US "family-on-demand" platform that addresses SDoH, including nutrition and social isolation, raised $150 million in Series D funding led by SoftBank Vision Fund 2, achieving unicorn status with a $1.4 billion valuation. Papa's model connects Medicare Advantage, Medicaid, and employer health plan members with trained "Papa Pals" who provide companionship, meal preparation assistance, grocery shopping, and transportation to medical appointments. The platform serves members across more than 40 states through partnerships with more than 65 health plans, including major insurers like Humana, Cigna, and Anthem. Papa's approach demonstrates the "Food as Medicine" thesis by addressing nutritional support alongside other social determinants, with studies showing Papa Pals reduce member loneliness by 68% while helping health plans identify and address food insecurity and medication adherence issues.

7.2.4.3 Outlook and Recommendations for Investors Cross-sector integration is poised for growth as payers assume more risk for the total cost of care. PE investors should do the following:

- Focus on measurable ROI: Strategies must demonstrate quantifiable returns to payers, e.g. proving that every dollar spent on meals saves three dollars in hospitalization costs.
- Build technology-enabled platforms: Scalability is key. Winning models will use tech to coordinate fragmented community providers. However, this presents a significant challenge, particularly in the social care sector. While there are providers capable of meeting the needs of hospitals worldwide, assembling systems that also serve social care remains a significant challenge. This is particularly important in the context of integrated care, which is now an economic necessity. As Nikki Walker, senior executive vice president at RLDatix, a PE-owned provider of healthcare risk and compliance management software, highlights, there is an absence of a truly global IT provider for social care operators:

> *In the United Kingdom, the situation is especially difficult for two reasons. First, social care is highly fragmented; beyond the main operators, there is a long tail of around 20,000 small providers, many of whom are not yet digital. This represents both a major opportunity for technology providers and an enormous undertaking. Second, IT budgets in social care are much lower than those in secondary or even tertiary care. However, things are beginning to change in some other parts of the world, such as Saudi Arabia and India.*

- Develop deep payer relationships: Success depends entirely on the ability to contract with large government and private payers and maintaining these relationships.
- Navigate the evolving policy landscape: Reimbursement models for SDoH are evolving; investors must adapt to changes in how these services are funded.

7.2.5 S11: International Expansion, Globalization, and Cross-border Arbitrage

PE-owned firms are more likely to internationalize because institutional owners provide not only capital but also internationalization expertise, managerial talent, and access to networks that facilitate rapid foreign expansion. Leveraging economies of scale across portfolios, PE investors help firms scale quickly and transform into multinationals. At the same time, their strong focus on financial returns encourages frequent reconfiguration of international operations, with firms entering and exiting markets more rapidly in pursuit of short-term performance (Cuervo-Cazurra et al., 2025).

This strategic category in PE covers a broad set of opportunities that leverage geographic, regulatory, and economic disparities across global healthcare markets. It involves building production platforms in multiple countries, exporting proven business models (e.g., Scandinavian digital health platforms rolled out in Latin America), and executing regulatory arbitrage or "vintage arbitrage"—acquiring assets in lower-valuation markets (like emerging Europe) to exit in higher-multiple Western markets.

7.2.5.1 The Pillars of International Healthcare PE Strategy

Leveraging International Network for Product Expansion This is the most straightforward situation: using a PE firm's global footprint to accelerate a portfolio company's growth.

Case Study: Quadrivio and MIR In 2025, Quadrivio's Silver Economy Fund acquired MIR to leverage its international offices (London, New York, Los Angeles, Hong Kong) for global expansion. Recognizing in particular the highly fragmented European medical devices market, Quadrivio planned to accelerate MIR's growth through strategic acquisitions and cross-border consolidation, capitalizing on local market leadership and financial backing to strengthen MIR's product offering and access new markets such as Germany and the United Kingdom (Caiazzo, 2025).

Figure 7.10 shows the successful international development of another company, focused on "omics."

7.2.5.2 Building Global Healthcare Platforms Traditional platform building involves establishing integrated delivery networks across multiple countries, leveraging operational expertise to standardize care models internationally. Europe provides a prominent case with its variety of national regulations and cultures. For example, Gimv has been investing in healthcare across Europe for over 40 years. Thomas Goudriaan explains how they leverage experience and dedicated pan-European healthcare teams to play a pivotal role in supporting innovative companies to realize better healthcare:

> *We do this by standing together with management teams, providing strategic reflections based on our knowledge of local stakeholders, but also the broader European context. Through this, we believe that PE can be part of*

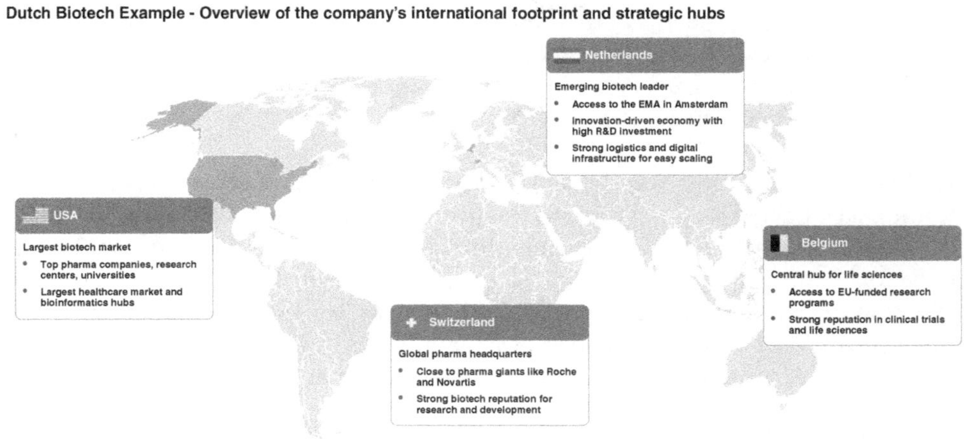

FIGURE 7.10 International expansion and globalization, networks for global reach.
Source: Candesic analysis.

the driving force to make healthcare more accessible, affordable and of higher quality. This will be essential to provide sustainable solutions to the challenges in healthcare today, but also for the next generations.

Case Study: CVC Capital Partners and Mehiläinen In 2018, CVC invested in Finland's Mehiläinen. By January 2025, Mehiläinen had acquired Lithuania's InMedica Group (89 facilities, €150 million revenue), Romania's Regina Maria (300 units, €400 million revenue), and Serbia's MediGroup (100 units, €150 million revenue), creating a pan-European network serving more than 4.5 million patients. This demonstrates true platform building through systematic geographic expansion and operational integration.

7.2.5.3 Digital Health Globalization and Technology Transfer This pillar leverages proven digital health solutions from advanced markets and deploys them globally, with localization for regulatory and cultural requirements.

Case Study: One Peak and DocPlanner Following an €80 million Series E led by One Peak Partners in 2019, DocPlanner expanded from Poland to 13 countries, including Germany, Turkey, and Latin America. The company localized its platform for diverse healthcare regulations, payment systems, and cultural preferences while maintaining unified technology infrastructure. By adapting its appointment platform to diverse payment systems and cultures while maintaining a unified tech infrastructure, DocPlanner scaled to process 18 million monthly bookings by 2024 for 2.5 million healthcare professionals globally, serving more than 100 million users annually. This demonstrates how PE-backed tech can capture global network effects (TechCrunch, n.d.).

7.2.5.4 Cross-border Operational Arbitrage This arbitrage focuses on improving the underlying operations of a healthcare business in one jurisdiction and then monetizing those enhancements in another. Unlike "Building Global Healthcare Platforms," which is about creating integrated networks and replicating full-service models across borders, operational arbitrage hones in on cost-effective markets where PE firms can drive efficiency gains—such as procurement, staffing, or localized service offerings—and then exit at developed-market multiples. Rather than a focus on platform scale, value is typically created by squeezing out operational delta between emerging- and developed-market cost structures.

Case Study: INVL Baltic Sea Growth Fund and InMedica Group INVL invested in Lithuania's InMedica Group in 2019 when it had €10 million revenue. By 2024, InMedica reached €150 million revenue through operational improvements, bolt-on acquisitions, and professionalization. The company scaled from 18 clinics in 2018 to 89 facilities serving over 2.7 million patient visits annually by 2024. INVL sold InMedica to CVC-backed Mehiläinen of Finland in early 2025, achieving developed-market multiples on an emerging-market asset—a landmark Baltic healthcare deal.

7.2.5.5 Emerging Strategies and Regulatory Risks This pillar encompasses nascent but rapidly growing approaches that extend beyond traditional models:

- Cross-border regulatory arbitrage: Capturing value by navigating differing regulatory regimes, approval processes, and reimbursement rules. Laurent Dethomas at Vivalto Partners highlighted that blindly trusting existing pricing structures without considering evolving reimbursement policies carries significant risk due to increasingly frequent and impactful changes. His firm's approach includes diversification across European markets to mitigate regulatory and funding risks:

  We have chosen to expand our French clinic group Vivalto Santé into Spain and Portugal, where healthcare budgets and service offerings still need strengthening, and private insurers cover 30 to 50% of costs.

  This cross-border strategy also includes Swiss ventures like Linnea, producing plant-based APIs, and OnO, which offers ophthalmologic services funded both publicly and through patients paying premiums for quality care.
- RegTech arbitrage: Acquiring regulatory-expert firms in one jurisdiction to streamline and accelerate global expansion.
- Cross-border listing arbitrage: This can be a pan-European approach that secures diverse financing sources and access to growing markets, enhancing resilience and patient care quality. This arbitrage operates at the intersection of regulatory compliance and capital markets—upgrading governance standards to qualify for listings on higher-multiple exchanges—which complements but remains distinct from operational improvements.
- Supply chain and manufacturing arbitrage: Building resilient, geographically diversified manufacturing and distribution networks.
- Telemedicine and remote care globalization: Scaling telehealth models internationally, particularly in underserved markets. This emphasizes regulatory adaptation, licensing, and cross-border clinical governance unique to remote care delivery, while "Digital Health Globalization and Technology Transfer" is about transplanting entire platform models and tech stacks across regions.

However, policy complexity is rising. Cross-border deals now face scrutiny from GDPR, HIPAA, and foreign investment reviews (CFIUS, EU screening). Post-pandemic resilience has also driven a shift toward localized manufacturing to mitigate supply chain risks, while US-China tensions have tightened oversight on biotech data transfers.

Outlook and Recommendations for Investors Aging demographics and healthcare digitization create compelling cross-border PE opportunities, particularly in Eastern Europe, Southeast Asia, and Latin America. PE firms should develop regulatory expertise across jurisdictions while prioritizing digital-first expansion strategies that enable rapid scaling without heavy physical infrastructure. Success requires strong local partnerships for compliance, integrating healthcare quality metrics into environmental, social, and governance (ESG) frameworks, and managing geopolitical risks in sensitive cross-border investments. Given evolving market conditions, investors should focus on mid-market opportunities with proven value creation potential while leveraging carve-out transactions and sector-focused strategies to navigate the complex international healthcare landscape.

7.2.6 S12: Human Capital

While workforce and talent have historically been operational value levers, they are increasingly recognized as strategic assets in PE. Bililies (2024) demonstrates that successful PE firms "manage talent differently" through systematic approaches that distinguish top-quartile performers. Bain & Company (2025c) credits talent with "a significant 71% of deal success" while leadership effectiveness shows positive impact on financial performance in portfolio companies. Various industry surveys confirm leadership quality as the main driver of deal success while positioning talent risk among the top three causes of portfolio underperformance.

Beyond traditional operational tweaks, top firms now view workforce as a differentiator in deal sourcing and value creation. This section outlines three dimensions of PE-driven human capital strategies.

7.2.6.1 Talent and Workforce Optimization (Innovative Staffing Models) PE sponsors are deploying novel staffing platforms and flexible labor models to improve capacity utilization, reduce agency costs, and scale headcount rapidly when needed.

Case Study: TPG Growth and Medical Solutions (2017) TPG acquired Medical Solutions to scale its tech-enabled platform, which uses algorithms to match traveling nurses with hospitals. By improving matching efficiency, TPG aimed to capture a larger share of the flexible clinical labor market, reducing reliance on less efficient traditional staffing models.

Risk Warning: KKR and Envision Healthcare KKR's 2018 take-private of Envision illustrates the risks. Envision deployed a mobile-first staffing platform across 25,000 clinicians, cutting agency costs by 18%. However, the 2022 No Surprises Act eliminated a critical revenue stream underpinning the model, contributing to bankruptcy in 2023. This underscores the need to align workforce models with regulatory landscapes.

7.2.6.2 Workforce Engagement and Resilience (Burnout Mitigation, Retention) High turnover and burnout plague healthcare operations, and PE owners have responded with structured engagement and support programs to stabilize critical teams (Figure 7.11).

Case Study: KKR and BrightSpring (2019) As detailed in its 2022 ESG report, KKR backed career-progression paths for 45,000 caregivers, including mental-health support initiatives. These programs reduced annual turnover by 15% and improved patient-satisfaction scores.

Case Study: Bain Capital and HCA (2006–2011) During this period, HCA launched its "Clinical Advancement Program," a tiered skills-training initiative for registered nurses, across its 180 hospitals. By offering clear progression pathways, the program cut RN turnover from 20% to 11%, saving an estimated $300 million annually in recruitment costs—reinforcing how staff development drives EBITDA.

7.2.6.3 Workforce Technology, Analytics, and Gamification PE firms are increasingly leveraging digital tools to optimize workforce performance, engagement, and compliance. By embedding analytics and carefully implemented gamification into learning and staffing platforms, sponsors drive measurable productivity gains while standardizing talent processes across portfolio companies.

Case Study: Clearlake Capital and Cornerstone OnDemand (2021) In 2021, Clearlake Capital took healthcare-adjacent Cornerstone OnDemand private for $5.2 billion to accelerate its shift to a subscription model and embed AI-driven analytics across

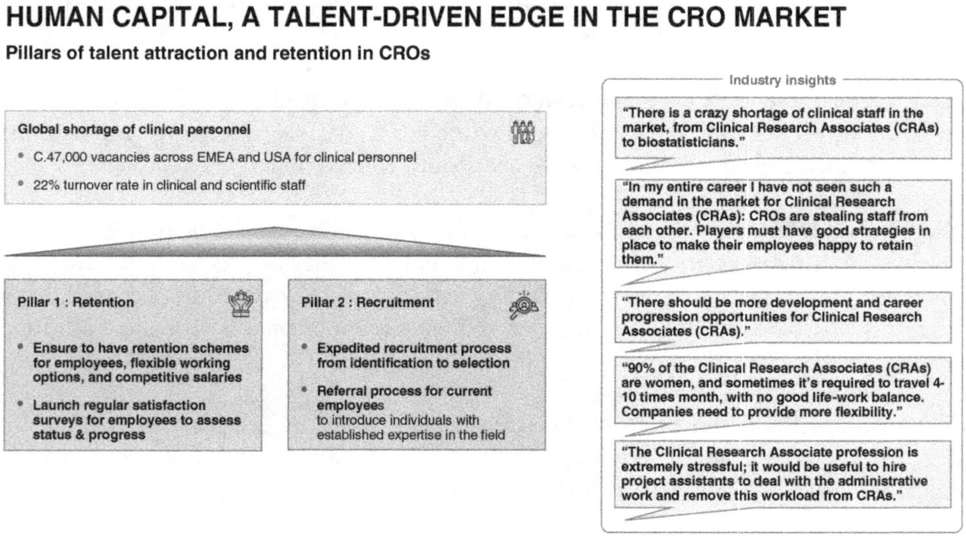

FIGURE 7.11 Human capital lever in CROs.
Source: Candesic interviews; Candesic analysis.

its talent platform. Mergermarket reported how Cornerstone rolled out enhanced compliance-training modules and personalized clinical-skills curricula for large hospital systems, using data to tailor learning paths and boost retention. Early results showed a 20% increase in course completion rates and a 15% reduction in time-to-competency for frontline clinical staff.

Case Study: Vista Equity and Relias Learning Relias Learning is not a pure PE example as it was acquired by Bertelsmann in 2014 after Vista Equity Partners' divestiture. But the approach was initiated by the PE owner. Relias's adaptive microlearning and gamified modules train more than 1 million clinicians. A 2023 outcomes report found learners completed courses 30% faster and retained 25% more knowledge compared to traditional LMS approaches. PE firms syndicate such platforms across clinical and administrative teams to enforce consistent onboarding, compliance, and professional development standards.

Additionally, sponsors are building flexible peer-to-peer staffing networks, AI-powered skills marketplaces, and performance-linked incentive dashboards. These platforms enable real-time shift swaps, micro-credential-based staff matching, and gamified compensation tied to productivity and quality metrics, driving higher utilization and stronger engagement.

7.2.6.4 Operating Partner with HR Specialization Leading sponsors now embed dedicated HR operating partners. For example, WCAS appointed a healthcare HR partner in 2025 who deployed standardized talent reviews, achieving a 20% retention uplift and a 15% rise in employee-engagement scores in six months. Similarly, TPG Capital added a chief people officer–level partner to its ValueHealth platform in 2023, establishing centralized HR centers of excellence that significantly reduced nurse turnover and unlocked estimated savings of $25 million, while stabilizing care delivery quality.

Embedding HR expertise at the operating level ensures that talent and culture initiatives move beyond one-off programs to become core value-creation levers throughout the investment life cycle.

7.2.6.5 Outlook and Recommendations To maximize impact in a tight labor market, PE investors should integrate talent analytics in diligence, build portfolio-wide leadership academies, and leverage gamified digital learning. Additionally, piloting AI-driven staffing marketplaces can flex capacity, while elevating the CPO role ensures alignment between people strategy and commercial goals.

7.2.7 S13: Payer-provider Partnerships and Risk Sharing

PE firms are increasingly aligning payors and providers through joint ventures that share both financial risks and rewards while embedding population health management capabilities within healthcare platforms. Such partnerships enable PE-backed platforms to capture upside from preventive and outcomes-driven care models while mitigating the decline in volume-based reimbursements. Outside of value-based healthcare strategies, public-private partnerships also allow public services to increase capacity, reduce waiting times, and allow patients to benefit from new technologies; PE-backed companies benefit from guaranteed, high volumes of patients against cutting costs (Figure 7.12).

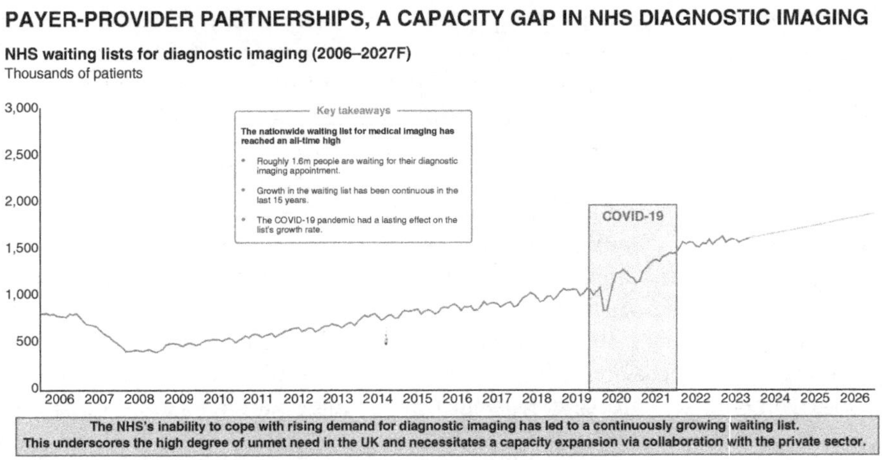

FIGURE 7.12 Payer-provider partnerships.
Source: Candesic analysis.

When risk-bearing arrangements by these platforms occurs, it typically take three forms: downside-protected shared savings through accountable care organizations (ACOs) or Medicare Advantage collaborations, full-risk capitation agreements in managed Medicaid and commercial contracts (paying a per-member-per-month rate for comprehensive care), and hybrid models that blend fee-for-service payments with performance incentives to ease the transition toward value-based care.

Real-world examples corroborate these approaches.

7.2.7.1 Case Study 1: Oak Street Health—Medicare Advantage Risk Model General Atlantic's 2015 minority investment in Oak Street Health, then a startup, helped expand its value-based primary care centers targeting high-need seniors through Centers for Medicare & Medicaid Services (CMS) Direct Contracting and Medicare Advantage risk models. Oak Street's capitated reimbursement structure and care coordination capabilities delivered stable margins and a reported 3:1 return on shared-savings bonuses. After its IPO in 2020, the company's successful execution of risk-based care led to its 2023 acquisition by CVS Health for approximately $10.6 billion, validating the PE-backed value-based care model.

7.2.7.2 Case Study 2: Alignment Healthcare—Tech-enabled Medicare Advantage Warburg Pincus invested $115 million in Alignment Healthcare in 2017 to support its tech-enabled Medicare Advantage platform. Alignment's capitated, population health-coordinated care model achieved medical-cost ratios below industry benchmarks by 2022, generating significant value-based revenue share. This case illustrates how PE can scale innovative payer-provider models that outperform traditional Medicare Advantage plans.

7.2.7.3 Case Study 3: Agilon Health—Physician-led Risk Platform As previously discussed, Agilon Health was formed by CD&R in 2016, receiving a significant growth investment in 2020 to scale its platform. The company enables independent physician groups to transition to full-risk, value-based care models for their senior patients. By 2023, Agilon was working with more than 2,000 primary care physicians managing more than 300,000 Medicare Advantage patients under these risk-sharing contracts. The company's successful IPO in 2021 and subsequent growth demonstrated PE's ability to create and scale physician-led, risk-bearing entities that are central to modern payer-provider partnerships.

These examples illustrate a strategic shift from volume-driven fee-for-service models to value-based payment frameworks. By sharing financial risk with payors, PE-backed platforms capture durable upside from cost control and quality improvements while absorbing downside risk tied to utilization variability. Success in these models depends on tightly aligning incentives across providers and payors, implementing sophisticated analytics for population health management, and delivering integrated care coordination. Such risk-sharing platforms provide competitive advantage and scalable returns within the evolving healthcare payment landscape.

7.2.8 S14: Behavioral Health Integration

Private investors are increasingly backing integrated models that embed mental and substance-use services within primary-care and specialty platforms, capitalizing on the shift toward holistic, value-based care. By funding capabilities that screen, triage, and treat behavioral-health conditions alongside physical health, PE-owned practices improve outcomes, capture care-coordination fees, and reduce costly downstream utilization.

These strategies typically involve embedding licensed therapists within primary-care clinics under collaborative-care protocols, partnering with tele-mental-health vendors to scale capacity without real-estate investments (Figure 7.13), and **structuring shared savings arrangements** with payors for reduced emergency-department visits.

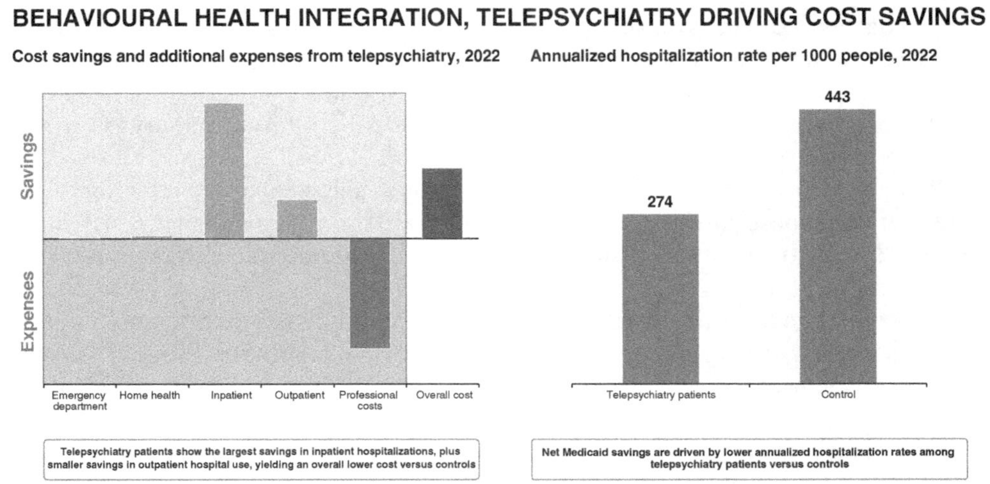

FIGURE 7.13 Telepsychiatry driving cost savings.
Source: JAMA; Candesic analysis.

7.2.8.1 Illustrative Transactions

Case Study 1: BC Partners & Acadia Healthcare (2016) In October 2016, BC Partners acquired a portfolio of 22 UK behavioral-health facilities divested by Acadia Healthcare for £300 million. Under BC Partners' ownership and according to their press release, the new platform co-located psychiatrists and primary-care providers, achieving a 15% reduction in avoidable readmissions and securing shared-savings bonuses under NHS value-based contracts.

Case Study 2: General Atlantic & Quartet Health (2019) General Atlantic led a $110 million Series C financing in Quartet Health in October 2019. Quartet's platform integrates primary-care referrals into a network of therapists and psychiatrists, enabling collaborative-care billing (e.g., CPT 99492–99494). According to Reuters, post-investment, Quartet reduced average wait times by 40% and improved therapy utilization by 25% across partner practices.

Case Study 3: KKR & BrightSpring Health Services (2019) KKR completed its acquisition of BrightSpring Health Services from Onex in March 2019 for $1.3 billion. BrightSpring, a leading provider of home- and community-based behavioral-health services, expanded under KKR's ownership to integrate tele-behavioral health and care navigation into primary-care networks, reducing inpatient psychiatric admissions by 12% and generating more than $100 million in shared-savings revenue in 2021.

7.2.8.2 Integration Models, Value Creation, and Implementation Challenges Omnichannel care models deliver coordinated, continuous treatment across in-clinic collaborative care, tele-behavioral health visits, and digital support tools. These platforms ensure seamless patient journeys and ongoing engagement.

AI-enabled triage platforms analyze patient-reported data and risk profiles to prioritize high-need cases, personalize outreach, and reduce no-show rates by up to 20% (Zhu et al., 2024).

By contrast, patient-acquisition and engagement platforms (S30) focus on funnel optimization and front-door technologies—digital marketing, scheduling, telehealth onboarding—to attract and convert new patients. In other words, omnichannel care models sustain long-term treatment journeys, while patient-facing acquisition strategies drive initial capture.

PE-backed behavioral platforms deliver returns through enhanced retention (integrated services boost patient lifetime value by 30–50%), cost avoidance (early interventions lower inpatient admissions by 10–20%), and revenue diversification via care-management fees

However, vendor fragmentation can disrupt workflows. Success requires integrated platforms offering intake, triage, and analytics in one solution, alongside robust change management. Compliance with privacy laws (HIPAA) and data governance is critical.

Dr. Michelle Tempest from Candesic warns investors about using open-source algorithms trained on non-specialized datasets: "The future winners are likely to have developed legally regulated clinical grade products from proprietary data which will be continually improved across multi modalities."

Looking forward, digital phenotyping via smartphones and wearables will enable proactive interventions. Investors should anticipate regulatory changes in mental-health parity and align portfolios around platforms that demonstrate measured reductions in total cost of care, which will increasingly command premium valuations.

7.3 CFO PLAYBOOK

(Financial operations, funding structures, and revenue-focused strategies)

7.3.1 S15: Real Estate Optimization (OpCo/PropCo)

For healthcare providers with significant real estate assets like hospital systems or nursing home chains, PE firms can create value by optimizing these assets through sale-leaseback arrangements or by creating separate real estate investment trusts (REITs). While not specific to healthcare, it is quite prevalent in the sector.[5]

This strategy involves separating the operating company (OpCo) from the property company (PropCo), each with its own distinct financial and operational structure. The OpCo focuses on the core healthcare business operations, such as providing medical services, managing staff, and handling day-to-day operations of healthcare facilities, while the PropCo owns and manages the real estate assets, leasing them back to the OpCo through long-term agreements. The PropCo may be structured as a REIT to optimize tax efficiency.

Separation allows investors to arbitrage the difference between healthcare and real estate valuations. It unlocks hidden asset value that may be underappreciated on a consolidated balance sheet and enables distinct capital structures: the PropCo can support higher leverage at lower rates due to stable rental income, while the OpCo becomes a "capital-light" service provider with improved ROIC. This division also attracts distinct investor bases, allowing the PropCo to be sold to yield-hungry real estate investors (e.g., REITs) while the OpCo appeals to growth-oriented healthcare investors.

A classic execution of this model is the Ardent Health Services transaction. PE sponsor WCAS sold Ardent's real estate assets to Ventas, a healthcare REIT, for $1.75 billion. Ventas retained the properties and leased them back to Ardent, which continued to operate the hospitals under separate ownership. This split allowed Ventas to secure inflation-protected cash flows while providing Ardent with substantial liquidity to fund clinical growth, aligning capital risk with the appropriate asset class (Appelbaum and Batt, 2020).

A further notable example of the OpCo/PropCo structure in healthcare services is the acquisition of Healthscope in Australia by Brookfield Asset Management that we described in Chapter 4. Healthscope owned both the operating hospital business and

[5] These strategies, particularly the REIT and tax benefits, are primarily applicable in the United States and may be less common or have different implications in the United Kingdom and Europe. They carry material reputational and regulatory risk when applied in publicly reimbursed care settings, as discussed in Chapter 8.

a substantial property portfolio they had been considering selling. In this case, real estate investors like NorthWest Healthcare and MPT were particularly interested in acquiring the property assets (often via dedicated property vehicles or REIT-like structures), while the operational healthcare business was targeted by PE groups. Brookfield acquired the company for an EV of $5.7 billion, with 22 properties forwarded on to MPT and Northwest. The deal illustrated how separating real estate into a PropCo unlocks intrinsic value and capital flexibility, giving the hospital group (OpCo) access to funds for operational improvements, expansion, or debt reduction—while the PropCo, frequently structured as a REIT, appeals to investors seeking inflation-protected, long-term cash flows. The Healthscope scenario also demonstrated how multiple investor groups can simultaneously realize value from different components of a healthcare business, reflecting varied risk appetites and specialized expertise.

This structure also provides important risk segmentation: The real estate assets typically offer stable, inflation-linked income and appeal to long-term institutional investors such as pension funds and REITs, whereas the operating company assumes operational, regulatory, and market risks inherent in healthcare delivery. Moreover, the separation can create tax efficiencies for the PropCo and unlock capital that would otherwise be tied up, facilitating investments in clinical improvements, technology upgrades, or acquisitions by the OpCo.

The Ardent-Ventas case, as well as the Healthscope transaction in Australia, show how this OpCo/PropCo separation is not merely a financing technique, but a strategic value creation tool. It allows PE sponsors to monetize "hidden" value in real estate holdings, improve capital efficiency, and align asset risk with specialized investor appetites—crucial factors in a complex, capital-intensive sector like healthcare.

Of course, there is no free lunch, and this strategy comes with its own challenges, including regulatory scrutiny, operational complexity when managing the relationship and lease agreements between OpCo and PropCo. There may also be concerns about the OpCo's commitment to long-term healthcare provision if it no longer owns its facilities. Typical examples of these are the recent discussions surrounding Emeis and Clariane. Combined with sector-specific regulatory issues, the two of the largest French care homes groups (EHPADs), have each planned more than $1.5 billion of real estate asset disposal (Figure 7.14).

Indeed, the main issue is that the OpCo must consider the long-term impact of lease obligations on its financial flexibility. A highly leveraged OpCo is exposed to the double burden of interest and rent payments with no control on the cash flows. A sudden reduction in reimbursements/tariffs can prevent the OpCo from fulfilling its financial obligations, breach covenants, and wipe out the equity.

One way to avoid this inflexibility is to structure the sale and lease back through a master lease that enables asset substitution or demolition rights, enabling the operator to gain some flexibility. For instance, an underperforming—or likely to be closed in the future—asset could be replaced by another one, future proof, in the portfolio. Likewise, an overperforming asset could potentially increase the rent paid to the landlord, while the rent of an underperforming assets would be decreased in parallel. The landlord would be satisfied as they would not lose out in the process, while the operator would decrease the volatility of their results post rent on an asset level basis. Another way could be to grant the operator buyback options on the assets, if their sustainability profile changes between the time of implementing

REAL ESTATE OPTIMISATION, AN OPERATOR TURNAROUND BUILT ON ASSETS

Overview of the financial and strategic considerations for Clariane and Emeis

NON-EXHAUSTIVE

	clariane	
Financial Restructuring and Recapitalisation	• Executed a €300m capital increase as part of a broader €1.5bn refinancing strategy • Included €1bn from asset disposals aimed at reducing leverage and shoring up liquidity	• Implemented a financial restructuring involving 3 capital increases totaling c.€5.4bn • Achieved a reduced gross debt of €5.3bn and a net cash position of c.€645m
Shareholder Structure and Share Consolidation	–	• Established a solid shareholder foundation, holding over 50% of the company's capital • A reverse share split adjusted the share count to c.160m
Financial Performance and Projections	• Experienced robust financial performance in 2023, with solid EBITDAR and marginal growths of c.2% in EBITDA • The 2024 guidance anticipates +5% organic revenue growth	• Displayed robust sales growth but faced challenges in maintaining profitability levels • Has ambitious targets for a 19% EBITDAR margin by 2026
Asset Strategy and Leverage Management	Has planned significant asset disposals as part of its €1.5bn refinancing strategy	Plans nearly €1.5 bn in disposals to manage debt and support financial projections
Market Positioning and Analyst Outlook	• Has managed to maintain a stable market position with plans for sustained growth • However, a new target price is set at €1.55, down from €3.55, due to increased share dilution expectations	• Analysts recommend holding Emeis shares, citing strategic restructuring initiatives as a basis for stability • A target price of €14.0 reflects cautious optimism
Valuation and Investment Considerations	• Valuation reflects the complexities of the aggressive financial maneuvers undertaken to stabilize its operations • Potential risks include further financial deterioration requiring additional capital and regulatory changes	–

FIGURE 7.14 An operator turnaround built on assets.
Source: Xerfi; Candesic analysis.

the sale and lease back and the new operational and economic environment, along the way. Two events such as the COVID-19 pandemic and the cost inflation induced by the invasion of Ukraine radically changed the performance of many European nursing homes, some of which were not being able to cover their rental costs in an appropriate manner. The buying back of the property from the landlord could enable the operator to reposition it, notably through CapEx, so that its operational performance could be improved.

The model's limitations are harshly illustrated by a series of prominent failures. Southern Cross Healthcare in the United Kingdom, under Blackstone's ownership, split off its property assets to landlords such as NHP (Nursing Home Properties plc), transforming itself into a pure OpCo with rent obligations that eventually proved unsustainable. When Southern Cross collapsed in 2011, unable to cover rental costs amid squeezed revenues, its collapse triggered a fatal chain reaction: NHP, whose income depended almost entirely on Southern Cross's rents, lost its main revenue source overnight. Highly leveraged, NHP defaulted on its own debt and was broken up, showing the PropCo can fall in the wake of an OpCo default (Appelbaum and Batt, 2020). Four Seasons Health Care, also in the United Kingdom, met a similar fate. After PE firm Terra Firma implemented an OpCo/PropCo structure, operational groups crumbled under their rent liabilities while the PropCo was left exposed during Terra Firma's continued ownership. The story was echoed in the United States with Sun Healthcare Group, whose separation of operations and property preceded both entities' subsequent downfall. Sometimes, this domino effect occurs after the PE sponsor has exited—such as the collapse of the OpCo at Gracewell Healthcare following Patron Capital's sale, demonstrating these structural risks can outlast PE's involvement.

While it is much more common for the OpCo to fail, there are prominent examples of the PropCo also collapsing as a direct result of the OpCo's failure. The most powerful and clear example is NHP (Nursing Home Properties plc), the primary landlord for Southern Cross in the United Kingdom. After Blackstone sold off Southern

Cross's properties, NHP's business became nearly entirely reliant on rental income from Southern Cross. When Southern Cross defaulted, NHP was left unable to service its own debt, saw its stock price plummet, breached loan covenants, and was ultimately broken up by its lenders—a vivid demonstration that real estate owners are not insulated from healthcare operator risk.

7.3.2 S16: Manufacturing Infrastructure and Capacity Expansion

This approach represents a foundational value creation strategy whereby PE firms provide dedicated capital to finance critical physical and operational infrastructure investments. This strategy enables portfolio companies to achieve production capacity aligned with their growth ambitions while securing supply chain and maintaining control over quality, logistics, and core competencies—all essential in a highly regulated and innovation-driven sector. In 2020, 11 notable transactions in the pharmaceutical industry exemplified this strategy (Figure 7.15).

The strategy encompasses five core and interconnected dimensions that collectively strengthen a company's manufacturing foundation.

Production capacity alignment ensures that manufacturing capabilities can support anticipated growth trajectories without creating bottlenecks that constrain revenue expansion. Production independence reduces reliance on third-party manufacturers, CDMOs or CMOs, thereby improving margin control and supply chain resilience. Quality infrastructure investments, particularly in good manufacturing practice (GMP) compliant facilities, establish the regulatory and operational standards necessary for healthcare and life sciences companies to maintain market access and competitive positioning. Logistics and storage optimization creates efficient material flow and inventory management capabilities that reduce costs and improve responsiveness to market demands. Finally, preserving specialized internal know-how ensures that critical manufacturing expertise remains within the organization rather than being outsourced to external partners, safeguarding critical processes and proprietary technologies.

ARCHIMED exemplifies this strategy through its targeted infrastructure investments across portfolio companies. The firm has financed the acquisition or construction

Year	Acquirer	Type	Target	Target location	Business Area	Rationale
2020	UNITHER	Bolt-on	I-Mab Biopharma			Unither is worldwide leader in sterile unit-doses manufacturing – this acquisition accelerates its development in China (2nd largest market), bringing manufacturers closer to customers.
	sanofi	Bolt-on	Principia			Strengthens Sanofi's core areas of autoimmune and inflammation diseases, giving them full control of small promising molecules. The Principia acquisition augments Sanofi small molecule research capabilities.
	CVC	Private Equity	Genetic Farmaceutica			CVC's investment allows Genetic to grow internationally, and strengthen its position in the respiratory and ophthalmology pharmaceutical markets.
	VETTER	Bolt-on	Rentschler			Strategic collaboration to expand services: Rentschler brings its experience in drug substance manufacturing - Vetter brings expertise in aseptic fill secondary packaging.
	TRILANTIC EUROPE	Private Equity	Dietopack			Trilantic Europe acquired 90% of Dietopack, an Italian familyowned CDMO, leader in dietary supplements, which is a resilient sector that helps supporting immune systems.
	AGC Biologics	Bolt-on	AstraZeneca			AGC Biologics acquired AstraZeneca's bioreactors facilities in Boulder (USA) to support its expansion due to an increasing demand for mammalian projects.
	Pfizer	Bolt-on	BIONTECH			Collaboration to accelerate Covid-19 vaccine development. Biontech provides clinical supply of vaccines, while Pfizer provides vaccine clinical research.
	Bora Pharmaceuticals	Bolt-on	GSK			Bora Pharmaceuticals has acquired GSK's Mississauga manufacturing facility in Canada to enter the North American market.
	Catalent BIOLOGICS	Bolt-on	MaSTherCell			Catalent acquired MaSTherCell to strengthen its European presence and to integrate its autologous and allogeneic cell therapy manufacturing capabilities into Catalent's service portfolio.
	Recipharm	Bolt-on	Consort Medical			Recipharm acquired Consort, to strengthen its presence in the UK, to expand its range of activities by offering an end-to-end services, and bring new dosage forms like inhalation products.
	GHO CAPITAL	Private Equity	Ardena			GHO capital acquires Ardena, a Belgian CDMO, from Mentha Capital as it intends to strengthen Ardena's position by leveraging organic and inorganic opportunities.

FIGURE 7.15 CDMO consolidation.
Source: Company websites; Annual reports; Mergermarket; Candesic analysis.

of advanced, scalable production facilities for several portfolio companies whose business models depend on robust, high-quality manufacturing capabilities. This tangible support has enabled these companies not only to accommodate significant growth but also to retain control over the technological and operational building blocks of their products.

As Ludovic Alonzi, partner at ARCHIMED, summarizes: "ARCHIMED invested between 2× and 10× the EBITDA of companies such as Xpress Bio, Clean Biologics, and Polyplus to secure independence and control over production processes, increase capacity, and ensure full compliance with quality standards."

Other notable examples include the following:

- KKR's acquisition and repositioning of Capsugel, a leading pharmaceutical capsule manufacturer. Capsugel made significant investments to expand and modernize its manufacturing capabilities. This included a $20 million expansion to enhance commercial manufacturing for spray-dried dispersions (crucial for improving drug solubility), a $25 million investment to increase capacity for vegetable-based capsules, and the acquisition of several US-based specialist companies (such as Bend Research, Powdersize, and Xcelience) to build out its technology base and service offering. Capsugel broadened its technical expertise, added new production technologies, improved quality systems, met strict regulatory benchmarks, and grew its global footprint. The outcome was a repositioning of Capsugel from a commoditized capsule supplier to an integrated provider of high-value drug delivery solutions and development services. KKR sold Capsugel to Lonza in 2017 for $5.5 billion.
- EQT's carve-out of three manufacturing sites from Recipharm in 2024 to form Bespak is another pertinent illustration. EQT supplied targeted funding and strategic resources to establish Bespak as an independent, end-to-end contract manufacturer of inhaled and nasal drug delivery systems. Investments included modernizing and scaling proprietary production lines to serve high-growth green propellant inhalers, ensuring GMP quality standards, and supporting international expansion. The emphasis has been on advanced infrastructure, vertical integration, and ownership of critical know-how and intellectual property.

The strategic rationale for manufacturing infrastructure investments extends beyond simple capacity expansion. PE firms recognize that manufacturing capabilities often represent the most significant constraint on portfolio company growth, particularly in regulated healthcare sectors. By providing dedicated capital for facility expansion, equipment upgrades, and process optimization, PE firms enable their investments to capture market opportunities that would otherwise be lost to capacity limitations.

In the biopharmaceutical sector, manufacturing infrastructure investments have become particularly critical as companies navigate complex regulatory requirements and supply chain challenges. The sector has experienced significant capacity constraints, particularly in specialized areas like cell and gene therapy manufacturing. Private equity firms have responded by investing heavily in specialized manufacturing capabilities, recognizing that control over production assets provides both operational flexibility and strategic value creation opportunities. These investments often involve constructing or acquiring GMP-compliant facilities that meet stringent regulatory standards while providing the scalability necessary for commercial success.

The medical device sector presents another compelling example of this strategy's application. Private equity-backed medical device companies frequently require significant manufacturing investments to scale production capabilities and meet quality standards required for regulatory approval and commercial success. These investments often involve establishing specialized cleanroom facilities, acquiring precision manufacturing equipment, and implementing quality management systems that ensure consistent product quality and regulatory compliance. The manufacturing infrastructure becomes a strategic asset that supports both organic growth and acquisition integration.

Manufacturing infrastructure and capacity expansion differs from traditional operational improvements in its focus on creating long-term competitive moats through physical assets and proprietary capabilities. While operational optimization strategies typically focus on efficiency improvements within existing facilities, infrastructure expansion creates new capabilities that enable market expansion, vertical integration, and enhanced value capture. This distinction makes infrastructure investment a foundational strategy that supports multiple other value creation approaches, from international expansion to product portfolio diversification.

For PE investors, manufacturing infrastructure investments require careful evaluation of market dynamics, regulatory requirements, and technology evolution. Successful implementation depends on understanding both current production constraints and future market opportunities, ensuring that infrastructure investments create lasting value rather than simply addressing short-term capacity limitations.

7.3.3 S17: Refinancing with Securitization

Although securitization has transformed several industries, including the financial sector (Chemla and Hennessy, 2014, 2016), few documented PE deals in healthcare have specifically used securitization as a primary financing mechanism. The scarcity of specific examples likely reflects several factors. First, securitization transactions involve complex structuring that may not be publicly disclosed in detail. Second, PE firms may prefer maintaining confidentiality around innovative financing structures. Third, many securitizations occur post-acquisition rather than as initial acquisition financing, making the PE connection less prominent in transaction documentation.

7.3.3.1 Trade Receivables Securitization The most common form appears to be trade receivables securitization, which Latham and Watkins describe as "now very widely used" in PE acquisition transactions. The typical pattern involves completing an acquisition using leveraged loans or high yield bonds, then later using proceeds from a trade receivables securitization to fund shareholder dividends. This structure allows PE firms to extract capital while maintaining lighter operating covenants than traditional debt facilities.

Italian healthcare securitization provides concrete examples where PE and specialized funds have securitized receivables owed by the Italian National Health Service to private healthcare providers. These deals capitalize on the Italian government's chronic payment delays, with investors earning returns enhanced by the European Central Bank rate plus 8% annual penalty that applies to late payments under EU Directive 2011/7/EU. However, these structures face increasing regulatory complexity, as evidenced by the 2020 Rilancio Decree requiring explicit debtor acceptance for certain healthcare receivables transfers.

7.3.3.2 Royalty and Revenue-based Financing The best theoretical case is probably that of EMI, albeit not in our chosen sector. In 2007, Terra Firma acquired the leading British music company, initially for £4 billion, with the brilliant plan to securitize the royalties from the best catalogue of music rights in the world and replace its expensive bridge loans. The Global Financial Crisis prevented it from happening and, for various reasons, Terra Firma lost the battle to turn around the business and its entire equity stake.

Healthcare royalties securitization has developed differently. Some PE firms specialize in acquiring royalty rights to approved drugs or late-stage drug candidates, providing lower-risk pharmaceutical sector exposure compared to early-stage drug development.

The healthcare royalty market has grown substantially, with transactions providing approximately $14 billion in annual deal flow. This includes both traditional royalty monetization and synthetic royalty transactions where companies sell portions of future product sales rather than existing royalty entitlements. Blue Owl Capital and other major PE firms have built dedicated life sciences teams investing in both credit and royalties. The Gibson Dunn analysis showed 102 publicly announced royalty transactions from 2020 to 2024 among major funds.

Beyond traditional securitization, PE firms increasingly use direct royalty and milestone-based financing structures as nondilutive alternatives to equity investments. Royalty-based financings reached approximately $3.4 billion in disclosed upfront volume in H1 2025 alone, as biotech companies responded to compressed equity valuations by embracing revenue interest financing (RIF) and milestone-based capital deployment tied to clinical trial phases or regulatory approvals.

Healthcare royalties differ fundamentally from music catalogs. Drug patents typically have finite lives (usually 10–20 years from approval), making cash flows more predictable but time-limited. Music royalties can theoretically continue indefinitely, making them more suitable for long-term securitization structures. Healthcare royalties are also tied to patient populations and treatment needs rather than consumer preferences, providing different risk characteristics.

The sector's innovation includes "synthetic royalties" where companies sell portions of future product sales rather than existing royalty entitlements, allowing earlier-stage companies without established royalty streams to access this financing model. These structures often combine upfront payments with contingent milestone payments, creating hybrid arrangements that provide immediate liquidity while aligning investor returns with development progress.

7.3.3.3 Clinical Trial Financing Through Securitization The most innovative development involves "megafunds" specifically designed to finance clinical trials through securitization structures. Fernandez et al. (2012) proposed a groundbreaking model where large biomedical portfolios ($5–15 billion) use securitization to issue "research-backed obligations." This structure would fund clinical trials across multiple biomedical programs, with senior tranches offering 5–8% returns to institutional investors and equity tranches targeting 8.9–11.4% returns (Fernandez et al., 2012) (Figure 7.16).

The MIT model employs special purpose vehicles to acquire biomedical assets and licenses, then issues multiple debt tranches based on the diversified cash flows from successful drug developments. While this remains largely theoretical, it represents a sophisticated application of securitization to clinical trial financing that could revolutionize biomedical innovation funding.

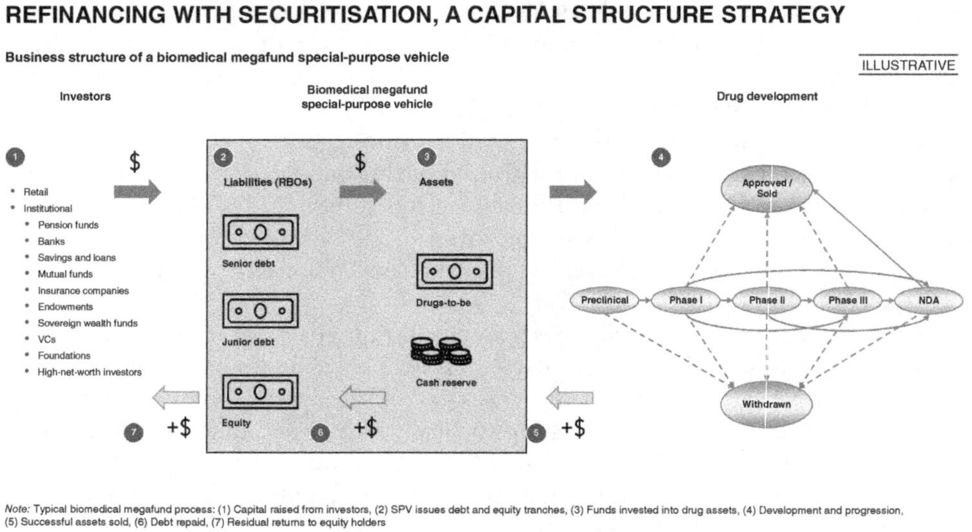

FIGURE 7.16 Refinancing with securitization.
Source: Candesic analysis.

Recent developments show this concept gaining traction. A 2025 PLOS One study proposed financing drug development through "adaptive platform trials" using similar securitization principles. The authors specifically reference the megafund securitization model as a method to "transfer the risk of drug development" by creating tranched securities appealing to different investor types.

The integration of PE and securitization appears most advanced in sectors with predictable cash flows—music royalties, student loans, equipment financing, and increasingly healthcare royalties. While dedicated clinical trial securitization funds have not yet materialized at scale, the theoretical framework exists and firms like Apollo and KKR have the infrastructure to execute such strategies when market conditions align.

7.3.3.4 Whole-business Securitization Whole-business securitization is another PE tool, where special purpose vehicles lend funds raised via rated debt securities secured over the target's entire asset base. The target group's cash flows service both the loans to the issuer and the rated securities to investors. Roark Capital's planned whole-business securitization for Subway represents a contemporary example, though this shows intent rather than completion. Such structures require stable cash flows, strong market positions, and high barriers to entry.

In 2006, General Healthcare Group (GHG) became the first UK hospital operator to execute a whole business securitization, with at least one tranche of £975 million. This transaction was arranged by Morgan Stanley shortly after GHG's £2.2 billion acquisition by a Netcare- and Apax Partners-led consortium from BC Partners. The deal securitized the entire hospital group's revenue streams, going beyond simple receivables and setting a precedent for UK hospital asset-backed securities. While healthcare receivables securitization was already established in the United States, Euromoney reported GHG's structure as an innovation for the UK market, allowing the PE-backed owners to refinance acquisition debt by monetizing the operational cash flows of the hospital group.

7.3.3.5 Why Is Securitization Rare in PE Healthcare Deals? In our discussions, we identified four healthcare-specific reasons, in addition to the generic ones:

a. Regulatory complexity: Healthcare receivables face unique challenges including Medicare/Medicaid anti-assignment provisions, complex reimbursement structures, and offset risks that require specialized lockbox arrangements and explicit regulatory compliance.
b. Valuation difficulties: Unlike other asset classes, healthcare receivables often have uncertain collection amounts due to contractual allowances, disputes, and variable reimbursement rates.
c. The NCFE legacy: National Century Financial Enterprises' collapse in 2002, involving $2.6 billion in investor losses and 275 healthcare provider bankruptcies, created lasting skepticism about healthcare receivables securitization. The fraud involved falsified receivables data and improper fund transfers between securitization programs, highlighting structural vulnerabilities in healthcare securitization.
d. Alternative financing: Most PE healthcare deals use traditional leveraged buyout structures, real estate sale-leasebacks, or revenue cycle management optimization rather than securitization.

7.3.3.6 Modern PE Usage of Asset-backed Securities A 2024 Dechert survey shows that 59% of PE firms globally now use asset-backed securities and structured products. Asia-Pacific PE firms are particularly active in ABS markets, though these typically involve other asset classes like equipment leases, auto loans, or consumer receivables rather than healthcare receivables.

The healthcare sector's complex regulatory environment, uncertain cash flows, and the cautionary tale of NCFE have generally steered PE firms toward more traditional financing structures for healthcare acquisitions, making securitization-based healthcare PE deals quite uncommon in practice.

Asset-based Lending as Alternative Recent trends show increased PE adoption of asset-based lending (ABL) rather than securitization. Walker Morris reported an "uptick in the use of ABL as a malleable, competitively priced, scalable financing option" in early 2025. ABL allows companies to leverage receivables, inventory, or equipment with borrowing capacity directly linked to asset values. It may represent a simpler and preferred alternative to complex securitization structures for working capital and acquisition financing needs.

7.3.4 S18: Revenue Cycle Optimization

While clinical excellence and strategic growth are high-profile value creation strategies, one of the most powerful and consistently applied operational levers in healthcare PE is *revenue cycle optimization*: Improving billing, coding, and collections. The revenue cycle management (RCM) process—the complex administrative and financial workflow that begins with patient registration and ends with final payment collection—is the financial lifeblood of any healthcare provider. In many independent or nonprofit-run organizations, this process is often inefficient, manual, and prone to errors, leading to significant revenue leakage.

For PE firms, RCM represents a prime opportunity for value creation. By applying data-driven analytics, investing in technology, and instilling operational discipline, sponsors can dramatically improve cash flow and expand EBITDA margins without altering the core clinical services. This strategy is particularly effective because it targets the administrative backbone of the business, unlocking value that is often trapped in inefficient processes. This section deconstructs the RCM optimization playbook into its three core pillars: front-end processes, mid-cycle clinical documentation, and back-end claims management.

7.3.4.1 The Three Pillars of RCM Optimization

Front-end Optimization: Preventing Denials Before They Happen The most effective way to improve revenue capture is to ensure accuracy at the very beginning of the patient journey, even before registration (Figure 7.17). Many claim denials and payment delays originate from simple errors made during patient registration and scheduling. PE firms focus on professionalizing these "front-end" processes:

- Automating insurance verification: Implementing software that automatically verifies a patient's insurance eligibility and coverage details in real time, preventing claims from being submitted to the wrong payer
- Streamlining prior authorization: Using technology and dedicated teams to manage the cumbersome process of obtaining prior authorization from insurers for specific procedures, a major source of administrative friction and claim denials
- Improving patient financial counseling: Establishing clear protocols for communicating with patients about their financial responsibility (co-pays, deductibles) upfront, which improves the likelihood of collection later in the cycle

By strengthening these foundational steps, sponsors can significantly reduce the number of claims that are denied for administrative reasons, immediately improving the "clean claim rate."

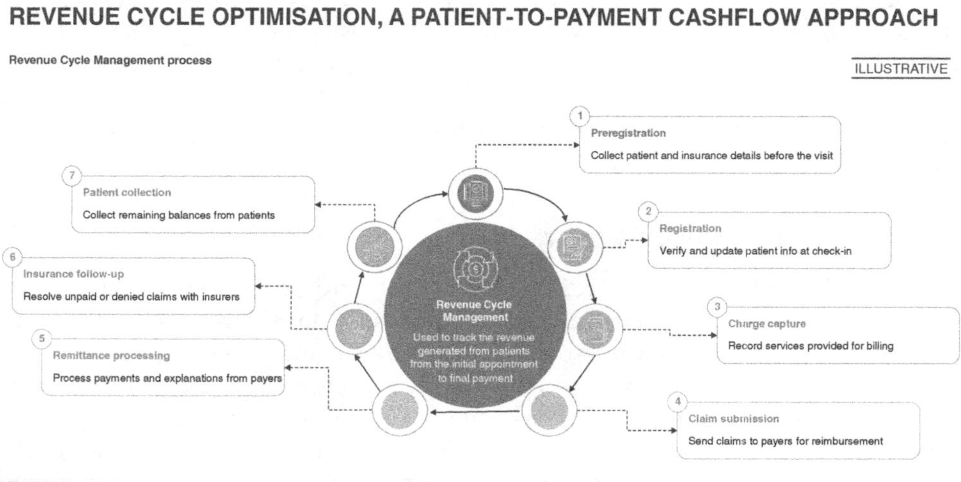

FIGURE 7.17 Patient-to-payment cashflow approach.
Source: Candesic analysis.

Mid-cycle Optimization: Accurate Coding and Documentation The "mid-cycle" phase involves translating the clinical services provided into standardized, billable codes. This is a highly complex area where accuracy is paramount for maximizing reimbursement. PE sponsors invest heavily in technology and expertise to improve this function:

- AI-powered and computer-assisted coding: Implementing AI-powered coding systems that analyze clinical documentation and suggest the appropriate medical codes. This increases coding accuracy, ensures compliance, and reduces the manual workload on coding staff.
- Clinical documentation improvement programs: Deploying specialists who work with physicians to ensure that their clinical notes are detailed and specific enough to support the highest appropriate level of coding for the patient's acuity.
- Integrating clinical and financial data: Investing in integrated IT systems that connect the EHR with billing platforms, reducing the need for manual data entry and reconciliation, which is a common source of errors.

These mid-cycle improvements ensure that the provider is fully and accurately compensated for the complexity of the care delivered.

Back-end Optimization: Data-driven Claims and Denial Management PE firms apply analytical rigor to the "back-end" revenue cycle—claims submission, denial management, and payment collection—transforming reactive processes into proactive systems. Rather than treating each denial as an isolated event, they deploy data analytics to identify root causes, whether a payer's rule changes, recurring coding errors, or documentation issues with specific providers. Sophisticated software automates appeals and resubmissions for routine denials, freeing staff to handle complex cases, while professionalized collection strategies use data to improve recovery of outstanding patient balances within consumer protection compliance. This systematic approach converts denial management from manual firefighting into continuous improvement driven by pattern recognition and automation.

7.3.4.2 Case Studies in Action

Case Study 1: Building a Technology-enabled RCM Platform (EQT VIII and CPPIB's Investment in Waystar) In 2019, EQT VIII and the Canada Pension Plan Investment Board acquired a majority stake in Waystar—then a fragmented collection of legacy billing platforms—for $2.7 billion, with Bain Capital retaining a meaningful minority position. Under new ownership, Waystar unified disparate systems into a single cloud-native platform, invested heavily in AI-driven prior-authorization workflows and denial-management tools, and standardized pricing and coding across client sites. These improvements reduced claim rejections by more than 40% and accelerated days-in-AR by two weeks on average, leading to a $968 million IPO in mid-2024 and a near-doubling of equity value (Waystar releases).

Case Study 2: Provider-side RCM Overhaul (KKR and Envision Healthcare) KKR's 2018 $9.9 billion take-private of Envision Healthcare centered on professionalizing and automating its complex physician-billing operations. The firm standardized coding practices, centralized collections, and introduced analytics to monitor out-of-network fee growth. However, the 2022 *No Surprises Act* capped out-of-network rates and eliminated surprise billing, eroding Envision's core RCM thesis. Despite operational gains, regulatory shifts led to cash-flow shortfalls and an eventual bankruptcy in 2023, underscoring the importance of aligning RCM strategies with evolving policy landscapes.

Case Study 3: Scaling a Technology-enabled RCM Champion (New Mountain Capital and Equian) New Mountain Capital acquired Equian—in 2016, backing its expansion from a single payment-integrity service into a full-service RCM outsourcing platform. Through bolt-on acquisitions of coding, contract-management and clinical-review specialists, plus the integration of predictive-analytics engines, Equian increased its average margin per claim by 25%. Axios reported that, in 2019, UnitedHealth Group's Optum acquired Equian for $3.2 billion, realizing a 3× multiple on invested capital and validating the playbook of building a technology-enabled RCM champion.

7.3.4.3 Outlook and Recommendations for Investors The importance of revenue cycle optimization as a value creation lever will only grow as reimbursement models become more complex and margins remain under pressure. The future of RCM will be defined by automation and intelligence. PE investors should do the following:

- Prioritize technology in due diligence: Assess a target's existing RCM technology stack as a core part of due diligence. Evaluate the level of automation in billing, the use of AI-powered coding, and the integration of financial and clinical reporting systems.
- Develop a portfolio-wide RCM playbook: For firms with multiple healthcare provider assets, create a standardized playbook for RCM that includes best-practice protocols and a list of preferred technology vendors.
- Focus on regulatory-resilient strategies: Ensure that RCM strategies are not overly reliant on aggressive or ethically questionable tactics (like out-of-network billing) that are vulnerable to regulatory changes.
- Invest in data analytics talent: Recruit or develop talent within operating partner teams who specialize in RCM data analytics to identify revenue leakage and drive continuous improvement across the portfolio.

By treating the revenue cycle with the same analytical rigor and technological focus as any other core business process, PE firms can continue to unlock significant and sustainable value in their healthcare investments.

7.3.5 S19: Other Opportunistic Competitive Moves

Some PE plays defy neat classification. They are about shrewd timing, rapid execution, and taking advantage of market wrinkles others miss. Opportunistic moves can arise from anticipating competitor exits, reacting to technological breakthroughs, or unlocking overlooked niches (Figure 7.18). They demand vigilance, deep sector intelligence, and a readiness to move before the window closes.

7.3.5.1 Anticipating Market or Corporate Events PE firms are often better placed than corporates to act when big shifts rattle the competitive landscape. Whether it is a

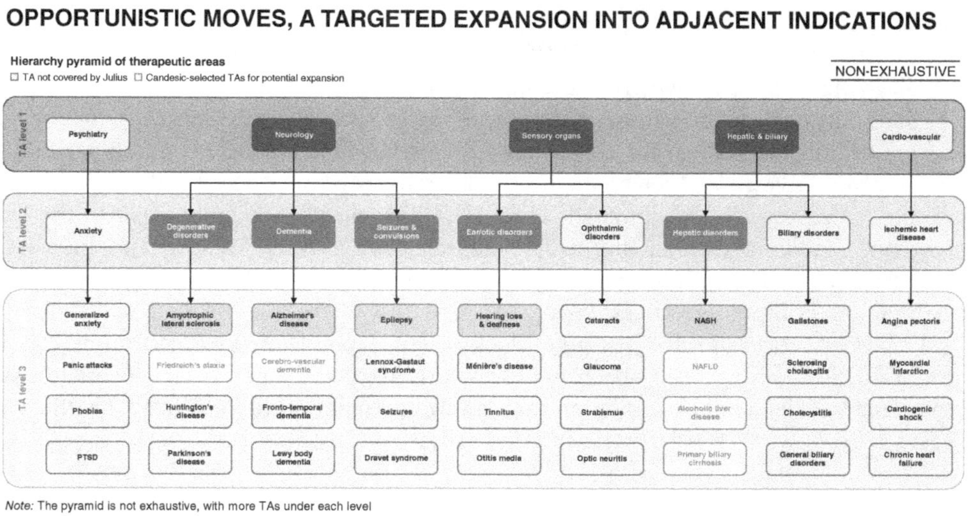

FIGURE 7.18 Example of opportunistic move.
Source: Candesic analysis.

divestment, a retrenchment, or an M&A misstep by a rival, these moments create opportunities to pick up valuable assets on terms incumbents cannot match. Acting fast, and occasionally boldly, can mean stepping into a vacuum created by slower-moving strategic buyers.

Example 1: Bain Capital and Softway Medical (2025) A possible example is the acquisition in 2025 by Bain Capital of Softway Medical, a leading hospital information system (HIS) provider in France, just as SAP was planning to exit the German hospital market by 2027, leaving 250 leading hospitals in Germany with the need to replace their HIS. Bain Capital timed the acquisition to position Softway Medical for cross-border expansion. According to Mergermarket, the move aligned with a broader European HIS market shift toward modular, cloud architectures—and exploited a two-year window before competitors could scale localized solutions.

Example 2: Bain Capital and HealthEdge (2025) Another example the same year is, again, Bain Capital's acquisition of HealthEdge, a major healthcare technology platform serving more than 115 health plans and more than 110 million members in the United States. The deal occurred as health plans faced mounting operational complexity and an urgent need to modernize their technology stacks. While some established vendors were slow to innovate or integrate next-generation solutions, Bain recognized HealthEdge's potential to become a mission-critical partner for payers transitioning to cloud-based, AI-enabled systems. By moving quickly, Bain Capital positioned HealthEdge to capture market share from legacy competitors and drive further consolidation in the healthcare IT sector.

Example 3: Blackstone and TeamHealth (2016–2017) Looking again at Blackstone's $6.1 billion acquisition of TeamHealth, we see a classic illustration of PE opportunism. The deal landed at a 33% premium over TeamHealth's market price, coming just as the hospital outsourcing sector was in the grip of consolidation and regulatory upheaval. Blackstone's previous ownership (2005–2009) gave it unique insights into the business, allowing it to move swiftly and confidently.

Post-acquisition, Blackstone steered rapid integration of IPC Healthcare (acquired for $1.6 billion in 2015, prior to the take-private by Blackstone), streamlined management, and invested in telemedicine to diversify revenue. TeamHealth's platform commanded about 19,000 clinicians across 3,400 facilities—roughly 20% of the US emergency medicine staffing market. By acting just as rivals AmSurg and Envision closed their own $10 billion merger, Blackstone strengthened TeamHealth's position and exploited competitive uncertainty.

This transaction did not just give Blackstone a second bite at a proven asset—it showcased how acting with speed, sector knowledge, and operational leverage can deliver market leadership and premium multiples in a rapidly shifting healthcare landscape.

Mid-market Examples Opportunism is not confined to megafunds. Mid-market PE firms have also demonstrated opportunism in biopharma and life sciences by acquiring companies that support testing, inspection, certification, or compliance—often as larger players retrench or refocus. Notable recent deals include WindRose Health Investors' acquisition of SubjectWell, a patient recruitment platform, capturing growth from increasing demand for technology-enabled clinical trial enrolment, GI Partners' acquisition of eClinical Solutions, a life sciences data management company—recognizing the accelerated digitization and decentralization of clinical research, and ARCHIMED's acquisition of FIM Medical to build a platform supplying occupational health testing equipment to doctors worldwide. The move appears timed with the ongoing consolidation of occupational health services across Europe. Rather than competing with other PEs acquiring OH providers, ARCHIMED could be positioning itself to serve these expanding, often PE-backed groups.

These investments were made as the sector shifted toward digital infrastructure and operational efficiency, with PE firms leveraging their specialized knowledge to act quickly when high-quality assets became available, sometimes before traditional strategic buyers could mobilize.

7.3.5.2 Anticipating a Technology Disruption Some firms prefer their opportunism in the form of early bets on emerging tech. These moves often involve highly specialized assets others dismiss as too risky or "too early" for PE.

Example: Summa Equity and Olink Proteomics (2019–2023) This opportunistic approach is highlighted by Yaoyao Wang of DC Advisory, who worked on multiple transactions with Summa Equity during her tenure at William Blair.

Summa Equity's acquisition of Olink Proteomics in 2019 exemplifies this strategy. Olink, a Swedish life sciences company, developed the Proximity Extension Assay technology, which enables researchers to measure hundreds of proteins using minimal sample volumes. This innovation reduces research costs and opens new avenues for therapeutic discovery. At the time, many PE investors were hesitant to invest in pre-profit life sciences tools, considering them too early stage. Summa Equity, however, recognized the growth potential and seized the opportunity.

In 2024, Summa Equity sold its shares in Olink to Thermo Fisher Scientific for $26 per share, valuing the company at approximately $3.1 billion. The transaction represented a substantial return on investment and was finalized on July 10, 2024, following a public cash tender offer initiated by Thermo Fisher.

In parallel, Summa Equity exited its investment in HyTest, a Finnish company specializing in antibodies and antigens for the in vitro diagnostics industry, in 2021. HyTest was acquired by Mindray Medical International for €545 million, providing a full exit after a relatively short holding period. This transaction benefited from the heightened interest in diagnostics and life sciences technologies during the COVID-19 pandemic.

7.3.5.3 Identifying a Neglected Area We illustrate this alternative opportunistic move with the case of Netsmart Technologies, a quiet pioneer in an overlooked segment that offered an opportunity to scale digital infrastructure for behavioral health.

Netsmart Technologies—Building a Leader in a Neglected Vertical Founded in the 1960s, Netsmart Technologies specialized in behavioral health and post-acute care software—sectors historically underserved by hospital IT giants like Epic or Cerner. Genstar Capital acquired Netsmart in 2010 to modernize its products and operations, then sold it in 2016 to GI Partners and Allscripts for around $950 million, with Allscripts contributing complementary intellectual property and GI providing capital to expand the behavioral health focus. In 2018, GI Partners teamed with TA Associates to acquire Allscripts' stake, betting on a market still in early digital adoption stages. Over the next six years, Netsmart expanded into home health, hospice, and care transitions through cloud-enabled platforms and multiple bolt-on acquisitions. By 2024, with over 750,000 clinicians on its platform and EBITDA near $250 million, GI and TA began a sale process targeting a $5 billion valuation, demonstrating the value potential in unglamorous healthcare IT segments.

Outlook and Recommendations for Investors Opportunistic competitive moves work best when underpinned by excellent market intelligence, rapid execution capacity, and a willingness to lean into sectors or technologies before consensus forms.

In the current market, this means the following:

- Tracking corporate portfolio reviews for carve-out opportunities before they hit auction
- Watching regulatory or competitive retreat signals that could create "replacement demand" surges
- Monitoring adjacent tech markets for assets with healthcare applicability (e.g., AI-native workflow platforms)
- Considering neglected verticals where digitization or value-based care pressures are just starting

For LPs, these investments carry higher binary risk but often deliver premium multiples when executed well. The skillful investor treats them as a calculated, finite allocation in a broader portfolio—the kind of sharp, well-timed moves that can materially lift a fund's overall performance.

7.3.6 S20: Contract Structuring and Bundled Payments

How can PE firms design payment contracts that align incentives, reduce cost variation, and drive value-based care across clinical episodes?

Private investors leverage episode-based bundles and shared-savings agreements to standardize pricing and capture margin improvements. By structuring provider networks under retrospective-risk and prospective-payment bundles—for procedures from joint replacement to chronic disease management—PE-backed platforms mitigate fee-for-service fragmentation and unlock operational efficiencies.

In the United States, these strategies typically reflect adaptation to payer-led reforms or collaboration with payers, rather than a proprietary PE strategy. They usually unfold in three key ways:

1. Participating in bundles under Center for Medicare & Medicaid Services' Bundled Payments for Care Improvement (BPCI) programs, designed to move from fee-for-services models to value-based care. Here, PE-backed operators are not designing unique bundles, but rather implementing mandated or incentivized government payment approaches. PE firms may help portfolio companies adopt these frameworks more efficiently and manage risk, yet the structure itself is payer driven. By encouraging efficient services and coordination that could lead to an overall cost-reduction, providers share savings as bonuses if actual costs fall below the target price.
2. Establishing prospective-payment agreements with commercial insurers for specific procedures, combining a fixed bundled fee with quality incentives.
3. Negotiating multi-payer bundled contracts that standardize episode pricing across Medicare, Medicaid, and commercial lines, creating scale and reducing administrative complexity.

Clarifying point: Beyond episode-based bundles, innovative revenue-share contracts are increasingly used to accelerate medical device adoption and align incentives between suppliers and providers. Instead of requiring high upfront capital expenditures, private practices acquire advanced equipment through shared-revenue agreements, where suppliers recoup costs via a portion of generated income. These arrangements extend the value-based alignment concept beyond traditional episodes to ongoing service and device utilization, moving toward broader outcome-focused partnerships. This structure mitigates financial risk, improves alignment of interests, and sustains quality through ongoing supplier involvement. For investors, such models enhance adoption rates, create recurring revenue streams, and enable tighter integration of device utilization with value-based care frameworks (Figure 7.19).

7.3.6.1 Illustrative Transactions

Case Study 1: GTCR and Cedar Gate Technologies (2018) In October 2018, GTCR acquired Global Healthcare Alliance (GHA) via Cedar Gate Technologies. GHA's Axia™ platform automates prospective bundled-payment adjudication for orthopedic and cardiac episodes, processing more than 2.25 million bundles. Post-deal, Cedar Gate became a leader in managing prospective bundles, securing contracts with three

CONTRACT STRUCTURING, A REVENUE-SHARE MODEL TO DRIVE ADOPTION

Traditional vs revenue-share models in medical device commercialization

Negated limiting factor	Traditional sales model	Revenue share model
Capital cost	Private solo practices **cannot afford highly expensive** ($150,000+) XTRAC Lasers: the devices are too expensive for solo private practices that have yet not consolidated their patient base	The private practice acquires the expensive laser for a minimal fee, circumventing the **prohibitive cost barrier**
Alignment of interests	After the sale of the device, **the transaction between the supplier and buyer is minimal**: the relationship maintained by expected customer service and the possibility of a resale	The supplier and buyer **enter a partnership with this model by sharing the generated revenue**: this synergetic relationship guarantees high quality customer service for the buyer
Risk allocation	**Buying an expensive device is risky for a solo private practice**: ROI may be low, payback period may be too long (3 years+), opportunity cost might be too high (can't afford other devices in return), etc.	Not allocating a great deal of financial resources to a single medical device **allows private clinics to invest in other opportunities**, e.g. medical devices with higher utility, a clinic in a more affluent location, etc.
Significant reduction in cost structure	The buyer has **significant cost drivers other than the initial acquisition price**: marketing costs, maintenance costs, software licensing costs, etc.	The entered partnership significantly reduces the private practices' costs as **the supplier fully or partially covers numerous cost items**

FIGURE 7.19 Example of contract structuring.
Source: Candesic analysis.

national health systems and generating 15% higher per-episode margins versus fee-for-service (GTCR press release, 2018).

Case Study 2: Linden Capital Partners and HOPCo (2020) Linden, Audax, and Frazier's portfolio company, HOPCo, acquired Stryker Performance Solutions' BPCI-Advanced business in October 2020. HOPCo now convenes musculoskeletal bundles—including joint replacement and spine care—across 50 health systems, delivering 12% net margins on 90-day episodes and expanding its post-acute care network by 40% (Linden press release, 2020).

Case Study 3: Mountain View Capital and Signify Health/Remedy Partners (2019–2021) Mountain View Capital owned Remedy Partners, a technology platform managing both retrospective and prospective bundled payment contracts. In 2019, Mountain View merged it with Signify Health, forming a leading value-based care platform coordinating home-based and post-acute services for joint replacement, cardiac care, and other episodes. The combined entity completed an IPO in 2021. Signify Health's scale and technology-enabled coordinated care have generated 12–15% net margins on 30- and 90-day CMS bundles, demonstrating effective risk-sharing and operational efficiency (Signify Health S-4, 2021).

Each transaction illustrates different approaches to risk allocation and contract design. Success hinges on aligning capital structures—equity tranches and risk corridors—with the chosen bundle model and ensuring robust data-analytics teams to monitor performance in real time.

7.3.6.2 Implementation, Operational Considerations, and Recommendations Bundling thrives where technology, clinical protocols, and financial governance converge. Successful implementation requires establishing standardized care pathways and training programs to ensure provider adherence to protocols, investing in real-time cost-and-quality dashboards with analytics infrastructure to track episode performance, and developing modular contract management templates that can be adapted across different payor segments.

Looking ahead, episode-based contracting is expected to expand into chronic care bundles for conditions like chronic obstructive pulmonary disease, congestive heart failure, and maternity care. PE investors should proactively monitor evolving CMS regulations, thoroughly map care continuums, and prepare capital reserves to manage financial risk. Real-world data on savings and improved outcomes will be foundational to scaling these models sustainably.

Investors are advised to develop flexible contract architectures encompassing both retrospective and prospective bundles, bolster analytics capabilities, and build portfolios around integrated care pathways paired with active payor collaboration. These elements will underpin sustained success in value-based care investments.

7.4 COO PLAYBOOK

(Operational efficiency, clinical quality, human capital, and patient experience)

7.4.1 S21: Cost and Supply Chain Optimization

While strategic repositioning and technological innovation are high-profile value creation strategies, one of the most reliable and impactful operational levers in healthcare PE is cost and supply chain optimization. The healthcare supply chain—encompassing everything from the procurement of pharmaceuticals and medical devices to the management of inventory and the outsourcing of noncore services—is notoriously complex and often inefficient. For PE firms, this complexity represents a significant opportunity to drive EBITDA margin expansion through operational discipline, the strategic use of technology, and the leveraging of scale.

This strategy is distinct from other operational levers; it is not about optimizing clinical pathways or revenue collection, but about systematically reducing nonlabor operating expenses and improving the efficiency of the administrative and physical supply chains. This section deconstructs this strategy into three core pillars: procurement and purchasing power, logistics and inventory management, and the strategic outsourcing of noncore functions.

7.4.1.1 The Core Pillars: Procurement, Logistics, and Outsourcing

Procurement and Group Purchasing Power PE firms professionalize procurement by leveraging scale. Key tactics include enrolling portfolio companies into GPOs to access volume discounts, implementing vendor consolidation to renegotiate contracts, and deploying spend analytics software to enforce compliance. This transforms procurement from an administrative task into a strategic function.

Logistics and Inventory Management Top-quartile firms optimize the physical flow of supplies to reduce waste and carrying costs. Initiatives include inventory tracking systems (barcoding), just-in-time (JIT) delivery models to free up working capital, and cold chain optimization to prevent spoilage of high-cost biologics.

Healthcare Services Outsourcing and Business Process Optimization A third, and increasingly strategic, pillar is the outsourcing of noncore clinical and administrative functions. By outsourcing these services to specialized, scaled providers, healthcare

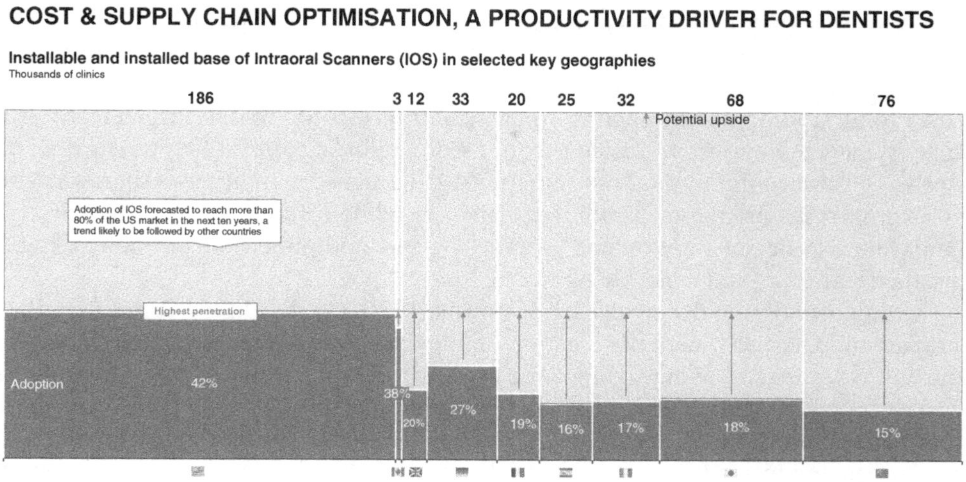

FIGURE 7.20 Adoption of IOS in selected geographies.
Source: National statistics; 3shape website; Candesic analysis.

organizations can convert fixed costs into variable costs, access specialized expertise, and focus on their core mission of patient care. PE firms often drive this by the following:

- Outsourcing lab services: Carving out or contracting with third-party diagnostic laboratories to manage a hospital's lab testing, leveraging the scale and efficiency of a dedicated provider
- Digitalizing services: Such as optimizing dental clinics costs by equipping dental practices with intra oral scanners (Figure 7.20).
- Business process outsourcing: Moving back-office functions such as IT, human resources, and even elements of revenue cycle management to specialized service providers.
- Investing in the outsourcing providers themselves: A key PE strategy is to acquire and build the very companies that provide these outsourced services, creating platforms that benefit from the broader trend of healthcare organizations seeking to improve efficiency.
- Right-sizing headquarters when growing (or failing to grow) operations: This intriguing idea was proposed by Stephane Pichon from YourCare. We illustrate it in our third case.

The outsourcing strategy allows portfolio companies to become leaner and more focused, while creating investment opportunities in the growing healthcare services ecosystem.

7.4.1.2 Case Studies in Action

Case Study 1: Outsourcing of Lab Services (EQT and Cerba HealthCare) The diagnostic laboratory sector exemplifies how PE firms create value through operational consolidation and supply chain optimization. Laboratory testing represents a classic outsourced clinical service where hospitals and clinics send specimens to specialized facilities rather than maintaining in-house capabilities. PE-backed laboratory consolidators achieve economies of scale by aggregating testing volumes across multiple client relationships, enabling bulk procurement of reagents and equipment at reduced unit costs. Total laboratory automation implementations can substantially increase productivity depending on the testing section, while reducing staffing requirements and improving turnaround times. These efficiency gains allow consolidated laboratories to offer competitive pricing to healthcare providers while maintaining margins through standardized processes, automated workflows, and optimized logistics networks for specimen transport and result delivery.

This consolidation occurred early, from the 1970s, in the United States first, then in Japan and Germany, with the creation of large platforms aggregating and automating routine testing, allowing significant economies of scale. In the 2000s, PE investors started to play a significant role, having observed and learned how to achieve these efficiencies. Some countries were late to adopt the model. France offers an interesting case, having instead initially industrialized esoteric (specialized) tests with central platforms developed by Cerba Healthcare and Biomnis. In the last 20 years, most European countries, including France, the United Kingdom, and Italy, have gone through an accelerated consolidation of routine labs with a hub-and-spoke model: central platforms and collection centers. Cerba and Eurofins Biomnis participated too, diversifying into routine labs.

In 2021, EQT replaced Partners Group as lead investor in Cerba for approximately €4.5 billion. However, EQT found value creation considerably more challenging than earlier PE owners, perhaps exposing the limits of PE involvement in a mature market. Opportunities for further operational enhancement had diminished. The situation worsened dramatically in 2024 as French government price cuts for laboratory testing tariffs eroded revenues faster than cost-cutting could offset, pushing leverage to unsustainable levels near 14× debt/EBITDA and forcing EQT to consider debt restructuring.

Case Study 2: IVC Evidensia's Veterinary Platform IVC Evidensia demonstrates comprehensive portfolio synergy execution across Europe's largest veterinary care network. Originally backed by EQT Private Equity in 2016 through its EQT VII fund, which merged it with Swedish veterinary group Evidensia in 2017, the platform welcomed minority investors Silver Lake and expanded participation from Nestlé in 2021. Operating more than 1,500 clinics and hospitals by then, with approximately 22,000 employees across 12 European countries, according to Mergermarket the company maintained a decentralized model promoting clinical freedom while integrating support functions such as procurement, veterinary advisors, and clinical boards. This integration approach, while typical of a roll-up strategy, enabled significant supply chain optimization and cost reductions across the network while accelerating onboarding for new acquisitions. The platform's shared services strategy demonstrated how operational synergies could maintain clinical excellence while achieving economies of scale across fragmented veterinary markets.

Case Study 3: Headquarters Right-sizing for Growing Operators When operators grow from a small base, one frequent trap is prematurely scaling central functions—legal, HR, finance, regulatory, quality—beyond what the network can sustain. Bruno Marie, founder of Almaviva Santé, a French hospital group, famously eliminated a central head office altogether, insisting that administrative infrastructure should never overshadow the frontline teams. By contrast, Dr. Jean-Claude Marian of Orpea estimated that a 3,000-bed threshold was the minimum to amortize headquarters overheads in nursing home operations. Medicharme, a French operator founded in 2015 and backed by PE firm G Square with real estate finance from BlackRock, illustrates this structural pitfall. Despite building a network of 43 nursing homes and 2,000 beds, its €7 million annual headquarter costs effectively erased the net profits of around 30 facilities. Debt pressures and insufficient scale led to its liquidation in 2024—a cautionary tale of how administrative ambition can outgrow the economic base. Getting this right is not simply about savings; it is about matching overhead elasticity to operational maturity. Lean central structures can free capital to fuel growth rather than fund bureaucracy.

7.4.1.3 Outlook and Recommendations for Investors Ingrid Mueller, COO at Evotec, believes that PE will secure medicine access by hardening supply chains—nearshoring critical steps, digitizing quality, and forecasting demand instead of reacting to it: "Decisive, because flexible, accountable capital can rewire global manufacturing networks in quarters, not budget cycles."

To succeed, investors must move beyond high-level procurement reviews to deep supply chain diligence. Priorities include leveraging technology for real-time visibility, systematically evaluating outsourcing opportunities for noncore functions, and establishing portfolio-wide GPOs to maximize negotiating power. Treating the supply chain as a strategic asset rather than a cost center is essential for sustainable value creation.

7.4.2 S22: Alternative Sites of Care

One of the most significant and durable value creation strategies in healthcare PE is the systematic shift of patient care away from high-cost, inpatient hospital settings to more efficient and convenient alternative sites of care. This thesis is not merely about cost arbitrage; it is a fundamental restructuring of care delivery, driven by technological advancements, evolving reimbursement models, and strong patient preference for accessible, specialized treatment. For PE firms, investing in the infrastructure and platforms that enable this shift—primarily ambulatory surgery centers (ASCs), home-based care, and telehealth—is a core strategy for building scalable, high-margin healthcare enterprises.

This strategy is distinct from simple specialization or vertical integration. Its central premise is the *de-institutionalization* of medicine: moving procedures, monitoring, and consultations out of the hospital and closer to the patient. This section deconstructs this strategy into its three core pillars: the ambulatory shift to outpatient centers, the expansion of care into the home, and the role of telehealth as a critical enabler.

7.4.2.1 The Three Pillars of the Alternative Care Site Strategy

The Ambulatory Shift: Outpatient Centers and ASCs The first pillar is the migration of surgical and diagnostic procedures from hospital operating rooms and departments to specialized, lower-cost outpatient facilities. ASCs, specialty clinics (e.g., cardiology, oncology, gastroenterology), and advanced diagnostic imaging centers can perform a growing number of procedures more efficiently and at a lower cost than a full-service hospital due to their lower overhead and more focused operating model. The PE playbook here is typically a buy-and-build strategy in these highly fragmented markets. Key initiatives include the following:

- Acquiring and consolidating practices: Building regional or national platforms of ASCs or specialty clinics to leverage scale in procurement, administrative functions, and payer contracting
- Physician partnerships: Aligning with physicians, often through joint-venture models, to drive case volume and ensure clinical quality
- Investing in technology and equipment: Upgrading facilities with the latest surgical and diagnostic technology to attract top physicians and enable more complex procedures to be performed safely in an outpatient setting

This shift allows PE-backed platforms to capture the significant reimbursement differential between hospital-based and freestanding site-of-service payments.

The Rise of Home-based Care The second pillar involves shifting care from facilities into patients' homes, one of healthcare's fastest growing segments driven by chronic disease management, aging populations, and the imperative to reduce costly hospitalizations. PE investment has been instrumental in scaling and professionalizing this sector through three main strategies. First, firms acquire and consolidate home health and hospice agencies to create scaled platforms capable of contracting with large payers, including Medicare Advantage plans. Second, they invest in hospital-at-home models and virtual wards that provide acute-level care in the home—a model that gained significant traction during COVID-19 (Kitten, 2025a) and is now supported by evolving reimbursement policies (Figure 7.21). Third, they build platforms delivering specialty

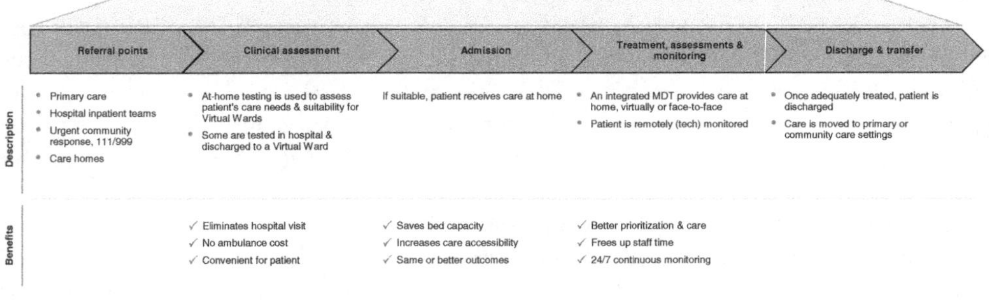

FIGURE 7.21 Virtual-ward model.
Source: NHS England; GIRFT; Candesic analysis.

drug infusions (for immunology or oncology, for instance) in the home, offering a lower-cost and more convenient alternative to hospital-based infusion centers.

This pillar aligns perfectly with the goals of value-based care, as effective home-based care has been shown to reduce emergency department visits and hospital readmissions.

The Virtual Front Door: Telehealth as an Enabler Telehealth provides the critical technology layer enabling and enhancing both ambulatory and home-based care models. While PE firms do invest in standalone telehealth platforms, a more common strategy integrates virtual care capabilities into their provider platforms to improve efficiency and access. This includes using telehealth for pre-operative consultations, post-operative follow-ups, and routine chronic care management, which frees up physical clinic space and improves patient accessibility. Remote patient monitoring (RPM) technologies allow clinicians to monitor patients with chronic conditions like heart failure or chronic obstructive pulmonary disease at home, enabling proactive intervention before deterioration occurs. By blending in-person and virtual visits, firms create hybrid care models that are more flexible, patient-centric, and cost-effective. Telehealth essentially acts as the "digital glue" allowing care to be delivered effectively and safely outside traditional hospital or clinic walls.

7.4.2.2 Case Studies in Action

Case Study 1: Building a Leading ASC Platform (KKR and Covenant Physician Partners) In 2017, KKR acquired Covenant Physician Partners, a company that develops and operates a network of physician practices and ambulatory surgery centers. The core of KKR's investment thesis was to accelerate the company's growth as a leading operator of ASCs, with a particular focus on ophthalmology and gastroenterology. Under KKR's ownership, Covenant pursued a classic buy-and-build strategy, acquiring smaller practices and ASCs and integrating them into its national platform. This strategy allowed the company to leverage its scale in payer negotiations and procurement, while providing its physician partners with capital and operational support. The investment is a clear example of PE driving the shift of surgical procedures from hospitals to more efficient, physician-aligned outpatient settings.

Case Study 2: Telehealth as a Strategic Enabler (Warburg Pincus and CityMD/Summit Health) We already presented the 2019 merger of CityMD, a leading urgent care provider, and Summit Medical Group, a large multi-specialty physician practice, backed by Warburg Pincus. A key element of the strategy for the combined entity, Summit Health, was the deep integration of telehealth. Instead of being a standalone service, telehealth was used to create a "virtual front door" for patients, allowing them to access care quickly for minor issues, get referrals to specialists within the network, and receive follow-up care without needing an in-person visit. This created a more integrated and seamless patient experience, driving patient volume to their physical urgent care and specialty sites. This case illustrates how PE firms use telehealth not just as a technology, but as a strategic tool to enhance and support a broader network of alternative care sites.

7.4.2.3 Outlook and Recommendations for Investors The strategic shift to alternative sites of care is a durable, long-term trend that will continue to offer significant investment opportunities. The convergence of payer pressure to reduce costs, patient demand for convenience, and technological innovation will only accelerate this migration. PE investors should do the following:

- Focus on platform integration: In a buy-and-build strategy, success will depend not just on acquiring assets, but on successfully integrating them onto a common technology and clinical platform to realize true synergies.
- Anticipate regulatory risks: Be mindful of potential changes in reimbursement policy, particularly the move toward "site-neutral payments," which could reduce the payment differential between hospitals and outpatient settings for the same service.
- Prioritize clinical quality: As more complex procedures move into alternative sites, the ability to demonstrate and maintain high standards of clinical quality and patient safety will be a key differentiator and a critical part of risk management.
- Invest in the enabling technology: Recognize that the most successful alternative site platforms will be those that effectively leverage technology—from telehealth and remote monitoring to patient engagement tools—to create a more efficient and integrated care model.

By focusing on these areas, PE firms can continue to build valuable and impactful companies that are at the forefront of the transformation of healthcare delivery.

7.4.3 S23: Clinical Excellence: Quality, Safety, and Pathway Optimization

Beyond traditional operational levers like supply chain management or revenue cycle optimization, a more sophisticated and increasingly critical value creation strategy is the direct pursuit of clinical excellence. This approach is rooted in the understanding that in healthcare, superior financial returns are often a direct consequence of superior patient outcomes. For PE firms, investing in clinical quality, safety, and pathway optimization is not an act of philanthropy; it is a strategic imperative that reduces risk, enhances reputation, aligns with value-based care models, and ultimately drives sustainable EBITDA growth.

This strategy moves beyond the assumption that quality and cost are in opposition. Instead, it operates on the principle that higher quality—defined by fewer errors, better outcomes, and standardized processes—is fundamentally more efficient. By eliminating waste caused by medical complications, re-admissions, and unnecessary variations in care, PE sponsors can achieve significant margin expansion. This section deconstructs this strategy into three core pillars: improving quality and safety, optimizing clinical pathways, and implementing data-driven clinical governance.

7.4.3.1 The Three Pillars of Clinical Excellence

Foundational Quality Improvement and Patient Safety The first pillar involves systematic reduction of preventable harm and implementation of evidence-based care standards, forming the foundational layer of risk mitigation and operational stability for PE investors. The focus is on measurable improvements in core safety metrics with direct financial impact. This includes reducing hospital-acquired infections through rigorous hygiene protocols and staff training to lower rates of central line-associated bloodstream infections and catheter-associated urinary tract infections, which carry significant nonreimbursed costs and penalties. Firms invest in post-discharge follow-up programs, patient education, and care coordination to prevent costly and often penalized 30-day readmissions. They also deploy technology and standardized protocols to reduce medication errors, a major source of patient harm and legal liability. These initiatives protect the core business from regulatory penalties and lawsuits while building trust with payers and patients, creating a more defensible and valuable asset.

Clinical Pathway Optimization The second pillar focuses on reducing unwarranted clinical variation—a major driver of both excess cost and inconsistent outcomes. By developing and implementing standardized clinical pathways for specific conditions or procedures (such as joint replacement, cardiac surgery, or cancer care), PE-backed companies achieve significant efficiencies. This involves working with clinical leaders to define best-practice guidelines for diagnosis, treatment, and recovery based on the best available evidence, then ensuring that staffing, medical supplies, and diagnostic tests are used consistently and appropriately according to the established pathway, eliminating waste. Standardization creates a more predictable care journey, allowing for better capacity planning, shorter lengths of stay, and smoother patient flow, ultimately increasing throughput.

Pathway optimization transforms care delivery from a bespoke, high-variance art into a reliable, high-quality science, which is essential for scaling healthcare services effectively. Figure 7.22 shows the impact of poor patient communication on cancellation rates.

Data-driven Clinical Governance The third pillar is the measurement and management layer enabling continuous improvement through robust clinical governance powered by data analytics. PE firms excel at implementing rigorous KPI monitoring, and applying this discipline to clinical metrics is a powerful value lever. This includes developing

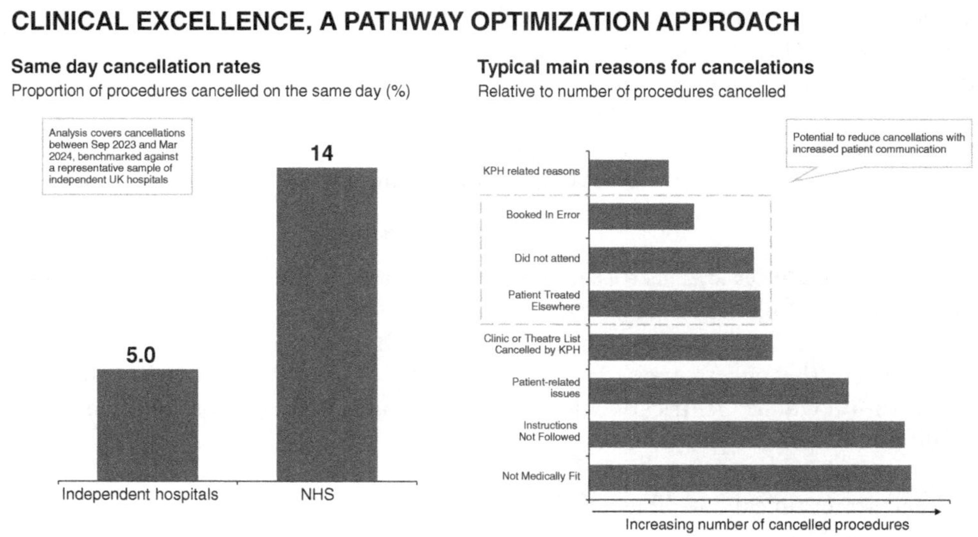

FIGURE 7.22 Pathway optimization.
Source: Acta Anaesthesiologica Scandinavica; Candesic analysis.

clinical KPI dashboards that track key quality, safety, and outcome metrics in real time to identify performance gaps and outliers. Physician performance benchmarking provides clinicians with confidential data on their performance relative to peers and evidence-based standards, driving behavioral change and adherence to best practices. Perhaps most importantly, firms create clear analytical links between improvements in clinical KPIs (such as a 10% reduction in readmissions) and their direct impact on EBITDA, making the return on clinical investment tangible and measurable.

This data-driven approach ensures that quality improvement is not a one-off project but an embedded, continuous part of the organization's operating model.

7.4.3.2 Case Studies in Action

Case Study 1: Quality and Safety in a Hospital Network (KKR and Max Healthcare) When KKR invested in Max Healthcare, one of India's largest hospital chains, in 2018 (see 7.2.1.2), a core part of the value creation plan was to instill a culture of clinical excellence and patient safety. The firm supported the implementation of a rigorous clinical governance framework focused on measurable quality improvements. Initiatives included deploying digital systems to track clinical KPIs, standardizing protocols across the network, and investing heavily in nurse training and infection control. As detailed in KKR's public ESG reports, these efforts led to a significant reduction in key metrics like medication errors and patient fall rates. This focus on quality was a key driver in improving the company's operational performance and reputation, contributing to its successful public listing in 2020 and a reported 4.5× return for KKR upon its exit.

Case Study 2: Pathway Optimization in Specialty Care (WCAS and the US Oncology Network) The creation in 2004 of the US Oncology Network, pioneered by WCAS, is a classic example of using clinical pathway optimization to drive value. By bringing together numerous independent community oncology practices into a single network, WCAS was able to provide the resources and scale needed to standardize complex cancer care. The network developed and implemented evidence-based treatment guidelines, known as "Level I Pathways," which helped to reduce variation in care, improve adherence to best practices, and manage the costs of expensive cancer drugs more effectively. This strategy not only improved the quality and consistency of care for patients but also created significant operational efficiencies and enhanced the network's negotiating power with payers, building a highly valuable national platform (US Oncology Network, n.d.).

7.4.3.3 Outlook and Recommendations for Investors As healthcare reimbursement continues to shift from volume to value, the ability to demonstrate and deliver clinical excellence will become a primary determinant of an investment's success. The era of driving returns solely through financial leverage or multiple expansion is over; sustainable value creation will be inextricably linked to quality and patient outcomes. PE investors should do the following:

- Integrate clinical due diligence: Move beyond financial and commercial diligence to include a rigorous assessment of a target's clinical quality, safety records, and data infrastructure. This should be led by experienced clinical operating partners or external experts.

- Build clinical KPI dashboards: For every healthcare portfolio company, implement a standardized dashboard to track a core set of clinical quality and safety metrics alongside financial KPIs.
- Link management incentives to quality: Ensure that a portion of the management team's compensation is directly tied to achieving pre-defined clinical excellence targets, not just financial ones.
- Invest in a clinical governance platform: For firms with multiple healthcare assets, consider investing in or building a portfolio-wide platform for sharing best practices, benchmarking performance, and deploying quality improvement tools at scale.

By embedding clinical excellence into the core of their investment thesis and operating model, PE firms can build more resilient, reputable, and ultimately more valuable healthcare enterprises.

7.4.4 S24: Regulatory Strategy and Policy Navigation

Effective regulatory strategy and policy navigation is a critical PE value lever, distinct from other investment themes in this book. It encompasses reactive adaptation to shifting rules, proactive policy engagement, arbitrage of regulatory regimes, and the cultivation of in-house regulatory expertise. These approaches—from basic and reactive to more strategic and advanced—turn complex healthcare regulations into systematic paths for value creation.

7.4.4.1 Reactive Regulatory Shifts and Deregulation In the United States over the years, regulatory changes have paved the way for increased PE investment in healthcare by removing barriers and fostering innovation. The Stark Law, introduced in 1989, initially restricted physicians from making referrals to entities in which they had a financial interest. Similarly, the Anti-kickback Statute, enacted in 1972, prohibited the exchange of remuneration for referrals involving federal healthcare programs. Regulatory reforms have repeatedly created fertile ground for PE investment in healthcare.

- Value-based arrangements: The 2011 Stark Law exceptions and subsequent Anti-kickback Statute safe harbors for ACOs enabled modern care platforms. Aledade, an ACO-enabling technology and services platform, raised about $670 million in 10 rounds of late-stage financing from 2014 to 2023. This allowed the company to ride these reforms to rapidly sign primary-care physician networks and ACOs into shared-savings contracts. As previously discussed, in 2015, General Atlantic, Harbour Point Capital and Quantum Strategic Partners invested $143 million growth-equity round in Oak Street Health, a value-based primary-care platform serving Medicare Advantage members. Oak Street's capitated contracts and quality incentives were enabled by CMS's Direct Contracting and Medicare Advantage value-based rules, driving rapid clinic expansion and improved outcomes. Oak Street was acquired by CVS Health in 2023 for an EV of $10.6 billion, demonstrating the success of this model.
- Certificate-of-need (CON) repeals: The relaxation of CON laws encouraged roll-ups of specialty clinics. Following Florida's partial repeal of CON requirements

in 2019, Revelstoke Capital Partners–backed Upstream Rehabilitation executed four bolt-on clinic chains acquisitions by 2021 and became the largest pure-play outpatient physical therapy provider in the United States, with more than 1,000 outpatient clinics.
- Telehealth waivers: COVID-19 accelerated regulatory flexibilities—interstate licensure reciprocity, reimbursement parity, and relaxed HIPAA enforcement. In May 2020, Amwell closed a $194 million Series C financing led by Allianz X and Takeda, coinciding with CMS's emergency COVID-19 telehealth waivers which drove Amwell's daily visit volume from approximately 10,000 pre-pandemic to around 45,000 at peak in June 2020 according to PitchBook.

7.4.4.2 Monopoly Plays from Deregulation Building on these reactive shifts, PE sponsors have exploited pockets of deregulation to create local monopolies. This strategy is similar to the niche market domination described earlier as a specialization strategy, but in a deregulation context.

- The US air ambulance industry illustrates this: under the Airline Deregulation Act of 1978, medical air transport prices were free from state controls, allowing American Securities and KKR to acquire Air Methods and Air Medical Response and control two-thirds of Medicare-paid helicopter volume by 2017.
- The 2023 FTC case against WCAS and its portfolio company US Anesthesia Partners (USAP) exemplifies regulatory scrutiny of PE roll-up strategies. The FTC accused the firm of orchestrating USAP's systematic acquisition of anesthesiology practices in Texas to create a monopoly and inflate prices. In May 2024, a federal judge dismissed Welsh Carson from the case, finding that its residual 23% minority stake did not constitute an ongoing antitrust violation. The FTC's case against USAP itself continues in federal court, while USAP separately settled with the Colorado Attorney General in 2024, divesting five hospital contracts. Welsh Carson accepted an FTC consent order in January 2025 restricting future anesthesia investments.
- Orphan-drug exclusivity extensions post-FDA approval have enabled PE owners of small biotechs to execute steep price hikes under monopoly protection. A frequently cited example is Marathon Pharmaceuticals, a firm backed by Valor Equity Partners. After securing a seven-year orphan drug exclusivity for Emflaza, a Duchenne muscular dystrophy treatment that families had been importing for ~$1,200 a year, Marathon launched it in 2017 at a list price of $89,000. The resulting public and political backlash forced the company to sell the drug's rights shortly after launch, illustrating a strategy that prioritized monopoly pricing over patient access. Antitrust agencies, constrained by a $111.4 million HSR threshold that exempts nearly 90% of PE transactions, often miss these smaller consolidations, tempting sponsors to build local market power.
- In Europe, a landmark example is Altor Fund III's 2009 acquisition of 206 former state pharmacies from Apoteket AB to form Apotek Hjärtat, immediately after Sweden lifted its 38-year-old pharmacy monopoly in April 2009. More recently, Medstop bought three pharmacy clusters from Apoteket AB in 2020, further consolidating market share under the new deregulated regime.

7.4.4.3 Changes in Reimbursement Policy and Rates Most healthcare companies are vulnerable to reimbursement policy shifts. Conversely, some companies, often with the backing of the PE owners, are able to spot the opportunity and position themselves ahead of an expected change, for example by designing or offering a product or service that meets the budgetary constraints of the payors.

Some dramatic cases of reimbursement changes have led to famous investment failures where PE shareholders have lost all their money, including HCR ManorCare in the United States, and Four Seasons Healthcare in the United Kingdom, both operators of nursing homes.

- Carlyle purchased ManorCare for $6.3 billion in 2007. The investment was premised on stable Medicare and Medicaid reimbursements for skilled nursing and rehabilitation services. Unfortunately, the US government implemented significant cuts to Medicare reimbursement rates for skilled nursing facilities, particularly in 2011, when the CMS reduced payments by 11.1%. Carlyle was unable to sell or recapitalize the business, and ManorCare ultimately filed for bankruptcy in 2018.
- Similarly, Terra Firma bought Four Seasons Healthcare in 2012 for up to £825 million. The leading UK nursing home group had approximately 80% of its revenue coming from local authorities and the NHS. In the years following the acquisition, the UK government implemented austerity measures that resulted in cuts or freezes to local authority fees paid to care homes. At the same time, the introduction of the national living wage increased staffing costs across the sector. By 2019, Four Seasons' holding companies were placed into administration, marking one of the largest insolvencies in the UK care home sector since the collapse of Southern Cross in 2011. Terra Firma was forced to write down £450 million on its investment, effectively losing most of its equity in the deal.

Alex Slack, co-founding partner at Lauxera Capital Partners in San Francisco, commented on the risks and opportunities surrounding changes in reimbursement policy and rates in the United States and European Union:

> *In the US, Medicare operates on an annual cycle of policy and rate changes, with Local Coverage Determinations (LCDs) providing additional, sometimes market-specific coverage guidelines. Private payors in the US lack standardized update schedules, while influential panels such as the National Comprehensive Cancer Network (NCCN) typically follow annual review cycles. Typically, major policy changes are extensively previewed through public comment periods, expert panels, and stakeholder interactions involving industry representatives, regulatory experts, and healthcare stakeholders.*
>
> *In European markets, healthcare policy approaches vary more complexly. While some countries centralize rate determinations, coverage policies can be either centrally coordinated or locally implemented, depending on the specific national healthcare system. The process of anticipating and analyzing potential policy changes represents a critical component of healthcare investment strategy, presenting both significant opportunities and risks across various healthcare subsectors, including tech-enabled services, traditional healthcare services, digital health, medical devices, and diagnostic technologies.*

In digital health, while some European nations like Germany and the Netherlands have relatively progressive reimbursement frameworks, others maintain more conservative approaches. Implementation can also be faulty. For instance, the German Digital Healthcare Act introduced in 2019 represented a breakthrough in digital health reimbursement, yet implementation remained inconsistent. There was also increased volatility in reimbursement rates, particularly in the wake of the COVID-19 pandemic. Technologies that gained emergency approval or temporary reimbursement during the pandemic faced significant scrutiny and potential rate reductions afterward. RPM solutions, telehealth platforms, and digital therapeutics have been particularly vulnerable to these policy shifts. Countries like France and Spain have implemented more stringent criteria for RPM reimbursement, effectively reducing the economic viability of previously promising digital health solutions. For instance, some RPM providers have seen reimbursement rates cut by 30–40% within a single fiscal year, challenging their existing business models and investment theses.

It is not all bad. According to Alex Slack, empirical analysis suggests that investment strategies can typically anticipate reimbursement and coverage directions with reasonable confidence for the initial three to five years of an investment. Moreover, long-term downside risks to reimbursement rates and coverage are often predictable, though the timing of potential rate increases remains less certain.

There are other ways to reduce vulnerability. According to our discussions with investors, in the case of European healthcare digital technologies, successful PE investment requires the following:

- Adaptive business models: Developing flexible revenue streams that are less dependent on direct reimbursement
- Regulatory intelligence: Maintaining deep insights into evolving healthcare policies across different European markets
- Value-based approach: Demonstrating clear clinical and economic value to justify reimbursement
- Multi-market strategy: Diversifying across different European healthcare systems to mitigate localized reimbursement risks

More often than not, PE investors have an eye for a good opportunity. In 2021, Lauxera strategically invested in Reapplix, a Danish medical technology company specializing in innovative wound care solutions for diabetic foot ulcers. These ulcers represent a critical and often underestimated healthcare challenge, characterized by their potential for severe complications. These chronic wounds pose a significant medical risk, with approximately 15% of diabetic patients developing foot ulcers, and up to 24% of these cases potentially leading to lower extremity amputation.

The US healthcare market presents a substantial opportunity in this domain, with more than one million new diabetic foot ulcer cases annually. Lauxera identified a strategic entry point by targeting the existing wound care reimbursement ecosystem, which was experiencing considerable market pressure and seeking innovative treatment solutions. By carefully positioning Reapplix's technology within the complex US wound care reimbursement "bundle," the firm was able to secure favorable reimbursement terms, potentially creating a compelling value proposition for healthcare providers and patients alike.

7.4.4.4 Strategic Regulatory Engagement and Arbitrage This sub-strategy focuses on harnessing regulatory expertise as a deliberate value-creation lever, guiding PE-owned companies through evolving policy landscapes and turning complex rulemaking into a source of competitive advantage by anticipating, influencing, and arbitraging regulation.

- Proactive policy engagement and coalition building
  Forward-looking PE sponsors increasingly engage regulators and industry associations to shape policy before final rules are issued. This involves detailed policy submissions, participation in public-private working groups, and funding of academic and trade-association research. Figure 7.23 highlights the long lead times of regulatory strategies.
- Scenario planning and rapid adaptation
  Leading PE firms maintain "regulatory war-rooms" to model potential rule changes—such as shifts in Medicare reimbursement, 340B program reforms, and surprise-billing legislation—and stress-test portfolio cash flows under alternative policy scenarios. This agility proved critical when the No Surprises Act (effective January 2022) mandated new dispute-resolution frameworks, prompting PE-owned urgent-care platforms to renegotiate payer contracts and adjust service mix.
- Regulatory sophistication and capability-building
  Some PE sponsors go beyond one-off advocacy and build permanent, in-house policy and regulatory affairs teams to stay ahead of evolving rules. These capability centers develop internal expertise in health economics, outcomes research, and government relations, enabling PE-owned companies to model policy impacts, draft comments during public consultations, and even pilot regulatory sandboxes. Though rare, this level of regulatory sophistication can turn prospective rule changes into competitive advantages by embedding policy know-how directly within the investment platform.

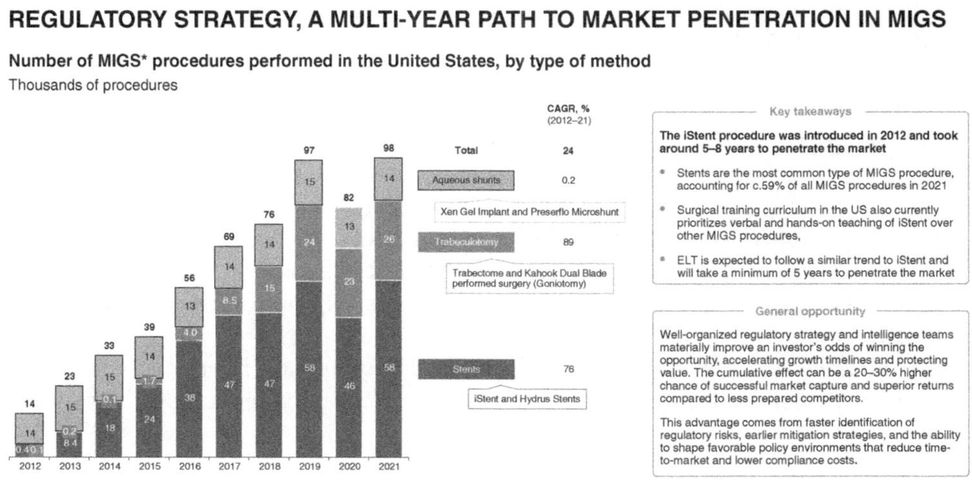

FIGURE 7.23 MIGS procedures in the USA.
Source: IRIS Registry; NIH; Candesic interviews; Candesic analysis.

- Cross-border policy network strategy
  As healthcare is often national or regional, top-tier PE sponsors build cross-border policy networks to anticipate and align with international regulatory trends, such as the EU's Medical Device Regulation roll-out in 2021 or China's evolving pricing and reimbursement guidelines for innovative drugs.
- Regulatory arbitrage in pharmaceutical development
  Complementing these strategies, PE firms can capture outsized gains by acquiring pharma assets with undervalued pipelines and deploying regulatory expertise to extend exclusivity or repurpose drugs. Such strategies exploit nuances in fast-track pathways, pediatric exclusivity, and priority review vouchers to maximize asset value ahead of exit.

Regulatory engagement can also take the form of systematically seeking gold standard approvals. The team at Quadria Capital sees regulation not as an obstacle but as a positive driver of value. They welcome the gradual harmonization of the regulatory landscape across Asia. "We certainly don't want to work in an unregulated or semi-regulated market because as a serious investor in high quality businesses, we welcome high quality regulation of products and services," says Abrar Mir.

In fact, increasingly, the businesses that they invest in aspire to gold standard regulatory approvals. Mir notes, "Not just the national regulatory standard but FDA approval for products and JCI approval for hospital operations. These benchmarks signal trust, quality, and global competitiveness, and they are integral to the way we define value creation."

To finish, we should also mention the option to provide the regulatory services directly, building a center of excellence. GHO's investment in Validant (2018–2021) is an example of successful healthcare PE execution in practice. The company provided regulatory remediation services, and the founder's decision to roll 40% equity into the fund demonstrated genuine alignment and conviction. Their "handshake deal" approach perfectly reflects the relationship-driven nature of successful healthcare investments.

Outlook and Recommendations Regulation will remain a decisive value axis. PE investors should do the following:

- Build dedicated regulatory intelligence teams to track federal, state, and international policy shifts.
- Conduct scenario planning for key rule proposals (e.g., drug pricing, telehealth parity) and integrate policy stress-tests into diligence.
- Engage proactively with stakeholders—regulators, payors, providers—to influence outcomes and secure safe harbors ahead of competitors.
- Seek arbitrage opportunities across jurisdictions, exploiting lags in regulation or differential reimbursement frameworks.
- Evaluate the merits of in-house policy capability centers for large platforms, recognizing that sustained regulatory expertise can create persistent competitive moats.

7.4.5 S25: Patient-centric and Experience-focused Models

As PE firms sharpen their focus on healthcare investment strategies, patient-centric and experience-focused models have emerged as important, distinct plays that complement but do not duplicate other strategies related to value-based care, technology, or clinical excellence. These models prioritize improving the patient's engagement, satisfaction, and loyalty as business drivers—whether within value-based care (VBC) frameworks or in more traditional settings.

7.4.5.1 VBC Initiatives VBC initiatives link provider reimbursement to quality, outcomes, and efficiency rather than service volume, rewarding healthcare organizations that improve population health, reduce chronic disease impact, and lower costs. PE firms increasingly invest in platforms and companies that facilitate these goals, such as population health management, care coordination, and hospital readmission reduction.

European examples include Waterland Private Equity's 2017 investment in Schönes Leben Gruppe, a leading elder care provider growing primarily through buy-and-build strategies emphasizing quality and accessibility. Palamon Capital Partners' investment in Prospitalia (2009–2016) saw the firm supporting a group purchasing organization that helped hospitals reduce costs while improving supply chain efficiency.

In the United States, TPG Capital's minority investment in Kelsey-Seybold Clinic Partners in 2019 exemplifies a VBC-oriented play that ultimately led to sale to UnitedHealthcare's Optum in 2022, illustrating the consolidation forces at work even among VBC-focused assets.

Market interest is illustrated by Kinderhook Industries' $500 million investment in Physician Partners—a value-based primary care group in Florida—and WCAS's $1.2 billion joint venture with Humana expanding CenterWell Senior Primary Care, a payer-agnostic VBC network for Medicare patients. CD&R's investment in Agilon Health (see "Specialization") similarly underscores PE's bet on companies partnering with physician groups in full-risk VBC arrangements.

These PE-led initiatives in VBC, specialty clinics, and eldercare together point to an enormous market opportunity. The US value-based healthcare services market alone was estimated to be worth more than $4 trillion in 2024, with the enterprise value of US value-based care assets on track to be above $1 trillion by 2030 (Figure 7.24). This scale reflects the growing shift toward patient-centered, outcome-driven care models and regulatory reforms that incentivize quality and efficiency over volume.

However, the shift toward VBC raises questions about whether it signals true transformation or simply another phase in provider consolidation. Ma et al. (2024) caution that the exit of PE firms from outpatient and specialty care to large insurers may concentrate market power, leading to rising costs rather than sustainable value. Moreover, PE's typical 3–7-year investment horizon may conflict with the longer-term cultural changes needed for authentic VBC success.

7.4.5.2 Other Engagement and Satisfaction Models Patient engagement and satisfaction go beyond reimbursement mechanics and can be pursued independently of VBC contracts. Many providers use engagement strategies within traditional fee-for-service frameworks—like patient portals, education programs, or shared decision-making tools—to boost adherence, loyalty, and reputation.

Hospitals and clinics often implement patient satisfaction programs with hospitality training, feedback surveys (e.g., HCAHPS), and service recovery protocols that drive ratings and market competitiveness, even if disconnected from value-based payments.

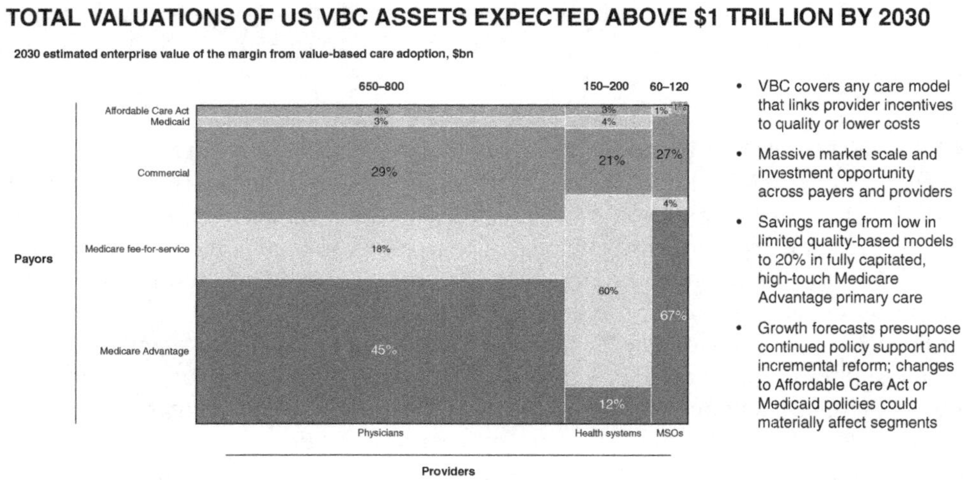

FIGURE 7.24 US VBC assets.
Source: Candesic research and analysis (inspired by McKinsey & Co, Investing in the new era of value-based care, 2022).

In competitive markets, patient loyalty models—featuring concierge services, branded experiences, or retention incentives—serve as business levers separate from clinical outcomes. Likewise, digital health and consumer engagement platforms (telemedicine apps, wellness trackers, remote monitoring) focus on usability and sustained adoption, monetizing through subscriptions, employer contracts, or direct payments rather than VBC.

Some managed-care and pay-for-performance (P4P) plans incorporate patient satisfaction metrics such as survey scores into provider bonuses, but these are often less comprehensive than VBC goals.

Innovative Engagement: Gamification An emerging frontier is the use of gamification—applying game-design elements like challenges, rewards, and social competition—to foster healthier behaviors and patient engagement. Some digital therapeutics and wellness platforms increasingly use gamification to improve treatment adherence and lifestyle changes. While few PE transactions explicitly highlight gamification, firms investing in digital health platforms may gain a competitive edge by enhancing user engagement through these techniques.

Outlook and Recommendations Patient-centric and experience-focused strategies will remain a critical piece of healthcare investing, especially as the market matures beyond pure VBC contracts. PE investors should do the following:

- Recognize that improving patient experience and engagement is a business driver independent of reimbursement shifts, especially under traditional fee-for-service or hybrid models.
- Explore digital health investments embedding gamification and other engagement-enhancing features, capitalizing on growing consumer demand for interactive, user-friendly health tools.

- Monitor consolidation risks that are inherent in some VBC investments, balancing financial returns with longer-term value creation that aligns with systemic healthcare goals.
- Partner with platforms that combine clinical excellence with patient experience innovations, realizing that sustainable value often depends on broad stakeholder alignment—patients, providers, and payors.
- Consider an active role in patient loyalty and retention models as complementary growth levers, particularly in competitive markets with high patient choice.

7.4.6 S26: Impact-driven Sustainability vs. ESG Compliance

Rather than a market adaptation, ESG is now foundational in deal selection and value creation.

In healthcare PE, impact defines the mission from day one—what firms choose to achieve—while ESG compliance describes the mandatory steps taken to satisfy external rules and stakeholder expectations. PE firms embed ESG principles deeply into healthcare platforms to drive operational efficiency, improve patient outcomes, and meet heightened stakeholder expectations. Impact is proactive: it shapes deal selection, deal structuring, and management incentives around clear social or environmental goals.[6] ESG compliance is reactive: it ensures minimum standards for energy use, waste management, workforce practices, and reporting. A value-creation strategy centered on impact weaves purposeful change into every phase of the investment life cycle; compliance alone merely checks boxes.

In healthcare PE, sustainability initiatives concentrate primarily on three pillars that were not historically interconnected.

Environmental stewardship under an impact lens means committing to transformative projects—such as developing carbon-negative hospital campuses powered by on-site solar and biogas—rather than simply upgrading to LED lighting and optimizing HVAC systems. It includes end-to-end pharmaceutical waste reduction programs that recover or neutralize active compounds, turning disposal liabilities into revenue streams. Compliance activities nonetheless remain important: they cover facility audits, emissions monitoring, and advanced recycling protocols to meet regulatory mandates.

Social impact moves beyond broad workforce well-being initiatives and reporting diversity metrics. Impact-focused sponsors launch permanent community-clinic networks, mobile health units, or telemedicine programs that measurably expand care access in underserved regions. They tie management incentives to specific targets—such as increasing rural patient volumes by 25% or reducing no-show rates in mental-health clinics by 40%. Compliance efforts still encompass employee training, safety protocols, and adherence to labor regulations, which are prerequisites for operating responsibly.

Governance excellence under impact involves creating stakeholder governance bodies—patient-advocate councils or public-health advisory boards—with real influence over strategic decisions. Investors embed these structures into governance frameworks

[6] Impact is foundational to deal selection and value creation, not just a market adaptation strategy, and could as well be moved to Section II (Other Structural Strategies).

at closing. Compliance activities include establishing transparent reporting frameworks aligned with Sustainability Accounting Standards Board (SASB) and Global Reporting Initiative (GRI) standards, rigorous audit processes, and linking ESG KPIs (energy use per patient, community-benefit investments) to executive compensation.

Illustrative Impact Transactions

- TPG's Rise Fund and Blue Cloud Pediatric Surgery Centers: From inception in 2016, Rise Fund structured the acquisition so that Blue Cloud would increase Medicaid-eligible pediatric surgeries by 30% within five years. Management bonuses were linked to expanding services in low-income areas, and the fund required quarterly reporting on access metrics, not just financial performance. Rise Fund also funded two new mobile surgery units deployed to rural counties in Alabama and Mississippi to reach children with special needs.
- EQT Healthcare Growth and Europa Biosite: In mid-2025, EQT's majority investment in this life-science reagent distributor included contractual milestones to cut Europa's distribution-network carbon intensity by 50% by 2030. EQT provided capital to build solar-powered warehouses in Germany and the United Kingdom, and financed a fleet of electric delivery vehicles, embedding these measures into the shareholder agreement rather than adding them later as an ESG afterthought.

By clearly distinguishing impact from compliance, we underscore that true value creation in healthcare PE arises when impact—the mission and measurable social or environmental objectives—drives every investment decision, with ESG compliance serving as the critical, but secondary, framework that ensures responsible execution. Through weaving ESG into their investment theses, PE-backed healthcare platforms secure cost savings, enhance brand value, and deliver tangible environmental and social returns alongside robust financial performance.

7.5 CHIEF TECHNOLOGY OFFICER PLAYBOOK

(Strategies driven by the adoption and development of novel technologies, data analytics, digital transformation, and scientific breakthroughs)

7.5.1 S27: Data Strategies: Analytics and Monetization

According to Grand View Research and MarketsandMarkets, healthcare data monetization represented a market valued between $500 million and $1 billion in 2024, with projected growth rates of 15% to 20% CAGR through 2030–2033 depending on research methodology, transforming how PE firms value healthcare assets and create competitive advantages through analytics-driven insights. Simultaneously, near-universal EHR adoption (>90%) and maturing AI tools have shifted healthcare from brick-and-mortar services to data-driven platforms, prompting PE firms to assign tech-style valuations to data assets.

PE firms increasingly recognize healthcare data as a strategic asset that fundamentally alters EBITDA multiples. Healthcare companies with proprietary datasets can command 15–25× EBITDA multiples rather than traditional healthcare service multiples of 8–12× EBITDA. For example, IQVIA's healthcare datasets (clinical data analytics) generate recurring, high-margin analytics revenue with minimal incremental costs. This is similar to the valuation arbitrage that separates software companies from brick-and-mortar operations. The difference? Data assets create scalable revenue streams without proportional cost increases—exactly the characteristics PE firms prize for multiple expansion.

PE strategies encompass both direct monetization (licensing proprietary data for premium EBITDA multiples) and indirect optimization (operational improvements through analytics that enhance traditional service margins while maintaining premium valuations). According to Iqvia and CB Insights, direct monetization generates revenue through subscription-based analytics dashboards ($50,000–500,000 annually per client), pharmaceutical market research services (selling anonymized patient journey insights for $100,000–$2 million per study), and API access to predictive models (usage-based pricing at $0.10–5.00 per query). Indirect optimization includes operational efficiency gains, risk reduction, and care pathway improvements that enhance existing revenue streams while maintaining premium EBITDA multiples. Radiology and labs have seen many AI driven innovations in the last 10 years, leading to almost fully autonomous diagnostic workflows. Radiotherapy, with AI contouring and dosage calculation are more recent examples that significantly reduce patient exposure to radiation, with the example of French company Therapanacea (Figure 7.25).

7.5.1.1 Population Health Management as Strategic Enabler PE-backed organizations leverage population health analytics to create dual value streams—operational efficiency and new revenue models. PHM transforms raw patient data into predictive insights for risk stratification, care pathway optimization, and value-based contract negotiations. PHM monetization occurs through shared savings contracts (capturing 20–50% of cost reductions), risk-adjusted capitation payments, clinical decision support licensing

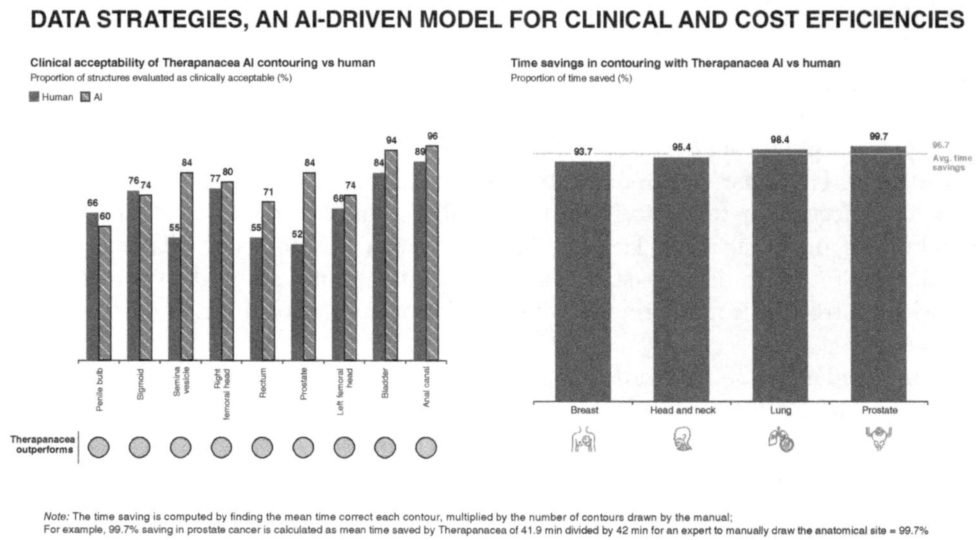

FIGURE 7.25 AI contouring in radiotherapy treatment planning for cancer care.
Source: Candesic analysis.

($25,000–$150,000 per health system annually), and actuarial insights sales to other payers. This data-driven approach enables identification of high-risk patients before costly interventions become necessary, generating measurable ROI ranging from –$244 to $1,592 per member per year (PwC, 2022). More importantly for PE investors, PHM platforms create proprietary datasets that command premium valuations and recurring revenue through analytics-as-a-service offerings.

7.5.1.2 Illustrative Transactions

Case 1: Envision Pharma In 2016, with the support of Candesic, Ardian and GHO Capital acquired Envision Pharma Group for its medical affairs software platform, systematically developing the iEnvision™ database through acquisitions and organic growth before Ardian exited in 2020 with a successful four-year value creation story. Ardian identified Envision as having "the highest potential for further growth" after analyzing the outsourced medical affairs services and software market. The investment thesis focused on the company's technology platform and blue-chip customer base in an attractive healthcare IT subsector.

With PE backing, Envision launched its comprehensive medical affairs technology platform encompassing its existing publication planning management, clearance approval, activity request management, workflow management for health economics outcomes research, and medical information enquiries. Envision also grew by acquisitions, acquiring Curo Consulting Ltd., adding specialized HEOR and Market Access software, dynamically matching datasets with payer needs and facilitating value narratives for different payer archetypes. These acquisitions expanded Envision's global reach into Asia-Pacific and diversified its communication services portfolio.

The platform generated revenue through scientific data communication services, technology licensing, and subscription-based access to proprietary medical affairs databases. Envision monetized client data through strategic publication planning, medical writing services, and evidence communication programs. This transaction has been widely observed by the PE community, with many investors trying to reproduce it in other segments.

Case 2: Surescripts In 2024, TPG acquired Surescripts, an electronic prescription network, paying a stunning 28× EBITDA multiple for $1.8 billion. It exemplifies workflow optimization through data analytics. This transaction demonstrates PE investment in healthcare IT infrastructure that monetizes prescription data flows across provider networks. According to FierceHealthcare (2024), unlike typical buyouts, existing shareholders including CVS Health, Express Scripts (Cigna), and pharmacy trade associations retained minority stakes. This unusual structure allowed TPG to capture majority control while maintaining industry relationships critical for network effects.

Case 3: Arcadia In 2025, Nordic Capital acquired majority ownership of Arcadia, a healthcare data platform integrating ecosystem data into actionable intelligence for providers, payers, and government organizations. The partnership demonstrates PE recognition of data platforms as infrastructure investments with recurring revenue potential.

7.5.1.3 Key Learnings Data Quality Drives Multiple Expansion: Successful monetization requires unique, instrumental data rather than fungible datasets. Healthcare organizations with comprehensive EHR integration, claims data, and real-world evidence can command 18–25× EBITDA multiples because they escape commodity service pricing.

PHM Creates Defensible Moats: Population health platforms generate proprietary insights impossible to replicate without comparable patient populations and longitudinal data. This creates sustainable competitive advantages that justify 20×+ EBITDA multiples rather than traditional healthcare service valuations.

Multi-stakeholder Revenue Structure: Successful analytics platforms monetize the same datasets across multiple customer segments—pharmaceutical companies pay for real-world evidence, medical device manufacturers buy outcomes data, health plans purchase comparative effectiveness research, and providers license clinical decision support tools.

Multiple Arbitrage Reality: Traditional hospital management companies trade at 8–10× EBITDA while healthcare technology platforms with proprietary data command 15–25× EBITDA multiples. PE firms capture this arbitrage by acquiring data-poor healthcare companies and transforming them into data-rich platforms worthy of technology valuations.

Regulatory Compliance Critical: HIPAA and state privacy regulations constrain monetization strategies. PE firms must implement robust encryption, anonymization, and access controls to protect patient information while extracting commercial value.

7.5.1.4 Outlook AI integration accelerates healthcare data value creation, with machine learning enabling predictive analytics for chronic disease management and operational optimization. Usage-based API monetization will become standard, with healthcare analytics companies charging per query for risk scores, predictive models, and clinical recommendations—creating recurring revenue streams that justify premium multiples. PE firms will increasingly target companies with proprietary datasets and proven analytics capabilities, particularly those serving pharmaceutical R&D and clinical decision support markets. The EBITDA multiple expansion from 10× to 20×+ represents the clearest financial incentive driving PE interest in healthcare data strategies.

7.5.2 S28: IP Monetization and Licensing

Intangible assets now account for roughly 90% of the total market value of S&P 500 companies, with patents, trademarks, proprietary data, and brand equity making up the vast majority. In healthcare and life sciences, drug and device patents, regulatory exclusivities, and clinical data represent a disproportionately large share of those intangible assets—explaining why PE firms target IP-rich biotech, pharma, and medtech companies.

Key strategic approaches include patent portfolio development and licensing revenue generation.

In the first case, PE firms implement aggressive patent-building strategies, including invention incentive programs ($1,000–3,000 per filing), IP audits, and continuation applications to maintain prosecution flexibility. Medical device companies particularly benefit from systematic patenting approaches covering both core technologies and potential infringement scenarios.

As for licensing, healthcare organizations monetize IP through exclusive/nonexclusive licensing, cross-licensing agreements, and rate card development for brand usage. Academic medical centers increasingly seek IP valuation for licensing and partnership negotiations, leveraging growing interest in technology transfer and collaborative innovation.

Additional strategic considerations include integrating data platforms with proprietary algorithms as IP assets, and monetization of real-world data through subscription-based analytics licensing models, increasingly important in healthcare decision-making.

7.5.2.1 Illustrative Transactions

- Life Sciences Royalty Financings—Sagard Healthcare Partners: Sagard Healthcare Partners is a leading fund specializing in life sciences royalty financing (in addition to credit), providing capital in exchange for rights to royalties on marketed and late-stage drugs. This fund exemplifies the growing trend of PE firms investing in asset-backed royalty streams with deal volumes exceeding $14 billion annually, growing at more than 40% CAGR. Sagard's portfolio includes royalties from diverse pharma assets, showcasing how PE structures nondilutive investments by monetizing future revenue streams secured by IP and regulatory exclusivities.
- EQT Healthcare Growth—Datavant & Ciox Health (2021–2023): EQT Growth led a $160 million round in Datavant, a tokenized real-world patient data connectivity leader. In 2023, EQT backed Datavant's $7 billion merger with Ciox Health, creating the largest neutral health data ecosystem in the United States. The combined platform enables ongoing out-licensing of tokenized patient data assets and analytics subscriptions to life sciences firms, driving 40% annual recurring revenue growth by monetizing proprietary data IP.
- KKR—Audax Royalty Corp Acquisition (2023): KKR participated in the acquisition of Audax Royalty Corp, a publicly traded royalty company focused on life sciences IP and royalty streams. This move illustrates KKR's approach to investing in royalty assets linked to patented pharmaceuticals and biotech products, aligning with nondilutive licensing and IP monetization strategies that generate stable cash flow tied to proven drug sales.
- CRISPR Patent Licensing—Vertex Pharmaceuticals and Editas Medicine (2023): The licensing deal, in which Vertex agreed to pay $50 million upfront, up to an additional $50 million in milestones, and up to $40 million in annual license fees through 2034 for nonexclusive rights to Editas' CRISPR-Cas9 gene-editing IP for ex vivo BCL11A-targeted editing in sickle cell disease and beta thalassemia, including Casgevy (not just "sickle cell therapy"), highlights the complexity of monetizing cutting-edge biotech patents. Though not directly a PE investment, this transaction exemplifies high-value IP licensing within the healthcare innovation ecosystem, often intersecting with PE-backed biotech companies as licensees or partners.

7.5.2.2 Success Factors and Key Challenges Early IP strategy implementation is critical. Life sciences startups and platforms with robust, enforceable patent protection attract higher valuations and better investment terms. PE firms increasingly prioritize patent portfolio strength and exclusivity during due diligence, recognizing IP as a durable competitive moat.

Brand value monetization is underexploited in healthcare. PE firms are introducing IP rate card strategies to monetize brand and trademark assets via licensing fees rather than relying solely on indirect brand exposure or joint ventures.

Rising patent quality standards driven by inter partes review proceedings require robust prosecution and enforceable IP portfolios. PE firms cannot rely on weak patents for enforcement or licensing leverage.

Life sciences IP monetization faces intricate regulatory hurdles, including FDA approval timelines, clinical trial dependencies, and synchronization of patent expiration with market exclusivity.

Going forward, we believe merging innovations such as patent-backed tokenization and blockchain-enabled IP exchanges will continue to offer novel monetization pathways for PE portfolios. The convergence of healthcare and high-tech IP management will create hybrid portfolio strategies, especially for AI-enhanced medical devices and therapeutics.

7.5.3 S29: Precision Medicine and Personalized Care

Healthcare is moving from a "one-size-fits-all" approach to treatments tailored for individual patients based on their genetic makeup, lifestyle, and environmental factors. For PE investors, this is another shift that presents both unprecedented opportunities and complex challenges. How can PE firms identify and capitalize on precision medicine investments while navigating the lengthy development timelines, regulatory uncertainties, and substantial capital requirements inherent in personalized healthcare?

The precision medicine market, valued at approximately $100 billion in 2024 by Precedence Research and Grand View Research, is projected to grow at 16% CAGR, reaching $250 billion by 2030. It represents a fundamental shift toward personalized healthcare that PE firms are aggressively pursuing through combinations of platform investments and strategic partnerships.

7.5.3.1 Market Drivers and Investment Thesis Technology convergence has created the foundation for precision medicine scalability. Next-generation sequencing costs have dropped from $100 million per genome in 2001 to under $1,000 in 2016 and under $300 in 2025, while AI analytics and big data integration enable comprehensive genetic profiling at unprecedented scale. PE firms target companies leveraging these technologies for therapeutic development, diagnostic tools, and clinical decision support.

Growing demand stems from rising chronic disease prevalence—affecting over 133 million Americans in 2024—and patient expectations for personalized treatment, creating expanding addressable markets. Regulatory support from FDA for precision medicine approaches reduces investment risk while accelerating approval pathways through breakthrough therapy designations and companion diagnostic approvals.

As a key takeaway for investors, precision medicine investments require understanding both technological capabilities and market readiness, with successful platforms combining proprietary datasets, AI capabilities, and established healthcare relationships.

7.5.3.2 Strategic Investment Approaches Platform strategies in precision medicine fall into three primary categories that PE firms must carefully evaluate. Data-driven platforms receive priority, with firms investing in companies possessing proprietary datasets, AI capabilities, and established healthcare relationships that combine comprehensive data collection with actionable clinical insights directly impacting patient outcomes. Service layer investments focus on companies providing precision medicine enablement services—clinical trial design, regulatory guidance, and biomarker development—rather than direct therapeutic development, offering more predictable revenue streams and shorter time-to-market cycles. Convergence strategies increasingly combine multiple precision medicine capabilities, such as AI-powered diagnostics paired with targeted therapeutics, or multi-omics platforms integrated with digital health monitoring and real-world evidence generation.

Note that successful precision medicine investments typically combine multiple value creation levers rather than relying on a single technological breakthrough.

7.5.3.3 Real-world Case Studies

Case Study 1: Caris Life Sciences—Comprehensive Genomic Profiling Platform Sixth Street led an $830 million growth equity financing in Caris Life Sciences at a $7.83 billion post-money valuation in 2021. Caris's Molecular Intelligence platform analyzes all 22,000 genes using whole exome sequencing, whole transcriptome sequencing, and proprietary AI models to guide oncology treatment decisions. The investment demonstrates PE confidence in comprehensive genomic profiling platforms that generate recurring revenue through test volume growth and expanded clinical applications.

Case Study 2: Precision Medicine Group—Infrastructure Play Blackstone completed a $2.3 billion investment and recapitalization of Precision Medicine Group in 2020, focusing on biomarker-based clinical trial services rather than direct therapeutic development. PMG's approach integrates deep therapeutic knowledge, data analytics, and regulatory expertise to enable precision medicine development for pharmaceutical clients. This transaction exemplifies PE preference for infrastructure investments with diversified client bases and predictable revenue streams.

Case Study 3: Parexel International—Adaptive Trial Design Specialist EQT Partners and Goldman Sachs acquired Parexel International for $8.5 billion in 2021 to capitalize on the growing demand for precision medicine trial capabilities. Parexel's expertise in adaptive trial designs and biomarker-stratified patient populations made it an attractive platform for serving biopharma clients developing targeted therapies. The deal highlights how PE firms are building comprehensive clinical research platforms to support personalized medicine development.

Case Study 4: BC Platforms—European Real-world Data Federation Jolt Capital led a $20 million growth financing in BC Platforms in 2022, supporting Europe's leading real-world data provider that enables personalized precision medicine through federated machine learning across healthcare networks. The investment targets the growing demand from pharmaceutical companies for clinically valuable data from European and Asian markets, serving more than 10 of the world's largest pharma companies.

7.5.3.4 Critical Investment Considerations and Risk Mitigation Precision medicine investments require patient capital with 5–10-year horizons, which can clash with typical PE fund life cycles. To bridge this gap, firms structure deals with milestone-based tranches, releasing additional capital as pipeline programs achieve predefined regulatory, clinical, or commercial milestones.

Dependence on pharmaceutical or health-system partnerships for data access and commercialization introduces concentration risk. Mitigation tactics include forming advisory boards of Key Opinion Leaders (KOLs) and industry veterans to validate strategy, diversify partnerships, and anticipate market shifts.

A PE investor in the segment notes: "As usual, the difficulty is in the balance, finding companies that can generate meaningful revenue and clinical impact within a PE timeframe while building platforms for long-term value creation."

Regulatory complexity—ranging from companion diagnostic approvals to evolving reimbursement frameworks—demands an expert regulatory advisory board and staged financing aligned with key regulatory filings (e.g., Investigational Device Exemption [IDE] submissions, Premarket Approval [PMA] filings). This ensures the company has the resources to navigate each phase without overcommitting upfront capital.

Market fragmentation creates "winner-take-all" dynamics. PE firms can reduce competitive risk by pursuing portfolio synergies, investing in multiple precision medicine platforms with complementary capabilities (e.g., one company specializing in genomics, another in AI-driven diagnostics) so that combined offerings strengthen market positioning.

By deploying milestone-based tranches, convening expert advisory boards, staging financing around regulatory and clinical milestones, and leveraging portfolio synergies, PE firms can manage the long horizons and high uncertainty inherent in precision medicine investments.

7.5.3.5 Future Implications and Outlook Looking ahead, several frontiers will define precision medicine's next chapter:

- Radiopharmaceutical *theranostics*—agents that diagnose and treat in one—will gain traction, with PE-backed pioneers like Aviko Radiopharmaceuticals advancing boron neutron capture therapy.
- AI-driven multi-omics platforms will unify genomics, transcriptomics, proteomics, metabolomics, and imaging data to power personalized treatment algorithms. CytoReason is a UK example that creates computational "digital twins" of human biology—essentially cell-level simulations of tissues and disease pathways built from large-scale single-cell RNA sequencing, bulk transcriptomics, and clinical data (Figure 7.26).

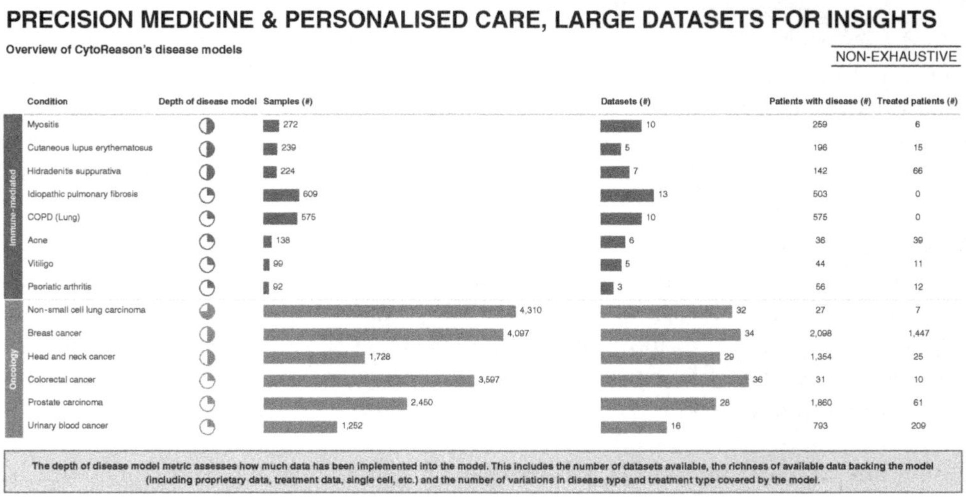

FIGURE 7.26 Insights from large datasets.
Source: Candesic analysis.

- Real-world evidence monetization will mature as VBC models reward outcomes, opening licensing revenue for longitudinal clinical data.
- Decentralized clinical trials, supported by telehealth and digital biomarkers, will lower costs and accelerate enrollment.
- Reimbursement innovation—indication-based pricing and outcomes-linked contracts—will unlock premium revenues for companion diagnostics and gene therapies.

We recommend future-focused investors keep an eye on long development cycles, map the end-to-end precision medicine value chain—radiopharmaceuticals, AI-multi-omics, real-world evidence, decentralized trials, and reimbursement models—and align their portfolios accordingly. They should also monitor adjacent technologies, evolving payer frameworks, and emergent therapeutic modalities that harness genetic and molecular insights. These trends will shape precision medicine investment opportunities for years to come.

7.5.4 S30: Patient Acquisition and Engagement (Patient Funnel Innovation/ Direct-to-consumerization, Digital Front Door)

Rising consumerization in healthcare—mirroring retail and fintech—has driven significant investment in patient acquisition technologies. As patients demand seamless, on-demand experiences, firms that master funnel optimization and unified digital front doors capture disproportionate market share and command premium valuations.

The global patient engagement market was valued at $22.5 billion in 2023 and is projected to reach $41.8 billion by 2028 (13.2% CAGR) according to MarketsandMarkets. This rapid growth underpins PE interest in digital front door platforms—consumer-centric solutions connecting patients and providers across the care continuum via smartphones and digital devices. These platforms integrate scheduling, telemedicine, EHR access, and patient navigation into a single interface that drives acquisition and deepens engagement.

Complementing digital front door, patient funnel innovation and direct-to-consumer (DTC) strategies serve as key PE value-creation levers. Patient funnel innovation uses data-driven marketing, personalized outreach, and digital engagement tools to guide prospects from awareness through conversion and retention. DTC models reduce friction by delivering services directly to consumers, bypassing traditional referral pathways. Together, they create a growth engine that increases new patient capture, boosts lifetime engagement, and strengthens loyalty—critical metrics for scalable healthcare businesses.

7.5.4.1 Illustrative Transactions

Case Study 1: Phreesia—Vista Equity Partners (2019) Vista Equity Partners acquired a majority stake in Phreesia in September 2019, expanding its digital front door and patient intake platform to more than 3,000 US clinics. Post-deal, Phreesia's subscription ARR grew from $50 to $200 million in two years, and Vista exited at a 20× EBITDA multiple when Phreesia went public in October 2019.

Case Study 2: TeleClinic—EQT Growth (2021) In March 2021, EQT Growth led a €100 million growth investment in Germany's TeleClinic, merging it with the digital prescription provider MedKit. Within 18 months, the combined platform tripled monthly patient consultations and improved EBITDA multiples from 8× to 18×, enabling EQT to begin a successful exit process in late 2022.

Case Study 3: One Medical—Hellman & Friedman (2020) Hellman & Friedman acquired a majority stake in One Medical for $2.7 billion in December 2020, transforming the membership-based primary care provider into a digital-first health platform. One Medical's DTC model and integrated app increased membership from 125,000 to 600,000 by 2022, leading to a successful IPO in January 2022 at a 15× revenue multiple.

Case Study 4: Gozio Health—Morgan Stanley Expansion Capital (2022) Morgan Stanley Expansion Capital invested in Gozio Health's patented wayfinding and digital engagement platform in July 2022. Gozio's mobile app now serves more than 50 hospital systems across North America, reducing patient wait times by 25% and achieving a 98% satisfaction score in KLAS surveys.

7.5.4.2 Technology Integration Models, Value-creation Levers, and Implementation Challenges

Two main forms of technology integration are serving patient acquisition and engagement. Omnichannel engagement relates to successful platforms providing unified experiences across multiple touchpoints. This includes web portals, mobile apps, telehealth platforms, and in-person visits. Integration with EHR systems and third-party applications creates seamless patient journeys. The other form is AI-powered optimization, whereas machine learning analyzes patient behavior, preferences, and outcomes to personalize engagement strategies and predict care needs. AI-driven search and chatbots act as invisible digital front doors, improving conversion and retention.

An elegant lesson emerges: top-performing platforms blend omnichannel reach with AI personalization, deepening engagement and optimizing funnel performance.

The value creation levers are multiple. Digital marketing and referral optimization through platform integration improve patient acquisition, with PE-backed organizations reporting 50–175× increases in telehealth patient volume. Automated scheduling, digital check-in, and self-service capabilities reduce administrative burden while improving patient satisfaction, decreasing no-show rates and improving appointment utilization. Enhanced patient engagement correlates with increased portal adoption, higher patient satisfaction scores, and improved revenue cycle management through digital payment processing, directly impacting financial performance.

Common implementation challenges include vendor fragmentation—where siloed point solutions hinder unified workflows—and change management, since cultural shifts and staff training often lag technology deployment. PE success depends on selecting companies that offer comprehensive digital front door orchestration and prioritizing workflow integration over standalone tools. Regulatory considerations around data privacy (HIPAA and state laws) require balancing personalization with compliance and managing liability risks from AI-driven triage and decision support through robust risk protocols.

Looking ahead, AI-driven patient engagement will become core healthcare infrastructure. As value-based care metrics evolve, consolidated digital front door platforms will unlock additional revenue streams and margin expansion. PE firms that back end-to-end solutions—combining funnel innovation, DTC models, and AI optimization—will capture leadership in consumerized healthcare.

We recommend future-focused investors anticipate continued market consolidation, map the full patient journey—from awareness through after-care—and align portfolios around platforms that integrate omnichannel engagement with AI-based personalization. Monitoring regulatory shifts in telehealth reimbursement and emerging privacy standards will be crucial to sustaining growth.

7.5.5 S31: Technology-enabled Care Delivery and Life Sciences Development Models

As mentioned in Chapter 6, PE investors actively foster digitalization in their portfolio companies by supporting the adoption of digital technologies to enhance operational efficiency, customer experience, and data-driven decision-making. By embedding digital talent, fostering a culture of innovation, and setting targeted digital transformation goals as part of the value creation plan, PE sponsors can accelerate growth and significantly increase exit valuations. Jannick Hunecke, managing director at DBAG, a leading German mid-market PE player, recognizes that there is a growing opportunity with the succession situations in the German Mittelstand:[7]

> *Many of these companies have yet to go digital. One area of value creation is focusing on optimizing sales with digital capabilities. We recently acquired such a business and merged it with a digital sale tech company to boost sales.*

7.5.5.1 Types of Innovation Innovation in healthcare and life sciences is often associated with early stage scientific breakthroughs—novel therapeutics, diagnostics, or digital health platforms—domains traditionally dominated by VC. PE plays an increasingly influential role in shaping how innovation is scaled, adopted, and embedded within health systems, extending beyond R&D to include innovations in care delivery, operational models, technology integration, and business processes.

PE's engagement with innovation is more systemic than scientific. While VC typically funds the creation of novel products, PE fuels the transformation of companies and systems that deliver those products. These firms often require substantial capital to scale operations, expand geographically, comply with regulations, or modernize aging infrastructure. In doing so, PE capital frequently enables **sustaining innovation:** improvements that enhance efficiency, expand access, or increase quality within the existing healthcare paradigm.

Examples of sustaining innovation include the digital transformation of primary care chains, standardization of diagnostics through platform consolidation, implementation of AI-driven tools in clinical workflows, and development of integrated service models in post-acute or behavioral health. In life sciences, PE often backs mid- to late-stage CDMOs, CROs, and healthtech infrastructure providers, driving innovation in process, delivery, and compliance rather than product discovery.

[7] Collective group of small and medium-sized enterprises (SMEs) in Germany, Austria, and Switzerland. Typically family-owned businesses, often passed down through generations. Widely considered the backbone of the German economy.

EQT VII's July 2017 acquisition of Certara for $850 million shows how sustaining innovation can boost productivity within established industry models. Certara's *in silico* modeling and regulatory-science tools optimize existing R&D workflows—improving dose selection, predicting clinical outcomes, and cutting late-stage failures—rather than creating entirely new paradigms. These enhancements yield up to 30% cost savings per program. Post-deal, EQT backed modular software upgrades and expanded Certara's global footprint.

By contrast, **disruptive innovation**—which upends existing models by introducing simpler, cheaper, or radically different solutions—is less frequently a target of traditional PE. Disruptive innovation often implies high regulatory risk, uncertain reimbursement, or immature market adoption. These factors are at odds with the return timelines and risk-adjusted strategies typical of growth and buyout funds. However, PE may support disruptive innovation indirectly by scaling early disruptors after they pass key inflection points. For instance, Hillhouse Capital co-led a $394 million funding round for WeDoctor (China's leading online medical booking platform) in 2015, while General Atlantic's $150 million investment in DocPlanner enabled the company to scale across 30+ markets globally, serving 50+ million patients and 500,000 practitioners by 2024.

PE can also play a role in reverse innovation, bringing to developed markets the technologies tested in developing markets (Chapter 9). But disruptive healthcare innovation carries extreme binary outcomes: many PE firms made costly bets on GLP-1 competitors and diabetes management companies that were disrupted by breakthrough drugs like Ozempic and Wegovy, leading to significant write-downs across portfolios focused on traditional diabetes care approaches.

PE can also drive **business model innovation**, which sits between sustaining and disruptive change. This includes new payment models (e.g., value-based care arrangements), vertical integration strategies, and data-driven personalization engines for care management. General Atlantic's investment in Oak Street Health exemplifies this: Oak Street pioneered a "concierge-style" Medicare Advantage model combining enhanced access, comprehensive care coordination, and full financial risk assumption through capitated contracts. The PE-backed company grew from a handful of clinics to more than 160 locations serving 200,000+ Medicare patients before CVS acquired it for $10.6 billion in 2023.

Overall, the dominant pattern is that PE in healthcare fosters sustaining innovation, with selective engagement in disruptive models once they reach commercial viability. This orientation reflects the strategic priorities of most PE firms: reducing waste, enhancing performance, standardizing quality, and improving margin scalability in complex and regulated environments. In life sciences, this often translates into platform roll-ups, service model optimization, or geographic expansion—innovations of integration and execution rather than scientific revolution.

Nevertheless, the line between sustaining and disruptive innovation is not fixed. In some cases, PE-backed scaling of a sustaining innovation—such as telemedicine or AI-enabled diagnostics—can create disruptive effects at the system level, changing the locus of care or the economics of delivery. As health systems globally face mounting pressure to do more with less, the distinction between operational excellence and strategic innovation may become increasingly blurred—and PE's role in that evolution more central.

7.5.5.2 AI in Healthcare AI has been reshaping healthcare for a while. This started before ChatGPT and the mass introduction of chatbots using large language models. First applications in healthtech included IBM Watson for Oncology decision support in the United States in 2015 after two years of pilot testing, which aimed to digest patient data and suggest treatment options but proved prohibitively expensive to scale.[8] Many early attempts collapsed, partially because the cost of developing reliable predictive models proved too high. That was part of the fate of Babylon Health, an ambitious British Healthtech that went full speed to the United States with its AI-driven offering, culminating with a $4 billion SPAC (special-purpose acquisition company) in 2021 (Kitten, 2026). The cash raised was less than expected, did not last, and the company collapsed in 2023, when the creditors called their loan. By that time, however, there were already many other established valuable AI contributions to healthcare, particularly in the treatment of data and signals (digital imaging, pathology automation, etc.). We can distinguish between contributions to the various stakeholders: patient outcomes, medical staff working conditions, and shareholder value. In ideal situations, AI contributes to all three, and not to one at the expense of another! These initiatives were often financed by VC, then PE money.

Examples include the following:

- Patient outcomes: In ophthalmology for instance, AI-powered platforms are revolutionizing early detection and disease management (Kitten and Ruffinoni, 2025). IDx-DR became the first FDA-approved autonomous AI diagnostic for diabetic retinopathy in 2018, enabling earlier detection and treatment and reducing vision loss.
- Medical staff: Aidoc's AI radiology triage platform, launched commercially in 2017, accelerates detection of critical findings (e.g., intracranial hemorrhage), cutting turnaround times by over 30%, with some institutions reporting reductions exceeding 60%. However, while AI has proven its diagnostic power in radiology and will be systematically used, its real-world impact remains limited. Adoption is slow due to resistance from radiologists and operators, patient skepticism, and integration challenges. Many hospitals also lack the radiologist time needed to test and adapt these tools, leaving most of AI's potential untapped. It makes it difficult for investors to time their investments, especially within a five-year horizon.
- Shareholder value: Butterfly Network's AI-powered handheld ultrasound, backed by PE and public markets via a 2021 SPAC merger, reached a $1.5 billion valuation, illustrating how AI-driven devices can unlock new capital-efficient growth pathways.[9] By 2022, the device was deployed in more than 2,500 healthcare facilities. The company invested heavily in AI and machine learning, developing specialized diagnostic algorithms and enhancing device connectivity with electronic health record systems.

---

[8] IBM ultimately sold Watson Health assets to PE firm Francisco Partners in 2021–2022, marking the end of the initiative.

[9] The valuation fell under $1 billion after 2022 as operating expenses increased faster than expected.

Beyond its impact on operations, AI fundamentally alters how investors evaluate the long-term durability of a business model. The central question is no longer just about market trends, but about a company's resilience to technological disruption. This shift is articulated by Eric Trüeb from eevolve: "The first question we ask ourselves is: Will the business model still be valid in five years considering the adoption of AI?"

A recent development is the use of AI in roll-up strategies, to make the operations of the combined companies more efficient. This started in VC, with firms including General Catalyst and Thrive Capital investing in startups that buy services businesses such as call center operators, merging them with similar companies, boosting sales while containing costs with AI tools. The approach is not new. PE has long identified companies for roll-up in sectors like professional services or home ownership association management that are slow to adopt technology. The introduction of the internet offered many opportunities. With AI, it can be faster and cheaper to extract synergies.

The Role of AI Agents The widespread launch of generative AI chatbots in late 2022 marked a pivotal moment, bringing AI capabilities to mainstream attention. This was quickly followed by the emergence of the first commercially viable AI agents in 2024, systems that moved beyond conversational text generation to autonomously perform complex, goal-directed tasks, through continuous learning and reasoning.

These agents go beyond traditional automation or predictive analytics by engaging in dynamic problem-solving, adapting to changing environments. For PE investors, this evolution requires a crucial mental shift: evaluating AI not merely as a cost-saving "tool," but as a new type of "digital teammate" capable of augmenting every level of an organization. Understanding the trajectory and impact of these agents is now essential for evaluating both risks and value creation opportunities.

As AI's scope in healthcare expands from diagnostics and administrative tasks to fully autonomous agents, the underlying infrastructure must evolve to support increasingly complex "world models." World models as the future of AI will require more computing power. Over the period 2019 to 2026, the performance of leading AI supercomputers has doubled every nine months. At the same time, their power requirements have doubled every 13 months. On the other hand, the cost of running text prompts is rapidly falling, with a 44× reduction in carbon footprint for the median Gemini apps text prompt over one year (Elsworth et al., 2025).

In Healthcare Delivery: From Administrative Relief to Autonomous Coordination Healthcare providers quickly began deploying AI agents to streamline administrative workflows and reduce the significant overhead that characterizes most health systems. One area of rapid adoption has been ambient clinical documentation. Pioneered by companies like Nuance (part of Microsoft) and startups like Abridge, these systems listened to doctor-patient conversations and automatically generated structured clinical notes. The effect on clinician productivity and the reduction of after-hours charting (so-called *pajama time*) has been significant, with solutions now embedded in major EHR systems in the United States and Europe. For investors, this reduces labor costs while increasing clinical throughput and revenue capture accuracy.

Another domain of active deployment has been patient triage and scheduling. AI agents increasingly handle initial symptom checking, directing patients to appropriate care settings (e.g., virtual vs. in-person), and managing appointment logistics. When accepted by patients, these systems reduce reliance on traditional call centers, lower barriers to access, and create a so-called *digital front door* for health systems. Meanwhile, in RCM, AI agents are being trained to navigate the complexity of insurance verification, coding, and prior authorization processes, tasks that historically required large administrative teams. While these agents still operate under human supervision (for how long?), their learning and adaptive capabilities improve reimbursement outcomes, accelerate cash conversion cycles, and reduce costly denials.

Looking ahead, the 2030s will likely see AI agents transition from administrative assistants to active coordinators of care. As interoperability improves, agents could begin to manage complex, multi-specialty care pathways—tracking patients across diagnostics, surgery, pharmacy, and rehabilitation settings. In oncology, for instance, an AI agent might autonomously coordinate tumor board decisions by pre-summarizing patient cases, schedule all subsequent scans and infusions based on real-time capacity data from the radiology and oncology departments, monitor treatment adherence via smart devices, and re-prioritize appointments dynamically based on clinical urgency and patient needs.

A transformative application is also emerging in VBC, as described earlier in this chapter. Imagine an AI agent assigned to manage a panel of 5,000 diabetic patients for a large accountable care organization. By continuously analyzing data from EHRs, pharmacy claims, and patient wearables (e.g., continuous glucose monitors), the agent could identify a patient whose data suggests an imminent risk of a hyperglycemic event. It could then autonomously dispatch a community health worker for an in-home visit and schedule a proactive telehealth consultation with a nurse practitioner, preventing a costly emergency department visit and improving the patient's long-term outcome. The entire organization needs to adapt to this shift from reactive treatment to proactive, automated population health management.

In Life Sciences: From Research Acceleration to Autonomous Discovery In the life sciences sector, AI agents are already improving the speed and accuracy of regulatory surveillance and clinical research support. Today, they are used to monitor scientific literature, regulatory agency updates, and safety signals across geographies, including analyzing unstructured data from social media and medical forums for potential adverse event reporting. This reduces the burden on regulatory and pharmacovigilance teams and improves time-to-response when rules or evidence shift. These applications are relatively mature and are being integrated into the workflows of large pharmaceutical companies and CROs.

AI agents are also increasingly involved in managing clinical trial data. In complex trials, platforms from providers like Medidata use agents to help clean and validate data, flag inconsistencies, and generate automated queries for site investigators—leading to faster database lock and higher-quality datasets. The financial impact is direct: shortening a late-stage trial by even a few weeks can save millions in operational costs and bring a blockbuster drug to market sooner. They are also used in patient stratification, where agents analyze real-world data to identify patients who are more likely to respond to treatment or meet inclusion criteria. These tools are particularly valuable in rare diseases or precision oncology, where recruitment bottlenecks can delay development timelines and erode investment returns.

Looking further ahead, AI agents are expected to play a central role in drug discovery and development by acting across multiple stages of the R&D life cycle. Already, early-stage agents are involved in gene or molecular simulation and target identification (Figure 7.27). Over the next decade, more sophisticated agents may manage iterative cycles of compound design, simulation, and validation—operating

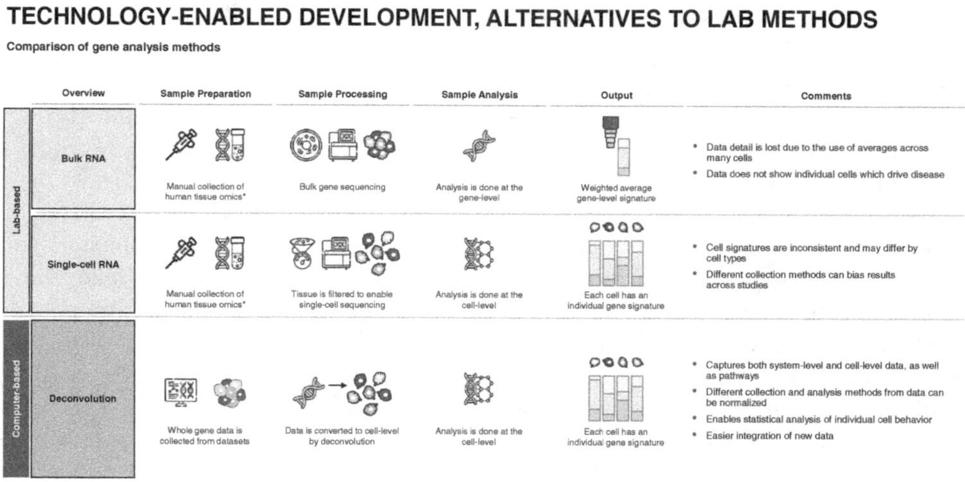

FIGURE 7.27 Alternatives to lab methods in gene analysis.
Source: Candesic analysis.

in closed-loop systems with laboratory robotics. This "self-driving lab," pursued by firms like Recursion Pharmaceuticals and Exscientia, aims to compress R&D timelines by having an AI agent hypothesize a molecule, instruct robots to synthesize and test it, analyze the results, and refine the hypothesis in a continuous cycle that runs 24/7.

Similarly, the logistics of personalized medicine will become a prime area for AI agent deployment. For complex cell therapies like CAR-T in the 2030s, an agent could manage the entire "vein-to-vein" supply chain. It would coordinate the patient's cell extraction (apheresis), orchestrate the cryopreserved shipping logistics, monitor the gene-editing manufacturing process, and schedule the patient's re-infusion appointment, all while maintaining a validated chain of identity on a blockchain to ensure patient safety and regulatory compliance.

Strategic Implications for Investors For PE sponsors, operational efficiencies from documentation, billing, and scheduling automation can quickly translate into EBITDA margin expansion within a typical three- to five-year investment horizon. In life sciences, while regulatory surveillance and trial automation offer near-term gains, the full impact of autonomous drug discovery may only emerge gradually, requiring longer holding periods and a venture-like mindset.

PE firms must evolve their due diligence to incorporate an "AI maturity" assessment, evaluating not just technology stack but data governance, integration capabilities, and organizational readiness to deploy digital teammates. The most successful strategies may involve creating platforms that combine data-rich assets with best-in-class AI agent providers, creating proprietary value-creation engines.

7.5.5.3 Quantum Computing In an article they published in May 2025,[10] Vimal Kapur and Rajeeb Hazra argued that the quantum era was no longer a distant prospect but

[10] Business Weekly, The Quantum era has already begun, May 5, 2025.

a present reality, with quantum computing already delivering tangible value across industries, especially in healthcare and pharmaceuticals. As mentioned by the authors, "You will not see a quantum computer for sale at Best Buy or a revolutionary app." Rather than a single "light bulb moment," quantum's impact is unfolding through incremental but significant breakthroughs, many of which are occurring behind the scenes in foundational sectors like drug discovery and healthcare systems.

It is always risky to assess the level of development of a new technology in a textbook. By the time it gets printed, the world has changed. It would be worse ignoring how this technology will transform healthcare in many ways. We can already see it revolutionizing drug discovery and development, enhancing clinical trials and personalized medicine, and optimizing operations and logistics.

Quantum computing is poised to transform pharmaceutical research by enabling simulation of complex molecular interactions at unattainable detail levels. This capability is crucial for accelerating drug discovery (modeling drug-protein interactions far more efficiently than classical systems, leading to faster compound identification) and solving complex biological problems (tasks like protein folding and ligand-protein binding that are computationally intensive). Quantum computers also optimize clinical trial design, patient stratification, and personalized treatment strategies, as well as hospital operations (bed allocation, supply chains, resource deployment). Figure 7.28 shows the expected impact of the acceleration and optimization of drug discovery and development.

Real partnership and transaction examples illustrate that quantum computing is moving beyond theoretical promise (Kitten, 2025b).

The Cleveland Clinic installed the IBM Quantum System One in 2023—the first quantum computer dedicated solely to healthcare research, supporting more than 50 projects focusing on protein structure prediction and imaging. Pfizer collaborates with IBM Quantum Network to accelerate antibiotics and antiviral development through molecular modeling. Merck partners with HQS Quantum Simulations to improve

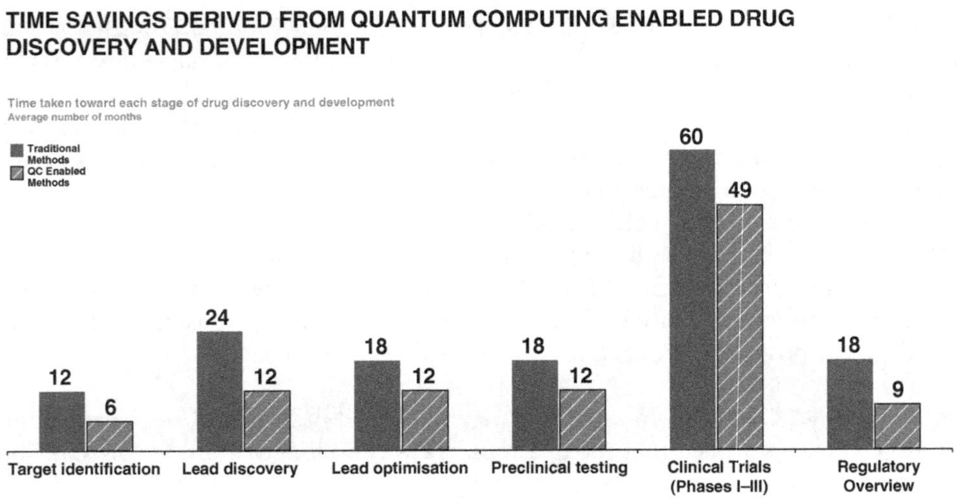

FIGURE 7.28 Expected time saving from quantum computing.
Source: Candesic analysis.

precision and speed in drug discovery, while Google's Quantum AI division works on oncology research by mapping cancer-related protein structures. Johnson & Johnson has teamed up with Pasqal and Qubit Pharmaceuticals to bring quantum simulations into early-stage drug discovery.

Novo Holdings has committed $200 million to establish a quantum life sciences hub in Denmark, and Israeli startup Classiq recently raised $110 million to serve clients across pharmaceuticals, automotive, and financial sectors.

While VC leads early quantum computing investments, PE is poised to engage post-profitability, targeting portfolio upgrades by embedding quantum tools in pharmaceutical and healthtech companies, acquiring quantum solution providers for healthcare operators, and creating shared quantum services across portfolios.

Two important warnings merit emphasis. First, current quantum hardware remains noisy and error-prone, requiring thousands of unstable "physical qubits" to produce a single reliable "logical qubit." Second, quantum technology raises regulatory and legal challenges, including data privacy risks under GDPR and HIPAA, and intellectual property complexities around machine-generated discoveries. According to Politico.eu (July 2025), Europe was drawing merely 5% of global private quantum funding, far behind the United States's 50% share and China's aggressive state-backed investments, suggesting faster implementations in those regions.

7.5.5.4 Robotization of Healthcare Robotization—the deployment of programmable, automated machines—is poised to be healthcare's defining transformation this century. Surgical robots enabling sub-millimeter precision, autonomous logistics systems, and robotic exoskeletons for rehabilitation are already proving their potential. This revolution works in concert with in vivo nanosensors, AI-driven diagnostics, CRISPR gene-editing, and 3D bioprinting to automate routine processes, accelerate innovation cycles, and unlock individualized care at scale.

Unlike other industries where robotics primarily replaced repetitive manufacturing tasks, healthcare robotics addresses uniquely complex challenges: sterile environments, precision handling of biological materials, 24/7 operational requirements, and the critical importance of error reduction in life-or-death situations.

Key Applications

- Hospitals: Robotic systems are increasingly used in surgery (da Vinci Surgical System[11]) and sterilization (UV-light disinfection robots). Perhaps the most transformative applications involve logistics: autonomous mobile robots transport medications, lab samples, surgical instruments, and waste throughout facilities 24/7 without breaks or errors.
- Pharmacies: Robotic dispensing units reduce errors and improve throughput, allowing pharmacists to focus on clinical roles. Systems often pay for themselves within two to three years.

[11]The da Vinci Surgical System, with more than 6,500 installations worldwide, demonstrates the market potential for surgical robotics, generating over $5 billion in annual revenue through equipment sales, consumables, and service contracts.

- Nursing homes and rehabilitation: Exoskeletons, robotic walkers, and companion robots offer physical and emotional support, mitigating staffing gaps. Rehabilitation robotics provide consistent, measurable therapy that adapts to patient progress.
- Pharmaceutical manufacturing and clinical laboratories: Robotization improves consistency and precision in both R&D and production. Sterile environments benefit from robotic arms under strict GMP conditions. Companies like Roche Diagnostics and Abbott have developed comprehensive laboratory automation platforms processing thousands of tests daily with minimal human intervention.
- Other areas include telepresence robotics for remote consultations.

The real inflection point emerges when robotization is combined with artificial intelligence. Intelligent and adaptive robots not only can perform physical tasks but can also make real-time decisions based on contextual data. A surgical robot guided by an AI algorithm trained on thousands of previous procedures can dynamically adapt to intraoperative complications. In nursing homes, emotionally intelligent robots are beginning to recognize facial expressions and speech patterns to better respond to resident needs. AI also enables predictive maintenance for robotic systems, ensuring higher uptime and better resource allocation across facilities.

Again, the expected combination with quantum computing promises to exponentially increase the power of these systems by accelerating simulation and optimization. For instance, robots used in drug synthesis or precision diagnostics may eventually integrate quantum-derived models to calculate optimal combinations or pathways in real time—something classical computers would take weeks to simulate. This could benefit fields like radiotherapy planning, pathology robotics, and real-time molecular diagnostics, where robotic execution needs to synchronize with vast computational demands.

Together, the convergence of robotization, AI, and quantum computing signals the arrival of *autonomous healthcare systems*—capable of continuous learning, adaptation, and physical intervention with minimal human oversight. Nico Prokop at AGIC reported the launch of a new autonomous, AI-powered robotic system that could design, execute, and verify biological experiments, all without human input. The system integrated LLMs, vision-language models, and modular robotics to act as a multiagent "AI biologist." Prokop noted:

> *This could mark a step-change in how biotech and pharma approach R&D, compressing months of benchwork into days through 24/7 autonomous wet labs, with the added potential of significantly lower R&D costs and faster iteration cycles.*

The Role of Private Equity PE is uniquely positioned to accelerate robotization deployment. The sector's long-term investment horizon matches the capital intensity and regulatory lead times of robotics development, while PE's operational focus aligns with the challenge of scaling from prototype to system-wide adoption. The recurring revenue model (robots requiring consumables, maintenance, software updates, and eventual replacement) is particularly attractive.

PE firms have made significant investments in healthcare automation and robotics across multiple sectors.

- In surgical robotics, PAI Partners successfully built Amplitude Surgical's lower-limb orthopedic robotics platform before selling it to Zydus Lifesciences for €530 million in 2025, while Permira-backed Corin Group acquired OMNI Orthopaedics to enter the robotic-assisted knee replacement market.
- Pharmacy automation has seen extensive PE activity, including Francisco Partners selling Aesynt to Omnicell in 2019 for $275 million, Blue Wolf Capital selling PSG's 340B Link business to Omnicell in 2020 for $225 million, and Frazier Healthcare selling Parata to BD in 2021 for $1.525 billion.
- Hospital workflow and revenue cycle management have attracted major deals like Veritas Capital and KKR's $11 billion recapitalization of Cotiviti in 2024, TowerBrook Capital and CD&R's acquisition of R1 RCM in 2024 for $8.9 billion, and New Mountain Capital's investment in Access Healthcare's transaction processing platform in 2025.
- Healthcare IT infrastructure investments include Francisco Partners' purchase of McKesson's entire pharmacy automation division back in 2013 (renamed Aesynt) and TPG's acquisition of Surescripts in 2024, which marked a strategic move to accelerate health data exchange innovation. While some robotic surgical platforms remain venture-funded (CMR Surgical) or corporate-backed (Verb Surgical), PE firms are increasingly targeting hospital logistics automation and pharmaceutical supply chain technologies.
- In elder care, PE-backed portfolios are integrating robotics into assisted living business models to reduce dependency on scarce human resources while maintaining standards of care.
- PE also plays a key role in the consolidation and globalization of manufacturing and service platforms. Robotics firms often emerge from narrow academic or industrial niches and require financial and managerial support to expand internationally, comply with multiple health systems, and integrate software and hardware stacks.

Healthcare technology consolidation extends beyond individual deals. According to Bain & Company (2025), 2024 healthcare PE deals reached $115 billion globally with 1,049 transactions in the United States alone, while robotics-focused deals generated more than $3.2 billion across 55 transactions.

This raises another question for investors. The operational cost of industrial and humanoid robots in manufacturing has now fallen to just $2–$10 per hour, and in some cases is expected to dip below $1 per hour within the next 10 years as mass production expands and technology improves. This rapid decline is primarily due to savings on wages, social costs, recruitment, training, and overhead that robots eliminate. If robot working speeds double through ongoing innovation, the cost per hour can drop to roughly 13–16% of that for a human employee, marking a dramatic transformation in manufacturing economics.

Dominik Schwartz, partner at Verdane, sees the hourly cost falling even more, in some cases to 30 cents, and reminds us that "offshoring or outsourcing on the basis of lower labor costs will become irrelevant. It's no longer a straightforward decision for the next five years of PE ownership. Moving operations to a low-cost country requires making a bet on the speed of robotization."

Finally, as the convergence with AI and quantum accelerates, PE can foster ecosystem plays, funding vertically integrated companies that combine robotic platforms with proprietary AI models and, eventually, quantum-native capabilities. This combination delivers real competitive advantages and drives platform value. The result? Strategic buyers circle, and IPO prospects sharpen in the emerging "intelligent automation" segments of healthtech.

Paul Tomasic observes that, "while the 2010s were all about offshoring and outsourcing, the 2020s have been about reshoring: relocalizing for strategic reasons and leveraging robotization and AI to benefit at home from the technological progress."

7.5.5.5 Blockchain in Healthcare Blockchain has emerged in healthcare not as a vehicle for disruptive business models, but as a critical enabler for solving deeply entrenched inefficiencies. Unlike in finance or logistics, where blockchain can replace intermediaries entirely, in healthcare it enhances trust, transparency, and verifiability across fragmented systems.

Healthcare faces persistent trust failures: an estimated $200 billion lost annually to drug counterfeiting (Statista estimate in 2020), $83 billion lost to fraud in the United States alone (NHCAA estimate in 2020), and delays in drug approvals due to inconsistent or tampered clinical data. Add to this the chronic problem of fragmented patient records, and it becomes clear that data integrity and traceability are not just IT issues—they are patient safety and cost issues.

Blockchain's core advantages—tamper-proof audit trails, permissioned access to data, and programmable compliance via smart contracts—target these issues directly. The COVID-19 pandemic further accelerated adoption, as it exposed the lack of trustworthy, interoperable systems for data exchange.

Deployment Examples Across healthcare sectors, blockchain applications have moved from experimental pilots starting from around 2017 to production deployments with measurable impact:

- Pharmaceutical supply chains: MediLedger and Chronicled, both backed by notable investors including Andreessen Horowitz and Mandra Capital, ensure product integrity from factory to pharmacy using shared ledgers.
- Clinical trials: Platforms like TrialChain help prevent data manipulation by timestamping clinical entries on a distributed ledger.
- Patient data management: Startups like Solve.Care and Hu-manity.co give patients ownership and monetization rights over their own data.
- Insurance and claims: Change Healthcare and Gem (now part of Blockdaemon) use blockchain to streamline adjudication and reduce fraud.
- Hospital IT systems: Integration with Epic Systems and Oracle Health highlights how blockchain can coexist with established EHR systems, enhancing rather than replacing them.

The global healthcare blockchain market, estimated at $1.4–$2.8 billion in 2023 (Towards Healthcare cites $1.37 billion, while other projections are higher), is expected to reach $15–25 billion by 2034, fueled by mandates like the FDA's serialization rules and the 21st Century Cures Act in the United States.

For PE investors, the opportunity lies in operationally mature businesses using blockchain infrastructure to reduce fraud, improve data liquidity, and enhance compliance rather than speculative crypto-assets. Francisco Partners' acquisition of IBM

Watson Health's assets illustrated this transition toward integrating blockchain into existing IT ecosystems.

7.5.5.6 Tokenization of Healthcare As discussed in Chapter 3, tokenization is the process of converting assets into tradable digital securities that carry a proof of ownership. While blockchain provides the foundational infrastructure for secure, verifiable, and decentralized data management in healthcare, tokenization builds on this foundation to unlock new forms of asset ownership, financing, and patient engagement (Cong and He, 2019). If blockchain is the plumbing, tokenization is the flow of value it enables. Whereas blockchain in healthcare typically targets operational issues—such as fraud prevention, data provenance, and interoperability—tokenization applies these same principles to restructure how healthcare assets, rights, and data are owned, exchanged, and monetized. The two are not mutually exclusive, but their roles, use cases, and strategic relevance—especially to PE—are distinct (Table 7.1).

TABLE 7.1 Comparing Blockchain and Tokenization in Healthcare

Dimension	Blockchain in Healthcare	Tokenization in Healthcare	Primary Purpose	Example Use Cases	Private Equity (PE) Relevance
Definition	A distributed ledger technology enabling immutable, transparent, and decentralized recordkeeping	The process of creating digital tokens that represent real-world healthcare assets	Security, transparency, compliance	Data sharing, drug traceability, smart contracts	Back end enhancement of portfolio companies
Focus	Operational improvement and compliance	Financing and ownership innovation	Integrity and auditability	Supply chains, clinical trial data integrity.	Enabling liquidity and new fundraising structures
Example Solutions	MediLedger, TrialChain, Solve.Care, Chronicled	Securitize Capital, KKR tokenized funds, Solve.Care (dual usage)	Infra-structure stability	EHRs, insurance processing, pharma track & trace.	Creating fractional ownership or direct access to assets
Benefits	Enhanced trust, data security, inter-operability	Liquidity, global investor access, fractionalization	Operational excellence	Reduced fraud, regulatory compliance.	Innovative funding, asset monetization
Risks	Scalability, privacy, regulatory adaptation	Volatility, regulatory uncertainty, complexity	Technology governance	Integration with legacy systems.	Legal risk in emerging financial models

Note: This table summarizes the differences and overlaps between blockchain and tokenization in healthcare, highlighting their use cases, benefits, and relevance to PE.

In 2025, BCG estimated that tokenized assets could reach $16 trillion by 2030, or 10% of global GDP. In healthcare, tokenization enables novel financial mechanisms, streamlined operations, and—most provocatively—patient empowerment.

How It Works Tokenization converts ownership rights (e.g., in healthcare startups, medical equipment, real estate, or even patient data) into **digital tokens** that can be exchanged on blockchain platforms. These can represent equity stakes (via **Security Token Offerings or STO**), data access rights, or usage rights for shared medical infrastructure.

The process typically includes the following:

- Token creation (e.g., fractional ownership of a biotech firm or MRI machine)
- Blockchain issuance and tracking (ensuring immutable, transparent ledgers)
- Market-based exchange and liquidity
- Smart contract–enabled governance (e.g., data consent, payments, usage rules)

Use Cases in Healthcare and PE Relevance

- Receivables, royalties, and IP-backed revenues: For example, hospitals or clinics can issue asset-backed tokens on claims to insurers or governments, improving liquidity. Biotech firms securitize future revenue streams from successful therapies. Tokenized claims on milestone-based payouts can enable clinical trial financing. Tokenization shortens payment cycles and improves access to alternative financing for all firms including small biotech firms. They will also enhance transparency for investors. Healthcare providers and biotech firms can tokenize receivables, future royalties, or IP-backed revenues, issuing digital tokens that represent fractional ownership or debt claims. Hospitals or clinics issue asset-backed tokens on claims to insurers or governments, improving liquidity. Meanwhile, biotech firms securitize future revenue streams from successful therapies.
- Patient data and consent: Patients tokenize consent rights for clinical trial participation or data monetization, creating new revenue models for healthcare providers. Beyond clinical trials, this should allow more efficient and secure management of health records, reducing the risk of data breaches and unauthorized access. It also gives patients greater control over their health data. PE firms could invest in platforms that allow patients to tokenize their health data, creating a marketplace where researchers or pharmaceutical companies can purchase access to this data. This could create new revenue streams for healthcare providers.
- Insurance and claims: Tokenization improves claim processing and transparency. It reduces administrative costs, prevents fraud, and ensures that all parties involved in a claim have access to accurate and up-to-date information.
- Cross-border healthcare services: Tokenization could facilitate easier payments and recordkeeping for international medical tourism or telemedicine services.

- Intellectual property rights: Tokenization of pharmaceutical patents or research findings could create new ways to fund drug development or monetize research outcomes.
- Pharmaceutical supply chains: Tokenizing pharmaceutical products can improve supply chain transparency, track authenticity, and prevent counterfeit drugs.
- Medical equipment: Tokenized leasing/rental of high-value equipment enables broader access, especially in emerging markets.
- Healthcare real estate: Platforms also allow fractional investment in clinics or hospitals, similar to REITs, but with greater liquidity.
- Financing startups: On the VC front, tokenized fundraising allows biotech or medtech firms to attract capital through STOs, providing liquidity and access to a global pool of investors. Notably, KKR and Securitize Capital launched a tokenized share class for part of their $4 billion Healthcare Strategic Growth Fund II in 2025—illustrating early but real institutional adoption.

Pros and Risks Tokenization enhances liquidity, transparency, security, and access. However, it comes with risks: regulatory uncertainty, privacy concerns (think twice, the data recording is immutable!), technological complexity, and market immaturity. Failed ICOs in the 2017–2019 cycle are cautionary tales, but newer models—backed by credible platforms and clear legal frameworks—are more resilient. Some early promising implementations include Solve.Care (Estonia/United States), a platform that has shown promise in tokenizing healthcare administration (Fang, 2021), and Clinicoin (United States), a wellness platform using tokens to incentivize healthy behaviors, which could be an interesting model for PE investment in preventive care.

In the United States, tokenization in healthcare is gaining traction. The US regulatory environment, including the SEC and the FDA, is gradually adapting to accommodate blockchain innovations, but challenges remain. Companies such as BurstIQ and Avaneer Healthcare are examples of early adopters using blockchain for healthcare data management and patient engagement.

In Europe, regulatory frameworks for blockchain and tokenization are also evolving, with initiatives like the European Blockchain Partnership and the General Data Protection Regulation (GDPR) influencing the development of blockchain solutions in healthcare.

In the United Kingdom, MedicalChain is one of many examples of companies offering to empower patients by giving them control over their medical records. Countries like Switzerland (Healthbank, HIT Foundation) and Estonia (Guardtime, Koos, Medifakt) are also emerging as leaders in healthcare tokenization initiatives. Outside of Europe, Singapore also presents some interesting experiments such as UHT's gamified health engagement model. Overall, DataM Intelligence forecasted the market to grow at 68% CAGR from 2024 to 2031.

The trajectory of healthcare tokenization, while promising, is contingent upon the interplay of several critical factors. Regulatory frameworks, in particular, will be pivotal; the development of clear and supportive guidelines by governing bodies worldwide could significantly accelerate adoption, whereas restrictive or ambiguous policies may impede progress. Concurrently, the maturation of blockchain technology itself, coupled with its seamless integration into existing healthcare informatics and operational systems, remains a fundamental prerequisite for widespread implementation. Beyond technological and regulatory hurdles, the ultimate success of tokenized healthcare models will hinge on their acceptance by key stakeholders—including healthcare providers, patients, and the investment community. The proliferation of validated use cases demonstrating tangible benefits, such as enhanced efficiency, improved data security, or novel financing mechanisms, will be instrumental in fostering this acceptance and driving broader market adoption.

For PE investors navigating this nascent field, a rigorous due diligence process is paramount. Investment theses must critically assess the robustness and scalability of the underlying technology. Equally important is ensuring strict alignment with evolving regulatory mandates, such as GDPR in Europe or SEC and HIPAA compliance in the United States, to mitigate legal and operational risks. The ability of tokenized solutions to interoperate with entrenched legacy healthcare systems is another crucial consideration, as this will dictate the feasibility and cost of implementation. Furthermore, PE investors should prioritize ventures with well-defined, sustainable business models that demonstrate clear healthcare use cases and pathways to recurring revenue.

The tokenization of healthcare thus presents a duality of compelling opportunities and significant challenges for PE. It unlocks novel investment avenues, from innovative healthtech platforms to new financial instruments for healthcare assets and offers the potential to drive substantial operational efficiencies within portfolio companies. However, capitalizing on these opportunities demands a sophisticated understanding of both the intricate healthcare ecosystem and the nuances of blockchain technology. Navigating the rapidly evolving regulatory landscape also requires specialized expertise and proactive risk management.

7.6 A FRAMEWORK FOR VALUE CREATION IN HEALTHCARE

7.6.1 Specificities of Healthcare

PE has long attracted scrutiny, but nowhere is the debate more charged than in healthcare. As highlighted in Chapter 8, the dynamics between stakeholders can lead to misaligned incentives and concerns about fairness. In most sectors, the discussion centers on the trade-off between financial returns and operational improvement. In healthcare, however, the stakes are dramatically higher. Here, value creation affects not only economic outcomes but also human lives. Decisions cannot be reduced to cost efficiency or productivity gains; they directly influence patients' health outcomes, with potential increases in disease burden (higher DALYs) or reductions in life expectancy and quality of life (lower QALYs). The consequences are significant, enduring, and emotionally charged.

This makes healthcare investing fundamentally multidimensional. Alongside financial performance (traditionally geared toward shareholders), investors must consider patient outcomes, strict regulatory compliance, and the well-being of clinical staff—an essential determinant of quality of care. Innovation adds a further layer of complexity: difficult to assess yet often decisive for sustainable value.

Balancing these competing priorities is the core constraint shaping every strategic decision discussed in this chapter. It also underpins the H.E.A.L. value-creation framework introduced for new investors approaching the healthcare sector. While experienced practitioners may intuitively navigate these trade-offs and "tricks of the trade," the framework highlights that in healthcare—more than in any other industry—the social and ethical costs of missteps are uniquely high.

Developing a tailored framework for healthcare PE is therefore highly valuable. For newcomers, it clarifies the complexity of the sector by identifying critical drivers, regulatory intricacies, and unique risks that should anchor investment decisions. For generalists entering healthcare, it offers a structured guide to avoid common pitfalls and identify sustainable growth opportunities. And even for seasoned investors, it serves as a practical checklist to strengthen diligence and strategy in a rapidly evolving environment. Ultimately, it improves decision-making discipline and helps ensure alignment between financial goals and the realities of healthcare delivery and innovation

Following, we recall the specifics of healthcare investing:

- **An ethical and highly regulated domain**
  Healthcare deals with life-and-death decisions and is therefore heavily regulated (e.g., FDA, EMA, national health authorities). Due diligence must rigorously assess compliance risks—clinical standards, billing practices, and data privacy (HIPAA, GDPR). Failures can trigger fines, litigation, or license withdrawal.
- **A hybrid B2B2C value chain**
  Three main stakeholders—providers and manufacturers, medical professionals, and patients—create a complex governance model in which influence is shared and decision power is distributed.
- **Three sources of financing**
  Social security (or NHS), private medical insurance, and out-of-pocket (vs. only two in most other sectors). Policy changes can dramatically impact margins. Hence, investors must assess payer mix, pricing models, and reimbursement sustainability.
- **Long-duration investment horizons**
  Drug development and large healthcare infrastructure take a decade or more to materialize, with hospitals and health systems operating on multi-decade cycles.
- **Capital-intensive business models**
  Hospitals can require hundreds of millions in capital; drug development and advanced healthtech can exceed the billion-dollar scale.
- **A lifelong service relationship**
  Unlike most consumer sectors, healthcare accompanies individuals from prenatal care to elder support, with evolving needs that require adaptive and continuous service provision.
- **Fragmented and locally governed markets**
  Regulation remains national or regional, creating both complexity and consolidation opportunities across highly fragmented landscapes.
- **Structurally rising demand**
  Ageing populations, chronic disease prevalence, and increased life expectancy provide resilience during economic downturns and drive long-term sector growth.

7.6.2 Introducing the H.E.A.L. Framework

7.6.2.1 Why Healthcare Needs a Different PE Lens Healthcare PE has expanded rapidly, yet the sector presents the unique set of complexities we described earlier: ethical responsibility, stringent regulation, hybrid B2B2C dynamics, fragmented and local

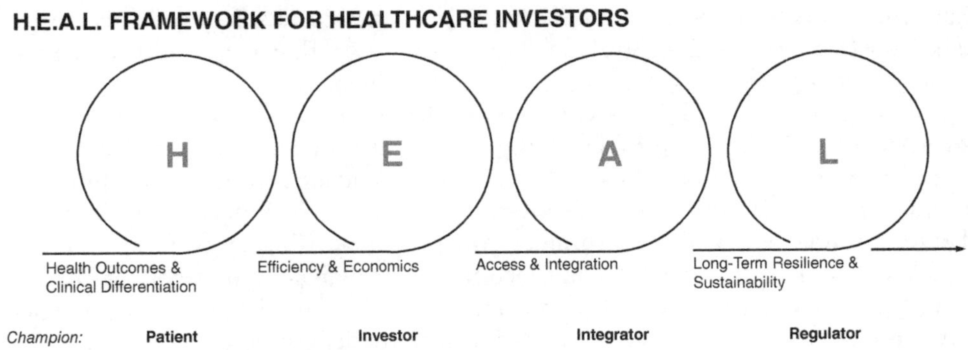

FIGURE 7.29 H.E.A.L. value creation framework.
Source: Kitten & Silvestri.

market structures, multi-payer systems, long investment horizons, and high capital requirements.

Traditional PE frameworks emphasize financial engineering—refinancing, tax optimization, cost takeout—which may be effective elsewhere but are insufficient in this industry. In healthcare, in fact, value depends not only on economics but also on clinical outcomes, regulatory compliance, and multi-stakeholder integration.

To address this gap, we introduce the **H.E.A.L. Value Creation Framework** (Figure 7.29), designed specifically for investors operating in healthcare environments.

H.E.A.L. stands for:

- H—Health Outcomes and Clinical Differentiation
- E—Efficiency and Economics
- A—Access and Integration
- L—Long-term Resilience and Sustainability

This four-dimensional model maps how PE investors create value in healthcare:

- **H** ensures clinical legitimacy and patient benefit. This reflects the ethical and regulatory nature of healthcare.
- **E** drives operating leverage and financial returns, which are essential for CapEx-heavy, fragmented, long-horizon healthcare investments.
- **A** expands reach in fragmented systems. It captures the hybrid B2B2C model and multi-payer financing structure.
- **L** future-proofs investments against regulation, policy shocks, and ESG pressures. It anchors the "20-year horizon" reality in drug/hospital/health system investing.

Moreover, each dimension aligns with a primary "champion" in the ecosystem:

- **H** centers on the *Patient*: the ultimate purpose and beneficiary of healthcare innovation and service.
- **E** reflects the *Investor's* mandate: seeking productivity, scale, and attractive returns.
- **A** embodies the *Integrator*—the catalyst for access and connectivity. In healthcare services, this is *the Provider*: clinicians, health systems, digital platforms, and network managers who connect care, data, and financing silos. They make integration real by scaling networks, aligning payers, and expanding reach—often

alongside PE partners. In life sciences, the *Innovator* plays this role, bridging labs, payers, and patients through science, technology, and data translation to bring therapies and platforms to market.

- L anchors the *Regulator* (or Steward Institution)—the agencies, payers, and public actors who keep investments sustainable, compliant, and policy-proof over decades. They set the guardrails that let investors and founders plan on long horizons without regulatory shocks.

7.6.3 Positioning the H.E.A.L. Framework

Most existing frameworks for value in healthcare build on the principles of value-based healthcare (VBHC), which defines value as clinical outcomes achieved relative to cost (Porter and Teisberg, 2006). VBHC has reshaped provider and payer strategies around effectiveness and accountability. However, it does not address how PE should structure its investments or manage assets in a sector where performance is both clinical and financial.

Similarly, previous research on PE in healthcare has primarily examined the consequences of ownership—on pricing, quality, and access—rather than equipping investors with a practical framework that helps balance financial objectives with clinical, regulatory, and ethical constraints.

The H.E.A.L. framework fills this strategic and conceptual gap. In contrast to general PE playbooks focused on capital structure optimization or cost reduction, H.E.A.L. embeds the four critical dimensions of healthcare value creation—Health

SIDEBAR—VBHC VS. H.E.A.L.: DIFFERENT TOOLS FOR DIFFERENT GOALS

Dimension	VBHC	H.E.A.L.
Primary Purpose	Improve clinical outcomes relative to the cost of care	Guide investment strategy and value creation in healthcare PE
Definition of "Value"	Patient outcomes/cost of delivering care	Four integrated dimensions: **Health, Efficiency, Access, Long-term Resilience**
Core Lens	Provider and payer performance in care delivery	Investor and portfolio company performance in regulated, mission-critical markets
Scope of Application	Clinical pathways, reimbursement, care models	Governance, operational strategy, and deal thesis in healthcare assets
Central Stakeholder	The patient	Patient + investor + integrator/ provider + regulator
Time Horizon	Continuous improvement in outcomes and cost efficiency	Long-cycle value creation in capital-intensive environments

Takeaway:

VBHC defines value **in care delivery.**

H.E.A.L. defines how to create value **when investing in care.**

outcomes, Efficiency, Access, and Long-term resilience—which collectively capture the distinct realities of investing in a highly regulated, mission-driven, and capital-intensive industry.

In doing so, H.E.A.L. complements VBHC by adding a clear investor perspective.[12] It offers PE funds a disciplined roadmap to pursue sustainable growth while reinforcing the core purpose of healthcare: delivering improved and equitable patient outcomes.

7.6.4 Mapping the 31 Value Levers in the H.E.A.L. Framework

We mapped the 31 common PE value levers identified earlier in this chapter onto the four dimensions of the H.E.A.L. framework, scoring each lever from 1 to 5 against Health outcomes (H), Efficiency (E), Access (A), and Long-term resilience (L).

Several patterns emerge:

Financial Engineering Plays (*Take-Private, Tax Arbitrage, Refinancing*): High **E**, low **H/A/L** → typically short-horizon and opportunistic

Clinical Differentiators (*Precision Medicine, Behavioral Health, Patient-centric Models*): High **H** and **L** → durable but capital-intensive

Integration & Access Models (*Health System Integration, Bundled Payments, Alternative Sites of Care*): Strong **A**, and often strong **H** and **E**, suggesting scalable transformation potential

Sustainability Enablers (*Regulatory Strategy, ESG, IP, Data*): Less visible to patients but critical for resilience and policy-proofing

To visualize these insights, we plot the 31 levers in a two-dimensional matrix/bubble chart:

X-axis: Efficiency & Economics (E)

Y-axis: Health Outcomes & Clinical Differentiation (H)

Color: Access & Integration (A)—e.g., Yellow = strong Access/Integration (payer-provider partnerships, international expansion, bundled payments), Gray = weak Access/Integration

Bubble size: Long-term Resilience (L)—Larger bubble = greater sustainability/regulatory alignment (ESG, IP, data strategies, regulatory robustness); Smaller bubble = opportunistic/shorter-term plays

The outcome reveals five natural clustering: short-term financial plays, operational plays, sustainability enablers, integrators, and clinical bets (Figure 7.30).

[12] While VBHC defines value = health outcomes/cost, H.E.A.L. extends this by asking: "What levers do investors have to influence both the numerator and denominator—while also accounting for access and resilience?" To this extent, H.E.A.L. can be described as the investor's VBHC, which could resonate with both clinicians and strategists.

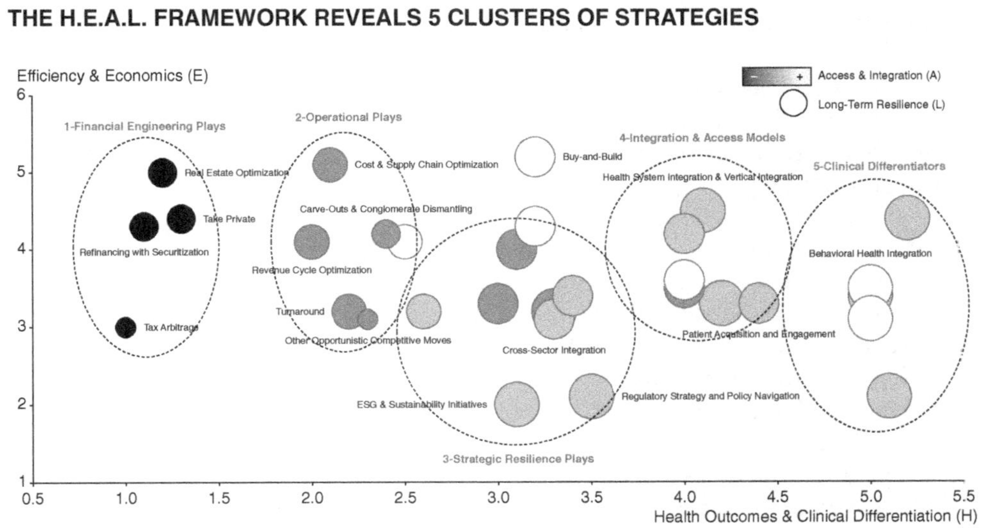

FIGURE 7.30 Five clusters of investment strategies.
Source: Kitten & Silvestri.

7.6.4.1 Five Clusters Emerge By mapping across Health (H), Efficiency (E), Access (A), and Long-term (L), we identify natural clusters of value-creation strategies:

1. **Financial engineering plays** (top left, small, pale bubbles): *Take-Private, Refinancing, Tax Arbitrage, Real Estate Optimization.* High on Efficiency, low on Health, Access, Long-term. They can generate quick IRR and support deal execution but do little to improve patient outcomes or access. If overused, they risk negative perception and may undermine trust in PE's role in healthcare.
2. **Operational plays** (next to financial plays, also small pale bubbles): *cost and supply chain, carve-out, revenue cycle, turnaround.* Close to financial plays on the map, these are more "hygiene factors" than differentiators. They strengthen the core economics of a business and are often necessary early in ownership, yet alone they rarely create sustainable competitive advantage in healthcare.
3. **Strategic resilience plays** (low middle, large bubbles): *Regulatory Strategy, ESG, Data Strategies, IP Monetization.* Moderate Health/Efficiency, but very high Long-term (bubble size). Often "enablers" that underpin sustainable success but are invisible to patients.
4. **Integration and access models** (center to top-right, darker bubbles): *Health System Integration, Payer-provider Partnerships, Bundled Payments, Alternative Sites of Care.* Strong Access and Integration, often mid-to-high Health and Efficiency. These represent the future of healthcare delivery—coordinated, value-based, scalable, and politically resilient.
5. **Clinical differentiators** (right, large, mid-color bubbles): *Precision Medicine, Behavioral Health, Clinical Excellence, Patient-centric Models.* High Health and Long-term, moderate Efficiency. They are strongly aligned with healthcare's mission and reputation, and while they may require substantial investment and talent, they build lasting value through improved outcomes and brand credibility.

7.6.4.2 Five Core Insights

1. **Tension Between Short-term IRR and Long-term Value**
   Value levers in the upper-left (E high, H low) quadrant (financial engineering) boost short-term returns but rarely contribute to sustainable healthcare transformation.
   Value levers in the right quadrants (H high, L large) build resilience and clinical legitimacy, but require patient capital (longer hold periods, more CapEx).
   Insight: The best-performing funds will combine near-term financial levers with long-term clinical and integration strategies.
2. **Access and Integration Is the Differentiator**
   Color (Access = A) reveals that most high-value, scalable models are darker bubbles (e.g., Payer-provider Partnerships, Alternative Sites of Care, Technology-enabled Care).
   In fragmented, local markets with multi-payer financing, integration is the bridge between efficiency and patient impact.
   Insight: Funds that specialize in payer/provider dynamics (contracting, bundled payments, population health) are better positioned than those relying on one-off arbitrage plays.
3. **Long-term Sustainability (L) Separates Winners**
   Larger bubbles (L high) often combine regulatory alignment, ESG, or clinical innovation.
   Value levers like *Precision Medicine, Patient-centric Models, ESG, Regulatory Strategy* are less "sexy" in short-term multiples, but they future-proof portfolios against reimbursement changes, litigation, and policy shocks.
   Insight: A resilient portfolio construction strategy needs a minimum "bubble size threshold"—i.e., each fund should ensure a baseline of high-L archetypes.
4. **Policy and Regulation Are Hidden Power Centers**
   Value levers like *Regulatory Strategy, ESG, IP, Data Monetization* may not score high on Health/Efficiency, but they disproportionately determine survivability in healthcare.
   Insight: Investors often undervalue these "silent enablers"—but in healthcare, they are existential risk mitigators.
5. **The Flywheel Effect: Archetypes Are Not Mutually Exclusive**
   Many companies can embody 2–3 archetypes simultaneously (e.g., *Tech-enabled Care Delivery* = Clinical + Efficiency + Access + Long-term).
   Insight: The most scalable investments create flywheels across H.E.A.L.—e.g., better patient experience (H) drives higher acquisition (A), which improves economics (E), underpinned by regulatory compliance (L).

7.6.4.3 Illustrative Applications of H.E.A.L. *Clarification: These are retrospective examples based solely on publicly available information. They illustrate how selected transactions align with the H.E.A.L. dimensions—and where value-creation plans could have been further enhanced. We make no claim that the investors applied this framework or executed the suggested actions, nor can we exclude that certain measures may have been implemented without public disclosure; rather, if they were implemented without public disclosure, we could not confirm them.*

H—Health Outcomes and Clinical Differentiation

Nordic Capital & Five Arrows → The Binding Site (sold to Thermo Fisher Scientific)

What happened:

In October 2022, Nordic Capital and Five Arrows announced the sale of the Binding Site—a UK-based specialist diagnostics company focused on multiple myeloma and immune-system disorders—to Thermo Fisher Scientific in a transaction valued at £2.25 billion.

Under private-equity ownership, the Binding Site scaled revenues five-fold, expanded global reach, invested in R&D and transformed from a research-bench model to a commercial diagnostics leader.

Prescriptive H.E.A.L. suggestion:
To maximize the **H** dimension (health outcomes and clinical differentiation), the value-creation plan could have included the following:

- The creation and publication of real-world evidence showing the impact of the company's diagnostics on time-to-diagnosis and patient survival outcomes.
- A tier-1 access program with public payers or under-served markets to ensure equitable deployment of the diagnostics, thus enhancing patient access and impact.
- Linking management incentives to clinical-outcome metrics (e.g., reduction in misdiagnoses, diagnostic turnaround time) as well as financial metrics—thereby aligning owner, management, and patient benefit more tightly.

E—Efficiency and Economics

Veritas Capital & Evergreen Coast Capital → Athenahealth

What happened:

In February 2019, Veritas Capital and Evergreen Coast Capital completed the acquisition of Athenahealth for approximately US$5.7 billion in cash. Subsequently, the company was combined with Virence Health under the Athenahealth brand. Later, in 2021/22, Bain Capital and Hellman & Friedman agreed to acquire Athenahealth for around US$17 billion.

Prescriptive H.E.A.L. suggestion:
To enhance the **E** dimension (efficiency and economics), the investment plan could have included the following:

- Provider-facing ROI dashboards showing key operational improvements (e.g., days in A/R, denial rates, clinician time saved) with data made available to major clients and linked to contract renewal incentives.

- Patient-impact KPIs integrated into the commercial model: e.g., portal adoption rates, refill-adherence improvements, patient-engagement scores.
- A customer charter publicly committing the business to aligned provider and patient outcomes, thus reinforcing alignment between financial performance and care value.

A—Access and Integration

KKR (via Radiant Life Care) → Max Healthcare Institute (India)

What happened:

In June 2019, Radiant Life Care, backed by KKR, completed the acquisition of 49.7% of Max Healthcare Institute from Life Healthcare (South Africa) for ~₹2,136 crore (~US$300 million). This transaction marked a major expansion of the Max hospital network in North India.

Prescriptive H.E.A.L. suggestion:
To fully harness the **A** dimension (access and integration), the value plan could have included:

- Formal payer-provider bundled-payment partnerships aligned with India's public health scheme and major private insurers, enabling risk-sharing and scale.
- A hub-and-spoke network model accelerating rollout into Tier-2/3 cities to extend reach to under-served populations and reduce referral burdens.
- Implementation of an interoperable data platform across hospitals and outpatient sites, with public reporting of key access metrics (wait-times, referral leakage, continuity of care) to build reputation and competitive positioning.

L—Long-term Resilience and Sustainability

Warburg Pincus & GTCR → Sterigenics International LLC (now part of Sotera Health)

What happened:

In January 2023, Sotera Health agreed to pay US$408 million to settle ~870 lawsuits in Illinois alleging ethylene-oxide emissions from sterilization facilities caused cancer and other health harms.

Prescriptive H.E.A.L. suggestion:
To strengthen the **L** dimension (long-term resilience and sustainability), the value plan could have included:

- Upfront environmental-control CapEx and continuous monitoring of emissions at sterilization sites, with real-time visibility and public reporting.
- Establishing community advisory councils around facilities, early-stage engagement with regulators, and proactive emission disclosures to reduce reputational risk.

- Incentive structures for management and investors tied to compliance, community metrics and regulatory performance, ensuring that long-term license-to-operate is baked into the value plan.

7.6.4.4 How to Use These Cases These examples show the shift from "if the deal works" to "why the deal should exist."

Investors can assess any value-creation plan by asking the following questions:

- Does it improve outcomes? (H)
- Does it scale sustainably? (E)
- Does it expand reach and coordination? (A)
- Does it endure through regulation and scrutiny? (L)

Investments that activate multiple H.E.A.L. dimensions are the most defensible—and the most transformative.

7.6.4.5 Conclusion: Value Creation Where It Matters Most PE will keep shaping the future of healthcare, which raises the question of where and how it creates value.

H.E.A.L. forces that choice into the open.

Funds that rely mainly on financial engineering may deliver strong short-term returns—but risk eroding trust in a sector where legitimacy is everything. Those that pair financial discipline with clinical differentiation, integration of care, and long-term resilience deliver stronger, more sustainable performance.

In healthcare, financial and human value are not opposing forces—they are mutually reinforcing. When investment improves outcomes, access, and reliability of care, it unlocks durable growth and stakeholder alignment.

The opportunity is clear:

Invest where value is created—and where lives are improved.

H.E.A.L. shows how.

CHAPTER 8

Owners, Other Stakeholders, and Society

Much of the academic corporate finance literature focuses on conflicts of interests between shareholders and other stakeholders (Tirole, 2006; Hart, 1995). Attention was first paid to how tensions between shareholders and debtholders affect capital structure and debt financing (Jensen and Mecking, 1976; Myers, 1977; Bolton and Scharfstein, 1990, 1996; Hart, 1995; Hart and Moore, 1994, 1995, 1998; Chemla and Milone, 2018), and these apply also to leveraged transactions such as buyouts. The academic literature then focused on conflicts between shareholders and managers (Tirole, 2006, Chapter 1), shareholders and workers or trading partners (Perotti and Spier, 1993; Chemla and Faure Grimaud, 2001), shareholders and policymakers (Miller, 1988; Laffont and Tirole, 1993; Iossa and Martimort, 2012, 2015), and different types of shareholders (Grossman and Hart, 1980, 1988; Myers and Majluf, 1984; Chemla et al., 2007; Edmans and Manso, 2011). The considerable corporate governance (Hart, 1995; Becht et al., 2003; Chemla, 2003, 2004, 2005; Pagano and Volpin, 2005a, b; Tirole, 2006; Chemla et al., 2007; Hart and Zingales, 2022) and mergers and acquisitions (Shleifer and Summers, 1988; Chemla, 2003, 2004, 2005) literatures have also largely evolved around these tensions. Private equity (PE) is no exception, with shareholders and general partners (GPs) often portrayed as the main villains. In this chapter, we explore the main controversies in PE. We then turn more specifically to the healthcare sector, where these tensions have attracted considerable attention.

The controversy surrounding private equity in healthcare is shaped by four selection effects. First, there is **segment selection**, with emphasis on LBOs and highly levered deals rather than the full range of PE strategies. Second, **exposure selection** concentrates on patient-facing care and drug access, where harm is most visible through prices, quality, and adverse events. Third, **event selection** further narrows attention to clearly problematic or abusive deals that attract headlines and academic scrutiny. Finally, **counterfactual selection** reflects the fact that we observe outcomes under PE ownership but not what would have happened otherwise, such as alternative buyers, ongoing under-investment, closure, or different consolidation paths.

The controversy surrounding PE primarily centers on LBOs and distressed deals due to the combination of debt financing and concentrated ownership by investors eager to implement operating improvement with a view to exit. Perhaps not surprisingly, many of the effects of buyouts on stakeholders have followed the analysis of corporate leverage on stakeholders in corporate finance. While high leverage serves as a powerful performance amplifier and imposes financial discipline on management, it also creates potential conflicts of interest. The pressure to service substantial debt obligations can incentivize firms to extract value from various stakeholders: workforce reductions and price increases become a quick path to cost savings (Perotti and Spier, 1993; Chevalier, 1995a, b; Kovenock and Phillips, 1997; Phillips, 1995; Chemla and Faure-Grimaud, 2001), supplier payments may be delayed to manage cash flow (Petersen and Rajan, 1997; Wilner, 2000; Cuñat, 2007), product quality might be compromised to maintain margins (Maksimovic and Titman, 1991; Mendes, 2024), and risks could be disproportionately shifted to lenders through aggressive financial engineering (Keys et al., 2010; Bolton and Oehmke, 2011; Chemla and Hennessy, 2014, 2016).

When combined with a short-term perspective due to a desire to exit early, the gain in efficiency due to concentrated ownership can also generate conflicts with stakeholders. In corporate finance, it is well established that liquidity motives alter incentives by reducing accountability, reducing commitment, and increasing short-term pressure (Tirole, 2006, Chapter 4; Bolton et al., 2006; Edmans et al., 2017). This short termism may lead firms to engage in operational improvements that sometimes result in higher prices, lower investments such as R&D, or job cuts. There is evidence, for example, that following non-PE mergers, hospitals do raise prices (Dafny, 2009; Dafny et al., 2019; Arnold et al., 2024).

PE is no different, although the disclosure requirements and short-term price fluctuations inherent to publicly listed firms have been shown to be more detrimental to long-term innovation than for private ownership (Bernstein, 2022). Privately held firms face largely heterogeneous financial constraints (Nanda and Philips, 2023). This chapter discusses existing findings that are mostly obtained after highly levered transactions such as LBOs.

Other PE segments such as growth capital or turnaround investments focus traditionally on operational improvements, organic growth, and buildup synergies. Indeed, growth capital provides expansion funding to promising businesses and turnaround investments aim to rehabilitate struggling companies through operational expertise rather than financial engineering.

In healthcare, controversies are generally concentrated in highly levered transactions in patient-facing care and drug access, where the concern regarding access to, and quality of, services has been the subject of an extant literature. Before we explore these controversies, we observe that they typically represent a small part of all transactions. When mapping five and a half years of PE transactions in healthcare by value (January 2020–September 2025), we find that highly levered transactions in patient facing care and in drug access account for about 13% of all PE transactions in healthcare (Figure 8.1). This is not the proportion of controversial transactions. Rather, this is certainly an upper bound. Controversial transactions may well account for 5–10% of this segment, including situations of blatant drug price gouging. This excuses in no way the abuses by some GPs. However, back of the envelope estimates suggest that transactions likely to be controversial account only for a small percentage of the transactions in healthcare by value.[1]

[1] Since we have included add-ons in the LBO segment, estimates based on the number of transactions would likely exaggerate the impact.

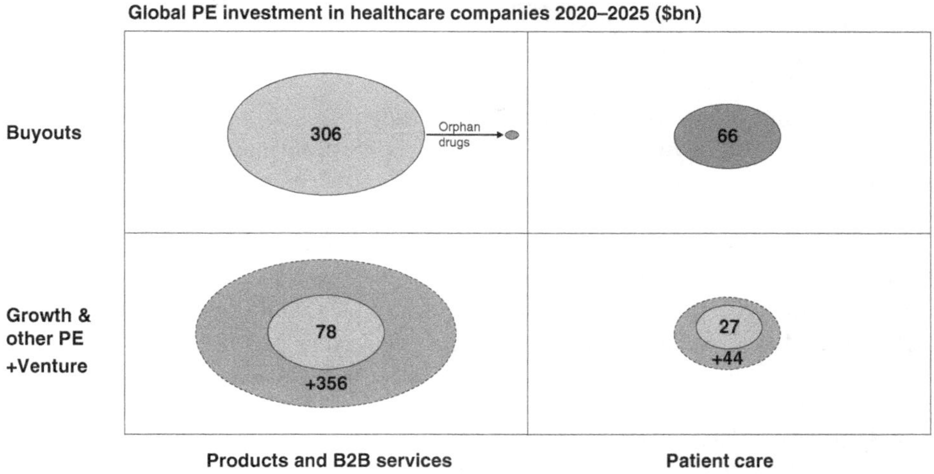

FIGURE 8.1 Public controversies are concentrated in a small segment of PE.
Source: Preqin (part of Blackrock); Candesic analysis (to September 2025).

Understandably, these are the transactions picked up in articles flagging abuse. They exemplify the event selection effect described above: attention concentrates on the most problematic cases. Moreover, in the absence of a clean counterfactual, we still do not know what would have happened had the PE investment not occurred.

Healthcare typically requires a long-term alignment between shareholders and other stakeholders, keeping a balance between financial and operational or societal value creation. According to Mike Mortimer from GHO, this is essential: "The healthcare companies we choose to invest in believe they are doing something good for the world."

Mortimer articulates how healthcare PE generally benefits from a natural mission alignment between investors, management teams, and societal needs. This alignment can significantly reduce agency costs and improve execution compared to other sectors where profit maximization may directly conflict with broader stakeholder interests:

> *Of course, as a GP we are committed to delivering high financial performance to our investors, but beyond that, we strive to excel. We create value alongside the portfolio company's management team. We want to have real impact: to deliver more affordable healthcare, achieve better patient outcomes, and to be known as best-in-class at exit.*

What about the agency problem between shareholders and management? In our discussions with GPs and LPs, fees were sometimes a concern, but management entrenchment, empire building, and managerial hubris, so widely discussed in the general corporate governance literature, have never been a common concern. The focus on value creation combined with the absence of distractions due to analyst coverage, public scrutiny, and regulatory compliance inherent to publicly listed firms shifts the potential for conflicts to those with various types of stakeholders. This includes limited partners (LPs), minority shareholders, lenders, but also the taxman, payors, local authorities, personal, suppliers, customers, as well as regulators and policy. In this chapter, we will first set the scene by exploring two owner perspectives: the original founder and the manager who acquires a stake in a buyout (whether a management buyout or buy-in). Then, we will turn to other stakeholders.

Estimating the cost of such possible conflicts is often highly challenging. When effects are short term, one can easily compare what happened to stakeholders after and before a buyout. When effects are long term, environments years after buyouts may well differ considerably to five those years before buyouts. When stakeholders are listed firms, one can also rely on so called event studies, which measure abnormal security price reactions at the announcement of a buyout (Chemla and Hennessy, 2022). When they are not listed, estimating the effect of buyouts would require an estimate of how well stakeholders would have been in the absence of a PE. Challenges to this so-called counterfactual analysis are the subject of abundant literature (Keane and Wolpin, 1997; Rust, 2010; Imbens and Rubin, 2015; Chemla and Hennessy, 2019, 2020, 2021, 2022, 2024).

8.1 PERSPECTIVES OF CORPORATE OWNERS

PE investors do more than just financing firms. They play a strategic role in the future of the business, partnering with "corporate owners" (Casamatta, 2003). We differentiate between three situations:

- Founders who bring external capital (minority investment) to finance the company growth and generally do not plan to relinquish control
- Founders who want to cash out and partner with an LBO fund to manage the transmission, sometimes with the understanding that the management team that succeeds them (internal promotion or external hiring) will get sweat equity and perhaps more
- Managers who take over from the founder with the help of the LBO fund and hope to raise their equity significantly (if successful) through the LBO, sometimes going through several LBOs raising their equity stake each time, eventually reaching a significant, sometimes controlling, stake

The abundance of private capital has enabled firms to grow significantly without/before going public. The considerable delayed timing of an initial public offering (IPO) speaks for itself: PE appears to be a more attractive financing route for founders and owners significantly longer than decades ago. There are several reasons for this. First, in early IPOs, investors capture a share of the value created by firms as they grow. Maksimovic et al. (2023) and Larraín et al. (2025) provide evidence that PE enables founders/owners to capture a much larger share of the value they create than earlier IPOs.

Second, LBO specialists play a big role in the firm's success, and particularly so when their expertise makes a difference. For example, after public to private LBOs, the board size is reduced, LBO sponsors often replace outside directors, and their presence on the board is higher for complex transactions (Cornelli and Karakas, 2012). Further, the presence of LBO sponsors on the board reduces CEO turnover, and its sensitivity to performance, but increases operating performance, which suggests that effective monitoring by PE reduces the reliance on short-term performance and allows for a longer term horizon for CEOs (Cornelli and Karakas, 2015). In contrast, boards in nonprofit hospitals appear to be larger, with more employee directors, but fewer external industry experts than for profit hospitals. They also feature CEO pay and turnover, acquisitions, and closures largely unresponsive to nonfinancial metrics. These hospitals are half as likely to be acquired or closed after bad financial performance than for-profit hospitals (Lewellen et al., 2025).

This section examines what it takes for owners to raise funds successfully.

8.1.1 Timing and Key Success Criteria

Timing and key success factors play a pivotal role for entrepreneurs aiming to secure venture or growth capital, especially in the healthcare sector. Securing investment goes beyond presenting a compelling business case; it requires aligning with the right market conditions and addressing critical investor expectations. Key performance indicators (KPIs) that resonate with investors—such as revenue growth, customer acquisition, customer lifetime value, and burn rate—are essential. Entrepreneurs who can demonstrate a clear trajectory toward profitability, even in the early stages, are more likely to instill confidence in potential investors. Milestones like regulatory approvals, strategic partnerships, and product launches can also act as significant drivers for fundraising success. Recognizing and integrating these factors into their strategy can greatly enhance an entrepreneur's ability to attract the necessary capital to scale their business.

In healthcare, the timing of fundraising is critical due to the sector's intricate regulatory framework and often lengthy development timelines. Entrepreneurs should align their capital-raising efforts with key milestones, such as concluding clinical trials, achieving regulatory approvals, or attaining notable market presence. Investors are typically drawn to companies at an inflection point, where additional funding is poised to deliver significant value creation. For early-stage ventures, seed or Series A funding often focuses on validating the business model, developing a minimum viable product (MVP), and building a core team. Later funding rounds typically aim to support product development, market expansion, and commercialization. Securing investment at pivotal moments, such as before a major clinical trial or during negotiations for a strategic partnership, can position the company for accelerated growth and increase its appeal to investors.

Market readiness is another crucial factor to consider. Entrepreneurs must evaluate whether the market is primed for their product or service, taking into account healthcare infrastructure, regulatory conditions, and competitive dynamics. Launching a fundraising campaign during periods of heightened market demand for innovative healthcare solutions or in response to favorable regulatory changes can significantly improve the chances of success. Additionally, staying attuned to broader economic trends is essential, as these can impact investor sentiment and the overall availability of capital.

Further, scalability is a paramount consideration for investors. Entrepreneurs need to present a clear path for scaling their business, which involves not only expanding their market reach but also ensuring that operations, supply chains, and regulatory strategies are built to support growth. Investors are particularly interested in ventures that can scale efficiently, leveraging technology, partnerships, and streamlined operations to maximize returns on investment. Entrepreneurs should demonstrate how their business model can adapt to increased demand and how additional capital will be used to accelerate growth while maintaining or improving margins.

8.1.2 Navigating the PE Investor's Requirements

Aligning with investors' requirements can significantly increase the likelihood of securing funding. Investors in healthcare and life sciences are often highly specialized, with a deep understanding of the sector's complexities. Entrepreneurs must demonstrate not only the potential of their business but also their ability to meet rigorous criteria regarding

- market opportunity,
- product viability,
- regulatory compliance, and
- management capability.

This process often involves a delicate balancing act between maintaining company vision and accommodating investor preferences.

The first step in navigating investors' requirements is to clearly articulate the market opportunity. Investors are looking for ventures that address significant unmet needs or that have the potential to disrupt existing markets. Entrepreneurs must provide a compelling narrative supported by robust data, showing that their solution addresses a critical pain point in healthcare. This includes a detailed analysis of market size, growth potential, and the competitive landscape. Investors want to see that the entrepreneur has a strong grasp of the market dynamics and that the business is positioned for sustainable growth.

Next, investors will closely scrutinize the product or service being offered, particularly its viability and differentiation. In the healthcare sector, this often involves a rigorous assessment of the technology or treatment's clinical efficacy, regulatory pathway, and intellectual property protection. Entrepreneurs need to demonstrate that their product not only works but also has a clear path to market. This includes having a well-thought-out regulatory strategy, evidence of clinical validation, and a timeline for achieving key milestones. The more tangible and de-risked the product development process appears, the more attractive the opportunity becomes to investors.

Another critical aspect investors evaluate is the quality and capability of the management team. In the healthcare sector, challenges are complex, and success often hinges on the expertise and experience of the team leading the venture. Investors are looking for teams with a proven track record in the industry, deep domain expertise, and the ability to execute on the business plan. Entrepreneurs should be prepared to showcase their team's credentials, including past successes, relevant industry experience, and the ability to adapt to challenges. Investors want to feel confident that the team has the necessary skills to navigate the intricate and often unpredictable healthcare landscape.

Lastly, entrepreneurs must be prepared to meet the financial expectations of investors, which often extend beyond just the capital requirements. Investors will assess the financial health of the business, its current and projected cash flow, and its ability to achieve profitability or a successful exit. This includes presenting a realistic financial model that outlines how the capital raised will be used to achieve specific milestones and how these milestones will increase the company's valuation. Entrepreneurs should also be prepared for discussions around deal structure, equity stakes, and exit strategies, ensuring alignment with investor expectations to foster a mutually beneficial partnership.

8.1.3 Choosing Investors

Early discussions, often called "fireside chats" or "coffee meetings" in the industry, are typically informal conversations with select prospective investors to gauge their interest. As the sale process advances, the pool of interested parties can grow significantly, ranging from 20 to as many as 50 potential buyers. Among these, a few may be strategic acquirers—larger companies seeking to expand through acquisitions. However, the majority are likely to be PE firms.

Throughout the years, we have interacted with many founders who sold their businesses to PE firms and C-level executives who later managed PE portfolio companies. A recurring theme is that many were not adequately prepared for the challenges involved—whether as founders in their original roles or as executives transitioning from family businesses or publicly listed companies.

For business owners in particular, it is critical to know how to evaluate investors as potential partners. How do you identify the right PE firm? What traits define a partner who will align with and support your business goals? These are pivotal questions to address when selecting the ideal buyer.

Quentin de Labarre, managing director at Merieux Equity Partners, observed how much more complex life sciences have become over the past 15 years, facing challenges from IP and regulation to market access and reimbursement. He stressed,

> *The right investor isn't just a source of capital, but a strategic partner with deep sector expertise to navigate this evolving landscape. The ability to combine operational know-how with specialist industry insight is now essential for companies seeking growth capital.*

To assist with this, we outline a series of key questions that experienced founders and executives recommend discussing with PE investors, whether as a founder considering an acquisition or as a manager preparing to join a newly acquired portfolio company.[2]

POSSIBLE QUESTIONS FROM A FOUNDER OR INCOMING CEO TO THE POTENTIAL PE INVESTOR

A. Performance of PE firm
   1. Do you have a specific investment approach or philosophy that differentiates you from other PE firms?
   2. How have your previous funds performed?
   3. What has your typical IRR been at the fund level?
   4. What has been the typical MOIC/TVPI at the fund level?
   5. Have your funds historically been top quartile?

(*Continued*)

[2]We found this useful list on the internet without attribution. We are grateful to the unknown author(s) and will be happy to quote them.

(Continued)

B. **Performance with similar investments**
   1. Give me examples of companies similar to this. How did they perform? Are there any lessons learned?
   2. What have been your typical IRR and MOIC/TVPI for similar companies?
   3. Do you already have an investment thesis for this company?

C. **Remuneration structure**
   1. What is the incentive equity for key executives in a portfolio company like this one?
   2. How does that incentive equity work under your various exit scenarios?
   3. Are there opportunities for me to invest?

D. **Relationship with management team**
   1. How do you work with your current portfolio companies?
   2. What is your rhythm with management?
   3. What is your governance philosophy?
   4. Can you tell me about the average tenure of your employees at the various levels?
   5. How typical is it for you to make changes in senior leadership?
   6. Can I speak with the CEO's references? One who succeeded and one who failed?

8.1.4 Who Is Usually Involved in Supporting Getting the PE Funding

Securing PE funding in the healthcare sector is a complex process that requires the involvement of various market players and advisors. These professionals provide critical support to entrepreneurs, helping them navigate the intricacies of fundraising, connect with the right investors, and position their business for successful capital acquisition. Understanding who these players are and how they contribute to the process is essential for entrepreneurs aiming to raise venture or growth capital effectively.

Investment bankers are often at the forefront of the fundraising process, acting as intermediaries between entrepreneurs and potential investors. These professionals have deep networks within the PE community and are skilled at identifying and approaching investors who are the best fit for the entrepreneur's business. They assist in preparing the company for the fundraising process, including valuing the business, structuring the deal, and negotiating terms. Investment bankers also help craft the narrative that will be presented to investors, ensuring that the business case is compelling and aligned with market expectations. Their expertise in deal structuring and market dynamics makes them invaluable partners in the capital-raising journey.

Legal advisors play a crucial role in ensuring that the fundraising process is conducted in compliance with all applicable regulations and that the interests of the entrepreneur are protected. Healthcare is a highly regulated industry, and raising capital in this space often involves navigating complex legal landscapes, including intellectual property rights, regulatory approvals, and compliance with healthcare laws. Legal advisors help draft and review term sheets, investment agreements, and other critical documents to ensure that the terms of the deal are clear, fair, and legally sound. They also provide guidance on structuring the company's governance and equity distribution to align with both the entrepreneur's and investors' long-term goals.

Accountants and financial advisors are key players in preparing the company's financials for investor scrutiny. They assist in creating detailed financial models that project the company's future performance, including revenue growth, profitability, and cash flow. These models are essential for demonstrating the business's potential to generate returns on investment, which is a primary concern for PE firms. Financial advisors also help entrepreneurs understand the financial implications of various deal structures, such as equity dilution and debt financing, allowing them to make informed decisions about which funding options align best with their business objectives.

Industry-specific consultants are another important group of advisors who provide specialized knowledge and insights into the healthcare market. These experts often have deep experience in healthcare subsectors, such as biotechnology, medical devices, or healthcare services, and can offer valuable perspectives on market trends, competitive dynamics, and regulatory challenges. Their input can be crucial in refining the business strategy and ensuring that the company is well-positioned to meet the expectations of PE investors. By leveraging the insights of industry consultants, entrepreneurs can better articulate their value proposition and demonstrate a strong understanding of the market environment.

8.1.5 Case Study: Interview of a Serial Entrepreneur

An insightful interview with Dr. Andrew Meikle, a healthcare entrepreneur backed by PE growth capital, conveys the nuanced relationship between founders and PE investors.[3] Dr. Meikle first cofounded dentalcare in Canada in 2011, a dental roll-up; by 2014, Imperial Capital Group and OPTrust invested CA$121 million to scale the platform, and by 2018 the company which had grown to CA$300 million revenue was sold to the US PE firm L Catterton at about CA$1.7 billion.[4] After this exit, Dr. Meikle launched the Fertility Partners in 2020, with roughly CA$90 million in equity and debt financing led by Peloton Capital Management (Toronto) and HEAL Partners Trust (Sydney), assembling a team to take a similar approach in the fertility clinic sector. Within the first year, he grew the Fertility Partners rapidly, capturing more than 20% of the Canadian fertility market by partnering with top clinics nationwide.

In this interview, Dr. Meikle emphasizes the critical importance of partnering with the right PE firm that respects the healthcare provider perspective and works collaboratively with clinical teams to improve patient outcomes. He notes that, unlike venture capital, PE investors often focus on operational scale, clinical quality, and sustainable growth over longer horizons, which suits the unique demands of healthcare service businesses and life sciences firms. This approach fosters true partnerships where entrepreneurial and clinical expertise aligns with financial and strategic support, driving value creation beyond mere cost-cutting.

---

[3] Inside Reproductive Health Podcast with Griffin Jones (2021, February 28). https://www.fertilitybridge.com/inside-reproductive-health/99-entrepreneurship-practice-valuation-private-equity-andrew-meikle.

[4] Dentalcorp went public in 2021. In 2025, GTCR took the company private at an EV of CA$3.3 billion.

8.2 TENSIONS BETWEEN INVESTORS

8.2.1 With LPs

In PE, conflicts between GPs and LPs commonly arise around several critical issues. First, LPs do not appear to always choose the PE investments that are best for them. This can be because the decision-makers at the LP level have objectives that differ from maximizing financial value or because they are subject to a familiarity bias. For example, LPs may choose PE investments geographically close to them (Hochberg and Rauh, 2013) or close to investment patterns they are familiar with. In particular, firms that invest significantly in R&D tend to have corporate defined benefit pension plans that invest more in PE, and particularly so in innovative projects (Atnasova and Chemla, 2026). Further, pension fund performance is often hampered by such geographical or professional bias.

Second, overvaluation of portfolio companies during fundraising can inflate asset values (Gornall and Strebulaev, 2020), benefiting GPs through higher fees but potentially disadvantaging LPs at entry or exit (Phalippou, 2021). Management fee manipulation and excessive fees have been notable concerns. For example, in 2016, Apollo agreed to a $52.7 million settlement following charges that it misled investors about fee practices and did not prevent a senior partner from charging personal expenses to clients. Conflicts of interest manifest in self-dealing practices where GPs engage in related-party transactions at unfair prices, exemplified by HCR ManorCare in 2018, where portfolio company resources were used for other investments. Other issues include preferential treatment of certain LPs (Lerner et al., 2007; Fang et al., 2015) or using portfolio company resources for other investments (US SEC, 2015).

When raising money from LPs, it is tempting to overvalue the previous fund or some initial investments. Research shows that GPs inflate net asset values by managing valuation assumptions (e.g., valuation multiples), influencing financial metrics (e.g., EBITDA and sales) reported by the portfolio firms, or both (Baik, 2022).

This can take the form of selectively choosing "comparable" companies with inflated metrics to justify higher valuations. In 2017, Outcome Health, a US healthtech company, inflated its revenue metrics to secure $500 million in investments, overstating the number of screens installed in doctors' offices, recognizing revenue for ads that were never actually delivered, and delaying disclosure of financial risks. Investigators found that the company also used fraudulent comparables to justify high valuations and misrepresented market potential.

There were examples of excessive fee collection too. Lincolnshire Management, a New York-based PE firm, was sued by investors for not distributing $44 million in fees and was accused of misappropriating nearly $8 million in wrongfully deducted fees, expenses, and interest in the United States around 2010. The lawsuit alleged that Lincolnshire improperly deducted fees and expenses related to a $99 million legal victory, resulting in investors receiving only $45 million instead of the expected $60 million. The SEC also charged Lincolnshire with misallocating expenses between funds, leading to a $2.3 million settlement in 2014.

One of our former clients, a relatively large PE firm, encountered significant challenges during the Global Financial Crisis. Their performance faltered, and there was no carry to be expected. In an attempt to reset their image, they changed their name. However, this rebranding did little to help them raise a subsequent fund. Instead, though they managed to continue overseeing their existing portfolio for several years. A more ethical course might have been to liquidate all investments and return capital to investors or, at the very least, offer investors an option to exit. Instead, the firm chose to continue collecting management fees. With a substantial amount of assets under management, receiving 2% in fees was still lucrative—especially while minimizing staff and adhering to minimal operational efforts.

8.2.2 With Minority Shareholders

Shareholder disputes will almost always involve minority shareholders. Controlling PE owners—here we would consider an aggregate of GP and LPs—can take advantage of minority shareholders in several ways. They often load the company with excessive debt to finance dividends and fees, increasing financial risk and reducing operational flexibility, which disproportionately affects minority shareholders who have little say in governance. PE owners may extract large management fees or "transaction fees" charged to the portfolio company, which minority shareholders indirectly bear but do not control or benefit from proportionally. They can engage in related-party transactions such as sale-leasebacks, where the PE firm sells company assets (like real estate) to a firm they control and then charges high rents, draining company resources. Governance manipulation is common: minority shareholders frequently have limited information, are excluded from key decisions, or face conflicts of interest where PE owners prioritize their exit strategies and returns over minority interests. Operationally, cost-cutting to improve short-term profits—often accompanied by underinvestment in quality or compliance—harms the company's long-term value and minority shareholders' equity. This multifaceted extraction and control strategy leaves minority shareholders with limited influence, disproportionate financial risk, and erosion of value despite any nominal dividends they receive.

Dominant GPs or sponsors may be tempted to use their discretionary control and the opacity embedded in their relationship with minority investors to reallocate value away from these shareholders. Academic evidence from contract design, continuation funds, side-letter governance, and fee extraction includes Kaplan and Stromberg (2003), Acharya et al. (2013), Phalippou (2018), and Lerner et al. (2022).

8.2.3 With Lenders

PE owners may be tempted to take advantage of the lenders in several ways:

- Loading the company with excessive debt to dilute existing debtholders and/or pay large dividend (dividend recaps) leaving it vulnerable to economic downturns or operational shocks
- Selling key assets and leaving a weakened shell company to bear the operational risks
- Transferring intellectual property, contracts, or other critical assets to separate entities controlled by the PE owners to siphon value away from the operating company

Since at least Warga and Welch (1993), several academic references have provided evidence that a small fraction of the value creation for sponsors and equity holders was at the expense of debtholders (creditors, lenders, or bondholders). Economically, this is a wealth transfer from debtholders to equity holders, often through leverage engineering, dividend recapitalizations, or asset shifting (Guo et al., 2011; Axelson et al., 2013; Hotchkiss et al., 2021).

In 2010, Cerberus acquired Caritas Christi Health Care, a Massachusetts-based nonprofit group of six financially troubled hospitals, through a leveraged buyout, rebranding it as Steward Health Care and converting it to a for-profit entity. It has been quite common for US and European nonprofit hospitals to struggle with the huge costs of modernizing outdated facilities and meeting ever-increasing regulatory compliance requirements, often pushing them to seek external funding or selling themselves to remain operational. For some observers, this reflected a broader trend where PE firms targeted financially vulnerable healthcare providers, often in underserved communities—a pattern shown to exacerbate healthcare inequities through asset-stripping and service reductions. Another reason was given by an obstetrician who used to work in Boston at the time. His point was that, while the hospitals in the region were generally profitable, the largest ones started to consolidate the local market in the 1990s to be able to negotiate with private medical insurers. Smaller hospitals were left out and were not in a position to negotiate with insurers and so were no longer options for the insured patients.

To finance this acquisition and subsequent expansions, Cerberus employed aggressive financial engineering, including a sale-leaseback arrangement in 2016, selling Steward's hospital properties to Medical Properties Trust (MPT), a real estate investment trust, in a typical OpCo/PropCo separation. This transaction generated immediate capital—$1.25 billion—but obligated Steward to substantial long-term lease payments, effectively mortgaging critical healthcare infrastructure—a practice criticized for prioritizing short-term investor returns over long-term community health needs. While these are standard practices, the high level of leverage made the company more sensitive to regulatory changes and economic conditions.

That same year, Steward paid $790 million in dividends to Cerberus and management despite a $300 million net loss, exemplifying what researchers describe as "wealth extraction mechanisms that destabilize safety-net institutions" (Eleogu, 2025).

In 2020, Cerberus exited its investment in Steward to a group of Steward's physician owners, leaving the hospital chain with potentially excessive financial obligations. Steward was already struggling with significant financial losses, including a $408 million loss during the COVID-19 pandemic. The situation worsened as interest rates unexpectedly rose in 2022, increasing Steward's debt servicing costs.

By May 2024, facing unsustainable financial pressures, Steward filed for bankruptcy, casting uncertainty over its hospitals' future and prompting legislative scrutiny of such PE practices. By the time of its bankruptcy filing, Steward owed $9 billion—a sum that represented an extraordinary level of debt for a hospital system of its size. Such a high degree of leverage not only far surpassed industry averages but also heightened the organization's exposure to financial distress, ultimately undermining its ability to provide stable healthcare services. The group announced that it planned to close two of its eight hospitals in Massachusetts: Carney Hospital and Nashoba Valley Medical Center.

It was not the first healthcare bankruptcy to ignite a wave of public fury, prompting US lawmakers to draft tough new curbs that were ultimately rejected at the end of 2024. Critics of the Massachusetts and California bills—the most advanced among state legislative efforts—argued that these measures unfairly targeted PE and real estate firms, ignoring broader systemic issues within the US healthcare industry.[5] One might also question the decision by the physician owners to acquire Cerberus's stake.

While 2024 state legislative efforts to curb PE practices failed, legal scholars argue that current regulatory frameworks inadequately protect healthcare as a public good and comprehensive federal reforms are needed, including the following:

- Mandatory community impact assessments for healthcare acquisitions
- Limitations on sale-leaseback transactions for essential medical facilities
- Requirements to reinvest percentage of profits into staff/equipment
- Transparent accounting of investor returns versus care expenditures (Eleogu, 2025)

Steward's bankruptcy also highlighted how, when things go wrong, the different types of investors start fighting for their part of the shrinking pie. During the bankruptcy proceedings, allegations emerged that Dr. de la Torre, Steward's CEO, may have prioritized the interests of certain stakeholders over others. Specifically, there were concerns that the financial maneuvers, including the substantial dividend payouts and sale-leaseback agreements, benefited the PE owners and certain lenders, potentially to the detriment of other creditors and the long-term viability of the hospital system. Conversely, disputes arose between Steward Health Care and its lenders, particularly Medical Properties Trust. Steward filed an "adversary complaint"—a lawsuit filed within a bankruptcy case—accusing MPT of speaking directly to potential buyers of Steward's assets without proper authorization, exacerbating tensions during the bankruptcy process.

8.2.4 With the Next Owners

PE investors are often praised for their ability to drive operational efficiencies, streamline costs, and enhance profitability. However, the intended exit may generate a focus on short-term financial performance that can sometimes come at the expense of long-term investments in research and development, infrastructure, technology, and other critical areas essential for sustainable growth and improved patient outcomes.

Although finding direct evidence of this is challenging, some findings appear to support this claim. Specifically, PE-backed IPOs generally tend to exhibit poor post-IPO operating performance, suggesting that the IPO itself may signal negative private information about the firm's prospects (Degeorge and Zeckhauser, 1993). Further, more than 70% of PE-backed IPOs between 2010 and 2014 underperformed their public benchmarks, with an average annualized total shareholder return 12 percentage points lower than the relevant index five years after listing, according to Private Equity Insights. The "lemon-squeezing" effect—where PE firms extract maximum value during their ownership period—leaves little room for further operational improvements or growth under new ownership.

[5] According to Mark Cuban, a television host, "We've turned hospitals and doctors into subprime lenders without assets." Because hospital emergencies must treat patients first and ask for payment later, they don't get paid a significant amount of times and inflate their prices to insurers to compensate. Insurers are happy to pass the price increases to employers and take an even larger profit. PE investors are sometimes accused of being complicit of this broken system.

This tension with future owners is particularly evident in healthcare, where robust infrastructure and continuous innovation are vital for maintaining quality of care and regulatory compliance. Healthcare entities such as hospitals and life sciences companies require significant capital expenditures to maintain state-of-the-art facilities, invest in R&D, and adapt to evolving regulatory standards. Yet, PE investors may be tempted to defer or minimize these investments to boost EBITDA and position the company for a lucrative exit. This strategy often leaves the burden of long-term capital needs to the next owner.

For example, when Apollo Global Management and ATP acquired LifePoint in 2018 to merge it with RCCH HealthCare, analysts observed a significant reduction in capital expenditure during the holding period. Maintenance CapEx fell below industry standards, which improved short-term EBITDA margins but created a backlog of deferred investments for future owners according to Finimize. Similarly, PE-owned hospitals may delay replacing outdated medical equipment like MRI machines or defer implementing electronic health record (EHR) systems to avoid large capital outlays. While these decisions enhance near-term profitability, they can compromise care quality and competitive positioning over time.

In life sciences companies, underinvestment is even more pronounced. A 2025 survey by BDO[6] reports that 55% of life sciences PE fund managers would like their portfolio companies to prioritize cost reduction in R&D. Laboratory equipment companies, for instance, can be tempted to delay replacing aging machinery to improve financial metrics temporarily but at the expense of long-term competitiveness.

The consequences of such underinvestment are profound. Inadequate infrastructure can lead to operational inefficiencies, regulatory violations, and even patient safety issues. For instance, research published in *Health Affairs* found that PE-owned nursing homes had higher rates of preventable patient harm compared to non-PE-owned facilities due to cost-cutting measures that reduced staffing levels and care quality (Zhu et al., 2024). In the life sciences sector, reduced R&D spending can stifle innovation and limit a company's ability to bring new therapies to market, eroding its long-term value.

This short-term focus on EBITDA optimization also creates challenges for the next owner—whether it be another PE firm, a strategic acquirer, or public market investors. The new owner often inherits a company with a lean cost structure but also with deferred capital needs and underinvested infrastructure. These challenges frequently become apparent post-exit.

Interestingly, infrastructure investors—who typically have longer investment horizons of 10–15 years compared to the 3–7 years typical of traditional PE—are often less prone to this short termism. The Infrastructure Investor Association's 2023 report highlighted that healthcare-focused infrastructure funds maintained capital expenditure rates closer to industry averages while still optimizing costs before exit. However, even these investors occasionally prioritize EBITDA enhancement over long-term value creation.

It is important to note that not all PE investments follow this pattern. Some specialized healthcare-focused PE firms recognize that sustainable value creation requires significant investments in infrastructure, technology, and human capital. For instance, EQT Partners has adopted an impact-investing approach in healthcare

[6]The 2026 Outlook on Private Equity Funding in Life Sciences, BDO USA.

by prioritizing measurable patient outcomes alongside financial returns. Such strategies demonstrate that it is possible for PE investors to balance profitability with long-term value creation.

While PE has the potential to bring much-needed efficiency and innovation to healthcare, its short-term focus on EBITDA optimization can lead to underinvestment in critical areas. This approach not only compromises care quality but also creates challenges for future owners and limits long-term performance—particularly evident in IPOs. As the healthcare sector continues to attract substantial PE investment, striking a balance between short-term gains and sustainable growth will remain a key challenge.

8.2.5 With Households

Since the early 2000s, household exposure to PE has expanded substantially—though mainly indirectly through pension funds, insurance companies, and mutual funds. Institutional allocations to PE have grown from less than 5% of portfolio assets in the 1990s to 12–15% in the 2020s (Lerner, 2023). This growth has, in turn, transmitted exposure to households participating in defined benefit and defined contribution pension plans.

Recent years have seen a regulatory and technological push toward democratizing PE. In the United States, the SEC expanded the definition of accredited investors in 2020, allowing more affluent households to participate directly before 401(k) accounts could include PE investments. Technology also broadens access. Platforms offering fractional PE investments and tokenized private funds, for example, Moonfare, Titanbay, and blockchain-based vehicles, have emerged.

Despite these trends, true retail penetration remains minimal outside wealthy investors. In the United States, the expansion of private capital markets over the last two decades correlated with the rise in income and wealth inequality (Gocmen et al., 2025), especially through the role of high-net-worth individuals. Further, this group's share of early-stage financing rose significantly, and the tax treatment of qualified small business stock amplified their participation, thereby influencing both firm decisions (to stay private) and inequality dynamics.

For ordinary households, PE investment can be a promising investment opportunity that is also likely to be a challenge. The opacity of decisions made by GPs, the illiquidity inherent to PE investment, and the complexity of investment products alongside hefty fees will likely be at least as much of a challenge as other asset classes (Campbell and Ramadorai, 2025).

8.3 TENSIONS WITH OTHER STAKEHOLDERS

8.3.1 The Dark Side

In Chapter 2, we discussed four common levers for increasing the equity value in an LBO. An additional unsung lever may see PE investors default on implicit contracts that managers entered between shareholders and stakeholders prior to a buyout (Shleifer and Summers, 1988; Chemla, 2004). These may include commitments to pay higher wages to older, more experienced workers and customary payment arrangements with suppliers. A new investor may disrupt the relationship with workers and suppliers.

The 2004 LBO of Mervyn's Department Store Chain in the United States is a popular example. A PE consortium acquired Mervyn's for $1.2 billion, spun its real estate into a separate entity, and imposed escalating rents that jumped $80 million in the first year alone to service LBO debt. The operating arm's $64 million loss in 2007 was dwarfed by annual rent obligations, and efforts to renegotiate leases failed. By 2008, Mervyn's filed for bankruptcy, owing suppliers more than $102 million and Levi Strauss $12 million, while 18,000 employees lost jobs, pensions, and benefits. Meanwhile, the investors walked away with substantial profits from property sales and tax advantages, despite the chain's collapse. In this case, it looks like all possible stakeholders were abused by the new shareholders: employees, suppliers, clients, taxman, local authorities, government, etc.

We do not know of such a blatant abuse in the healthcare sector, but there have been numerous stories of financial engineering that prioritised investor returns at the direct expense of other stakeholders. A well-documented UK example is HC-One, the largest care home operator in Britain with over 300 homes and approximately 20,000 elderly residents. In 2012, a vehicle backed by Safanad, a Gulf-based PE investor, assembled HC-One from the ruins of Southern Cross Healthcare and immediately structured it using an OpCo/PropCo separation: the operating company paid rent to a property vehicle, creating a fixed cash drain that was senior to any expenditure on staffing or maintenance. Intercompany loans and management fees flowed to holding companies registered in the Cayman Islands, and HC-One paid virtually no UK corporation tax for several years despite growing revenues—a pattern documented by Tax Watch UK and raised in parliamentary hearings on care home funding.

With rent, debt service, and intercompany charges absorbing the bulk of cash generation, the only remaining variable was labour. CQC inspection reports during this period recorded persistent concerns about staffing ratios, staff turnover above 40%, and inadequate training—consequences that are structurally inseparable from the financial architecture rather than attributable to operational mismanagement. When COVID-19 arrived, homes with the highest debt burdens and lowest staffing ratios recorded the worst mortality outcomes. By 2020, HC-One carried net debt exceeding £400 million against revenues of approximately £700 million—leverage that left no buffer for any adverse shock. Throughout this period, roughly 70% of HC-One's revenues derived from local authority and NHS contracts, meaning that the rent, interest, and fees extracted through the ownership structure were ultimately funded by the UK taxpayer.

This case illustrates the darker side of PE's financial engineering in social care. Implicit commitments to residents, staff, and the public health system were subordinated to the financial architecture from day one—not as an unfortunate consequence of bad luck, but as a designed outcome. In healthcare, where residents cannot choose to leave a failing provider, these trade-offs carry direct and measurable human consequences.

We did not find a specific healthcare deal in Asia, Latin America, or the Middle East that reaches the level of systematic stakeholder abuse seen in Brookdale's or Mervyn's cases. This may reflect either better regulatory oversight in Asian healthcare markets, different PE operating models in the region, or simply that such cases have not been as well-documented publicly.

What other investor behaviors are detrimental to financial stakeholders? We identify four main ones. The first is quick flips because they provide potentially an asymmetrical benefit for the managers over everyone else. The second is leverage recaps because they boost the IRR very artificially. The third is too many successive LBOs, where we see companies go through a third or fourth, or even a fifth, LBO, which adds unnecessary costs that continue to pile up.[7] And, finally, the constant delisting and re-listing of the company on a stock exchange may be considered detrimental to financial stakeholders. This happens at a premium each time, and there are also the listing costs.

Various other hidden costs can also hit stakeholders. These include the direct costs linked to setting up the transaction, such as paying management, performing due diligence, and paying more carry to the GPs. Then there is the cost of uncalled capital, such as that which was invested in hedge funds in 2008. There are also opportunity costs, for example, when there is a lack of reinvestment opportunity. And lastly there is the so-called denominator effect, where, for example, a pension fund invests less in public equity, and more and more in PE, and needs to divest at a high discount.

In the healthcare sector too, PE firms often employ a well-worn playbook to maximize EBITDA in the short term. This includes reducing overhead costs, renegotiating supplier contracts, optimizing staffing levels, and implementing revenue cycle management improvements. Increased fees will hit directly the patients when they pay out of pocket or will be passed on by the private insurance to the employers.

Having considered some of the weaknesses in regulation before and during the financial crisis, we now consider some examples of where certain companies and individuals took advantage of the weaknesses in the rules and broke the rules for their own gain. And then let's examine some of the ethical issues raised by all this.

In PE-backed healthcare, outright fund misappropriation has been less publicized than in other sectors, but one stark case is the collapse of Abraaj Group's $850 million Growth Markets Health Fund. Between 2016 and 2018, Abraaj allegedly diverted more than $230 million of LP capital—intended for clinics and diagnostics in Africa and South Asia—to shore up its Dubai parent company, delaying or cancelling investments, leaving staff unpaid and facilities under-equipped, and ultimately forcing the fund into liquidation while executives insulated themselves from losses.

Collusion often begins with insider trading, and numerous instances have been documented both during the Global Financial Crisis and in more recent times. In 2024, executives from PE firms Warburg Pincus and GTCR faced insider trading allegations related to Sotera Health Company. The lawsuit claimed that these executives engaged in securities fraud by trading on nonpublic information, selling $675 million in stock at prices inflated by their scheme to conceal the carcinogenic and neurotoxic nature of ethylene oxide produced by a subsidiary.

In 2023, a Delaware Chancery Court case revealed deceptive practices involving healthcare executive April Anthony and PE professionals from Nautic Partners and Vistria Group. They were found to have engaged in covert actions to establish what became VitalCaring, an in-home care provider and a competitor to her then employer Encompass Health, leading to significant legal penalties.

Collusion extends beyond insider trading to include corruption, often manifesting as "pay-to-play" schemes where financial contributions are exchanged for preferential access or opportunities. This is more likely to happen in developing countries that lack some of the regulatory safeguards that protect investors. But it is not limited to them,

---

[7] Successive LBOs make sense when the company gets transferred to a "better" owner, who brings new ideas, relationships, talent and impetus. It can also be justified by the fact that the company has become too large relatively to the size of the portfolio of the previous investor.

especially considering the bulk of the PE activity is concentrated in developed economies. For example, in the 2000s, nineteen PE firms were awarded advisory mandates by pension funds as a reward for donations to the campaigns of elected officials in the United States. This resulted in a $20 million SEC fine in 2009.

Other serious breaches that cross legal boundaries often involve manipulating data to gain an unfair advantage over stakeholders. The most egregious abuses include misrepresenting asset values or performance metrics, typically aimed at fundraising or distributing profits.

In all fairness, it happens that the offender can be the advisor, not the principal. In the case of Rural/Metro, a US fire protection and emergency medical services, now part of Global Medical Response, RBC Capital Markets exhibited serious conflicts of interest while advising Rural on its sale to PE firm Warburg Pincus for $438 million in 2011. RBC deliberately structured a flawed sales process to pursue its own interests: it ran Rural's sale in parallel with the sale of its competitor Emergency Medical Services Corporation ("EMS"). In doing so, it gained lucrative buy-side financing work from EMS bidders, while simultaneously offering financing to Warburg in the Rural deal. This dual role led RBC to share confidential information about Rural's process with Warburg and manipulate its valuation analysis to make Warburg's offer appear more attractive. The Delaware Court found that RBC's undisclosed conflicts and misleading conduct created an "informational vacuum" that led Rural's board to unknowingly approve a sale to Warburg that significantly undervalued the company, resulting in RBC being held liable for $76 million in damage for aiding and abetting the board's breach of fiduciary duties (Morris James LLP, 2024).

8.3.2 Patients and Health Outcomes

In healthcare, PE firms face an additional stakeholder: the patient. For Elena Coluccelli, co-head M&A Healthcare at Rothschild, "M&A in healthcare contributes to make innovation financing possible and create operational efficiency in the interest of all stakeholders, notably patients." While PE investors aim to drive returns for their LPs, the consequences of ownership decisions often land directly on the quality, safety, and accessibility of care. This duality—between financial efficiency and clinical excellence—lies at the heart of the debate on PE in healthcare. How can PE win in healthcare by doing better for patients? Can PE align outcomes with returns?

8.3.2.1 Academic Findings and Challenges in Causal Inference Much of the academic scrutiny of PE in healthcare has come from physicians and public health researchers concerned about rising costs and diminished care. A meta-analysis in *BMJ* (Borsa et al., 2023), reviewing over 50 studies, concluded that PE acquisitions were "most consistently associated with increases in costs to patients or payers" and that impacts on clinical outcomes ranged from neutral to negative, particularly in hospitals and care homes. In the United States, studies linked PE ownership of hospitals with higher rates of hospital-acquired conditions such as infections and falls. In dental and fertility care, similar findings emerged, particularly in the form of reduced staffing or procedural overuse.

Yet causality is difficult to establish. In many instances, PE steps in precisely when public systems or nonprofits are exiting. Whether they exit because financial and/or non-financial performance is poor or because capital needs to be invested in more capital-intensive, perhaps more innovative, activities begs the question of the overall health service provided by capital. The lack of adequate counterfactuals limits the robustness of these conclusions.

8.3.2.2 Why Outcomes Matter Commercially PE firms are exceptionally effective at operational transformation. The challenge—and opportunity—lies in aligning that capability with better patient outcomes. PE is not designed to be a philanthropic enterprise. But in healthcare, strong outcomes and financial success are not contradictory—they are often co-dependent. Poor care creates legal, reputational, and operational risks. Conversely, providers that improve outcomes often secure pricing power, regulator trust, and payer loyalty.

Poor clinical quality leads to lawsuits, penalties, and revenue clawbacks. Providers failing to meet safety or performance thresholds may lose public contracts or face corrective action—damaging enterprise value. Conversely, as insurers and health systems shift toward outcome-contingent payment models, only providers with validated performance data can participate. This creates a direct revenue advantage for those who excel. Moreover, many quality improvements actually reduce costs: fewer infections reduce average length of stay, effective chronic disease management cuts emergency admissions, and digitized workflows reduce errors and rework—all of which enhance both care and margins.

Buyers are increasingly drawn to companies with demonstrable performance advantages. In medtech, validated outcomes support faster market access. In services, payer-aligned models command higher multiples. High-quality operators also attract better clinicians. Lower staff turnover enhances care continuity and lowers recruitment costs. Culture and clinician engagement are now factored into commercial due diligence—especially post-COVID-19.

8.3.2.3 Building Outcomes into the Investment Thesis To embed outcomes into the investment cycle, PE firms must start at acquisition. They should assess material outcome metrics alongside financial KPIs. In hospitals, these may include mortality rates, staffing ratios, or surgical complications. In medtech, device accuracy and usability are key. During ownership, investors should link these metrics to financial performance—for example, a reduction in readmissions may reduce penalties and improve payer bonuses. Digitized diagnostics that increase throughput can raise revenue while reducing per-unit costs.

Incentivizing management is also critical. Management contracts and bonus schemes should include clinical performance targets such as patient satisfaction scores, reductions in medication errors, or adherence to treatment guidelines. Investors should also direct capital toward areas where return on investment and outcomes intersect—such as electronic medical records, nurse training, or clinical audit systems. These are often capital intensive but generate long-term value.

8.3.2.4 Case Examples: Outcomes and Financial Performance Several cases illustrate the link between outcomes and financial performance. Max Healthcare in India, backed by KKR, improved operating margins from under 10% to over 25% within four years by investing in clinical governance, reducing unnecessary procedures, and standardizing hospital workflows. The investment generated a reported 5× return while improving care quality. Netsmart in the United States, backed by GI Partners and TA Associates, built a digital platform for behavioral health and post-acute care providers. By focusing on underserved populations, they expanded care access and coordination, driving EBITDA growth and achieving a strong exit valuation.

In an era of increasing scrutiny on PE's role in healthcare, the $18 billion acquisition of Hologic by Blackstone and TPG in 2025 represents a compelling case study where profit motives and social benefit may converge. PE firms identified women's health as a significantly underserved market opportunity, recognizing both the substantial economic potential and the genuine healthcare gaps that needed addressing. Hologic's focus on cervical and breast cancer screening, along with uterine health devices, positions it to serve a demographic that has historically received less-effective treatments and poorer care than male patients. The economic case is substantial: eliminating gender-based healthcare disparities could contribute $1 trillion to the global economy by 2040, according to estimates by McKinsey and the World Economic Forum, largely by recovering the seven days per year the average woman loses to ill health. Medicine has long overlooked fundamental sex-based physiological differences—from cardiovascular function to respiratory capacity—resulting in treatments like standard asthma inhalers being far less effective for women. Beyond addressing conditions affecting both sexes, the market opportunity in female-specific conditions is enormous, with endometriosis treatments representing a potential $180–220 billion market and menopause treatments valued between $120–230 billion. While PE's acquisition of Hologic at 14 times 2024 EBITDA—one-third below the average for large healthcare deals—reflects their characteristic ability to identify undervalued opportunities, the transaction also demonstrates how market forces can align with healthcare equity. The industry's expertise in consolidating smaller companies through roll-up acquisitions may enable Hologic to invest and innovate more effectively in women's health technologies. Though reducing sex-based medical inequities may not be the primary driver, this case illustrates how recognizing and addressing healthcare market gaps can simultaneously advance both financial returns and population health outcomes.

Not all outcomes are positive. Envision Healthcare, also PE-owned, leaned heavily on out-of-network billing and failed to adjust to regulatory bans on surprise billing. Poor alignment between care quality and the financial model led to its bankruptcy in 2023—one of the largest in PE healthcare history. We discuss it in detail at the end of the chapter.

8.3.2.5 Sector-specific Considerations The sectoral context also matters. In hospitals, aged care, and primary care, performance metrics are closely watched by regulators and payers. Investors in these spaces should aim for standardized protocols, real-time monitoring, and margin improvements based on productivity—not staff cuts. In biopharma and diagnostics, real-world effectiveness underpins market access and pricing power. Investors should promote the generation of post-market evidence and patient engagement. In medtech, clinical validation drives adoption. Usability, outcome metrics, and integration with hospital systems support both sales growth and exit valuations.

8.3.2.6 Performance Is the Best Defense PE's role in healthcare will continue to face scrutiny. Headlines questioning the social impact of PE deals are unlikely to stop. However, the most sustainable way to respond is to deliver consistently better performance—for patients and investors alike.

Firms that prioritize measurable health outcomes reduce exit risk, secure better payer terms, and retain stronger clinical teams. In an increasingly competitive healthcare investment landscape, the firms that win will be those that prove—not just promise—that doing good care is good business.

In healthcare, good business means doing good. And doing good, when structured correctly, can be very good business indeed.

8.3.2.7 PE in Nursing Homes An influential early paper by Stevenson and Grabowski (2008) found little evidence that the quality of care in nursing homes significantly worsens after being purchased by PE firms. While not finding harm, the study concluded that the trend of PE acquisitions still raises important, unanswered questions about the general oversight and accountability for all types of nursing home owners.

This perspective on financial health was later reinforced by Cadigan et al. (2015). Their national study investigates the impact of private investment on the financial health of US nursing homes, using a large panel dataset of 163,214 facility-year observations from Medicare Cost Reports and OSCAR data between 1998 and 2010. The authors employ a fixed-effects differences-in-differences regression model to mitigate potential selection bias by controlling for pre-existing differences between facilities. The study addresses selection directly, finding that private investment firms tend to acquire nursing home chains that are already in good financial health. It also highlights the role of leverage, noting that a key PE strategy involves targeting firms with major real estate holdings, separating those assets from operations, and then leveraging them to help finance the acquisition. The principal finding is that there was little statistically significant impact on the financial health, costs, or revenue of nursing homes following their purchase. The authors conclude that while PE buyouts did not appear to harm the financial performance of these already-healthy facilities, the trend necessitates greater ownership oversight and transparency across the sector.

Furthering the argument that PE's negative effects may be misinterpreted, Huang and Bowblis (2019) focused specifically on methodological rigor. They investigate the relationship between PE ownership and the quality of care for long-stay residents, focusing explicitly on correcting for statistical biases that previous literature may have overlooked. Using resident-level minimum dataset (MDS) and facility-level Ohio Medicaid Cost Report data for all for-profit nursing homes in Ohio from 2005 to 2010, the paper employs a two-stage residual inclusion (2SRI) regression, a form of instrumental variables analysis. To address the critical issue of nonrandom resident selection, the methodology uses the differential distance from a resident's home to the nearest PE and non-PE facility as a valid instrument. The results indicate that PE ownership is not associated with a deterioration in quality of care. The analysis of 17 quality measures shows that after correcting for selection bias, PE-owned facilities provide care of at least a similar quality to that of other for-profit homes. The authors conclude that ignoring resident selection leads to a systematic underestimation of the quality provided by PE-owned nursing homes, suggesting that theoretical concerns about PE's aggressive financial models may not translate into poorer resident outcomes in this specific context.

In direct contrast to the more benign view, a substantial and growing body of evidence challenges this neutral stance, pointing to significant declines in care quality and patient welfare following PE acquisition.

Early signs of these issues were identified by Harrington et al. (2012), who investigated quality of care at the 10 largest US for-profit nursing home chains from 2003 to 2008, comparing them to other ownership groups and examining changes in chains acquired by PE. Using federal OSCAR data and generalized estimation equation (GEE) panel regression models, the research found that the top 10 for-profit chains had lower registered nurse and total nurse staffing hours than government facilities. Furthermore, these large chains received 36% more deficiencies and 41% more serious deficiencies than their government-owned counterparts, indicating a significantly lower quality of care. A key sub-analysis of chains purchased by PE companies during this period showed little change in staffing levels after the acquisition. However, it revealed an increase in the number of both total and serious deficiencies in some post-purchase years when compared to the pre-purchase period, suggesting that PE ownership was associated with a decline in regulatory compliance.

Similarly, another study focusing on for-profit chains by Pradhan et al. (2014) found troubling shifts in care structure. Using a longitudinal dataset from 2000 to 2007 that combines five national and state-level data sources, their random effects analysis indicates that PE-owned nursing homes have significantly lower registered nurse (RN) staffing intensity and a lower RN skill mix compared to the control group of non-PE for-profit chain facilities. While many other quality measures were similar, PE-owned homes were found to perform significantly worse in terms of regulatory deficiencies. The study concludes that these results highlight the need for increased policy focus on transparency and accountability for PE investments in the nursing home sector.

More recent national studies have linked PE ownership not just to staffing and compliance issues but to direct adverse patient events and increased costs. A major cohort study by Braun et al. (2021) examined US nursing homes from 2000 to 2018. The study compared 9,632 residents in 302 newly PE-acquired facilities against nearly 250,000 residents in 9,562 other for-profit homes. The findings show a statistically significant decline in quality and an increase in costs following PE buyouts. Specifically, PE acquisition was associated with an 11.1% relative increase in emergency department visits and an 8.7% relative increase in hospitalizations for conditions sensitive to ambulatory care. Furthermore, total quarterly Medicare costs rose by 3.9%, amounting to an additional $1,081 per resident annually. While the study found no significant changes in the rates of antipsychotic use, severe pain, or pressure ulcers, the primary results suggest that the PE model, potentially driven by debt from LBOs and pressure for high short-term profits, leads to adverse outcomes and higher taxpayer spending, warranting more stringent oversight.

Perhaps more strikingly, Gupta et al. (2024) not only confirmed adverse patient outcomes but also identified specific financial mechanisms driving them. Their study employed a large-scale longitudinal dataset from the Centers for Medicare and Medicaid Services (CMS) covering approximately 12,400 for-profit facilities, 1,674 of which were acquired by PE firms, and 4.2 million unique patients between 2000 and 2017. To address significant selection bias from both non-random facility targeting and changes in patient composition post-buyout, the authors used a differences-in-differences methodology enhanced by an instrumental variables (IV) strategy with patient-to-facility distance as an instrument. Findings indicate a statistically significant and substantial negative impact on patient health; the IV estimates reveal that PE ownership leads to an 11% increase in the 90-day patient mortality rate, corroborated by declines in other quality measures such as patient mobility and pain management. The paper distinguishes the PE effect from general corporatization by highlighting how value is extracted via financial engineering rather than operational improvements. Specifically, PE buyouts lead to a more than 200% increase in interest payments, reflecting a sharp rise in leverage, alongside higher monitoring and lease fees, which drain facility resources without changing reported net income.

Earlier studies on the impact of PE-ownership on nursing houses (e.g., Huang and Bowblis, 2019; Gandhi et al., 2020) were often restricted to specific geographic sample or small sample span. For instance, Huang and Bowblis studied PE acquisition of five nursing homes in Ohio between 2005 and 2010 and found little evidence of quality declines but did not explore mortality. According to the paper, Gandhi, Song, and Upadrashta related market structure with PE acquisition of nursing homes and found positive effects of it on nurse availability when the market is competitive but negative effects in a concentrated market. Using a unique comprehensive data spanning almost two decades and a robust methodology, Gupta et al. (2024) provides striking results on the impact of PE-ownership of care houses in the United States: They find that on average, patients' mortality rate increases by 0.3 pp, almost 2% of the mean. However, after controlling for patients' natural preference for nearby nursing homes, they document an increase of 11% in mortality rate. In fact, post-LBO, PE-owned facilities receive a lower risk pool of patients. Surprisingly, they still fail to maintain the quality of care. Three main channels help explain the increase in mortality: First, PE acquisition reduces nurse availability, the most important determinant of mortality as known in this literature, according to the authors. They find that the number of hours per patient-day decrease by 3% due to a reduction in low-skilled but crucial staff that are responsible for day-to-day caregiving. This is reflected in the higher mortality rate of low-risk patients who are retained for a longer period, but with poorer quality of care, by PE-owned facilities (which would maximize their profits). However, PE-owned facilities appear to maintain quality for high-risk patients. This may be the result of an increase in the number of qualified staff (RNs) who are responsible for most medicalized aspects of treatment. Second, the CMS Five Star rating, a measure of quality-of-care in nursing homes constructed by the Centres for Medicare and Medicaid Services, a US federal agency, declines for PE-owned facilities after the buyout. But the literature (Grabowski and Town, 2011; Werner et al., 2012) found no demand response to this rating, reflecting information friction in this market. Finally, patients' well-being, indicated by three standard measures of the CMS of patients' well-being decline. OLS (IV) return a decrease in mobility by 6% (3%), an increase in ulcer development of 8.5% (0%), and an increase in pain intensity of 10.5% (8.3%).

Since much of the revenues from nursing homes come from the government (75%), authors investigate PE financial strategies and the costs borne by taxpayers. They find that when using an instrumental variable method, the amount billed to Medicare per stay increase by 8%. However, a simple ordinary least square regression documents a small decline in the costs billed due to lower risk pool of patients. Furthermore, the three types of costs associated with PE all went up: monitoring fees charged to portfolio companies by PE funds, lease payments after the PE funds sell off the real estate of the nursing homes to generate cash, and interest payments (which increases by more than 200% on average). PE-owned facilities with more financial liabilities, and especially those that are focused in the healthcare sector, drive most of the decrease in quality-of-care. These findings point to the unique operational and financial strategies of PE as being negative for patients. The authors conclude that, in partial equilibrium, restricting PE ownership of nursing homes would likely save lives. However, they recognize the needs for further studies. In fact, such restriction could also affect nursing homes owners' incentives, affecting overall health of elderly.

8.3.2.8 PE in Hospitals PE firms do not acquire healthcare facilities at random; they select targets with specific characteristics and then strategically reshape their operations to maximize financial returns.

Offodile et al. (2021) provides a systematic, descriptive overview of PE acquisitions of US short-term acute care hospitals from 2003 to 2017, identifying 42 deals involving 282 unique hospitals. This research conducts a comparative analysis to characterize the financial and operational differences between hospitals that were acquired by PE and those that were not. The analysis reveals that PE firms systematically acquire a distinct type of hospital. Even before being acquired, these target hospitals were already larger (more beds, discharges, and staff) and significantly more profitable (higher operating margins and charge-to-cost ratios) than their nonacquired counterparts. Furthermore, the study finds that this gap in profitability between PE-acquired and nonacquired hospitals widened over the study period, which demonstrate that PE firms select for larger, more profitable hospitals, which motivates further research by policymakers to evaluate the downstream impacts of these acquisitions on patient care and costs.

Once a hospital is acquired, evidence suggests that PE firms actively manage the hospital's clinical offerings to enhance profitability. The Offodile et al. study further investigates how PE acquisition influences the mix of clinical services offered by hospitals, using a difference-in-differences approach to compare changes at PE-acquired hospitals to a control group of nonacquired facilities. The analysis reveals that PE ownership is associated with a strategic restructuring of service lines to maximize profitability. Relative to control hospitals, PE-acquired facilities had a significantly higher probability of adding profitable hospital-based services, such as interventional cardiac catheterization and labor and delivery, as well as lucrative technologies like robotic surgery. Furthermore, the study found that PE hospitals were more likely to add services that have recently become financially attractive, such as mental health services, while simultaneously being less likely to add or continue services with unreliable revenue streams, like outpatient psychiatry. These findings suggest that PE firms actively manage hospital service offerings to focus on areas with the highest financial opportunity, shifting the provision of care toward more profitable procedures and technologies.

The central debate revolves around what these profit-driven strategies mean for patients and the healthcare system. One side of the argument posits that PE brings operational discipline that can cut waste without harming key clinical outcomes, while the opposing view argues these changes lead to higher costs, compromised patient care, and negative economic spillovers.

The effects of PE's operational changes on patients are more nuanced, however. Some studies find targeted efficiencies and even improvements in care. Gao et al. (2024) compare 281 for-profit hospital acquisitions from 2001 to 2018 to both a matched control group and hospitals acquired by other for-profit firms over a long, eight-year post-acquisition window. Exploiting changes in state-level regulations as a quasi-experimental shock, the authors find that PE ownership brings a unique form of operational restructuring. PE-acquired hospitals do not have a higher closure rate; instead, they significantly cut costs by reducing their administrative workforce by 20%

in the long run. Crucially, the number of core medical workers (doctors, nurses) temporarily declines but returns to pre-acquisition levels within five to eight years. This operational pattern is unique to PE, as other for-profit acquirers tend to reduce core staff while leaving administrative staff unchanged. From the patient perspective, the study finds no significant increase in inpatient prices, no shift toward healthier or wealthier patients, and no deterioration in key health outcomes such as patient mortality or readmission rates. However, patient satisfaction does decline, an effect also seen in hospitals acquired by other for-profit entities.

Further supporting a more mixed or even positive view on clinical outcomes, Cerullo et al. (2022) investigate the association between PE acquisition of short-term acute care hospitals and patient outcomes for more than 21 million Medicare beneficiaries from 2001 to 2018. Using a generalized difference-in-differences approach with robust fixed effects, the research compared changes in outcomes for five acute medical conditions at PE-acquired versus non-PE-acquired hospitals. The findings present a mixed picture: for most conditions and outcomes, including readmission rates and 30-day spending, PE acquisition was not associated with any significant differences. However, for patients admitted with an acute myocardial infarction (AMI), PE acquisition was associated with a statistically significant and moderate improvement in patient mortality, specifically a 1.1 percentage point greater decrease in in-hospital mortality and a 1.4 percentage point greater decrease in 30-day mortality compared to non-PE hospitals. The study concludes that while PE ownership has no substantial association with most patient-level outcomes, it is linked to improved survival for elderly patients hospitalized for a heart attack.

The effects observed in the complex inpatient hospital setting may not translate to all areas of PE investment. A study on Ambulatory Surgical Centers (ASCs) by Bruch et al. (2022) investigates the association between PE acquisition of ASCs and key outcomes using a novel, manually assembled dataset of 148 ASC acquisitions (91 PE, 57 non-PE) from 2011 to 2014, linked to a national sample of Medicare claims from 2009 to 2017. Employing a quasi-experimental difference-in-differences design with a two-way fixed-effects model, the research compared changes in quality, cost, and volume at PE-acquired ASCs relative to a control group of ASCs acquired by non-PE entities. The analysis found no statistically significant relative changes in the primary outcomes following PE acquisition. Specifically, there was no significant association with the probability of a seven-day unplanned hospital visit, total costs per encounter, or the total volume of patient encounters. While the authors conclude that these findings show no signal of decreased quality of care for the period studied, they highlight limitations such as the sample size and focus on Medicare and call for increased transparency in ownership and financial reporting for ASCs.

In sharp contrast, a growing body of recent evidence documents significant negative consequences for patients, from higher costs and worse experiences to measurable increases in preventable harm and mortality.

On the financial front, PE ownership has a significant impact on prices. Liu (2022). This study investigates the effects of PE ownership on the US hospital market by developing and estimating a structural model of hospital-insurer price bargaining, using a novel, large-scale dataset of private insurance claims from 2013 to 2019 covering more than 5,000 hospitals. To overcome the endogenous selection of PE targets, the study uses state-level changes in corporate practice of medicine (CPOM) regulations as an instrumental variable. Descriptively, the research finds that PE buyouts lead to a ~32%

increase in negotiated prices with private insurers, without a significant change in service utilization, and also create spillover effects that raise prices at rival hospitals by 8.1%. The structural model quantifies the channels driving these effects, finding that superior PE bargaining skills (43%) and financial engineering (40%)—specifically the credible threat of bankruptcy due to high leverage—are the primary mechanisms. A counterfactual analysis shows that restricting PE ownership would reduce regional health spending by 11% and that current regulatory models for merger reviews, which ignore unique PE features, may underestimate post-merger price hikes by as much as 10 percentage points.

Beyond costs, patient-reported experiences also appear to decline. Bhatla et al. (2025) investigates the impact of PE on patient experience, using a difference-in-differences analysis of Hospital Consumer Assessment of Healthcare Providers and Systems survey data from 2008 to 2019. The research compared 73 PE-acquired hospitals against 293 matched control hospitals, examining patient-reported outcomes from three years before to three years after the acquisition. The study found a statistically significant decline in global measures of patient experience following PE buyouts. Compared to control hospitals, the percentage of patients giving a top overall hospital rating decreased by 2.4 percentage points, and the percentage who would definitely recommend the hospital fell by 2.1 percentage points. This negative effect on patient satisfaction grew over time, reaching its largest point three years post-acquisition. Among secondary measures, there was also a significant decline in the responsiveness of hospital staff. The findings indicate that patient-reported care experience, an important dimension of quality, worsened after PE acquisition of US hospitals.

Most concerning are findings that link PE ownership to direct patient harm. Kannan et al. (2023) examine the impact of PE acquisition on hospital quality, using a difference-in-differences analysis of 100% Medicare claims data from 2009 to 2019. It compares more than 662,000 hospitalizations at 51 PE-acquired hospitals to more than 4 million hospitalizations at 259 matched control hospitals. The primary finding is that PE acquisition was associated with a statistically significant 25.4% increase in hospital-acquired conditions (preventable adverse events), driven by a 27.3% rise in patient falls and a 37.7% increase in central line–associated bloodstream infections. This decline in patient safety occurred despite evidence that PE hospitals began admitting a lower-risk patient population (younger and less likely to be dually eligible for Medicare and Medicaid). While there was a small relative decrease in in-hospital mortality, this potential benefit disappeared by 30 days post-discharge, suggesting it was an artifact of patient selection and transfer patterns rather than a true improvement in care quality. Overall, the study concludes that PE acquisition was associated with a significant increase in preventable patient harm, indicating a poorer quality of inpatient care.

Culminating these concerns, Kannan et al. (2025) links PE-driven operational changes to mortality in high-acuity settings. This study examines the effects of PE acquisition on hospital Emergency Departments (EDs) and Intensive Care Units (ICUs), using a matched difference-in-differences analysis of 100% Medicare claims and cost report data from 2009 to 2019. The research compared more than 1 million ED visits and 121,000 ICU hospitalizations at 49 PE-acquired hospitals to millions more at 293 matched control hospitals. Following acquisition, PE hospitals significantly reduced salary expenditures in the ED by 18.2% and the ICU by 15.9%, as part of broader hospital-wide cuts to staffing and salaries. These reductions in high-acuity departments were associated with a statistically significant 13.4% relative increase in patient mortality in the ED. While ICU mortality did not change significantly, patients in PE hospitals were transferred out to other hospitals more frequently from both the ED (a 4.2% increase) and the ICU (a 10.6% increase). The study concludes that PE buyouts led to reduced staffing and resources in critical care areas, which may explain the observed increase in ED mortality and the greater reliance on transferring patients to other facilities.

The price hikes at PE-acquired hospitals have tangible consequences for the surrounding community. Aghamolla et al. (2025) investigate the broader economic consequences of rising healthcare costs, using PE acquisitions of hospitals as a quasi-exogenous shock to local economies. Employing a difference-in-differences framework on data from 1993 to 2023, the research traces the impact from PE buyouts to local business outcomes. The authors first document that after a PE hospital acquisition, local businesses face a significant 4.0–8.2% increase in health insurance premiums, confirming that higher hospital prices are passed on to employers. This surge in costs has significant negative spillover effects on the local economy. The study finds that counties affected by a PE hospital buyout experience a 6.9% increase in total business bankruptcies, an increase in business loan volume (suggesting financial strain), and significantly lower growth in employment, new business establishments, and innovation. The research concludes that PE involvement in the hospital sector, by driving up local healthcare costs, imposes substantial harm on the wider local business community, stifling economic growth and increasing financial distress.

Beyond facilities, PE's influence extends to critical pre-hospital services, where different regulatory environments can lead to unique and concerning strategies. A recent study by Ellis and Esson (2024) on ambulance services found that PE firms exploited regulations to boost profits by shifting costs to public providers, a strategy that directly resulted in severe negative public health consequences. This was achieved through a "cream-skimming" mechanism where PE-owned companies fired higher-cost paramedics, making them unable to respond to unprofitable advanced life support calls. These calls were then offloaded onto local fire departments, allowing the PE firm to capture more profitable basic life support calls. This strategy led to a 48% increase in operating profit but was also associated with a 15% increase in fatal traffic accidents in their service areas, resulting in an estimated 200 additional deaths in Arizona during the study period (2010–2017). A national analysis confirmed a 7% increase in traffic fatalities, suggesting that PE firms exploited regulations to boost profits by shifting costs to public providers, a strategy that directly resulted in a significant increase in traffic-related deaths.

At a broader level, the PE model's approach to labor is driven by efficiency. Analyzing all US PE buyouts, Herkenhoff et al. (2025) find that affected workers experience a 20% average earnings loss three years after an acquisition. The research rejects two common explanations for this: that PE firms use local labor market power (monopsony) or that they target specific groups like managers for cuts. Instead, the study concludes these negative labor outcomes are a consequence of efficiency-driven restructuring, where PE managers strategically downsize less productive plants and reallocate key workers to more productive ones to increase overall firm productivity.

8.3.3 Staff Well-being

As discussed in the previous section, PE owners are notoriously good at extracting efficiency gains. Could this be at the expense of labor and employee health? Garcia-Gomez et al. (2020) investigate the link between employee health and labor outcomes after buyouts in all sectors in the Netherlands by matching social security data and buyout data. They argue that the increase of productivity in target firms can come at the expense of some employees. They document an average loss of approximately €1,300/year by the fourth calendar year after buyouts, with about half of that loss replaced by transfers of the social security system. They also find that employees on cardiovascular medication before the transactions lose another €2,500/year and those on antidepressants €2,000/year relative to matched control employees. The authors do not find evidence of PE buyout effects on employees who remain in the firm post-transaction. This result contrasts with other studies (Bach et al., 2025), which found that M&A restructuring affects employees' mental health, which suggests that M&A restructuring creates a more stressful environment than PE buyouts.

Some argue that in the health sector specifically, the improvement in productivity can come at the expense of the satisfaction, the well-being, and labor market outcomes of the medical staff. In our own ongoing survey-based research, we found that many physicians actually value the PE-led organization that minimizes the time they spend on administrative tasks, allowing them to focus on the patient. In a short survey conducted among European dental groups, we observed that practitioners who transitioned from individual practice to group structures—often supported by PE or similar investors—generally benefited from greater clinical and nonclinical staffing, improved access to medical equipment such as intraoral scanners, enhanced team dynamics, and, in some cases, better workplace safety. While it remains difficult to attribute these improvements specifically to PE involvement rather than to the broader effects of consolidation, the findings suggest that cost mutualization in a fragmented environment can yield tangible benefits.

8.3.4 Payors

It has long been established that following LBOs, firms experience increases in operating income (Kaplan, 1989; Smith, 1990), reductions in capital expenditures (Kaplan, 1989), increases in total factor productivity (Lichtenberg and Siegel, 1990), decreases in white collar employment and compensation (Lichtenberg and Siegel, 1990) and R&D (Long and Ravenscraft, 1993), and also increases in prices (Chevalier, 1995a, b). How about in the health sector?

PE owners are often accused of maximizing the money they receive from payors, whether for healthcare services or for prescription drugs. In a difference-in-differences event study of 578 PE-acquired dermatology, gastroenterology, and ophthalmology physician practices and 2,874 similar independent practices in the United States, Singh et al. (2022) found that spending increased differentially compared with controls. Compared with the control practices, the PE-acquired physician practices exhibited an average increase of 20.2% charged per claim and 11.0% in the allowed amount per claim. New and unique patient volume as well as total encounters also increased, including for established patients. No statistically significant changes in patient risk scores were found.

We present a couple of cases with alleged pricing abuse.

8.3.4.1 H.I.G. Capital and CIS In January 2021, mental health company Community Intervention Services (CIS) filed for bankruptcy amid ongoing litigation alleging fraud by H.I.G. Capital as the owner of the company. H.I.G. had created CIS in 2012 as a platform to acquire mental health companies, starting with South Bay Mental Health Center (SBMHC).

The Massachusetts Attorney General had filed a lawsuit against SBMHC in 2018, accusing the company of fraudulently billing the state's Medicaid program for mental health services delivered by staff who were unlicensed, unqualified, and lacked proper supervision at 17 clinics statewide. In a notable development, the attorney general also included H.I.G., who controlled the board, as a defendant in the case, alleging that H.I.G. "knew that SBMHC was providing services in violation of regulatory requirements and did not bring SMBHC operations into compliance or make any attempts to repay the money owed to MassHealth, as required by law."

In October 2021, H.I.G. agreed to pay $20 million to settle the claims—then the largest amount a PE firm had paid to resolve fraud allegations based on its oversight of a healthcare portfolio company. SBMHC executives agreed to pay an additional $5 million to conclude the case.

8.3.4.2 Cinven, Hg, and Advanz Pharma Advanz Pharma was created through the merger of two companies acquired by PE firms, including Cinven, with the intent to consolidate niche pharmaceutical products. The company, as the sole UK supplier of liothyronine—a vital thyroid hormone—raised the drug's price in the United Kingdom from £20 to £248 per box between 2009 and 2017. While some price increases occurred before Cinven's ownership starting in 2013, the UK Competition and Markets Authority (CMA) ruled that the overall steep price hikes constituted an abuse of a dominant market position, especially harmful because the NHS is a publicly funded health system. Unlike private insurance markets, where price negotiations differ, the NHS's monopoly buyer status and patient reliance mean such exploitative pricing harms taxpayers directly.[8] The CMA imposed significant fines on Advanz and its former PE owners for charging excessive and unfair prices with no substantial justification like innovation or cost increases. The result was a £52 million fine for Cinven and over £6 million for Hg, which had earlier owned one of the merged units. UK regulators went further, considering the disqualification of Cinven's co-heads, arguing that the conduct crossed from aggressive pricing into outright exploitation of the NHS. This case illustrates the high-risk PE owners face in markets tied to public health systems where exploitative pricing can trigger legal action, including heavy fines and director disqualifications, reaffirming that in the United Kingdom, raising drug prices excessively in these circumstances is illegal, not just penalized as a deterrent. This protection is specific to the NHS context, where taxpayer funding necessitates regulatory oversight on pricing fairness.

These cases serve as a cautionary precedent: regulatory scrutiny and liability may extend beyond the portfolio company to include the PE sponsor itself. We now turn to another case of a high-stakes bet that unraveled.

---

[8] In the United Kingdom, it is not inherently illegal for a drug company to raise prices; however, the law steps in when such price increases constitute an abuse of a dominant market position, especially for essential medicines with little or no competition. The CMA has enforced competition law to prevent "excessive and unfair pricing," which it defines as charging prices significantly above a fair level, without justification such as innovation or increased costs.

8.3.5 Government

8.3.5.1 At the Expense of the Taxman PE-backed healthcare firms may engage in tax inversion strategies to enhance profitability and align operations with global tax efficiencies. Tax inversions were more common in the 2012–2016 period, often involving mergers between US companies and those based in Ireland, the United Kingdom, or the Netherlands. While these countries remain attractive for their favorable tax structures and pro-business environments, increased scrutiny from regulators, particularly after high-profile cases like Pfizer-Allergan and subsequent changes to US tax regulations made these transactions more difficult to execute.

Many multinational pharmaceutical companies operate globally from the United Sates or the United Kingdom but manage taxation through subsidiaries in jurisdictions with more favorable tax regimes. This, however, is not by any means specific to PE.

There are not many examples of tax reversion for healthcare companies that were orchestrated by PE owners. In the case of Mallinckrodt, PE played only a secondary role. In 2013, after separating from its US-based parent, Covidien, Mallinckrodt moved its tax base to Ireland, acquiring PE-backed Cadence Pharmaceuticals. Though Mallinckrodt's operational headquarters remained largely in the United States, the move to Ireland allowed it to relocate its tax domicile there to benefit from a more favorable corporate tax regime.

8.3.5.2 At the Expense of Public Health The possible effect of PE on health outcomes has attracted attention from policymakers. In the United States, by 2024, the Federal Trade Commission, the Department of Justice, and the US Department of Health jointly launched a cross-government public inquiry into PE's increasing control over healthcare. While the general regulatory sentiment has shifted again under the Trump administration, there are also state-level legislations that affect PE investment in healthcare. For example, California enacted two new statutes (SB 351 and AB 1415) effective January 1, 2026, specifically designed to limit the control of PE on clinical practice and increase the oversight of changes in ownership. This may require regulatory diligence both as part of the Investment Process in Chapter 4 or the CEO Playbook in Chapter 7. In Europe, rather than restrictions on PE, indirect constraints such as national rules, professional constraints, and competition policy may also require attention. Overall, policy regarding PE in healthcare is not yet very developed.

8.3.5.3 At the Expense of the Local Authority PE investors, driven by return targets and short fund cycles, may negotiate aggressively with local or regional administrations to obtain permits, land, tax incentives, or subsidies. These authorities usually compete to attract investment and jobs, and that rivalry can be quietly leveraged. A recurring pattern is "jurisdictional arbitrage": PE sponsors play neighboring local authorities against each other, securing better land prices or tax holidays by hinting at relocation possibilities. Once one authority offers preferential conditions, others feel compelled to match or exceed them, even when the underlying investment would have proceeded anyway.

Another form of opportunism arises after the initial deal closes. Once the PE fund controls the company or project, it may delay or cancel commitments made to the local community. These can include promised real estate developments, training programs, or job creation targets. The fund may argue that market conditions have changed or that the commitments were "best efforts" rather than binding obligations. In many cases, the municipality lacks the legal leverage—or political appetite—to litigate, especially if it fears losing future investment.

A classic illustration comes from industrial redevelopments where land was sold below market price on the condition of local employment. PE owners sometimes resell parcels at higher value for logistics or housing, pocketing large gains while creating few of the promised jobs. Local administrators face public criticism, while the fund exits profitably. The moral or social contract implicit in the initial negotiation—support for regional development in exchange for favorable terms—effectively collapses.

Sometimes, these tactics extend to timing and communication. Funds might withhold closure decisions until after local elections or release optimistic press statements that buy silence from officials. By the time the reality emerges, the deal's economics are irreversible. This asymmetry of time horizons—four years between elections versus three-year hold periods—works to the PE investor's advantage.

To mitigate this, some administrations have begun including clawback clauses, performance-linked incentives, or reversion rights over real estate in their contracts. Yet enforcement remains patchy, and smaller municipalities often lack the technical expertise to draft such mechanisms. The imbalance in legal and financial sophistication remains a structural weakness exploited by seasoned PE investors.

8.3.6 PE and the Environment

Recent research examines the environmental impact of PE. Although we are not aware of studies specific to the healthcare sector, several papers point to interesting effects.

Bellon (2025) asks whether PE ownership improves or worsens firms' environmental performance and to which extent results depend on regulatory and legal incentives. He combines US plant-level pollution data (EPA) with PE buyout information and applies difference-in-differences designs that exploit variation in environmental liability risk, enforcement intensity, and expected litigation exposure.

He finds that PE ownership reduces pollution when environmental liability risk is high. In jurisdictions or sectors where firms face strong legal or regulatory consequences for emissions, PE-backed firms emit less after buyouts. Further, PE ownership can increase pollution when liability risk is low. Where enforcement is weak, PE incentives tilt toward cost-cutting and cash-flow extraction rather than environmental investments. The results reject a blanket "PE is bad for the environment" view and instead show strong state-dependence: PE amplifies existing incentives embedded in the regulatory environment. The paper reframes PE not as inherently short termist or green, but as highly incentive-responsive. Environmental outcomes depend critically on whether pollution is priced—through regulation, courts, or expected penalties. This links PE governance to the broader literature on law, enforcement, and real outcomes, and explains why empirical findings on PE and ESG are often mixed.

Andonov and Rauh (2025) ask who owns electricity generation assets in the United States, how ownership has shifted over time, and examine the consequences for investment, efficiency, and the energy transition. The authors assemble a comprehensive asset-level dataset covering US power plants, tracking ownership changes across utilities, PE funds, infrastructure investors, and other financial owners, combined with plant characteristics and operating outcomes.

They find that financial investors including PE and infrastructure funds now own a substantial share of US generation capacity, especially in natural gas, wind, and solar. New financial owners are more likely to build new plants and improve the operational efficiency of acquired plants relative to traditional utility ownership. Deregulation plays a key role: ownership shifts and efficiency gains are strongest in restructured electricity markets, where profit incentives and operational flexibility are greater. Rather than emphasizing emissions directly, the paper highlights capital allocation and operational efficiency as central channels through which financial ownership affects the energy sector. It positions PE and related investors as active reallocators of capital toward newer and more efficient technologies, helping explain their growing role in gas and renewables alongside divestment from older coal assets.

Hence, Bellon (2025) explains when PE ownership improves environmental outcomes: when regulation and liability make pollution costly. In contrast, Andonov & Rauh (2025) explain where and how PE operates in energy markets: reallocating capital, improving efficiency, and reshaping the generation mix. Taken together, they suggest that PE can contribute to cleaner energy indirectly (via efficiency and asset turnover) and directly (via emissions reductions), but only when institutional incentives are aligned.

Bai and Wu examine plant-level emissions and energy efficiency after PE buyouts of US fossil-fuel electricity generators. They merge granular EPA power-sector emissions/operations data with PE buyout data and estimate stacked matched difference-in-differences models. Their key move is to decompose "emissions per MWh" (output-scaled emissions) into (i) an input-emissions rate (emissions per unit of heat input—linked to scrubbers/controls) and (ii) the heat rate (heat input per MWh—an inverse measure of energy efficiency/fuel use per output).

They find that output-scaled CO_2 and NO_x emissions fall after PE buyouts (they report average declines of about 4.2% for CO_2 and 9.0% for NO_x in the SSRN version). The improvement is driven primarily by lower heat rates (better thermal efficiency/less fuel burned per MWh), i.e., energy-consumption efficiency gains, rather than broad reductions in input-scaled emissions via new abatement equipment.

They find little average effect on production scale or retirement decisions, and effects are stronger in corporate divestiture deals and non-add-on buyouts—settings where PE has more scope to change operations. In this setting, PE can look "greener" mainly when profit-motivated operational engineering overlaps with fuel-saving efficiency—but the paper is more cautious about PE incentives to fund privately costly, socially beneficial pollution-control investments. While Bai and Wu hold scale roughly fixed and study within-plant efficiency, Andonov and Rauh allow entry, exit, and technology switching, and Bellon allows scale responses conditional on enforcement.

In a separate piece, Wu provides a conceptual and measurement framework for assessing PE's climate impact rather than a single reduced-form estimate. The paper clarifies why PE portfolios are difficult to evaluate using standard financed-emissions metrics, emphasizing opaque ownership chains, frequent asset turnover, leverage, and incomplete Scope 1–3 disclosures at portfolio companies. Wu distinguishes between intensive-margin effects (changes in emissions intensity via operational efficiency or abatement at existing assets) and extensive-margin effects (entry, exit, brown-to-brown transfers, and technology reallocation), arguing that net climate impact depends on both. The paper reviews emerging empirical evidence—highlighting that observed emissions reductions often arise from energy-efficiency improvements or regulatory pressure rather than voluntary internalization of externalities—and warns that "brownspinning" can reduce reported portfolio emissions without reducing economy-wide emissions. Overall, Wu concludes that credible evaluation of PE's carbon footprint requires asset-level, life cycle–consistent measurement and explicit accounting for scale, ownership transitions, and regulatory context, and that policy and disclosure rules are central to aligning PE incentives with climate objectives. Although studies on the environmental impact of PE are in their infancy, one may expect more studies to be written in the future.

8.3.7 Public Funding and Economic Sovereignty

Government-backed development financial institutions (DFIs) have become major players in venture capital and PE. They participate in roughly one in six venture capital (VC) deals worldwide, primarily as limited partners, with mandates to build VC ecosystems, support entrepreneurship and firm growth, foster innovation, and promote sustainability. Andonov et al. (2025) find that DFIs are generally more risk-averse than conventional VCs: they invest less in first-time funds, new general partners, early-stage startups, and high-tech industries. DFI-backed firms perform similarly to conventionally backed firms in terms of growth, profitability, and employment but do not exhibit superior innovation or sustainability outcomes and tend to attract less follow-on private capital. The authors find that their impact is more evident in developing economies, where DFIs focus more on high-externality sectors and improve market transparency while their effects are muted in developed countries. Organizational structure matters: subnational and bank-affiliated DFIs underperform, whereas direct DFI investments are more effective in achieving developmental objectives. Overall, despite their scale and mandates, DFIs' VC and PE investments often fall short of funding superior firm growth.

The fact that sovereign funds invest in PE suggests that at least some PE investments are of sovereign nature, be it for their risk-return properties or for the strategic sectors that some PE funds invest in. The sovereign importance of PE lies in its increasing role as both a strategic policy instrument and a financial intermediary linking state interests, global capital flows, and long-term investment in productive assets. Sovereign importance can be understood along at least three main dimensions: (1) macroeconomic stability and industrial policy, (2) the participation of sovereign institutions such as sovereign wealth funds (SWF) and fiscal diversification, and (3) geopolitical and developmental strategy (Bolton et al., 2012). A country hence needs a sufficient financial infrastructure with institutions that can finance PE in order to invest in strategically important firms. This can be achieved by relationships between PE groups and specific LPs or directly through SWFs.

The International Forum of Sovereign Wealth Funds (IFSWF) report on SWF investments in private markets notes that they are primarily invested in growth equity, which typically includes technology, healthcare, and newer infrastructure sectors. And indeed, many reports indicate that SWFs invest in such sectors and in particular in a wide range of healthcare services and facilities, including hospitals, ambulatory care, medical devices, insurance, managed care, pharmaceuticals, and biotech (Yunis, 2021; Al Hammadi, 2024; SWFI, 2025).

8.4 IMPACT OF INNOVATION ON THE RELATIONSHIPS BETWEEN STAKEHOLDERS

8.4.1 Performance and Controversies in Life Sciences: Innovation

Innovation is at the core of value creation in life sciences, whether in pharma or in medtech, and more so than in healthcare where stringent regulatory requirements can slow the rate of change (the primary focus is on patient safety, quality of care, and compliance with health regulations, which may limit the scope for rapid, disruptive innovations in service delivery). The impact of PE ownership on innovation in life sciences companies is mixed, and whether it promotes or sabotages innovation depends on the specific circumstances and strategies employed by the investor. This controversy is generally centered around LBOs, suspected of prioritizing the servicing of the debt. Growth capital, like venture capital, is associated with minority investments and without the trauma of financial engineering. On balance, LBO investors can promote innovation by providing financial and operational support to life sciences companies (capital for R&D, scaling potential, identifying market needs, bridging the gap between research and viable commercial application), especially when aligned with long-term growth strategies. However, their focus on short-term returns and financial engineering, including—perhaps counterintuitively—their risk aversion when already exposed to financial leverage, can damage innovation if it stifles investment in risky but potentially groundbreaking R&D.

Herb Hooper from Ampersand shared how PE can contribute significantly to healthcare innovation ecosystems. In 2015, the Ampersand team identified that gene therapy clinical trials had reached an inflection point. Focused on rare diseases with efficacy data available early in trials, the field could progress quickly to Phase 3. However, insufficient viral vector supply capacity threatened innovation pace. Their 2015 investment in Brammer Bio targeted a gene therapy; CDMO focused on viral vectors, initially carved from University of Florida (which had hired faculty around 2005 to develop the capability). Catalized by an early partnership with Biogen, the company expanded from one facility generating $15 million revenue to three facilities producing more than $200 million in only four years, becoming the market leader involved in one-third of all gene therapy clinical trials. Thermo Fisher acquired Brammer Bio for $1.7 billion in 2019.

Here we can see how PE's ability to react quickly, deploy capital efficiently, assemble talent, and execute buildouts accelerated innovation timelines that might otherwise have stalled. This contrasts with slower traditional funding mechanisms.

We find many other positive cases like WuXi AppTec, founded in China in 2000, a leading global provider of R&D and manufacturing services to the life sciences industry. During critical phases of its expansion, it received backing from VC and PE firms, including Ally Bridge Group and Hillhouse Capital. In 2015, as part of a consortium of PE firms, they backed the founder and took the company private in a $3.3 billion deal. These firms provided capital, strategic guidance, and industry connections. This included the expansion of services to cover the entire drug development pipeline, significant investments in cutting-edge technologies, and the establishment of advanced manufacturing facilities and global R&D hubs that enabled WuXi to scale internationally, create a global network, and ultimately play a critical role in accelerating drug development.

Conversely, a notable example of a life sciences company where PE ownership may have hindered innovation is BenevolentAI. Established in the United Kingdom in 2013, the company set out to transform the pharmaceutical sector by leveraging AI to expedite drug development. Over time, BenevolentAI secured substantial investments from venture capital and PE firms like Temasek, eventually achieving a valuation exceeding $2 billion. However, the company shifted its focus to developing its own pharmaceuticals, a resource-intensive strategy that marked a departure from its original AI-driven platform approach. This pivot strained resources and drew attention away from advancing its core AI technology. The strategic change, driven by investor demands for higher returns, resulted in reduced funding for AI advancements, increased operational complexity, and diminished innovation in both areas. Following its public listing in 2022, the company's share price dropped 95% after two years, highlighting investor concerns about its strategy and ability to innovate. In 2024, tech entrepreneur and company founder Ken Mulvany rejoined the board after an activist campaign and initiated a significant restructuring effort aimed at realigning the company with its foundational mission of AI-powered drug discovery.

After all, the net effect depends heavily on the PE firm's investment philosophy, the company's innovation stage, and the broader market context. Some PE-backed firms thrive as innovation leaders, while others struggle under the weight of financial constraints and short-term pressures. One thing is sure: the investment horizon of PE is about five years. Any investment in innovation needs to show a positive return by the time of the exit.

8.4.2 Performance and Controversies in Healthcare: Innovation

In healthcare services, innovation is generally associated with new or adjusted business models. This often raises the suspicion of the medical staff, naturally anxious about getting abused in a transfer of wealth to the PE owners.

However, the industry faces criticism regarding provider consolidation (many US states now limit M&A pace following negative stories about provider buildups, including recent anesthesia PE controversies) and supply chain exploitation where investors arbitrage pricing opportunities.

In Germany in 2025, a case involving AOK Nordost, a major statutory health insurance provider, illustrated the recurring tension between healthcare system innovation and entrenched interests. AOK Nordost restructured its procurement model for incontinence products—such as adult diapers and absorbent pants—by signing new contracts with experienced, nationwide mail-order suppliers. The model prioritizes measurable quality, reliable multi-channel access (including phone and online support, with in-home assistance where needed), lower costs for the insurer, and clearly defined service levels. This represents a shift toward more efficient, patient-centered procurement practices. However, the reform has met resistance: local pharmacies have opposed the new system, spreading claims of reduced quality, and pharmacy associations have exerted political pressure. Despite these reactions, the initiative does not represent a decline in care standards; rather, it aims to improve outcomes and value for patients and the healthcare system. The case underscores a broader lesson for PE investors in healthcare: optimizing procurement and service delivery based on evidence and return on investment often clashes with legacy structures and vested interests.

8.5 CASE STUDY: KKR AND ENVISION HEALTHCARE

8.5.1 Building a Physician Services Giant

Envision Healthcare was born from the consolidation of two major US healthcare companies: AmSurg and Envision Healthcare Holdings. In 2016, the two firms merged to create one of the largest physician services organizations in the country, with operations spanning emergency medicine, anesthesiology, radiology, and ASCs.

AmSurg had built its reputation on outpatient surgery—operating more than 250 ASCs across the United States—while Envision was best known for staffing emergency departments, particularly in hospitals that outsourced 24/7 physician coverage. Together, the merged entity represented a sprawling infrastructure of clinicians, often in specialties with round-the-clock needs.

At its peak, Envision Healthcare employed more than 25,000 physicians and advanced practitioners and operated in nearly every US state. It had grown rapidly through acquisitions, using leverage to roll up small and mid-sized physician groups. The company's scale gave it strong negotiating power with hospitals, but its business model also leaned heavily on a controversial practice: out-of-network billing, particularly in emergency medicine.

This approach allowed Envision to bill patients (or their insurers) at higher, non-contracted rates when care was delivered in facilities not covered by their insurance plans. The strategy was profitable, but it drew increasing scrutiny from regulators and the media. By 2017, Envision had become a flashpoint in the national debate over "surprise billing"—situations where patients received unexpectedly high bills for out-of-network care they did not knowingly choose.

8.5.2 KKR Steps In: The Largest Healthcare LBO of the Decade

In October 2018, PE firm KKR & Co. acquired Envision Healthcare in a $9.9 billion leveraged buyout, making it the largest healthcare PE deal of the decade. The transaction involved approximately $7 billion in debt, and the equity was contributed from KKR's flagship PE fund.

At the time, Envision's stock had declined due to mounting public scrutiny and weaker-than-expected earnings. However, KKR viewed the company as a distressed opportunity: with its scale, national footprint, and dominant position in physician staffing, Envision seemed like a strong platform that could be stabilized and eventually expanded. KKR also believed that private ownership would provide the flexibility needed to navigate the political environment without quarterly investor pressure.

The investment thesis focused on several levers: improving revenue cycle management, restructuring unprofitable contracts, growing the ambulatory business, and enhancing relationships with payers to reduce out-of-network exposure. But most critically, KKR had to bet on its ability to manage regulatory risk.

8.5.3 The Surprise Billing Cliff

Unfortunately for KKR, that risk materialized quickly. In 2020, bipartisan momentum in the US Congress began to coalesce around legislation to end surprise billing. In 2021, the No Surprises Act was passed and took effect in early 2022, effectively banning the kind of out-of-network billing that had underpinned much of Envision's profitability.

The Act mandated that disputes between providers and insurers be resolved through arbitration, pegging payments to in-network rates. This dramatically reduced Envision's revenue in EDs and other settings where it had previously relied on higher out-of-network charges.

At the same time, Envision was dealing with rising labor costs, COVID-related pressures, and mounting debt service obligations. Despite efforts to restructure contracts and cut costs, the company's cash flow deteriorated. Its ambulatory surgery business, AmSurg, was more stable but could not offset the collapse in the physician staffing division.

8.5.4 Collapse and Bankruptcy

By 2023, Envision was in financial freefall. The company had been downgraded by credit rating agencies and was struggling to make interest payments on its increasing debt, by then reaching $7.9 billion. In May 2023, Envision Healthcare filed for Chapter 11 bankruptcy protection, becoming one of the highest-profile failures of a PE-backed healthcare company in the United States.

Under the restructuring plan, AmSurg was spun out into a separate entity, while the physician services business—once the crown jewel of the platform—was effectively wiped out. The majority of the company's debt was converted to equity in the reorganized business, and KKR's equity stake was largely lost.

The collapse sent shockwaves through the healthcare investment community and reignited debates about PE's role in essential services like emergency care. It also underscored the risks of aggressive leverage combined with heavy regulatory exposure—especially when core revenues depend on billing strategies vulnerable to policy change.

8.5.5 Lessons from the Envision Deal

Envision Healthcare is a cautionary tale about the limits of scale and financial engineering in complex, politically sensitive sectors. While KKR was not responsible for creating the underlying billing model, its investment was premised on a belief that regulatory obstacles could be managed or delayed. That assumption proved incorrect.

The failure also highlights how quickly a company with national reach, thousands of employees, and real clinical infrastructure can unravel when core revenue levers are shut off. Even with operational improvements, there was no viable path to offset the structural blow delivered by the No Surprises Act.

Envision reminds investors that in healthcare—especially in areas like emergency medicine and insurance billing—policy risk can be just as material as market risk. And when deals are highly leveraged, there may be little room to adapt once the assumptions underpinning the investment thesis begin to collapse.

8.6 CHAPTER SUMMARY

The chapter synthesizes academic corporate finance insights on conflicts between shareholders, debtholders, managers, workers, policymakers, and different investor types, emphasizing how these conflicts intensify in LBOs. While PE's concentrated ownership and debt can drive operational discipline and efficiency, this often comes at the expense of various stakeholders, such as workforce reductions, price increases, delayed supplier payments, diminished product quality, and elevated financial risks for lenders.

Key learnings include the following:

- PE ownership intensifies traditional shareholder and stakeholder conflicts, especially in leveraged buyouts with high debt.
- Healthcare PE controversy centers on patient care and drug access, with significant ethical stakes.
- Financial engineering by PE can harm minority shareholders, lenders, and other stakeholders through debt, asset sales, and related-party transactions.
- Innovation in life sciences is a double-edged sword—PE can spur growth but also cut R&D and defer investment for short-term gain.
- Regulatory risk is a critical factor for healthcare PE outcomes and may cause rapid financial distress.
- Sustainable healthcare value requires alignment among investors, management, clinicians, and society.
- Envision Healthcare's bankruptcy highlights risks associated with aggressive billing practices and excessive leverage amid tightening regulation.

CHAPTER 9

Private Equity in Emerging and Developing Markets

Private equity in emerging and developing markets (often categorized as low- and middle-income countries, or LMICs, by the World Bank) presents unique opportunities and challenges ...

First, we note the distinction between "emerging" and "developing" markets—here developing markets include countries like China, Brazil, and India, while emerging markets refer, for example, to countries like Ghana. For the sake of brevity, we will follow private equity (PE) industry practice and often use the term "emerging" as a shorthand to refer to both categories. In addition, both emerging and developing markets are distinct from "developed" markets, which include countries and regions such as North America, Western Europe, Australia and New Zealand, Japan, South Korea, Singapore, and Hong Kong.

Emerging markets are a small but promising part of the PE industry. Although they were once a slow growth area of PE, they have shown some momentum all over the world in recent years, and they are largely viewed as the next big opportunity.

This chapter presents some of the biggest players and examines both opportunities and risks and challenges faced by PE investors when working in emerging markets. It will also present several examples and explore issues specific to particular regions and countries.

9.1 FUNDRAISING

Figure 9.1 shows funds raised in emerging and developing markets by strategy, including buyouts, growth capital, and other types of funds such as funds of funds, turnaround and distressed. It also includes venture capital, which is the dominant strategy for fundraising and the largest segment in aggregate capital raised. Growth is the second largest segment. Leverage buyouts (LBOs) are more difficult to assess because LBO fundraising largely takes place outside of the developing markets. While emerging markets were once dominated by large American firms such as Carlyle and Warburg Pincus, a growing number of large local players, like buyout funds in China—some raising more than $10 billion—become increasingly important. Yet PE activity remains dominated by venture capital and growth as access to debt is extremely limited.

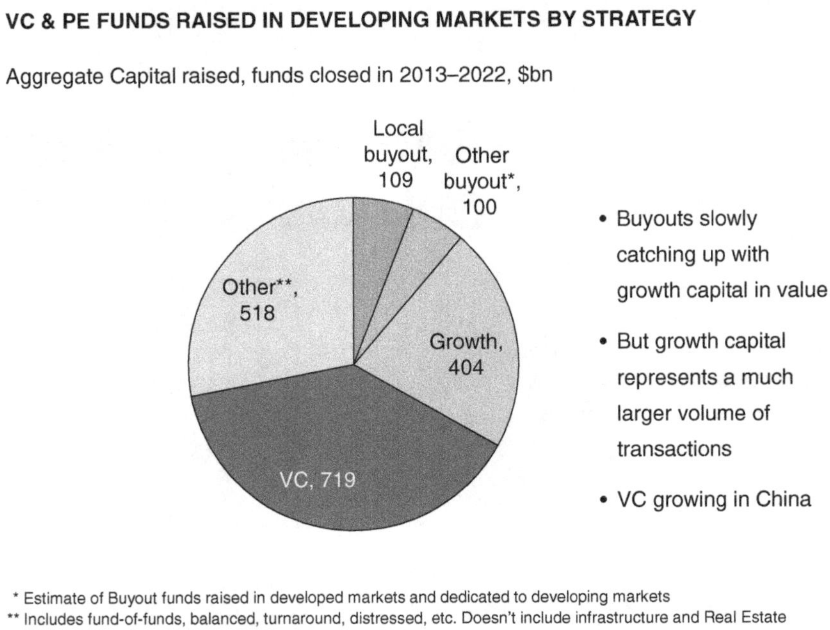

FIGURE 9.1 Fundraising in developing markets by PE strategy.
Source: Preqin (part of Blackrock).

9.2 INVESTMENT

Figure 9.2 (AsiaPac's Share of AuM) shows the share of global venture and growth capital allocated to the Asia-Pacific region, i.e., Asia and Australasia. China accounts for the majority of this allocation. The figures show particularly strong growth in venture capital, followed by growth equity, with buyouts growing more modestly. In buyouts locally domiciled funds account for about half of LBO activity; the remainder is made by funds located in Western financial centers.

9.2.1 Risks

PE investments in emerging markets involve a range of risks. At the macro-level, key exposures include political risk, currency volatility, and regulatory risk. Investors also need to account for micro-level risks—company and firm-specific factors that can affect access to information, execution, protection of intellectual property, governance, and returns. As a result, due diligence in emerging markets is crucial.

Take Carlyle's investment in China Forestry Holdings, a company that had a fast-growth forestry business model based on extracting greenhouse gas credits by planting trees in China. Carlyle invested about US$55 million beginning in early 2008 and at one point held roughly an 11% stake. The company listed on the Hong Kong stock exchange in December 2009.

Subsequent investigations alleged extensive falsification across both operations and financial reporting, including materially overstated turnover and plantation assets, as well as falsified supporting documents (e.g., bank statements and forestry-right certificates).

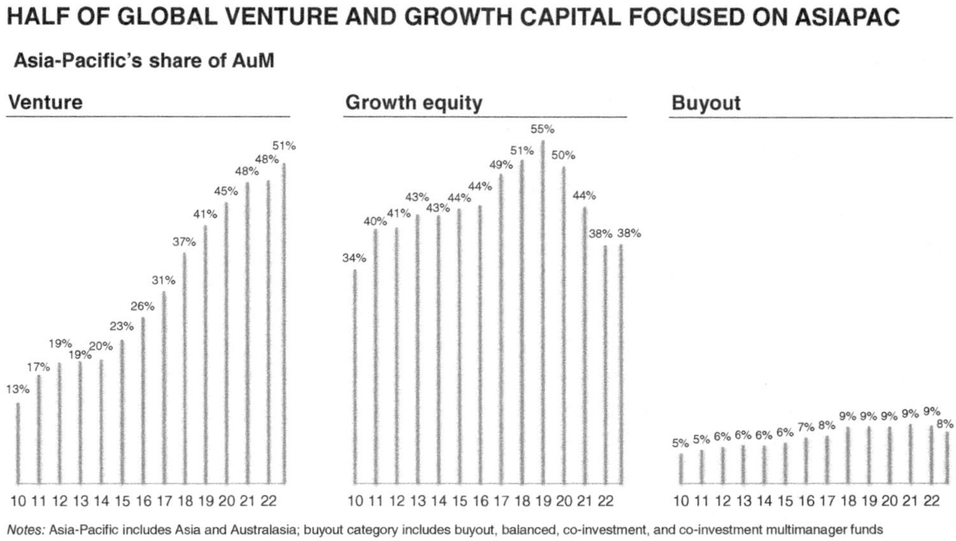

FIGURE 9.2 AsiaPac's share of assets under management (AuM).
Source: Preqin (part of Blackrock).

A significant portion of reported customers never existed. These issues went undetected publicly for an extended period, despite the involvement of institutional investors and external audit. Trading in the shares was suspended on January 26, 2011, after "serious irregularities" were discovered by KPMG, the company's then auditors, which led to criminal proceedings against management.

One important micro-level risk in emerging markets is corporate governance. In practice, there are at least five areas to assess and address. First, the company needs a robust management information system and tight financial controls—capabilities that are often underdeveloped at the time of entry—along with tight financial control. Second, governance effectiveness depends on the board. One needs to understand how it is constituted, whether it has real oversight, and the rights investors actually have. Third, the capital structure should include investor protection; for example, preferred equity can provide liquidation preference and improve downside protection. Fourth, anti-dilution provisions matter; without them, follow-on issuances can erode ownership materially and weaken control and economics. Finally, the deal should include clear performance incentives and remedies for underperformance—such as vesting, earn-outs, or other contractual penalties—because misalignment after a liquidity event can reduce execution intensity and divert capital away from value creation.

9.2.2 Investment Process of a Limited Partner

This process is common to all investments, but in emerging markets, the strategic asset allocation stage will be slightly different.

We briefly outline the six-step investment process a limited partner (LP) typically follows when evaluating a PE fund in emerging markets. While the overall process is broadly consistent across geographies, the strategic asset allocation stage tends to differ somewhat for emerging markets.

Institutional LPs rarely follow a strictly linear sequence. Instead, they iteratively weigh trade-offs, revisit assumptions, and adjust decisions as market conditions evolve. The process is shaped by risk assessment and feedback loops rather than a fixed checklist.

9.2.2.1 Strategic Asset Allocation Start with the core question: what role should PE play in the overall portfolio? From there, assess the macro backdrop—whether returns are likely to be driven by cyclical swings, volatility, or longer-term structural trends—alongside local growth fundamentals such as the GDP trajectory and other demand drivers. Incorporate liquidity and pricing signals from valuation metrics before committing capital.

Before allocating a single dollar, pressure-test local market frictions that can dominate outcomes: corporate governance standards, cultural and business practices that affect control and enforcement, and foreign-exchange volatility. These factors frequently determine whether value can be realized at exit.

9.2.2.2 Opportunity Mapping and Risk Scanning Map regions and sectors for genuine opportunity—distinguishing credible growth narratives from local boosterism. Benchmark targets against practical constraints: market liquidity, viable exit routes, and the intensity of competing PE capital. Screen early for regulatory tripwires, agency and governance risks that may not be obvious upfront, and the depth of local capital markets.

Treat foreign exchange as an investability question, not an afterthought. Hedge only where instruments are available, affordable, and scalable; in many emerging markets, effective hedging is limited or impractical.

9.2.2.3 Manager and Deal Identification Screen fund managers for true local expertise, not just expat CVs or imported "best practices." Good general partners (GPs) have networks, real operational stories, and have navigated local pitfall-laden landscapes. Insist on transparent governance and alignment of interest, since agency problems have more room to flourish here.

9.2.2.4 Dynamic Portfolio Construction Build out a portfolio to balance exposure across geographies, sectors, and stages. Diversification is less "nice to have" and more "defensive bunker" in regions prone to outsized shocks or dislocations.

9.2.2.5 Adaptive Investment Structuring Tailor deal terms, currency exposure, and governance requirements to local market conditions. In some jurisdictions, headline valuations and even legal enforceability can prove unreliable, so it is prudent to rely on flexible structures and contingent protections—such as staged funding, downside preferences, and enforceable control and information rights.

9.2.2.6 Ongoing Monitoring and Risk Reactivity Monitor with vigilance: expect regulation, political context, and currency moves to change the rules mid-game. Update risk assessments and respond actively—emerging markets rarely reward "wait and see" approaches.

This process tells a more honest story: investing in emerging market PE is a revolving door of risk assessment, not a tidy set of checkboxes. If an LP tries to treat it as such, they could find themselves caught by surprises markets routinely throw.

It is important to understand the underlying macro environment and whether it is cyclical. The environment includes the structural drivers for expected PE returns and to what extent they are linked to the GDP, the relative evaluation metrics, the cultural drivers in PE, which can be agency relationships, and the standards of governance in place. Finally, foreign exchange risk also needs to be estimated.

9.2.3 Other Factors of PE in Emerging Markets

To start with, in addition to PE firms, there are two alternative funding sources in emerging markets. First, sovereign wealth funds, such as ADIA, Sammar, and CIC, have recently increased their investments in PE and represent about 10% of all commitments. Second, developing finance institutions now also play an important role. They can be national or multilateral or supranational. They typically promote development through projects, and they will intervene particularly when there is no alternative private investment available. They are essential for the development of small and medium enterprises in emerging markets. These institutions are a side entry for those who want to work in PE. The work they do is very similar to what they would do in a PE fund, and sometimes they switch to PE funds.

Ultimately, the know-how is difficult to import from one country or region to another (Figure 9.3).

The essential factors for PE investing all depend on the rules, regulations, and cultures of the particular country one is investing in. For example, it is important to have a strong mastery of country-specific accounting, tax, and legal issues; to be able to enforce legal rights in the territory, to disclose and follow due diligence standards, and to comply with public markets, for exits and to get access to them. One also needs to assess the extent of the equity culture in the region. Do people understand what an equity investment is? Are they entrepreneurial? Are there investment opportunities? And are there experienced investors?

As the managing partner of a large international PE fund states, to execute in a certain country, you need a team there. And that is particularly true in emerging markets.

What are some other reasons PE funds might have a local operation in an emerging market? Obviously, relationships are essential, and reputation and culture are also

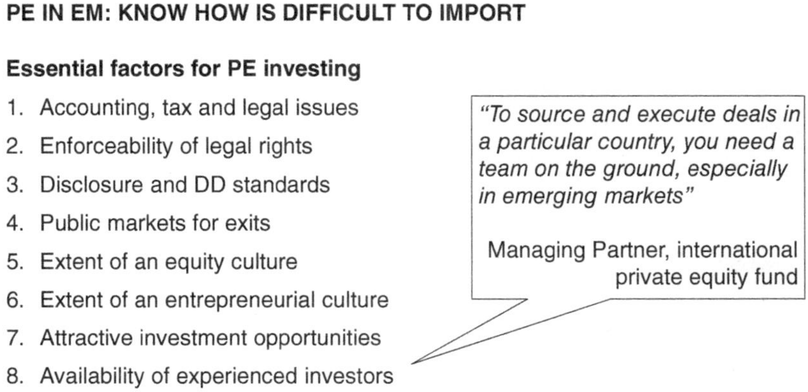

FIGURE 9.3 Essential factors for PE investing in emerging markets.
Source: IESE.

important reasons. And in cases where funds originally come from developed markets, the local executives in emerging markets need to be given the power to make the decisions, otherwise they will quickly leave. And it is very difficult to rebuild this level of trust.

We should also mention some of the typical structures in emerging markets. Often, PE firms go for minority investments as they are an easier risk to manage. In addition, we generally do not have access to mezzanine financing, and it will be difficult to put in place anti-dilution provisions. In terms of the legal environment, the general tradition in most countries with emerging markets is the common law. This law provides more contractual protections, and this is something that's important for larger deals.

9.3 EXIT

Issues relating to exits in emerging markets include a volatile and sometimes significant proportion of write-offs (Figure 9.4). This chart does not provide the full picture: most of the write-offs and bankruptcies in 2017–2021 actually happened in the venture capital (VC) segment. It is however a useful reminder that emerging markets function differently.

In emerging markets, there is a very strong preference for strategic buyers. In particular, the markets are not mature enough to provide secondary LBO exits. Initial public offerings (IPOs) can be frequent but will often take place abroad on a foreign exchange because the local exchanges tend to be too small, illiquid, and prone to manipulation. Moreover, the way the exit can be managed is not always straightforward and transparent. As a foreign investor, we would, for example, want to be able to repatriate the proceeds of our sale, and that would be something to add to our exit process.

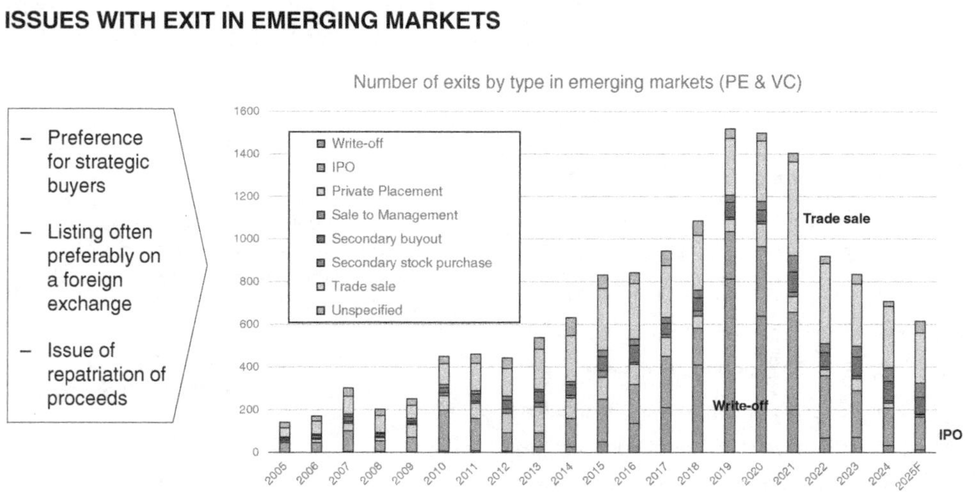

FIGURE 9.4 Number of exits by type in emerging markets.
Source: Preqin (part of Blackrock).

9.4 HEALTH SPECIFICITIES

Emerging markets present a unique set of challenges and opportunities for PE investors in healthcare and life sciences. These markets—characterized by rapid urbanization, growing middle classes, and fragmented healthcare systems—operate under distinct constraints and dynamics. We list some of these specificities PE investors need to factor in.

9.4.1 Resource Constraints and Infrastructure Gaps

Emerging markets often lack robust healthcare infrastructure. Rural areas may have limited access to hospitals, diagnostic facilities, or even basic utilities. For example, in sub-Saharan Africa, 70% of the population lives in rural areas, yet 80% of healthcare resources are concentrated in urban centers. This disparity forces innovators to develop decentralized, low-cost, and durable solutions—qualities that later make some of them attractive for adoption in cost-conscious developed markets. This can happen through a process known as reverse innovation or frugal innovation.

9.4.2 Demographic and Epidemiologic Pressures

Emerging markets face a dual burden: persistent infectious diseases alongside rising noncommunicable diseases. PE investors must balance investments in traditional care delivery with preventive and chronic disease management.

9.4.3 Regulatory Fragmentation and Policy Risks

Healthcare regulation is often inconsistent or underdeveloped. PE firms must navigate local compliance hurdles and intellectual property risks, adapting to shifting policies and weak IP enforcement.

9.4.4 Talent Shortages and Task-shifting

Physician scarcity has spurred models that redistribute responsibilities to nonspecialists. For example, Narayana Health in India trains nurses for pre- and post-operative care, freeing doctors for complex surgeries—a model now replicated in Western markets. Yet, scarcity is exacerbated by the fact that developed markets attract legions of doctors and nurses from emerging markets.

9.4.5 Payment Systems and Affordability

With limited insurance penetration, patients often pay directly for care, driving demand for microinsurance, subscription-based telemedicine, and outcome-based financing.

Instead of merely replicating Western models, PE investors must recognize that emerging market constraints have sparked the rise of innovative, scalable, and affordable healthcare solutions—many now driving competitive advantage globally. Success requires not just capital, but strategic flexibility, operational grit, and a readiness to back business models that can leapfrog legacy systems and set new industry standards.

9.5 REVERSE OR FRUGAL INNOVATION—LOW-TECH SOLUTIONS FROM EMERGING MARKETS TO DEVELOPED HEALTHCARE SYSTEMS

The traditional model of healthcare innovation, dominated by high-income countries, sometimes is being upended by a powerful countertrend: solutions developed in resource-constrained emerging markets that could be adopted in wealthier countries. This phenomenon, known as "reverse innovation," has the potential to reshape global health systems' approach to cost-efficiency, access, and scalability.

In emerging markets, the scarcity of resources and infrastructure compels healthcare providers and entrepreneurs to develop lean, robust, and user-centric solutions. These innovations are not simply stripped-down versions of Western technologies; they represent a fundamental reimagining of care delivery, emphasizing affordability, adaptability, and accessibility.

Youssef at Eckuity confirms that reverse innovation is becoming increasingly relevant in healthcare:

> *We're starting to see highly cost-efficient diagnostic tools, AI triage systems, and remote monitoring solutions developed for resource-constrained environments proving valuable in OECD markets, particularly as payors seek to manage costs and improve access.*

One of the most celebrated examples is the Aravind Eye Care System in India, which pioneered a high-throughput, low-cost cataract surgery model through process innovation, task-shifting, and in-house production of intraocular lenses (Lewallen and Thulasiraj, 2010; Mehta and Shenoy, 2012). This approach has inspired efficiency improvements in the United States and Europe. Similarly, the GE MAC 400, a rugged, battery-operated ECG machine developed for rural India, was later adopted in developed markets for its portability and affordability. GE's "frugal" ultrasound machines and baby warmers, initially designed for emerging markets, have also found use in Western healthcare settings.

NephroPlus is another affordable healthcare model that can be exported to wealthier markets. It began in India and has grown to become Asia's largest dialysis network. Today, it is already expanding into the Gulf Cooperation Council and is preparing to enter Eastern and Western Europe—exporting not capital-intensive infrastructure, but a model of efficiency and access.

By contrast, hospital business models are harder to export. They inevitably run into political obstacles. For Abrar Mir from Quadria Capital,

> *... in much of the Western world, healthcare too quickly becomes a political conversation—framed as left versus right, pro-Obamacare or anti-Obamacare—rather than a practical discussion on how to deliver the highest quality care to the greatest number of people at the lowest possible cost.*

Asia's models prove that affordability and efficiency can transcend politics, and that is what makes them so valuable globally.

In healthcare logistics, Zipline International, founded in California in 2014, pioneered medical drone delivery in Rwanda (2016) and Ghana (2019), where it now serves more than 2,000 health centers and handles 75% of blood deliveries outside Kigali. Operating in all weather and covering up to 160 kilometer per sortie, Zipline's fixed-wing drones dispatch life-saving supplies within 15–45 minutes at roughly $1 per drop—one-fifth the cost of ground transport. After logging 70 million autonomous miles without human-related incidents, FDA emergency waivers in 2021 cleared the way for US rollouts in North Carolina, Utah, and Arkansas, as well as pilot programs with Walmart. By refining its tech in resource-constrained settings, Zipline turned an African success into a scalable, cost-effective US healthcare solution, exemplifying reverse innovation's power to "drone" traditional logistics in favor of rapid, reliable care.

Diagnostic innovation has followed a similar path. Cepheid's GeneXpert, originally deployed for TB control in Africa and Asia, demonstrated how low-cost, point-of-care molecular diagnostics could disrupt centralized lab testing. The technology gained traction in rural US areas, especially during the COVID-19 pandemic.

Other notable examples include mPedigree, a mobile-based drug authentication system from Ghana, and Zipline, a US-based drone delivery company that launched its first large-scale operations in Rwanda before expanding to rural America. Telemedicine platforms like India's Apollo Telemedicine Networking Foundation and Mexico's MedicallHome have inspired similar models in developed countries, addressing rural healthcare deserts and reducing unnecessary emergency visits.

As much as we would hope to see this phenomenon solve the issue of the broken Western health systems, the initiatives so far have only had a marginal impact. Souleymane Ba from Leapfrogs explains that emerging-market innovations like Zipline's drone-delivery model are tailored to very young populations—Africa's median age is just 19.3 years—so they focus on maternal health, pediatric vaccines, and trauma response for road-traffic injuries. Europe's median age, by contrast, is about 42.8 years, meaning its healthcare priorities skew toward chronic disease management, geriatric care, and long-term home monitoring. A delivery network optimized for rapid blood and vaccine drops within 15–45 minutes at $1 per sortie may excel under Africa's youthful, acute-care demands but requires significant adaptation—such as temperature-controlled payloads for biologics and integration with elder-care workflows—to meet Europe's aging population needs. Thus, reverse innovators must recalibrate both technology and service design to bridge vastly different demographic health profiles.

But these cases illustrate that innovation is increasingly bidirectional. The rigorous testing of solutions in low-resource environments often makes them more scalable and adaptable when transferred to developed markets. The process is just not that straightforward; regulatory barriers and differing patient expectations can slow adoption. Nevertheless, as developed countries face mounting cost and access pressures, the appetite for proven, cost-effective solutions is growing.

For PE investors, reverse innovation is both a challenge and an opportunity. Identifying and supporting scalable, high-impact solutions from emerging markets can yield not only strong returns abroad but also valuable models for developed-market portfolios. As the global flow of innovation becomes truly two-way, the lessons and ingenuity of emerging markets are increasingly vital for the future of healthcare worldwide.

9.6 REGIONAL OUTLOOKS

We now look at some of the characteristics and challenges of PE in a few specific regions and countries. We had to make difficult choices as we could not cover all regions of the world. As one might expect, Asia is on the verge of becoming the most important region in terms of healthcare spending and hence we cover it first. While many parts of Asia like Japan and the "Asian tigers" of the 1980s have been considered developed markets for a while, the bulk of Asia is still developing or emerging. As stated by Abrar Mir from Quadria Capital in his foreword, by 2030, Asia's total healthcare spending will exceed \$5 trillion—surpassing today's combined outlays of the United States and Europe. Although Asia is home to about one-third of the global population, it bears over 55% of the world's disease burden, with the highest rates of diabetes, cancer, and cardiovascular illness. At the same time, the region's economic ascent will place more than two-thirds of the world's middle-class consumers in Asia by 2030. This intersection of chronic illness and growing affluence ensures that healthcare demand in Asia will not only rise but accelerate rapidly. Says Abrar:

> *We firmly believe that the Asia healthcare story is the investment opportunity of our lifetime. The global center of gravity of the healthcare industry is shifting from the West to the East, with 10 to 15% top line annual growth in Asia.*

Already by the end of this decade, total healthcare spend in Asia is going to be larger than in the United States and Europe combined today.

On the other hand, the markets are undersupplied. Asian governments invest 2–3% of their budget in healthcare and cannot do more in funding and in provision. WHO estimates there's something like \$80 billion of healthcare underspend each year, for decades, even now, just to meet minimum healthcare standards in Asia.

The private sector must lead the way, and PE plays a crucial role in funding and helping drive the democratization of healthcare in Asia. Eight out of ten of all new hospital beds in Asia are being built by the private sector. Asia is also becoming the manufacturing hub for the world. Almost 70% of all pharmaceutical products that are being prescribed in the United States and Europe, by volume, are manufactured in Asia. It will be true by value within a decade. Today, Asia has more FDA-approved facilities than the whole of the United States and Europe combined.

Abrar makes a strong case for the Asian opportunity:

> *As PE investors, we are always searching for the combination of strong growth dynamics, predictability and reliability of that growth. Healthcare in Asia offers all three in abundance. It is a sector that delivers extraordinary growth, often in the double digits. This character—stability and growth—makes Asian healthcare a compelling investment opportunity.*

Equally important, the sector is shaped by forces that create a favorable environment for private capital. While corruption may be endemic in many parts of Asia, healthcare has been comparatively insulated, largely because of its political salience. Access to healthcare is viewed as a national priority, and this political intent acts as a safeguard, ensuring greater transparency and oversight.

Abrar adds:

Moreover, Quadria's focus is squarely on the private sector, where the drivers of efficiency, accountability, and governance are strongest. We are not encumbered by the complexities of state bureaucracy. Instead, we partner with private operators who are motivated to innovate, scale and deliver measurable improvements in access, affordability and quality. This alignment of purpose and capital allows us to channel investment where it can have the greatest multiplier effect—creating both economic returns and societal impact.

For a firm like Eckuity, Asia offers both a market opportunity and a partnership ecosystem—particularly in areas like medical devices, clinical outsourcing, and AI-enabled healthcare delivery. They see Asia not just as a destination for capital, but as a source of innovation and efficiency, often setting benchmarks for value-based care models that the rest of the world will follow.

9.6.1 China

China's PE market has leapt from zero to become the world's third largest—trailing only North America and Europe—in just 20 years. Early on, concerns about corruption, opaque regulations, and government intervention threatened to shave up to half of deal value, yet global sponsors pressed on, confident that local expertise and deep networks could unlock opportunity.

Central to that local advantage is *guanxi*—the trust-based relationships essential for fast access to decision-makers and off-market deals. Without it, due diligence drags, approvals stall, and strategic conversations rarely progress beyond polite introductions.

Despite reform efforts—such as streamlining foreign capital entry and tightening enforcement to shore up the court system—investors still navigate a landscape of shifting rules, tighter capital controls, and sporadic geopolitical frictions. Domestic firms, by contrast, benefit from direct pipelines to local funding sources, priority access to IPO markets, and on-the-ground operational capabilities that foreign players must strive years to build.

GUANXI (关系): THE CENTRALITY OF RELATIONSHIPS

In China, business relationships are shaped by the cultural concept of guanxi, or connections, which rests on the foundation of trust. Trust is historically rooted in family and community ties, where familiarity and loyalty take precedence over engagement with outsiders. In practice, this makes trust-building an essential precursor to business. Shared meals, social ritual, and personal introductions are central for acceptance and collaboration and to consolidate agreements and confirm partnerships.

A 2011 report by Wharton described the Chinese court system as weak and unreliable, posing serious enforcement risks for investors. While regulatory reforms introduced in the subsequent years suggested a shift toward a more PE-friendly legal environment, the investment climate became increasingly challenging after 2020, even for domestic investors and entrepreneurs. This shift coincided with intensified regulatory scrutiny, tighter capital controls, and geopolitical tensions that collectively constrained cross-border investment activity.

Bo Shi, former head of China for Terra Firma, discussed with our students a recent positive development: "In China, we are now more ready to change the CEO. It is still difficult to change the strategy compared to Western markets, but I am confident it is progressing too."

During China's PE expansion, several sizable domestic players emerged, some of whom originated from diversified conglomerates. For example, the author's advisory firm, Candesic, collaborated with Fosun, a fast-growing corporate investor often likened to a smaller version of Samsung. China also witnessed the rise of successful growth equity funds. CDH China, for instance, delivered a 93% net internal rate of return on its 2002 vintage fund,[1] and numerous other local firms have generated strong returns in recent years.

9.6.1.1 Localization A notable trend has been the introduction and localization of Western consumer brands and medical technologies. Firms such as Hony Capital pioneered this model by facilitating the Chinese expansion of global names like Pizza Express and WeWork. In healthcare, PE investors have played a similarly strategic role, bringing in foreign innovations, enabling localization, and scaling operations within China. Following are three illustrative transactions.

CDH and Sirtex In 2018, CDH Investments, alongside Hong Kong-listed Grand Pharmaceutical, acquired 100% of Australian liver cancer device maker Sirtex for A$1.9 billion (approx. RMB 9.5 billion). CDH controlled 51% through its vehicle CDH Genetech Limited, while Grand held 49% via its subsidiary, with the deal funded by an $850 million syndicated loan and Grand's capital contribution. The acquisition centered on Sirtex's flagship technology, the Y-90 resin microspheres—a targeted radiotherapy for liver cancer approved in more than 40 countries. To localize this innovation, Sirtex China was established, multi-center clinical trials were conducted with leading hospitals like Peking Union Medical College Hospital and Shanghai Changhai Hospital, and a regulatory strategy was implemented to reclassify the product as a medical device to shorten approval timelines. A GMP-certified production line was later built in Suzhou, significantly reducing costs. As a result, Y-90 was included in national treatment guidelines and is now widely adopted for advanced liver cancer care in China.

C-Bridge and UCB China In 2024, C-Bridge Capital acquired UCB's China operations for $680 million, in partnership with Mubadala, a major Middle Eastern sovereign wealth fund. They established a new company, NeuroGen Pharma, to run and scale the acquired portfolio. The acquisition included five mature drugs: Keppra,

[1] A reminder that this is not a true rate of return, but probably still impressive performance.

Vimpat, Neupro, Zyrtec, and Xyzal (€131 million in China sales in 2023), as well as UCB's manufacturing site in Zhuhai. C-Bridge applied its investor-operator model to streamline production using digital supply chain systems, targeting an 18% cost reduction. It also leveraged its local market expertise to expand access, especially in primary care settings. The transaction localized important therapies for neurological and allergic diseases while supporting broader healthcare access in China.

Fosun and Gland Pharma In 2017, Fosun Pharma, part of the Fosun conglomerate, acquired a 74% stake in India-based Gland Pharma for $1.1 billion, including a performance-based earn-out. Fosun purchased 57.9% from KKR and Gland's founding shareholders, with the remainder held through convertible preferred shares and other existing stakeholders. Gland Pharma, India's first injectable manufacturer approved by the US FDA, brought extensive GMP certifications and global regulatory experience. By integrating Gland's injectable technologies into subsidiaries like Yaoyou Pharmaceutical, Fosun improved supply chain synergies and formulation capacity. The results were significant: injectable exports rose from $120 million in 2017 to $870 million by 2023. Gland also acquired European contract development and manufacturing organization, Cenexi in 2023, establishing localized production in Europe and expanding its' and Fosun's competitive reach in the global injectable market.

Together, these cases highlight how PE funds are helping bridge innovation from global companies into China's dynamic healthcare system by injecting capital, accelerating localization, and building strong commercial and operational infrastructure.

Alongside inbound investment, a growing trend is the export of Chinese healthcare innovation to global markets. This is especially visible in biotechnology and advanced health technologies, where Chinese firms are no longer just recipients of capital and know-how, but are increasingly shaping international pipelines. This creates a very different competition–opportunity dynamic for PE investors, with implications for valuation, deal structuring, and long-term portfolio strategy. A recent example is GSK's $12 billion oncology deal with Jiangsu Hengrui, which secured global rights (ex-China) to camrelizumab and 12 other pipeline assets.

9.6.1.2 Take-China Private Another distinct feature of Chinese PE was the "take-China-private" strategy, whereby Chinese companies listed in the United States were taken private by PE sponsors and subsequently relisted on domestic exchanges—typically in Hong Kong or mainland China—to benefit from higher valuations and friendlier regulatory environments. One early example was Morgan Stanley Private Equity's involvement in the relisting of Sihuan Pharmaceutical Holdings Group between 2009 and 2011. This strategy became less prevalent in later years, particularly as Chinese authorities began actively encouraging "homecoming listings" for Chinese firms listed abroad. By the mid-2020s, that window of opportunity had mostly closed.

It is worth mentioning the risks associated with this take-China-private approach. Lots of the small to medium-sized enterprises that had been listed in the United States through reverse takeovers, like that of China Fire & Security (Gromb and Kitten, 2016), suffered from accounting issues and credibility concerns, which eroded investor trust and complicated relisting efforts elsewhere. Structurally, many of these deals relied on offshore holding companies, raising concerns around cash flow repatriation, regulatory approvals, and debt servicing. Key questions emerged: Will the operating company upstream sufficient cash to the offshore structure? Will Chinese regulators authorize such transfers? Will the bank accept the credit risk associated with offshore vehicles? These challenges introduced significant legal and financial uncertainties.

More recently, a new phenomenon appeared in the local market. In 2025, the economic downturn in China led to a wave of PE sponsors acquiring controlling stakes in listed companies, often at very attractive discounts. Discounts of 40–50% to net asset value were common in the secondary PE market, and some distressed or block transactions in listed companies traded at substantial discounts as well. Appetite among LPs remained robust for these opportunities, as some investors were able to double their investment value within a year—though this outcome was more the exception than the rule and usually required significant restructuring or strategic change.

9.6.1.3 The PEBCI Model: A Chinese Innovation Going Global Schulman et al. (2017) identify a defining theme in modern China: rapid, M&A-driven expansion in fragmented sectors. Their case on China Hospitals Inc. (CHI) illustrates the early phase of this evolution: CHI expanded by acquiring public hospitals and shifting to a mixed-ownership model, typically 30% government and 70% private ownership. While this structure enabled operational flexibility and financial discipline, the "private" stake was not specifically composed of PE funds, but rather a broad mix of nongovernmental investors.

A more sophisticated evolution is the "PE + Listed Company" model, introduced in Chapter 2 under the PEBCI acronym. This partnership formally combines a public company's industrial strength with a PE firm's financial capabilities. While its individual components exist globally, the model's formalization and application at scale represent a significant recent Chinese financial innovation, born from a unique set of market conditions. Its initial success is now inspiring adoption in other fast-growing economies, particularly across Asia.

The model's core logic is an "incubate-and-acquire" strategy. An off-balance-sheet fund acquires and develops target companies, shielding the public partner from initial M&A risk. Once de-risked and profitable, these assets are sold to the listed company in a pre-arranged exit. This process typically unfolds in four stages: establishing a leveraged fund, making strategic investments aligned with the public company, driving value through direct operational integration, and finally, exiting the investment via acquisition by the listed entity.

Aier Eye Hospital, China's largest ophthalmic group, exemplifies this model's execution,[2] using it to build a network of more than 800 hospitals, across China and overseas. In partnership with PE firms like CITIC, Aier created M&A funds that could execute ambitious deals, famously leveraging a €15 million investment to acquire Spain's Clínica Baviera for ~€150 million to secure advanced technology. Following the acquisition, Aier drove value through "industrial empowerment," implementing its signature "day surgery model" to boost efficiency and using its scale for centralized procurement to cut supply costs by 30%. As reported by CITIC Capital, this systematic value creation paved the way for a successful exit, where Aier's listed company acquired the matured asset, allegedly delivering a 22% annualized return to the fund's investors and demonstrating the model's power to amplify returns while containing risk.

[2] Fujinhui Mergers and Acquisitions Research Institute, 2025.

The advantages of this model are evident:

- It allows public companies to pursue aggressive M&A without compromising their financial ratios.
- It offers PE firms a de-risked, planned exit.
- It aligns both parties through industrial synergies rather than just financial engineering.

Despite its power, the model carries significant risks. As usual, the high financial leverage that drives returns can also magnify losses. More specifically here, divergent interests between risk-averse LPs seeking capital preservation and the growth-seeking corporate partner can create conflict. Furthermore, operational integration poses a major challenge, as a standardized business model may face cultural or market resistance, especially in cross-border deals. Finally, intense competition for assets can lead to inflated valuations and regulatory scrutiny, demanding disciplined execution.

Remarkably, the PEBCI model may become a dominant strategy in China as an elegant solution to local challenges, such as volatile IPO markets and the need to de-risk M&A for public shareholders. These same drivers—the need for exit certainty and a tool for rapid, managed industry consolidation—are now making it an increasingly popular strategy in other parts of Asia, notably India, Vietnam, and Indonesia, where rapid growth, regulatory uncertainty, and family business succession issues present similar structural hurdles. It provides a powerful playbook for market leaders in economies undergoing rapid transformation, underscoring the universal principle that financial innovation is most powerful when it enhances—not replaces—operational excellence and strategic clarity.

9.6.1.4 The Three Phases of the PE Cycle According to Bo Shi at Pall Mall Capital, China's PE market faces significant challenges with poor exit conditions and difficult fundraising environments, though opportunities remain in heavy asset investments. The regulatory landscape has evolved to become more welcoming to foreign capital over the past decade, actively seeking to attract international investors. Local PE firms maintain competitive advantages through superior access to domestic funding sources, local IPO markets, and on-the-ground operational capabilities. Shi highlighted a successful investment in a South Korean touch screen manufacturer with 90% of operations in China, acquired for $400 million with $40 million in net income and sold through a shell company at a 30× PE ratio after growing net income to $60 million within 12 months. Looking ahead, AI, healthcare, and semiconductors are drawing the most investor interest, while the sector's future trajectory over the next five to ten years will likely be shaped by increased government funding, state-backed general partners, and a strategic shift toward domestic replacement of foreign technologies and services.

As 2024 drew to a close, market analysis from Dealogic revealed an unprecedented situation: none of the major international PE firms with Chinese investments had completed either an IPO or full divestment through acquisition during the year. This marked a historic first in recent memory, though exit activity had already diminished following regulatory changes in 2021 that affected Chinese listings. As reported by the *Financial Times*, the data showed these leading PE firms had deployed around $137 billion throughout the 2014–2024 period yet only managed to realize approximately $38 billion in exits. Moreover, their appetite for new Chinese investments had significantly decreased, with only $5 billion invested between 2022 and 2024.

Overall, China-focused fundraising fell from approximately $75 billion in 2017 to $22 billion in 2023, and its proportion of Asia PE fundraising fell from over 80% to less than a third in that period (McKinsey & Company, 2024). Besides cyclical reasons (there being abundant dry powder from previous fundraising activity), capital flight in general after COVID-19 and regulatory constraints limiting nonfinancial entities' borrowing to invest in PE funds, doubtless played a role in this phenomenon.

In 2025, Reuters reported that China Investment Corporation (CIC)—the country's sovereign wealth fund—planned to divest around $1 billion of PE fund interests managed by eight US general partners, further signaling the widening disengagement between Chinese and Western capital.

Despite these impediments, China continues to invest heavily in AI, with a focus on applied technologies rather than foundational models. The premise is that economic value will accrue primarily to those who deploy AI effectively rather than to the model developers. Investment is not limited to capital alone, as policy incentives, government support, and large-scale talent programs are being rolled out at every level. National strategies including the annual Two Session and Five-year Plans, have consistently underlined AI as "high quality productive forces" central to economic development, and Chinese PE firms are being invited to support and benefit.

In 2025, Kai-Fu Lee, a well-known tech entrepreneur based in Beijing, suggested that by the time artificial general intelligence (AGI) emerges, China may hold an advantage over the United States due to its strong ecosystem of social platforms, search engines, AI agents, and hardware infrastructure. Lee contended that China's early-mover advantage in scaling user bases and accumulating vast datasets would create a *defensive advantage*—making it difficult for Western competitors to catch up, much like TikTok's dominance in short-form video, which rivals have struggled to challenge.

9.6.1.5 Comparing with Japan Japan and China display distinct landscapes in PE despite their economic clout in Asia. China has become and remains the largest economy and has built a vast PE market fueled by a tech surge and a booming consumer sector. However, since 2021, regulatory tightening, geopolitical friction, and capital controls have restrained foreign PE activity and complicated exits, especially IPOs, while restricting large minority or majority stakes. Meanwhile, Japan's PE market has matured into a reform-driven, carve-out friendly environment that global PE firms favor. In 2025, Japan's deal value hit record levels, driven by large-scale buyouts from legacy conglomerates, supported by government policies enhancing corporate governance and shareholder returns (Figure 9.5).

Healthcare and life sciences highlight these contrasts sharply. Japan's aging population and steady reforms have made healthcare a vibrant sector for PE. KKR's acquisition and expansion of Panasonic's healthcare business, PHC, with subsequent purchases of Bayer's diabetes care unit and Thermo Fisher Scientific's pathology business, remain hallmark examples. More recently, Blackstone's 2025 majority stake purchase of CMIC, a leading clinical trial firm, and Bain Capital's $5.6 billion investment in R1 RCM, a health data and payments platform, underscore ongoing PE interest. These deals thrive within Japan's transparent regulatory regime and accessible exit routes, helping consolidate fragmented healthcare providers into global players.

By contrast, China's healthcare sector faces tough regulatory scrutiny and geopolitical uncertainties that limit foreign PE scale. While the domestic market grows, many firms attract minority investments mostly from local funds, with exits complicated by tighter public market conditions. Foreign PE treats China's overall

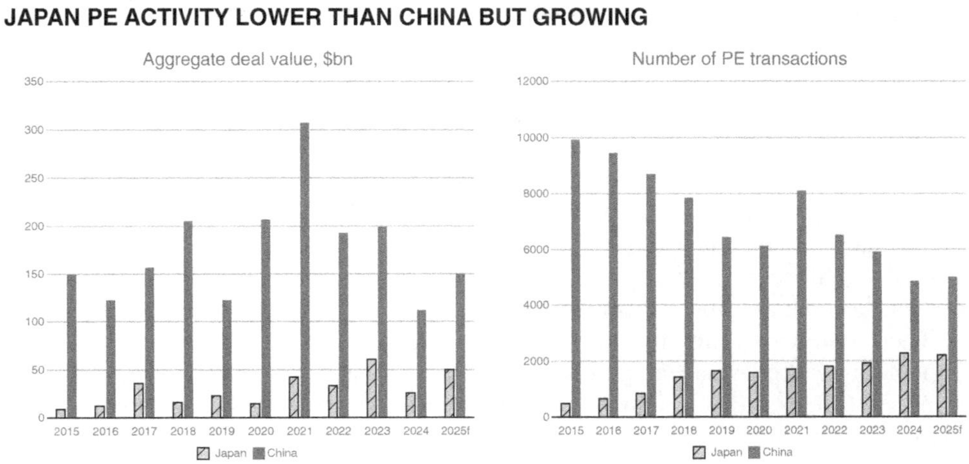

FIGURE 9.5 Comparing Japan and China PE activity.
Source: Preqin, part of Blackrock (all PE and VC transactions).

market and healthcare space with more caution than the mature, governance-focused Japanese environment. China remains massive and evolving but now calls for specialized, domestically focused investment approaches due to stricter regulation and geopolitical challenges.

9.6.1.6 What About Healthcare in China? Despite the aforementioned challenges, China's healthcare and life sciences sector continues to attract substantial PE interest, albeit with evolving strategies and risk profiles. Growth has been propelled by demographic shifts, rising demand for quality care among the middle class, and government initiatives such as "Healthy China 2030," which prioritize healthcare innovation and accessibility.

Government Policy This policy context has only deepened in recent years, where healthcare is emphasized as a pillar of national strategy that is linked directly with innovation, AI integration, and accelerated biotech development. Government priorities shape regulation, reimbursement, and even investment flows to a degree unmatched elsewhere. For this reason, investors cannot rely on secondary market signals alone.

POLICY DIRECTION IS THE ULTIMATE MARKET DRIVER

Above all, the most important stakeholder in China is government. State priorities, regulatory frameworks, and policy directives shape both public and private sectors, and investors must navigate this environment carefully. Successful engagement requires alignment with government objectives and an acceptance of China's guiding principle: national interest comes first. Because China always acts in its own interest, foreign investors, companies, or even universities must work on a win–win basis. where the Chinese partner is seen to benefit first. This principle runs through both regulation and daily operations, such as the requirement to partner locally in order to establish an entity in China.

Ruby Wang, director at LINTRIS Health, a consultancy bridging East and West, says: "Whether we are advising industry on market access or investors on long-term opportunity, the starting point is always alignment with policy, because in China, governance sets the rules of the game."

One of our former students shared her experience working at a local government guidance fund in China. In the high-potential healthcare sector, PE operates by a distinct set of rules centered on a "public-private partnership" between government capital and market-driven institutions. As key players, local government guidance funds offer value that extends far beyond financial investment. Understanding policy motivations has become as critical as analyzing financial statements in this context.

Their uniqueness lies in "resource enablement." For example, when investing in an innovative pharmaceutical company, a government fund can leverage its local resources to help it quickly establish operations in an industrial park, secure policy incentives, and gain access to clinical resources, thereby significantly reducing operational risks. In restructuring a struggling hospital, it acts as a "lubricant" between the public and private sectors, smoothing regulatory processes—an advantage that purely commercial capital cannot easily replicate.

However, this model also faces inherent tensions. The socioeconomic objectives of the government often need to be balanced against the financial return requirements of investors, which can complicate decision-making processes and introduce nonmarket considerations during exit strategies.

Growth and Buyouts in Healthcare Growth equity has remained the dominant PE strategy in Chinese healthcare, targeting high-growth areas such as biopharmaceuticals, medical devices, diagnostics, and digital health. Notable examples include the 2023 strategic financing of Sangon Biotech, a leading life sciences tools manufacturer, which raised $290 million led by GL Capital Group. This investment supported Sangon's expansion in reagents and biological engineering, aligning with China's ambitions to reduce reliance on imported medical technology. Similarly, in the VC segment, QL Biopharm, a developer of recombinant protein drugs, raised $28 million in a Series B+ round in 2023 to advance therapies for oncology and autoimmune diseases, reflecting the sector's innovation focus.

True LBOs of Chinese healthcare companies remain relatively rare. The LBO model, which relies heavily on using the target company's own assets and cash flows as collateral for debt, faces specific challenges in China: acquiring control of healthcare assets often requires complex, time-consuming regulatory approvals; the high-yield debt market used to finance Western LBOs is less mature and accessible; and founding families or state-owned enterprises are often reluctant to cede control to financial sponsors, making true buyouts rarer than minority growth investments.

For about 10 years, things have started to change. Several examples illustrate the model's applicability across hospitals, medtech, and pharma. In 2014, Carlyle Group and CITIC Capital took AmCare Healthcare private in a roughly RMB 3 billion transaction, using sponsor equity and secured bank debt to acquire control of Shanghai's leading obstetrics and women's health hospital chain. In 2016, Hillhouse Capital completed a take-private of Sinopharm's Logan Pharma retail pharmacies for an estimated RMB 2.2 billion, funding the deal with high-yield notes and a term loan secured against Logan's nationwide network. More recently, Hony Capital executed an LBO of Winhealth Medical, a specialty children's hospital operator, for approximately

RMB 1.8 billion, layering asset-backed financing secured by hospital receivables atop traditional leveraged loans. In the pharma sector, Trustar Capital's China buyout fund completed a leveraged acquisition of Guilong Pharmaceutical—maker of Guilong and Manyanshuning throat medicines—in 2024, marking one of the few true pharmaceutical LBOs in China. These transactions demonstrate that, when sponsor alignment, asset scale and cash-flow visibility converge, PE firms can successfully deploy LBO structures across China's healthcare spectrum.

While China has long emphasized universal health coverage through its public system, it is now increasingly recognizing parallel public-private pathways as the most effective way to reach its vast and wealthier population. Regulatory changes are increasingly favoring would-be private investors.

The National Reimbursement Drug List (NRDL) is the central instrument through which China manages drug affordability and access. Its mechanism of action is the volume-based procurement (VBP) scheme, which uses centralized purchasing to drive down prices and expand coverage. While this has reduced healthcare costs, it has also compressed margins across generic drugmakers and medtech suppliers. The NRDL framework was inspired by international health technology assessment models such as the UK's NICE, and since 2018 it has matured into a more transparent and predictable system. Yet foreign companies still face hurdles in securing inclusion. This is less for technical reasons than because of China's "China-for-China" approach, which favors domestic innovation and alignment with national priorities. In parallel, data governance concerns continue to complicate deal structuring for digital health platforms, particularly those reliant on cloud-based patient data. In 2024, a liberalization initiative reported by the China National Health Commission broadened scope for 100% foreign ownership of hospitals in nine major cities (Beijing, Shanghai, Guangzhou, Shenzhen, Tianjin, Nanjing, Suzhou, Fuzhou, and Hainan) from a previous 70%. Also, to address the problem of high out-of-pocket costs in general for private healthcare, gradual changes have been made such as greater tax deductions for commercial health insurance premia and allowing dependents to share employee health insurance benefits. This has encouraged greater health insurance penetration, albeit slowly.

This private health sector support was underscored by the July 2025 national launch of the Commercial Insurance Innovative Drug List (CIIDL), which expands access to new therapies through private reimbursement channels. For PE investors, this evolution opens up opportunities across hospital services, insurance-linked models, and healthcare delivery platforms aligned with both public and private demand. At the same time, it introduces new complexity: strategies must navigate between government priorities and private market incentives, with the balance between the two shaping both risk and return.

Cross-border activity has also played a role in shaping the market. In 2024, Singapore-based CBC Group and UAE-based Mubadala acquired UCB Pharma's Chinese neurology and allergy portfolio for $680 million, a move that highlights global firms' willingness to localize operations in response to regulatory uncertainty and shifting market dynamics. Conversely, Chinese PE firms have pursued overseas acquisitions to access advanced manufacturing and healthcare know-how, as seen in GL Capital's investments in life sciences assets across Asia, Europe, and other regions.

Geography also plays an important role: policy adjustments are occurring alongside regional investment strategies. One focal point has been the "Greater Bay Area," spanning Guangdong, Hong Kong, and Macau, where concentrated innovation ecosystems, economic integration, and designated investment zones are drawing significant capital. Other regions are also emerging as priorities under national strategy, for example, the Yangtze River Delta and Hainan's Free Trade Port, each promoted as hubs for international healthcare collaboration, medical tourism, and advanced clinical trials. These regional dynamics add another layer of opportunity for PE investors, while also underscoring the close alignment between national policy and geographic capital flows.

The distinction between growth equity and LBOs in China's healthcare sector is perhaps even more pronounced than elsewhere. Most growth equity deals have a strong late-stage VC flavor. They are typically minority investments in innovative, high-growth companies, often at earlier stages, and are closely aligned with government priorities around R&D and technology. LBOs, meanwhile, focus on consolidation and operational improvement of more mature businesses, such as hospital groups and device manufacturers, where scale and efficiency can drive returns.

Nonetheless, the sector faces significant valuation and liquidity risks. Average healthcare deal sizes in China rose by more than 50% between 2018 and 2023, driven by investor competition and government-backed enthusiasm for biotech, often outpacing revenue fundamentals. At the same time, exit routes have narrowed, with regulatory tightening on overseas listings and stricter IPO criteria on the STAR Market and HKEX. The impact has been felt across the sector: exit proceeds declined by more than 60% year-on-year between 2021 and 2024, with life sciences deals particularly affected (AVCJ, 2024).

Biotech remains the flagship subsector, but with important distinctions from elsewhere. Chinese biotechs are increasingly "future-proofed" from the outset. Many are dual-listed, operate dual-source manufacturing and supply chains, and cultivate deep regional networks across China. This positioning de-risks them geopolitically and gives them a stronger forward trajectory than even some multinational pharma players, which face growing instability. Importantly, the expansion of innovative pipelines (from oncology to rare disease drugs) carries direct implications for patient outcomes, moving China from a follower to a global contributor in clinical impact.

Health AI has emerged as the other fast-accelerating subsector, particularly the rapid rise of large language models (LLMs) in clinical decision support and hospital operations. While still early in terms of proven business models, state backing and vast datasets have created immense momentum. Both biotech and health AI offer PE firms powerful, long-term growth stories but also require careful calibration to valuation cycles, exit constraints, and evolving regulation.

Looking forward, growth equity is expected to continue driving innovation, supported by substantial government funding for healthcare infrastructure in lower-tier cities. In AI diagnostics, China has become a world leader, with platforms such as DeepSeek and Alibaba's Qwen and DAMO Academy, advancing cutting-edge applications that are already being deployed at scale. Surgical robotics is another area of high-tech innovation where China is moving quickly from follower to global competitor, with local players offering systems that challenge imported technologies on both cost and capability. Elder care, by contrast, is being pushed less by consumer demand and more by top-down urgency. As the population ages and workforce resilience becomes a critical concern for the state, policy is driving preventative strategies and long-term care pilots. Yet the sector remains split: public programs dominate in lower-income settings, while private consumer-facing products are targeted largely at urban, wealthier families.

LBOs are likely to focus on hospital consolidation and cross-border medtech acquisitions, leveraging operational expertise and scale. Domestic strategics such as Fosun and Mindray are also reshaping the market, using their integration capabilities and access to low-cost capital to compete with both local and foreign PE sponsors.

While China's healthcare PE landscape presents formidable challenges, including exit risk and regulatory opacity, it also offers substantial upside. The sector's alignment with national priorities and demographic trends ensures that it will remain a central focus for both domestic and international investors. The ability to balance local relationship-building (guanxi), sector expertise, and regulatory navigation will be key to unlocking value in this complex but dynamic market.

9.6.2 India

India is a continent, which means a lot of opportunities, but they come with a lot of regional and local complexities. In spite of the significant size of the Indian market, most companies are small, and large transactions are few, neither in buyouts nor in growth capital (Figure 9.6).

Like China, India also has lots of issues—nepotism, red tape, corruption—but also lots of investment restrictions for foreigners. The market conditions have not been ideal: not particularly high growth, very poor corporate governance, and not very promising returns. There have not been significant profits in India so far, compared to China. However, India provides a robust venture capital segment, and we have seen a surge in internal PE funds from large corporations.

Still, owing to a humming GDP growth engine driven by favorable population demographics, India remains an attractive destination for investors, especially in healthcare. Insurance penetration has also increased after and catalyzed by the COVID-19 pandemic, with a surge of 17.8% in health insurance coverage in 2023.

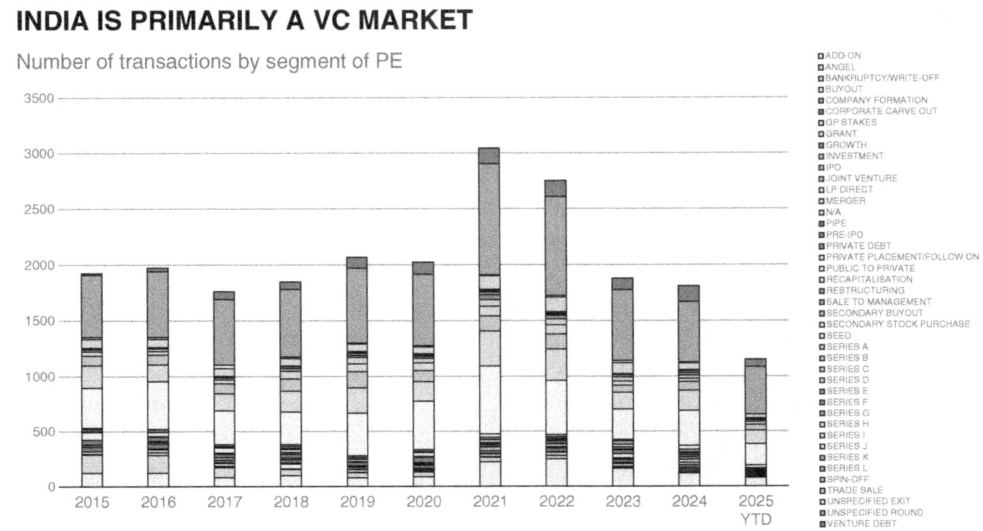

FIGURE 9.6 Number of transactions by PE segment in India.
Source: Preqin (part of Blackrock).

This has been helped by regulatory developments improving the inclusivity of insurance cover, such as a loosening of age caps and improvement of cover for pre-existing illnesses and chronic conditions. Insurance distribution has also benefited from technological advancements such as digital marketing.

The market has seen significant consolidation activity among healthcare providers—Max Healthcare being a prime example we develop hereafter, but also Manipal hospitals, Apollo hospitals, Aster DM, etc. In 2024, India became the largest market in the Asia-Pacific region by deal volume, accounting for approximately 26% of the region's total transactions. Notably, India demonstrated greater resilience to downturns in deal activity compared to its regional counterparts. While buyout volumes across Asia-Pacific declined by nearly 49% from 2023, India's buyout volumes decreased by only 18% over the same period. This relative stability underscores India's growing significance and robustness as a destination for PE investments within the region (Bain & Company, 2025).

To illustrate the specificities of the Indian market, we selected two transactions that we think are representative and that we have some familiarity with.

9.6.2.1 Case Study 1: Max Healthcare—Building India's Second-largest Hospital Chain

A Fragmented Beginning with Strategic Ambition Max Healthcare began its journey in 2000 as part of Max India Group, a diversified conglomerate led by entrepreneur Analjit Singh. The company opened its first hospital in New Delhi and aimed to bring high-quality, private, multi-specialty care to India's growing urban middle class. Over the next decade, Max steadily expanded across North India, developing a network of tertiary and secondary care hospitals focused on cardiology, oncology, orthopedics, and diagnostics.

By the mid-2010s, Max Healthcare had become one of the top private hospital chains in India, but its footprint was still relatively concentrated in Delhi-NCR and Punjab. It faced increasing competition from national players like Apollo Hospitals and Fortis Healthcare, and its margins were under pressure due to inefficient operations, underutilized capacity, and high administrative costs. At the same time, the broader Indian hospital sector was experiencing consolidation, driven by rising demand, constrained public infrastructure, and interest from international investors and PE firms.

A key turning point came in 2018, when Radiant Life Care—a hospital platform backed by PE firm KKR—began discussions to merge with Max Healthcare. Radiant was smaller but operated two prominent tertiary care facilities: BLK Hospital in Delhi and Nanavati Hospital in Mumbai. While Max had broader reach, Radiant had stronger profitability and a PE sponsor with global experience in healthcare turnarounds. The proposed merger offered a path to create a scaled, pan-India network.

KKR Takes Control: Merger and Platform Creation In December 2018, KKR announced that it would acquire a controlling stake in Max Healthcare through a complex deal involving Radiant Life Care and the Max Group. As part of the transaction, KKR invested approximately $900 million and merged Radiant with Max Healthcare, resulting in a combined entity with more than 3,400 beds across 17 hospitals. Abhay Soi, who had led Radiant, became the chairman and managing director of the new Max Healthcare platform.

Through this structure, KKR and Soi effectively took over the business, holding operational control. Their thesis was to streamline operations, drive margin improvement, and prepare the platform for long-term scalability in India's fragmented hospital market.

The Turnaround: Margin Expansion and Operational Focus The transformation under KKR was rapid and decisive. The new management introduced hospital-level profit-and-loss responsibility, rationalized the vendor base, renegotiated procurement contracts, and implemented strict cost controls across staffing and support services. They also consolidated administrative functions and invested in data systems that allowed real-time visibility into hospital performance.

Crucially, the strategy focused not just on cost but also on improving operating metrics: increasing average revenue per occupied bed (ARPOB), reducing average length of stay (ALOS), and enhancing case mix by bringing in more complex, higher-value procedures.

These initiatives paid off. Between FY2019 and FY2022, Max Healthcare's EBITDA margin rose from 9.7 to over 27%, among the highest in the Indian hospital sector. Revenues grew at a compound annual rate of over 32%, and the business became consistently profitable—a rare feat in a sector often plagued by thin margins and regulatory uncertainty.

Max also benefitted from the COVID-19 pandemic, which boosted demand for critical care and diagnostics. But unlike many providers, Max used this period not just to ride the revenue wave but to invest in long-term clinical capacity, IT infrastructure, and strategic partnerships.

Clean Exit, Strong Returns By 2022, with the turnaround complete and financial performance stabilized, KKR began exiting the investment. In a secondary sale worth approximately INR 9,185 crore (around $1.1 billion), the firm sold its remaining 27.5% stake in Max Healthcare to a mix of institutional and retail investors through block trades on the Indian stock exchange.

This exit marked one of the most successful PE outcomes in Indian healthcare. From its initial $900 million investment, KKR reportedly generated a return of over 5×, making it a landmark case in platform-building and operational turnaround.

Post-exit, Max Healthcare remains listed on the Bombay Stock Exchange and continues to pursue expansion through brownfield development and tuck-in acquisitions, now with a reputation for disciplined execution and strong margins.

Lessons from the Max Healthcare Deal The Max Healthcare case demonstrates the potential of PE to drive operational excellence in healthcare delivery—a sector traditionally viewed as difficult to scale due to regulatory complexity, labor intensity, and localization of care. By combining KKR's capital and strategic expertise with Abhay Soi's leadership and hands-on execution, the investment turned a moderately performing provider into a national leader.

It also underscores the importance of timing and structure. Rather than buying a stake in a single operator, KKR effectively created a platform by merging two assets with complementary strengths. The result was not just cost savings but a reshaped corporate culture, a more integrated business model, and a strong value proposition for future growth—all achieved in under five years.

9.6.2.2 Case Study 2: Carlyle's Majority Acquisition of SeQuent in India: Public or Private? You should be aware of a few interesting aspects of the animal health industry. For example, there is a large diversity of animal species. When one works in human blood testing, there is only one species. There is a long list of complex tests, but everyone can use all these tests. In the animal world, it's very different. You have a series of tests for bovine, for instance, but then every species has its own specific test. This means the animal health industry sometimes operates on a smaller scale. The industry also has a strong dependence on veterinarians, who are the prescribers of these products.

In addition, it is important to note that there is a lot of information asymmetry in this industry, which makes it quite interesting for PE. You will find this asymmetry in many sectors, due to limited transparency—but compared to human healthcare, the animal healthcare industry is much less standardized in terms of data collection and reporting practices. PE investors like asymmetry because they can position themselves in such a way as to take advantage of it.

Some people say that animal health presents the best of both worlds because it has a need for R&D, relatively high regulatory barriers, and some intellectual property barriers, and it benefits a lot from local know-how and a need for local information availability. That makes it a typical example of a *"glocal"* business.

The market for animal health has become highly concentrated in recent years, with only a handful of dominant players shaping the global landscape. Currently, roughly five major companies stand out as absolute giants in the sector (Figure 9.7). Globally, fewer than 10 companies generate revenues approaching or exceeding one billion dollars. At the lower end of this spectrum is Sequent Scientific, which, with a turnover of $169 million, may still rank within the top 20 companies worldwide. This limited number of medium and smaller firms illustrates the high degree of consolidation in the industry. Having collaborated with many companies in the space, I continue to observe the recurring presence of the same well-established names.

Sequent Scientific, an Indian company, has notably rebranded its animal health division as Alivira. The remainder of Sequent's operations constitutes a contract research organization (CRO) network, with subsidiaries predominantly operating under the Alivira brand across multiple countries. Since 2017, Sequent has strategically focused exclusively on animal health, positioning itself as a pure-play entity within this specialization. This decision reflected the recognition that the human and animal

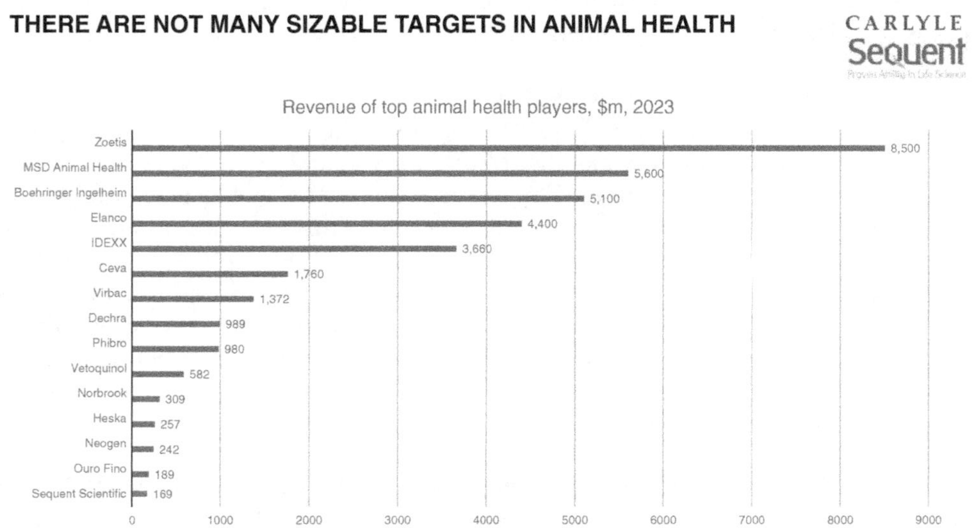

FIGURE 9.7 Revenue of top animal health players globally.
Source: Candesic research.

health businesses are fundamentally distinct and not synergistic—an insight shared by most pharmaceutical firms, many of which have divested their animal health units to enhance overall corporate value.

PE investors maintain a strong interest in cultivating a new leader within the animal health market. However, the majority of large animal health companies are publicly traded, making acquisitions challenging without taking these entities private. Such transactions are often prohibitive due to the high valuations driven by robust growth opportunities within the sector.

Consequently, PE investment opportunities remain limited. Sequent Scientific stands as a notable exception, where Carlyle negotiated the purchase of shares held by so-called promoters—the largest shareholders in Indian companies holding a specific status. Remarkably, Carlyle acquired a 74% stake at a price only about 7% above the trading share price. Regulatory requirements in India mandate that acquiring more than 25% ownership in a listed company triggers an open offer to purchase an additional 26% of shares from the public, which partially explains the deal structure. This acquisition exemplifies the creative approaches PE firms must deploy to invest in attractive yet difficult-to-access markets.

9.6.2.3 Practical Implications and Strategies Indian healthcare PE is entering a new phase of maturity, shaped by evolving market dynamics, regulatory shifts, and lessons from transformative deals. The sector remains highly fragmented, with around 70% of hospital beds in standalone facilities or small partnerships. This fragmentation creates inefficiencies, inconsistent quality, limited access to capital, and difficulty attracting and retaining talent. For PE, this represents a multi-decade opportunity for consolidation. The winners will be operators who integrate acquisitions into unified networks while preserving clinical standards and local relevance, as demonstrated by Max Healthcare and HCG.

At the same time, diagnostics and outpatient services are emerging as high-growth areas. Digital platforms, home testing, and advanced diagnostics are reshaping patient expectations, favoring scale operators that combine physical infrastructure with digital capabilities. Chains like Vijaya, Thyrocare, and SRL are capturing market share by offering convenience, technology-enabled care, and advanced testing. Outpatient and preventive care models—day-care surgery centers, dialysis, fertility clinics, physiotherapy, and primary care networks—offer attractive margins, rapid scalability, and meet rising demand for convenient access, complementing traditional hospital infrastructure.

Rising health consciousness, expanding insurance coverage, and the prevalence of chronic diseases are also driving interest in preventive, digital, and precision medicine. Genomics, AI-enabled diagnostics, and digital therapeutics remain nascent but carry transformative potential. Success in these areas requires patient capital, operational engagement, and integration with clinical practice rather than pure research plays.

Operating successfully in India demands long-term capital horizons, often extending well beyond typical PE cycles. Building hospital capacity, establishing clinical reputation, training staff, securing regulatory approvals, and developing referral networks all take years. Deals like CVC's investment in HCG highlight the importance of patience and long-term planning. Value creation is rarely achieved through financial engineering alone; operational improvements in procurement, technology, talent, and clinical workflows drive sustainable returns, as seen in KKR's Max Healthcare turnaround.

Clinical governance, quality, and ESG considerations are inseparable from financial performance. Strong clinical outcomes, patient safety, regulatory compliance, and accreditation build reputational and operational resilience. Environmental sustainability, social responsibility, and robust governance not only enhance reputation but also improve operational efficiency and community trust. Exceptional talent is critical: hospital administrators, laboratory leaders, pharma executives, and digital health specialists shape the success of investments. PE firms must invest in recruiting, developing, and retaining skilled leaders, and create organizational cultures that retain talent over time.

Many leading Indian healthcare businesses are family-owned or promoter-led, requiring partnerships built on trust, respect, and alignment of values. Founders bring credibility, local networks, and commitment, but their involvement necessitates sensitivity and careful governance structures that balance influence with professional oversight. Across subsectors, hospitals, diagnostics, pharmaceuticals, and digital health each demand unique approaches. Successful investors either specialize deeply in specific areas or build dedicated teams with sector expertise.

Practical strategies for PE include adopting extended fund horizons, prioritizing operational excellence, supporting consolidation with disciplined integration, and diversifying across higher-margin segments like diagnostics, outpatient services, and precision medicine. Proactive regulatory engagement is essential, as is developing proprietary deal sourcing and rigorous clinical due diligence. Effective exits often involve secondary sales, strategic partnerships, or recapitalizations rather than IPOs. ESG (or "impact") should be viewed as a genuine lever for value creation, encompassing environmental efficiency, social impact, and strong governance. Ultimately, the most successful healthcare investors treat their portfolio companies as enduring institutions, focusing on sustainable growth, clinical integrity, and meaningful patient impact rather than short-term financial gains. Those who combine patient capital with operational expertise, regulatory insight, and a commitment to improving healthcare delivery are best positioned to generate transformative impact and superior long-term returns.

9.6.3 Southeast Asia

Excluding South Korea, Southeast Asia's PE market is small, young, but dynamic and rapidly evolving, shaped by compelling demographics, economic growth, and increasing demand for high-quality healthcare. Singapore's prime minister reminds us that Singapore used to be called "the Balkans of Asia" for its historical instability. A very diverse and highly complex region, with numerous ethnicities, languages, religions, political and economic systems, Singapore has been able to maintain relative peace since the end of the Vietnam war. A lot of the credit goes to ASEAN.

The region recorded $20 billion in PE and VC deals in 2024, with a rebound in deal volume and transaction size expected as valuations adjust and investor optimism returns. Singapore continues to top the region as an investment destination, followed by Indonesia, Malaysia, Thailand, Vietnam, and the Philippines (Figure 9.8). In particular, while Vietnam has seen a flurry of activity in provider M&A as well as a growth in medtech and pharmaceuticals, Thailand remains strong in medical tourism, and Indonesia experiments with special economic zones attracting foreign players. Key sectors drawing PE attention include healthcare, digital and physical

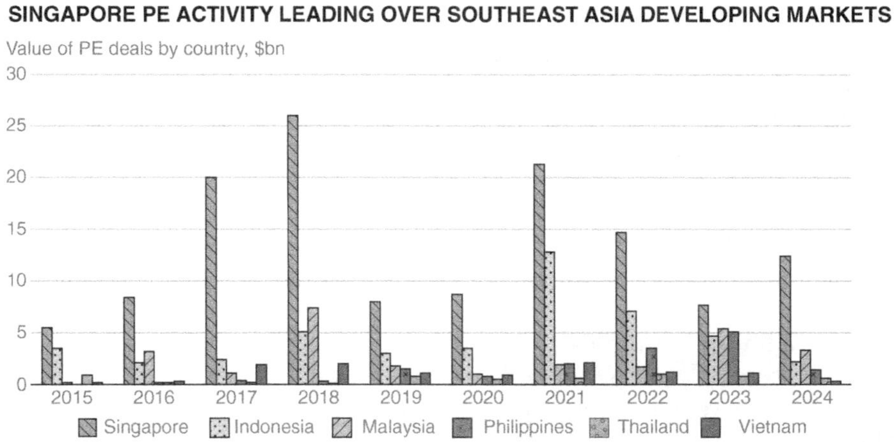

FIGURE 9.8 PE deals in value by country in Southeast Asia.
Source: Preqin (part of Blackrock)—South Korea not included.

infrastructure, and clean energy, as investors respond to the needs of a growing middle class, urbanization, and government support for foreign capital and public-private partnerships (PPPs).

9.6.3.1 Leading Southeast Asian PE Markets and Key Examples Singapore is the region's financial hub and a magnet for healthcare PE, with strong deal flow and successful exits. Indonesia and the Philippines are seeing increased PE activity, particularly in hospital and primary care expansion, while Malaysia, Thailand, and Vietnam attract their share of investment in both healthcare delivery and life sciences. Notable recent deals include the attempted 80% stake sale valued at about $3 billion in Metro Pacific Hospital Holdings, the largest private hospital operator in the Philippines. Global PE firms like Warburg Pincus, TPG and CVC were reported to compete in 2024. The same year, IHH Healthcare's $900 million acquisition of Island Hospital in Malaysia (see next section) and Mitsui's co-investment alongside Rohto Pharmaceutical in Singapore-based Eu Yan Sang International—in a deal valued about USD 600 million—underscore the scale and internationalization of healthcare PE in the region. Quadria Capital, one of Asia's leading healthcare-focused PE firms, is actively investing in Southeast Asia, with a $1.5 billion commitment across South and Southeast Asia, targeting hospitals, diagnostics, pharmaceuticals, and medical devices.

PE Segments and Institutional Coordination

- VC: Active in digital health, telemedicine, and healthtech, but remains a smaller segment compared to growth capital and buyouts
- Growth capital: The dominant PE segment, funding the expansion of hospital chains (e.g., Metro Pacific Hospitals), diagnostics, and scalable healthtech platforms
- Buyouts: Increasingly common in hospital and healthcare services consolidation, as seen in the Philippines and Malaysia
- Turnaround: Less frequent but emerging in underperforming hospital assets and supply chains, often with support from development finance institutions (DFIs)

DFIs such as the World Bank, Asian Development Bank, and multilateral funds play a significant role, providing patient capital and supporting PPPs to bridge infrastructure and access gaps. Governments are generally welcoming of foreign investment, with PPP models expanding in Indonesia, the Philippines, and Thailand to address public sector capacity constraints.

9.6.3.2 The Three Phases of PE in Southeast Asia

Fundraising Fundraising is supported by a mix of institutional investors, DFIs, pension funds, and family offices, with healthcare-focused funds like Quadria's third fund reaching a first close of $500 million in 2023, and more than $1 billion by 2025. However, fundraising is challenged by global market volatility, the "denominator effect," and a relatively shallow local LP base, especially outside Singapore. DFIs provide crucial patient capital and are more tolerant of longer holding periods and delayed distributions. Sovereign wealth funds have traditionally played an outsize role here—for example Singapore's GIC and Temasek allocated between 7% and 9% of their deal value in 2022–2023 to healthcare (Bortolotti et al., 2023). However, in recent years, regional and global PE funds like Quadria Capital and Warburg Pincus have increased their presence with significant deals.

Investing Due diligence in Southeast Asia is complicated by market fragmentation, inconsistent regulatory environments, and the lack of robust management information systems, especially outside Singapore and Malaysia. Many healthcare providers are concentrated in urban areas, leaving rural populations underserved and requiring PE investors to address infrastructure and talent shortages. PE firms often need to professionalize management, implement new governance structures, and invest in digitalization and operational upgrades to unlock value. A good example is provided by CVC Capital in medtech. CVC has been active in consolidating Southeast Asian medical technology suppliers since 2022, leveraging cross-border operations to improve supply chain resilience, regulatory compliance, and innovation diffusion. The focus on enhancing local manufacturing capabilities and distribution networks aligns with regional governments' healthcare self-sufficiency goals underscored by pandemic disruptions. CVC's investments enabled portfolio companies to achieve financial scale while fostering technology upgrades, particularly in critical care devices.

Case Study 1: Quadria Capital and Hermina Hospitals, Indonesia When Quadria invested in Hermina in 2020, it had 32 hospitals. By 2025, it had scaled to 51 hospitals across 36 cities and 17 provinces—a footprint unmatched in Indonesia. What makes this particularly powerful is that over 40% of its hospitals are in Tier II and Tier III cities,[3] areas often underserved by infrastructure and medical talent. Hermina became the only large hospital group with full accreditation under Indonesia's universal health insurance scheme, BPJS, enabling it to provide affordable care to millions of patients who previously had no access to specialist services. In 2025, around 78% of Hermina's 711,000 annual inpatient admissions and nearly three-quarters of its 8.8 million outpatient visits were covered under BPJS.

[3]While there is no single classification, Asian cities with populations >4 million as often considered Tier I, 1–4 million as Tier II, and 0.1–1 million as Tier III.

The company has also expanded its clinical excellence, launching new Centers of Excellence in oncology, cardiology, and emergency care, with pediatrics and urology on the way. This not only improves the quality of care available domestically but positions Hermina as a referral hub for higher-acuity cases. At the same time, Hermina has implemented a group-wide digitization program, integrating enterprise resource planning, hospital information systems, and electronic patient records. These digital investments had streamlined workflows, improved bed turnover, and lifted margins from 25% in 2023 to nearly 30% in 2024.

Abrar Mir added:

> *The impact goes beyond financial performance. Hermina has awarded 26 scholarships to promising healthcare professionals, created over 6,200 new jobs (with 85% held by women), and delivered nearly 1 million hours of staff training. It is also collaborating with the government on new schemes to expand coverage, while simultaneously reducing its environmental footprint—from cutting operational plastic waste by 40% to planting trees across 787,000 m^2 of green space.*

Hermina is a remarkable case study because it shows what makes Asian healthcare unique: a huge, underserved population, governments constrained by limited budgets, and the private sector stepping up to democratize access at scale. It is not just a hospital chain—it is proof that in Asia, financial success and social impact are mutually reinforcing.

Case Study 2: IHH Healthcare and Island Hospital, Malaysia IHH Healthcare's $900 million acquisition of Island Hospital, a 600-bed premium medical institution in Penang, Malaysia, in 2024, marked a strategic move to capture the lucrative medical tourism market and expand specialty care services. The deal, valued at approximately 24.6× EV/EBITDA, positioned IHH to build on Island Hospital's established reputation for high standards and patient care, with an eye toward expanding capacity via adjacent land with a potential additional 400 beds. The acquisition not only reflects Malaysia's growing healthcare infrastructure ambitions but also IHH's regional consolidation strategy to scale hospitals with premium offerings. Island Hospital's recent net profits and EBITDA growth underscore the success of blending operational excellence, location advantage, and strategic capacity expansion.

Case Study 3: Quadria Capital and Soho Pharmaceuticals, Indonesia The Indonesian pharmaceutical manufacturer Soho represented a distinct value creation opportunity in the country. Despite being a 60-year-old company with $300 million of revenue, the business remained domestically focused with limited innovation capacity. "With a $300 million revenue base, you can't put a billion dollars to work in innovating a single molecular drug," Managing Partner Abrar Mir observed.

Quadria's solution leveraged their network to secure drug licensing deals: "With our know-how, we'll bring you five or six new drugs through our relationships, through in-licensing that are going to be exclusive to you in Indonesia." This focused approach delivered exceptional results, bringing 26 new drugs and doubling revenue from $300 million to $600 million over five years, during the ownership period.

Exiting Exits remain a challenge, with public markets less favored due to volatility and past disappointments (e.g., Grab's SPAC lost 20% on first trading day after initially rising 21%, PropertyGuru did not curb losses after its NYSE listing and was ultimately acquired by EQT for $1.1 billion in December 2024, representing a 40% discount from its $1.8 billion listing valuation—still providing a reasonable exit for some investors). The infrastructure for traditional IPO exits remains weak, with Southeast Asia recording "no IPOs in 2024" according to Bain's analysis. Trade sales (80%) and secondary sales (15%) are the most common exit routes, with middle-market transactions dominating the landscape. Successful exits, such as the sale of Metro Pacific Hospital stakes, demonstrate the potential for strong returns.

Despite selective success stories and higher exit values in 2024, overall distributions to paid-in ratios remain constrained. Asian funds show distributions to paid-in ratios 15–25% lower than Western funds, and this liquidity challenge directly impacts fundraising. Managers face pressure to return capital but are hampered by limited public-market exit opportunities, as well as the "denominator effect," where falling public valuations inflate private-asset weights in LP portfolios, thereby throttling new PE fundraising.

9.6.3.3 How Healthcare Issues Differ in Southeast Asia Southeast Asia faces a dual burden of infectious diseases and rapidly rising noncommunicable diseases (NCDs) such as diabetes and obesity, alongside persistent challenges in maternal and child health. Public healthcare expenditure is low in many countries, with private out-of-pocket spending accounting for over half of total health expenditure in Indonesia, Vietnam, and the Philippines. Access to care is highly unequal, with rural and remote areas suffering from a lack of infrastructure, medical professionals, and affordable services. Medical inflation and cost escalation are major issues, and more than 80% of the population cannot afford advanced medical care. Private health insurance penetration is patchy and generally low (<10% in most countries). Governments are increasingly turning to the private sector and PPPs to fill these gaps, as seen in the Philippines' UP-PGH Cancer Center PPP and Thailand's new PPP hospital models. Many private healthcare providers in Southeast Asia remain family-owned or physician-founder led and are of particular interest as buyout targets.

MergerMarket reported in 2025 that Vietnam's healthcare sector showed strong growth potential beyond traditional corporate M&A, increasingly drawing PE interest across pharmaceuticals, hospitals, and clinics. Deal volume hit almost a billion dollars that year. Key investors like Warburg Pincus, CVC, GIC, and KKR were actively acquiring stakes, driven by rising private healthcare demand, an expanding middle class, and favorable regulatory reforms. Market fragmentation and new land restrictions further spur consolidation, with foreign investors encouraged to acquire majority stakes to fast-track growth and innovation.

9.6.3.4 Specificities of PE Phases in Healthcare and Life Sciences In healthcare and life sciences, PE fundraising is characterized by strong DFI and impact investor participation, with funds like Quadria Capital explicitly targeting scalable, market-leading businesses that deliver both financial returns and measurable social impact. Investing requires a hands-on approach: PE firms must often address weak management, insufficient digital infrastructure, and fragmented operations, especially when expanding hospital networks or scaling diagnostics and medtech businesses. For example, investments in Metro Pacific Hospitals and IHH Healthcare have focused on both operational excellence and expanding access to underserved populations. Due diligence is made more complex by inconsistent data quality and regulatory fragmentation, necessitating on-the-ground assessments and close collaboration with local stakeholders. Exiting healthcare investments typically relies on trade sales to strategic buyers or secondary sales to other PE funds, as public market exits remain limited outside Singapore. Successful exits require demonstrating operational improvements, scalability, and alignment with government health priorities, often after longer holding periods than in more developed markets.

Like India, Southeast Asia is seen as a group of dynamic, youthful, and reform-driven PE markets with international LP attention, while China is becoming more insular, mature, and volatile—though still very large. Put simply, China is big but cautious; SE Asia and India are smaller but growing fast and playing nicer with foreigners.

In summary, Southeast Asia's PE market in healthcare and life sciences is vibrant but challenging, driven by demographic forces, government openness to private capital, and a pressing need to bridge healthcare access and quality gaps. While Singapore, Malaysia, and the Philippines lead in deal activity and exits, the entire region is seeing increased PE interest, with funds like Quadria Capital and TVM Capital Healthcare at the forefront of transformational investments. Success in this market depends on the ability to navigate regulatory complexity, address operational deficits, and partner with governments and DFIs to deliver both financial returns and meaningful health outcomes.

9.6.3.5 Implications for Private Equity Operators in Southeast Asia Success in Southeast Asia healthcare PE requires adapting to the region's diversity and healthcare system complexity. Extended holding periods beyond typical PE time horizons are common to realize operational turnaround, scale, and quality improvements, particularly in hospital platforms and specialty care. The Metro Pacific deal exemplifies how global PE firms like KKR leverage capital and expertise to consolidate and strengthen fragmented hospital markets, improving clinical outcomes and capturing growing demand. Active operational engagement is critical. Investments in digital transformation, as seen in Hermina Hospitals, increase efficiency and margins while also expanding patient access via national insurance providers. Digital health platforms like Grab Health and Teladoc illustrate the increasing integration of technology to bridge urban-rural gaps and improve care delivery models.

Clinical quality governance and regulatory navigation are paramount, given uneven regulatory oversight. Investments in pharmaceutical manufacturing, exemplified by Soho Pharmaceuticals, show how patient capital combined with licensing partnerships fuels innovation in emerging markets constrained by policy complexities. Diversification across healthcare subsectors—hospitals, diagnostics, pharmaceuticals, digital health, and animal health—is essential. Firms must build specialized sector knowledge and networks to unlock value in these heterogeneous segments. ESG principles increasingly influence investment decisions, aligning financial returns with social impact—especially key in markets with significant healthcare access inequities.

Successful PE investment in Southeast Asia's healthcare market demands a tailored, nuanced approach that aligns with the region's economic, demographic, and structural realities. Firms must embrace a long-term capital horizon, often extending well beyond the conventional PE cycle, to allow investments in hospitals, diagnostics, digital health, and pharmaceuticals sufficient time to build scale, clinical excellence, and regulatory compliance. Rapid expansion without deep operational foundations risks value erosion in this complex environment.

Developing in-market operational capabilities is critical. Southeast Asia's fragmented healthcare infrastructure and diverse regulatory frameworks mean that strong local expertise—ranging from clinical governance and talent management to supply chain optimization and IT modernization—is vital to drive sustainable improvements in portfolio companies. Investors should build dedicated health sector operating teams or partner with regional specialists who understand country-specific challenges and nuances. Given rising competition and market maturation, active portfolio management centered on operational excellence is essential. This includes embedding robust clinical KPIs, enhancing physician engagement, and harnessing technology-driven care models to improve patient outcomes and experiences. The successful scaling of players like Hermina Hospitals underscores the value of combining digitalization with clinical innovation.

9.6.4 MENA

The MENA region's PE market is anchored by the Gulf states, especially Saudi Arabia (KSA) and the United Arab Emirates (UAE), and Egypt, with these countries accounting for the overwhelming majority of deal flow and capital deployment.

- KSA, driven by Vision 2030, is undergoing a historic privatization of its healthcare sector, with more than 290 hospitals and 2,300 health institutions transitioning to private operation, and a surge in digital health, pharmaceuticals, and insurance.
- The UAE continues to lead in digital health innovation, hospital consolidation, and cross-border healthcare investments.
- Egypt's large population, economic reforms, regulatory reforms, and new tax incentives have positioned it as a regional magnet for PE activity, particularly in hospital and pharmaceutical growth, particularly from Gulf sovereign wealth funds, and despite ongoing macroeconomic challenges. Regulatory enhancements, such as the shift to pre-merger approval and streamlined procedures, are making the environment more investor friendly.
- The rest of the Gulf, including Qatar, Oman, and Kuwait, is also experiencing increased PE activity, especially in hospital infrastructure and PPP models, although on a smaller scale than KSA and the UAE.
- Morocco, while a smaller and less liquid market, is emerging as a North African healthcare investment hub, with notable deals and successful exits, but its scale remains modest compared to the Gulf and Egypt.

9.6.4.1 Leading MENA PE Markets and Key Examples Saudi Arabia is the undisputed leader in healthcare PE, with the sector valued at $68.3 billion in 2025 and projected to more than double by 2034 according to Dimension Market Research. The Kingdom's market is characterized by large-scale privatization, a $1.5 billion telemedicine boom driven by digital health investments under the Vision 2030 agenda, and robust IPO activity, including Almoosa Health's $450 million listing in 2025. Major PE-backed expansions include Abeer Medical Company in 2021 and Sulaiman Al Habib Group in 2024, both supported by GII, as well as the Jada Fund of Funds' $250 million commitment to healthcare platforms in 2024.

The UAE's TVM Capital Healthcare Partners has pioneered investments in rehabilitation, long-term care, and digital health, with successful exits such as ProVita International Medical Center's sale to NMC Health in 2015 for approximately $160 million. Gulf Capital, another UAE-based PE firm, invested in the Middle East operations of IVI-RMA, the world's largest assisted reproduction group, by acquiring ART Fertility Clinics in January 2020 for more than $100 million. This acquisition was a corporate carve-out of IVI-RMA's Middle Eastern clinics. Under Gulf Capital's ownership, ART Fertility expanded from a UAE-focused business to a regional platform with 15 clinics across the UAE, Saudi Arabia, and India. The firm invested heavily in science, research, and infrastructure, launching a genetic testing lab in Abu Dhabi and achieving high IVF success rates. In 2025, Gulf Capital successfully exited its majority stake in ART Fertility Clinics' Middle East operations through a sale to KKR-backed IVI-RMA Global.

In Egypt, Alta Semper completed its exit from Macro Group Pharmaceuticals via a successful IPO in 2022, which is notable for demonstrating PE's ability to build scalable pharma/derma platforms in emerging markets and realize returns through public markets.

Egypt's Akdital Group, while based in Morocco, is illustrative of the region's cross-border appetite: under Mediterrania Capital Partners, Akdital expanded from 5 to 35 hospitals and achieved the largest IPO on the Casablanca Stock Exchange since 2008, delivering a 9× return for its PE backer after full exit in 2025. In Morocco itself, the private sector is growing. The market remains a fraction of the Gulf's size but has its success stories. In addition to Akdital, medtech distributor IM Alliance, initially developed by CIG, a local PE player, sold to Helios in 2021 and became part of the largest and most diversified medtech platform in Francophone Africa with revenues exceeding $100 million.

Creating a pan-MENA player—Development Partners International (DPI), a British PE investor, partnered with British International Investment (BII), and the EBRD to found Kelix Bio in 2020, with operational headquarters in Dubai.

Together with other DFIs and institutional investors, they invested more than $450 million to create and scale the first pan-MENA and pan-emerging-markets biopharmaceutical platform. Their capital funded strategic acquisitions in Egypt, Morocco, Malta, and India enabled rapid expansion into cross-market distribution and supported the development of new specialty generic drugs for more than 50 countries. The investors played a transformative role by mobilizing growth capital, institutional expertise, and supporting leadership to build out Kelix's integrated multinational manufacturing network, increasing revenues to well above $150 million.

In 2024, DPI, BII, and EBRD sold 100% of their shares in Kelix Bio to Mubadala Investment Company of Abu Dhabi in a landmark exit—the largest African pharma PE deal in two decades—at a price that remains undisclosed but was widely recognized for its scale and impact.

In terms of PE segments, VC in MENA is vibrant in healthtech and digital innovation, but most healthcare PE activity is concentrated in growth capital and buyouts. Growth capital dominates, funding the scaling of hospital networks, diagnostics, and digital health platforms—exemplified by the expansion of telemedicine in Saudi Arabia and the UAE. Buyouts are increasingly common in the Gulf and Egypt, where hospital consolidation and medtech roll-ups are underway. Turnaround investments are less frequent but are emerging in distressed pharma and underperforming hospitals, often with DFI support. Across the region, sovereign wealth funds (such as Saudi's PIF and Abu Dhabi's ADQ), development banks, and government initiatives play a central role in de-risking investments, providing blended finance, and driving PPPs to address infrastructure and service gaps. Charitable organizations and international aid, while less prominent than in sub-Saharan Africa, support capacity building and public health initiatives, especially in Egypt and Morocco.

9.6.4.2 The Three Phases of PE in MENA Fundraising in the Gulf and Egypt is buoyed by sovereign wealth funds, a growing local investor base, and strong government support for healthcare privatization and digitalization. In Morocco, fundraising is more challenging, with a smaller pool of institutional investors and greater reliance on international DFIs and specialized Africa-focused funds. Investing in the region is shaped by the need for rigorous due diligence, yet challenges persist—especially outside the Gulf—in the form of limited management information systems, fragmented data, and regulatory complexity. PE firms often need to implement new governance, budget, and reporting systems post-investment, as seen in Akdital's transformation in Morocco. Exiting is increasingly feasible in the Gulf and Egypt, with active IPO markets, trade sales to multinationals, and secondary PE deals. In Morocco, successful exits like Akdital's IPO are still the exception rather than the rule, with most exits occurring through trade sales or gradual buybacks.

9.6.4.3 How Healthcare Issues Differ in MENA MENA's healthcare landscape is marked by rapid population growth, high rates of NCDs (especially diabetes and cardiovascular conditions), and persistent gaps in infrastructure. As reported by the Praxis Global Alliance in 2025, Saudi Arabia faces an urgent need for 84,000 new hospital beds by 2030, while the UAE and Qatar are investing heavily in digital health and hospital capacity. Insurance reforms in Saudi Arabia and Egypt are expanding coverage and creating new demand for private healthcare. Talent shortages are significant, with the Gulf relying heavily on expatriate medical professionals, while Egypt and Morocco face challenges in retaining skilled staff. Regulatory complexity persists, but the Gulf states are streamlining processes to attract foreign capital, and Morocco is modernizing its legal and compliance frameworks to facilitate PE investment.

9.6.4.4 Specificities of PE Phases in Healthcare and Life Sciences In healthcare and life sciences, PE fundraising in the Gulf and Egypt is characterized by the strong presence of sovereign and government-linked funds, which provide both capital and credibility to new investments. In Morocco, PE funds must often blend DFI, international, and local capital, with a focus on demonstrating both financial returns and measurable improvements in healthcare access and quality. Investing in the region's healthcare sector demands a hands-on approach: PE firms are frequently required to address operational inefficiencies, upgrade management teams, and implement robust information systems. This is especially true in Morocco, where Akdital's partnership with Mediterrania Capital Partners resulted in a tripling of bed capacity, major job creation, and the professionalization of governance and budgeting processes. Due diligence is often more complex outside the Gulf, requiring on-the-ground assessments and close collaboration with local stakeholders to overcome data and infrastructure gaps. Exiting healthcare investments is increasingly viable in the Gulf and Egypt, where IPOs and trade sales are more common, while in Morocco, success stories like Akdital's IPO are still rare but signal growing maturity. Across the region, longer holding periods are typical, especially where operational transformation and alignment with national health priorities are required to realize full value.

9.6.4.5 Implications for PE Operators in MENA Success in developing the MENA healthcare PE sector hinges on leveraging public-sector reform momentum and the region's growing digital health ecosystem. With substantial privatization underway in Saudi Arabia and supportive regulatory reforms in Egypt, PE firms can capitalize on expanding hospital networks, telemedicine adoption, and insurance market growth. The UAE's push into specialty care and rehabilitation, alongside Morocco's emerging private healthcare market, offer complementary opportunities for regional diversification. However, investors must navigate complexities such as fragmented data, talent shortages, and regulatory variance while building operational capabilities post-investment to unlock long-term value. This phased, hands-on approach is key to capturing growth in MENA's rapidly evolving healthcare landscape.

In summary, while Saudi Arabia, the UAE, Egypt, and the wider Gulf dominate the MENA region's PE landscape in healthcare and life sciences—with deep capital pools, ambitious reform agendas, and active exit markets—Morocco is emerging as a dynamic but smaller player, offering compelling case studies in hospital expansion and successful PE exits, yet still facing scale and liquidity constraints relative to the larger economies in the region.

9.6.5 Sub-Saharan Africa

PE in sub-Saharan Africa is predominantly growth-oriented, shaped by demographic expansion, rising consumer demand, and significant infrastructure gaps. DFIs such as the African Development Bank and International Finance Corporation provide a substantial share of capital, often through blended finance models that combine public, private, and philanthropic resources. While consumer goods, fintech, and energy attract considerable investment, healthcare and life sciences are increasingly recognized as high-impact sectors, offering both strong financial returns and measurable social outcomes. However, investors must navigate challenges ranging from currency volatility and political instability to fragmented markets and regulatory uncertainty.

9.6.5.1 Leading SSA PE Markets and Key Examples South Africa stands out as the region's most advanced PE market, with a robust financial ecosystem and regulatory framework. It is home to initiatives such as Bioventures, the first life sciences-focused VC fund in sub-Saharan Africa, launched in 2000, which has backed medical technology innovators like Disa Vascular.

Nigeria has seen growth capital support integrated healthcare providers such as Hygeia Limited in 2016, AfyA Care in 2022 and the transformation of Lagoon Hospitals by Iwosan Investments from 2021.

Kenya has emerged as a hub for digital health innovation, with PE-backed Lapaire Glasses expanding affordable eye care across six countries and MYDAWA securing a $20 million growth investment from Alta Semper in 2023, marking a flagship regional expansion in digital primary care and e-pharmacy.

Ghana is gaining prominence due to regulatory reforms and projects such as mPharma, which raised $35 million in 2022 and is transforming pharmaceutical supply chains to systematically address medication distribution and affordability across Africa. These markets benefit from urbanization, a growing middle class, and strong partnerships with DFIs, but they still face significant obstacles, including talent shortages and infrastructure deficits.

9.6.5.2 PE Segments and Institutional Coordination VC is a major driver of early-stage innovation in sub-Saharan Africa, accounting for a majority of deal volume but facing funding slowdowns in recent years. VC is especially active in digital health and healthtech, though it is challenged by small ticket sizes and long development cycles. Growth capital remains the dominant PE segment, targeting scalable business models such as Africa Healthcare Network, the largest provider of dialysis services in the region, often with DFI backing. Buyouts are less common due to the fragmented nature of the market but are starting to emerge in hospital consolidation, as seen with South Africa's Life Healthcare. Turnaround investments are typically applied to distressed assets, such as supply chain rehabilitation, and often involve partnerships with NGOs or public health organizations. Development banks and philanthropic organizations play a critical role in de-risking investments, providing guarantees, and funding pilot projects. The Transform Health Fund, a $111 million blended finance initiative, exemplifies how public and private capital can be coordinated to scale health enterprises in SSA.

9.6.5.3 The Three Phases of PE in Sub-Saharan Africa As mentioned, fundraising in sub-Saharan Africa relies heavily on DFIs, but also on impact-focused LPs, with first-time fund managers—such as Bioventures—targeting niche areas like biotech but often struggling to balance financial and social returns. The fundraising environment is complicated by currency risks, a limited local investor base, and geopolitical instability. The investing phase is marked by significant due diligence challenges, as reliable data and management information systems are often lacking. In healthcare, for example, the vast majority of providers do not have digitized records, forcing PE firms to conduct manual audits and rely on fragmented information. Operational improvements are a central focus, with PE investors working to professionalize management, strengthen governance, and upgrade systems. Companies like Insta Products, which produces therapeutic foods, have expanded regionally after receiving operational and strategic support from PE backers. Capital and strategic backing allowed Insta Products to become the largest manufacturer of therapeutic foods in East Africa and a top five global UNICEF supplier, enabling it to distribute lifesaving nutrition to drought-affected regions in Kenya, Somalia, South Sudan, and Uganda.

LeapFrog's investment in Goodlife was a bold bet not just on formalizing East Africa's fragmented pharmacy market, but on recognizing that pharmacies are the true front line of healthcare in these markets, where up to 90% of care is paid for out of pocket. It paid off handsomely, with broad sector transformation and tidy returns for everyone not allergic to profit or a good case study.

Goodlife's appeal to PE was clear. Back in 2016, the sector was highly fragmented, predominantly informal, and plagued by substandard or counterfeit drugs. There was a gap for a trusted, branded chain offering quality and access and a chance to strengthen healthcare systems at scale. The thesis was asset-light retail expansion built on a deep understanding of consumer needs.

LeapFrog began by truly studying the market, then designing products and formats to fit it. They developed four distinct store models, each tailored to its location, local demographics, and ability to pay. Every SKU and every service offering was curated for that setting. When customers walked in, they wanted every need met. If they didn't have a prescription, telemedicine gave them one. Once that ecosystem worked, they created a brand that felt familiar, not intimidating or overly polished, but just right for each community.

Access was everything. Some formats were compact container pharmacies, small but perfectly suited to reach underserved areas. On the supply side, they streamlined procurement and distribution, cutting out layers of middlemen that had inflated prices three to five times over. That not only reduced costs but safeguarded integrity and eliminated substandard drugs.

LeapFrog built Goodlife as a one-stop shop for health, integrating retail, diagnostics, and telemedicine under one roof. They didn't just fund the vision. They led on governance, recruited an entirely new leadership team, implemented a rigorous environmental and social framework, and developed the concept of community health hubs.

The outcomes were dramatic, even by impact funds' standards. Store count grew from 19 to nearly 150, reaching more than 3 million customers annually by 2025. Emerging consumers served rose from 400,000 to 1.5 million. Quality standards were enforced through rigorous supplier checks and only sourcing from compliant manufacturers.

The innovation they brought also helped address the ability to pay. They partnered with Safaricom on M-Pesa credit products and worked with several of the top insurance companies to introduce insurance coverage so that people could still afford their medications even when they didn't have cash on hand. Along the way, they used various forms of catalytic capital, including DFI debt, which accelerated their expansion. Two years before exit, LeapFrog brought in CFAO with a partial payout, allowing them to learn the business and prepare for a smooth full acquisition in 2025, the largest PE-led pharmacy exit in sub-Saharan Africa. Financial returns were positive, but perhaps more impressive is the sectoral wake—formal retail chains are now recognized as the backbone for safe, affordable care in the region.

As Dr. Felix Olale, who led the Goodlife investment for LeapFrog, explains: "You shouldn't be afraid to get operationally involved. In emerging markets, value creation happens on the ground—in the systems, people, and execution. At the outset, build for the right exit path and align on return expectations early. That's what creates both commercial success and lasting impact."

Exits in sub-Saharan Africa are dominated by trade sales, with multinational companies acquiring scaled healthcare businesses. Secondary sales—particularly PE-to-PE transactions—are becoming more common, especially in digital health, while IPOs remain rare due to the limited liquidity of local capital markets, with South Africa being a notable exception.

9.6.5.4 Healthcare Challenges Specific to Sub-Saharan Africa Sub-Saharan Africa faces a unique set of healthcare challenges. The region bears a disproportionate share of the global disease burden, accounting for 20% of worldwide illness and 94% of malaria deaths. Infrastructure is severely lacking, with fewer than five ICU beds per 100,000 people—compared to more than 30 in Europe—and more than 80% of the population lacking access to basic medical services. Talent shortages are acute, particularly in rural areas, and there is a persistent brain drain, as seen in Nigeria where a majority of doctors emigrate. Regulatory fragmentation further complicates the landscape, with inconsistent drug approval processes and underfunded agencies slowing the distribution of essential medicines. Financial barriers are also significant, with half of all health spending coming out-of-pocket, pushing millions into poverty each year.

A partner at LeapFrog shared his recommendations to other PE investors in African healthcare:

> *Don't fear sector formalisation, provided the right operational support and digital backbone are in place. Value comes not just from scale but from building trust and standards in a market prone to informality and risk. Healthcare in Africa isn't just about clinics and hospitals; retail infrastructure is a lever for both financial and development gains—if managed with discipline and a dash of courage.*

Specificities of PE Phases in Healthcare and Life Sciences The PE process in healthcare and life sciences in sub-Saharan Africa is shaped by a need for blended finance, patient capital, and a strong focus on impact. Fundraising for healthcare PE funds often involves a mix of development finance, philanthropic contributions, and private investment, with a particular emphasis on attracting LPs who value both financial returns and measurable outcomes such as patient reach or improvements in health infrastructure.

Investing in this sector requires a hands-on approach, as PE firms frequently encounter companies with underdeveloped management teams, weak governance, and a lack of reliable management information systems. Due diligence is therefore more complex and time-consuming, often necessitating on-the-ground assessments and close collaboration with local stakeholders. Once invested, PE firms typically prioritize operational improvements, professionalizing management, implementing robust information systems, and expanding access to care. For example, Lapaire Glasses has leveraged PE support to scale its affordable eye care model across multiple countries, while Africa Healthcare Network has expanded its dialysis services through strategic partnerships and operational upgrades.

Exiting investments in healthcare and life sciences also presents unique challenges. Trade sales to strategic buyers, such as multinational healthcare companies, are the most common exit route, but secondary sales to larger PE funds are becoming more frequent as the sector matures. IPOs are rare due to the illiquidity of most local stock exchanges, with South Africa being a partial exception. Overall, the PE life cycle in healthcare and life sciences in sub-Saharan Africa requires longer holding periods, adaptive strategies to mitigate local risks, and close coordination with governments and NGOs to align with broader public health and universal coverage goals.

This overview highlights how PE in sub-Saharan Africa, particularly in healthcare and life sciences, must navigate a complex and challenging environment. Success depends on innovative financing, operational rigor, and partnerships that bridge the gap between commercial returns and transformative social impact.

9.6.6 Latin America

Latin America's PE landscape is diverse and dynamic, not a monolithic market. The region's economies vary greatly in size, governance, and maturity. Although many countries share cultural ties, differences in regulation, politics, and market structure mean that PE performance can differ sharply by country. In general, Brazil, Mexico and Colombia have been the most active PE markets (together accounting for roughly 90% of regional healthcare PE deal volume in 2015–2024), while smaller markets like Chile, Peru, or Central American countries have seen far fewer deals. Brazil's large economy and population give it scale, Mexico's proximity to the United States and manufacturing base make it attractive, and Colombia's recent reforms and stability have drawn investors. In contrast, countries like Argentina or Guatemala remain more volatile or opaque, limiting interest despite occasional high-return opportunities.

As shown in Figure 9.9, Latin America's largest PE deals (2015–2024) were dominated by Brazilian companies.

Healthcare and life sciences PE deals account for 5–15% of all deals (average 10%), in line with the proportion of GDP. Similarly, veteran pan-Latin American PE firm Southern Cross, founded 1998, invested in 33 platform companies over 25 years (only 6 operate in Brazil), of which 4 where in healthcare, social care, and life sciences.

Brazil's deals have historically dominated regional PE activity in deal count too, in healthcare as across sectors (Figure 9.10). This reflects Brazil's market scale and sectoral

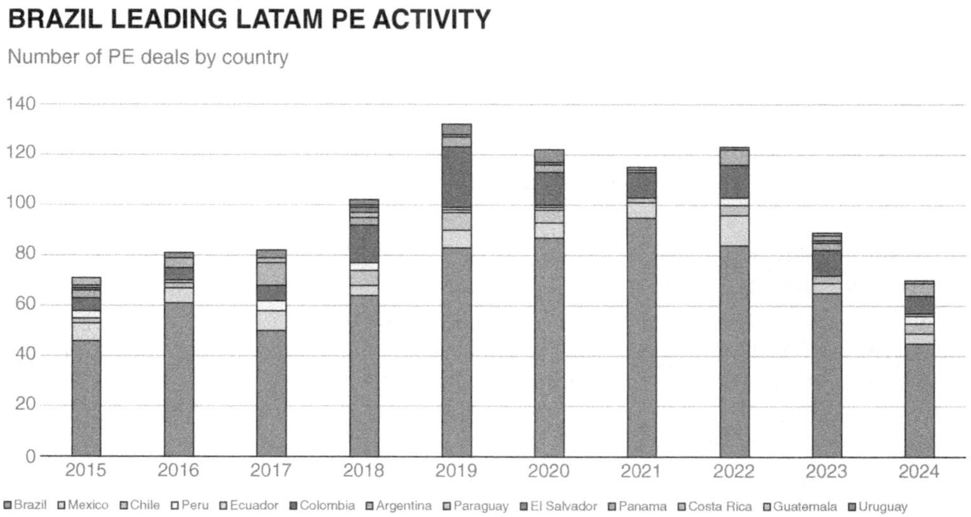

FIGURE 9.9 Number of PE deals by country in Latin America.
Source: MergerMarket.

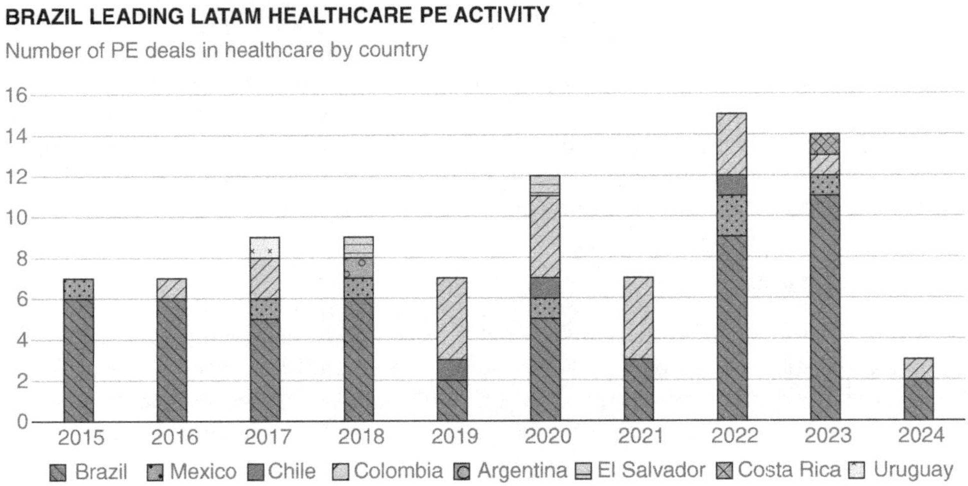

FIGURE 9.10 Number of PE deals in healthcare by country in Latin America.
Source: MergerMarket.

diversity, but it also brings challenges. Brazil's economy grew steadily in the 2010s and attracted many PE firms, yet investors have often struggled with complex exit routes and economic volatility. For example, Brazil's largest hospital chain, Rede D'Or, was backed by global PE (Carlyle) and achieved a successful public exit in 2020 at a $22 billion valuation, demonstrating the potential for large-scale healthcare exits in the region. At the same time, macroeconomic and regulatory uncertainty (high inflation, currency swings, policy shifts) have frequently weighed on deal sizes and timing.

9.6.6.1 Brazil: Scale with Complexity Brazil is by far the largest and most mature PE market in Latin America. Its population (more than 200 million) and middle class mean strong domestic demand for health and life-science products. Local capital markets are deeper, and many large Brazilian PE funds and family offices have been active for decades. This has led to a surge of deals (Brazil has accounted for about 60% of Latin America PE deals in 2015–2024) but also to tough competition. Bain notes that Brazilian PE investors must often target "insulated" sectors (healthcare, education, agribusiness) to hedge against economic swings. Investors cite difficulties in finding suitable exit paths, since IPOs and strategic buyers can be unpredictable. In healthcare specifically, Brazil's universal SUS public system coexists with a large private market (private insurance covers ~25% of population). PE interest has focused on consolidating private providers: hospital chains, clinical laboratories, and diagnostic networks. Beyond the prominent example of Rede D'Or's consolidation and IPO, the sector has seen significant activity in diagnostic lab networks and specialized provider chains.

Major hospital and clinic consolidations have attracted substantial PE investment. The success of Rede D'Or's public exit has inspired similar consolidation strategies across the sector.

PE firms have also invested in large lab networks and specialty clinics. Brazil's sizeable pharmaceutical industry (especially generics) and growing medtech manufacturing (though still limited) also attract deals. However, investors must navigate stringent regulation (ANVISA approvals can be lengthy) and local bureaucracy and be prepared for inflation and currency risk.

Diagnostic lab chains and consolidated clinic networks (dental, ophthalmology, etc.) are other targets. PE investors work to professionalize management, upgrade equipment, and standardize operations across outlets.

9.6.6.2 Mexico: Growth and Fragmentation Mexico has seen fast PE growth, though its deal share remains much smaller (around 10% of regional deals). Its advantages include proximity to the United States, strong manufacturing and fintech sectors, and trade integration (USMCA). Mexican PE deals have concentrated in consumer, industrial, tech and increasingly healthcare services. The growing middle class and rising health spending encourage private hospital chains, specialty clinics and diagnostics to expand. However, Mexico's healthcare system is highly fragmented. Public coverage is split among multiple schemes: IMSS (social security for private employees), ISSSTE (for public workers), and what was Seguro Popular/INSABI for the uninsured. Around half the population are covered by government programs, and less than 10% have private insurance. At the same time, the private sector (self-pay clinics, insurance) accounts for more than 50% of total health spending. For PE investors, this means navigating multiple regulators (e.g., COFEPRIS drug approvals) and co-pay systems. Security concerns, shifting policies, and bureaucratic delays also affect deal timelines. Nevertheless, Mexico's stable rule of law and opening reforms have made it attractive; PE funds have achieved notable success, exemplified by General Atlantic's $160 million investment in MAC Hospitals in 2023, Mexico's second-largest hospital chain by volume, which focuses on affordable private medical services across 17 cities in underserved markets, though hospital investments remain more fragmented.

PE firms have invested in chains of outpatient facilities (e.g., imaging centers, dialysis clinics) and smaller hospital groups, especially in major cities. Regulatory complexity is a challenge—deals often face long approval processes and require local legal expertise. The overall environment favors investors with strong local partnerships and knowledge of the multi-tier system.

9.6.6.3 Colombia and Other Andean Markets Colombia (22% of deals) and its neighbors Chile and Peru have smaller but growing PE markets. Colombia has become particularly attractive due to its recent peace dividend, improving infrastructure, and pro-investment policies. More than 95% of Colombians now have health coverage through Law 100 (a contributory regime for formal workers and a subsidized regime for the poor), creating near-universal insurance and growing demand for private care. However, the sector faces significant regulatory turbulence. In 2024, the government assumed administrative control of major EPS health insurers including Sanitas EPS (owned by Keralty, Colombia's second largest with 6 million members) and Nueva EPS (the largest with 10 million members), reflecting systemic financial pressures and policy reforms under President Petro's administration. PE funds have financed expansions of private clinics, imaging centers and laboratory chains, often focusing on major cities. Growth has also come in infrastructure (hospital construction) and health-focused service providers. Chile's economy is highly stable and transparent, with a robust private pension system that invests in PE. Its healthcare sector (ISAPRE insurance and private providers) has seen some consolidation by PE, though the market is relatively small. Peru's PE market benefits from firms like Linzor Capital Partners, which has raised more than $1.4 billion since 2006 and maintains active healthcare investments across the region, including recent successful exits in adjacent infrastructure sectors that support healthcare digitization.

Investors in Colombia, Chile and Peru have backed clinic networks and specialty-care providers, though regulatory complexity varies significantly. Colombia's current healthcare system interventions create both risks and opportunities for PE investors, while Chile and Peru offer more stable regulatory environments with strong institutional frameworks supporting private investment. These markets benefit from stronger institutions and, in Chile's case, deep capital pools (pension funds), but face limited domestic exit options. Colombia's blend of regulated insurance and private provision means PE deals often involve public-private contracts or enabling new services for insured patients. Argentina, by contrast, has seen only opportunistic PE deals. Its turbulent economy and policy shifts keep many international investors on the sidelines, so any healthcare deals there are usually small, local carve-outs.

9.6.6.4 Common Challenges in Healthcare PE Across Latin America, PE investors in healthcare and life sciences face familiar hurdles:

- **Regulatory complexity:** Each country has its own health regulators and frequent rule changes. Approvals for new drugs, devices, or facility upgrades can be slow and opaque. Funds must budget extra time for compliance (e.g., multi-year drug registration by ANVISA in Brazil, or multiple state/national permits in Mexico).
- **Bureaucracy and red tape:** Setting up hospitals or medical device plants involves many licenses. Delays and inconsistent enforcement raise costs.
- **Macro and political volatility:** Inflation, currency swings, and politics hit all PE sectors. Healthcare can be sensitive because prices and reimbursement (public tariffs or insurance rates) are often regulated, so devaluations rapidly erode local currency margins.
- **Market fragmentation and informal payments:** Many systems still rely on out-of-pocket payments or supplemental insurance. Understanding patient payment behavior and how doctors refer patients is crucial. Local practice patterns (e.g., preference for face-to-face medicine, or reliance on smaller doctors' networks) can limit uptake of new technologies or services.
- **Infrastructure gaps:** Outside major urban centers, roads, internet, and logistics are weaker. This can hinder expansions (e.g., telemedicine or remote clinics in rural areas) and increase costs.

Despite these challenges, Latin America's fast-growing middle class and underserved markets continue to attract PE. Investors who combine international best practices with local know-how and take a long view often find success.

9.6.6.5 PE Investment Areas: Healthcare and Life Sciences Private capital is increasingly present in Latin American healthcare and life sciences. Broadly, funds target two categories:

- **Health and Social Care:** PE-backed health services are expanding across the region through diverse consolidation and growth strategies. In Brazil, beyond the successful Rede D'Or hospital chain consolidation and IPO, PE firms have targeted diagnostic lab networks, dental clinic chains, and specialized provider networks across multiple therapeutic areas. In Mexico, General Atlantic's \$160 million investment in MAC Hospitals in 2023 exemplifies the sector's appeal—supporting expansion of Mexico's second-largest hospital chain by

volume across 17 cities, focusing on affordable private medical services in underserved markets. Colombia presents a complex regulatory environment, with private health insurers (EPS) like Keralty's Sanitas facing government intervention in 2024, though Keralty itself continues expanding internationally, including a joint $120 million investment with AXA to build 50 medical centers in Mexico. Chile's stable private insurance system (ISAPREs) supports investments in clinics, surgical centers, and telemedicine providers. Peru has attracted specialized growth capital through firms like Linzor Capital Partners, which has successfully executed infrastructure deals (such as WIN Internet's fiber network serving more than 527,000 clients) that support healthcare digitization and rural connectivity. Even Argentina has seen some PE investment in niche services (often smaller hospital groups or tech-driven healthcare startups), though volume is low. Social care (e.g., elder care facilities meeting international standards) is a very nascent but emerging theme across countries.
- **Life Sciences (Pharma and Medtech):** The region's biotechnology sector has gained significant momentum, with biotech ranking among Latin America's top 10 tech verticals by deal volume and more than 1,200 healthtech startups emerging regionally. Brazil alone attracted more than $650 million in digital health funding by 2022, with biotech investments increasing by 60% over the past decade. Many medium-sized pharma companies are family controlled; PE has entered via buyouts or growth investments aimed at consolidation, professionalization, and export expansion. Distribution networks and CROs have also attracted investment, as regional R&D and clinical trials grow. In medical devices, most local activity is distribution of imports. A notable exception is Costa Rica, which has become a regional hub for medical device manufacturing (attracting FDI and specialized funds), along with smaller device factories in Mexico and Brazil. Success stories like NotCo and Bioceres (each valued at more than $500 million), and recent acquisitions such as Neoprospecta by bioMérieux, demonstrate the sector's growing international recognition. PE deals often target device distributors or producers with niche expertise. Specialized biotech-focused venture capital firms, such as SP Ventures and Kaszek Ventures in Brazil, and emerging funds across the region, are providing crucial early stage financial support to companies developing everything from agricultural biotech to precision medicine solutions. Overall, health and life-science companies in Latin America remain largely family owned. PE transactions usually involve buying a stake and working with the owners on succession planning, governance, and aggressive growth (often via add-on acquisitions or expansion into other countries).

9.6.6.6 Key Lessons for Healthcare PE Experience to date (pre-2025) suggests a few **general lessons** for Latin America healthcare investors:

- **Local expertise is essential:** Every successful deal has deep local management and advisors. Understanding the health system's nuances, as well as having relationships with regulators and doctors, is nonnegotiable.
- **Value creation focus:** Funds must bring more than capital. Improving clinical operations, IT systems, and corporate governance (often weak in family firms) is critical to drive growth and exit value.

- **Currency and macro risk management:** Inflation and devaluation are constant threats. Useful strategies include pricing in local currency where possible, matching revenues and costs, and judicious use of local-currency financing.
- **Patient, long-term approach:** Returns may take longer than in developed markets. Flexibility is required as regulations or politics shift. Investors often plan for longer holding periods or build in contingencies.
- **ESG and social impact:** Healthcare PE is under scrutiny for patient outcomes and equity. Funds are increasingly integrating ESG: improving patient care standards, fair pricing, and governance transparency. Strong ESG practices (e.g., quality accreditation, broad access strategies) can actually enhance returns and exit options in this sector.

9.6.6.7 Outlook Looking ahead into 2030, the prospects for PE in Latin American healthcare remain a mix of opportunity and caution.

On the plus side, underlying growth drivers are strong. Latin America's population is aging, and its middle class is expanding, raising demand for medical services and pharmaceuticals. Many countries still spend well below the WHO-recommended levels (PAHO suggests ~6% of GDP on health, yet only a few like Cuba or Uruguay reach that), implying room for increased private investment. Digital health continues to expand rapidly: biotech now ranks among Latin America's top 10 tech verticals by deal volume, with more than 1,200 healthtech startups emerging regionally and Brazil alone seeing over $650 million of digital health funding in 2022. Telemedicine and wellness services are widely embraced post-COVID (e.g., 86% of Uruguay's early COVID-19 cases were managed via telehealth). These trends play to PE's strengths in scaling tech-enabled healthcare models.

Several themes will likely draw continued PE interest: consolidation of fragmented provider markets (hospitals, clinics, labs, diagnostics, dental chains), growth of specialized facilities (e.g., high-end oncology centers, imaging centers), expansion of pharma manufacturing (generics and specialty drugs), and digital health platforms (telemedicine, e-records, health-insurance tech). Life-science manufacturing (pharma and devices) may also attract funds looking to export to other LatAm markets.

A special consideration should be given to frugal innovation, particularly in Brazil, which alongside India has played a significant role in democratizing access to essential services such as mobile telephony and blood testing. This has been achieved through the development of scalable infrastructure and digital platforms tailored to the needs of emerging and developing markets. In healthcare, Brazil's large population and resource constraints have fostered the creation of cost-effective, high-impact solutions—ranging from low-cost diagnostics to telehealth models—that not only improve access and efficiency domestically but also have the potential to inspire or be exported to developed healthcare systems seeking greater value and sustainability.

As demonstrated by the broader regional innovation ecosystem, with success stories like NotCo and Bioceres achieving $500 million+ valuations and the emergence of specialized biotech venture funds across multiple countries, frugal innovation is not merely about cost-cutting; it involves rethinking processes, products, and delivery models to achieve more with less, often leveraging digital technology and local ingenuity. For PE investors, Latin America represents fertile ground for scaling these innovations regionally and, increasingly, transferring proven models to more mature markets facing their own cost and access challenges.

However, significant hurdles remain. Macroeconomic volatility (high inflation, volatile exchange rates) and political instability may persist in countries like Argentina (although, surprisingly, Argentina may finally get its act together), and occasionally in larger markets too. Regulatory environments can shift dramatically, as demonstrated by Colombia's 2024 interventions in its EPS health insurance system, affecting major players like Keralty/Sanitas and creating new uncertainties for private healthcare investors. Global cost pressures or trade policies (e.g., shifting US tariffs or supply chains) can affect Latin firms. Overall risk factors—uncertain exit markets, currency risk, and governance issues—will keep some capital on the sidelines.

Country-specific outlooks diverge: Brazil and Mexico should continue to capture the lion's share of PE capital due to sheer size, despite inherent complexities. Colombia faces near-term regulatory uncertainty following healthcare system interventions, though its underlying market fundamentals remain attractive for patient capital. Chile and Peru will likely be seen as relatively lower-risk, moderate-growth markets (offering "balanced" risk-reward) with their more stable macro environment. Argentina will remain a market for opportunistic or domestic investors willing to shoulder high risk in pursuit of large returns. Costa Rica is expected to continue leveraging its strong life-sciences manufacturing base (especially medical devices) to attract specialized growth investment.

In conclusion, Latin America's healthcare sector offers significant long-term potential for PE, driven by demographic and structural trends, but success depends on skillfully navigating local realities. Funds that blend international best practices (efficient operations, digital tools, strong governance) with deep local insight—as demonstrated by successful regional players like Linzor Capital Partners and international investors like General Atlantic—are most likely to thrive. Achieving sustainable growth will also require attention to ESG—ensuring that investment translates into better patient care and accessible services—which increasingly shapes both investor decisions and public policy in the region.

9.6.7 Central and Eastern Europe

Central and Eastern Europe (CEE), for the purposes of this analysis, encompass a diverse group of countries, including the Visegrád nations (Poland, Czech Republic, Slovakia, Hungary), the Baltic states (Estonia, Latvia, Lithuania), Southeastern European countries such as Romania and Bulgaria, and other nations in the Balkan region. Historically, Russia had been a significant market in the broader Eastern European context; however, by the early 2020s, geopolitical shifts and ensuing sanctions effectively removed it as a viable option for most international PE firms.

Milan Kulich, director and head of CEE at Advent International:

> *The CEE region is great. There are many good companies driven by people with a "can-do" attitude and we are keen to keep investing in these assets. Similarly to the broader European region, there have been fewer exits for larger assets in CEE recently where one needs more creative ideas including various partnerships next to IPO as an alternative.*

Within this redefined CEE, Ukraine stood out due to its large population and, theoretically, substantial untapped market potential in healthcare. However, even before the major escalation of conflict in 2022, the country presented a complex and challenging investment environment.

The remainder of Central Europe, having undergone significant waves of privatization and economic reforms since the late twentieth century, had developed a more mature, albeit still relatively small, PE market. Healthcare, in particular, saw varied levels of PE penetration across these nations, often correlated with the extent and nature of healthcare system reforms and privatization efforts.

9.6.7.1 Ukraine: Navigating PE Investment in a High-hurdle Environment Ukraine, prior to the 2022 conflict, was viewed by some investors as a frontier market with long-term healthcare investment potential given its large domestic market and nascent private sector. However, PE activity remained limited due to several intertwined hurdles that significantly impacted the investment climate.

The legal and regulatory environment was perceived as unstable and unpredictable, with frequent legislative changes and concerns about consistent rule of law application and judicial independence creating significant uncertainty. Corruption remained pervasive, adding risk and complexity. Healthcare reforms were ongoing, but their implementation and direction weren't always clear, making it difficult to assess investment viability—for instance, a PE firm considering diagnostic laboratories faced uncertainty from shifting licensing rules or unpredictable reimbursement rate changes. Significant bureaucratic hurdles, lengthy approval processes, and lack of administrative transparency delayed investments and increased operational costs, with processes like obtaining clinic permits or importing medical devices proving extraordinarily lengthy and opaque.

The legacy of state-dominated healthcare influenced public perception and operations. While demand for private services was growing, building trust and changing patient pathways took time, and developing managerial skills aligned with PE operational standards proved challenging. Geopolitical tensions even before 2022 demanded higher risk premiums, and the events of February 2022 fundamentally altered the risk calculus, rendering large-scale PE investments exceptionally challenging for the foreseeable future. Despite these hurdles, some small-scale PE and growth capital investments occurred, often from local entrepreneurs or specialized funds with high-risk tolerance focusing on niche segments or asset-light models.

9.6.7.2 The State of Healthcare and Life Sciences in the Region

Sector Development and PE Involvement in CEE (Excluding Ukraine) Across many CEE countries, the decades following the fall of the Berlin Wall saw substantial healthcare reforms. Privatization of state-owned assets, including clinics, hospitals, and pharmaceutical enterprises, opened doors for private investment. PE firms played a role in this transformation by consolidating fragmented markets—investing in and merging smaller private clinics, diagnostic centers, and dental practices to create larger, more efficient chains. They injected capital to upgrade medical equipment and facilities while introducing new medical specialties, developed private hospitals and specialized treatment centers (in cardiology, oncology, and elderly care), and invested in local pharmaceutical manufacturers (often focusing on generics or niche products) and medical technology companies including distribution networks. Poland, the Czech Republic, and Romania saw notable PE activity in private clinic chains, diagnostic imaging, and laboratory services, though Poland experienced surprise reimbursement reductions that impacted private healthcare providers like Nu-Med radiology clinics.

The Baltic states also attracted investment, particularly in specialized medical services and healthtech.

Focus on Ukraine: A Nascent Private Sector with Pockets of Strength Ukraine's healthcare system was historically state dominated, with a private sector that remained relatively underdeveloped and fragmented compared to Central European neighbors. Most private providers were small, often family-owned clinics or individual practices. Private multidisciplinary clinics and dental practices were the most visible segments, while investment in private hospitals was rare due to significant public sector competition and high capital requirements. Social care, particularly private elder care, was an emerging but very nascent field. Ukraine had a domestic pharmaceutical manufacturing base focused primarily on generic drugs, with many enterprises remaining family-owned or controlled by local business groups, while the distribution sector was more consolidated. Medtech was characterized by distributors of international equipment with limited local manufacturing at scale attracting PE interest, though recognized potential existed in healthtech IT solutions and CROs leveraging a well-educated medical workforce for clinical trials. PE involvement in Ukrainian healthcare and life sciences prior to 2022 was opportunistic and limited, with deals typically smaller and international PE firms often partnering with local players or focusing on companies with significant export potential to mitigate domestic market risks.

9.6.7.3 PE Investment in Action: Lessons from the CEE Healthcare Corridor Specific, publicly detailed accounts of failed PE investments in CEE healthcare were rare, but common success factors emerged from regional investment experiences. Strong local management teams who understood market nuances, regulatory landscapes, and cultural context proved crucial. Successful PE investors implemented best practices in financial management, operational efficiency, and corporate governance beyond just providing capital. Platform buy-and-build strategies—acquiring a platform company and making add-on acquisitions to achieve scale—proved effective in fragmented sectors like private clinics or dental care. Understanding and aligning investment theses with national healthcare reforms and reimbursement systems unlocked significant growth, while focusing on underserved niches or specialized services where private provision offered clear value propositions often yielded better results than competing directly with established public systems.

Common pitfalls included regulatory risk, as unexpected changes in healthcare regulations, reimbursement rates, or licensing requirements could significantly impact profitability—a persistent concern across the region. Integration challenges in buy-and-build strategies often proved more complex and time-consuming than anticipated, especially with legacy systems and differing company cultures. Over-reliance on original founders or key medical professionals in smaller, founder-led businesses posed post-acquisition risks if departures weren't carefully managed. Healthcare investments carried inherent reputational risks, requiring high standards of patient care, ethical practices, and transparent operations to avoid public backlash and regulatory scrutiny. The exit landscape proved challenging, with strategic buyers not always readily available and IPOs viable only for larger, well-established companies, making secondary buyouts to other PE firms an increasingly common exit route.

Marek Rodak, partner at MidEuropa, a leading PE investor in healthcare in the CEE region, reckons:

Unlike in the German Mittelstand, many children of successful Polish entrepreneurs have an Anglo-Saxon education and started their career at prestigious professional services firms. While some return to take over the family business—particularly in the case of larger enterprises—there are also instances where founding families consider selling to professional investors to ensure business continuity. This trend is especially evident among small and medium-sized companies.

For Ukraine specifically, the overriding lesson was the profound impact of geopolitical risk and the foundational importance of rule of law and institutional stability for attracting and retaining long-term PE investment.

9.6.7.4 Key Players: Regional PE Firms and Family Offices The CEE healthcare PE landscape was populated by international PE firms with CEE-focused funds, dedicated regional players, and increasingly, local family offices. Several PE firms had significant CEE presence and included healthcare within their investment mandates, such as Enterprise Investors (a long-standing CEE player with investments in major Polish private healthcare providers), Abris Capital Partners (focused on mid-market CEE opportunities with healthcare services as a target area), Horizon Capital (particularly active in Ukraine and Moldova with experience navigating challenging environments), and BaltCap (a leading Baltic states investor with healthcare in its portfolio). Most firms did not exclusively focus on healthcare but considered it opportunistically as part of broader CEE strategies, with specialist healthcare-focused PE funds being less common than in Western Europe or North America. Local and regional family offices played a growing though less visible role, participating as co-investors alongside PE firms or making direct investments into smaller healthcare businesses, sometimes with longer investment horizons and different risk appetites, leveraging their deep local networks.

9.6.7.5 The Perceived Trajectory of PE in CEE Healthcare Looking back from the early to mid-2020s, the outlook for PE investment in CEE healthcare was one of cautious optimism, albeit with significant regional disparities.

For Central European countries, particularly those within the European Union, the trajectory appeared set for continued, albeit moderate, growth. Drivers included aging populations, rising disposable incomes leading to increased demand for private healthcare options, and ongoing needs for modernization and efficiency in healthcare delivery. PE was expected to continue playing a role in market consolidation, service specialization, and the introduction of innovative healthcare models, including digital health solutions. The primary challenges revolved around navigating evolving national regulatory landscapes, managing labor costs, and ensuring sustainable reimbursement models.

For Ukraine, the outlook was starkly different and far more uncertain. Prior to the major escalation of conflict in 2022, there had been hopes that ongoing reforms and a gradual improvement in the investment climate might attract more PE capital, particularly into areas like private clinics, diagnostics, local pharma manufacturing, and healthtech. However, the war effectively put most, if not all, traditional PE investment on hold. Any future PE engagement in Ukrainian healthcare became contingent upon the cessation of hostilities, massive reconstruction efforts, and fundamental improvements in security, governance, and the rule of law. The focus shifted from growth equity to humanitarian aid and, eventually, the immense task of rebuilding the nation's healthcare infrastructure, a task where DFIs and impact investors were anticipated to play a more immediate role than traditional PE.

Across the entire CEE region, the development of robust capital markets and a more diverse range of exit opportunities remained important factors for the long-term maturation of the healthcare PE segment. The overarching lesson was that while demographic and economic fundamentals could signal opportunity, political stability, transparent governance, and a predictable regulatory environment were the bedrock upon which sustained PE investment in the critical healthcare sector could be built.

9.7 PE IN AUTOCRACIES

The possibility of a shrinking share of democracies and liberal economies globally raises a crucial question: can PE continue to thrive as autocratic regimes grow in economic influence? This topic warrants serious consideration given the shifting geopolitical and economic landscape.

We have discussed how China has been a major focal point for PE activity, fueled by rapid economic growth and the partial liberalization of specific sectors. However, the regulatory crackdowns in the 2020s have provided a clear reminder of the unique—and at times unpredictable—risks associated with investing in such environments. It is worth noting that not all autocracies are created equal: investor risk profiles in China, Saudi Arabia, Vietnam, and Russia can differ dramatically, especially in what counts as presidential "whim."

PE can develop in autocracies, but its growth and operating model often diverge substantially from its trajectory in democracies. In some autocratic regimes, centralized authority and the absence of frequent elections can reduce day-to-day regulatory volatility, facilitating certain types of investments and quick state-led approvals. PE firms may benefit from more direct lines to decision-makers, a less burdensome bureaucracy, and, more cynically, an ability to side-step public debate. However, the same concentration of power brings material risks: ad hoc policy reversals, arbitrary asset seizures, and "rule by law" rather than rule of law. Major success may bring unwanted official attention, and entire sectors can suddenly become off-limits—or retroactively subject to new rules. Limited transparency, inconsistent contract enforcement, and institutionalized favoritism (or outright rent-seeking) further erode long-term predictability for investors. Ultimately, the economic logic of a deal can be neutralized overnight by the political calculus of an autocrat.

In democracies, PE activity typically flourishes within a more transparent, rules-based order. Legal protections for investors, contract enforcement mechanisms, and judicial independence encourage sustained capital deployment. However, PE firms must navigate more comprehensive regulation—labor standards, competition policy, and environmental compliance—each of which can delay or complicate deals and sometimes serves more to protect incumbents than to ensure true competition. Public scrutiny and media attention are rarely trivial hurdles, especially in high-profile or politically sensitive sectors. Still, democracies offer a generally higher degree of legal recourse, making contract stability and property rights less vulnerable to overnight reversals, even as the legislative process can sometimes feel glacial.

The dichotomy is imperfect. While PE can operate in both systems, democracies usually provide greater certainty and due process, supporting longer investment horizons. Autocracies may present lucrative, fast-moving opportunities, but investors are well advised to carry a second passport and keep the engine running. Sustainable success in autocratic contexts relies on shrewd political risk analysis, robust local partnerships, and a willingness to play by rules that may shift without warning.

On this note, it is important to note that PE is actively deployed by some developing-country governments as a tool for economic modernization—not only as a profit engine for private investors. For example, PE investments were instrumental in the explosive growth of India's mobile telecom sector, providing capital, management expertise, and competitive pressure; the result was among the world's fastest network expansions. China's 2004 sale of an 18% stake in Shenzhen Development Bank to Newbridge Capital was another explicit attempt to import international private-sector discipline (and perhaps to send a signal about openness that was, in hindsight, partially reversible).

To conclude, the temptation to chase big returns in emerging markets is obvious, but investors would be wise not to confuse potential with inevitability. Historically, PE needed 40 years to reach maturity in the United States, with Europe lagging by another generation. Today's enthusiasm for rapid growth may just as easily fizzle, especially in countries where transparency and regulatory consistency are still works in progress. Hype rarely builds real institutions overnight, and there's little evidence that these markets will break the historical speed limit toward professionalization. Anyone looking for a shortcut is likely to get lost.

9.8 CASE STUDY: CVC AND THE GREEK HOSPITALS

You may be surprised that we chose Greece to illustrate this chapter on emerging markets.

After the 2008 Global Financial Crisis, Greece faced severe economic distress, coming close to bankruptcy. The state's ability to provide public healthcare diminished sharply, with nearly 20% of public hospital beds disappearing. The private healthcare sector stepped in but remained underfunded. Recognizing an opportunity, CVC, a leading European PE firm, acquired several hospitals, culminating in the creation of the Hellenic Healthcare Group (HHG). By 2018, HHG became Greece's largest private hospital chain, capturing about 30% of the private healthcare market (Kitten, 2021).

The case study examines whether CVC would be a good owner if it pursued acquiring Henri Dunant hospital in Athens and how it might create value. Though it was a large and well-established hospital, Henri Dunant struggled with very low occupancy rates (dropping to about 25% in 2012), declining revenues (from €96.5 million in 2009 to €24.7 million in 2012), and significant negative EBITDA (around –33.6%). CVC was a professional PE investor known for disciplined investment, thorough due diligence, and partnering with competent management teams. They had successfully built and exited Spain's largest private hospital group and were performing well with their Greek hospitals, making them a strong potential owner for Henri Dunant.

As summarized in Figure 9.11, value creation could involve prioritizing strategic capital expenditures, optimizing operations, and reducing procurement costs. (CVC

HOW CVC WAS LIKELY TO CREATE VALUE WITH HENRY DUNANT

What CVC achieved with their hospital acquisitions in Greece:

- Synergies: ~20% boost of profit
  - Half in product tenders
  - Rest mostly in services: IT, catering, laundry
  - Some revenue synergies from Insurance partnerships
- Shift to insurance (50% of revenue) and corporate contracts (5%)
- Public revenue (20%) is low margin but payments now <6 months (vs. 5 years!)
- Market recovery has happened to be faster than expected
- Multiple arbitrage: Hygeia at 12× (vs. Metropolitan at 8×)
- Other opportunities in acquisitions, primary care, public hospital contracts ...

FIGURE 9.11 CVC's value creation plan.

had previously reduced such expenses by 20% in their own hospitals.) Synergies could be realized by consolidating procurement across hospitals for consumables, drugs, and equipment. Attracting medical tourists might also be considered, although this was likely premature given Greece's economic climate at the time.

Notably, CVC publicly committed not to reduce the workforce despite tempting cost-saving opportunities. Low wages and ambitious growth plans meant retaining staff was essential. They also recognized that attempting workforce reductions would be unlikely to succeed legally or socially and could alienate public opinion.

They anticipated synergies that could increase profits by 20%, primarily from product tenders but also from shared services like IT, catering, and laundry, along with insurance partnerships. By transitioning the hospital group toward insurance coverage, approximately 50% of their revenue came from private insurance, with around 5% from corporate contracts. Public revenue was maintained at a low 20%, contributing to fixed costs and becoming more affordable as government payment delays shortened to under six months—a major improvement from the five-year delays seen between 2009 and 2012.

The healthcare market was rebounding, with expectations of acceleration. CVC's acquisition strategy reflected this: they did not go for Henri Dunant, paid 12× EBITDA for the more stable Hygeia hospital and secured the Metropolitan hospital, which required modernization, at a lower multiple (8×), with plans to invest up to bring its value to par.

These strategies exemplify how CVC might have created value from acquiring Henri Dunant through synergy capture, operational improvements, and leveraging market recovery (Spoiler: CVC decided against acquiring it).

9.9 CHAPTER SUMMARY

Emerging and developing markets offer PE investors a compelling but structurally distinct opportunity set—higher growth potential, but compressed exit options, thinner institutional infrastructure, and governance risk that demands local expertise and patience. The Greek hospitals case, while geographically anomalous, illustrates how crisis-driven dislocation can briefly recreate emerging-market dynamics even in developed economies.

PE in emerging and developing markets is not simply a lower-cost version of the developed-market playbook—it is a different game, with different rules at every stage of the cycle. Fundraising is harder, with fewer institutional LPs and shallower domestic capital pools. Deal sourcing relies more heavily on proprietary networks and local intermediaries than on competitive auction processes. And exits remain the most persistent structural constraint: shallow public markets, limited strategic buyer appetite, and unpredictable regulatory environments all compress realised returns and extend holding periods beyond standard fund timelines.

Within this landscape, China stands apart—not merely as the largest market but as the most institutionally sophisticated emerging PE market, having produced outsized returns for growth capital funds across a compressed 15-year window. India has followed a different trajectory, with PE creating value through operational transformation of fragmented service businesses, as illustrated by the Max Healthcare and SeQuent cases. Southeast Asia, MENA, Sub-Saharan Africa, Latin America, and CEE each present their own risk-return profiles, shaped by regulatory fragmentation, currency risk, and varying degrees of political stability.

Across all regions, one factor consistently differentiates winning from losing investments: local knowledge. Not just local presence, but genuine on-the-ground expertise in regulatory navigation, talent management, payer dynamics, and stakeholder relationships. PE firms that attempt to manage emerging-market portfolios from London or New York with periodic travel tend to underperform those with embedded local teams and culturally fluent leadership.

The Greek hospitals case, while technically an outlier in a chapter on emerging markets, is instructive precisely because of its anomalous character. Greece after 2010 demonstrated how a developed-economy healthcare system, under severe fiscal stress, can exhibit the information asymmetries, distressed valuations, and governance deficits more typically associated with frontier markets—and how a disciplined PE investor can create value in exactly those conditions.

The convergence question—how long before emerging markets reach developed-market institutional depth—is worth posing carefully. For China and India, the trajectory is well established, even if periodically disrupted by geopolitical or regulatory reversals. For Sub-Saharan Africa and parts of Southeast Asia, the honest answer is that the structural preconditions—rule of law, functioning capital markets, credible exit pathways—are still being built. Decades, not years, is the right unit of measurement. The implication for PE is not to wait, but to invest with a strategy explicitly designed for that institutional gap rather than one that assumes it will close before the exit.

CHAPTER 10

Industry Outlook and Career Opportunities

In the first part of this chapter, we will discuss developments and trends in the private equity (PE) industry, covering everything from fundraising and investments to some of the current approaches toward fees, and some of the key drivers of change in the industry going forward.

In the second part, we will discuss the key players in the world of PE healthcare specialists, and in the third part give you a better idea of the kind of work that PE professionals do day in and day out. We will also share the testimonies from some people who work in the industry, to get insider perspectives.

But first, let's look at who the main players of PE are nowadays. The landscape has somehow changed since the 1980s, the foundational years of the industry. At that time, PE was an American affair. How has it changed 40 years later? In the United States at least, still the largest market in the world, not that much. Figure 10.1 shows the largest PE investors there. They remain mostly American.

10.1 DEVELOPMENTS TO WATCH

In this part, we describe some key developments in PE and consider what the future might hold. We indicated earlier on that following the financial crisis, after 2010, we went back to healthier market conditions, with a very long bull market, cash-rich fund managers and generally content investors, until 2022. 2014 in particular was a record year for the PE asset class, followed by many more record years, especially 2021—and that was in spite of the COVID-19 pandemic.

But what about the future? There is still a lot of potential for PE, but general partners (GPs) and limited partners (LPs) also face significant challenges from high inflation, energy and environmental issues, political and technological disruptions, and their impacts on globalization and supply chains. In addition, while investors have been enjoying the liquidity delivered to them by ongoing high levels of distributions, the market has started to show signs of saturation from 2022, with a record number of funds seeking capital. More than ever, investors face the challenge of identifying the best investment opportunities. Finally, fund managers are confronted with intense competition, not only with fundraising, but also in finding attractive deal entry prices, sometimes sacrificing safety for yield, with increased demands from both investors and regulatory bodies.

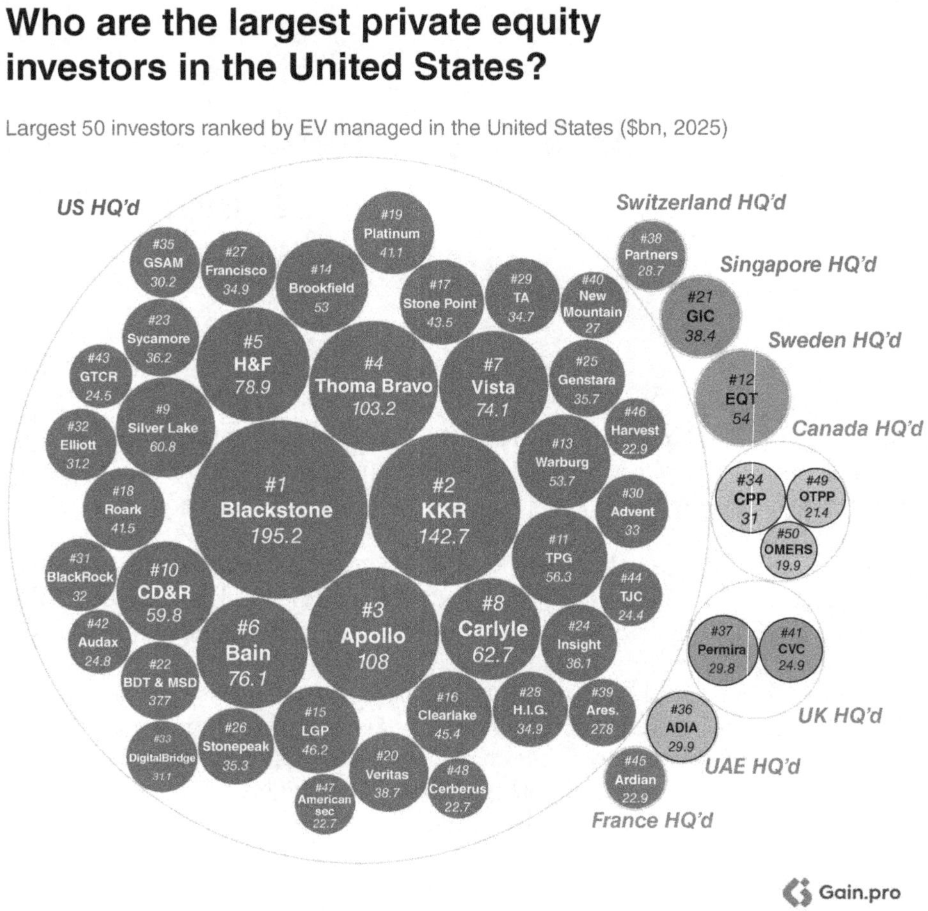

FIGURE 10.1 Largest PE investors in the United States.
Source: Gain.pro

10.1.1 Fundraising

Since the onset of the COVID-19 pandemic, PE fundraising has experienced notable fluctuations reflecting broader economic uncertainties, shifting investor priorities, and evolving market dynamics. Fundraising activity declined sharply in 2020 as the pandemic's shock led to heightened caution among limited partners and slower dealmaking. However, a strong rebound emerged in 2021, fueled by abundant liquidity, low interest rates, and strong investor confidence. This recovery was characterized by a surge in mega-funds and sector-focused vehicles, particularly in healthcare, biotech, and cleantech, reflecting renewed interest in resilient and high-growth industries. From 2022 onward, fundraising growth slowed amid rising inflation, tighter monetary policies, and geopolitical tensions, leading to a more selective and elongated fundraising environment. Despite a muted backdrop with declines in capital raised year-over-year through 2024 and into 2025, PE firms have demonstrated resilience by shifting focus toward value preservation, operational improvements, and strategic sector positioning. Increasingly, fundraisings now emphasize ESG (environmental, social, governance), digital transformation, and thematic sectors as firms prepare for an evolving investment landscape. The PE industry stands at a crossroads, balancing cautious optimism with structural changes that will shape opportunities and challenges in the coming decade. This evolving environment will critically shape deal sourcing, portfolio management, and exit strategies discussed in this final chapter on the outlook for PE. The sections that follow explore eight interrelated themes shaping recent fundraising dynamics.

10.1.1.1 First-time Funds: An Uphill Battle with Notable Exceptions Let's start with a definition. "First-time funds" are the inaugural funds launched by new GP teams, typically facing the sharpest capital-raising constraints due to limited operational track record and heightened perceived risk. "Emerging managers," by contrast, are a broader group: they include all GPs managing their first, second, or even third fund, or whose assets under management remain relatively modest—often under $1 billion. All first-time funds are emerging managers, but not all emerging managers are first timers. This distinction matters for investors and fund managers alike, shaping due diligence, access to LP allocation programs, fee structures, and the odds of raising a successor fund. In today's market, where capital is increasingly concentrated among industry giants and fundraising timelines for newcomers are longer than ever, being clear about these categories may not open doors—but at least you will know which ones to knock on.

The challenges facing first-time funds stem from fundamental LP concerns: without a proven track record, these managers represent higher perceived risk, unknown execution capabilities, and uncertain returns. LPs typically prefer established relationships with managers who have demonstrated consistent performance across market cycles.

Across all segments of private capital, emerging managers have seen their share of fundraising steadily decrease over 25 years (Figure 10.2). First-time funds typically represent less than 15% of all PE funds raised (7% in 2013 and 2014) and face

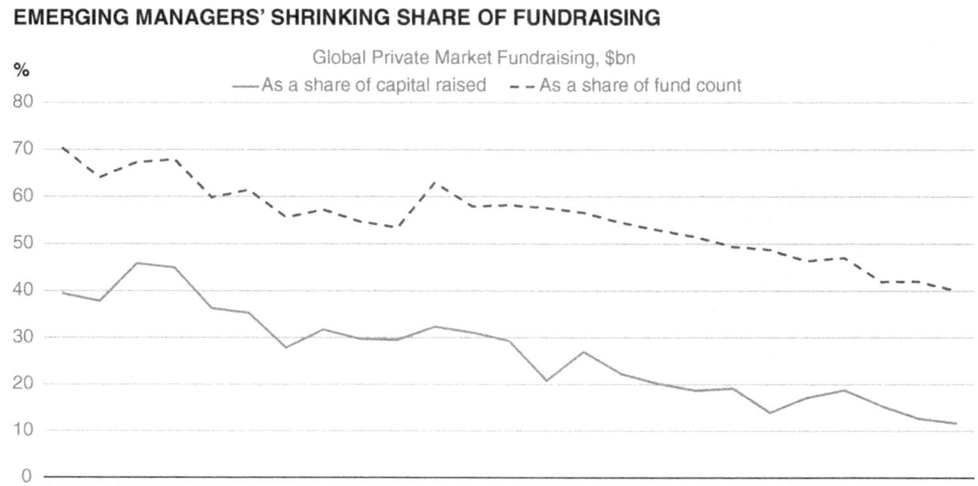

FIGURE 10.2 Evolution of global private market fundraising.
Source: PitchBook.

significant challenges attracting institutional investors. These difficulties intensified from early 2022, as first-time funds and other emerging PE managers encountered some of the toughest fundraising conditions in recent memory.

These challenging conditions persisted into 2024. By that year, first-time mid-market PE funds ($1–5 billion) managed only $34 billion worldwide—the lowest tally since 2013 (McKinsey & Company, 2025). Smaller funds (those under $1 billion) spent five more months "in market" than in prior years, and the number of closed funds fell to the lowest in a decade (McKinsey & Company, 2025).

While $100 million remains a plausible target for first-time PE funds in developed markets—notably Europe—rising setup and administration costs make sub-$50 million funds economically unviable (Gen II Fund Services, 2020). Even with $2–3 million tickets, fixed costs can now devour returns before the first deal even closes.

The economics are challenging: Negotiating the traditional 2% management fee is usually impossible for first timers: most settle for less, sometimes below 1.5%. Add a placement agent's 1–2% cut and managers may spend their early years cash-flow negative, which is a bad look even for the most patient LPs. Timelines stretch out: first-time PE funds take 14 months to close (versus 13 for established rivals) and require more than 100 investor meetings to get to a final close (Gen II Fund Services, 2020).

Therefore, only by skipping the agent and securing a full 2% fee on $100 million can a duo or trio of experienced partners operate viably without financial strain. However, this approach faces significant challenges given LPs' concerns about key-person risk.

That does not mean companies needing growth capital will starve. Family offices, high-net-worth individuals, and angels have stepped into the breach—ranging from absentee funders to hyper-involved would-be board members. In healthcare specifically, this alternative funding landscape has become increasingly important for early-stage medical device companies, digital health platforms, and specialized service providers seeking growth capital.

The fundraising market presents intense competition. Despite these challenges, notable exceptions exist: Albion River, for instance, raised $400 million in aerospace/defense in just 12 months, while Eagle Merchant Partners secured $265 million for a southern US strategy (PitchBook, 2023).

What sets the rare winners apart? Track records as independent sponsors, actually doing deals during the capital raise (instead of just waving term sheets), granting co-investment rights, and offering surgical-sector specialization (PitchBook, 2023). In healthcare, this sector specialization has proven particularly valuable, as LPs recognize the complexity and regulatory requirements that demand deep domain expertise. Patient Square Capital's $3.9 billion debut (Q1 2023) set the all-time record for a first-time PE fund as well as for healthcare PE.

The stakes for first-time funds are particularly high, as performance directly determines future fundraising prospects. For most, however, the failure rate is sobering: more than half of first-time PE funds do not make it to Fund II. Performance quartile is destiny:

- Top quartile first-time funds have a 90%+ chance of raising a second.
- Second quartile: 50–60% odds.
- Third/fourth: only 10–30% succeed.

(Kaplan and Schoar, 2005; Preqin, 2017; Harris et al., 2014)

However, several important caveats apply: definitions shift, data are patchy, and LPs are notorious for short-term memory loss anytime the market sours. That top-quartile badge might mean little come next cycle.

Somewhat contradicting the gloom, research on first-time buyout funds shows they outperformed established managers in 12 of 13 years from 2000 to 2012, with top-quartile hit rates of 34% versus 25% for established shops, and an average annual return edge of 250bps (Preqin, 2016; Natixis Investment Managers, 2024). Perhaps this is why LPs—tired of bland returns from "brand name" funds—are trickling back toward emerging managers with an actual story or specialty.

Looking ahead, industry consensus expected challenging forces for newcomers from 2025: LPs still gravitate toward size and "track record," crowding big shops and ignoring the lone wolves. But there was cautious optimism for specialists and managers with demonstrable day-one capabilities (McKinsey & Company, 2025).

Deal-by-deal raises have thus become the norm. "Reducing blind pool risk is especially effective in a market swamped with thousands of managers competing for investor dollars," as PitchBook observes (PitchBook, 2023). If you cannot show something real, do not expect LPs to bother with the imaginary.

10.1.1.2 Fees An important development in the PE industry has been the pressure on fees, especially after the Global Financial Crisis (GFC). We mentioned that discounts and the rise of fee-free co-investments have effectively reduced fees in percentage of AuM, some say by half over a decade. Let's take the example of Altas Partners, a Canadian buyout fund.[1] Imagine they are targeting a mid-size, $600-million fund as a debut. They are trying to find a compromise between the typical approach and the deal-by-deal approach. They decide that they will still charge 20% carry after the usual 8% hurdle, but that they are giving up on the usual 2% management fee. Instead, the firm will get a 1% "one-time distribution" on invested equity, as well as an annual payment equal to 1% of invested capital. Altogether, that will amount to less than 2%, perhaps 1.2%, 1.3%, depending on the time they keep the money. That, coupled with an option for co-investment, effectively lowers the fees for LPs, who are not going to pay the fees on the uninvested capital, which is a big issue in the industry in general. Altas is committing to invest over four years, but with an additional 10-year potential ownership period. So, this will help to improve the fees over a potentially longer period.

Another example of the pressure on fees is the trend toward so-called predefined budgets and progressive carried interest, which means the carried interest will grow with the performance rather than being a simple percentage based on the assets under management.

The PE industry also see its largest players like Blackstone and Apollo targeting retail investors, less willing to pay high fees, but less likely to get the best investment opportunities. This may lead the way to a segment of low-cost PE that will dilute the average fee level. Blackrock, the largest asset manager in the world, could accelerate this with low-cost PE indices.

[1] We couldn't retrieve the original author of this example but will be happy to mention them if they could let us know.

On the other hand, the fees may not decrease much more. There are at least three reasons for that. First, many firms are exposed to increasing regulation and disclosure requirements, which requires them to invest heavily in IT. Those system expenditures require a certain level of fees. The second reason is the weight of all regulations, both financially and over time. And a third reason is the need for an extensive track record of fund managers. All of that tends to favor the largest fund managers. Investors are queueing up to jump on.

10.1.1.3 Co-investment Another prominent development back in the 2010s was the increase in co-investment. This trend was partly driven by the need to extend capital deployment cycles and preserve liquidity during slower fundraising periods. It offers LPs an option to invest selectively in certain assets without paying the fees. At the same time, co-investments allowed managers to support portfolio companies without immediately returning to the fundraising market, which remained difficult for many after the GFC.

We saw a growing demand that stretched into smaller deals, including mid-cap and small-cap deals. Now these smaller transactions, according to academic research, have historically underperformed the larger deals. But, as you can see, the percentage of US leverage buyout (LBO) deals that included co-investment went from 5% before the crisis to 20% after the crisis (Figure 10.3).

In recent years, LPs have pushed even further toward co-investment and other direct approaches to portfolio exposure. With slower distributions and higher pressure on returns, many are no longer content to remain passive in blind pool structures. Instead, they are increasingly using co-investment vehicles and continuation funds to gain selective exposure to individual assets while cutting down on management fees and carried interest. PitchBook data show that co-investment fundraising surpassed $30 billion in both Q1 and Q2 2025, confirming that what began as a necessity in the 2010s has evolved into a structural feature of the PE landscape.

At the same time, continuation funds—both single- and multi-asset—have become another major pathway for LPs to exercise discretion over specific assets.

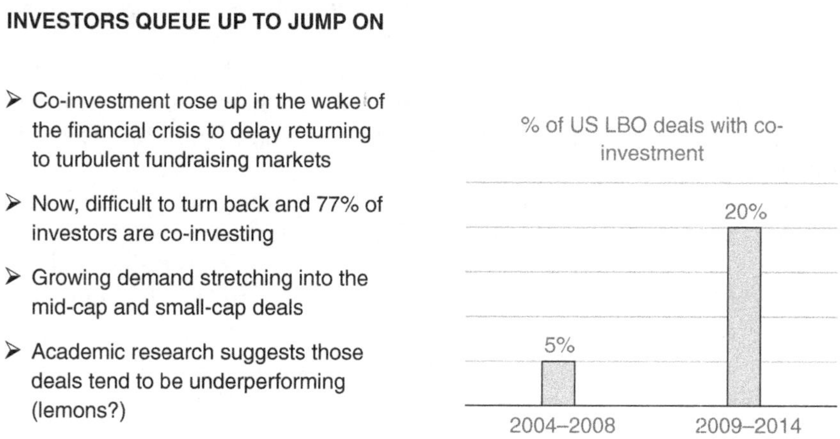

FIGURE 10.3 Proportion of US LBO deals with co-investment.
Source: Financial News 2015; Palico; Harvard.

This shift reflects not only cost sensitivity but also a strategic desire for more targeted exposures, as noted by investment heads at firms like Federated Hermes and Neuberger Berman.

However, the trend is not frictionless. Mid-sized LPs often lack the internal teams or bandwidth needed to evaluate and lead such deals. For many, deal access depends on their existing GP relationships rather than pure capital availability.

This pattern extends the post-crisis rise of co-investment noted earlier. Today, that early adaptation has matured into a broader rethink of how LPs deploy capital, marking a shift from passive fund allocation toward direct portfolio construction.

10.1.1.4 Fund Life and Longer Life Funds

Origins and Strategic Advantages The PE landscape has witnessed a significant evolution with the emergence of longer-life funds, a model that traces its origins to family offices. Unburdened by the pressure to return capital within conventional time frames, family offices pioneered an approach that affords them a distinct advantage in negotiations with both portfolio company management and potential sellers. Their ability to position themselves as truly patient capital creates immediate credibility in an industry often criticized for short-termism.

Traditional PE firms have taken notice, increasingly adopting elements of this patient capital approach while typically stopping short of embracing the full evergreen structures we introduced in Chapter 4.

Market Adoption and Leading Examples Industry response to these challenges has manifested as extended-life cycle closed-end funds with durations sometimes extending to 20 years—double the traditional PE timeline. Market leaders including CVC, KKR, Blackstone, and Carlyle have all explored or implemented these structures, developing modified fee arrangements specifically designed for 15+ year investment horizons. Abraaj Capital in the Middle East similarly pursued this strategy prior to its collapse from unrelated governance issues.

Castik Capital provided a particularly instructive example of this trend. Founded in 2014, the German firm deliberately constructed its investment vehicles with 10-year investment horizons—not merely 10-year fund lives—based on the pragmatic recognition that optimal investment entry points cannot be predicted with precision. Their founding thesis acknowledged that "you never know if the next two to three years are the best time to invest," while identifying a pervasive industry problem: the premature divestiture of high-quality assets to demonstrate returns necessary for subsequent fundraising cycles.

Key Characteristics and Target Investments Longer-life PE funds represent a distinct evolution from traditional PE structures. While conventional PE typically operates on 10-year fund cycles with three to five years holding periods, these extended vehicles embrace 15- to 20-year investment horizons. Their target investments reflect this patience: economically resilient, established companies that may not fit the rapid value-creation template of traditional PE, but offer compelling potential for steady, compounded returns across extended time frames.

This approach delivers several structural advantages, including reduced portfolio turnover, lower fee erosion, and expanded co-investment opportunities. Perhaps most significantly, the extended ownership period enables comprehensive implementation of operational improvements (as well as ESG initiatives), providing sufficient runway for these programs to mature and deliver measurable impact.

Investor Alignment and Economic Structure From the investor perspective, these extended-duration vehicles align advantageously with the liability profiles of pension funds and insurance companies, while satisfying growing institutional demand for stable performance with reduced volatility. The economic structures typically reflect this more patient approach, featuring the following:

- Lower hurdle rates (often around 5%)
- Reduced carried interest percentages
- Modified management fee structures

These adjustments acknowledge the reduced pressure for rapid value creation and exit. However, this approach introduces its own trade-offs, including less frequent liquidity events and heightened organizational risks associated with potential staff turnover and key person dependencies over the extended investment period.

Comparison with Infrastructure Funds The positioning of longer-life PE funds becomes clearer when contrasted with infrastructure funds, as both serve investors seeking extended investment horizons but operate with fundamentally different objectives and asset focuses.

Infrastructure funds concentrate exclusively on essential physical assets—transportation networks, energy facilities, utilities, and communications infrastructure. These investments naturally align with long-term horizons due to their extensive operational lifespans and ability to generate stable, inflation-linked cash flows. The sector has progressively moved from PE-style fund structures with 7- to 10-year durations toward longer-term or open-ended vehicles that better match the inherent longevity of infrastructure assets.

The distinctions between these fund types are consequential. Longer-life PE funds invest in operating companies across diverse sectors, employing moderate leverage while emphasizing sustainable growth trajectories. Infrastructure funds concentrate on physical assets providing essential services within monopolistic frameworks, often operating in regulated environments with predictable return profiles. This fundamental difference creates distinct risk-return characteristics: infrastructure investments typically offer lower risk due to their essential nature and regulatory frameworks, while longer-life PE investments involve higher operational complexity.

Investment Thesis and Portfolio Construction The investment thesis for longer-life PE centers on patient capital deployment to extract maximum value from high-quality businesses through sustained operational improvements and strategic positioning. Infrastructure investing focuses on acquiring critical assets with natural competitive advantages that deliver predictable yields across economic cycles.

For institutional investors constructing diversified portfolios, these vehicles serve complementary roles—infrastructure providing stable, bond-like returns with inflation protection, and longer-life PE offering enhanced yields through operational value creation without the exit pressure inherent in traditional PE.

10.1.1.5 Damaged Track Record and Zombie Funds Since 2022, rising interest rates and market uncertainty have made it increasingly difficult for many PE funds to exit investments acquired at elevated multiples. As holding periods lengthen, there has been growing anticipation of a natural "Darwinian" cleansing in the industry. Guy Semmens of Gyrus Capital noted in 2025 at PE Insights:

> *In the coming years, expect many GPs to disappear who have too many mediocre assets in portfolio. Consolidation and Darwinism have been talked about for 30 years but there are signs that it is actually happening now.*

One immediate consequence of this evolution is that raising new funds without a strong track record has become near impossible. In such situations, what options exist for firms struggling to secure fresh capital?

The first survival method for such firms—often described as "running on empty"—involves leveraging **secondary market transactions** and **continuation fund restructurings**. Many firms that raised funds before or during the GFC found themselves unable to raise new vehicles due to market dislocation or legacy underperformance. For example, Doughty Hanson, a large and well-known firm, navigated this challenge by securing capital from HarbourVest as part of a secondary transaction in 2015. Similarly, Magnum Capital, a Spanish mid-sized firm with a 2007 fund, undertook a restructuring of its investor base after the crisis. According to the *Wall Street Journal*, Magnum "reached a deal to overhaul some of its old investor base and kick-start its operations," entering into discussions to provide a "liquidity event" for existing investors. These actions, involving secondary sales and asset recapitalization, are consistent with early continuation fund structures that became widespread later in the decade.

A second way for firms unable to raise new funds to survive is **deal-by-deal financing**. Rather than seeking a traditional fundraise, these firms seek investor commitments on a per-deal basis, reminiscent of the earliest days of the leveraged buyout industry. This approach is riskier—absent standout opportunities, investor appetite may wane—but firms with strong teams and market access have successfully used it to stay active and rebuild track records. For instance, Duke Street Capital adopted this route following the GFC, aided by a minority investment from Tikehau in the management company. Starr Capital Partners similarly pursued deal-by-deal agreements to maintain momentum after setbacks. Such recoveries have encouraged more firms to adopt deal-by-deal strategies, which often serve as bridge paths back to traditional fund structures.

10.1.1.6 The Rise of the Independent Sponsor Model The independent sponsor, or deal-by-deal, model has been gaining momentum as a flexible alternative to traditional "blind pool" PE funds (Table 10.1). Once seen as a fallback for GPs unable to raise blind-pool capital, it is increasingly adopted by choice. Sponsors source deals individually and raise capital per transaction, attracting LPs seeking greater selectivity, faster deployment, and a cleaner return profile. In contrast to blind pools, this model allows investors to assess each opportunity, aligning capital more closely with individual asset risk.

This shift has been catalyzed by three core drivers: prolonged difficulties in traditional fundraising, rising LP appetite for co-investments and direct exposure, and the increasing cost and complexity of fund compliance—especially under AIFMD,

TABLE 10.1 Comparative Overview: Blind-pool Funds vs. Independent Sponsor Model

Feature	Blind-pool Fund	Independent Sponsor Model
Fundraising Approach	Capital raised upfront via commitments	Capital raised deal-by-deal
Capital Deployment	Discretionary by GP across multiple deals	Only after LP due diligence on each deal
Speed of Execution	Fast—committed capital allows immediate execution	Slower—fundraising needed for each transaction
LP Involvement	Limited during investment period	High—LPs choose specific deals
Fees and Economics	2% management fee + 20% carry (typically)	One-off deal fee, monitoring fee, tiered carry (20%+)
GP Team Size	Larger teams, fixed cost base	Lean teams, fewer mouths to feed
Regulatory Burden	High—subject to AIFMD, ESG, investor reporting	Lower—outside scope of many fund regulations
Preferred By	Institutional investors seeking diversification	Family offices, high net worth individuals, selective institutional LPs
Attractive For	Large-scale strategies with deal pipelines	Niche strategies, new GPs, mid-market healthcare
Key Drawback	Pressure to deploy capital within investment period	Execution risk; slower fundraising per deal

Brexit-era regulation, and ESG mandates. In addition, the model offers sponsors reduced bureaucracy and greater economics, often featuring one-off deal fees, monitoring fees tied to EBITDA, and tiered carried interest that may exceed 20% depending on performance.

The model's appeal has grown among entrepreneurial LPs such as family offices, but institutional players are entering as infrastructure matures. Placement agents, legal advisors, and credit providers now support independent sponsor transactions, and intermediaries are creating terms surveys and forums to standardize practices. While fundraising remains deal-by-deal and slower than with a committed fund, LPs appreciate the transparency and control, especially when backing emerging managers or niche strategies.

For healthcare, this model is particularly relevant for specialist operating partners or clinical experts who can source proprietary deals but may lack the track record to raise a large, diversified fund. It provides a viable pathway to leverage deep sectoral knowledge on a targeted, deal-by-deal basis.

Execution risk and team retention remain key challenges—GPs must fundraise for each transaction, risking delays or LP withdrawal. Yet for mid-market and healthcare investors, the model offers valuable flexibility, particularly when blind-pool deployment pressure could lead to misaligned investments.

As the strategy continues to institutionalize, especially in the United States and increasingly in Europe, it is seen not just as a stopgap, but as a lasting alternative.

10.1.1.7 The Time of the Global Alternative Asset Managers In Figure 10.4, we mapped the evolution of the structure of assets under management at the top five diversified PE firms for your perusal. See how fast they have grown and how they have grown beyond PE, especially Blackstone, which reached half a trillion dollars of assets under

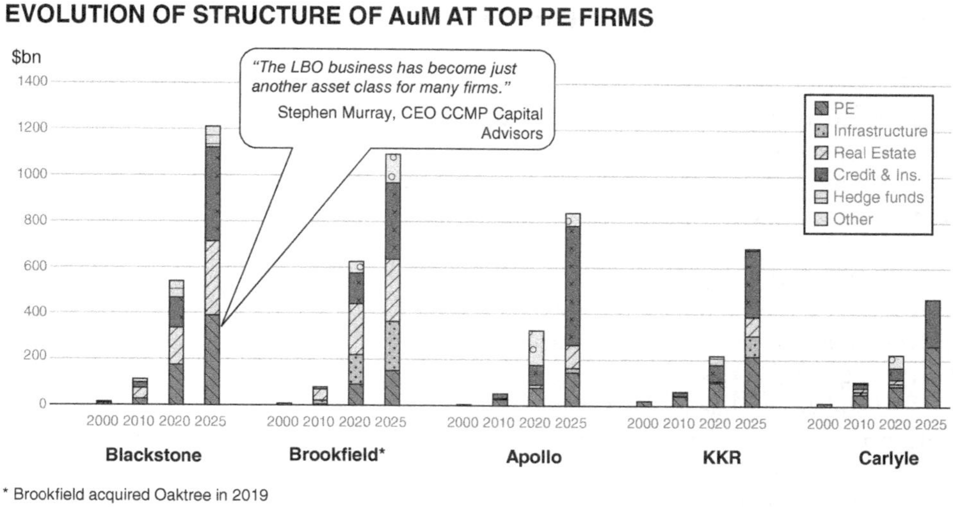

FIGURE 10.4 Evolution of the structure of AuM at the top four PE firms.
Source: Candesic research.

management by 2020, and a trillion dollars just four years later. Note also how PE represents only about 30% of the total alongside credit, real estate, hedge funds (increasingly renamed multi-assets strategies), as well as insurance in the case of KKR.

The expansion of these global alternative asset managers across multiple investment classes represents a structural transformation of the investment management industry driven by both demand-side pressures and supply-side synergies. This diversification strategy has been catalyzed by institutional investors' prolonged search for yield in extended low-interest-rate environments during the 2010–2021 period, demographic shifts toward defined-contribution pension schemes requiring long-duration assets, and regulatory developments facilitating individual investor access to previously institutional-only asset classes. The integration of PE, credit, real estate, and infrastructure strategies within single management platforms generates substantial operational efficiencies through shared investor relations infrastructure, cross-asset deal origination networks, and transferable operational expertise that creates competitive advantages in both fundraising and deployment. These synergies are particularly pronounced in client management, where established relationships can support multi-product sales, and in operational capabilities, where due diligence, portfolio monitoring, and value creation expertise translate across asset classes. Looking forward, the industry's trajectory toward an estimated $65 trillion in private market assets by 2032 (Bain & Company, 2024b) suggests continued consolidation around diversified alternative platforms that can offer comprehensive investment solutions. The convergence of regulatory reform enabling broader retail access, technological infrastructure supporting scaled distribution, and institutional demand for diversified alternative exposure positions these multi-strategy managers to capture disproportionate market share in the evolving investment landscape.

10.1.1.8 Democratization of Private Equity The "democratization" of PE is accelerating—new digital platforms, products with tiny minimums, and regulatory nudges are lowering barriers faster than ever. While access is widening, longstanding institutional safeguards and investor protections are coming under pressure. Is the future genuinely inclusive, or are we tiptoeing toward risks best left to professionals?

We covered this aspect in detail in Chapter 4 (expanding investor access) and Chapter 7 (tokenization). In 2025, Private Equity International highlighted the plethora of new products targeting wealth and retail investors "from customizable public-private models to infrastructure offerings with entry tickets as low as $500" and published a comprehensive special report[2] to address regulatory and valuation challenges. Like it or not, they argue, this democratization will only continue, in spite of the concerns around liquidity and risk. As highlighted in a PitchBook article, however, the real problem is not access itself but the confusion between access and liquidity, with semi-liquid and evergreen wrappers at risk of manufacturing an illusion of liquidity that can transmit stress into other asset classes when redemptions are constrained (Tarhuni, 2026).

"Private equity has long sparked fascination—and for good reason," says Estelle Dolla, president and co-founder of Private Corner, a leading French platform dedicated to private markets. "Its resilience through crises, its capacity to generate value over the long term, and the depth of opportunities across geographies and strategies have made it a cornerstone of institutional portfolios. It's time it became a structural component of individual wealth allocation as well."

For Private Corner, three reasons explain why digital platforms like theirs are here to stay. First, the long-term appeal of PE remains strong, especially in uncertain times where diversification and real economic exposure are critical. Second, the structural evolution of wealth management—toward independence, transparency, and global allocation—calls for platforms that can bridge the gap between asset managers and financial advisors. And third, technology has fundamentally changed the game, making access smoother, reporting clearer, and onboarding faster, all while preserving regulatory integrity.

Blackrock's CEO even wrote to his shareholders: "We see an opportunity to do for the public-private market divide what we did for index vs. active." There is little doubt wealthy individuals will multiply their access points. The launch of PISCES in the United Kingdom reinforced it and may open the door to similar initiatives.

Dolla is careful to emphasize the distinction between expanding access and lowering standards:

> *[W]e believe in opening the doors of institutional-grade PE to private investors—but without compromising on the fundamentals that make this asset class so powerful. Not all models follow this approach. Some are moving toward a mass retail logic, which drifts away from the asset class's original DNA.*

The Fundamental Distinction: Sophisticated vs. Retail Investors A key regulatory fault line runs through the difference between "sophisticated" (accredited) investors and retail. Sophisticated investors—institutions, endowments, funds—are presumed to have enough financial expertise and resources to understand illiquidity and loss, and to negotiate protection. Retail investors, by contrast, are protected by stricter rules for

[2] Private Equity International. (2025, May). Democratisation of private equity. www.privateequityinternational.com/democratisation.

a reason: their savings are more vulnerable, and most lack the knowledge or scale to properly evaluate PE products.

The Temptation to Reach Retail Investors In the United States, the debate about 401(k) plans and PE remains fierce. The Trump administration's Department of Labor approved the inclusion of select PE vehicles within DC plans in 2020, a move Biden officials questioned but did not reverse. Meanwhile, proposals for mandatory or quota-based allocations to "alternative assets" (including PEs) keep resurfacing on both sides of the Atlantic. In the United Kingdom, the Mansion House Accord has been seeking to channel at least 10% of DC default funds into private markets—a move reinforced by legal powers to mandate such allocations if targets are not met. In August 2025, President Trump issued a new executive order that aimed to allow more PE and other alternative assets in 401(k) retirement accounts. Each initiative reflects PE's hunger for a new capital source and policymakers' search for higher returns—sometimes at the expense of retail risk awareness.

Arguments for expanding access often highlight "democratization" and "inclusion." In reality, the shift increases the risk of mis-selling, hidden fees, and a mismatch between asset illiquidity and investor liquidity needs. Pension plan members (effectively retail) could see their retirement tied up in illiquid, expensive funds with opaque valuation. In extreme cases, the gains of democratization are privatized for GPs and early LPs, while risks are socialized among the uninitiated.

Retail investors should remain under the protection of their local regulators. Orlando Bravo, co-founder of buyout firm Thoma Bravo, worried in the *Financial Times* that there was a risk that retail investors could end up being sold funds invested in companies that nobody else wanted. Tony Tutrone, head of private markets at Neuberger Berman, also warned in the *Financial Times* in late 2025 about the reputation risk: "there will be some bad stories which will reflect poorly on the entire industry," emphasizing that as evergreen private market vehicles expand access to retail investors, evidence of effective past conflict management remains crucial to protect both investors and the sector's reputation.

The Asymmetric Information Dilemma There are reasons to be concerned. The surge of initiatives aimed at expanding PE access to retail investors in the 2020s has sparked critical questions. Are GPs pressured by LPs, genuinely innovating to broaden exit opportunities-or is there a darker narrative at play?

Consider this unsettling hypothesis: What if GPs (and LPs) recognize that the net asset value (NAV) of their holdings is overstated by 20%, yet offer these assets to distributors at a 10% discount? Distributors could then market the investment to retail clients as an immediate "paper gain" of 11%, masking the underlying valuation gap. Over time, as retail investors hold these illiquid assets, the transient discount advantage evaporates, leaving less impressive if not lackluster returns in its wake. Time will tell.

The Critical Policy Challenge The most concerning development is the shift from market-driven expansion of PE access to government-mandated allocations, particularly in DC pension systems. While sophisticated investors can independently evaluate PE risks, compulsory pension allocations effectively compel retail investors into illiquid strategies regardless of circumstance. This could socialize losses and privatize GP fees—hardly the democratization retail savers imagine.

Finally, this democratization of PE may be the signal of another change beyond just fundraising: the separation between two segments of private markets, a point we will address in our conclusions.

10.1.2 Investment

This section explores some of the ways PE firms are adapting their approaches to sourcing, managing, and exiting investments to navigate today's complex market and capitalize on emerging opportunities.

10.1.2.1 Recent Developments in Private Equity Deal Activity: Post-COVID and Inflationary Environment (2022–2024) Deal wise, the PE landscape experienced significant turbulence following the unprecedented growth witnessed during the early 2020s. After reaching historic peaks in deal activity during 2020–2021, the PE industry confronted a dramatic shift in market conditions beginning in 2022. The confluence of rising interest rates, persistent inflation, geopolitical uncertainties, and evolving post-pandemic economic conditions fundamentally altered the dealmaking environment, leading to substantial declines in transaction volumes and values across most segments of the market (McKinsey & Company, 2023a).

Overall Market Decline and Key Drivers The PE deal market experienced a sharp contraction starting in 2022, marking the end of an unprecedented growth cycle. Global PE deal value decreased by 26% to $2.4 trillion in 2022, with deal count dropping 15% from the prior year (McKinsey & Company, 2023a). This downturn continued into 2023, with PE deal value falling to $508 billion—a 38% year-over-year decline—while deal counts fell 31%, marking the steepest annual contraction since the GFC (Bain & Company, 2025c).

The US Federal Reserve's aggressive monetary policy response to inflation contributed to the market contraction. Rising interest rates fundamentally altered the economics of leveraged buyouts. Additionally, inflation pressures compressed operating margins for portfolio companies while simultaneously raising labor and input costs, making target companies less attractive at prevailing valuations (McKinsey & Company, 2023a).

The exit environment became particularly challenging as LPs starved for distributions pull back new allocations from all but the largest, most reliable GPs (Bain & Company, 2025c). This created a cascading effect where limited liquidity reduced available capital for new investments while simultaneously pressuring valuations downward.

Geographic Distribution North American markets, particularly the United States, bore the brunt of the dealmaking decline. US PE deal value fell by approximately 45% in 2023, dropping to levels not seen since 2016. European markets experienced similar pressures but showed slightly more resilience in certain sectors, with deal value rising 54% in 2024 compared to 2023, making it the only region to show growth over the past five years (Bain & Company, 2025c). Asian markets demonstrated mixed performance depending on local economic conditions and regulatory environments, with China representing half of Asia-Pacific deal value as recently as 2020 but falling to just over 25% by 2024 (Bain & Company, 2025c).

Deal Size Segmentation Larger deals were disproportionately affected by the market downturn. Mega-deals (transactions exceeding $1 billion) became increasingly rare as financing became more expensive and complex. However, this trend reversed dramatically in 2024, with PE firms completing 18 megadeals valued at $5 billion or higher—more than double the prior year's total. The average deal size in 2024 jumped to $849 million, the second-highest value historically, with deals worth $1 billion or more making up 77% of total deal value (Bain & Company, 2025c). Middle-market transactions showed greater resilience throughout the downturn, though still experienced significant volume declines. Smaller deals in the lower middle market demonstrated relative stability, as these transactions typically require less leverage and face fewer financing constraints.

Sector Performance Variations Traditional sectors that had driven PE growth in previous decades faced particular challenges. Technology companies, which had commanded premium valuations during the 2020–2021 period, experienced sharp valuation corrections but maintained their position as PE's staple sector, representing 33% of buyout deals by value and 26% by volume in 2024. Consumer discretionary sectors suffered from changing spending patterns and supply chain disruptions. Industrial sectors initially faced resistance from inflation and global trade uncertainties but rebounded strongly in 2024, with deals rising 81% year-over-year. Financial services also showed remarkable recovery, with deal value jumping 92% year-over-year in 2024 (Bain & Company, 2025c).

Conversely, certain defensive sectors showed relative resilience throughout the period. Healthcare services, utilities, and essential consumer goods maintained more stable transaction activity, though still experienced volume declines compared to peak periods (McKinsey & Company, 2023a).

Market Recovery Indicators and Developments in the Mid-2020s Signs of market stabilization began emerging in 2024, though recovery remained tentative initially. Global M&A activity grew 13% in deal value to $3.6 trillion in 2024, with buyout's share of the market growing to 19% by value, up from 16% in 2023. More significantly, buyout investment value rose by 37% year-over-year to $602 billion in 2024, excluding add-on deals, reversing sharp declines in the two previous years. Global exit value jumped 34% year-over-year to $468 billion, while exit count climbed 22% to 1,470, marking signs of a tentative but welcome thaw in the exits environment (Bain & Company, 2025c).

The recovery was characterized by increased selectivity among investors, with firms focusing on higher-quality assets and more conservative leverage structures. Public-to-private deals continued to dominate the high-end of the PE market, increasing to $250 billion globally and representing almost half of deals over $5 billion in North America (Bain & Company, 2025c). The average PE holding period had reached a 20-year high of 7.1 years in 2023, indicating that firms were adapting to the new environment by extending investment horizons and focusing on operational improvements rather than financial engineering (McKinsey & Company, 2024a).

Future Outlook Looking forward, industry experts anticipate continued recovery in PE deal activity, though the timeline and pace remain subject to macroeconomic and geopolitical developments. More than 60% of survey respondents expected deal volume to rise in 2025, suggesting cautious optimism among market participants, though

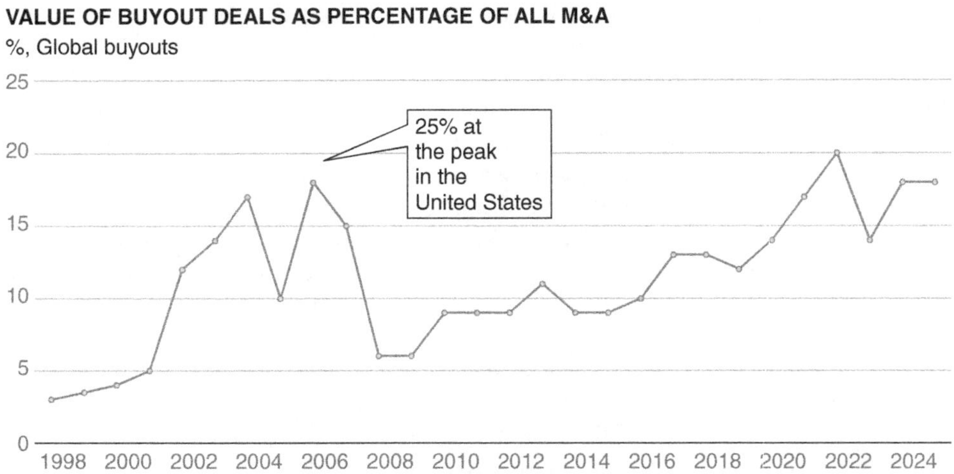

FIGURE 10.5 Buyout deals as percentage of all M&A deals in value.
Source: Dealogic.

this optimism was tempered by ongoing uncertainties regarding inflation trends, interest rates, trade policy, and geopolitical factors (Bain & Company, 2025c).

Private equity buyouts have experienced substantial growth as a proportion of global M&A activity since the 1990s (Figure 10.5). From representing approximately 5% of global M&A volume during the GFC, buyouts have steadily expanded their market share, reaching nearly 20% in peak years. This growth trajectory reflects the increasing institutionalization and scale of the PE industry.

This expansion represents more than cyclical variation—it signals a structural shift in the M&A landscape. PE firms have evolved from niche players to major market participants with significant capital deployment capabilities and sophisticated operational expertise. Their permanent establishment in the M&A ecosystem is evidenced by the changing attitudes of investment banks, which have repositioned PE firms from secondary clients to primary relationship targets, actively pursuing their advisory mandates and financing business.

The sustained growth in PE's M&A market share suggests this elevated level of participation—approaching 20% in favorable market conditions—represents a new baseline rather than a temporary peak. As institutional investors continue allocating capital to private markets and PE firms expand their sector expertise and deal origination capabilities, their role as permanent fixtures in the global M&A landscape appears firmly established.

Several positive drivers are expected to sustain growth opportunities in the healthcare sector over the coming years. Continued demographic trends, technological innovation, and the ongoing need for operational efficiency improvements in healthcare delivery should sustain investment interest. As Hugh MacArthur, chairman of Bain & Company's global Private Equity practice, noted:

> *The industry is anxious to make deals, GPs are finding creative ways to boost liquidity, more dollars should flow in from sovereign wealth funds and private wealth and, returns remain strong. But deal appetite is still tempered by the uncertainties keeping markets on edge.*

For the broader PE market, success in the evolving environment will likely require adaptation to new realities including higher cost of capital, extended holding periods, and greater emphasis on operational value creation rather than financial engineering. The industry's evolution during this period represents a maturation process, with market participants adapting strategies and expectations to align with a more normalized economic environment following the exceptional conditions of the early 2020s.

10.1.2.2 Is VC Moving into PE? There are multiple signs that the traditional boundaries between VC and PE (PE understood as excluding VC) are dissolving as leading VC firms transform themselves into multi-asset investment platforms. This shift represents a significant structural change in private markets and has been happening for over a decade.

The Regulatory Gateway: RIA Status as Liberation The most visible manifestation of this evolution is the wave of prominent VC firms registering as Registered Investment Advisors (RIAs). As reported by Bloomberg, Lightspeed Venture Partners completed its RIA registration in 2025, joining a growing list that includes Andreessen Horowitz (2019), Sequoia Capital, General Catalyst, Bessemer, Thrive Capital, and at least 18 other major firms.

This regulatory shift is transformative. Traditional VC firms face a 20% cap on nonqualifying investments—meaning 80% of their capital must flow into direct startup equity. RIA status eliminates these constraints, allowing firms to invest freely in public stocks, secondary shares, buyouts, crypto assets, and even acquire entire companies.

Structural Innovation: From Fund Cycles to Evergreen Models Sequoia Capital's 2021 restructuring exemplifies this transformation most dramatically. The firm abandoned the traditional 10-year fund cycle in favor of "The Sequoia Fund"—a single evergreen vehicle that can hold public stocks, PE, and other assets indefinitely. This $19.6 billion fund serves as the sole LP for Sequoia's sub-funds (seed, venture, growth), creating a continuous capital recycling system.

The evergreen model addresses a fundamental inefficiency in traditional VC: "cash drag" and reinvestment risk. When portfolio companies exit via IPO or acquisition, proceeds from traditional funds often sit idle while managers seek new investments. Evergreen structures automatically recycle capital into new deals, maintaining higher average allocation to private markets and potentially delivering superior compounded returns.

The Extreme Case: General Catalyst's Complete Transformation General Catalyst has taken this evolution furthest, no longer calling itself a VC firm but rather a "transformation company." Under CEO Hemant Taneja, the firm has acquired Summa Health for $485 million through its Health Assurance Transformation Corporation (HATCo) subsidiary, launched a wealth management division, built AI companies in-house rather than just investing in them, and created a network of 20 health systems across 43 US states to serve as testing grounds for portfolio innovations. This shift from passive capital provider to active industry transformer combines investment with operational control and in-house company building.

Market Forces Driving Convergence Several factors explain this convergence:

1. Market saturation and competition
   The explosive growth of VC over the last 15 years has created capital oversupply for the best deals. Firms need new terrains: secondary markets, public equities, buyouts, and operational control to differentiate and deploy growing fund sizes.
2. Extended private company life cycles
   Companies now stay private longer, with secondary markets "eating" public markets. Firms want flexibility to support portfolio companies through later stages, including post-IPO holdings.
3. Asset class blurring
   The line between late-stage VC and growth PE has blurred. Crossover funds and growth equity strategies naturally lead to PE-style minority buyouts and operational involvement.
4. Returns pressure
   With traditional VC returns under pressure from competition, firms seek alpha in adjacent strategies: distressed investing, roll-ups, operational improvement, and multi-asset approaches.

This transformation carries profound implications:

- For LPs: Traditional asset allocation buckets (VC vs. PE vs. hedge funds) become meaningless when a single firm spans all three. LPs gain diversification but lose precision in portfolio construction.
- For portfolio companies: Firms can now provide continuity capital across all growth stages, eliminating the traditional "handoff" from VC to PE. This creates stronger founder relationships but also concentrates risk.
- For competition: Traditional PE firms face new competition from VC-origin players with deeper technology expertise and founder networks. Meanwhile, the barrier to entry for "mega-deals" has lowered as VC firms gain PE capabilities.

The Future Landscape This convergence appears irreversible and accelerating. The traditional VC partnership model—small, focused, relationship-driven—is evolving into diversified asset management platforms resembling investment banks or family offices more than classic venture partnerships.

However, the transformation is not without risks. Compliance costs for RIAs are roughly eight times higher than traditional exempt advisors. Cultural challenges emerge as firms blend different investment philosophies and time horizons. Some firms may find their expansion dilutes their core competency rather than enhancing it.

The most successful firms will likely be those that maintain their investment edge while scaling operational capabilities—using their platform breadth to create unique value propositions rather than simply chasing larger AuM. As General Catalyst's approach demonstrates, the future belongs to firms that can seamlessly integrate capital, operational expertise, and transformational vision across the entire business life cycle.

10.1.2.3 Specific Outlook for Healthcare and Life Sciences The healthcare and life sciences sector has demonstrated remarkable resilience and sustained growth over the past two decades, building upon dramatic expansion documented since 2000. Historical analysis shows PE healthcare investments grew from less than $5 billion annually in 2000 to $100 billion in 2018—a 20-fold increase, with 70% of cumulative investments occurring since 2010 (Appelbaum and Batt, 2020). A new historical record was set in 2021 with $200 billion PE deals in healthcare (Figure 10.6). We introduced earlier how the healthcare and life sciences sector demonstrated remarkable resilience throughout this period of market contraction, building upon the strong foundation established in previous decades. As documented in historical context, PE investments in healthcare had already shown dramatic growth, and this trend continued even during the challenging 2022–2024 period, though at moderate levels.

Global healthcare PE deal value fell slightly to an estimated $115 billion in 2024. North America continued to be the largest market, representing 65% of global deal value, with Europe and Asia-Pacific accounting for 22% and 12%, respectively (Bain & Company, 2025b).

Healthcare deal value remained relatively high after the peak of 2021 (Figure 10.7). Healthcare deal volume activity maintained relative stability compared to other sectors for several structural reasons. First, the sector's defensive characteristics provided cash flow stability during economic uncertainty. Government reimbursement programs, which account for approximately 40% of healthcare spending, offered predictable revenue streams that were less susceptible to cyclical economic pressures and were projected to grow at 5.4% annually through 2026 (Appelbaum and Batt, 2020). Second, demographic trends continued to drive long-term demand growth regardless of macroeconomic conditions. An aging population and increased healthcare utilization created sustained investment opportunities that remained attractive even in a higher interest rate environment (Boston Consulting Group, 2024).

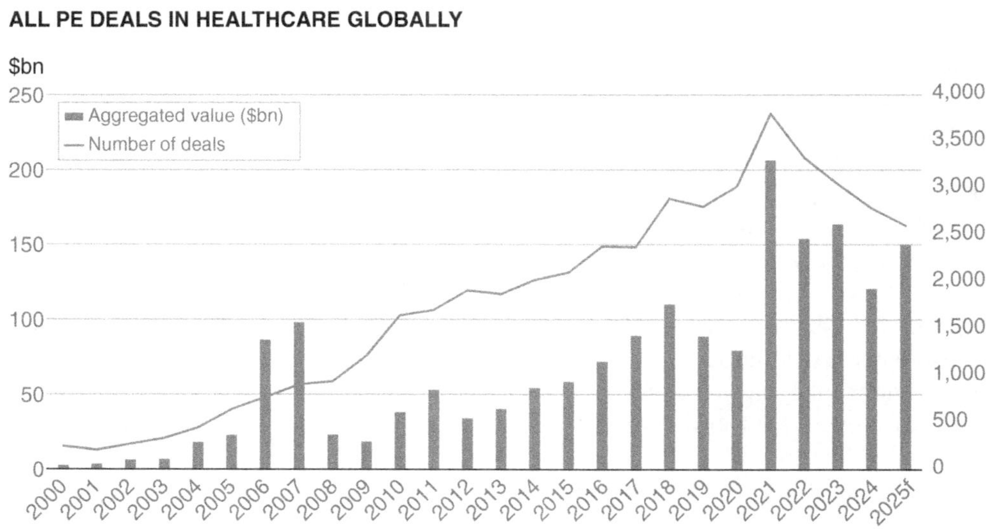

FIGURE 10.6 Volume and value of PE deals in healthcare globally.
Source: Preqin (buyouts, growth and other PE, excluding VC).

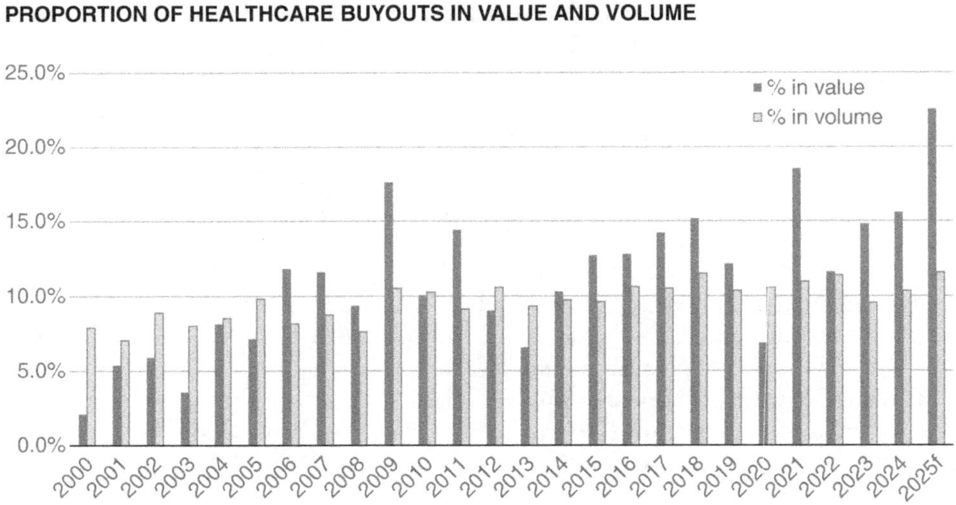

FIGURE 10.7 Share of healthcare PE deals in volume and value.
Source: Preqin.

Third, the fragmented nature of many healthcare subsectors continued to present consolidation opportunities. However, the regulatory landscape has evolved significantly, with federal and state authorities implementing new oversight mechanisms that create compliance burdens and challenge established business models. State-level scrutiny has intensified particularly in 2025, with Oregon implementing the nation's most stringent law restricting management services organization (MSO) models, Massachusetts expanding notice requirements and investor liability, and California pursuing similar legislative efforts. Despite challenges from increasing regulatory scrutiny and high interest rates, PE firms maintained steady investment in the US healthcare space in 2024, albeit at lower levels than in 2023. The Private Equity Stakeholder Project tracked 1,049 PE-backed healthcare deals in the United States in 2024, representing a 7.6% decrease from 2023 levels. This included 262 growth/expansion investments, 166 leveraged buyouts, and 621 add-on acquisitions to 383 unique platform companies.

The biopharma segment within healthcare showed particularly strong performance (Figure 10.8), leading all other healthcare segments in deal value in 2024 (Bain & Company, 2025). This growth was fueled by investments in clinical trial IT infrastructure and manufacturing capabilities, exemplified by notable transactions (not just PE) such as Novo Holdings' $16.5 billion purchase of Catalent to bolster manufacturing capacity for GLP-1 therapies. Healthcare IT also experienced significant activity, with investments targeting core systems of record and revenue cycle management within the provider space as well as AI applications, which accounted for nearly a third of all healthcare investment in the first half of 2025 and grew approximately twofold since 2022 according to SVB.

European dealmaking in healthcare rebounded to record highs in 2024, with deal volume surging past its 2021 peak, boosted by a focus on smaller deals and strategic investments in biopharma and medtech sectors that can easily scale across the region (Bain & Company, 2025a). However, Asia-Pacific healthcare deals faced challenges,

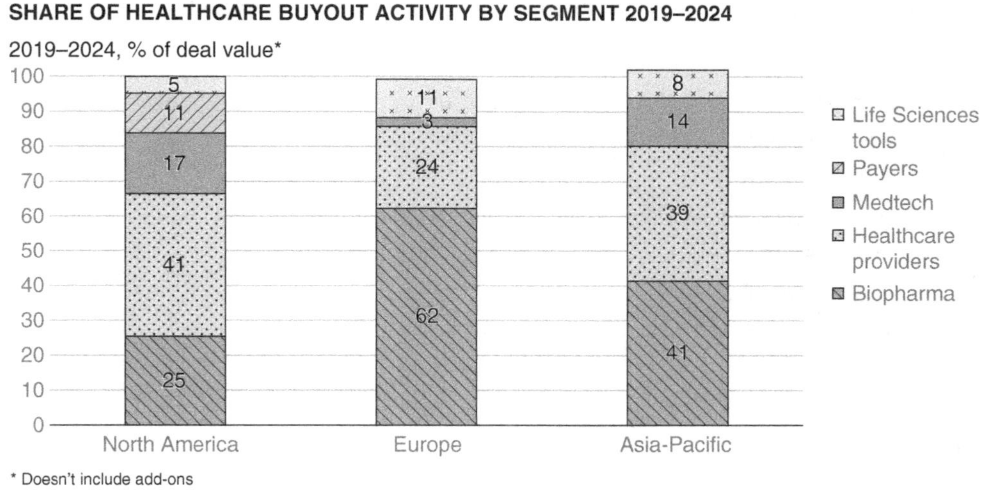

FIGURE 10.8 Share of healthcare buyout activity by PE segment.
Source: Dealogic.

with deal volume declining 49% year-over-year, primarily due to China's macroeconomic slowdown and regulatory uncertainties.

10.1.2.4 Minority Deals An important development we have seen in PE is the pursuit of new investment opportunities through minority deals. This is because there are not enough majority deals. For example, many good firms will accept a minority stake in a Chinese company because they do not really have an alternative; they might design a structure that would allow them to take control later. For example, I have worked with clients who have considered investing 49% in a deal, but with a few agreements and clauses that say that if the management were to change, the investors would have an option to buy another 2% and take the control. The advantage of that is, if there is a less formal option, you are at less risk of overpaying—this was particularly the case when there was not a significant performance differential over the period 2008–2014 between minority and majority deals.

Figure 10.9 illustrates the proportion of minority deals as a percentage of all global deals grew a lot when you compare the years before and after the financial crisis. By 2014, minority deals represented over a quarter of all deals, showing that many investors were ready to consider giving up on control, at least then.

10.1.2.5 European Bolt-ons in the United States ... and US Investors Eyeing Europe Those looking to find new investment opportunities have also been gravitating toward the West. In other words, some funds want to go to America in particular. PE-backed firms need bolt-on acquisitions. We have discovered that they need to grow, but organic growth is too slow most of the time. Acquisitions are a way to grow fast, and also sometimes a way to hide the fact that the organic performance is lacking. Confronted by very stagnant economic growth in Europe after the crisis, European funds have been trying to grow their European businesses with foreign subsidiaries, or by buying bolt-ons in foreign countries. And the United States has traditionally been their first destination, as it has a very large market with plenty of opportunities.

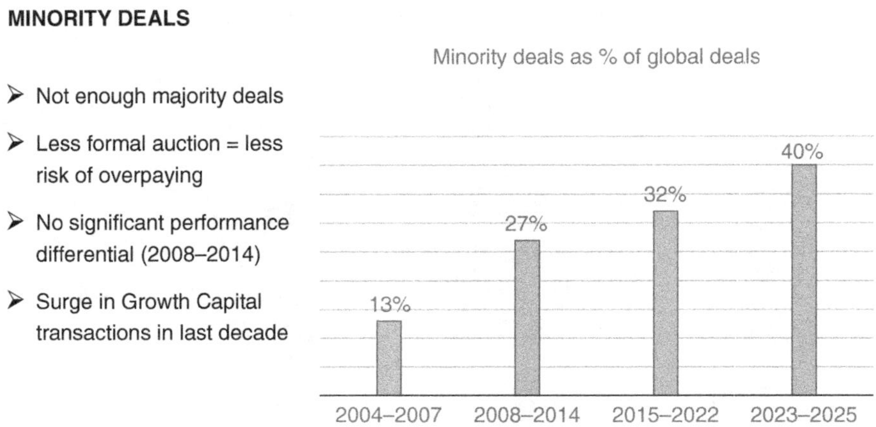

FIGURE 10.9 Share of minority deals.
Source: Boston Consulting Group: ECI Partners; White & Case; Candesic research.

At least until 2025, when US investors started to realize that Europe was probably undervalued. For Guy Semmens, co-founder of Gyrus Capital,

> *Traditionally, you succeed in sourcing a good opportunity, having a good plan to develop it, and finding a buyer who wants or needs the asset. But the international dynamic is changing by the day and that's new. Europe has been less attractive than the US for 10–20 years, things have now changed. The announcement by Blackstone [in 2025] that they plan to invest massively in Europe is a strong indicator that a lot of value will be there for the years to come.*

10.1.2.6 NAV Lending Many LPAs allow follow-on investments in the range of 20–30% of committed capital. GPs will often borrow to pay for these investments rather than using uncalled capital or other financing mechanisms. The borrowed money is secured against the value of its entire portfolio of companies. This is called NAV lending. The NAV loans may be used to top up equity in leveraged underperforming portfolio companies, when the original LBO lenders are asking for deleveraging. But they may be the same who are going to make the NAV loans, effectively shifting the leverage from individual company exposure to fund level exposure.

GPs utilize NAV loans for four primary reasons. First and foremost, they provide much-needed liquidity to support underperforming or over-leveraged companies within a fund, injecting equity to stabilize these assets and prevent default scenarios. Second, GPs may use NAV loans to avoid the reputational or operational consequences of issuing capital calls to LPs, particularly during times of economic uncertainty when LPs may face their own liquidity constraints. Third, borrowing at the fund level can be used to optimize fund performance metrics such as the internal rate of return (IRR), as the capital can accelerate growth or recovery across the portfolio. Finally, NAV loans can create liquidity for secondary investments or other opportunities without forcing the GP to sell existing assets at potentially distressed valuations.

The NAV lending market is serviced by a diverse group of capital providers. Traditional lenders, such as established banks, are frequent participants, but specialist private credit funds have become increasingly active, offering more bespoke and flexible financing solutions, typically at a higher cost.

A critical dynamic, however, involves the transformation of risk. A particularly interesting situation arises when the original lenders from a portfolio company's LBO also provide the NAV loan. This can lead to significant concentration of leverage where the risk is not mitigated. It is merely shifted from the company level to the fund level. For instance, a lender might demand deleveraging from a single struggling company while simultaneously extending new credit to the fund that holds it. While this approach dilutes the lender's exposure to any single asset failure, it amplifies the overall fund-level risk, concentrating exposure and potentially threatening the stability of the entire fund if portfolio recovery fails to materialize.

You guessed it, this shifting of risk, combined with a lack of transparency, has made NAV lending a controversial practice. The core ethical concern is that it can be used to obscure problems rather than solve them. For example, GPs might use NAV loans to artificially boost fund performance metrics ("window dressing"), creating a misleading representation of fund health. In other cases, leveraging the fund to rescue a single failing investment could transfer significant risk to LPs without their explicit consent. This creates potential conflicts of interest, especially if the same institution benefits from fees on both the original LBO debt and the new NAV loan.

This dynamic has drawn sharp criticism from industry observers. Professor Ludovic Phalippou of Oxford's Saïd Business School notes:

> *Even though I was always amazed by all the leeway given to GPs in most LPAs ... I had never thought that so many GPs would borrow on behalf of LPs to pay them. I must confess that this is a level of audacity that I had not conceived. And it gets better if it is a private credit fund making the NAV loan because the LPs then give the money to the PC fund who then give it to the GP who give it back to the LP minus all the fees from all these wealth creators. It is really stunning.*

From the LP's perspective, the primary concerns are undisclosed risk and cost. LPs will naturally view NAV lending unfavorably when it increases fund-level risk without commensurate returns. Transparency about the use of borrowed capital is therefore critical to maintaining trust.

Guy Semmens of Gyrus Capital identifies another key issue for LPs: the cost and timing of these loans. He notes,

> *NAV financing is fine as a tool but expensive at low double-digit interest rates. The issue is that it tends to be used at the tail end of funds, for businesses that are on average less attractive. LPs should be worried that the GPs are giving away their return to a third party.*

This highlights the risk that LPs are paying high interest rates to support the fund's weakest assets, with the primary benefit flowing to the lender and the GP, not the investor.

Whatever the controversies, NAV lending has become a global phenomenon. Initially prevalent in the mature US market, the practice has been widely adopted since the early 2020s by European and Asian PE funds, spurred by the growth of private credit markets.

Ultimately, NAV loans are a powerful tool for PE funds, providing liquidity and strategic flexibility. However, they also carry significant risks and ethical challenges. For LPs and regulators, the emphasis must be on robust governance, clear disclosures, and aligning GP incentives with long-term fund health. The global expansion of NAV lending highlights the urgent need for consistent industry standards to mitigate these associated risks.

10.1.3 Exits

Building on the evolving fundraising landscape and shifting investment strategies, this section delves into recent trends and a few ways PE firms are navigating the delicate balance of unlocking liquidity, managing portfolio quality, and timing exits amid ongoing market uncertainties, offering insights into what exit dynamics may look like in the near term.

10.1.3.1 Seven-year Cycles Figure 10.10 offers some key information about buyout-backed exits since just before the GFC. Based on this data, it seems that there is a surge in exit activity every seven years. After 2007, 2014, and 2021, massive amounts of dry powder drummed up deals between sponsors. While strategic sales remained by far the largest channel, soaring public markets led to a burst in IPO activity, rising stock prices and better-than-expected economic growth. Remember, 2021 was during the COVID-19 pandemic. This all gave corporate buyers ample currency for strategic deals. In the years after 2021, exits dropped drastically due to the high discount rates hitting the valuations of the investments of the previous years.

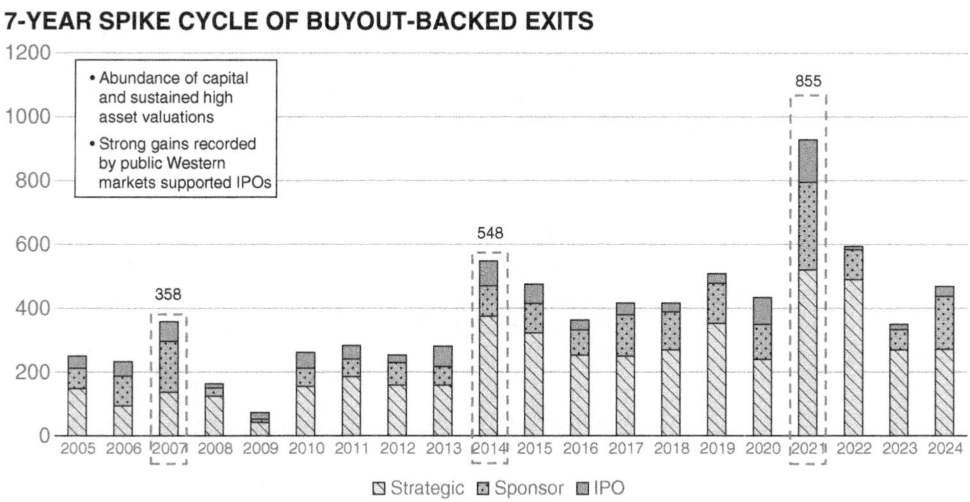

Notes: Includes partial and full exits; bankruptcies excluded; IPO value represents offer amount and not market value of company

FIGURE 10.10 Seven-year spike cycle of buyout-backed exits.
Source: Dealogic.

10.1.3.2 Quick Flips Quick flip deals, where buyout-backed companies are sold within 18 months of investment, tend to fluctuate in frequency based on broader market conditions. For example, 2014 recorded the lowest proportion of quick flips alongside a record six-year median holding period (Figure 10.11). This was largely a consequence of accumulated investments that funds could not exit readily during or immediately after the GFC, leading to longer holds and fewer rapid sales. Quick flips generally become more prevalent during strong economic cycles and buoyant markets when PE firms can capitalize on heightened valuations and shorter turnaround times. Conversely, in periods of market uncertainty or downturns, holding periods lengthen as exit opportunities diminish, and funds focus on operational improvements rather than quick sales. Research suggests quick flips often correlate with experienced funds and larger transactions but remain a small proportion of total deals, reflecting a broader preference for value creation over rapid asset turnover in PE.

10.1.3.3 Steeper Net Cash Flow J-curves This analysis by Pitchbook (Figure 10.12) highlighted how 2019 and 2020 vintages faced steep negative cash flows, surpassing even the historically slow 2006 vintage at comparable stages. These funds endured the pandemic early in their life cycle, aggressive investments at high valuations during the first two years, and the subsequent impact of rising interest rates in years four and five, which had challenged those valuations. In 2023, exit activity remained subdued throughout the year as GPs awaited lower interest rates and a revival of the IPO market. This stagnation created challenges across the PE ecosystem. LPs, receiving limited distributions, had less capital to commit to new funds, making fundraising harder for GPs.

In contrast, despite the difficult exit environment, the 2016 vintage had achieved notable distributions, highlighting the importance of timing in investment strategies. These funds benefited from acquiring assets at more moderate valuations compared to the inflated prices of 2020–2021, enabling stronger exit opportunities.

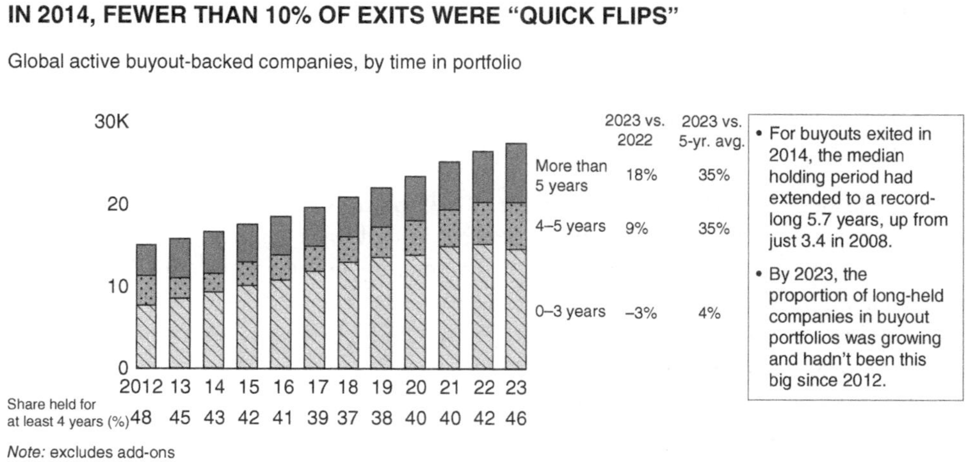

FIGURE 10.11 Evolution of number of years in portfolio.
Source: PitchBook (Bain report).

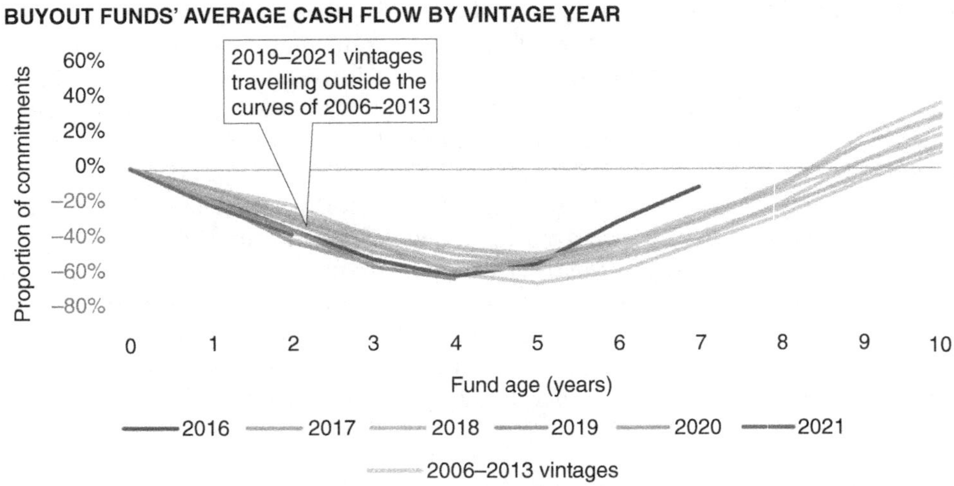

FIGURE 10.12 Buyout funds' average cash flow by vintage year.
Source: PitchBook, Behind the J-curve, April 2024.

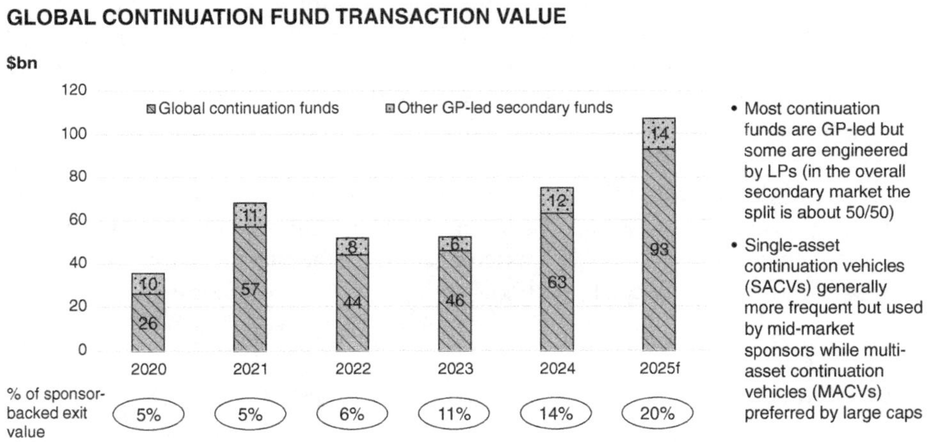

FIGURE 10.13 Global continuation fund transaction value.
Source: Jefferies Global Secondary Market Review, Evercore.

10.1.3.4 Continuation Funds In December 2024, Bain & Co. highlighted a massive backlog of some $3 trillion in aging deals that needed to be sold in the coming years. Continuation funds played a small part in engineering some exits. Jefferies estimated that they reached $63 billion that year, accounting for a record 14% of all PE exits. In 2025, the proportion reached 20%. In comparison, they represented only 5% of exits during the peak year of 2021 (Figure 10.13).

Continuation funds are not direct successors to the zombie funds of 2009 (see Chapter 2) but rather represent an evolution of the PE market's ability to address long-term illiquidity challenges. They are intended to reflect increased sophistication, transparency, and alignment in PE, contrasting sharply with the negative connotations and governance issues associated with zombie funds. While both tackle the challenge of extended asset holding periods, continuation funds focus on maximizing value and providing liquidity options for investors, whereas zombie funds were typically a by-product of market distress and mismanagement.

That said, many LPs view continuation funds as a necessary evil and would have preferred successful proper redemptions during the original fund's lifetime. While continuation funds offer an opportunity to exit, it is generally at a discount to the expected price. A conflict of interest can arise as GPs oversee both sides of the deal. For those LPs who are allowed to and choose to reinvest, provided the asset receives proper valuation and GP incentives remain well-aligned, these structures can deliver appealing opportunities for ongoing exposure to high-performing companies with reduced fee and carry arrangements.

Guy Semmens from Gyrus Capital reminds us:

> *The real risk in PE is liquidity. So, what LPs should be looking for is the ability to realize and exit investments. There was a shift post Covid when the cost of capital was no longer close to zero, and the liquidity fell even more. The history of PE is a story of illiquidity: we started by developing businesses to sell them to trade buyers. We then increasingly sold to other PE investors in secondary deals. Later we sold to secondary funds, then to ourselves with continuation funds!*

Recent primary research confirms that single-asset continuation vehicles (CVs)—which frequently include healthcare assets—accounted for the majority of reviewed CV transactions in both 2023 (60%) and 2024 (57%). Technology, industrials, and notably healthcare (8.6%) were leading sectors for CV deployment in these years, with healthcare's share demonstrating both the sector's complexity and attractiveness to GPs.

The market has seen a steep increase in overall transaction volume and size: 2024 saw a 48% year-over-year growth in GP-led transaction volume and a 139% jump in the median total enterprise value (TEV) of single-asset CVs, rising to $1.4 billion from $582 million the year before. This explosion in deal size was partly attributable to larger premium healthcare assets being rolled into CVs rather than exited outright.

Healthcare-specific examples are underrepresented in public summaries due to confidentiality, but Houlihan's tombstone data lists several leading multi-asset transactions involving large portfolio transfers across legacy healthcare and energy services funds. One such example in the healthcare space is the continuation fund for Prolacta Bioscience, a life sciences company focused on human-milk-based nutritional products.

Structurally, 2024 brought further innovation: the use of purchase price deferrals and earn-outs increased, with 19% of CVs reviewed including deferred consideration and 8% including earn-outs, according to Houlihan Lokey. For healthcare platforms—often facing regulatory or revenue hurdles—such tools allow parties to bridge pricing gaps while aligning incentives around milestone achievements or post-close performance. This trend reflects the need to tailor exits and liquidity events to the idiosyncratic risks of healthcare assets.

Pricing in the CV market remained robust: in 2024, 75% of all CVs reviewed—we must assume the sample is representative—occurred at or above 90% of NAV, with a median of 93.6% according to Houlihan Lokey. Single-asset CVs—especially those involving high-quality healthcare assets—tended to trade at higher prices than multi-asset vehicles, though younger portfolio ages commanded better pricing. Most notably, more than 90% of deals included substantial unfunded capital commitments, designed to fund growth (such as clinical trial expansion or M&A) in portfolio companies.

Market best practice is evolving toward greater governance rigor. Regulatory focus on conflicts—particularly from the SEC and, from 2025, the UK FCA—has heightened expectations that sponsors secure independent fairness opinions and more robust LP election mechanics. Yet, practical implementation remains patchy: only 17% of recent CV deals offered LPs a "true status quo" reinvestment option, with most LPs still opting to cash out rather than roll over, highlighting the ongoing centrality of liquidity for investors.

Yes, most investors chose in recent years to sell rather than remain invested when PE firms transferred portfolio companies into CVs, with between 75% and 80% doing so in 2024, rising to more than 85% in 2025, according to Houlihan Lokey and as reported by the *Financial Times*. Kastiel and Nili (2024) observed that most investors declined the option to roll over their stakes, even though the continuation fund was "run by the same PE firm with which they have cultivated relationships for years."

But it did not stop there. By 2025, a new and controversial term had entered the PE lexicon: "CV-squared." As some of the first-generation CVs approached maturity—often structured as 5+1+1-year funds—the promised liquidity event remained elusive. In many cases, the underlying assets, particularly in complex sectors like healthcare and life sciences, had not yet reached exit readiness due to regulatory delays, clinical trial setbacks, or shifting market dynamics. To address this, some sponsors floated a bold idea: a continuation fund on top of a continuation fund, a strategy that blurred the lines between long-term value realization and perpetual rollover.

While the terminology gained prominence in 2025, the practice itself had earlier precedents. The most notable early example of this type of "cross-fund transaction" was Nordic Capital's 2023 transaction, which involved transferring multiple healthcare assets—including ArisGlobal and Advanz Pharma—from a 2018 continuation vehicle (Fund IX CV1) into a second continuation fund, backed by Coller Capital, Goldman Sachs Asset Management, and Glendower Capital, among others according to Secondaries Investor. Nordic justified the move on the basis that the assets still had substantial upside potential and required further time and capital to realize full value. However, critics viewed it as a warning signal: an emblem of exit avoidance, valuation layering, and GP–LP misalignment.

These CV-on-CV structures raised several serious concerns. First, they compounded liquidity challenges for LPs, who now faced successive rollovers, often under pressure and with little leverage. Second, they created valuation complexity: when the same GP is buying and selling the same assets in successive internal transactions, the risk of circular pricing and misaligned incentives increases. Third, they reset fees and carry, potentially creating disproportionate upside for GPs while legacy LPs face narrowing paths to liquidity.

Mike Mortimer from GHO recognized potential market timing issues, with continuation vehicles becoming overused as financing tools rather than genuine value creation mechanisms:

> *Unlike some PE firms, we decided we would do only one continuation vehicle per fund, always with two independent valuations. LPs are increasingly concerned when they see several continuation funds in a single vintage. There's lots of financial engineering happening right now, and it will eventually catch up with you.*

Proponents argued that such structures might be appropriate for sectors with unusually long time horizons, such as advanced therapeutics, AI diagnostics, or gene therapy platforms—where even 15-year fund horizons may fall short. But even among sympathetic investors, concerns remain about transparency, governance, and the erosion of discipline around exits.

Ultimately, the emergence of CV-squared reflects a broader structural tension in PE: as firms move deeper into science-based and infrastructure-heavy sectors, the mismatch between traditional fund cycles and real-world timelines is becoming acute. Whether CV-squared is an adaptive innovation or an unsustainable workaround remains an open question—but it has undoubtedly become a litmus test for GP–LP trust in the 2020s.

10.1.4 Sustainability

In recent years, the ESG push has been accompanied by significant regulatory changes that reshaped PE to a different extent in Europe, the United Kingdom and the United States. The ILPA-Bain ESG Survey 2022 report already identified significant differences (Bain & Company, 2022).

10.1.4.1 European Push Europe led the way with the adoption and implementation of the Sustainable Finance Disclosure Regulation (SFDR) in March 2021. It mandated ESG disclosures from all fund managers targeting EU investors, compelling a widespread integration of ESG principles into investment strategies. By 2023, Invest Europe reported that approximately 84% of new vintage funds were classified as Article 8 or 9.[3]

Major PE houses across Europe, such as EQT and CVC, have had long established robust ESG frameworks. These firms have employed dedicated ESG teams, issued detailed sustainability reports, and built Article 8 and Article 9 funds that explicitly promoted environmental or social characteristics. With pressure from LPs, ESG integration has become directly correlated with fundraising success. Many of these large funds were able to raise capital faster and at larger ticket sizes by advertising their sustainable investing credentials.

Mid-market managers, typically controlling between €500 million and €5 billion, had been slower to react before 2021. However, following the introduction of SFDR

[3] Article 8 funds promote environmental or social characteristics, while Article 9 funds have a sustainable investment objective.

and increased LP scrutiny, most adopted ESG frameworks, published formal ESG policies, and set measurable climate and DEI targets, tracking KPIs such as emissions, gender diversity, and governance scores. ESG had increasingly become a lever for value creation, enabling stronger governance, higher productivity, and in some cases, a valuation premium upon exit.

Firms managing below €300 million had initially defaulted to basic SFDR compliance, mostly filing Article 6 funds with no specific ESG characteristics. Yet by 2024, even these players had begun adopting simplified ESG processes, driven by increasing pressure from funds of funds, bank lenders, and institutional LPs. A growing number signed up to the UN's Principles for Responsible Investment (PRI), viewing ESG not as a regulatory burden but as an operational advantage that improved transparency, mitigated reputational risk, and helped them compete against larger houses.

10.1.4.2 The United Kingdom's Journey Beyond EU Rules Post Brexit, the United Kingdom chose to diverge from EU regulatory frameworks. It began developing its own ESG regime, primarily through the Task Force on Climate-related Financial Disclosures (TCFD), which became mandatory for large companies in 2022, and the UK Sustainability Disclosure Requirements (SDR), which rolled out anti-greenwashing rules in 2024 and fund sustainability labels in 2025.

Large UK-based PE firms, including Permira and Apax, had closely mirrored their EU peers by embedding ESG across portfolio management, fund structuring, and investor reporting. They prepared extensively for SDR rules by aligning internal ESG systems to match both UK and EU standards, ensuring continued access to European LPs. Many had launched climate-focused and gender-equity funds, viewing ESG as essential for both capital raising and long-term portfolio value creation. Bain and Company noted that, by 2025, sustainability-themed PE funds in the United Kingdom consistently outperformed their traditional counterparts on internal rates of return (Bain & Company, 2025c).

UK mid-market players, such as Inflexion and LDC, accelerated ESG adoption after 2021. These firms created ESG leads, implemented portfolio-level ESG reporting, and introduced deal-level covenants tied to ESG KPIs including energy efficiency and board diversity. BVCA guidance documents, which were widely adopted in the United Kingdom, helped standardize these practices across the market. Many mid-market funds cited improved LP relationships and smoother due diligence processes as tangible benefits of their ESG investment.

Smaller UK funds, which often focused on growth equity or venture strategies, had made more modest strides. Initially, many adopted ESG primarily to satisfy bank lenders or win over development finance institutions. However, by 2026, they increasingly saw ESG integration as a branding opportunity, especially in sectors like fintech, digital health, and climate tech. Several early adopters saw inbound demand from LPs and family offices interested in mission-aligned capital.

10.1.4.3 The United States: From Voluntary to Essential ESG integration in US PE has relied on voluntary frameworks such as the UN PRI, SASB, and ILPA guidelines rather than a formal SFDR-style regulation. US LPs, especially public pensions and university endowments, have increasingly demanded ESG data, driving significant market shifts. However, political tensions have persisted, with more than 20 states having introduced or passed anti-ESG laws by 2025, restricting ESG considerations in public fund investments and state contracts. This has created a fragmented regulatory environment, forcing managers to navigate conflicting demands from global LPs and local political pressures.

Major US players such as Blackstone, KKR, and Carlyle have embraced ESG through global coordination, publishing sustainability reports aligned with TCFD and referencing SFDR standards for certain products. These firms have also raised substantial capital through sustainability-linked loans and dedicated impact strategies, focusing on energy transition, green real estate, and healthcare access. ESG-linked lending has become widespread, with debt pricing increasingly influenced by portfolio companies' emissions or diversity metrics.

US mid-market managers began prioritizing ESG as LP demands grew, often relying on third-party ESG consultants for due diligence and reporting. ESG performance is now a factor in valuations, with exit buyers scrutinizing climate risk, supply chain ethics, and employee welfare during M&A due diligence.

Smaller US managers, particularly in traditional sectors, have shown weaker ESG maturity, but many have adopted basic exclusion lists and portfolio-level carbon data to meet minimum requirements. Growing pressure from auditors, commercial banks, and secondaries buyers has pushed even the smallest firms to implement some ESG basics. Despite the backlash, most managers continue to integrate ESG practices to satisfy global LPs and regulatory requirements, even as some downplay the term "ESG" in politically sensitive markets.

10.1.4.4 Impact on Healthcare ESG is generally considered particularly relevant in healthcare because the sector faces unique challenges, including reducing carbon footprints, ensuring equitable access to care, managing patient safety, and meeting evolving regulatory expectations, all of which directly impact public health outcomes and investor priorities.

Sustainability in healthcare and life sciences, as in most sectors, is about balancing current needs with the well-being of future generations. It requires a focus on environmental stewardship, social equity, economic viability, and governance, ensuring that advancements in these sectors contribute positively to both human health and the planet.

From an environmental perspective, the healthcare sector is responsible for approximately 4–5% of global greenhouse gas emissions due to energy-intensive facilities, waste generation, and transportation, while pharmaceutical manufacturing, especially in life sciences, contributes heavily to emissions and water pollution through the disposal of chemical by-products. Green hospitals, efficient waste management, and sustainable supply chains are three key initiatives promoted by most PE investors. While there is no direct public pressure like in public markets, it is a wise choice to be prepared before new regulation hits, especially in Europe. There is also the exit consideration, especially in the case of an IPO, but also when selling to an investor with their own requirements.

From a social perspective too, life sciences companies and healthcare systems play a vital role in improving equitable access to treatments and services. There is growing focus on addressing healthcare disparities, including providing affordable medicines to underserved populations, on developing therapies and technologies that address pressing health challenges (e.g., antibiotic resistance, pandemics, chronic diseases) in a sustainable manner, and on promoting preventive healthcare and wellness initiatives to reduce disease burden, which can lessen the strain on healthcare systems and the environment.

Moreover, proper governance is vital in healthcare and life sciences to address ethical concerns, ensure transparency and accountability in operations, and build public trust in the development of new treatments and technologies.

PE plays a pivotal role in advancing ESG objectives within healthcare and life sciences by providing the capital and strategic oversight necessary to drive sustainable innovation and operational improvements. Many other investors—public sector, family businesses, nonprofit organizations—sometimes lack the necessary resources. Many PE investors tell us they invest in scaling green technologies, such as energy-efficient healthcare facilities and sustainable pharmaceutical manufacturing practices, while supporting companies in reducing waste and emissions. They promote social equity by backing businesses that enhance access to affordable care, develop life-saving therapies, and address health disparities in underserved populations. Additionally, PE firms are typically sophisticated players that embed robust governance frameworks, fostering ethical practices, regulatory compliance, and transparency in clinical trials, drug development, and digital health innovations. If they achieve to align profitability with ESG principles, PE investors have the power to catalyze transformative growth in these sectors, ensuring long-term value creation for stakeholders and society.

Most PE firms of all sizes now report annually on their sustainability efforts. This includes of course listed firms like KKR and CVC's *Sustainability Report* and Bain Capital's *ESG Report*, but most private firms too, like Ardian's *Public Transparency Report*, ARCHIMED's *Sustainability and Impact Report*, GHO's *Annual Responsible Investing Report* and TA Associates *Responsible Investment Report*, all publicly available and that we invite you to compare. Many became a signatory to the UN-supported Principles for Responsible Investment, launched in 2006. Partners Group and Permira were among the first large ones to sign in 2008. CD&R, H.I.G. and Hellman and Friedman joined in 2023.

10.2 HEALTHCARE SPECIALIST INVESTORS

The Healthcare Private Equity Association (HCPEA) highlights the dramatic rise of PE involvement in healthcare by serving as the industry's first and only sector-specific trade group. Established in 2010, HCPEA is a nonprofit association with a mission to foster knowledge-sharing, professional growth, and collaboration among its members—ultimately aiming to build the relationships and expertise needed to support enduring, innovative healthcare businesses. Its activities include educational programming, industry conferences, networking events, and resources covering emerging trends and regulatory issues.

Membership spans the spectrum from boutique firms to industry giants, bringing together most of the famous houses such as Bain Capital, Blackstone, Clayton Dubilier & Rice, KKR, TPG, Thomas H. Lee Partners, and Warburg Pincus. As of 2025, the association encompassed more than 100 member firms and more than 1,200 investment professionals, collectively managing upward of $4.3 trillion in assets (not all of them in healthcare!) with investments across more than 1,500 healthcare companies. That was a stark increase compared to just $200 billion in revenue across 500 companies at the time of its founding. HCPEA has helped cement healthcare's place at the top of the PE agenda by facilitating connections between capital and care and by backing initiatives focused on access, quality, and innovation in the industry.

While generalist PE funds have historically invested in healthcare, specialized healthcare and life sciences funds began gaining prominence in the early 2000s, with significant acceleration after the 2008 GFC, driven by the combined impact of demand, technology and regulation:

- Growing demand for healthcare due to aging populations, rising chronic diseases, and global healthcare access initiatives require mastering complex and dynamic economic models.
- Technological advancements in biotech, pharmaceuticals, medical devices, and digital health create attractive investment opportunities for those who can better assess the likelihood of success and the pace of adoption.
- Complex regulatory environments and long development cycles require more specialized knowledge.

Specialization in healthcare and life sciences is driven by the sector's unique complexity, requiring deep expertise to navigate intricate regulatory landscapes, such as FDA and EMA approvals granted to new drugs, biologics, and gene/cell therapies, or JCI Accreditation for international hospital certification, as well as scientific innovations that generalist funds may not effectively manage. Understanding clinical trials, reimbursement models, and intellectual property rights is critical for successful investments in these fields. Specialized funds excel in identifying niche opportunities, such as emerging therapies or innovative healthcare delivery models, while providing operational and strategic support to portfolio companies. They are also better equipped to mitigate risks, including trial failures and regulatory setbacks. Additionally, these funds leverage strategic partnerships with industry experts, healthcare providers, and research institutions to accelerate the growth and success of their investments.

Laurent Dethomas from Vivalto Partners emphasized how vital it is to rely on dedicated specialists:

> *For an LP seeking exposure to healthcare, the advantage of partnering with a sector-focused PE firm is the ability to gauge on the ground, through its networks, the real utility of services, devices, or drugs. Our investment in Delbert Pharma reflects our commitment to preserving critical, injectable hospital medicines manufactured in Europe, ensuring continuity in areas where public health spending is increasingly selective.*

Figure 10.14 shows the main specialist players in the United States and in Europe. Like many trends in PE, it started in the United States. We mentioned earlier how WCAS, founded in 1979, began specializing in healthcare by the mid-1980s, setting a precedent for sector-specific expertise. Before that, healthcare became a strategic focus at Warburg Pincus under the leadership of Lionel Pincus and John Vogelstein, who directed the firm's operations from 1966 through 2002. The duo developed a growth-oriented investment philosophy that spanned multiple industries, with healthcare emerging as a sector offering exceptional prospects for sustainable value building. Warburg Pincus reports on their website that, since inception in 1966, while remaining a generalist investor, it has invested over $17 billion in more than 180 healthcare companies, including Summit

FIGURE 10.14 Main healthcare-focused PE firms.
Source: Candesic.

Health, Modernizing Medicine, Ensemble Healthcare Partners, and Global Healthcare Exchange, and has been an active investor in life sciences, with notable investments in Polyplus, Norstella, Sotera Health, and Bausch + Lomb, among others.

The first pure players appeared in the 1990s. We introduced Ampersand Capital Partners, founded in 1988 but pivoting to focus primarily on healthcare in the 1990s and becoming a prominent player in mid-market healthcare investments, with \$3 billion AuM in 2025. Ampersand emphasizes growth equity investments in business-to-business segments of diagnostics, biopharma services, and medical technology, with a track record of building value through sector expertise. Waud Capital started as a one-person team in 1993, to reach \$5 billion 30 years later, focusing on healthcare services and software and technology, with particular expertise in healthcare supply chain. BPOC followed in 1996 with a focus on providers, outsourced services, products and distribution, and pharmacy and pharmaceutical services.

The 2000s saw the emergence of more specialized healthcare-focused firms. Arsenal Capital Partners was founded in New York in 2000, focusing equally on healthcare and industrials. Formed in 2003, Altaris "targets companies that are on 'the right side of healthcare.' That is, companies selling products and services that improve patient outcomes, enhance the care experience, increase system efficiency and transparency, and enable access and affordability." Founded the same year, Webster Equity Partners has been investing in "purpose driven, patient-centric healthcare organizations dedicated to providing best of class clinical care and service to their patients." Water Street Healthcare Partners, founded in 2005 by former healthcare executives, exemplified a trend toward operators-turned-investors leading specialized firms, reaching \$6 billion capital under management in 2024. Large generalist buyout firms stepped in too. Cressey & Company launched in 2008 in Chicago. TPG Healthcare Partners was launched in 2018 as an extension of their healthcare franchise and reached \$7 billion AuM in 2025. Patient Square Capital may show the most impressive growth in the industry. Founded in 2020 in California, it was managing \$17 billion in healthcare assets five years later. VC boutique firms focusing exclusively on healthcare and life sciences began to emerge, like OrbiMed (splitting from Mehta & Isaly) and Aisling Capital in the United States.

In Europe too, specialized healthcare investors emerged, like Gilde Healthcare (1982), initially focused on VC but later expanding in growth, SHS in Germany (1993), Apposite Capital (2006), G Square Private Equity (2007), and Mérieux Equity Partners (2009).

GHO Capital, founded in 2014, brought a global perspective to European healthcare investing. The firm's focus on healthcare specialty services and pharmaceuticals, combined with their transatlantic approach, has resulted in notable successes like FairJourney Biologics (10× exit in 2024), Sterling Pharma Solutions (quadrupling earnings in four years), BioAgilytix (6× exit when sold to Cinven in 2021), and Quotient Sciences (transformation of a local UK player into an international integrated contract research organization and contract development and manufacturing organization player). Their rapid growth to managing close to $10 billion by end of 2025 reflects the increasing sophistication of healthcare-focused investing. In May 2026, GHO and CBC announced their merger to form the largest healthcare-focused PE firm with $21 billion AuM.

ARCHIMED, also founded in 2014 by Denis Ribon after leaving 3i, pioneered a multi-strategy approach to healthcare investing and grew as fast, reaching €8 billion AuM after 10 years. ARCHIMED pursued a unique strategy by focusing on small to mid-cap healthcare businesses across Europe, often supporting founder-led companies to expand internationally. Some notable investments include Polyplus (see Chapter 4), a leader in gene therapy reagents, acquired for less than €10 million in 2016 and sold to Sartorius Stedim in 2023 for €2.4 billion, and BOMI Group, sold to UPS in 2022 for about €600 million EV. According to Preqin data, ARCHIMED's first fund and original buyer for Polyplus is ranked the best performing buyout fund on a global level for its 2014 vintage year, returning some seven times invested capital:

> *Even without Polyplus, MED I would have easily qualified as a top quartile performer, with its six other investments returning a combined three times invested capital.*

The team has continued to perform with its next two funds, small cap-focused MED II (€315 million raised in 2018) and mid-cap-focused MED Platform I (€1.5 billion raised in 2019), which were both top decile performers.

The 2010s have seen increasing specialization within healthcare PE. Firms have developed expertise in specific subsectors This specialization has been driven by the increasing complexity of healthcare business models and regulation.

Recent years have seen the emergence of even more specialized investors focusing on specific healthcare subsectors such as medical devices (Linden Capital Partners) or healthcare software (MTIP). Vistria invests in healthcare and other segments that deliver lasting societal impact. Similarly, specialized growth equity firms like Oak HC/FT and Keensight have emerged to target the intersection of healthcare and technology. GENUI, founded in 2014 in Germany, adds environmental transformation to this cocktail. While some established firms have recently reinforced their dedicated specialist teams in life sciences (Eurazeo), healthcare IT (Francisco Partners, Thoma Bravo), or contract research organizations (GTCR), new specialized healthcare investors continue to emerge, like Lauxera Capital Partners in 2020 in the United States and France (focus on business-to-business, no direct exposure to patients), as well as "generalist" healthcare investors like Evolve Healthcare Partners in Spain in 2020 and Vivalto Partners in France with their first €700 million fund raised in 2024. That same year, EQT's Healthcare Growth Strategy was formed to fill the space between EQT

Life Sciences, formed in 2022 after EQT's acquisition of venture capital firm LSP (Life Sciences Partners) and EQT's existing PE strategy (Thunell, 2024).

In Asia, the trend is more recent but there are already a few large players like CBC and Quadria Capital. Abrar Mir, cofounder of Quadria, explains that their industrial approach has consistently allowed them to invest at valuations below market multiples, and it is one of the defining reasons why their portfolio companies have grown faster than the market:

> *Healthcare may be a competitive and expensive sector, but we believe our edge is clear.*
>
> *We have built one of the largest and most specialized investment teams in the region. Alongside them stands our Value Optimization team, supported by a full healthcare ecosystem and an unparalleled bench of operating partners—former CEOs of some of the largest healthcare companies in Asia and around the world, who work exclusively with us.*
>
> *Equally important is the discipline of our playbook. We do not apply a generic approach; we bring tailored frameworks—one designed for hospital groups, another for pharmaceutical companies, others for medical devices and consumer health. Each playbook is rigorous, measurable, and adaptable, ensuring that in every investment we make, execution is guided by discipline and amplified by experience.*

Overall, we could identify at least 25 healthcare specialist PE firms with more than $2 billion AuM allocated to healthcare[4] (Figure 10.15). Bear in mind this does

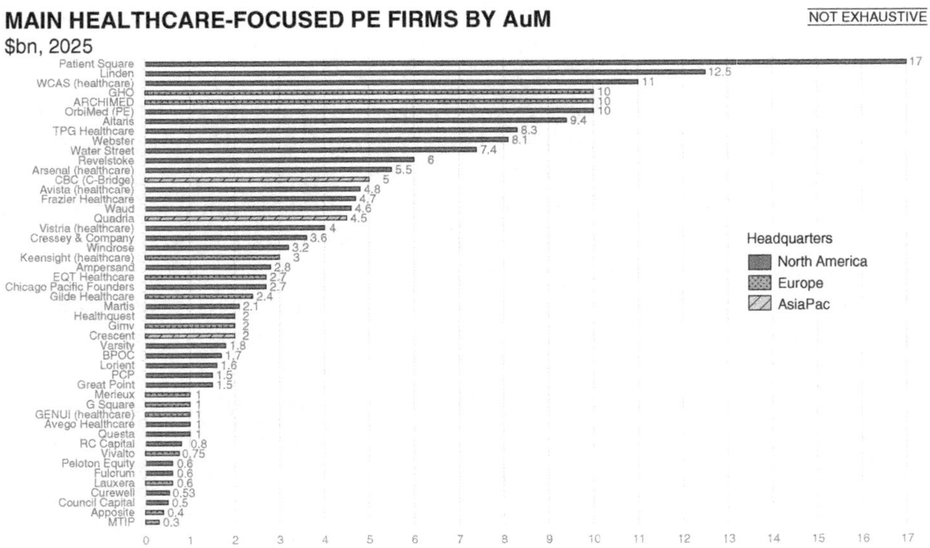

FIGURE 10.15 Main healthcare-focused PE firms by AuM.
Source: Candesic research (PE firms with 50% of AuM or more allocated to healthcare).

---

[4] In May 2026, GHO and CBC announced their merger to form the largest healthcare-focused PE firm with $21 billion AuM. Note also that Novo Holdings ($30bn non strategic investments) is not included.

not give an exhaustive view of PE investing in healthcare. In particular, it misses most large generalist buyout firms. Most of them have significant investments in healthcare. It also misses VC firms that venture into growth capital as well.

The creation of specialized PE funds in healthcare and life sciences reflects the need for expertise in navigating complex, high-growth industries. Their superior business model—characterized by sector-specific knowledge, focused investment strategies, and resilience to market cycles—offers a compelling advantage over generalist funds, enabling them to deliver better outcomes for investors and portfolio companies alike. Many LPs have been historically attracted to their track record in achieving outsized returns and their ability to weather economic volatility.

Over 2015–2020, mid-market healthcare funds—defined as those with AuM between $0.5 and $4 billion—outperformed large-cap funds. Although they made up only 15% of total fund AuM in the period, they represented roughly 25% of funds in the top performance quartile (Bain & Company, 2025). This may point to stronger performance dynamics in the mid-market segment, though it could also reflect the particularly favorable opportunities available in healthcare compared to other industries.

And yet, focus is not a guarantee for superior performance, as demonstrated with 2018–2020 vintage funds that invested predominantly in 2020–2021, when healthcare investments required historically high multiples and were exposed to the subsequent years of high inflation. Specialist funds seem to have been hit even harder than generalist ones. As mentioned in a Pitchbook analysis,[5]

> *While specialist funds have tended to reach net cash flow positive values more quickly than generalist funds historically, current distributions as a percentage of NAV flip that narrative on its head, with generalist funds returning 16.1% and specialist funds returning just 9.8% through 2023. Exits have slowed for healthcare and IT buyout funds in particular.*

Private equity investment in healthcare and life sciences has evolved from a peripheral strategy to a core focus for many firms. Pure players like WCAS, Waud, BPOC, Ampersand, Altaris, Webster, Water Street, Linden, Apposite, GSquare, Merieux, GHO, ARCHIMED, MTIP, Lauxera and Vivalto have demonstrated the value of sector specialization, while large generalist firms continue to leverage scale and capital to execute transformative deals. In 2025, the top 25 healthcare specialist PE firms[6] by AuM allocated to healthcare accounted for $161 billion or about 13% of the estimated amount allocated to healthcare by buyout and growth funds, including $1 trillion by generalist funds (Figure 10.16). Ten years earlier, some of today's main firms did not exist or had just raised their first fund. They accounted then for about $31 billion AuM in healthcare, that is about 6% of the buyout and growth capital allocated to healthcare at the time. As global healthcare needs grow, specialist PE firms are poised to play an even more significant role in shaping the future of the industry.

While healthcare-focused PE firms have multiplied significantly (comparing 2025 to 2010 shows dramatic growth), many concentrate on providers. Ampersand chose

[5] Pitchbook (2024, June). Generalist fund managers beat specialists in returning cash to LPs.

[6] We roughly defined healthcare specialist PE firms as having at least 50% of their AuM allocated to healthcare buyouts and growth capital. For these firms, we counted the AuM allocated to healthcare only. We estimate that, globally, they manage close to $200 billion AuM in healthcare.

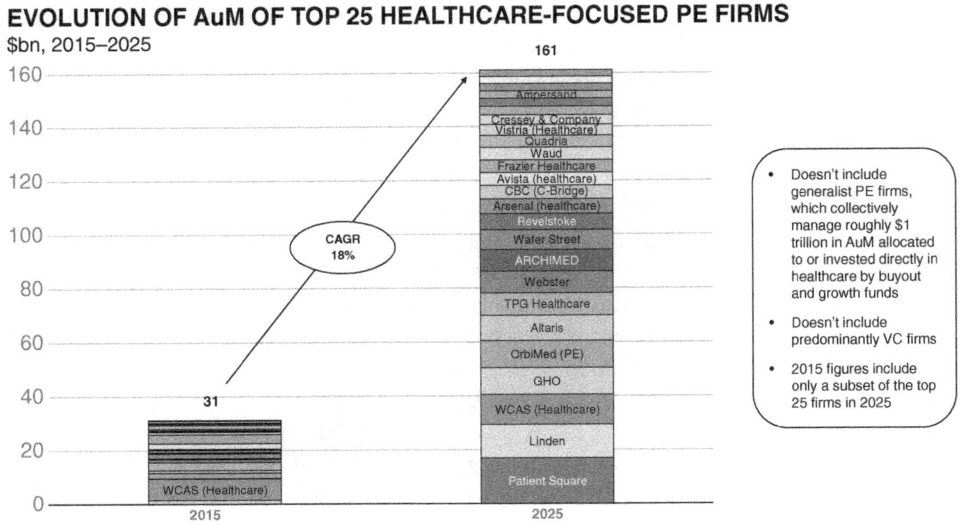

FIGURE 10.16 Evolution of AuM of top 25 healthcare-focused PE firms.
Source: Candesic research.

a different path, expanding to Europe and maintaining a focus on smaller companies. A notable example is their 2019 investment in Vibalogics, a German viral vector company where they helped build capabilities and expand operations to the United States, even relocating headquarters to the Boston area. Unlike peers who have diversified into multiple fund strategies including credit strategies in some cases, Ampersand maintains focus on equity investments through a single fund strategy targeting mid-market opportunities.

Some European healthcare investors like ARCHIMED, GHO, or Merieux rapidly expanded to the United States, setting up local offices and investing locally, which is not a surprise when you consider the size of the US market for life sciences products: around 40% of the global market in value. It is less common for US healthcare investors to settle in Europe, with the exception of Ampersand.

We recognize however that the focus on specialist investors can be misleading. Generalists like Bain Capital, Nordic Capital, Montagu, or Astorg have developed a true capability to invest in healthcare and play at the level of the specialists. Noe Richard makes it clear that Astorg knows the sector:

> *We believe PE can play a transformative role in advancing healthcare when applied with focus and high conviction. At Astorg, [within healthcare,] we deliberately concentrate on a narrow set of subsectors—pharmaceutical services and technology, MedTech and MedTech services, life science tools, and diagnostics. Our investment approach is highly specialised yet continuously informed by new scientific and technological developments. This dynamic focus allows us to identify emerging opportunities, foster innovation, and anticipate change across the healthcare ecosystem. By partnering with Healthcare leaders, we aim to build enduring businesses that enhance the efficiency of healthcare delivery and create sustainable value for patients, partners, and investors alike.*

10.3 ROLES AND CAREERS

You should bear in mind that most PE funds are typically small enterprises. They will have a partnership of a few people, and below that a few operating experts and some fund managers, and perhaps only a couple of analysts and some support staff.

10.3.1 Activities of PE Investment Professionals

But what kinds of things do these people do? The following list shows some of the key tasks PE professionals are involved with on a day-to-day basis. You might want to pause here to read through them all. These tasks relate to the cycle of PE, including fundraising, investing, and exiting. A PE professional, especially a senior one, will have to be good at all three of those jobs. Most of the team will focus on sourcing, executing deals, and managing the PortCo.

1. Assess opportunities, source deals, and identify managers
2. Review teasers and business plans
3. Meet with management teams and bankers
4. Conduct or coordinate due diligence
5. Structure and negotiate financings
6. Lead or coordinate with other investors
7. Oversee portfolio companies, work closely with management
8. Manage portfolio strategy and exits
9. Contribute to the administration of the fund (cash calls, distributions, etc.)
10. Raise capital, contribute to managing LP relations

It is easy to forget that the role evolves significantly with tenure and experience. A second-year associate at a large buyout fund provided a reality check: according to them, junior PE roles are not true "investing"—and neither are mid-level ones. This testimony highlights a pervasive misconception about PE hierarchy and decision-making authority that extends well beyond junior roles. True investing authority in PE emerges only at the partner level, with organizational incentives systematically discouraging independent thought at all junior and mid-level positions—regardless of actual competence. We have heard this often enough to consider that, while not universal, it represents a common occurrence, especially in less entrepreneurial large-cap funds.[7]

Sooner or later, the time will come to stand in your own shoes. Dr Bruno Ladriere, Managing Director at Ardian, remembers his first outing: "*I'll never forget facing the investment committee for the first time—nervous, overconfident, and sure my deck would win them over. Now, decades later, I can spot the same rookie mistakes and blind spots in new proposals that I once made myself. Experience has a way of sharpening your eye for recycled optimism.*"

There is little doubt that junior staff primarily build financial models targeting predetermined IRRs, create presentation materials, coordinate advisors, and support deal execution. But the associate believes this limitation extends upward: principals and vice presidents—despite being experienced 30+ year-old professionals—function

[7] Anna Silvestri reminds us that this is why juniors are encouraged to carefully investigate the type of fund, its culture, and the specific role and responsibilities before joining.

similarly as intermediaries rather than true decision-makers. Many of these mid-level PE professionals are actually skilled investors but may remain strategically silent. The risk-reward calculus discourages dissent: partners propose deals, investment committees decide, and challenging a partner's view offers minimal upside with significant career downside. Consequently, there is a risk principals will focus on directing associates to model outcomes that support partners' preferences rather than expressing independent investment judgment.

There is another potential institutional dynamic: at mega-funds, even partners face investment committee oversight, which may create layered deference that suppresses authentic investment debate throughout the organization. This environment would allow weaker performers to hide behind process while genuine talent remains underutilized. Hopefully this remains anecdotal.

Another current topic is the impact of AI. Like in investment banks, AI automation of data room analysis and basic modeling significantly reduces PE firms' reliance on junior-level personnel, potentially reshaping traditional hierarchical structures by eliminating much of the manual analytical work currently performed by associates and analysts. The pyramid may become senior-heavy again, as it used to be a few decades ago, or in diamond shape, with most of the work done by managers and principals.

10.3.2 On-cycle vs. Off-cycle Recruitment

10.3.2.1 Navigating On-cycle and Off-cycle Pathways PE recruitment is a highly competitive process that typically targets candidates with backgrounds in investment banking, strategy consulting, or transaction services. While the allure of PE roles is strong, the pathways into the industry are structured and demanding, often requiring prior experience in related fields.

PE offers both on-cycle and off-cycle pathways for candidates. While on-cycle recruitment provides early access to prestigious firms, it requires swift decision-making and thorough preparation. Off-cycle recruitment, on the other hand, allows for a more measured approach, accommodating candidates who have accrued relevant experience post-graduation.

10.3.2.2 On-cycle Recruitment: The Fast-paced Entry Point On-cycle recruitment refers to the accelerated hiring process initiated by large PE firms, often targeting investment banking analysts early in their careers. This process is characterized by its unpredictability, with start dates varying annually, typically during the summer. Once initiated, it triggers a rapid sequence of interviews and offers, compelling candidates to make swift decisions about roles that may commence up to two years later. Despite its intensity, on-cycle recruitment accounts for a relatively small portion of total PE hiring, estimated at around 10%.

This frenzied process is highly visible—and increasingly controversial. While it may account for only around 10% of annual PE hiring, it draws outsize attention due to its speed, secrecy, and the caliber of firms involved. It is, however, a very visible and irritating process for investment banks, torn between the opportunity to place their juniors at potential clients and customers and the hassle of losing their brightest minds just at the point where they have been trained and are starting to start adding significant value. As reported by *Business Insider* (2024), executives like JPMorgan's Jamie Dimon have gone so far as to call the practice "unethical," and some banks have tried—with limited success—to shield their analysts from early PE poaching.

10.3.2.3 Off-cycle Recruitment: A More Flexible Approach In contrast, off-cycle recruitment offers a more extended and flexible timeline, allowing candidates to apply for positions as they become available. This pathway is particularly prevalent among middle-market PE firms and accommodates candidates who may not have participated in the on-cycle process or who have gained additional experience post-graduation. Off-cycle recruitment emphasizes a candidate's developed skills and readiness, often leading to roles that commence within a few months of the hiring decision.

10.3.2.4 Preferred Backgrounds: Investment Banking and Strategy Consulting Generalist PE firms predominantly recruit individuals with experience in investment banking or strategy consulting. Candidates from Big Four Transaction Services are also in demand, particularly for their strong financial due diligence (FDD) skills. These backgrounds provide candidates with the analytical skills, deal exposure, and strategic thinking necessary for success in PE roles. Investment bankers bring expertise in financial modeling and transaction execution, while consultants offer insights into business strategy and operational improvement. This preference for experienced professionals over direct university hires stems from the immediate value they can add to lean PE teams.

At specialist firms, relevant sector experience is a key differentiator and sometimes a prerequisite. Healthcare specialist firms have a high share of medical doctors, biomedical engineers, and life sciences PhDs. The combination with investment banking or consulting experience makes attractive candidates. Mike Mortimer from GHO Capital emphasizes that

> *... particularly in healthcare, you want to demonstrate real subject expertise—it's a key differentiator. Nothing is more off-putting than a meeting with a PE investor who only wants to know the financials and won't talk about the fundamentals: the customers, the differentiation of the products.*

This insight reveals a critical flaw in how some generalist PE firms approach healthcare deals. Technical expertise becomes table stakes when competing for quality opportunities in specialized sectors where operational knowledge matters as much as financial engineering: "My advice is to develop real healthcare expertise or experience before moving into PE—you'll be much better positioned with that baseline experience."

For Herb Hooper, managing partner of Ampersand, "for graduate students targeting healthcare PE, developing sector expertise takes priority over pure technical skills." The recommendation emphasizes reading extensively, analyzing public companies, and leveraging freely available resources, including analyst calls. Many technically proficient candidates lack crucial sector knowledge that distinguishes successful healthcare investors.

But Mike also values the strategic perspective, both in the investment team and in the PortCos' management teams: "The big issue with many people we hire is they see the company as it is now, not what it could become or how it will be tomorrow. They don't think strategically."

Youssef at Eckuity sees it both ways:

For those aspiring to enter healthcare PE, I always emphasize depth before breadth. Develop a strong grounding in either healthcare operations or investment fundamentals—and then build cross-disciplinary fluency. Curiosity, empathy, and patience are critical. This is not an industry driven purely by numbers; it's about understanding science, regulation, and the human dimension of care. The best investors in healthcare are those who can bridge innovation with compassion and business with purpose.

10.3.2.5 Preparation and Strategic Considerations Candidates aiming for PE roles must be deliberate in their preparation. Engaging in the on-cycle process without adequate readiness can be detrimental, as firms are unlikely to reconsider candidates who underperform in initial interviews. Therefore, it's advisable for individuals to assess their technical proficiency and industry knowledge before entering the recruitment process. Utilizing resources such as financial modeling courses and case study preparations can enhance readiness. Moreover, candidates should clearly define their sector interests, preferred firm sizes, and geographic locations to align with potential employers' expectations.

10.3.3 Buyout Skill Set

This next list shows a view on the skillset required to work on buyouts specifically. In particular, you will need to have stamina and be able to cope with stress. And more and more you'll be required to show either strategic or operational expertise, or even both:

- Savvy buyers at auction
- Good sense of hidden value
- Project team leadership skills (lawyers, accountants, consultants)
- Love for deal-making and negotiation
- "Financial engineering" skills
- Eye for detail ... patience
- Stamina—ability to cope with stress
- Increasingly, strategic and operational expertise

A managing director at KKR said: "You need a taste, view and judgment on operations of the company where you invest (the ability to convince the CEO), as well as financial skills and creativity to structure deals."

Now, a few words of advice for associates who are trying to work their way up the ladder. First, do the hard stuff! This means establishing early on that you can do the tough things, the things that many others might try to avoid. Everyone wants to be on the hot new deal, but if you can help fix the losers, people will remember you for that.

The second recommendation is to focus on portfolio companies and one good piece of advice here is to develop a good relationship with the CEOs and CFOs of the companies you manage. You might even get more mentorship from them than your PE boss.

Third, play nice. Do not be arrogant. Be humble. There will be situations where people will not take advantage of you if you have been playing nice. Sometimes you will have to bite your tongue and bide your time because you will be working with people much more senior who believe they know better than you.

And lastly, think long and hard about whether you really want to have a PE career. Because your job as an associate will be very different from what you can expect your role as a partner to be in 15 or 20 years. And you need to be sure that you can do more than just manage a deal. You need to be good at fundraising, managing investors, and managing the fund itself—that will be necessary to get promoted. If you think you are effective in all those areas, then maybe this is the career for you.

A WORD FROM ABRAR MIR, COFOUNDER OF QUADRIA CAPITAL

My advice to graduate students who want to enter private equity, particularly in healthcare, is not to worry about having every technical skill from the outset. You can learn financial modelling, industry frameworks and domain knowledge as you go. What really matters at the start is curiosity, humility and the hunger to learn. I began life as a lawyer and the only way was up after that!

What you do need to bring with you is mindset. This is an industry where discipline and resilience matter as much as intelligence. You have to be willing to roll up your sleeves, immerse yourself in businesses and learn. The ability to ask the right questions, to earn trust and to build credibility will take you far.

In healthcare private equity, the stakes are higher still, because at the other end of every investment are human lives. That means you need to approach the work with empathy and a sense of purpose. Returns are important, but the true test of whether you are succeeding is whether you are improving lives.

If you carry that mindset—curiosity, humility, discipline, and purpose—you will not only become a better investor, you will also find yourself part of a mission far larger than your own career. And that, in my experience, is where the real fulfilment lies.

10.3.4 Gender Representation

Now, what does that mean gender-wise? Research on gender representation in the US PE industry in 2024 delivered statistics very similar to our own research in Europe back in 2007, but for a much larger sample of 661 PE firms managing over $4 trillion. Women still represented only 22% of all investment professionals, 27% of junior, 20% of mid-level, and 6% of senior roles (Ewens et al., 2024). The authors defined the roles in three ranks, shown in Table 10.2.

Perhaps more striking, 31% of all firms—mostly the smaller ones—had no women across all investment professionals. The research also showed that the largest PE firms by AuM had the highest fraction of women across all ranks so, once again, size matters.

TABLE 10.2 Investment Roles in Private Equity

Seniority	Investment Roles	Additional Contextual Information
Senior	• Chairman • Chief executive officer • Founder • Founding partner • Senior managing partner • Managing partner • General partner • Managing principal • Chief investment officer • Senior partner • Partner • Senior managing director • Managing director	• Leadership of investment team • Leadership of the firm, excluding noninvestment roles, such as operations, financial, investor relations, human resources, administration, legal, finance, accounting, and technology • Responsible for final investment and divestment decisions • Responsible for sourcing, evaluating, and executing deals
Mid	• Director • Principal • Senior vice president • Vice president	• Responsible for sourcing, evaluating, and executing deals • Noninvestment roles were excluded, such as operations, investor relations, human resources, administration, legal, finance, accounting, and technology
Junior	• Senior associate • Associate • Private equity associate • Analyst	• Supports senior and mid investment professionals • Noninvestment roles were excluded such as operations, investor relations, human resources, administration, legal, finance, accounting, and technology

In another article on carried interest in the United Kingdom (Advani et al., 2024), men made up 85% of carry recipients and received 96% of all carry in the period 2017–2023.

Assuming more gender diversity is better for the performance (actually a controversial area of research) and the firm culture, this raises two main questions: how can PE firms attract more women as investment professionals, and how can they promote and retain them?

10.3.5 Compensations

Are PE professionals rich? On average, they are well remunerated, but they work hard, and there are significant variations. The managing partner of a $10 billion AuM PE firm confided:

> *[W]hen I started working in the 80s, PE was still a niche industry. It was easy money: financial leverage, de-conglomeration, asset stripping, some operational effectiveness, I didn't have to work very long hours. Today, I see our analysts working 80-hour weeks, as much as they did in their previous job in investment banking. It's a much more competitive environment. Too much money chasing too few deals.*

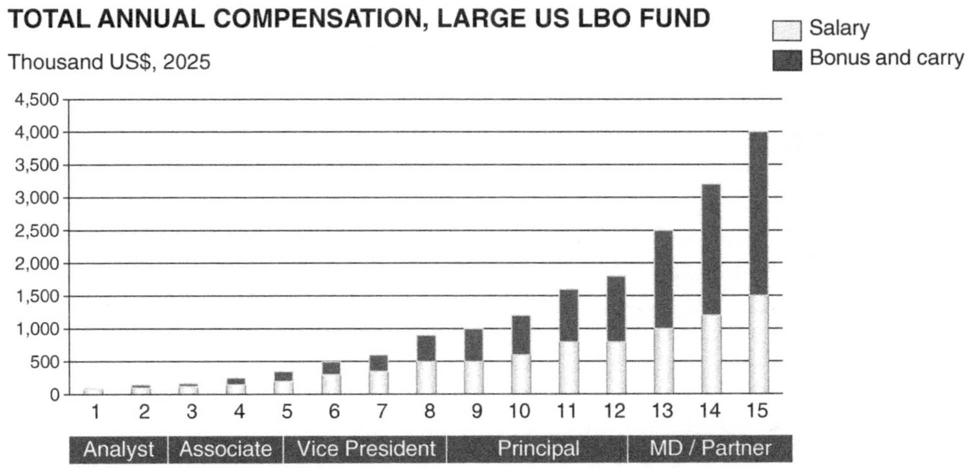

FIGURE 10.17 Total annual compensation by seniority at large US LBO firms.
Source: CFI; Mergers & Inquisitions; Candesic interviews.

Many websites track remunerations in the PE industry. While the numbers shown are consistent, they tend to focus on the United States and on the mid to large LBO funds. From the principal (or director) level, compensation differ substantially. We show in Figure 10.17 an indicative yearly progression at a large and well performing US LBO fund for salary only and for total compensation, including bonus and carry (note there will not be much carry for the lower quartiles). Everything else being equal, smaller funds (growth capital) and funds with lower management fees (funds of funds, secondaries, infrastructure) pay logically less.

The same article on carry, focused on the United Kingdom but allegedly similar to the US situation, shows how "carried interest is extremely concentrated among a small number of top executives. The top 30 individuals alone received around a quarter of all carry in 2023, totaling £1 billion—an average of over £33 million each. The top 100 received a total of £1.8 billion, almost half (45%) of all carry in that year. Even aggregating over a seven-year period from 2017 to 2023 [...] the top 100 still received more than a third (36%) of all carry, an average of £90 million per person over the period" (Advani et al., 2024).

This can be misleading, however. While the top earners benefit significantly from the carry, it makes up a small share of total pay for most recipients. For 68% of them, carry represented less than half of their total compensation. For the bottom 35% of carry recipients who received less than £1 million in total pay, carry accounted for only 30% of their total compensation.

Is it different in healthcare? Investments in healthcare and life sciences often require specialized knowledge due to the complexities of medical research, regulatory hurdles, and scientific advancements. The transactions can be significantly larger and more complex due to the need for regulatory compliance, intellectual property valuation, and specialized due diligence. As a result, PE firms in these areas may offer higher compensation packages to attract and retain professionals with deep industry expertise, including medical, regulatory, and scientific backgrounds. Investors may also be compensated with higher risk premiums, given the longer timelines and higher uncertainty associated with drug development, clinical trials, healthcare regulations, and market adoption.

THE UNTOLD PE LIQUIDITY CRUNCH

Rumors are swirling through industry circles about a "hidden" liquidity crunch in PE—more whispered at conferences than dissected in whitepapers. PE professionals are taking on leveraged loans to cover GP co-invest commitments, usually 1–3% of total expected compensation over the fund's life, not just base salary. With most investments marked held to maturity, this gives the illusion of stability as distributions dry up and hefty interest payments (often 8–12%) come due. For many mid to senior staff, net worth is locked in the firm and tough to access, leading to forced sales and mounting stress when markets stall.

The system inadvertently creates leveraged employees unable to manage downturns, pushing some firms to adopt phantom carry and deferred equity vesting in response. Meanwhile, top PE houses keep paying out, but elsewhere even senior team members are left choosing between illiquidity and punishing loans—evidence that what was meant to align incentives now mostly screens for the already wealthy. This crisis is very real, even if you'll only hear about it in whispers, not in GP pitchbooks.

Looking ahead, whether in healthcare or other sectors, compensation in PE is closely tied to industry performance. Buyout firms typically divest approximately 20% of their investments annually, a long-standing average in the history of PE. However, the *Financial Times* reported that 2024 marked the third consecutive year of disappointing payouts to investors, with distributions in that year at just half the historical average. According to Cambridge Associates, funds collectively fell approximately $400 billion short in payments to investors over the three years. This shortfall has directly affected compensation within PE firms, particularly the carried interest, which is tied to fund performance. Bonuses for junior staff, often reliant on surplus revenues beyond management fees, have also been impacted, highlighting the broader ripple effects of subdued exit activity.

10.3.6 Fundraising and Investor Relations

For Alessandra Mazzuchelli from Soledar Partners, if you are thinking about working in PE fundraising or investor relations, here are two solid paths—both demanding but rewarding.

While fundraising and investor relations were once tightly linked, today they're often treated as distinct disciplines. Capital formation teams focus on bringing in commitments, while investor relations (IR) is more about managing relationships post-close, coordinating reporting, and offering transparency around portfolio development.

That said, the best professionals in either role understand both sides. Successful fundraising often starts with strong investor trust—which is built through thoughtful, consistent investor communications long after a fund is raised.

10.3.6.1 Placement Agent: Independent and Broad

- **What you do:** Work with several GPs across fund sizes and geographies to raise capital
- **What you gain:** Exposure to a variety of strategies and LP types (high net worth individuals, family offices, pension funds, banks)
- **Challenges:** High pressure, variable deal flow, and limited control over fund quality

Strong placement agents often become trusted extensions of their clients' IR teams—deeply embedded in the pitch and the strategy.

10.3.6.2 In-house IR: Embedded and Strategic

- **What you do:** Manage investor communications, due diligence, fundraising planning, and co-investment processes
- **What you gain:** Deep firm knowledge, job stability, and long-term LP relationships
- **Trade-offs:** Less variety than a placement agent; tied to one team and one strategy

10.3.6.3 What Both Roles Require

- **Being real and credible:** Investors value honesty and consistency.
- **Strong analytical skills:** Know your numbers—from fund structures to IRRs and benchmarks.
- **Cultural and social adaptability:** You will be meeting investors from all over the world, each with different expectations.
- **Languages and travel readiness:** You will be on the road—physically and metaphorically—more than you expect.

10.3.7 Company Managers and Advisors

Historically, PortCo managers known as "guns for hire" were brought in by PE firms for specific projects, transformations, or crisis management roles at portfolio companies, operating as freelancers who were not on the PE firm's payroll and often working with several firms at once, typically compensated only by the portfolio company for the length of their engagement and never with any formal or exclusive affiliation with the sponsor. Over time, however, a growing number of firms have shifted toward retaining these managers directly as part of an internal operating partner group, keeping them formally on the firm's payroll and moving them flexibly between PortCos as operational needs arise—sometimes for the full holding period, sometimes for short-term assignments—allowing the firm to deploy experienced leadership rapidly, ensure alignment on strategic and value creation goals, and build institutional know-how. These retained experts now occupy roles that blend functional expertise, project management, and embedded transformation oversight, marking a significant evolution from ad hoc engagements to a more organized, retained, and strategic talent model in PE.

We invite you to refer to Chapter 6, where we discuss the specific roles of the operating partners. They are part of the internal team.

Working as a financial or strategic advisor provides partial but direct exposure to the PE industry. For many professionals, it is enough exposure, but for many others it is the next coveted role. Indeed, a few years in investment banking, transaction services, or strategy consulting provide an ideal foundation for a career in PE. A quick review of the composition of the investment teams shows that about half the people took that path. These roles teach how to analyze companies in depth, model cash flows under pressure, and identify value creation levers—skills that directly translate to deal analysis and portfolio management. Bankers gain hands-on experience negotiating and structuring transactions; consultants learn to dissect business models and operational drivers; and transaction advisors become fluent in due diligence and financial review. Recruiters in PE firms value this early-career training because it builds both technical excellence and commercial judgment—two rare commodities when real money is at stake. That said, positions in PE are limited, and competition is fierce. Not every candidate from investment banking, transaction services, or consulting will land their dream job in PE—there are simply fewer seats than applicants. Visibility matters almost as much as ability. A previous internship in a PE firm, direct exposure to PE clients while working on a transaction, or well-timed conversations with specialized headhunters can make the difference between being noticed or forgotten. In short, the right background opens the door, but staying visible gets you through it.

10.4 CHAPTER SUMMARY

Hopefully this chapter gave you a clearer sense of the directions in which PE is heading as an industry and of some of the key drivers of change within the sector. And whether you work in PE already or are planning to work there, we hope you now have a better understanding of the key firms involved, what it takes to work as a PE professional, and whether it is the right fit for you, either now or in the longer term.

We hope to see some of you working in the industry in future. Either way, well done on reading this book—assuming you did not start from the last page like someone we know—and good luck!

10.5 CONCLUSIONS

Private equity, at its core, is defined by **illiquidity**—a structural feature that shapes its investment cycle, challenges its methods of measuring performance, and increasingly drives its evolution in the face of technological and market innovation.

1. **The investment cycle: beyond linear thinking**

   Allow us to return to the metaphor introduced in Chapter 1: fulfilment in life comes from being able to anticipate joy, experience it in the moment, and remember it fondly, all at once. In PE, this maps neatly to fundraising, investing, and exiting. These are not discrete, sequential steps but overlapping processes, each influencing the others in real time. The best PE professionals understand this. They fundraise while investing, invest with exits in mind, and exit in ways that reinforce their fundraising narrative. The cycle is circular, not linear, and it demands a mindset capable of navigating multiple temporalities simultaneously.

2. **Performance: misunderstood metrics**

   Second, PE performance is notoriously opaque to the untrained eye. Metrics like IRR and MOIC dominate pitch decks and press releases, yet their limitations are well known to insiders. IRR can flatter returns when capital is returned early—even if total value creation is modest—while MOIC says nothing about time or risk. These figures, often presented without context, lend themselves to misunderstanding and, at times, to manipulation. They are tools, not truths. A sophisticated LP must look beyond headline numbers to understand the assumptions, timing, and risks underlying the performance story.
3. **Evolution: from illiquid to optional**

   The industry's relationship with illiquidity is undergoing rapid transformation. Traditional closed-end funds are now supplemented by secondaries, continuation funds, evergreen vehicles, and semi-liquid structures targeting retail investors. Platforms like iCapital and Moonfare promise accessibility; listed firms like Blackstone and KKR provide visibility; continuation vehicles offer flexibility in holding onto prized assets. All of this represents an effort to make PE more liquid, scalable, and democratic—and, perhaps, more commercial.
4. **Evolution of private healthcare markets: a bifurcated future**

   While we believe Asia will be the main driver of PE activity in healthcare, demand in developed markets will continue to grow. We believe there is a fundamental structural divergence happening in the private healthcare capital landscape. While traditional healthcare enterprises, including family-owned clinics, specialist practices, and regional care operators, will remain anchored in relationship-based, illiquid ownership structures that prioritize control and community ties, sophisticated private capital markets are converging toward public market characteristics through institutionalization, digitization, and enhanced liquidity mechanisms. Large PE-backed healthcare platforms are increasingly adopting the financial transparency, operational reporting, and risk management frameworks typically associated with publicly listed firms, enabled by technological advances in tokenization, blockchain registries, and AI-enhanced due diligence. Yes, this convergence remains partial and constrained by the inherent illiquidity of healthcare assets, complex regulatory requirements, and the heterogeneous nature of medical enterprises that resist standardization, but the result is a bifurcated healthcare capital market where institutional PE will increasingly exhibit public market-like characteristics—including faster capital rotation, broader investor access, and more responsive pricing—while traditional healthcare ownership will preserve its emphasis on long-term control, local knowledge, and relationship-driven capital allocation. This structural division fundamentally reshapes how healthcare enterprises access capital, with profound implications for innovation funding, consolidation patterns, and the balance between financial optimization and patient care delivery.

Whether these developments signal maturity or decadence is an open question. On one hand, they broaden participation, improve capital efficiency, and modernize the asset class. On the other, they risk commodifying a model that once stood apart for its discipline, patience, and alignment. The challenge ahead is to retain what made PE effective—its long-term perspective, its hands-on ownership, its clarity of purpose—while adapting to the expectations of a more liquid, transparent, and inclusive investment world.

TOUCHING ONE BILLION LIVES

If there is one thing I would add about private equity in Asian healthcare, it is that success ultimately rests on trust. In volatile markets, consistency is the true currency of trust, and we have built our strategy around that principle: DPI-led, IRR-first, with a relentless focus on repeatability in process and outcomes.

We also believe alpha must be institutionalized, not improvised. Instinct alone is not enough in healthcare. That is why we built Quadria iQ, our proprietary Artificial Intelligence platform for sharper diligence, smarter value creation and real-time KPI tracking. It elevates both performance and impact from anecdote to measurable data. In Asia, financial returns and social outcomes are not separate ambitions—they are one mission, what we call "impact with integrity."

Our approach is industrial, not financial. Returns here are created through operating excellence, clinical quality, digitization and tailored playbooks for every subsector. We aim to build ecosystems, not isolated assets—platforms that link hospitals, diagnostics, manufacturing, and financing so that quality improves with scale.

All of this depends on culture. A high-performance, accountable culture is what allows strategy to scale across geographies. Today, our companies touch 300 million lives; by 2030, our ambition is to reach one billion. But the real measure is not the headline number—it is the steady cadence of improvements in access, affordability and quality. That is how we intend to compound both returns and trust.

—Abrar Mir, Quadria Capital

Glossary of Private Equity and Healthcare

Note: we decided to mix definitions from the two universes we are tackling: private equity and healthcare.

21 CFR Part 11 FDA regulations for electronic records and signatures in pharmaceutical and medical device companies.

510(k) Clearance FDA premarket notification process for medical devices demonstrating substantial equivalence to predicate devices.

A

Angel investor or business angel An individual investor who provides early stage funding to startups, often serving as a precursor to formal venture capital or private equity investment rounds.

Abbreviated New Drug Application (ANDA) Simplified FDA approval process for generic drugs.

ABL Asset-based lending.

ABS Asset-backed security.

Accountable Care Organization (ACO) A formal designation in the United States for a group of doctors, hospitals, and other providers who agree to be held accountable for the quality, cost, and overall care of a population of patients, typically those in the traditional, fee-for-service Medicare program.

Accredited investor (or certified investor) An investor who meets specific regulatory criteria that qualifies them to participate in private investments and purchase unregistered securities (securities that are not closely regulated by the financial authorities).

Active pharmaceutical ingredient (API) The active component in medications.

Add-on Supplementary acquisition made by private equity funds to their existing portfolio companies to drive growth and increase value. Similar to "bolt-on" acquisition.

Adjusted present value (APV) A valuation methodology commonly used in private equity for determining portfolio company value by calculating it as fully equity-financed and incorporating the present value of leverage benefits and tax shields.

Administrative Services Only (ASO) Healthcare service model where companies provide administrative services without assuming insurance risk.

Allocated capital The portion of committed capital designated by private equity funds for specific investments, portfolio companies, or strategic initiatives.

Ambulatory surgery center (ASC) Outpatient surgical facilities.

Anchor investor An institutional investor who commits early and substantially to a private equity fund, providing credibility and encouraging other limited partners to participate in the fund.

Anti-dilution Protective clauses in private equity investment agreements that safeguard investors against reductions in their equity ownership percentage when portfolio companies issue new shares.

Antibody–drug conjugate (ADC) Targeted cancer therapy that links a monoclonal antibody to a cytotoxic payload via a linker to deliver the drug directly to tumor cells.

Aseptic processing Manufacturing under sterile conditions to prevent microbial contamination, often used for injectable products and biologics.

Asset stripping A private equity strategy involving the acquisition of undervalued companies, separating their assets into components and selling them individually to maximize returns for fund investors.

Asset-light model Business strategy minimizing capital-intensive assets while focusing on intellectual property and services.

Assets under management (AuM) Represents the total capital managed by private equity firms across their fund portfolio.

Autoinjector/pen device Patient-operated drug delivery devices that enable self-administration (e.g., for GLP-1s); typically combine a prefilled cartridge, dose mechanism, and needle system.

B

Biologic License Application (BLA) FDA approval pathway for biological products.

Biomarker Measurable indicator of biological processes or treatment response.

Blind-pool capital Capital committed by private equity limited partners to funds without knowledge of the specific investments the general partners will make, relying on the fund manager's track record and strategy rather than disclosed deal pipeline. This is the common case.

Bolt-on see *Add-on*

Bond Debt security.

Book see *Investment memorandum*

Bridge finance Short-term financing provided by private equity firms to portfolio companies to satisfy liquidity requirements while permanent financing solutions are arranged.

Build-up A more strategic and operationally intensive version of a roll-up. While it also involves acquiring multiple companies, the focus is on creating a single, cohesive, and market-leading company. You are not just making it bigger; you are making it *better*.

Bullet loan (typically a tranche B) A specialized debt instrument commonly used in private equity transactions featuring complete capital holidays with principal repayment at maturity, often used in leveraged buyout structures.

Bundled payments Single payments covering all services related to specific medical episodes or conditions.

Business development (BD) Activities to win new customers, expand key accounts, and form partnerships; in CRO/CDMO, includes RFP response and contracting.

Business development companies (BDCs) Publicly traded, closed-end investment funds created by Congress in 1980 to democratize access to private company investing. They pool capital from retail and institutional investors to provide debt and equity financing to small and mid-market US businesses, typically those valued under $250 million, much like PE funds but with liquidity available on public exchanges.

Business plan (BP) A comprehensive document that private equity firms require from portfolio companies outlining strategic objectives and execution strategies for value creation.

Buy and build A core private equity strategy that starts with the acquisition of a platform company, which is then expanded through strategic add-on acquisitions to accelerate growth, achieve synergies, and increase overall enterprise value for eventual exit.

Buy-in management buyout (BIMBO) A private equity transaction combining characteristics of both management buy-in (MBI) and management buyout (MBO), where PE funds collaborate with both existing and external management teams to acquire companies.

C

CapEx/Opex Capital expenditures (long-term investments in assets) vs. operating expenses (day-to-day costs).

Capital call A formal request by private equity general partners to limited partners for a portion of their committed capital to fund new investments or support existing portfolio companies.

Capitation Fixed payment per patient regardless of services provided.

Captive fund A private equity investment vehicle where shares are restricted from transfer outside the fund structure, preventing limited partners from selling holdings to external parties.

Carried interest or "carry" The performance-based compensation that private equity general partners receive, typically 20% of fund profits above the hurdle rate, aligning GP interests with LP returns.

Carve-out Transaction involving the acquisition of a business unit that a parent company separates from its core operations, often presenting attractive investment.

Cash sweep A mechanism in private equity portfolio companies requiring excess cash flow to be directed toward debt repayment ahead of schedule, maximizing leverage optimization and returns.

Catch-up clause A provision in private equity fund waterfalls enabling general partners to receive accelerated profit distributions after limited partners achieve their preferred return.

CE marking From the French Conformité Européenne, meaning "European Conformity"; a mandatory regulatory certification indicating that a product—including medical devices, pharmaceuticals, and other regulated goods—complies with all applicable European Union health, safety, and performance requirements and may be legally marketed throughout the European Economic Area. For medical devices, the CE mark confirms that the manufacturer has completed the appropriate conformity assessment process under the Medical Device Regulation (MDR) or In Vitro Diagnostic Regulation (IVDR), implemented a quality management system aligned with ISO 13485, and produced technical documentation demonstrating safety and clinical efficacy.

Cell and gene therapy (C&GT) An advanced biotechnology sector encompassing therapeutic approaches that modify or replace defective genes and utilize living cells to treat diseases, representing a high-growth investment area for private equity firms targeting companies developing innovative treatments for previously incurable conditions including genetic disorders, cancers, and autoimmune diseases through cutting-edge cellular engineering and genetic modification technologies.

Change of control provision Contractual clauses in private equity investments specifying rights and obligations when portfolio companies undergo ownership changes or exit transactions.

Chemistry, manufacturing, and controls (CMC) Regulatory discipline covering how a drug is made, tested, and controlled across its life cycle.

Clawback A provision requiring private equity general partners to return previously distributed carried interest if the fund's overall performance falls below agreed thresholds.

Cleanroom Controlled environment with low levels of particulates; classified by ISO grade and designed for aseptic operations.

Clinical Trial Application (CTA) Regulatory submission to begin human clinical trials.

Clinical trials (CT) Research studies that private equity-backed healthcare companies conduct to develop and validate new medical treatments, representing significant value creation opportunities.

Closed-end fund The predominant private equity fund structure that raises capital through fixed commitments at inception rather than continuous fundraising.

Closing The milestone events in PE fundraising where investor commitments become legally binding, including initial closing (first investor commitments enabling fund operations) and final closing (completion of all capital commitments). Also used when the fund finalizes an acquisition.

Club deal A transaction where multiple private equity firms collaborate to co-invest in large buyout opportunities, sharing risks and expertise.

Co-GP structure Partnership arrangements where multiple general partners share management responsibilities and carried interest in private equity funds.

Co-investment Direct investments by limited partners alongside their private equity fund commitments, typically offering reduced fees and increased exposure to specific deals.

Collateral Assets that private equity firms and their portfolio companies pledge to secure acquisition financing and credit facilities.

Commercial due diligence (CDD) A critical component of private equity investment analysis, involving comprehensive evaluation of target companies' market position, competitive dynamics, and growth prospects.

Committed capital The total amount that limited partners have legally committed to contribute to a private equity fund over its investment period.

Compound annual growth rate (CAGR) The annualized rate of return that an investment or financial metric (such as revenue or EBITDA) would need to achieve each year to grow from its beginning value to its ending value over a specified period, assuming profits are reinvested and growth compounds. It smooths out volatility to provide a single, consistent percentage for comparing long-term performance across investments or business metrics.

Computerized systems validation (CSV) Validation of GxP-relevant software and digital systems to ensure they are fit for intended use and compliant.

Consumer health/over-the-counter (OTC) Nonprescription medicines and health products sold directly to consumers without a prescription.

Continuation fund A specialized private equity vehicle designed to acquire assets from existing funds, extending holding periods for portfolio companies requiring additional development time.

Contract development and manufacturing operator (CDMO) A pharmaceutical services company that private equity firms often target for investment, providing outsourced development and manufacturing capabilities to healthcare clients.

Contract manufacturing operator or organization (CMO) A company manufacturing the products of other pharma or medtech companies.

Contract research organization (CRO) A pharmaceutical services company frequently targeted by private equity investors, providing outsourced research capabilities to healthcare companies.

Controlled auction A competitive sale process that private equity firms conduct when exiting portfolio companies, involving selected strategic and financial buyers.

Convertible debt A hybrid financing instrument used in private equity transactions that converts to equity under specified conditions, providing downside protection with upside participation.

Cornerstone investor A large institutional investor who commits to significant participation in private equity fund fundraising before the formal marketing process begins.

Corporate venture capital (CVC) Investment vehicles funded by large corporations that often compete with traditional private equity funds for growth-stage opportunities.

Corrective and preventive action (CAPA) Quality system mechanism to address root causes of deviations and prevent recurrence.

Covenant Financial and operational restrictions that private equity firms impose on portfolio companies through debt agreements and shareholder arrangements.

Cross-fund investing When private equity management companies invest multiple funds in the same portfolio company, requiring careful conflict management and limited partner approval.

Crossover fund A private equity investment vehicle that maintains positions in both publicly traded and privately held companies, providing flexible capital deployment across different stages of company development.

Crowdfunding An alternative funding mechanism that typically precedes institutional private equity investment in startup and growth companies.

Current Good Manufacturing Practice (cGMP) FDA manufacturing quality standards.

Custodian Financial institutions that private equity funds employ to safeguard fund assets and facilitate secure transaction processing.

CV-squared Continuation fund on a continuation fund. A form of "cross-fund transaction."

D

De Novo Classification FDA pathway for novel medical devices without predicate devices requiring new regulatory classifications.

Deal by deal A private equity fund waterfall structure where profit distributions are calculated separately for each portfolio company investment.

Deal flow The rate at which private equity firms receive and evaluate potential investment opportunities from various sourcing channels.

Deal sourcing The systematic process private equity firms use to identify, evaluate, and originate potential portfolio company investments.

Debottlenecking Targeted changes (process, equipment, staffing) that relieve the rate-limiting step to increase throughput.

Delisting The process of removing a company from a public stock exchange, typically occurring in private equity take-private transactions.

Dental service organizations (DSO) Organizations that private equity firms increasingly target for investment, representing companies that acquire dental practices and manage their operations, administration, and support services.

Department of Health and Human Services (HHS) In the United States, the federal agency responsible for health policy, Medicare and Medicaid administration, and oversight of agencies like the FDA and CDC.

Development capital Private equity investment focused on providing growth capital to established companies seeking expansion, often involving minority stakes.

Development finance institutions (DFI) Institutions such as the World Bank, the Asian Development Bank.

Device/containment Primary containers (vials, syringes, cartridges) and delivery devices (pens, autoinjectors) that store/administer a drug.

Digital therapeutics (DTx) Software-based interventions for medical conditions.

Dilution The reduction in private equity fund ownership percentages when portfolio companies issue new equity, potentially impacting investment returns.

Direct primary care (DPC) Healthcare delivery model with direct patient-physician relationships bypassing traditional insurance.

Direct secondaries Private equity transactions involving the sale of directly held ownership interests in individual portfolio companies from existing institutional investors to new investors, distinct from LP interest transfers or full company buyouts, typically representing noncontrol stakes that provide liquidity alternatives for original private equity investors seeking partial or complete exits from specific portfolio company positions. Also called secondary directs, GP-led secondaries, secondaries direct GPs, or sometimes direct managers.

Disability-adjusted life year (DALY) A comprehensive health metric that quantifies disease burden by combining years of life lost due to premature death with years lived with disability, representing one year of healthy life lost due to illness or injury—commonly used by private equity firms in healthcare investments to assess population health impacts, evaluate preventive medicine opportunities, and measure the societal value of medical interventions and treatments developed by portfolio companies.

Discount rate The required rate of return private equity investors use in DCF valuations, typically reflecting higher risk premiums than public market investments.

Discounted cash flow (DCF) The primary valuation methodology private equity professionals use to assess portfolio companies and determine appropriate investment prices.

Distribution Cash or securities that private equity funds return to limited partners from portfolio company exits, dividend recapitalizations, or other realizations, representing the primary mechanism for delivering investment returns.

Distributions to Paid-in Capital ratio (DPI) A key private equity fund performance metric measuring actual cash distributions to limited partners relative to called capital.

Divestment or divestiture Typically used to describe the sale of a division by a corporate.

Dividend recap A financial engineering technique where private equity firms have portfolio companies issue special dividends funded by additional debt.

Down round A fundraising scenario where private equity portfolio companies receive valuations lower than previous investment rounds.

DQ/IQ/OQ/PQ Qualification stages for equipment and systems—Design, Installation, Operational, and Performance Qualification.

Drag-along rights Contractual provisions enabling private equity majority shareholders to force minority stakeholders to participate in exit transactions.

Drawdown The process by which GPs call committed capital from LPs to fund new investments and operational expenses.

Drug discovery The research and development process that pharmaceutical companies undertake to identify new therapeutic opportunities.

Drug substance/drug product (DS/DP) The DS is the active ingredient, and the DP is the finished dosage form delivered to patients.

Dry powder Immediately deployable cash reserves and highly liquid assets that private equity firms maintain for swift investment deployment, representing capital that has already been called from limited partners and is ready for immediate use—distinct from overhang which represents future committed but uncalled capital that creates potential market pressure over time.

Due diligence (DD) The comprehensive investigative process private equity firms conduct before making investments, covering financial, commercial, legal, and operational aspects.

E

Earnings before interest and tax (EBIT) A key profitability metric private equity firms use to evaluate portfolio company performance.

Earnings before interest, tax, depreciation, and amortization (EBITDA) The primary valuation multiple used in private equity transactions.

Earnings per share (EPS) A metric private equity firms track for public portfolio companies and during IPO preparations.

Earnout A deal structure mechanism in private equity exits where sellers receive additional payments based on portfolio company performance post-transaction.

Electronic batch record (EBR) Digital record of manufacturing steps, materials, and tests for a lot; enables review-by-exception and data analysis.

Electronic health record (EHR) Systems that private equity firms often target as investment opportunities in healthcare IT sectors. See *Electronic batch record.*

EMR/EHR integration Electronic medical/health record system connectivity.

Enterprise value (EV) The total value metric private equity firms use for portfolio company valuations, including both equity and debt components.

Envy ratio The ratio comparing equity purchase prices between private equity investors and management teams in buyout transactions.

Equity kicker Additional equity participation rights that private equity lenders receive alongside debt investments in portfolio companies.

Escrow account A secure account structure used in private equity transactions to hold purchase price adjustments and warranty claims.

eSource/eClinical Digital capture and management of clinical trial source data and workflows (e.g., eCRFs, eConsent, ePRO).

European Medicines Agency (EMA) A regulatory body that private equity-backed pharmaceutical and biotechnology companies must navigate for drug approvals and market authorization throughout the European Union.

Evergreen fund A permanent capital structure that some private equity firms adopt, eliminating traditional fund life cycles and capital return requirements.

Expansion capital Private equity investment in established companies with proven business models seeking capital for growth initiatives and geographic expansion. Typically, a minority investment.

Extension period Additional time frames that private equity funds may request to extend their standard 10–12 years life cycles, typically requiring limited partner approval and justified by market conditions, outstanding litigation, or portfolio company development needs.

F

Factory Acceptance Testing (FAT) Pre-shipment testing of equipment at the vendor site to confirm it meets specifications before installation.

Fairness opinion Independent valuation assessments that private equity firms obtain for significant portfolio company transactions and conflict situations.

Fast Track Designation or Status FDA expedited review for drugs addressing unmet medical needs in serious conditions.

Feeder fund A tax-efficient structure private equity funds use to accommodate different investor types (taxable and tax-exempt) through separate investment vehicles.

Feeder-master structure Tax-optimized fund architecture separating different investor types through multiple feeder funds investing into a single master fund.

Fill and finish Final steps where a sterile drug product is filled into containers (vials, syringes, cartridges) and finished for distribution.

Finder's fund A flexible private equity structure allowing limited partners to evaluate each investment opportunity individually before committing capital. Also known as pledge fund or deal-by-deal fund.

Food and Drug Administration (FDA) US regulatory body that private equity-backed healthcare companies must navigate for product approvals.

For cause Legal provisions in private equity partnership agreements that allow limited partners to remove general partners or terminate fund operations due to specific wrongdoing, fraud, or material breaches of fiduciary duty.

Formulary List of covered medications by insurance plans/PBMs.

Fund administrator Third-party service providers that handle operational, accounting, and reporting functions for private equity funds.

Fund of funds (FoF) Investment vehicles that provide limited partners with diversified private equity exposure by investing across multiple underlying funds.

Fund recap A financial restructuring where private equity management companies borrow against fund assets to provide early returns to limited partners.

G

Gatekeeper Institutional consultants who advise limited partners on private equity fund selection and portfolio construction.

General Data Protection Regulation (GDPR) A comprehensive EU law enacted in May 2018 that governs how organizations within and outside the European Union collect, process, store, and protect the personal data of EU residents. The regulation establishes strict principles—including lawfulness, data minimization, accuracy, storage limitation, and accountability—and grants individuals enhanced privacy rights such as the right to access, rectify, erase, and port their data. Organizations failing to comply face penalties of up to €20 million or 4% of global annual revenue, whichever is higher.

General partner (GP) The private equity firm professionals who manage funds, make investment decisions, and bear unlimited liability for fund operations. The general partner is associated with the management company of the investment fund.

Glucagon-like peptide-1 (GLP-1) Hormone-based drug class used in Type 2 diabetes and obesity; current demand stresses pen/device and aseptic capacity.

Good manufacturing practice (GMP) Regulatory quality standards that private equity-backed pharmaceutical and medical device companies must maintain to ensure product safety and compliance with healthcare authorities.

Growth capital Private equity investment in established companies focused on accelerating growth through expansion capital rather than leveraged buyouts. Typically, a minority investment.

Guarantee of assets (representations) Contractual assurances in private equity acquisition agreements where sellers warrant the accuracy of asset valuations, ownership rights, and condition of company assets being acquired.

Guarantee of liabilities (warranties) Seller commitments in private equity transactions providing protection against undisclosed or understated liabilities, typically backed by escrow accounts and indemnification provisions.

H

Harvesting "Selling the PortCos." The exit phase where private equity funds realize returns by selling portfolio companies through various divestiture strategies.

Health Economics and Outcomes Research (HEOR) Evidence demonstrating drug value and cost-effectiveness.

Health information exchange (HIE) Sharing of health information across systems.

Health Technology Assessment (HTA) Systematic evaluation process determining healthcare intervention value for reimbursement decisions.

High yield bond Debt securities that private equity firms often use to finance leveraged buyouts and provide portfolio companies with flexible capital structures.

HIPAA Compliance Healthcare data privacy and security requirements affecting private equity healthcare investments.

Holdback *See Escrow*

Holding period The duration private equity funds maintain ownership of portfolio companies, typically ranging from 3–7 years.

Horizon IRR A projected internal rate of return calculation private equity funds use to estimate future performance based on current portfolio valuations. Uses the beginning net asset values as an initial cash outflow and net asset values at the period end as the terminal cash flow.

Hurdle rate (preferred return) The return that a fund must realize for its investors before the management of the investment fund can share in the added value of the fund. Approximately 80% of private equity funds set hurdle rates at 8%.

I

Inclusion/exclusion criteria Patient eligibility requirements for clinical trials.

Indemnification Legal protections private equity firms negotiate in acquisition agreements to safeguard against undisclosed liabilities and warranty breaches.

Initial public offer (IPO) A primary exit strategy where private equity firms take portfolio companies public through stock exchange listings.

Institutional investor Large investment entities (pension funds, endowments, insurance companies) that serve as limited partners in private equity funds.

Internal rate of return (IRR) The compounded rate of return on an investment or series of investments. It reflects the performance of a PE fund by taking into account the size and timing of its cash flows (capital calls and distributions) and its net asset value at the time of the calculation.

Interoperability Healthcare IT systems' ability to seamlessly exchange, integrate, and utilize clinical and administrative data across different platforms and organizations, representing a critical technical requirement for private equity investments in health information technology, electronic health records, and care coordination platforms that rely on standardized protocols including FHIR (Fast Healthcare Interoperability Resources) and HL7 (Health Level 7) to enable data sharing and improve patient outcomes.

Interval fund A specialized fund structure that some private equity managers use, offering periodic liquidity opportunities to investors at predetermined intervals rather than traditional closed-end fund structures.

Investigational New Drug (IND) FDA authorization to test experimental drugs in humans.

Investment (or Offering or Sale) Memorandum (IM) Basically, a detailed marketing document presenting the company and its business plan.

Investment committee (IC) The decision-making body within private equity firms that evaluates, approves, and monitors portfolio investments.

Investment horizon The target timeframe private equity funds establish for making investments and achieving exits, typically 10–12 years total. There are two types of funds in terms of horizon: open-end (no horizon) and closed-end.

J

J-curve A visual representation of the plain fact that sometimes things will get worse before they get better. An initial decline in performance followed, at least theoretically, by a steep improvement in performance.

K

Key-man clause Fund provisions protecting limited partners by suspending investment activities if crucial general partners leave the firm.

L

Lead investor The private equity firm that originates and manages significant investment opportunities, often in syndicated deals.

Leaver provision A "good and bad leaver" clause in shareholder agreements seek to treat the valuation of a party's shares differently depending on their circumstances of departure. They are therefore triggered by an event that compels the shareholder to offer their shares for sale in a company.

Letter of Intent (LOI) Largely nonbinding document entered into by the potential sellers and buyers of a company, with two primary objectives: establish a value and secure some form of exclusivity.

Leveraged build-up (LBU) A private equity strategy combining leveraged buyouts with add-on acquisitions to create larger, more valuable platform companies.

Leveraged buy-in (LBI) A private equity transaction where external management teams acquire companies using significant debt financing.

Leveraged buyout (LBO) A transaction in which a significant portion of the purchase price is financed through debt. LBOs are common in both management buyouts and management buy-ins.

Life cycle management Strategies to extend product commercial viability.

Limited partnership (LP) Anglo-Saxon funds are often set up as tax transparent limited partnerships with limited liability for the investors (the limited partners or LPs). These limited partnerships are often offshore partnerships for maximum legal flexibility.

Limited Partnership Agreement (LPA) The foundational legal document governing private equity funds, establishing rights and obligations between general partners and limited partners, including investment terms, fee structures, and governance provisions.

Liquidation preference Investment agreement provisions specifying how private equity investors receive proceeds upon portfolio company sales or liquidations.

Lock-up period The time frame during which private equity limited partners cannot withdraw committed capital or transfer fund interests.

M

Managed care organization (MCO) A healthcare entity that integrates financing and delivery of medical services to enrolled members through structured provider networks and utilization management protocols, representing a significant investment category for private equity firms targeting health insurance companies, health maintenance organizations, preferred provider organizations, and point-of-service plans that generate returns through risk-based contracting, cost management, and population health strategies.

Management buy-in (MBI) An external management team is brought in to acquire and run the company. This can be ideal for companies in need of transformative leadership, such as in cases of underperformance or preparation for an IPO.

Management buyout (MBO) The company's existing management team acquires a controlling stake, leveraging their familiarity with the business. This is often suitable for continuity and stability.

Management fees Annual fees (typically 2%) that private equity limited partners pay to general partners for fund management services.

Management presentation (MP) Intensive sessions where private equity firms evaluate portfolio company management teams during due diligence. Typically 2 to 6 hours being grilled by a potential buyer and their advisors.

Market access Strategy to ensure patient access to treatments through payers.

Marketing Authorization Application (MAA) European drug approval application.
Master Batch Record (MBR) Approved, master version of the batch instructions from which executed batch records are created.
Medical affairs A functional area within private equity-backed healthcare companies managing clinical data and regulatory compliance.
Medical communications (MedComms) Healthcare service companies that private equity firms target for investment opportunities in medical information and education sectors.
Medicines and Healthcare products Regulatory Agency (MHRA) UK regulatory authority.
Mergers and acquisitions (M&A) A source of deal flow and primary exit strategy for private equity portfolio companies.
Mezzanine An intermediate form of financing that has some of the characteristics of equity and some of the characteristics of debt. This can technically take the form of convertible debt, preferred shares or debt with warrants.
Minimum advertised price (MAP) Policy setting the lowest publicly advertised price a retailer may display
Modality Class of therapeutic approach (e.g., small molecules, mAbs, ADCs, CGT) with distinct process and capacity requirements.
Money in Capital calls and investments private equity funds make into portfolio companies.
Money out Distributions and exits private equity funds generate from portfolio company sales and dividends.
Monoclonal antibodies (mAbs) Laboratory-produced antibodies targeting specific diseases.
Multiple on invested capital (MOIC) Measure of the multiple of money returned to investors (realized plus unrealized) relative to the amount of capital they invested. Unlike TVPI, MOIC can refer to individual investments or the overall fund, and it doesn't distinguish between realized and unrealized value.
Multiple Valuation metrics (EV/EBITDA, P/E) private equity professionals use to assess and compare investment opportunities and exit pricing.

N

National Medical Products Administration (NMPA) Formerly known as the China Food and Drug Administration (CFDA) and State Food and Drug Administration (SFDA), serves as China's primary regulatory authority overseeing pharmaceuticals, medical devices, food safety, and cosmetics—a critical regulatory body that private equity firms must navigate when investing in healthcare companies seeking market access in China or Chinese companies preparing for international expansion.
National Venture Capital Association (NVCA) A nonprofit trade organization founded in 1973 that represents US venture capital firms, entrepreneurs, and industry partners.
Net asset valuation (NAV) A business is not profitable or carries out an activity that is essentially involved with purchase and management of assets (such as a property investment company) they may be valued by reference to their net tangible assets. Goodwill created by the acquisition should normally be excluded along with certain other intangible assets. As in an earnings valuation based on market comparators, a discount is typically applied to the tangible asset valuation.
Net asset value loan (NAV Loan) Credit facilities that private equity general partners secure using fund portfolio values as collateral.
NewCo New company structures private equity firms create to facilitate complex acquisition transactions and optimize tax efficiency.
New Drug Application (NDA) FDA submission for new drug approval.
No fault divorce clause Provisions allowing private equity partners to dissolve relationships without proving wrongdoing, protecting fund stability.
Non-binding offer (NBO) Preliminary proposal submitted by a buyer in a transaction, setting out key terms like price and structure without creating legal obligations to complete the deal. The NBO is closely linked to the LOI. After reviewing the NBO, both parties may agree to move forward and develop a more detailed LOI, which outlines finer terms and intentions for the deal. The LOI is still nonbinding (except for select sections like exclusivity or confidentiality), but it usually follows the NBO and contains more specifics.
Nondisclosure agreement (NDA) Confidentiality contract, executed before sharing sensitive company information.
Nonrecourse debt Acquisition financing where private equity portfolio company assets serve as sole collateral, limiting fund liability exposure.

O

Omics The comprehensive study of biological molecules (genomics, proteomics, metabolomics) that private equity firms target through investments in precision medicine, diagnostics, and personalized healthcare companies.

On shoring/"China plus one" Strategy to localize or diversify supply chains away from single country dependence.

Open-ended fund Less common private equity fund structures allowing continuous capital raising and redemptions, unlike traditional closed-end formats.

Operating company/property company (OpCo/PropCo) A private equity structuring strategy separating operating businesses from real estate assets to optimize valuations and exit strategies.

Operating debt Working capital facilities that private equity portfolio companies use for day-to-day business operations.

Operating partner Senior professionals hired by private equity firms to work directly with portfolio companies to drive operational improvements and value creation.

Orphan Drug Medication for rare diseases affecting fewer than 200,000 patients.

Over-the-counter (OTC) products Healthcare products and medications available without prescription that private equity firms may target through consumer healthcare, pharmaceutical retail, and wellness sector investments.

Overall Equipment Effectiveness (OEE) Composite metric of availability × performance × quality that reflects equipment productivity.

Overhang The total amount of committed but uncalled capital across private equity funds that represents future investment demand, creating potential market pressure as funds compete to deploy remaining commitments over their investment periods—distinct from dry powder which represents immediately deployable liquid capital.

P

Patent cliff A period when major products lose exclusivity, risking rapid revenue decline from generic/biosimilar entry.

Payer or payor Entity (insurer, government program, employer) that pays for healthcare services and drugs.

Payment in Kind (PIK) Fixed-income securities that generate interest in the form of additional debt instead of a sum of money. The final interest is only payable on the final maturity date. Typically unsecured. (Sometimes called "Pay-If-you-Kan.")

PE-backed Corporate Incubation (PEBCI) Refers to a model sometimes called "PE + Listed Company," a hybrid approach combining PIPE-like arrangements, SPV fund incubation, and roll-up style consolidation developed mostly in Asia.

Pen assembly Assembly process for drug delivery pens (mechanisms, cartridges, needles), often a capacity bottleneck for GLP-1s.

Personalized medicine Treatments tailored to individual genetic profiles.

Pharmaceuticals and Medical Devices Agency (PMDA) Japanese regulatory authority.

Pharmacovigilance Drug safety monitoring activities that private equity-backed pharmaceutical companies must maintain for regulatory compliance.

Pharmacy benefit manager (PBM) Third-party administrators that negotiate drug prices and rebates with manufacturers, manage formularies for insurers and employers, and process prescription drug claims.

Phase I-IV Trials Sequential stages of clinical drug development.

Placement agent Financial intermediaries that private equity firms engage to assist with fund fundraising from institutional limited partners.

Placement memorandum (PPM) The offering document private equity funds provide to prospective limited partners during fundraising.

Pooled return Aggregate performance metrics private equity funds report across their entire portfolio rather than individual investment returns.

Population health management Coordinated care for defined patient groups.

Portfolio company (PortCo) Companies owned by private equity funds that represent the core investments generating fund returns.

Post-money value Portfolio company valuations immediately after private equity investment rounds, used for ownership percentage calculations.

Pre-emption right Rights allowing existing private equity investors to maintain ownership percentages when portfolio companies issue additional equity.

Pre-money value Portfolio company valuations before new private equity investment rounds, establishing baseline values for deal negotiations.

Preferred equity Equity that pays a fixed dividend (as opposed to common equity) and sits behind debt but ahead of common equity in a company's capital structure. Often includes some form of upside participation, which could take several forms, including warrants, a conversion feature, or an attached common equity co-investment.

Preferred provider model Contracting approach where sponsors direct a large share of work to a small set of scaled vendors in return for SLAs and pricing.

Preferred return (rate) The minimum return threshold limited partners receive before private equity general partners participate in profit distributions.

Price/earnings (PE) ratio Multiple used by private equity firms for portfolio company valuations and public market exit planning.

Priority review Accelerated FDA review timeline (6 months vs. 10 months).

Private investment in public equities (PIPE) Investment strategy where private equity firms acquire stakes in publicly traded companies through private placements.

Private placement The investment approach private equity funds use to acquire securities directly from companies without public market transactions.

Process performance qualification (PPQ) A stage in process validation that demonstrates the commercial process operates within control to consistently produce a quality product.

Protocol Detailed clinical trial design and procedures.

Q

Quality management system (QMS) Integrated set of processes, procedures, and responsibilities to ensure product quality and compliance (e.g., SOPs, CAPA, change control).

Quality-adjusted life year (QALY) Metric combining life expectancy and quality of life.

Quartile Performance ranking system used to compare private equity fund returns against industry peers, with first quartile representing top 25% performers and fourth quartile representing bottom 25%.

R

Ratchets Mechanisms designed to adjust the proportional ownership among various shareholder groups are known as ratchets. These tools can allow management to gain a larger equity stake in a company if its performance meets or exceeds expectations. Conversely, ratchets can also safeguard an investment fund's ability to maximize its returns if the company's performance falls short.

Real-world evidence (RWE) Clinical evidence from actual patient usage data.

Recapitalization (Recap) Financial restructuring transactions where private equity firms modify portfolio company capital structures to optimize returns.

Registered Investment Advisor (RIA) A status in the United States for a firm or individual that provides investment advice and/or manages client assets for compensation and is registered with either the US SEC or state securities regulators.

Regulatory affairs A critical function in private equity-backed healthcare companies managing regulatory compliance and product approval processes.

Revenue cycle management (RCM) Healthcare financial processes from patient registration through final payment collection.

Revolver Revolving credit facilities that private equity portfolio companies use for working capital and operational flexibility.

Right First Time (RFT) Doing work without errors or rework; key driver of yield and lead time.

Roll-up Primarily a financial and scale-driven PE strategy. The core idea is to acquire multiple small companies (add-ons) in a fragmented market and combine them under a single larger entity (the platform). A roll-up specifically denotes the consolidation of many small players within a single niche, whereas buy-and-build is a broader approach applicable across industries and strategies.

Round of financing Sequential investment stages that companies progress through, in venture capital or growth capital.

Royalty monetization/revenue interest financing Nondilutive funding where future product revenues or royalties are pledged/sold in exchange for upfront capital.

Rx drug A prescription pharmaceutical product that requires authorization from a licensed healthcare provider before dispensing, representing a significant investment category for private equity firms targeting pharmaceutical companies, specialty pharmacies, and healthcare services organizations that develop, manufacture, or distribute regulated medications under FDA oversight.

S

SaaS net retention Annualized metric for software platforms indicating revenue growth within an existing customer base (expansion minus churn/contraction).

Sales and Purchase Agreement (SPA) The definitive legal contract for private equity portfolio company acquisitions and exits.

Second-lien debt Subordinated debt instruments private equity firms use in leveraged buyout capital structures, ranking below senior debt.

Secondaries The market for existing private equity fund interests and portfolio company stakes, where limited partners sell their positions to specialized secondary buyers, providing liquidity before traditional fund exits.

Secondary buyout Exit transactions where private equity funds sell portfolio companies to other private equity firms rather than strategic buyers.

Secured debt Priority debt instruments backed by portfolio company assets, commonly used in private equity leveraged buyout transactions.

Seed investing Early-stage venture capital investment that often precedes later private equity growth funding rounds.

Senior debt The highest-priority debt in private equity leveraged buyout capital structures, typically provided by banks and institutional lenders.

Separation/Transition Services Agreement (TSA) Temporary services provided by a seller to a carved-out business (IT, HR, finance) until it becomes standalone.

Shareholder agreement Comprehensive contracts governing relationships between private equity investors and portfolio company management teams.

Side letter Customized agreement between private equity funds and specific limited partners modifying standard partnership terms.

Skin in the game Unwritten principle for ensuring alignment of interest according to which the management team should use its own funds to acquire a significant investment of its own in the fund. The typical investment amount for fund management is in the range of 1–3% (Source: Moonfare).

Small and medium enterprises (SMEs) Often targeted by private equity firms for buyout and growth capital investments.

Software as a Medical Device (SaMD) Software applications intended for medical purposes requiring FDA oversight and validation.

Special Purpose Vehicle (SPV) Separate legal entities private equity firms create for specific investments, tax optimization, and risk isolation.

Special-purpose acquisition company (SPAC) shell company established to merge with or acquire a private company, enabling it to go public without undergoing the traditional IPO process.

Spin off Separation of a business into an independent public company, distributing shares to the parent's shareholders.

Sponsorless Private equity transactions where management teams acquire companies without traditional private equity backing, often utilizing alternative financing sources and maintaining greater operational control.

Stage of financing See *Round of financing*.

Stapled debt package A package of loans in various forms and with different degrees of subordination, ranging from mezzanine to junior and senior debt, organized by the vendor to expedite the process.

Stark Law Compliance US federal regulations governing physician self-referrals in healthcare transactions.

Statistical Process Control (SPC) Use of control charts and statistics to detect process drift and maintain quality.

Stepdown Scheduled reductions in interest rates or other financial terms in private equity debt structures upon achieving performance milestones.

Sterile injectables Parenteral drugs requiring sterility assurance; include small molecules and biologics.

Sweat equity To align the interests of management with those of the investment fund and provide motivation, management is often granted the opportunity to invest in the target company under preferential terms. Typically, the per-share contribution required from management is lower than the amount paid by the investment fund. The relative difference between the effective price paid by management and the price paid by the investment fund is commonly referred to as the "envy ratio." Note that "Sweet equity" isn't a standard financial term, though it is sometimes used as a play on words to describe equity that is particularly valuable or well-positioned.

Syndication The process where multiple lenders collaborate to provide large debt facilities for private equity leveraged buyout transactions.

T

Tag along right Minority shareholder protections allowing portfolio company management to participate in private equity exit transactions.

Take-private Private equity transactions acquiring publicly listed companies and removing them from stock exchange trading.

Tech transfer (technology transfer) A structured process of moving a product/process from development to a manufacturing site or between sites.

Term loan A (TLA) Amortizing senior debt facilities commonly used in private equity leveraged buyout financing packages.

Term sheet Nonbinding preliminary agreements outlining key commercial terms for private equity investments and exits.

Theranostics An emerging healthcare sector combining therapeutic and diagnostic capabilities that private equity firms increasingly target, representing companies developing personalized medicine solutions that diagnose and treat conditions simultaneously.

Throughput Rate at which a system produces output; in manufacturing, units or batches per period.

Time-weighted return (TWR) A performance calculation methodology that private equity funds use to measure returns independent of capital call timing.

Total value to paid-in (TVPI) A comprehensive private equity fund performance metric combining realized distributions with unrealized portfolio values. While DPI measures distribution as a percentage of paid-in capital, TVPI measures total value as a percentage of paid-in capital. Both are measures of value per $.

Tranche Separate portions of debt facilities with different risk profiles, interest rates, and repayment terms.

Transitional service agreement (TSA) Post-closing contracts where private equity sellers provide temporary services to buyers during portfolio company integration.

Turnaround Private equity investment strategy focusing on distressed companies with cheap equity requiring operational and financial restructuring.

U

Utilization Percentage of available capacity that is used; a key driver of CDMO economics.

V

Value-based care (VBC) Healthcare payment model based on patient outcomes.

Value-based insurance design (VBID) Insurance structures aligning patient cost-sharing with clinical value of services.

Value-based pricing Drug pricing based on demonstrated clinical outcomes.

Vendor loan Seller financing that private equity buyers sometimes negotiate to bridge valuation gaps in portfolio company acquisitions.

Venture capital (VC) Early stage private equity investing in startup and emerging growth companies, typically preceding later stage buyout investments.

Vesting of carry The gradual earning process for private equity general partner carried interest rights over fund performance periods.

Vintage year The year private equity funds begin making investments, used for performance comparison and industry analysis.

Virtual data room (VDR) Secure online platform where the vendor puts all the confidential documents available to the potential investors under NDA during due diligence processes.

W

Waterfall distribution The sequential profit allocation mechanism determining how private equity fund returns flow between limited partners and general partners.

Write down Portfolio company valuation reductions that private equity funds implement when investment prospects deteriorate.

Write-off Complete elimination of portfolio company values when private equity investments become worthless.

Write up Portfolio company valuation increases that private equity funds recognize when investment performance exceeds expectations.

Z

Zombie funds Funds that continue operating beyond their intended lifespan due to inability to successfully exit remaining portfolio investments.

Main Resources

Candesic
ION/MergerMarket
ION/Dealogic
Preqin (part of Blackrock)
PitchBook
HBI
Real Deals
PE International
Gain.pro
Private Equity Insights

List of Companies Mentioned

CORPORATES (293)

21st Century Oncology · 23andMe · Acadia Healthcare · Access Healthcare · Acteon · Active Care Group · Advanz Pharma · Aesynt · AfyA Care · AGC Biologics · Aier Eye Hospital · Agilon Health · AIG (Asia Institute of Gastroenterology) · Akdital Group · Alignment Healthcare · Alliance Boots / Walgreens Boots Alliance · Allocate Software · Allscripts · Almoosa Health · Almus · AmCare Healthcare · AmSurg · Amgen · Amwell · Amplitude Surgical · Anthem · Apollo Telemedicine Networking Foundation · Aravind Eye Care System · Ardena · Ardent Health Services · ArisGlobal · Arranta Bio Holdings · ART Fertility Clinics · Aster DM Healthcare · AstraZeneca · Athenahealth · AtlasEdge · Avaneer Healthcare · Babylon Health · Bausch & Lomb · BC Platforms · Belron · Berkshire Hathaway · Bespak · Binding Site, The · BioAgilytix · Biogen · BioClinica (later Clario) · BioVendor Group · Blue Cloud Pediatric Surgery Centers · BOMI Group · Bora Pharma · Brammer Bio · BrightSpring Health Services · BTG Specialty Pharmaceuticals · Bupa · Butterfly Network · Capital Cell · Cardinal Health · Caris Life Sciences · Caritas Christi Health Care · Catalent · Cedar Gate Technologies · CenterWell · Cenexi · Cerba Healthcare · Certara · Cetus Corporation · CFAO · Change Healthcare · China Biologic Products (CBPO) · China Forestry Holdings · Cigna / Evernorth · Cipla · CIS (Community Integrated Services) · CityMD · CMIC · CMR Surgical · Consort Medical · CordenPharma · Cornerstone OnDemand · Corin Group · Covenant Physician Partners · CVS Health · D'Ieteren Group · Datavant / Ciox Health · Dedienne Santé · Dentalcorp · DigitalBridge · Digital Equipment Corporation (DEC) · Doctolib · DocPlanner · Duomed Group · Ecolab · Eden Biopharma · Elsan · Elysium Healthcare · EMC · Ensemble Healthcare Partners · Envision Healthcare · Epic Systems · Europa Biosite · Evotec AG · Express Scripts · Fairchild Semiconductor · FairJourney Biologics · Famar · Fareva · Fertility Partners · FIM Medical · Flatiron Health · Fortis Healthcare · Fosun Pharma · Four Seasons Health Care · Gastro Health · Genentech · General Electric · GenesisCare · Gibson Greetings · Gland Pharma · GL Capital Group · Global D · Goodlife Pharmacy · Gozio Health · Grab Health · Gracewell Healthcare · Guardant Health · Guangzhou Pharmaceuticals Corporation · Guilong Pharmaceutical · Hahnemann University Hospital · HC-One · HCA Healthcare · Heinz · Hermina Hospitals · Hologic · HOPCo · Houdaille Corp · Humana · HyTest · Hygeia · IHH Healthcare · IM Alliance · Immunex · InBrain Neuroelectronics · Igenomix · InMedica Group · Intech · Intuitive Surgical / da Vinci · IPC Healthcare · IQVIA · Island Hospital · IVI-RMA Global · IVC Evidensia · Izasa Scientific · Kadiant · Kelix Bio · Kiddicare · Kinetic Concepts · Labco · Leading Edge Data Centres · Life Healthcare (South Africa) · LifeCare Holdings · LifePoint Health · Livongo · Logan Pharma · LogistiCare Solutions · MAC Hospitals · ManorCare (HCR ManorCare) · MaSTherCell · Max Healthcare · MC Medical · McLean Industries · Medical Solutions · Medica Group · Medline · Mediwound · Mehiläinen · MedKit · Menix · Meribel Pharma Solutions · Mervyn's Department Store Chain · Metropolitan Hospital · Metro Pacific Hospitals · Mindray Medical International · MIR · MindMaze · Modernizing Medicine · Mylan · Nanavati Hospital · Narayana Health · Nanjing Pharmaceutical · NeuroGen Pharma · Netsmart Technologies · NHP (Nursing Home Properties) · NMC

Health · Noom · Norstella · Oak Street Health · OM Scott · Omnicell · One Medical · Olink Proteomics · Opella · Oracle Health · Oscar Health · Outcome Health · Oxford Biomedica · Palex Medical · Pan-Atlantic Steamship Company · Parexel International · Pastel Health · PCI Pharma Services · Peptomyc · Phreesia · Precision Medicine Group · Quartet Health · Quaker Oats · Quotient · R1 RCM · Radiant Life Care · Ramsay Health Care · RCCH HealthCare · Recipharm · Relias Learning · Remedy Partners · Resolve Surgical · RJR Nabisco · RLDatix · Safeway · Sangon Biotech · Sartorius Stedim Biotech · Scala Data Centers · Sealy Corporation · SERF · SERB Pharmaceuticals · SeQuent Scientific · Signify Health · Simtra BioPharma · Sinopharm · Sirtex · Snapple Beverage Corporation · Softway Medical · Soho Pharmaceuticals · Sobi (Swedish Orphan Biovitrum) · Sotera Health / Sterigenics · Southern Cross Healthcare · Spire Healthcare · STADA Arzneimittel · Sterling Pharma Solutions · Steward Health Care · Stryker · Sulaiman Al Habib Group · Summit Health · Summit Medical Group · Surescripts · Surgery Partners · Synlab · Syncona · Synerlab · TeamHealth · Teladoc · Teva · Thermo Fisher Scientific · TXU / Energy Future Holdings · Tyber Medical · U.S. Bank · UnitedHealth / Optum · UPS · Upstream Rehabilitation · US Anesthesia Partners (USAP) · US Oncology Network · ValueHealth · Vantage Data Centers · Ventas · Vibalogics · Virence Health · Vitrolife · Vivalto Santé · VNV Global · Waystar · Werfen · WuXi PharmaTech · Y-mAbs Therapeutics · Zelis · Zipline International · Zydus Lifesciences

INVESTMENT FIRMS (264)

3G Capital · 3i Group · ADIA · AEA Investors · Abraaj Group · Abris Capital Partners · Active Ownership Capital · Adams Street Partners · Advent International · Alchemy Special Opportunities · AlbaCore Capital · Allianz X · Alpinvest (Carlyle) · Alta Semper Capital · Altas Partners · Alta Life Sciences · Altaris Capital · Altor Fund · Ampersand Capital Partners · Antin Infrastructure Partners · Apollo Management · Apposite Capital · ARCHIMED · Ardian · Arsenal Capital Partners · Asabys Partners · Astorg · Athyrium Capital · ATP · Audax Private Equity · Avista Capital Partners · Avenue Capital · AXA IM Alts · Bain Capital · BC Partners · Bear Stearns · Berkshire Partners · BGH Capital · BII (British International Investment) · Blackstone · Blue Owl · Blue Wolf Capital · Boyu Capital · BPI France · Bridgepoint Capital · Brookfield Asset Management · C-Bridge Capital · CAIS · CalPERS · Cambridge Associates · Castik Capital · Centurium Capital · CITIC Capital · Cobepa · CPPIB · CapVest · Carlyle Group · CarVal · CBC Group · CD&R · CDPQ · CDH Investments · Centre Lane Partners · Cerberus Capital Management · CIC · Chicago Pacific Founders · CIG · Cinven · Clearlake Capital · Coliseum Capital Management · Coller Capital · CPP Investments · CQS · Cressey & Company · CRG · Cross Atlantic Capital Partners · CVC Capital Partners · Darwin PE · DBAG (Deutsche Beteiligungs AG) · Deerfield Management · Development Partners International · DigitalBridge · Duke Street Capital · ECM Partners · Eckuity Capital · ECI Partners · eevolve · Elliott Management · EMZ Partners · Endless LLP · EQT Partners · Equistone Partners Europe · Eurazeo · Evergreen Capital · Everstone Capital · Evoco · Five Arrows (Rothschild) · Francisco Partners · Frazier Healthcare Partners · Fremman Capital · Fulcrum · Gen II Fund Services · GENUI · General Atlantic · Genstar Capital · GHO Capital · GIC · GI Partners · Gilde Healthcare · Gimv · Glendower Capital · Goldman Sachs Capital Partners · Groupe Crédit Agricole · GSO (Blackstone credit) · GTCR · Gulf Capital · Gyrus Capital · H.I.G. Capital · Hamilton Lane · HarbourVest · Harbour Point Capital · Harvest Partners · Hayfin · HealthQuad · Hellman & Friedman · Helios Investment Partners · Hg Capital · Hillhouse Capital · Hony Capital · HPS Investment Partners · iCapital Network · IK Partners · Imperial Capital Group · InfraVia Capital Partners · Insight Venture Partners · Intel Capital · INVL Baltic Sea Growth Fund · Iwosan Investments · JPMorgan Partners · J.W. Childs · Jolt Capital · Kaszek Ventures · Keensight Capital · Kleiner Perkins · KKR · Lauxera Capital · LBO Partners ·

LeapFrog Investments · Leonard Green & Partners · Lexington Partners · LGT · Lightspeed Venture Partners · Linden Capital Partners · MACSF · Macquarie Group · Madison Dearborn Partners · Magnum Capital · Martis Capital · Mediterrania Capital Partners · Medical Properties Trust · Mentha Capital · Merieux Equity Partners · MidEuropa · MidOcean (formerly DLJ Merchant Bank) · Miura · Montagu Private Equity · Moonfare · Morgan Stanley Expansion Capital · Mountain View Capital · MTIP · Mubadala · Nautic Partners · Naxicap Partners · New Enterprise Associates · New Mountain Capital · Newbridge Capital · Nordic Capital · Nordic Alpha Partners · NorthWest Healthcare Properties REIT · Nova · Novo Holdings · Oaktree Capital Management · OMERS Private Equity · One Equity Partners · One Peak · Ontario Teachers' Pension Plan · Onex Corporation · OrbiMed · OPTrust · PAG · PAI Partners · Pall Mall Capital · Palamon Capital Partners · Pantheon Ventures · Partners Group · Patient Square Capital · Patron Capital · Peloton Capital Management · Peloton Equity · Permira · PIF (Saudi Public Investment Fund) · Ping An Insurance · Private Corner · Providence Equity Partners · PSP Investments · Quadria Capital · Quadrivio · Quantum Strategic Partners · Questa · Quilvest · RC Capital · Revelstoke Capital Partners · RIT Capital Partners · Roark Capital · Sagard Healthcare Partners · Sands Capital Life Sciences · Securitize · Sequoia Capital · SFC Capital · SHS · Silver Lake Partners · Sofinnova Partners · Soledar Partners · SoftBank Vision Fund 2 · SP Ventures · Starr Capital Partners · Starwood · StepStone · Stone Point Capital · Summa Equity · Summit Partners · Swiss Life Asset Managers · Sycamore Partners · TA Associates · Temasek · Tempo · Terra Firma Capital Partners · Thomas H. Lee Partners · Thoma Bravo · Three Hills Capital · Tikehau Capital · Titanbay · TJC · TowerBrook Capital Partners · TPG · Triton Partners · Turenne Capital · TVM Capital Healthcare · Varsity Crescent · Vauban Infrastructure Partners · Verdane · Veritas Capital · Vestar Capital Partners · Vista Equity Partners · Vistria Group · Vivalto Partners · Warburg Pincus · Water Street Healthcare Partners · Waterland Private Equity · Waud Capital Partners · Webster Equity Partners · Welsh Carson Anderson & Stowe · Wesray Capital Corporation · WindRose Health Investors · York Capital · Yieldstreet

About the Website

Thank you for purchasing this book.

You may access the following additional complementary resources provided for your use by visiting: www.candesic.com/WileyPEhealth

The companion website extends the book from a static text into a practical, regularly updated workspace. It is where you download the hospital leverage buyout (LBO) model, quiz yourself on each chapter, and follow how private equity markets evolve long after the ink on this edition is dry.

- At the center of the site is the fully built hospital LBO model presented in Chapter 5 of the book. You can adjust assumptions on both the operating and the financial model—pricing, activity, reimbursement, CapEx, or leverage—and immediately see the impact on returns and exit outcomes. The model combines the standard building blocks of an LBO with healthcare-specific features so that readers can experiment with realistic hospital dynamics rather than generic case studies.
- Each chapter is accompanied by a short Q&A set available on the website. These questions move from basic comprehension checks to more applied, transaction-style problems that require you to connect concepts across chapters. Concise solutions highlight the most common conceptual and numerical errors, making the Q&As suitable for self-study, classroom use, or interview preparation.
- Because PE markets move faster than publishing cycles, the website also hosts a few brief, regularly updated comments on current developments. These notes concentrate on themes that matter for deals and valuation—fundraising conditions, interest rate and credit environments, regulation, and structural shifts in healthcare delivery and reimbursement. The aim is not to forecast markets but to show how the analytical tools developed in the book can be used to interpret new data points and headlines.
- Finally, the site offers an open channel for readers' questions. You can email queries on the model, conceptual issues in private equity and healthcare, or points of disagreement with the book. A selection will be answered in detail and posted (anonymized upon request), gradually building a living FAQ that reflects the problems real readers actually encounter rather than an idealized exam.

Bibliography

Acharya, V. V., and Xu, Z. (2017). Financial dependence and innovation: The case of public versus private firms. *Journal of Financial Economics*, 124(2), pp. 223–243. https://doi.org/10.1016/j.jfineco.2017.02.002

Acharya, V. V., Gottschalg, O. F., Hahn, M., and Kehoe, C. (2013). Corporate governance and value creation: Evidence from private equity. *Review of Financial Studies*, 26(2), pp. 368–402. https://doi.org/10.1093/rfs/hhs117

Advani, A., Alemu, A., and Wren-Lewis, L. (2024, October). *Policy brief: Ten key facts about carried interest.* CenTax.org.uk. https://centax.org.uk/policy-brief-ten-key-facts-about-carried-interest/

Aghamolla, C., Jain, J., and Thakor, R. T. (2025). *When private equity comes to town: The local consequences of rising healthcare costs.* https://papers.ssrn.com/sol3/papers.cfm?abstract_id=4491104

Aghion, P., Askenazy, P., Berman, N., Cette, G., and Eymard, L. (2012). Credit constraints and the cyclicality of R&D investment: Evidence from France. *Journal of the European Economic Association*, 10(5), pp. 1001–1024. https://doi.org/10.1111/j.1542-4774.2012.01093.x

Aid, R., Chemla, G., Porchet, A., and Touzi, N. (2011). Hedging and vertical integration in electricity markets. *Management Science*, 57(7), pp. 1438–1452.

Al Hammadi, H. (2024, July 22). *How sovereign and private capital can help develop healthcare infrastructure.* World Economic Forum.

Alekseeva, L., Dalla Fontana, S., Genc, C. and Rashidi Ranjbar, H., 2022. *From in-person to online: the new shape of the VC industry.* Available at SSRN 4198138.

Alvarez and Marsal. (2023). *Private equity shared services centers: Global performance benchmark report.* https://www.alvarezandmarsal.com/expertise/private-equity-performance-improvement

Andonov, A., Li, A., and Smeets, P. (2025). *Do Development financial institutions create impact through venture capital investments*? Available at SSRN 5101408.

Andonov, A. and Rauh, J. D. (2025). The shifting finance of electricity generation (Working paper).

Ang, A., Chen, B., Goetzmann, W. N., and Phalippou, L. (2018). Estimating private equity returns from limited partner cash flows. *Journal of Finance*, 73(4), pp. 1751–1783.

Angrist, J. D., and Pischke, J.-S. (2009). *Mostly harmless econometrics: An empiricist's companion.* Princeton University Press.

Appelbaum, E. and Batt, R. (2020). *Private equity buyouts in healthcare: Who wins, who loses*? (Institute for New Economic Thinking Working Paper Series 1–115). https://doi.org/10.36687/inetwp118

Arnold, D., Dafny, L., Ho, K., and Lee, R. S. (2024). Hospital consolidation and prices: A review and directions for future research. *Review of Industrial Organization*, 65(1–2), 1–34. https://doi.org/10.1007/s11151-024-09989-9

Astorg.com (2022). *Astorg to acquire leading Pharmaceutical Contract Development and Manufacturing Organization CordenPharma from ICIG.* https://www.astorg.com/news/corden-news

Atanasova, C. and Chemla, G. (2026). Does familiarity breed alternative investment? Evidence from corporate defined-benefit pension plans. *Review of Finance*, revised and resubmitted (third round).

AVCJ. (2024). China healthcare private equity and venture capital report 2024. *Asia Venture Capital Journal.* https://www.avcj.com

Axelson, U., Jenkinson, T., Strömberg, P., and Weisbach, M. S. (2013). Borrow cheap, buy high? The determinants of leverage and pricing in buyouts. *Journal of Finance*, 68(6), pp. 2223–2267.

Axelson, U., Strömberg, P., and Weisbach, M. S. (2009). Why are buyouts levered? The financial structure of private equity funds. *Journal of Finance*, 64(4), pp. 1549–1582.

Bach, L., Baghai, R., Bos, M., & Silva, R. (2021). How do acquisitions affect the mental health of employees?. *Swedish House of Finance Research Paper*, (21-21).

Bai, X., and Wu, Y. (2024). *Private equity and gas emissions: Evidence from electric power plants* (Working paper). SSRN. https://doi.org/10.2139/ssrn.4364437

Baik, B. K. (2022). Private equity fund valuation management during fundraising. *SSRN Electronic Journal*. https://doi.org/10.2139/ssrn.4199605

Baik, B. K., Chen, W., and Srinivasan, S. (2024). *Private equity and the adoption of digital technologies* (No. 24-070). Harvard Business School Working Paper.

Bain & Company. (2022). *Limited partners and private equity firms embrace ESG*. https://www.bain.com/insights/limited-partners-and-private-equity-firms-embrace-esg/

Bain & Company. (2023a). *Life sciences: White-hot competition to win the right deals*. https://www.bain.com/insights/life-sciences-healthcare-private-equity-and-ma-report-2023/

Bain & Company. (2023b). *Private equity outlook 2024: Industry trends*. https://www.bain.com/insights/private-equity-outlook-liquidity-imperative-global-private-equity-report-2024/

Bain & Company. (2024a). *Healthcare private equity market 2023: Year in review and outlook*. https://www.bain.com/insights/year-in-review-global-healthcare-private-equity-report-2024/

Bain & Company. (2024b). The data imperative in private equity: From intuition to evidence. *Global Private Equity Report*.

Bain & Company. (2025a). *Global healthcare private equity and M&A report 2025: Year in review and outlook*. https://www.bain.com/insights/year-in-review-and-outlook-global-healthcare-private-equity-report-2025/

Bain & Company. (2025b). *Healthcare private equity market 2024: Year in review and outlook*. https://www.bain.com/insights/year-in-review-and-outlook-global-healthcare-private-equity-report-2025/

Bain & Company. (2025c). Private equity outlook 2025: Is a recovery starting to take shape? https://www.bain.com/insights/outlook-is-a-recovery-starting-to-take-shape-global-private-equity-report-2025/

Barber, B. M., Morse, A., and Yasuda, A. (2021). Impact investing. *Journal of Financial Economics*, 142(2), pp. 697–718.

Barber, F. and Goold, M. (2007). The strategic secret of private equity. *Harvard Business Review*, 85(9), pp. 108–117.

Becht, M., Bolton, P., and Röell, A. A. (2003). Corporate governance and control. In G. M. Constantinides, M. Harris, and R. M. Stulz (Eds.), *Handbook of the economics of finance: Corporate finance* (Vol. 1A, pp. 1–109). North-Holland Publishing Company.

Bellon, A. (2025). Does private equity ownership make firms cleaner? The role of environmental liability risks. *The Review of Financial Studies*, 38(9), pp. 2517–2556. https://doi.org/10.1093/rfs/hhaf035

Bernstein, S. (2022). The effects of public and private equity markets on firm behavior. *Annual Review of Financial Economics*, 14(1), pp. 295–318.

Bettignies, J.-E. and Chemla, G. (2008). Corporate venture capital: The upside of failure and competition for talent. *Management Science*, 54(3), pp. 505–521.

Bhardwaj, A., Gupta, A., and Howell, S. T., (2025). *Leveraged payouts: How using new debt to pay returns in private equity affects firms, employees, creditors, and investors*. US Census Bureau, Center for Economic Studies.

Bhatla, A., Bartlett, V. L., Liu, M., Song, Z., and Bruch, J. D. (2025). *Changes in patient care experience after private equity acquisition of US hospitals. JAMA*, 333(6), pp. 490–497. https://doi.org/10.1001/jama.2024.23450

Bililies, T. (2024). Successful private equity firms manage talent differently. *Harvard Business Review*. https://hbr.org/2024/12/successful-private-equity-firms-manage-talent-differently

Bolton, P. and Oehmke, M. (2011). Credit default swaps and the empty creditor problem. *The Review of Financial Studies*, 24(8), pp. 2617–2655. https://doi.org/10.1093/rfs/hhr002.

Bolton, P. and Scharfstein, D. S. (1990). A theory of predation based on agency problems in financial contracting. *American Economic Review*, 80(1), pp. 93–106. https://doi.org/10.1257/aer.80.1.93

Bolton, P. and Scharfstein, D. S. (1996). Optimal debt structure with multiple creditors. *Journal of Political Economy*, 104(1), pp. 1–26.

Bolton, P. Samama, F., and Stiglitz, J. E. (2012). *Sovereign wealth funds and long-term investing*. Columbia University Press.

Borsa, A., Bejarano, G., Ellen, M., and Bruch, J. D. (2023). Evaluating trends in private equity ownership and impacts on health outcomes, costs, and quality: Systematic review. *British Medical Journal*, 382, e075244. https://doi.org/10.1136/bmj-2023-075244

Bortolotti, B., Loss, G., and van Zwieten, R. W. (2023). The times are they a-changin'? Tracking sovereign wealth funds' sustainable investing. *Journal of International Business Policy*, 6, pp. 276–305. https://pmc.ncbi.nlm.nih.gov/articles/PMC10187512/

Bos, A. and Harrington, C. (2017). What happens to a nursing home chain when private equity takes over? A longitudinal case study. *INQUIRY: The Journal of Health Care Organization, Provision, and Financing*, 54, 46958017742761. https://doi.org/10.1177/0046958017742761

Bos, A., Kruse, F. M., and Jeurissen, P. P. T. (2020). For-profit nursing homes in the Netherlands: What factors explain their rise? *International Journal of Health Services*, 50(4), pp. 431–443. https://doi.org/10.1177/0020731420915658

Boston Consulting Group. (2014). *Maximizing value: Choose the right exit route*. BCG Insights.

Boston Consulting Group. (2023, July 7). *A CEO's first 1,000 days begins with the first 100*. https://www.bcg.com/publications/2023/impact-of-ceo-first-100-days

Boston Consulting Group. (2024). *The 2024 outlook for private equity in US health care*. https://www.bcg.com/publications/2024/private-equity-in-health-care-2024

Boston Consulting Group, H. M., and Liechtenstein, H. (2008). *Get ready for the private equity shakeout*. https://www.iese.edu/media/research/pdfs/ST-0313-E.pdf

Bound, J., Brown, C., and Mathiowetz, N. (2001). Measurement error in survey data. In *Handbook of econometrics* (Vol. 5, pp. 3705–3843). Elsevier.

Braun, R. T., Jung, H. Y., Casalino, L. P., Kim, J., and Mostashari, F. (2021). Association of private equity investment in US nursing homes with the quality and cost of care for long-stay residents. *JAMA Health Forum*, 2(11), e213817. https://doi:10.1001/jamahealthforum.2021.3817

Braun, R. T., Lelli, G. J., Pandey, A., Zhang, M., Winebrake, J. P., and Casalino, L. P. (2024). Association of private equity firm acquisition of ophthalmology practices with Medicare spending and use of ophthalmology services. *Ophthalmology*, 131, pp. 360–369. https://doi.org/10.1016/j.ophtha.2023.09.029

Braun, R. T., Stevenson, D. G., and Unruh, M. A. (2021). Acquisitions of hospice agencies by private equity firms and publicly traded corporations. *JAMA Internal Medicine*, 181, pp. 1113–1114. https://doi.org/10.1001/jamainternmed.2020.6262

Braun, R. T., Yun, H., Casalino, L. P., Myslinski, Z., Kuwonza, F. M., Jung, H.-Y., and Unruh, M. A. (2020). Comparative performance of private equity–owned US nursing homes during the COVID-19 pandemic. *JAMA Network Open*, 3(10), e2026702. https://doi.org/10.1001/jamanetworkopen.2020.26702

Braun, R., Jenkinson, T., and Stoff, I. (2017). How persistent is private equity performance? Evidence from deal-level data. *Journal of Financial Economics*, 123(2), pp. 273–291. https://doi.org/10.1016/j.jfineco.2016.01.033

Brill, D., Luo, S., Sridhar, J., and Williams, B. K. Jr. (2022). Private equity in ophthalmology: Lessons from other specialties. *Current Opinion in Ophthalmology*, 33, pp. 352–361. https://doi.org/10.1097/ICU.0000000000000876

Brown, G., Harris, B., Jenkinson, T., Kaplan, S., and Robinson, D. (2020). Private equity: Accomplishments and challenges. *Journal of Applied Corporate Finance*, 32(3), pp. 8–20.

Bruch, J. D., Borsa, A., Song, Z., and Richardson, S. S. (2022a). Expansion of private equity involvement in women's health care. *JAMA Internal Medicine*, 180, pp. 1542–1545. https://doi.org/10.1001/jamainternmed.2020.3567

Bruch, J. D., Foot, C., Singh, Y., Song, Z., Polsky, D., and Zhu, J. M. (2023). Workforce composition in private equity-acquired versus non-private equity-acquired physician practices. *Health Affairs (Millwood)*, 42, pp. 121–129. https://doi.org/10.1377/hlthaff.2022.00308

Bruch, J. D., Gondi, S., and Song, Z. (2020). Changes in hospital income, use, and quality associated with private equity acquisition. *JAMA Internal Medicine*, 180(11), 1428. https://doi.org/10.1001/jamainternmed.2020.3552

Bruch, J. D., Nair-Desai, S., Orav, E. J., and Tsai, T. C. (2022b). Private equity acquisitions of ambulatory surgical centers were not associated with quality, cost, or volume changes. *Health Affairs (Millwood)*, 41, pp. 1291–1298. https://doi.org/10.1377/hlthaff.2021.01904

Bruch, J., Zeltzer, D., and Song, Z. (2021). Characteristics of private equity–owned hospitals in 2018. *Annals of Internal Medicine*, 174(2), pp. 277–279. https://doi.org/10.7326/m20-1361

Buchak, G., Matvos, G., Piskorski, T., and Seru, A. (2024). *The secular decline of bank balance sheet lending* (NBER Working Paper No. w32176).

Burkart, M., Gromb, D., and Panunzi, F. (1997). Large shareholders, monitoring, and the value of the firm. *Quarterly Journal of Economics*, 112(3), pp. 693–728.

Burkart, M., Gromb, D., and Panunzi, F. (1998). Why higher takeover premia protect minority shareholders. *Journal of Political Economy*, 106(1), pp. 172–204.

Business Insider. (2025). *How to get ahead of the coming PE recruiting cyclone.* https://www.businessinsider.com/private-equity-recruiting-on-cycle-prepare-career-jamie-dimon-2025-4.

Cadigan, R. O., Stevenson, D. G., Caudry, D. J., and Grabowski, D. C. (2015). Private investment purchase and nursing home financial health. *Health Services Research*, 50(1), pp. 180–196. https://doi:10.1111/1475-6773.12212

Cai, C., and Song, Z. (2023). A policy framework for the growing influence of private equity in health care delivery. *Journal of the American Medical Association*, 329, pp. 1545–1546. https://doi.org/10.1001/jama.2023.2801

Caiazzo, V. (2025, February 4). *MIR's top-notch technology, strategic positioning key selling points for Quadrivio—Deal Focus.* Mergermarket. https://mergermarket.ionanalytics.com/content/1004170153

Campbell, J. Y. and Ramadorai, T. (2025). *Fixed: Why personal finance is broken and how to make it work for everyone.* Princeton University Press.

Capital Cell. (2024). *Capital cell: Europe's equity crowdfunding platform for biotech and life sciences.* Retrieved November 9, 2025, from https://capitalcell.com/en

Casalino, L. P. (2020). Private equity, women's health, and the corporate transformation of American medicine. *JAMA Internal Medicine*, 180, pp. 1545–1546. https://doi.org/10.1001/jamainternmed.2020.3564

Casalino, L. P., Saiani, R., Bhidya, S., Khullar, D., and O'Donnell, E. (2019). Private equity acquisition of physician practices. *Annals of Internal Medicine*, 170, pp. 114–115. https://doi.org/10.7326/M18-2363

Casamatta, C. (2003). Financing and advising: Optimal financial contracts with venture capitalists. *Journal of Finance*, 58(5), pp. 2059–2085.

Casamatta, C. and Haritchabalet, C. (2014). Dealing with venture capitalists: Shopping around or exclusive negotiation. *Review of Finance*, 18(5), pp. 1743–1773.

Cerullo, M., Kaili Yang, K., McDevitt, R. C., Joynt Maddox, K., Roberts, J. W., and Offodile, A. C. 2nd. (2023). Research: What happens when private equity firms buy hospitals? *Harvard Business Review.* https://hbr.org/2023/03/research-what-happens-when-private-equity-firmsbuy-hospitals

Cerullo, M., Lin, Y.-L., Rauh-Hain, J. A., Ho, V., and Offodile, A. C. (2022). Financial impacts and operational implications of private equity acquisition of US hospitals: Study examines the impacts and operational implications of private equity acquisitions of US hospitals. *Health Affairs*, 41(4), pp. 523–530. https://doi.org/10.1377/hlthaff.2021.01284

Cerullo, M., Yang, K. K., Roberts, J., McDevitt, R. C., and Offodile, A. C. (2021). Private equity acquisition and responsiveness to service-line profitability at short-term acute care hospitals: Study examines private equity acquisition at short-term acute care hospitals. *Health Affairs*, 40(11), pp. 1697–1705. https://doi.org/10.1377/hlthaff.2021.00541

Cerullo, M., Yang, K., Joynt Maddox, K. E., McDevitt, R. C., Roberts, J. W., and Offodile, A. C. (2022). Association between hospital private equity acquisition and outcomes of acute medical conditions among Medicare beneficiaries. *JAMA Network Open*, 5(4), e229581. https://doi.org/10.1001/jamanetworkopen.2022.9581

Chemla, G. (2003). Downstream competition, foreclosure and vertical integration. *Journal of Economics and Management Strategy*, 12(2), pp. 261–289.

Chemla, G. (2004a). Pension fund investment in private equity and venture capital: Canada vs. the U.S. *Journal of Private Equity*, 1–8 (Lead article).

Chemla, G. (2004b). Takeover threats and the dynamics of information flows. *International Journal of Industrial Organization*, 22(4), pp. 575–590.

Chemla, G. (2005). Hold-up, stakeholders, and takeover threats. *Journal of Financial Intermediation*, 14(3), pp. 376–397.

Chemla, G., and Faure-Grimaud, A. (2001). Dynamic adverse selection and debt. *European Economic Review*, 45, pp. 1773–1792.

Chemla, G., Habib, M. A., and Ljungqvist, A. (2007). An analysis of shareholder agreements. *Journal of the European Economic Association*, 5(1), pp. 93–121.

Chemla, G. and Hennessy, C. (2014). Skin in the game and moral hazard. *Journal of Finance*, 69(4), pp. 1597–1641.

Chemla, G. and Hennessy, C. (2016). Government as borrower of first resort. *Journal of Monetary Economics*, 84, 1–16 (Lead article).

Chemla, G. and Hennessy, C. (2019). Controls, belief updating, and bias in medical RCTs. *Journal of Economic Theory*, 184(C), 104929.

Chemla, G. and Hennessy, C. (2020). Rational expectations and the paradox of policy-relevant experiments. *Journal of Monetary Economics*, 114, pp. 368–381.

Chemla, G. and Hennessy, C. (2021). Equilibrium counterfactuals. *International Economic Review*, 62(2), pp. 639–669.

Chemla, G. and Hennessy, C. (2022). Signaling, instrumentation, and CFO decision-making. *Journal of Financial Economics*, 144(3), pp. 849–886.

Chemla, G. and Hennessy, C. (2025). *Discretionary choice, information production, and the SUTVA*. SSRN working paper 4409947.

Chemla, G. and Milone, M. (2018). Oliver Hart ou la genèse de la finance d'entreprise moderne. In A. Albouy, and G. Charreaux (Eds.), *Les grands auteurs de la finance* (pp. 529–554). EMS Management and Sociétés.

Chemla, G., Islam, Q. and Li, S. (2026) *Strategic and financial requirements for a sovereign AI infrastructure*. SSRN working paper 6296919.

Chemla, G. and Tena, V. (2025). *AI adoption, incentives, and firm value in general equilibrium*. SSRN working paper. 5997775.

Chemla, G. and Tinn, K. (2020). Learning through crowdfunding. *Management Science*, 66(5), pp. 1783–1801 (Lead article).

Chemla, G. and Tinn, K. (2021). How wise are crowds on crowdfunding platforms? In R. Rau, R. Waldrop, and L. Zingales (Eds.), *The Palgrave handbook of technological finance* (Ch. 16). Cambridge University Press.

Chemla, G. and Tinn, K. (2026) Digital ownership: The tokenization of real-world assets. SSRN, 1 May. Available at: https://ssrn.com/abstract=6693219.

Chemla, G., Rivera, A., and Shi, L. (2025). Too much, too soon, for too long: The dynamics of competitive executive compensation. *Journal of Finance*, 80(5): 2921–2970.

Chen, E. M., Cox, J. T., Begaj, T., Armstrong, G. W., Khurana, R. N., and Parikh, R. (2020). Private equity in ophthalmology and optometry: Analysis of acquisitions from 2012 through 2019 in the United States. *Ophthalmology*, 127, 445455. https://doi.org/10.1016/j.ophtha.2020.01.007

Chevalier, J. A. (1995a). Do LBO supermarkets charge more? An empirical analysis of the effects of LBOs on supermarket pricing. *The Journal of Finance*, 50(4), pp. 1095–1112.

Chevalier, J. A. (1995b). Capital structure and product-market competition: Empirical evidence from the supermarket industry. *The American Economic Review*, 85, pp. 415–435.

Chevalier, J. A. and Scharfstein, D. S. (1995). Liquidity constraints and the cyclical behavior of markups. *The American Economic Review*, 85(2), pp. 390–396.

Christodoulou, T. K. (2021). *What are the pros and cons of private equity in healthcare*? (Master's thesis). Erasmus Universiteit Rotterdam.

Cochrane, J. H. (2005). The risk and return of venture capital. *Journal of Financial Economics*, 75(1), pp. 3–52. https://doi.org/10.1016/j.jfineco.2004.03.006

Colonnelli, E., Lerner, J., Cruz, M. and Pereira Lopez, M.D.L.P. (2025) *How do emerging markets investors make decisions? Evidence from venture capital and private equity*. Working paper, 30 November.

Colonnelli, E., Li, B. and Liu, E. (2024). Investing with the government: A field experiment in China. *Journal of Political Economy*, 132(1), pp. 248–294.

Compass Carter Osborne. (2025). *Why people strategy is now a financial imperative: CPO roundtable report*. https://www.compasscarterosborne.com/news/why-people-strategy-is-now-a-financial-imperative/

Cong, L. W., and He, Z. (2019). Blockchain disruption and smart contracts. *Review of Financial Studies*, 32(5), pp. 1754–1797.

Cong, L. W., Li, Y., and Wang, N. (2021). Tokenomics: Dynamic adoption and valuation. *Review of Financial Studies*, 34(3), pp. 1105–1155. https://doi.org/10.1093/rfs/hhaa113

Cornelli, F., and Karaka , O. (2012). *Corporate governance of LBOs: The role of boards*. Available at SSRN 1875649.

Cornelli, F., and Karaka , O. (2015). *CEO turnover in LBOs: The role of boards*. Available at SSRN 2269124.

CoStar. (2022). *Blackstone limits investor withdrawals from $145 Billion REIT*. https://www.costar.com/article/1465250437/blackstone-limits-investor-withdrawals-from-145-billion-reit-as-economic-concerns-grow

Creadore, A., Desai, S., Li, S. J., Lee, K. J., Bui, A.-T. N., Villa-Ruiz, C., Lo, K., Zhou, G., Joyce, C., Resneck, J. S., Seiger, K., and Mostaghimi, A. (2021). Insurance acceptance, appointment wait time, and dermatologist access across practice types in the US. *JAMA Dermatology*, 157(2), 181. https://doi.org/10.1001/jamadermatol.2020.5173

Cuervo-Cazurra, A., Grosman, A., Mol, M. J., and Wood, G. (2025). The impact of ownership on global strategy: Owner diversity and non-financial objectives. *Global Strategy Journal*, 15(1), pp. 3–33.

Cumming, D. and Monteiro, P. (2023). Sovereign wealth fund investment in venture capital, private equity, and real asset funds. *Journal of International Business Policy*, 6, pp. 330–355.

Cumming, D. and Walz, U. (2010). Private equity returns and disclosure around the world. *Journal of International Business Studies*, 41(4), pp. 727–754.

Cuñat, V. (2007). Trade credit: Suppliers as debt collectors and insurance providers. *Review of Financial Studies*, 20(2), pp. 491–527.

Dafny, L. S. (2009). Estimation and identification of merger effects: An application to hospital mergers. *Journal of Law and Economics*, 52(3), pp. 523–550. https://doi.org/10.1086/596511

Dafny, L. S., Ho, K., and Lee, R. S. (2019). The price effects of cross-market hospital mergers. *RAND Journal of Economics*, 50(2), pp. 286–325. https://doi.org/10.1111/1756-2171.12263

De Fontenay, E., and Nili, Y. (2022). *Side letter governance*. Washington University Law Review, 100, 907.

Degeorge, F. and Zeckhauser, R. (1993). The reverse LBO decision and firm performance: Theory and evidence. *The Journal of Finance*, 48(4), pp. 1323–1348.

Deloitte. (2023). *Data-driven deal sourcing in private equity*. Deloitte Insights.

Driessen, J., Lin, T.-C., and Phalippou, L. (2012). A new method to estimate risk and return of nontraded assets from cash flows: The case of private equity funds. *Journal of Financial and Quantitative Analysis*, 47(3), pp. 511–535. https://doi.org/10.1017/S002210901200016X

Eaton, C., Howell, S. T., and Yannelis, C. (2020). When investor incentives and consumer interests diverge: Private equity in higher education. *The Review of Financial Studies*, 33(9), pp. 4024–4060.

Edmans, A. (2014). Blockholders and corporate governance. *Annual Review of Financial Economics*, 6(1), pp. 23–50.

Edmans, A., Fang, V. W., and Lewellen, K. A. (2017). Equity vesting and investment. *The Review of Financial Studies*, 30(7), pp. 2229–2271.

Edmans, A. and Manso, G. (2011). Governance through trading and intervention: A theory of multiple block holders. *Review of Financial Studies*, 24(7), pp. 2395–2428. https://doi.org/10.1093/rfs/hhq145

Eleogu, E. (2025). Private equity drive health care inequality: Regulatory guardrails for private equity investment in health care. *Columbia Black Pre-Law Journal*. https://blackprelaw.studentgroups.columbia.edu/news/private-equity-drives-health-care-inequity-regulatory-guardrails-private-equity-investment

Ellis, C. and Esson, M. (2024). *Price regulation and cream-skimming: How private equity competes with government-backed firms*. https://papers.ssrn.com/sol3/papers.cfm?abstract_id=4792828

Elsworth C., Huang K., Patterson D., Schneider I., Sedivy R., Goodman S., Townsend B., Ranganathan P., Dean J., Vahdat A., Gomes B., and Manyika J. (2025). *Measuring the environmental impact of delivering AI at Google Scale*. Google. https://paperreading.club/page?id=332703

Ercan, E. Y., Kaplan, S. N., and Strebulaev, I. A. (2025). *Interim valuations, predictability, and outcomes in private equity* (No. w33637). National Bureau of Economic Research.

European Federation of Pharmaceutical Industries and Associations. (2023). *The pharmaceutical industry in figures: Key data 2023*. Brussels: EFPIA. https://www.efpia.eu

Evotec AG. (2010, March 23). *MandA advisor global healthcare turnaround company of the year*. https://www.evotec.com/en/news/ma-advisor-global-healthcare-turnaround-company-of-the-year

Ewens, M., and Farre-Mensa, J. (2020). The deregulation of the private equity markets and the decline in IPOs. *The Review of Financial Studies*, 33(12), pp. 5463–5509.

Ewens, M., and Farre-Mensa, J. (2022). Private or public equity? The evolving entrepreneurial finance landscape. *Annual Review of Financial Economics*, 14(1), pp. 271–293.

Ewens, M., Fink, J. and Manku, G. (2024) *Female investment professionals in US private equity: A numerical analysis and opportunities for further exploration*. Research report. New York: Level 20, Columbia Business School and Three Cairns Group, September.

Ewens, M., Gupta, A., and Howell, S. T. (2022). *Local journalism under private equity ownership* (No. w29743). National Bureau of Economic Research.

Ewens, M., Jones, C. M., and Rhodes-Kropf, M. (2013). The price of diversifiable risk in venture capital and private equity. *The Review of Financial Studies*, 26(8), pp. 1854–1889.

EY. (2024a). *Harnessing data for portfolio value creation*. EY Private Equity Pulse.

EY. (2024b, September 2). *EY on private equity AI playbook*. https://www.ey.com/en_ch/insights/strategy-transactions/ai-in-private-equity

Fang, H. S. A. (2021). Commercially successful blockchain healthcare projects: A scoping review. *Blockchain in Healthcare Today*, 4, pp. 10–30953. https://doi.org/10.30953/bhty.v4.166

Fang, L. H., Goldman, J., and Roulet, A. (2022). *Private equity and pay gaps inside the firm* (INSEAD Working Paper No. 2023/04/FIN/EPS). http://dx.doi.org/10.2139/ssrn.4306840

Fang, L., Ivashina, V., and Lerner, J. (2015). The disintermediation of financial markets: Direct investing in private equity. *Journal of Financial Economics*, 116(1), pp. 160–178.

Feldman, E. R. (2021). Restructuring and divestitures. In *Strategic management: State of the field and its future*. Oxford University Press.

Fernández Tamayo, B., Braun, R., Lopez-de-Silanes, F., Phalippou, L., and Sigrist, N. (2023). Limited partners versus unlimited machines; artificial intelligence and the performance of private equity funds. *SSRN Electronic Journal*. https://doi.org/10.2139/ssrn.4490991

Fernandez, J. M., Stein, R. M., and Lo, A. W. (2012). Commercializing biomedical research through securitization techniques. *Nature Biotechnology*, 30(10), pp. 964–975.

Financial Times. (2019, April 22). *The rise of "super carry" unsettles private equity investors.*

Financial Times. (2022). *Blackstone limits withdrawals from $125bn real estate fund*. https://www.ft.com/content/e1ddc6f0-eb0a-4d52-8971-b1d9c2cb5c02

Fogel, A. L., Hogan, S., and Dover, J. (2022). Surgical dermatology and private equity: A review of the literature and discussion. *Dermatologic Surgery*, 48, pp. 339–343. https://doi.org/10.1097/DSS.0000000000003363

Forbes. (2021). *Turnaround specialist behind Indian hospital chain becomes India's newest billionaire*. https://www.forbes.com/sites/anuraghunathan/2021/08/31/indias-newest-billionaire-is-turnaround-specialist-owner-of-hospital-chain-battling-covid-19/

Frances, C. (2019). Private equity investment in health care. *Journal of the American Medical Association*, 322, 468. https://doi.org/10.1001/jama.2019.7844

Franzoni, F., Nowak, E., and Phalippou, L. (2012). Private equity performance and liquidity risk. *Journal of Finance*, 67(6), pp. 2341–2373.

Fraser-Sampson, G. (2007). *Private equity as an asset class*. John Wiley and Sons.

Frésard, L., and Phillips, G. M. (2024). Product markets, competition and corporate finance: A review and directions for future research. In *Handbook of corporate finance* (pp. 591–646).

FTI Consulting Report. (2024). AI takes center-stage for value creation in private equity firms.

Gadiesh, O., and McArthur, H. (2008). *Lessons from private equity any company can use (Memo to the CEO)*. Harvard Business Press.

Gandhi, A., Song, Y., and Upadrashta, P. (2020). Have private equity owned nursing homes fared worse under COVID-19? *SSRN Electronic Journal*. https://doi.org/10.2139/ssrn.3682892

Gandhi, A., Song, Y., and Upadrashta, P. (2025). *Private equity, consumers, and competition: Evidence from the nursing home industry* (No. w34306). National Bureau of Economic Research.

Gao, H., Hsu, P. H., and Li, K. (2018). Innovation strategy of private firms. *Journal of Financial and Quantitative Analysis*, 53(1), pp. 1–32.

Gao, J., Kim, Y., and Sevilir, M. (2025). Private equity in the hospital industry. *Journal of Financial Economics*, 171, 104107.

Garcia-Gomez, P., Maug, E. G., and Obernberger, S. (2020). Private equity buyouts and employee health. *Management Science*, forthcoming.

Gargano, A., Rossi, A. G., and Wermers, R. (2017). The freedom of information act and the race toward information acquisition. *Review of Financial Studies*, 30(6), pp. 2179–2228. https://doi.org/10.1093/rfs/hhw035

Gen II Fund Services. (2020). *Emerging manager report 2020*. Gen II Fund Services, LLC.

Gen II Fund Services. (2023). *Emerging manager report 2023*. Gen II Fund Services, LLC.

Genesis Biomed. (2021, October 27). *Crowdfunding and venture capital: Two complementary systems for private funding in the health sector*. https://genesis-biomed.com/crowdfunding-venture-capital-two-complementary-systems-private-funding-health-sector/

Gilligan, J. and Wright, M. (2020). *Private equity demystified: An explanatory guide*. Oxford University Press. http://doi:10.1093/oso/9780198866961.001.0001

Gocmen, A., Martínez-Toledano, C., and Mittal, V. (2025). *Private capital markets and inequality*. Available at SSRN 5166981.

Gompers, P. A., Kaplan, S. N., and Mukharlyamov, V. (2016). What do private equity firms say they do? *Journal of Financial Economics*, 121(3), pp. 449–476. https://doi.org/10.1016/j.jfineco.2016.06.003

Gompers, P. and Lerner, J. (2001). The venture capital revolution. *Journal of Economic Perspectives*, 15(2), pp. 145–168. https://doi.org/10.1257/jep.15.2.145

Gompers, P., Kaplan, S. N., Gornall, W., and Strebulaev, I. (2020). What do venture capitalists make decisions? *Journal of Financial Economics*, 135(1), pp. 169–190.

Gompers, P., Kovner, A., Lerner, J., and Scharfstein, D (2008). Venture capital investment cycles: The impact of public markets. *Journal of Financial Economics*, 87(1), pp. 1–23.

Gondi, S. and Song, Z. (2019). Potential implications of private equity investments in health care delivery. *Journal of the American Medical Association*, 321(11), pp. 1047–1048. https://doi.org/10.1001/jama.2019.1077

Gong, J. J. and Wu, S. Y. (2011). CEO turnover in private equity sponsored leveraged buyouts. *Corporate Governance: An International Review*, 19(3), pp. 195–209. https://doi.org/10.1111/j.1467-8683.2010.00834.x

Gornall, W. and Strebulaev, I. A. (2020). Squaring venture capital valuations with reality. *Journal of Financial Economics*, 135(1), pp. 120–143. https://doi.org/10.1016/j.jfineco.2018.04.015

Grabowski, D.C. and Town, R.J. (2011). Does information matter? Competition, quality, and the impact of nursing home report cards. *Health Services Research*, 46(6 Pt 1), pp. 1698–1719.

Gredil, O. R., Griffiths, B., and Stucke, R. (2023). Benchmarking private equity: The direct alpha method. *Journal of Corporate Finance*, 81, 102360. https://doi.org/10.1016/j.jcorpfin.2023.102360

Gromb, D. and Kitten, M. (2016). *Bain Capital's "take private" of China fire (Case* No. 116-0020-1). HEC Paris. The Case Centre. https://www.thecasecentre.org/products/view?id=133859

Grossman, S. J. and Hart, O. D. (1980). Takeover bids, the free-rider problem, and the theory of the corporation. *Bell Journal of Economics*, 11(1), pp. 42–64. https://doi.org/10.2307/3003400

Grossman, S. J. and Hart, O. D. (1988). One share/one vote and the market for corporate control. *Journal of Financial Economics*, 20(1–2), 175–202. https://doi.org/10.1016/0304-405X(88)90044-X

Guo, S., Hotchkiss, E. S., and Song, W. (2011). Do buyouts (still) create value? *Journal of Finance*, 66(2), pp. 479–517. https://doi.org/10.1111/j.1540-6261.2010.01639.x

Gupta, A., Howell, S. T., Yannelis, C., and Gupta, A. (2024). Owner incentives and performance in healthcare: Private equity investment in nursing homes. *Review of Financial Studies*, 37(4), pp. 1029–1077. https://doi:10.1093/rfs/hhad082

Hammer, B., Marcotty-Dehm, N., Schweizer, D., and Schwetzler, B. (2022). Pricing and value creation in private equity-backed buy-and-build strategies. *Journal of Corporate Finance*, 77, 102285. https://doi.org/10.1016/j.jcorpfin.2022.102285

Harford, J. and Kolasinski, A. (2014). Do private equity returns result from wealth transfers and short-termism? Evidence from a comprehensive sample of large buyouts. *Management Science*, 60(4), pp. 888–902.

Harrington, C., Olney, B., Carrillo, H., and Kang, T. (2012). Nurse staffing and deficiencies in the largest for-profit nursing home chains and chains owned by private equity companies. *Health Services Research*, 47(1 pt 1), 106–128. https://doi.org/10.1111/j.1475-6773.2011.01311.x

Harris, R. S., Jenkinson, T., and Kaplan, S. N. (2014). Private equity performance: What do we know? *Review of Financial Studies*, 27(7), pp. 1401–1435.

Hart, O. (1995). *Firms, contracts, and financial structure*. Clarendon press.

Hart, O. D. and Moore, J. (1994). A theory of debt based on the inalienability of human capital. *The Quarterly Journal of Economics*, 109(4), pp. 841–879. https://doi.org/10.1162/003355394555851

Hart, O. D., and Moore, J. (1995). Debt and seniority: An analysis of the role of hard claims in constraining management. *American Economic Review*, 85(3), pp. 567–585.

Hart, O. D. and Moore, J. (1998). Default and renegotiation: A dynamic model of debt. *Quarterly Journal of Economics*, 113(1), pp. 1–41. https://doi.org/10.1162/003355398555496

Hart, O. D. and Zingales, L. (2022). The new corporate governance. *University of Chicago Business Law Review*, 1(1), pp. 195–216.

Heckman, J. J. (1979). Sample selection bias as a specification error. *Econometrica*, 47(1), pp. 153–161.

Hennessy, C. A. and Whited, T. M. (2005). Debt dynamics. *Journal of DFinance*, 60(3), pp. 1129–1165.

Herkenhoff, K. F., Lerner, J., Phillips, G. M., Rebelo, F., and Sampson, B. (2025). *Private equity and workers: Modeling and measuring monopsony, implicit contracts, and efficient reallocation* (NBER Working Paper No. 33942). https://www.nber.org/papers/w33942

Hernán, M. A. (2010). The hazards of hazard ratios. *Epidemiology*, 21(1), pp. 13–15.

Hernán, M. A. and Robins, J. M. (2020). *Causal inference: What if*. Chapman and Hall/CRC.

Higson, C. and Stucke, R. (2012). The performance of private equity. *SSRN Electronic Journal*. https://doi.org/10.2139/ssrn.2009067

HolonIQ. (2023, February 1). *HealthTech unicorns: The world's leading health technology startups valued at over $1 billion*. HolonIQ. https://www.holoniq.com/healthtech-unicorns

Hotchkiss, E. S., Smith, D. C., and Strömberg, P. (2021). Private equity and the resolution of financial distress. *Review of Financial Studies*, 34(12), pp. 5573–5618. https://doi.org/10.1093/rfs/hhab07

Huang, S. S. and Bowblis, J. R. (2019). Private equity ownership and nursing home quality: An instrumental variables approach. *International Journal of Health Economics and Management*, 19(3–4), 273–299. https://doi.org/10.1007/s10754-018-9254-z

Hurduzeu, G. and Popescu, M.-F. (2015). The history of junk bonds and leveraged buyouts. *Procedia Economics and Finance*, 32, pp. 1268–1275. https://doi.org/10.1016/s2212-5671(15)01504-x

Imbens, G. W. and Rubin, D. B. (2015). *Causal inference in statistics, social, and biomedical sciences.* Cambridge University Press.

Insurance Journal. (2023, December 27). *SPAC mania's ugly end yields $46 billion of investor losses in 2023.* https://www.insurancejournal.com/news/national/2023/12/27/753320.htm

Ioannidis, J. P. A. (2005). Why most published research findings are false. *PLoS Medicine*, 2(8), e124.

Iossa, E. and Martimort, D. (2012). Risk allocation and the costs and benefits of public–private partnerships. *RAND Journal of Economics*, 43(3), pp. 442–474. https://doi.org/10.1111/j.1756-2171.2012.00181.x

Iossa, E. and Martimort, D. (2015). The simple microeconomics of public–private partnerships. *Journal of Public Economic Theory*, 17(1), pp. 4–48. https://doi.org/10.1111/jpet.12114

Ivashina, V. and Kovner, A. (2011). The private equity advantage: Leveraged buyout firms and relationship banking. *Review of Financial Studies*, 24(7), pp. 2462–2498.

JDSupra. (2024, September 5). *Royalty financings and similar revenue monetizations surge in life sciences.* https://www.jdsupra.com/legalnews/royalty-financings-and-similar-revenue-1023035/

Jenkinson, T., Sousa, M., and Stucke, R. (2013). *How fair are the valuations of private equity funds*? Oxford University Working Paper.

Jensen, M. C. and Meckling, W. H. (1976). Theory of the firm: Managerial behavior, agency costs and ownership structure. *Journal of Financial Economics*, 3(4), pp. 305–360. https://doi.org/10.1016/0304-405X(76)90026-X IDEAS/RePEc+1

Johnston-Ross, E., Ma, S., and Puri, M. (2025). Private equity and financial stability: Evidence from failed-bank resolution in the crisis. *Journal of Finance*, 80(1), pp. 163–210.

Kannan, S., Bruch, J. D., and Song, Z. (2023). Changes in hospital adverse events and patient outcomes associated with private equity acquisition. *Journal of the American Medical Association*, 330(24), pp. 2365–2375. https://doi:10.1001/jama.2023.23147

Kannan, S., Bruch, J. D., Zubizarreta, J. R., Stevens, J., and Song, Z. (2025). Hospital staffing and patient outcomes after private equity acquisition. *Annals of Internal Medicine*, 178(11), pp. 1529–1538. https://doi:10.7326/ANNALS-24-03471

Kaplan, S. (1989). The effects of management buyouts on operating performance and value. *Journal of Financial Economics*, *24*(2), 217–254.

Kaplan, S. N. and Schoar, A. (2005). Private equity performance: Returns, persistence, and capital flows. *Journal of Finance*, 60(4), pp. 1791–1823.

Kaplan, S. N. and Sensoy, B. A. (2015). Private equity performance: What do we know? *Journal of Finance*, 70(6), pp. 1791–1823.

Kaplan, S. N. and Strömberg, P. (2003). Financial contracting theory meets the real world: An empirical analysis of venture capital contracts. *Review of Economic Studies*, 70(2), pp. 281–315. https://doi.org/10.1111/1467-937X.00245

Kaplan, S. N. and Strömberg, P. (2009). Leveraged buyouts and private equity. *Journal of Economic Perspectives*, 23, pp. 121–146. https://doi.org/10.1257/jep.23.1.121

Kaplan, S. N., Martel, F., and Strömberg, P. (2007). How do legal differences and experience affect financial contracts? *Journal of Financial Intermediation*, 16(3), pp. 273–311.

Kastiel, K. and Nili, Y. (2023). The rise of private equity continuation funds. *University of Pennsylvania Law Review*, 172, 1601.

Keane, M. P. and Wolpin, K. I. (1997). The career decisions of young men. *Journal of Political Economy*, 105(3), pp. 473–522. https://doi.org/10.1086/262077

Kerr, W. R., Nanda, R., and Rhodes-Kropf, M. (2014). Entrepreneurship as experimentation. *Journal of Economic Perspectives*, 28(3), pp. 25–48.

Keys, B. J., Mukherjee, T., Seru, A., and Vig, V. (2010). Did securitization lead to lax screening? Evidence from subprime loans. *Quarterly Journal of Economics*, 125(1), pp. 307–362.

Khetpal, S., Lopez, J. and Steinbacher, D. M. (2021). Private equity in plastic surgery: A nine-year analysis. *Plastic and Reconstructive Surgery*, 148, 1088e–1090e. https://doi.org/10.1097/PRS.0000000000008536

Khetpal, S., Lopez, J., and Steinbacher, D. M. (2021). Trends in private equity deals in oral and maxillofacial surgery and dentistry. *Journal of Oral and Maxillofacial Surgery*, 79, pp. 513–515. https://doi.org/10.1016/j.joms.2020.10.010

Kirkpatrick, S. A. and Locke, E. A. (1996). Direct and indirect effects of three core charismatic leadership components on performance and attitudes. *Journal of Applied Psychology*, 81(1), pp. 36–51.

Kitten, M. (2018). *Rocket internet how long can we continue to lose money*? (Case No. 318-0322-1). EDHEC Business School. The Case Centre. https://www.thecasecentre.org/products/view?id=158014

Kitten, M. (2021). *Midas Asclepius and Oizys—The tale of CVC and the Greek hospitals (Case No. 121-0015-1)*. Imperial Business School. The Case Centre. https://www.thecasecentre.org/products/view?id=175124

Kitten, M. (2025a). *Doctor Care Anywhere goes to Australia* (Case No. 126-0049-1). Imperial Business School. The Case Centre. https://www.thecasecentre.org/products/view?id=213161

Kitten, M. (2025b). *Quantum computing in healthcare and life sciences*. LaingBuisson. https://www.laing-buisson.com/product/quantum-computing-in-healthcare-and-lifesciences/

Kitten, M. (2026). *Babylon's SPAC opera* (Case No. 126-0011-1). UCL Global Business School for Health. The Case Centre.

Kitten, M. and Mazevet, M. (2026). *The global dental market: A sector in transition, not in decline*. LaingBuisson.

Kitten, M. and Ruffinoni, F. (2025). *The future is in sight. Revolutionising eye care products and services*. LaingBuisson. https://candesic.com/wp-content/uploads/2025/03/1741691764493.pdf

Klausner, M. and Ohlrogge, M. (2022). Was the SPAC crash predictable? *JREG Bulletin*, 40, 101.

Konda, S., Patel, S., and Francis, J. (2023). Private equity: the bad and the ugly. *Dermatologic Clinics*, 41(4), pp. 597–610. https://doi.org/10.1016/j.det.2023.04.004

Korteweg, A. (2019). Risk adjustment in private equity returns. *Annual Review of Financial Economics*, 11(1), pp. 131–152.

Korteweg, A. and Nagel, S. (2016). Risk-adjusting the returns to venture capital. *The Journal of Finance*, 71(3), pp. 1437–1470.

Korteweg, A. and Westerfield, M. M. (2022). Asset allocation with private equity. *Foundations and Trends® in Finance*, 13(2), pp. 95–204.

Korteweg, A. and Nagel, S. (2025). Risk-adjusted returns of private equity funds: A new approach. *Review of Financial Studies*, 38(9), pp. 2557–2601.

Kovenock, D. and Phillips, G. M. (1997). Capital structure and product market behavior: An examination of plant exit and investment decisions. *Review of Financial Studies*, 10(3), pp. 767–803.

KPMG and Wharton School. (2022). *The big breakup: The math behind giant divestitures*. KPMG.

KPMG. (2022). *AI in due diligence: Accelerating insights in private equity*. KPMG Global PE Outlook.

Kunz, J. S., Propper, C., Staub, K. E., and Winkelmann, R. (2024). Assessing the quality of public services: For-profits, chains, and concentration in the hospital market. *Health Economics*, 33(9), pp. 2162–2181.

La Forgia, A., Bond, A. M., Braun, R. T., Yao, L. Z., Kjaer, K., Zhang, M., and Casalino, L. P. (2022). Association of physician management companies and private equity investment with commercial health care prices paid to anesthesia practitioners. *JAMA Internal Medicine*, 182(4), 396. https://doi.org/10.1001/jamainternmed.2022.0004

La France, A., Batt, R., and Appelbaum, E. (2021). Hospital ownership and financial stability: A matched case comparison of a nonprofit health system and a private equity–owned health system. In *The contributions of health care management to grand health care challenges* (Vol. 20, pp. 173–220). Emerald Publishing Limited.

Laffont, J.-J., and Tirole, J. (1993). *A theory of incentives in procurement and regulation*. MIT Press.

Landier, A. and Thesmar, D. (2009). Financial contracting with optimistic entrepreneurs. *Review of Financial Studies*, 22(1), pp. 117–150. https://doi.org/10.1093/rfs/hhn060

Larraín, B., Phillips, G., Sertsios, G., and Urzúa, F. (2025). The real effects of going public: Evidence from firm dynamics and innovation. *Review of Financial Studies*, forthcoming.

Lerner, J. (2023). Private equity and long-term capital. *Journal of Applied Corporate Finance*, 35(1), pp. 10–23.

Lerner, J., Mao, J., Schoar, A., and Zhang, N. R. (2022). Investing outside the box: Evidence from alternative vehicles in private equity. *Journal of Financial Economics*, 143(1), pp. 359–380.

Lerner, J. and Nanda, R. (2020). Venture capital's role in financing innovation: What we know and how much we still need to learn. *Journal of Economic Perspectives*, 34(3), pp. 237–261.

Lerner, J. and Nanda, R. (2023). Venture capital and innovation. In *Handbook of the economics of corporate finance*, 1(1), pp. 77–105). North-Holland.

Lerner, J. and Schoar, A. (2004). The illiquidity puzzle: Theory and evidence from private equity. *Journal of Financial Economics*, 72(1), pp. 3–40.

Lerner, J., Schoar, A., and Wan, W. (2007). Smart institutions, foolish choices: The limited partner performance puzzle. *Journal of Finance*, 62(2), pp. 731–764. https://doi.org/10.1111/j.1540-6261.2007.01222.x

Lerner, J., Sorensen, M., and Strömberg, P. (2011). Private equity and long-run investment: The case of innovation. *Journal of Finance*, 66(2), pp. 445–477.

Lerner, J., Sorensen, M., and Strömberg, P. (2021). *Private equity and data analytics: The next frontier*. Harvard Business School Working Paper No. 21-054.

Leshin, B. (2023). Private equity: The good. *Dermatologic Clinics*, 41(4), pp. 589–596. https://doi.org/10.1016/j.det.2023.04.003

Lewallen, S. and Thulasiraj, R. D. (2010). Eliminating cataract blindness—how do we apply lessons from Asia to Sub-Saharan Africa? *Global Public Health*, 5(6), pp. 639–648. https://doi.org/10.1080/17441692.2010.503551

Lewellen, K., Phillips, G. M., and Sertsios, G. (2025). *Control without ownership: Governance of nonprofit hospitals* (No. w34132). National Bureau of Economic Research.

Lewis, M. (2023a, November 27). *Tokenization in private equity is creating new markets*. Kaleido. https://www.kaleido.io/blockchain-blog/tokenization-in-private-equity

Lewis, R. (2023b, August 3). *Medica scouts for new therapeutic add-ons after IK Partners take-private-sponsor*. Mergermarket. https://mergermarket.ionanalytics.com/content/1003571560

Lewis, R. (2025, February 20). *Montagu's three-way portfolio merger bets on OEM outsourcing trends—Deal Focus*. Mergermarket. https://mergermarket.ionanalytics.com/content/1004157504

Lichtenberg, F. R. and Siegel, D. (1990). The effects of leveraged buyouts on productivity and related aspects of firm behavior. *Journal of financial economics*, 27(1), 165–194.

Liu, T. (2022). *Bargaining with private equity: Implications for hospital prices and patient welfare*. https://papers.ssrn.com/sol3/papers.cfm?abstract_id=3896410

Lo, A. W. and Naraharisetti, V. S. (2022). *Healthcare finance: Modern financial analysis for accelerating biomedical innovation*. Princeton University Press.

Lo, A. W. and Thakor, R. T. (2022). Financing biomedical innovation. *Annual Review of Financial Economics*, 14(1), pp. 231–270.

Long, W. F. and Ravenscraft, D. J. (1993). *The financial performance of whole company LBOs* (Vol. 93, No. 16). Bureau of the Census.

Lucas, D. and Zeldes, S. P. (2006). *Valuing and hedging defined benefit pension obligations—the role of stocks revisited*. Northwestern University and Columbia University, working paper, September.

Lundy, D. W. (2019). A day at the office: Private practice and private equity. *Clinical Orthopaedics and Related Research*, 477, pp. 955–957. https://doi.org/10.1097/CORR.0000000000000758

Ma, L. W., Buckman, C., Shah, S. A., and Schulman, K. (2024). Healthcare Private Equity: A Qualitative Review of Investments in Healthcare Services and the Impact of the No Surprises Act of 2020. *Health Management, Policy and Innovation*, 9(2).

Maksimovic, V., Phillips, G., and Yang, L. (2023). Do public firms respond to investment opportunities more than private firms? *Review of Finance*, 27(2), pp. 359–407. https://doi.org/10.1093/rof/rfac008

Matthews, S. and Roxas, R. (2022). Private equity and its effect on patients: A window into the future. *International Journal of Health Economics and Management*, 23(4), pp. 673–684. https://doi.org/10.1007/s10754-022-09331-y

Maurin, V., Robinson, D. T., and Strömberg, P. (2023). A theory of liquidity in private equity. *Management Science*, 69(10), pp. 5740–5771.

McKinsey and Company. (2019). *From pure investor to entrepreneurial owner: How private-equity firms can master the shift*. McKinsey and Company. https://www.mckinsey.com/~/media/McKinsey/Industries/Private%20Equity%20and%20Principal%20Investors/Our%20Insights/From%20pure%20investor%20to%20entrepreneurial%20owner%20How%20private%20equity%20firms%20can%20master%20the%20shift/From-pure-investor-to-entrepreneurial-owner.pdf

McKinsey and Company. (2023a). *McKinsey global private markets review 2023: Private markets turn down the volume*. https://www.mckinsey.com/industries/private-capital/our-insights/mckinseys-private-markets-annual-review-2023

McKinsey and Company. (2023b). *The power of goodbye: How carve-outs can unleash value*. McKinsey Insights. https://www.mckinsey.com/capabilities/strategy-and-corporate-finance/our-insights/the-power-of-goodbye-how-carve-outs-can-unleash-value

McKinsey and Company. (2024a). *Bridging private equity's value creation gap*. McKinsey and Company. https://www.mckinsey.com/industries/private-capital/our-insights/bridging-private-equitys-value-creation-gap

McKinsey and Company. (2024b). *Global private markets report 2024: Private markets—A slower era*. McKinsey and Company. https://www.mckinsey.com/~/media/mckinsey/industries/private%20equity%20and%20principal%20investors/our%20insights/mckinseys%20private%20markets%20annual%20review/2024/mckinsey-global-private-markets-review-2024.pdf

McKinsey and Company. (2024c). *How private equity funds can use M&A to create outsize returns*. McKinsey Insights. https://www.mckinsey.com/capabilities/m-and-a/our-insights/how-private-equity-funds-can-use-m-and-a-to-create-outsize-returns

McKinsey and Company. (2025). *Global private markets report 2025: Private equity emerging from the fog*. McKinsey and Company. https://www.mckinsey.com/industries/private-capital/our-insights/global-private-markets-report

Mehta, P., and Shenoy, S. (2012). *Infinite vision: How Aravind became the world's greatest business model for curing blindness*. HarperCollins. https://www.harpercollins.com/products/infinite-vision-pavan-mehta?variant=31862478581862

Meikle, A. (2021, February 28). *Entrepreneurship, practice valuation, and working with private equity [Interview]*. Fertility Bridge. https://www.fertilitybridge.com/inside-reproductive-health/99-entrepreneurship-practice-valuation-private-equity-andrew-meikle

Mendes, D. (2024). *Financing constraints and product market decisions: The role of production cycles* (Swedish House of Finance Research Paper 20-19).

Mergermarket. (2025) Vietnam healthcare M&A spurs amid regulatory, market tailwinds. 25 September.

Meskarpour Amiri, M., Kazemian, M., Motaghed, Z., and Abdi, Z. (2021). Systematic review of factors determining health care expenditures. *Health Policy and Technology*, 10(2), 100498. https://doi.org/10.1016/j.hlpt.2021.01.004

Miller, M. H. (1988). The Modigliani-Miller propositions after thirty years. *Journal of Economic Perspectives*, 2(4), pp. 99–120. https://doi.org/10.1257/jep.2.4.99

MJ Hudson. (2021). *Private equity fund terms research*. MJ Hudson.

Morris James LLP. (2024). *The Delaware Supreme Court Upholds $76 Million Judgment Against RBC for Rural/Metro Sale*. https://www.morrisjames.com/p/102jgvt/the-delaware-supreme-court-upholds-76-million-judgment-against-rbc-for-rural-met/ [Accessed 21 February 2026].

Moses, H., Matheson, D. H. M., Cairns-Smith, S., George, B. P., Palisch, C., and Dorsey, E. R. (2015). The anatomy of medical research: US and international comparisons. *JAMA*, 313(2), pp. 174–189. https://doi.org/10.1001/jama.2014.15939.

Moskowitz, T. J. and Vissing-Jørgensen, A. (2002). The returns to entrepreneurial investment: A private equity premium puzzle? *American Economic Review*, 92(4), pp. 745–778.

Myers, S. C. (1977). Determinants of corporate borrowing. *Journal of Financial Economics*, 5(2), pp. 147–175. https://doi.org/10.1016/0304-405X(77)90015-0 EconPapers+1

Myers, S. C. and Majluf, N. S. (1984). Corporate financing and investment decisions when firms have information that investors do not have. *Journal of Financial Economics*, 13(2), pp. 187–221. https://doi.org/10.1016/0304-405X(84)90023-0

Nanda, R. and Phillips, G. (2023). Small firm financing: Sources, frictions, and policy implications. In *Handbook of the Economics of Corporate Finance* (Vol. 1, No. 1, pp. 107–135). North-Holland.

Natixis Investment Managers. (2024, October 3). *Private equity: The surprising outperformance of emerging managers*.

Nie, J., Demkowicz, P.C., Hsiang, W., Umer, W., Chen, E.M., McMahon, G., Kenney, P.A., Breyer, B.N., Parikh, R., and Leapman, M.S. (2022). Urology practice acquisitions by private equity firms from 2011–2021. *Urology Practice*, 9, pp. 17–24. https://doi.org/10.1097/UPJ.0000000000000269

Nie, J., Hsiang, W., Lokeshwar, S.D., McMahon, G., Demkowicz, P.C., Kenney, P.A., Breyer, B.N., and Leapman, M.S. (2022). Association between private equity acquisition of urology practices and physician Medicare payments. *Urology*, 167, pp. 121–127. https://doi.org/10.1016/j.urology.2022.03.045

Nie, J., et al. (2022). Access to urological care for Medicaid-insured patients at urology practices acquired by private equity firms. *Urology*, 164, pp. 112–117. https://doi.org/10.1016/j.urology.2022.01.055

O'Donnell, E. M., Lelli, G. J., Bhidya, S., and Casalino, L. P. (2020). The growth of private equity investment in health care: Perspectives from ophthalmology. *Health Affairs (Millwood)*, 39, pp. 1026–1031. https://doi.org/10.1377/hlthaff.2019.01419

Offodile II, A. C., Cerullo, M., Bindal, M., Rauh-Hain, J. A., and Ho, V. (2021). Private equity investments in health care: An overview of hospital and health system leveraged buyouts, 2003–17. *Health Affairs*, 40(5), pp. 719–726. https://doi.org/10.1377/hlthaff.2020.01535

Olson, L. K. (2022). *Ethically challenged: Private equity storms US health care*. JHU Press.

P+P Pöllath + Partners. (2016). *Current developments in fund terms of private equity funds*. Fund Year Book 2017. https://www.pplaw.com/sites/default/files/2020-07/av-tam-2016-fyb-current-developments-fund-terms-pe-funds.pdf

Pagano, M. and Volpin, P. F. (2005a). The political economy of corporate governance. *American Economic Review*, 95(4), pp. 1005–1030. https://doi.org/10.1257/0002828054825646

Pagano, M. and Volpin, P. F. (2005b). Managers, workers, and corporate control. *Journal of Finance*, 60(2), pp. 841–868. https://doi.org/10.1111/j.1540-6261.2005.00748.x

Paine, F., Townsend, R.R. and Xu, T. (2025) *Should governments restrict foreign investments in startups?* (NBER Working Paper No. w33803). Cambridge, MA: National Bureau of Economic Research.

Patwardhan, S., Sutton, M., and Morciano, M. (2022). Effects of chain ownership and private equity financing on quality in the English care home sector: Retrospective observational study. *Age and Ageing*, 51, afac222. https://doi.org/10.1093/ageing/afac222

Perotti, E. and Spier, K. E. (1993). Capital structure as a bargaining tool: The role of leverage in contract renegotiation. *American Economic Review*, 83(5), pp. 1131–1141.

Petersen, M. A. and Rajan, R. G. (1997). Trade credit: Theories and evidence. *Review of Financial Studies*, 10(3), pp. 661–691.

Petersone, S., Tan, A., Allmendinger, R., Roy, S., and Hales, J. (2022). *A data-driven framework for identifying investment opportunities in private equity*. arXiv. https://arxiv.org/abs/2204.01852

Pfitzer, E., Giger, O., Kausch, C., and Kowatsch, T. (2025). Success factors and measures for scaling patient-facing digital health technologies from leaders' insights. *BMC Health Services Research*, 25, 632. https://doi.org/10.1186/s12913-025-12748-z

Phalippou, L. (2009). Beware of venturing into private equity. *Journal of Economic Perspectives*, 23(1), pp. 147–166.

Phalippou, L. (2014). Performance of buyout funds revisited? *Review of Finance*, 18(1), pp. 189–218. https://doi.org/10.1093/rof/rft002

Phalippou, L. (2018). Private equity portfolio company fees. *Journal of Corporate Finance*, 50, pp. 539–564.

Phalippou, L. (2020). An inconvenient fact: Private equity returns and the billionaire factory. *SSRN Electronic Journal*. https://doi.org/10.2139/ssrn.3623820

Phalippou, L. (2021). *Private equity laid bare* (Version 3.0). Independently Published. https://pelaidbare.com/

Phalippou, L. (2025). *Apples and oranges: Benchmarking games and the illusion of private equity outperformance*. Available at SSRN 5278859.

Phalippou, L. and Gottschalg, O. (2009). The performance of private equity funds. *Review of Financial Studies*, 22(4), pp. 1747–1776. https://doi.org/10.1093/rfs/hhn014

Phillips, G. M. (1995). Increased debt and industry product markets an empirical analysis. *Journal of Financial Economics*, 37(2), pp. 189–238.

Phillips, G. M. and Sertsios, G. (2017). Financing and new product decisions of private and publicly traded firms. *Review of Financial Studies*, 30(5), pp. 1744–1789.

Phillips, G., and Sertsios, G. (2013). How do firm financial conditions affect product quality and pricing? *Management Science*, 59(8), pp. 1764–1782.

Pictet Group. (2025). *Private equity comes to grips with AI [Megatrending 2025 report]*. Pictet Group. https://www.pictet.com/content/dam/www/documents/corporate-publications/Megatrending-2025-final-EN_WEB.pdf.coredownload.pdf

PitchBook. (2023). *How first-time fund managers can gain fundraising edge*. PitchBook News. https://pitchbook.com/news/articles/first-time-fund-managers-fundraising-tips

PitchBook. (2024a). *Healthcare PE investors proceed with caution in 2024*. https://pitchbook.com/news/articles/healthcare-private-equity-deal-activity-2024

PitchBook. (2024b). *Q3 2024 analyst note: Quantifying PE investment in healthcare providers*. https://pitchbook.com/news/reports/q3-2024-pitchbook-analyst-note-quantifying-pe-investment-in-healthcare-providers

PitchBook. (2024c). *The evergreen evolution: The growth of evergreen funds, perpetual capital, and private wealth investment in private markets*. https://pitchbook.com/news/reports/2024-evergreen-evolution-analyst-note

PitchBook Data Inc. (2024d). *Private equity fundraising data*. PitchBook. https://pitchbook.com

Porter, M. E. and Teisberg, E. O. (2006). *Redefining health care: creating value-based competition on results*. Harvard Business Press.

Pradhan, R., Weech-Maldonado, R., Harman, J. S., Laberge, A., and Hyer, K. (2013). Private equity ownership and nursing home financial performance. *Health Care Management Review*, 38(3), pp. 224–233. https://doi.org/10.1097/hmr.0b013e31825729ab

Pradhan, R., Weech-Maldonado, R., Harman, J. S., and Hyer, K. (2014). Private equity ownership of nursing homes: Implications for quality. *Journal of Health Care Finance*, 42.

Preqin. (2016). *Preqin special report: Making the case for first-time funds*. Preqin Ltd.

Preqin. (2017). *Private equity fund manager performance Q2 2017*. Preqin Ltd.

Primack, D. (2019, April 23). *Big-name private equity firms are asking for bigger cuts of investment profits*. Axios. https://www.axios.com/2019/04/23/private-equity-super-carry-investment-profits

Private Equity International. (2021). *Fundraising report 2021*. PEI Group. https://www.privateequityinternational.com/fundraising-reports/

Private Equity International. (2025). *Democratisation of private equity.* https://www.privateequityinternational.com/democratisation/

Private Equity Stakeholder Project. (2025). *Private equity healthcare deals: 2024 in review.* https://pestakeholder.org/reports/healthcare-deals-2024-in-review/

PwC. (2022). *Population health management.* https://www.pwc.com/us/en/technology/alliances/library/salesforce-population-health-management.html

Research America. (2022). *US Investments in medical and health R&D, 2016–2020* (TEConomy Partners). https://www.researchamerica.org/ (see pp. 4–6 for funder shares).

Resneck, J. S. Jr. (2018). Dermatology practice consolidation fueled by private equity investment: Potential consequences for the specialty and patients. *Journal of the American Medical Association Dermatology*, 154, pp. 13–14. https://doi.org/10.1001/jamadermatol.2017.5558

Reuters. (2023). *KKR-backed envision healthcare files for bankruptcy.* https://www.reuters.com/markets/deals/kkr-backed-envision-healthcare-files-bankruptcy-2023-05-15/

Risner, C. (2025, April 25). *Montreux's GBP 425m healthcare fund enters liquidation, though investor keeps raising capital.* ION Analytics | Mergermarket. https://mergermarket.ionanalytics.com/content/1003721272?source=news

Robbins, C. J., Rudsenske, T., and Vaughan, J. S. (2008). Private equity investment in health care services. *Health Affairs (Millwood)*, 27, pp. 1389–1398. https://doi.org/10.1377/hlthaff.27.5.1389

RobinAI. (2025). *AI in private markets.* https://robinai.com/ai-in-private-markets

Robinson, D. T. and Sensoy, B. A. (2013). Do private equity fund managers earn their fees? Compensation, ownership, and cash flow performance. *Review of Financial Studies*, 26(11), pp. 2760–2797.

Robinson, D. T. and Sensoy, B. A. (2016). Cyclicality, performance measurement, and cash flow liquidity in private equity. *Journal of Financial Economics*, 122(3), pp. 521–543. https://doi.org/10.1016/j.jfineco.2016.09.008

Ross, S. A., Westerfield, R. W., Jaffe, J. F., and Roberts, G. S. (2002). Valuation and capital budgeting for the levered firm. In *Corporate finance* (6th ed., pp. 490–494). McGraw-Hill Primis.

Rust, J. (2010). *Structural econometric modeling: Rationality, learning, and complexity.* In D. Acemoglu, K. Rogoff, and M. Woodford (Eds.), *Handbook of macroeconomics* (Vol. 2, pp. 1875–1960). Amsterdam: Elsevier. https://doi.org/10.1016/B978-0-444-53238-1.00015-3

Schuhmacher, A., Hinder, M., Dodel, A., Gassmann, O., and Hartl, D. (2023). Investigating the origins of recent pharmaceutical innovation. *Nature Reviews Drug Discovery*, 22(10), pp. 781–782. https://doi.org/10.1038/d41573-023-00102-z

Schulman, K., Xiao, Y., and Ariel, H. (2017). *China Hospitals Inc.: The Growth of Private Hospitals in China* (Case No. 317-104). Harvard Business School Case, pp. 317–104.

Sharfstein, J. M. and Slocum, J. (2019). Private equity and dermatology—First, do no harm. *JAMA Dermatology*, 155, pp. 1007–1008. https://doi.org/10.1001/jamadermatol.2019.1322

Shleifer, A. and Summers, L. H. (1988). Breach of trust in hostile takeovers. In A. J. Auerbach (Ed.), *Corporate takeovers: Causes and consequences* (pp. 33–68). University of Chicago Press. https://doi.org/10.7208/9780226032160-004

Silicon Valley Bank. (2025). *Healthcare industry trends 2025 mid-year report.* https://www.svb.com/trends-insights/reports/healthcare-investments-and-exits/

Singh, Y., Aderman, C. M., Song, Z., Polsky, D., and Zhu, J. M. (2024). Increases in Medicare spending and use after private equity acquisition of retina practices. *Ophthalmology*, 131(2), pp. 150–158. https://doi.org/10.1016/j.ophtha.2023.07.031

Singh, Y., Reddy, M., and Zhu, J. M. (2024). Life cycle of private equity investments in physician practices: An overview of private equity exits. *Health Affairs Scholar*, 2(4), qxae047. https://doi.org/10.1093/haschl/qxae047

Singh, Y., Song, Z., Polsky, D., Bruch, J. D., and Zhu, J. M. (2022). Association of private equity acquisition of physician practices with changes in health care spending and utilization. *JAMA Health Forum*, 3(9), e222886. https://doi.org/10.1001/jamahealthforum.2022.2886

Singh, Y., Zhu, J. M., Polsky, D., and Song, Z. (2022). Geographic variation in private equity penetration across select office-based physician specialties in the US. *JAMA Health Forum*, 3, e220825. https://doi.org/10.1001/jamahealthforum.2022.0825

Smith, A. (1990). The effects of leveraged buyouts. *Business Economics*, pp. 19–25.

Sola, D., and Couturier, J. (2014). *How to think strategically: Your roadmap to innovation and results.* Palgrave Macmillan.

Sovereign Wealth Fund Institute. (2025, May 23). *In-depth: Sovereign wealth funds invest in health outcomes*. SWFI.

SSandC Intralinks. (2025). *The dynamics of due diligence*. https://www3.intralinks.com/rs/414-BKN-706/images/SSandC-Intralinks-The-Dynamics-of-Due-Diligence-Report.pdf

Stevenson, D. G. and Grabowski, D. C. (2008). Private equity investment and nursing home care: Is it a big deal? *Health Affairs*, 27(5), pp. 1399–1408. https://doi.org/10.1377/hlthaff.27.5.1399

Stewart, J. B. (1992). *Den of thieves*. Simon and Schuster.

Stucke, R. (2011). Updating history. *SSRN Electronic Journal*. https://doi.org/10.2139/ssrn.1967636

Tarhuni, N. (2026). The problem isn't democratizing private markets. It's confusing access with liquidity. PitchBook News, 24 February. https://finance.yahoo.com/news/problem-isnt-democratizing-private-markets-014527535.html.

Tasi, M. C., Keswani, A., and Bozic, K. J. (2019). Does physician leadership affect hospital quality, operational efficiency, and financial performance? *Health Care Management Review*, 44(3), pp. 256–262.

Tempest, M. and Funa, D. (2024). *From tradition to transformation—the time is ripe for primary care*. LaingBuisson.

Thunell, C. (2024, January 10). *Private equity spotlight: EQT healthcare growth strategy to fill the gap between VC and PE strategies*. Mergermarket. https://mergermarket.ionanalytics.com/content/10037 21272?source=news

Tirole, J. (2006). *The theory of corporate finance*. Princeton University Press.

Todd, P. E. and Wolpin, K. I. (2023). Ex-post policy evaluation and selection bias. *Journal of Economic Literature*, 61(1), pp. 1–63.

TVM Capital. (2010). *TVM capital portfolio company, Evotec AG, named M&A advisor global healthcare turnaround company of the year [PDF]*. https://www.evotec.com/uploads/download-files/6f395b01c6 3bbe8239e01c95e7278579.pdf

US SEC. (2015). SEC charges KKR with misallocating broken deal expenses (Press Release 2015-131).

Vandoros, S. (2020). Excess mortality during the Covid-19 pandemic: Early evidence from England and Wales. *Social Science & Medicine*, 258, 113101.

Vandoros, S., Hessel, P., Leone, T., and Avendano, M. (2013). Have health trends worsened in Greece as a result of the financial crisis? A quasi-experimental approach. *The European Journal of Public Health*, 23(5), pp. 727–731.

Wall Street Journal. (2028). *Private-equity giant Abraaj files for liquidation*. https://www.wsj.com/articles/private-equity-giant-abraaj-files-for-liquidation-1528979610

Warga, A. and Welch, I. (1993). Bondholder losses in leveraged buyouts. *The Review of Financial Studies*, 6(4), pp. 959–982.

Werner, R. M. and Norton, E.C. and Konetzka, R. T. and Polsky, D. (2012). Do consumers respond to publicly reported quality information? Evidence from nursing homes. *Journal of Health Economics*, 31(1), pp. 50–61.

Wilner, B. S. (2000). The exploitation of relationships in financial distress: The case of trade credit. *Journal of Finance*, 55(1), pp. 153–178.

Winblad, U., Blomqvist, P., and Karlsson, A. (2017). Do public nursing home care providers deliver higher quality than private providers? Evidence from Sweden. *BMC Health Services Research, 17*(1), 487. https://doi.org/10.1186/s12913-017-2403-0

World Bank Group. (2017). *The evolution of the Canadian pension model: practical lessons for building world-class pension organizations*. Washington, DC: World Bank. https://hdl.handle.net/10986/28828

World Economic Forum. (2025). *How tech innovations are transforming private equity*.

Wu, Y. (2023). Carbon footprint of private equity. In *The Palgrave Encyclopedia of Private Equity* (forthcoming). Working paper. https://doi.org/10.2139/ssrn.4533377

Xu, X. E. (2004). A comparative study of venture capital performance in the US and Europe. *Journal of Entrepreneurial Finance*, 9(4), pp. 284–299.

Yunis, H. (2021, June 4). *Sovereign wealth fund investment in the global healthcare industry*. McDermott Will & Schulte LLP/Lexology.

Zhu, J. M., Greenberg, E., King, M., and Busch, S. (2024). Geographic penetration of private equity ownership in outpatient and residential behavioral health. *JAMA Psychiatry*, 81(7), pp. 732–735. https://doi.org/10.1001/jamapsychiatry.2024.0825

Zhu, J. M., Hua, L. M., and Polsky, D. (2020). Private equity acquisitions of physician medical groups across specialties, 2013–2016. *JAMA*, 323, pp. 663–665. https://doi.org/10.1001/jama.2019.21844

Index

Note: Page numbers in *italics* and **bold** refers to figures and tables respectively.

Q

R